11th Edition

UNDERSTANDING COMPUTERS:

TODAY A[...]

COMPREHENSIVE

DEBORAH MORLEY
CHARLES S. PARKER

2007 Update

THOMSON
COURSE TECHNOLOGY

Australia • Canada • Mexico • Singapore • Spain • United Kingdom • United States

Understanding Computers: Today and Tomorrow, 11th Edition, 2007 Update
is published by Thomson Course Technology

Acquisitions Editor:
Kristina Matthews

Senior Product Manager:
Kathy Finnegan

Product Managers:
Brianna Hawes,
Katherine T. Pinard

Associate Product Manager:
Brandi Henson

Editorial Assistant:
Leigh Robbins

Senior Marketing Manager:
Joy Stark

Marketing Coordinator:
Jennifer Hankin

Developmental Editor:
Pam Conrad

Senior Content Project Manager:
Jennifer Goguen McGrail

Composition:
GEX Publishing Services

Text and Cover Designer:
Joel Sadagursky

Printed in the United States of America

1 2 3 4 5 6 7 8 9 BM 11 10 09 08 07

For more information, contact Thomson Course Technology, 25 Thomson Place, Boston, Massachusetts, 02210.

Or find us on the World Wide Web at: www.course.com

ISBN-13: 978-1-4239-0636-0
ISBN-10: 1-4239-0636-5

PREFACE

In today's computer-oriented society, computers and technology impact virtually everyone's life. *Understanding Computers: Today and Tomorrow, 11th Edition, 2007 Update* will ensure that students are current and informed in order to thrive in our technologically oriented, global society. With this new edition, students not only learn about relevant cutting-edge technology trends, but also gain a better understanding of technology in general and the important issues surrounding technology today. This information will give students the understanding they need to succeed in today's world.

This nontechnical, introductory text explains in straightforward terms the importance of learning about computers, the various types of computer systems and their components, the principles by which computer systems work, the practical applications of computers and related technologies, and the ways in which the world is being changed by these technologies. The goal of this text is to provide the reader with a solid knowledge of computer fundamentals, an understanding of the impact of our computer-oriented society, and a framework for using this knowledge effectively in their lives.

KEY FEATURES

Just like its previous editions, *Understanding Computers: Today and Tomorrow, 11th Edition, 2007 Update* is current and comprehensive. Flexible organization and an engaging presentation combined with learning tools in each chapter help the student master important concepts. Numerous marginal notations lead students to the Understanding Computers Web site where they can access numerous **Interactive Activities**, **Testing Activities**, and **Study Tools/Additional Resources**.

Currency and Accuracy

The state-of-the-art content of this book and its Web site reflect the latest technologies, trends, and classroom needs. Throughout the writing and production stages, enhancements were continually made to ensure that the final product is as current and accurate as possible.

Comprehensiveness and Depth

Accommodating a wide range of teaching preferences, *Understanding Computers: Today and Tomorrow, 11th Edition, 2007 Update* provides comprehensive coverage of traditional topics while also covering relevant, up-to-the minute new technologies and important societal issues, such as dual-core CPUs, nanotechnology, blue laser and hybrid CD/DVD discs, holographic storage, OLED displays, 3D displays, and other new and emerging types of hardware; biometric access systems, e-tokens, laser visas, and other access technologies; new software, such as Windows Vista, as well as Linux and other open source software programs that are growing in importance; new communications technologies, such as RFID, mesh networks, broadband over power lines (BPL), WiMAX, Mobile-Fi, Voice over IP (VoIP), Voice over W-Fi, m-commerce, and presence technology; new and growing Internet applications, such as digital data distribution, place-shifting, blogs, podcasting, online music, mobile TV, video-on-demand (VOD), and legal P2P file sharing; security and privacy issues, such as war driving, spyware, identity theft, phishing, pharming, electronic health records (EHSs), e-mail hoaxes, data security, and data privacy; new Web development technologies, such as XML, XHTML, AJAX, behavioral targeting, and rich media advertising; GISs, robotics, Application Lifecycle Management (ALM), and other developing systems applications; and important societal issues, such as software piracy, digital counterfeiting, digital rights management (DRM), Internet addiction, and green computing.

Readability

We remember more about a subject if it is presented in a straightforward way and made interesting and exciting. This book is written in a conversational, down-to-earth style—one designed to be accurate without being intimidating. Concepts are explained clearly and simply, without the use of overly technical terminology. Where complex points are presented, they are explained in an understandable manner and with realistic examples from everyday life.

Chapter Learning Tools

TECHNOLOGY AND YOU

1. **Outline, Learning Objectives, and Overview:** For each chapter, an **Outline** of the major topics covered, a list of student **Learning Objectives**, and a **Chapter Overview** help instructors put the subject matter of the chapter in perspective and let students know what they will be reading about.
2. **Boldfaced Key Terms and Running Glossary:** Important terms appear in boldface type as they are introduced in the chapter. These terms are defined at the bottom of the page on which they appear and in the end-of-text glossary.
3. **Chapter Boxes:** In each chapter, a **Trend** box provides students with a look at current and upcoming developments in the world of computers; an **Inside the Industry** box provides insight into some of the practices that have made the computer industry unique and fascinating; a **How it Works** box explains in more detail how a technology or product works; and a **Technology and You** box takes a look at how computers and technology are used in your everyday life.
4. **Marginal Tips: TIP** marginal elements feature time-saving tips or ways to avoid a common problem or terminology mistake, or present students with interesting additional information related to the chapter content.

TIP

There are numerous online blog search engines and directories—such as BlogStreet.com—to help you find blogs that meet your interests.

5. **Illustrations and Photographs:** Instructive, current full-color illustrations and photographs appear throughout the book to help illustrate important concepts. Figures and screenshots feature the latest hardware and software products and are carefully annotated to convey important information.

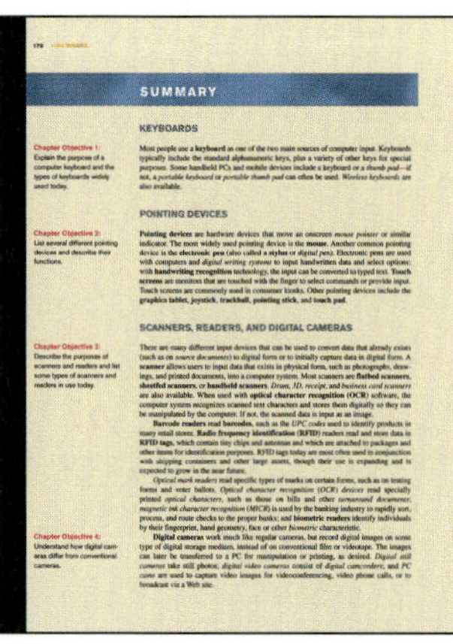
SUMMARY

KEYBOARDS

POINTING DEVICES

SCANNERS, READERS, AND DIGITAL CAMERAS

6. **Summary and Key Terms:** The end-of-chapter material includes a concise, section-by-section **Summary** of the main points in the chapter. The chapter's Learning Objectives appear in the margin next to the relevant section of the summary so that students are better able to relate the Learning Objectives to the chapter material. Every boldfaced key term in the chapter also appears in boldface type in the summary.
7. **Review Activities and Projects:** End-of-chapter activities allow students to test themselves on what they have just read. A matching exercise of selected **Key Terms** helps students test their retention of the chapter material. A **Self-Quiz** (with the answers listed at the end of the book) consists of ten true-false and completion questions. Five additional easily graded matching and short-answer **Exercises** are included for instructors who would like to assign graded homework. A **Discussion Question** for each chapter provides a jumping off point to get classroom discussion started. End-of-chapter **Projects** require students to extend their knowledge by

doing research and activities beyond merely reading the book. Organized into six types of projects (Hot Topics, Short Answer/Research, Hands On, Writing About Computers, Presentation/Demonstration, and Group Discussion), the projects feature explicit instructions so that students can work through them without additional directions from instructors. Special marginal icons denote projects that require Internet access.

8. **Understanding Computers Web Site:** Throughout each chapter, **Further Exploration** marginal elements direct students to the Understanding Computers Web site where they can access collections of links to Web sites containing more in-depth information on a given topic from the text. At the end of every chapter, students are directed to the Understanding Computers Web site to access a variety of **Interactive Activities**, **Testing Activities,** and **Study Tools/Additional Resources**.

FURTHER EXPLORATION

For links to further information about CPUs, go to www.course.com/uc11/ch02

References and Resources Guide

A **References and Resources Guide** at the end of the book brings together in one convenient location a collection of computer-related references and resources, including a Computer History Timeline, Coding Charts, and a Guide for Buying a PC.

KEY FEATURES OF THIS EDITION

NEW 2007 Update Section

A 40-page 2007 Update section has been added to this text and contains the following elements:

- **Chapter-by-Chapter Update Guide**—An easy-to-use two-page spread for each chapter provides students with currency updates for the chapter content, as well as an overview of related new and emerging technology trends. Many new illustrative color photographs are also included.
- **Expert Insight**—a new "Expert Insight on Windows Vista" feature with a Senior Product Manager from the Microsoft Windows Vista Group discussing the impact of Windows Vista and trends for the future.
- **Windows Vista and You**—An up-close look at the exciting new release of the world's most popular operating system.
- **Tech News Video Projects**—Two new video projects based on CNET TV videos (available via the Understanding Computers Web site) are included.

Streamlined Introduction Chapter

To help get students up and running even faster, this edition features a single consolidated introductory chapter containing the key topics previously contained in Chapters 1 and 2.

"Network and Internet Security" Chapter

To better cover the vast number of important issues related to network and Internet security today, these topics are in their own chapter—**Chapter 9**, **"Network and Internet Security**," which is located at the end of the **Networks and the Internet** module. Additional security topics related to computers are still discussed, along with privacy, intellectual property rights, ethics, health, access, and the environment, in the **Computers and Society** module.

Expert Insight

In this exciting new feature located at the end of each module, industry experts provide students with personal insights on topics presented in the book, including their personal experiences with technology, key points to remember, and advice for the future. The experts, professionals from these major companies—**Microsoft, Nokia**, **Hewlett Packard**, **Novell**, **The Hanover Insurance Group**, **Yahoo!**, **Best Buy**, and **Dell**—provide a unique perspective on the module content and how the topics discussed in the module impact their lives, their industry, what it means for the future, and more!

Expanded Web Site Content

The **Understanding Computers Web site** includes a wealth of information at your fingertips to help enhance the classroom experience and to help students master the material covered in the book. Some of the content featured on the site includes new and updated **Self-Quizzes**, **Exercises**, **and Practice Tests**. The site also features interactive activities, such as **Student Edition Labs** and **Tech News Video Projects**. In addition, many other resources, including **Online Study Guides**, **Online Glossary**, **Online Crossword Puzzles**, **Further Exploration** links, and **Online References and Resources Guide** content, are available for use.

Student and Instructor Support Materials

Understanding Computers: Today and Tomorrow, 11th Edition, 2007 Update, is available with a complete package of support materials for instructors and students. Included in the package are the Understanding Computers Web site, Instructor Resources (available on CD and online), and SAM Computer Concepts.

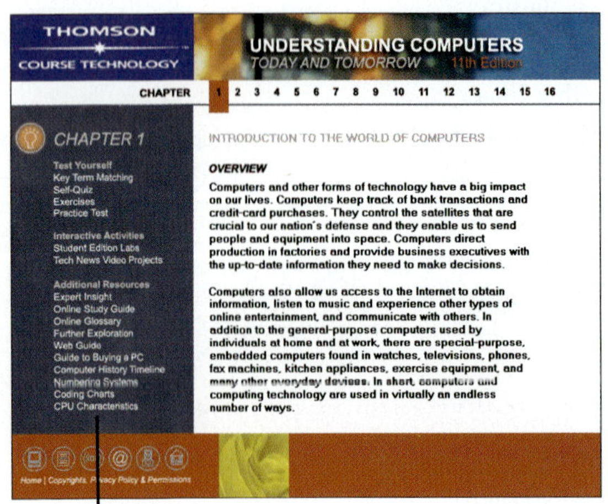

Click any link in the navigation bar on the left to access any of the online resources described below.

The Understanding Computers Web Site

The Understanding Computers Web site is located at **www.course.com/uc11** and provides media-rich support for each chapter of the book.

The Web site includes the following:

- **Key Terms Matching**—this feature allows students to test their knowledge of selected chapter key terms by matching the terms with their definitions.
- **Self-Quiz**—this feature allows students to test their retention of chapter concepts.
- **Exercises**—this feature reviews the concepts and terms covered in the chapter.
- **Practice Test**—this feature allows students to test how ready they are for upcoming exams.
- **Crossword Puzzles**—this feature incorporates the key terms from each chapter into an online interactive crossword puzzle.
- **Student Edition Lab**—this feature reinforces and expands the concepts covered in the chapters.
- **Tech News Video Project**—this feature includes the complete **Tech News Video Project** associated with the chapter, as well as a link to watch the appropriate video.

- **Additional Resources**—this feature includes a wide range of additional resources, such as an **Online Study Guide** and **Online Glossary** for each chapter; **Further Exploration** links, a **Web Guide**, a **Guide to Buying a PC**, and a **Computer History Timeline**; more information about **Numbering Systems**, **Coding Charts**, and **CPU Characteristics**; and much, much more!

Instructor Resources

Course Technology instructional resources and technology tools provide instructors with a wide range of tools that enhance teaching and learning. These tools can be accessed from the Instructor Resources CD or at www.course.com.

Electronic Instructor's Manual

The Instructor's Manual is written to provide instructors with practical suggestions for enhancing classroom presentations. For each of the 16 chapters in the text, the Instructor's Manual provides: **Instructor Notes**, **Troubleshooting Tips**, **Quick Quizzes**, **Classroom Activities**, **Discussion Questions**, **Key Terms**, a **Chapter Quiz**, and more!

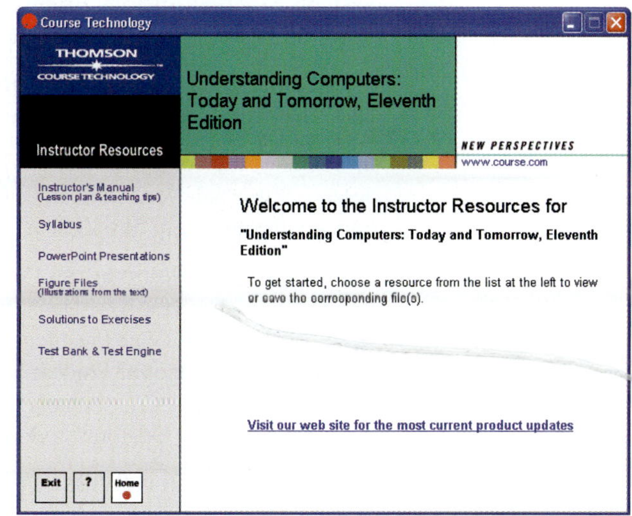

ExamView Test Bank

This textbook is accompanied by ExamView, a powerful testing software package that allows instructors to create and administer printed, computer (LAN-based), and Internet exams. ExamView includes over 2,400 questions that correspond to the topics covered in this text, enabling instructors to create exams mapping exactly to the content they cover. The computer-based and Internet testing components allow instructors to administer exams over the computer and also save by grading each exam automatically.

PowerPoint Presentations

This book comes with **Microsoft PowerPoint slides** for each chapter. These are included as a teaching aid for classroom presentation, to make available to students on the network for chapter review, or to be printed for classroom distribution. Instructors can customize these presentations to cover any additional topics they introduce to the class. **Figure Files** for all figures in the textbook are also available for instructor use.

Blackboard and WebCT content

We offer a full range of content for use with Blackboard and WebCT to simplify the use of Understanding Computers in distance education settings. Contact your sales representative for more details.

SAM Computer Concepts

Instructors who have chosen to use SAM Computer Concepts (assessment and training software) in their courses have access to hands-on assessment and interactive training simulations that reinforce lessons presented in this text.

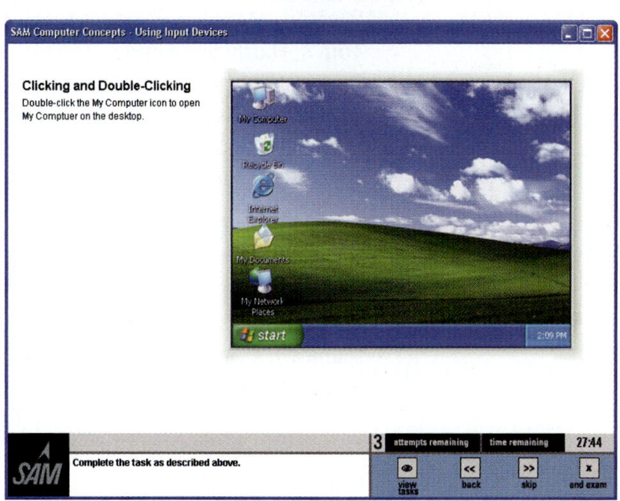

ACKNOWLEDGEMENTS

We would like to extend a special thank you to all of industry professionals who reviewed module content and who provided their expertise for the new **Expert Insight** feature:

Introduction Module: Vipul Mehrotra, Director, Technology and Portfolio Management, Nokia
Hardware Module: John Janakiraman, Research Manager for Data Center Architecture, HP Labs
Software Module: Aaron Weber, Product Marketing Manager, Novell
Networks and the Internet Module: Jeffrey Bardin, Chief Information Security Officer, The Hanover Insurance Group.
Web Applications Module: Christopher Allen, Head of Product Strategy, Yahoo! Music
Systems Module: Anthony Briggs, Business Information Officer, Best Buy
Computers and Society Module: Frank Molsberry, Technologist, Dell Inc.

New to the 2007 Update Edition

2007 Update: Graham Watson, Senior Product Manager, Vista Group, Microsoft

In addition, the following past and present industry expert and educational reviewers of this text deserve a special word of thanks for their thoughtful suggestions that have helped to define and improve the quality of this text over the years.

Industry Expert Reviewers–11th Edition, 2007 Update

Bernie Spang, Director IBM Data Servers, IBM Corporation
Hugh Taylor, CISM, Vice President, Marketing, SOA Software
David Hauck, Director of Product Marketing, Borland Software Corporation
Jeff Rush, Advocacy Coordinator, Python Software Foundation
Nels Jewell-Larsen, Doctoral student, University of Washington

Industry Expert Reviewers–11th Edition

Janice K. Mahon, Vice President of Technology Commercialization, Universal Display Corporation
Dr. Nhon Quach, Next Generation Processor Architect, AMD
Jos van Haaren, Department Head Storage Physics, Philips Research Laboratories
Terry O'Kelly, Technical Communications Manager, Memorex
Randy Culpepper, Texas Instruments RFID Systems
Aaron Newman, CTO and Co-Founder, Application Security Inc.
John Nash, Vice President of Marketing, Visible Systems
Dr. Maressa Hecht Orzack, Director, Computer Addiction Study Center

Industry Expert Reviewers–Previous Editions

Alan Charlesworth, Staff Engineer, Sun Microsystems; Khaled A. Elamrawi, Senior Marketing Engineer, Intel Corporation; Timothy D. O'Brien, Senior Systems Engineer, Fujitsu Software; John Paulson, Manager, Product Communications, Seagate Technology; Omid Rahmat, Editor in Chief, Tom's Hardware Guide; Jeremy Bates, Multimedia Developer, R & L Multimedia Developers; Charles Hayes, Product Marketing Manager, SimpleTech, Inc.; Rick McGowan, Vice President & Senior Software Engineer, Unicode, Inc.; Russell Reynolds, Chief Operating Officer & Web Designer, R & L Multimedia Developers; Rob Stephens, Director, Technology Strategies, SAS; Dave Stow, Database Specialist, OSE Systems, Inc.

Educational Reviewers

Beverly Amer, Northern Arizona University; James Ambroise Jr., Southern University, Louisiana; Virginia Anderson, University of North Dakota; Robert Andree, Indiana University Northwest; Linda Armbruster, Rancho Santiago College; Michael Atherton, Mankato State University; Gary E. Baker, Marshalltown Community College; Richard Batt, Saint Louis Community College at Meremec; Luverne Bierle, Iowa Central Community College; Fariba Bolandhemat, Santa Monica College; Jerry Booher, Scottsdale Community College; Frederick W. Bounds, Georgia Perimeter College; James Bradley, University of Calgary; Curtis Bring, Moorhead State University; Brenda K. Britt, Fayetteville Technical Community College; Cathy Brotherton, Riverside Community College; Chris Brown, Bemidji State

University; Janice Burke, South Suburban College; James Buxton, Tidewater Community College, Virginia; Gena Casas, Florida Community College, Jacksonville; Thomas Case, Georgia Southern University; John E. Castek, University of Wisconsin-La Crosse; Mario E. Cecchetti, Westmoreland County Community College; Jack W. Chandler, San Joaquin Delta College; Alan Charlesworth, Staff Engineer, Sun Microsystems; Jerry M. Chin, Southwest Missouri State University; Edward W. Christensen, Monmouth University; Carl Clavadetscher, California State Polytechnic University; Vernon Clodfelter, Rowan Technical College, North Carolina; Joann C. Cook, College of DuPage; Laura Cooper, College of the Mainland, Texas; Cynthia Corritore, University of Nebraska at Omaha; Sandra Cunningham, Ranger College; Marvin Daugherty, Indiana Vocational Technical College; Donald L. Davis, University of Mississippi; Garrace De Groot, University of Wyoming; Jackie Dennis, Prairie State College; Robert H. Dependahl Jr., Santa Barbara College, California; Donald Dershem, Mountain View College; John DiElsi, Marcy College, New York; Mark Dishaw, Boston University; Eugene T. Dolan, University of the District of Columbia; Bennie Allen Dooley, Pasadena City College; Robert H. Dependahl Jr.; Santa Barbara City College; William Dorin, Indiana University Northwest; Mike Doroshow, Eastfield College; Jackie O. Duncan, Hopkinsville Community College; John Dunn, Palo Alto College; John W. Durham, Fort Hays State University; Khaled A Elamrawi, Senior Marketing Engineer, Intel Corporation; Hyun B. Eom, Middle Tennessee State University; Michael Feiler, Merritt College; Terry Felke, WR Harper College; J. Patrick Fenton, West Valley Community College; James H. Finger, University of South Carolina at Columbia; William C. Fink, Lewis and Clark Community College, Illinois; Ronald W. Fordonski, College of Du Page; Connie Morris Fox, West Virginia Institute of Technology; Paula S. Funkhouser, Truckee Meadows Community College; Janos T. Fustos, Metropolitan State; Gene Garza, University of Montevallo; Timothy Gottleber, North Lake College; Dwight Graham, Prairie State College; Wade Graves, Grayson County College; Kay H. Gray, Jacksonville State University; David W. Green, Nashville State Technical Institute, Tennessee; George P. Grill, University of North Carolina, Greensboro; John Groh, San Joaquin Delta College; Rosemary C. Gross, Creighton University; Dennis Guster, Saint Louis Community College at Meremec; Joe Hagarty, Raritan Valley Community College; Donald Hall, Manatee Community College; Jim Hanson, Austin Community College; Sallyann Z. Hanson, Mercer County Community College; L. D. Harber, Volunteer State Community College, Tennessee; Hank Hartman, Iowa State University; Richard Hatch, San Diego State University; Mary Lou Hawkins, Del Mar College; Ricci L. Heishman, Northern Virginia Community College; William Hightower, Elon College, North Carolina; Sharon A. Hill, Prince George's Community College, Maryland; Alyse Hollingsworth, Brevard College; Fred C. Homeyer, Angelo State University; Stanley P. Honacki, Moraine Valley Community College; L. Wayne Horn, Pensacola Junior College; J. William Howorth, Seneca College, Ontario, Canada; Mark W. Huber, East Carolina University; Peter L. Irwin, Richland College, Texas; John Jasma, Palo Alto College; Nicholas JohnRobak, Saint Joseph's University; Elizabeth Swoope Johnson, Louisiana State University; Jim Johnson, Valencia Community College; Mary T. Johnson, Mt. San Antonio College; Susan M. Jones, Southwest State University; Amardeep K. Kahlon, Austin Community College; Robert T. Keim, Arizona State University; Mary Louise Kelly, Palm Beach Community College; William R. Kenney, San Diego Mesa College; Richard Kerns, East Carolina University, North Carolina; Glenn Kersnick, Sinclair Community College, Ohio; Richard Kiger, Dallas Baptist University; Gordon C. Kimbell, Everett Community College, Washington; Mary Veronica Kolesar, Utah State University; Robert Kirklin, Los Angeles Harbor Community College; Judith A. Knapp, Indiana University Northwest; James G. Kriz, Cuyahoga Community College, Ohio; Joan Krone, Denison University; Fran Kubicek, Kalamazoo Valley Community College; Rose M. Laird, Northern Virginia Community College; Robert Landrum, Jones Junior College; Shelly Langman, Bellevue Community College; James F. LaSalle, The University of Arizona; Linda J. Lindaman, Black Hawk College; Chang-Yang Lin, Eastern Kentucky University; Alden Lorents, Northern Arizona University; Paul M. Lou, Diablo Valley College; Deborah R. Ludford, Glendale Community College; Kent Lundin, Brigham Young University-Idaho; Barbara J. Maccarone, North Shore Community College; Donna Madsen, Kirkwood Community College; Wayne Madison, Clemson University, South Carolina; Donna L. Madsen, Kirkwood Community College; Randy Marak, Hill College; Gary Marks, Austin Community College, Texas; Kathryn A. Marold, Ph.D., Metropolitan State College of Denver; Cesar Marron, University of Wyoming; Ed Martin, Kingsborough Community College; Vickie McCullough, Palomar College; James W. McGuffee, Austin Community College; James McMahon, Community College of Rhode Island; William A. McMillan, Madonna University; Don B. Medley, California State Polytechnic

University; John Melrose, University of Wisconsin—Eau Claire; Dixie Mercer, Kirkwood Community College; Mary Meredith, University of Southwestern Louisiana; Marilyn Meyer, Fresno City College; Carolyn H. Monroe, Baylor University; William J. Moon, Palm Beach Community College; Marilyn Moore, Purdue University; Marty Murray, Portland Community College; Don Nielsen, Golden West College; George Novotny, Ferris State University; Timothy D. O'Brien, Senior Systems Engineer, Fujitsu Software; Richard Okezie, Mesa Community College; Joseph D. Oldham, University of Kentucky; Dennis J. Olsen, Pikes Peak Community College; Bob Palank, Florissant Community College; John Paulson, Manager, Product Communications, Seagate Technology; James Payne, Kellogg Community College; Lisa B. Perez, San Joaquin Delta College; Savitha Pinnepalli, Louisiana State University; Delores Pusins, Hillsborough CC; Mike Rabaut, Hillsborough CC; Omid Rahmat, Editor in Chief, Tom's Hardware Guide www.tomshardware.com; Robert Ralph, Fayetteville Technical Institute, North Carolina; Herbert F. Rebhun, University of Houston-Downtown; Arthur E. Rowland, Shasta College; Kenneth R. Ruhrup, St. Petersburg Junior College; John F. Sanford, Philadelphia College of Textiles and Science; Kammy Sanghera, George Mason University; Carol A. Schwab, Webster University; Larry Schwartzman, Trident Technical College; Benito R. Serenil, South Seattle Community College; Allanagh Sewell, Southeastern Louisiana University; Tom Seymour, Minot State University; John J. Shuler, San Antonio College, Texas; Gayla Jo Slauson, Mesa State College; Harold Smith, Brigham Young University; Willard A. Smith, Tennessee State University; David Spaisman, Katherine Gibbs; Elizabeth Spooner, Holmes Community College; Timothy M. Stanford, City University; Alfred C. St. Onge, Springfield Technical Community College, Massachusetts; Michael L. Stratford, Charles County Community College, Maryland; Karen Studniarz, Kishwaukee College; Sandra Swanson, Lewis &Clark Community College; Tim Sylvester, Glendale Community College; Semih Tahaoglu, Southeastern Louisiana University; William H. Trueheart, New Hampshire College; Jane J. Thompson, Solano Community College; Sue Traynor, Clarion University of Pennsylvania; James D. Van Tassel, Mission College; James R. Walters, Pikes Peak Community College; Joyce V. Walton, Seneca College, Ontario, Canada; Diane B.Walz, University of Texas at San Antonio; Joseph Waters, Santa Rosa Junior College, California; Liang Chee Wee, University of Arizona; Merrill Wells, Red Rocks Community College; Fred J. Wilke, Saint Louis Community College; Charles M. Williams, Georgia State University; Roseanne Witkowski, Orange County Community College; David Womack, University of Texas, San Antonio; George Woodbury, College of the Sequoias; Nan Woodsome, Araphoe Community College; James D. Woolever, Cerritos College; Patricia Joann Wykoff, Western Michigan University; A. James Wynne, Virginia Commonwealth University; Robert D. Yearout, University of North Carolina at Asheville; Israel Yost, University of New Hampshire; and Vic Zamora, Mt. San Antonio College.

We would also like to thank the people on the Course team—their professionalism, attention to detail, and enormous enthusiasm makes working with them a pleasure. In particular, we'd like to thank Kristina Matthews, Rachel Goldberg, Amanda Young Shelton, Brianna Hawes, Pam Conrad, Kitty Pinard, and Jennifer Goguen McGrail for all their ideas, support, and tireless efforts during the design, writing, rewriting, and production of this book. Thanks to Joseph Gorzynski and Tim Reczek for managing the development of the Understanding Computers Web site, Brandi Henson and Shana Rosenthal for managing the Instructor's Resource package, Rebecca Padrick and Janine Tangney for all their assistance, and Joy Stark for her efforts on marketing this text. We would also like to thank Joel Sadagursky for working on the new interior and cover design. Thanks also to Kristen Duerr and Nicole Pinard.

We are also very appreciative of the numerous individuals and organizations that were kind enough to supply information and photographs for this text.

We sincerely hope you find this book interesting, informative, and enjoyable to read. If you have any suggestions for improvement, or corrections that you'd like to be considered for future editions, please send them to deborah.morley@thomson.com.

Deborah Morley
Charles S. Parker

BRIEF CONTENTS

Preface

MODULE Introduction 2

Chapter 1
Introduction to the World of Computers 4

Expert Insight on Personal Computers 50

MODULE Hardware 52

Chapter 2
The System Unit: Processing and Memory 54

Chapter 3
Storage 96

Chapter 4
Input and Output 132

Expert Insight on Hardware 178

MODULE Software 180

Chapter 5
System Software: Operating Systems and Utility Programs 182

Chapter 6
Application Software 220

Expert Insight on Software 262

MODULE Networks and the Internet 264

Chapter 7
Computer Networks 266

Chapter 8
The Internet and World Wide Web 310

Chapter 9
Network and Internet Security 362

Expert Insight on Networks and the Internet 406

MODULE Web Applications 408

Chapter 10
Multimedia and the Web 410

Chapter 11
E-Commerce 448

Expert Insight on Web-Based Multimedia and E-Commerce 482

MODULE Systems 484

Chapter 12
Information Systems and System Development 486

Chapter 13
Program Development and Programming Languages 530

Chapter 14
Databases and Database Management Systems 574

Expert Insight on Systems 614

MODULE Computers and Society 616

Chapter 15
Computer Security and Privacy 618

Chapter 16
Intellectual Property Rights, Ethics, Health, Access, and the Environment 658

Expert Insight on Computers and Society 702

2007 Update U-1

Expert Insight on Windows Vista U-34

References and Resources Guide R-1

Credits C-1

Glossary/Index I-1

CONTENTS

Preface iii

MODULE Introduction 2

Chapter 1 Introduction to the World of Computers 4

Overview 5

Computers in Your Life 6

> Why Learn About Computers? 6
> Computers in the Home 7
> Computers in Education 7
> Computers in the Workplace 8
> Computers on the Go 10

What Is a Computer and What Does It Do? 11

> Data vs. Information 12
> Computers Then and Now 12
> Hardware 15
> Software 16
> Computer Users and Professionals 19

Computers to Fit Every Need 20

> Mobile Devices 20
> Personal Computers 21
> Midrange Servers 28
> Mainframe Computers 28
> Supercomputers 28

Computer Networks and the Internet 30

> What Are the Internet and the World Wide Web? 31
> Accessing a Network or the Internet 31
> Surfing the Web 35
> Searching the Web 36
> E-Mail 37

Computers and Society 38

> Benefits of a Computer-Oriented Society 38
> Risks of a Computer-Oriented Society 39
> Differences in Online Communications 40
> The Anonymity Factor 41
> Information Integrity 41

Summary 42

Review Activities 44

Projects 46

Web Activities 49

TECHNOLOGY AND YOU Wired Med Students 9

TREND Mobile TV 22

INSIDE THE INDUSTRY PC Modding 24

HOW IT WORKS Setting Up a New PC 27

Expert Insight on Personal Computers 50

MODULE Hardware 52

Chapter 2 The System Unit: Processing and Memory 54

Overview 55

Data and Program Representation 55

> Digital Data Representation 55
> Representing Numerical Data: The Binary Numbering System 56
> Coding Systems for Text-Based Data 57
> Coding Systems for Other Types of Data 58
> Representing Programs: Machine Language 61

Inside the System Unit 62
> The Motherboard 63
> The CPU 63
> Memory 67
> Fans, Heat Sinks, and Other Cooling Components 69
> Expansion Slots and Cards 69
> Buses 70
> Ports 72
How the CPU Works 75
> Typical CPU Components 75
> The System Clock and the Machine Cycle 78
Making Computers Faster and Better Now and in the Future 81
> Improving the Performance of Your System Today 81
> Strategies for Making Faster and Better Computers 83
> Future Trends 86
Summary 88
Review Activities 90
Projects 92
Web Activities 95

HOW IT WORKS MP3 Compression 61
TECHNOLOGY AND YOU CPUs and Running Shoes 64
INSIDE THE INDUSTRY Moore's Law 77
TREND High-Tech Investigators 78

Chapter 3 Storage 96
Overview 97
Storage Systems Characteristics 97
> Storage Devices and Storage Media 97
> Volatility 98
> Random vs. Sequential Access 98
> Logical vs. Physical Representation 99
> Magnetic Disks vs. Optical Discs 100
Magnetic Disk Systems 100
> Floppy Disks and Drives 100
> Hard Disk Drives 102
> High-Capacity Removable Magnetic Disks and Cartridges 108
Optical Disc Systems 109
> Read-Only Discs: CD-ROM and DVD-ROM Discs 110
> Recordable Discs: CD-R, DVD-R, DVD+R, and DVD+R DL Discs 112
> Rewritable Discs: CD-RW, DVD-RW, DVD+RW, DVD-RAM, and Blue Laser Discs 112
Flash Memory Systems 114
> Flash Memory Media 115
> Flash Memory Drives 116
Other Types of Storage Systems 117
> Remote Storage Systems 117
> Smart Cards 119
> Holographic Storage 120
> Storage Systems for Large Computer Systems and Networks 120
> Magnetic Tape Systems 122
Comparing Storage Alternatives 122
Summary 124
Review Activities 126
Projects 128
Web Activities 131

INSIDE THE INDUSTRY Data Recovery Experts 105
HOW IT WORKS Business Card CDs and DVDs 111
TREND Automated Optical Disc Carousels 113
TECHNOLOGY AND YOU Smart Card IDs 118

Chapter 4 Input and Output 132
Overview 133
Keyboards 133
Pointing Devices 135
> The Mouse 135
> Electronic Pens 137
> Touch Screens 139
> Other Pointing Devices 139
Scanners, Readers, and Digital Cameras 141
> Scanners 141
> Readers 144
> Digital Cameras 149
Audio Input 152
> Voice Input Systems 152
> Music Input Systems 153
Display Devices 154
> Display Device Characteristics 154
> Flat-Panel Display Technologies 160
> Data and Multimedia Projectors 162
Printers 163
> Printer Characteristics 163
> Laser Printers 165
> Ink-Jet Printers 165
> Special-Purpose Printers 166
> Multifunction Devices 168
Audio Output 168
Summary 170
Review Activities 172
Projects 174
Web Activities 177

TREND Virtual Input Devices 136
TECHNOLOGY AND YOU Body Scanners: Fitting Room of the Future? 144
INSIDE THE INDUSTRY RFID 150
HOW IT WORKS E-Paper 156

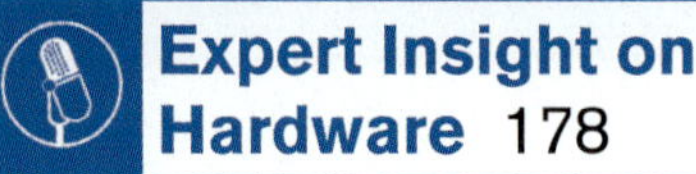
Expert Insight on Hardware 178

MODULE Software 180
Chapter 5 System Software: Operating Systems and Utility Programs 182
Overview 183
System Software vs. Application Software 183
The Operating System 184
> Functions of an Operating System 185
> Processing Techniques for Increased Efficiency 188
> Differences Among Operating Systems 191
Operating Systems for Desktop PCs and Servers 194
> DOS 194
> Windows 194
> Mac OS 198
> UNIX 199
> Linux 199
> NetWare 201
> Solaris 201
Operating Systems for Handheld PCs and Mobile Devices 201
> Embedded and Mobile Versions of Windows 201
> Palm OS 203
> Embedded Linux 203
> Symbian OS 204
Operating Systems for Larger Computers 204
Utility Programs 204
> File Management Programs 206
> Search Tools 208
> Diagnostic and Disk Management Programs 208
> File Compression Programs 208
> Uninstall Utilities 209
> Backup and Recovery Utilities 210
> Antivirus, Antispyware, Firewalls, and Other Security Programs 210
The Future of Operating Systems 211

Summary 212
Review Activities 214
Projects 216
Web Activities 219

INSIDE THE INDUSTRY Jellyvision's Interactive Conversation Interface (iCi) 192
TECHNOLOGY AND YOU Smart Cars 202
HOW IT WORKS Downloading and Installing Programs 205
TREND Desktop Searching 209

Chapter 6 Application Software 220
Overview 221
The Basics of Application Software 221
> Software Ownership Rights 221
> Installed vs. Web-Based Software 224
> Software Suites 227
> Desktop vs. Mobile Software 228
> Common Software Commands 229
Word Processing Concepts 232
> What Is Word Processing? 232
> Creating a Word Processing Document 233
> Tables, Graphics, and Templates 234
> Word Processing and the Web 235
Spreadsheet Concepts 236
> What Is a Spreadsheet? 236
> Creating a Spreadsheet 236
> Charts and What-If Analysis 239
> Spreadsheets and the Web 239
Database Concepts 239
> What Is a Database? 240
> Creating a Database 241
> Queries and Reports 242
> Databases and the Web 243
Presentation Graphics Concepts 243
> What Is a Presentation Graphic? 243
> Creating a Presentation 244
> Finishing a Presentation 245
> Presentation Graphics and the Web 246
Graphics and Multimedia Concepts 246
> Graphics Software 246
> Audio Editing Software 248
> Video Editing and DVD Authoring Software 248
> CD and DVD Burning Software 249
> Media Players 249
> Graphics, Multimedia, and the Web 249
Other Types of Application Software 251
> Desktop and Personal Publishing Software 252
> Educational, Entertainment, and Reference Software 252
> Accounting and Personal Finance Software 252
> CAD and Other Types of Design Software 252
> Project Management and Collaboration Software 253
> Note Taking and Personal Productivity Software 253
Summary 254
Review Activities 256
Projects 258
Web Activities 261

INSIDE THE INDUSTRY Open Source Software 223
TREND Software Kiosks 226
HOW IT WORKS Managing and Archiving Digital Photos 250
TECHNOLOGY AND YOU Taking Digital Classroom Notes 253

Expert Insight on Software 262

MODULE Networks and the Internet 264

Chapter 7 Computer Networks 266

Overview 267
What Is a Network? 267
Networking and Communications Applications 268
> Mobile Phones 268
> Paging and Messaging 269
> Global Positioning Systems (GPSs) 270
> Monitoring Systems 270
> Satellite Radio 272
> Videoconferencing 272
> Collaborative Computing 273
> Telecommuting 274
> Digital Data Distribution 274
> Telemedicine 276
Types of Networks 277
> Network Topologies 277
> Network Architectures 278
> LANs, WANs, and Other Types of Networks 279
How Does Data Travel Over a Network? 281
> Data Transmission Characteristics 281
> Wired vs. Wireless Connections 283
> Wired Network Transmission Media 284
> Wireless Network Transmission Media 286
Communications Protocols 288
> Ethernet 289
> Token Ring 290
> Wi-Fi (802.11) 291
> Mesh Networks, WiMAX, Mobile-Fi, and xMax 292
> Bluetooth and Ultra Wideband (UWB) 293
> TCP/IP and Wireless Application Protocol (WAP) 294
> Phoneline and Powerline Networks 297
Networking Hardware 297
> Network Adapters 297
> Modems 298
> Hubs, Switches, and Other Networking Hardware 300
Summary 302
Review Activities 304
Projects 306
Web Activities 309

TREND New Mobile Phone Applications: Celebrity Walking Tours and Park-by-Phone 269
INSIDE THE INDUSTRY Smart Dust 273
TECHNOLOGY AND YOU Multimedia Place Shifting 275
HOW IT WORKS Setting Up a Home Network 296

Chapter 8 The Internet and World Wide Web 310

Overview 311
Evolution of the Internet 311
> From Arpanet to Internet2 312
> The Internet Community Today 314
> Myths About the Internet 317
Getting Set Up to Use the Internet 318
> Type of Device 318
> Type of Connection and Internet Access 319
> Selecting an ISP and Setting Up Your PC 323
Searching the Internet 325
> Search Sites 326
> Search Strategies 328

> Evaluating Search Results 330
> Citing Internet Resources 331
Beyond Browsing and E-Mail 332
> Discussion Groups, Instant Messaging, and Other Types of Online Communications 332
> Online Shopping and Investing 334
> Online Entertainment 337
> Peer-to-Peer File Sharing 340
> Online News and Research 340
> Online Education and Writing 344
Censorship and Privacy Issues 347
> Censorship 347
> Web Browsing Privacy 349
> E-Mail Privacy 353
The Future of the Internet 353
Summary 354
Review Activities 356
Projects 358
Web Activities 361

HOW IT WORKS Voice over IP (VoIP) 334
INSIDE THE INDUSTRY RSS Feeds 341
TECHNOLOGY AND YOU P2P Legal Implications for College Students 342
TREND Personal Biometrics: Finger Payment Systems 347

Chapter 9 Network and Internet Security 362
Overview 363
Why Be Concerned About Network and Internet Security? 363
Unauthorized Access, Unauthorized Use, and Computer Sabotage 364
> Hacking 364
> Interception of Communications 367
> Computer Sabotage 367
Protecting Against Unauthorized Access, Unauthorized Use, and Computer Sabotage 372
> Access Control Systems 372
> Firewalls and Antivirus Software 376
> Encryption and Other Security Tools 378
> Take Caution with Employees 382
Online Theft, Fraud, and Other Dot Cons 383
> Theft of Data, Information, and Other Resources 384
> Identity Theft 384
> Online Auction Fraud 385
> Internet Scams, Spoofing, and Phishing 386
> Spyware 388
Protecting Against Online Theft, Fraud, and Other Dot Cons 389
> Protecting Against Identity Theft 389
> Protecting Against Other Dot Cons 391
> Protecting Against Spyware 392
> Using Digital Signatures and Digital Certificates 393
Personal Safety Issues 395
> Cyberstalking 395
> Online Pornography 395
Protecting Against Cyberstalking and Other Personal Safety Concerns 396
> Safety Tips for Adults 396
> Safety Tips for Children 396
Network and Internet Security Legislation 396

Summary 398
Review Activities 400
Projects 402
Web Activities 405

TECHNOLOGY AND YOU E-Tokens on Campus 375
HOW IT WORKS Private Key Encryption 380
TREND Pharming 387
INSIDE THE INDUSTRY Getting a Free Online Credit Report 390

Expert Insight on Networks and the Internet 406

MODULE Web Applications 408

Chapter 10 Multimedia and the Web 410
- Overview 411
- What Is Web-Based Multimedia? 411
  - > Web-Based Multimedia Applications 411
  - > Advantages and Disadvantages of Using Web-Based Multimedia 413
- Multimedia Elements 414
  - > Text 414
  - > Graphics 415
  - > Animation 418
  - > Audio 420
  - > Video 420
- Multimedia Web Site Design 421
  - > Basic Design Principles 421
  - > Determining the Intended Audience and Objectives 423
  - > Using Flowcharts, Page Layouts, and Storyboards 424
  - > Navigational Design Considerations 426
  - > Access Considerations 428
- Multimedia Web Site Development 429
  - > Creating the Multimedia Elements 430
  - > Creating the Web Site 430
  - > Testing, Publishing, and Maintaining the Site 437
- The Future of Web-Based Multimedia 438
- *Summary 440*
- *Review Activities 442*
- *Projects 444*
- *Web Activities 447*

TECHNOLOGY AND YOU Digital Worlds 413
TREND 3D Browsers 423
INSIDE THE INDUSTRY Creating Animated Films 426
HOW IT WORKS Publishing a Web Site 439

Chapter 11 E-Commerce 448
- Overview 449
- What Is E-Commerce? 449
  - > Advantages of E-Commerce 450
  - > Disadvantages of E-Commerce 452
- Types of E-Commerce Web Sites 454
  - > Manufacturer and E-Tailer Web Sites 454
  - > Brokerage Sites 454
- E-Commerce Business Models 456
  - > Business to Consumer (B2C) 456
  - > Business to Business (B2B) 458

> Consumer to Consumer (C2C) 458
> Business to Government (B2G) 458
> Intermediary Hubs 459

Implementing Web-Based E-Commerce 459

> Step 1: Select Appropriate Business Models and Types of Web Sites 460
> Step 2: Select the Desired E-Commerce Applications 460
> Step 3: Develop Procedures for Handling Electronic Financial Transactions 461
> Step 4: Design and Develop an Effective Web Site 467
> Step 5: Implement Appropriate Sales and Marketing Strategies 468

Security Issues 473

Summary 474

Review Activities 476

Projects 478

Web Activities 481

TECHNOLOGY AND YOU M-Commerce and U-Commerce: Steps Towards a Cashless Society 451

HOW IT WORKS Music Downloads 457

TREND Cell Phone Coupons 464

INSIDE THE INDUSTRY Banner Ads and Behavioral Targeting 472

Expert Insight on Web-Based Multimedia and E-Commerce 482

MODULE Systems 484

Chapter 12 Information Systems and System Development 486

Overview 487

What Is an Information System? 487

Who Uses Information Systems? 488

> Executive Management 489
> Middle Management 489
> Operational Management 489
> Nonmanagement Workers 489

Types of Information Systems 489

> Office Systems 491
> Transaction Processing Systems 492
> Management Information Systems (MISs) 495
> Decision Support Systems (DSSs) 495
> Geographic Information Systems (GISs) 496
> Enterprise-Wide and Inter-Enterprise Systems 496
> Design and Manufacturing Systems 501
> Artificial Intelligence Systems 502

Responsibility for System Development 508

> The Information Systems Department 508
> Outsourcing Companies 510

The System Development Life Cycle (SDLC) 511

> Preliminary Investigation 512
> System Analysis 513
> System Design 515
> System Acquisition 516

> System Implementation 518
> System Maintenance 520
Approaches to System Development 520
> The Traditional Approach 520
> Prototyping 521
> End-User Development 521
Summary 522
Review Activities 524
Projects 526
Web Activities 529

TECHNOLOGY AND YOU Laundry Room and Roller Coaster Information Systems 490
TREND Fingerprint Payment Systems 493
HOW IT WORKS UPS DIAD IV Delivery System 500
INSIDE THE INDUSTRY The Turing Test and Loebner Prize 502

Chapter 13 Program Development and Programming Languages 530
Overview 531
Approaches to Program Design and Development 531
> Structured Programming 531
> Object-Oriented Programming (OOP) 532
> Aspect-Oriented Programming (AOP) 533
The Program Development Life Cycle (PDLC) 534
> Problem Analysis 534
> Program Design 535
> Program Coding 542
> Program Debugging and Testing 545
> Program Implementation and Maintenance 550
Tools for Facilitating Program Development 551
> Application Lifecycle Management (ALM) Tools 551
> Application Generators 552
> Software-Asset Management Tools 553
> Device Software Development Tools 553
Programming Languages 553
> What Is a Programming Language? 554
> Categories of Programming Languages 554
> Popular Programming Languages 556
Summary 566
Review Activities 568
Projects 570
Web Activities 573

INSIDE THE INDUSTRY The Original Program “Bug” 546
HOW IT WORKS Visual Basic 561
TREND DVD Game Programming 563
TECHNOLOGY AND YOU Java-Based Systems for Personal Safety 564

Chapter 14 Databases and Database Management Systems 574
Overview 575
What Is a Database? 575
> Relational Databases: A Simple Example 576
> Individuals Involved with a Database Management System 578

> The Evolution of Databases 578
> Advantages and Disadvantages of the Database Approach 579
Data Concepts and Characteristics 581
> Data Hierarchy 581
> Entity Relationships 581
> Data Definition 582
> The Data Dictionary 584
> Data Integrity, Security, and Privacy 584
> Data Organization 588
Database Classifications 589
> Single-User vs. Multiuser Database Systems 589
> Client-Server Database Systems 590
> N-Tier Database Systems 590
> Centralized vs. Distributed Database Systems 591
> In-Memory Databases 591
Database Models 591
> The Hierarchical and Network Database Models 593
> The Relational Database Model 593
> The Object-Oriented Database Model 599
> Multidimensional Databases 601
Databases and the Web 601
> Examples of Web Databases in Use 601
> How Web Databases Work 605
Summary 606
Review Activities 608
Projects 610
Web Activities 613

INSIDE THE INDUSTRY File Management Systems 580
TECHNOLOGY AND YOU Databases and College Portals 587
TREND Innovative New Search Possibilities 602
HOW IT WORKS Web-Based Customer Service and Package Tracking 604

Expert Insight on Systems 614

MODULE Computers and Society 616
Chapter 15 Computer Security and Privacy 618
Overview 619
Why Be Concerned About Computer Security? 619
Hardware Loss, Damage, and System Failure 620
> Hardware Loss 620
> Hardware Damage 620
> System Failure and Other Disasters 620
> Protecting Against Hardware Loss, Damage, and System Failure 621
Software Piracy and Digital Counterfeiting 627
> Software Piracy 627
> Digital Counterfeiting 628

> Protecting Against Software Piracy and Digital Counterfeiting 629
Why Be Concerned About Information Privacy? 630
Databases, Electronic Profiling, Spam, and Other Marketing Activities 631
> Databases and Electronic Profiling 631
> Spam and Other Marketing Activities 634
> Protecting the Privacy of Personal Information 636
Electronic Surveillance and Monitoring 640
> Computer Monitoring Software 640
> Video Surveillance 641
> Employee Monitoring 643
> Presence Technology 646
> Protecting Personal and Workplace Privacy 647
Computer Security and Privacy Legislation 648
Summary 650
Review Activities 652
Projects 654
Web Activities 657

TECHNOLOGY AND YOU E-Voting 622
HOW IT WORKS Protecting Your PC 626
TREND Digital Health Records 632
INSIDE THE INDUSTRY High-Tech Border Control 644

Chapter 16 Intellectual Property Rights, Ethics, Health, Access, and the Environment 658
Overview 659
Intellectual Property Rights 659
> Copyrights 659
> Trademarks 661
> Patents 662
Ethics 663
> Ethical Use of Copyrighted Material 664
> Ethical Use of Resources and Information 666
> Computer Hoaxes and Digital Manipulation 669
> Ethical Business Practices and Decision Making 671
Computers and Health 675
> Physical Health 675
> Emotional Health 679
Access to Technology 682
> The Digital Divide 683
> Assistive Technology 686
Environmental Concerns 689
> Green Computing 689
> Recycling and Disposal of Computing Equipment 690
Related Legislation 693
Summary 694
Review Activities 696
Projects 698
Web Activities 701

HOW IT WORKS Digital Rights Management 660
TECHNOLOGY AND YOU E-Mail Hoaxes 671
TREND Digital Implants 688
INSIDE THE INDUSTRY Digital Republishing 691

Expert Insight on Computers and Society 702

2007 Update

Introduction U-1

MODULE Introduction
Chapter 1
Introduction to the World of Computers U-2

MODULE Hardware
Chapter 2
The System Unit: Processing and Memory U-4
Chapter 3
Storage U-6
Chapter 4
Input and Output U-8

MODULE Software
Chapter 5
System Software: Operating Systems and Utilities U-10
Chapter 6
Application Software U-12

MODULE Networks and the Internet
Chapter 7
Computer Networks U-14
Chapter 8
The Internet and World Wide Web U-16
Chapter 9
Network and Internet Security U-18

MODULE Web Applications
Chapter 10
Multimedia and the Web U-20
Chapter 11
E-Commerce U-22

MODULE Systems
Chapter 12
Information Systems and System Development U-24
Chapter 13
Program Development and Programming Languages U-26
Chapter 14
Databases and Database Management Systems U-28

MODULE Computers and Society
Chapter 15
Computer Security and Privacy U-30
Chapter 16
Intellectual Property Rights, Ethics, Health, Access, and the Environment U-32
Windows Vista and You U-36
Tech News Video Projects U-39

Expert Insight on Windows Vista U-34

References and Resources Guide R-1
Computer History Timeline R-2
Coding Charts R-8
> ASCII and EBCDIC R-8
> Unicode R-9
Guide to Buying a PC R-10
> Analyzing Needs R-10
> Listing Alternatives R-11
> System Troubleshooting and Upgrading R-13
E-Mail Fundamentals R-15
> Sending E-Mail R-15
> Receiving E-Mail R-15
> Managing E-Mail R-15
Answers to Self-Quiz R-17

Credits C-1

Glossary/Index I-1

11th Edition

UNDERSTANDING COMPUTERS:

TODAY AND TOMORROW

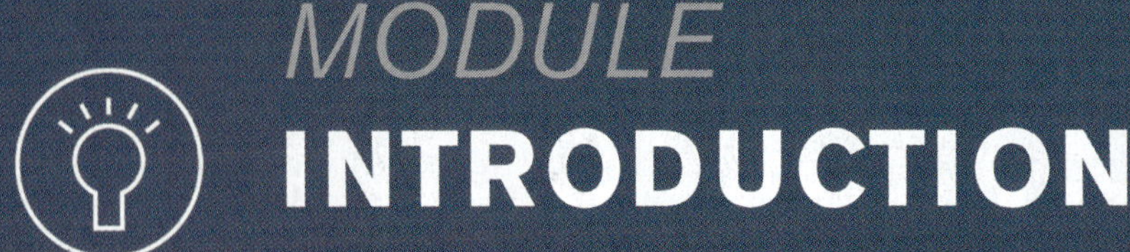

MODULE INTRODUCTION

We live in an age of computers. People today use computers to pay bills, shop, manage investments, communicate with others, prepare taxes, play games, research products, download and listen to music, make travel arrangements, check current news and weather, look up phone numbers, map locations, modify and print digital photos, and perform other important daily tasks. Businesses, government agencies, and other organizations use computers and related technologies to facilitate day-to-day transactions, provide better services to customers, and assist managers in making good decisions. Because they are so embedded in our society today, it is essential to know something about computers and what they can do.

This module introduces you to computers and some of their uses. Chapter 1 helps you to understand what computers are, how they work, and how people use them. In addition, Chapter 1 presents important terms and concepts that you will encounter throughout this text and in discussions about computers with others. It also includes a brief look at how to use a computer to perform basic tasks and to access resources on the Internet and the World Wide Web.

“. . . today we are a digital society. Mobile devices will transform the society further and our life will be increasingly mobile. Students today should embrace mobility . . .”

For more comments from Guest Expert Vipul Mehrotra of Nokia North America, see the Expert Insight on . . . Personal Computers feature at the end of the module.

IN THIS MODULE

Chapter 1 Introduction to the World of Computers 4

Overview 5

Computers in Your Life 6

What Is a Computer and What Does It Do? 11

Computers to Fit Every Need 20

Computer Networks and the Internet 30

Computers and Society 38

1 CHAPTER Introduction to the World of Computers

OUTLINE

- Overview
- Computers in Your Life
  - Why Learn About Computers?
  - Computers in the Home
  - Computers in Education
  - Computers in the Workplace
  - Computers on the Go
- What Is a Computer and What Does It Do?
  - Data vs. Information
  - Computers Then and Now
  - Hardware
  - Software
  - Computer Users and Professionals
- Computers to Fit Every Need
  - Mobile Devices
  - Personal Computers
  - Midrange Servers
  - Mainframe Computers
  - Supercomputers
- Computer Networks and the Internet
  - What Are the Internet and the World Wide Web?
  - Accessing a Network or the Internet
  - Surfing the Web
  - Searching the Web
  - E-Mail
- Computers and Society
  - Benefits of a Computer-Oriented Society
  - Risks of a Computer-Oriented Society
  - Differences in Online Communications
  - The Anonymity Factor
  - Information Integrity

LEARNING OBJECTIVES

After completing this chapter, you will be able to:

1. Explain why it is essential to learn about computers [illegible] and discuss several ways computers are integrated into our business and personal lives.
2. Define a computer and describe its primary operations.
3. List some important milestones in computer evolution.
4. Identify the major parts of a personal computer, including input, processing, output, storage, and communications hardware.
5. Define software and understand how it is used to instruct the computer what to do.
6. List the five basic types of computers, giving at least one example of each type of computer and stating what that computer might be used for.
7. Explain what a network, the Internet, and the World Wide Web are, as well as how computers, people, and Web pages are identified on the Internet.
8. Describe how to access a Web page.
9. Discuss the societal impact of computers, including some benefits and risks related to their prominence in our society.

OVERVIEW

Computers and other forms of technology impact our lives daily. We encounter computers in stores, restaurants, and other retail establishments. We use computers and the Internet regularly to obtain information, listen to music and experience other types of online entertainment, buy products and services, and communicate with others. Many of us carry a computer, cell phone, or other electronic device with us at all times so we can remain in touch with others on a continual basis and access Internet information as we need it. It is even becoming more common to use these portable devices to pay for purchases, play online games with others, watch TV and movies, and much, much more. Businesses use computers to keep track of bank transactions, inventories, sales, and credit card purchases; control robots and other machines in factories; and provide business executives with the up-to-date information they need to make decisions. The government uses computers to control the satellites that are crucial to our nation's defense and that are used to send people and equipment into space. In addition to the *general-purpose computers* used by individuals, there are special-purpose, *embedded computers* found in watches, televisions, telephones, game set-top boxes, kitchen appliances, exercise equipment, cars, and scores of other everyday devices. In short, computers and computing technology are used in an endless number of ways.

Fifty years ago, computers were used primarily by researchers and scientists. Today, computers are an integral part of our lives. Experts call this trend *pervasive computing*, in which few aspects of daily life remain untouched by computers and computing technology. With pervasive computing—also referred to as *ubiquitous computing*—computers are found virtually everywhere. Embedded computing technology is integrated into scores of devices to give those devices additional functions or to enable them to communicate with other devices on an on-going basis. Because of the prominence of computers in our society, it is important to understand what a computer is, a little about how a computer works, and the implications of living in a computer-oriented society.

Understanding Computers: Today and Tomorrow is a guide to computers and related technology. It will provide you with a comprehensive introduction to computer concepts and terminology and give you a solid foundation for future study. It will also provide you with the basic knowledge you need to understand and use computers in school, on the job, and in your personal life.

Chapter 1 is designed to help you understand what computers are, how they work, and how people use them. It introduces the important terms and concepts that you will encounter throughout this text and in discussions about computers with others, as well as provides an overview of the history of computers. It gives an explanation of the various categories of computers that today's users may encounter, as well as takes a brief look at how to use a computer to perform basic tasks and to access resources on the Internet and the World Wide Web. The chapter closes with a look at the societal impact of computers. Most of the computer concepts introduced in this chapter are discussed in more detail in subsequent chapters of this text, but Chapter 1 is intended to give you an overall understanding of what a computer is and the knowledge, skills, and tools necessary to use a computer and the World Wide Web to complete the projects and online activities that accompany this textbook. ■

COMPUTERS IN YOUR LIFE

Why Learn About Computers?

Prior to about 1980, computers were large and expensive, and few people had access to them. Most computers used in organizations were equipped to do little more than carry out high-volume paperwork processing, such as issuing bills and keeping track of product inventories. The average person did not need to know how to use a computer for his or her job, and it was uncommon to have a computer at home. Furthermore, the use of computers generally required a lot of technical knowledge. Because there were so few good reasons or opportunities for learning how to use computers, the average working person was unfamiliar with them.

Suddenly, in the early 1980s, things began to change. *Microcomputers*—inexpensive personal computers that you will read about later in this chapter—were invented and computer use increased dramatically. Today, more than 60% of all U.S. households include a personal computer, and most individuals use a computer of some sort or another on the job. Whether you become a teacher, attorney, doctor, salesperson, professional athlete, musician, artist, manager, executive, or skilled tradesperson, you will likely use a computer to obtain and evaluate information and to communicate with others. Today's computers, with their almost dizzying speeds and high levels of accuracy and reliability, are very useful tools for these purposes; they are also continually taking on new roles in our society, such as providing a means of entertainment and facilitating the tasks we need to accomplish in day-to-day life. In fact, computers and traditional devices we use everyday—such as the telephone, television, stereo, and music player—have begun to *converge* into single units with multiple capabilities. As a result of this *convergence* trend, the computer has moved beyond being primarily a productivity tool into a personal entertainment and communications hub that can be used to help individuals obtain information from the Internet, organize and access multimedia content, communicate with others, and more (see Figure 1-1).

FIGURE 1-1

Convergence. Today's computers typically take on the role of multiple devices.

HANDHELD DEVICES
Typically include the functions of a telephone, organizer, music player, gaming device, Web browser, and digital camera.

HOME COMPUTERS
Can often be used as a telephone, television, and stereo system, in addition to their regular computing functions.

Just as you can learn to drive a car without knowing much about car engines, you can learn to use a computer without understanding the technical details of how a computer works. However, a little knowledge gives you a big advantage. Knowing something about cars can help you to make wise purchases and save money on repairs. Likewise, knowing something about computers can help you buy the right one for your needs, get the most efficient use out of it, and have a much higher level of comfort and confidence along the way. Therefore, basic **computer literacy**—knowing about and understanding computers and their uses—is an essential skill today for everyone. The next few sections illustrate how computers are currently used in the home, at school, in the workplace, and while you are on the go.

>**Computer literacy.** The knowledge and understanding of basic computer fundamentals.

Computers in the Home

Home computing has increased dramatically over the last few years as computers and Internet access have become less expensive and an increasing number of computer-related consumer activities have become available. Use of the Internet at home to look up information, exchange *e-mail* (electronic messages), shop, download music and movies, research products, pay bills and manage bank accounts, check news and weather, store and organize digital photos, play games, plan vacations, and so forth has grown at an astounding pace. Home computing for work purposes is also increasing rapidly. Checking office e-mail from home or otherwise working at home in the evening is normal for many jobs. Working entirely from home, such as *telecommuting* for a company or working from home as a consultant or other self-employed individual, is more acceptable today as a result of fast Internet access and the wide use of e-mail, telephone calls, teleconferencing, and videoconferencing for business communications. Wireless networking connections have added to the convenience of home computing, allowing the use of computers in places other than traditional locations, such as a home office. For instance, e-mail can be answered from the backyard or living room, recipes can be looked up in the kitchen, games can be played on the patio, and so forth (see Figure 1-2).

Computing technologies also make it possible to have *smart appliances*—traditional appliances with some type of built-in computer or communications technology. For instance, the smart oven shown in Figure 1-2 both refrigerates and cooks and can be controlled by the user via a telephone or the Internet. *Smart homes*—in which household tasks (such as watering the lawn, turning the air conditioning on or off, making coffee, monitoring the security of the home and grounds, and managing Internet access and home entertainment devices) are controlled by a main computer in the home—are also becoming closer to reality.

Computers in Education

Today's youths could definitely be called the *computing generation*. Baby boomers may have been introduced to computers at college or on the job, and older Americans may never have used a computer until after retirement, if at all, but many of today's young people have been brought up with computing technology. From video games to computers at school and home,

REFERENCE, EDUCATION, AND COMMUNICATIONS
Many individuals today have access to the Internet at home; retrieving information, playing online games, and exchanging e-mail are popular home computer activities.

ENTERTAINMENT AND SHOPPING
Computers and the Internet offer a host of entertainment and online shopping activities.

DIGITAL MEDIA DELIVERY
Computers are becoming a central hub for delivering digital media (such as digital photos, downloaded music, and recorded TV shows) to home entertainment systems.

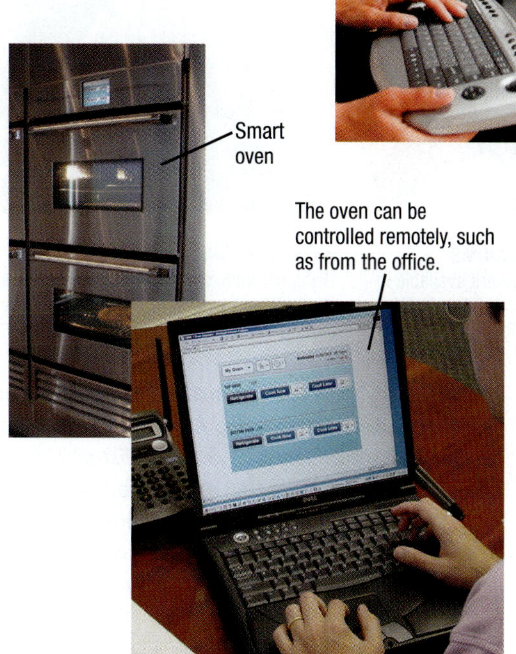

Smart oven

The oven can be controlled remotely, such as from the office.

SMART APPLIANCES
Smart appliances (such as the smart oven shown here that is controlled via a telephone or the Internet) are regular appliances with some type of built-in computer technology.

FIGURE 1-2
Computer use at home.

most children and teens today have been exposed to computers and related technology all their lives. Although the amount of computer use varies from school to school, students in elementary and secondary schools typically have access to computers either in the classroom or in a computer lab, and virtually all colleges have some sort of computing facility available for student use.

With the increased availability of computers and Internet access, the emphasis on computer use in K–12 schools has evolved from straight drill-and-practice programs to using the computer as an overall student-based learning tool. Today, students use multimedia programs to enhance learning; productivity software—such as *word processors* and *presentation software*—for creating papers and electronic presentations; and the Internet for research. K–12 teachers also typically use computers for a variety of tasks, such as creating lesson plans, researching topics, and submitting daily attendance reports and other required school information.

At colleges and universities, computer use is typically much more integrated into daily classroom life than in K–12 schools. Computers are commonly found in classrooms (see Figure 1-3), computer labs, dorms, and libraries. A growing number of college campuses have *wireless hotspots* on campus that allow students to use their PCs to connect wirelessly to the college network and the Internet from anywhere on campus. College students today are typically expected to use the Internet for research, as well as to use computers to prepare papers and classroom presentations and to access online course materials. In fact, some institutions require a computer for enrollment. For a look at how handheld computers are being used by medical school students, see the Technology and You box.

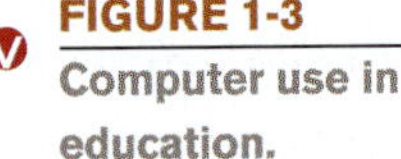

FIGURE 1-3
Computer use in education.

COMPUTER LABS AND CLASSROOMS
Many schools today have computers available in a lab or the library, as well as computers or Internet connections in classrooms for student use.

PRESENTATIONS
Using computers and projection equipment, both students and teachers can deliver effective classroom presentations.

DISTANCE LEARNING
With distance learning, students—such as this U.S. Marine—can take classes from home or wherever they happen to be at the moment.

Most college instructors use computers to prepare handouts and exams, to prepare and deliver classroom presentations and lectures, and to create and maintain course Web pages. Many colleges also offer *distance learning*—a common alternative to traditional classroom learning that allows students to participate from their current location (via their computers and Internet connections) instead of physically going to the educational institution. Distance learning students can do coursework and participate in class discussions from home, work, or wherever they happen to be at the moment. Consequently, distance learning gives students greater flexibility to schedule class time around their personal, family, and work commitments. Distance learning also allows students, such as individuals located in very rural areas or stationed at military posts overseas, to take courses when they are not able to physically attend classes.

Computers in the Workplace

Although computers have been used in the workplace for years, their role is continually evolving. Originally used as a research tool for computer experts and scientists, and then as a productivity tool for office workers, the computer is used today by all types of employees

TECHNOLOGY AND YOU

Wired Med Students

From Stanford University to the University of Florida to the University of Cambridge, medical students are going high-tech. Although some medical schools strongly recommend that their med students acquire a handheld PC, many now require their use—particularly for third- and fourth-year students. Handheld PCs are also beginning to be required for students in dental, nursing, and pharmacological programs.

Medical students today commonly use handheld PCs to access class-specific materials, medical dictionaries, and drug databases; view high-resolution digital images, such as X-rays and microscope images; and communicate with classmates and instructors. If the hospital system supports it, medical residents can also view and update patient files, and physicians can access any patient's record at any time—a convenience, as well as an immense time-saver. For example, one family practice center in Oregon that supplied handheld PCs to its physicians and residents for patient data access found that the time required for reviewing charts, lab results, and other data dropped from 6.3 hours per week to 2.7 hours per week per physician—less than half the time it took before.

Although a little slow to embrace handheld PCs in the past, the medical community is quickly catching up. New useful medical applications designed for handheld PCs—such as those that perform medical calculations or allow physicians to quickly look up drug dosages and possible interactions—are rapidly changing the practice of medicine. When doing rounds in the hospital, chart information can be entered into the handheld PC and, assuming the handheld PC is connected to a wireless network, this information can be transferred automatically to the main computer systems for the hospital and the physician's office. Handheld PCs can also be used to send prescriptions electronically to the appropriate pharmacy. In addition to reducing errors—a Harvard study found that using electronic prescriptions reduced errors by 55 percent—electronic prescriptions also allow the patient records to be checked automatically for drug allergies, potential problems with other medicine the patient is currently taking, and other important concerns. For closer monitoring of critical hospital patients, some hospitals use electronic monitors to transmit clinical data—such as heart rate, respiration, blood pressure, and even photographs of the patient—to the attending physician via his or her handheld PC on a continual basis. For example, Miami Children's Hospital uses Palm PCs and a continuous monitoring system to allow physicians to check on children before and after surgery at any time of the day or night. PDAs are also being used to fulfill the continuing education required of all physicians, allowing them to take online courses via their handheld PCs.

Despite the late start, handheld use in the medical community has now passed that of the general population. According to Forrester Research and the American Medical Association, well over half of all physicians own handheld PCs. While some physicians and hospitals use tablet PCs instead, the ability to carry a handheld PC in a lab coat pocket is a big advantage. This portability factor, along with the trend of medical schools and hospitals requiring handheld PC use, points to increased growth in this area. Thanks to handheld PCs and prescription software, even one of the oldest standing doctor jokes—illegible handwriting—may soon become irrelevant.

in all types of businesses—from the CEO of a multinational corporation, to the check-out clerk at the grocery store, to the traveling sales professional, to the police officer on patrol, to the insurance adjuster in the field, to the doctors and nurses at the local hospital, to the auto mechanic at the local garage. In essence, the computer has become a universal tool for on-the-job decision making, productivity, and communications (see Figure 1-4).

One of the fastest growing new uses for workplace computing is in the service industry, in which service professionals—such as food servers, repair technicians, and delivery people—use portable computers to record and process customer orders (a technique referred to as *linebusting*), as well as to capture customer signatures for purchases, deliveries, and other provided services. Some computers are even small enough to be embedded in clothing or worn on the body. For instance, *wearable PCs* available today

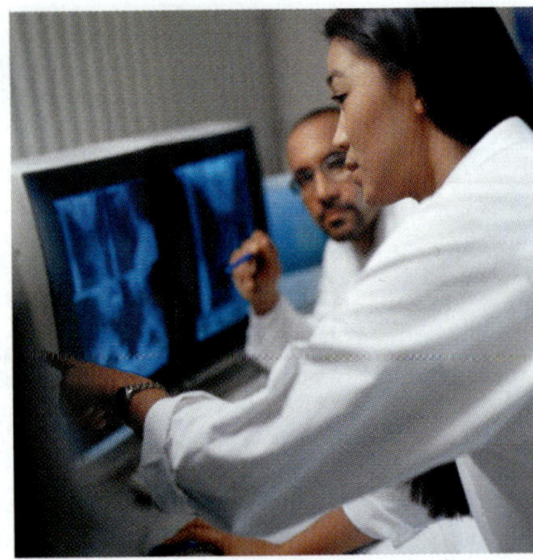

PRODUCTIVITY AND DECISION MAKING
Many individuals today use a computer at work to perform on-the-job tasks efficiently and accurately, as well as to help them evaluate alternatives and make decisions.

CUSTOMER SERVICE
Service professionals frequently use computers to process orders and store customer signature authorizations.

COMMUNICATIONS
Handheld or wearable computers are used by employees who need to record data or access remote data when they are out of the office.

FIGURE 1-4
Computer use in the workplace.

are small enough to be worn on a belt (see the rightmost photo in Figure 1-4) and can use a *microdisplay*—a tiny display screen often fitted into glasses or goggles—to display images close to the eye to simulate viewing images on a large monitor. Wearable PCs are currently used by employees in a variety of industries, such as warehouse and construction workers, police and fire personnel, delivery and other types of service workers, doctors and nurses, and telephone repair personnel.

Computers are also used extensively by military personnel for communications and navigational purposes, as well as to control missiles and other weapons, identify terrorists and other potential enemies, and perform other necessary tasks. To update their computer skills, when needed, employees in all lines of work today may take computer training classes or enroll in computer certification programs.

FURTHER EXPLORATION

For links to information about computer certification programs, go to www.course.com/uc11/ch01

Computers on the Go

In addition to using computers in the home, at school, and in the workplace, most people encounter and use all types of computers in other aspects of day-to-day life—from depositing or withdrawing money at an ATM machine, to using an ID card to gain access to a local gym, to using a *smart card* or other device to pay for gas or parking, to using a portable *global positioning system* (*GPS*) for navigation while traveling or hiking. As they become more integrated into our society, computers are becoming easier to use. For example, electronic *kiosks*—small self-service computer-based stations providing information or other services to the public—usually include a screen that is touched with the finger to select options and request information. Kiosks are commonly placed in hotels, conference centers, retail stores, and other public locations to allow consumers to look up information or purchase products. Some kiosks allow individuals to copy color photographs or print photos taken with a *digital camera*; others enable individuals to check themselves out at a retail store, or print a ticket or boarding pass at the airport (see Figure 1-5).

For Internet access while on the go, computers and *Wi-Fi hotspots* (Internet access points that enable consumers to connect wirelessly to the Internet using their portable computers) are being installed increasingly in a wide variety of public locations, such as libraries, airports, health clubs, coffeehouses, hotels, taxis, parks, restaurants, and *Internet cafés*. Some of these locations charge for access; others offer free access as a courtesy to customers, such as the unlimited access some hotels offer guests or the free access some McDonald's locations offer customers making a minimum purchase. It is also becoming increasingly common for individuals to carry Web-enabled cell phones, handheld computers, or similar portable devices to remain electronically in touch with others and to obtain stock quotes, driving directions, airline flight updates, movie times, and other needed information while on the go via their cellular providers.

WHAT IS A COMPUTER AND WHAT DOES IT DO?

A **computer** can be defined as a programmable, electronic device that accepts data, performs operations on that data, presents the results, and can store the data or results as needed. Being *programmable*, a computer will do whatever the instructions—called the *program*—tell it to do. The programs being used with a computer determine the tasks the computer is able to perform.

The four operations described in this definition are more technically referred to as *input*, *processing*, *output*, and *storage*. These four primary operations of a computer can be defined as follows:

- **Input**—entering data into the computer.
- **Processing**—performing operations on the data.
- **Output**—presenting the results.
- **Storage**—saving data, programs, or output for future use.

PORTABLE COMPUTERS
Many people today carry a portable PC with them at all times or when they travel in order to remain in touch with others and Internet resources.

SELF-SERVICE KIOSKS
Electronic kiosks are widely available to view conference or gift registry information, print photographs, order products or services, facilitate self check-in and check-out, and more.

GPS APPLICATIONS
Computers and handheld devices with built-in GPS capabilities can be used for navigational purposes, such as to show users their exact geographical location or to plan the most efficient route to a destination.

HOTELS AND COFFEEHOUSES
Many hotels and restaurants offer free or fee-based Internet access to their customers, either via installed computers or wireless access (as in the Athens location shown here).

FIGURE 1-5
Computer use while on the go.

For example, let's assume that we have a computer that has been programmed to add two numbers. As shown in Figure 1-6, *input* occurs when data (in this example, the numbers 2 and 5) is entered into the computer; *processing* takes place when the computer program adds those two numbers; and *output* happens when the sum of 7 is displayed on the monitor. The *storage* operation occurs any time the data, program, or output is saved for future use.

For an additional example, let's look at a supermarket barcode reader to see how it fits this definition of a computer. First, the grocery item being purchased is passed over the barcode reader—*input*. Next, the description and price of the item are looked up—*processing*. Finally, the item description and price are displayed on the cash register and printed on the receipt—*output*—and the inventory, ordering, and sales records are updated—*storage*.

This progression of input, processing, output, and storage is sometimes referred to as the *IPOS cycle* or the *information processing cycle*. In addition to these four primary computer operations, today's computers typically also perform *communications* functions,

>**Computer.** A programmable, electronic device that accepts data input, performs processing operations on that data, and outputs and stores the results. >**Input.** The process of entering data into a computer; can also refer to the data itself. >**Processing.** Performing operations on data that has been input into a computer to convert that input to output. >**Output.** The process of presenting the results of processing; can also refer to the results themselves. >**Storage.** The operation of saving data, programs, or output for future use.

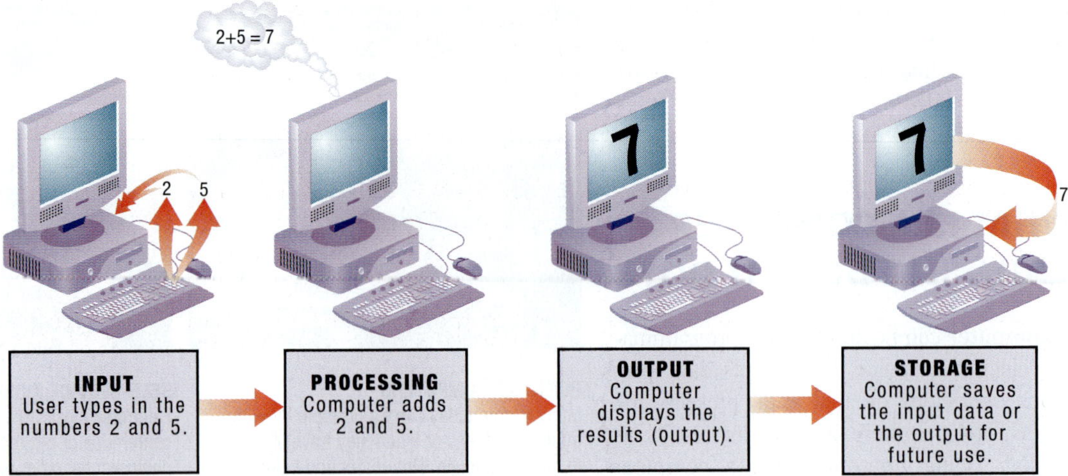

FIGURE 1-6
The information processing cycle.

such as retrieving data via the Internet, updating information located in a shared company database, or exchanging e-mail messages. Therefore, **communications**—technically an input or output operation, depending on which direction the information is going—is increasingly considered the fifth primary computer operation.

Data vs. Information

As just discussed, a user inputs **data** into a computer, and then the computer processes it. Almost any kind of fact or set of facts can become computer data—the words in a letter to a friend, the text and pictures in a book, the numbers in a monthly budget, a photograph, a song, or the facts stored in a set of employee records. Consequently, data can exist in many forms, such as to represent *text* (words consisting of standard alphabetic, numeric, and special characters), *graphics* (illustrations or photographs), *audio* (sound, such as music or voice), or *video* (live video or video clips). When data is processed into a meaningful form, it becomes **information**.

Information is frequently generated to answer some type of question. An individual might want to know, for example, how many of a firm's employees earn more than $100,000, how many seats are available on a particular flight from Los Angeles to San Francisco, or what Babe Ruth's home run total was during a particular baseball season. Of course, you don't need a computer system to process data into information. Anyone can go through an employee file and make a list of people earning a certain salary. By hand, however, this work would take a lot of time, especially for a company with thousands of employees. Computers, however, can perform such tasks almost instantly with accurate results.

Information processing (the conversion of data into information) is a vital activity today because the success of many businesses depends heavily on the wise use of information. Because better information often improves employee decisions and customer service, many companies today regard information as one of their most important assets and consider the creative use of information a key competitive strategy.

Computers Then and Now

The basic ideas of computing and calculating are very old, going back thousands of years. However, the computer in the form in which it is recognized today is a fairly recent invention.

>**Communications.** The transmission of data from one device to another. >**Data.** Raw, unorganized facts. >**Information.** Data that has been processed into a meaningful form.

In fact, personal computers have only been around since the late 1970s. The history of computers is often referred to in terms of *generations*, with each new generation characterized by a major technological development. The next sections summarize some early calculating devices and the different computer generations.

Precomputers and Early Computers (before approximately 1945)

Based on archeological finds, such as notched bones, knotted twine, and hieroglyphics, experts have concluded that ancient civilizations had the desire to count and compute. The *abacus* is considered by many to be the earliest recorded calculating device. Believed to have been invented by the Babylonians sometime between 500 B.C. and 100 B.C., the abacus and similar types of counting boards were used primarily as an aid for basic arithmetic calculations.

Other early computing devices include the *slide rule*, the *mechanical calculator*, and Dr. Herman Hollerith's *Punch Card Tabulating Machine and Sorter*. This device (see Figure 1-7) was the first electromechanical machine that could read *punched cards*—special cards with holes punched in them to represent data. In the first successful case of an information processing system replacing a paper-and-pen-based system, Hollerith's machine was used to process the 1890 U.S. Census data and was able to complete the task in two and a half years, instead of the decade it usually took to process the data by hand. Hollerith's company eventually became *International Business Machines* (*IBM*).

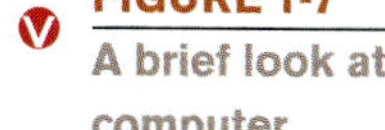

FIGURE 1-7
A brief look at computer generations.

PRECOMPUTERS AND EARLY COMPUTERS
Dr. Herman Hollerith's Punch Card Tabulating Machine and Sorter is an example of an early computing device. It was used to process the 1890 U.S. Census in about one-quarter of the time usually required to tally the results by hand.

FIRST-GENERATION COMPUTERS
First-generation computers, such as ENIAC shown here, were large, bulky, used vacuum tubes, and had to be physically wired and reset to run programs.

SECOND-GENERATION COMPUTERS
Second-generation computers, such as the IBM 1401 mainframe shown here, used transistors instead of vacuum tubes so they were physically smaller, faster, and more reliable than earlier first-generation computers.

THIRD-GENERATION COMPUTERS
The integrated circuit marked the beginning of the third generation of computers. These chips allowed the introduction of smaller computers, such as the DEC PDP-8 shown here, which was the first commercially successful minicomputer.

FOURTH-GENERATION COMPUTERS
Fourth-generation computers, such as the original IBM PC shown here, are based on microprocessors. Most of today's computers fall into this category.

First-Generation Computers (approximately 1946–1957)

The first computers were enormous, often taking up entire rooms. They were powered by thousands of *vacuum tubes*—glass tubes that look similar to large, cylindrical light bulbs—that needed replacing constantly, required a great deal of electricity, and generated a lot of heat. *First-generation computers* could solve only one problem at a time since they needed to be physically rewired with cables to be reprogrammed (see Figure 1-7), which typically took several days (sometimes even weeks) to complete and several more days to check before the computer could be used. Usually paper punched cards and paper tape were used for input, and output was printed on paper.

Two of the most significant examples of first-generation computers were *ENIAC* and *UNIVAC*. ENIAC, shown in Figure 1-7, was the world's first large-scale, general-purpose computer. Although it was not completed until

1946, ENIAC was developed during World War II to compute artillery-firing tables (the settings to be used when firing different weapons under various conditions) for the U.S. Army. Instead of the 40 hours required for a person to compute the optimal settings for a single set of conditions and a single gun using hand calculations, ENIAC could complete the same calculations in less than two minutes. UNIVAC, released in 1951, was initially built for the U.S. Census Bureau and was used to analyze votes in the 1952 U.S. presidential election. Interestingly, its correct prediction of an Eisenhower victory only 45 minutes after the polls closed was not publicly aired because the results were not trusted. Despite this initial mistrust of its capabilities, UNIVAC did go on to become the first computer to be mass produced for general commercial use.

TIP

For a more detailed timeline regarding the development of computers, see the "Computer History Timeline" located in the References and Resources Guide at the end of this book.

Second-Generation Computers (approximately 1958–1963)

The second generation of computers began when the *transistor*—a small device made of semiconductor material that acts like a switch to open or close electronic circuits—started to replace the vacuum tube. Transistors allowed *second-generation computers* to be physically smaller, more powerful, cheaper, more energy-efficient, and more reliable than first-generation computers. Typically, programs and data were input on punched cards and magnetic tape, output was on punched cards and paper printouts, and magnetic tape and disks were used for storage (see Figure 1-7). *Programming languages* (such as *FORTRAN* and *COBOL*) were also developed and implemented during this generation.

Third-Generation Computers (approximately 1964–1970)

The replacement of the transistor with *integrated circuits* (*ICs*) marked the beginning of the third generation of computers. Integrated circuits incorporate many transistors and electronic circuits on a single tiny silicon *chip*, allowing *third-generation computers* to be even smaller and more reliable than computers in the earlier computer generations. Instead of punched cards and paper printouts, keyboards and monitors were introduced for input and output; magnetic disks were typically used for storage. An example of a third-generation computer is shown in Figure 1-7.

Fourth-Generation Computers (approximately 1971–present)

A technological breakthrough in the early 1970s made it possible to place an increasing number of transistors on a single chip. This led to the invention of the *microprocessor* in 1971, which ushered in the fourth generation of computers. In essence, a microprocessor contains the core processing capabilities of an entire computer on one single chip. The original IBM PC (see Figure 1-7) and Apple Macintosh, and most of today's modern computers, fall into this category. *Fourth-generation computers* typically use a keyboard and mouse for input, a monitor and printer for output, and magnetic disks and optical discs for storage. This generation also witnessed the development of *computer networks*, *wireless technologies*, and the *Internet*.

FURTHER EXPLORATION

For links to further information about the history of computers, go to www.course.com/uc11/ch01

Fifth-Generation Computers (now and the future)

Although some people believe that the fifth generation of computers has not yet begun, most think it is in its infancy stage. *Fifth-generation computers* have no precise classification, since experts tend to disagree about the definition for this generation of computers. However, one common opinion is that fifth-generation computers will be based on *artificial intelligence*, allowing them to think, reason, and learn. Voice recognition will likely be a primary means of input, and computers may be constructed differently than they are today, such as in the form of *optical computers* that process data using light instead of electrons.

FIGURE 1-8
Typical computer hardware.

Hardware

The physical parts of a computer (the parts you can touch, as shown in Figure 1-8 and discussed next) are collectively referred to as **hardware**. The instructions or programs used with a computer—called *software*—are discussed in a later section.

Hardware components can be *internal* (located inside the main box or *system unit* of the computer) or *external* (located outside of the system unit). External hardware components typically plug into connectors called *ports* located on the exterior of the system unit. There are hardware devices associated with each of the five computer operations previously discussed (input, processing, output, storage, and communications), as summarized in Figure 1-9.

Input Devices

An *input device* is any piece of equipment that is used to input data into the computer. The most common input devices today are the *keyboard* and *mouse* (shown in Figure 1-8). Other possibilities include *scanners*, *touch screens*, *digital cameras*, *electronic pens*, *touch pads*, *fingerprint readers*, *joysticks*, and *microphones*. Input devices are discussed in more detail in Chapter 4.

>**Hardware.** The physical parts of a computer system, such as the keyboard, monitor, printer, and so forth.

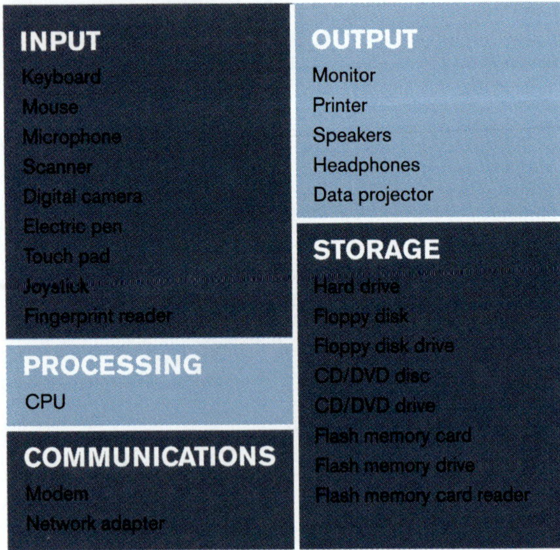

FIGURE 1-9 Common hardware listed by operation.

Processing Devices

The main *processing device* for a computer is the *central processing unit (CPU)*. The CPU is a chip located inside the system unit that performs the calculations and comparisons needed for processing; it also controls the computer's operations. For these reasons, the CPU is often considered the "brain" of the computer. Also involved in processing are various types of *memory*—additional chips located inside the system unit that the computer uses to temporarily store data and instructions while it is working with them. The CPU, memory, and processing are discussed in more detail in Chapter 2.

Output Devices

An *output device* accepts processed data from the computer and presents the results to the user, most of the time on the computer screen (*monitor*), on paper (via a *printer*), or though a *speaker*. Other possible output devices include *headphones* and *data projectors* (which project computer images onto a projection screen). Output devices are covered in more detail in Chapter 4.

Storage Devices

Storage devices are hardware used to store data on or access data from *storage media*, such as *floppy disks*, *CD discs*, *DVD discs*, or *flash memory cards*. The storage hardware featured in Figure 1-8 includes a *hard drive*, a *floppy disk drive*, a *DVD drive*, a *flash memory card reader*, floppy disks, CD discs, DVD discs, and flash memory cards. Storage devices are used to save data, programs, or output for future use and can either be installed inside the computer, attached to the computer as an external device, or accessed remotely through a network or wireless connection. Storage is discussed in more detail in Chapter 3.

Communications Devices

Communications devices allow users to communicate electronically with others and to access remote information via the Internet or a home, school, or company network. The two most common types of communications hardware are *modems* (used to connect a computer to the Internet) and *network adapters* (used to connect a computer to a computer network). A variety of modems and network adapters are available because there are different ways to connect to the Internet and computer networks, such as via telephone lines or a *cable*, *satellite*, *cellular network*, or *Wi-Fi* connection. Communications hardware and computer networks are discussed in more detail in Chapter 7.

Software

The term **software** refers to the programs or instructions used to tell the computer hardware what to do. Software is generally purchased on a CD or DVD or downloaded from the Internet. In either case, once the program has been obtained, it usually needs to be *installed* on a computer before it can be used. An alternative is running programs directly from the Internet without installing them on your computer. Instead, the programs are accessed via Web pages. Installing and using software programs is discussed in Chapters 5 and 6.

Computers use two basic types of software: *system software* and *application software*. The differences between these types of software are discussed next.

>**Software.** The instructions, also called computer programs, that are used to tell a computer what it should do.

INT

System Software

The programs that allow a computer to operate are collectively referred to as *system software*. The main system software program is the **operating system**, which starts up the computer and controls its operation. Common operating system tasks include setting up new hardware, allowing users to run other types of software, and allowing users to manage the documents stored on their computers. Without an operating system, a computer cannot function at all. Common operating systems are *Windows*, *Mac OS*, and *Linux*, which are all discussed in more detail in Chapter 5.

To begin to use a computer (assuming that the computer is already out of the box and the cables are correctly connected), the user first turns on the power by pressing the power button, and then the computer begins to **boot**. During the *boot process*, part of the computer's operating system is loaded into memory, the computer does a quick diagnostic on the computer, and then it launches any programs—such as an *antivirus* or *instant messaging* (*IM*) program—designated to run each time the PC starts up.

Once a computer has finished the boot process, it is ready to be used and waits for input from the user. The manner in which an operating system or any other type of program interacts with its users is known as its *user interface*. Older software programs used a text-based *command line interface*, which required the user to type precise instructions indicating exactly what the computers should do. Most programs today use a *graphical user interface* or *GUI* (pronounced "goo-ey"), which uses graphical objects (such as *icons* and *buttons*) that are selected with the mouse to tell the computer what to. For instance, the Windows **desktop** (the user's basic workspace—the place where documents, folders, programs, and other objects are displayed when they are being used) shown in Figure 1-10 contains the following objects.

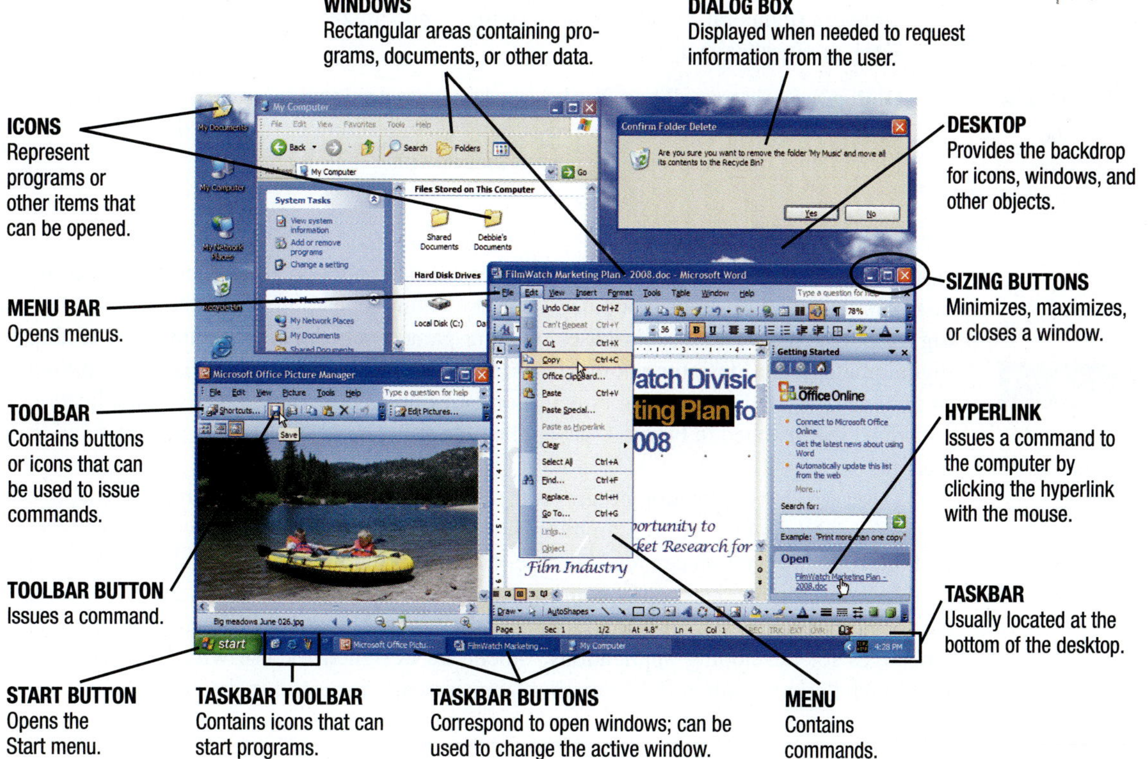

FIGURE 1-10
The Windows desktop. Icons, buttons, menus, and other objects can be used to issue commands to the computer.

>**Operating system.** A type of system software that enables a computer to operate and manage its resources and activities. >**Boot.** To start up a computer. >**Desktop.** The background work area displayed on the screen in Microsoft Windows.

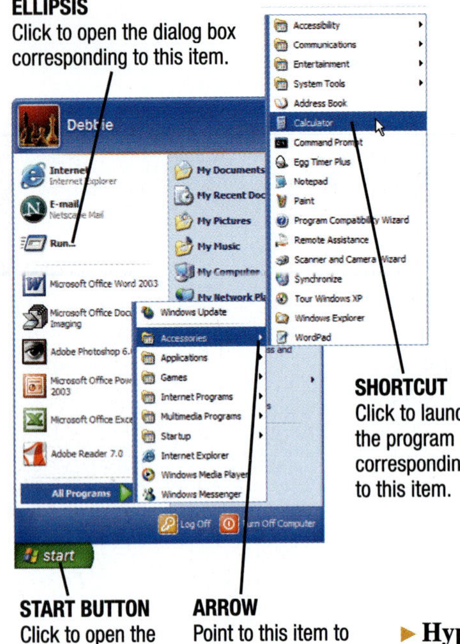

FIGURE 1-11
The Windows Start menu.

- **Windows**—rectangular areas in which programs, documents, and other content is displayed on the desktop.
- **Icons**—small pictures located on the desktop, a toolbar, or in a window that represent programs, documents, or other elements that can be opened.
- **Menus**—text-based lists that appear at the top of many windows and can be used to issue commands to that program. Items contained on a menu either display another, more specific, menu; open a dialog box to prompt the user for more information; turn a feature on or off; or execute a command.
- **Toolbars**—sets of icons or buttons, called *toolbar buttons*, that can be clicked with the mouse to issue commands, such as printing or saving a document.
- **Taskbar**—a bar located along the bottom of the desktop which houses the *Start button* at the left edge (used to open the *Start menu*—shown in Figure 1-11—which is used to launch programs), *taskbar toolbar* and *taskbar buttons* in the center (used to launch programs and switch between open windows), and a clock and other indicators in the *system tray* at the far right edge.
- **Hyperlinks**—text or images (located on the desktop, a Web page, or a program option) that are clicked to display more information; hyperlinks found on Web pages are discussed in more detail later in this chapter.
- **Sizing buttons**—small buttons located at the top-right corner of each window that are used to resize the window, such as to *maximize* (enlarge as big as possible), *minimize* (temporarily hide), *restore* (return a maximized window to its previous size), or *close* (exit) it.
- **Dialog boxes**—a small box displayed whenever additional input is needed from the user, such as to specify the desired options when printing or saving a document. Menu items with ellipses (. . .) next to them display dialog boxes.

TIP

Point to the clock located in the system tray at the right edge of the Windows taskbar to see the current date; double-click it to view a calendar or to adjust the date or time.

TIP

Taskbar buttons can also be used to minimize, maximize, restore, or close windows. Right-click a taskbar button to see the available options.

Application Software

Application software consists of programs designed to allow people to perform specific tasks or applications using a computer, such as creating letters, preparing budgets, managing inventory and customer databases, playing games, scheduling appointments, editing digital photographs, designing homes, making travel plans, viewing Web pages, recording or playing CDs, and exchanging e-mail. Some examples of common types of application software are illustrated in Figure 1-12; application software is discussed in greater detail in Chapter 6.

There are also application programs that help users write their own programs using a *programming language*. A programming language is a set of commands written in a form that the computer system can read and use, once the program is written and prepared correctly. Programming languages come in many varieties—for example, *BASIC*, *Visual Basic*, *Pascal*, *COBOL*, *C++*, and *Java*. Some languages are traditional programming languages for developing applications; others are designed for use with Web pages or multimedia programming. Programming languages are discussed in detail in Chapter 13.

>Window. A rectangular area in which programs, documents, and other content are displayed. **>Icon.** A small graphical image that invokes some action when selected. **>Menu.** A set of options (usually text-based) used to issue commands to the computer. **>Toolbar.** A set of icons used to issue commands to the computer. **>Taskbar.** The bar located at the bottom of the Windows desktop that contains the Start button, task buttons, and the system tray. **>Hyperlink.** Text or an image that is linked to a Web page or other type of document. **>Sizing button.** Small buttons located at the top-right corner of a window used to resize the window. **>Dialog box.** A window that requires the user to supply additional information. **>Application software.** Programs that enable users to perform specific tasks on a computer, such as writing a letter or playing a game.

FIGURE 1-12

Application software. Application software can help individuals work more productively at their jobs, as well as provide entertainment.

Computer Users and Professionals

In addition to hardware, software, data, and *procedures* (the predetermined steps to be carried out in particular situations), a computer system includes people. The people involved in a computer system include both the people who make the computers work and those who use them.

Computer users, or *end users*, are the people who use a computer to obtain information. Anyone who uses a computer is a computer user, including an accountant electronically preparing a client's taxes, an office worker using a word processing program to create a letter, a shop-floor supervisor using a computer to check and see whether workers have met the

>**Computer user.** A person who uses a computer.

day's quotas, a college student analyzing science lab data, a child playing a computer game, and a person bidding at an *online auction* over the Internet.

Programmers, on the other hand, are computer professionals whose primary job responsibility is to write the programs that computers use. Although some computer users may do small amounts of programming to customize the software on their desktop computers, the distinction between a computer user and a programmer is based on the work that the person has been hired to do. In addition to programmers, organizations may employ other *computer professionals*. For instance, *systems analysts* design computer systems to be used within their companies. *Computer operations personnel*, in contrast, are responsible for the day-to-day operations of large computer systems. Computer operations personnel are also often employed to help train users or assist them with their desktop computers and to troubleshoot user-related problems. Computer professionals and computer careers are discussed in more detail in Chapter 12.

COMPUTERS TO FIT EVERY NEED

The types of computers available today vary widely from the pocket-sized computers that do a limited number of computing tasks, to the powerful and versatile *desktop computers* and *portable PCs* found in homes and businesses, to the superpowerful computers used to control the country's defense systems. Computers are generally classified in one of five categories, based on size, capability, and price.

- *Mobile devices*—cellular phones and other communications devices with computer or Internet capabilities.
- *Personal computers*—conventional *desktop*, *notebook*, *tablet*, and *handheld computers*.
- *Midrange servers*—computers that host data and programs available to a small group of users.
- *Mainframe computers*—powerful computers used to host a large amount of data and programs available to a wide group of users.
- *Supercomputers*—extremely powerful computers used for complex computations and processing.

In practice, classifying a computer into one of these five categories is not always easy or straightforward. For example, some high-end personal computers are as powerful as midrange servers, and some personal computers today are nearly as small as a Web-enabled cell phone or other mobile device. In addition, technology changes too fast to have precisely defined categories. Nevertheless, these five categories are commonly used to refer to groups of computers designed for similar purposes.

FIGURE 1-13
Mobile devices.

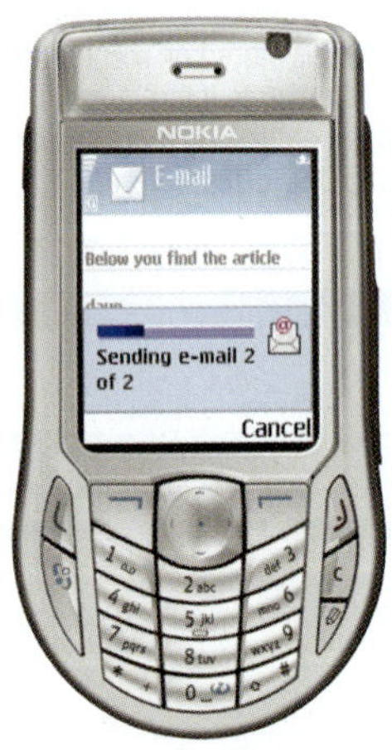

SMART PHONE

SMART WATCH

Mobile Devices

A **mobile device** (see Figure 1-13) is loosely defined as a very small device that has some built-in computing or Internet capability. Mobile devices today are typically based on cellular phones; these devices are often referred to as *smart phones*. Smart phones can be used to access the Web and e-mail wirelessly, take digital photos, play games, and access calendars, address books, and other personal productivity features, in addition to performing their regular telephone functions. Mobile devices based on wristwatches are called *smart*

>**Programmer.** A person whose primary job responsibility is to write, maintain, and test computer programs. >**Mobile device.** A very small device, usually based on a wireless phone, that has some type of built-in computing or Internet capability.

watches. Smart watches can download weather, sports scores, news headlines, and other content wirelessly from the Internet; some can be used to transfer personal files, store and play music files, or store voice recordings.

Because of their typically small screen size and tiny, crowded keyboards, today's mobile devices are most appropriate for individuals wanting constant e-mail and messaging ability—as well as occasional updates on stock prices, weather, directions, and other timely information—rather than general Web browsing and computing. This is expected to change in the future, however, as cell phones, mobile devices, and portable computers continue to converge and wireless capabilities continue to improve. In some countries, this has already happened more than in the United States. For instance, smart phones currently available in Japan can be used for videoconferencing, storing gym IDs and concert tickets in digital form, purchasing products (via a built-in *digital wallet* into which users can transfer cash values), and even unlocking apartment doors. For a look at an emerging mobile device application available in the United States—*mobile TV*—see the Trend box.

Personal Computers

A **personal computer (PC)** or **microcomputer** is a small computer system designed to be used by one person at a time. PCs are small enough to fit on a desktop, inside a briefcase, or even inside a shirt pocket and are widely used in homes, small businesses, and large businesses alike. For instance, an individual might use a PC at home to play games, pay bills, prepare his or her taxes, exchange e-mail, and access Web pages. A small business might use its PCs for a variety of computing tasks, including tracking merchandise, preparing correspondence, creating marketing material, billing customers, responding to customer e-mails, updating the company Web site, and completing routine accounting chores. A large business might use PCs as productivity tools for office personnel and as analysis tools for decision makers, to name just two important applications. Office PCs are also commonly connected to a company *computer network* to provide access to company files, as well as to the company's Internet connection. Personal computers are available in a variety of configurations, as discussed next.

Desktop PCs

Conventional PCs are often referred to as **desktop PCs** because the complete computer system (system unit, monitor, keyboard, mouse, and so forth) fits on or next to a desk. The most common style of desktop PC today is with a *tower case*; that is, with a system unit that is designed to sit vertically, typically on the floor (see Figure 1-14). Desktop PCs can also have a *desktop case* that is designed to be placed horizontally on a desk's surface, usually with the monitor sitting on top of the system unit, as shown in Figure 1-14, although it is more common today for desktop cases to be used with *mini PCs*—very tiny desktop PCs that sit on the desk next to the monitor. A third possibility is the *all-in-one* desktop PC case, which incorporates the monitor and system unit into a single piece of hardware. While the conventional appearance of a desktop PC is a fairly large white or black box, desktop PCs are getting smaller and are now available in a variety of colors and designs. For a look at an emerging industry trend regarding PC appearance—*PC modding*—see the Inside the Industry box.

Desktop PCs typically cost between $500 and $2,500 and usually conform to one of two standards: *PC-compatible* or *Macintosh*. PC-compatibles (sometimes referred to as *Windows PCs* or *IBM-compatible PCs*) evolved from the original IBM PC—the first personal computer widely accepted for business use—and are the most common type of

TIP

For more tips on buying a PC, see the "Guide to Buying a PC" in the References and Resources Guide located at the end of this book.

>**Microcomputer.** A type of computer based on a microprocessor and designed to be used by one person at a time; also called a **personal computer** or **PC**. >**Desktop PC.** A PC designed to fit on or next to a desk.

TREND

Mobile TV

The entertainment factor of mobile phones just went up a big notch. In addition to the games and Web access that smart phones already provide, a hot new application is *mobile TV* (see the accompanying figure). Live television programming delivered via cell phones is now available in a number of countries, including the United States. One of the leaders is this area is *MobiTV*, which offers over 20 channels of news, music videos, comedies, and cartoons, including content from MSNBC, ABC News, FOX Sports, ToonWorld TV Classics, C-SPAN, and The Discovery Channel. The service costs less than $10 per month and is available through a number of wireless providers, including Sprint, Verizon, and Cingular. Content is even being developed specifically for mobile TV. For example, Twentieth Century Fox has created a new series of one-minute dramas based on its hit show *24*. The episodes–called *mobisodes*, short for "mobile episodes"–are based on the characters and actors in the TV show and became available in 2005.

A related alternative to live mobile TV is *mobile video-on-demand*–video clips that are delivered to a cell phone on demand, whenever the user requests it. Mobile video-on-demand typically includes short news clips, music videos, TV show updates, and more. Content is available 24/7 and the video clips are updated throughout the day in order to offer breaking news stories and up-to-date sports scores as they happen. Two examples of mobile video-on-demand providers are *GoTV* and Verizon's *Vcast* service.

Mobile TV is just beginning, but is expected to soon develop into a major market. For example, the ARC Group research company projects that, by 2008, 250 million consumers worldwide will be watching some form of mobile TV or video, generating more than $5 billion in annual revenues.

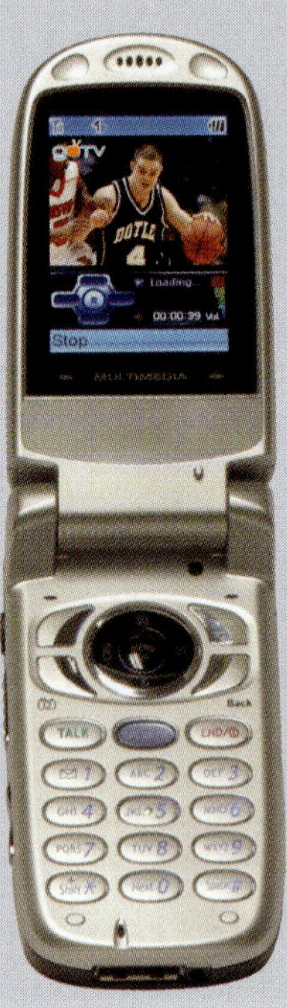

FIGURE 1-14
Typical styles for desktop PCs.

TOWER CASE

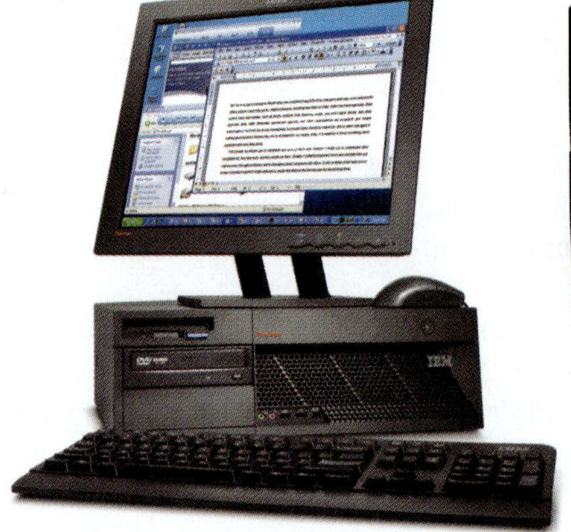

DESKTOP CASE

ALL-IN-ONE CASE

personal computer used today. In general, PC-compatible hardware and software are compatible with all brands of PC-compatible computers—such as those made by Dell, Hewlett-Packard, NEC, Acer, Fujitsu, and Gateway—and these computers typically run the Microsoft Windows operating system. Macintosh computers are made by Apple, use the Mac OS operating system, and often use different hardware and software than PC-compatible computers. Although PC-compatible computers are by far the most widely used, the Mac is traditionally the computer of choice for artists, designers, and others who require advanced graphics capabilities. But because there are virtually no Macintosh-compatible computers on the market to help drive down the price, Macs tend to cost more than PC-compatible computers with comparable hardware. A user who is deciding between these two *platforms* must consider what the computer will be used for and if it needs to be compatible with any other PCs, such as a school or office computer. For a brief introduction to the steps involved in setting up a new desktop PC, see the How it Works box on page 27.

Portable PCs

Portable PCs are computers that are designed to be easily carried around, such as in a carrying case, briefcase, purse, or pocket, depending on their size. Portable computers are essential for many workers, such as salespeople who need to make presentations or take orders from clients off-site, agents who need to collect data at remote locations, and managers who need computing and communications resources as they travel. For workers who need computer access on the go but do not have their hands free, wearable computers can be used. Portable PCs today usually come with built-in communications capabilities, so the PCs can be easily connected to an office network or the Internet. Increasingly, individuals are buying portable PCs as their primary computer; in fact, monthly sales of portable *notebook PCs* (a type of portable PC discussed next) surpassed monthly sales of desktop PCs for the first time in May 2005, according to the research firm Current Analysis.

Two types of portable PCs that are about the size of a standard paper notebook or ruled tablet are *notebook computers* and *tablet PCs* (see Figure 1-15). Both are designed for users who need a fully functioning computer that they can easily take with them wherever they go, but have different physical characteristics.

FIGURE 1-15 Notebook and tablet PCs.

>**Portable PC.** A small personal computer, such as a notebook, tablet, or handheld PC, designed to be carried around easily.

INSIDE THE INDUSTRY

PC Modding

Similar to hot-rodders, who create custom cars, *PC modders* modify high-performance PCs into functional works of art. Often the goal is a case design that reflects the modder's personality or interests. Sometimes the reason to modify a PC is to increase its functionality for specific power-hungry tasks, such as PC gaming.

Most PC modders build their PCs completely from the ground up, beginning with the motherboard and adding the newest and fastest components. Although most modified PCs still contain similar components to conventional PCs—such as a motherboard, hard drive, expansion cards, RAM, cabling, and fans—often the components need to be connected in an unconventional manner to fit inside the desired case design. Some interesting case components used by PC modders include furniture, BBQs, toys, old radios, coffeemakers, fishtanks, model cars (see the accompanying photos), and custom-made fiberglass and acrylic cases. Often custom cutouts in the system unit case and custom lighting add to the overall effect; custom paint jobs are the norm. Some PC modders create PCs just for their own enjoyment or to display at computer shows; others sell their creations to friends or as a business. Companies that sell PC-modding supplies (such as clear cases, glow-in-the-dark cables, fan sculptures, and water cooling systems) also sometimes sell kits for the beginning modder.

While not everyone may be ready for a PC that looks like the Starship Enterprise or a LEGO creation, with the increased amount of time people are spending with their PCs, it is becoming more common to want a computer that is fun to look at. Along this line of thought, some PC manufacturers are designing PCs with style in mind. For example, the two retail PCs in the accompanying photo are more mod than a conventional computer, but are available for sale to the general public.

CUSTOM MODDED PCS

RETAIL PCS

TIP

PCs that allow pen input—such as tablet PCs—are convenient in crowded situations, as well as in places where the clicking of a keyboard would be annoying to others.

Notebook computers (also called *laptops*) are fully functioning computers that open to reveal a screen and keyboard. Most notebooks follow the traditional *clamshell* design in which the monitor is on the inside top half of the PC, and the keyboard and touch pad are on the inside bottom half, as shown in Figure 1-15. **Tablet PCs** can use either a *slate* or a *convertible tablet PC* design. Slate tablets include what looks like just the top half of a notebook PC. Typically slate tablets are not used with a keyboard; instead, a special pen is used to select objects and write electronically on the screen (the handwritten text can later be converted to typed text, if desired). Convertible tablet PCs are essentially a combination of a notebook computer and a slate tablet PC. In its notebook format, a convertible tablet PC is used just the same as a notebook PC; that is, with keyboard and touch pad input.

>**Notebook computer.** A fully functioning portable PC that opens to reveal a screen and keyboard. >**Tablet PC.** A portable PC about the size of a notebook that is designed to be used with an electronic pen.

When the screen is rotated and then closed with the screen facing out, the device resembles a slate tablet PC, and just pen input is used. Although similar in capabilities to their desktop cousins, notebook computers and tablet PCs tend to cost more, have smaller screens, and use denser keyboard arrangements (if a keyboard exists). Most notebook computers and tablet PCs are designed to run on rechargeable batteries, although many come with adapters that allow them to be plugged into a power outlet, as well. Both notebook computers and tablet PCs also tend to use alternative pointing devices (such as an electronic pen or a touch pad) instead of a mouse, although a mouse can be connected to the computer, if it has an available *mouse port*.

Handheld computers (sometimes called *pocket computers*) are about the size of a paperback book or pocket calculator. Handheld computers have a built-in keyboard, a *thumbpad* (such as on the BlackBerry handheld computer shown in Figure 1-16), or—like tablet PCs—the screen is touched with an electronic pen to provide input. Handheld PCs are typically battery powered and are sometimes referred to as *personal digital assistants*, or *PDAs*, since they usually provide personal organizer functions (such as a calendar, appointment book, and address book), as well as messaging, electronic mail, and other communications functions. As the capabilities of handheld PCs have improved—for instance, the tiny, fully functioning Oqo PC shown in Figure 1-16 runs Windows XP and Windows applications—they are becoming increasingly practical for day-to-day tasks. In fact, fully functioning handheld computers with telephone and Internet capabilities can conceivably replace both a desktop PC and cell phone.

For individuals who choose to use both a desktop and a portable computer, the ability to share information and synchronize data between the two computers is an important consideration. Some handheld PCs come with a cradle that attaches via a cable to the user's primary PC. After the user docks the handheld PC by inserting it into the cradle, the data on the two PCs can be updated (see Figure 1-17). Other portable PCs come with *infrared* capabilities that allow the user to "beam" data from that device to his or her primary PC. Still others can store data on flash memory cards, which can then be inserted into a desktop PC's flash memory card reader to retrieve the data. And with some types of *wireless networking* technology, it is possible for portable and desktop PCs to be in communication with each other and to synchronize data whenever they are within a specific range. Some services can even sync a handheld computer or mobile device to a desktop PC via the Internet on a continual basis, so changes made to your schedule or contact list on your primary PC are automatically reflected on your portable PC or device.

For users who prefer to use a portable PC as their primary PC but want the features of a desktop computer when working at home or in the office, *docking stations* and *notebook stands* can be used. Docking stations connect a portable PC (typically a notebook or tablet PC) to *peripheral devices*, such as a monitor, keyboard, mouse, and printer. The peripheral devices are always attached to the docking station, so as soon as the PC is connected to the docking station (via a special slot or connector), it can be used as a regular desktop PC (see Figure 1-17). Notebook stands raise a notebook PC up to an appropriate height, so the notebook's screen can be used instead of an external monitor. Some notebook stands include connectors for a keyboard and mouse; if not, those devices can be connected directly to the notebook PC.

BLACKBERRY HANDHELD PC

OQO FULLY FUNCTIONING PC

FIGURE 1-16
Handheld computers.
Handheld computers come in a variety of sizes and capabilities.

INT

FURTHER EXPLORATION

For links to further information about personal computers, go to www.course.com/uc11/ch01

Thin Clients and Internet Appliances

Most personal computers today are sold as stand-alone, self-sufficient units that are equipped with all the necessary hardware and software to operate independently. In other words, they can perform input, processing, output, and storage without being connected to a network,

>**Handheld computer.** A portable PC about the size of a paperback book or pocket calculator.

CRADLES
Handheld PCs are often docked into a special cradle to synchronize the data on the handheld PC with the data on the primary PC.

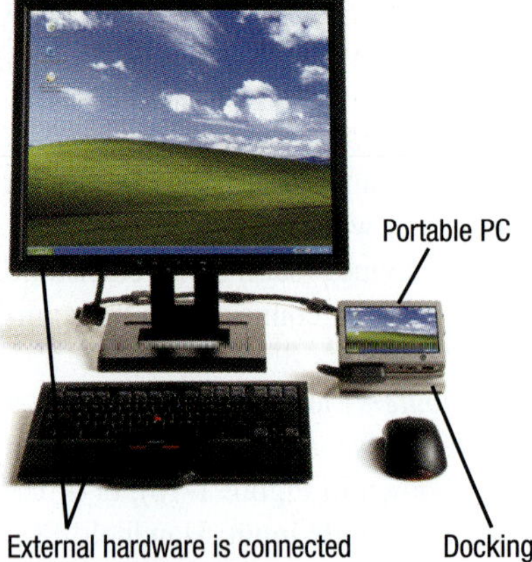

DOCKING STATIONS
Once a portable PC is connected to a docking station, the monitor and other hardware connected to the docking station can be used.

FIGURE 1-17
Docking portable PCs.

although they can be networked if desired. In contrast, a device that must be connected to a network to perform processing or storage tasks is referred to as a *dumb terminal*. Somewhere between a PC and a dumb terminal are devices that may be able to perform a limited amount of independent processing but are designed to be used with a network. Two examples of these are *thin clients* and *Internet appliances*.

A **thin client**—also called a *network computer (NC)*—is designed to be used in conjunction with a company network. Instead of using their own local disk drives for storage and their own CPUs for processing, these computers utilize a network server for those tasks. The primary advantage of thin clients is lower cost of hardware and software, as well as easier maintenance, since all software is located on the server. Disadvantages include having limited or no local storage (although this is an advantage for companies with highly secure data that need to prevent data from leaving the facility) and not being able to function as a stand-alone computer when the network is not working.

Network computers or other devices designed primarily for accessing Web pages and/or exchanging e-mail are called **Internet appliances** (sometimes also referred to as *Internet devices*, *information appliances*, or *Web pads*). As shown in Figure 1-18, these devices can take on a variety of configurations. Some look like a small PC but cannot run any software other than their Web browser or e-mail programs and so cannot be used as general-purpose computers. Some are designed to be located in the home and connect to the Internet via a standard telephone line; others (such as the portable Internet appliance shown in Figure 1-18) are portable and designed to access the Internet via a cell phone network. In addition to portability, some portable Internet appliances—such as the one in Figure 1-18—have a fairly large screen size, so Web pages display more like they do on conventional PCs, instead of only showing limited, modified content as is needed on many smart phones and portable PCs. Some Internet appliances—such as the MSN TV 2 device shown in Figure 1-18—take the form of a *set-top box* that connects to a TV. Increasingly, these devices facilitate the delivery

FIGURE 1-18
Thin clients and Internet appliances. These devices are designed to be used only with company networks or the Internet.

THIN CLIENT

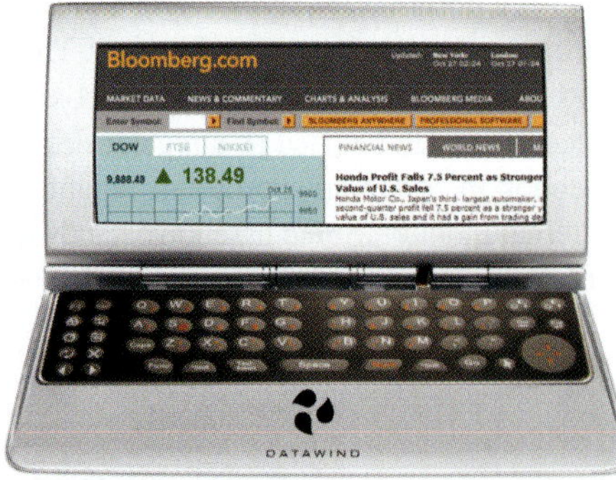

PORTABLE INTERNET APPLIANCE

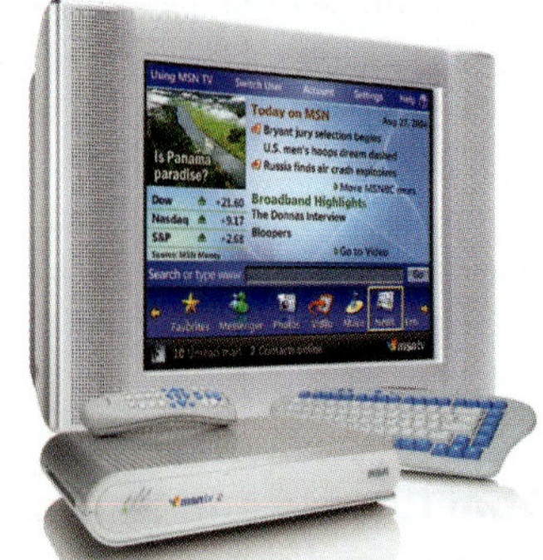

SET-TOP BOX INTERNET APPLIANCE

>**Thin client.** A PC designed to access a network for processing and data storage, instead of performing those tasks locally; also called a network computer (NC). >**Internet appliance.** A specialized network computer designed primarily for Internet access and/or e-mail exchange.

HOW IT WORKS

Setting Up a New PC

Before setting up a new PC, it is a good idea to give a little thought to its location. It should be close to a telephone jack (if one is needed), and it should have its own power outlet. In addition, the location should have enough room for ventilation, and it should not be in direct sunlight. Although set-up procedures vary from system to system, the basic steps involved in setting up a typical desktop PC are shown in the accompanying illustration. In a nutshell, you need to unpack and connect the components, install additional software, set up your initial connection, and then you are good to go.

After your system is up and running, you will need to back up your data periodically so it will not be lost if your computer fails. If you computer does malfunction, you can restore the PC to its original setup using the system backup and then restore your data from your backup medium. Some new PCs come with a *restore disc* for this purpose and some operating systems, such as Windows XP, also automatically create *restore points* to which your computer settings can be rolled back if there is ever a problem with your computer. Even though using the operating system's system restore option usually does not alter your data files, it is still good practice to back up your data on a regular basis. You will also want to back up any application software that was preinstalled on your PC but not supplied on disc, and back up any programs that you download from the Internet. Some PCs include some type of "Make discs" option to easily perform this task.

1. Unpack all components and locate the installation guide to refer to during the setup process.

2. Plug all cables (for the monitor, mouse, keyboard, printer, speakers, and so on) into the appropriate port on the system unit. For speakers, usually just one speaker is connected to the system unit; the second speaker connects directly to the first speaker.
   For conventional modems, the cord from the telephone wall jack is plugged into the appropriate port on the system unit; the second telephone port on the PC can be used for a telephone, if desired.

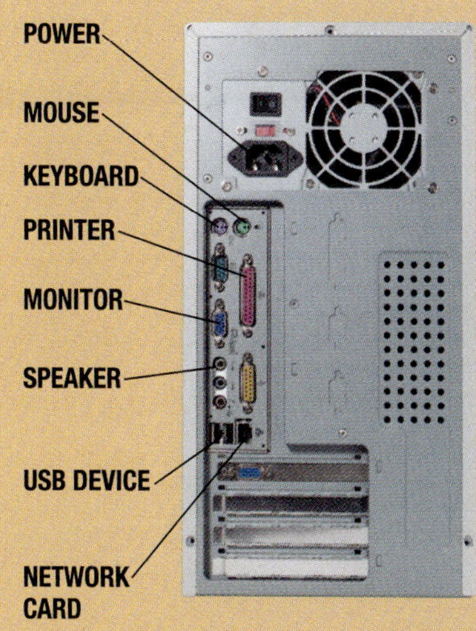

3. Plug all power cords (for the system unit, monitor, printer, scanner, powered subwoofer, and so on) into a surge suppressor power strip, then turn the power on.

4. Install any additional software you have obtained, set up your Internet or network connection, and customize the desktop display.

5. Back up your PC and any programs that were preinstalled on your PC but not supplied on disc. Store the discs in a safe place and enjoy your new PC!

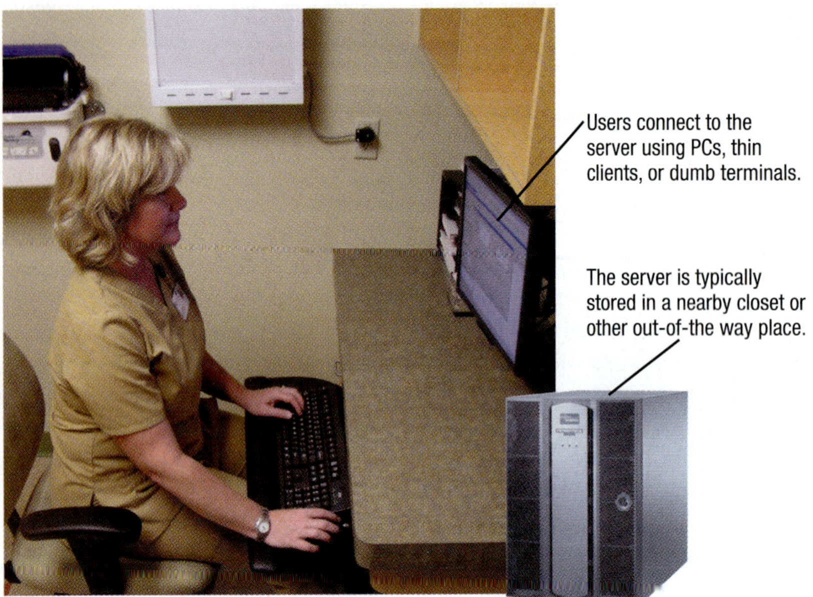

FIGURE 1-19
Midrange servers. Midrange servers are used to host data and programs on a small network, such as a school computer lab or medical office network.

of other types of digital content (such as digital photos, recorded television shows, and downloaded movies and music), in addition to Web pages and e-mail.

Midrange Servers

A **midrange server**—also sometimes called a *minicomputer* or *midrange computer*—is a medium-sized computer used to host programs and data for a small network. Typically larger, more powerful, and more expensive than a desktop PC, a midrange server is usually located in a closet or other out-of-the way place and can serve many users at one time. Users connect to the server through a network, using their desktop computer, notebook PC, thin client, or a dumb terminal consisting of just a monitor and keyboard (see Figure 1-19). Midrange servers are often used in small- to medium-sized businesses, such as medical or dental offices, as well as in school computer labs.

Some midrange servers consist of a collection of individual *circuit boards* called *blades*; each blade contains the hardware necessary to provide the complete processing power of one PC. These servers—called *blade servers*—are much easier to expand and upgrade than traditional servers, and are more secure. With some blade servers, the processing power of the blades is shared among users. With others, each user has his or her own individual blade, which functions as that individual's PC, but the blades are locked in a secure location instead of having that hardware located on each employee's desk. In either case, the hardware designed specifically for user access to a blade server is often called a *blade PC*.

Mainframe Computers

A **mainframe computer** (see Figure 1-20) is the standard choice for large organizations—such as hospitals, universities, large businesses, banks, and government offices—that need to manage large amounts of centralized data. Larger, more expensive, and more powerful than midrange servers, mainframes usually operate 24 hours a day, serving thousands of users connected to the mainframe via PCs, thin clients, or dumb terminals, in a manner similar to the way users connect to midrange servers. During regular business hours, a mainframe runs multiple programs as needed to meet the different needs of its wide variety of users. At night, it commonly performs large processing tasks, such as payroll and billing. Today's mainframes are sometimes referred to as *high-end servers* or *enterprise-class servers* and usually cost at least several hundred thousand dollars each.

Supercomputers

Some applications require extraordinary speed, accuracy, and processing capabilities—for example, sending astronauts into space, controlling missile guidance systems and satellites, forecasting the weather, exploring for oil, and assisting with some kinds of scientific

>**Midrange server.** A medium-sized computer used to host programs and data for a small network. >**Mainframe computer.** A computer used in large organizations (such as hospitals, large businesses, and colleges) that need to manage large amounts of centralized data and run multiple programs simultaneously.

research. **Supercomputers**—the most powerful and most expensive type of computer available—were developed to fill this need. Some relatively new supercomputing applications include hosting extremely complex Web sites and decision-support systems for corporate executives, and three-dimensional applications, such as 3D medical scans, image projections, and architectural modeling. Unlike mainframe computers, which typically run multiple applications simultaneously to serve a wide variety of users, supercomputers generally run one program at a time, as fast as possible.

FIGURE 1-20
Mainframe computers.
Mainframes computers, such as the one shown here, are usually located in a climate-controlled room; users connect to the mainframe via PCs, thin clients, or dumb terminals.

Conventional supercomputers can cost several million dollars each. To reduce the cost, it has become more common to build less-expensive supercomputers by connecting hundreds of smaller computers—increasingly midrange servers running the Linux operating system—into a *supercomputing cluster* that acts as a single computer. The computers in the cluster usually contain several CPUs each and are dedicated to processing cluster applications. The resulting supercomputer is often referred to as a *massively parallel processor (MPP)* computer. For example, one of the fastest supercomputers in the world, IBM's *Blue Gene/L* (shown in Figure 1-21), contains 65,536 nodes containing two CPUs each for a combined total of 131,072 CPUs. This supercomputing cluster, built for the U.S. Department of Energy, was installed at Lawrence Livermore National Laboratories in mid-2005. It cost approximately $100 million, will perform about 360 *teraflops* (trillions of *floating point operations per second*) when fully installed and configured (only one-half the machine was installed initially), runs the Linux operating system, and is used primarily to conduct nuclear weapons simulations to help ensure the safety, security, and reliability of the nation's nuclear weapon stockpile.

A concept related to cluster computing is *grid computing*—a growing trend of utilizing the unused processing power of a large number of computers—typically PCs—connected through the Internet to work together on a single task, on demand. For instance, consumers can volunteer their PCs to be used for scientific or medical research purposes and their PCs' processing power will be tapped (via the Internet) when needed by the research organization. New grid computing services are beginning to be offered to provide companies with immense processing power on demand, similar to the way electricity is delivered as it is needed. For instance, businesses can form a grid of their employee's PCs and sell that processing power during off-hours (whenever employees are not at work) to those who need it.

BLUE GENE/L SUPERCOMPUTER
Here the supercomputer is partially installed; the racks containing the circuit boards are visible on some units.

BLUE GENE/L CIRCUIT BOARDS
Each rack holds several circuit boards; each circuit board contains four processors.

FIGURE 1-21
The Blue Gene/L supercomputer.
Supercomputers are used for specialized situations in which immense processing speed is required.

>**Supercomputer.** The fastest, most expensive, and most powerful type of computer.

COMPUTER NETWORKS AND THE INTERNET

Many computers today are connected to a *computer network*. A **computer network** is a collection of hardware and other devices that are connected together so that users can share hardware, software, and data, as well as electronically communicate with each other. As shown in Figure 1-22, many networks use a *network server* to manage the data flowing through the network devices and the resources on a network. For example, a network server might control access to shared printers and other shared hardware, as well as to shared programs and data. The other computers on a network that access network resources through the network server are called *clients*.

Computer networks exist in many sizes and types. For instance, a home network might connect two computers inside the home to share a single printer and Internet connection, as well as to exchange files. A small office network of five or six computers might be used to enable workers to access the company database, communicate with other employees, and access the Internet. A large corporate network might connect all of the offices or retail stores in the corporation, creating a network that spans several cities or states. A public wireless network—such as those available at some coffeehouses, restaurants, public libraries, and parks—might be used to provide Internet access to customers or the general public. Chapter 7 discusses networks in greater detail.

FIGURE 1-22
Example of a computer network.

>**Computer network.** A collection of computers and other hardware devices that are connected together to share hardware, software, and data, as well as to communicate electronically with one another.

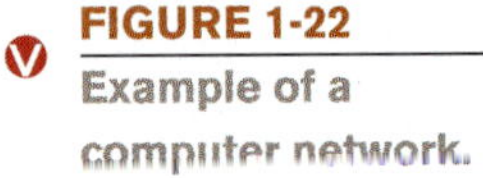

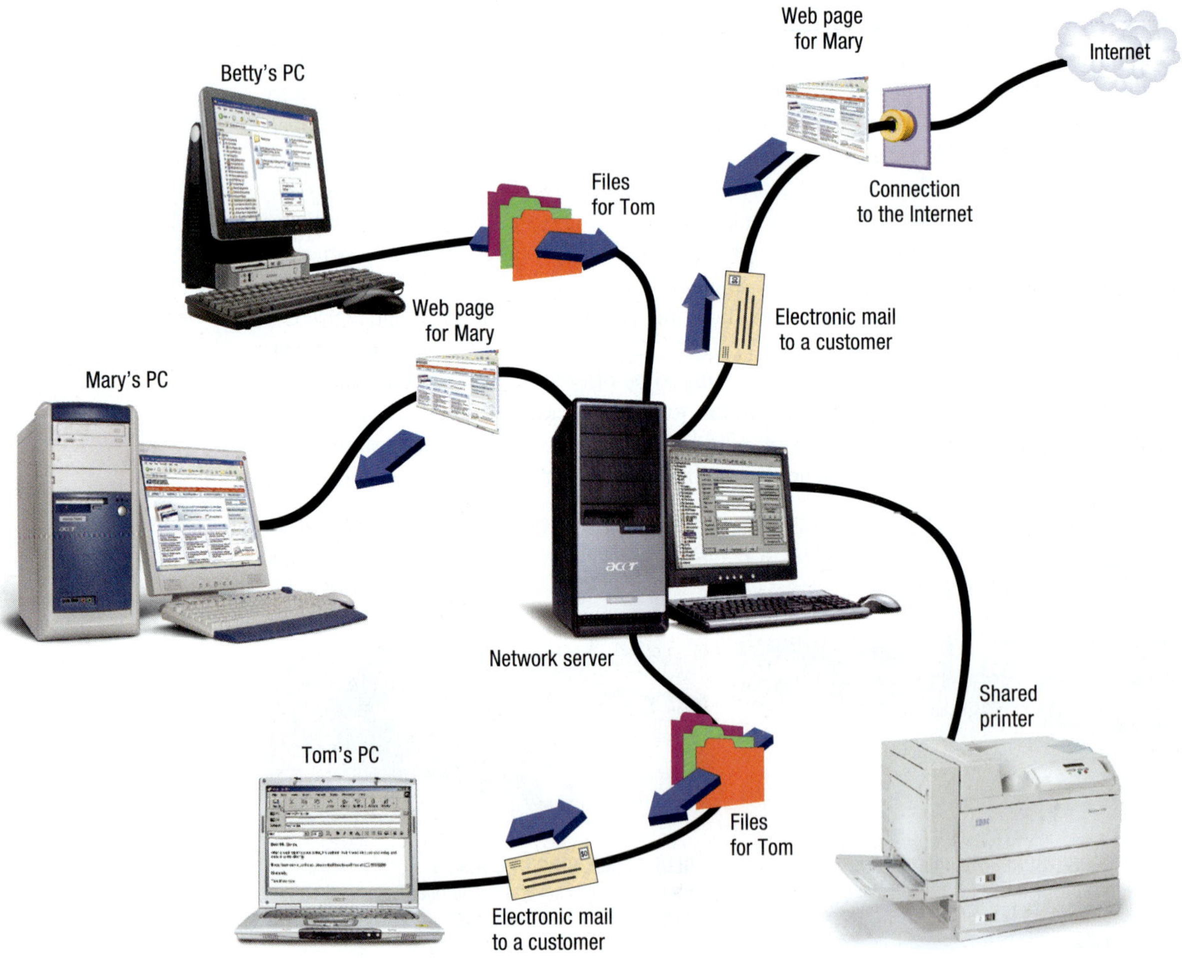

What Are the Internet and the World Wide Web?

The **Internet** is the largest and most well-known computer network in the world. It is technically a network of networks, since it consists of thousands of networks that can all access each other via the main *backbone* infrastructure of the Internet. Typically, individual users connect to the Internet by connecting to computers belonging to an **Internet service provider** (**ISP**)—a company that provides Internet access, usually for a fee. ISP computers are continually connected to a larger network, called a *regional network*, which, in turn, is connected to onc of the major high-speed networks within a country, called a *backbone network*. Backbone networks within a country are connected to each other and to backbone networks in other countries. Together they form one enormous network of networks—the Internet. ISPs function as a gateway or onramp to the Internet, providing Internet access to their subscribers. Most ISPs charge a monthly fee for Internet access, although there are some ISPs that offer free Internet access in exchange for onscreen advertising. If you connect to the Internet using a school or company network, the school or company acts as your ISP. If you connect using a smart phone, PDA, or other handheld device, your wireless provider is usually your ISP. Home PC users typically use a national ISP (such as *America Online* (*AOL*), *EarthLink*, *AT&T WorldNet*, *StarBand*, or *RoadRunner*) that provides Internet service to a large geographical area, or a local ISP that has a more limited service area. Tips for choosing and getting set up with an ISP are included in Chapter 8.

Millions of people and organizations all over the world are connected to the Internet. Two of the most common Internet activities today are exchanging e-mail and accessing the *World Wide Web* (*WWW*). While the term "Internet" refers to the physical structure of that network, the **World Wide Web** refers to one resource—a collection of documents called **Web pages**—available through the Internet. A group of Web pages belonging to one individual or company is called a **Web site**. Web page files are stored on computers (called **Web servers**) that are continually connected to the Internet, so they can be accessed at any time by anyone with a computer (or other Web-enabled device) and an Internet connection. A wide variety of information is available via Web pages, such as news, weather, airline schedules, product information, government publications, music downloads, maps, telephone directories, movie trailers, and much, much more. You can also use Web pages to shop, bank, trade stock, and perform other types of online financial transactions, as well as to listen to music, play games, and perform other entertainment-oriented activities. Web pages are viewed using a **Web browser**, such as *Internet Explorer*, *Netscape Navigator*, *Safari*, *Opera*, or *Firefox*.

INT

TIP

Although some people use the terms "Internet" and "Web" interchangeably, technically the Web–the collection of Web pages available over the Internet–is only one resource available via the Internet.

FURTHER EXPLORATION

For links to information about Web browsers, go to www.course.com/uc11/ch01

Accessing a Network or the Internet

To access a computer network (such as a home network, company network, or the Internet), you need a modem or a network adapter to physically connect your computer to the network. Communications software (either built into your operating system or installed as a separate program) allows you to connect to and *log on* to the network, if needed, so that you can access network resources. Sometimes a *username*, *user ID*, or *login ID* and a password are required to log on to a network—typically you will be asked to supply them each time you boot the computer. After providing the correct information, you will have access to network resources, and you can select the program you want to run.

To access the Internet, you must be connected to it. Many computers today are continually connected to the Internet (called a *direct* or *always-on connection*), in which the computer or other device being used to access the Internet is continually connected to the ISP's computer. With a direct connection, you only need to open your browser (using the desktop icon for your browser, the desktop icon for your ISP, or the appropriate Start menu item) to

>Internet. The largest and most well-known computer network, linking millions of computers all over the world. **>Internet service provider (ISP).** A business or other organization that provides Internet access to others, typically for a fee. **>World Wide Web.** The collection of Web pages available through the Internet. **>Web page.** A document, typically containing hyperlinks to other documents, located on a Web server and available through the World Wide Web. **>Web site.** A collection of related Web pages usually belonging to an organization or individual. **>Web server.** A computer that is continually connected to the Internet and hosts Web pages that are accessible through the Internet. **>Web browser.** A program used to view Web pages.

begin using the Internet. With a *dial-up connection*, the PC or device must dial up and connect to the ISP's computer via a telephone line when Internet access is needed. Most national dial-up ISPs include a desktop icon or Start menu item that opens your browser and dials your telephone together as a single step; smaller, regional dial-up ISPs may require you to open your browser and start the *dialing program* installed on your PC as two separate steps. You may also be asked to enter your username and password before being connected to the Internet; these will have been assigned or chosen during your ISP setup procedure. Once connected to the Internet, you can open a Web browser program and begin to view Web pages.

In order to request a Web page or other resource located on the Internet, you need to use its *Internet address*. **Internet addresses** are numerical or text-based addresses used to identify resources accessible through the Internet, such as computers, Web pages, and people. Each Internet address is unique and is assigned to one—and only one—person or thing. The most common types of Internet addresses are *IP addresses* and *domain names* (to identify computers); *URLs* (to identify Web pages); and *e-mail addresses* (to identify people).

TIP

To see if a particular domain name is available for registration, visit the InterNIC Web site at www.internic.net and use the *Whois* search function.

IP Addresses and Domain Names

IP addresses and their corresponding **domain names** are used to identify computers available through the Internet. IP (short for *Internet Protocol*) addresses are numeric, such as *207.46.138.20*, and are commonly used by computers to refer to other computers. A computer that hosts information available through the Internet (such as a Web server hosting Web pages) usually has a unique text-based domain name (such as *microsoft.com*) that corresponds to the host computer's IP address to make it easier for people to remember the address to use to access that information. IP addresses and domain names are unique; that is, there cannot be two computers on the Internet using the exact same IP address or exact same domain name. To ensure this, specific IP addresses are allocated to each network to be used with the computers on that network, and there is a worldwide registration system for domain name registration. Domain names are typically registered on an annual basis; the required fee varies from registrar to registrar. When a domain name is registered, the IP address of the computer that will be used with that domain name is also registered, so the computer can either be accessed using its domain name or corresponding IP address.

Domain names typically identify who owns that computer and either the type of entity (such as a school, a commercial business, the government, or an individual person) or the computer's location. A period separates the different parts of a domain name. The rightmost part of the domain name (beginning with the rightmost period) identifies the type of the organization or its location and is called the *top-level domain* (*TLD*). There were seven original TLDs used in the United States (see Figure 1-23). Since then, over 240 additional two-letter *country code TLDs* have been created to represent countries or territories (*.us* for United States and *.jp* for Japan, for instance). Because of the high demand for domain names, new top-level domains are periodically proposed to *ICANN* (*Internet*

FIGURE 1-23
Some top-level domains (TLDs).

ORIGINAL TLDS	INTENDED USE
.com	Commercial businesses
.edu	Educational institutions
.gov	Government organizations
.int	International treaty organizations
.org	Noncommercial organizations
.net	Network providers and ISPs
.mil	Military organizations
NEW TLDS	**INTENDED USE**
.biz	Businesses
.info	Resource sites
.name	Individuals
.museum	Museums
.pro	Licensed professionals
.aero	Aviation industry
.coop	Coop organizations

>**Internet address.** What identifies a computer, person, or Web page on the Internet, such as an IP address, domain name, or e-mail address. >**IP address.** A numeric Internet address used to uniquely identify a computer on the Internet. >**Domain name.** A text-based Internet address used to uniquely identify a computer on the Internet.

Corporation for Assigned Names and Numbers), the nonprofit organization responsible for Internet IP address allocation and domain name management. Seven new TLDs have been approved and recently implemented; there are also 10 additional TLDs under consideration.

Some TLDs—such as .gov, .edu, and .mil—are *restricted TLDs* and can only be registered by a qualifying organization; *unrestricted TLDs*—such as .com, .net, .biz, .name, and .us—can be registered by any person or type of organization. However, only the legitimate holder of a trademarked name can use that trademarked name as a domain name. Some sample domain names are shown in Figure 1-24. Although many domain names consist solely of two parts, additional parts can be used to identify an organization more specifically, as in the last example in Figure 1-24. When this occurs, all of the pieces of the domain name are separated by periods.

DOMAIN NAME	ORGANIZATION	TYPE/LOCATION OF ORGANIZATION
microsoft.com	Microsoft Corporation	Commercial business
stanford.edu	Stanford University	Educational institution
fbi.gov	Federal Bureau of Investigation	Government organization
navy.mil	United States Navy	Military organization
royal.gov.uk	The British Monarchy	Government organization in the United Kingdom

FIGURE 1-24
Examples of domain names.

Uniform Resource Locators (URLs)

Similar to the way an IP address or domain name uniquely identifies a computer on the Internet, a **uniform resource locator** (**URL**) uniquely identifies a Web page. URLs consist of information identifying the Web server hosting the Web page (typically the *computer name* assigned to that computer by the organization's system administrator to uniquely identify that computer within the organization's domain name), the name of any folders in which the Web page file is stored, and the Web page's filename. For example, looking at the URL for the Web page shown in Figure 1-25 from right to left, we can see that the Web page is called *index.html*, and that file is stored in a folder called *arthur* on a Web server named *www* in the *pbskids.org* domain.

Some characteristics of the URL shown in Figure 1-25 are common to most URLs. The letters *http* stand for *Hypertext Transfer Protocol*—the protocol typically used to display Web pages. Web pages are the most common Internet resource accessed with a Web browser. If a different type of Internet resource is requested, a different protocol indicator is used. For example, URLs beginning with *ftp://* use *File Transfer Protocol*—a protocol used to upload and download files—and URLs beginning with *https://* use *Secure Hypertext Transfer Protocol*—the protocol used to display *secure Web pages*; that is, Web pages that can safely be used to transmit sensitive information, such as credit card numbers. The *www* at the beginning of the domain name in Figure 1-25 is a very common computer name for a Web server. The file extension *.html* stands for *Hypertext Markup Language*—the language usually used to create Web pages. Other file extensions,

FIGURE 1-25
A Web page URL.

>Uniform resource locator (URL). An Internet address, usually beginning with http://, that uniquely identifies a Web page.

TIP

Be sure that any Web page used to send sensitive data (such as your social security number or credit card information) is secure. Look for a URL that starts with *https* instead of *http* and a locked padlock icon on the browser status bar.

such as *.htm* (another abbreviation for Hypertext Markup Language) and *.asp* (for *Active Service Pages*, which are commonly used with Web pages that are created dynamically based on user input), are also frequently used with Web pages.

E-Mail Addresses

To contact people using the Internet, you most often use their **e-mail addresses**. An e-mail address consists of a **username** (an identifying name), followed by the @ symbol, followed by the domain name for the computer that will be handling that person's e-mail (called a *mail server*). For example,

jsmith@thomson.com
maria_s@thomson.com
sam.peterson@thomson.com

are the e-mail addresses assigned respectively to jsmith (John Smith), maria_s (Maria Sanchez), and sam.peterson (Sam Peterson), three hypothetical employees at Thomson Learning, the publisher of this textbook. Usernames are typically a combination of the person's first and last names and sometimes include periods, underscores, and numbers, but cannot include blank spaces. To ensure a unique e-mail address for everyone in the world, usernames must be unique within each domain name. So, even though there could be a *jsmith* at Thomson Learning using the e-mail address *jsmith@thomson.com* and a *jsmith* at Stanford University using the e-mail address *jsmith@stanford.edu*, the two e-mail addresses are unique. It is up to each organization with a registered domain name to ensure that one—and only one—exact same username is assigned under its domain. Using e-mail addresses to send e-mail messages is discussed later in this chapter.

Pronouncing Internet Addresses

Because Internet addresses are frequently given verbally, it is important to know how to pronounce them. A few guidelines are listed next, and Figure 1-26 shows some examples of Internet addresses and their proper pronunciations.

- If a portion of the address forms a recognizable word or name, it is spoken; otherwise, it is spelled out.
- The @ sign is pronounced *at*.
- The period (.) is pronounced *dot*.
- The forward slash (/) is pronounced *slash*.

FIGURE 1-26
Pronouncing Internet addresses.

TYPE OF ADDRESS	SAMPLE ADDRESS	PRONUNCIATION
Domain name	berkeley.edu	berkeley dot e d u
URL	microsoft.com/windows/ie/default.asp	microsoft dot com slash windows slash i e slash default dot a s p
E-mail address	president@whitehouse.gov	president at whitehouse dot gov

>**E-mail address.** An Internet address consisting of a username and computer domain name that uniquely identifies a person on the Internet.
>**Username.** A name that uniquely identifies a user on a particular network.

Surfing the Web

Once you have an Internet connection, you are ready to begin *surfing the Web*—that is, using a Web browser to view Web pages. In addition to being used to display Web pages, most Web browsers today can be used to perform other Internet tasks, such as downloading files, exchanging e-mail, accessing *discussion groups*, and participating in *chat sessions*. The ability to perform a variety of Internet tasks, either as part of the browser program itself or using a separate companion program that is opened automatically when needed, has made the Web browser a universal tool for exploring and using the Internet.

The first page that your Web browser displays when it is opened is your browser's starting page—or *home page*. Often this is the home page for the Web site belonging to your browser, school, or ISP. However, you can change your browser's home page to any page—such as a *search site* (a Web site that helps you find Web pages containing the information that you are seeking) or a news site—that you plan to visit regularly. The browser's *Options* or *Preferences* dialog box typically includes an option for changing the browser's home page. From your browser's home page, you can move to any Web page you desire, as discussed next.

INT

TIP

The *home page* for a Web site is the starting page of that particular site; the *home page* for your browser is the Web page designated as the first page you see each time the browser is opened.

Using URLs and Hyperlinks

To navigate to a new Web page for which you know the URL, type that URL in the browser's *Address bar* and press Enter (see Figure 1-27). You can either edit the existing URL or delete it and type a new one, but be sure to match the spelling, capitalization, and punctuation exactly. If you do not know the exact URL to type, you can type the URL for a *search site* to display the search site's home page and then use that site to search for the Web page, as discussed shortly.

Web pages are connected by hyperlinks, which can be graphics or text. When a hyperlink is clicked with the mouse, the Web page associated with that hyperlink is displayed (when you point to a hyperlink, the *status bar* displays the URL of the page that will load if the hyperlink is clicked, as shown in Figure 1-27). Hyperlinks can be either text-based or image-based and are often underlined, although hyperlinks may also be displayed in a different color than the rest of the text on the page or underlined only when the mouse points to them. To more easily identify hyperlinks, the mouse pointer typically changes to a pointing hand when a hyperlink is pointed to; the pointing hand pointer indicates that the item being pointed to is, indeed, a hyperlink. When a hyperlink is clicked, the Web page associated with

TIP

If you get an error message when trying to load a Web page, check the spelling of the URL and then press Enter to try to load the page again. As a last resort, edit the URL to remove any folder or filenames and press Enter to try to load the home page of that site.

FIGURE 1-27
Surfing the Web.
URLs, hyperlinks, and favorites can be used to display Web pages.

that hyperlink is displayed, regardless of whether the new page is located on the same Web server as the original page, or on a Web server in an entirely different state or country. In addition to Web pages, hyperlinks can also be linked to other types of files, such as to enable Web visitors to view or download images, listen to or download music files, view video clips, or download software programs.

To return to the previous Web page, you can use the Back button on your browser's toolbar. To print the current Web page, click the browser's Print button or select *Print* from the browser's File menu.

Using Favorites and the History List

TIP

To save time when browsing on your own PC, add the URL for any Web page you plan to visit regularly to your *Favorites* list.

Virtually all browsers have a feature (called *Favorites* in Internet Explorer and *Bookmarks* in Netscape Navigator) that you can use to save Web page URLs. This feature allows you to return to Web pages easily at a later time. To add the URL for the page you are currently viewing to your Favorites list, select the *Add to Favorites* option from your browser's Favorites menu. Once the URL for a page is saved as a favorite, you can redisplay that page again by selecting its link from the Favorites list (see Figure 1-27). Because a *Favorites list* can get large and unwieldy, typically an option on the Favorites menu allows you to delete outdated items from the list or move items into folders to keep them organized.

Most browsers also maintain a *History list*, which is a record of all Web pages visited in the last few weeks (how long a page stays in the History list depends on your browser settings). If you want to revisit a page you have been to recently that is not on your Favorites list, click the History button (if one is available on your browser), or look for a *History* option on the menu to display the History list, and then select the desired page.

FURTHER EXPLORATION

For links to further information about search and reference Web sites, go to www.course.com/uc11/ch01

Searching the Web

While casual surfing is a popular Web pastime, people often turn to the Internet to find specific types of information. When you know generally what you want but do not know which URL to use to find that information, one of your best options is to perform an *Internet search*. There are a number of special Web pages, called *search sites*, available to help you locate what you are looking for on the Internet. One of the most popular search sites—Google—is shown in Figure 1-28. Searching the Web is discussed in more detail in Chapter 8, but you typically type one or more *keywords* into the search box on a search site, and a list of links to Web pages matching your search criteria will be displayed. There are also numerous *reference sites* available on the Web to look up addresses, telephone numbers, ZIP codes, maps, and other information. To find a reference site, type the information that you are looking for (such as "ZIP code lookup" or "topographical maps") in a search site's search box to see links to sites supplying that type of information.

FIGURE 1-28
The Google search site.

E-Mail

Electronic mail (more commonly called **e-mail**) is the process of exchanging electronic messages between computers over a network—usually the Internet. It is one of the most widely used Internet applications—Americans alone send billions of e-mail messages daily. If you are connected to the Internet (via a desktop computer, portable computer, or mobile device), then you can send an e-mail message to anyone who has an Internet e-mail address. As illustrated in Figure 1-29, e-mail messages typically travel from the sender's PC to his or her ISP, and then through the Internet to the recipient's ISP. When the recipient logs on to the Internet and requests his or her e-mail, it is sent to the PC he or she is currently using. Because e-mail is stored for an individual until he or she requests it, the sender and the receiver do not have to be online at the same time to exchange e-mail. In addition to text, e-mail messages can include attached files, such as photos and other documents. Some e-mail systems today allow for video transmission, as well—sometimes called *video e-mail*.

In order to send or receive e-mail, you typically use an *e-mail program* (such as *Netscape Mail*, *Microsoft Outlook Express*, *Microsoft Outlook*, or a proprietary mail program used by your ISP) that is set up with your name, e-mail address, incoming mail server, and outgoing mail server information. Once your e-mail program has been set up successfully, you do not need to specify this information again, unless you want to retrieve

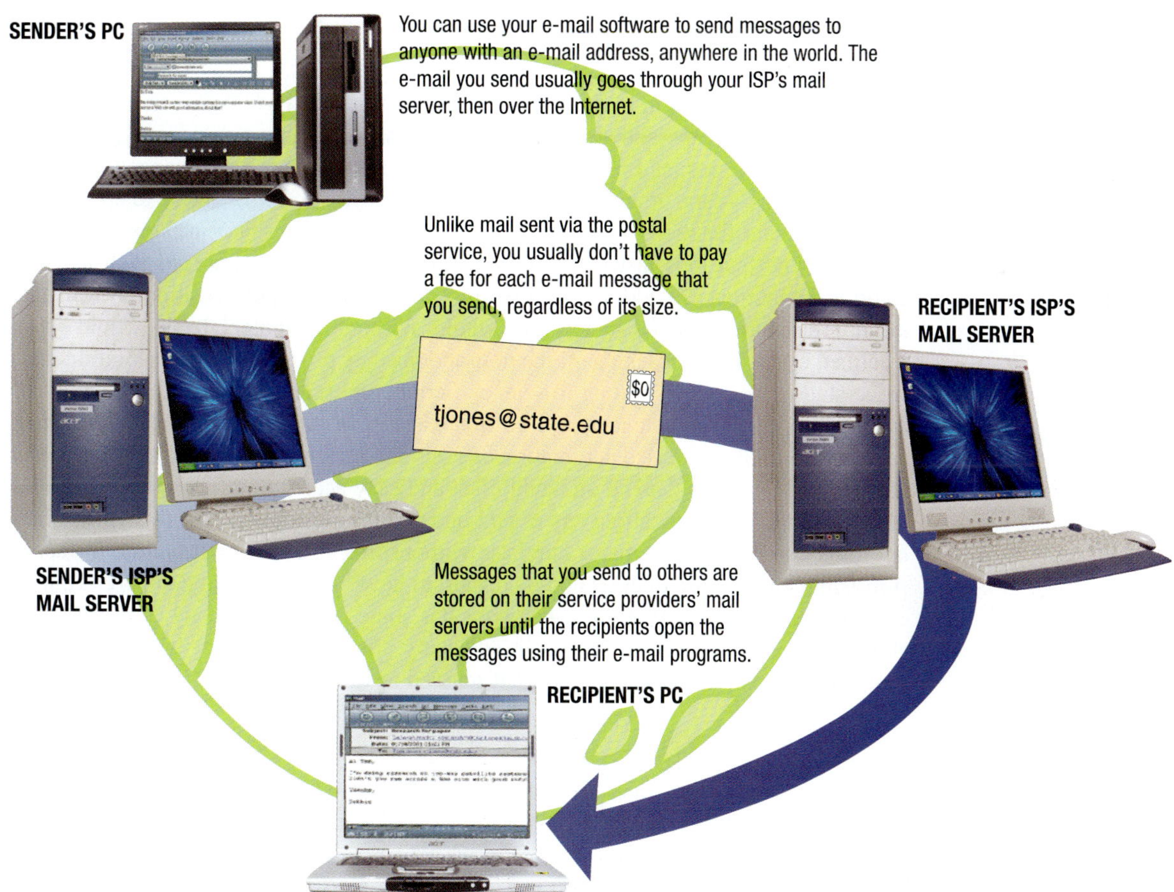

FIGURE 1-29
How conventional e-mail works.

>**Electronic mail (e-mail).** Electronic messages sent from one user to another over the Internet or other network.

TIP

For a closer look at how to send, receive, and manage e-mail messages, see the "E-Mail Fundamentals" section of the References and Resources Guide located at the end of this book.

e-mail sent to a different e-mail account, you want to check your e-mail from a different PC, or you change ISPs. Some browsers allow multiple e-mail accounts (such as both a personal and school account) to be set up at one time. Others support only one e-mail account at a time, so the settings must be changed to check a different e-mail account.

Virtually all ISPs used with desktop and portable PCs include e-mail service in their monthly fee and do not charge additional fees for sending or receiving e-mail messages. However, many plans from wireless providers (such as those used with handheld PCs and smart phones) include a limited number or size of e-mail messages that can be sent or received during a billing period; messages after that point result in additional fees. With conventional e-mail, messages are usually downloaded to the user's PC and viewed using an e-mail program. With *Web-based e-mail*, e-mail messages stay on the mail server and are viewed using a Web browser. Web-based e-mail is offered by some ISPs, and free Web-based e-mail is available from some Web-based e-mail providers, such as *Hotmail*, *Yahoo! Mail*, and *Google Gmail*. Web-based e-mail is more flexible than conventional e-mail, since a user's e-mail can be accessed from any computer with an Internet connection. The user does not have to change his or her e-mail settings in order to view e-mail messages from a different PC, and all e-mail messages in the user's Inbox can be viewed from any computer. However, Web-based e-mail is typically slower than conventional e-mail and raises some privacy concerns, since your e-mail messages are stored on a Web server instead of on your PC.

COMPUTERS AND SOCIETY

The vast improvements in technology over the past decade have had a distinct impact on daily life, both at home and at work. Computers have become indispensable tools in our homes and businesses, and related technological advancements have changed the way our everyday items—cars, microwaves, coffee pots, toys, exercise bikes, telephones, and more—look and function. As computers and everyday devices become smarter, they tend to do their normal jobs faster, better, and more reliably than before, as well as take on additional functions. In addition to affecting individuals, computerization and advancing technologies have changed society as a whole. Without computers, banks would be overwhelmed by the job of tracking all the transactions they process, moon exploration and the space shuttle would still belong to science fiction, and scientific advances, such as DNA analysis and gene mapping, would be nonexistent. In addition, individuals are getting accustomed to the increased automation of everyday activities, such as shopping, banking, and travel. Many also depend on having fast and easy access to information via the Internet, and rapid communications via e-mail and instant messaging. And many of us would not think about making a major purchase without first researching it online. In fact, it is surprising how fast the Internet and its resources have become an integral part of our society. But despite all its benefits, *cyberspace* has some risks. How many of us really think about how our online activities might adversely affect us? Some of the most important societal implications of cyberspace are discussed next.

Benefits of a Computer-Oriented Society

The benefits of having such a computer-oriented society are numerous, as touched on throughout this chapter. The capability to virtually design, build, and test new buildings, cars, and airplanes before the actual construction begins helps professionals create safer end products. Technological advances in medicine allow for earlier diagnosis and more effective treatment of diseases than ever before. The benefit of beginning medical students performing virtual surgery using a computer instead of performing actual surgery on a patient is obvious. The ability to shop, pay bills, research products, participate in online courses, and look up vast amounts of information 24 hours a day, 7 days a week, 365 days a year via the Internet is a huge convenience. In addition, a computer-oriented society generates new opportunities. For example, technologies, such as speech recognition software and Braille input and output devices, enable physically or visually challenged individuals to perform necessary job tasks and communicate with others more easily.

In general, technology has also made a huge number of tasks in our lives go much faster. Instead of experiencing a long delay for a credit check, an applicant can get approved for a loan or credit card almost immediately. Documents and photographs can be e-mailed or faxed in mere moments, instead of taking at least a day to be physically mailed. And you can download information, programs, music files, and more on demand when you want or need them, instead of having to order them and then wait for delivery or physically going to a store to purchase the desired items.

Risks of a Computer-Oriented Society

Although there are a great number of benefits from having a computer-oriented society and a *networked economy*, there are risks as well. A variety of problems have emerged in recent years, ranging from stress and health concerns, to personal security and privacy issues, to ethical dilemmas. Many of the security and privacy concerns stem from the fact that so much of our personal business takes place online—or at least ends up as data in a computer database somewhere—and the potential for misuse of this data is enormous. Another concern is that we may not have had time to consider all the repercussions of collecting such vast amounts of information. Some people worry about creating a "Big Brother" situation, in which the government or another organization is watching everything that we do. Although the accumulation and distribution of information is a necessary factor of our networked economy, it is one area of great concern to many individuals. And some Internet behavior, such as downloading music or movies from an unauthorized source or viewing pornography on a school or office PC, can even get you sued or fired.

Security Issues

One of the most common online security risks today is your PC becoming infected with a *computer virus*—a malicious software program designed to change the way a computer operates. Computer viruses often cause damage to the infected PC, such as erasing data or bogging down the computer so it does not function well. Viruses can be attached to a program (such as one downloaded from the Internet), as well as attached to, or contained within, an e-mail message. To help protect your computer from viruses, never open e-mail attachments from someone you do not know or that have an executable *file extension* (the last three letters in the filename preceded by a period), such as *.exe*, *.com*, or *.vbs*, without first checking with the sender to make sure the attachment is legitimate. It is also crucial to install an *antivirus program* on your PC and set it up to scan all e-mail messages, attachments, and files before they are downloaded to make sure they are virus-free, as well as to scan your entire PC periodically for viruses. If a virus is found in an e-mail message (see Figure 1-30), the antivirus program will delete the infected file before the message appears in your Inbox; if a virus is found on your PC, the antivirus program will try to remove it.

Another growing security problem is *identity theft*—in which someone else uses your identity, typically to purchase goods or services. Identity theft can stem from personal information discovered from offline means—like discarded papers—or from information found online. *Phishing*—in which identity thieves send fraudulent e-mails to people masquerading as legitimate businesses to obtain social security numbers or other information needed for identity theft—is also a major security issue today. Common security concerns and precautions, such as protecting your PC from viruses and protecting yourself from identity theft, are discussed in more detail in Chapter 9.

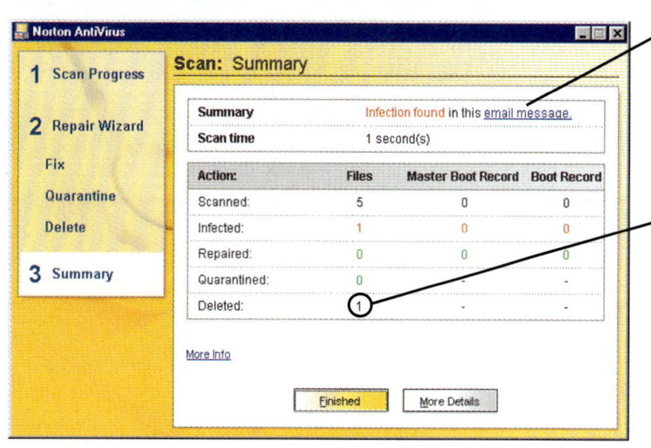

FIGURE 1-30
Antivirus software. Antivirus software is crucial for protecting your PC from computer viruses.

Privacy Issues

Some individuals view the potential risk to personal privacy as one of the most important issues regarding our networked society. As more and more data about our everyday activities is collected and stored in databases, our privacy is at risk because the potential for privacy violations increases. Today, data is collected about practically anything we buy online or offline, although offline purchases may not be associated with our identity unless we use a credit card or a membership or loyalty card. At issue is not that data is collected—with virtually all organizations using computers for recordkeeping, that is just going to happen—but rather how the collected data is used and how secure it is. Data collected by businesses may be used only by that company or, depending on the businesses' *privacy policy*, may be shared with others. Data shared with others often results in *spam*—unsolicited e-mails. Spam is an enormous problem for individuals and businesses today, and it is considered by many to be a violation of personal privacy. Privacy concerns and precautions are discussed in more detail in Chapter 15.

TIP

Use a *throw-away e-mail address*–a free e-mail address from Yahoo! or another free e-mail provider that you can change easily when shopping. This will help protect your privacy and cut back on the amount of spam delivered to your regular e-mail account.

Differences in Online Communications

There is no doubt that e-mail, instant messaging, and other online communications methods have helped speed up both personal and business communications and have made them more efficient (no more telephone tag, for instance). As you spend more and more time communicating online, you will probably notice some differences between online communications methods (e-mail, chat, and discussion groups, for example) and traditional communications methods (such as telephone calls and written letters). In general, online communications tend to be much less formal. This may be because people usually compose e-mail messages quickly and just send them off, without taking the time to reread and consider their message content or check their spelling or grammar. However, you need to be careful not to be so casual—particularly in business—that your communications appear unprofessional or become too personal with people you do not know.

To help in that regard, a special etiquette—referred to as **netiquette**—has evolved to guide online behavior. A good rule of thumb is always to be polite and considerate of others and to refrain from offensive remarks. This holds true whether you are asking a question via a company's e-mail address, posting a discussion group message, or chatting with a friend. When the communication involves business, you should also be very careful with your grammar and spelling, to avoid embarrassing yourself. Some specific guidelines are listed in Figure 1-31.

FIGURE 1-31

Netiquette. Use these netiquette guidelines and common sense when communicating online.

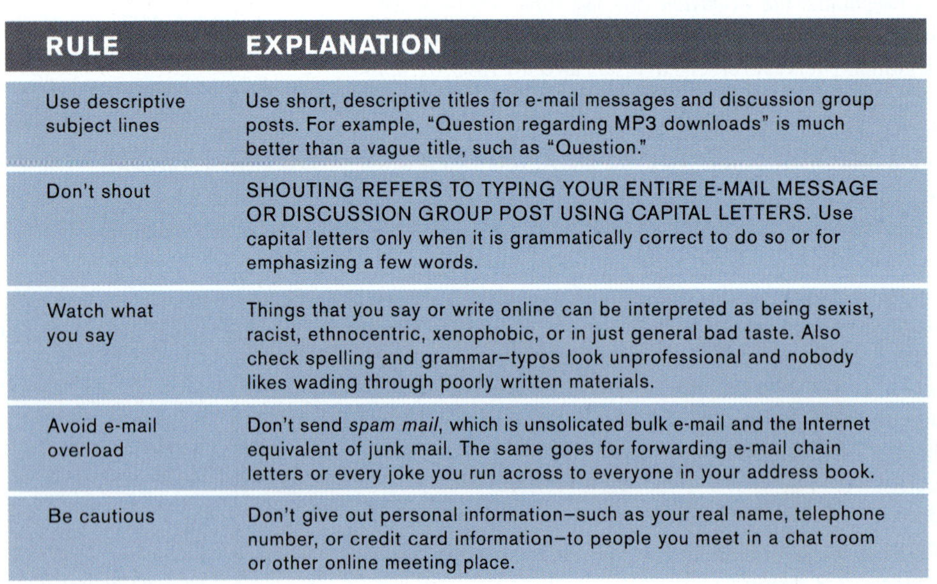

RULE	EXPLANATION
Use descriptive subject lines	Use short, descriptive titles for e-mail messages and discussion group posts. For example, "Question regarding MP3 downloads" is much better than a vague title, such as "Question."
Don't shout	SHOUTING REFERS TO TYPING YOUR ENTIRE E-MAIL MESSAGE OR DISCUSSION GROUP POST USING CAPITAL LETTERS. Use capital letters only when it is grammatically correct to do so or for emphasizing a few words.
Watch what you say	Things that you say or write online can be interpreted as being sexist, racist, ethnocentric, xenophobic, or in just general bad taste. Also check spelling and grammar–typos look unprofessional and nobody likes wading through poorly written materials.
Avoid e-mail overload	Don't send *spam mail*, which is unsolicated bulk e-mail and the Internet equivalent of junk mail. The same goes for forwarding e-mail chain letters or every joke you run across to everyone in your address book.
Be cautious	Don't give out personal information–such as your real name, telephone number, or credit card information–to people you meet in a chat room or other online meeting place.

Another trend in online communications is the use of abbreviations and *emoticons*. Abbreviations or *acronyms*, such as BTW for "by the way," are commonly used to save time in all types of communications today. They are being used with increased frequency in text messaging and e-mail exchanged via

>Netiquette. An etiquette for guiding online behavior.

wireless phones to speed up the text entry process. Emoticons—also sometimes called *smileys*—allow people to add an emotional tone to written online communications. Without these symbols, it is sometimes difficult to tell if the person is serious, joking, or being facetious, since you cannot see the individual's face or hear his or her tone of voice. Emoticons are illustrations of faces showing smiles, frowns, and other expressions that are created with keyboard symbols, such as the popular smile emoticon :-) (tilt your head to the left to view it). With some programs, emoticons are changed into actual faces, such as ☺. While most people would agree that these abbreviations and symbols are fine to use with personal and casual communications, they are not usually viewed as appropriate for formal business communications.

The Anonymity Factor

By their very nature, online communications lend themselves to *anonymity*. Since recipients usually do not hear senders' voices or see their handwriting, it is difficult to know for sure who the sender is. Particularly in discussion groups and chat rooms, where individuals use made-up names instead of real names, there is an anonymous feel to being online.

Being anonymous gives many individuals a sense of freedom, which makes them feel able to say or do anything online. This sense of true freedom of speech can be beneficial. For example, a reserved individual who might never complain about a poor product or service in person may feel comfortable lodging a complaint by e-mail. In political newsgroups or chat discussions, many people feel they can be completely honest about what they think and can introduce new ideas and points of view without inhibition. Anonymous e-mail is also a safe way for an employee to blow the whistle on a questionable business practice, or for an individual to tip off police to a crime or potential terrorist attack.

But, like all good things, online anonymity can be abused. Using the Internet as their shield, some people use rude comments, ridicule, profanity, and even slander to attack people, places, and things they do not like or agree with. Others may use multiple online identities (such as assuming two or more different usernames in a discussion group) to give the appearance of increased support for their points of view. Still others, feeling that their identities are protected, may use multiple identities to try to manipulate stock prices (by posting multiple negative messages or false information about a company to drive the price down, for instance), to get buyers to trust an online auction seller (by posting fictitious positive feedback comments about themselves), or to commit other types of illegal or unethical acts.

It is possible to hide your true identity while browsing or sending e-mail by removing personal information from your browser and e-mail program or by using a cloaking service, such as the *Anonymizer* service available for about $30 per year. But, in fact, even when personal information is removed, ISPs and the government may still be able to trace communications back to a particular computer when a crime has occurred, so it is difficult—perhaps impossible—to be completely anonymous online.

Information Integrity

As stated time and time again, the World Wide Web contains a vast amount of information on a wide variety of topics. While much of the information is factual, other information may be misleading, biased, or just plain wrong. As more and more people turn to the Web for information, it is crucial that they take the time to determine if the information they obtain and pass on to others is accurate. There have been numerous cases of information intended as a joke being restated on a Web site as fact, statements being quoted out of context, which changed the meaning from the original intent, and hoaxes circulated via e-mail. Consequently, use common sense when evaluating what you read online, and double-check information before passing it on to others.

TIP

To check if a story you hear about or receive via e-mail is a hoax or chain letter, try the Hoaxbusters site at hoaxbuster.ciac.org.

One of the most direct ways of evaluating online content is by considering the source. If you obtain information from a news source that you trust, you should feel confident that the accuracy of its online information is close to that of its offline counterpart. For information about a particular product or technology, go to the originating company. For government information, government Web sites have more objective information than other Web sites that may have a bias.

SUMMARY

COMPUTERS IN YOUR LIFE

Chapter Objective 1:
Explain why it is essential to learn about computers today and discuss several ways computers are integrated into our business and personal lives.

Computers appear almost everywhere in today's world, and most people need to use a computer or a computerized device frequently on the job, at home, at school, or while on the go. **Computer literacy**, which is being familiar with basic computer concepts, helps individuals feel more comfortable using computers and is a necessary skill for everyone today.

Computers abound in today's homes, schools, workplaces, and other locations. Increasingly, students and employees need to use a computer for productivity or research. Individuals often use computers at home and/or carry portable computers or devices with them to remain in touch with others or to use Internet resources on a continual basis.

WHAT IS A COMPUTER AND WHAT DOES IT DO?

Chapter Objective 2:
Define a computer and describe its primary operations.

A **computer** is a *programmable* electronic device that accepts **input**; performs **processing** operations; **outputs** the results; and provides **storage** for data, programs, or output when needed. Most computers today also have **communications** capabilities. This progression of input, processing, output, and storage is sometimes called the *information processing cycle.*

Data is the raw, unorganized facts that are input into the computer to be processed. Data that the computer has processed into a useful form is called **information**. Data can exist in many forms, representing *text*, *graphics*, *audio*, and *video*.

Chapter Objective 3:
List some important milestones in computer evolution.

One of the first calculating devices was the *abacus*. Early computing devices that predate today's computers include the *slide rule*, the *mechanical calculator*, and Dr. Herman Hollerith's *Punch Card Tabulating Machine and Sorter*. *First-generation computers*, such as *ENIAC* and *UNIVAC*, were powered by *vacuum tubes*; *second-generation computers* used *transistors*; and *third-generation computers* were possible because of the invention of the *integrated circuit* (*IC*). Today's *fourth-generation computers* use *microprocessors* and are frequently connected to the *Internet* and other *networks*. Some people believe that *fifth-generation computers* will likely be based on *artificial intelligence*.

Chapter Objective 4:
Identify the major parts of a personal computer, including input, processing, output, storage, and communications hardware.

A computer is made up of **hardware** (the actual physical equipment that makes up the computer system) and **software** (the computer's programs). Common hardware components include the *keyboard* and *mouse* (*input devices*), the *CPU* and *memory* (*processing devices*), *monitors* and *printers* (*output devices*), and *storage devices* and *storage media* (such as *floppy disks*, *CDs*, and *flash memory cards*). Most computers today also include a *modem* or other type of *communications device*.

Chapter Objective 5:
Define software and understand how it is used to instruct the computer what to do.

All computers need *system software*, namely an **operating system** (usually *Windows*, *Mac OS*, or *Linux*), to function. The operating system assists with the **boot** process, and then controls the operation of the computer, such as to allow users to run other types of software and to manage their files. Most software programs today use a *graphical user interface* (*GUI*), which typically displays information in **windows** on the **desktop**. The Windows **taskbar** contains the *Start button*, *taskbar buttons* and *taskbar toolbars*, and the *system tray*. Common features found on windows include **menus**, **toolbars**, **icons**, **dialog boxes**, and **sizing buttons**. **Hyperlinks**, sometimes found in windows, are clicked to display another document, Web page, or other information.

Application software consists of programs designed to allow people to perform specific tasks or applications, such as word processing, Web browsing, photo touch-up, and so on. Software programs are written using a *programming language*. Programs are written by **programmers**; **computer users** are the people who use the computer system.

COMPUTERS TO FIT EVERY NEED

Chapter Objective 6:
List the five basic types of computers, giving at least one example of each type of computer and stating what that computer might be used for.

Mobile devices are small devices typically used for accessing Web page data and e-mail. Mobile devices are used by individuals to maintain communications with the office while on the road, as well as for quick checks of weather forecasts, stock prices, flight information, and other Internet resources available for that particular device.

Small computers used by individuals at home or work are called **personal computers (PCs)** or **microcomputers**. Most PCs today are either **desktop PCs** (with a *desktop*, *tower*, or *all-in-one case*) or **portable PCs (notebook computers, tablet PCs,** or **handheld computers)** and typically conform to either the *PC-compatible* or *Macintosh* standard. Tablet PCs come in both *slate* and *convertible* tablet *PC* formats. **Thin clients** are designed solely to access a network; **Internet appliances** are designed specifically for accessing the Internet and e-mail.

Medium-sized computers, or **midrange servers**, are used in small- to medium-sized businesses to host data and programs that can be accessed by the company network. The powerful computers used by most large businesses and organizations to perform the information processing necessary for day-to-day operations are called **mainframe computers**. The very largest, most powerful computers, which typically run one application at a time, are classified as **supercomputers**.

COMPUTER NETWORKS AND THE INTERNET

Chapter Objective 7:
Explain what a network, the Internet, and the World Wide Web are, as well as how computers, people, and Web pages are identified on the Internet.

Computer networks are used to connect individual computers and related devices so that users can share hardware, software, and data as well as communicate with one another. The **Internet** is a worldwide collection of networks. Typically, individual users connect to the Internet by connecting to computers belonging to an **Internet service provider (ISP)**—a company that provides Internet access, usually for a fee. One resource available through the Internet is the **World Wide Web**—an enormous collection of **Web pages** located on **Web servers**. The starting page for a **Web site** (a related group of Web pages) is called the *home page* for that site. Web pages are viewed with a **Web browser**, are connected with hyperlinks, and can be used to retrieve news and product information, download music and movies, play online games, shop, and a host of other activities.

To access a computer network, you need some type of *modem* or *network adapter*. To access the Internet, an *Internet service provider* (*ISP*) is also used.

Chapter Objective 8:
Describe how to access a Web page.

Internet addresses are used to identify resources on the Internet and include numerical **IP addresses** and text-based **domain names** (used to identify computers), **uniform resource locators** or **URLs** (used to identify Web pages), and **e-mail addresses** (a combination of a **username** and domain name that is used to send an individual e-mail messages).

Once you are connected to the Internet and have opened your browser, Web pages can be displayed by clicking hyperlinks or by typing the appropriate URLs in the browser's *Address bar*. *Search sites* can be used to locate Web pages matching certain criteria, and **electronic mail (e-mail)** is used to send electronic messages over the Internet.

COMPUTERS AND SOCIETY

Chapter Objective 9:
Discuss the societal impact of computers, including some benefits and risks related to their prominence in our society.

Computers and devices based on related technology have become indispensable tools for modern life, making ordinary tasks easier and quicker than ever before and helping make today's worker more productive than ever before. However, there are many societal implications related to our heavy use of the Internet and the vast amount of information available through the Internet. Issues include privacy and security risks and concerns, the differences in online and offline communications, the anonymity factor, and the amount of unreliable information that can be found on the Internet. In addition, a special etiquette—referred to as **netiquette**—has evolved to guide online behavior.

REVIEW ACTIVITIES

KEY TERM MATCHING

Instructions: Match each key term on the left with the definition on the right that best describes it

a. computer
b. hardware
c. hyperlink
d. Internet
e. operating system
f. software
g. storage
h. supercomputer
i. uniform resource locator (URL)
j. Web site

1. ______ A collection of related Web pages usually belonging to an organization or individual.
2. ______ An Internet address, usually beginning with http://, that uniquely identifies a Web page.
3. ______ A programmable, electronic device that accepts data input, performs processing operations on that data, and outputs and stores the results.
4. ______ A type of system software that enables a computer to operate and manage its resources and activities.
5. ______ Text or an image located on a Web page or other document that is linked to a Web page or other type of document.
6. ______ The operation of saving data, programs, or output for future use.
7. ______ The fastest, most expensive, and most powerful type of computer.
8. ______ The instructions, also called computer programs, that are used to tell a computer what it should do.
9. ______ The largest and most well-known computer network, linking millions of computers all over the world.
10. ______ The physical parts of a computer system, such as the keyboard, monitor, printer, and so forth.

SELF-QUIZ

Instructions: Circle **T** if the statement is true, **F** if the statement is false, or write the best answer in the space provided. **Answers for the self-quiz are located in the References and Resources Guide at the end of the book.**

1. **T F** A mouse is one common input device.
2. **T F** Software includes all the physical equipment in a computer system.
3. **T F** A computer can run without an operating system if it has good application software.
4. **T F** One of the most common types of home computers is the midrange server.
5. **T F** An example of a domain name is *microsoft.com*.
6. ______ is the operation in which data is entered into the computer.
7. A(n) ______ PC can come in convertible or slate form.
8. Web pages are connected using ______, which can be either text or images.
9. Electronic messages sent over the Internet that can be retrieved by the recipient at his or her convenience are called ______.

10. Write the number of the term that best matches each of the following descriptions on the blank to the left of its description.

a. ________ Allows access to resources located on the Internet.
b. ________ Supervises the running of all other programs on the computer.
c. ________ Helps prepare written documents, such as letters and reports.
d. ________ Allows an individual to create application programs.

1. Word processing program
2. Operating system
3. Programming language
4. Web browser

EXERCISES

1. For the following list of computer hardware devices, indicate the principal function of each device by writing the appropriate letter—I (input device), O (output device), S (storage device), P (processing device), or C (communications device)—in the space provided.

a. CPU ________ **d.** Keyboard ________ **g.** Speakers ________
b. Monitor ________ **e.** Hard drive ________ **h.** DVD drive ________
c. CD drive ________ **f.** Modem ________ **i.** Microphone ________

2. Supply the missing words to complete the following statements.

 a. The starting page for a Web site is called the site's ________.

 b. For the e-mail address *jsmith@course.com*, *jsmith* is the ________ and *course.com* is the ________ name.

 c. The e-mail address pronounced *bill gee at microsoft dot com* is written ________.

 d. One of the most common online security risks today is a computer becoming infected with a(n) ________, which is a software program designed to change the way a computer operates without the permission or knowledge of the user and which often causes damage to the PC.

3. What is the difference between a tablet PC and a notebook PC?

4. List two reasons why a business may choose to network its employees' computers.

5. If a computer manufacturer called Apex created a home page for the Web, what would its URL likely be? Also, supply an appropriate e-mail address for yourself, assuming that you are employed by that company.

DISCUSSION QUESTION

The ubiquitous nature of cell phones today brings tremendous convenience to our lives, but will misuse of new improvements to this technology result in the loss of that convenience? For instance, camera phones being used to take photos in changing rooms has resulted in a ban on camera phones in many fitness centers, park restrooms, and other similar facilities. Cell phones being used to cheat on exams by taking photos of the exam to give to other students in a later class or to exchange answers during the test via text messaging has led to a ban on cell phones in many classrooms during exam periods. Do you think these reactions to cell phone misuse are justified? Is there another way to ensure the appropriate use of cell phones without banning their use for all individuals? Should there be more stringent consequences for those who use technology for illegal or unethical purposes?

PROJECTS

HOT TOPICS

1. **Mobile TV** As discussed in the Trend box, TV is one of the newest entertainment options available for cell phones. From live TV shows to video clips to reruns of TVs shows and movies, mobile TV is taking off.

   For this project, investigate the mobile TV options available today. Find at least two services and compare features, such as cost, compatibility, channels, and programming. Do your selected services offer live TV, video-on-demand, or both? If you have a cell phone, are any of the services available through your cellular provider? Have you ever watched TV on a cell phone? Would you want to? Why or why not? At the conclusion of your research, prepare a one-page summary of your findings and submit it to your instructor.

SHORT ANSWER/ RESEARCH

2. **24 Hours** Computers have a tremendous impact on our daily lives. They can be used to generate information or facilitate transactions. They can also be embedded in devices or appliances. On a daily basis, many computers are used by consumers, or on behalf of consumers, to carry out everyday tasks.

   For this project, take notice of and record all encounters you have with computing devices for the next 24 hours. Be sure to include both the computers that you use and ones that are used on your behalf. You should note both positive and negative impacts of these devices, and what your daily routine might be like without them. At the conclusion of the 24 hours, prepare a one-page summary of your observations and submit it to your instructor.

3. **Your ISP** As discussed in the chapter, ISPs are used to connect to the Internet. You may have a limited number of options for an ISP, depending on where you live and how much you are willing to spend on Internet service.

   For this project, research what options you have to connect to the Internet from where you live. For conventional dial-up Internet service, either call a local service provider listed in your telephone book or go to the Web site for America Online, EarthLink, Juno, or another large ISP and determine which ones have a local telephone access number for your area. For faster Internet service, your telephone company should be able to tell you if they offer any types of Internet service (such as *DSL* or *ISDN*) in your area and what the costs are. If you have access to cable, check with your local cable provider for information on cable Internet. If DSL, ISDN, and cable are not available to you, check into satellite service (such as from StarBand or DirecPC). After you have completed your research, summarize your findings in a one-page paper, including the cost and estimated speed for each service, any limitations on e-mail (such as number of e-mail addresses, mailbox size, or size of attachments), and whether or not each service ties up your telephone line. Be sure to include your opinion as to which service you would choose to use and why.

HANDS ON

4. **Buying a New PC** New PCs are widely available directly from manufacturers, as well as in retail, computer, electronic, and warehouse stores. Some stores carry only standard configurations as set up by the manufacturers; others allow you to customize a system.

   For this project, assume that you are in the market for a PC for your personal use. Make a list of your hardware and software requirements (refer to the "Guide for Buying a PC" in the References and Resources Guide at the end of this textbook, if needed), being as specific as possible. By researching newspaper ads, manufacturer Web sites, and/or systems for sale at local stores, find three systems that meet your minimum requirements. Prepare a one-page comparison chart, listing each requirement and how each system meets or exceeds it. Also include any additional features each system has, and information regarding the brand, price, delivery time, shipping, sales tax, and warranty terms for each system. On your comparison sheet, mark the system that you would prefer to buy and write one paragraph explaining why. Turn in your comparison sheet and summary to your instructor, stapled to copies of the printed ads, specifications printed from Web sites, or other written documentation that you collected during this project.

5. **The Internet** The Internet and World Wide Web are handy tools that can help you research topics covered in this textbook, complete many of the projects, and perform the online activities located on the textbook's Web site.

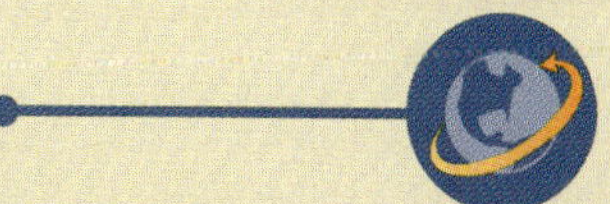

For this project, find an Internet-enabled computer on your campus, at home, or at your public library. Follow the directions provided by your instructor or lab aide to access the Understanding Computers Web site located at www.course.com/uc11. Once you are at the site, note the types of information and activities that are available to you as a student and select a few of them by using your mouse to click the hyperlinks—usually underlined or otherwise highlighted text or graphical buttons—corresponding to the options you want to explore. At the conclusion of this task, prepare a one-page summary describing the resources available through this textbook's Web site and submit it to your instructor.

WRITING ABOUT COMPUTERS

6. **Online Education** The amount of distance learning available through the Internet and World Wide Web has exploded in the last couple of years. A few years ago, it was possible to take an occasional course online—now, a college degree can be earned online.

For this project, look into the online education options available at your college or university and at least two other colleges or universities. Compare and contrast the programs in general, including such information as whether or not the institution is accredited, the types of courses available online, whether or not an entire certificate or degree can be earned online, and the required fees. After you have completed your general research, select one online course that interests you and research it more closely. Find out how the course works in an online format, including whether or not any face-to-face class time is required, whether assignments and exams are submitted online, which software programs or *plug-ins* (programs that give extra capabilities to a Web browser) are required, and other class requirements. Summarize your findings in a two- to three-page paper. Be sure to include your opinion as to whether or not you would be interested in taking an online course and why.

7. **E-Mail Options** If you have access to the Internet, you can exchange electronic messages—including digital photos and other types of files—with any other person who has an e-mail address. This exchange can be accomplished using your computer or a PC available through your home, school, public library, or other location, provided that computer is connected to the Internet.

For this project, research what e-mail options are available to the students at your school through the school's e-mail server as well as through free e-mail services available online, such as Hotmail, Yahoo! Mail, or Google Gmail. Compare features, such as mailbox size and any limitations on attachments, of the available services. Select one free online e-mail provider and sign up for an account. Send yourself one e-mail to experience the service and evaluate the features available through that online e-mail provider. Share your findings with the class in the form of a short presentation. The presentation should not exceed 10 minutes and should make use of one or more presentation aids, such as the chalkboard, handouts, overhead transparencies, or a computer-based slide presentation (your instructor may provide additional requirements). If possible, demonstrate the e-mail service you selected to the class. You may also be asked to submit a summary of the presentation to your instructor.

GROUP DISCUSSION

8. **New Technology: Benefits vs. Risks** As illustrated throughout this chapter, new technology adds convenience to our daily lives, helps many employees become more productive, and can increase the length and quality of our lives. However, there is usually a positive side and a negative side to each new technological improvement. Agricultural advancements help farmers grow more food more economically, but many people are concerned that heavy pesticide use and genetic engineering of crops and animals are dangerous to their health. Nuclear energy generates a very clean source for power, but it also has the possibility of tremendous destruction. The Internet allows users to obtain information very quickly and efficiently and to communicate with others at their convenience, but it also permits unscrupulous individuals to find out private information about others and commit fraud in ways that are easier than any that existed before. It is good to carefully consider the benefits vs. the risks of new technologies as they are made available to you.

   For this project, think of a technology, product, or service that you use (such as desktop PCs, handheld computers, cell phones, distance learning, online shopping, online banking, ATM machines, e-mail, electronic signature devices, music CDs, digital cameras, or DVD players). Consider the following questions: What benefits does this technology offer me? Does it bring any potential risks to my health, privacy, or security? If so, what can I do to minimize these risks? If this product or service did not exist, how would my life be different? If I don't use this technology, will I be at a disadvantage? Form an opinion about the benefits and risks of using this product or service and be prepared to discuss your position (in class, via an online class discussion group, or in a class chat room, depending on your instructor's directions). You may also be asked to write a short paper expressing your opinion.

INT

WEB ACTIVITIES

The *Understanding Computers* Web site located at **www.course.com/uc11** features many resources to help reinforce your understanding of the chapter content and help you prepare for exams. Your instructor may also assign specific activities to be completed that will count toward your final grade in the course.

Instructions: Go to **www.course.com/uc11/ch01** to work the following online activities.

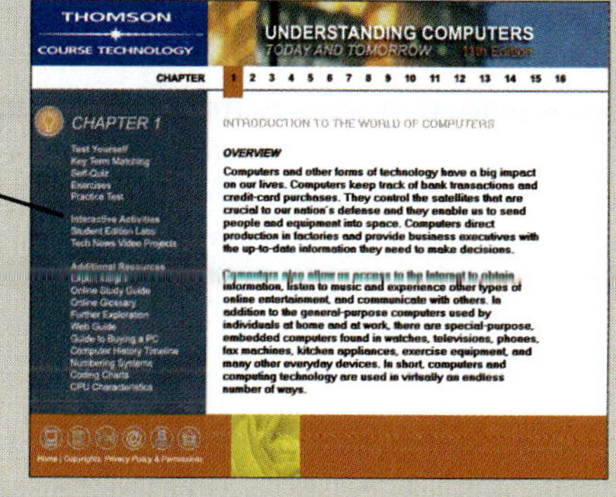

Click any link in the navigation bar on the left to access any of the online resources described below.

INTERACTIVE ACTIVITIES

1. **Crossword Puzzle** Practice your knowledge of the key terms in Chapter 1 by completing the interactive Crossword Puzzle.
2. **Tech News Video Project** Watch the **"High-Tech Climbing"** video clip that features professional mountain climber Ed Viesturs who brings a variety of high-tech gear (such as a notebook computer, digital camera, satellite phone, solar panels to recharge the equipment, and an all-in-one digital barometer, thermometer, altimeter, and wind gauge) on his climbs. After watching the video online, complete the corresponding project.
3. **Student Edition Labs** Reinforce the concepts you have learned in this chapter by working through the interactive **Using Windows** and **E-Mail** labs.

Student Edition Labs

TEST YOURSELF

1. **Key Term Matching** Test your knowledge of selected chapter key terms by matching the terms with their definitions.
2. **Self-Quiz** Test your retention of chapter concepts by taking the Self-Quiz.
3. **Exercises** Work these short exercises to review the concepts and terms covered in the chapter.
4. **Practice Test** Test how ready you are for an upcoming exam by completing the online Practice Test.

STUDY TOOLS/ ADDITIONAL RESOURCES

The Understanding Computers Web site has a wide range of additional resources, including an **Online Study Guide** (containing study tips, a chapter outline with room to add your own notes, and a chapter checklist of the activities to complete when the chapter is covered in class and when you are preparing for a test) and an **Online Glossary** for each chapter; **Further Exploration** links; a **Web Guide**, a **Guide to Buying a PC**, and a **Computer History Timeline**; more information about **Numbering Systems**, **Coding Charts**, and **CPU Characteristics**; and much, much more!

EXPERT INSIGHT ON . . .
Personal Computers

NOKIA

A conversation with **VIPUL MEHROTRA**
Director, Technology and Portfolio Management for Nokia North America

My Background . . .

From an early age I was very interested in science (Dad is an Aeronautical Engineer). In undergraduate college I took Information Sciences Engineering as my field of study. I have been lucky enough to work with computers, workstations, services, software, and networks right from the beginning of my career. I gained experience in the IT industry before I moved to the telecom industry which attracted me due to the immense growth potential of mobility and communication.

> **"The power of mobility has transformed the way people live their lives, in addition to the way they communicate."**

It's Important to Know . . .

The different kinds of computers available today. Computers are rapidly evolving, and new technology and terminology is surfacing faster than before. The risk is that people can get lost. Chapter 1 gives students a clear understanding and a good starting point to navigate through the world of computers.

What the Internet can be used for. I think this is a key point because our society today revolves around the Internet and we are highly dependent on it. The Internet is increasingly going mobile and in five years we will see mobile Internet becoming more popular.

The power of mobile devices. Mobile devices have expanded from just voice capabilities to imaging, games, entertainment, media, and many other exciting applications. Today a cellular phone can be built with a computer-like functionality to take pictures, play games, read news, stream videos, and much more. The power of mobility has transformed the way people live their lives, in addition to the way they communicate. People are more connected to their friends and family, as well as to information, media, entertainment, etc., while they are mobile. Students should understand how they can use this power to their advantage, such as to become better informed, communicate more easily, and share information.

How I Use this Technology . . .

I regularly use computers to search for information, to read and write e-mail including remote e-mail (when I am traveling), to share pictures, to keep in touch with family and friends, to pay bills, etc. I use my mobile phone (Nokia 9300 and Nokia 6682) to be connected (via voice and text messaging) with my friends, family, colleagues, and customers, as well as to read the news, exchange e-mail, share images, and download video clips. I also use my mobile phone as an alarm clock and calculator.

Vipul Mehrotra is currently the Director, Technology and Portfolio Management for Nokia North America. He is part of the Customer and Market Operations team engaged in technology marketing with key customers and the analysts, and portfolio analysis and development. In his 12 years working in this industry, he has worked for Nokia in the United States, Finland, and India. Vipul holds college degrees in both Engineering and Business.

. . . the mobile phone has the potential to become the one personal device with which one can communicate, share information, transact, stream video and music, and so forth.

What the Future Holds . . .

Computers will be faster, smaller, full of rich media applications, will use wireless connections instead of cables, and could be the main information and entertainment device at home. As cellular phones are evolving from a voice only device to a voice device combined with a rich software platform, the mobile phone has the potential to become the one personal device with which one can communicate, share information, transact, stream video and music, and so forth. It will be the preferred device while on the go. Future evolution of mobile devices will see them interoperate with other devices at home—for example, to share images with TVs or PCs via Wi-Fi. Mobile video applications (such as video sharing, video streaming, video downloads, and video phone calls) have a lot of potential for the future as mobile devices and the communications infrastructure continue to become increasingly capable of handling such powerful applications/services.

Computers in general have transformed our society and today we are a digital society. Mobile devices will transform the society further and our life will be increasingly mobile. Students today should embrace mobility and use it for more than voice. They should use mobility to become a more informed person and to connect with other people and applications.

My Advice to Students . . .

Use technology to become a better informed person and use the information gained to become a responsible person. Use technology as an enabler to achieve your goals and improve your life and the lives of others.

Discussion Question

Vipul Mehrotra views the mobile phone as the platform of choice for the future. Think about which computing tasks you use your mobile phone for today and which ones you cannot. What changes need to be made in the future in order to perform all of these tasks on a mobile phone? Will the changes be primarily hardware changes? Software changes? Is the mobile phone the computer of the future? Be prepared to discuss your position (in class, via an online class discussion group, or in a class chat room, depending on your instructor's directions). You may also be asked to write a short paper expressing your opinion.

>For more information on Nokia and Nokia products, visit www.nokia.com.

MODULE HARDWARE

When most people think of computer systems, images of hardware usually fill their minds. Hardware includes the keyboard, monitor, and all of the other interesting pieces of equipment you take out of the box when you buy a computer system. This module explores the rich variety of computer hardware available today. But as you already know, hardware needs guidance from software in order to function. Hardware without software is like a car without a driver or a canvas and paintbrush without an artist.

This module divides coverage of hardware into three subject areas. Chapter 2 describes the hardware located inside the main box of the computer, which is called the system unit—the location where most of the work of a computer is performed. Chapter 3 discusses storage devices, which are the types of hardware that provide an indispensable library of resources for the computer. Chapter 4 covers the wide variety of hardware that can be used for input and output.

"Computers will get woven, invisibly in many cases, into many more aspects of life, such as in maintaining a healthy lifestyle, education, the environment, and government services."

For more comments from Guest Expert John Janakiraman of HP Labs, see the Expert Insight on . . . Hardware feature at the end of the module.

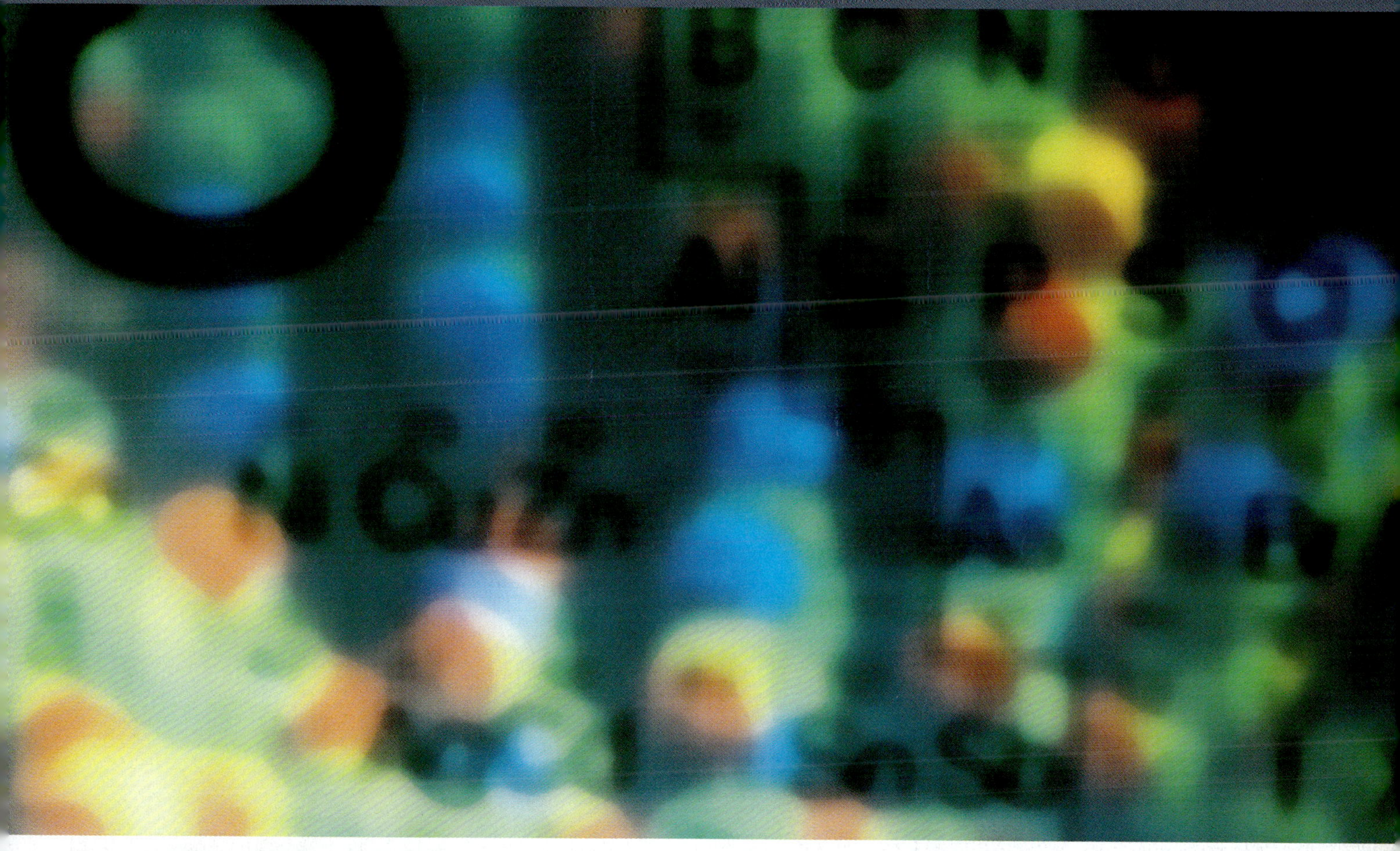

IN THIS MODULE

Chapter 2 The System Unit: Processing and Memory 54

Overview 55

Data and Program Representation 55

Inside the System Unit 62

How the CPU Works 75

Making Computers Faster and Better Now and in the Future 81

Chapter 3 Storage 96

Overview 97

Storage Systems Characteristics 97

Magnetic Disk Systems 100

Optical Disc Systems 109

Flash Memory Systems 114

Other Types of Storage Systems 117

Comparing Storage Alternatives 122

Chapter 4 Input and Output 132

Overview 133

Keyboards 133

Pointing Devices 135

Scanners, Readers, and Digital Cameras 141

Audio Input 152

Display Devices 154

Printers 163

Audio Output 168

The System Unit: Processing and Memory

OUTLINE

Overview
Data and Program Representation
- Digital Data Representation
- Representing Numerical Data: The Binary Numbering System
- Coding Systems for Text-Based Data
- Coding Systems for Other Types of Data
- Representing Programs: Machine Language

Inside the System Unit
- The Motherboard
- The CPU
- Memory
- Fans, Heat Sinks, and Other Cooling Components
- Expansion Slots and Cards
- Buses
- Ports

How the CPU Works
- Typical CPU Components
- The System Clock and the Machine Cycle

Making Computers Faster and Better Now and in the Future
- Improving the Performance of Your System Today
- Strategies for Making Faster and Better Computers
- Future Trends

LEARNING OBJECTIVES

After completing this chapter, you will be able to:

1. Understand how data and programs are represented to a computer and be able to identify a few of the coding systems used to accomplish this.
2. Explain the functions of the hardware components commonly found inside the system unit, such as the CPU, memory, buses, and expansion cards.
3. Describe how peripheral devices or other hardware can be added to a PC.
4. Understand how the computer system's CPU and memory components process program instructions and data.
5. Name and evaluate several strategies that can be used today for speeding up the operations of a computer.
6. List some technologies that may be used in future PCs.

OVERVIEW

The system unit of a computer is sometimes thought of as a mysterious "black box" that makes the computer work, and often the user does not have much understanding of what happens inside the computer. In this chapter, we demystify the system unit by looking inside the box and closely examining the functions of the parts inside. In doing so, the chapter gives you a feel for how the CPU, memory, and other devices commonly found within the system unit work together to process data into meaningful information.

To start, we discuss how a computer system represents data and program instructions. Here we talk about the codes that computers use to translate data back and forth from symbols that the computer can manipulate to symbols that people are accustomed to using. These topics lead into a discussion of how the CPU and memory are arranged with other processing and storage components inside the system unit, and then how a CPU carries out processing tasks. Finally, we look at strategies that are used today to speed up a computer, plus some strategies that may be used to create faster and better computers in the future.

While most of you reading this chapter will apply its contents to conventional personal computer systems–such as desktop and notebook PCs–keep in mind that the principles and procedures discussed in this chapter cover a broad range of computer products. These products include microprocessors embedded in toys, household appliances, and other devices, as well as processors located in powerful servers, mainframes, and supercomputers. ■

DATA AND PROGRAM REPRESENTATION

In order to be understood by a computer, data and programs need to be represented appropriately. There are *coding systems* (also called *coding schemes*) that are used to represent numeric, text-based, and multimedia data, as well as to represent programs. These concepts are discussed in the next few sections.

Digital Data Representation

Most computers today—such as the mobile devices, microcomputers, midrange servers, mainframes, and supercomputers discussed in Chapter 1—are *digital computers*. Digital computers can understand only two states, usually thought of as *off* and *on* and represented by the digits 0 and 1. Consequently, all data processed by a computer must be in digital form (0s and 1s) for it to be processed and stored. The process of representing data in digital form so it can be used by a digital computer is called *digital data representation*.

The 0s and 1s used with digital devices can be represented in a variety of ways, such as with an open or closed circuit, the absence or presence of an electronic charge, the absence or presence of a magnetic spot or depression on a storage medium, and so on. This two-state, or *binary*, nature of electronic devices is illustrated in Figure 2-1. Regardless of their physical representations, these 0s and 1s are commonly referred to as *bits*, a

FIGURE 2-1
Ways of representing 0 and 1. Digital computers recognize only two states–off and on–usually represented by 0 and 1.

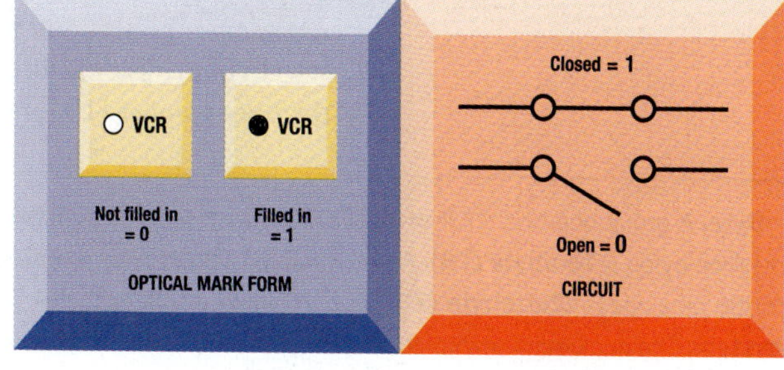

computing term derived from the phrase *binary digits*. A bit is the smallest unit of data that a digital computer can recognize, so the input you enter via a keyboard, the software program you use to play your MP3 files, and the term paper stored on your PC are all just groups of bits. Consequently, binary can be thought of as the computer's "native language."

People, of course, do not speak binary language. For example, you are not likely to go up to a friend and say,

0100100001001001

which translates into the word "HI" using one binary coding system. People communicate with one another in their *natural languages*, such as English, Chinese, Spanish, and French. For example, this book is written in English, which uses a 26-character alphabet. In addition, most countries use a numbering system with 10 possible symbols—0 through 9. As already mentioned, however, computers understand only 0s and 1s. For us to interact with a computer, a translation process from our natural language to 0s and 1s and then back again is required. When we enter data into a computer system, the computer translates the natural-language symbols we input into binary 0s and 1s. After processing the data in digital form, the computer translates and outputs the resulting information in a form that can be understood by the user.

A bit by itself typically represents only a fraction of a piece of data. Consequently, bits are usually grouped together to form letters and other characters, documents, program files, graphics files, and more. Eight bits grouped together are collectively referred to as a **byte**. It is important to be familiar with this concept because "byte" terminology is frequently used in a variety of computer contexts. For example, document size and storage capacity are measured in bytes, based on the amount of data that is contained in the document or that can be stored on the storage medium. In fact, the size of any item—such as a computer program, written document, photograph, or music file—stored on a storage medium is measured in bytes. Prefixes are commonly used with the term *byte* to represent larger amounts of data (see Figure 2-2). A **kilobyte (KB)** is equal to 1,024 bytes, but is usually thought of as approximately 1,000 bytes. A **megabyte (MB)** is about 1 million bytes; a **gigabyte (GB)** is about 1 billion bytes; a **terabyte (TB)** is about 1 trillion bytes; a **petabyte (PB)** is about 1,000 terabytes (2^{50} bytes); an **exabyte (EB)** is about 1,000 petabytes (2^{60} bytes); a **zettabyte (ZB)** is about 1,000 exabytes (2^{70} bytes); and a **yottabyte (YB)** is about 1,000 zettabytes (2^{80} bytes). Therefore, 5 KB is about 5,000 bytes, 10 MB is approximately 10 million bytes, and 2 TB is about 2 trillion bytes.

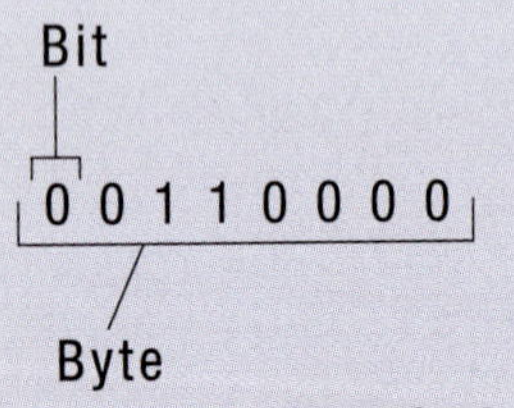

Computers represent programs and data through a variety of binary-based coding schemes. The coding system used depends primarily on the type of data needing to be represented. Coding systems for numerical, text-based, and a few other types of data are discussed in the next few sections.

Bit

0 0 1 1 0 0 0 0

Byte

Abbreviation	Approximate Size
KB	1,024 bytes
MB	1 million bytes
GB	1 billion bytes
TB	1 trillion bytes
PB	1,000 terabytes

FIGURE 2-2
Bits and bytes.
Document size, storage capacity, and memory capacity are all measured in bytes.

Representing Numerical Data: The Binary Numbering System

A *numbering system* is a way of representing numbers. The numbering system we commonly use is called the *decimal* (or *base 10*) *numbering system* because it uses 10 symbols—the digits 0, 1, 2, 3, 4, 5, 6, 7, 8, and 9—to represent all possible numbers. Numbers greater than nine, such as 21 and 683, are represented using combinations of these 10 symbols. The **binary numbering system** uses only two symbols—the digits 0 and 1—to represent all possible numbers. Consequently, computers use the binary numbering system to represent numbers and perform math computations.

In both systems, the position of each digit determines the power, or exponent, to which the *base number* (10 for decimal or 2 for binary) is raised. In the decimal numbering system,

>Byte. A group of 8 bits. **>Kilobyte (KB).** 1,024 bytes. **>Megabyte (MB).** Approximately 1 million bytes. **>Gigabyte (GB).** Approximately 1 billion bytes. **>Terabyte (TB).** Approximately 1 trillion bytes. **>Petabyte (PB).** Approximately 1,000 terabytes. **>Exabyte (EB).** Approximately 1,000 petabytes. **>Zettabyte (ZB).** Approximately 1,000 exabytes. **>Yottabyte (YB).** Approximately 1,000 zettabytes. **>Binary numbering system.** The numbering system that represents all numbers using just two symbols (0 and 1).

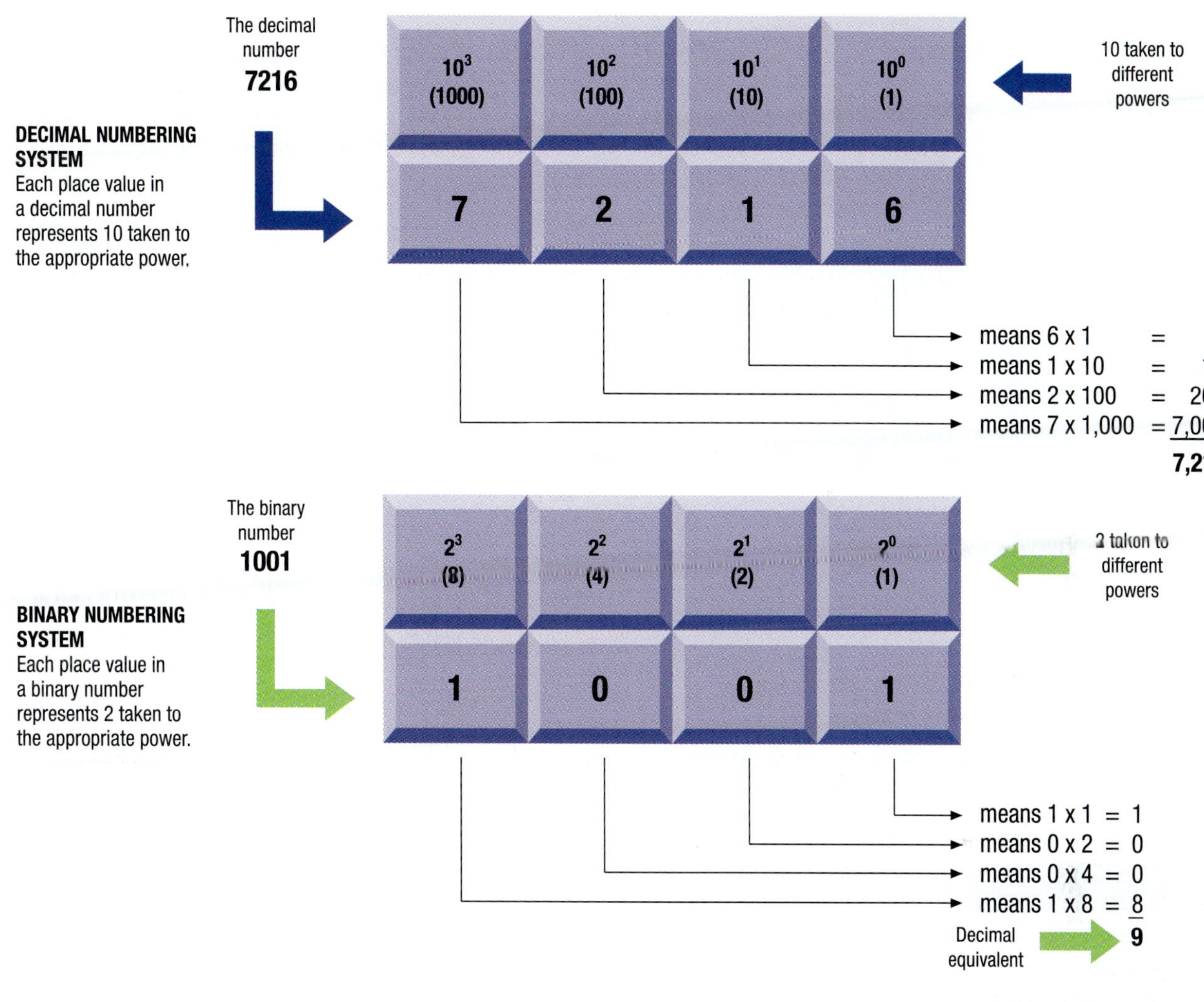

FIGURE 2-3
Examples of using the decimal and binary numbering systems.

going from right to left, the first position or column (ones column) represents 10^0 or 1; the second position (tens column) represents 10^1, or 10; the third position (hundreds column) represents 10^2, or 100; and so forth. Therefore, as Figure 2-3 shows, the decimal number 7,216 is understood as $7 \times 10^3 + 2 \times 10^2 + 1 \times 10^1 + 6 \times 10^0$ or 7,000 + 200 + 10 + 6 or 7,216. In binary, the concept is the same but the columns have different place values. For example, the first column is the ones column (for 2^0), the second column is the twos column (2^1), the third column is the fours column (2^2), and so on. Therefore, as illustrated in the bottom half of Figure 2-3, although 1001 represents "one thousand one" in decimal notation, in the binary numbering system 1001 equals "nine" ($1 \times 2^3 + 0 \times 2^2 + 0 \times 2^1 + 1 \times 2^0$ or 8 + 1 or 9).

FURTHER EXPLORATION

For links to further information about data representation, go to www.course.com/uc11/ch02

Coding Systems for Text-Based Data

While numeric data is represented by the binary numbering system, text-based data is represented by fixed-length binary coding systems specifically developed for text-based data—namely, *ASCII*, *EBCDIC*, and *Unicode*. Such codes represent all characters on the keyboard that can appear in text data—numeric characters, alphabetic characters, and special characters, such as the dollar sign ($) and period (.).

CHARACTER	ASCII	EBCDIC
0	00110000	11110000
1	00110001	11110001
2	00110010	11110010
3	00110011	11110011
4	00110100	11110100
5	00110101	11110101
A	01000001	11000001
B	01000010	11000010
C	01000011	11000011
D	01000100	11000100
E	01000101	11000101
F	01000110	11000110
+	00101011	01001110
!	00100001	01011010
#	00100011	01111011

FIGURE 2-4
Examples from the ASCII and EBCDIC codes. These common fixed-length binary codes represent all characters as unique strings of 8 bits.

ASCII and EBCDIC

ASCII (American Standard Code for Information Interchange) is the coding system traditionally used with PCs. **EBCDIC (Extended Binary-Coded Decimal Interchange Code)** was developed by IBM, primarily for mainframe use. Both ASCII and EBCDIC represent each character as a unique combination of 8 bits (see Figure 2-4), although the original version of ASCII was a 7-digit code. One group of 8 bits (one byte) allows 256 (2^8) unique combinations, so an 8-bit code can represent up to 256 characters, including the 26 uppercase and 26 lowercase characters used in the English alphabet, the 10 decimal digits, the other characters usually found on a keyboard, and many special characters not included on a keyboard, such as mathematical symbols, drawing characters, additional punctuation marks, and *dingbats* (small illustrations often inserted into documents or Web pages). Many computer systems can work with both ASCII and EBCDIC.

Unicode

Unicode is a newer code, now widely used for Web pages and in recent versions of popular software programs, such as Windows XP, Mac OS X, Netscape Navigator, and Internet Explorer. Unlike ASCII, which is limited to only the Latin alphabet used with the English language, Unicode is a universal coding standard designed to represent text-based data written in any language, including those with different alphabets, such as Chinese, Greek, and Russian. It is a longer code (32 bits per character is common) and can represent over one million characters—more than enough unique combinations to represent the standard characters in all the world's current written languages, as well as thousands of mathematical and technical symbols, punctuation marks, and dingbats. The biggest advantage of Unicode is that it can be used worldwide with consistent and unambiguous results. It is expected that Unicode will eventually replace ASCII as the primary text-coding system.

TIP

For examples of Unicode, as well as a more complete ASCII and EBCDIC chart, see the "Coding Charts" section in the References and Resources Guide at the end of this book.

Coding Systems for Other Types of Data

So far, our discussion of data coding schemes has focused on numeric and text-based data, which consist of alphanumeric symbols and special symbols, such as the comma and semicolon. Graphics, audio, and video data must also be represented in binary form in order to be used with a computer. Just as with text-based data, standardized coding systems are needed so that different computers can interpret the data correctly. Some common coding schemes used with these types of data are discussed next.

Graphics Data

Graphics data consists of still images, such as photographs or drawings. One of the most common methods for storing graphics data is in the form of a *bitmap*—a grid of hundreds of thousands of dots, called *pixels* (short for *picture elements*), arranged to represent an image. The color to be displayed at each pixel is represented by some combination of 0s and 1s, and the number of bits required to store the color for one pixel is called *bit depth.*

A *monochrome* graphic, which is the simplest type of bitmapped image, has only two possible colors. Suppose that these colors are black and white, and that the color white is represented by a 1 and the color black is represented by a 0. Using this scheme, the graphic would be represented to the PC as a black-and-white bitmap, such as the one shown in the top part of Figure 2-5, and the binary representation of that image would use a bit depth of 1 (and require one bit of storage space per pixel).

>**ASCII.** A fixed-length, binary coding system widely used to represent text-based data for computer processing on many types of computers. >**EBCDIC.** A fixed-length, binary coding system widely used to represent text-based data on IBM mainframe computers. >**Unicode.** A coding system for text-based data using any written language.

MONOCHROME GRAPHICS
With monochrome graphics, the color of each pixel is represented by a single bit, either 0 or 1.

ORIGINAL IMAGE

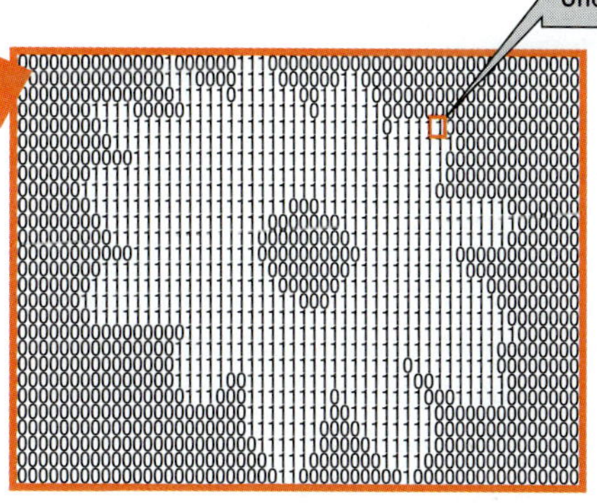

BITMAP

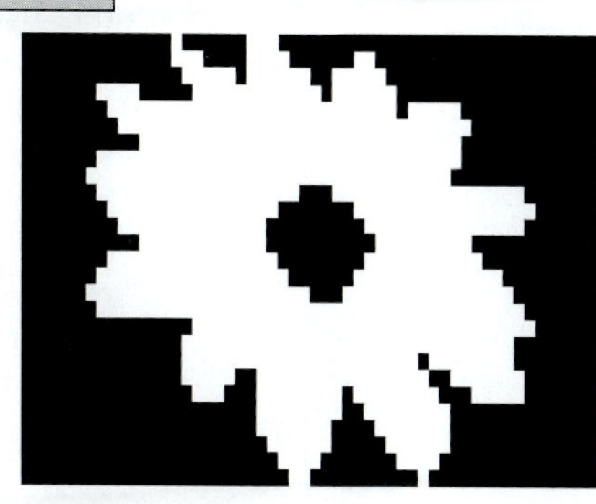
DISPLAYED IMAGE

HW

GRAYSCALE GRAPHICS
With 256-shade grayscale graphics, the color of each pixel is represented by one byte, such as 01101110. Different byte values represent black, white, and 254 different shades of gray.

COLOR GRAPHICS
Color images can be 16-color, 256-color, or photographic quality. The more colors used, the better the image quality.

16-COLOR IMAGE
The color of each pixel is represented using one half byte (4 bits).

256-COLOR IMAGE
The color of each pixel is represented using one byte (8 bits).

PHOTOGRAPHIC-QUALITY (TRUE COLOR) IMAGE (16.8 million colors)
The color of each pixel is represented using three bytes (24 bits).

FIGURE 2-5
Representing graphics data. With bitmapped images, the color of each pixel is represented by bits; the more bits used, the better the image quality.

More realism can be achieved using a *grayscale* image. In grayscale images, each pixel can be not only pure black or pure white but also any of the 254 shades of gray in between. Therefore, each pixel could appear in any of 256 possible states. It takes 8 bits (one byte) to represent 256 (2^8) states, so grayscale images use a bit depth of 8 (and require one byte of storage per pixel). For example, 11111111 might represent one pure white pixel, 00000000 might represent one pure black pixel, and any byte pattern in between—such as 11001000 and 00001010—would represent one particular shade of gray (see the middle part of Figure 2-5).

With *color* images, a variety of bit depths are possible, including 4, 8, and 24 bits to represent 16, 256, or 16,777,216 colors respectively. In a 16-color image, one-half byte (4 bits, such as 0000, 1111, or some combination in between) is assigned to each pixel to represent the color to be displayed in that pixel. In a 256-color image, 1 byte (8 bits) is assigned to each pixel to represent its color. Finally, in a 16.8-million-color (called photographic quality or *true color*) image, 3 bytes (24 bits) are used to store the color data for each pixel in the image (see the bottom part of Figure 2-5). Some digital cameras today support 48-bit (6-byte) color images, in order to enable more precise color adjustments of digital photos taken with that camera.

Theoretically, the higher number of bits used in color coding, the higher the image quality. In practice, however, it is sometimes difficult for the human eye to tell much of a quality difference between low-end and high-end color images, unless the images have been enlarged. Because using fewer colors results in a smaller file size and a faster download time, Web developers often reduce true-color images to 256-color or 16-color images for use on Web pages. This is typically accomplished by a process called *dithering*. Dithering produces colors not available on a limited color palette by coloring neighboring pixels with two available colors that appear to blend together to make a different color. For example, your eye will see a lime green color on the screen when several yellow and green pixels are placed adjacent to one another.

TIP

Most Web page images today are 8-bit color images, and most digital cameras take 24-bit true color images.

Although bitmapped images are widely used, they are not the best choice when images need to be resized because the existing pixels are just made larger or smaller (no new pixels are added). This results in the image looking distorted or blurry. A better choice in this situation is *vector-based* images, which use mathematical formulas to represent images instead of a map of pixels; vector-based images can be resized without losing quality.

Audio Data

Like graphics data, *audio data*—such as a song or the sound of someone speaking—must be in digital form in order to be stored on a storage medium or processed by a PC. To convert analog sound to digital sound, several thousand *samples*—digital representations of the sound at a particular moment—are taken every second. When the samples are played back in order, they recreate the sound of the voice or music. For example, audio CDs record sound using 2-byte samples sampled at a rate of 44,100 times per second (the minimum number of times in order to maintain sound quality). When these samples are played back at a rate of 44,100 per second, the human ear cannot distinguish them, and they collectively sound like continuous voice or music. With so many samples per second, sound files take up a great deal of storage space—about 32 MB for a 2-minute stereo song (44,100 times × 2 bytes × 180 seconds × 2 channels).

Because of its large size, when audio data is transmitted over the Internet it is often compressed to shorten the download time. For example, files that are *MP3-encoded*—that is, compressed with the MP3 compression algorithm—are about 10 times smaller than their uncompressed digital versions, so they download 10 times faster and take up one-tenth of the storage space. For a look at how MP3 compression works, see the How It Works box.

HOW IT WORKS

MP3 Compression

The *MP3 format* is a compression system for music. It is used to reduce the number of bytes in a song without sacrificing musical quality. MP3 is officially *MPEG Audio Layer 3*, an *MPEG* (*Moving Pictures Experts Group*) compression standard. Each MPEG layer uses a different sampling rate to obtain different compression results. MP3 (Layer 3)–the norm for digital music today–typically compresses a CD-quality song to about one-tenth of its original size. For example, the 32 MB Norah Jones song shown in the accompanying illustration compresses to less than 3 MB after it is converted to an MP3 file. Because of its efficiency, the MP3 format is widely used for music downloaded from the Internet, as well as when music is copied from a CD to a PC or digital music player. Because of their smaller file sizes, MP3 files can be downloaded in minutes rather than hours, and hundreds of MP3 files can be stored on a single storage medium.

MP3 utilizes two compression techniques. The first technique uses the principle of *perceptual coding*; that is, removing the parts of the song that the human ear would not hear anyway, such as sounds that occur in frequencies too high or too low to be perceived by the human ear or soft sounds that are played at the same time as louder sounds. Although data is lost by this compression technique, the lost data is considered superfluous, so the size of the song is reduced without significantly altering the quality of the song. The second compression technique, called *Huffman coding*, substitutes shorter strings of bits for frequently used larger strings. Since the bits are reconstructed when the song is played, no information is lost during this process. The resulting MP3 file–saved with the file extension *.mp3*–can then be played on a PC using media player software, burned onto a CD, or copied to a digital music player.

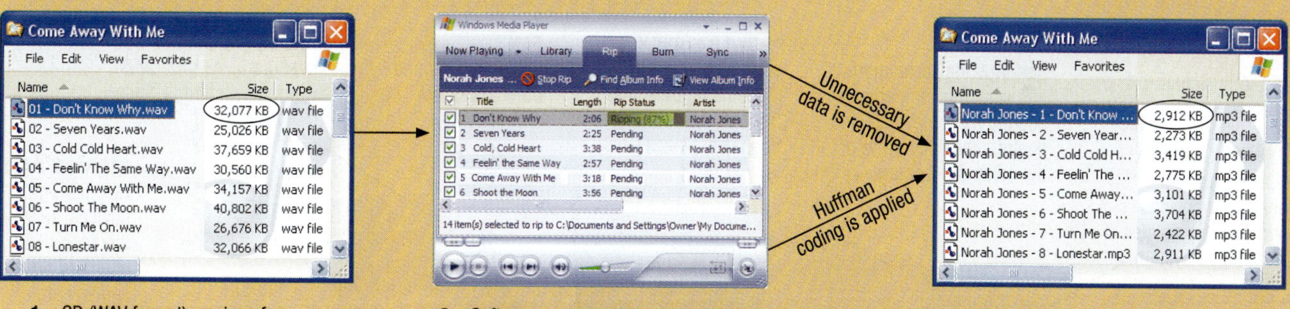

1. CD (WAV format) version of song: 32 MB.
2. Software removes the unnecessary parts of the song and codes the song in the MP3 format.
3. MP3 version of song: 2.9 MB.

Video Data

Video data—such as home movies, feature films, and television shows—is displayed using a collection of frames; each frame contains a still graphical image. When the frames are projected one after the other—typically at a rate of 30 frames per second—the illusion of movement is created. With so many frames, the amount of data involved in showing a two-hour feature film can be substantial. For instance, one frame containing a single 256-color image shown on a 640-by-480-pixel display requires 307,200 bytes. When you multiply that figure by 30 frames per second, 60 seconds per minute, and 120 minutes, you get more than 66 gigabytes of information for a typical two-hour movie. Fortunately, like audio data, video data can be compressed to reduce it to a manageable size. For example, a two-hour movie can be compressed to less than 8.5 GB to fit on a single DVD disc.

Representing Programs: Machine Language

Just like data, which must be represented by 0s and 1s, programs also need to be represented in binary form. Before a computer can execute any program instruction, such as requesting input from the user, moving a block of data from one place to another, or opening a new window on the screen, it must convert the instruction into a binary code known as **machine language**. An example of a typical machine language instruction is:

01011000011100000000000100000010

A machine language instruction might look like a meaningless string of 0s and 1s, but it actually represents specific operations and storage locations. The 32-bit instruction shown here, for instance, moves data between two specific memory locations on one type of computer system. Similar instructions transfer data from memory to other locations, add or subtract values in memory, and so on. Early computers required programs to be written in machine language, but today's programs are not. Instead, the programs are translated into machine language in order to be understood by the computer. Programming languages and *language translators* are discussed in more detail in Chapter 13.

INSIDE THE SYSTEM UNIT

The **system unit** is the main case of a computer. It houses the processing hardware for that computer, as well as a few other devices, such as disk drives, memory, the power supply, and cooling fans. The system unit for a desktop PC often looks like a rectangular box, although other shapes and sizes are available, such as the all-in-one PC illustrated in Figure 1-14 and the modified PCs shown in the Chapter 1 Inside the Industry box. The inside of a system unit for a typical desktop PC system is shown in Figure 2-6. In general, the system unit contains one or more *CPUs*, several types of *memory*, interfaces to connect external *peripheral*

FIGURE 2-6
Inside a typical system unit. The system unit houses the CPU, memory, and other important pieces of hardware.

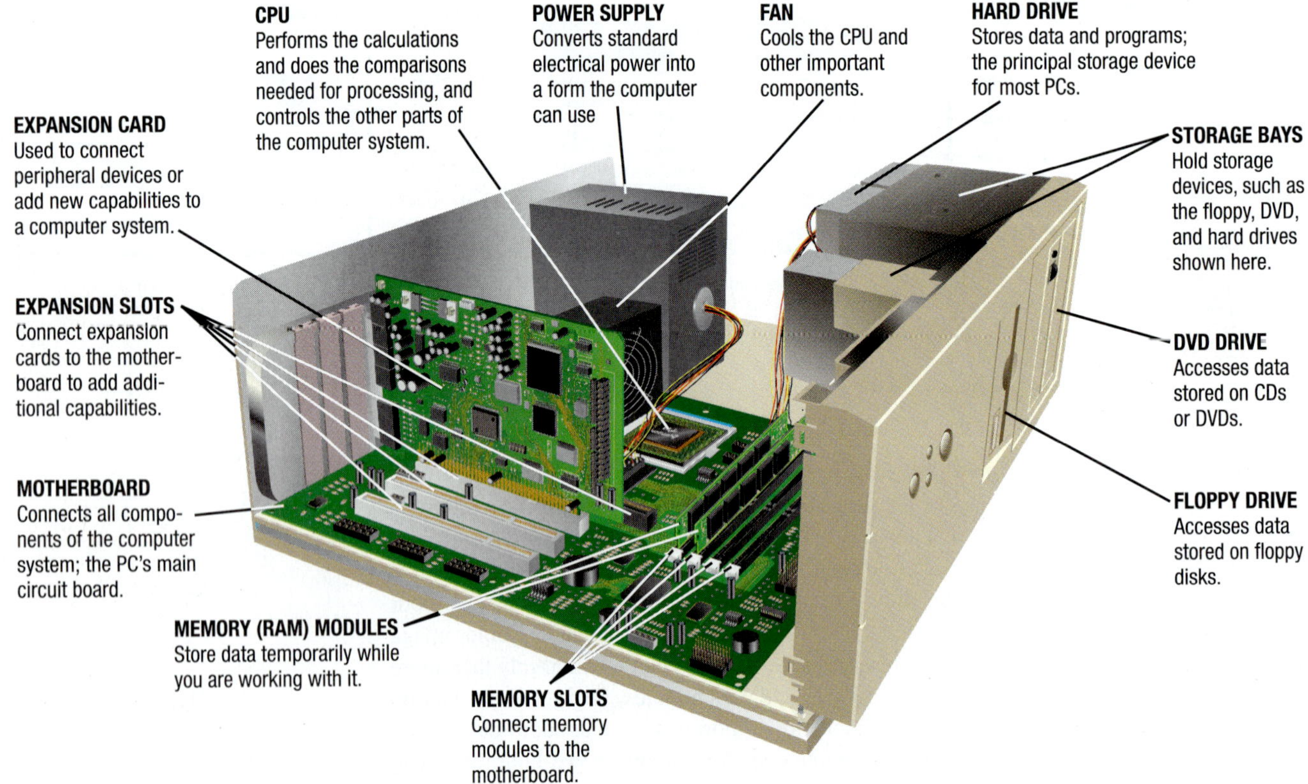

>Machine language. A binary-based language for representing computer programs that the computer can execute directly. **>System unit.** The main box of a computer that houses the CPU, motherboard, memory, and other devices.

devices (such as printers), and other components all interconnected through sets of wires called *buses* on the *motherboard*. All of these components are discussed in the next few sections. Portable PCs have similar components, but many of the components are smaller and the system unit is typically combined with the computer screen to form a single piece of hardware.

The Motherboard

A *circuit board* is a thin board containing *chips*—very small pieces of silicon or other semiconducting material onto which *integrated circuits* are embedded—and other electronic components. The main circuit board inside the system unit is called the **motherboard** or *system board*. As shown in Figure 2-6, the motherboard has a variety of chips and boards attached to it; in fact, all devices used with a computer need to be connected in one way or another to the motherboard. Typically, *external* devices (such as monitors, keyboards, mice, and printers) connect to the motherboard by plugging into a *port*—a special connector exposed through the exterior of the system unit case. The port is either built directly into the motherboard, or it is created via an *expansion card* inserted into an *expansion slot* on the motherboard. A wireless device typically has a *transceiver* that plugs into a port to transmit data between the device and the motherboard. Ports and system expansion are discussed in more detail later in this chapter.

The CPU

The **central processing unit (CPU)** consists of a variety of circuitry and components packaged together on one chip, which is plugged directly into the motherboard. The CPU—also called the **microprocessor** (when talking about PCs) or just the **processor** (when speaking in general terms for any computer)—does the vast majority of the processing for a computer.

Most PCs today use CPUs manufactured by Intel or Advanced Micro Devices (AMD); some examples of their processors are shown in Figure 2-7. CPUs commonly used with desktop PCs include the Intel *Pentium 4* and AMD *Athlon 64*. Newer *dual-core CPUs* (CPUs that contain the processing components—or *cores*—of two separate, independent processors on a single CPU) include the Intel *Pentium D* and AMD *Athlon 64 X2*. Lower-end home PCs may use a CPU belonging to the Intel *Celeron* or AMD *Sempron* microprocessor families. Typically, portable computers use either desktop PC CPUs or similar microprocessors designed for portable PC use, such as the Intel *Pentium M* or AMD *Turion 64*. Among other things, processors designed for portable PC use typically run a little slower than comparable desktop CPUs, but run cooler and consume less power to allow the portable PCs to run

FIGURE 2-7

CPUs. Shown here are the Pentium D and Athlon 64 (for desktop PCs) and the Pentium M (for portable PCs).

INTEL PENTIUM D

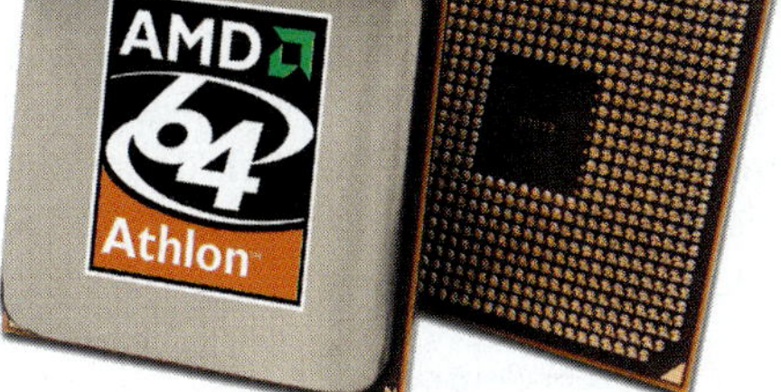

AMD ATHLON 64

INTEL PENTIUM M

>**Motherboard.** The main circuit board of a computer, located inside the system unit, to which all computer system components connect.
>**Central processing unit (CPU).** The chip located inside the system unit of a computer that performs the processing for a computer.
>**Microprocessor.** A central processing unit (CPU) for a microcomputer. Also called processor. >**Processor.** Another name for central processing unit (CPU).

TECHNOLOGY AND YOU

CPUs and Running Shoes

We all know that CPUs are incorporated into all PCs and many other electronic devices, but running shoes?

Yes, if the new Adidas smart running shoe takes off. This shoe—called the *Adidas 1*—uses a processor in conjunction with a sensor and motorized system (see the accompanying photo) to automatically adjust the shoes' cushioning to adapt to the surface the runner is currently on. For example, the cushion becomes more rigid on dirt trails and softer on pavement or when the runner is walking. Sensor readings are taken on a continual basis (at a rate of about 1,000 readings per second), and the cushioning is adjusted when the shoe is in midair. The shoe's processor is capable of making five million calculations per second and is controlled by software also built into the shoe.

The Adidas 1 runs on replaceable batteries that are estimated to have a life of about 100 hours of running. Users can override or turn off the shoe's adjustment feature, when desired. The shoe also stops adjusting the cushioning if the runner walks more than 10 minutes. According to Adidas, the changes are so gradual and automatic that they are not noticeable to the runner—he or she just notices that the shoe feels right during an entire run. Now that is one smart shoe.

FURTHER EXPLORATION

For links to further information about CPUs, go to www.course.com/uc11/ch02

longer on battery power without a recharge. Powerful *workstations* (powerful PCs designed for users running engineering and other applications requiring extra processing capabilities) and servers use more powerful microprocessors, such as Intel's *Xeon* and *Itanium 2*, AMD's *Opteron*, IBM's *Power5*, and Sun's *UltraSPARC* microprocessors. Apple Macintosh computers traditionally use *PowerPC* processors—CPUs, such as the *G5*, that were originally developed through the cooperative efforts of Apple, Motorola, and IBM. However, Apple has announced that it will begin using Intel microprocessors for at least some Macs beginning in 2006. Selected CPUs introduced since 2000 are summarized in Figure 2-8; the characteristics listed in Figure 2-8 are discussed next.

In addition to computers, CPUs are incorporated into a number of other devices, such as appliances, cars, game boxes, and more. These CPUs are typically different from the ones used in computers. For instance, the CPU designed for the Sony PlayStation 3 is a powerful new processor named *Cell*. Cell is designed to process large volumes of high-definition content. It has nine cores and operates at 256 billion *floating point operations per second* (256 *gigaflops*)—as fast as a 1990's era supercomputer and 40 times faster than the CPU in the Sony PlayStation 2. The Cell microprocessor is not initially expected to be used for conventional PCs, but Sony and Toshiba have announced plans to incorporate the Cell processor into high-definition TVs and other home entertainment and media devices. For a look at an unusual product that uses a CPU—running shoes—see the Technology and You box.

Processing Speed

One measurement of the speed of a CPU is the *CPU clock speed*, which is rated in *megahertz (MHz)* or *gigahertz (GHz)*. A higher CPU clock speed means that more instructions can be processed per second than the same CPU with a lower CPU clock speed. For instance, a Pentium 4 microprocessor running at 3.6 GHz would be faster than a Pentium 4 running at 2.8 GHz, if all other components remained the same. CPUs for the earliest PCs ran at less than 5 MHz; today's fastest CPUs run at 3.8 GHz. Although CPU clock speed is

Type of Processor	Year Introduced	Name	Manufacturer	Clock Speed	Word Size	Cache Memory			Maximum Bandwith
						Level 1	Level 2	Level 3	
DESKTOP	2005	Athlon 64 X2 (dual core)	AMD	2–2.4 GHz	64 bit	256 KB	1–2 MB	n/a	14.4 GB/s
	2005	Pentium D (dual core)	Intel	2.8–3.2 GHz	64 bit	32 KB*	2 MB	n/a	6.4 GB/s
	2005	Turion 64	AMD	1.6–2.2 GHz	64 bit	128 KB	512 KB–1 MB	n/a	9.6 GB/s
	2004	Sempron	AMD	1.5–2.0 GHz	32 bit	128 KB	128–512 KB	n/a	9.6 GB/s
	2004	Athlon 64-FX	AMD	2.4–2.8 GHz	64 bit	128 KB	1 MB	0–2 MB	14.4 GB/s
	2003	Pentium 4EE	Intel	3.2–3.733 GHz	32–64 bit	8–16 KB*	512 KB–2 MB	n/a	8.5 GB/s
	2003	Athlon 64	AMD	1.8–2.4 GHz	64 bit	128 KB	512 KB–1 MB	n/a	14.4 GB/s
	2003	PowerPC G5	Apple/IBM	1.6–2.7 GHz	64 bit	96–192 KB	512 KB–1 MB	n/a	28 GB/s
	2003	Pentium M	Intel	1.3–2.13 GHz	32 bit	64 KB	1–2 MB	n/a	4.3 GB/s
	2002	Celeron (Pentium 4-based)	Intel	1.6–3.2 GHz	32–64 bit	8–16 KB*	128–256 KB	n/a	4.3 GB/s
	2001	Athlon XP	AMD	1.33–2.25 GHz	32 bit	128 KB	256–512 KB	n/a	3.2 GB/s
	2000	Pentium 4	Intel	1.3–3.8 MHz	32–64 bit	8–16 KB*	256 KB–2 MB	n/a	6.4 GB/s
SERVER	2005	Opteron (dual core)	AMD	1.8–2.2 GHz	64 bit	256 KB	2 MB	n/a	30.4 GB/s
	2003	Opteron	AMD	1.4–2.6 GHz	64 bit	128 KB	1 MB	n/a	30.4 GB/s
	2002	Itanium 2	Intel	900 MHz–1.6 GHz	64 bit	32 KB	256 KB	1.5–9 MB	10.6 GB/s
	2002	Xeon MP	Intel	1.4–3.66 GHz	32–64 bit	8–16 KB*	256 KB–1 MB	0–8 MB	5.33 GB/s
	2001	Xeon (Pentium 4-based)	Intel	1.4–3.6 GHz	32–64 bit	8–16 KB*	256 KB–2 MB	0–2 MB	6.4 GB/s

* Plus room for 12,000 microcoded instructions

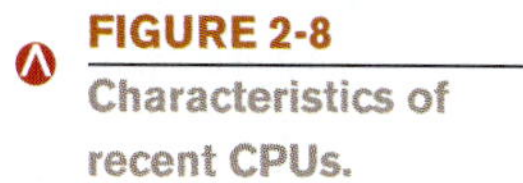

FIGURE 2-8
Characteristics of recent CPUs.

an important factor in computer performance, other factors (such as the amount of *RAM* and *cache memory*, the speed of external storage devices, and the *bus width* and *bus speed*) greatly affect the overall *processing speed* of the computer. As a result, computers today are beginning to be classified less by CPU clock speed and more by the computer's overall processing speed or performance. For a more universal measurement of processing speed, the number of instructions the CPU can process per second—such as *megaflops*, *gigaflops*, and *teraflops* (millions, billions, and trillions of floating-point operations per second, respectively)—can be used instead of clock speed. It is also common for computer journals and other independent organizations to test the performance of CPUs during a variety of similar tasks. These tests—called **benchmark tests**—typically run the same series of programs on the same computer system (except for the CPU) and measure how long each task takes to determine the overall relative performance of the CPUs being tested.

Word Size

A computer *word* is the amount of data (measured in bits or bytes) that a CPU can manipulate at one time. CPUs today use either 32-bit words (referred to as *32-bit processors*) or 64-bit words (referred to as *64-bit processors*). Usually, a larger word size allows faster processing in a computer system.

Cache Memory

Cache memory is a special group of very fast memory chips located on or close to the CPU. Cache memory is used to speed up processing by storing the data and instructions that may be needed next in handy locations. In theory, it works the same way you might work at your desk; that is, with file folders or documents you need most often placed within an arm's length and with other useful materials placed farther away but still within easy reach. The computer works in a similar manner. Although it can access materials (data, instructions, and programs, for instance) in its main memory (RAM) relatively quickly, it can work much faster if it places the most urgently needed materials into areas—cache memory—that allow even faster access. When cache memory is full and the CPU calls for a new instruction or data, the system overwrites as much data in cache memory as needed for the new instruction or data. This allows the data and instructions that are most likely to still be needed to remain in cache memory.

Cache memory today is usually *internal cache* (built right into the CPU chip). In the past, some cache memory was *external cache* (located close to, but not inside, the CPU) but that is less common today because the continued miniaturization of CPU components allows for more room inside the CPU. Cache memory level numbers indicate the order in which the various caches are accessed by the CPU when it requires new data or instructions. *Level 1 cache* (which is the fastest type of cache but holds less data than other levels of cache) is checked first, followed by *Level 2 cache*, followed by *Level 3 cache* if it exists. If the data or instructions are not found in cache memory, the computer looks for them in RAM, which is slower than cache memory. If the data or instructions cannot be found in RAM, then they are retrieved from the hard drive—an even slower operation. Typically more cache memory results in faster processing.

Bus Width and Bus Speed

A **bus** is an electronic path over which data can travel. You can picture a bus as a highway with several lanes; each wire in the bus acts as a separate lane, transmitting one bit at a time. The number of bits being transmitted at one time is dependent on the *bus width*—the number of

---

>**Benchmark test.** A test that measures the performance of a computer system to evaluate certain hardware or software components. >**Cache memory.** A group of fast memory chips located on or near the CPU to help speed up processing. >**Bus.** An electronic path on the motherboard or within the CPU or other computer component along which data is transferred.

wires in the bus over which data can travel. Just as a wider highway allows more cars to travel at one time, a wider bus allows more data to be transferred at one time. The bus speed can also vary. The bus width and bus speed together determine the bus's *throughput* or *bandwidth*; that is, the amount of data that can be transferred via the bus in a given period of time.

Memory

The term *memory* refers to chip-based storage used by the computer. This is in contrast to *storage media* (discussed in Chapter 3), which are typically disk-based and are used more actively by the user. It is important to use the terms *memory* and *storage* properly. In general, "memory" refers to chip-based storage—usually the amount of the computer's main memory (*random access memory* or *RAM*), which is located inside the system unit. In contrast, "storage" refers to the amount of long-term storage available to a PC—usually in the form of the PC's hard drive or removable storage media, such as floppy disks and CDs, all discussed in the next chapter.

In addition to RAM, computer users should be aware of four other types of computer memory. Two of these—*cache memory* and *registers*—are volatile, similar to RAM; *read-only memory* (*ROM*) and *flash memory* are nonvolatile. Cache memory has already been discussed; the other types of memory are explained next.

HW

TIP

To avoid confusion, when you are referring to the amount of room on your hard drive, use the proper term–"storage" space, not "memory."

Random Access Memory (RAM)

RAM (random access memory), also called *main memory*, is used to store the essential parts of the operating system while the computer is running, as well as programs and data that the computer is currently using. When someone uses the term *memory* in reference to computers, that person is usually referring to RAM. Since RAM is volatile, its content is lost when the computer is shut off. Data in RAM is also deleted when it is no longer needed, such as when the program using that data is closed. If you want to have the option of retrieving a document at a later time, you need to save the document on a storage medium before closing the program you are using to create the document. Although the document in RAM is lost when the program is closed, the document can be retrieved from the storage medium (if it has been saved) whenever it is needed again.

Like the CPU, RAM consists of circuits etched onto chips. These chips are arranged onto circuit boards called *memory modules* (see Figure 2-9), which in turn, are plugged into the motherboard. More specifically, memory modules are referred to as *single in-line memory modules* (*SIMMs*), *dual in-line memory modules* (*DIMMs*), or *Rambus in-line memory modules* (*RIMMs*), depending on the type of memory and type of circuit board used. DIMMs are currently the most common format. Most—but not all—desktop PCs sold today come with empty memory slots, so the user can add additional memory modules, if needed. For example, in the motherboard shown in Figure 2-6, there are two memory modules already installed and room to add an additional two modules, if necessary.

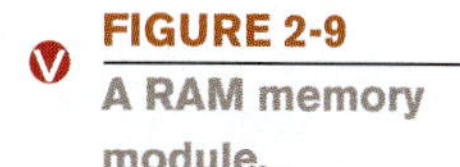

FIGURE 2-9
A RAM memory module.

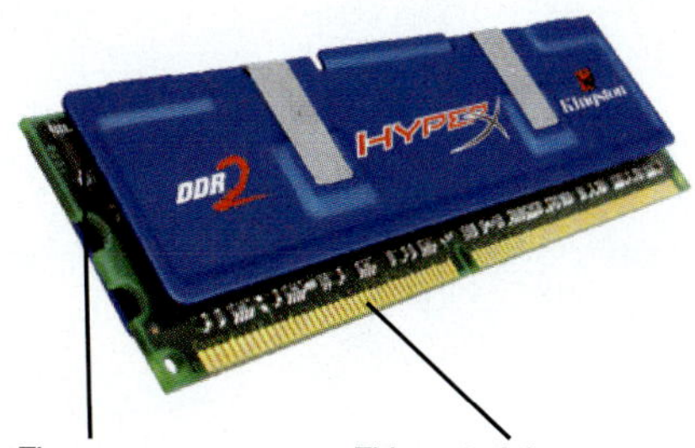

RAM capacity is measured in bytes. Conventional 32-bit CPUs can address up to 4 GB of RAM in theory, but typically address only about 2 or 3 GB. Most desktop PCs sold today have either 512 MB or 1 GB of RAM; servers and workstations typically have between 1 and 4 GB of RAM. Computers using 64-bit processors (which can address a virtually unlimited amount of RAM) can use higher amounts of RAM, so the typical amount of RAM for computers in the near future may be higher as 64-bit CPUs become more common. It is important for a PC to have enough RAM to run the necessary applications (minimum RAM requirements are

>**RAM (random access memory).** Chips connected to the motherboard that provide a temporary location for the computer to hold data and program instructions while they are needed.

almost always stated on a software program's packaging), as well as to work efficiently (more RAM allows more programs to be opened at one time).

The most common type of RAM is *SDRAM* (*synchronous dynamic RAM*). Several versions of SDRAM exist—the most common, called *double-data rate* (*DDR*) *SDRAM*, sends data twice as often as ordinary SDRAM to increase throughput. In addition to the original DDR SDRAM, *double-data rate-II* (*DDR-II*) *SDRAM* (which can transmit twice as much data in the same period of time as the original DDR SDRAM) is available. *Double-data rate-III* (*DDR-III*) *SDRAM* is under development. Most desktop PCs today use either DDR SDRAM or DDR-II SDRAM. To further improve memory performance, memory today is increasingly using a *dual-channel memory architecture*, which has two paths that go to and from memory and so can transfer twice as much data at one time as *single-channel memory* of the same speed. It is possible that some memory architectures in the near future will have four paths (called *quad-channel memory architecture*).

An emerging type of RAM is *magnetic* (or more precisely, *magnetoresistive*) *RAM* (*MRAM*). While RAM as we know it today is volatile, MRAM is nonvolatile. MRAM is nonvolatile because it uses magnetic technology rather than electrical technology, which requires a constant stream of electricity to retain data. MRAM chips are expected to be physically smaller than conventional memory chips, but store more data and access it faster. They are also expected to be less expensive to make than *flash memory* chips (flash memory is discussed shortly). As an added bonus, MRAM chips will allow PCs to become instant-on devices, similar to a light switch or television. In the future, it is possible that MRAM will replace SDRAM as the main memory for a computer. It is even possible that a type of nonvolatile memory like MRAM could replace all memory and storage in a PC.

Regardless of the type of RAM used, the CPU must be able to find data and programs located in memory when they are needed. To accomplish this, each location in memory has an *address*. Whenever a block of data, instruction, program, or result of a calculation is stored in memory, it is stored in one or more consecutive addresses, depending on its size (each address typically holds only one byte). The computer system sets up and maintains directory tables that keep track of where data is stored in memory, in order to facilitate the retrieval of data. When the computer has finished using a program or set of data, it frees up that memory space to hold other programs and data. Therefore, the content of each memory location constantly changes. This process can be roughly compared with the handling of the mailboxes in your local post office: the number on each P.O. box (memory location) remains the same, but the mail (data) stored inside changes as patrons remove their mail and as new mail arrives (see Figure 2-10).

FIGURE 2-10
Memory addressing.

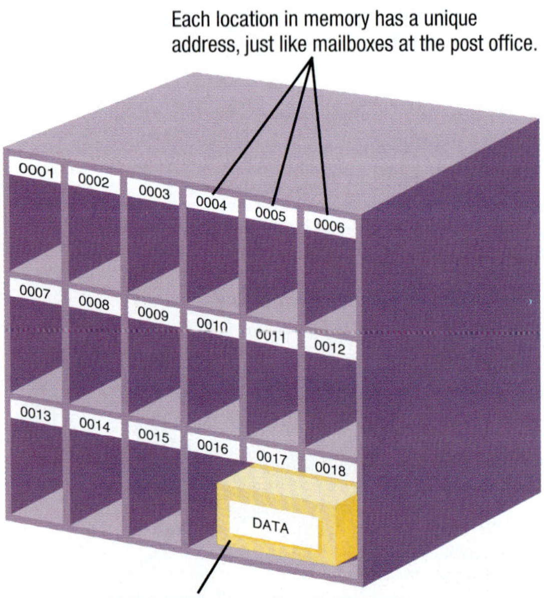

Registers

A **register** is high-speed memory built into the CPU. Registers are used by the CPU to temporarily store data and intermediary results during processing. Registers are the fastest type of memory used by the CPU, even faster than Level 1 cache. Generally, the more data a register can contain at one time, the faster the CPU performs. Register size usually matches word size and so it is usually 32 bits today, although 64-bit CPUs, such as the Itanium 2, Opteron, Athlon 64, and Power 5, use 64-bit registers. Most CPUs contain many registers; registers are discussed in more detail later in this chapter.

>**Register.** High-speed memory built into the CPU that temporarily stores data during processing.

Read-Only Memory (ROM)

ROM (read-only memory) consists of nonvolatile chips that permanently store data or programs. Like RAM, these chips are attached to the motherboard inside the system unit, and the data or programs are retrieved by the computer when they are needed. An important difference, however, is that you can neither write over the data or programs in ROM chips (which is the reason ROM chips are called *read-only*), nor destroy their contents when you shut off the computer's power.

FURTHER EXPLORATION

For links to further information about memory, go to www.course.com/uc11/ch02

Flash Memory

Flash memory (sometimes called *flash RAM*) is a type of nonvolatile memory into which data can be stored and retrieved. Data is stored in flash memory in blocks, which are erased in a single action or *flash*. Flash memory chips (see Figure 2-11) have begun to replace ROM for storing system information, such as a PC's *BIOS* or *basic input/output system*—the sequence of instructions the PC follows during the boot process. For instance, one of the computer's first activities when you turn on the power is to perform a *power-on self-test* or *POST*. The POST takes an inventory of system components, checks each component for proper functioning, and initializes system settings, which produces the beeps you hear as your PC boots. Traditionally, the instructions for the POST have been stored in ROM. By storing this information in flash memory instead of ROM, the BIOS information can be updated as needed.

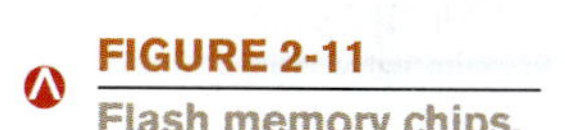

FIGURE 2-11
Flash memory chips.

HW

In addition to PCs, devices such as portable PCs, cell phones, digital cameras, MP3 players, and other small devices can contain built-in flash memory. While some built-in flash memory chips are used only by the computer, other flash memory chips are designed to be used by the user for storage purposes. Flash memory chips used for storage are either built directly into a device (such as a PC, cell phone, digital cameras, MP3 player, or other small device) or incorporated into removable *flash memory cards* or *flash memory drives*. Flash memory storage devices and media are discussed in more detail in Chapter 3.

Fans, Heat Sinks, and Other Cooling Components

One byproduct of packing an increasing amount of technology in a smaller system unit is heat, a continuing problem for CPU and computer manufacturers. Since heat can damage components and cooler chips can run faster, virtually all computers today employ *fans*, *heat sinks* (small components typically made out of aluminum with fins that help to dissipate heat), or other methods to cool the CPU and system unit. One of the newest cooling methods being used with PCs uses liquid-filled tubes that act as radiators to draw heat away from processors. For example, *water cooling systems* are now available. Although initially expensive, difficult to install, and complicated to use, these systems are now available in simpler and less expensive formats. An added bonus of water-cooled PCs is that they are quieter than conventional systems.

Expansion Slots and Cards

Most desktop PCs have **expansion slots** located on the motherboard into which **expansion cards** (also called *add-in boards*, *interface cards*, and *adapter boards*) can be inserted. Expansion cards are used to give the PC additional capabilities, such as to add network or Internet connectivity or to connect a monitor or set of speakers to the computer. Today, many basic capabilities are being integrated directly into the motherboard. When this occurs—such as with *integrated sound* or *integrated graphics*—an expansion card is not

>**Read-only memory (ROM).** Nonerasable chips located on the motherboard into which data or programs have been permanently stored.
>**Flash memory.** A type of nonvolatile memory that can be erased and reprogrammed; commonly implemented in the form of sticks or cards.
>**Expansion slot.** A location on the motherboard into which expansion cards are inserted. >**Expansion card.** A circuit board that can be inserted into an expansion slot on a PC's motherboard to add additional functionality or to attach a peripheral device.

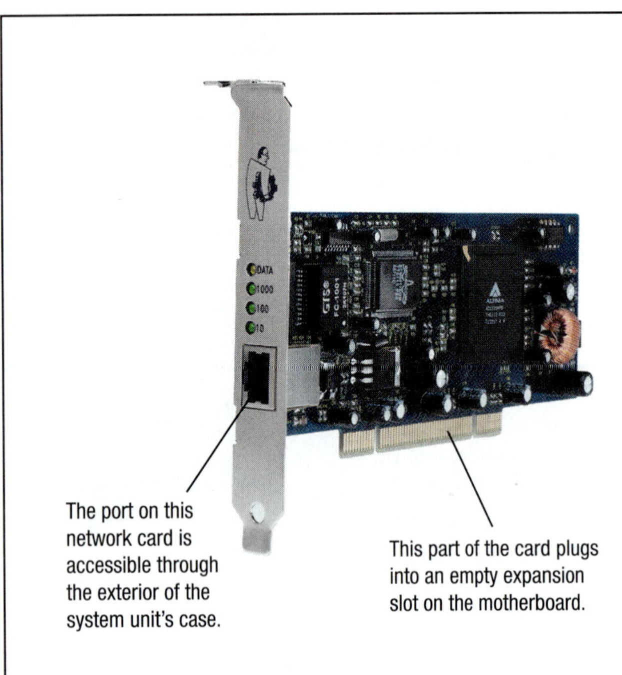

COMMON EXPANSION CARDS	
Card Type	**Purpose**
Accelerator board	Uses specialized processor chips that speed up overall processing.
Disk controller card	Enables a particular type of disk drive to interface with the PC.
Modem card	Provides communications capabilities to connect to a network or the Internet.
Network interface card	Enables a PC to connect to a network.
Sound card	Enables users to attach speakers to a PC and provides sound capabilities.
TV tuner card	Allows a PC to pick up television signals.
USB or FireWire card	Adds one or both of these ports to the PC.
Video capture board	Allows video images to be input into the computer from a video camera.
Video graphics board	Enables the connection of a monitor; may provide additional graphics capabilities.

FIGURE 2-12
Expansion cards for desktop PCs.

needed. Most new desktop PCs come with a few empty expansion slots on the motherboard so that new capabilities can be added, when needed. Figure 2-12 shows a typical expansion card and lists some examples of common expansion cards. As shown in this figure, expansion cards designed to connect external devices (such as a monitor, printer, scanner, or networking cable) have a *port* that is exposed through the case of the system unit to connect that device. Ports are discussed in more detail shortly.

Buses

As already discussed, a bus is an electronic path within a computer over which data travels. A variety of buses are used to tie the CPU to memory and to peripheral devices. The bus that moves data back and forth between the CPU and memory is typically called the *system bus*. Usually a *chipset* is used between the CPU and RAM (see Figure 2-13); if so, the part of the system bus between the CPU and the chipset is called the *frontside bus* (*FSB*). If external cache exists, the *backside bus* (*BSB*) transfers data between that cache and the CPU. Many CPUs today have 64-bit system buses, although the speed of the system bus varies. Generally a faster system bus indicates a faster PC, and a faster frontside bus creates less of a bottleneck in the overall performance of the system.

The buses that connect the CPU to peripheral (typically input and output) devices are usually referred to as **expansion buses**. Expansion buses are etched onto the motherboard and vary in width and speed. They either connect the CPU directly to *ports* on the system unit case or to expansion slots on the motherboard (some of the most common expansion buses and expansion slots are illustrated in Figure 2-13). It is important to realize that expansion slots are not interchangeable—each type of expansion slot is designed for a specific type of expansion card, such as *PCI*, *PCI Express* (*PCIe*), or *AGP*. Some of the most common types of expansion buses are discussed next.

TIP

The various PCI and PCI Express expansion slots are different sizes, and neither the slots nor the cards are interchangeable. Be sure to check the format of any empty expansion slot in your PC before buying a new expansion card.

>**Expansion bus.** A bus that connects the CPU to peripheral devices.

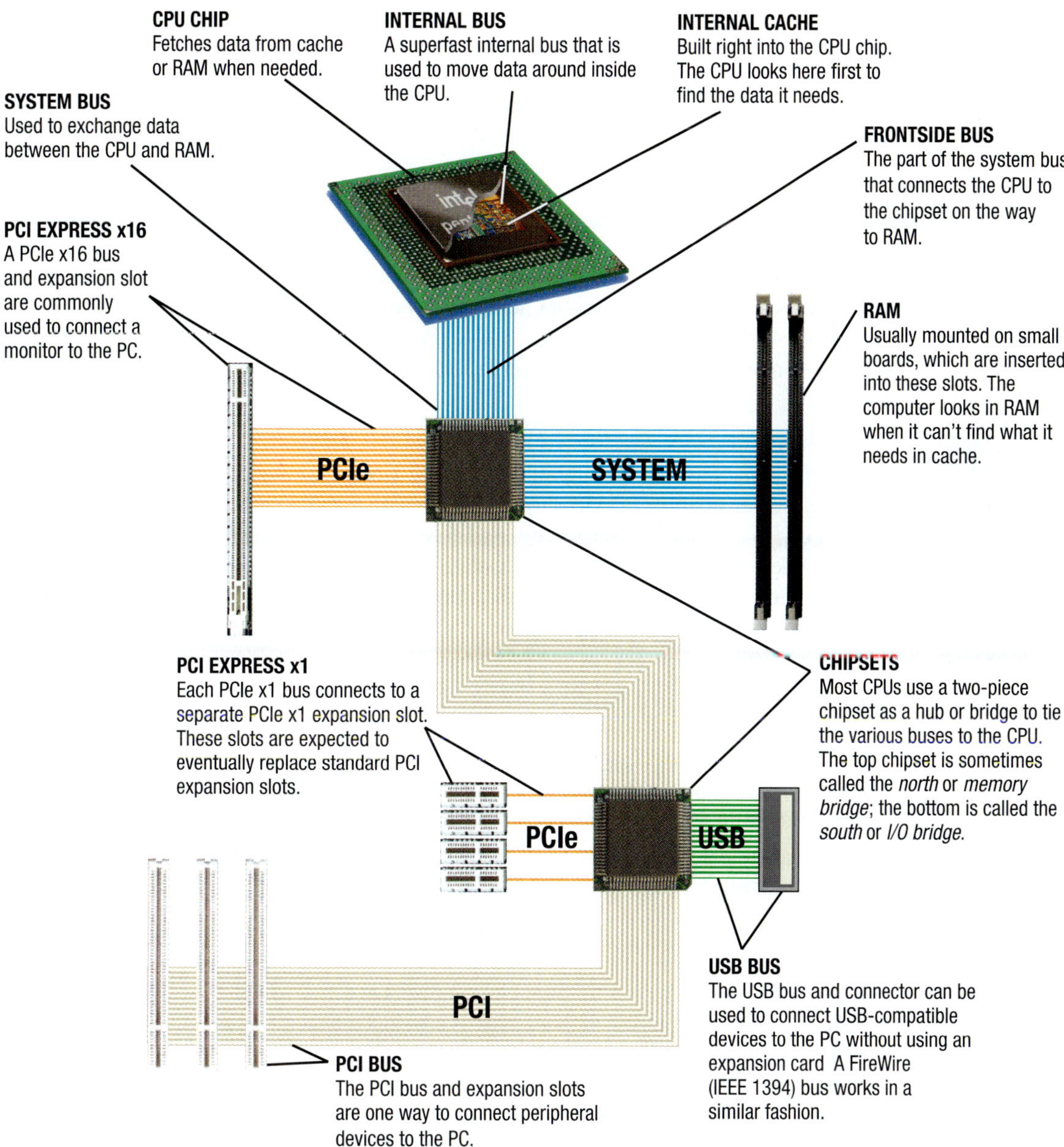

FIGURE 2-13

Buses. Buses transport bits and bytes from one component to another, including the CPU, cache, RAM, and peripheral devices.

PCI and PCI Express Bus

The *PCI* (*Peripheral Component Interconnect*) bus has been one of the most common types of expansion buses in past years. It can be implemented as a 64-bit bus, but most PCs use a 32-bit PCI bus that has a bandwidth of 133 *MBps* (*megabytes per second*). The newest version of PCI is called **PCI Express (PCIe)**, formally known as *3GIO* for *third-generation input output*. A 16-bit version of PCIe (referred to as *PCIe x16*) is commonly used with *video cards* (to connect a monitor to a PC); other peripherals usually use a 1-bit PCIe bus (referred to as *PCIe x1*). PCIe is extremely fast—the 1-bit PCIe bus, at 500 MBps, is approximately four times faster than a regular PCI; PCIe x16 is significantly faster at 8 GBps.

>**PCI Express (PCIe).** One of the buses most commonly used to connect peripheral devices.

AGP Bus

The *AGP* (*Accelerated Graphics Port*) bus was originally developed to provide greater performance for graphics display. AGP provides a fast, 32-bit, dedicated interface for the video card, operating at over 2 GBps. However, the AGP bus is now being replaced by the even faster 16-bit PCIe.

HyperTransport Bus

A newer bus, invented by AMD, is *HyperTransport*. The 32-bit HyperTransport bus has a bandwidth of over 22 GBps—roughly 165 times as fast as the standard PCI bus. The HyperTransport bus is fairly versatile—in addition to being used today on the motherboard to connect the CPU chipsets to each other and to the CPU, it is also used for the paths between CPUs in computers with multiple processors as well as other nonmotherboard applications.

TIP

When buying a desktop PC, check to see how many available (nonused) expansion slots the PC has and what types they are. You should also have at least two USB ports to add additional hardware available in USB format.

USB Bus

One of the more versatile bus architectures is the **Universal Serial Bus (USB)**. The USB standard enables up to 127 devices to be connected to a computer's PCI bus through a single port on the computer's system unit. At 1.5 MBps, the original USB standard was fairly slow. The newer *USB 2* standard supports data transfer rates of 60 MBps—still slower than PCI, but the convenience and universal support of USB have made it one of the most widely used standards for peripherals today.

FireWire/IEEE 1394 Bus

FireWire (also known as *IEEE 1394*) is a fairly recent bus standard developed by Apple. Like USB, FireWire can connect multiple external devices to the PCI bus via a single port. FireWire is fast and is commonly used with digital video cameras and other multimedia peripherals for both Apple and IBM-compatible computers. The original FireWire format supports data transfer rates of up to 40 MBps; the newer *FireWire 2* (*IEEE 1394b*) standard supports data transfer rates up to 100 MBps.

TIP

PC Cards come in a variety of thicknesses–from *Type I* (the thinnest) to *Type III* (the thickest). It is a good idea to verify the size and number of PC Cards your notebook computer can support before buying a PC Card.

CardBus

The traditional expansion bus for portable computers is *CardBus*, which transmits data from *PC Cards* (cards that conform to the standards developed by the *Personal Computer Memory Card International Association* or *PCMCIA*) inserted into the PC's *PCMCIA card slot*. Common types of PC Cards include hard drives, flash memory card readers, modems, USB, and networking cards. It is expected that CardBus will not be needed in the future, since new PC Cards—like the new *ExpressCard* PC Cards—connect via the USB or PCI Express bus.

Ports

As already mentioned, **ports** are the connectors located on the exterior of the system unit that are used to connect external hardware devices. Each port is attached to the appropriate bus on the motherboard so that when a device is plugged into a port, the device can communicate with the CPU. Typical ports for a desktop PC are shown in Figure 2-14. As shown in this figure, there are unique connectors for each type of port on a computer system. When connecting cables to the system unit, it is important to pay attention to the *gender* of the port, in addition to the shape, pin count, and pin configuration. *Male* connectors have the pins extended and connect to *female* connectors with matching holes. If a port is of the proper

>**Universal Serial Bus (USB).** A universal bus used to connect up to 127 peripheral devices to a computer without requiring the use of additional expansion cards. >**FireWire.** A bus standard often used to connect digital video cameras to a PC. >**Port.** A connector on the exterior of a PC's system unit to which a device may be attached.

type (such as serial), but is the wrong gender or has the wrong number of pins, adapters or special cables can sometimes be used to convert the connector to the desired configuration.

If you want to add a new device to your PC and there is an available port for the device you want to add, then you just need to plug it in (shut down the computer first, unless the device uses a USB or FireWire port). Most computers today support the *Plug and Play* standard, in which the computer automatically configures new devices as soon as they are installed. If the appropriate port is not available, you need to either insert the appropriate expansion card to create one or use a USB or FireWire version of the device, if you have one of those two ports available on your PC. Because a wide variety of hardware is available in USB format today, most recent PCs come with at least two USB ports. In fact, it is becoming common to see multiple USB ports located on the front of a system unit for easier access, such as to connect a digital camera or USB flash memory drive on a regular basis. Front slots for the flash memory cards used with digital music players and digital cameras are also common today (see Figure 2-15). USB and FireWire devices can be plugged into USB and FireWire ports while the computer is powered up; they are recognized by the computer as soon as they are connected to it and can be used right away.

Some of the most common ports are discussed next; some of the oldest types—such as *serial* and *parallel* ports—are increasingly being referred to as *legacy ports* and are being phased out on newer PCs.

- *Serial ports* can transmit data only a single bit at a time. However, they use very inexpensive cables, and they can send data over long distances reliably. Serial ports can be used for such devices as keyboards, mice, and modems, although most systems today come with dedicated ports to attach the mouse and keyboard, as shown in Figure 2-14. *Serial connectors* typically have 9 or 25 pins and are referred to as *DB-9* or *DB-25 connectors*, respectively.

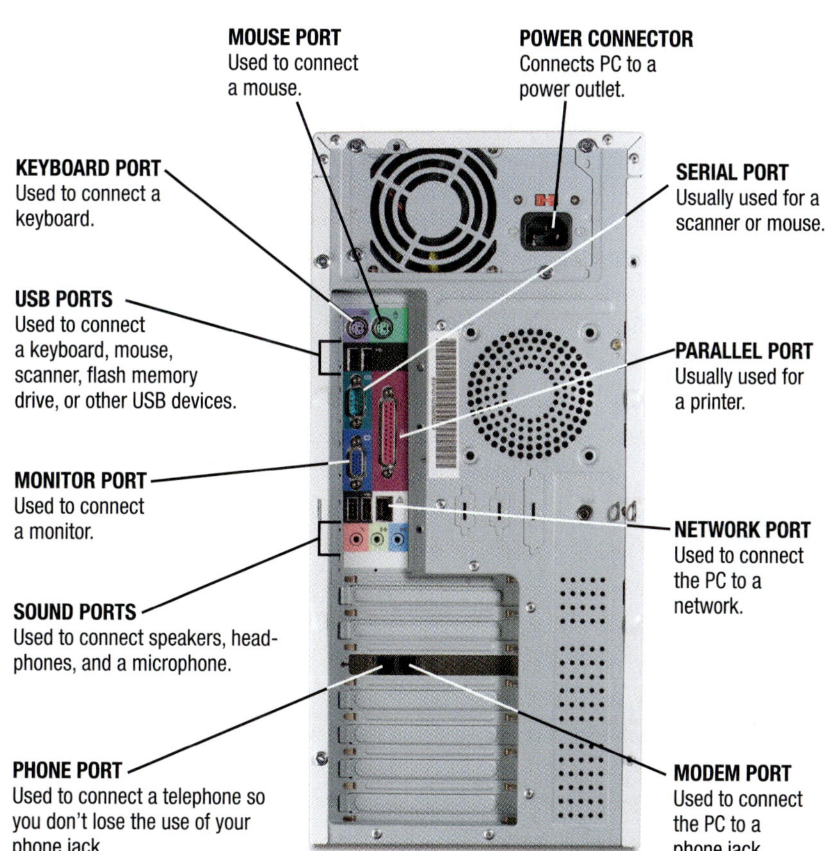

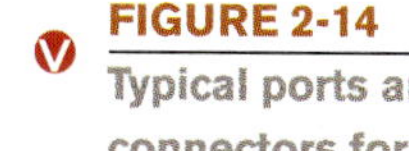

FIGURE 2-14
Typical ports and connectors for a desktop PC.

CONNECTORS

Power plug

USB plug

FireWire plug

PS/2 plug for mouse or keyboard

Serial plug

Monitor plug

Parallel plug

Telephone plug for modem and telephone

Network (RJ-45) plug

Network (Fiber-optic) plug

HW

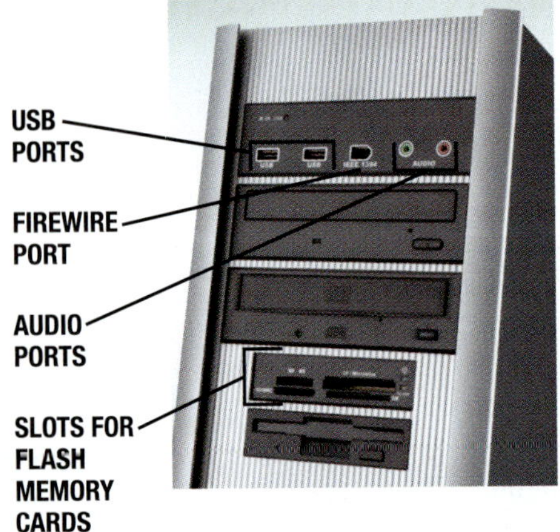

FIGURE 2-15
Front ports. Many computers today come with a variety of ports on the front of the system unit for easy access.

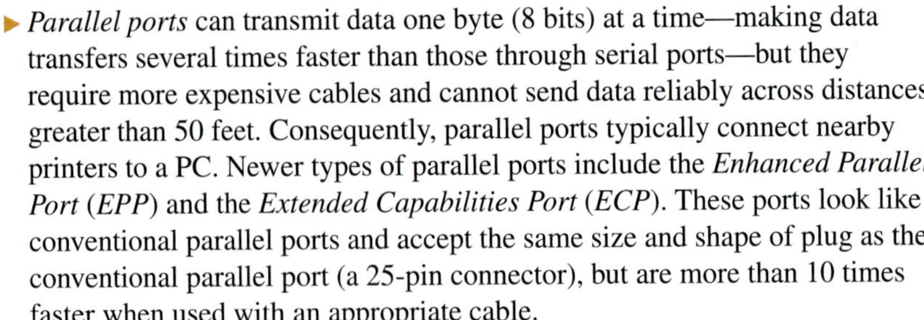

- *Parallel ports* can transmit data one byte (8 bits) at a time—making data transfers several times faster than those through serial ports—but they require more expensive cables and cannot send data reliably across distances greater than 50 feet. Consequently, parallel ports typically connect nearby printers to a PC. Newer types of parallel ports include the *Enhanced Parallel Port* (*EPP*) and the *Extended Capabilities Port* (*ECP*). These ports look like conventional parallel ports and accept the same size and shape of plug as the conventional parallel port (a 25-pin connector), but are more than 10 times faster when used with an appropriate cable.
- *Network ports* are used to connect a PC to a local area network. Most network cards contain a port that accepts an *RJ-45 connector*, which looks similar to a telephone connector but is larger. Coaxial cable or fiber optic connectors can be used for network connections, as well. Networks are discussed in more detail in Chapter 7.
- The *keyboard port* and the *mouse port* typically use a *PS/2 connector* and are used to connect the keyboard and mouse to the system unit. Some mice and keyboards today connect via a USB port instead.
- The *monitor port* is used to connect the monitor to a PC. Some computers also come with an *S-video* port that can be used to connect the computer to a television or other S-video device.
- The *modem port* and *phone port* are used to connect the PC to a phone outlet and then connect a telephone to the phone jack, respectively.
- *SCSI* (*Small Computer System Interface*) *ports* are high-speed parallel ports generally used to attach printers, scanners, and hard drives.
- A *MIDI port* is used to connect a *MIDI* (*musical instrument digital interface*) device to the computer. MIDI devices include music keyboards and other instruments that can be connected to the computer to compose music to be stored electronically. A MIDI port usually looks similar to a keyboard port.
- An *IrDA* (*Infrared Data Association*) *port* receives infrared transmissions from such devices as wireless keyboards, wireless mice, and portable devices. Since the transmission is wireless, the port does not use a plug. With infrared transmission, there cannot be anything blocking the infrared light waves, so newer wireless mice and keyboards tend to use radio wave transmission instead. However, IrDA ports are commonly used to "beam" data from a handheld PC or other portable device to another PC. Another wireless port is a *Bluetooth port*, which uses Bluetooth technology and radio waves to transmit data between devices. Wireless data transmission is discussed in more detail in Chapter 7.

FIGURE 2-16
USB hubs. A USB hub can be used to connect multiple USB devices to a single USB port.

- A *game port* is used to connect a joystick, game pad, steering wheel, or other device commonly used with computer game programs.
- *USB ports* are used to connect USB devices to the computer. Most new PCs come with at least two USB ports, but a *USB hub*—a device that plugs into your PC's USB port to convert one port into several USB ports (see Figure 2-16)—can be used to connect multiple USB devices to a single USB port, when necessary. In addition, USB devices are *hot-swappable*, meaning that they can be attached and removed while the computer is turned on.
- *FireWire* (*IEEE 1394*) *ports* are used to connect FireWire devices to the computer. Similar to USB, a *FireWire hub* can be used to connect multiple devices to a single port, and FireWire devices are hot-swappable.

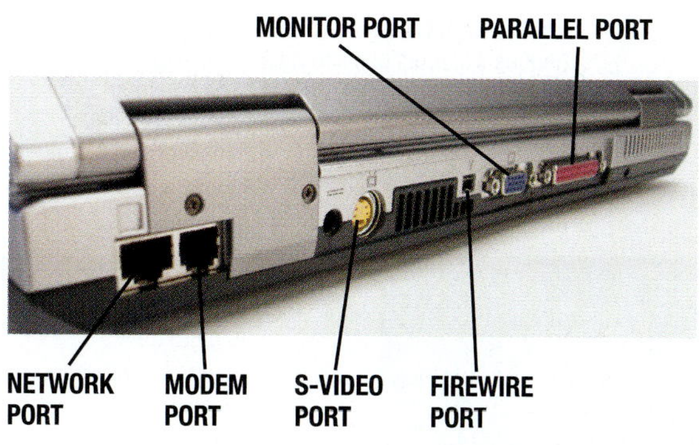

FIGURE 2-17
Notebook ports. Shown here are typical ports on the back (left) and side (right) of a typical notebook PC.

HW

Notebook computers have ports similar to desktop PCs, but usually they do not have as many. One type of port found on notebook computers but not on desktop PCs is a port used to connect a *port replicator*. A port replicator is a hardware device containing additional ports (such as serial, parallel, PS/2, USB, and networking ports) that can be used with the notebook computer whenever the port replicator is connected to it (some port replicators connect via a USB or PC card slot instead). Some typical notebook ports are illustrated in Figure 2-17.

Most handheld PCs and mobile devices have a limited amount of expandability, but usually come with at least one built-in expansion slot that can be used to attach peripheral devices, such as modems, networking adapters, MP3 players, digital cameras, fingerprint readers, barcode scanners, and GPS receivers. Most often, the expansion slot is an *SD slot*, which can be used with both the postage-stamp-size *Secure Digital* (*SD*) flash memory cards and with hardware adhering to the *Secure Digital Input/Output* (*SDIO*) standard (see Figure 2-18). Some handheld PCs support additional types of flash memory cards or have a proprietary expansion slot designed only for hardware made for that device; a few include a PC card slot. More commonly, portable PCs are coming with an *ExpressCard port* that supports the new type of ExpressCard PC cards that are expected to eventually replace PCMCIA PC cards. Many portable PCs and some smart phones also have a port to connect a special portable keyboard designed for the device.

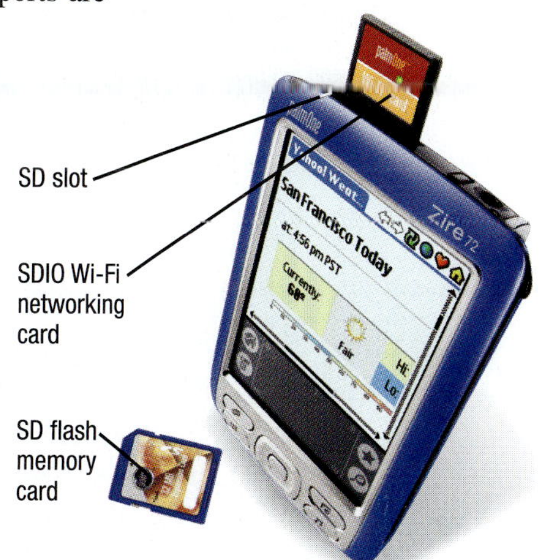

FIGURE 2-18
Handheld PC expansion. Most handheld PCs and smart phones have at least an SD-compatible expansion slot for expansion.

HOW THE CPU WORKS

As already discussed, a CPU consists of a variety of circuitry and components packaged together. The key element of the microprocessor is the *transistor*—a device made of semiconductor material that acts like a switch controlling the flow of electrons inside a chip. Today's CPUs contain hundreds of millions of transistors, and the number doubles approximately every 18 months. This phenomenon is known as *Moore's Law* and is explained in the Inside the Industry box. The primary components of a typical CPU are discussed next.

Typical CPU Components

To begin to understand how a CPU works, you need to know how the CPU is organized and what components it includes. This information will help you understand how electronic impulses move from one part of the CPU to another to process data. The architecture and components included in a CPU (referred to as *microarchitecture*) vary from microprocessor to microprocessor. A simplified example of the principal components that might be included in a typical CPU is shown in Figure 2-19 and discussed next. For a look at the companies that are used to examine the parts of a CPU or other computer component to gather evidence for patent lawsuits, see the Trend box.

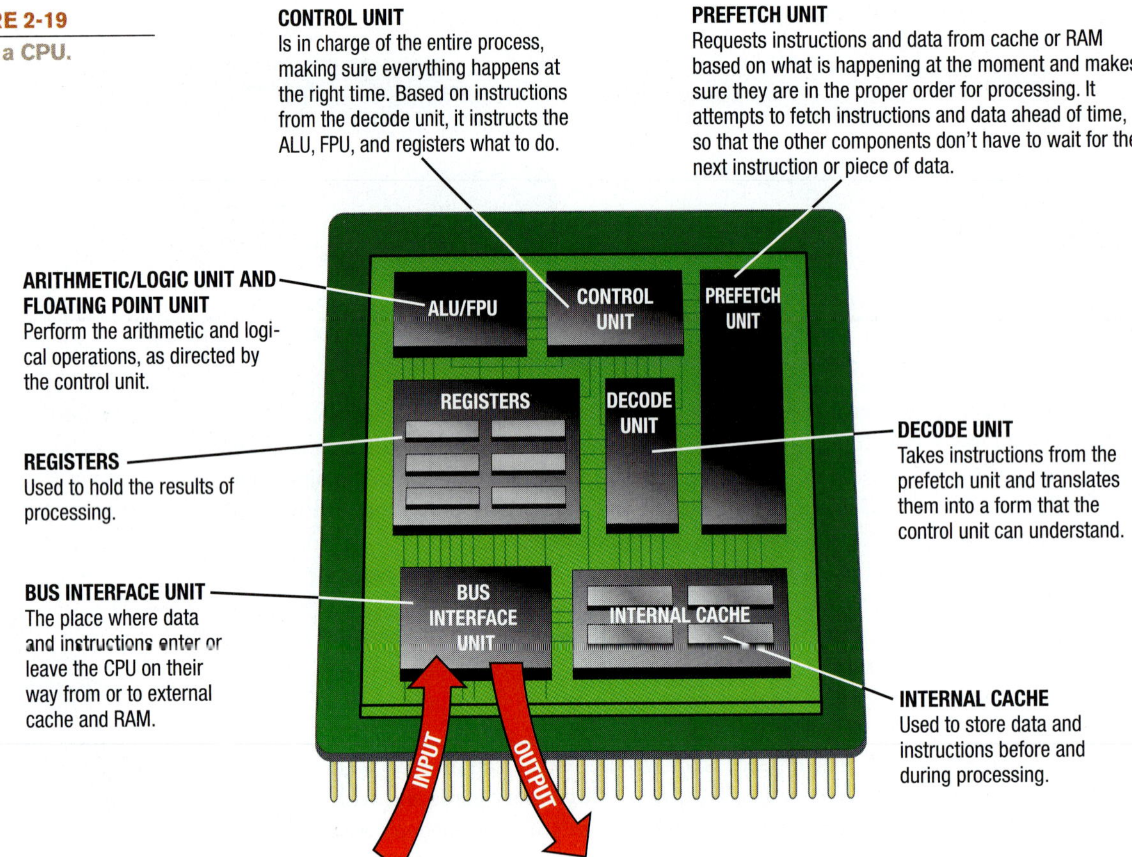

FIGURE 2-19
Inside a CPU.

Arithmetic/Logic Unit (ALU) and Floating Point Unit (FPU)

The **arithmetic/logic unit (ALU)** is the section of the CPU that performs arithmetic (addition, subtraction, multiplication, and division) involving integers and logical operations (such as comparing two pieces of data to see if they are equal or determining if a specific condition is true or false). Arithmetic requiring decimals is usually performed by the **floating point unit (FPU)** instead. Arithmetic operations are used both for actual mathematical calculations requested by the user, as well as for other everyday tasks. For example, editing a digital photograph in an image editing program, running the spelling checker in a word processing program, and burning a music CD are all performed by the ALU, with help from the FPU when needed, using only arithmetic and logical operations. Most CPUs today have multiple ALUs and FPUs that work together to perform the necessary operations.

Control Unit

The **control unit** coordinates and controls the operations and activities taking place within the CPU, such as retrieving data and instructions and passing them on to the ALU or FPU for execution. In other words, it directs the flow of electronic traffic within the CPU, much like a traffic cop controls the flow of vehicles on a roadway. Essentially, the control unit tells the ALU and FPU what to do and makes sure that everything happens at the right time in order for the appropriate processing to take place.

>**Arithmetic/logic unit (ALU).** The part of the CPU that performs logical operations and integer arithmetic. >**Floating point unit (FPU).** The part of the CPU that performs decimal arithmetic. >**Control unit.** The part of the CPU that coordinates its operations.

INSIDE THE INDUSTRY

Moore's Law

In 1965, Gordon Moore, the cofounder of Intel, observed that the number of transistors per square inch on chips had doubled every year since the integrated circuit was invented. He then made a now-famous prediction–that this doubling trend would continue for at least 10 more years. Here we are, 40 or so years later, and, although the pace has slowed down a bit, transistor density still doubles about every 18 months (see the accompanying figure). Due to technological breakthroughs, *Moore's Law* has been maintained for far longer than the original prediction and most experts, including Moore himself, expect the doubling trend to continue for at least another decade. In fact, Intel states that the mission of its technology development team is to continue to break barriers to Moore's Law.

Interestingly, other computer components also follow Moore's Law. For example, storage capacity doubles approximately every 20 months, and chip speed doubles about every 24 months. Consequently, the term "Moore's Law" has been expanded and is now used to describe the amount of time it takes components to double in capacity or speed.

Many experts predict that, eventually, a physical limit of the number of transistors that can be crammed onto a chip will end Moore's Law. But the end is not yet in sight.

GORDON MOORE (1970)

Microprocessor	Year of Introduction	Transistors
4004	1971	2,300
8008	1972	2,500
8080	1974	4,500
8086	1978	29,000
Intel286	1982	134,000
Intel386™ processor	1985	275,000
Intel486™ processor	1989	1,200,000
Intel® Pentium® processor	1993	3,100,000
Intel® Pentium® II processor	1997	7,500,000
Intel® Pentium® III processor	1999	9,500,000
Intel® Pentium® 4 processor	2000	42,000,000
Intel® Itanium® processor	2001	25,000,000
Intel® Itanium® 2 processor	2003	220,000,000
Intel® Itanium® 2 processor (9MB cache)	2004	592,000,000

TRANSISTOR GROWTH

Prefetch Unit

The **prefetch unit** orders data and instructions from cache or RAM based on the task at hand. The prefetch unit tries to predict what data and instructions will be needed and retrieves them ahead of time, in order to help avoid delays in processing.

Decode Unit

The **decode unit** takes the instructions fetched by the prefetch unit and translates them into a form that can be understood by the control unit, ALU, and FPU. The decoded instructions go to the control unit for processing.

>**Prefetch unit.** The part of the CPU that attempts to retrieve data and instructions before they are needed for processing, in order to avoid delays. >**Decode unit.** The part of the CPU that translates instructions into a form that can be processed by the ALU.

TREND

High-Tech Investigators

With the high value of technology today and claims of stolen technology and patent infringements happening all the time, what can companies in the computer industry do to find out the truth? Increasingly, they turn to reverse engineering companies, such as Taeus International. Short for "Tear Apart Everything Under the Stars," Taeus is a leader in the area of applying engineering skills and industry knowledge to analyze products to evaluate patent claims. In a nutshell, companies like Taeus tear products apart to hunt for patented technologies that should not be there. Just as with criminal investigations, patent infringement claims require physical proof, and Taeus engineers inspect and photograph critical elements of a product (see the accompanying photo) to compare that product to existing patents.

In just the past few years, Taeus has helped to settle numerous patent infringement claims. For instance, it helped Intel avoid litigation when they were sued by Digital Equipment Corporation (DEC) for a share of its Pentium CPU profits. After Taeus found patented Intel technology inside DEC's servers, the case was settled with no money changing hands. They also do preemptive work helping tech companies avoid patent liabilities by searching through existing patents to determine which technology patents are enforceable before a problem arises.

At a rate of $100,000 to reverse engineer one computer chip, services such as the one Taeus provides are not cheap, but with patent lawsuits often exceeding $100 million, for tech companies that use Taeus services and avoid litigation, it is money well spent.

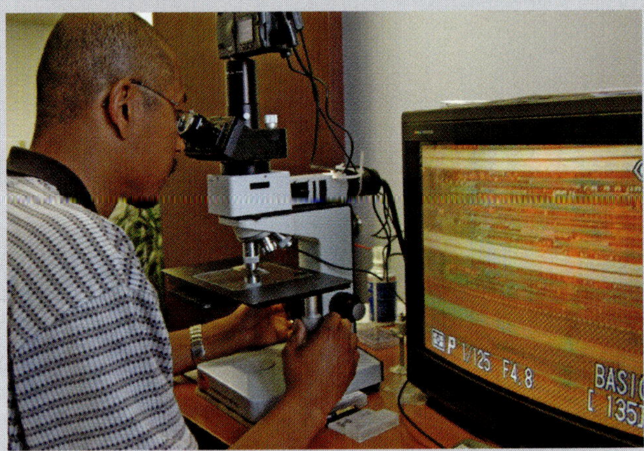

A Taeus engineer at work.

Internal Cache and Registers

As mentioned earlier, internal cache (such as Level 1 and Level 2 cache) is used to store instructions and data for the CPU, to avoid retrieving them from RAM or the hard drive, and registers are groups of high-speed memory located within the CPU that are used during processing. The ALU and FPU use registers to temporarily store data, intermediary calculations, and the final results of processing. CPUs today typically have a variety of registers—for example, the Intel Itanium 2 has a total of 328 different registers. As directed by the control unit after processing, the results located in the registers can be sent from the CPU to RAM or an output device, depending on the instructions received.

Bus Interface Unit

The **bus interface unit** is the place where instructions and data flow in and out of the CPU. It connects the CPU to the system bus so it can communicate with external cache, RAM, and the rest of the computer.

The System Clock and the Machine Cycle

As mentioned at the beginning of this chapter, every instruction that you issue to a computer—either by typing a command or clicking something with the mouse—is converted

>**Bus interface unit.** The part of the CPU where instructions and data flow in and out of the CPU.

into machine language. In turn, each machine language instruction in a CPU's *instruction set* (the collection of basic machine language commands that the CPU can understand) is broken down into several smaller, machine-level instructions called *microcode*. Microcoded instructions, such as moving a single piece of data from one part of the computer system to another or adding the numbers located in two specific registers, are built into the CPU to provide its basic instructions.

In order to synchronize the computer's operations, a **system clock**—a quartz crystal located on the motherboard—is used. The system clock sends out a signal on a regular basis to all other computer components, similar to a musician's metronome or a person's heartbeat. Each signal is referred to as a *cycle*. The number of cycles per second is measured in *hertz (Hz)*. One megahertz (MHz) is equal to one million ticks of the system clock. Many PCs today have a system clock that runs at 200 MHz, and all devices that are synchronized with the system clock can run at this speed or can run faster or slower by running at a multiple of or a fraction of the system clock speed. For example, to reach a CPU clock speed of 2 GHz, a multiplier of 10 is used, meaning that the CPU clock essentially "ticks" 10 times during each system clock tick. During each CPU clock tick, the CPU usually executes one or more pieces of microcode. Most computers today can process more than one piece of microcode at one time—a characteristic known as *superscalar* or being able to process multiple *instructions per cycle (IPC)*. A CPU with a higher clock speed processes more instructions per second than the same CPU using a lower clock speed.

Whenever the CPU processes a single piece of microcode, it is referred to as a **machine cycle**. Each machine cycle consists of the four general operations illustrated in Figure 2-20 and discussed next.

1. *Fetch*—the program instruction is fetched.
2. *Decode*—the instructions are decoded so the control unit, ALU, and FPU can understand them.
3. *Execute*—the instructions are carried out.
4. *Store*—the original data or the result from the ALU or FPU execution is stored either in the CPU's registers or in memory, depending on the instruction.

Because a machine cycle processes only a single instruction, many seemingly simple commands (such as multiplying two numbers) might require more than one machine cycle, and a computer might need to go through thousands, millions, or even billions of machine cycles to complete a user command or program instruction. A simplified example of how a CPU might process the command *2 + 3* is illustrated in Figure 2-21. In this example, four machine cycles are used, as follows:

1. The number 2 is fetched from RAM using the appropriate address and is sent to the decode unit, where it is determined that the number needs to be stored in register X. The control unit then stores the number in register X.

FIGURE 2-20

A machine cycle. A machine cycle is typically accomplished in four steps.

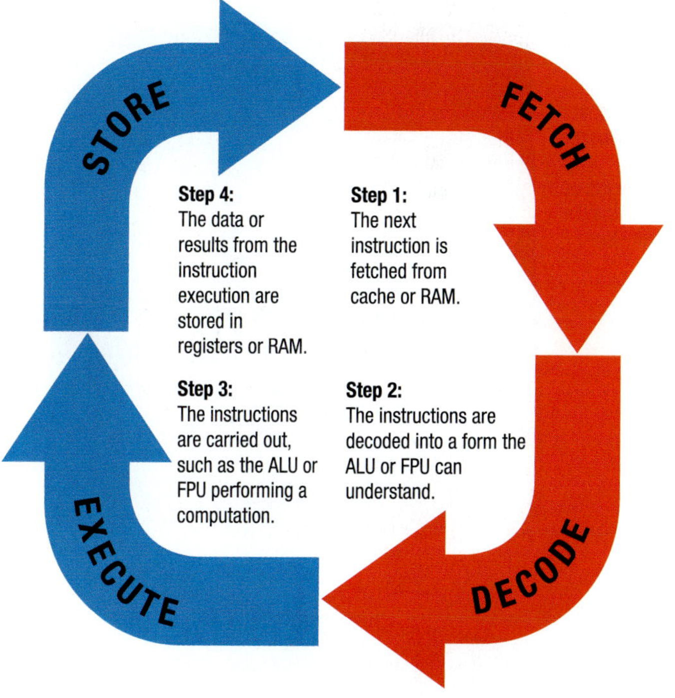

HW

>System clock. The timing mechanism within the computer system that synchronizes the computer's operations. **>Machine cycle.** The series of operations involved in the execution of a single machine level instruction.

MACHINE CYCLE 1: The number 2 is input and stored.

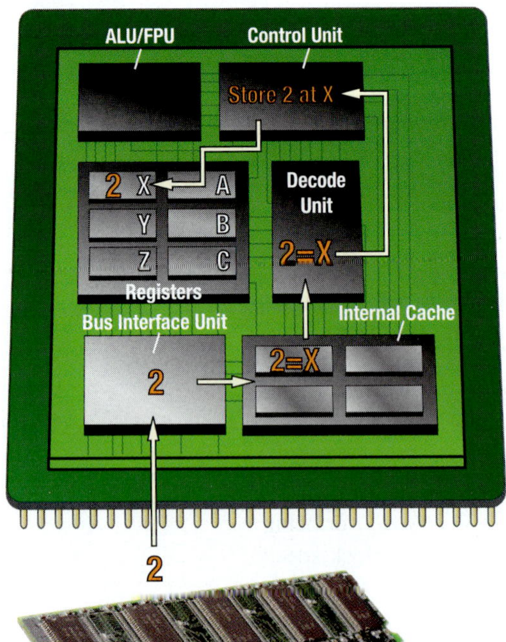

MACHINE CYCLE 2: The number 3 is input and stored.

MACHINE CYCLE 3: The addition command is input, causing the two numbers to be added and the result stored.

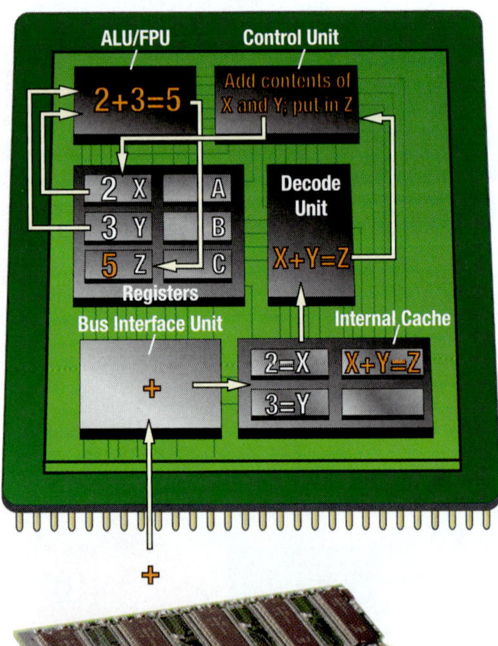

MACHINE CYCLE 4: The equal sign is input, causing the sum to be output.

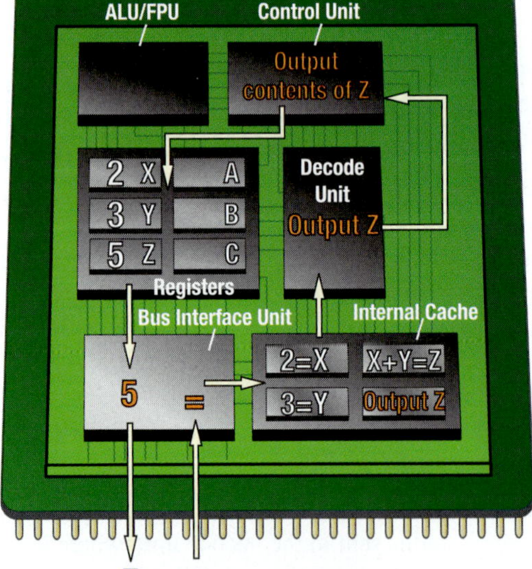

FIGURE 2-21

Machine cycle examples. This example, adding two numbers, requires 4 machine cycles.

2. The number 3 is fetched from RAM using the appropriate address and is sent to the decode unit, where it is determined that the number needs to be stored in register Y. The control unit then stores the number in register Y.
3. The addition symbol is fetched from RAM using the appropriate address and is sent to the decode unit, where it is determined that the numbers in registers X and Y need to be added and the sum stored in register Z. The control unit then instructs the ALU to add the two numbers, and then stores the result in register Z.
4. The equal sign is fetched from RAM using the appropriate address and is sent to the decode unit, where it is determined that the sum in register Z needs to be output. The control unit then sends the sum located in register Z to the appropriate location in RAM.

MAKING COMPUTERS FASTER AND BETTER NOW AND IN THE FUTURE

Over the years, computer designers have developed a number of strategies to achieve faster, more powerful, and more reliable computing performance. Researchers are also constantly working on ways to improve the performance of computers of the future. There are several ways computer users can speed up their computers today, and a number of technologies being developed by manufacturers to improve computers both today and in the future.

Improving the Performance of Your System Today

Several strategies you can use to try to improve the performance of your current computer are discussed next.

Add More Memory

With today's graphic-intensive interfaces and applications, much more memory is required than was necessary even a couple of years ago. If your computer is just a few years old and slows down significantly when you have multiple programs open, you should consider adding more memory to your system to bring it up to a minimum of 512 MB. Be sure to check inside your PC first to determine if there is room for more memory modules, and then check with your PC manufacturer to determine the appropriate type and speed of RAM that your PC uses. Some memory modules must be added in pairs. If you do not have enough empty RAM slots in your PC, you will need to remove some of the old modules and replace them with newer, higher capacity ones, in order to add more memory to your system.

TIP

Before opening your PC's system unit, be sure to turn it off and unplug it, then carefully remove the cover. Before touching any components inside the PC, touch the power supply to discharge any static electricity contained within your body.

Perform System Maintenance

As you work and use your hard drive to store and retrieve data, and as you install and uninstall programs, most PCs tend to become less efficient. One reason for this is because as large documents are stored, retrieved, and then stored again, they often become *fragmented*—that is, not stored in contiguous (adjacent) storage areas. Because the different pieces of the document are physically located in different places, it takes longer for the computer to retrieve or store it. Another reason a computer might become inefficient is that when programs are uninstalled, pieces of the program are sometimes left behind or references to these programs are left in operating system files. Yet another reason is that as a hard drive begins to get full, it takes longer to locate and manipulate the data stored on the drive. All of these factors can result in a system performing more slowly than it should.

FURTHER EXPLORATION

For links to further information about system maintenance, go to www.course.com/uc11/ch02

FIGURE 2-22

Uninstalling programs. Always uninstall programs properly, such as by using the Windows Control Panel *Add or Remove Programs* option.

To avoid some of these problems, regular *system maintenance* should be performed. Some system maintenance tips every computer user should be aware of are as follows:

- Uninstall any programs that you no longer want on your computer in order to free up space on your hard drive. Be sure to use the designated removal procedure for your operating system, such as the Add/Remove Programs option in the Windows Control Panel (see Figure 2-22) or an "Uninstall" option for that program located on the Start menu, to remove the program for Windows PCs.
- If you have large files (such as digital photos or other graphical images) stored on your computer that you do not need on a regular basis, consider moving them to a removable storage medium, such as a CD or DVD disc. Once copied onto the new medium, the files can be deleted from your hard drive to free up space. If the files are important, you might want to make two copies, just to be safe. Be sure to open the files from the storage medium to confirm that the transfer was successful before deleting the files from your hard drive, and store multiple discs containing the same files in different locations. Copying files, deleting files, and types of storage media will be discussed in more detail in later chapters.
- Delete the temporary files stored by your Web browser (choose *Internet Options* from the Tools menu, if you are using Internet Explorer; select *Preferences* from the Edit menu, and then choose *Advanced* and *Cache* in Netscape Navigator). Web browsers tend to store a large amount of data—it is not unusual to have over 1,000 temporary Internet files, including your browsing history and copies of Web pages you have recently visited. If you no longer need this information, deleting the files will make room on your hard drive. Deleting temporary Internet files can also speed up your Internet browsing. There are also *utility programs*, such as the Windows Disk Cleanup program, that can help you locate and delete temporary files left over from installing programs, uninstalling programs, and browsing the Internet.
- Open the Recycle Bin (or similar location holding deleted files on your PC) and empty it. As long as you are sure that none of the files in the Recycle Bin need to be restored, those files are taking up room on your hard drive needlessly.

FIGURE 2-23

The Windows Task Manager. The Windows Task Manager can be used to shut down processes manually, if necessary.

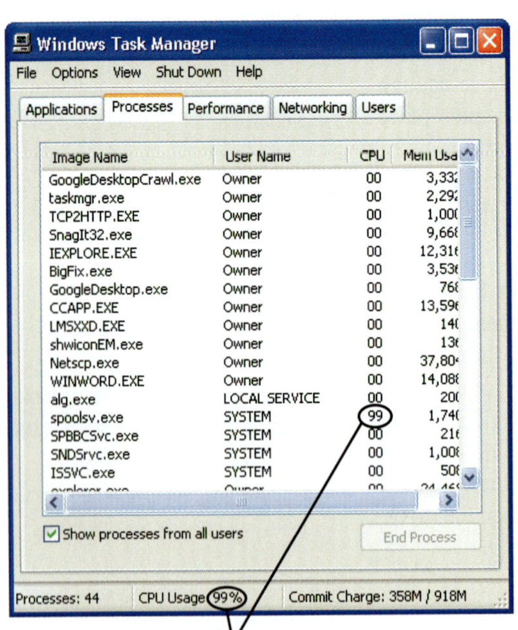

A continued high CPU usage for a process may indicate a problem.

- Scan for *computer viruses* and *spyware* regularly. A computer that suddenly slows down might be the result of extra workload created by a computer virus, spyware program, or other threat. *Antivirus* and *antispyware programs* can help detect and correct these problems and are discussed in more detail in Chapter 9. If you are using Windows XP, you can also check the current CPU load any time by pressing the Ctrl+Alt+Delete key combination one time. The resulting Windows Task Manager screen can be used to view all open programs and processes, as shown in Figure 2-23. If the CPU load stays very high for a long period of time, look for a process with a high CPU percentage. Some processes, such as *print spoolers*, occasionally *hang* (stay running) after they should be finished; if this happens, the process can be shut down manually using this screen. But be sure you know what a process does (use an Internet search site to research it, if needed) before shutting it down to avoid creating problems with your PC.
- Use a utility program, such as the Windows Disk Defragmenter program, to arrange the files on your hard drive more efficiently. On large hard drives, this may need to be done during the night because of the time required to defragment the drive. Utility programs are discussed more in Chapter 5.

Buy a Larger or Second Hard Drive

As already mentioned, hard drives get less efficient as they fill up. If your hard drive is almost full and you do not have any data or programs that you can remove, you should consider buying and installing a second hard drive. The new drive can be an internal hard drive if you have an empty storage bay inside your computer. It can also be an external USB hard drive if you have a free USB port. Alternatively, you can replace your existing hard drive with a larger one, although the data transfer process will be a little more complicated. Hard drives are discussed in more detail in Chapter 3.

Upgrade Your Internet Connection

If your system seems slow primarily when you are on the Internet, the culprit might be your Internet connection. If you are using standard dial-up access, you may wish to investigate the faster connection options available in your area. Switching to cable, satellite, DSL, or another fast type of Internet service is more expensive than dial-up, but is significantly faster. The differences between these and other types of Internet connections are described in Chapters 7 and 8.

TIP

Using an external USB hard drive to store your data makes it very fast and easy to move your data to a different computer, when needed. It also protects your data from being lost if the main hard drive on your PC stops working or if you need to restore your computer's main hard drive back to its original state.

Upgrade Your Video Card

If you are a gamer, computer artist, graphical engineer, or otherwise use 3D-graphic-intensive applications, consider upgrading your video card to one that better supports 3D graphics or has more memory (called *video memory*) located on the card. If you do not use 3D applications, upgrading your video card may not improve your speed. However, if your PC uses integrated video (in which some of your computer's RAM is used for video memory), installing a separate video card, if the motherboard allows it, may speed up your system since it will free up the RAM currently being used for video memory.

Strategies for Making Faster and Better Computers

There are several strategies that researchers and manufacturers are using today to continue to build faster and better PCs. Some relate to technology in general; others are techniques used specifically to speed up the CPU. Some of these strategies are described in the next few sections.

Improved Architecture

Computer manufacturers continually work on improving the basic architecture of the PC, such as to make it faster, cooler, quieter, more energy efficient, and more reliable. For example, new designs for motherboards and CPUs are being developed, and computer components are continually being built smaller, so more power and capabilities can be contained in the same size package. In fact, today's CPUs—which are formed using a process called *lithography* that imprints patterns on semiconductor materials—typically contain transistors that are 50 *nanometers* (*nm*) in size; transistors as small as 10 nm have been created in lab settings. As lithography techniques continue to improve, transistors will likely continue to shrink, allowing more transistors to fit on the same-sized CPU. Creating components smaller than 100 nm fits the definition of *nanotechnology*, which is discussed in more detail shortly.

Other improvements include faster memory and faster bus speeds to help speed up processing and to help reduce or eliminate bottlenecks, and creating CPUs with multiple cores (such as the dual-core CPUs that are currently available and the *quad-core* CPUs that are expected by 2007). Improvements to CPU instruction set designs are also being made to expand the instruction set design for new applications—particularly growing multimedia applications, such as editing digital movies and photos, burning music CDs, and more—are continually being developed. For example, *MMX* (*Multimedia Extensions*) is a set of 57 multimedia instructions for handling many common multimedia operations, and *streaming SIMD extensions* (*SSEs*), *SSE2*, and *SSE3* help CPUs perform floating-point-intensive applications (such as video and audio handling, 3D modeling, and physical simulations) much more quickly than before, provided the software being used supports the extensions being used.

Improved Materials

Traditionally, CPU chips used aluminum circuitry etched onto a silicon backing. As the limit of the number of aluminum circuits that can be packed onto a silicon chip without heat damage or interference approached, chip makers began to look for alternate materials. Copper was one of the next choices since it is a far better electrical conductor, and it can produce chips containing more circuitry at a lower price. A more recent development is *SOI* (*silicon on insulator*). SOI chips use a thin layer of insulating material over the silicon to reduce heat and power consumption. This results in being able to place the circuits closer together than is possible without the insulating material. Another possibility sometimes used today in conjunction with SOI is *strained silicon*. With this technique, the silicon is "stretched out" or "strained" so that the atoms in silicon are further apart. Because of this, the electrons experience less resistance and flow up to 70% faster, which can lead to chips that are up to 35% faster without changing the size of the transistors.

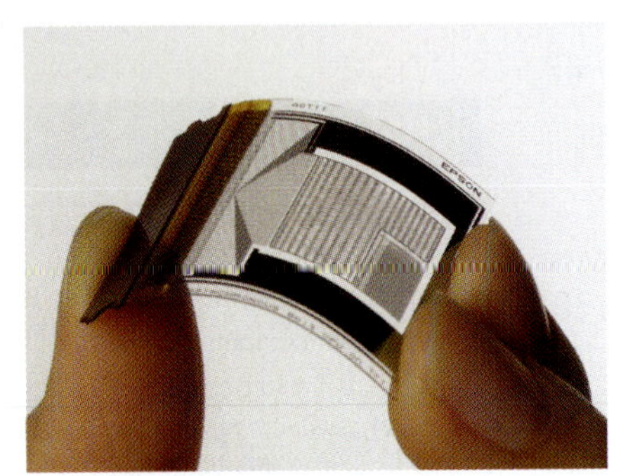

FIGURE 2-24
Flexible microprocessors.

For integration into clothing and other flexible materials, a number of companies are developing flexible electronic components, such as the flexible microprocessor shown in Figure 2-24. In addition to the ability to be bent without damaging the circuitry, flexible microprocessors are thinner, lighter, generate little heat, and consume significantly less energy than conventional microprocessors.

Another possibility currently in the testing stages is replacing the CPU entirely with *field-programmable gate arrays* (*FPGAs*). An FPGA is a type of chip that can be programmed and reprogrammed as needed. To replace a CPU, groups of FPGA chips would need to work together to process several tasks at the same time. While it is possible that FPGAs will replace CPUs in future PCs, they are currently being used in storage devices, networking hardware, cell phones, and digital cameras.

Pipelining

In older PC systems, the CPU had to completely finish processing one instruction before starting another. Today's PCs, however, can process multiple instructions at one time. One way this is accomplished is through **pipelining**. With pipelining, a new instruction begins executing as soon as the previous one reaches the next stage of the machine cycle. Figure 2-25 illustrates this process with a 4-stage pipeline. Notice that while the pipelined CPU is executing one instruction, it is simultaneously fetching and getting the next instruction ready for execution. Without a pipeline, the ALU and FPU would be idle while an instruction is being fetched and decoded.

Pipelines for CPUs today usually have between 10 and 20 stages, and the machine cycle is broken down in as many parts as needed to match the number of stages used. For example, with a 10-stage pipeline, the 4 steps of the machine cycle would be broken down into a total of 10 steps so that all stages of the pipeline can be used at one time. Pipelining increases the number of machine cycles completed per second, which increases the number of instructions performed per second, which improves performance.

>**Pipelining.** A CPU feature designed to begin processing a new instruction as soon as the previous instruction completes the first stage of the machine cycle.

Stages

Fetch Instruction 1	Decode Instruction 1	Execute Instruction 1	Store Result Instruction 1	Fetch Instruction 2	Decode Instruction 2	Execute Instruction 2

WITHOUT PIPELINING
Without pipelining, an instruction finishes an entire machine cycle before another instruction is started.

Stages

Fetch Instruction 1	Fetch Instruction 2	Fetch Instruction 3	Fetch Instruction 4	Fetch Instruction 5	Fetch Instruction 6	Fetch Instruction 7
	Decode Instruction 1	Decode Instruction 2	Decode Instruction 3	Decode Instruction 4	Decode Instruction 5	Decode Instruction 6
		Execute Instruction 1	Execute Instruction 2	Execute Instruction 3	Execute Instruction 4	Execute Instruction 5
			Store Result Instruction 1	Store Result Instruction 2	Store Result Instruction 3	Store Result Instruction 4

WITH PIPELINING
With pipelining, a new instruction is started when the preceding instruction moves to the next stage of the machine cycle.

FIGURE 2-25
Pipelining. Pipelining streamlines the machine cycle by executing different stages of multiple instructions at the same time, so the different parts of the CPU are idle less often.

HW

Multiprocessing and Parallel Processing

While the vast majority of desktop PCs are still driven by single CPUs, using more than one CPU is becoming more common, such as dual-core PCs that have the processing components of two CPUs contained on a single CPU. When two or more CPUs are located within a single computer, techniques that perform operations simultaneously—such as *multiprocessing* (most often used with desktop PCs, midrange servers, and mainframe computers) and *parallel processing* (most often used with supercomputers)—are possible.

With **multiprocessing**, each CPU typically works on a different job. Because multiple jobs are being processed simultaneously, they are completed faster than with a single processor. With **parallel processing**, multiple processors work together to make one single job finish sooner; as shown in Figure 2-26, a *control processor* assigns a portion of the processing for that job to each CPU. Two of the most common designs are *symmetric multiprocessing (SMP)* and *massively parallel processing (MPP)*. With SMP, a single copy of the operating system is in

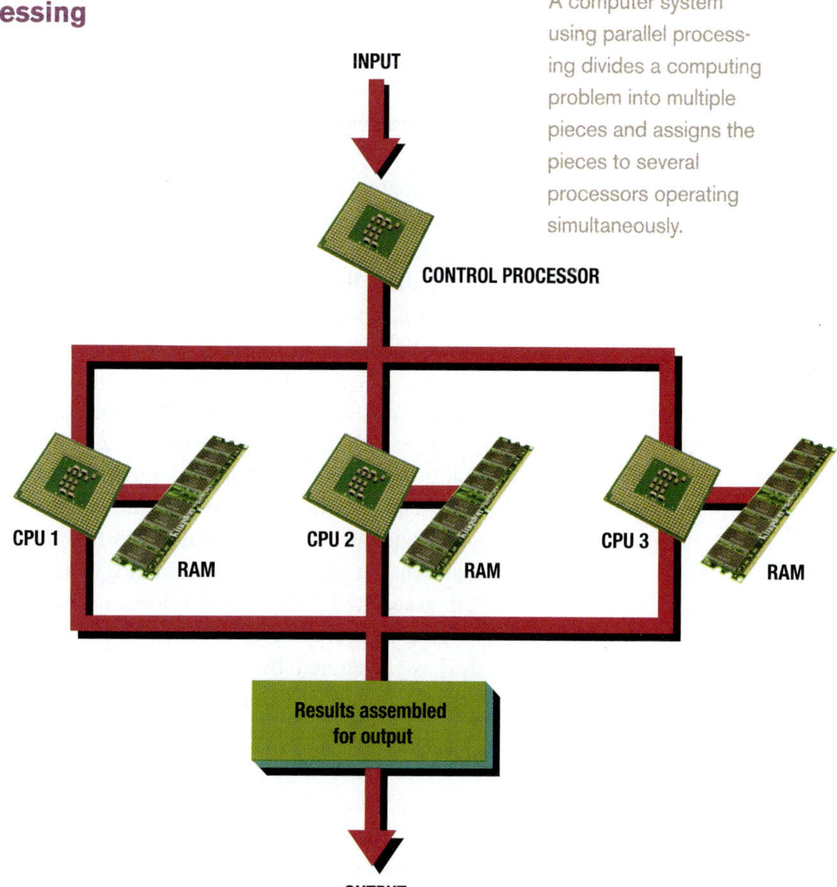

FIGURE 2-26
Parallel processing. A computer system using parallel processing divides a computing problem into multiple pieces and assigns the pieces to several processors operating simultaneously.

>**Multiprocessing.** The capability of an operating system to use multiple processors in a single computer, usually to process multiple jobs at one time faster than could be performed with a single processor. >**Parallel processing.** A processing technique that uses multiple processors simultaneously in a single computer, usually to process a single job as fast as possible.

charge of all the processors and the processors share memory. Typically, SMP systems do not exceed 64 processors. MPP systems, in contrast, can use hundreds or thousands of microprocessors and each processor has its own copy of the operating system and its own memory. MPP systems are typically more difficult to program than SMP systems.

The use of multiprocessing and parallel processing can increase astronomically the number of calculations performed in any given time period. For example, IBM's Blue Gene/L supercomputer (shown in Figure 1-21 in Chapter 1) uses 131,072 processors and will operate at approximately 360 teraflops when fully installed. In other words, it will be able to process about 360 trillion operations per second (most desktop PCs today operate slightly faster than 1 gigaflop).

A concept related to multiprocessing is *Hyper-Threading Technology*—a technology developed by Intel to enable software to treat a single processor as two processors. Since it utilizes processing power in the chip that would otherwise go unused, this technology lets the chip operate more efficiently, resulting in faster processing, provided the software being used supports Hyper-Threading.

Future Trends

Some of the strategies discussed in the prior sections are currently being used, but some ideas are further from being implemented. Selected trends we will likely see more of in the near future are discussed next.

Nanotechnology

Although there are varying definitions, most agree that **nanotechnology** involves creating computer components, machines, and other structures that are less than 100 nanometers in size—one *nanometer* (*nm*) is one-billionth of a meter. As already discussed, today's CPUs contain components that fit the definition of nanotechnology. But some experts believe that, eventually, current technology will reach its limits. At that point, transistors and other computer components may need to be built at the atomic and molecular level—starting with single atoms or molecules to construct the components. Prototypes of computer products built in this fashion include a single switch that can be turned on and off like a transistor but is made from a single organic molecule and tiny nickel-based *nanodots* that would, theoretically, allow about 5 TB of data to be stored on a hard drive roughly the size of a postage stamp. Carbon *nanotubes*—tiny, hollow tubes made up of carbon atoms—are also being evaluated as a possible replacement for CPU transistors.

Possible future applications of nanotechnology include improved military uniforms that protect against bullets and germ warfare, microscopic robots that can enter the bloodstream and perform tests or irradiate cancerous tumors, and computers and sensors that are small enough to be woven into the fibers of clothing or embedded into paint and other materials. In addition, nanotechnology may eventually solve much of the toxic waste problem associated with *e-trash* (electronic waste, such as old computer equipment) by rearranging dangerous components, at the atomic level, into inert substances. Some of the devices generated by nanotechnology research may contain or be constructed out of organic material. Complete *organic computers* are a long way off in the future, but researchers have already created biological computing devices—such as one interactive DNA-based system that can play tic-tac-toe and has never lost at that game.

>**Nanotechnology.** The science of creating tiny computers and components by working at the individual atomic and molecular levels.

Quantum Computing

The idea of **quantum computing** emerged in the 1970s, but it has received renewed interest lately. Quantum computing applies the principles of quantum physics and quantum mechanics to computers, going beyond traditional physics to work at the subatomic level. Quantum computers differ from conventional computers in that they utilize atoms or nuclei working together as quantum bits or *qubits*. Qubits function simultaneously as both the computer's processor and memory, and each qubit can represent more than just the two states (one and zero) available to today's electronic bits; a qubit can even represent many states at one time. Quantum computers can perform computations on many numbers at one time, making them, theoretically, exponentially faster than conventional computers. Physically, quantum computers in the future might consist of a thimbleful of liquid whose atoms are used to perform calculations as instructed by an external device.

While quantum computers are still in the pioneering stage, working quantum computers do exist. For instance, in 2001 the researchers at IBM's Almaden Research Center created a 7-qubit quantum computer (see Figure 2-27) composed of the nuclei of seven atoms that can interact with each other and be programmed by radio frequency pulses. This quantum computer successfully factored the number 15—not a complicated computation for a conventional computer, but the fact that it was possible to supply a quantum computer with the problem and have it compute the correct answer is viewed as a highly significant event in the area of quantum computer research. Hewlett-Packard scientists have developed a *crossbar latch*—a switch just a single molecule thick that can store binary data and might one day function as a transistor in a quantum computer.

Quantum computing is not well suited for general computing tasks but is ideal for, and expected to be widely used in, the areas of encryption and code breaking.

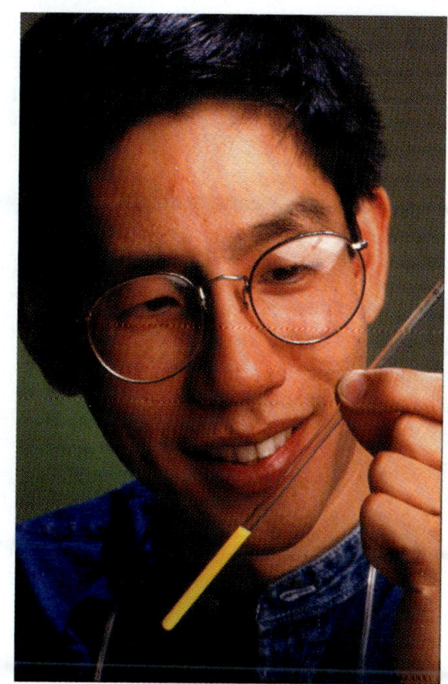

FIGURE 2-27

Quantum computers. The vial of liquid shown here contains the 7-qubit computer used by IBM researchers in 2001 to perform the most complicated computation by a quantum computer to date–factoring the number 15.

HW

Optical Computing

Optical chips, which use light waves to transmit data, are also currently in development. A possibility for the future is the **optical computer**—a computer that uses light, such as from laser beams or infrared beams—to perform digital computations. Because light beams do not interfere with each other, optical computers can be much smaller and faster than electronic PCs. For instance, according to one NASA senior research scientist, an optical computer could solve a problem in one hour that would take an electronic computer 11 years to solve. While some researchers are working on developing an all-optical computer, others believe that a mix of optical and electronic components—or an *opto-electronic computer*—may be the best bet for the future. Opto-electronic technology is already being used to improve long-distance fiber-optic communications. Initial opto-electronic PC applications are expected to be in the area of speeding up communications between PCs and other devices, as well as between PC components. In fact, prototypes of chips that have both optical and electrical functions combined on a single silicon chip—a feat that was thought to be impossible until recently—already exist.

3D Chips

Three-dimensional (3D) chips are another technique for packing an increasing number of components onto small chips. With 3D chips, the transistors are layered, which cuts down on the surface area required. 3D chips are now available for some applications—such as video cards—and are expected to be used for other multimedia applications in the near future.

>**Quantum computing.** A technology that applies the principles of quantum physics and quantum mechanics to computers to direct atoms or nuclei to work together as quantum bits (qubits), which function simultaneously as the computer's processor and memory. >**Optical computer.** A computer that uses light, such as from laser beams or infrared beams, to perform digital computations.

SUMMARY

DATA AND PROGRAM REPRESENTATION

Chapter Objective 1:
Understand how data and programs are represented to a computer and be able to identify a few of the coding systems used to accomplish this.

The electronic components of a *digital computer* work in a two-state, or *binary*, fashion. It is convenient to think of these binary states in terms of 0s and 1s. Computer people refer to such 0s and 1s as *bits*. Converting data to these 0s and 1s is called *digital data representation*.

Computers use the **binary numbering system** to represent numbers and perform numeric computations. Text-based data can be represented with one of several fixed-length binary codes. Two popular coding schemes are **ASCII (American Standard Code for Information Interchange)** and **EBCDIC (Extended Binary-Coded Decimal Interchange Code)**. These systems represent single characters of data—a numeric digit, alphabetic character, or special symbol—as strings of eight bits. Each string of bits is called a **byte**. **Unicode** is another binary code used with text-based data that can represent text in all written languages, including those that use alphabets different from English, such as Chinese, Greek, and Russian.

The storage capacity of computers often is expressed in **kilobytes (KB)**, or thousands of bytes; **megabytes (MB)**, millions of bytes; **gigabytes (GB)**, billions of bytes; and **terabytes (TB)**, trillions of bytes. Other possibilities are the **petabyte (PB)**, about 1,000 terabytes; the **exabyte (EB)**, about 1,000 petabytes; the **zettabyte (ZB)**, about 1,000 exabytes; and the **yottabyte (YB)**, about 1,000 zettabytes.

The binary system can represent not only text but graphics, audio, and video data, as well. **Machine language** is the binary-based code through which computers represent program instructions. A program must be translated into machine language before the computer can execute it.

INSIDE THE SYSTEM UNIT

Chapter Objective 2:
Explain the functions of the hardware components commonly found inside the system unit, such as the CPU, memory, buses, and expansion cards.

PCs typically contain a variety of hardware components located inside the **system unit**. For instance, *chips* are mounted onto *circuit boards*, and those boards are positioned in slots on the **motherboard** or *system board*—the main circuit board for a PC. Every PC has a **central processing unit (CPU)**—also called a **processor** or **microprocessor** when referring to PCs—attached to its motherboard that performs the processing for the computer. CPU chips differ in many respects, such as what types of PCs the CPU is designed for, its *clock speed*, and *word size*. Another difference is the amount of **cache memory**—memory located on or very close to the CPU chip to help speed up processing. Other important differences are the general architecture of the CPU and the bus speed and width being used. The overall *processing speed* of the computer determines its performance. One of the most consistent measurements of overall performance is a **benchmark test**.

The main memory chips for a PC are commonly referred to as **RAM (random access memory)**. RAM is volatile and used to temporarily hold programs and data while they are needed. RAM is available in different types and speeds. **ROM (read-only memory)** are memory chips that store nonerasable programs. **Flash memory** is nonvolatile memory that can be erased and reprogrammed in blocks. Flash memory chips can be found in PCs and mobile devices; flash memory chips can also be used for storage with portable PCs, digital cameras, and other smaller devices. **Registers** are memory built into the CPU chip to hold data before or during processing.

Most desktop PCs contain internal **expansion slots**, into which users can insert **expansion cards** to give the computer added functionality. A computer **bus** is an electronic path along which bits are transmitted. The *system bus* moves data between the CPU and RAM, and **expansion buses** connect the CPU to peripheral devices. Common buses include *PCI*, **PCI Express (PCIe)**, *AGP*, *HyperTransport*, **USB (Universal Serial Bus)**, **FireWire**, and *CardBus*.

System units typically have external **ports** that are used to connect peripheral devices to the computer. Notebook and tablet PCs may have fewer ports than desktop PCs. Handheld PC and mobile device users often add new capabilities with *Secure Digital (SD) cards* or other types of flash memory cards. In addition, some handheld PCs and mobile devices include a PC card slot or proprietary expansion system.

Chapter Objective 3:
Describe how peripheral devices or other hardware can be added to a PC.

HW

HOW THE CPU WORKS

CPUs include at least one **arithmetic/logic unit (ALU)**, which performs integer arithmetic and logical operations on data, and at least one **floating point unit (FPO)**, which performs decimal arithmetic. The **control unit** directs the flow of electronic traffic between memory and the ALU/FPU and also between the CPU and input and output devices. Registers—high-speed temporary holding places within the CPU that hold program instructions and data immediately before and during processing—are used to enhance the computer's performance. The **prefetch unit** requests data and instructions before or as they are needed, the **decode unit** decodes the instructions input into the CPU, internal cache stores frequently used instructions and data, and the **bus interface unit** inputs data and instructions from RAM.

The CPU processes instructions in a sequence called a **machine cycle**, consisting of four basic steps. Each machine language instruction is broken down into several smaller instructions called *microcode*, and each piece of microcode corresponds to an operation (such as adding two numbers located in the CPU's registers) that can be performed inside the CPU. The computer system has a built-in **system clock** that synchronizes all of the PC's activities.

Chapter Objective 4:
Understand how the computer system's CPU and memory components process program instructions and data.

MAKING COMPUTERS FASTER AND BETTER NOW AND IN THE FUTURE

There are several possible remedies for a computer that is performing too slowly, including adding more memory, performing system maintenance to clean up the PC's hard drive, buying a larger or additional hard drive, and upgrading the computer's Internet connection or video card, depending on the primary role of the computer and where the processing bottleneck appears to be. To make computers work faster over all, computer designers have developed a number of strategies over the years, and researchers are continually working on new strategies. Some of the strategies already being implemented include improved architecture, **pipelining**, **multiprocessing**, **parallel processing**, and the use of improved materials.

Chapter Objective 5:
Name and evaluate several strategies that can be used today for speeding up the operations of a computer.

One possibility for future computers is **nanotechnology** research, which focuses on building computer components at the individual atomic and molecular levels. **Quantum computing** and **optical computers** are other possibilities being researched, along with *three-dimensional (3D) chips*.

Chapter Objective 6:
List some technologies that may be used in future PCs.

REVIEW ACTIVITIES

KEY TERM MATCHING

Instructions: Match each key term on the left with the definition on the right that best describes it.

a. ASCII
b. binary numbering system
c. byte
d. central processing unit (CPU)
e. control unit
f. motherboard
g. nanotechnology
h. parallel processing
i. random access memory (RAM)
j. Universal Serial Bus (USB)

1. ______ A processing technique that uses multiple processors simultaneously in a single computer, usually to process a single job as fast as possible.

2. ______ A fixed-length, binary coding system widely used to represent text-based data for computer processing on many types of computers.

3. ______ A group of 8 bits.

4. ______ A universal bus used to connect up to 127 peripheral devices to a computer without requiring the use of additional expansion cards.

5. ______ Chips connected to the motherboard that provide a temporary location for the computer to hold data and program instructions while they are needed.

6. ______ The chip located inside the system unit of a computer that performs the processing for a computer.

7. ______ The main circuit board of a computer, located inside the system unit, to which all computer system components connect.

8. ______ The numbering system that represents all numbers using just two symbols (0 and 1).

9. ______ The part of the CPU that coordinates its operations.

10. ______ The science of creating tiny computers and components by working at the individual atomic and molecular levels.

SELF-QUIZ

Instructions: Circle **T** if the statement is true, **F** if the statement is false, or write the best answer in the space provided. **Answers for the self-quiz are located in the References and Resources Guide at the end of the book.**

1. **T F** A storage medium that can hold 256 GB can hold about 256 billion characters.
2. **T F** ASCII is the coding system used by a computer to perform mathematical computations.
3. **T F** Cache memory is typically built into a CPU.
4. **T F** A bus is a pathway, such as on the motherboard or inside the CPU, along which bits can be transferred.
5. **T F** Computers that process data with light are referred to as quantum computers.
6. The binary number 1101 is equivalent to the decimal number ______.
7. The main memory the computer uses to temporarily store programs and data it is working with is ______.
8. A(n) ______ is a connector on the exterior of a computer's system unit into which a peripheral device may be plugged.
9. With ______, the CPU is able to begin executing a new instruction as soon as the previous instruction finishes the first stage of the machine cycle.

10. Number the following terms from 1 to 10 to indicate their size from smallest to largest.

a. _______ Petabyte	**d.** _______ Yottabyte	**g.** _______ Zettabyte
b. _______ Kilobyte	**e.** _______ Exabyte	**h.** _______ Terabyte
c. _______ Gigabyte	**f.** _______ Byte	**i.** _______ Megabyte

---

EXERCISES

1. What do each of the following acronyms stand for?

a. KB _______	**d.** USB _______
b. RAM _______	**e.** PCIe _______
c. ROM _______	**f.** CPU _______

2. Using the ASCII code chart in this chapter or in the References and Resources Guide at the end of the book, decode the following word. What does it say?

01000011	01000001	01000110	01000101
_______	_______	_______	_______

3. Assume you have a USB mouse, USB keyboard, and USB printer to connect to a PC, but you have only two USB ports. Explain one solution to this problem that does not involve buying a new mouse, keyboard, or printer.

4. If your PC seems sluggish, list two things you could do to try to speed it up without resorting to purchasing an entirely new system.

5. Match the picture to its name and write the corresponding number in the blank to the left of each name.

a. _______ memory module	**c.** _______ keyboard port
b. _______ expansion card	**d.** _______ USB port

1.

2.

3.

4.

DISCUSSION QUESTION

In addition to being used with computers and consumer products, there are also processors and other similar components designed to be implanted inside the human body. One of the most prominent is the *VeriChip*—a tiny chip about the size of a grain of rice that is implanted under a person's skin. The VeriChip is intended to be used in conjunction with a database to provide identification data, such as to provide hospital emergency room personnel with health information about an unconscious patient. Another implantable device that is currently in development uses an implantable wafer containing medication in conjunction with a processor to deliver the medication at the appropriate time and dosage without patient intervention. And *brain-to-computer interfacing (BCI)* involves implanting electrodes directly into the human brain to restore lost functionality or to facilitate the communications of severely disabled individuals, such as by enabling them to move a mouse cursor or direct it to click an object using only their thoughts. What do you think about these implantable chip applications? Are the benefits worth the risk of something going wrong with the chips implanted inside your body? Are there any privacy risks? Would you consider using an implanted device? Why or why not?

PROJECTS

HOT TOPICS

1. **USB Gadgets** As discussed in the chapter, computers today usually come with several USB ports, often on the front of the PC for easy access. In addition to being used with conventional peripheral devices and external storage devices, a growing number of gadgets are being developed for use with an empty USB slot. Some—such as keyboard vacuums and ionizers—have practical applications; others—such as fake aquariums and disco balls—are more for entertainment purposes.

   For this project, locate several USB gadgets that are currently on the market. Research these products to determine their purpose and cost, and classify the gadgets as practical or entertaining. At the conclusion of your research, prepare a one- to two-page summary of your findings and submit it to your instructor. Be sure to mention which gadgets you think are worthwhile and which ones you would choose not to use and why.

SHORT ANSWER/ RESEARCH

2. **Adding Memory** Adding additional RAM to a PC is one of the most common computer upgrades. Before purchasing additional memory, however, a little research is in order to make sure that the purchased memory is compatible with the PC.

   For this project, select a computer to which you might want to add memory. It does not matter if you own the computer or not, but it needs to be one you can find out information about, such as your own PC, a school PC if there is someone to whom you can ask questions about the computer, or a computer for sale at a local store. For your selected PC, determine the following: manufacturer and model number, CPU, current amount of memory, total memory slots, and the number of available memory slots. (If you look inside the PC, be sure to unplug the power cord first and do not touch any components inside the system unit.) For a school PC, you may be able to find some of the information on the front of the PC; you will have to ask someone in charge of that PC for the rest of the information. For a PC at a local store, determine what you can from an advertisement or by looking at the PC in a store, then ask a salesperson (either in person or over the telephone) questions to determine any missing information. Once you have the necessary information, call a local store or use your information and a memory supplier's Web site to determine the appropriate type of memory needed for your selected PC. What choices do you have in terms of capacity and configuration? Can you add just one memory module, or do you have to add memory in pairs? Can you keep the old memory modules, or do they have to be removed? At the conclusion of your research, prepare a one-page summary of your findings and submit it to your instructor.

3. **In Review** It is a good idea to start the process of expanding or upgrading your computer by reading hardware reviews in offline or online computer journals, such as Computerworld, PC World, or MacWorld, or on tech news sites, such as CNET.com or ZDNet.com. Reviews available online are often organized by category, providing you with the latest information about compatibility, performance, cost, reliability, and overall value.

   For this project, select a piece of hardware that you would like to upgrade on your PC or add to your computer system (if you do not have a PC, just assume that you do). Some possible options include adding a new video board, modem, sound card, scanner, digital camera, printer, DVD drive, CD-R drive, network interface, or flash memory reader. Research specific brands and models of your selected product, then select the one that would best suit your needs, noting why you selected the model you did over its competitors. In your findings, be sure to identify how the device will be connected to your PC. If an expansion card is required, identify which slot the card would need to be inserted into and make certain that there is an empty slot of that type on your PC. If there is not an available slot, check whether the product is available in a format compatible with your PC, such as in a USB format. At the conclusion of your research, prepare a one-page summary of your findings and submit it to your instructor.

HANDS ON

4. **Ports** As mentioned in the chapter, external hardware connects to the computer via ports located on the exterior of the system unit. Conventional ports include parallel, serial, PS/2 (keyboard/mouse), sound, and monitor ports. Newer ports include USB 2 and FireWire (IEEE 1394) ports. Many PCs today also have a modem and/or networking port. Some of the older ports—particularly parallel and serial—are beginning to be referred to as "legacy ports." They are being omitted from some new computers today, and many people predict that they will eventually be replaced by newer types of ports.

   For this project, select one computer (such as at home, your school, public library, or a computer store) and make sure you can look at the exterior of the entire system unit. Draw a sketch of all four sides of the PC case, including all of its ports. On your sketch, label each port with a note about what that port is being used for (for the ports in use) or might be used for (for the available ports) on that particular PC. Does the PC you selected use legacy ports? If you wanted to add a flash memory drive or reader that plugs into a USB port, would you be able to use it with your selected PC? Why or why not? Turn in your labeled sketch along with the answers to these questions to your instructor.

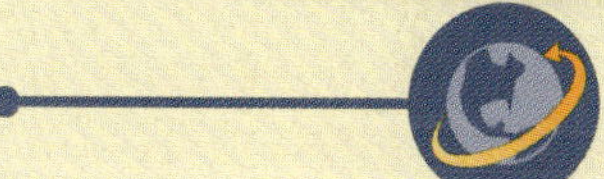

5. **Intel Museum Tour** Intel Corporation has a great deal of interesting information about microprocessors and related technology on its Web site, including information available through its online museum.

   For this project, go to the Intel Museum at www.intel.com/museum/index.htm (if this URL no longer works at the time you do this project, go to the Intel home page at www.intel.com and search for "Intel Museum" using the site's search feature). Once you are at the Intel Museum home page, select an Online Exhibit related to microprocessors, such as *How the Transistor Works*, *How the Microprocessor Works*, *How Chips Are Made*, or *Clean Room*, and then tour the exhibit. As you tour, make a note of at least three interesting facts you learned. At the conclusion of this task, prepare a short summary listing the tour you took and the interesting facts you recorded and submit it to your instructor.

WRITING ABOUT COMPUTERS

6. **Wearable PCs** As mentioned in Chapter 1, wearable computers are computers that are small enough to be worn on a belt or wrist, like a portable MP3 player or Walkman. Although they have been available in some form for commercial applications for several years, their entry into the consumer market is just beginning. Some current features of wearable PCs, such as corded components and using an eye-piece display device that some individuals view as unattractive, may make today's wearable PCs less desirable than those that are expected to become available in the future.

   For this project, write a short essay expressing your opinion about wearable computers. Try to find a photo of a wearable computer geared toward consumer use—would you be willing to wear one in public today? Why or why not? If not, how (if at all) would wearable computers need to be changed in order for you to be willing to wear one? As they become smaller, wireless, and controllable by your voice, do you think their use by consumers will increase? Will their use be looked at as any different from wearing a Walkman or MP3 player in public? Think about your chosen profession—is wearable or portable computer use needed or useful today? What advantages and disadvantages do you see regarding wearable computer use in that profession? Submit your opinion on this issue to your instructor in the form of a short paper, not more than two pages in length.

PRESENTATION/ DEMONSTRATION

7. **Binary Conversions** As discussed in the chapter, all numbers processed by the CPU must be represented in a binary format. The conversion from decimal (base 10) to and from true binary (base 2) format is a fairly straightforward process and can be accomplished with basic arithmetic. The conversion from true binary format to hexadecimal (base 16) format is also a fairly straightforward process and is generally used to conserve memory whenever possible.

   For this project, research how to convert a three-digit decimal number to both binary and hexadecimal and back again, without the use of a calculator (refer to the "A Look at Numbering Systems" feature located on this book's Web site at www.course.com/uc11 if needed). Next, use your knowledge of binary and decimal numbering systems to determine how to represent the decimal number 10 in base 3. Share your findings with the class in the form of a short presentation, including a demonstration of the conversions between binary and hexadecimal and the representation of the decimal number 10 in base 3. The presentation should not exceed 10 minutes and should make use of one or more presentation aids such as the chalkboard, handouts, overhead transparencies, or a computer-based slide presentation (your instructor may provide additional requirements). You may also be asked to submit a summary of the presentation to your instructor.

GROUP DISCUSSION

8. **People Chips** The *VeriChip* is a tiny chip about the size of a grain of rice that is designed to be implanted under a person's skin, such as on the forearm. Each VeriChip contains a unique verification number that can be read when a proprietary scanner is passed over the implanted chip. Although the VeriChip does not contain any personal data at the present time, it can be used in conjunction with a database to access data, such as to provide hospital emergency room personnel with health information about an unconscious patient. According to the company that invented VeriChip, future versions could be used for access control to secure facilities, personal computers, cars, and homes, as well as to authenticate users for ATM and credit card transactions. Versions of the VeriChip with GPS capabilities could also be used to find missing individuals, such as kidnap victims and lost Alzheimer's patients. These VeriChip versions would be similar to the clip-on and wristwatch monitoring systems available today that allow for continuous location information to be broadcast to a proprietary receiver. Electronic payments are also another possibility—for example, one version of the VeriChip is already being used by some regular patrons at a nightclub in Barcelona, Spain, to charge their food and beverages to their house accounts. Although privacy-rights advocates worry that a chip like the VeriChip could someday be used by the government to track citizens, others view the chip no differently than a medical ID bracelet, and they are not concerned because it is available on a purely voluntary basis. What do you think? Would you be willing to have a VeriChip implanted under your skin if it made some tasks (such as unlocking your home or car) easier or some types of transactions (such as withdrawing money from your bank account or shopping online) more secure? Do you think it would make these tasks easier or more secure?

   For this project, form an opinion of the use of human-implantable chips and be prepared to discuss your position (in class, via an online class discussion group, or in a class chat room, depending on your instructor's directions). You may also be asked to write a short paper expressing your opinion.

HW

WEB ACTIVITIES

The *Understanding Computers* Web site located at **www.course.com/uc11** features many resources to help reinforce your understanding of the chapter content and help you prepare for exams. Your instructor may also assign specific activities to be completed that will count toward your final grade in the course.

Instructions: Go to **www.course.com/uc11/ch02** to work the following online activities.

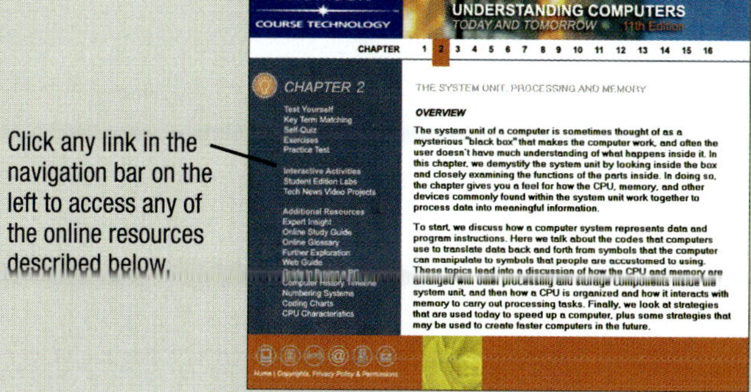

INTERACTIVE ACTIVITIES

1. **Crossword Puzzle** Practice your knowledge of the key terms in Chapter 2 by completing the interactive Crossword Puzzle.
2. **Tech News Video Project** Watch the **"High-Tech Helmets"** video clip that features a new helmet sensor system developed by sports medicine researchers at Virginia Tech University. The sensors measure the physical impacts (in G-forces) experienced by each player to evaluate his condition on an on-going basis in order to help make football a little safer. After watching the video online, complete the corresponding project.
3. **Student Edition Labs** Reinforce the concepts you have learned in this chapter by working through the interactive **Binary Numbers** and **Understanding the Motherboard** labs.

TEST YOURSELF

1. **Key Term Matching** Test your knowledge of selected chapter key terms by matching the terms with their definitions.
2. **Self-Quiz** Test your retention of chapter concepts by taking the Self-Quiz.
3. **Exercises** Work these short exercises to review the concepts and terms covered in the chapter.
4. **Practice Test** Test how ready you are for an upcoming exam by completing the online Practice Test.

STUDY TOOLS/ ADDITIONAL RESOURCES

The Understanding Computers Web site has a wide range of additional resources, including an **Online Study Guide** (containing study tips, a chapter outline with room to add your own notes, and a chapter checklist of the activities to complete when the chapter is covered in class and when you are preparing for a test) and an **Online Glossary** for each chapter; **Further Exploration** links; a **Web Guide**, a **Guide to Buying a PC**, and a **Computer History Timeline**; more information about **Numbering Systems**, **Coding Charts**, and **CPU Characteristics**; and much, much more!

3 CHAPTER Storage

OUTLINE

Overview
Storage Systems Characteristics
Storage Devices and Storage Media
Volatility
Random vs. Sequential Access
Logical vs. Physical Representation
Magnetic Disks vs. Optical Discs
Magnetic Disk Systems
Floppy Disks and Drives
Hard Disk Drives
High-Capacity Removable Magnetic Disks and Cartridges
Optical Disc Systems
Read-Only Discs: CD-ROM and DVD-ROM Discs
Recordable Discs: CD-R, DVD-R, DVD+R, and DVD+R DL Discs
Rewritable Discs: CD-RW, DVD-RW, DVD+RW, DVD-RAM, and Blue Laser Discs
Flash Memory Systems
Flash Memory Media
Flash Memory Drives
Other Types of Storage Systems
Remote Storage Systems
Smart Cards
Holographic Storage
Storage Systems for Large Computer Systems and Networks
Magnetic Tape Systems
Comparing Storage Alternatives

LEARNING OBJECTIVES

After completing this chapter, you will be able to:

1. Explain the difference between storage systems and memory.
2. Name several general characteristics of storage systems.
3. Identify the two primary types of magnetic disk systems and describe how they work.
4. Discuss the various types of optical disc systems available and how they differ from each other and from magnetic systems.
5. Explain what flash memory media and flash memory drives are and how they are used today.
6. List at least three other types of storage systems.
7. Summarize the storage alternatives for a PC, including which storage systems should be included on a typical PC and for what applications other storage systems are appropriate.

OVERVIEW

In Chapter 2, we discussed the role of RAM, the computer's main memory. RAM *temporarily* holds program instructions, data, and output while they are needed by the computer. For instance, when you first create a letter or other word processing document on your computer, the word processing program and the document are both temporarily stored in RAM. But when the word processing program is closed, the computer no longer needs to work with the program or the document, and so they are erased from RAM. Consequently, anything (such as your word processing document) that needs to be preserved for future use needs to be stored on a more permanent medium. *Storage systems* fill this role.

We begin this chapter with a look at the characteristics common among storage systems. Then, storage systems based on magnetic disks (namely floppy disks and hard drives) are discussed. From there, we turn to optical discs and discuss how optical discs work and the various types of CDs and DVDs available today. Next, we discuss flash memory storage systems, followed by a look at other types of storage systems that can be used for some applications, such as remote storage, smart cards, holographic storage, and storage systems used with large computer systems and networks. The chapter concludes with a summary and comparison of the portable storage devices covered in the chapter. ■

STORAGE SYSTEMS CHARACTERISTICS

All storage systems have specific characteristics, such as consisting of a *storage device* and a *storage medium*, *portability*, *volatility*, how data is accessed and represented, the type of storage technology used, and so on. These characteristics are discussed in the next few sections.

Storage Devices and Storage Media

There are two parts to any storage system: the **storage device** and the **storage medium**. A storage medium is the hardware where data is actually stored (for example, a *floppy disk*, *CD*, or *flash memory card*); a storage medium is inserted into the appropriate storage device (such as a *floppy drive*, *CD drive*, or *flash memory card reader*) to be read from or written to. Usually the storage device and storage medium are two separate pieces of hardware (that is, the storage medium is *removable*), although with some systems—such as a *hard drive*—the two parts are permanently sealed together to form one piece of hardware (called a *fixed-media* storage system). Fixed-media storage systems generally provide higher speed and better reliability at a lower cost than removable-media alternatives, but removable-media storage systems have the advantages of a virtually unlimited storage capacity (by purchasing more of the proper storage medium), being able to be easily transported from one location to another (to share data with others, transfer data between a

FURTHER EXPLORATION

For links to further information about removable storage devices and media, go to www.course.com/uc11/ch03

>**Storage device.** A piece of hardware, such as a floppy drive or CD drive, into which a storage medium is inserted to be read from or written to.

>**Storage medium.** The part of a storage system where data is stored, such as a floppy disk or CD disc.

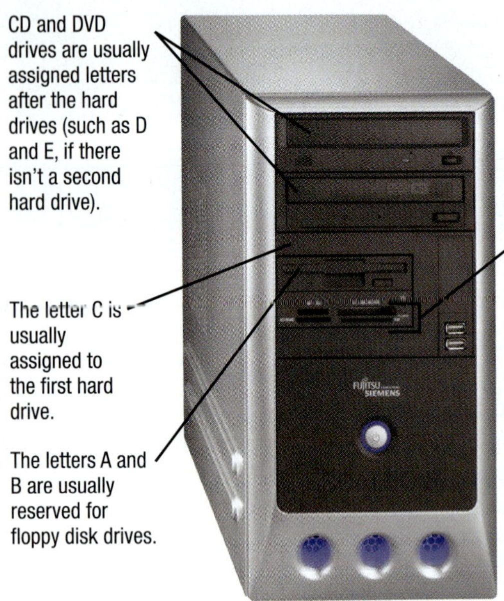

FIGURE 3-1
Storage device identifiers. To keep track of storage devices in an unambiguous way, the computer system assigns letters of the alphabet or names to each of them.

work and home PC, or take digital photos to a photo store, for instance), and being able to be stored in a secure area, such as for backup purposes or to protect sensitive data.

Storage devices can be *internal* (located inside the system unit), *external* (plugged into an external port on the system unit), or *remote* (located on another computer, such as a network server). Internal devices have the advantage of requiring no additional desk space and are often faster than their external counterparts. External devices can be used with multiple computers or added to a PC that has no room left inside its system unit. Remote devices are accessed over a network; in the case of the *online storage systems* accessed via the Internet, they have the additional advantage of being able to be accessed from any PC that has an Internet connection.

Regardless of how storage devices are connected to a computer, letters of the alphabet and/or names are typically assigned to each storage device, so the devices can be identified when they need to be used (see Figure 3-1). Some drive letters, such as for a floppy drive (*A*) and the first hard drive (*C*), are typically consistent from computer to computer and do not usually change even if more storage devices are added to a PC. The rest of the drive letters on a PC may change as new devices are added either permanently (like when an additional hard drive is installed inside the PC) or temporarily (like when a flash memory drive or digital camera is connected to the PC)—the computer just assigns and reassigns drive letters as needed, as often as needed.

Volatility

Storage media are **nonvolatile**. This means that when you shut off power to a storage device, the data stored on that device's storage medium will still be there when you turn the device back on. This feature contrasts with RAM, which is **volatile**. As discussed previously, programs and documents held in RAM are erased once they are no longer needed or the power to the computer is turned off.

Random vs. Sequential Access

When the computer system receives an instruction that requires data or programs located in storage, it must go to the designated location on the appropriate storage medium and retrieve the requested data or programs. This procedure is referred to as access. Two basic access methods are available: random and sequential.

Random access, also called *direct access*, means that data can be retrieved directly from any location on the storage medium, in any order. Most PC storage devices—including hard disk drives, floppy disk drives, and CD/DVD drives—are random access devices. They work like audio CD players or movie DVD players—the user can jump directly to a particular selection or location on the CD or DVD, as needed. Media that allow random access are sometimes referred to as *addressable* media. This means that the storage system can locate each piece of stored data or each program at a unique *address*, which is determined by the computer system. With *sequential access*, however, the data can only be retrieved in the

---

>**Nonvolatile.** Describes a storage medium that retains its contents when the power is shut off. >**Volatile.** Describes a medium whose content is erased when the power is shut off.

order in which it is physically stored on the medium. One type of PC storage device that uses sequential access is a *tape drive*. Computer tapes work like audio cassette tapes or videotapes—to get to a specific location on the tape, you must play or fast forward through all of the tape before it.

Logical vs. Physical Representation

Anything (such as a program, letter, digital photograph, or song) stored on a storage medium is referred to as a **file**. Data files are also sometimes called *documents*. When a document that was just created (such as a memo or letter in a word processing program) is saved, it is stored as a new file on the storage medium that the user designates. During the storage process, the user is required to give the file a name, called a **filename**; the user uses that filename whenever he or she wants to open the file again.

To keep files organized, related documents are often stored in **folders** (also called *directories*) located on the storage medium. For example, one folder might contain memos to business associates while another might hold a set of budgets for a specific project (see Figure 3-2). To further organize files, you can create *subfolders* (*subdirectories*) within a folder. For instance, you might create a "Letters" folder that contains one subfolder for letters sent to friends and a second subfolder for letters sent to potential employers. In Figure 3-2, both *Budgets* and *Memos* are subfolders inside the *My Documents* folder.

Although both the user and the computer use drive letters, folder names, and filenames to save and retrieve documents, a user typically views how data is stored (what has been discussed so far in this section and what appears in the *Windows Explorer* file management program screen shown in Figure 3-2) using *logical file representation*. That is, individuals view a document stored as one complete unit in a particular folder on a particular drive. Computers, however, use *physical file representation*; that is, they access data stored on the storage media using its physical locations. For example, the ABC Industries Proposal Memo file shown in Figure 3-2 is *logically* located in the Memos folders in the My Documents folder on the hard drive C, but the content of this file could be *physically* stored in many different pieces scattered across that hard drive. When this occurs, the computer keeps track of the various physical locations as well as the logical representations (filename, folder names, and drive letter) used to identify that file. Fortunately, users do not have to be concerned with how files are physically stored on a storage medium because the computer keeps track of that information and uses it to retrieve files whenever they are requested.

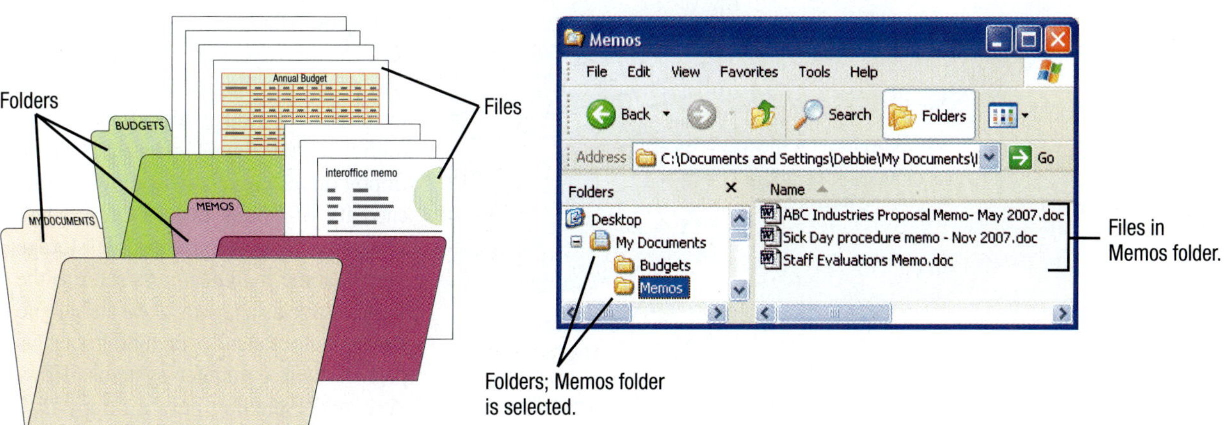

FIGURE 3-2
Organizing data.
Folders can be used to organize related items on a storage medium.

>File. Something stored on a storage medium, such as a program, document, or image. **>Filename.** A name given to a file by the user that is used to retrieve the file at a later time. **>Folder.** A named place on a storage medium into which files can be stored to keep the files stored on that medium organized.

TIP

Use the term *discs* when referring to optical media; use the term *disks* when referring to magnetic media.

Magnetic Disks vs. Optical Discs

Data is stored *magnetically* or *optically* on most storage media. With magnetic media, such as floppy disks, data is stored magnetically, which means the data (0s and 1s) is represented using different magnetic alignments. The magnetic alignment on the disk can be changed, so the data on magnetic disks can be erased and overwritten as needed. Optical storage media (such as CDs and DVDs) store data optically using laser beams. On some optical media, the laser burns permanent marks into the surface of the medium so the data cannot be erased or rewritten. With *rewritable* optical media, the laser changes the reflectivity of the medium but does not permanently alter the disc surface so that the reflectivity of the medium can be changed back again. Consequently, the data stored on the disc can be erased or overwritten.

Some storage systems use a combination of magnetic and optical technology. Others use a different technology altogether, such as flash memory media that represent data using *electrons*. Some of the most widely used storage systems are discussed in the remainder of the chapter.

MAGNETIC DISK SYSTEMS

Speedy access to data, relatively low cost, and the ability to erase and rewrite data make **magnetic disks** one of the most widely used storage media on today's computers. With magnetic storage systems, data is written by *read/write heads* which magnetize particles a certain way on a medium's surface to represent the data's 0s and 1s. The particles retain their magnetic orientation until the orientation is changed again, so files can be stored, rewritten to the disk, and erased, as needed. Storing data on a magnetic disk is illustrated in Figure 3-3. The most common type of magnetic disk is the *hard disk*; another common type of magnetic disk is the *floppy disk*.

FIGURE 3-3
Storing data on magnetic disks.

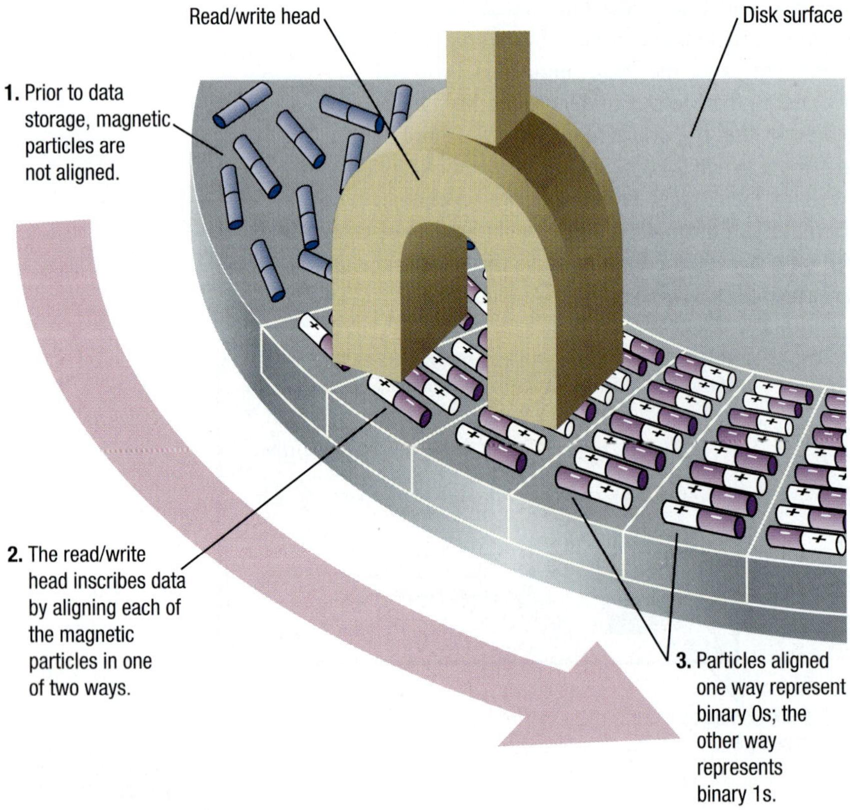

Floppy Disks and Drives

PCs have traditionally been set up to use a **floppy disk**—sometimes called a *diskette* or *disk*—to meet removable storage needs. Floppy disks are written to and read by **floppy disk drives** (commonly called *floppy drives*). Because floppy drives are relatively slow and the capacity of floppy disks is very small compared to newer removable storage media, some manufacturers refer to the floppy drive as a *legacy drive* and are no longer automatically including one as part of their computer systems. However, understanding how a floppy disk works will help you to understand how magnetic disks in general work.

>**Magnetic disk.** A storage medium that records data using magnetic spots on disks made of flexible plastic or rigid metal. >**Floppy disk.** A low-capacity, removable magnetic disk made of flexible plastic permanently sealed inside a hard plastic cover. >**Floppy disk drive.** A storage device that reads from and writes to floppy disks.

Floppy Disk Characteristics

A floppy disk consists of a round piece of flexible plastic (hence the name "floppy disk") coated with a magnetizable substance. The disk is protected by a square, rugged plastic cover lined with a soft material that wipes the disk clean as it spins (see Figure 3-4). The surface of a floppy disk is organized into circular rings, called **tracks**, and pie-shaped **sectors**. On most PC systems, the smallest storage area on a disk is a **cluster**—the part of a track that crosses a specific number of adjoining sectors (see Figure 3-5). Tracks, sectors, and clusters are numbered by the computer so it can keep track of where data is stored. The PC uses a *file system* to record where each file is physically stored and what filename the user has assigned to it. When the user requests a document (always by filename), the computer uses its file system to retrieve it. Since a cluster is the smallest addressable area on a disk, everything stored on a disk always takes up at least one cluster of space on the disk.

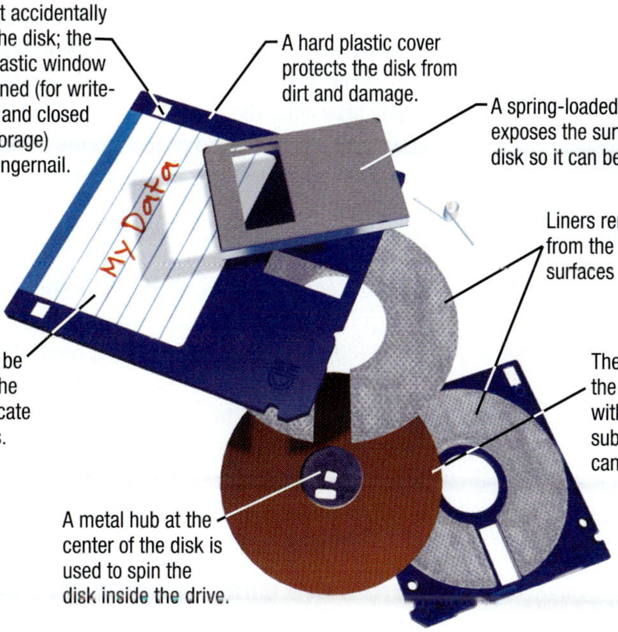

A write-protect square can prevent accidentally writing to the disk; the square's plastic window can be opened (for write-protection) and closed (for data storage) with your fingernail.

A hard plastic cover protects the disk from dirt and damage.

A spring-loaded shutter exposes the surface of a disk so it can be read from.

Liners remove dirt from the disk's surfaces as it spins.

A label can be placed on the disk to indicate its contents.

The plastic surfaces of the disk are coated with a magnetizable substance so that data can be recorded.

A metal hub at the center of the disk is used to spin the disk inside the drive.

FIGURE 3-4
The anatomy of a floppy disk.

Most floppy disks in use today measure 3½ inches in diameter and can store 1.44 MB of data, which is sufficient to store about 500 pages of double-spaced text or one or two digital photos, depending on the photo settings used. Floppy disks typically cost about 25 cents each. Music files, large numbers of digital photos, and documents containing a lot of images usually require a higher-capacity removable storage media—such as a CD, a DVD, or flash memory media; these types of storage media are discussed shortly.

Using Floppy Disks

To use a floppy disk, it must first be inserted into a floppy drive (face up and with the disk shutter closest to the drive door, as illustrated in Figure 3-6). When it is completely inserted, the disk clicks into place, the metal shutter is moved aside to expose the surface of the disk, and the *eject button* on the front of the drive pops out. Before data can be stored on a floppy disk, the disk must be *formatted*. Most floppy disks sold today are already formatted for either IBM-compatible or Macintosh computers and are, therefore, ready to use. If a disk is not formatted, the user must format it first before it can be used. Users can also format floppy disks to quickly erase them for reuse—formatting a disk that already contains data erases everything on the disk.

FIGURE 3-5
Magnetic disks (such as floppy disks) are organized into tracks, sectors, and clusters.

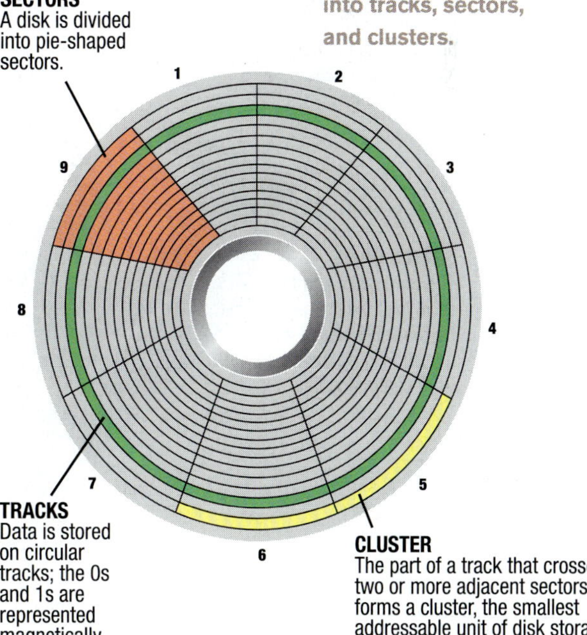

HW

>**Track.** A concentric path on a disk where data is recorded. >**Sector.** A pie-shaped area on a disk surface. >**Cluster.** The part of a track on a disk that crosses a fixed number of contiguous sectors; it is the smallest addressable area of a disk.

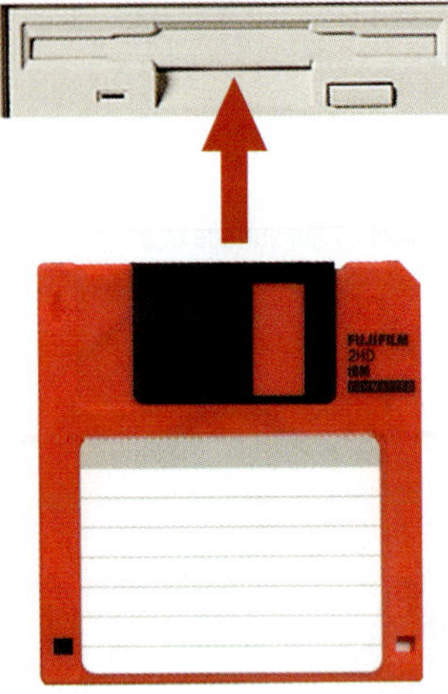

FIGURE 3-6
Inserting a floppy disk into a floppy drive. Disks go into a drive only one way—right side up, with the disk shutter facing the drive door.

When the floppy disk in the floppy drive needs to be accessed, the drive begins to rotate the disk within its plastic cover. The drive's read/write head can read (retrieve) data from or write (store) data onto the actual surface of the disk while the disk is spinning. The read/write heads move in and out over the surface of the disk, allowing the read/write heads access to all tracks on that disk. While the disk is spinning, the drive's indicator light goes on—do not remove the floppy disk while this light is on. To remove the disk, wait until the light goes off, and then press the eject button to remove the disk.

Hard Disk Drives

With the exception of computers designed to use only network storage devices (such as network computers and some Internet appliances), virtually all PCs come with a **hard disk drive** (commonly referred to as a **hard drive**) that is used to store most programs and data. *Internal hard drives* (those located in the system unit) are not designed to be removed, unless they need to be repaired or replaced. *External hard drives* typically connect to a computer via a USB port. In addition to being used with computers, hard drives are also increasingly being incorporated into other consumer products, such as *digital video recorders (DVRs)*, *game consoles*, *portable media players*, digital camcorders, cars, and more.

Hard Drive Characteristics

Similar to floppy drives, hard drives store data magnetically; they use read/write heads to store and retrieve data; and their disks are organized into tracks, sectors, and clusters. However, the disks used with a hard drive are made out of metal and are permanently sealed (along with the read/write heads and access mechanisms) inside the hard drive to avoid contamination and to enable the disks to spin faster. One drive may contain a stack of several hard disks, as shown in Figure 3-7.

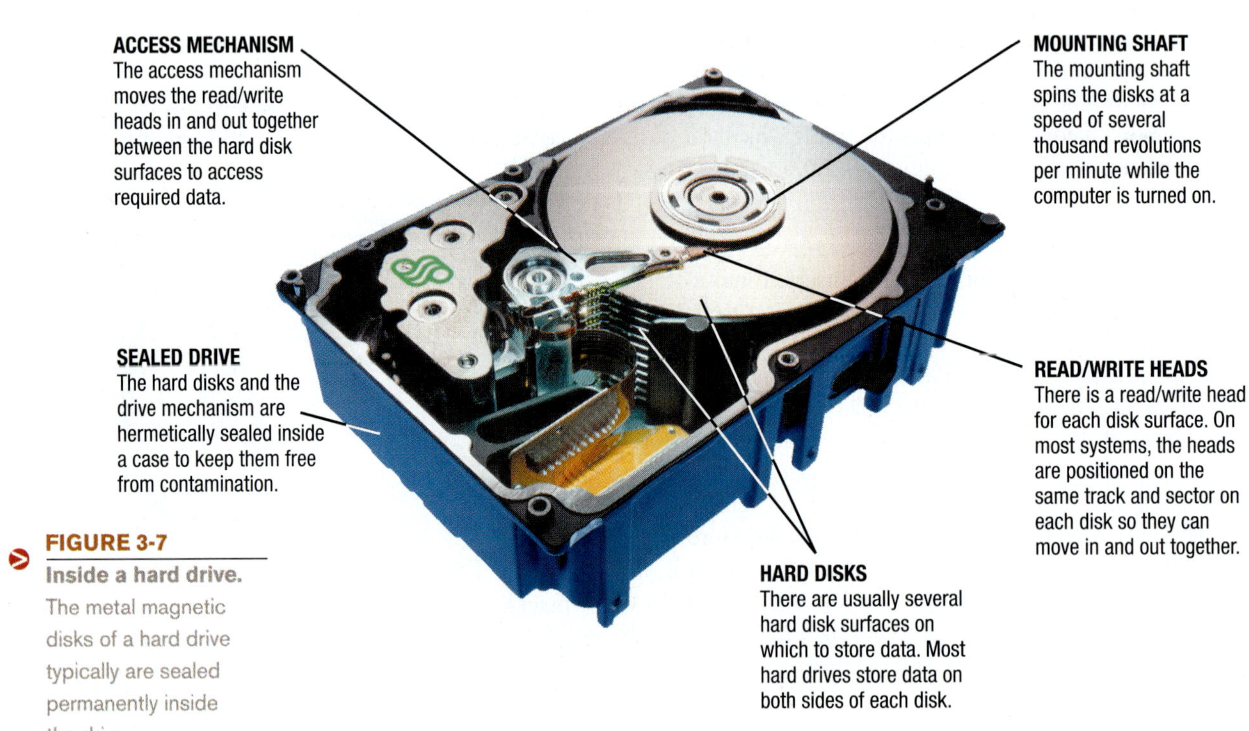

FIGURE 3-7
Inside a hard drive. The metal magnetic disks of a hard drive typically are sealed permanently inside the drive.

>**Hard disk drive.** A storage system consisting of one or more metal magnetic disks permanently sealed with an access mechanism inside its drive. Also called a **hard drive**.

In addition to tracks, sectors, and clusters, hard drives also have **cylinders**. A cylinder is the collection of one particular track, such as the first track or the tenth track, on each disk surface. In other words, it is the area on all of the hard disks inside the hard drive that can be accessed without moving the read/write access mechanism, once it has been moved to the proper position. For example, the four-disk system in Figure 3-8 contains eight possible recording surfaces (using both sides of each disk), so a cylinder on that system would consist of eight tracks, such as track 13 on all eight surfaces. Hard drives commonly have anywhere from a few hundred to a few thousand cylinders. The number of tracks on a single disk is equal to the number of cylinders in the disk system.

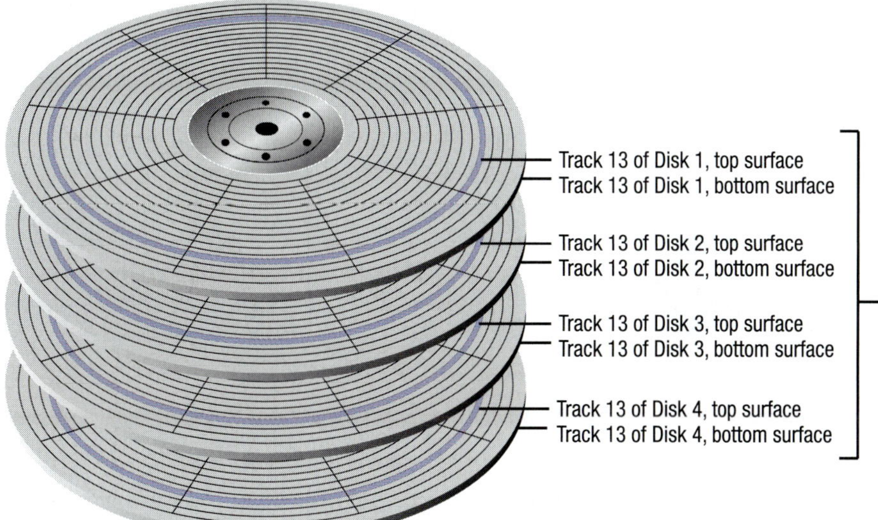

FIGURE 3-8

A disk cylinder. Hard drives use cylinders, in addition to tracks, sectors, and clusters, to keep track of where data is stored.

HW

Virtually all hard drives are formatted at the factory before they are sold, so they are ready to be used as soon as they are installed. Because reformatting a disk erases everything on the disk, hard drives are rarely reformatted. This task is only performed if errors are preventing the hard drive from operating properly and there is no other option. To retrieve or store data, most hard drives have at least one read/write head for each recording surface. These heads are mounted on an *access mechanism*; this mechanism moves the heads in and out over the tracks together, similar to the way the heads move over a floppy disk. Because all the heads move together, all the tracks in the cylinder containing the data can be accessed at the same time.

TIP

Be very careful when formatting any type of storage media, since formatting erases all data stored on the media.

It is important to realize that a hard drive's read/write heads never touch the surface of the hard disk at any time, even during reading and writing. If the read/write heads do touch the surface—such as if the PC is bumped while the hard drive is spinning or a foreign object gets onto the surface of the disk, a *head crash* occurs, which may do permanent damage to the hard drive. Because the heads are located extremely close to the surface of the disk—less than one millionth of an inch above the surface—the presence of a foreign object the width of a human hair or even a smoke particle (about 2,500 and 100 millionths of an inch, respectively) on the surface of a hard disk is like placing a huge boulder on a road and then trying to drive over it with your car (see Figure 3-9). One never knows when a hard drive will crash—there may be no warning whatsoever—which is a good reason for keeping the drive backed up regularly. *Backing up* a computer system—that is, creating a second copy of important files—is discussed in more detail in Chapter 5. When hard drives containing critical data become damaged, *data recovery firms* may be able to help out, as discussed in the Inside the Industry box.

Internal PC hard drives today hold between 80 to 500 GB, and their storage capacity is continually growing. External hard drive storage capacity is even larger—up to 2 TB at the time of this writing. Some hard drives today come with built-in security features, such as a *fingerprint reader* that allows only authorized users access to the drive. Others—called

>**Cylinder.** The collection of tracks located in the same location on a set of hard disk surfaces.

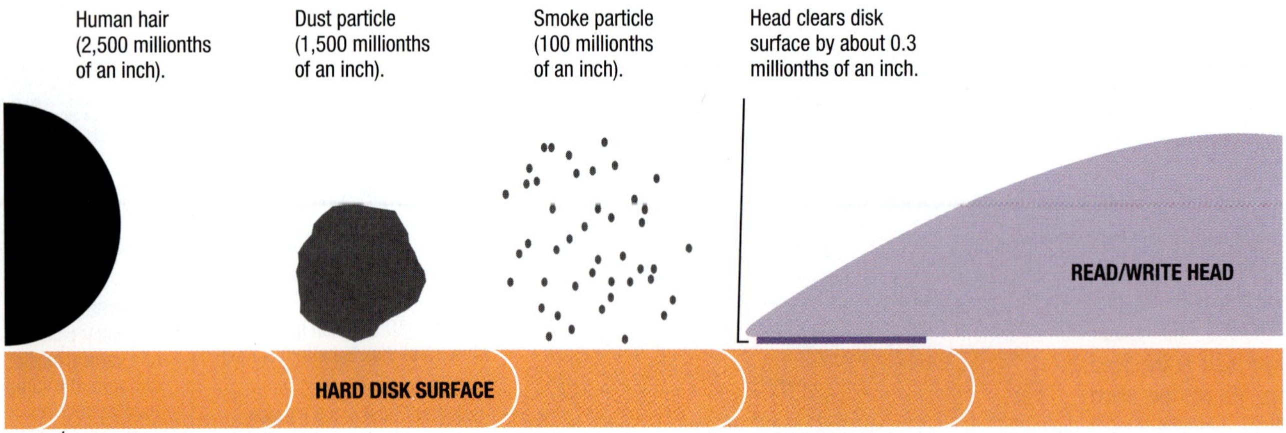

Human hair (2,500 millionths of an inch).

Dust particle (1,500 millionths of an inch).

Smoke particle (100 millionths of an inch).

Head clears disk surface by about 0.3 millionths of an inch.

READ/WRITE HEAD

HARD DISK SURFACE

FIGURE 3-9

Obstacles on a hard disk surface. A human hair or even a smoke particle on a fast-spinning hard disk surface can damage both the surface and the read/write head.

wireless hard drives—are accessed from up to 100 yards away from the computer using a *Wi-Fi* wireless networking connection.

Hard Drive Speed and Caching

Because of their construction and the fact that their disks typically spin continually at a rate of 5,400 to 15,000 revolutions per minute, hard drives provide fast access to data. The total time that it takes for a hard drive to read or write data is called the **disk access time** and requires the following three steps:

1. Move the read/write heads to the cylinder that contains (or will hold) the desired data—called *seek time*.
2. Rotate the disks into the proper position so that the read/write heads are located over the part of the cylinder to be used—called *rotational delay*.
3. Move the data, such as reading the data from the disk and transferring it to memory, or transferring the data from memory and storing it on the disk—called *data movement time*.

A typical disk access time is around 10 milliseconds (ms). To minimize disk access time, drives usually store related data on the same cylinder. This strategy sharply reduces the seek-time component and improves the overall access time. Another strategy for speeding up hard drive performance is *disk caching*.

A *cache* (pronounced *cash*) is a place to store something temporarily. For instance, in Chapter 2 we learned that *cache memory* is a group of very fast memory chips used by the CPU to store data and instructions that might be needed in order to speed up processing. *Disk caching* is similar in concept—it stores data or programs that might be needed soon in memory chips in order to avoid having to retrieve the data or programs from the hard drive when they are requested. Since retrieving data from memory is much faster than from the hard drive, disk caching can speed up performance.

The memory used for disk caching can be a designated portion of RAM or memory chips located on the circuit board inside the hard drive. In either case, it is called the **disk cache**. When a hard drive uses disk caching (as most do today), any time the hard drive is accessed the computer copies the requested program and data, as well as extra programs or data located in neighboring areas of the hard drive (such as the entire track or cylinder), to the disk cache. The theory behind disk caching is that neighboring data will likely have to be read soon anyway (research indicates that there is an 80% to 90% chance the next

>**Disk access time.** The time it takes to locate and read data from (or position and write data to) a storage medium. >**Disk cache.** A dedicated part of RAM used to store additional data adjacent to data retrieved during a disk fetch to improve system performance.

INSIDE THE INDUSTRY

Data Recovery Experts

It happens far more often than most people imagine. A hard drive quits working the day before a big report is due, a laptop is dropped in the parking lot and then run over by a car, or a business burns down taking the PC containing the only copy of the company records with it. If the data on the drive was recently backed up, the data can be installed on a new drive with just a little expense and a short delay. When critical data was not backed up and is located on a potentially destroyed hard drive, it is time to seek a professional data recovery expert.

Data recovery firms, such as DriveSavers in California, specialize in recovering data from severely damaged storage media (see the accompanying photos). The damaged drives are taken apart in a clean room (an airtight room similar to the ones in which computer chips are manufactured), cleaned, put back together, and the data is copied onto a server. Then, if the file directory is not recovered, engineers try to match the jumbled data to file types in order to reconstruct the original files. DriveSavers clients have included Barbara Mandrell, whose musical director's hard drive containing several months of work and more than 1,200 orchestra charts needed for a concert nine days away stopped working; the executive producer of "The Simpsons," whose computer crashed taking scripts for 12 episodes of the show with it; an individual whose notebook PC was trapped for two days beneath a sunken cruise ship in the Amazon River; and a Fortune 500 company, which lost all its financial data and stockholder information when its Unix server went down. In all four cases, DriveSavers was able to recover all of the lost data.

Data recovery firms stress the importance of backing up data. According to Scott Gaidano, president of DriveSavers, "The first thing we tell people is back up, back up, back up. It's amazing how many people don't back up." It is also important to make sure the backup procedure is working. For instance, the Fortune 500 company mentioned previously performed regular backups and kept the backup media in a fire-resistant safe, but when they went to use the backup after their server crashed, they discovered that the backup media were all blank.

Because potentially losing all the data on a drive can be so stressful and traumatic, DriveSavers has its own data-crisis counselor, a former suicide hotline worker. Fortunately for their clients, DriveSavers has a 90% recovery rate. The services of data recovery experts are not cheap, but when the lost data is irreplaceable, they are a bargain.

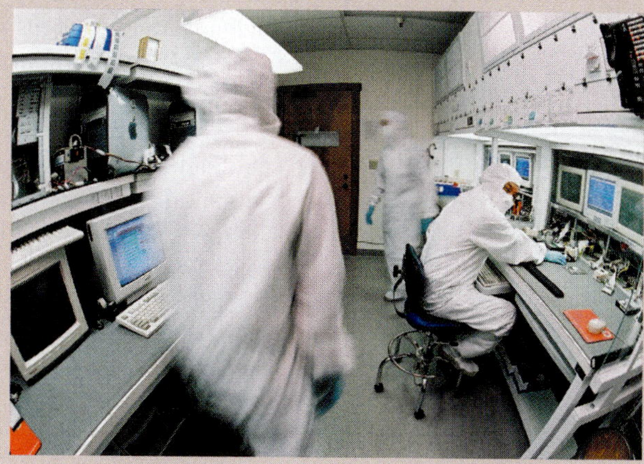

Data recovery. All the data located on the hard drive of this computer (left) that was virtually destroyed in a fire was recovered by data recovery experts in less than 24 hours. Recovery takes place in a clean room (right).

request will be for data located adjacent to the data last read), so the computer reduces the number of times the hard drive is accessed by copying that data into the disk cache before it is needed. When the next data is requested, the computer checks the disk cache first to see if the data it needs is already there. If it is, the data is retrieved for processing; if not, the computer retrieves the requested data from the hard drive (see Figure 3-10). Disk caching saves not only time but also wear and tear on the hard drive. In portable computers, it can also extend battery life.

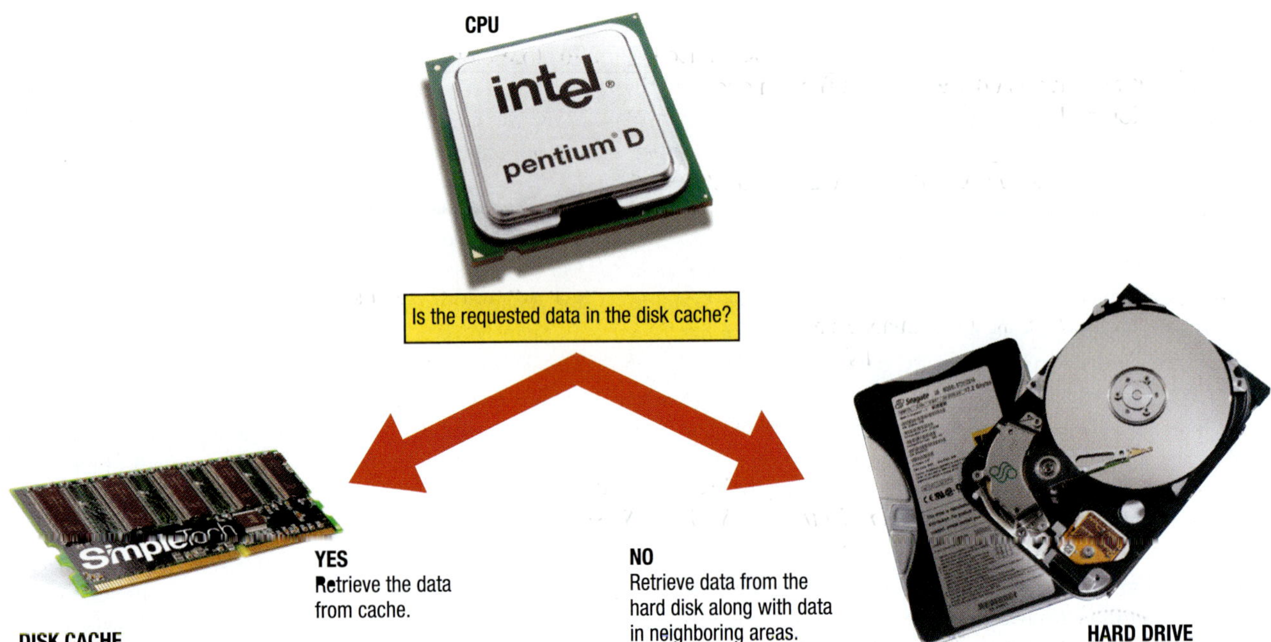

FIGURE 3-10

Disk cache. Disk cache is either a special area of RAM or memory chips located inside the hard drive case used to store small amounts of hard drive data, in order to speed up the retrieval of that data.

Partitioning and File Systems

Partitioning a hard drive enables you to logically divide the physical capacity of a single drive into separate areas, called *partitions*. Partitions look and act like independent disk drives and are sometimes referred to as *logical drives* since they are labeled as separate drives, such as a C drive and a D drive, but they are still physically one drive. One or more partitions are created when a hard drive is first formatted. Users can create additional partitions if desired, although this action usually destroys any data in the partitions being changed. Consequently, you should back up data stored on that drive to another storage medium before you repartition that hard drive, and then copy the data back onto the repartitioned hard drive. Some operating systems have a limit to the number of partitions that can be used.

While today's PCs do not usually need partitions to function (older operating systems could only address hard drives up to 512 MB, so hard drives larger than that limit had to use multiple partitions), partitioning a large drive can make it function more efficiently. This is because operating systems typically use a larger cluster size with a larger hard drive. When a large cluster size is used, disk space is often wasted because even tiny files have to use up one entire cluster of storage space. When a hard drive is partitioned, each logical drive can use a smaller cluster size, since each logical drive is smaller than the original drive. The cluster size, maximum drive size, and maximum file size are determined by the file system being used. For instance, the Windows *FAT32 file system* is more efficient than the original FAT system because FAT32 systems allow smaller cluster sizes, which cuts down on wasted storage space. The FAT32 file system also supports larger hard drives than the FAT file system. The recommended file system for Windows XP computers is the newer *NTFS* file system, which supports much larger drives and files than either the FAT or the FAT32 file systems, and includes better security capabilities.

Many computers today are set up with one partition for the main hard drive and another partition for a *recovery partition* that contains the data necessary to restore the hard drive back to its state at the time of purchase, if the computer malfunctions. Another reason for partitioning a hard drive is to be able to use two different operating systems on the same hard drive—such as Windows and Linux. You can then decide which operating system you will run each time you boot your computer. Creating the appearance of having separate hard drives for file management, multiple users, or other purposes is another common reason for partitioning a hard drive. Some users choose to install their programs on one partition of the hard drive (usually the one named C) and to store their data on a second partition (such as D). Storing data files on one partition and program files on a different partition makes it easier for the user to locate data files. It also enables users to back up all data files simply by backing up the entire data partition. Operating systems and backing up data are discussed in more detail in Chapter 5.

FURTHER EXPLORATION

For links to further information about hard drives, go to www.course.com/uc11/ch03

Hard Drive Interface Standards

Hard drives connect, or interface, with a computer using one of several different standards. These standards determine performance characteristics, such as the density with which data can be packed onto the disk, the disk access speed, the storage capacity, and the way the disk drive interfaces with other hardware.

The most common *hard drive interface standards* for desktop PCs today are *serial ATA* (*SATA*) and *serial ATA II* (*SATA II*), which are replacing earlier parallel standards, such as *parallel ATA* and *IDE*. The *SCSI* (for *small computer system interface* and pronounced "skuzzy") and the newer *serial attached SCSI* (*SAS*) standards are commonly used with servers. Another hard drive interface standard used with high-end servers is *Fibre Channel*—a reliable, flexible, and very fast standard geared for long-distance, high-bandwidth applications (hard drives used with larger computers and networks are discussed later in this chapter). Emerging standards for storage devices that are accessed via the Internet or another network that uses the *TCP/IP* networking standard to communicate include *Internet SCSI* (*iSCSI*) and *Fibre Channel over IP*. *External hard drives* today typically connect instead via a USB or FireWire port.

External and Portable Hard Drive Systems

Although hard drives are typically located inside the system unit, *external hard drives* (see Figure 3-11)—which typically connect to a PC via a USB port, a FireWire port, or a wireless networking connection—are also available. External hard drives can be used to transport a large amount of data from one PC to another (by moving the entire drive to another PC) or can be used with a single PC for backup or as a second hard drive.

While external drives can be moved from PC to PC when needed, *portable hard drives* are specifically designed for that purpose. One example of a portable *mini hard drive* is shown in Figure 3-11. This 1-inch portable hard drive—also referred to as a *pocket hard drive*—holds 5 GB. Because of their small physical size, portable mini hard drives are designed to be used with handheld PCs, digital music players, and other portable devices, in addition to being used to transfer data from one PC to another. *Internal mini hard drives* are also beginning to be built into portable devices to increase

FIGURE 3-11
External and portable hard drives.

USB EXTERNAL HARD DRIVE
This drive holds 250 GB and connects via a USB port.

WI-FI EXTERNAL HARD DRIVE
This hard drive holds 160 GB and connects via a wireless Wi-Fi connection.

USB POCKET HARD DRIVE
This hard drive holds 5 GB, connects via a USB port, and can be carried in a pocket.

PC CARD HARD DRIVE
This hard drive holds 5 GB and connects via a PC Card slot.

their storage capacity. For instance, the Apple iPod comes with either a 20 GB or a 60 GB built-in mini hard drive and Palm's new LifeDrive handheld computer contains a 4 GB built-in mini hard drive. Notebook PCs can have built-in internal conventional or mini hard drives, but often use a removable *PC Card hard drive* (such as the one shown in Figure 3-11) instead.

High-Capacity Removable Magnetic Disks and Cartridges

There are some high-capacity removable magnetic storage systems available for users who need portability or the ability to store media in a secure location. These products fall into two categories: *superdiskettes* and *hard disk cartridges*.

Superdiskettes

Superdiskettes are high-capacity removable storage media that are usually *proprietary*; that is, can only be used with their respective drives. The most widely used type of superdiskette is the *Zip disk*, introduced by Iomega Corporation in 1995. Zip disks are high-capacity magnetic disks that can be read from and written to using only *Zip drives*. Zip disks are similar in size and in appearance to floppy disks (see Figure 3-12), but they have a capacity of 100, 250, or 750 MB and cannot be used in a conventional floppy disk drive. Zip drives can be internal or external and are *downward compatible*, meaning the higher-capacity Zip drives can read Zip disks with a matching or lower storage capacity. Zip drives are most appropriate for users who need to back up large files or transfer large files between PCs or other users that have a Zip drive. Because Zip drives were one of the first high-capacity removable storage solutions, they are still in use, although it is likely that they will eventually be replaced by other types of high-capacity removable media, such as optical discs and flash memory drives, that are not proprietary.

FIGURE 3-12
High-capacity removable magnetic disk systems.

ZIP DISKS
Zip disks can be used only with Zip drives and hold up to 750 MB per disk.

REV HARD DISK CARTRIDGES
REV cartridges can be used only with REV drives and hold up to 35 GB (or up to 90 GB of compressed data) per cartridge.

Hard Disk Cartridges

Some hard drive systems are designed to use removable *hard disk cartridges*. With these systems, the hard drive remains attached to the PC and the hard disk cartridges are inserted into and removed from the drive, similar to a floppy disk or superdiskette system. The advantage over other types of removable storage media is capacity—for instance, the Iomega REV system shown in Figure 3-12 holds 35 GB (or up to 90 GB with compression). Like superdiskettes, hard disk cartridges are proprietary, so they can only be used with their respective drives. Consequently, they are not appropriate for sharing data with a large group of users, but they are useful for storing and backing up very large files, transporting large files from one PC to another, and for exceptionally secure facilities—such as government and research labs—that require all hard drives to be locked up when not in use. They are also commonly used for complete system backups.

OPTICAL DISC SYSTEMS

Optical discs (such as *CDs* and *DVDs*) store data *optically*—using laser beams—instead of magnetically, like floppy and hard disks. Optical discs are made out of plastic and are typically 4½ inches in diameter, although smaller discs are sometimes used. Data can be stored on one or both sides of an optical disc, depending on the disc, and some discs use multiple layers to increase capacity. To keep data organized, optical discs are divided into tracks and sectors like magnetic disks but use a single grooved spiral track beginning at the center of the disc (see Figure 3-13), instead of a series of concentric tracks. (To avoid confusion with the *tracks* or songs on an audio CD, the track on an optical disc is sometimes referred to as a *groove*.) Data is written to an optical disc by stamping or molding the surface of the disc (for commercial CDs and DVDs) or by changing the reflectivity of the disc with a laser (for CDs and DVDs that are recorded using a CD or DVD drive). In either case, the disc is read with a laser and the reflection of the laser off of the disc indicates the data's 1s and 0s.

To accomplish this with molded or stamped CD and DVD discs, tiny depressions (when viewed from the top side of the disc) or bumps (when viewed from the bottom) are molded into the disc's surface. These bumps are called *pits*; the areas on the disc that are not changed are called *lands*. Although many people believe that each individual pit and land represents a 1 or 0, that is not completely accurate—it is the transition between a pit and land that represents a 1. When the disc is read, the angle of reflection of the laser beam inside the CD or DVD drive changes when it reaches a transition between a pit and a land, and when the drive detects a transition, it is interpreted as a 1; no transition for a specific period of time indicates a 0. With a CD or DVD that is recorded using a CD or DVD drive, the recording laser beam changes the reflectivity of the appropriate areas on the disc to represent the data stored there—dark, nonreflective areas are pits; reflective areas are lands, as illustrated in Figure 3-13—but the transition between a pit and a land still represents a 1 and no transition represents a 0.

The process of recording data onto an optical disc is called *burning*. To burn a CD-R or DVD-R disc, special hardware and software is needed. Many commercial burning programs are available, and many recent operating systems, such as Windows XP, include CD burning capabilities.

Optical discs can be made into a variety of sizes and shapes—such as a heart, triangle, irregular shape, or the hockey-rink shape commonly used with *business card CDs*—because the track starts at the center of the

FIGURE 3-13
How recorded optical discs work.

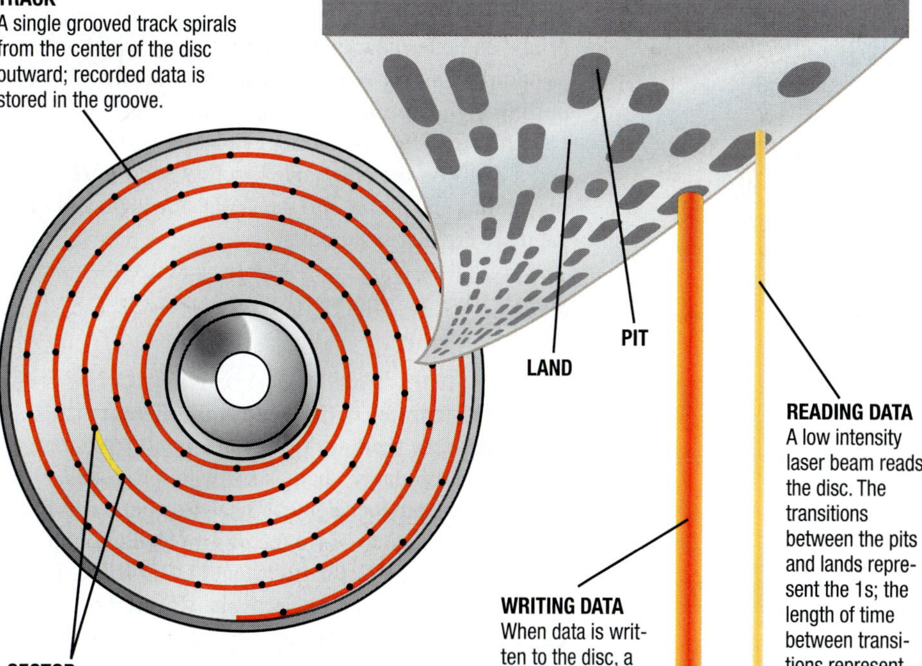

>**Optical disc.** A type of storage medium read from and written to using a laser beam.

FIGURE 3-14

Custom shaped optical discs. Optical discs can be made in a variety of shapes and sizes, such as the business card CD shown here.

disc and the track just stops when it reaches the outer edge of the disc. Standard shapes are molded and less expensive; custom shapes—such as those that match a key product or service being sold (a soda can, musical instrument, saw blade, candy bar, or house, as in Figure 3-14)—are custom cut and are more costly. The practice of using optical discs to replace ordinary objects, such as business cards, is becoming more common. For a closer look at business card CDs and DVDs, see the How it Works box.

CD and DVD discs are read by *CD* and *DVD drives*. The speed of a CD or DVD drive is rated as a number followed by the "×" symbol to indicate how fast the drive is compared to the first version of that drive. For instance, a 52× CD drive is 52 times faster than the original CD drive, and a 16× DVD drive is 16 times faster than the original DVD drive. Drives that can both read and write to discs typically state the speed for each type of operation separately. Many optical discs have a title and other text printed on one side; if so, they are inserted into the drive with the printed side facing up, and the data is stored on the bottom, nonprinted side of the disc.

One of the biggest advantages of CDs and DVDs is their large capacity—standard-sized 4½-inch CD discs hold either 650 MB or 700 MB, standard-sized DVD discs can hold 4.7 GB (single-layer discs) or 8.5 GB (double-layer discs), 3-inch mini CD discs hold about 200 MB, business-card-sized CD discs hold 50 MB, and business-card-sized DVD discs hold 325 MB. Other advantages include their small size and durability—optical discs are more durable than magnetic media and don't degrade with use, like some magnetic media does. However, the discs should be handled carefully and stored in *jewel cases* when they are not in use, to protect the recorded surfaces of the discs from scratches, fingerprints, and other marks that can interfere with the usability of a disc. Optical discs are the standard today for software delivery; they are also commonly used for storing and transporting high-capacity music and video files, and for backup. For added versatility, *hybrid CD/DVD* discs are becoming available, with a CD on one side (such as for audio content) and a DVD on the other side (such as for a DVD movie). The CD side of a hybrid disc is played in a CD player and the DVD side is played in a DVD player. Specific types of optical discs are discussed next.

For a look at one new way to organize the giant stacks of CDs and DVDs many individuals have on hand, see the Trend box.

Read-Only Discs: CD-ROM and DVD-ROM Discs

CD-ROM (compact disc read-only memory) discs and **DVD-ROM (digital versatile disc read-only memory) discs** are *read-only* storage media and come prerecorded with commercial products, such as software programs, clip art and other types of graphics collections, and product demos. The data on a CD-ROM or DVD-ROM cannot be erased, changed, or added to, since the pits molded into the surface of the disc when the disc is produced are permanent. CD-ROM and DVD-ROM discs are designed to be read by *CD-ROM* and *DVD-ROM drives*, respectively. CD-ROM drives can usually play both data and audio CDs; DVD-ROM drives can typically play data and audio CDs, DVD-ROM discs, and DVD movies.

>**CD-ROM (compact disc read-only memory) disc.** An optical disc, usually holding about 650 MB, that can be read from, but not written to, by the user. >**DVD-ROM (digital versatile disc read-only memory) disc.** An optical disc, usually holding 4.7 GB, that can be read from, but not written to, by the user.

HOW IT WORKS

Business Card CDs and DVDs

With computers so common in businesses and homes today, use of business card CDs is on the rise. Business card CDs are similar to conventional CDs, but they are physically smaller, come in different shapes, and hold less data. They can, however, be played using CD and DVD drives, just like any other CD. Business card CD-R discs can be recorded using a standard recordable CD or DVD drive, but are more commonly mass-produced once a master CD has been developed. For higher capacity, business card DVDs can be used.

Business card CDs and DVDs today can contain a wide variety of content, such as résumés in Word or PDF format, multimedia presentations, portfolio material (such as copies of ad campaigns created by advertising executives, digital images created by graphic artists, Web sites created by Web site designers, or photographs of an artist's or architect's work), catalogs, and copies of the company Web site—virtually any type of information an individual wants to distribute to others. The accompanying figure takes a closer look at one business card CD; as in this example, it is becoming common for business card CD content to be developed using a multimedia authoring program so that the content, along with animated effects to catch the user's interest, can be incorporated into a professional-looking presentation that is automatically played after the CD is inserted into a PC's CD or DVD drive. Blank business card CD-R discs cost about 50 cents each; professionally prepared business card CDs and DVDs cost between 50 cents and $2 each, depending on format, capacity, and shape.

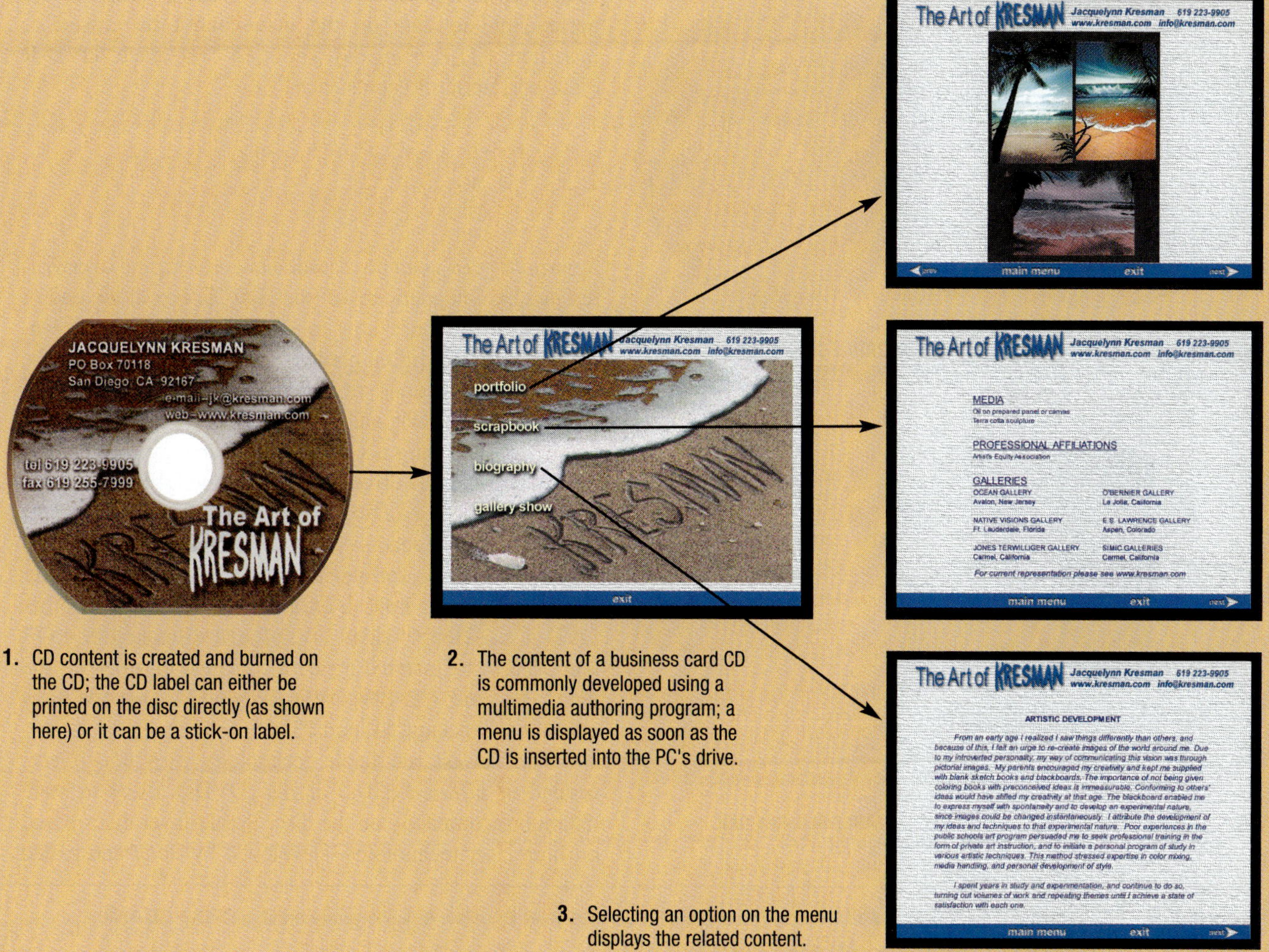

1. CD content is created and burned on the CD; the CD label can either be printed on the disc directly (as shown here) or it can be a stick-on label.

2. The content of a business card CD is commonly developed using a multimedia authoring program; a menu is displayed as soon as the CD is inserted into the PC's drive.

3. Selecting an option on the menu displays the related content.

Recordable Discs: CD-R, DVD-R, DVD+R, and DVD+R DL Discs

Recordable discs can be written to, but the discs cannot be erased and reused. Recordable CDs are typically **CD-R discs**; recordable DVDs are either **DVD-R discs** or **DVD+R discs**. Recordable CDs and DVDs are written to using an appropriate optical drive, such as a *CD-R drive* for CD-R discs and a *DVD-R drive* for DVD-R discs. Some optical drives support multiple types of discs; for instance, a drive might be able to record on both DVD-R and DVD+R discs. Virtually all recordable DVD drives can record on recordable CDs, in addition to recordable DVD discs. Once recorded, CD-R discs can be read by most types of CD and DVD drives; recorded DVD-R and DVD+R discs can be read by most DVD drives.

Recordable CDs are commonly used for backing up files, sending large files to others, and creating custom music CDs (for example, from MP3 files legally downloaded from the Internet or from songs on CDs the user owns). DVD-Rs can be used for similar purposes when more storage space is needed, such as for large backups and for storing home movies and other video files. The newest recordable DVDs (**DVD+R DL discs**) are *dual-layer* discs (also called *double-layer* discs), which means they use two recording layers on a single disc, resulting in a capacity of 8.5 GB (see Figure 3-15). One company has developed a similar six-layer DVD disc that holds 15 GB, but this product is not yet on the market.

Instead of having physically molded pits, recordable discs contain an organic light-sensitive dye located in the spiral grooved track and embedded between the plastic and reflective layers. When data is written to the disc, the recording laser inside the CD-R or DVD-R drive burns the dye, creating nonreflective burned areas that function as pits. These burn marks are permanent, so data on the disc cannot be erased or rewritten. CD-R discs cost about 15 cents each; DVD-R discs cost about 50 cents each.

FIGURE 3-16
Recordable and rewritable CDs and DVDs.

RECORDABLE DVD+R DL DISC
Dual-layer disc—holds 8.5 GB.

REWRITABLE CD-RW DISC
Single-layer disc—holds 650 MB.

REWRITABLE DVD-RAM DISC
Holds 9.4 GB.

REWRITABLE BLU-RAY DISC
Holds 23.3 GB.

Rewritable Discs: CD-RW, DVD-RW, DVD+RW, DVD-RAM, and Blue Laser Discs

Rewritable discs can be recorded on, erased, and overwritten just like magnetic disks (the How To box at the end of Chapter 6 illustrates how to store data—such as downloaded music or digital photos—on rewritable discs). The most common types of rewritable optical media are **CD-RW**, **DVD-RW**, and **DVD+RW discs**. CD-RW discs are written to using a *CD-RW drive* and can be read by most CD and DVD drives. DVD-RW and DVD+RW discs are recorded using a *DVD-RW* or *DVD+RW drive*, respectively, and can be read by most DVD drives. An additional rewritable DVD format is DVD-RAM. Single-layer **DVD-RAM** discs hold 4.7 GB and look similar to other DVD discs. Double-sided DVD-RAM discs hold 9.4 GB and need to be inserted inside a cartridge in order for the disc to be used. CD-RW, DVD-RW, and DVD-RAM discs cost about 50 cents, $1, and $3, respectively.

The newest rewritable technology uses *blue lasers* instead of *infrared* (CDs) or *red* (DVDs) *lasers* to store data more compactly on the disc. Single-layer discs based on blue laser technology—developed by Sony and called

>**CD-R disc.** A recordable CD. >**DVD-R/DVD+R discs.** Recordable DVDs. >**DVD+R DL disc.** A dual-layer recordable DVD. >**CD-RW.** A rewritable CD. >**DVD-RW/DVD+RW/DVD-RAM discs.** Rewritable DVDs.

TREND

Automated Optical Disc Carousels

Have you ever wasted valuable time searching for a CD or DVD? If you are like most people, the answer would be a resounding "Yes!" New products–such as the *automated disc carousel*–are becoming available to take care of this growing problem.

Automated disc carousels are CD and DVD storage systems that typically hold about 100 discs each. The carousel is connected to a PC and inserting a disc into the carousel launches an interface program that records the name, description, and user-supplied data about the disc. The disc is then allocated a storage slot inside the carousel. Once a disc has been inserted, retrieving it again is easy. Using the interface, the user browses or searches for the desired disc, and then the carousel ejects that disc so the user can insert it in his or her CD or DVD drive. When the user inserts the disc back into the carousel, the carousel stores the disc again, so it is ready for the next time it is requested. Automated carousels usually work with all kinds of optical discs, including computer, music, movie, and game discs.

One available product–Imation's *Disc Stakka*–is shown in the accompanying photograph. Each Disc Stakka holds up to 100 discs, and up to five units can be stacked for a total capacity of 500 discs without needing additional cabling or desk space. In addition to organizing your disks, the Disc Stakka and other similar products protect discs from the damage that can be caused by mishandling, such as stacked on a shelf, stored without a jewel case, or piled on a desk.

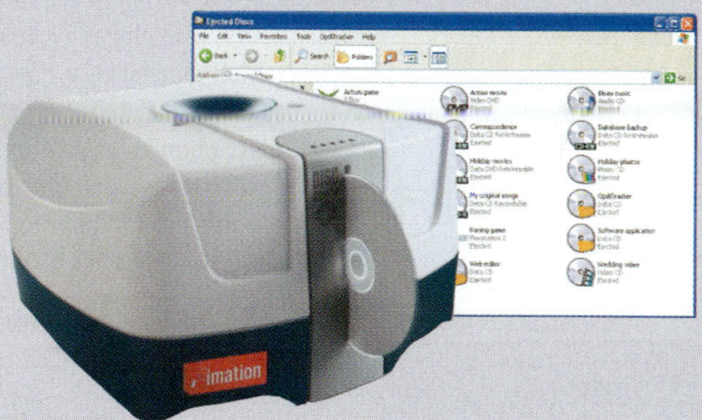

Blu-ray Discs (*BD*)—hold 23 GB. Dual-layer BD discs that hold 50 GB are in development, and a prototype of a four-layer BD disc that holds 100 GB was demonstrated in 2005. A similar, but competing, blue laser format developed by Toshiba and NEC is *high-definition DVD* (*HD-DVD*). This format, previously known as *Advanced Optical Disc* (*AOD*), is currently capable of storing up to 30 GB of data on a dual-layer disc and 45 GB on a triple-layer disc.

Blue laser discs were originally developed to enable recording, rewriting, and playback of high-definition content (such as HDTV shows and high-definition movies HD), as well as for storing large amounts of data. Blu-ray and HD-DVD are not compatible, and it has yet to be determined which format will be supported most by PC manufacturers and movie studios. But it is certain that a high-capacity optical disc format will be needed as high-definition content increases. Although recordable and rewritable conventional DVD drives are now available to record television shows and store home movies, a high-definition movie requires three or four of today's regular DVD discs. With blue laser discs, the same content would fit on a single disc. Blue laser discs are viewed by many as the next generation DVD format; in fact, Sony has announced that the upcoming PlayStation 3 game console will have a Blu-ray drive. Although originally only a rewritable format, read-only and recordable Blu-ray Discs (*BD-ROM* and *BD-R discs*, respectively) are also in development.

To record and erase rewritable optical discs, *phase-change* technology is used. With this technology, the recordable CD or DVD disc is coated with layers of a special metal alloy compound that has two different appearances once it has been heated and then cooled, depending on the temperature reached during the heating process. With one temperature, the surface is reflective; with a higher temperature, it is not. Before any data is written to a disc, the disc is completely reflective. To record data on the disc, the recording

FURTHER EXPLORATION

For links to further information about DVD technology, go to www.course.com/uc11/ch03

laser heats the metal alloy in the appropriate spots on the spiral grooved track to the appropriate temperature to create nonreflective areas (pits); unburned areas (lands) remain reflective. To erase the disc, the appropriate temperature is used to change the areas to be erased back to their original reflective state.

It is important to realize that recordable and rewritable DVDs have not yet reached a single standard, so there are competing formats that are not necessarily compatible with each other. Luckily, most DVD drives today support more than one format. It is expected that, eventually, some type of DVD drive will replace the CD drive.

FLASH MEMORY SYSTEMS

Unlike magnetic and optical storage systems, **flash memory storage systems** have no moving parts—a property that makes them a *solid-state storage system*. Because they have no moving parts, flash memory storage systems require much less power than conventional drives, and they are resistant to shock and vibration. In addition, flash memory media (which consist of chips and other circuitry) are very small and so are especially appropriate for use with digital cameras, digital music players, handheld PCs, notebook computers, smart phones, and other types of portable devices (see Figure 3-16), as well as for transporting data from one place to another in a briefcase or pocket. Flash memory media is rewritable and has a longer expected life than removable magnetic media. Although flash memory media are relatively expensive per gigabyte, their convenience and universal compatibility make them an appealing storage option for many purposes. Today, flash memory

FIGURE 3-16

Flash memory uses. Flash memory media are used in conjunction with a variety of devices, such as digital cameras, digital music players, PCs, smart phones, and more.

DIGITAL CAMERAS

Flash memory drive

DIGITAL MUSIC PLAYERS

Secure Digital (SD) card

DESKTOP COMPUTERS

NOTEBOOK COMPUTERS

HANDHELD COMPUTERS

CELL PHONES

>**Flash memory storage system.** A storage system that uses flash memory media.

is most often found in the form of *flash memory media* and *flash memory drives*. Flash memory chips are also integrated directly into a variety of consumer products—such as portable computers, digital music players, and even sunglasses—to store MP3 files.

Flash Memory Media

The main type of *flash memory media* is the **flash memory card**—a small card containing flash memory chips and metal contacts to connect the card to the device or reader that it is being used with. Flash memory cards can be inserted into computers or other devices (such as handheld PCs, digital cameras, portable music players, and so forth) for storage purposes and come in a variety of formats, such as *CompactFlash*, *Secure Digital* (*SD*), *MultiMedia Card* (*MMC*), *xD*, and *Memory Stick* (see Figure 3-17). CompactFlash and Secure Digital (SD) cards are the most widely used type of flash memory media at the present time. Many computers and mobile devices today contain a built-in *flash memory card reader* that can read and write to at least one type of flash memory media; when an appropriate port is not built into the device, an external flash memory card reader can be used. Typically, flash memory media is purchased blank, but some flash memory-based software is available, such as games, encyclopedias, language translators, and more. The capacity of flash memory cards is continually growing and ranges from 64 MB to 8 GB at the present time.

Flash memory media can be inserted into a reader only one way, similar to a floppy disk. To help with this, many flash memory readers have directional hints imprinted next to each slot—look for these before inserting a flash memory card to insure you are using the proper card orientation and also make sure the slot is the proper size.

FIGURE 3-17

Flash memory cards. Shown here are four of the most widely used types of flash memory cards and a multicard reader.

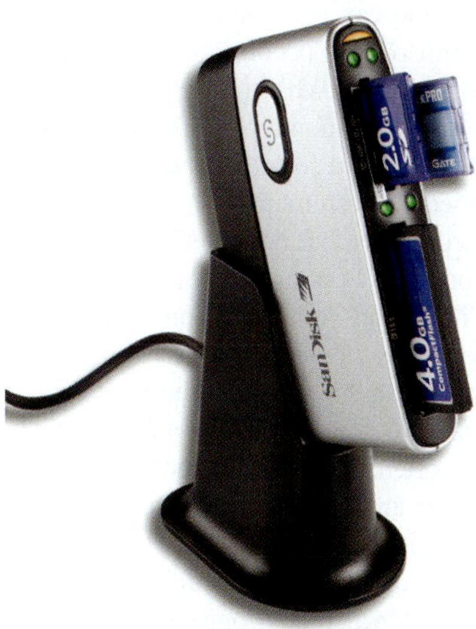

FLASH MEMORY CARD READER
This reader connects to a USB port and can be used with several different types of flash memory media.

COMPACTFLASH CARD

XD PICTURE CARD

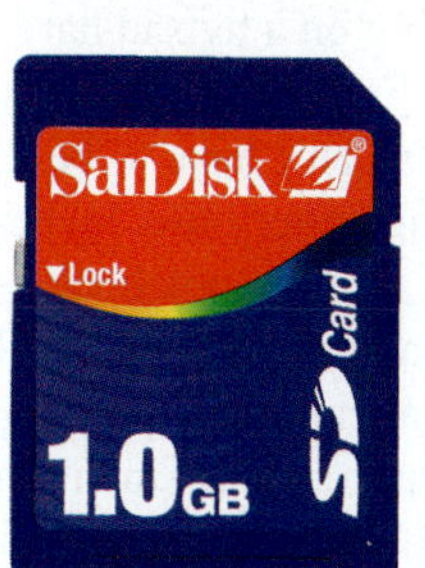

SECURE DIGITAL (SD) CARD

MEMORY STICK

>Flash memory card. A small, rectangular flash memory media, such as a CompactFlash or Secure Digital card.

FLASH MEMORY DRIVE WITH NECKCHAIN

CONVENTIONAL FLASH MEMORY DRIVE

FLASH MEMORY WATCH

FIGURE 3-18

Flash memory drives. USB flash memory drives are becoming increasingly popular for portable personal storage.

TIP

To avoid data loss when you are finished using a flash memory drive, first double-click the Safely Remove Hardware icon in the system tray, and then stop the drive before removing it from the USB slot.

Flash Memory Drives

Flash memory drives (sometimes called *USB mini drives*, *USB flash drives*, *thumb drives*, *jump drives*, and *key drives*) consist of flash memory media and a reader in a single self-contained unit. Most flash memory drives are designed to be very portable and so are small enough to fit in a pocket or be carried on a keychain or around the neck (see Figure 3-18). Some flash memory drives today are built into watches (a retractable cord is used to connect the watch to a PC when needed); one is even built into a Swiss Army knife. To read from or write to a flash memory drive, the user plugs it into a PC's USB port, and then the flash memory drive is assigned a drive letter by the computer, like any other type of drive attached to a PC. Files can be read from or written to the drive until it is unplugged from the USB port. Some flash memory drives have their flash memory media permanently sealed inside; others use standard flash memory cards and can be opened to replace the drive with a new memory card when the original is full or if it becomes damaged. The capacity of flash memory drives today typically ranges from 128 MB to 8 GB.

While portable USB flash memory drives are the most common type of flash memory drive, there are also *flash memory hard drives* (sometimes called *solid state memory disks* or *SSDs*) that use flash memory instead of magnetic media. Flash memory hard drives are much more expensive than conventional magnetic hard drives, but can boot a PC almost instantly, use much less battery power when used in portable PCs, and are much less susceptible to physical damage. *Hybrid hard drives* (*HHDs*), consisting of a combination of magnetic disks and flash memory, are under development. For instance, Samsung and Microsoft are collaborating on a hybrid hard drive that includes 1 GB flash memory along with the usual magnetic disks. Data to be written to the hard drive is cached in flash memory so the magnetic disks don't have to be accessed as often, saving wear-and-tear on the disks, as well as extending battery life. Hybrid hard drives are expected to begin to replace conventional hard drives in some notebook computers and tablet PCs by 2006.

In addition to convenient file transfers, flash memory drives can have additional capabilities, such as to automatically synchronize files with a PC when it is connected to it or to recreate the user's PC environment (including appearance, e-mail, contact lists, calendar, browser favorites, documents, and other designated files) on any PC to which the drive is connected. Some can even be used to lock a PC, password-protect data stored on the drive, issue Web site passwords, and even delete all Web-usage history when the user issues the command to stop the device. Others include *biometric features*—such as a built-in fingerprint reader—to allow only authorized individuals access to the data stored on the drive or to the PC the flash drive is being used with.

>**Flash memory drive.** A small drive that usually plugs into a PC's USB port and contains flash memory media.

OTHER TYPES OF STORAGE SYSTEMS

Other types of storage systems include *remote storage*, *smart cards*, and *holographic storage*. There are also storage systems and technologies designed for large computer systems and networks.

Remote Storage Systems

Remote storage refers to using a storage device that is not connected directly to the user's PC system; instead, the device is accessed through a local network or through the Internet. Using remote storage devices and media works similarly to using *local storage* (the storage devices and media that are directly attached to the user's PC)—the user just selects the appropriate remote storage device (such as a hard drive attached to a network server), and then stores data on or retrieves data from it. When the remote device is accessed through a local network, it is sometimes referred to as *network storage*; the term *online storage* most commonly refers to storage accessed via the Internet. Two examples of online storage sites are shown in Figure 3-19.

FIGURE 3-19

Online storage.

Online storage services allow you to upload and download files from any PC or device with Internet access; some services have the option of password protecting access to your files.

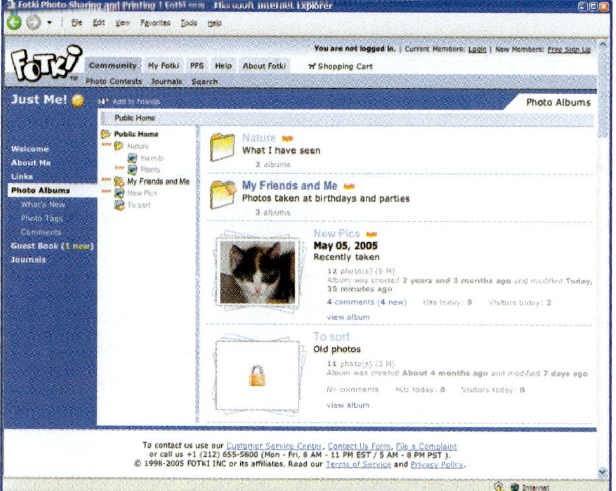

ONLINE PHOTO SHARING COMMUNITY
This site is designed to host online photo albums to be shared with others. Although albums can be password protected, many, such as the one shown here, are set up to be viewed by anyone.

LOGGING ON
This site requires users to log on before seeing their personal files stored on the site's server.

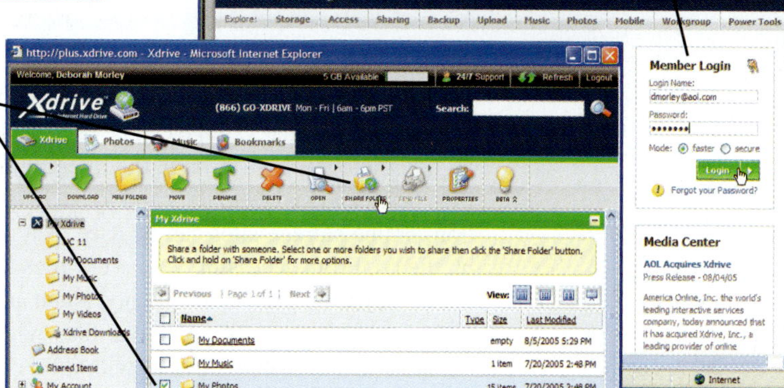

SHARING FILES
The contents of the marked folder will be shared with a specific individual, once his or her e-mail address is supplied.

SECURE ONLINE STORAGE
This site is designed to securely store files for backup or to be shared with others. After logging on, users can upload, download, or delete files, as well as designate who is allowed to access files.

>**Remote storage.** A storage device that is not directly a part of the PC being used, such as network storage or online storage.

TECHNOLOGY AND YOU

Smart Card IDs

At Pikeville College in Kentucky, the traditional school ID card has become much more than just an ID card. It has gotten smart. The new student ID cards are smart cards, which contain a built-in chip (see the accompanying photograph) that can hold digital cash values to be used at vending machines, printers, in the cafeteria, and at other places on campus to make purchases. When the cash stored in the card is depleted, the card can be reloaded at a card value center. Other uses for the Pikeville smart ID card include identifying students for exams and meal service, and providing access to secure areas, such as labs and residence halls. It may also be used as an ATM card in the future.

Smart card ID systems like this are not unique on college campuses today. Many colleges and universities across the country have either replaced or augmented their conventional student ID cards with smart card technology. The convenience of smart ID cards is a good fit with college students. They need to carry their student ID around anyway, and this smart card ID allows students to buy lunch, a soda, do laundry, or make copies without having to worry about how much cash they have on hand. In 2005, a college in Japan became the first college to use a smart card in conjunction with a *vein recognition system* (a noncontact biometric authentication system that verifies an individual's identity based on the veins in his or her palm) to authorize access to personal data, such as academic transcripts.

Other ID cards that are beginning to use smart card technology are national ID cards, driver's licenses, passports, and other important documents. Following the terrorist attacks in the United States on 9/11 and the subsequent attacks in other countries, there has be a strong push to create more secure identification documents to strengthen national security. In the United States, it is expected that new revamped driver's licenses will be used as a national ID card, and smart passports are being considered by both the United States and the United Kingdom. Hospitals in the United Kingdom are also beginning to use smart cards to restrict access to patient records to authorized individuals.

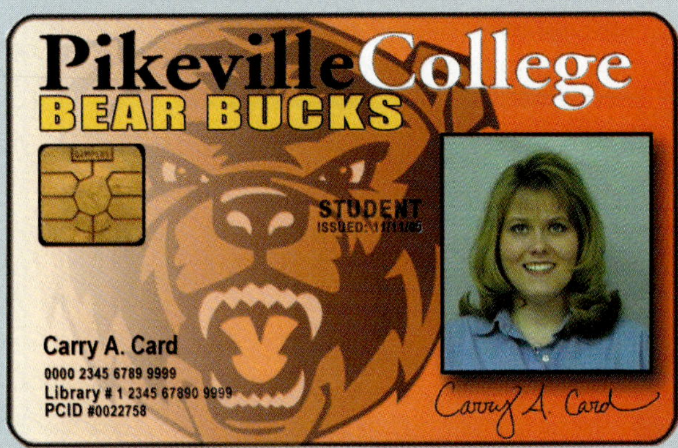

The Pikeville College smart ID card can be used for a wide variety of on-campus activities.

Individuals and businesses can use online storage Web sites for a variety of purposes. For instance, online storage can be used by individuals who want to share files—particular digital photographs—through the Internet. Online storage sites can also be used to transfer files between two computers and to back up files in case of a fire or other disaster. In addition, online storage sites can be used as a place to store content you want to access while on the go. From accessing your work files and contact information, to playing your digital music stored online via any device (such as a portable PC or smart phone), online storage allows you to virtually take your files with you. For some Internet appliances, network computers, and mobile devices with little or no local storage capabilities, online storage is especially important. Some Web sites dedicated to online storage offer the service for free to individuals; others charge a small fee, such as $5 or $10 per month for up to 5 GB of storage space (business accounts typically cost more).

Although some sites allow access to anyone, most online storage sites require users to log on with usernames and passwords to limit access to authorized individuals. Some sites allow you to e-mail links to others to download specific files in your online collection without having to supply a password. Other online storage sites contain an automatic back up option in which the files in designated folders on your PC are uploaded to your online account at regular specified intervals.

Smart Cards

A **smart card** is a credit card-sized piece of plastic that contains some computer circuitry—typically a processor, memory, and storage. Smart cards today are used to store a small amount of data (typically about 256 KB or less) for payment or identification purposes. For example, a smart card can store a prepaid amount of *digital cash* for purchases using a smart card-enabled vending machine or PC, and the amount of cash available on the card will be reduced as the card is used. Smart cards are also commonly used with national and student ID cards (see the Technology and You box); credit and debit cards; and cards that store loyalty system information (frequent flyer points, for example), identification data for accessing facilities or computer networks, or an individual's medical history and insurance information for fast treatment and hospital admission in an emergency. Although these applications have used conventional *magnetic stripe* technology in the past, the microprocessor in a smart card can perform computations—such as to authenticate the card and *encrypt* the data on the card to protect its integrity and secure it against unauthorized access—and data can be added to the card or modified on the card as needed.

To use a smart card, it must be inserted into a *smart card reader* built into or attached to a PC, keyboard, vending machine, or other device (see Figure 3-20). Once a smart card has been verified by the card reader, the transaction—such as making a purchase or unlocking a door—can be completed. For an even higher level of security, some smart cards today store *biometric data*—such as the characteristics of a fingerprint—in the card and use that data to ensure the authenticity of the card's user before authorizing the smart

CONVENTIONAL SMART CARDS
Used to store and retrieve personal information, as well as pay for items using digital cash loaded onto the card.

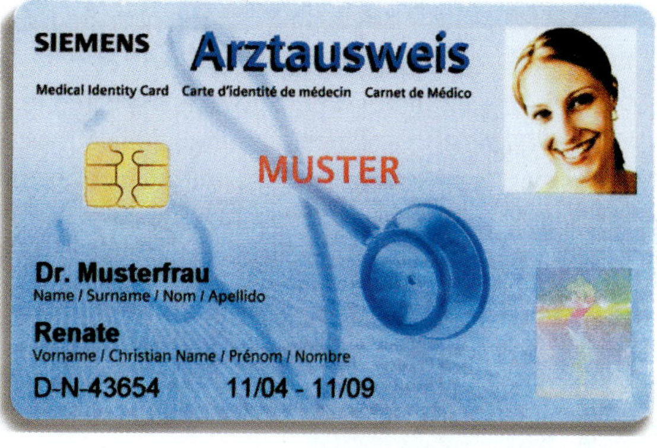

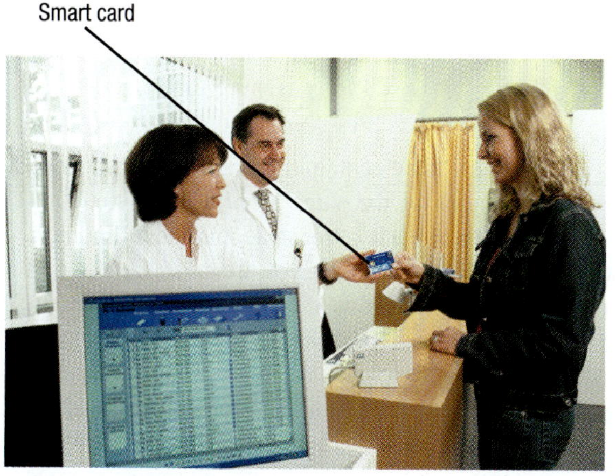

HIGH-CAPACITY SMART CARDS
The StorCard smart card shown here contains a magnetic disk inside the card to increase storage capacity to 100 MB.

>**Smart card.** A credit card-sized piece of plastic containing a chip and other circuitry into which data can be stored.

card transaction (biometrics, encryption, and other security procedures are discussed in more detail in Chapter 9). For applications that require more data storage, smart cards with an embedded magnetic disk are now available. For instance, the *StorCard* smart card shown in Figure 3-20 can be read by standard smart card readers, but holds 100 MB; storage capacities up to 5 GB are expected in the future.

FIGURE 3-21

Holographic storage. This recordable holographic drive and disc is expected to become available in 2006; each disc holds 300 GB.

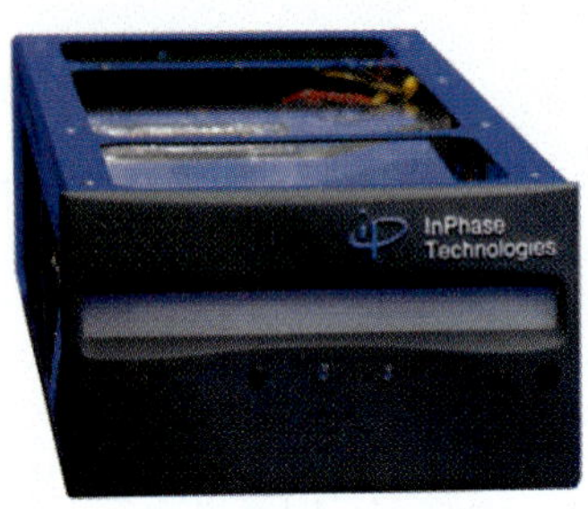

HOLOGRAPHIC DRIVE

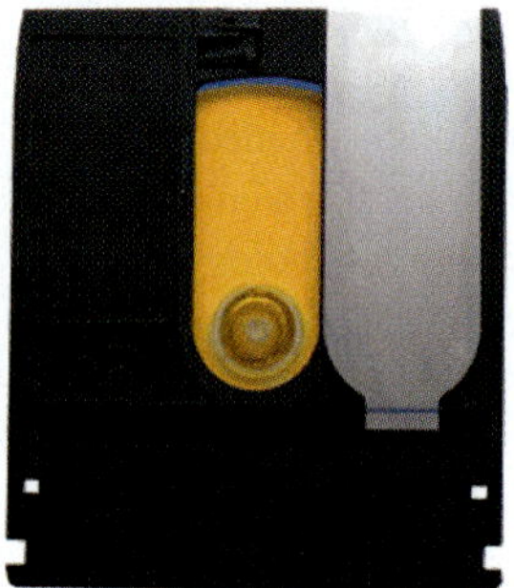

HOLOGRAPHIC DISC

Holographic Storage

Storing information in three dimensions is far from a new idea. DVDs use multiple layers to store more data on the same size disc as a CD, and 3D memory chips have been developed. One technology for 3D storage systems that, after many years of research and development, is now a reality is **holographic storage**. Holographic storage systems use two intersecting blue laser beams to store data through the entire thickness of the medium, which means that much more data can be stored on a holographic disc than on a CD of the same physical size. In fact, thousands of holographic files can be stored in an overlapping manner in the same area of the disc—a different angle or wavelength is used for each file so that each individual file can be retrieved when needed. The first generation of holographic drives (see Figure 3-21) is scheduled to be released by InPhase Technologies in 2006 and will utilize recordable discs with a capacity of 300 GB—enough room for almost 150 million pages of text, or 300,000 photos, or 21 hours of high-definition video. Rewritable holographic drives are expected to become available by early 2008, and the capacity of holographic discs is expected to reach 1.6 TB by 2009.

Potential initial applications for holographic data storage systems include high-speed digital libraries and image processing for medical, video, and military purposes—that is, for any application in which data needs to be stored or retrieved quickly in large quantities but rarely changed.

FIGURE 3-22

Storage servers for larger computer systems. Storage systems for larger computers are usually scalable so additional hard drives can be added as needed.

HARD DRIVES
Each drive chassis can have up to 40 individual hard drives that can hold up to 147 GB each.

STORAGE SERVER
This server can manage up to 2,560 hard drives located in up to 8 cabinets like the one shown here, for a total capacity of 384 TB in a single system.

Storage Systems for Large Computer Systems and Networks

Large computer systems (such as those containing mainframe computers and midrange servers) utilize much of the same storage hardware, standards, and principles as PCs but on a much larger scale. Instead of finding a single hard drive installed within the system unit, you are most likely to find a **storage server**—a separate piece of hardware containing multiple high-speed hard drives—connected to the computer system. Large storage servers typically contain racks of hard drives for a large total capacity. For instance, the storage server shown in Figure 3-22 can include up to 2,560 hard drives that hold 147 GB each for a total capacity of over 384 TB. These types of storage systems—also referred to as *enterprise storage systems*—typically use fast Fibre Channel connections and are *scalable*, meaning that more racks of drives can be added as needed up to the maximum capacity. In addition to being used as stand-alone storage for large computer systems, storage servers may also be used in *network attached storage (NAS)*, *storage area network (SAN)*, and *redundant arrays of independent disks (RAID)* storage systems. Most storage systems are based on magnetic disks, although *magnetic tape storage systems* are also possible.

>**Holographic storage.** An emerging type of storage technology that uses multiple blue laser beams to store data in three dimensions.

>**Storage server.** A hardware device containing multiple high-speed hard drives.

Network Attached Storage (NAS) and Storage Area Networks (SANs)

Storage servers are often used to provide storage for computer networks. With the vast amounts of data that many companies need to manage and store today, network-based storage has become increasingly important. One possibility is a **network attached storage (NAS)** device. NAS devices are high-performance storage servers that are individually connected to a network to provide storage for the computers connected to that network. **Storage area networks (SANs)** also provide storage for a network, but consist of a separate network of hard drives or other storage devices. That storage area network is, in turn, attached to the main network. The primary difference between NAS and SANs is how the storage devices interface with the network—that is, whether the storage devices act as individual network nodes, just like PCs, printers, and other devices on the network (NAS), or whether they are located in a completely separate network of storage devices that is accessible to the main network (SAN). However, in terms of functionality, the distinction between NAS and SANs is blurring, since they both provide storage services to the network. Both NAS and SAN systems are usually scalable, so new devices can be added as more storage is needed, and devices can be added or removed without disrupting the network.

HW

RAID

RAID (redundant arrays of independent disks) is a method of storing data on two or more hard drives that work in combination to do the job of a larger drive (see Figure 3-23). Although RAID can be used to increase performance, it is most often used to protect critical data on a storage server. Because RAID usually involves recording redundant (duplicate) copies of stored data, the copies can be used, when necessary, to reconstruct lost data. This helps to increase the *fault tolerance*—the ability to recover from an unexpected hardware or software failure, such as a system crash—of a storage system.

There are six different RAID designs or levels (0 to 5) that use different combinations of RAID techniques. For example, RAID level 0 uses *disk striping*, which spreads files

FIGURE 3-23

RAID. The two main benefits of RAID are increased speed and the ability to recover easily from a disk crash.

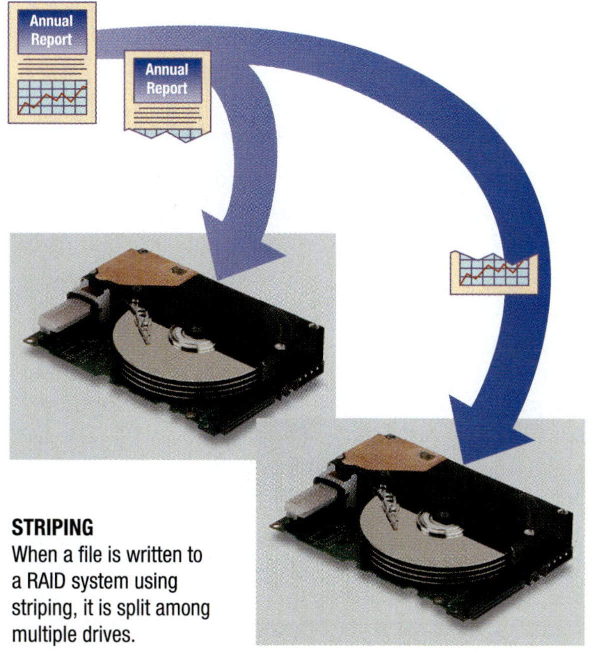

STRIPING
When a file is written to a RAID system using striping, it is split among multiple drives.

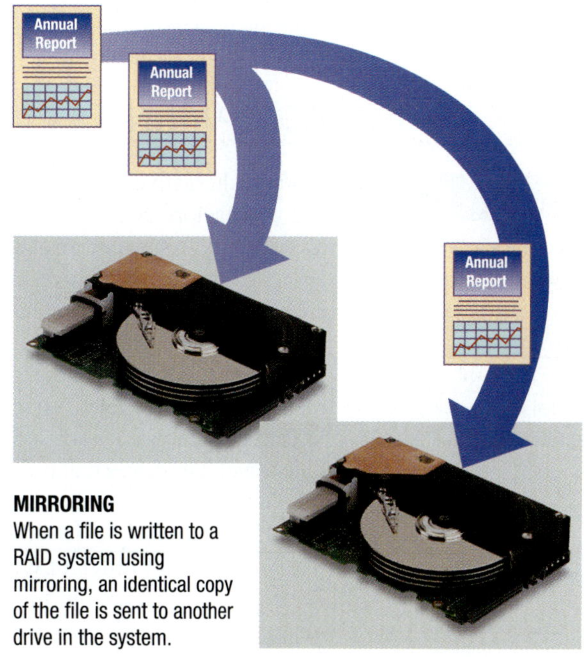

MIRRORING
When a file is written to a RAID system using mirroring, an identical copy of the file is sent to another drive in the system.

>Network attached storage (NAS). A high-performance storage server individually connected to a network to provide storage for computers on that network. **>Storage area network (SAN).** A network of hard drives or other storage devices that provide storage for another network of computers. **>RAID (redundant arrays of independent disks).** A storage method that uses several small hard disks in parallel to do the job of a larger disk.

over several disk drives (see the leftmost part of Figure 3-23). Although striping improves performance, since multiple drives can be accessed at one time to store or retrieve data, it does not provide fault tolerance. Another common RAID technique is *disk mirroring*, in which data is written to two duplicate drives simultaneously (see the rightmost part of Figure 3-23). The objective of disk mirroring is to increase fault tolerance—if one of the disk drives fails, the system can instantly switch to the other drive without any loss of data or service. RAID level 1 uses disk mirroring. Levels beyond level 1 use some combination of disk striping and disk mirroring, with different types of error correction provisions.

Because using RAID is significantly more expensive than just using a traditional hard drive storage system, it has traditionally been reserved for use with network and Internet servers. However, recently RAID has become more popular with PC users looking for increased performance. One test by *PC World* magazine showed that two RAID-connected drives completed some tasks in 40% less time than one drive of the same type. To implement RAID on a desktop PC, a RAID expansion card must be used.

Magnetic Tape Systems

Magnetic tape consists of plastic tape coated with a magnetizable substance that represents the bits and bytes of digital data, similar to magnetic disks. Although tape is no longer used for everyday storage applications because of its sequential-access property, it is still used today for data archiving and backup. One advantage of magnetic tape is its low cost per megabyte.

Most computer tapes today are in the form of *cartridge tapes*, which look similar to video or audio tapes. Computer tapes are read by *tape drives*, which can be either an internal or an external piece of hardware. Tape drives contain one or more read/write heads over which the tape passes to allow the drive to read or write data. Just as with other magnetic storage technologies, the 1s and 0s stored on magnetic tape are represented magnetically.

There are a variety of sizes and formats of cartridge tapes, and sizes and formats of tapes are not generally interchangeable. A typical tape cartridge holds between 40 GB and 240 GB. When a larger capacity is needed, some tape drives are designed to be used with multiple tape cartridges, increasing the potential storage capacity to well over 2 TB.

COMPARING STORAGE ALTERNATIVES

TIP

Virtually all computer users today need at least one USB port, in order to connect external hard drives, flash memory drives, and other storage hardware. If your PC doesn't have one, you can install an expansion card to add a USB port.

Storage alternatives are often compared by weighing a number of product characteristics and cost factors. Some of these product characteristics include speed, compatibility, storage capacity, convenience, and the portability of the media. Keep in mind that each storage alternative normally involves trade-offs. For instance, most systems with removable media are slower than those with fixed media, and external drives are typically slower than internal ones. Although cost is a factor when comparing similar devices, it is often not the most compelling reason to choose a particular technology. For instance, although the flash memory drives are relatively expensive per GB, many users find them essential for transferring files between work and home or for taking presentations or other files with them as they travel. For drives that use a USB interface, the type of USB port is also significant. For instance, storage devices that connect via the original USB port transfer data at up to 1.5 MB per second; devices that connect via a USB 2.0 port are about 40 times faster.

With so many different storage alternatives available, it is a good idea to research which devices and media are most appropriate for your personal situation. In general, most users today need a hard drive (for storing programs and data), some type of CD or DVD drive (for

>**Magnetic tape.** A plastic tape with a magnetizable surface that stores data as a series of magnetic spots; typically comes as a cartridge.

installing programs, backing up files, and sharing files with others), and a flash memory card reader (for transferring photos, music, and other content between portable devices and the PC). Some users may choose to include an additional drive for a particular type of high-capacity removable media, such as Zip disks, if they only need to use the disks in their PC or a PC that has a drive compatible with that medium. Users who plan to transfer music, digital photos, and other multimedia data on a regular basis between several different devices—such as a PC, digital camera, handheld PC, and printer—will want to select and use the flash memory media that is most compatible with the devices they are using and obtain the necessary adapter for their PC, if it does not include a built-in flash memory port. Some of the most common types of portable storage media are compared in Figure 3-24.

FIGURE 3-24
Portable storage alternatives. When comparing portable storage media, look at storage capacity, speed, cost, and device compatibility.

Media	Maximum Capacity	Approximate Cost (each)*	Approximate Cost (per GB)*	Can Be Read By	Best For
Conventional 3½-inch floppy disk	1.44 MB	$0.25	$175.00	Conventional floppy drive, SuperDisk drive	Transferring small files between users
Zip 750 disk	750 MB	$12.50	$17.00	Zip 750 drive	Archiving files or transferring large files between Zip users
CD-R disc	700 MB	$0.15	$0.20	Most CD and DVD drives	Transferring large files between users; archiving large files; making music CDs
CD-RW disc	700 MB	$0.50	$0.70	CD-RW drives, some other CD drives, most DVD drives	Transferring large files between users; archiving large files
DVD-R disc	4.7 GB	$0.50	$0.10	Most DVD drives	Transferring large files between users; archiving large files; backup; making home movie DVDs
DVD+RW	4.7 GB	$1.00	$0.20	Most DVD drives	Transferring large files between users; archiving large files; backup; making home movie DVDs
DVD+R DL	8.5 GB	$5.00	$0.60	DVD+R DL drives	Transferring large files between users; archiving large files; backup; making home movie DVDs
DVD-RAM	4.7 GB	$3.00	$0.60	DVD-RAM drives	Transferring large files between DVD-RAM users; archiving large files; backup
Flash memory drive (USB)	8 GB	**	$30.00	Any device with a USB port	Transferring small to medium-sized files between users or PCs
REV hard disk cartridge	35 GB	$40.00	$1.00	Proprietary drive to which that cartridge belongs	Archiving large files; securing sensitive data; backup
Portable hard drive (USB or PC card)	2 TB	**	$0.50	Any device with a USB port or PC card slot, respectively	Extending PC storage; securing sensitive data; backup
Flash memory cards	8 GB	**	$40.00	Compatible flash memory reader	Transferring small- to medium-sized files between users, PCs, or multimedia devices (digital cameras, MP3 players, etc.)

*Cost as of 2005 **Varies with capacity

SUMMARY

STORAGE SYSTEM CHARACTERISTICS

Chapter Objective 1:
Explain the difference between storage systems and memory.

Chapter Objective 2:
Name several general characteristics of storage systems.

Storage systems make it possible to save programs, data, and processing results for later use. They provide **nonvolatile** storage, so when the power is shut off, the data stored on the storage medium remains intact. This differs from RAM, which is **volatile**.

All storage systems involve two physical parts: A **storage device** and a **storage medium**. The most common types of storage media are magnetic disks and optical discs, which are read by the appropriate type of drive. Drives can be *internal*, *external*, or *remote*. Drives are typically assigned letters by the computer; these letters are used to identify the drive. Storage devices can record data either on *removable* media, which provide access only when inserted into the appropriate storage device, or *fixed media*, in which the media is permanently located inside the storage device. Removable media provide the advantages of unlimited storage capacity, transportability, safer backup capability, and security. Fixed media have the advantages of higher speed, lower cost, and greater reliability.

Sequential access allows a computer system to retrieve the records in a file only in the same order in which they are physically stored. *Random access* (also called *direct access*) allows the system to retrieve records in any order. In either case, **files** (sometimes called *documents*) stored on a storage medium are given a **filename** and can be organized into **folders**. This is referred to as *logical file representation*. *Physical file representation* refers to how the files are physically stored on the storage medium by the computer.

MAGNETIC DISK SYSTEMS

Chapter Objective 3:
Identify the two primary types of magnetic disk systems and describe how they work.

Magnetic disk storage is most widely available in the form of *hard disks* and *floppy disks*. Computer systems originally used **floppy disks** because they provided a uniform removable storage system at a low cost. Each side of a floppy disk holds data and programs in concentric **tracks** encoded with magnetized spots representing 0s and 1s. **Sector** boundaries divide a floppy disk surface into pie-shaped pieces. The part of a track crossed by a fixed number of contiguous sectors forms a **cluster**. To use a floppy disk, it is inserted into a **floppy disk drive**.

Hard disk drives (also called **hard drives**) are the main storage medium for most PCs. They offer faster access than floppy disks and much greater storage capacity. A hard drive contains one or more *hard disks* permanently sealed inside along with an *access mechanism*. A separate read/write head corresponds to each disk surface, and the access mechanism moves the heads in and out among the tracks to read and write data. All tracks in the same position on all surfaces of all disks in a hard drive form a disk **cylinder**. Hard drives can be divided into multiple *partitions* (logical drives) for efficiency or to facilitate multiple users or operating systems. Hard drives can be *internal* or *external*.

The total time it takes for a hard drive to read from or write to disks is called **disk access time**. A **disk cache** strategy, in which the computer fetches program or data contents in neighboring disk areas and transports them to RAM whenever disk content is retrieved, can help to speed up access time. Hard drives connect to a computer using one of several standards, such as *serial ATA* (*SATA*), *serial ATA II* (*SATA II*), or USB. If portability is required, portable hard drives, in which either the entire drive or a removable hard drive cartridge can be moved to another PC, are available. Hard drives for notebook PCs can be internal, external, or in a PC card format. *Mini hard drives* are commonly integrated in mobile devices and consumer electronic products.

OPTICAL DISC SYSTEMS

Optical discs store data *optically* using laser beams, and they can store data much more densely than magnetic disk technology. They are divided into tracks and sectors like magnetic disks, but use a single grooved spiral track instead of concentric tracks. Optical discs are available in a wide variety of *CD* and *DVD* formats and are read by *CD* or *DVD drives*. **CD-ROM (compact disc read-only memory) discs** come with data already stored on the disc. Data is represented by *pits* and *lands* permanently formed in the surface of the disk. CD-ROM discs cannot be erased or overwritten—they are *read-only*. **DVD-ROM (digital versatile disc read-only memory) discs** are similar to CD-ROM discs, but they hold much more data (4.7 GB instead of 700 MB). *Recordable discs* (**CD-R, DVD-R, DVD+R,** and **DVD+R DL discs**) and *rewritable disks* (**CD-RW, DVD-RW, DVD+RW, DVD-RAM,** and *blue laser discs*) can all be written to, but only recordable discs can be erased and rewritten to, similar to a floppy disk or hard drive. Recordable CDs and DVDs store data by burning permanent marks onto the disc, similar to CD-ROM and DVD-ROM discs; rewritable discs typically use *phase-change* technology to temporarily change the reflectivity of the disc to represent 1s and 0s. It is expected that, eventually, some form of DVD disc will eventually replace CDs as the optical disc standard.

Chapter Objective 4:
Discuss the various types of optical disc systems available and how they differ from each other and from magnetic systems.

HW

FLASH MEMORY SYSTEMS

Flash memory storage systems have no moving parts. **Flash memory cards**, the most common type of *flash memory media*, are commonly used with digital cameras, portable PCs, and other portable devices, as well as with desktop PCs. Flash memory cards come in a variety of formats—the most common are *CompactFlash* and *Secure Digital* (*SD*) *cards*. **Flash memory drives** typically connect to a PC via a USB port and are a convenient method of transferring files between computers.

Chapter Objective 5:
Explain what flash memory media and flash memory drives are and how they are used today.

OTHER TYPES OF STORAGE SYSTEMS

Remote storage—using a storage device that is not directly a part of your PC system—typically involves using a *network storage* device or an *online storage service*. Online storage services enable users to share files with others over the Internet, access files while on the road, and backup documents. **Smart cards** are credit card-sized pieces of plastic that contain a chip or other circuitry usually used to store data or a monetary value. **Holographic storage**, which uses multiple blue laser beams to store data in three dimensions, is becoming available for high-speed data retrieval applications.

Storage systems for larger computers implement many of the same standards as PC-based hard drives. Instead of finding a single set of hard disks inside a hard drive permanently installed within a system unit, however, a **storage server** is often used. **Network attached storage** (**NAS**) and **storage area networks** (**SANs**) are commonly used to provide storage for a business network. **RAID (redundant arrays of independent disks)** technology can be used to increase *fault tolerance* and performance. **Magnetic tape** systems store data on plastic tape coated with a magnetizable substance. Magnetic tapes are usually enclosed in cartridges and are inserted into a *tape drive* in order to be accessed.

Chapter Objective 6:
List at least three other types of storage systems.

COMPARING STORAGE ALTERNATIVES

Most PCs today include a hard drive, some type of CD or DVD drive, and a flash memory card reader. The type of optical drive and any additional storage devices are often determined by weighing a number of product characteristics and cost factors. These characteristics include speed, compatibility, capacity, removability, and convenience.

Chapter Objective 7:
Summarize the storage alternatives for a PC, including which storage systems should be included on a typical PC and for what applications other storage systems are appropriate.

REVIEW ACTIVITIES

KEY TERM MATCHING

Instructions: Match each key term on the left with the definition on the right that best describes it.

a. disk cache
b. DVD-ROM disc
c. file
d. flash memory card
e. flash memory drive
f. folder
g. hard disk drive
h. nonvolatile
i. RAID
j. remote storage

1. ______ A dedicated part of RAM used to store additional data adjacent to data retrieved during a disk fetch to improve system performance.

2. ______ A named place on a storage medium into which files can be stored to keep the files stored on that medium organized.

3. ______ An optical disc, usually holding 4.7 GB, that can be read from, but not written to, by the user.

4. ______ A small drive that usually plugs into a PC's USB port and contains flash memory media.

5. ______ A small, rectangular flash memory media, such as a CompactFlash or Secure Digital card.

6. ______ A storage device that is not directly a part of the PC being used, such as network storage or online storage.

7. ______ A storage method that uses several small hard disks in parallel to do the job of a larger disk.

8. ______ A storage system consisting of one or more metal magnetic disks permanently sealed with an access mechanism inside its drive.

9. ______ Describes a storage medium that retains its content when the power is shut off.

10. ______ Something stored on a storage medium, such as a program, document, or image.

SELF-QUIZ

Instructions: Circle **T** if the statement is true, **F** if the statement is false, or write the best answer in the space provided. **Answers for the self-quiz are located in the References and Resources Guide at the end of the book.**

1. **T F** A computer system with a C drive and a D drive must have two physical hard drives.
2. **T F** The smallest amount of space a file on a disk can take up is one cluster.
3. **T F** External hard drives typically connect via a flash memory reader.
4. **T F** A CD-R is a type of read-only optical disc.
5. **T F** Most PCs today include a hard disk drive.

6. A storage medium is ______ if it loses its content when the power is shut off.
7. A single-sided, single-layer DVD disc typically holds ______.
8. A(n) ______ looks similar to a credit card but contains a chip and other circuitry into which data can be stored.
9. Secure Digital (SD) cards are one type of ______ medium.

10. Match the storage device to the drive letter that it would most likely be assigned on a typical PC, and write the corresponding number in the blank to the left of each drive letter.

a. _______ A:	1. CD/DVD drive
b. _______ C:	2. Floppy disk
c. _______ D:	3. Hard drive

EXERCISES

1. Assume, for simplicity's sake, that a kilobyte is 1,000 bytes, a megabyte is 1,000,000 bytes, and a gigabyte is 1,000,000,000 bytes. You have an 80-gigabyte hard drive with the following content:

ITEM	STORAGE SPACE USED
Operating system	65 MB
Office suite	85 MB
Other software	250 MB
Digital photos	3.5 GB
Other documents	10 MB

Approximately how much room is left on the drive? _______

2. Match the image to its name, and write the corresponding number in the blank to the left of its name.

a. _______ Hard drive	c. _______ Optical disc	e. _______ Flash memory drive
b. _______ Floppy disk	d. _______ Smart card	f. _______ Flash memory card

1\. 

2\. 

3\. 

4\. 

5\. 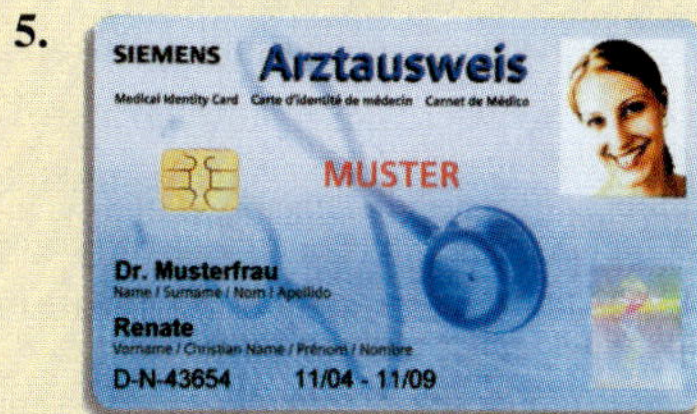

6\. 

3. Explain why CD-ROM discs are not erasable, but CD+RW discs are.
4. What does the term "solid-state drive" mean? List one storage device to which this term applies.
5. Which types of storage media would be appropriate for someone who needed to exchange large (5 MB to 75 MB) files with another person? List at least three different types, stating why each might be the most appropriate under specific conditions.

DISCUSSION QUESTION

People send their digital photos over the Internet in different ways. For instance, digital photos are often e-mailed to others, posted on an online storage site, or uploaded to a server (such as one belonging to SnapFish, Walmart, or Costco) in order to order prints, enlargements, or other photo-based items. If you have ever sent photos over the Internet, were you concerned about someone other than the intended recipient intercepting or viewing your photo files? If you have ever uploaded files to a processing service for printing, did you check to see if the Web server being used was secure? Should individuals be concerned about sending their personal photos over the Internet? There are a number of advantages, but are there privacy risks, as well?

PROJECTS

HOT TOPICS

1. **Blue Laser Discs** As mentioned in the chapter, an emerging optical technology that uses blue lasers can increase the capacity of a standard-sized DVD disc significantly. At the time of this writing, Sony Blu-ray DVD drives were only available in Japan and were extremely expensive. Another blue laser standard, competing against and incompatible with Blu-ray, is Advanced Optical Disc.

   For this project, research the current state of blue laser DVDs. Are there any products available in the United States? Has the blue laser standard war been settled, or is there still more than one competing standard? What is the current capacity of discs using blue laser technology? At the conclusion of your research, prepare a one- to two-page summary of your findings and submit it to your instructor.

SHORT ANSWER/ RESEARCH

2. **Smart IDs** The chapter Technology and You box discusses the growing use of smart cards as campus ID cards. Some credit cards are now being issued as smart cards, and smart cards have been proposed to replace conventional drivers' licenses, medical insurance cards, and other important documents. Some countries have already implemented smart-card-based national ID cards. The ability of a smart card to hold a larger amount of personal data than a conventional magnetic stripe card and to confirm online credit card orders via a smart card reader attached to your PC is viewed as a benefit by some. The additional information potentially available through a card (such as an individual's medical history or purchasing record), however, is viewed as a privacy risk to others.

   For this project, consider the points raised in the previous paragraph and write a short essay expressing your opinion about using smart cards to replace conventional magnetic stripe cards. If it is not already, would you want your campus ID card to be a smart card? Why or why not? Do you think smart cards will be used any differently by consumers in the future than conventional magnetic stripe cards are used at the present time? List any pros and cons of replacing magnetic stripe cards with smart cards and provide a concluding paragraph stating other possible uses for smart cards that would be beneficial and/or accepted by the general public. Submit your opinion on this issue to your instructor in the form of a one-page paper.

3. **Auto Backup** For those of us who forget to back up our files on a regular basis, there is an alternative—using an automatic backup utility that performs this task for you on a regular basis. Many backup programs offer this option, and some online storage sites have the option of uploading your designated files or folders to the online storage site on a regular basis. In addition, some companies that sell storage devices with removable media include this software for free with the purchase of the device.

   For this project, research a few of the options that are available for performing automatic backups, and summarize the alternatives that you find. At the conclusion of your research, prepare a one-page summary of your findings and submit it to your instructor.

HANDS ON

4. **Storage Evaluation** Most PCs have multiple storage devices, such as a hard drive, floppy drive, CD or DVD drive, and so on.

   For this project, find one computer (such as at home, your school, or a public library) that you are allowed to use, preferably the one you will use most often for this course. By looking at the outside of the PC, as well as by using a file management program (such as Windows

Explorer), identify each storage device on your selected PC. For each device, list the type of storage device (such as floppy disk drive, CD drive, or hard drive) and its assigned drive letter. In Windows Explorer, right-click each hard drive icon and select Properties to determine the size of the drive and how much room is left. At the conclusion of this task, prepare a one-page summary of your observations and submit it to your instructor.

5. **Online Storage** There are a number of online storage services (such as Xdrive, Yahoo! Briefcase, and IBackup) designed to allow users to backup and share files with others; specialty online storage services designed for digital photo sharing include Fotki and Yahoo! Photos.

   For this project, visit at least one online storage site designed for backup and file exchange, and at least one site designed for digital photo sharing. You can try the sites listed above or use a search site to find alternative sites. Tour the sites you select to determine what features each service offers, what it costs, the amount of storage space available, and your options for sending your uploaded files to others. Do the sites you selected password protect your files, or are they available for anyone with an Internet connection to see? What are the benefits for using these types of online storage services? Can you think of any drawbacks? Would you want to use any of the online storage sites you visited? Why or why not? At the conclusion of this task, prepare a short summary containing the information and answers to the questions listed above, and then submit it to your instructor.

HW

WRITING ABOUT COMPUTERS

6. **Storage Solutions** The selection of an appropriate storage solution is usually based on the computer being used and the individual's storage requirements.

   For this project, consider the storage requirements for each of the following three scenarios, and determine an appropriate storage solution for each one.

   Scenario 1: A home computer where several family members will be using the computer for homework, shopping, taxes, downloading and playing music, playing multimedia games, and surfing the Web.

   Scenario 2: A small accounting company that has only one computer and is using it to support all the administrative and information needs of the company.

   Scenario 3: A two-person video editing and multimedia production company that has two computers and specializes in recording and producing videos of weddings and other special occasions.

   Feel free to modify or clarify the three scenarios defined above in order to make your storage solutions match more closely with the diverse number of possibilities and storage options available today. Submit your recommendations to your instructor in the form of a short paper, not more than two pages in length. Be sure to include why you choose each storage solution.

PRESENTATION/ DEMONSTRATION

7. **Flash Cards** The number of uses for flash memory cards has been growing at a tremendous rate. Primarily developed for use with digital cameras, today's possibilities include storage for portable and desktop PCs and a variety of other devices, as well as providing programs and peripheral devices for some PCs.

   For this project, research the various uses for flash memory cards. Find at least two examples of flash memory products in each of the following three categories: user storage, software, and an interface for a peripheral device. Share your findings with the class in the form of a short presentation, including the products that you found and their specifications, as well as your opinion regarding the flash card market in the future. Be sure to include any current or potential application you find in your research in addition to the three categories listed here. The presentation should not exceed 10 minutes and should make use of one or more presentation aids, such as the chalkboard, handouts, overhead transparencies, or a computer-based slide presentation (your instructor may provide additional requirements). You may also be asked to submit a summary of the presentation to your instructor.

GROUP DISCUSSION

8. **Big Brother?** Some of the storage technology used today, such as smart cards, can help facilitate faster and more secure access to locked facilities, protect against the use of stolen credit card numbers, and, when used in conjunction with a biometric characteristic, unequivocally identify a user to a computer system. They can also be used for employee monitoring, informing a business where each employee carrying or wearing his or her smart card is located at all times. While some people find benefits to the applications just discussed, others worry that smart cards and other devices will be used to track our movements. Is the convenience of smart card technology worth the possibility that information about you and your actions will be recorded in a database somewhere? Do you think employers or the government have the right to track individuals' movements? If so, under what conditions do they have this right? What are some advantages and disadvantages for the government and your employer always knowing where you are? Have you ever used a smart card or been identified with a biometric system? If so, how do you rate the experience?

   For this project, form an opinion of the use of smart cards and similar technology to identify individuals for various applications and be prepared to discuss your position (in class, via an online class discussion group, or in a class chat room, depending on your instructor's directions). You may also be asked to write a short paper expressing your opinion.

WEB ACTIVITIES

The *Understanding Computers* Web site located at **www.course.com/uc11** features many resources to help reinforce your understanding of the chapter content and help you prepare for exams. Your instructor may also assign specific activities to be completed that will count toward your final grade in the course.

Instructions: Go to **www.course.com/uc11/ch03** to work the following online activities.

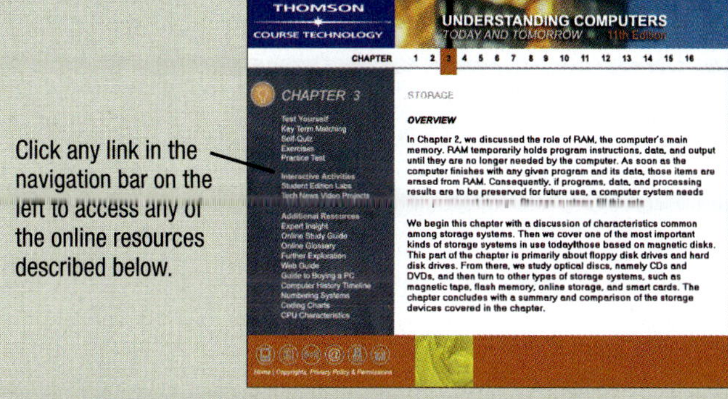

INTERACTIVE ACTIVITIES

1. **Crossword Puzzle** Practice your knowledge of the key terms in Chapter 3 by completing the interactive Crossword Puzzle.
2. **Tech News Video Project** Watch the **"Online Storage Options"** video clip that takes a look at the growing use of online storage, which allows you to upload files and then access them from any computer anywhere you have an Internet connection. After watching the video online, complete the corresponding project.
3. **Student Edition Labs** Reinforce the concepts you have learned in this chapter by working through the interactive **Managing Files** lab.

TEST YOURSELF

1. **Key Term Matching** Test your knowledge of selected chapter key terms by matching the terms with their definitions.
2. **Self-Quiz** Test your retention of chapter concepts by taking the Self-Quiz.
3. **Exercises** Work these short exercises to review the concepts and terms covered in the chapter.
4. **Practice Test** Test how ready you are for an upcoming exam by completing the online Practice Test.

STUDY TOOLS/ ADDITIONAL RESOURCES

The Understanding Computers Web site has a wide range of additional resources, including an **Online Study Guide** (containing study tips, a chapter outline with room to add your own notes, and a chapter checklist of the activities to complete when the chapter is covered in class and when you are preparing for a test) and an **Online Glossary** for each chapter; **Further Exploration** links; a **Web Guide**, a **Guide to Buying a PC**, and a **Computer History Timeline**; more information about **Numbering Systems**, **Coding Charts**, and **CPU Characteristics**; and much, much more!

CHAPTER 4 Input and Output

OUTLINE

Overview
Keyboards
Pointing Devices
- The Mouse
- Electronic Pens
- Touch Screens
- Other Pointing Devices

Scanners, Readers, and Digital Cameras
- Scanners
- Readers
- Digital Cameras

Audio Input
- Voice Input Systems
- Music Input Systems

Display Devices
- Display Device Characteristics
- Flat-Panel Display Technologies
- Data and Multimedia Projectors

Printers
- Printer Characteristics
- Laser Printers
- Ink-Jet Printers
- Special-Purpose Printers
- Multifunction Devices

Audio Output

LEARNING OBJECTIVES

After completing this chapter, you will be able to:

1. Explain the purpose of a computer keyboard and the types of keyboards widely used today.
2. List several different pointing devices and describe their functions.
3. Describe the purposes of scanners and readers and list some types of scanners and readers in use today.
4. Understand how digital cameras differ from conventional cameras.
5. Explain how audio input is accomplished.
6. Describe the characteristics of a display device.
7. List several types of printers and explain their function.
8. Understand which hardware devices are used for audio output.

OVERVIEW

In Chapter 2, we learned how data is processed by a computer. The focus of Chapter 4 is on the hardware designed for inputting data into the computer, and then outputting results to the user after the data has been processed. We begin with a look at input. First we discuss the most common *input devices* used with personal computers to enter commands or data into the PC–mainly, keyboards and pointing devices (such as a mouse). Next, hardware designed for capturing data in electronic form, such as scanners, barcode readers, and digital cameras, is discussed, followed by a look at two types of audio input.

The second part of this chapter explores the different types of *output devices*–hardware that can be used for output. Typically, output occurs on the screen (via a display device) or paper (via a printer). Display devices are covered first, including their basic properties and the various types of display devices in use today. Next, we discuss printers and devices used for audio output. Keep in mind that this chapter describes only a sample of the input and output equipment available today. In fact, there are thousands of input and output products, and they can be combined together in many ways to create a computer system to fit almost any conceivable need. ■

KEYBOARDS

Most PCs today are designed to be used with a **keyboard**. Virtually all desktop PCs are used in conjunction with either a wired or wireless keyboard. Wired keyboards are connected via a cable to the computer's system unit; *wireless keyboards* are powered by batteries and send wireless signals to a receiver that is usually plugged into the computer's serial or USB port. Although earlier wireless keyboards used *infrared signals* and needed to be within *line of sight* of their receivers, newer models use *radio waves* and, therefore, do not require line of sight transmission, although there is a limit on the allowable distance between the keyboard and the receiver. Some of the newest wireless keyboards are *Bluetooth-compliant*, meaning they communicate with the PC via a Bluetooth wireless networking connection. Bluetooth and wireless networking are covered in more detail in Chapter 7.

Most keyboards today (refer to the typical desktop PC keyboard shown in Figure 4-1) contain the standard alphanumeric keys found on all keyboards and typewriters along with a *numeric keypad* (used for entering numbers), *function keys* (used to issue commands in some programs), *Delete* and *Backspace keys* (used to delete characters from the screen), *Control* and *Alternate keys* (used in conjunction with other keys on the keyboard to issue commands, such as Ctrl+S to save the current document, in some programs), and *directional keys* (used to move around within a document). Some keyboards also contain additional keys for a specific purpose or software program, such as to open the Windows Start menu, control the speaker volume, launch an e-mail program or favorite Web site, or

TIP

Some keys on a keyboard, like the Caps Lock and Number Lock keys, are *toggle* keys, which are pressed once to turn the feature on and again to turn the feature off. If you ever find yourself typing in all caps or the numeric keypad does not work, check the status of these keys.

>**Keyboard.** An input device containing numerous keys, arranged in a configuration similar to that of a typewriter, that can be used to input letters, numbers, and other symbols.

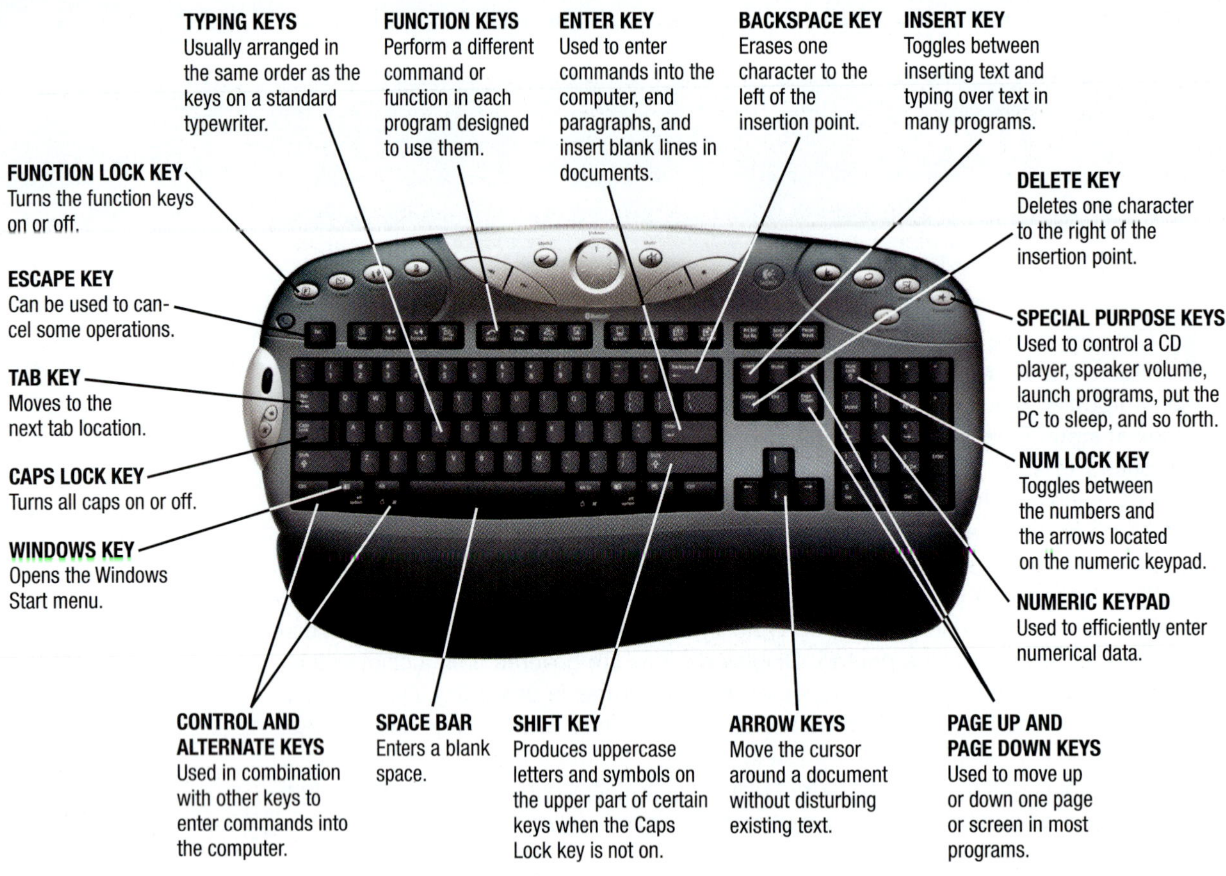

FIGURE 4-1
A typical desktop keyboard.

perform specific tasks in the Microsoft Office software programs. When buying a PC or replacement keyboard, look carefully at the keyboard to be sure it fits your needs.

Notebook PCs usually have a keyboard that is smaller and contains fewer keys than a desktop PC keyboard, and the keys are typically placed closer together. Because of this, notebook buyers should try out the keyboard before buying, whenever possible, to ensure that the size, layout, and feel of the keyboard meet their needs. Notebook computer users can also connect and use a conventional keyboard, when needed, if the notebook contains a keyboard or USB port.

Many handheld PCs and mobile devices today have a built-in keyboard or *thumb pad* (a keyboard designed to be pressed with just the thumbs, as shown in Figure 4-2), but the layout may be different than a conventional keyboard, and the keyboard layout may vary from device to device. For instance, some smart phones have several letters assigned to a single key, and the key is pressed multiple times to

FIGURE 4-2
Keyboards for handheld PCs and mobile devices.

FLIP-OPEN THUMB PAD

BUILT-IN KEYBOARD

FOLDABLE KEYBOARD

indicate the desired letter. Others, like the smart phone with a built-in keyboard shown in Figure 4-2, contain separate keys for each letter of the alphabet but they are in a different order than on a typical keyboard. If the device does not have a built-in keyboard, often a special *portable keyboard* or *portable thumb pad* can be used with the device for easier data entry. Portable keyboards designed for handheld PCs typically fold or roll up (see Figure 4-2); thumb pads slip over the bottom of a handheld PC or smart phone. Full-sized keyboards can also be used with portable computers, if the proper connector is built into the PC. Portable computers that do not support a keyboard or thumb pad typically rely on *pen input* or *touch input* instead, as discussed shortly.

POINTING DEVICES

In addition to a keyboard, most PCs today have some type of **pointing device**. Unlike keyboards, which are used to enter characters at the *insertion point* (sometimes called the *cursor*) location, pointing devices are used to move an onscreen *mouse pointer*—usually an arrow. Once that pointer is pointing to the desired object on the screen, that object can be selected (usually by pressing a button on the pointing device) or otherwise manipulated. Some common types of pointing devices are the *mouse*, *electronic pen*, and *touch screen*.

The Mouse

A **mouse** rests on the desk or other flat surface close to the user's PC and is moved across the surface with the user's hand in the appropriate direction to point to and select objects on the screen. Older *mechanical mice* have a ball exposed on the bottom surface of the mouse to control the pointer movement. Most mice today are *optical mice* that track movements with light. Newer *laser mice* (such as the one shown in Figure 4-3) use laser beams to track movement and are even more accurate—one study found them to be 20 times more accurate—than conventional optical mice. While mechanical mice require regular cleanings to operate properly, optical and laser mice do not. Mice are commonly used to start programs; open, move around, and edit documents; draw or edit images; and more. A list of common mouse commands is included in Figure 4-3.

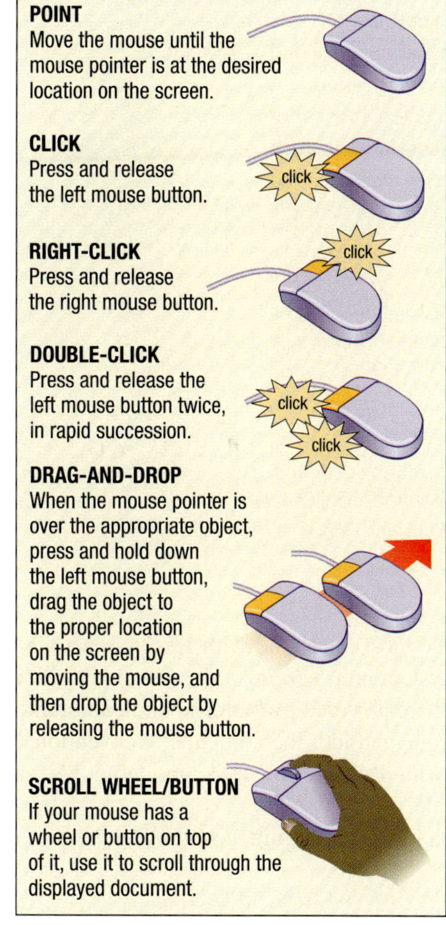

COMMON MOUSE OPERATIONS

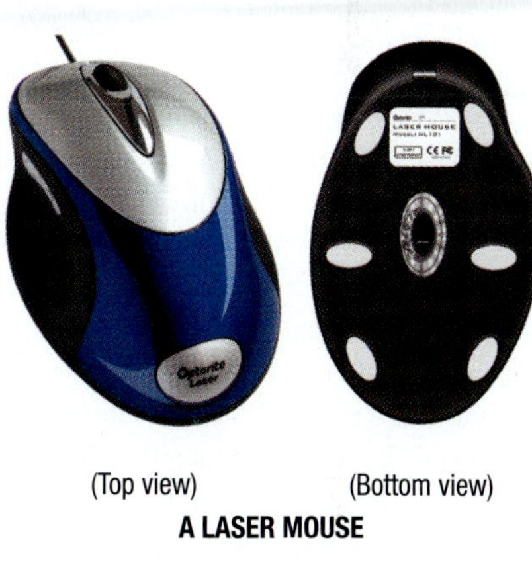
(Top view) (Bottom view)

A LASER MOUSE

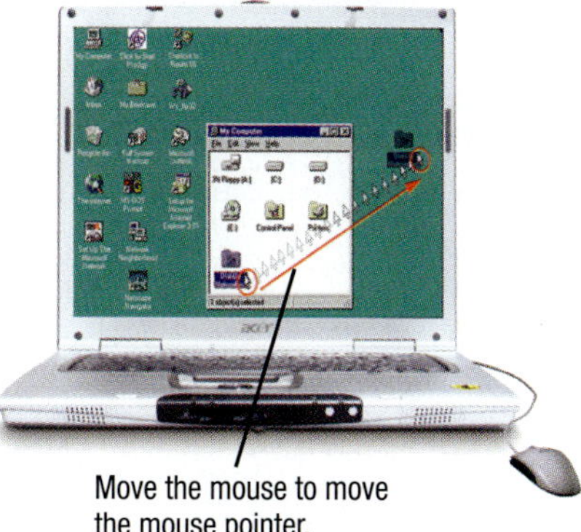

USING A MOUSE

FIGURE 4-3
Using a mouse.

>**Pointing device.** An input device that moves an onscreen pointer, such as an arrow or insertion point, to allow the user to select objects on the screen. >**Mouse.** A common pointing device that the user slides along a flat surface to move a pointer around the screen and clicks its buttons to make selections.

TREND

Virtual Input Devices

There is an ongoing trend to continue to make input methods and devices easier and more natural to use. Voice recognition is one strong possibility. Other possibilities include more *virtual*, less physical, devices that use projections or gestures instead of more conventional methods of input.

One emerging input device being developed for use with portable PCs and mobile devices is the *virtual keyboard*. A virtual keyboard uses a projector and camera—the projector projects a keyboard image onto a flat surface and the camera translates motion on that projected image back to the computer as input. Virtual keyboard capabilities are expected to soon be built into cell phones, portable PCs, and other portable devices to allow input via a standard keyboard layout without requiring actual keyboard hardware (see the accompanying photo). A related emerging application is the use of projected images for consumer kiosks. Instead of requiring floor space, kiosk images are displayed on a wall or the floor using a wall-mounted projector and a camera tracks the user's interactions with the projected images as input.

Other possibilities for the future are *gesture-based input devices*—input devices that are controlled by gestures, such as hand movements. One example of a gesture-based input system is the EyeToy system used with some Sony PlayStation games. This system uses a special video camera in conjunction with software to enable the player to control the game using only body movements. For computer input, some companies are working toward a noncontact gesture interface, similar to the one used by Tom Cruise's character in *Minority Report* to change the images on his display by just gesturing with his hands. Although such an interface might be far in the future, more than one company has already developed a *motion-controlled* interface for mobile devices, in which users can rotate a smart phone or other device to change the orientation of the display image, tip the device forward or backward to zoom in or out, tip the device left or right to change songs on a music playlist, tilt the device to scroll, and more, allowing the user to operate the device with one hand. One interface even enables users to "write" in the air with the phone and have the phone recognize and input the letters or numbers being written.

A virtual keyboard.

While most mice sold with PCs connect via a serial, USB, or PS/2 port on the computer's system unit, *wireless mice* are also available. Similar to wireless keyboards, wireless mice are powered by batteries and communicate wirelessly with the system unit via a receiver plugged into the computer. Conventional, wireless, and small travel mice can all be used with desktop, notebook, and tablet PCs, as desired, as long as an appropriate port is available.

For a look at emerging *virtual input devices*, see the Trend box.

>**Electronic pen.** An input device that is used to write electronically on the display screen; also called a **stylus** or *digital pen*.

Electronic Pens

An **electronic pen** is a pointing device that can be used instead of a mouse to select objects, as well as to draw or write electronically on the screen. Also called a **stylus** or *digital pen*, electronic pens are typically wireless and look similar to a ballpoint pen. Handheld PCs, tablet PCs, and other devices that accept pen input typically use a stylus. *Pen-based PCs* and other devices that use electronic pens are discussed next. The idea behind pen-based input and *digital writing* in general is to make using a computer as convenient as writing with a pen, while adding the extra capabilities the computer can provide, such as converting the pen-based text input to editable typed text or retrieving handwritten electronic documents by keywords or the document contents.

Pen-Based PCs

Although their capabilities depend on the type of computer and software being used, electronic pens can be used with a variety of computer types (see Figure 4-4). Most often, electronic pens are used with handheld or tablet PCs to input handwritten text and sketches, as well as to manipulate objects (such as to select an option from a menu, select a group of text, or resize an image). Depending on the software being used, handwritten input can be stored as an image, stored as handwritten characters that can be recognized by the computer, or converted to editable, typed text. For the latter two options, software with **handwriting recognition** capabilities must be used.

FIGURE 4-4

Pen-based PCs. Users of pen-based PCs can typically use their stylus to input handwritten data and instructions, as well as to select menu items, check boxes, and command buttons.

HANDHELD PC

TABLET PC

DESKTOP PC

Some handwriting recognition systems require the handwritten input to conform to a specific handwriting style (such as the *Palm Graffiti* alphabet used with Palm handheld PCs); others can accept handwritten input written in the users' personal style. Just as with *speech recognition*—in which the computer accepts spoken input—handwriting recognition usually requires some training for the PC to adjust to the particular style of the user, and the input is not always interpreted correctly. For a look at how handwriting recognition works, see Figure 4-5.

One area of recent growth is the use of *digital forms*—such as the patient assessment form shown in Figure 4-5—in conjunction with handwriting recognition. This application is expected to continue to grow in the near future as companies continue to move towards digital records and digital documents.

>**Handwriting recognition.** The ability of a device to identify handwritten characters.

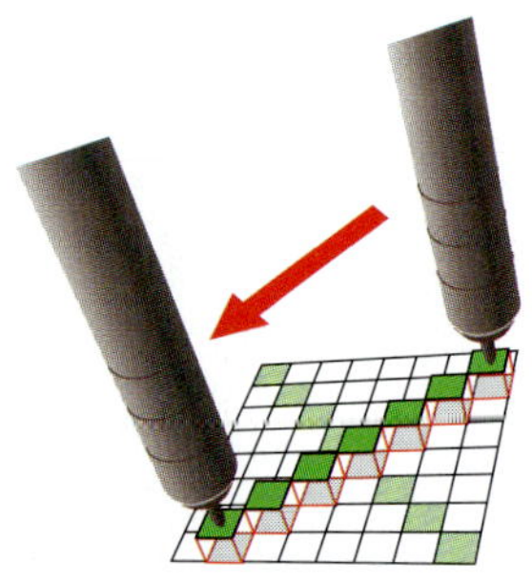

1. As the pen moves, the computer continually calculates its position, instructing the pixels it passes over to turn on.

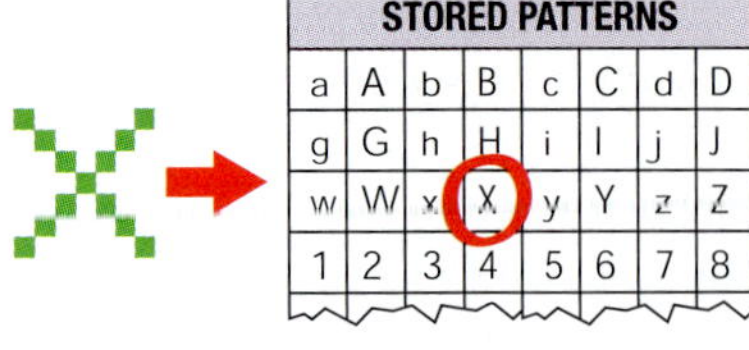

2. The computer then compares the pattern that was input to other patterns it has stored. It makes allowances within certain limits for imprecision.

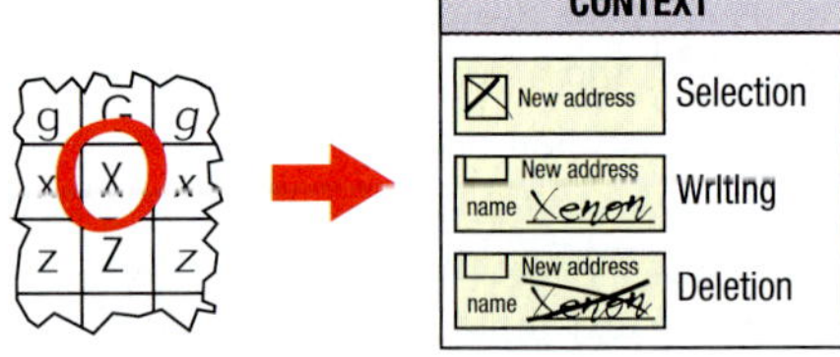

3. After a pattern is recognized, the computer looks at the context in which the pattern was made before it decides what to do. For instance, an "X" in a check box means selecting a certain action, whereas an "X" over filled-in text implies a deletion operation.

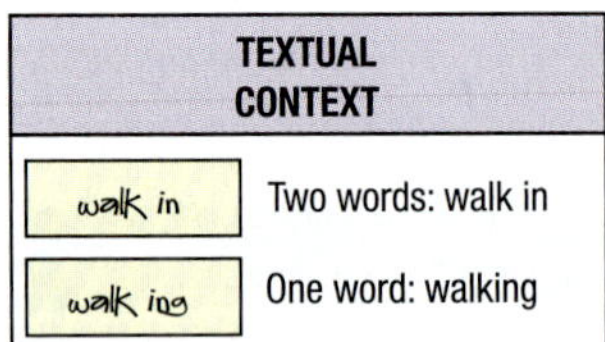

4. For text input, the computer looks at surrounding words, consults dictionaries, and uses grammar rules to determine the most likely intended input.

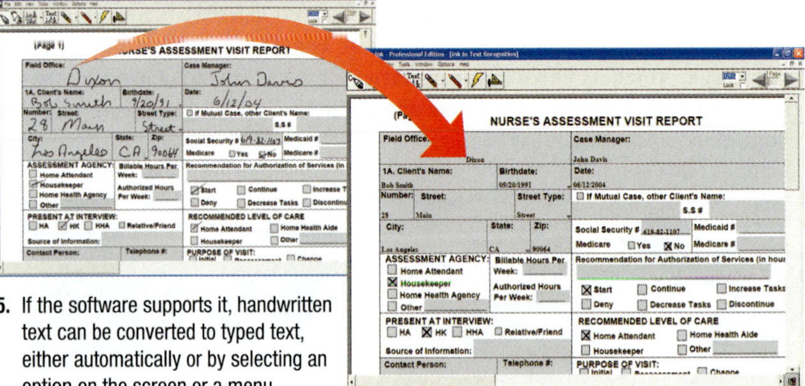

5. If the software supports it, handwritten text can be converted to typed text, either automatically or by selecting an option on the screen or a menu.

FIGURE 4-5
How handwriting recognition works. Pen-based computers usually use contextual clues, dictionaries, grammar rules, and more to make the best determination of what the user wrote, instead of strictly interpreting content letter by letter.

Digital Writing Systems

Other types of electronic pens used with PCs include those designed solely to capture handwritten input as it is written and then transfer that input to the PC after the pen is docked in its cradle attached to the PC. Alternatively, the input can be transmitted wirelessly to a PC as it is being written. Typically, these *digital writing systems* require the use of special paper, and anything written on that paper can be transferred to a PC (see Figure 4-6).

Graphics Tablets

A **graphics tablet**—also called a *digitizing tablet*—is a flat, touch-sensitive tablet used in conjunction with a stylus (see Figure 4-6). Anything drawn or written on the graphics tablet is automatically transferred to the connected PC in graphic form. Graphics tablets are often used by graphic artists, photographers, and other graphics professionals in conjunction with *image editing software* to create original images or to modify digital photographs.

Signature Capture Devices

Another type of pen-based input device is the *signature capture device* (see Figure 4-6). These devices are commonly attached to point-of-sale equipment, so they can electronically record signatures used to authorize credit card purchases. Delivery companies,

>**Graphics tablet.** A flat, rectangular input device that is used in conjunction with a stylus to transfer drawings, sketches, and anything written on the device to a PC in graphic form.

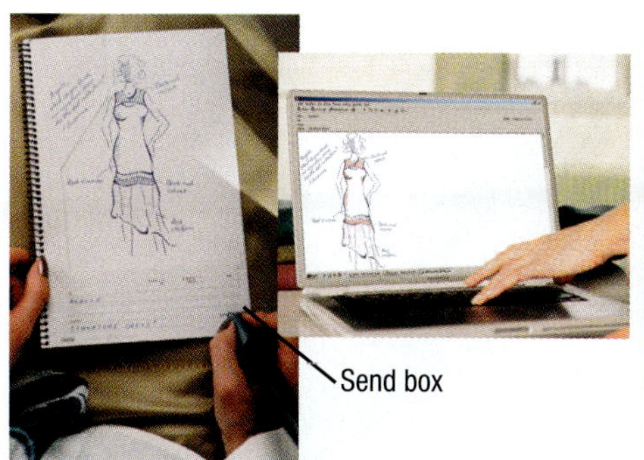

DIGITAL WRITING SYSTEM
When the Send box on the paper is selected, the document content is transferred wirelessly to the computer.

GRAPHICS TABLET
All input written on the graphics tablet is transferred in real time to the computer.

SIGNATURE CAPTURE DEVICE
When a signature is entered and the appropriate confirmation box is tapped, the signature is recorded.

FIGURE 4-6
Other uses for electronic pens.

restaurants, retail stores, and other service businesses may also use a signature capture device—or a handheld or tablet PC with appropriate software—to record authorizing signatures.

Touch Screens

As PCs have become more integrated into the lives of consumers, **touch screens** have become increasingly more prominent. With a touch screen, the user touches the screen with his or her finger to select commands or otherwise provide input to the computer with which the touch screen is being used (see Figure 4-7). Touch screen kiosks are found in a variety of locations—such as retail stores, movie theaters, courthouses, fast-food restaurants, and airports—to allow for more self-service applications, including self-check-in. According to the IHL Consulting Group, U.S. consumers spent $123 billion at consumer kiosks in 2003—an 80% jump from the year before—and purchases made via kiosks are expected to surpass $1 trillion by 2007. Touch screens are also used in *point-of-sale (POS) systems*—systems that record sales transaction data at the point where the product or service is purchased, such as a checkout or sales counter—and are useful for on-the-job applications (such as factory work) that require users to wear gloves, or where using a keyboard or mouse is otherwise impractical.

FIGURE 4-7
Touch screens. Touch screens are commonly used in consumer kiosks and point-of-sale systems.

Other Pointing Devices

A few other common pointing devices are described next and shown in Figure 4-8. There are also pointing devices specifically designed for users with limited mobility. These pointing devices—along with *ergonomic keyboards*, *Braille keyboards*, and other types of input devices designed for users with special needs—are discussed in Chapter 16.

AIRLINE SELF-CHECK-IN

RESTAURANT ORDER-ENTRY SYSTEM

>**Touch screen.** A display device that is touched with the finger to issue commands or otherwise generate input to the connected PC.

FIGURE 4-8
Other common pointing devices.

JOYSTICK
Used most often in computer games.

TRACKBALL
Takes up less desk space than a mouse and is easier for some users to manipulate.

POINTING STICK
Found on some notebook PCs. The stick is pushed in different directions to move the onscreen pointer.

TOUCH PAD
Commonly found on notebook PCs, keyboards, or as a stand-alone device.

Joysticks and Other Gaming Devices

A **joystick**, which looks similar to a car's gearshift, is most often used with computer games. The movement of the joystick's stick controls an onscreen object, such as a player or vehicle in a game. Buttons on the joystick are usually assigned functions, such as jumping or firing a weapon, by the program being used. Today, some games can be used with gloves containing built-in sensors, enabling the computer to detect hand movements directly. Other gaming input devices include *gamepads* that are held in the hand and contain buttons similar to those on a joystick and *steering wheels* for driving games.

Trackballs

Similar to an upside-down mechanical mouse, a **trackball** has the ball mechanism on top, instead of on the bottom. The ball is rotated with the thumb, hand, or finger to move the onscreen pointer. Because the device itself does not need to be moved, trackballs take up less space on the desktop than mice; they also are easier to use for individuals with limited hand or finger mobility.

>Joystick. An input device that resembles a car's gear shift and is often used for gaming. **>Trackball.** An input device, similar to an upside-down mouse, that can be used to control an onscreen pointer and make selections.

Pointing Sticks

A **pointing stick** (also called a *touch stick*) is the pencil eraser-shaped device found in the middle of many notebook computer keyboards. It works similarly to a trackball, except that the thumb or finger pushes the stick in the appropriate direction, instead of rolling the ball, and the stick is pushed down to perform mouse clicks.

Touch Pads

A **touch pad** is a rectangular pad across which a fingertip or thumb slides to move the onscreen pointer. The buttons that appear next to the touch pad surface are used to perform clicks and other mouse actions; often the pad can be tapped to make selections, as well. Although most often found on notebook computer keyboards, touch pads are also available as stand-alone devices to be used with desktop computers.

SCANNERS, READERS, AND DIGITAL CAMERAS

Some input devices are designed either to convert data that already exists in physical form to digital form or to capture data initially in digital form. Documents containing data that already exists in physical form—such as an order form, photograph, invoice, check, or price label—are referred to as *source documents*. There are various types of scanners and readers that can be used to capture data from a source document and convert it into input that the computer can understand. Capturing data directly from a source document (called *source data automation*) saves time and is usually more accurate than inputting the data via a keyboard or other manual input device. It also allows the people who know the most about the events that the data represents to be the ones who input the data, which helps ensure accuracy during the data-entry process. For instance, an insurance adjuster or auto mechanic entering data directly into a computer about the condition of a car involved in an accident will likely have fewer input errors than if he or she recorded that data on paper and then it was later keyed into a PC by an assistant; and a pharmacist electronically verifying the identity of a prescription medicine against a customer's record and prescription before giving it to the customer can help reduce prescription errors (see Figure 4-9).

Many of the most common devices used in source data automation are *scanning* or *reading devices*; that is, devices that read printed text, codes, or graphics, and then translate the results into digital form that can be used by a computer. The next few sections discuss several different types of scanning and reading devices, followed by a look at *digital cameras*, which capture data initially in digital form.

FIGURE 4-9

Source data automation. Recording data initially in digital form or capturing data directly from a source document can both help reduce data input errors and save time.

RECORDING DATA DIRECTLY INTO A PC

CAPTURING DATA FROM ITS SOURCE DOCUMENT

Scanners

A **scanner**, more officially called an *optical scanner*, captures the image of a usually flat object (such as a printed document, photograph, or drawing) in digital form and then transfers that data to a PC. Typically, the entire document (including both text and images) is input as a single graphical image that can be resized, inserted into other documents, posted on a Web page, e-mailed to someone, printed, or otherwise

>**Pointing stick.** An input device shaped like a pencil eraser that appears in the middle of some notebook computer keyboards and is used as a pointing device. >**Touch pad.** A small rectangular-shaped input device, often found on notebook computers, that is touched with the finger or thumb to control an onscreen pointer and make selections. >**Scanner.** An input device that reads printed text and graphics and transfers them to a computer in digital form.

treated like any other graphical image. The text in the image, however, cannot be edited unless **optical character recognition (OCR)** software is used in conjunction with the scanner to input the scanned text as individual text characters.

Types of Scanners

Scanners exist in a variety of configurations (see Figure 4-10). A **flatbed scanner** is designed to scan flat objects one page at a time. Flatbed scanners work in much the same way that photocopiers do—whatever is being scanned remains stationary while the scanning mechanism moves underneath it to capture the image. Some scanners can scan slides and film negatives, in addition to printed documents; scanners designed for high-volume processing come with automatic document feeders so that large quantities of documents can be scanned with one command. Businesses are increasingly converting their paper documents to electronic form for both archival purposes and to send electronically to clients. As more document processing is being carried out via e-mail and fax, high-volume scanning is becoming more important.

With a **sheetfed scanner**, documents are inserted into the top of the scanner, similar to the way paper is inserted into a fax machine. This design reduces the amount of desk space required. However, the feature also prevents the scanner from scanning bound-book pages or other items thicker or larger than a standard sheet of paper. Sheetfed scanners are most often used in mobile settings with a portable PC.

Handheld scanners are useful for capturing short newspaper or magazine articles, as well as Web addresses, names, and telephone numbers. Most handheld scanners (such as the *C-Pen* scanner shown in Figure 4-10) are designed to be used away from the computer. The scanned text is stored in the scanner and can be transferred to a PC (via a cable or a wireless connection) when needed. Data that will be needed while on the go (such as phone numbers, e-mail addresses, and so on) can also be stored in the scanner for retrieval at a later time. Other handheld scanners are designed to stay connected to the PC so that the user can scan data while working at his or her computer. Some handheld scanners can scan text in a variety of languages and come with built-in dictionaries to allow the text to be translated, or words defined, while the text is being scanned.

Applications requiring the most professional results may require the use of a *drum scanner*. A drum scanner is much more expensive and more difficult to operate than the other types of scanners discussed here. When a drum scanner is used, the documents to be scanned are mounted on a glass cylinder, which is then rotated at high speeds around a sensor located inside the scanner. Multimedia and medical applications may require the use of a *three-dimensional (3D) scanner*, which can scan an image or person in 3D. Task-specific scanners, such as *receipt scanners* and *business card scanners*, are also available.

For a look at how scanning is beginning to be used in conjunction with clothes shopping, see the Technology and You box.

Scanning Quality and Resolution

The quality of scanned images is indicated by *optical resolution*, typically measured in the number of *dots per inch (dpi)*. When a document is scanned using either an application program (such as a word processing program) or scanning software, the resolution to be used with the scanned image can often be specified. The resolution of scanned images can also be specified when the image is first saved or if it is modified at a later time using an *image editing program*. Scanners today usually scan at between 3,200 × 6,400 dpi and

>**Optical character recognition (OCR).** The ability of a scanning device to recognize handwritten or typed characters and convert them to electronic form as text, not images. >**Flatbed scanner.** An input device that scans flat objects one at a time. >**Sheetfed scanner.** A scanner that can accept a single sheet of paper at one time. >**Handheld scanner.** A small, handheld optical scanner.

identifying data, such as to uniquely identify a product, shipped package, or other item—can be retrieved. *Fixed* barcode readers are frequently used in point-of-sale (POS) systems (see Figure 4-11); *portable* barcode readers are also available. Portable barcode readers (either dedicated barcode reading devices or portable PCs with built-in barcode reading capabilities) are used by workers who need to scan barcodes while on the go, such as while walking through a warehouse or at a variety of different retail locations.

The most familiar barcode is *UPC* (*Universal Product Code*), the barcode commonly found on packaged goods in supermarkets. Businesses and organizations can also create and use custom barcodes to fulfill their unique needs. For instance, shippers, such as FedEx, UPS, and the U.S. Postal Service, use their own barcodes to mark and track packages; hospitals use custom barcodes to match patients with their charts and medicines; libraries and video stores use barcodes for checking out and checking in materials, such as books and movies; researchers use barcodes to tag and track the migration habits of animals; and law enforcement agencies use barcodes to mark evidence. In fact, any business with a barcode printer and appropriate software can create custom barcodes for use with its products or to classify items used within its organization, such as client or employee files, computers, office equipment, sales receipts, and more. The most popular barcode for these types of nonfood use is Code 39, which can encode both letters and numbers. Examples of a UPC code, Code 39 barcode, and POSTNET code (used by the U.S. Postal Service to represent a ZIP or postal code for sorting purposes) are shown in Figure 4-11.

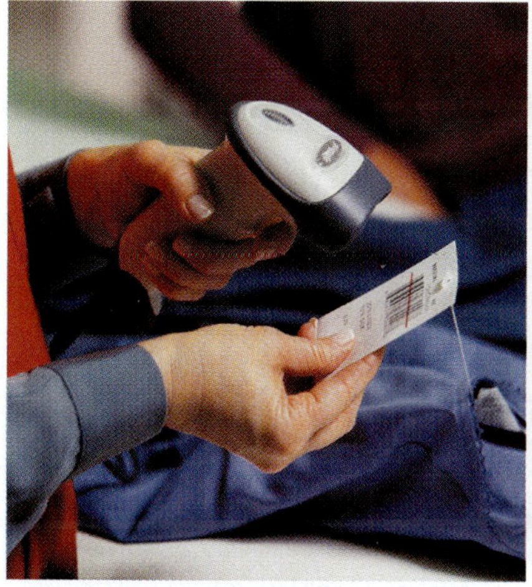

FIXED BARCODE READERS
Used most often in retail point-of-sale applications.

PORTABLE BARCODE READERS
Used when portability is needed.

INTEGRATED BARCODE READERS
Built into or added to portable PCs.

BARCODES
Uniquely identify a product or other item.

UPC (UNIVERSAL PRODUCT CODE)

CODE 39

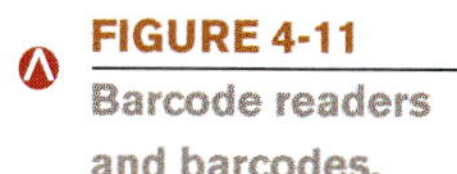

POSTNET CODE

FIGURE 4-11
Barcode readers and barcodes.

Radio Frequency Identification (RFID) Readers

Radio frequency identification (RFID) is a technology that can store and transmit data located in **RFID tags**. RFID tags, which contain tiny chips and radio antennas, can be attached to objects that need to be tracked. Many RFID tags today are *passive*, which require a reader to "wake them up" so they can broadcast data; *active RFID tags* include a battery, so they broadcast data on a continual basis. Some RFID applications already in use include tracking the movement of inventory pallets and shipping containers, tracking or locating livestock and other animals, and tagging tractors and other large assets to keep

>**Radio frequency identification (RFID).** A technology used to store and transmit data located in RFID tags. >**RFID tag.** A device containing tiny chips and radio antennas that is attached to objects that will be identified using RFID technology.

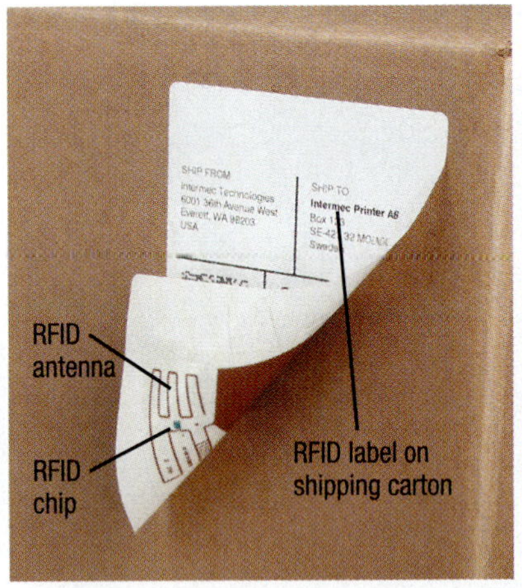

RFID TAGS
RFID tags, containing a built-in chip and an antenna, are often included in shipping labels today.

RFID READERS
This portal RFID reader reads all of the RFID tags on a palette at one time, as it passes between the readers.

FIGURE 4-12
RFID readers and tags.

track of their locations. Recently, the Department of Defense, Wal-Mart, Target, and a number of other major retailers across the globe began requiring suppliers to start using RFID tags on delivered items, the Social Security Administration (SSA) is beginning to use RFID tags to track orders for SSA forms and pamphlets, and the FDA has recommended the use of RFID tags for prescription drugs to prevent counterfeiting. In addition, Delta Air Lines has been testing RFID luggage tags with amazing results—baggage tagged with RFID tags arrived at the proper destination nearly 100% of the time, whereas barcoded luggage typically arrived with only 80% to 85% accuracy. RFID is also extensively used by the military, primarily for asset tracking, although the technology is also being used to track wounded soldiers, civilians, and POWs (via wristbands with built-in RFID chips) in at least one Navy hospital located in the Iraqi desert. The U.S. Army is also installing RFID tags on military vehicles located in Iraq to allow convoys to be tracked (via the tags and GPS technology), and redirected, if necessary.

Unlike barcode systems, data can be stored in an RFID tag before it is attached and that data can be updated via the antenna after the tag is attached to its designated item—for instance, to record information about the product's origin, shipping history, or final destination. RFID tags are also read by radio waves, instead of by light. This is an advantage over barcodes because radio waves do not require line of sight, can be read from a distance of up to 15 feet if an *ultra-high frequency RFID tag* is used, and can pass through materials such as cardboard and plastic. These characteristics enable all the RFID tags attached to all items located inside a shipping container to be read at one time as the container passes by a *portal RFID reader* or is picked up by an *RFID-enabled forklift* (an RFID tag and portal RFID reader are shown in Figure 4-12). RFID-equipped products and store shelves can even keep track of inventory, automatically reorder products (according to ordering criteria previously set up) when supplies run low, notify employees when items need restocking or wind up in the wrong aisle, and help employees quickly find recalled products.

RFID is also being used in conjunction with several types of electronic payment systems. Special key fobs or wands containing RFID chips allow customers to pay for gas or fast food by waving the wand close to a special reader (for security purposes, *high-frequency RFID chips* are used in electronic payment applications, so the wand has to be within a few inches of the reader), and the purchase amount is automatically deducted from a checking account or charged to a credit card, depending on the customer's preference when registering to use the RFID payment system. Some credit cards—such as Chase's *Blink* cards—are also RFID-enabled, allowing consumers to more quickly authorize credit card transactions by simply waving the card in front of a special reader. An increasing number of U.S. highways are using RFID tags placed on cars for automatic toll collection. Singapore has gone a step further by using the RFID tags to collect different toll prices at different times of the day, in the hope that this will encourage drivers to stay off busy roads during rush times.

For a closer look at how RFID technology works and a peek at its possible future, see the Inside the Industry box, beginning on page 150.

Optical Mark Readers (OMRs)

Optical mark readers (*OMRs*) input data from special forms to score or tally exams, questionnaires, ballots, and so forth. Typically, users use a pencil to fill in small circles or other shapes on the form to indicate their selections, and then the forms are inserted into an optical mark reader (see Figure 4-13) to be scored or tallied. Filled-in responses reflect the light, and those responses are recorded by the OMR. If it is an exam or some other type of objective instrument, a form containing the correct responses is input first, and then the OMR can indicate any wrong answers and print the total correct on each exam form; surveys and other subjective forms are usually just tallied and the results printed on a tally sheet. In either case, the results can be input to a computer system, or the data can be stored on a disk or other storage medium, if the optical mark reader is connected to a computer.

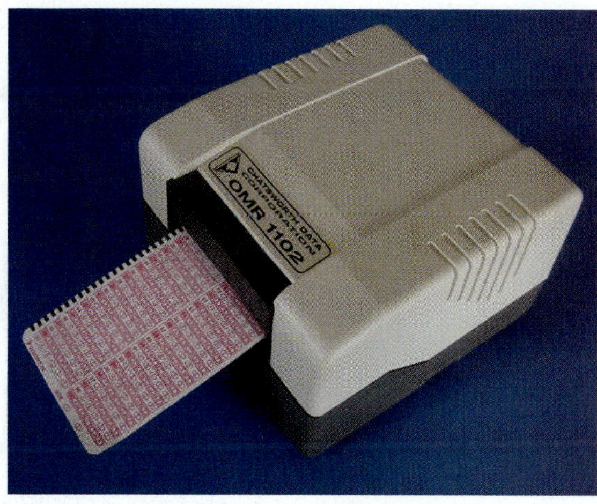

FIGURE 4-13
Optical mark readers. OMR readers are commonly used to score tests and tally questionnaires.

Optical Character Recognition (OCR) Devices

Optical characters are characters specifically designed to be identifiable by humans as well as by some type of *optical character recognition* (*OCR*) device. Optical characters conform to a certain font design, such as the one shown in Figure 4-14. The optical reader shines light on the characters and converts the reflections into electronic patterns that the machine can recognize. The OCR device can identify a character only if it is familiar with the font used. Today, most machines are designed to read several standard OCR fonts, even when these fonts are mixed in a single document.

Optical characters are widely used in processing *turnaround documents*, such as the monthly bills for credit card, utility, and cable-TV companies (see Figure 4-14 for a sample utility bill that uses OCR fonts). These documents contain optical characters in certain places on the bill to aid processing when consumers send it back with payment—or "turn it around." Sometimes it is easy to spot the optical characters on a document. Today, however, many OCR fonts look so much like normal text that it is hard for an ordinary person to tell which parts the computer system can read and which parts it cannot.

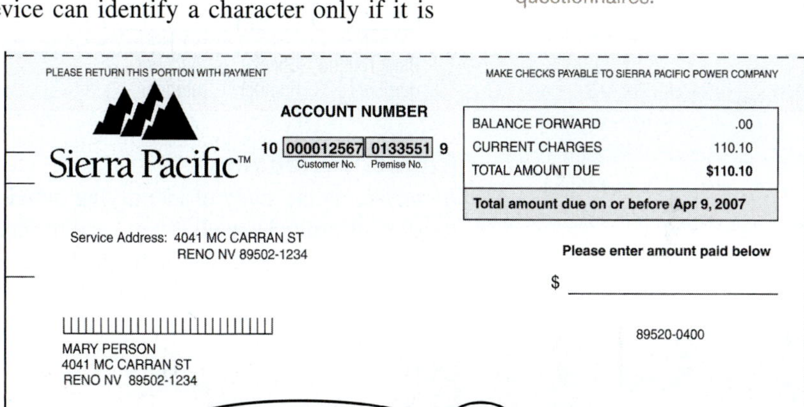

PLEASE RETURN THIS PORTION WITH PAYMENT

MAKE CHECKS PAYABLE TO SIERRA PACIFIC POWER COMPANY

Sierra Pacific™

ACCOUNT NUMBER
10 000012567 0133551 9
Customer No. Premise No.

BALANCE FORWARD	.00
CURRENT CHARGES	110.10
TOTAL AMOUNT DUE	$110.10
Total amount due on or before Apr 9, 2007	

Service Address: 4041 MC CARRAN ST
RENO NV 89502-1234

Please enter amount paid below
$

89520-0400

MARY PERSON
4041 MC CARRAN ST
RENO NV 89502-1234

10000012567013355190000011010 0000011010 0 007

OPTICAL CHARACTERS
These OCR characters indicate the customer account number and amount due and can be read by both computers and humans.

FIGURE 4-14
Optical characters. The most common use of optical characters is in turnaround documents, such as on the utility bill shown here.

Magnetic Ink Character Recognition (MICR) Readers

Magnetic ink character recognition (*MICR*) is a technology confined primarily to the banking industry, where it is used to facilitate high-volume processing of checks. Figure 4-15 illustrates a check encoded with MICR characters and a reader/sorter that processes such checks. The standard font adopted by the banking industry contains only 14 characters—the 10 decimal digits (0 through 9) and four special symbols. MICR characters are inscribed on checks with magnetic ink by a special machine. As people write and cash checks, the recipients deposit them in the banking system. At banks, reader/sorter machines magnetically read and identify the MICR-encoded bank and account information on the check, magnetically encode the amount of the check onto the check, and sort the checks. Images of the checks can then be captured and routed to the appropriate bank for processing.

FIGURE 4-15
Magnetic ink character recognition (MICR).

MICR READER
This device that reads and sorts checks and other MICR-encoded documents can process around 500 documents per minute (dpm); faster units can process up to 2,000 dpm.

MICR-ENCODED CHECK
MICR characters on the bottom of the check respectively identify the bank, check number, account number, and check amount. The characters on the left are put on when checks are preprinted; the numbers representing the check amount are added when the check is cashed.

FIGURE 4-16
Biometric readers. Biometric readers can be either stand-alone (left) or built into another piece of hardware (right).

Biometric Readers

Biometrics is the study of identifying individuals based on measurable biological characteristics. **Biometric readers** are used to input biometric data about a person into a computer system so that the individual can be identified based on a particular unique physiological characteristic (such as a fingerprint, hand geometry, face, or iris of the eye) or personal trait (such as a voice or signature). Emerging biometric readers can identify individuals by their skin, gait, or the veins in their hand. As shown in Figure 4-16, a biometric reader can be stand-alone or built into another piece of hardware, such as a keyboard or mouse. Some handheld computers, notebook PCs, and storage devices (such as external hard drives and flash memory drives) today have built-in fingerprint readers to allow only authorized users access to the PC or data stored on the device. Biometric input devices are increasingly being used to restrict access to facilities or computer systems, authorize electronic payments, log on to

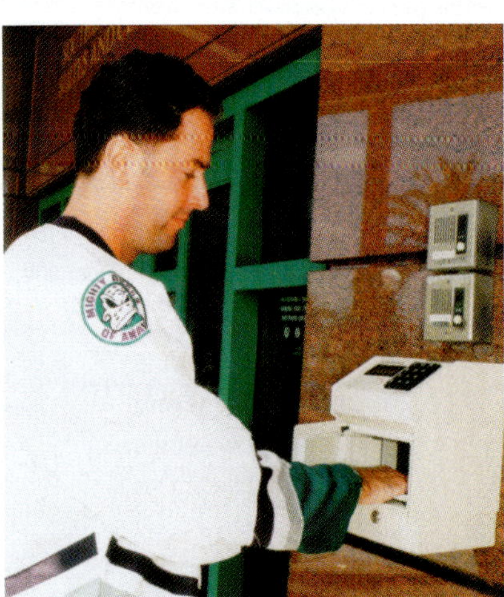

STAND-ALONE HAND GEOMETRY READER
Often used for access control, such as to authenticate NHL Mighty Ducks players at the Anaheim Pond arena shown here.

BUILT-IN FINGERPRINT READER
Often used for access control or to authorize electronic financial transactions.

>**Biometric reader.** A device used to input biometric data.

secure Web sites, punch in and out of work, and more. Biometrics for access control is covered in more detail in Chapter 9.

HW

Digital Cameras

Digital cameras work much like conventional film cameras, but instead of recording images on film they record them on some type of digital storage medium, such as a flash memory card, digital tape cartridge, or DVD disc. Digital cameras are usually designated either as *still* cameras (which take individual still photos) or *video* cameras (which capture moving video images). Many still cameras can take a limited amount of video, and many video cameras can capture still images, but the quality may not be as good. This may change in the future, however, as digital camera manufacturers begin to design digital cameras that incorporate both capabilities. For example, Samsung's DuoCam digital camera, released in 2005, contains the technology (including two separate lenses) to take both high-quality still photos and high-quality video.

Digital Still Cameras

Digital still cameras are available in a wide variety of sizes and capabilities. For instance, you can get an inexpensive (less than $100) consumer stand-alone, point-and-shoot model; a professional digital camera with removable lenses; a *digital camera watch*; or a digital camera integrated into your handheld PC or mobile phone (see Figure 4-17). The primary appeal of digital still cameras is that the images are immediately available for viewing or printing, instead of having the film developed first. Digital still cameras typically use flash memory for storage, in the form of either removable flash memory cards or built-in flash memory chips. The number of digital photos that can be stored in the camera at one time depends on the capacity of the storage medium being used and the resolution of the photos being taken (many cameras let you select the resolution to be used). At any time, the photos can be transferred to a PC or printer, usually by removing the flash memory card and inserting it into the PC or printer, by connecting the camera to a PC via a cable, or by attaching the camera to a special docking station attached to the printer or PC. Once the photos have been transferred to a PC, they can be retouched with image editing software, saved, printed, posted to a Web page, or burned onto a CD or DVD disc, just like any other digital image. The images on the storage medium can be deleted at any time to make room for more photos.

FIGURE 4-17
Digital still cameras. Digital still cameras, which record images on digital media instead of on film, are available in many shapes and sizes.

PROFESSIONAL DIGITAL CAMERA

PREVIEWS
Virtually all digital cameras let you display and erase images while shooting.

STORAGE MEDIA
Some cameras use removable storage media in addition to, or instead of, built-in storage.

TYPICAL CONSUMER DIGITAL CAMERA

DIGITAL CAMERA INTEGRATED INTO A MOBILE PHONE

>**Digital camera.** An input device that takes pictures and records them as digital data (instead of film or videotaped) images.

INSIDE THE INDUSTRY

RFID

RFID is a technology that uses radio waves to automatically identify objects. The RFID chip inside an RFID tag stores information about the object to which it is attached. One of the fastest-growing RFID applications is to identify retail goods. RFID tags can be made in a variety of shapes and sizes, including tags designed to be attached to end products, shipping palettes, and shipping labels (see the accompanying figure). Whenever an RFID-tagged item is within range of an RFID reader, the tag's built-in antenna allows the information located within the RFID chip to be sent to the reader. For supply chain applications, additional information can be stored in the RFID chip during the life of the product–such as manufacturing and origin data, shipping time, and the temperature range the item has been exposed to–which can be read at the final destination.

To use RFID as a replacement for barcodes, a unique identifying product code referred to as an *Electronic Product Code* (*EPC*) is typically assigned to each product and stored in its RFID tag. This code, currently in its second generation of development, can be used in conjunction with a database to determine additional product information, such as the pricing information needed in order for the RFID tag to be used at checkout. Because RFID technology can read numerous items at one time, it is possible that, someday, *low-frequency RFID tags* (tags with a reading range of approximately 3 feet) will be used to allow consumers to shop, bag their items, and have all the items rung up at the checkout station at one time.

Despite all its advantages, there are a number of privacy and security issues that need to be resolved before RFID gains widespread use at the consumer end. Precautions against fraudulent use–such as using high-frequency tags that need to be within a few inches of the reader and requiring a PIN code, signature, or other type of authorization when an RFID payment system is used–are being developed. Privacy advocates are concerned about linking RFID tag data with personally-identifiable data contained in corporate databases, as well as the possibility of using RFID tags to track the movements or shopping habits of consumers. A proposed solution to the latter concern is to allow consumers to either remove or deactivate a tag after purchase so it can no longer be read. In the meantime, at least two states have introduced legislation to place limits on the use of RFID technology.

TIP

When comparing the zoom capabilities of a digital camera, look for *optical zoom*, not *digital zoom*, specifications. Optical zoom specifications reflect how much the camera can zoom without losing image quality.

One factor affecting digital camera quality is the number of pixels (measured in *megapixels* or millions of pixels) used to store the data for each image. Today's cameras are typically between 2 and 12 megapixels. Although other factors—such as the quality of the lens and the technology used inside the camera to capture and process images—also affects the quality of digital photographs, the number of pixels does impact how large the digital photos can be printed. For instance, a 2-megapixel camera can produce 4-inch by 6-inch prints; to print high-quality 8-by-10-inch prints, a 3- or 4-megapixel camera is needed.

1. RFID tags are created in various formats and attached to end products, shipping cartons, or other items to be tracked. Some tags, such as the ones on the orange crates shown here, are reusable; others, such as the ones shown on the shipping label and tire, are designed to be disposable.

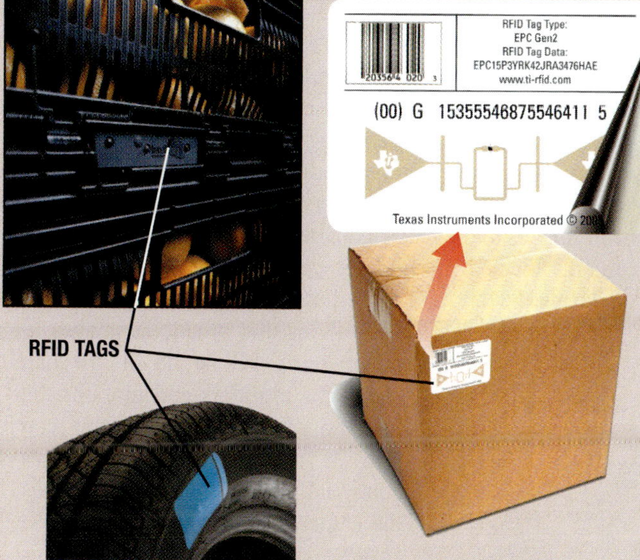

2. Data is stored in the RFID tag when the tag is created or attached and then can be updated as needed during the life of the product. Tags can be read automatically as palettes move through portal RFID readers or are lifted by RFID-enabled forklifts to keep track of products during shipping and to receive them easily into inventory at the final destination.

3. At the final destination, product history can be read and products can be restocked and reordered when supplies run low. If reusable RFID tags or RFID-tagged shipping containers are used (such as the orange crates shown here), they are cleaned and returned to the grower or supplier.

4. In the future, retail stores may use RFID-enabled checkout systems to ring up all of the products in a shopping cart at one time.

Some digital cameras today are Wi-Fi enabled, so digital photos can be e-mailed to others directly from the camera. Another recent improvement in digital cameras is a decrease in the delay between when the user presses the button and when the camera takes the photo, which is especially important when taking action shots. Although not yet as quick as conventional film cameras, the delay typically associated with digital cameras is continually being made shorter. Consumer digital cameras start at about $100; professional digital cameras cost $1,000 or more.

FURTHER EXPLORATION

For links to further information about digital cameras and digital photography, go to www.course.com/uc11/ch04

Digital Video Cameras

Digital video cameras include *digital camcorders* and small *PC video cameras* (see Figure 4-18). Digital camcorders are similar to conventional *analog* camcorders, but they store images on digital media—typically either on mini digital video (DV) tape cartridges or rewritable DVDs, although hard drive digital camcorders are now available. Once the video is recorded, it can be transferred to a PC, edited with software as needed, and saved to a DVD or other type of storage medium.

PC video cameras—commonly called PC cams—are designed to transmit video images over the Internet, such as during a *videoconference* or *video phone call*. Although video phone calls can be one-way (with only one person sending video and only one person receiving it), usually during a videoconference each person has a PC video camera attached to his or her PC to transmit images to the participant, as in Figure 4-18. Some one-way applications include PC cameras located in childcare centers that allow parents to watch live video of their children during the day, and surveillance cameras set up in homes and offices that broadcast images to the owner's PC so he or she can check for intruders and monitor the location remotely. PC cameras can also be used to broadcast images continually to a Web page, such as the cameras frequently found in zoo animal exhibits, on top of mountains, or other locations of interest to the general public. In this type of application, the video camera is referred to as a *Web cam*.

Digital video cameras can also be used for identification purposes, such as with face recognition technology to authorize access to a secure facility or computer resource. These and other types of security applications are discussed in more detail in Chapter 9.

DIGITAL CAMCORDER
Typically allows you to view video during and after it is recorded; digital media, such as the DVD shown here, are used for storage instead of videotape.

Video camera

PC VIDEO CAMERA
Commonly used to deliver video over the Internet, such as in the family videoconference shown here.

FIGURE 4-18
Digital video cameras. Common types include digital camcorders and PC video cameras.

AUDIO INPUT

Audio input is the process of entering audio data into the computer. Types of audio input include voice and music.

Voice Input Systems

A system used to input spoken words and convert them to digital form is known as a **voice input system**. All voice input systems (also called *speech recognition systems* and *voice recognition systems*) consist of a *microphone* or *headset* (a set of *headphones* with a built-in microphone) and appropriate software, such as *IBM ViaVoice* or *ScanSoft NaturallySpeaking*. Voice input can also be used to dictate text or commands the computer will recognize, as an

>**Voice input system.** A system that enables a computer to recognize the human voice.

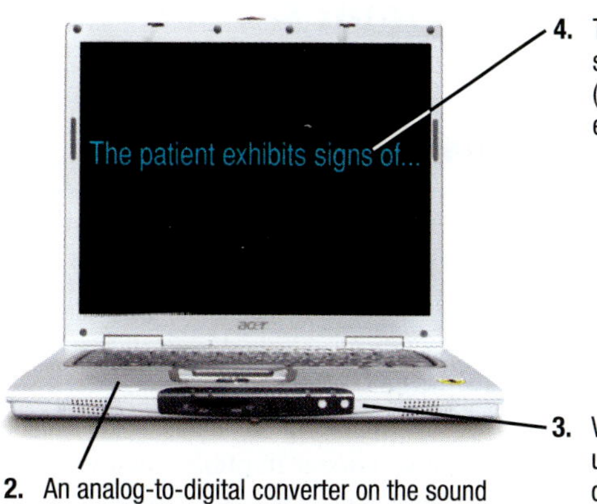

1. The user speaks into a microphone that cancels out background noise and inputs the speech into the computer.

2. An analog-to-digital converter on the sound card located inside the PC converts the spoken words to phonemes, the fundamental sounds in the language being used, and digitizes them.

3. Voice recognition software matches up the phoneme combinations to determine the words that were spoken. Sentence structure rules are used to select one word if it is a questionable match or a word with a homonym.

4. The spoken words appear on the screen in the application program (such as a word processor or an e-mail program) being used.

FIGURE 4-19
How a voice input system works.

alternative to mouse or keyboard input. Voice input systems are used by individuals who cannot use a keyboard, as well as by individuals who prefer not to use a keyboard or who can generate input faster via a voice input system. For instance, medical and legal transcription is the most frequently used voice input application at the present time. Voice input systems are also increasingly being incorporated into portable PCs, mobile devices, cells phones, GPS systems, and so on for hands-free operation. Specialty voice recognition systems are also used to control machines, robots, and other electronic equipment, such as by surgeons during surgical procedures.

Here's a quick look at how a typical voice input system might work (see Figure 4-19). First, a microphone is used to input the spoken words into the PC, and then the sounds are broken into digital representations of *phonemes*—the basic elements of speech, such as *duh*, *aw*, and *guh* for the word "dog." (The English language contains about 50 phonemes.) Next, the voice recognition software analyzes the content of the speech to convert the phonemes to words. Once words are identified, they are displayed on the screen. If a match is questionable or a homonym is encountered (such as the choice between "their," "there," and "they're"), the program analyzes the context in which the word is used in an attempt to identify the correct word. If the program inserts an inappropriate word while converting the user's voice input to text, the user can usually override it. To increase accuracy, most voice recognition software can be trained by individual users to allow the program to become accustomed to the user's speech patterns, voice, accent, and pronunciation.

FIGURE 4-20
A combination PC/MIDI keyboard.

Music Input Systems

Musical input can be recorded for use in music arrangements, to accompany a multimedia presentation, or to create a custom music CD. Music can be input into a PC via a CD, a DVD, or a Web download. For original compositions, a *MIDI* (*musical instrument digital interface*) device, such as a MIDI keyboard with piano keys instead of, or in addition to, alphanumeric keys (see Figure 4-20), can be used. Once the music is input into the computer, it can be saved, modified, played, inserted into other programs, or burned onto a CD or DVD, as necessary.

DISPLAY DEVICES

A **display device**—the most common form of output device—presents output visually, such as on some type of computer screen. Because the output appears temporarily on a display device, it is sometimes referred to as *soft copy*. The display device for a desktop PC is more formally called a **monitor**. With all-in-one PCs, notebook computers, handheld PCs, and other devices for which the screen is built into the unit, the term **display screen** is often used instead. In addition to being used with computers, display screens are also built into home entertainment devices, *portable media players* (which play music, videos, and other multimedia content), *digital picture frames* (which display images uploaded via a PC or cell phone), remote controls, gaming devices, and other consumer products (see Figure 4-21). Display devices also appear in public locations in the form of electronic *e-paper* signs (see the How it Works box), on kiosks, and to target advertising to consumers when they are waiting in a check-out line, riding in an elevator or taxi, in the restroom, or some other location where they are captive for a few minutes—a trend referred to as *captive marketing*.

Display Device Characteristics

There are several characteristics and features that differentiate one type of display device from another. The following sections discuss a few of the most significant characteristics.

FIGURE 4-21
Uses for displays.

COMPUTERS

SMART PHONES

HOME ELECTRONICS

PORTABLE MEDIA PLAYERS

DIGITAL PICTURE FRAMES

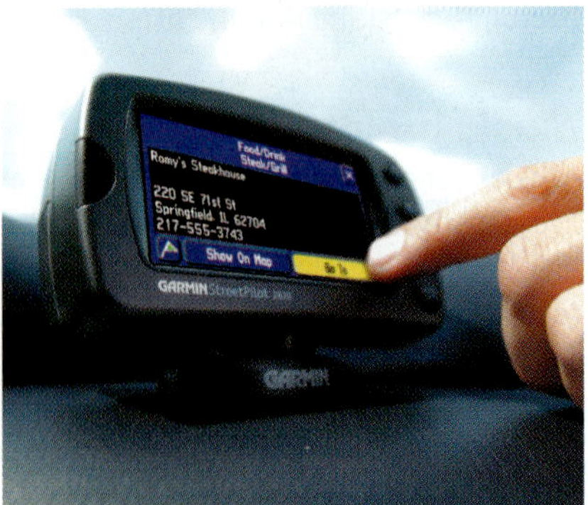

CAR NAVIGATION SYSTEMS

>**Display device.** An output device that contains a viewing screen. >**Monitor.** A display device for a desktop PC. >**Display screen.** A display device built into a notebook computer, handheld PC, or other device.

Color vs. Monochrome Displays

Display devices form images by lighting up the proper configurations of *pixels*. *Monochrome displays* use only two colors (usually black and white or black and green) and are not commonly used today as monitors although they still appear on some consumer products. *Color displays* are the norm and form colors by mixing combinations of only three colors—red, green, and blue (see Figure 4-22). When a display device blends red, green, and blue light of varying intensities, it can produce an enormous spectrum of colors.

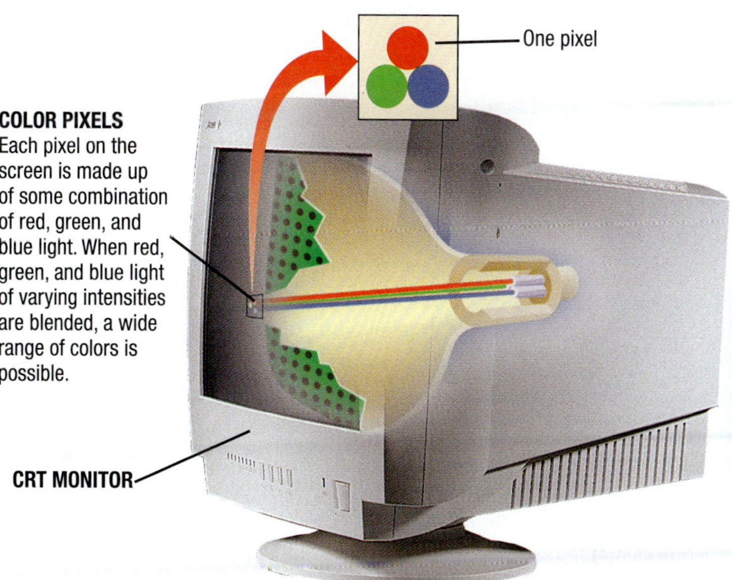

FIGURE 4-22
A color CRT monitor.

CRT vs. Flat-Panel Monitors

The traditional type of monitor for a desktop PC is the **CRT monitor**, such as the one shown in Figures 4-22. CRTs use *cathode-ray tube* technology to display images, so they are large, bulky, and heavy like conventional televisions. To form images on the screen of a CRT monitor, an electron gun sealed inside a large glass tube fires at a phosphor-coated screen to light up the appropriate pixels in the appropriate color to display the images, similar to a conventional television. Because the phosphors glow for only a limited amount of time, the monitor image must be redrawn (*refreshed*) on a continual basis, relighting each pixel in the appropriate color—typically this occurs between 60 and 85 times per second.

Thinner and lighter *flat-panel displays* form images by manipulating electronically charged chemicals or gases sandwiched between thin panes of glass (or other transparent material) instead of firing a bulky electron gun (flat-panel technology is discussed in more detail shortly). Flat-panel displays are almost always used on portable computers and mobile devices, and they are frequently also used with desktop PCs. In fact, the sale of flat-panel monitors surpassed that of CRT monitors for the first time in 2004, and, according to the research firm IDC, flat-panel monitors are expected to make up about 80% of the display market by 2007. Flat-panel monitors have the advantage of taking up less desk space and consuming less power, although the images displayed on a flat-panel display sometimes cannot be seen clearly when viewed from certain angles. As shown in Figure 4-23, the smaller footprint of a flat-panel display makes it possible to use multiple monitors working together to increase the amount of data the user can view at one time.

Another difference between CRT monitors and flat-panel displays is that most flat-panel displays use digital signals to display images, while CRT monitors use analog signals. Digital signals allow for much sharper images.

FIGURE 4-23
Flat-panel displays.
The smaller footprint of a flat-panel display makes it possible to use multiple monitors together to increase productivity.

>**CRT monitor.** A display device that projects images onto a display screen using a technology similar to the one used with conventional TVs.

HOW IT WORKS

E-Paper

Electronic paper (*e-paper*) consists of a display device onto which written content is displayed in electronic form, but that is thinner and more paper-like than other types of display devices. E-paper products are being developed by a number of companies, such as Gyricon Media, Xerox, and E Ink. Practical applications for e-paper from an environmental standpoint include any documents that only need to be kept for a short time, such as newspapers and retail display signs. Instead of being discarded when their useful life has ended, e-paper versions of these documents could be erased and then reused.

Electronic paper is becoming a viable replacement for some traditional paper and ink applications. For instance, one of the first areas in which e-paper has been applied is retail signs, such as those found in department stores and other retail establishments, as well as hotels, conference centers, schools, and more. These *e-signs* look like ordinary paper signs, but their text can be changed wirelessly (two examples of e-signs are included in the accompanying photographs). Consequently, instead of continually having to print new paper signs, e-signs can be changed electronically to be reused, which saves the time and expense of printing, delivering, and setting up new signs, as well as the time, cost, and waste associated with disposing of the old ones. Their low power consumption means that e-signs can run off of battery power for an extended period of time without attention. Other retail applications currently in development include e-paper shelf price tags that can electronically communicate with the store's database to always display the current price, and newspaper dispenser boxes that are updated periodically during the day to reflect the latest headlines or a featured section of the newspaper.

So how does e-paper work? One type of e-paper technology uses two sheets of very thin transparent plastic with millions of very small beads sandwiched between them. Each bead is smaller than a grain of sand and sealed inside a tiny pocket surrounded by liquid (these beads and their liquid are sometimes referred to as *electronic ink* or *e-ink*). Each bead (see the close up photo of e-ink in the accompanying photos) has two colors—such as half white and half black—and can rotate within its pocket only when an electrical signal is received. To change the text or images displayed on the e-paper, electronic signals are sent to the e-paper via a wireless transmission. These electronic signals instruct each bead to rotate appropriately to display either its black side or white side in order to form the proper text and images, similar to the way pixels are used to display images on a monitor. The content remains displayed until another transmission changes the pattern, such as changing all the beads to display their white sides to "erase" the e-paper. Current e-paper products can be written to and erased electronically thousands of times, but in the near future that number is expected to increase to several million times.

As e-paper technology improves, it is expected that the e-paper will more easily support the smaller text needed for personal printouts. Types of e-paper expected in the future include regular-sized e-paper that can be inserted into a special computer printer to be printed electronically and then reused over and over again; regular and newspaper-sized e-papers that can wirelessly download new content from the Internet; and *e-books* that look and feel like real paper books, but whose content can be rewritten to display the content of a different book when directed by the user.

Improvements that need to be made before e-paper and other e-ink applications become more commonplace include color capabilities, lower cost, and increased life span, as well as thinner and more flexible e-paper. Future possibilities for e-ink include its use on billboards, T-shirts, and even paint for easy redecorating. *Conductive e-ink* currently in development can carry electricity after it is printed; conductive e-ink will potentially enable keyboards to be printed onto military uniform sleeves, light switches to be printed onto wallpaper, and radio circuitry and controls to be printed onto clothing and other everyday objects.

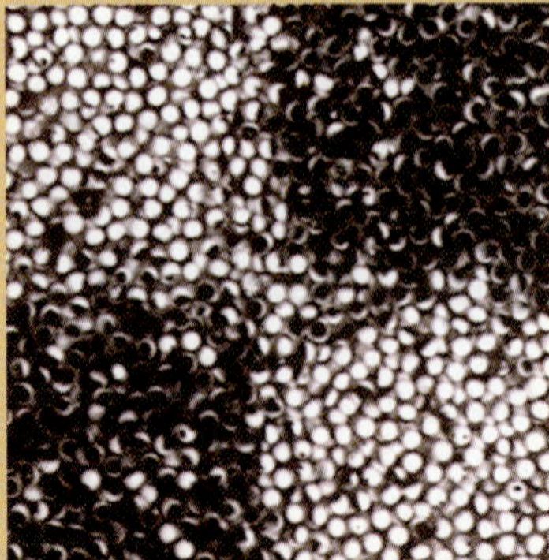

E-paper products, such as the e-signs shown here (right) are written electronically using tiny beads (left) and can be erased and rewritten over and over again.

Size

Monitor size is measured diagonally from corner to corner, similarly to the way TV screens are measured. It is important to realize, however, that the actual viewing area of a CRT monitor is almost always smaller than the stated monitor size. For example, one 17-inch monitor might have a *viewable image size* (*VIS*) of 16 inches, while another 17-inch monitor might have a viewable image size of 15.7 inches. Although 0.3 inches may not sound like much of a difference in size, small size variations can be noticeable and are important to keep in mind when comparing the quality and price of two CRT monitors (there typically is no difference between the stated size and the VIS of flat-panel displays). Most desktop PC monitors today are between 15 and 24 inches for desktop PCs; notebook and tablet displays are usually between 13 and 17 inches. To better view DVDs and other multimedia content, some monitors today are *widescreen displays*, which conform to the 16:9 aspect ratio of widescreen televisions, instead of the conventional 4:3 aspect ratio.

Screen Resolution

Regardless of the technology used, the screen of a display device is divided into a fine grid of small areas or dots—pixels. The number of pixels used on a display screen determines the *screen resolution*, which affects the amount of information that can be displayed on the screen at one time. When a high resolution is selected, such as 1,280 pixels horizontally by 1,024 pixels vertically (written as 1,280 × 1,024 and read as *1280 by 1024*), more information can fit on the screen, but everything will be displayed smaller than with a lower resolution, such as 800 × 600 or 1,024 × 768 (see Figure 4-24). The screen resolution on most computers today can be changed by users to match their preferences and the software being used (on Windows PCs, display options are changed using the Control Panel). Very high-resolution monitors are available for special applications, such as viewing digital X-rays.

FIGURE 4-24

Screen resolution. A higher screen resolution (measured in pixels) displays everything smaller than a lower screen resolution.

800 × 600

1,024 × 768

1,280 × 1,024

Video Cards and Ports

The video card or integrated video component built directly into the motherboard on a PC is used to connect a display device to the computer. The type of video card or component used determines such display characteristics as the screen resolutions available, the number of bits used to store color information about each pixel (called the *bit depth*), the total number of colors that can be used to display images, how many monitors can be connected to the PC, the types of connectors that can be used to connect the monitor to the PC, whether or not you can receive TV broadcasts or connect a digital video recorder (DVR) to the computer, and so forth.

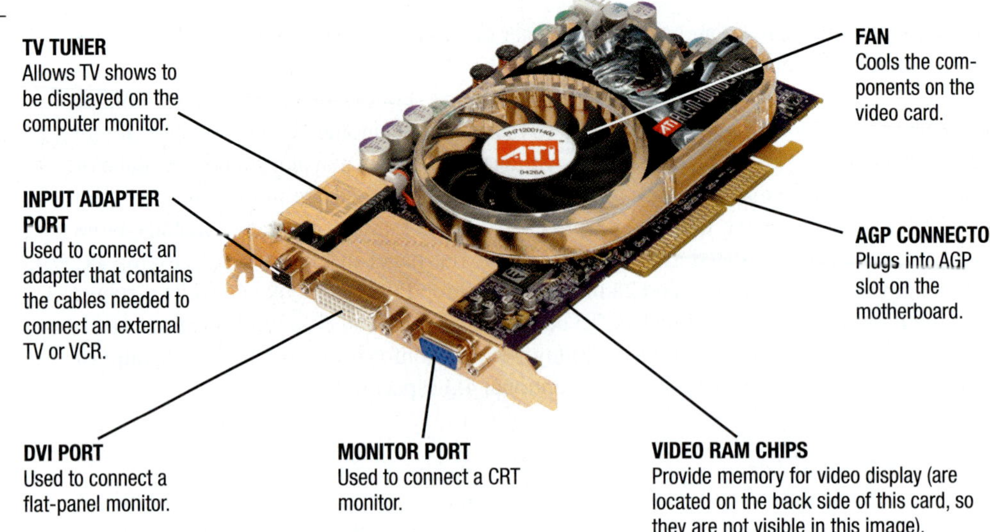

FIGURE 4-25
Video cards. Video cards provide a connection to a monitor, as well as determine video capabilities.

Video cards also contain memory chips (typically called *video RAM* or *VRAM*) to support graphics display, although some systems use a portion of the PC's regular RAM as video RAM instead. To support higher resolutions, higher bit depths, and a greater number of colors, a sufficient amount of video RAM is required. Most video cards today contain between 128 and 256 MB of video RAM.

CRT monitors typically connect to a video card via a conventional monitor port and connector. Flat-panel displays usually have the option of connecting via a *Digital Visual Interface* (*DVI*) port, if that port exists on the video card being used. A DVI connection allows the flat-panel monitor to receive digital signals directly from the computer, creating a clearer, more reliable signal than if the conventional monitor connection was used. For the video card shown in Figure 4-25, a monitor can connect via either a conventional monitor port or a DVI port. This video card also has a built-in TV tuner, which can be used to display TV shows as well as enable the computer to act as a digital video recorder (DVR). It also can connect to an external VCR or TV, has 256 MB of video RAM, can support screen resolutions of 640 × 480 up to 2,048 × 1,536, and can display screen images in true color (16.7 million colors).

Wired vs. Wireless Monitors

Most monitors today are *wired monitors*; that is, monitors that are physically connected to the system unit via a cable. Some monitors, however, are designed to be wireless. *Wireless monitors*—sometimes called *smart displays*—are portable monitors that are wirelessly connected to a desktop PC, so they can access that PC from anywhere within a home or office, as long as the monitor is within the required range of the PC. Although similar in appearance to a tablet PC, an important difference is the location of the computing hardware. Unlike a tablet PC, which contains all processing hardware inside the tablet and is independent of any other device, a smart display is designed to always be used in conjunction with its associated PC and cannot function independently when the PC is off or the monitor is too far away from the PC. Smart displays typically use a wireless *Wi-Fi* networking connection (discussed in more detail in Chapter 7) to connect the display to the system unit whenever both pieces of hardware are within range of the same wireless network. Wireless monitors often come with some type of stand or docking station. Typically, the mouse and keyboard attached to the docking station are used when the smart display is connected to its docking station, and touch or pen input is used when the smart display is undocked.

FURTHER EXPLORATION

For links to further information about display devices, go to www.course.com/uc11/ch04

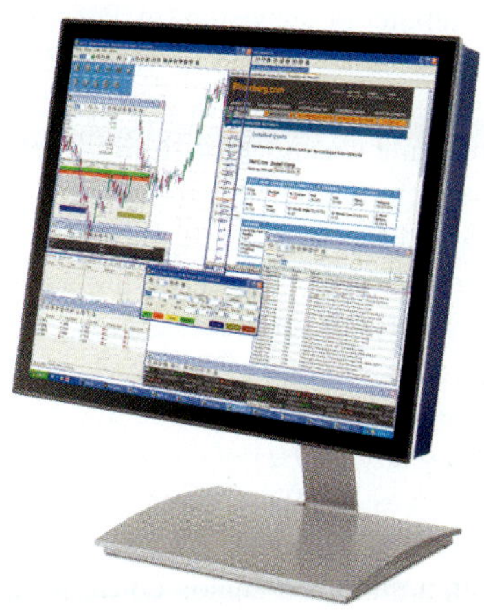

3D FLAT-PANEL DISPLAY
This 3D monitor uses multiple layers to display images in different depths at one time and can display input from more than one PC at one time.

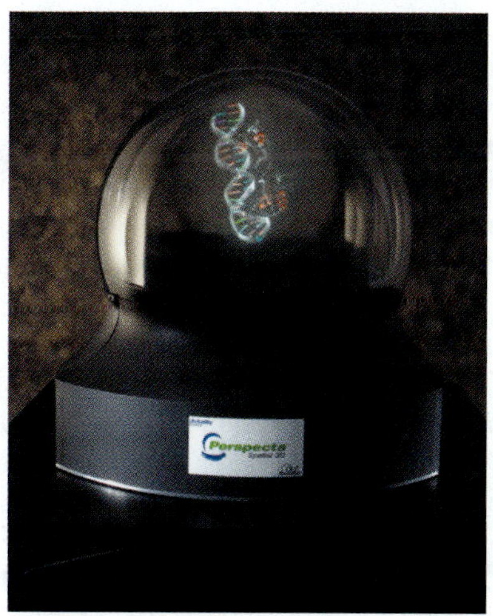

3D DOME DISPLAY
This 20-inch dome allows a 360° view of images, such as the DNA image shown here.

WEARABLE PERSONAL DISPLAY
The sunglasses shown here include a display screen that projects images: the images appear equivalent to those projected on a 14-inch monitor.

FIGURE 4-26
3D output devices.

2D vs. 3D Displays

Recent improvements in flat-screen display technology and graphics processing have led to several emerging *three-dimensional (3D)* output devices, including *3D display screens* for computers (see Figure 4-26), as well as cell phones, digital cameras, car navigation systems, and other small devices. Unlike traditional 3D applications that require special 3D glasses, the newest 3D products use filters, prisms, and other techniques to create the 3D effect using only the display screen. In addition to their appeal for games, movies, and other consumer PC applications, 3D displays are an important improvement for scientists, physicians, architects, and other professionals who routinely view detailed graphics or diagrams in the course of their work.

In addition to conventionally shaped and sized 3D displays, alternative 3D display shapes—such as the dome-shaped 3D display shown in Figure 4-26—are beginning to become available. *3D projectors*, such as those used to display *holograms*, are also in the works. In fact, researchers at Tokyo University have developed a holographic device that uses a 360-degree digital camera to scan a person's head and then that data can be sent over telephone lines to a special display device that projects a 3D image of the person. Another emerging display option is the *wearable personal display*, such as the display sunglasses shown in Figure 4-26. Similar to the *head-mounted displays* used by soldiers, surgeons, and other individuals who require a hands-free display while working, wearable personal displays project the image from a PC or other device with video output (such as a digital camera or portable DVD player) to a display screen located close to the eye, but the display screen is built into the glasses and the glasses are designed for personal use.

Digital TV and HDTV

Digital television (DTV) is a set of 18 broadcasting standards for delivering TV programming using digital signals, instead of conventional analog TV signals. In the United States, all commercial broadcasters are required today to broadcast some programs in digital form, but they must continue analog broadcasts until the end of 2006. At this time, analog broadcasts are scheduled to be replaced completely with digital broadcasts, but this deadline is expected to be extended in at least some areas of the United States until 85% of the homes in that area have TV sets capable of displaying digital TV programming.

In addition to increased quality, digital TV technology can also be used to transmit large amounts of other data into the home to be accessed via a computer or television set. Possibilities include *video-on-demand* (renting movies online that are downloaded to your PC or DVR instead of physically picking them up at a movie rental store) and *interactive TV* (television with some interactive activities that you can perform while watching the show). These applications, currently delivered via the Internet, are discussed in more detail in Chapter 8.

HDTV (*high-definition television*) is a high-resolution type of digital television that results in an even clearer, sharper picture than regular digital TV. Computer monitors and televisions that have a built-in HD tuner and can receive HDTV broadcasts today are referred to as *HD-capable* or *HD-integrated*. All TV sets that are sold after July 1, 2006 and are larger than 24" are required to have a built-in HD tuner, and it is expected that similar requirements will be set for computer monitors. *HD-ready* or *HD-compatible* computer monitors and TVs require an external HD source (such as an HD receiver or a cable or satellite set-top box containing an HD tuner) in order to receive digital TV broadcasts. To watch digital TV broadcasts on an older analog TV set, a digital-to-analog converter is required, and the quality will be analog quality.

TIP

The term *HDTV monitor* is another name for an HD-ready display device and does not refer to its ability to be used as a computer monitor.

Flat-Panel Display Technologies

Flat-panel displays form images by manipulating electronically charged chemicals or gases sandwiched between thin panes of glass instead of using a bulky electron gun like CRT monitors. The most common flat-panel technologies are *liquid crystal display* (*LCD*), *organic light emitting diode* (*OLED*), and *gas plasma*. Monitors using each of these technologies are shown in Figure 4-27.

Liquid Crystal Displays (LCDs)

A **liquid crystal display (LCD)** uses charged liquid crystals located between two sheets of clear material (usually glass or plastic) to light up the appropriate pixels to form the image on the screen. Several layers of liquid crystals are used, and, in their normal state, the liquid crystals are aligned so that light passes through the display. When an electrical charge is applied to the liquid crystals (via an electrode grid layer contained within the LCD panel), the liquid crystals change their orientation or "twist" so that light cannot pass through the display, and the liquid crystals at the charged intersections of the electrode grid

FIGURE 4-27
Flat-panel displays.

LCD DISPLAYS
The most common type of computer monitor and flat-panel television.

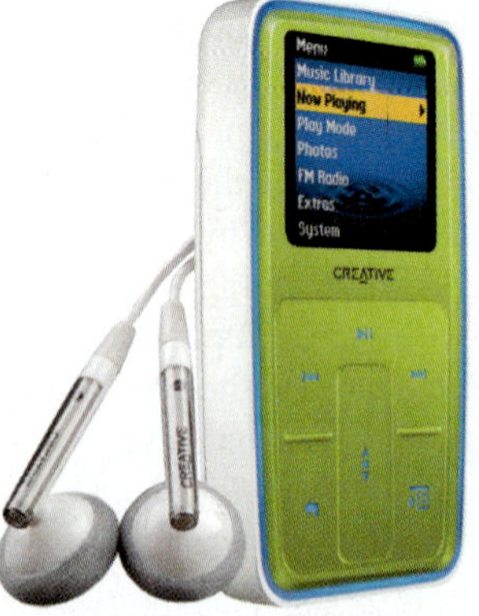

OLED DISPLAYS
Used primarily with smaller displays, like digital cameras and handheld PCs.

PLASMA DISPLAYS
Used primarily with large computer monitors and TVs.

>**Flat-panel display.** A slim type of display device that uses electronically charged chemicals or gases instead of an electron gun to display images. >**Liquid crystal display (LCD).** A type of flat-panel display that uses charged liquid crystals to display images.

appear dark. Color LCD displays use a color filter that consists of a pattern of red, green, and blue *subpixels* for each pixel, and the voltage used controls the orientation (twisting) of the liquid crystals and the amount of light that gets through, affecting the color and shade of that pixel—the three different colors blend to make the appropriate colored pixel.

Just as with other products (such as digital watches and appliances) that use LCD display technology, unless light is built into the display, it can be viewed only with reflective light. Consequently, LCD panels used with computer monitors typically include at least one fluorescent light inside the panel, usually at the rear of the display—a technique referred to as *backlighting*. LCDs are the most common type of flat-panel technology used for small- to medium-sized computer monitors (typically up to only about 23 inches). Larger flat-panel displays typically use another type of technology (such as *gas plasma* today) and it is expected that, someday, LCD monitors may be completely replaced by newer technologies, such as *OLED*, discussed next.

TIP

Display devices and printers designed for visually impaired PC users and other users with special needs are discussed in Chapter 16.

Organic Light Emitting Diode (OLED) Displays

Organic light emitting diode (OLED) displays also use layers, but there is a distinct difference between OLEDs and LCDs. While LCDs are *nonemissive*, which means they do not produce light and so they require backlighting, OLEDs use a layer of organic material which, when electric current is applied, emits a visible light. Therefore, OLEDs do not use backlighting, which makes them more energy efficient and lengthens the battery life of portable devices using OLED displays. In order to produce color output, there must be blue, red, and green organic material, as shown in Figure 4-28. In addition, there are other advantages of OLEDs over LCDs. For instance, OLEDs are even thinner (Samsung unveiled a 40-inch OLED television in 2005 that is only about one inch thick), they have a wider viewing angle visible from virtually all directions, and their images are brighter and sharper. OLED displays are beginning to be incorporated into digital cameras and mobile phones; over the next few years, their use is expected to be expanded to other portable consumer electronic devices, as well as car dashboard displays, television sets, and other products.

There are also a few special types of OLEDs, which lead to applications not possible with CRT or LCD technology. For instance, *flexible OLED (FOLED)* displays—a technology developed by Universal Display Corporation—are OLED displays built on flexible surfaces, such as plastic or metallic foil. Flexible displays using FOLED technology—such as displays that can roll up when not in use—are being developed by several companies. Other possible uses for flexible screens include making lighter desktop and portable PC monitors, enabling pullout displays

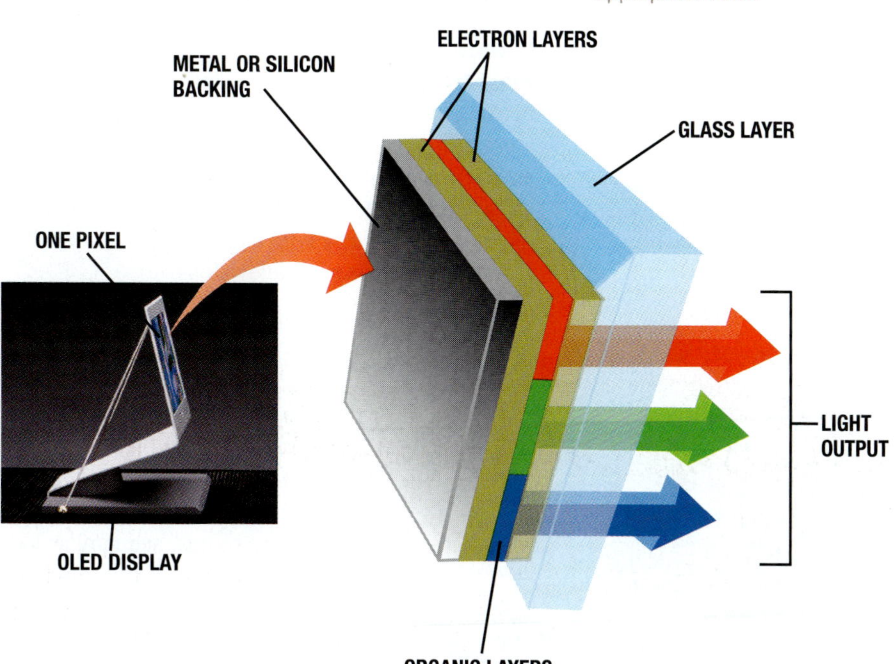

FIGURE 4-28

How OLED displays work. Each pixel on an OLED display emits light in the appropriate color.

>**Organic light emitting diode (OLED) display.** A type of flat-panel display that uses emissive organic material to display brighter and sharper images.

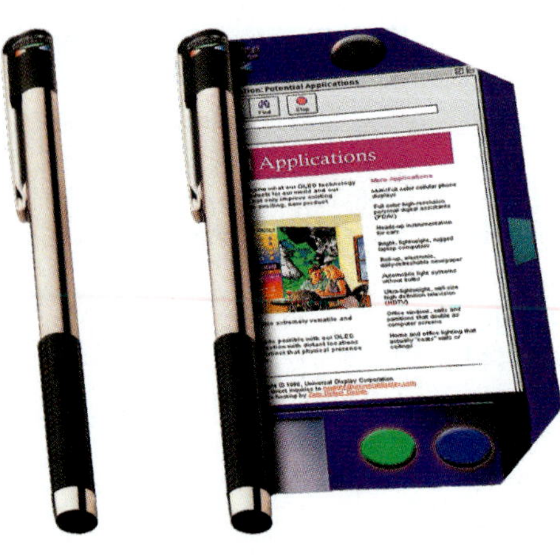

FOLEDS
Used to create flexible displays on plastic or another type of flexible material.

TOLEDS
Used to create transparent displays.

FIGURE 4-29
Special types of OLEDs.

(see Figure 4-29) to be used in conjunction with handheld PCs and mobile devices, integrating displays on military uniform sleeves, and allowing retractable wall-mounted big screen televisions and monitors. The flexibility of FOLED displays also adds to their durability, and their thinness makes FOLED technology extremely suitable for mobile devices.

Another form of OLED developed by Universal Display Corporation is *transparent OLED (TOLED)*. TOLED displays are transparent and can emit light towards the top and bottom of the display surface. The portion of the display that does not currently have an image displayed (and the entire display device when it is off) is nearly as transparent as glass, so the screen can be seen through (see Figure 4-29). TOLEDs open up the possibility of displays on home windows, car windshields, helmet face shields, and other transparent items. A third type of OLED is *Phosphorescent OLED* or *PHOLED*. The term *phosphorescence*, also referred to as *electrophosphorescence*, is a process that results in much more conversion of electrical energy into light instead of heat. When used with PHOLEDs, this process makes the efficiency of a PHOLED up to four times higher than a conventional OLED. Consequently, PHOLED technology is very appropriate for use on mobile devices, consumer electronics, and other devices where power consumption is an important concern.

Plasma Displays

Plasma displays use a layered technology like LCD and OLEDs, but they use a layer of gas between two plates of glass, instead of liquid crystals or organic material. Similar to CRTs, a phosphor-coated screen (with red, green, and blue phosphors for each pixel) is used, but an electron grid layer and electronic charges are used (as in LCD displays) to make the gas atoms light up the appropriate phosphors to create the image on the screen. Plasma technology is used primarily with larger displays (typically over 40 inches), such as large computer monitors and big screen televisions.

FIGURE 4-30
Data projectors. Data projectors are frequently used for both business and classroom presentations.

Data and Multimedia Projectors

A **data projector** connects to a computer, and any output that is sent to the computer monitor is also projected through the projector onto a wall or projection screen (see Figure 4-30). Most data projectors today (sometimes referred to as *data/video projectors*, *multimedia projectors*, or *digital projectors*) can project video, in addition to computer output. In classrooms, conference rooms, and similar locations, projectors are often permanently mounted onto the ceiling. Portable projectors are also available, either as freestanding units or small panels used in conjunction with a standard overhead projector. Portable projectors are commonly used for business presentations that occur out of the office. While most data projectors connect via cable to a PC, *wireless projectors* that use a Wi-Fi connection are available.

>**Plasma display.** A type of flat-panel display that uses layers of gas to display images; most often used on large displays. >**Data projector.** A display device that projects all computer output to a wall or projection screen.

PRINTERS

Instead of the temporary, ever-changing soft copy output that a monitor produces, **printers** produce *hard copy*; that is, a permanent copy of the output on paper. Most desktop PCs are connected to a printer; portable PCs can use printers as well.

Printer Characteristics

Printers differ in a number of important respects, such as the technology used, size, speed, and quality. Some general printer characteristics are discussed next, followed by a look at the most common types of printers.

Impact vs. Nonimpact Printing

Printers produce images through either impact or nonimpact technologies. *Impact printers*, like old ribbon typewriters, have a print mechanism that actually strikes the paper to transfer ink to the paper. For example, a *dot-matrix printer* uses a print head consisting of pins that strike an inked ribbon to transfer the ink to the paper. As illustrated in Figure 4-31, the appropriate pins are extended (and, consequently, strike the ribbon) as the print head moves in order to form the appropriate words or images. When the pins press into the ribbon, dots of ink are transferred onto the paper. Impact printers are primarily used today for producing multipart forms, such as invoices, packing slips, and credit card receipts.

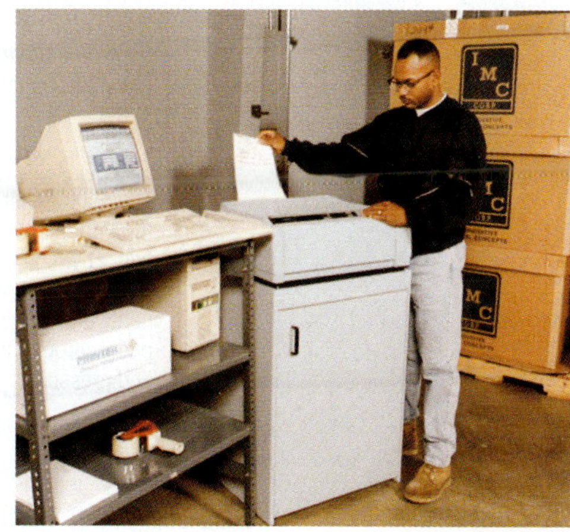

The extended pins print dots on the paper.

As the print head moves from left to right, specific pins are extended to form the text and images.

FIGURE 4-31
Dot-matrix printers. Dot-matrix printers are impact printers; today they are typically high-speed printers used in manufacturing, shipping, or similar applications.

Most printers today are *nonimpact printers*, meaning they form images without the print mechanism actually touching the paper. Nonimpact printers (such as the *laser* and *ink-jet printers* discussed shortly) usually produce higher-quality images and are much quieter than impact printers. Both impact and nonimpact printers form images with dots, similarly to the way monitors display images with pixels. Because of this, printers are very versatile and can print text in virtually any size, as well as print photos and other graphical images. In addition to paper, both impact and nonimpact printers can print on transparencies, envelopes, mailing labels, and more.

Color vs. Black and White

Both *color printers* and *blank-and-white printers* are available. Color printers work similarly to black-and-white printers, except they use at least four different colors of ink—cyan (blue), magenta (red), yellow, and black—instead of only black ink. Color printers either apply all of the colors in one pass, or they go through the entire printing process multiple times, applying one color during each pass. Color printers are often used in homes (to print photographs, greeting cards, flyers, and more); businesses may use black-and-white printers for output that does not need to be in color (since it is less expensive and faster to print in black and white) and color printers for output that needs to be in color.

>**Printer.** An output device that produces output on paper.

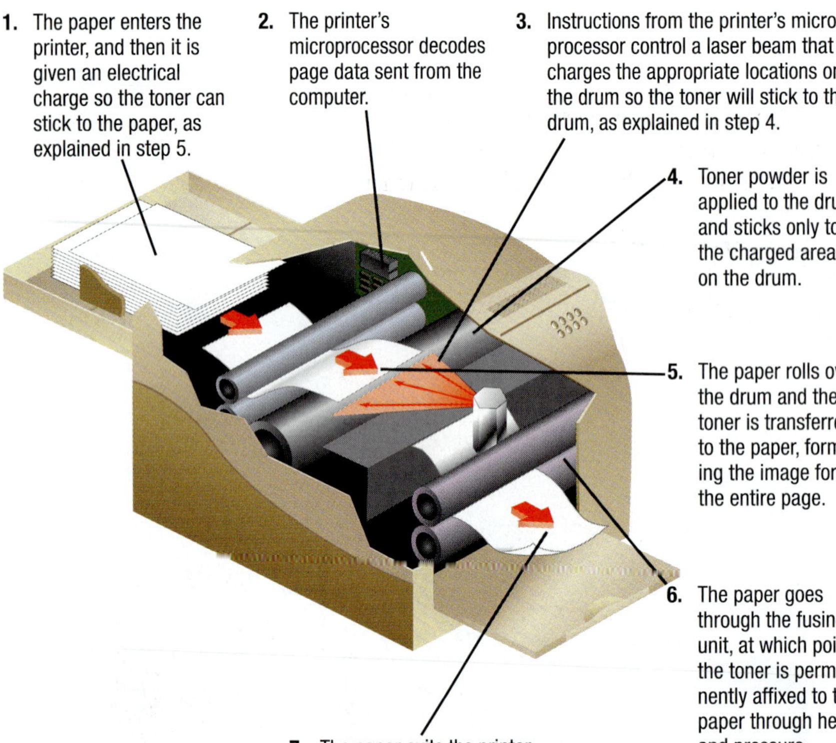

NETWORK LASER PRINTER

PERSONAL LASER PRINTER

FIGURE 4-32
How laser printers work.

TIP

To save money, consider buying *recharged* (refilled) toner cartridges when your laser printer cartridge runs out of toner powder. Recharged cartridges typically cost about one-third less than new cartridges and last at least as long.

Personal vs. Network Printers

Most printers found in homes and small businesses today are commonly referred to as *personal printers*—that is, printers designed to be connected to one computer and not shared with others. *Network printers*, in contrast, are printers designed to be shared by multiple users. Although multiple users can share a personal printer through a home or office network, network printers are specifically designed for high-volume, high-speed printing (both a personal printer and a network printer are shown in Figure 4-32), network printers are usually larger than personal printers, work up to about 10 times faster than personal printers, and cost anywhere from \$500 to \$10,000 or more. Some network printers are *line printers* (which print one line of text at a time), but most are *page printers* (which print a full page of output at a time). Some high-end network printers can also collate and staple.

Print Resolution

Most printing technologies today form images with dots of liquid ink or flecks of ink toner powder. The number of *dots per inch* (*dpi*)—called the *print resolution*—affects the quality of the printed output. Printers with a higher print resolution tend to produce sharper and cleaner text and images than printers with a lower resolution. Although other factors (such as the technology and number of colors used) affect the quality of a printout, guidelines for acceptable print resolution are typically 300 dpi for general-purpose printouts, 600 dpi for higher-quality documents, 1,200 dpi for photographs, and 2,400 dpi for professional applications.

Print Speed

Print speed is typically measured in *pages per minute* (*ppm*). How long it takes a document to print depends on the actual printer being used, the selected print resolution, and the content being printed. For instance, pages containing photographs or other images typically take longer to print than pages containing only text, and full-color pages take longer to print than black-and-white pages. Common speeds for personal printers today range from about 6 to 25 ppm; network printers typically print from 45 to 100 ppm.

Laser Printers

Laser printers are the standard for business documents and come in both personal and network styles. To print a document, the laser printer first uses a laser beam to charge the appropriate locations on a drum to form the page's image, and then *toner powder* (powdered ink) is released from a *toner cartridge* and sticks to the drum. The toner is then transferred to a piece of paper when the paper is rolled over the drum, and a heating unit fuses the toner powder to the paper to permanently form the image (see Figure 4-32). Laser printers print one entire page at a time and are typically faster and have better quality output than *ink-jet printers*, discussed next. Common print resolution for laser printers is between 600 and 2,400 dpi; speeds for personal laser printers range from about 6 to 25 ppm. Black-and-white laser printers start at about $150; color laser printers start at about $400.

Ink-Jet Printers

Ink-jet printers form images by spraying tiny drops of liquid ink onto the page, one printed line at a time (see Figure 4-33). Some printers print with one single-sized ink droplet; others print using different-sized ink droplets by using multiple nozzles or varying electrical charges for more precise printing. Because they are relatively inexpensive, have

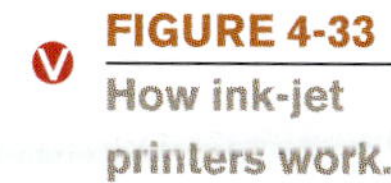

FIGURE 4-33
How ink-jet printers work.

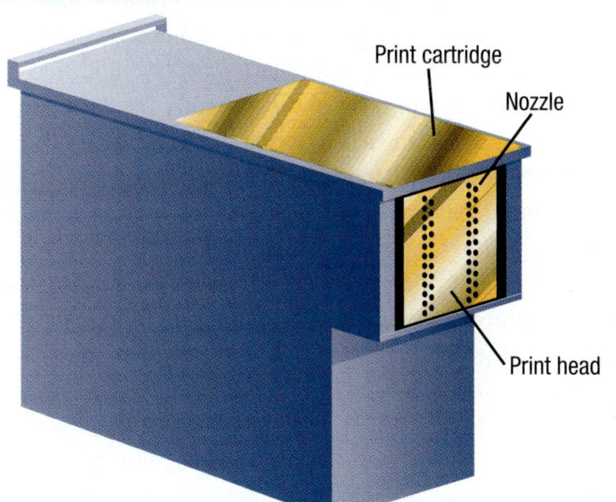

HOW INK-JET PRINTERS WORK
Color ink-jet printers create colors by mixing different combinations of four colors of ink—magenta, cyan, yellow, and black. The different colors can be in one or multiple cartridges. Each cartridge is made up of 300 or more tiny ink-filled firing chambers, each attached to a nozzle smaller than a human hair. To print images, the appropriate color ink is ejected through the appropriate nozzle.

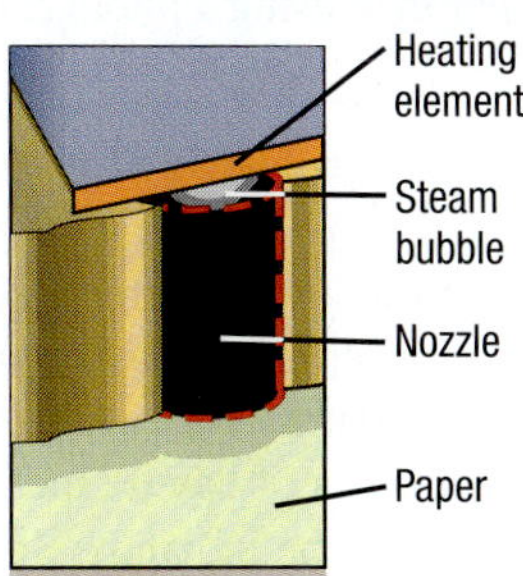

1. A heating element makes the ink boil, which causes a steam bubble to form.

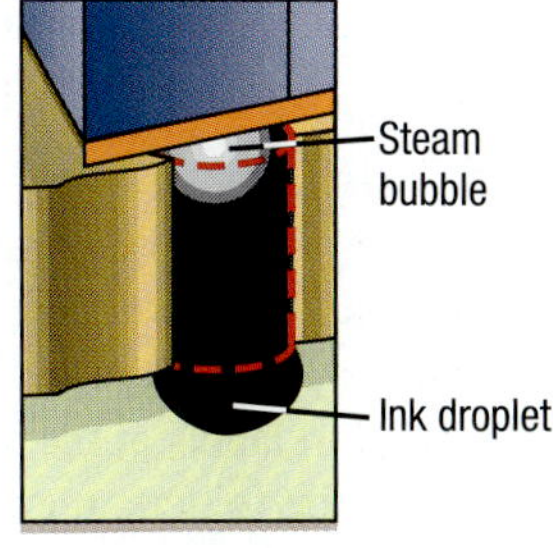

2. As the bubble expands, it pushes ink through the nozzle.

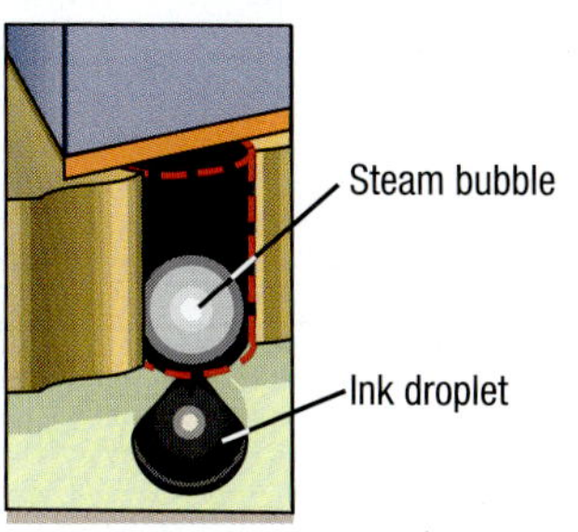

3. The pressure of the bubble forces an ink droplet to be ejected onto the paper. When the steam bubble collapses, more ink is pulled into the print head, so it is ready for the next steam bubble.

>**Laser printer.** An output device that uses toner powder and technology similar to that of a photocopier to produce images on paper. >**Ink-jet printer.** An output device that sprays droplets of ink to produce images on paper.

good-quality output, and can print in color, ink-jet printers are usually the printer of choice for home use. With the use of special photo paper, *photo-quality ink-jet printers* can also print photograph quality digital photos. At around $100 or less for a simple home printer, ink-jet printers are affordable, although the cost of the replaceable ink cartridges can add up, especially if you do a lot of color printing.

In addition to being used in computer printers, ink-jet technology is also being used in the development of a number of emerging applications unrelated to current ink-jet printers, such as dispensing liquid metals, aromas, computer chips and other circuitry, and even "printing" human tissue and other organic materials for medical purposes.

Special-Purpose Printers

Although printers can typically print on a variety of media, such as sheets of labels, envelopes, transparencies, photo paper, and even fabric, some printers are designed for a particular purpose. Some of the most common *special-purpose printers* are discussed next and illustrated in Figure 4-34.

Photo Printers

Photo printers are color printers designed to print photographs. Photo printers have become increasingly popular as digital cameras have become the norm. Although many photo printers are connected to a PC to print photos stored on the hard drive or modified using image editing software, most photo printers also can print photos directly from a digital camera or a storage medium without transferring them first to a computer, typically by using a cable, flash memory card slot, or camera docking station to connect the camera or storage medium to the printer. Often, photo printers have a preview screen (see Figure 4-34) to allow for minor editing and cropping before printing, but it is usually more efficient to do extensive editing via a PC. Some photo printers can print a variety of photo paper sizes; others—sometimes called *snapshot printers*—print only on standard 4 × 6-inch photo paper.

Photo printers today usually use either ink-jet technology, like conventional ink-jet printers, or a *thermal-transfer* technology, such as *thermal-wax transfer* or *dye-sublimation*. Thermal-wax transfer printers use heat to melt dots of wax from a ribbon onto the paper. Dye-sublimation printers use heat to transfer dye from a ribbon to form the image on special paper. Both technologies produce a better image than an ink-jet printer, but at a greater expense. Although photo printers offer the convenience of printing digital photos at home and whenever the need arises, the cost per photo is typically higher than using a photo printing service at a retail store or an Internet photo printing service.

TIP

In addition to printing digital photo prints, many retail and Internet photo services can print your digital photos on shirts, mugs, playing cards, calendars, mouse pads, even valid U.S. postage stamps.

Barcode and Label Printers

Barcode printers enable businesses and other organizations to print custom barcodes on price tags, shipping labels, and other documents for identification or pricing purposes. Most barcode printers can print labels in a variety of barcode standards; some can also encode RFID tags embedded in labels at the same time. For other types of labels, such as for envelopes, packages, and file folders, regular *label printers* may come in handy. Some special-purpose label printers can print *electronic postage* (sometimes called *e-stamps* or *PC postage*). E-stamps are valid postage stamps that can be printed once a postage allotment has been purchased via the Internet or from an e-stamp vendor; postage values are deducted from your allotment as you print the e-stamps. Some e-stamp services also allow stamps to be printed directly onto shipping labels and envelopes using laser or ink-jet printers, as well.

>**Photo printer.** An output device designed for printing digital photographs. >**Barcode printer.** An output device that prints barcoded documents.

PHOTO PRINTERS
Used to print digital photographs, such as those taken with a digital camera.

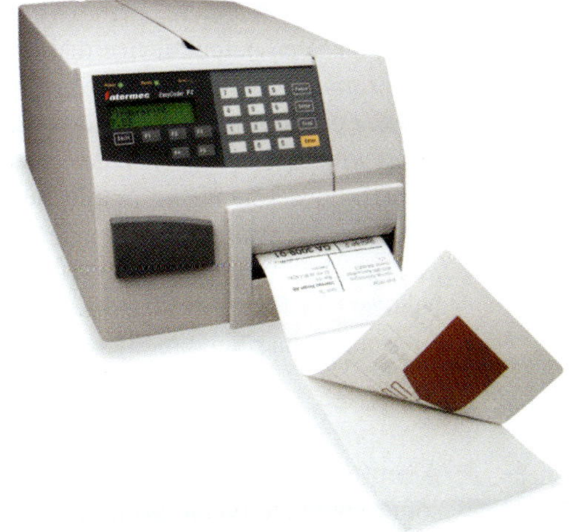

BARCODE PRINTERS
Used to print barcoded labels. This printer can also program RFID tags, when they are embedded inside the barcoded labels.

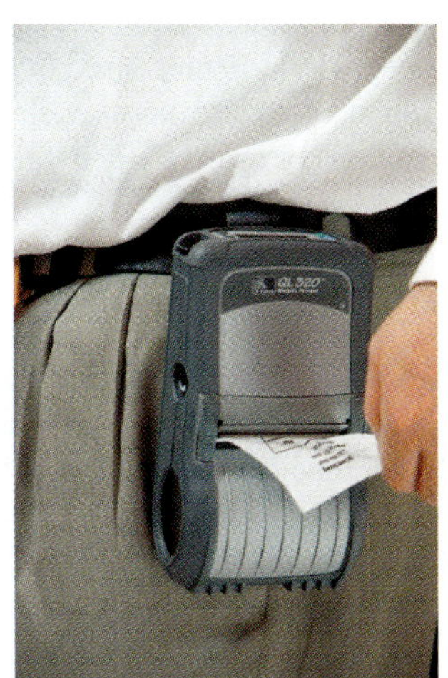

PORTABLE PRINTERS
Used to print from a portable PC or while on the go.

WIDE-FORMAT PRINTERS
Used for printouts that are too big for a standard-sized printer.

FIGURE 4-34
Special-purpose printers.

Portable Printers

Portable printers are small, lightweight printers that can be used on the go, such as with a notebook computer, handheld PC, or smart phone. Some portable printers need to be physically connected to the computer; others can receive documents to be printed using wireless transmission. Portable printers are used by businesspeople while traveling, as well as to print receipts and other needed documents while on the job. Some snapshot printers today are also small enough to be considered portable. The portable printer featured in Figure 4-34 is designed for printing receipts, barcodes, and other small items; some portable printers can print on regular-sized (8½-by-11-inch) paper.

Plotters and Wide-Format Ink-Jet Printers

A *plotter* is an output device that is designed primarily to produce charts, drawings, maps, blueprints, three-dimensional illustrations, and other forms of large documents. *Electrostatic plotters* create images using toner in conjunction with a matrix of tiny wires to charge the paper with electricity. When the charged paper passes over the toner bed, the toner adheres to it and produces an image. While these types of plotters were commonly used in the past and a few are still available, it is more common today to use an *ink-jet plotter* (also called a *wide-format ink-jet printer*) for large documents, including color posters, signs, and advertising banners (see Figure 4-34). Although typically used to print on paper, some wide-format ink-jet printers can print directly on fabric and other types of materials.

Multifunction Devices

A **multifunction device** (sometimes called a *multifunction printer*) is a device that offers some combination of printing, copying, scanning, and faxing capabilities. Most commonly, these types of devices are based on color ink-jet printer technology, although laser multifunction devices are available. The advantage of using a multifunction device is that it takes up less space and is less expensive than purchasing multiple machines. The disadvantages include possibly not being able to find a multifunction device that has exactly the components you would get if you bought them separately, and the risk that when the device breaks down, you will lose all of its functions if the device needs to be repaired off site. Although multifunction devices have traditionally been desktop units used in small offices and home offices, larger workgroup multifunction devices are now available that are designed for multiple users, either as stand-alone stations or as networked units.

AUDIO OUTPUT

Audio output is output in the form of voice or music. *Speakers* and *headsets* are the most common types of audio output hardware. **Speakers** connect to a PC and provide audio output for computer games, music, video, TV, videoconferencing, and other applications that have audio output. *Voice output* can also occur when a computer (such as your PC or the Web server hosting a Web page you are viewing) talks to you. These types of voice output systems—sometimes also referred to as *text-to-speech systems*—typically either use prerecorded sentences stored in digital form (such as a greeting or instruction) or prerecorded

>**Multifunction device.** A device that offers multiple functions (such as printing, scanning, and faxing) in a single unit. >**Speakers.** Output devices that produce sound.

words or sounds used to create sentences extemporaneously (such as when quoting an account balance).

Computer speaker systems resemble their stereo system counterparts and are available in a wide range of prices. Some speaker systems consist of only a pair of speakers. Others include a subwoofer for better bass tones (see Figure 4-35), and still others are capable of surround sound effects. Many speakers have a *headphone jack*, which allows a *headphone* or *headset* to be used so the sound will not disturb others (such as in a school computer lab or public library); if not, there is almost always a headphone port on the outside of the system unit (coming from the sound card or integrated sound component). Instead of being stand-alone units, the speakers for some desktop PCs are built directly into, or permanently attached to, the monitor. Portable PCs and mobile devices almost always have speakers and headphone jacks integrated into the device, but there are external speakers designed for these devices to boost their sound when at home or another fixed location. For instance, a speaker system designed to be used with the iPod digital music player is shown in Figure 4-35.

FIGURE 4-35
Speakers.

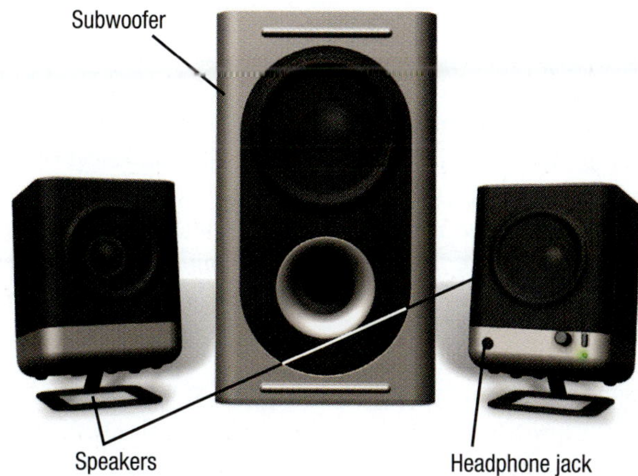

COMPUTER SPEAKERS
Many speaker systems today come with a subwoofer, in addition to the standard two speakers.

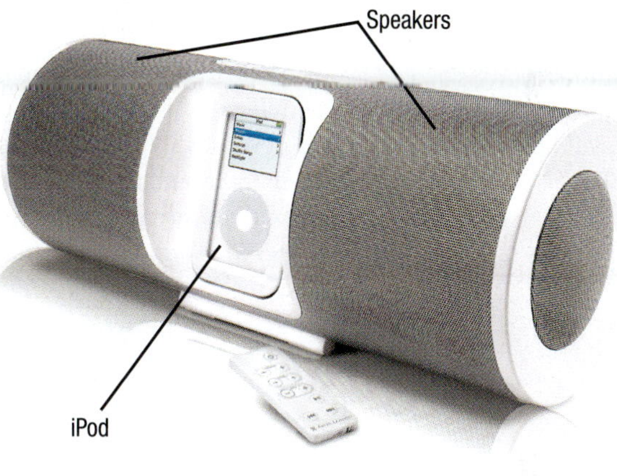

IPOD SPEAKERS
External speakers are also available for use with mobile devices to increase quality, such as the iPod speakers shown here.

SUMMARY

KEYBOARDS

Chapter Objective 1:
Explain the purpose of a computer keyboard and the types of keyboards widely used today.

Most people use a **keyboard** as one of the two main sources of computer input. Keyboards typically include the standard alphanumeric keys, plus a variety of other keys for special purposes. Some handheld PCs and mobile devices include a keyboard or a *thumb pad*—if not, a *portable keyboard* or *portable thumb pad* can often be used. *Wireless keyboards* are also available.

POINTING DEVICES

Chapter Objective 2:
List several different pointing devices and describe their functions.

Pointing devices are hardware devices that move an onscreen *mouse pointer* or similar indicator. The most widely used pointing device is the **mouse**. Another common pointing device is the **electronic pen** (also called a **stylus** or *digital pen*). Electronic pens are used with computers and *digital writing systems* to input handwritten data and select options; with **handwriting recognition** technology, the input can be converted to typed text. **Touch screens** are monitors that are touched with the finger to select commands or provide input. Touch screens are commonly used in consumer kiosks. Other pointing devices include the **graphics tablet**, **joystick**, **trackball**, **pointing stick**, and **touch pad**.

SCANNERS, READERS, AND DIGITAL CAMERAS

Chapter Objective 3:
Describe the purposes of scanners and readers and list some types of scanners and readers in use today.

There are many different input devices that can be used to convert data that already exists (such as on *source documents*) to digital form or to initially capture data in digital form. A **scanner** allows users to input data that exists in physical form, such as photographs, drawings, and printed documents, into a computer system. Most scanners are **flatbed scanners**, **sheetfed scanners**, or **handheld scanners**. *Drum*, *3D*, *receipt*, and *business card scanners* are also available. When used with **optical character recognition (OCR)** software, the computer system recognizes scanned text characters and stores them digitally so they can be manipulated by the computer. If not, the scanned data is input as an image.

Barcode readers read **barcodes**, such as the *UPC codes* used to identify products in many retail stores. **Radio frequency identification (RFID)** readers read and store data in **RFID tags**, which contain tiny chips and antennas and which are attached to packages and other items for identification purposes. RFID tags today are most often used in conjunction with shipping containers and other large assets, though their use is expanding and is expected to grow in the near future.

Optical mark readers read specific types of marks on certain forms, such as on testing forms and voter ballots. *Optical character recognition* (*OCR*) *devices* read specially printed *optical characters*, such as those on bills and other *turnaround documents*; *magnetic ink character recognition* (*MICR*) is used by the banking industry to rapidly sort, process, and route checks to the proper banks; and **biometric readers** identify individuals by their fingerprint, hand geometry, face or other *biometric* characteristic.

Chapter Objective 4:
Understand how digital cameras differ from conventional cameras.

Digital cameras work much like regular cameras, but record digital images on some type of digital storage medium, instead of on conventional film or videotape. The images can later be transferred to a PC for manipulation or printing, as desired. *Digital still cameras* take still photos; *digital video cameras* consist of *digital camcorders*; and *PC cams* are used to capture video images for videoconferencing, video phone calls, or to broadcast via a Web site.

AUDIO INPUT

Voice input systems, which enable computer systems to recognize spoken words, are one means of audio input. Voice input technologies offer tremendous work-saving potential in the legal and medical fields, such as for transcription. *MIDI* devices can be used to input original music compositions into a PC. Music can also be input via a CD, DVD, or Web download.

Chapter Objective 5:
Explain how audio input is accomplished.

DISPLAY DEVICES

Display devices (also called **monitors** and **display screens**) are the most common of the output devices for a computer; they are also incorporated into a wide variety of other electronic devices. Monitors are available in a wide variety of sizes and are generally either **CRT monitors** or **flat-panel displays**. Flat-panel displays are most often **liquid crystal displays (LCDs)** or **plasma displays**, but these technologies are expected to be someday replaced by **organic light emitting diode (OLED) displays**. OLED displays generate their own light so they do not require *backlighting*, are more energy efficient, and produce sharper and brighter images. Special types of OLEDs (such as *flexible*, *transparent*, and *Phosphorescent OLEDs*) are emerging for special applications. Regardless of the technology used, the screen of a display device is divided into a fine grid of small areas or dots—**pixels**. Monitors can be *wired* or *wireless*, some support 3D images, and some can display *HDTV* broadcasts and other types of *digital television*. **Data projectors** connect to a PC and project any output sent to the PC's monitor through the projector onto a wall or projection screen.

Chapter Objective 6:
Describe the characteristics of a display device.

PRINTERS

Printers produce *hard copy* output through either *impact* or *nonimpact* printing technology. Most printers today form images as matrices of dots, although with many technologies, the dots are too small to be visible. Quality of printers is usually measured in *dots per inch* (*dpi*); speed is typically measured in *pages per minute* (*ppm*). Both *personal* and *network printers* are available; some printers print in color and others in just black and white.

The most common printers are **laser printers** and **ink-jet printers**. Special-purpose printers include **photo printers**, **barcode printers**, *portable printers*, *plotters*, and *wide-format ink-jet printers*. **Multifunction devices** incorporate the functions of multiple devices—typically a printer, scanner, and fax machine—into a single unit.

Chapter Objective 7:
List several types of printers and explain their function.

AUDIO OUTPUT

Audio output devices include **speakers**, to output music or spoken voice, and *voice output* systems, which enable computer systems to play back or compose spoken messages from digitally stored words, phrases, and sounds. *Headphones* or *headsets* can be used to prevent the sound from disturbing other people.

Chapter Objective 8:
Understand which hardware devices are used for audio output.

REVIEW ACTIVITIES

KEY TERM MATCHING

Instructions: Match each key term on the left with the definition on the right that best describes it.

a. digital camera
b. electronic pen
c. handwriting recognition
d. laser printer
e. mouse
f. optical character recognition (OCR)
g. OLED display
h. RFID tag
i. scanner
j. touch screen

1. ______ A common pointing device that the user slides along a flat surface to move a pointer around the screen and clicks its buttons to make selections.

2. ______ A device containing tiny chips and radio antennas that is attached to objects that will be identified using RFID technology.

3. ______ A display device that is touched with the finger to issue commands or otherwise generate input to the connected PC.

4. ______ An input device that reads printed text and graphics and transfers them to a computer in digital form.

5. ______ An input device that is used to write electronically on the display screen; also called a stylus or digital pen.

6. ______ An input device that takes pictures and records them as digital data (instead of film or videotaped) images.

7. ______ An output device that uses toner powder and technology similar to that of a photocopier to produce images on paper.

8. ______ A type of flat-panel display that uses emissive organic material to display brighter and sharper images.

9. ______ The ability of a device to identify handwritten characters.

10. ______ The ability of a scanning device to recognize handwritten or typed characters and convert them to electronic form as text, not images.

SELF-QUIZ

Instructions: Circle **T** if the statement is true, **F** if the statement is false, or write the best answer in the space provided. **Answers for the self-quiz are located in the References and Resources Guide at the end of the book.**

1. **T F** A keyboard is an example of a pointing device.
2. **T F** Most digital cameras store photos on conventional floppy disks.
3. **T F** UPC is a type of barcode.
4. **T F** Consumer kiosks located in retail stores commonly use touch screens for input.
5. **T F** An ink-jet printer normally produces a better image than a laser printer.

6. With ______ software, pen-based PCs can convert handwritten text into editable, typed text.
7. A(n) ______ can be used to convert flat printed documents, such as a drawing or photograph, into digital form.
8. The smallest colorable area in an electronic image (such as a scanned document, digital photograph, or image displayed on a display screen) is called a(n) ______.

9. Portable PCs virtually always use ______ displays, while desktop PCs may use the larger, more bulky ______ monitors.

10. Match each input device to its input application, and write the corresponding number in the blank to the left of the input application.

a. ______ Gaming	1. RFID tag
b. ______ Pen-based computing	2. Keyboard
c. ______ Consumer kiosk	3. Stylus
d. ______ Text-based data entry	4. Joystick
e. ______ Access a secure facility	5. Biometric reader
f. ______ Tracking goods	6. Touch screen

HW

EXERCISES

1. For the following list of computer input and output devices, write the appropriate abbreviation (I or O) in the space provided to indicate whether each device is used for input (I) or output (O).

a. ______ Biometric reader	f. ______ Digital camera
b. ______ Graphics tablet	g. ______ Pointing stick
c. ______ Speaker	h. ______ Microphone
d. ______ Photo printer	i. ______ OLED monitor
e. ______ Flat-panel display	j. ______ Joystick

2. Write the number of the type of printer that best matches each of the printing applications in the blank to the left of each printing application. Note that all types of printers will not be used.

   a. ______ To print inexpensive color printouts for a wide variety of documents.
   b. ______ To print all output for an entire office.
   c. ______ To print receipts for jet-ski rentals at the beach.
   d. ______ To print high-quality black-and-white business letters and reports at home.

1. Personal laser printer	5. Barcode printer
2. Network laser printer	6. Plotter
3. Color laser printer	7. Ink-jet printer
4. Photo printer	8. Portable printer

3. List three advantages of RFID technology over barcode technology.

4. Would an OLED display or an LCD display use more battery power? Explain why.

5. List one personal or business application that you believe is more appropriate for a dot-matrix printer, instead of another type of printer, and explain why.

DISCUSSION QUESTION

The choice of an appropriate input device for a product is often based on both the type of device being used and the target market for that device. For instance, a device targeted to college students and one targeted to older individuals may use different input methods. Suppose that you are developing an Internet appliance being marketed to senior citizens. What type of hardware would you select as the primary input device? Why? What are the advantages and disadvantages of your selected input device? How could the disadvantages be minimized?

PROJECTS

HOT TOPICS

1. **E-Paper** The chapter Trend box discusses electronic paper (e-paper)—an erasable, reusable alternative to traditional paper and ink for computer output. Although currently in its early stages, some experts predict that it will become a viable product for many personal applications in the very near future. One of the first widespread applications for e-paper is retail signs. The obvious benefit of e-paper is reducing the use of traditional paper and ink and the resources needed to create and dispose of paper and ink. Two disadvantages at the current time are longevity (the medium is not designed to display an image for long periods of time) and expense.

   For this project, research the current state of e-paper. What products are available now? Are additional products expected to become available in the near future? When more products become available, do you think businesses or individuals will choose to use these types of products if the only incentive is a cleaner environment? Or will there need to be an economic incentive, such as savings on the cost of paper and ink surpassing the cost of using e-paper? What applications do you think are the most appropriate and exciting for the use of e-paper technology? At the conclusion of your research, prepare a one-page summary of your findings and submit it to your instructor.

SHORT ANSWER/ RESEARCH

2. **New Keyboards** The design and capability of keyboards continue to evolve to meet new user needs. Newer keyboards offer special features, such as ergonomic design, Internet buttons, wireless connections, multimedia control buttons, and built-in fingerprint and smart card readers.

   For this project, research a variety of keyboards designed for use with a desktop PC that are currently for sale. Select at least three different models and identify the special features and cost of each. At the conclusion of your research, prepare a one-page summary of your findings and submit it to your instructor. Be sure to include whether or not you would consider purchasing one of your selected keyboards and why.

3. **Printer Shopping** Printers today have many more features than a few years ago. These features may include improved quality, more memory, photo printing capabilities, digital camera connectivity, built-in flash memory card readers, and faster speed.

   For this project, suppose you are in the market for a new printer, primarily for personal and school applications. Make a list of the most important features needed to meet your needs, and then research printers currently on the market to identify which one you feel would be the best printer for your needs. Be sure to take into consideration both the price of the printer and the price of consumables (such as paper, ink cartridge/toner—both the cost and disposal of) in your evaluation process. At the conclusion of your research, prepare a one-page summary of your findings and submit it to your instructor.

HANDS ON

4. **Will it Fit?** Many new PCs today come with very large—such as 17-inch or 19-inch—monitors. Although they make output much easier to see, sometimes it may be difficult to get the monitor to fit on your desk.

   For this project, find two 17-inch and two 19-inch CRT monitors made by different manufacturers and determine their physical size (most manufacturers have size and other specifications listed by model on their Web sites, although you may also use newspaper or magazine ads or research systems for sale at your local stores). Next, select the desk or table at home that you would use for your PC and measure it. Draw a sketch to scale of the top surface of the desk (bird's-eye view) and then add each monitor (drawn to scale) to your sketch to illustrate how well each one would fit. Are there any significant size differences among the models sold by the manufacturers you selected? Would you need to eliminate any of these models due to lack of space? Next, find two 17-inch and two 19-inch flat-panel monitors made by different manufacturers and determine their physical size. How much difference is there between these models and the CRT models you researched earlier? Compare the prices of the eight monitors. Do you think the price difference justifies a larger monitor size? The convenience of a smaller footprint? Prepare a summary of your findings to turn in to your instructor along with your sketch.

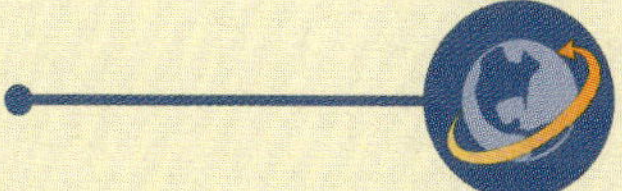

5. **Keyboarding Speed Test** Although voice input and other alternative means of input are emerging, most of the time input is a matter of entering large amounts of data via the keyboard. Proper keyboarding technique and practice can help increase both your speed and accuracy. Keyboarding tests are available online to evaluate your keyboarding ability; keyboarding tutorials are available both online and in software form.

   For this project, find a site (such as Typingtest.com) that offers a free online typing test (often the test requires your browser to have Java compatibility). Take the available typing test to test your keyboarding speed and accuracy. At the conclusion of the test, rate your keyboarding ability and determine whether a keyboarding course or tutor program, or just keyboarding experience, will help bring you up to speed if you do not already keyboard at least 20 correct words per minute (cwpm). Take the test one more time to see if your speed improves now that you are familiar with how the test works. If your speed is fast, but your accuracy is low, take the test one more time, concentrating on accuracy. If you test less than 20 correct words per minute on all tests, use a search site to locate a site with a free typing tutor and evaluate it to see if it would be helpful to increase your speed and accuracy. At the conclusion of this task, prepare a short summary of your experience, including the typing test site used and your best score.

HW

WRITING ABOUT COMPUTERS

6. **Assistive Computing** In addition to the conventional input and output hardware mentioned in the chapter, there are a variety of *assistive* input and output devices that physically challenged individuals can use to make computing easier and more efficient.

   For this project, select one type of disability, such as being blind, deaf, paraplegic, quadriplegic, or having the use of only one arm or hand. Research the hardware and software options that could be used with a new PC for someone with the selected disability. Make a list of potential limitations of any standard PC hardware and the assistive hardware and software that would be appropriate for this individual to use to overcome the limitation of that hardware. Research each possibility, comparing such factors as ease of use, cost, and availability and then prepare a recommendation for the best computer system for your selected hypothetical situation. Summarize your findings in a two- to three-page paper.

PRESENTATION/DEMONSTRATION

7. **Instant Photos** Digital cameras are becoming very common for both consumers and professionals, and there are many options for printing digital photographs.

   For this project, research the options for printing photos taken with digital cameras. Select one personal printer capable of printing good-quality photos and determine the cost of the printer, as well as the printing cost per photograph (include the cost of ink and photo-quality paper). Also locate two businesses (either physical stores in your area or online services) that will print digital photos. For each location, determine the cost per photo, waiting time, and options available for submitting the photos. Share your findings with the class in the form of a short presentation. The presentation should not exceed 10 minutes and should make use of one or more presentation aids, such as the chalkboard, handouts, overhead transparencies, or a computer-based slide presentation (your instructor may provide additional requirements). You may also be asked to submit a summary of the presentation to your instructor.

GROUP DISCUSSION

8. **Biometrics and Personal Privacy** Biometric input devices, such as the use of fingerprint readers, hand geometry readers, or iris scanners, are increasingly being used for security purposes. Common activities that some employees are required to use at work include using a biometric reader to clock in and out of work or to obtain access to locked facilities, a computer, or a computer network. Other uses of biometric technology are more voluntary, such as expedited airport-screening programs used by some frequent travelers. While viewed as a time-saving tool by some, other individuals may object to their biometric characteristics being stored in a database for this purpose. Is convenience worth compromising some personal privacy? What about national security? Would you be willing to sign up for a voluntary program, such as an airport-screening system or a payment system that enabled you to purchase goods and services (automatically charged to your credit card or deducted from your bank account) at retail stores and restaurants using only your fingerprint? Would you work at a job that required you to use a biometric input device on a regular basis? Do you think a national ID card (such as a standard hard-to-forge national driver's license containing a thumbprint or other biometric data) could help prevent terrorist attacks, such as the September 11, 2001 attacks? If so, do you think most Americans would support their use?

   For this project, form an opinion of the use of biometric input devices and any potential impact their use may have on personal privacy. Be sure to consider the questions mentioned in the previous paragraph and be prepared to discuss your position (in class, via an online class discussion group, or in a class chat room, depending on your instructor's directions). You may also be asked to write a short paper expressing your opinion.

WEB ACTIVITIES

The *Understanding Computers* Web site located at **www.course.com/uc11** features many resources to help reinforce your understanding of the chapter content and help you prepare for exams. Your instructor may also assign specific activities to be completed that will count toward your final grade in the course.

Instructions: Go to **www.course.com/uc11/ch04** to work the following online activities.

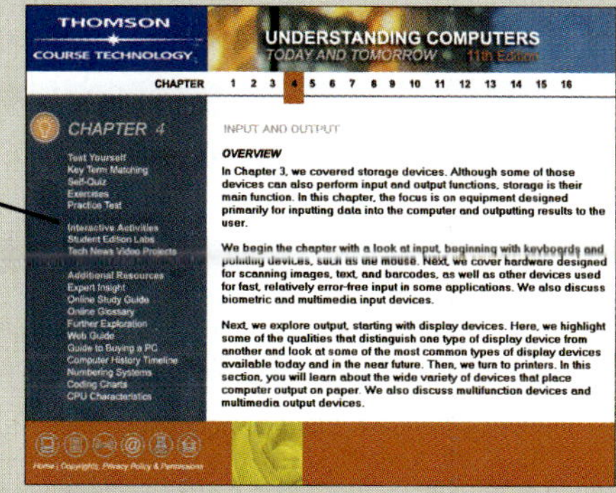

Click any link in the navigation bar on the left to access any of the online resources described below.

INTERACTIVE ACTIVITIES

1. **Crossword Puzzle** Practice your knowledge of the key terms in Chapter 4 by completing the interactive Crossword Puzzle.
2. **Tech News Video Project** Watch the **"Predicting Huge Surf"** video clip that features a system that uses various types of input regarding weather and the surf to determine, often only hours in advance, when the surf will be huge so that the Mavericks Surf Contest can take place. After watching the video online, complete the corresponding project.
3. **Student Edition Labs** Reinforce the concepts you have learned in this chapter by working through the interactive **Using Input Devices** and **Peripheral Devices** labs.

TEST YOURSELF

1. **Key Term Matching** Test your knowledge of selected chapter key terms by matching the terms with their definitions.
2. **Self-Quiz** Test your retention of chapter concepts by taking the Self-Quiz.
3. **Exercises** Work these short exercises to review the concepts and terms covered in the chapter.
4. **Practice Test** Test how ready you are for an upcoming exam by completing the online Practice Test.

STUDY TOOLS/ ADDITIONAL RESOURCES

The Understanding Computers Web site has a wide range of additional resources, including an **Online Study Guide** (containing study tips, a chapter outline with room to add your own notes, and a chapter checklist of the activities to complete when the chapter is covered in class and when you are preparing for a test) and an **Online Glossary** for each chapter; **Further Exploration** links; a **Web Guide**, a **Guide to Buying a PC**, and a **Computer History Timeline**; more information about **Numbering Systems**, **Coding Charts**, and **CPU Characteristics**; and much, much more!

HW

EXPERT INSIGHT ON . . .
Hardware

A conversation with **JOHN JANAKIRAMAN**

Research Manager for Data Center Architecture, HP Labs

My Background . . .

I studied engineering since I always enjoyed solving problems. I got fascinated by the creativity in building electronic/computing devices and pursued graduate studies in computer science to prepare for a career in this field. I now lead a team researching how the next generation of servers must be architected and managed. My primary responsibility is to create a future where the architecture and management of servers enable a range of applications (e.g., digital movie rendering, searching the Web, and voice-over-IP) to be performed much more reliably, efficiently, and easily.

> "Students in all fields should become computer-literate and keep abreast of developments in the field of computing."

It's Important to Know . . .

Basic computer concepts. For instance, that the engine of the computer is the processor that executes computer instructions provided by the programmer. Storage such as disks maintain all permanent data in the computer, while memory and caches are actually used to temporarily store instructions and data close to the processor. All computer users should be aware of these concepts.

Computer designers are not focused only on the performance of computers these days. Their designs increasingly focus on non-performance objectives such as lowering power consumption, improving reliability, and improving usability. The industry is also envisioning new ways of using processors to improve the way we live. Computers can be embedded in medicines for health applications, in the environment for ecological applications, and so on.

Computing appliances must be able to interact with each other. For instance, a PDA must be able to communicate with a PC. So, computer hardware and software vendors must actively develop standards in every aspect of computing so that computers can work together. Creating standards while simultaneously building unique products is an important business challenge for the computer industry.

How I Use this Technology . . .

I use my computers at home to interact with family and friends (e.g., through e-mail and VoIP phone calls), to follow news, to shop and pay bills, to work from home, and to maintain my personal content (e.g., photos and financial documents). I maintain a wireless network which allows me to roam around the house while still being connected to the Internet through my broadband provider. I maintain most of my content on storage devices and back them up periodically. I use a photo-quality printer to print photos and other documents. In addition to my digital camera/camcorder, I use my computer to record audio

John Janakiraman is currently the Research Manager for the Data Center Architecture group at HP Labs. He is leading research on the architecture and management of the server infrastructure in data centers, where his team is researching virtualization and automation techniques to improve the efficiency, reliability, and manageability of data centers. He and his team have developed many technologies that have influenced HP products, industry standards, and open-source community projects. John has a Ph.D. in Computer Science.

Future advances in hardware technology and their decreasing costs can have a beneficial impact on society in many ways, such as to improve the quality of personal life, improve economic opportunity in developing regions, and improve environment management.

HW

and video of my family. Like other individuals, I also invisibly use computers integrated into devices, such as in cars and in the garden sprinkler system.

What the Future Holds . . .

Computer hardware will decrease in cost while becoming more powerful, compact, and power-efficient. Advances in computer hardware will enable pervasive wireless connectivity, permit more of the human experience to be captured in digital form, and provide richer entertainment. Computers will get woven, invisibly in many cases, into many more aspects of life, such as in maintaining a healthy lifestyle, education, the environment, and government services.

Future advances in hardware technology and their decreasing costs can have a beneficial impact on society in many ways, such as to improve the quality of personal life, improve economic opportunity in developing regions, and improve environment management. Technology also imposes some societal responsibilities, such as the appropriate handling of used computer parts (e.g., recycling) so that they do not contaminate the environment.

My Advice to Students . . .

A career in the intersection between technology and some other field (as diverse as, for example, medicine, library management, or geology) can give you an edge. Getting real-world experience through internships in related jobs is also key. To rise to a position of leadership, solid verbal and written communication skills and the ability to influence people's thinking are also critical.

Students in all fields should become computer-literate and keep abreast of developments in the field of computing. This knowledge can enable them to use computing to advance their field by conceiving new solutions and tools. It will also equip them to reason about the risks and rewards of specific computing applications and to influence the development of governance policies.

Discussion Question

John Janakiraman views the appropriate handling of used computer parts so that they do not contaminate the environment one of the responsibilities involved with the use of technology. Think about all of the computing refuse you create—such as old printouts, depleted toner cartridges, broken hardware, and so forth. What do you feel is your responsibility for making sure this refuse is disposed of properly? Does the manufacturer share any of that responsibility? Some states—such as California—are beginning to charge a recycling fee on some hardware, such as computer monitors, to help pay for the cost of properly disposing of that hardware. Do you agree with this trend? What should individuals be required to do to help alleviate the computing refuse problem? Is there a long-term solution to this problem? Be prepared to discuss your position (in class, via an online class discussion group, or in a class chat room, depending on your instructor's directions). You may also be asked to write a short paper expressing your opinion.

>For more information on HP, visit www.hp.com. For more information on HP Labs, visit www.hpl.hp.com. Some good industry association references are www.acm.org and www.ieee.org.

MODULE SOFTWARE

In Chapter 1, we looked at the basic software concepts needed to get a computer system up and running. We continue that focus in this module, discussing in more depth both system software—the software used to run a computer—and application software—the software that performs the specific tasks that users want to accomplish using a computer.

System software, the subject of Chapter 5, consists of the programs that enable the hardware of a computer system to operate and run application software. Chapter 6 offers a brief introduction to some of the most common types of application software, such as word processing, spreadsheet, database, presentation graphics, and multimedia software.

"... eventually we'll stop talking about how computers are changing our society, and focus more on using them to get on with our lives and be part of society."

For more comments from Guest Expert Aaron Weber of Novell, Inc., see the Expert Insight on . . . Software feature at the end of the module.

IN THIS MODULE

Chapter 5 System Software: Operating Systems and Utility Programs 182

Overview 183

System Software vs. Application Software 183

The Operating System 184

Operating Systems for Desktop PCs and Servers 194

Operating Systems for Handheld PCs and Mobile Devices 201

Operating Systems for Larger Computers 204

Utility Programs 204

The Future of Operating Systems 211

Chapter 6 Application Software 220

Overview 221

The Basics of Application Software 221

Word Processing Concepts 232

Spreadsheet Concepts 236

Database Concepts 239

Presentation Graphics Concepts 243

Graphics and Multimedia Concepts 246

Other Types of Application Software 251

System Software: Operating Systems and Utility Programs

OUTLINE

Overview
System Software vs. Application Software
The Operating System
- Functions of an Operating System
- Processing Techniques for Increased Efficiency
- Differences Among Operating Systems

Operating Systems for Desktop PCs and Servers
- DOS
- Windows
- Mac OS
- UNIX
- Linux
- NetWare
- Solaris

Operating Systems for Handheld PCs and Mobile Devices
- Embedded and Mobile Versions of Windows
- Palm OS
- Embedded Linux
- Symbian OS

Operating Systems for Larger Computers
Utility Programs
- File Management Programs
- Search Tools
- Diagnostic and Disk Management Programs
- Uninstall Utilities
- File Compression Programs
- Backup and Recovery Utilities
- Antivirus, Antispyware, Firewalls, and Other Security Programs

The Future of Operating Systems

LEARNING OBJECTIVES

After completing this chapter, you will be able to:

1. Understand the difference between system software and application software.
2. Explain the different functions of an operating system and discuss some ways that operating systems can differ from one another.
3. List several ways in which operating systems enhance processing efficiency.
4. Name today's most widely used operating systems for desktop PCs and servers.
5. State several devices other than desktop PCs and servers that require an operating system and list one possible operating system for each type of device.
6. Discuss the role of utility programs and outline several duties that these programs perform.
7. Describe what the operating systems of the future might be like.

OVERVIEW

All stand-alone computers require some sort of software to run the computer system. For instance, software is needed to translate your commands into a form the computer can understand, to open and close other software programs, to manage your stored files, to help to keep your computer running smoothly and efficiently, and to locate and set up new hardware as it is added to the PC.

The type of software used to perform these tasks is system software—the focus of this chapter. System software runs in the background at all times, making it possible for you to use your computer. It is also responsible for a variety of tasks that need to be carried out as you work. For example, when you issue the command for your PC to store a document on your hard drive, the system software must make sure that such a drive exists, look for adequate space on the hard drive, write the document to this space, and finally update the hard drive's directory with the filename and disk location so that the document can be retrieved again when needed. When you click an icon to start a software program, the system software must first determine which program is associated with that icon and where the program is stored on the hard drive in order to verify that the program file exists in that location, and then it launches that program. In addition to managing your local computer, the system software may perform additional tasks if you are connected to a network, such as checking the validity of your user ID or password before granting you access to network resources and ensuring that you have permission to access the data or programs you are requesting.

System software is usually divided into two categories: operating system software and utility programs. We begin this chapter by taking a look at the difference between system software and application software, and then examining the operating system—the primary component of system software. We discuss what operating systems do, in general, and then explore the operating systems most widely used today. Next, we cover utility programs. Utility programs typically perform support functions for the operating system, such as allowing you to manage your files, perform maintenance on your computer, check your PC for viruses, or uninstall a program you no longer want on your PC. Chapter 5 closes with a look at what the future of operating systems may hold. ■

SW

SYSTEM SOFTWARE VS. APPLICATION SOFTWARE

Computers run two general types of software: system software and application software.

- **System software** consists of the "background" programs (namely, the operating system and utility programs) that run a computer system and allow you to use your computer. These programs enable the computer to boot, to launch application programs, and to facilitate important jobs, such as transferring files from one storage medium to another, configuring your computer system to work with a specific brand

>**System software.** Programs, such as the operating system, that control the operation of a computer and its devices, as well as enable application software to run on the PC.

of printer or monitor, managing files on your hard drive, and protecting your computer system from unauthorized use.

- **Application software** includes all the programs that allow a user to perform certain specific tasks on a computer, such as writing a letter, preparing an invoice, viewing a Web page, listening to an MP3 file, checking the inventory of a particular product, playing a game, preparing financial statements, designing a home, and so forth. Application software is discussed in detail in Chapter 6.

In practice, the difference between system and application software is not always clear cut. Some programs, such as those used to burn DVDs, were originally viewed as utility programs. Today, these programs typically contain a variety of features (including the ability to transfer videos and digital photos to a PC, edit videos and photos, create DVD movies, copy CDs and DVDs, and create slide shows) in addition to burning CDs and DVDs, and so now more closely fit the definition of an application program. Also, system software often contains application software components. For example, the *Microsoft Windows* operating system contains several application programs, including a Web browser, calculator, painting program, and text editor. A program's classification as system or application software usually depends on the principal function of the program, and the distinction between the two categories is not always clear.

THE OPERATING SYSTEM

A computer's **operating system** is a collection of programs that manage and coordinate the activities taking place within a computer system. The operating system boots the computer, launches application software programs, and ensures that all actions requested by a user are valid and processed in an orderly fashion. It also manages the computer system resources to perform those operations with efficiency and consistency, and it facilitates connections to the Internet and other networks. When you are ready to print a document or save it onto your hard drive, the operating system assists with those tasks, as well.

In general, the operating system serves as an intermediary between the user and the computer (see Figure 5-1) and is the most critical piece of software installed on the computer. Without an operating system, no other program can run, and the computer cannot function. Many tasks performed by the operating system, however, go unnoticed by the user because the operating system works in the background much of the time.

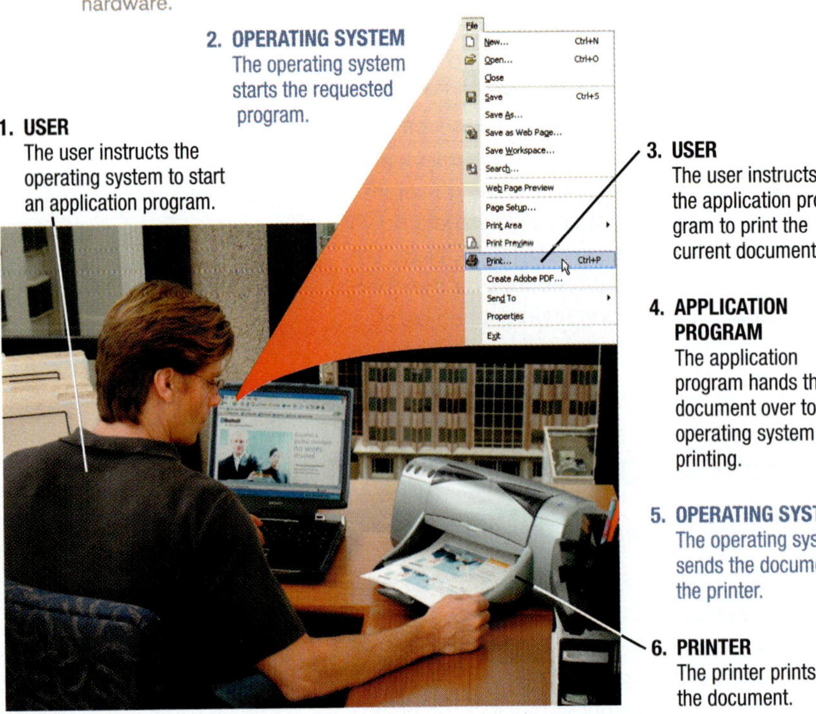

FIGURE 5-1
The intermediary role of the operating system. The operating system acts as a middleman between the user and the computer, as well as between application software programs and the computer system's hardware.

>**Application software.** Programs that enable users to perform specific tasks on a computer, such as writing a letter or playing a game.

>**Operating system.** The main component of system software that enables the computer to manage its activities and the resources under its control, run application programs, and interface with the user.

Functions of an Operating System

Operating systems have a wide range of functions—some of the most important are discussed next.

> **TIP**
>
> Press Ctrl+Alt+Delete to bring up the Task Manager screen shown in Figure 5-2.

Interfacing with Users

As Figure 5-1 suggests, one of the principal roles of every operating system is to translate user instructions into a form the computer can understand. In the other direction, it translates any feedback from the hardware—such as a signal that the printer has run out of paper or the scanner is turned off—into a form that the user can understand. The means by which an operating system or any other program interacts with the user is called the *user interface*; user interfaces can be *text-based* or *graphics-based*, as discussed in more detail shortly. Most, but not all, operating systems today use a *graphical user interface* or *GUI*.

Booting the Computer

As discussed in Chapter 1, the first task your operating system performs when you power up your PC is to *boot* the PC. During the boot process, certain parts of the operating system (called the *kernel*) are loaded into memory. The kernel remains in memory the entire time the PC is on so that it is always available; other parts of the operating system are retrieved from the hard drive and loaded into memory when they are needed. Before the boot process ends, the operating system determines which hardware devices are connected and properly configured, and it reads an opening batch of instructions. These instructions—which the user can customize to some extent when necessary—assign tasks for the operating system to carry out before the current session begins; for instance, checking for computer viruses or starting up a few programs (such as a security program or instant messaging program) to continually run in the background. Typically, many programs are running in the background at any one time, even before the user launches any application software (see Figure 5-2). In Windows, the system configuration information is stored in the *registry* files, which should be modified only by the Windows program itself or advanced Windows users.

FIGURE 5-2
Even with no application programs open, many programs–launched by the operating system during the boot process–run in the background.

TASK MANAGER These programs are running, even before any application programs are launched by the user.

SYSTEM TRAY ICONS These programs were launched during the boot process and will show up in the system tray unless they are closed by the user.

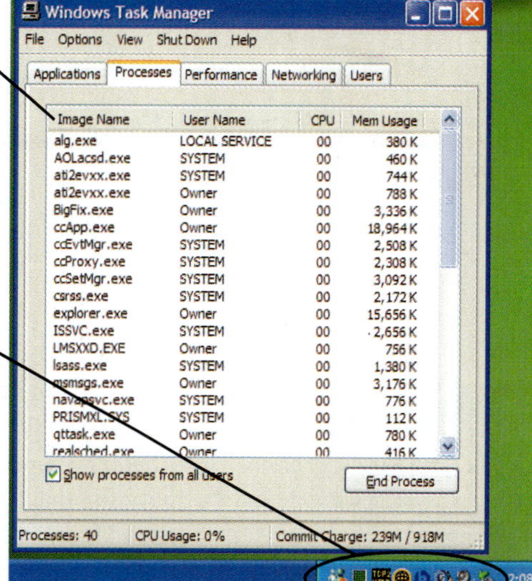

Configuring Devices

The operating system is also used to configure the devices connected to a computer system. Small programs called **device drivers** (or just *drivers*) are used to communicate with peripheral devices, such as monitors, printers, and scanners. Most operating systems today include the drivers needed for the most commonly used peripheral devices. In addition, drivers often come on a disk or a CD packaged with the peripheral device, or they can be obtained from the manufacturer's Web site. Most operating systems today look for new devices each time the PC boots and recognize new devices as they are connected to the PC. If a new device is found, the operating system will typically try to install the appropriate driver automatically in order to get the new hardware ready to use (see Figure 5-3)—a feature called *Plug and Play*. Because USB and FireWire devices can be connected to a PC when the computer is running, those devices will be recognized and configured, as needed, whenever they are plugged into the PC.

FIGURE 5-3
Finding new hardware. Most operating systems are designed to detect new hardware and automatically try to configure it.

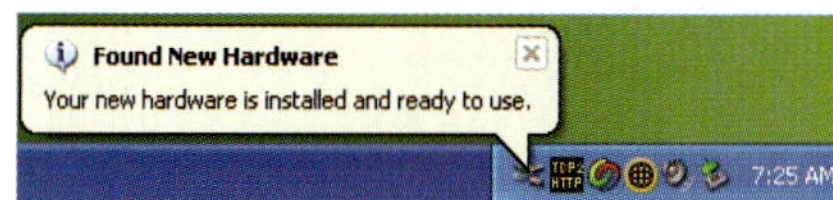

>**Device driver.** A program that enables an operating system to communicate with a specific hardware device.

Once a device and its driver have been properly installed, they usually work fine. If the device driver file gets deleted or becomes corrupted, however, it will no longer work. Usually, the operating system detects this during the boot process and notifies the user that the driver needs to be reinstalled. The user can then reinstall the driver either by using the initial installation disk for that hardware or by downloading a new installation file from the manufacturer's Web site. Device drivers also frequently need to be updated after you *upgrade* your operating system to a newer version. Some operating systems, such as *Windows*, have options to automatically check for operating system updates—including updated driver files—on a regular basis.

FIGURE 5-4

Program malfunctions. When a problem occurs, most operating systems attempt to close only the programs or tasks causing the problem, rather than requiring a full reboot.

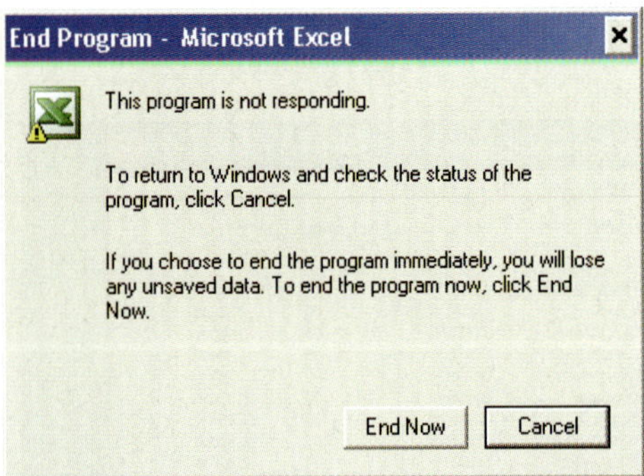

Managing and Monitoring Resources and Jobs

As you work on your PC, the operating system is in charge of managing *system resources* (such as software, disk space, and memory) and making them available to devices and programs when they are needed. If a problem occurs—such as a program stops functioning or too many programs are open for the amount of memory available—the operating system notifies the user and tries to correct the problem, sometimes by closing the offending program (see Figure 5-4). If the problem cannot be corrected by the operating system, the user typically needs to reboot the computer.

Along with assigning system resources, the operating system performs a closely related process: scheduling user jobs to be performed using those resources. *Scheduling routines* in the operating system determine the order in which jobs (such as documents to be printed and files to be retrieved from a hard job) are carried out, as well as which commands get executed first if the user is working with more than one program at a time or if the computer being used supports multiple users.

TIP

When a program stops functioning in an operating system with an error reporting system (such as Windows or Linux), click the option to report the problem, if you are connected to the Internet. After doing so, you may be given a link to information available to correct that problem, such as a software patch or update.

File Management

Another important task that the operating system performs is *file management*—keeping track of the files stored on a PC so that they can be retrieved when needed. As discussed in Chapter 3, operating systems organize the files on a disk or hard drive into *folders* to simplify file management. Usually the operating system files are stored in one folder, and each application software program is stored in its own separate folder. Other folders may be created by the user for storing and organizing files. Folders can contain both files and other folders (called *subfolders*).

Files and folders are usually viewed in a hierarchical format; the top of the hierarchy for any storage medium is called the *root directory* (such as C:\ for the root directory of the hard drive C shown in Figure 5-5). The root directory almost always contains both files and folders. To access a file, you generally navigate to the folder containing that file by opening the appropriate drive, folder, and subfolders. Alternatively, you can type the *path* to a file's exact location. For example, as Figure 5-5 shows, the path

C:\My Documents\Letters\Mary

leads through the root directory of the C drive and the *My Documents* and *Letters* folders to a file named *Mary*. A similar path can also be used to access the files *John* and *Bill*. As discussed in Chapter 3, users specify a filename for each file when they initially save the file on a storage medium; there can be only one file with the exact same filename in any particular folder on a storage medium.

Filename rules vary with each operating system. For instance, all current versions of Windows support filenames that are from 1 to 255 characters long and may include numbers, letters, spaces, and any special characters except \ / : * ? “ < > and |. Filenames almost always contain a *file extension* at the end of the filename. File extensions are generally three characters preceded by a period and are automatically added to a filename by the program in which that file was created, although sometimes the user may have a choice of file extensions supported by a program. Some common file extensions are listed in Figure 5-6.

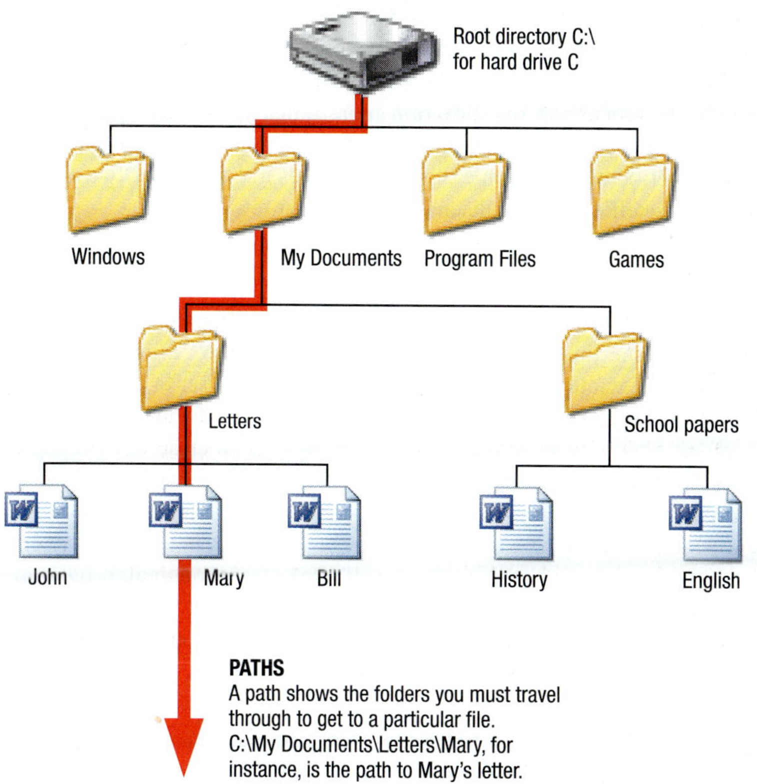

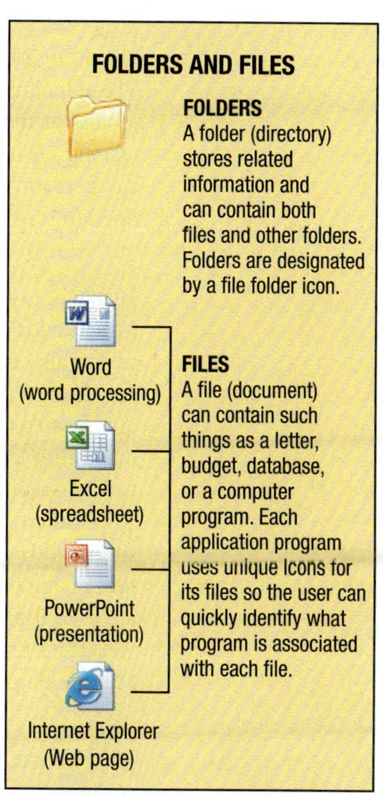

FIGURE 5-5
A sample hard drive organization.

File extensions should not be changed by the user because the operating system uses them to identify the program that should be used to open the document. For instance, if you give the command in a *file management program* (a program, such as *Windows Explorer*, that allows you to perform file management) to open a file named *Letter to Mom.doc*, the document will open using the Microsoft Word program because the *.doc* file extension is typically associated with the Microsoft Word word processing program. Depending on how your PC and file management program are set up, you may or may not be able to see file extensions; they are typically hidden by default, although that setting can be changed by the user. If the file to be opened does not have a file extension that your operating system recognizes, the operating system will ask you which program should be used to open the file.

File management programs can be used to open, move, copy, rename, or delete files, and to create new folders. The Windows Explorer file management program and other utilities typically included in an operating system are discussed near the end of this chapter.

FIGURE 5-6
Common file extensions.

WIDELY USED FILE EXTENSIONS
DOCUMENTS
.doc .txt .htm .html .mht .mhtml .xml .xls .mdb .ppt .rtf .pdf
PROGRAMS
.com .exe
GRAPHICS
.bmp .tif .jpg .eps .gif .png .pcx .svg
AUDIO
.wav .au .mp3 .snd .aiff .midi .aac .wma .ra
VIDEO
.mpg .mov .avi .mpeg .rm .wmv .asf
COMPRESSED FILES
.zip .sit .sitx .tar

Security

A computer's operating system can protect against unauthorized access by using *passwords*, *biometric* characteristics (such as fingerprints), or other security procedures to prevent outsiders from accessing system resources that they are not authorized to access. Most operating systems have other security features available, such as an integrated *firewall* to protect against unauthorized access via the Internet or an option to automatically download and install *security patches* (small program updates that correct known security problems) from the operating system's manufacturer on a regular basis. Operating system passwords can also be used to set up different accounts on a single PC to control access and capabilities; for example, to control children's access so they cannot install programs or change system settings. Passwords, biometrics, and other security issues related to networks and the Internet are discussed in much more detail in Chapter 9.

Processing Techniques for Increased Efficiency

Operating systems often utilize various processing techniques to operate more efficiently. These techniques usually involve either processing multiple programs at the same time or almost at the same time, or processing one program more quickly. Consequently, these techniques increase system efficiency and the amount of processing the computer system can perform in any given period of time. Some of the techniques most commonly used by operating systems to increase efficiency are discussed in the next few sections.

Multitasking

Multitasking refers to the ability of an operating system to work with more than one program (also called a *task*) at one time. For example, multitasking allows a user to edit a spreadsheet file in one window while loading a Web page in a Web browser in another window, or to retrieve new e-mail messages while editing a word processing document. Without the ability to multitask, an operating system would require the user to close one program before opening another. Virtually all of today's operating systems support multitasking.

Although multitasking enables multiple programs to be open and used at one time, a single CPU cannot work on all of the tasks at one time. Consequently, it rotates between processing tasks, but it works so quickly that to the user it appears as though all programs are executing at the same time.

The term *multitasking* is most commonly used in reference to single-user operating systems. Multitasking with a multiuser operating system is usually referred to as *multiprogramming*.

Multithreading

A *thread* is a sequence of instructions within a program that is independent of other threads. Examples might include spell checking, printing, and opening documents in a word processing program. Operating systems that support *multithreading* have the ability to run multiple threads for a program at one time (similar to the way multitasking is used to run multiple programs at one time) so that processing is completed faster and more efficiently. Most current operating systems support multithreading. Some CPU architectures—such as Intel's Hyper-Threading Technology—are designed to take advantage of multithreading.

Multiprocessing, Parallel Processing, and Coprocessing

As discussed in Chapter 2, both **multiprocessing** and **parallel processing** involve using two or more CPUs in one computer system to perform work more efficiently. The primary difference between these two techniques is that, with multiprocessing, each CPU typically works on a different job; with parallel processing, the processors usually work together to make one job finish sooner. In either case, all CPUs perform tasks *simultaneously* (at precisely the same instant), in contrast with multitasking and multithreading, which use a single CPU and process programs or tasks *concurrently* (by taking turns). Figure 5-7 illustrates the difference between concurrent and simultaneous processing.

Multiprocessing is supported by most operating systems and is traditionally used with servers and mainframe computers, although the *dual-core CPUs* discussed in Chapter 2 are bringing multiprocessing to the desktop PC user. Parallel processing is used most often with supercomputers and supercomputer clusters.

Coprocessing is another way of increasing processing efficiency. Coprocessing utilizes special-purpose processors (called *coprocessors*) to assist the CPU with specialized chores. For example, a *math coprocessor* performs mathematical computations, and a *graphics coprocessor* performs high-speed calculations for fast screen graphics display.

>**Multitasking.** The capability of an operating system to work with more than one programs at one time. >**Multiprocessing.** The capability of an operating system to use multiple processors in a single computer, usually to process multiple jobs at one time faster than could be performed with a single processor. >**Parallel processing.** A processing technique that uses multiple processors simultaneously in a single computer, usually to process a single job as fast as possible.

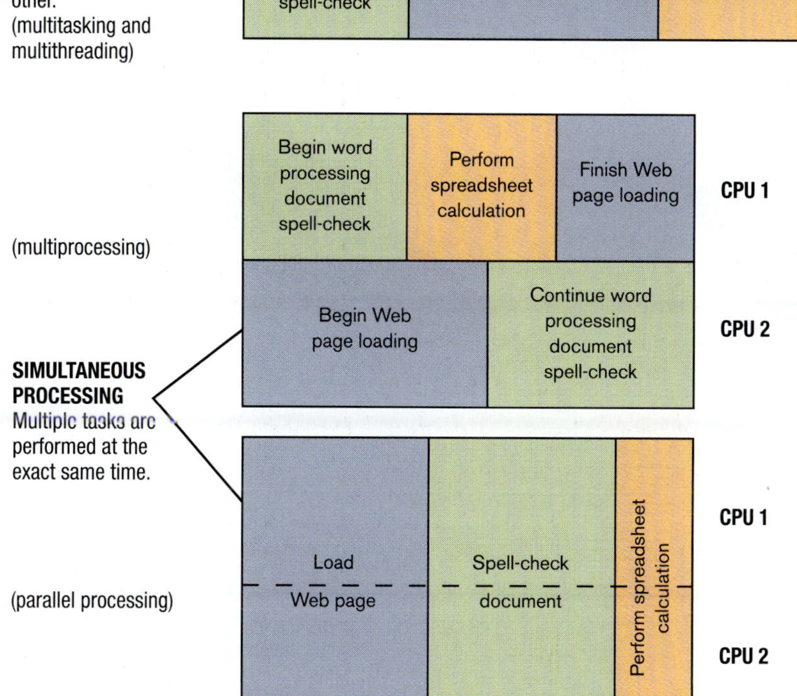

CONCURRENT VS. SIMULTANEOUS PROCESSING
With concurrent processing, tasks are performed one right after another; with simultaneous processing, multiple tasks are performed at exactly the same time. The tasks shown here are more typical of a desktop PC; typical tasks for multiprocessing and parallel processing computers would be more complex.

FIGURE 5-7
Concurrent vs. simultaneous processing.

Memory Management

Another key function of the operating system is *memory management*, which is optimizing the use of main memory (RAM). The operating system allocates RAM to programs as needed and then reclaims that memory when the program is closed. With today's memory-intensive programs (Windows XP requires a minimum of 64 MB of RAM, although 128 MB is recommended, and each open program requires additional RAM), good memory management can help speed up processing.

One memory management technique frequently used by operating systems is **virtual memory**, which uses a portion of the computer's hard drive as additional RAM. Programs and data ready for processing are stored in the virtual memory area of the hard drive (sometimes called the *swap file*). There, the content of virtual memory is divided into either fixed-length *pages* or variable-length *segments*, depending on the operating system being used. For example, a program that requires 20 MB of memory might be divided into 10 pages of 2 MB each. As the computer executes the program, it stores only some of the pages in RAM and the rest in virtual memory. As it requires other pages during program execution, it retrieves them from virtual memory and writes over the pages in RAM that are no longer needed (pages in RAM containing data not yet in virtual memory are copied to virtual memory before they are overwritten in RAM). All pages remain intact in virtual memory as the computer processes the program, so any page that was overwritten in

TIP

Although memory used by a program or process is supposed to be released when it is no longer needed, this does not always happen. Referred to as *memory leaking*, this problem can cause your computer to run out of memory temporarily. When this occurs, reboot the computer to refresh your RAM.

>**Virtual memory.** A memory-management technique that uses hard drive space as additional RAM.

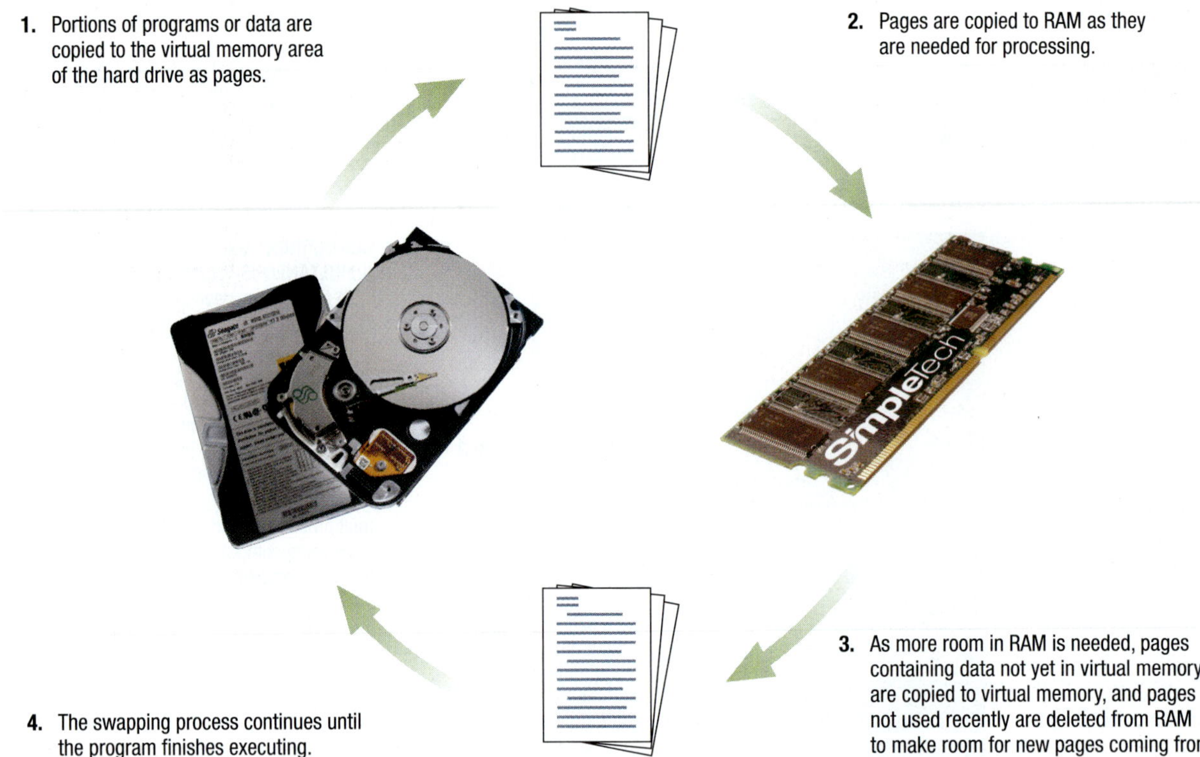

FIGURE 5-8

Virtual memory. With virtual memory, the operating system uses a portion of the hard drive as additional RAM.

RAM can be readily fetched from virtual memory again when needed. This process—sometimes called *swapping* or *paging*—continues until the program finishes executing (see Figure 5-8). Virtual memory allows you to use more memory than is physically available on your computer, but using virtual memory is slower than just using RAM. Most operating systems today allow the user to specify the total amount of hard drive space to be used for virtual memory.

Buffering and Spooling

Some input and output devices are exceedingly slow, compared to today's CPUs. If the CPU had to wait for these slower devices to finish their work, the computer system would face a horrendous bottleneck. For example, suppose a user just sent a 50-page document to the printer. Assuming the printer can output 10 pages per minute, it would take 5 minutes for the document to finish printing. If the CPU had to wait for the print job to be completed before performing other tasks, the PC would be tied up for 5 minutes.

To avoid this problem, most operating systems use two techniques—buffering and spooling. A **buffer** is an area in RAM or on the hard drive designated to hold input and output on their way in or out of the system. For instance, a *keyboard buffer* stores a certain number of characters as they are entered via the keyboard, and a *print buffer* stores documents that are waiting to be printed. The process of placing items in a buffer so they can be retrieved by the appropriate device when needed is called **spooling**. The most common use of spooling and buffering is for print jobs. It allows multiple documents to be sent to the printer at one time, and they will print, one after the other, in the background while the computer and user are performing other tasks. The documents waiting to be printed are said to be in a *print queue*, which designates the order the documents will be printed. While in the

>**Buffer.** An area in RAM or on the hard drive designated to hold input and output on their way in or out of the system. >**Spooling.** The process of placing items in a buffer so they can be retrieved by the appropriate device (such as a printer) when needed.

print queue, some operating systems allow the order of the documents to be rearranged, as well as the cancellation of a print job (see Figure 5-9).

Although originally used primarily for keyboard input and print jobs, most PCs and operating systems today use several other buffers to speed up operations. For instance, it is common today to use buffers to assist in redisplaying screen images and buffers in conjunction with burning CDs and DVDs.

All print jobs currently in the queue.

Print job being cancelled.

Print job currently printing.

FIGURE 5-9

A print queue.

Differences Among Operating Systems

There are different types of operating systems available to meet different needs. Some of the major distinctions between operating systems include the type of user interface utilized, whether the operating system is targeted for personal or network use, and what type of processing and CPU the operating system is designed for.

Command Line vs. Graphical User Interface

Most PC operating systems today use a **graphical user interface** (**GUI**). The older *DOS* operating systems and some versions of the *UNIX* and *Linux* operating systems use a **command line interface** (see Figure 5-10), although graphical versions of UNIX and Linux are available. With a command line interface, commands to the computer are typed using the keyboard; as explained in Chapter 1, graphical user interfaces allow the user to issue commands by selecting icons, buttons, menu items, and other graphical objects with a mouse or other pointing device. Operating systems for larger computers, such as mainframes, tend to use command line interfaces.

For a look at the interactive graphical user interface used in the popular *You Don't Know Jack* computer game, see the Inside the Industry box.

FIGURE 5-10

Command line vs. graphical user interfaces.

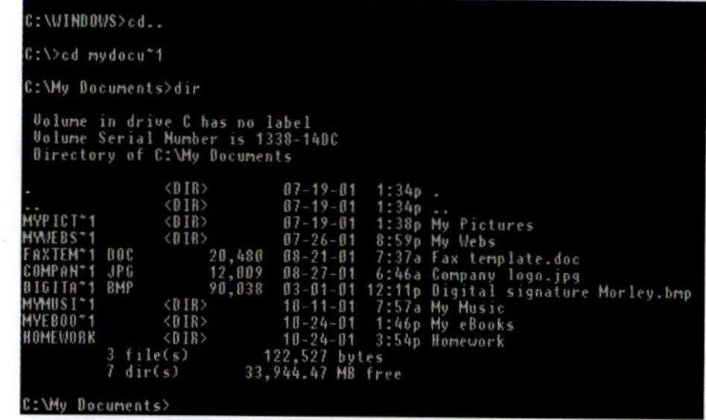

COMMAND LINE INTERFACE

Commands are entered using the keyboard.

GRAPHICAL USER INTERFACE

Icons, buttons, menus, and other objects are selected with the mouse to issue commands to the PC.

Personal vs. Server Operating Systems

Most operating systems are designated as either single-user **personal** (*desktop*) **operating systems** or multiuser **server** (*network*) **operating systems**. Although most personal operating systems today include some networking capabilities—such as to create a home network—they are designed to be installed on user PCs; server operating systems are designed to be installed on network servers. Many operating systems—such as Windows, *Mac OS*, and Linux—come in both a personal version and a server version (see Figure 5-11).

On a server-based network, a server operating system is installed on the server, and each PC attached to the network has its own personal operating system installed, just as with a stand-alone PC. The PCs may also need special *client* software to access the network and issue requests to the server. The server operating system—*Novell NetWare*, for example—controls access to network resources, while the personal operating system (such as Microsoft Windows, Mac OS, or Linux) controls the activity on the local PC. For instance, when you boot a PC connected to the network, the server operating system asks for your username and password, verifies your identity based on

>**Graphical user interface (GUI).** A graphically based interface that allows a user to communicate instructions to the computer easily. >**Command line interface.** A user interface in which commands are typed on a keyboard. >**Personal operating system.** A type of operating system designed to be installed on a PC. >**Server operating system.** A type of operating system designed to be installed on a network server.

INSIDE THE INDUSTRY

Jellyvision's Interactive Conversation Interface (iCi)

Beginning with its release in 1995, Jellyvision's *You Don't Know Jack* adult trivia game (see the accompanying screen shot) has been a huge success. Key to the program is Jellyvision's concept of "Interactive Conversation" that relies on a user interface called the *Interactive Conversation Interface* (*iCi*). The goal of iCi is to create the illusion of conversation between the player (a person) and the game host (a software program). To accomplish this, writers, designers, and other individuals work together to script and record realistic answers to every possible situation the player will encounter during the game and every response he or she will make to a question, and then they develop the program so that the proper responses will be delivered for each possible player action. Several factors crucial to the success of this process include ensuring the dialog is appropriate and doesn't repeat, giving the user only one task to do at a time with a limited number of choices, and keeping the pace steady by responding appropriately if the user does not answer a question. For instance, not answering a question quickly enough in the *You Don't Know Jack* program might cause the host's next assigned line to be "OK, sleepy, let's try that again" or "Excuse me, we've got a game to play!"–in the same manner as a real game show host would prod a contestant who failed to act in a timely manner during a live game show. Adding to the appeal of the *You Don't Know Jack* program is the chatty background atmosphere of a game show studio, catchy music and graphics, lots of animation, funny trivia questions, and a host whose casual, but intimate, conversation is funny, as well as sarcastic at times.

In addition to being used with computers games, iCi can be used for a variety of other applications, such as for an interactive tour with a guide who gives you advice via a cell phone as you travel by asking and responding to questions, for customized news delivery, for interactive customer service support, for educational applications, and more.

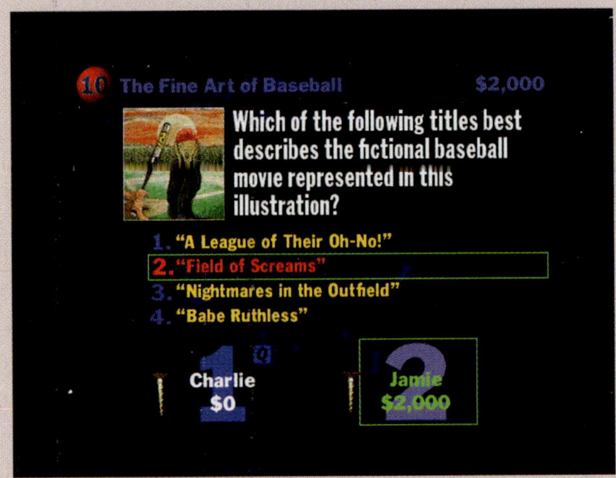

Jellyvision's best-selling YOU DON'T KNOW JACK games use iCi to create realistic conversations between the player and the host.

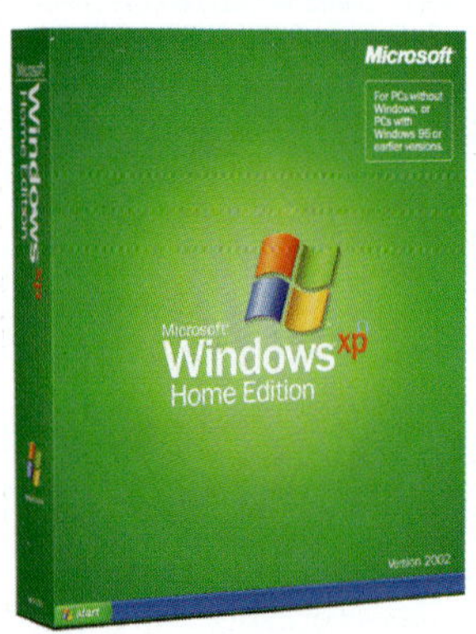

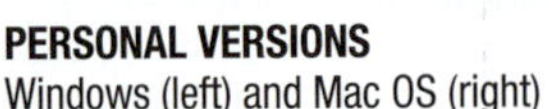

PERSONAL VERSIONS
Windows (left) and Mac OS (right)

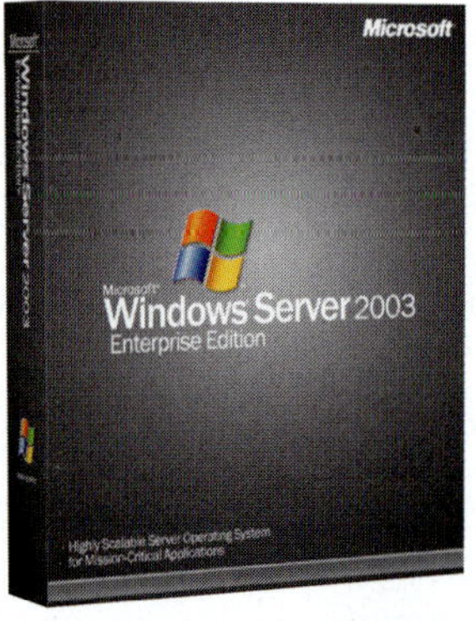

SERVER VERSIONS
Windows (left) and Mac OS (right)

FIGURE 5-11
Many operating systems have both a personal version and a server version.

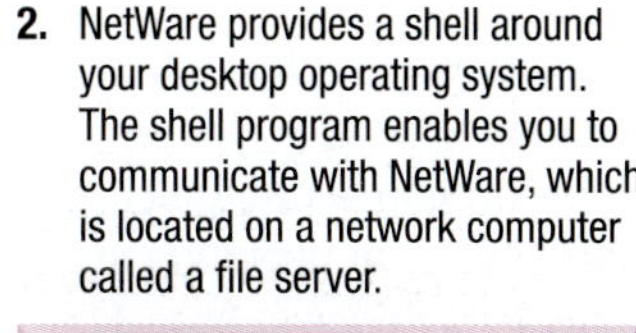
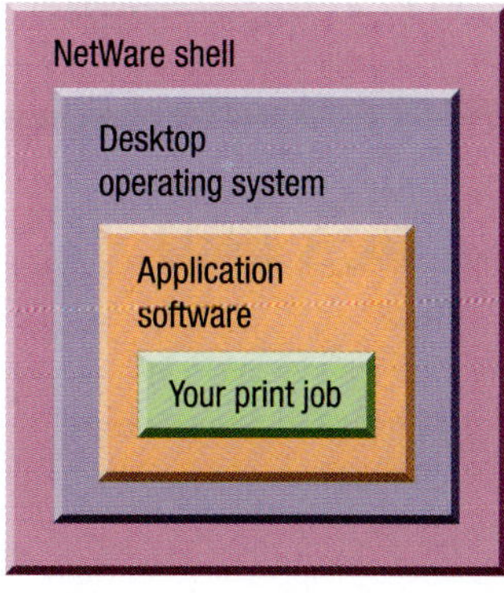
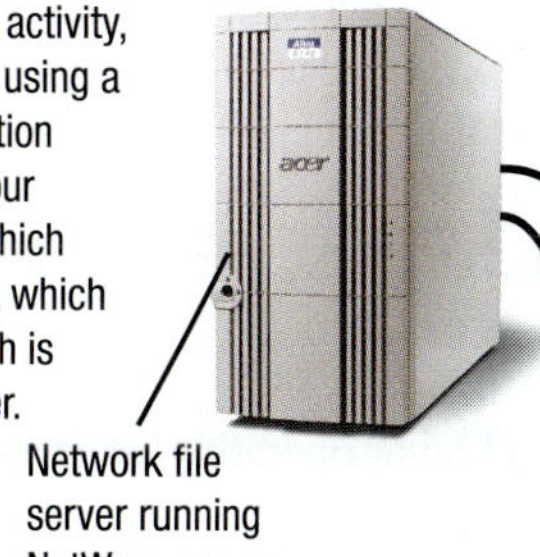

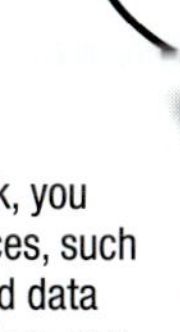
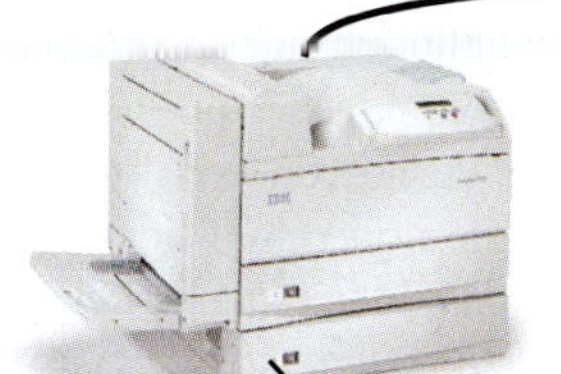

FIGURE 5-12
How a server operating system works. This example uses NetWare; other server operating systems work in a similar manner.

this supplied data, and then grants you access to the network resources you are authorized to access, such as launching programs or opening documents stored on the network server, or printing a document on a shared printer. Network resources (such as a shared network hard drive or printer) generally look like local (non-network) resources. For instance, a network hard drive would be listed with its own identifying letter (such as F or G) along with the drives included on your PC, and a network printer would be included on your list of available printers whenever you open a Print dialog box, provided you are connected to and logged on to the network. If you do not log on to the network or if the network is down, you cannot access network resources, such as to launch a program located on the network server, save a document to a network hard drive, or print using a shared printer. However, the personal operating system installed on your PC will allow you to work locally on that computer, just as you would on a stand-alone PC.

An overview of a typical NetWare scenario is illustrated in Figure 5-12; many other server operating systems work in a manner similar to this example. In addition to personal operating systems and server operating systems, there are also *mobile operating systems* and *embedded operating systems*. These operating systems are usually based on a personal operating system and are installed on consumer kiosks, cars, cash registers, cell phones, handheld PCs, and other non-PC-based devices.

The Types of Processors Supported

Most operating systems today are designed to be used with specific types of processors, such as Intel and AMD desktop CPUs, or Intel's Itanium processor. In addition, most operating systems today are designed for either 32-bit or 64-bit CPUs. As discussed in Chapter 2, typical desktop PC microprocessors are 32-bit processors, but the use of 64-bit processors is growing. Because their word size is twice as large, 64-bit processors can process up to twice as much data per clock cycle as a 32-bit processor (depending on the extent to which the application being used supports 64-bit processing), and they can address more than 4 GB of RAM. Both of these factors help to speed up processing in some applications, if a 64-bit operating system is being used. Operating systems that support 64-bit CPUs often include other architectural improvements that together may result in a more efficient operating system and, consequently, faster operations. At least some versions of Windows, Mac OS, Linux, and other widely used operating systems are 64-bit operating systems. Details about these and other operating systems are discussed next.

OPERATING SYSTEMS FOR DESKTOP PCS AND SERVERS

As previously discussed, operating systems today are usually designed either for desktop PCs or network servers and many operating systems are available in both personal and server versions. The most widely used personal and server operating systems are discussed next.

DOS

During the 1980s and early 1990s, **DOS** (**Disk Operating System**) was the dominant operating system for microcomputers. DOS traditionally used a command line interface, although newer versions of DOS support a menu-driven interface. A sampling of DOS commands is provided in Figure 5-13.

There were two primary forms of DOS: *PC-DOS* and *MS-DOS*. Both were originally developed by Microsoft Corporation, but PC-DOS was created originally for IBM microcomputers (and is now owned by IBM), whereas MS-DOS was used with IBM-compatible PCs. Neither version is updated any longer, but an alternative version of DOS originally created by Digital Research and called *DR-DOS* is still available and being marketed for use with thin clients and devices that use embedded operating systems. DOS, in any of its forms, is not widely used with personal computers today because it does not utilize a graphical user interface and does not support modern processors and processing techniques.

Windows

There have been many different versions of the Microsoft **Windows** operating system over the last several years. The next few sections chronicle the main developments of the Windows operating system.

Windows 1.0 through Windows 2000

Microsoft created the original version of Windows—*Windows 1.0*—in 1985 in an effort to meet the needs of users frustrated by having to learn and use DOS commands. Windows 1.0 through *Windows 3.x* (*x* stands for the version number of the software, such as Windows 3.0, 3.1, or 3.11) were not, however, full-fledged operating systems. Instead, they were *operating environments* for the DOS operating system; that is, graphical shells that operated around the DOS operating system designed to make DOS easier to use. Windows 3.0 was the first widely used version of Windows and allowed DOS to address more than 1 MB of RAM, perform multitasking, and run several built-in utility applications—such as a card file, calendar, and paint program. Still, the shortcomings of DOS limited the effectiveness of Windows 3.x.

>DOS (Disk Operating System). The operating system designed for and widely used on early IBM and IBM-compatible PCs. **>Windows.** The primary PC operating system developed by Microsoft Corporation; the most recent version is Windows XP.

```
C:\WINDOWS>cd..

C:\>cd mydocu~1

C:\My Documents>dir

 Volume in drive C has no label
 Volume Serial Number is 1338-140C
 Directory of C:\My Documents

.              <DIR>        07-19-01  1:34p .
..             <DIR>        07-19-01  1:34p ..
MYPICT~1       <DIR>        07-19-01  1:38p My Pictures
MYWEBS~1       <DIR>        07-26-01  8:59p My Webs
FAXTEM~1 DOC        20,480  08-21-01  7:37a Fax template.doc
COMPAN~1 JPG        12,009  08-27-01  6:46a Company logo.jpg
DIGITA~1 BMP        90,038  03-01-01 12:11p Digital signature Morley.bmp
MYMUSI~1       <DIR>        10-11-01  7:57a My Music
MYEBOO~1       <DIR>        10-24-01  1:46p My eBooks
HOMEWORK       <DIR>        10-24-01  3:54p Homework
         3 file(s)        122,527 bytes
         7 dir(s)      33,944.47 MB free

C:\My Documents>
```

FIGURE 5-13

DOS. Even though DOS has become technologically obsolete, some PCs still use it. This table lists some of the most commonly used DOS commands, and the screen shows DOS in action.

COMMAND	DESCRIPTION	EXAMPLE	EXPLANATION
COPY	Copies individual files	**COPY BOSS A:WORKER**	Makes a copy of the file BOSS located in the current directory on the current disk and stores it on the disk in the A drive using the filename WORKER.
DIR	Displays the names of files on a disk	**DIR A:**	Displays names of files stored on the disk in the A drive.
DEL	Deletes individual files	**DEL A:DOLLAR**	Deletes the file DOLLAR from the disk in the A drive.
REN	Renames individual files	**REN SAM BILL**	Changes the name of the file SAM located in the current directory on the current disk to BILL.
CD	Changes to a new directory	**CD HOMEWORK**	Changes the current directory to HOMEWORK, located one level down from the current location on the current disk.
FORMAT	Prepares a disk for use, erasing what was there before	**FORMAT A:**	Formats the disk in the A drive.

In 1994, Microsoft announced that all versions of Windows after 3.11 would be full-fledged operating systems instead of just operating environments. The next several versions of Windows are listed next:

- *Windows 95* (released in1995) and *Windows 98* (released in 1998)—both used a similar GUI to the one used with Windows 3.x, but they were easier to use, and supported multitasking, long filenames, a higher degree of Internet integration, more options for customizing the desktop user interface, improved support for large hard drives, and support for both DVD and USB devices.
- *Windows 98 Second Edition* (*SE*)—an update to Windows 98 released in 1999. Although Windows 98 is no longer sold, there is still an installed base of older PCs running Windows 98 SE.
- *Windows NT* (*New Technology*)—the first 32-bit version of Windows designed for high-end workstations and servers. Windows NT was built from the ground up using a different basic code base or kernel than the other versions of Windows.

TIP

When a new version of a program that you use (such as an operating system or application program) becomes available, you can typically buy an *upgrade* version of that program that installs over your existing version, if you want to move to the new version. Upgrades are almost always less expensive than buying a new full version.

- *Windows Me (Millennium Edition)*—the replacement for Windows 98 and Windows 98 SE. Designed for home PCs, Windows Me supported improved home networking and a shared Internet connection; it also featured improved multimedia capabilities, better system protection, a faster boot process, and more Internet-ready activities and games. Windows Me was the last version of Windows that used the original Windows 95 kernel.
- *Windows 2000*—released in 2000 to replace Windows NT for workstation use. Windows 2000 was geared towards high-end business workstations and servers and included support for wireless devices and other types of new hardware.

These earlier versions of Windows have all been replaced by *Windows XP* (a personal operating system) and *Windows Server 2003* (a server operating system). Versions of *Windows Vista*, when available, will replace both Windows XP and Windows Server 2003. These three versions of Windows are discussed next.

Windows XP

Windows XP is the latest personal version of Windows and replaces both Windows 2000 (for business use) and Windows Me (for home use). It is based on Windows NT technology and is more stable and powerful than earlier versions of Windows built on the Windows 9x kernel. Windows XP has a slightly different appearance than earlier versions of Windows (see Figure 5-14), but the basic elements (Start menu, taskbar, menu bars, and so forth) are still present. In addition, users have the option of using the classic Windows interface—the one used in Windows 2000, Me, and 98—instead of the new interface, if they prefer. Some of the newest features of Windows XP are related to multimedia and communications, such as improved photo, video, and music editing and sharing; the ability to switch between user accounts without closing open windows; the ability to access a PC remotely via a network; improved networking capabilities; and support for handwriting and voice input.

FIGURE 5-14

Windows XP. Most versions of Windows XP look like the Professional edition (left); Windows XP Media Center (right), however, has a different appearance.

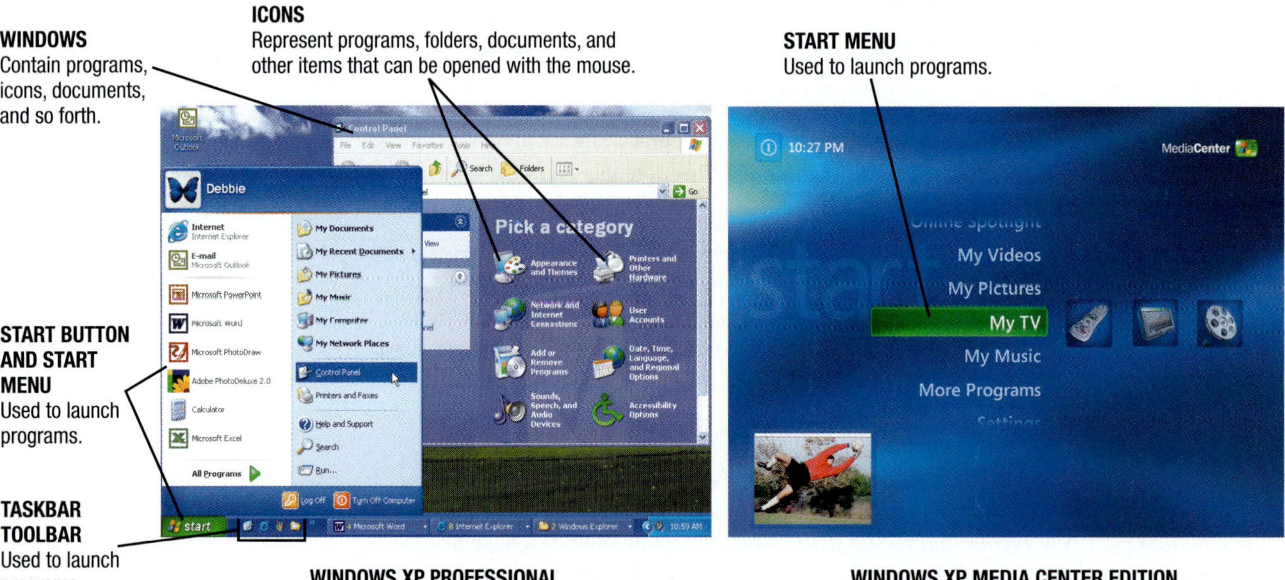

>**Windows XP.** The latest personal version of Windows; designed to replace both Windows Me and Windows 2000.

Windows XP is available in the five different versions listed next. All of the versions except *Windows XP Media Center Edition* use a similar interface (refer again to Figure 5-14). In addition, there are special versions of Windows XP Home Edition that contain fewer features and are designed for first-time home users with lower-end PCs in a variety of countries other than the United States. One of these *Windows XP Starter Editions* is shown in Figure 5-15.

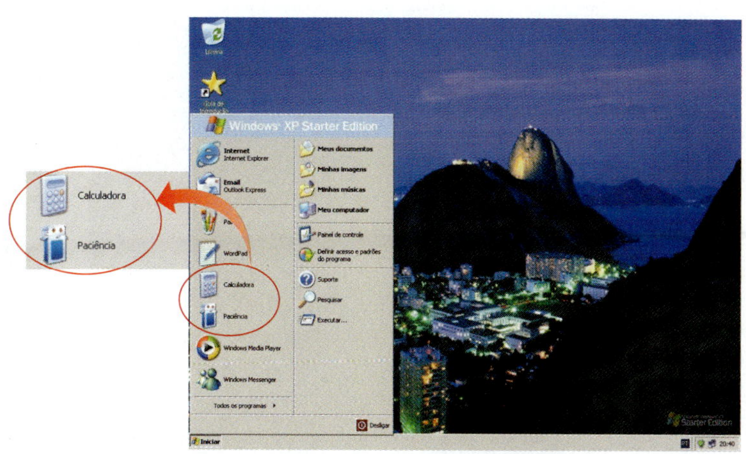

FIGURE 5-15

Windows XP Starter Editions. There are Windows XP Starter Editions for a variety of countries, such as the Brazilian version shown here.

- *Windows XP Home Edition*—designed for home PCs. Includes improvements for working with digital photographs, playing digital music, making home movies, and communicating with others.
- *Windows XP Professional*—designed for business users and advanced home computing. In addition to the features included in the Home Edition, Windows XP Professional has additional security and privacy features, improved ability to connect to large networks, and the ability to remotely access one PC from another.
- *Windows XP Professional x64 Edition*—designed specifically for high-end business PCs using 64-bit CPUs and users who require large amounts of memory and processing speed, such as for movie special effects, 3D, animation, engineering, and scientific applications.
- *Windows XP Tablet PC Edition*—designed for use with tablet PCs and includes extended pen and speech input capabilities, as well as improved wireless connectivity. This version of Windows is only available already installed on a tablet PC.
- *Windows XP Media Center Edition*—designed for living room PCs and other PCs designated as Windows Media Center PCs. Combines computing, television, and multimedia capabilities; incorporates additional features for watching live TV, recording TV shows, watching DVDs, and managing music, video, and photo collections on a PC or TV display. This version of Windows is only available already installed on a Windows Media Center PC.

Windows Server 2003

Windows Server 2003 is the most recent version of Windows designed for server use. It builds on the server version of Windows 2000 but is designed to be easier to deploy, manage, and use. It also incorporates Microsoft *.NET* technology for connecting information, people, systems, and devices. Windows Server 2003 comes in four versions: *Standard Edition* for small to medium networks with standard workloads; *Enterprise Edition* for larger, more mission-critical servers; *Datacenter Edition* for high-level servers requiring the highest levels of scalability and reliability; and *Web Edition* for dedicated Web servers. In 2005, Microsoft released 64-bit *x64* versions of the Standard, Enterprise, and Datacenter editions.

>**Windows Server 2003.** The most recent version of Windows designed for server use.

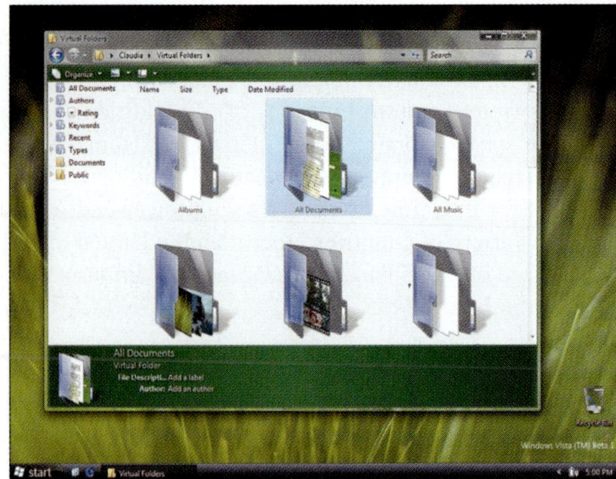

FIGURE 5-16

Windows Vista. The beta version shown here reveals some slight differences in appearance from Windows XP, but the core functionality seems to remain the same.

Windows Vista

The next major release of Windows is **Windows Vista** (previously code-named *Longhorn*). Beta testing of Windows Vista began in 2005, and both a personal and server version of the new Windows is expected to be available by 2007. Previews of Windows Vista reveal a new graphical interface that has the core functionality of the Windows XP interface but a slightly different appearance (see Figure 5-16). Windows Vista is expected to include more visual features and to have intuitive file management capabilities that allow documents to be created or organized based on characteristics, such as author, subject, keyword, category, artist, song title, and so forth. Beta versions of Vista also include improved search capabilities and better support for peer-to-peer searches and file sharing. In addition, Vista is expected to directly support DVD burning, and Microsoft has announced that it will be more secure, easier to manage and update, and it will support advanced document technologies, such as *XML (extensible markup language)*. XML is discussed in more detail in Chapter 10.

Mac OS

Mac OS is the proprietary operating system for computers made by Apple Corporation. It is based on the UNIX operating system (discussed shortly) and originally set the standard for graphical user interfaces. Many of today's operating systems follow the trend that Mac OS started and, in fact, use interfaces that highly resemble the one used with Mac OS.

There have been a number of different versions of Mac OS since the original Apple Macintosh computer debuted in 1984. The latest personal and server versions of the operating system are version 10.4 of **Mac OS X**, also known as *Tiger*. Like earlier versions of Mac OS X, Tiger (see Figure 5-17) allows multithreading and multitasking; it also supports dual 64-bit processors and a high level of multimedia functions and connectivity. New features include a new search feature, called *Spotlight*, which allows users to search through documents, folders, e-mail messages, and programs based on a variety of criteria, and then continues to update those searches and add related files as the user works. A new *Dashboard* feature hosts a variety of mini applications called *widgets* that can be used to receive timely information from the Internet, such as stock quotes, weather forecasts, flight updates, phone numbers, and more. Tiger also supports handwritten and voice input.

>**Windows Vista.** The upcoming version of Windows (previously known as Longhorn) that is designed to replace Windows XP. >**Mac OS X.** The most recent version of the operating system used on Apple computers.

FIGURE 5-17
Mac OS X Tiger.

UNIX

UNIX was originally developed in the late 1960s at AT&T Bell Laboratories as an operating system for midrange servers. UNIX is a multiuser, multitasking operating system. Computer systems ranging from microcomputers to mainframes can run UNIX, and it can support a variety of devices from different manufacturers. This flexibility gives UNIX an advantage over competing operating systems for many types of applications. However, UNIX is more expensive, requires a higher level of PC knowledge, and tends to be harder to install, maintain, and upgrade than most other commonly used operating systems.

There are many versions of UNIX available and many operating systems based on UNIX. These operating systems—such as Mac OS and Linux—are sometimes referred to as *UNIX flavors*. In fact, the term "UNIX," which initially referred to the original UNIX operating system, has evolved to refer today to a group of similar operating systems based on UNIX. Many UNIX flavors are not compatible with each other, which creates some problems when a program written for one UNIX computer system is moved to another computer system running a different flavor of UNIX. A new universal UNIX specification is expected to be used with upcoming versions of UNIX-based operating systems to alleviate this incompatibility problem. In fact the *Open Group* open source consortium is a working group dedicated to the development and evolution of the *Single UNIX Specification*—a standardized programming environment for UNIX applications. Both personal and server versions of UNIX-based operating systems are available.

Linux

Linux is a flavor of UNIX originally developed by Linus Torvalds in 1991 when he was a student at the University of Helsinki in Finland. The operating system was released to the public as *open source software*; that is, a program whose *source code* is available to the public and can be modified to improve it or to customize it to a particular application. Over the years, Linux has obtained a loyal band of followers, and volunteer programmers from all over the world have collaborated to improve it, sharing their

>**UNIX.** An operating system developed in the 1970s for midrange servers and mainframes; many variations of this operating system are in use today. >**Linux.** A version (flavor) of UNIX that is available without charge over the Internet and is increasingly being used with PCs, servers, mainframes, and supercomputers.

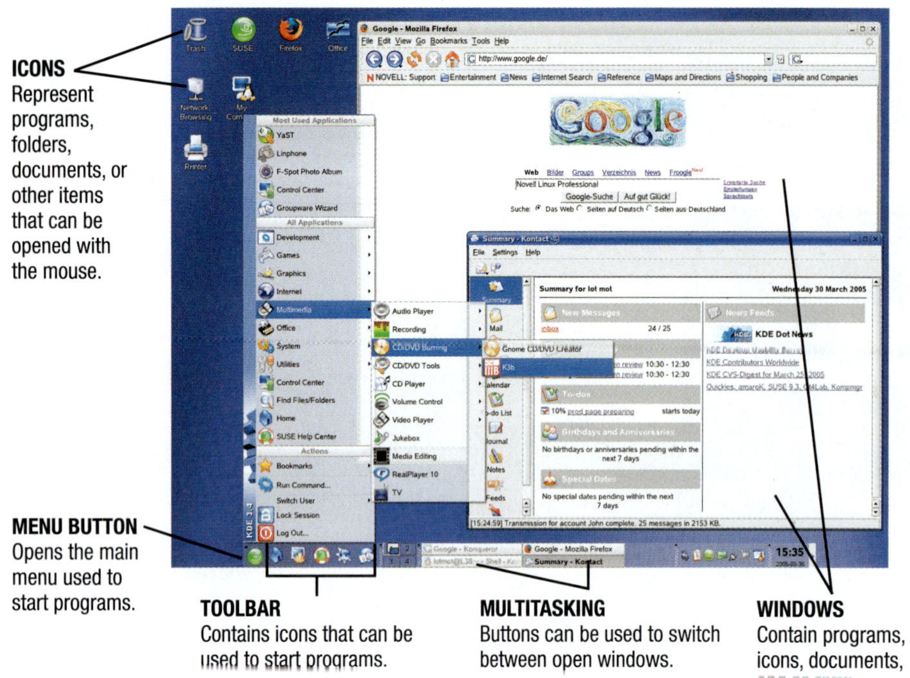

FIGURE 5-18

Linux. Linux is a rapidly growing alternative to Windows and Mac OS that is available free of charge over the Internet. Purchased versions are also available, such as the one shown here.

modified code with others over the Internet. Some versions of Linux are available as free downloads from the Internet; companies are also permitted to customize Linux and sell it as a retail product. Some of the most widely known commercial versions of Linux are from Red Hat and Novell.

Although Linux originally used a command line interface, most recent versions of Linux programs use a graphical user interface (see Figure 5-18). These interfaces are generally built around either the *KDE* or *GNOME* desktop environments, products of the KDE Internet project and the GNOME project and foundation, respectively. Both organizations are committed to developing free, easy-to-use desktop environments and powerful application frameworks for Linux and other operating systems based on UNIX. Purchased Linux operating systems usually come with more support materials than the versions downloaded for free. Linux is available in personal, professional, and server versions.

In the past few years, Linux has grown from an operating system used primarily by computer techies who disliked Microsoft to a widely accepted operating system with strong support from mainstream companies, such as Sun, IBM, HP, and Novell. For instance, many large companies, including Charles Schwab & Co, use Linux to run their data centers; the city of Munich, Germany, has switched to Linux; and several large cities in Brazil are running only Linux software. The primary reason companies are switching to Linux and other open source software is cost. Typically, using the Linux operating system and a free or low-cost office suite, Web browser program, and e-mail program can enable a business to work competitively while at the same time saving several hundreds of dollars per computer user. For instance, Microsoft Windows XP Professional Edition retails for $299 while Linux can be downloaded for free or a retail version purchased for around $50, and the standard edition of Microsoft Office 2003 retails for $400 while the similar *OpenOffice.org* office suite is free and Sun's *StarOffice 7* costs $80. Although most of these programs do not incorporate as many features as Microsoft Office, many users find them adequate for their needs, and the cost savings can be significant. Another reason some companies are moving to Linux is dissatisfaction with Microsoft products, the need for only a limited number of employee applications (such as retail store computers that are set up to do a limited number of tasks), as well as companies employing programmers, engineers, and other technical workers who are already familiar with Linux or UNIX. Many Linux supporters maintain that personal computers running Linux crash less often, are more secure and less prone to viruses and other security hazards, and are easier to run on older equipment. In addition to the growing use on servers and desktop PCs, it has been suggested that the next biggest growth area for the Linux operating system might be in lower-end personal computers, Internet appliances, and point-of-sale terminals.

NetWare

NetWare—developed by Novell during the mid-1980s—is one of the most widely used operating systems today for networks and competes directly with the server versions of Windows and Mac OS. As discussed earlier and illustrated in Figure 5-12, NetWare provides a shell around your personal desktop operating system through which you can interact with network resources, such as a shared hard drive or printer. The latest version of NetWare is *NetWare 6.5*. NetWare is also incorporated in Novell's new Open Enterprise Server product that combines NetWare and Novell's server version of Linux (*SUSE Linux Enterprise Server*) into a single suite to allow businesses to use NetWare, Linux, or a combination of both technologies.

FURTHER EXPLORATION

For links to further information about operating systems, go to www.course.com/uc11/ch05

Solaris

Solaris is a UNIX-based operating system developed by Sun Microsystems for Sun computers. The Solaris operating system can run on desktop systems and servers, as well as on some supercomputers. There is also a Solaris operating environment that can be used to bring enhanced stability and functionality to UNIX machines. The latest version of Solaris—*Solaris 10*—is designed to run across a variety of platforms in a safe, efficient, and stable manner. Some new features include diagnostic tools to detect and fix bottlenecks and errors before they cause a failure and a new *container* system that allows a server to be partitioned into as many as 8,000 secure partitions. In 2005, Sun released some of the Solaris code to create a new open source project called *OpenSolaris*.

SW

OPERATING SYSTEMS FOR HANDHELD PCS AND MOBILE DEVICES

Handheld PCs, as well as smart phones, pagers, and other mobile devices, usually require a different operating system than a desktop PC. Typically, the operating system used is one designed for mobile devices in general or is a proprietary operating system designed solely for that specific device. In many mobile devices, the operating system is embedded into the device using flash RAM chips or similar hardware. Operating systems are also embedded into everyday objects, such as home appliances, game boxes, digital cameras, toys, watches, navigation systems, home medical devices, voting terminals, portable media players, and cars. The most widely used operating systems for handheld PCs and mobile devices are discussed next.

Embedded and Mobile Versions of Windows

There are both embedded and mobile versions of Windows targeted for handheld PCs, smart phones, and other mobile devices, called *Windows Embedded* and *Windows Mobile*, respectively.

Windows Embedded

Windows Embedded is a family of operating systems based on Windows that is designed primarily for nonpersonal computer-based devices, such as cash registers, ATM machines, thin clients, and consumer electronic devices. The Windows Embedded family includes *Windows CE 5.0* (designed for devices requiring multimedia capabilities, such as DVD

>**NetWare.** A widely used operating system for PC-based networks. >**Windows Embedded.** A family of operating systems based on Windows and designed for nonpersonal computer devices, such as cash registers and consumer electronic devices.

TECHNOLOGY AND YOU

Smart Cars

Computers have been integrated into cars for years to perform tasks such as regulating fuel consumption, controlling emissions, assisting with gear shifting and braking, and more. Lately, however, the use of computers in cars has skyrocketed. It is estimated that over 20% of the components in today's cars are electronic, and that figure is expected to reach 40% in the near future. Essentially, cars are getting smart and these new digital improvements help to make cars smarter and safer. Some features, such as GPS navigation systems and smart air bag systems that adjust the deployment of an air bag based on the weight of the occupant, are fairly standard today. Some new and emerging trends in smart cars include the following:

- Volvo has developed a *blind spot information system (BLIS)* that uses a digital camera mounted on the driver's side mirror to detect vehicles in the driver's blind spot (see the accompanying photo). The camera takes 25 photos per second and an onboard computer analyzes the photos to determine when there is a moving car or motorcycle in the blind spot—a yellow warning light near the mirror tells the driver that something is in the blind spot. This feature is available as an option on 2006 models.
- Select Audi models now have the option of a *keyless entry and ignition system*, in which the user's fingerprint is used to unlock and start the car.
- Ford, BMW, and Mercedes are all working to develop *adaptive cruise control systems*. These systems, available now on select Mercedes models, use a radar system installed on the front of the car to detect the speed and distance of the vehicle ahead of it, and then automatically decrease or increase the speed of the car up to the driver's selected cruise control speed to maintain a safe distance from the vehicle ahead of it.
- IBM has developed a *voice recognition system* that uses both video and audio input to understand more accurately the driver's voice commands. In tests, the dual-input system improved performance by 80%.
- In addition to being used to lock, unlock, arm, and disarm the car, the remote for Dodge Viper's new security system is a *two-way remote* that blinks and chimes to notify the owner whenever the car's alarm system goes off.

One of the biggest challenges for smart car technologies is the safe use of all the smart gadgets being incorporated into cars. The concern stems from studies consistently showing that distracted drivers are the cause of the vast majority of crashes—nearly 80%, according to a 2005 study. Voice controlled digital dashboards, cell phones, and other devices help because they are hands-free, although studies have found that your risk of an accident requiring a trip to the hospital quadruples when you are talking on a cell phone—hands-free or not.

Volvo's BLIS system. This system notifies the driver when a moving vehicle is in the driver's blind spot.

players, digital cameras, and other consumer electronic devices) and *Windows XP Embedded* (a more powerful operating system used with retail point-of-sale terminals, thin clients, and advanced gaming boxes). There is also a version of Windows CE called *Windows Automotive*, which is an embedded operating system used in cars. For a look at some of the features now available in *smart cars*, see the Technology and You box.

Windows Mobile

Windows Mobile is the version of Windows designed for handheld PCs, smart phones, and portable media players. Windows Mobile has some of the look and feel of the larger desktop versions of Windows (see Figure 5-19) and can be used with *pocket* versions of a number of Microsoft desktop computer software products, such as Word, Excel, Outlook, Messenger, Internet Explorer, and more. The most recent version is *Windows Mobile 5.0*.

Palm OS

Palm OS is the operating system designed for Palm handheld devices (see Figure 5-20). The philosophy behind Palm OS was to design an operating system specifically for mobile devices, instead of trying to convert an entire desktop operating system into a smaller package. Consequently, Palm OS was designed to use memory and battery power very efficiently. Palm OS is developed by PalmSource, a subsidiary of Palm, Inc., and the latest version is *Palm OS Cobalt 6.1*. In addition to being used on Palm handheld PCs, Palm OS has been increasingly used by other manufacturers of handheld PCs, smart phones, and mobile devices.

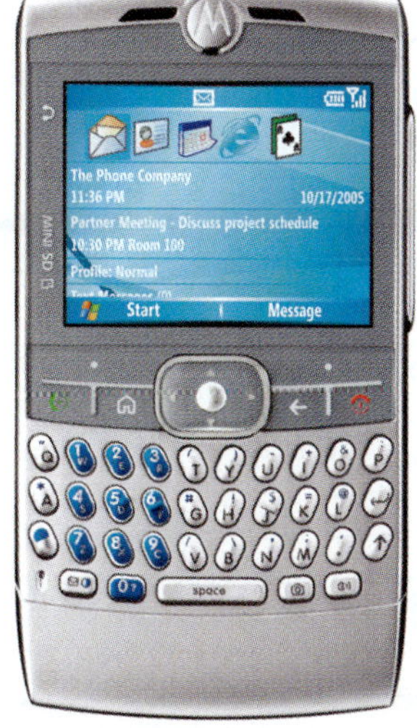

HANDHELD PC

PORTABLE MEDIA PLAYER

FIGURE 5-19
Windows Mobile. Mobile versions of Windows resemble desktop versions of Windows, but on a smaller scale.

Embedded Linux

Embedded Linux is another alternative for use with handheld PCs and mobile devices. In addition to existing versions of embedded Linux, Palm announced in 2005 the intent to develop a version of the Palm OS based on a version of embedded Linux. A Wi-Fi Internet tablet using embedded Linux is shown in Figure 5-20. This product, from Nokia, connects to the Internet via a Wi-Fi network or a Bluetooth-compatible mobile phone. Other embedded Linux products include the TiVo DVR and the TouchTunes touch screen digital jukeboxes.

FIGURE 5-20
Palm OS, embedded Linux, and Symbian OS.

A HANDHELD PC RUNNING PALM OS

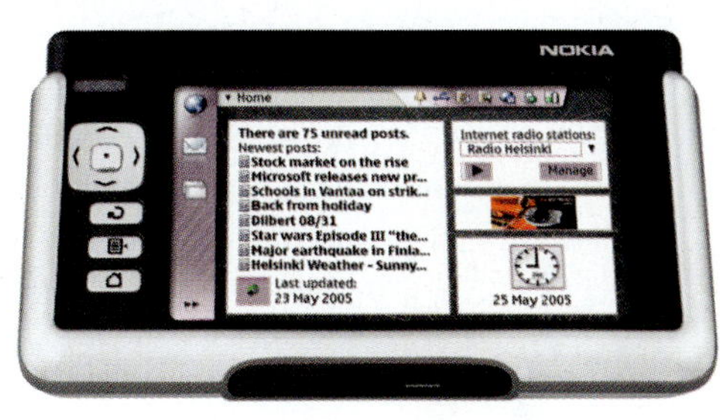

A WI-FI INTERNET TABLET RUNNING EMBEDDED LINUX

A SMART PHONE RUNNING SYMBIAN OS

>**Windows Mobile.** A family of operating systems based on Windows and designed for handheld PCs, smart phones, and other mobile devices. >**Palm OS.** The operating system designed for Palm handheld PCs. >**Embedded Linux.** A version of Linux designed for handheld PCs and mobile devices.

Symbian OS

Symbian OS is one of the leading operating systems for smart phones, and it is based on the *EPOC* operating system developed by the UK technology company Psion. Symbian OS was initially released in 1998 by the private company Symbian, which was established by Psion and several wireless industry leaders, including Nokia, Ericsson, and Motorola. Symbian OS is an advanced, multithreaded, multitasking operating system that includes support for Web browsing, e-mail, handwriting recognition, synchronization, and a range of other applications designed for mobile communications and computing. Symbian OS has a flexible user interface framework that enables mobile phone manufacturers to develop and customize user interfaces to meet the needs of their customers. A smart phone using Symbian OS Version 7.0 and one possible user interface is shown in Figure 5-20.

OPERATING SYSTEMS FOR LARGER COMPUTERS

Larger computer systems—such as high-end servers, mainframes, and supercomputers—sometimes use operating systems designed solely for that type of system. For instance, IBM's *z/OS*, *OS/390*, and *MVS* operating systems are designed for their various mainframes, and many larger Sun computers are powered by the Solaris operating system. Conventional operating systems, such as Windows, UNIX, and Linux, are also used with both mainframes and supercomputers. Linux is increasingly being used with both mainframes and supercomputers; often a group of Linux PCs are linked together to form what is referred to as a *Linux supercluster* supercomputer. For example, the world's fastest supercomputer—Blue Gene/L (shown in Figure 1-21 in Chapter 1)—runs Linux. Larger computer systems may also use a customized operating system based on a conventional operating system; for instance, many IBM mainframes use *AIX*, a version of UNIX developed by IBM.

UTILITY PROGRAMS

A **utility program** is a type of software program that performs a specific task, usually related to managing or maintaining the computer system. Many utility programs—such as programs for finding files, diagnosing and repairing system problems, cleaning up a hard drive, viewing images, playing multimedia files, and backing up files—are built into operating systems. There are also many stand-alone utility programs available as an alternative to the operating system's utility programs (such as a *search tool* or *backup program* containing additional features) or to provide additional utility features not usually built into operating systems (such as an *antivirus* or *file compression* program). Stand-alone utility programs are often available in a *suite* of related programs (such as a collection of security programs or maintenance programs, as shown in Figure 5-21). Some of the most commonly used integrated and stand-alone utility programs are discussed next. For a look at how to download and install a new utility program from the Internet, see the How it Works box.

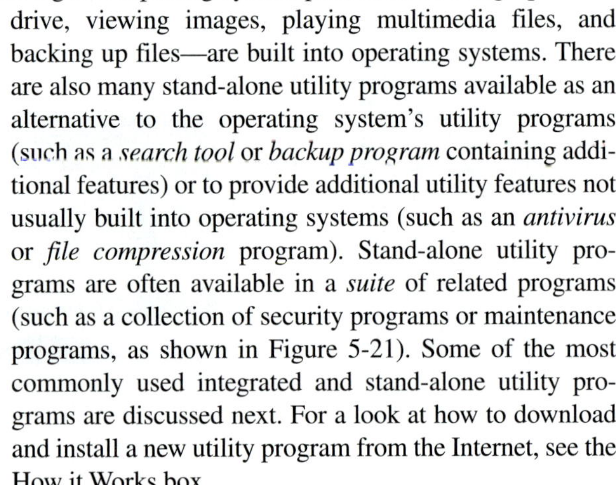

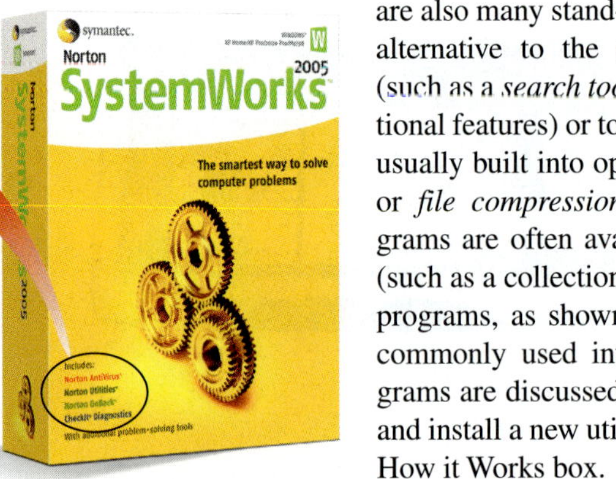

FIGURE 5-21
Utility suites. Utility suites contain a number of related utility programs.

>**Symbian OS.** A leading operating system for smart phones. >**Utility program.** A type of software that performs a specific task, usually related to managing or maintaining the computer system.

HOW IT WORKS

Downloading and Installing Programs

Many software programs are available to download via the Web. To download a program, generally a hyperlink is clicked and then the file is downloaded to your PC in the location that you specified. To start the installation process for a downloaded file, locate the file on your hard drive and open it. With some installations, you can specify the location in which the program will be installed on your PC. Many installations require that you accept the terms of a license agreement before the program will be installed; if the product was purchased, some also require you to type in the *registration code* that was provided after your payment was processed. Once the installation process has been completed, the program can be launched. This procedure is illustrated in the accompanying illustration.

DOWNLOADING THE PROGRAM

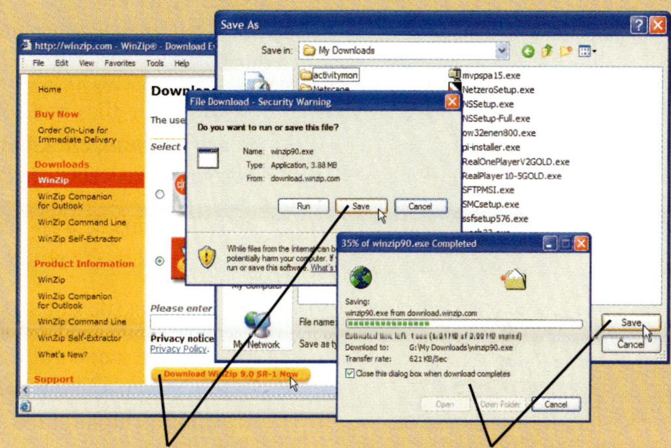

1. Click the download link, then click Save to download the program.
2. Specify the download location, then click Save to download the installation file.

INSTALLING THE PROGRAM

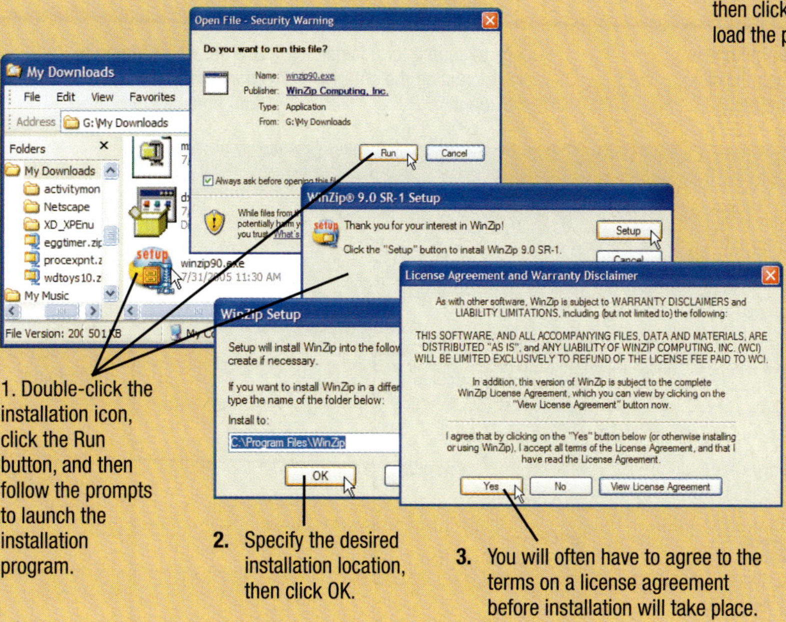

1. Double-click the installation icon, click the Run button, and then follow the prompts to launch the installation program.

2. Specify the desired installation location, then click OK.

3. You will often have to agree to the terms on a license agreement before installation will take place.

USING THE INSTALLED PROGRAM

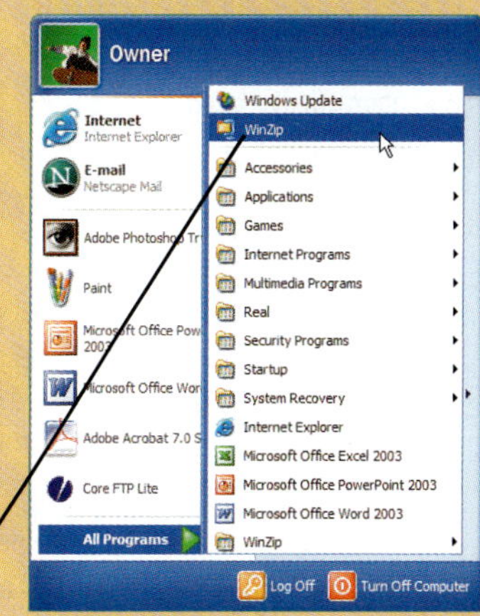

Click the program name on the Start menu to launch the installed program

File Management Programs

File management programs allow you to perform such file management tasks as formatting a disk; looking at the contents of a storage medium; and copying, moving, deleting, and renaming folders and files. The primary file management program included with Windows XP is *Windows Explorer*. Common file management tasks using this program are summarized next; since there is generally more than one way to perform each of the following tasks, one commonly used method is described for each task.

Looking at the Contents of a PC

Once a file management program is open, you can look at the files and folders stored on your PC.

- To see the files and folders stored on your floppy disk, hard drive, or any other storage medium, click the appropriate letter or name for that medium (some programs or setups may require you to double-click instead of single-click); see Figure 5-22.
- To look inside a folder, double-click the folder. To close that folder and go back up one level in the structure, click the Up toolbar button.
- To open a file in its associated program, double-click it.
- To create a new folder in the current location, select *New* and then *Folder* from the File menu, and then enter the name for the new folder while the default name *New Folder* is highlighted.

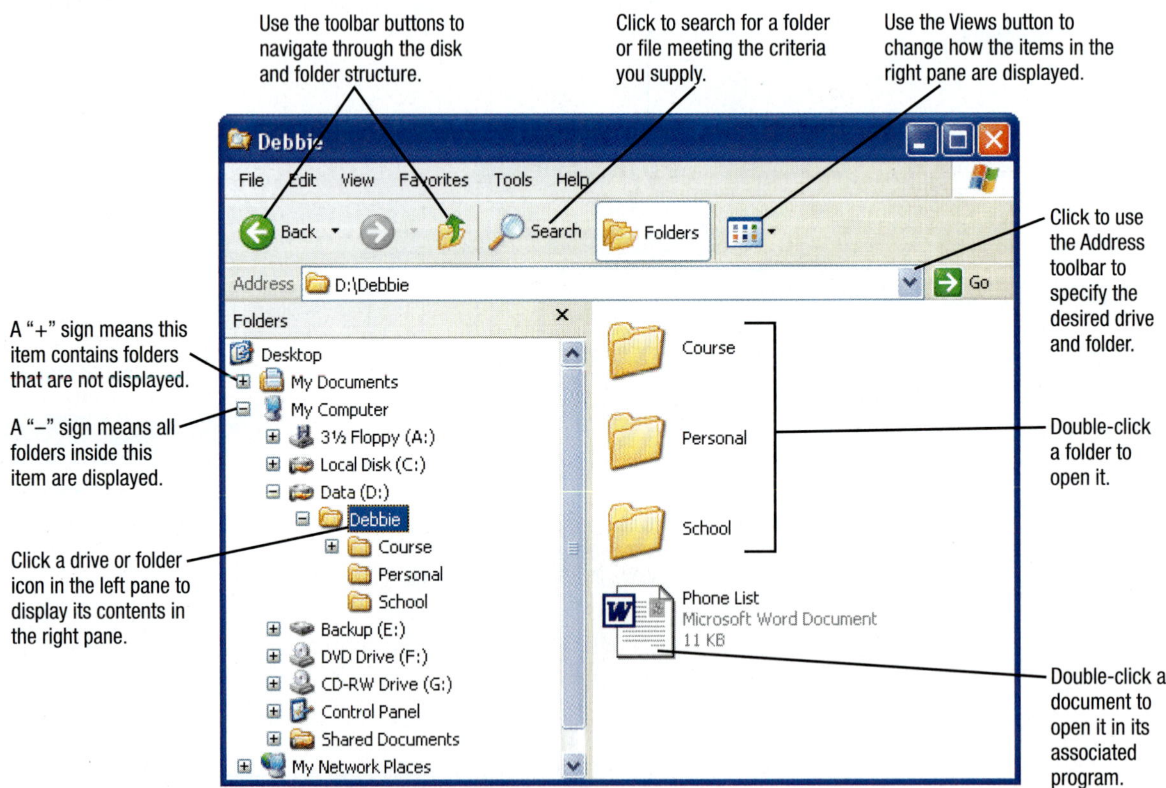

FIGURE 5-22
Using Windows Explorer to look at the contents of a PC.

>**File management program.** A utility program that enables the user to perform file management tasks, such as copying and deleting files.

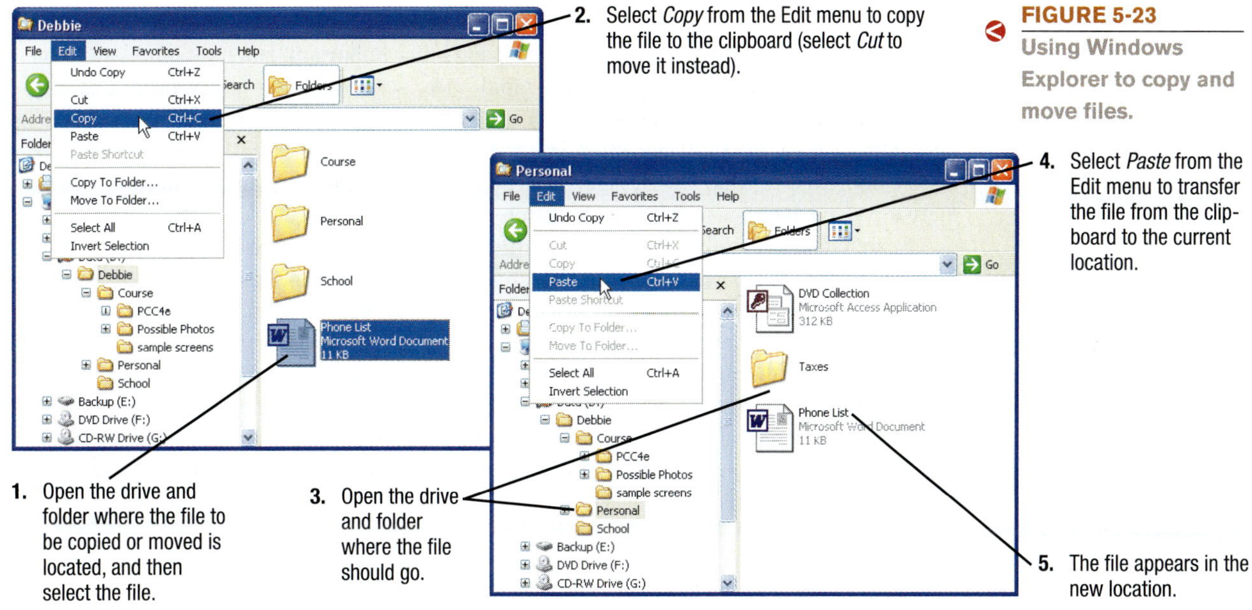

FIGURE 5-23
Using Windows Explorer to copy and move files.

Copying, Moving, and Renaming Files and Folders

You can also copy or move files using a file management program. (To copy or move an entire folder, use the same procedure, but select the folder instead of a file.)

1. Open the drive and folder where the file is located.
2. Select the desired file.
3. Select *Copy* from the Edit menu (see Figure 5-23) to copy the file to a temporary storage area called the *clipboard*. (If you want to move the file instead of copying it, select *Cut* instead of *Copy*).
4. Open the drive and folder where you want the file to go, and then select *Paste* from the Edit menu to transfer the item from the clipboard to the new location.

To change the name of a file or folder:

1. Open the drive and folder where the item to be renamed is located.
2. Select the item you want to rename.
3. Choose *Rename* from the Edit menu, or click a second time on the filename or folder name.
4. When the name is highlighted, either type the new file or folder name or click the highlighted name to display an insertion point, and then edit the name.

Deleting Files and Folders

Files can be deleted using a file management program. (To delete an entire folder, use the same procedure, but select the folder instead of a file.)

1. Open the drive and folder where the item to be deleted is located.
2. Select the item you want to delete, and then press the Delete key on the keyboard.
3. At the Confirm File/Folder Delete dialog box, select *Yes* to delete the file or folder. (Deleting a folder will delete all the files and folders contained within the folder being deleted. To cancel the deletion of a file or folder, select *No* at the Confirm File/Folder Delete dialog box.)

TIP

You can also copy, move, rename, or delete a file or folder in Windows Explorer by right-clicking the item and selecting the desired action.

TIP

To *restore* a file or folder deleted from your PC's hard drive, open your PC's *Recycle Bin* and restore the file to its original location. Files and folders deleted from removable media cannot be restored in this manner, but there are special utility programs available to help you recover deleted files from flash memory cards and drives, as long as you have not written anything to the card or drive since the files were deleted.

Search Tools

As the amount of e-mail, photos, documents, and other important data individuals store on their PCs today continues to grow at a rapid pace, **search tools**—utility programs that search for documents and other files on a user's hard drives—are becoming more important. Although search tools are often integrated into file management programs (and are highly improved in Mac OS X Tiger and, purportedly, in the upcoming Windows Vista), there are also a number of third-party search tools available.

Search tools typically are used to find files located somewhere on the specified storage medium that meet a particular pattern, such as being in a certain folder, including certain characters in the filename, being of a particular type (song, digital photo, or spreadsheet, for instance) and/or having a particular modification date. Some search tools update the results of specified searches on a continual basis, but most are designed to perform a new search command each time new results are desired. Search tools can typically include all of the drives (including local hard drives, network hard drives, CD/DVD drives, and flash memory drives) that a user has access to. For a look at an emerging search tool—desktop searching—see the Trend box.

Diagnostic and Disk Management Programs

Diagnostic programs evaluate your system, looking for problems and making recommendations for fixing any errors that are discovered. *Disk management programs* diagnose and repair programs related to your hard drive. Diagnostic and disk management utilities included in the Windows operating system can perform such tasks as checking the Windows registry for errors, cleaning out extra system files that are no longer needed, checking your hard drive for errors, recovering damaged or erased files, and optimizing your hard drive (by rearranging the data on the hard drive so all files are stored in contiguous locations—called *disk defragmentation*) so it works more efficiently.

File Compression Programs

File compression programs reduce the size of files so they take up less storage space on a storage medium or can be transmitted faster over the Internet. The most common format for user-compressed files in the Windows environment is the *.zip* format, created by file compression programs such as the *WinZip* program shown in Figure 5-24. Mac users typically use *StuffIt* or a similar program instead, although many file compression programs can open files compressed with other programs. A file compression program is required to both compress (*zip*) and decompress (*unzip*) files, unless the zipped file is made *executable*. Executable zipped files have the extension *.exe* and decompress automatically when they are opened, even if the appropriate file compression program is not installed on the recipient's PC. File compression programs can compress either a single file or a group of files into a single compressed file. When multiple files are compressed, they are separated back into individual files when the file is decompressed.

FIGURE 5-24

File compression. File compression can be used with both image and text files, though image files generally compress more efficiently.

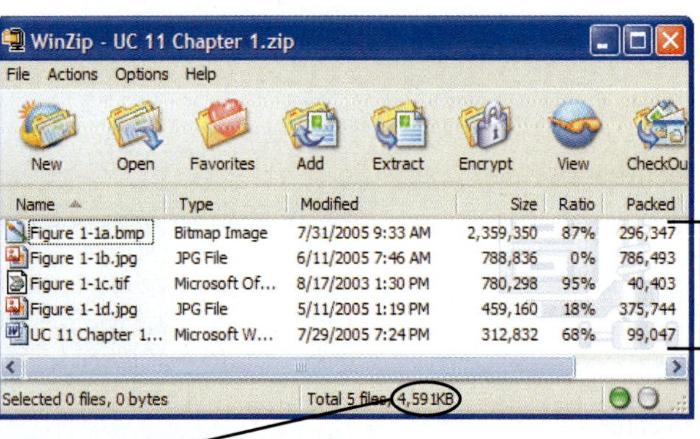

COMPRESSION RATIOS
Certain image file formats (such as *.bmp* and *.tif*) compress more than others (such as *.jpg*, which is already in a compressed format). Text files (such as *.doc*) fall somewhere in between.

FILE SIZE
The 5 files, totalling over 4.5 MB, are zipped into a single 1.6 MB *.zip* file.

>Search tool. A utility program designed to search for files on the user's hard drive.

TREND

Desktop Searching

Many Internet search companies—such as Google, Microsoft, Yahoo, AOL, and Ask Jeeves—are developing desktop search tools that apply the technology used in their Internet search tools. For example, the *Google Desktop Search* program (see the accompanying figure) is currently free and searches through files, e-mail and chat messages, cached Web pages, and other content stored on the user's hard drive to find the items that match the user's supplied search terms. Most of these search tools create an index of the content of the PC first, so that searches can be carried out quickly and efficiently. In fact, if you choose to have Google Desktop Search run in the background on a continuous basis, it will update the index anytime PC processing power is available to keep your searches up-to-the-moment current. An enterprise version of Google Desktop Search is also available that extends searching capabilities to the company network.

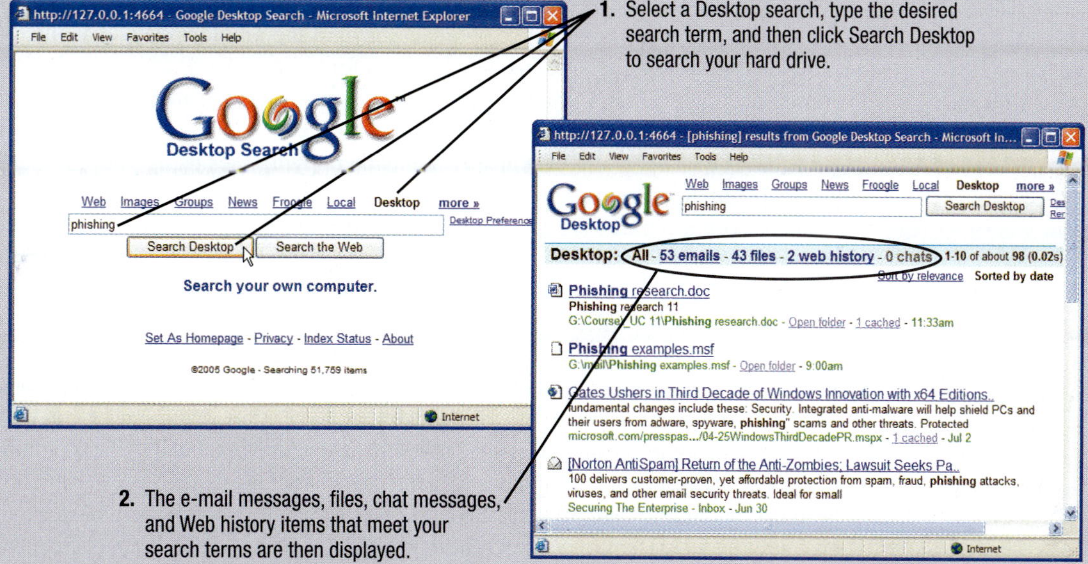

Google's Desktop Search feature allows you to quickly find files, e-mail messages, cached Web pages, and other content stored on your PC.

Uninstall Utilities

When programs are *uninstalled* (removed from the hard drive), small pieces of the programs can be left behind on the hard drive or in system files unless an *uninstall utility* is used. If a user removes programs by deleting the program's folder (which is not the recommended method for removing programs), a large amount of extraneous data can accumulate on the hard drive over time. Uninstall utilities remove the programs themselves, along with all references to those programs in your system files. Some uninstall capabilities are built into most operating systems; uninstall utility programs are also available as stand-alone programs, and sometimes an uninstall option is included in a program's folder when that program is originally installed.

TIP

Windows users should be cautious when uninstalling programs; if an uninstall utility asks you whether to keep or delete a system file (such as a *.dll* file) that it says might be needed by another program, it is safer to keep it.

TIP

Be sure to save your documents frequently as you work, in case the power goes out. Creating a copy of a document with a different filename (by using the *Save As* option of the File menu, for example) before editing a document is another good idea, so you can return to the original version, if needed.

Backup and Recovery Utilities

Virtually every computer veteran will warn you that, sooner or later, you will lose some critical files. Maybe a storm will knock down power lines, causing your electricity to go out—shutting off your PC and erasing the document that you have not saved yet. Perhaps your PC will stop working in the middle of finishing that term paper that is due tomorrow. Or, more likely, you will accidentally delete or overwrite an important file or the file just will not open properly anymore. And do not forget major disasters—a fire or flood can completely destroy your PC and everything that is stored on it.

Creating a **backup** means making a duplicate copy of important files so that when a problem occurs, you can restore those files using the backup copy. You can back up your entire PC (so it can be restored at a later date, if needed) or you can just back up data files. Depending on their size, backup data can be placed on a floppy disk, recordable or rewritable CD or DVD disc, second hard drive, or virtually any other storage medium. Good backup procedures can help protect against data loss.

It is critical for a business to have backup procedures in place that back up all data on a frequent, regular basis—such as every night. A rotating collection of backup media should be used so it is possible to go back beyond the previous day's backup, if needed. Individuals, however, tend to back up in a less formal manner. Personal backups can be as simple as copying an important document to a floppy disk or e-mailing that document to a second PC you have access to, or as comprehensive as backing up the entire contents of your PC. You can perform backups by manually copying files using your file management program, but there are *backup utility* programs that make the backup process easier. Standalone backup programs are available; most operating systems have some sort of backup capabilities, as well, such as the *Windows Backup* program shown in Figure 5-25. Using the Internet for backup is becoming another viable option, especially for storing duplicates of important selected files.

TIP

To make backing up your data easier, as well as to protect your data if the hard drive containing your operating system and program crashes, consider using a second hard drive just for data. Your system can be rolled back or your operating system can be reinstalled without jeopardizing your data, and the data hard drive can be moved to a new PC, if a major PC problem occurs.

It is also a good idea to create a backup of your entire PC once all programs have been installed and the PC is configured correctly, so your system can be restored to that configuration quickly if something goes wrong with your PC at a later time, which saves you the time and bother of having to reinstall all your programs and settings manually. The Windows *System Restore* program, shown in Figure 5-25, exists for that purpose. Once your entire system has been backed up, you can just back up data from that point on, unless you make enough major changes to your system to warrant a new full system backup. For convenience, many backup programs can be scheduled to back up specified files, folders, or drives on a regular basis (such as every Friday night). To protect against fires and other natural disasters, backup media should be stored in a different physical location than your PC or inside a fire-resistant safe. Backups and *disaster recovery* are discussed in more detail in Chapter 15.

Antivirus, Antispyware, Firewalls, and Other Security Programs

A *computer virus* is a software program that is designed to cause damage to the computer system or perform some other malicious act, and *spyware* is a software program installed without the user's knowledge that secretly collects information and sends it to an outside party via the user's Internet connection. Other security concerns today include *phishing* schemes that try to trick users to supply personal information that can be used for credit card fraud, *identity theft*, and other criminal acts. Because of these threats, it is critical that all computer users today protect themselves and their computers—there are many *security utility programs* designed for this purpose. For instance, *antivirus* programs can protect against getting a virus in the first place (by checking files and e-mail messages being

>**Backup.** A duplicate copy of data or other computer content in case the original version is destroyed.

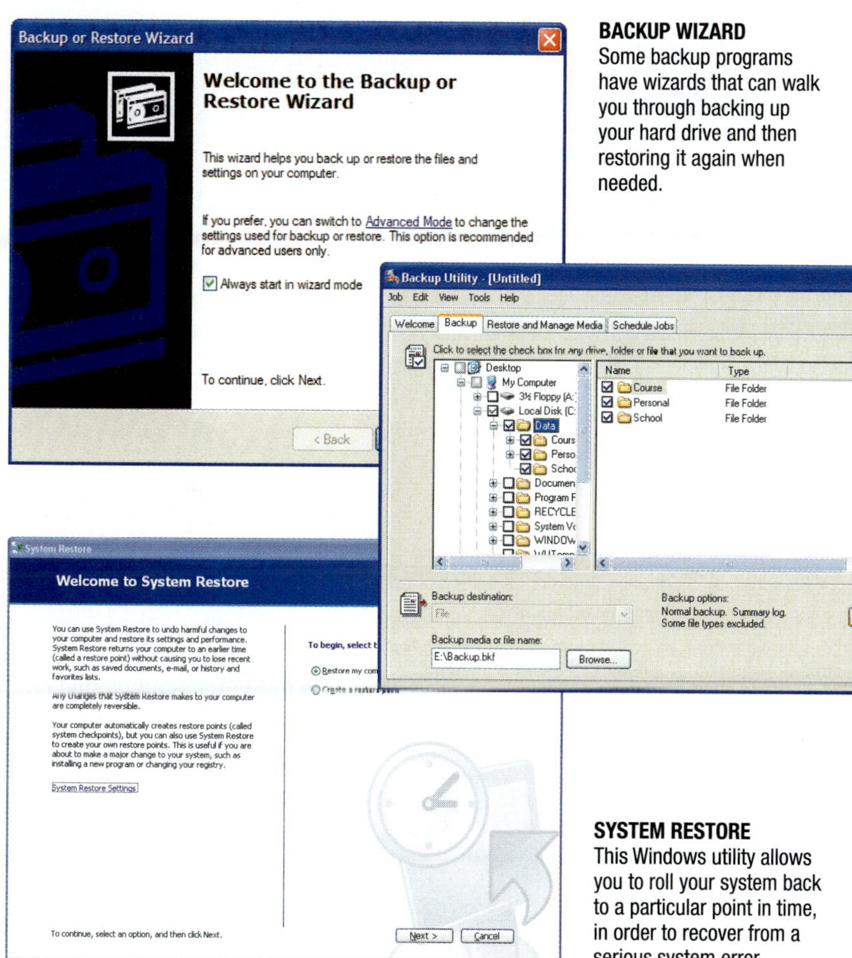

BACKUP WIZARD
Some backup programs have wizards that can walk you through backing up your hard drive and then restoring it again when needed.

MANUAL BACKUP
Many backup programs allow you to select just the files you want backed up. In this example, just the checked folders will be backed up to a CD+RW disc in the E drive.

SYSTEM RESTORE
This Windows utility allows you to roll your system back to a particular point in time, in order to recover from a serious system error.

FIGURE 5-25
Backup and recovery utilities. Most backup utilities, such as the Windows Backup program shown here, allow you to back up an entire hard drive or just specific folders and files; Windows XP also includes a System Restore utility.

SW

downloaded to your PC before they are stored on your PC), as well as detect and remove any viruses that may find their way onto your PC; *antispyware programs* can detect and remove any spyware programs installed on your PC; and *firewalls* can protect against someone accessing your PC via the Internet. Because network and Internet security is such an important topic today, Chapter 9 is dedicated to these topics.

FURTHER EXPLORATION

For links to further information about utility programs, go to www.course.com/uc11/ch05

THE FUTURE OF OPERATING SYSTEMS

The future configuration of operating systems is anyone's guess, but it is expected that they will continue to become more user-friendly and, eventually, be driven primarily by a voice interface. Operating systems are also likely to continue to become more stable and self-healing, repairing or restoring system files as needed. In addition, they will likely continue to include improved security features and to support multiple processors and other technological improvements.

With the pervasiveness of the Internet, operating systems in the future may be used primarily to access software available through the Internet or other networks, instead of accessing software on the local device. Improvements will almost certainly continue to be made in the areas of synchronizing and coordinating data and activities between a person's various computing and communications devices, such as his or her desktop PC, handheld PC, and smart phone.

SUMMARY

SYSTEM SOFTWARE VS. APPLICATION SOFTWARE

Chapter Objective 1:
Understand the difference between system software and application software.

System software consists of the programs that coordinate the activities of a computer system. The basic role of system software is to act as a mediator between **application software** (programs that allow a user to perform specific tasks on a computer, such as word processing, playing a game, preparing taxes, browsing the Web, and so forth) and the computer system's hardware, as well as between the PC and the user.

THE OPERATING SYSTEM

Chapter Objective 2:
Explain the different functions of an operating system and discuss some ways that operating systems can differ from one another.

A computer's **operating system** is the primary system software program that manages the computer system's resources and interfaces with the user. The functions of the operating system include booting the computer, configuring devices and **device drivers**, communicating with the user, managing and monitoring computer resources, file management, and security. To manage the enormous collection of files typically found on a PC's hard drive, *file management programs* allow the user to organize files hierarchically into folders. To access a file in any directory, the user can specify the *path* to the file; the path identifies the drive and folders the user must navigate through in order to access the file.

Chapter Objective 3:
List several ways in which operating systems enhance processing efficiency.

A variety of processing techniques can be built into operating systems to help enhance processing efficiency. **Multitasking** allows concurrent execution of two or more programs for a single user, and **multiprocessing** and **parallel processing** involve using two or more CPUs to perform work at the same time. Operating systems typically use **virtual memory** to extend conventional memory by using a portion of the hard drive as additional memory, and **spooling** frees up the CPU from time-consuming interaction with input and output devices, such as printers, by storing input and output on the way in or out of the system in a **buffer**.

Some of the differences among operating systems center around whether it uses a **graphical user interface (GUI)** or **command line interface**, whether it is a **personal operating system** designed for individual users or a **server** (*network*) **operating system** designed for multiple users, and the types and numbers of processors supported.

OPERATING SYSTEMS FOR DESKTOP PCS AND SERVERS

Chapter Objective 4:
Name today's most widely used operating systems for desktop PCs and servers.

One of the original operating systems for PCs was **DOS (Disk Operating System)**, which is still in existence, but not widely used. Most desktop PCs today run a version of **Windows**. *Windows 3.x*, the first widely used version of Windows, was an *operating environment* that added a GUI shell to DOS, replacing the DOS command line interface with a system of menus, icons, and screen boxes called *windows*. *Windows 95*, *Windows 98*, *Windows 98 Second Edition* (*SE*), *Windows NT*, *Windows Me*, and *Windows 2000*—all successors to Windows 3.*x*—included an increasing number of enhancements, such as multitasking, a better user interface, and more Internet, multimedia, and communications functions. The current personal version of Windows is **Windows XP**, which has a variety of versions to meet specific needs and types of PCs. The successor to Windows XP and the current network version of Windows, **Windows Server 2003**, is **Windows Vista**, which is expected to be available by 2007.

Mac OS X is the most recent version of *Mac OS*, the operating system used on Apple computers. **UNIX** is a flexible, general-purpose server operating system that works on mainframes, midrange computers, PCs used as network servers, graphics workstations, and even desktop PCs. A *flavor* (version) of UNIX called **Linux** has gathered popularity because it is distributed free over the Internet and can be used as an alternative to Windows and Mac OS. Linux has earned support as a mainstream operating system in recent years and is being used in computer systems of all sizes, from desktop PCs to supercomputers. **NetWare** is a widely used server operating system, and *Solaris* is used on Sun computers.

OPERATING SYSTEMS FOR HANDHELD PCS AND MOBILE DEVICES

Handheld PCs and mobile devices usually require a different operating system than a desktop PC. For handheld PCs, mobile versions of Windows (such as **Windows Embedded** and **Windows Mobile**) and **Palm OS** (the operating system designed for Palm handheld PCs) are widely used. **Embedded Linux** is another operating system used with handheld PCs and mobile devices; smart phones sometimes use the **Symbian OS**, which is designed around the *EPOC* operating system. Other everyday devices—such as cars—that contain a computer use an operating system, as well.

Chapter Objective 5:
State several devices other than desktop PCs and servers that require an operating system and list one possible operating system for each type of device.

SW

OPERATING SYSTEMS FOR LARGER COMPUTERS

High-end servers, mainframes, and supercomputers may use an operating system designed specifically for that type of system, but are increasingly using customized versions of conventional operating systems, such as Windows, UNIX, and Linux.

UTILITY PROGRAMS

A **utility program** is a type of system software program written to perform specific tasks usually related to maintaining or managing the computer system. **File management programs** enable users to perform file management tasks, such as copying, moving, and deleting files. **Search tools** are designed to help users find files on their hard drives; *diagnostic* and *disk management programs* deal primarily with diagnosing and repairing PC problems, such as hard drive errors and accidentally deleted files, as well as maintenance tasks, such as performing *disk defragmentation*. *Uninstall utilities* allow programs to be removed from a hard drive without leaving annoying remnants behind, *file compression* programs reduce the stored size of files so they can be more easily archived or sent over the Internet, and **backup** programs make it easier for users to back up the contents of their hard drive. There are also a number of security-oriented utility programs, such as *antivirus*, *antispyware*, and *firewall* programs.

Chapter Objective 6:
Discuss the role of utility programs and outline several duties that these programs perform.

THE FUTURE OF OPERATING SYSTEMS

In the future, operating systems will likely become even more user-friendly, voice-driven, and stable, repairing themselves when needed and causing errors and conflicts much less frequently.

Chapter Objective 7:
Describe what the operating systems of the future might be like.

REVIEW ACTIVITIES

KEY TERM MATCHING

Instructions: Match each key term on the left with the definition on the right that best describes it.

a. backup
b. device drive
c. Linux
d. Mac OS X
e. multiprocessing
f. operating system
g. spooling
h. utility program
i. virtual memory
j. Windows Mobile

1. _______ A duplicate copy of data or other computer content for use in the event that the original version is destroyed.
2. _______ A family of operating systems based on Windows and designed for handheld PCs, smart phones, and other mobile devices.
3. _______ A memory-management technique that uses hard drive space as an extension to a PC's RAM.
4. _______ A program that enables an operating system to communicate with a specific hardware device.
5. _______ A type of software that performs a specific task, usually related to managing or maintaining the computer system.
6. _______ A version (flavor) of UNIX that is available without charge over the Internet and is increasingly being used with PCs, servers, mainframes, and supercomputers.
7. _______ The capability of an operating system to use multiple processors in a single computer, usually to process multiple jobs at one time faster than could be performed with a single processor.
8. _______ The main component of system software that enables the computer to manage its activities and the resources under its control, run application programs, and interface with the user.
9. _______ The most recent version of the operating system used on Apple computers.
10. _______ The process of placing items in a buffer so they can be retrieved by the appropriate device (such as a printer) when needed.

SELF-QUIZ

Instructions: Circle **T** if the statement is true, **F** if the statement is false, or write the best answer in the space provided. **Answers to the self-quiz are located in the References and Resources Guide at the end of the book.**

1. **T F** Microsoft Windows XP is an example of an operating system.
2. **T F** Most operating systems today use a command line interface.
3. **T F** The principal reason so many people like UNIX is that it is much easier to use than competing operating systems.
4. **T F** Solaris is an operating system designed for smart phones.
5. **T F** Linux can be used on mainframe and supercomputers, in addition to PCs and servers.
6. System software consists of _______ software and _______ programs.
7. _______ is a popular version of UNIX available for free over the Internet.
8. To decrease the size of a file, a(n) _______ utility program can be used.
9. To guard against losing your data if a computer problem occurs, you should _______ your data files on a regular basis.

10. Match each device to the most appropriate operating system and write the corresponding number in the blank to the left of the device.

a. ______ Home office PC
b. ______ Mainframe computer
c. ______ Smart phone
d. ______ Business network server
e. ______ Handheld PC
f. ______ Living room PC

1. Symbian OS
2. NetWare
3. Windows XP Professional
4. Windows XP Media Center Edition
5. Palm OS
6. UNIX

EXERCISES

1. For the following path, identify the drive the document is located on, the name of the file, and whether or not the document is stored inside a folder. If the file is stored inside one or more folders, list the folder name(s).

   C:\My Documents\Resume.doc

2. Match each program or processing technique with the appropriate term and write the corresponding number in the blank to the left of each term.

   a. ______ Zipped file
   b. ______ Server operating system
   c. ______ Swap file
   d. ______ Folder
   e. ______ Printer
   f. ______ Simultaneous processing
   g. ______ Command line interface
   h. ______ Fragmentation

   1. DOS
   2. NetWare
   3. File management program
   4. Virtual memory
   5. Multiprocessing
   6. Spooling
   7. File compression program
   8. Disk management program

3. Would a notebook PC typically have Windows 3.1, Windows XP, Windows Mobile, or Windows Server 2003 installed as its operating system? Explain your answer.

4. What type of utility program can be used to make a duplicate copy of your hard drive?

5. Identify the purpose of each of the following types of utility programs.

   a. File management program ______
   b. Search tool ______
   c. Uninstall utility ______
   d. File compression program ______
   e. Antivirus program ______

SW

DISCUSSION QUESTION

As discussed in the chapter, more and more everyday devices—including cars and other vehicles—are being controlled by operating systems. Even large transportation systems, such as subway trains, are increasingly becoming automated. There are advantages, such as avoiding possible driver errors and the ability to change the speed of or reroute trains to avoid collisions or to run the system more efficiently. But are there potential risks, as well? For example, Thailand's Finance Minister once had to be rescued from inside his limousine after the onboard computer malfunctioned, leaving the vehicle immobilized. With the door locks, power windows, and air conditioning not functioning, the Minister and his driver were in growing danger until a guard freed them by smashing one of the vehicle's windows with a sledgehammer 10 minutes later. Do you think the benefits of increased automation of devices that could put us in danger if they malfunction outweigh the risks? What types of safeguards do you think should be incorporated into computer-controlled cars, subway trains, and other automated vehicles? What about medication dispensers and other automated medical devices?

PROJECTS

HOT TOPICS

1. **Autonomic Computing** *Autonomic computing* is a term coined by IBM to refer to computers that can operate on their own with little need of attention from a person. To facilitate this, autonomic computers are expected to have built-in self-diagnostics and other types of utilities, as well as other appropriate software. Autonomic computers will have the ability to recognize, isolate, and recover from problems, with as little human intervention as possible. Some see autonomic computing as a natural progression for computing, similar to the way the telephone system evolved from using a human switchboard operator to a system that automatically routes calls on its own; others are more skeptical.

   For this project, research the current state of autonomic computing. Has the definition of an autonomic computer changed since this project was written? How do the autonomic computing systems being tested today compare in terms of reliability and the ability to recover from errors to conventional computer systems? Are there any autonomic computer systems available in the United States? Do you think all computers in the future will be autonomic? Do you see any disadvantages of autonomic computing? At the conclusion of your research, prepare a one- to two-page summary of your findings and submit it to your instructor.

SHORT ANSWER/ RESEARCH

2. **Suit Happy** Beginning with the lawsuit filed against Microsoft by Apple Corporation in the late 1980s, claiming that the Windows interface stole the look and feel of the Apple OS, there have been a number of lawsuits involving operating systems. Some more recent legal actions include the antitrust lawsuit filed against Microsoft in 1998 by the Justice Department, the suit filed in 2002 against Microsoft by Sun Microsystems regarding the inclusion of their Java program in the Windows operating system, and the lawsuit filed in 2003 against IBM by the SCO Group (formerly Caldera Systems) regarding UNIX and Linux.

   For this project, select a lawsuit that involved an operating system product (either one of those mentioned in the previous paragraph or a more recent example) and research it. Be sure to find out what the initial claim was, the defending company's response, and the result of the lawsuit, if it was settled. If it hasn't yet been settled, provide an update of the current status of the suit. If it was settled, do you agree with the ruling? Why or why not? At the conclusion of your research, prepare a one-page summary of your findings and submit it to your instructor.

3. **Compression** As described in the chapter, compression programs can be used to make more efficient use of disk space and speed up the delivery of files over the Internet. They also come in handy for large files—such as digital photographs or other types of graphical images—that you want to archive. The most common compression programs create files with the file extensions *.zip*, *.sit*, and *.exe*. Compression programs usually allow you to create both compressed files and self-extracting compressed files. Self-extracting files automatically decompress when you download them, while compressed files must be decompressed by running a version of the program that compressed them.

   For this project, identify compression programs associated with each of the file extensions listed above and determine which extensions represent a self-extracting format, as well as which extensions are associated with the Windows and Mac OS operating systems. For the type of PC you use most often, find at least two compression programs that you might use and compare their costs and capabilities. At the conclusion of your research, prepare a one-page summary of your findings and submit it to your instructor.

HANDS ON

4. **File Practice** As discussed in the chapter, all operating systems have at least one program you can use to manage your files; typically, they work similarly to the Windows Explorer program illustrated in Figures 5-22 and 5-23.

   For this project, obtain a blank floppy disk or other removable storage medium (such as a USB flash memory drive) appropriate for the computer you will be using most often, insert it into the PC, and perform the following tasks.

   a. Open the file management program (such as Windows Explorer for Windows PCs). Once the program is open, click or double-click the icon for the removable storage medium being used (such as the letter *A* for a floppy drive) to display the content of your storage medium (if a message stating that the floppy disk needs to be formatted appears, select the option to format the disk and then continue with the rest of the steps in this project, provided you know the disk doesn't contain any data, since formatting will erase the disk). Are there any files on the storage medium? By looking at the status bar at the bottom of the file management program's window, or by right-clicking the drive icon and selecting *Properties*, determine how much room is available on the storage medium.

   b. Open any word processing program available on your PC (such as Word, WordPerfect, or WordPad). Create a new document consisting of just your name. By using the appropriate toolbar button or File menu option, save the document onto your storage medium (be sure to change the save location to the appropriate drive and give the document an appropriate name, such as your last name). Return to your file management program and view the content of your storage medium. Is your new document stored there? If so, how big is it and how much room is left on your storage medium now? If it is not there, use your word processor's *Save As* option to save the file again, making sure you are storing it on your storage medium.

   c. Prepare a short summary of your work to submit to your instructor, listing the software programs used, the name of the file you saved on your storage medium, the size of the file, and the amount of space left on your storage medium once the file was stored on it.

   d. Return to your file management program, display the content of your storage medium, and delete the file you stored there.

SW

5. **How Stuff Works: System Software** The How Stuff Works Web site has a number of interesting articles and tutorials explaining how some computer-oriented hardware, software, and technologies work.

   For this project, go to the How Stuff Works Web site at www.howstuffworks.com and use either the search option or browse through the computer topics to locate an article related to operating systems or utility programs, such as one explaining how operating systems, file compression, screensavers, virtual memory, or computer viruses work. Read through the article, making note of at least three new things you learned about your chosen topic. At the conclusion of the article, prepare a short summary for your instructor, including the name of the article and the new information you learned from reading it.

WRITING ABOUT COMPUTERS

6. **Operating System Bugs** Most software, including operating systems, is not error-free when it is first released. Some programs, in fact, contain thousands of problems, called *bugs*. Some are annoying; others leave security holes in your system that can make it vulnerable from attack by a computer virus or unscrupulous individual.

   For this project, identify one recently discovered security hole in a current operating system or a program included with that operating system, such as a utility or Web browser. You may want to review recent computer journals or search the Internet for the information. Once you have identified your hole or bug, find out what the potential problem was, how the problem can be fixed, and where an individual would go to download the appropriate *security patch* or upgrade. Does the security patch fix just that one problem, or does it address multiple bugs? Is there a charge for it? If someone bought a PC today with that operating system installed, would it contain the bug? What is the easiest way for Windows users to keep their operating system up-to-date? Submit this project to your instructor in the form of a short paper, not more than two pages in length.

PRESENTATION/ DOCUMENTATION

7. **OS Support** No matter which operating system you have, it's likely you will eventually need to get some help resolving a system-related hardware or software problem. Support for most popular operating systems includes the following: searchable knowledge bases, technical support phone numbers and e-mail addresses, online support chat sessions, FAQs, and user discussion groups.

For this project, first find out what type of help each support option listed in the previous paragraph can be used for. Next, select one operating system and research the support options available for that program, including the options available through the Web site of the program's manufacturer. Select one support option and determine in more detail how it would be used and what type of information can be obtained. Share your findings with the class in the form of a short presentation. The presentation should not exceed 10 minutes and should make use of one or more presentation aids, such as the chalkboard, handouts, overhead transparencies, or a computer-based slide presentation (your instructor may provide additional requirements). You may also be asked to submit a summary of the presentation to your instructor.

GROUP DISCUSSION

8. **Teaching Computer Viruses** When the University of Calgary announced plans to offer a new course in the Fall 2003 semester that included instruction on writing computer viruses, it unleashed a huge round of criticism and objections from the computer industry. Although the course was to delve into the ethics and legalities surrounding viruses, the students would also be coding actual viruses, which worried many industry leaders. At Calgary, planned precautions included only allowing fourth year students to take the course, not having a network connection in the classroom, and prohibiting the removal of disks from the classroom. Do you think these precautions are sufficient? Should virus-coding be allowed as part of a computer degree curriculum? The University's premise is that students need to know how viruses work to be able to develop antivirus software; however, the antivirus industry disagrees, and most antivirus professionals were never virus writers. Who do you think is right? Will including teaching illegal and unethical acts in college classes help to legitimize the behavior in society? Research whether or not the University of Calvary ever offered the class as planned. Do you agree with that decision?

For this project, form an opinion of the inclusion of virus-writing instruction in college classes and its potential impact on society and the computer industry and be prepared to discuss your position (in class, via an online class discussion group, or in a class chat room, depending on your instructor's directions). You may also be asked to write a short paper expressing your opinion.

WEB ACTIVITIES

The ***Understanding Computers*** Web site located at **www.course.com/uc11** features many resources to help reinforce your understanding of the chapter content and help you prepare for exams. Your instructor may also assign specific activities to be completed that will count toward your final grade in the course.

Instructions: Go to **www.course.com/uc11/ch05** to work the following online activities.

Click any link in the navigation bar on the left to access any of the online resources described below.

INTERACTIVE ACTIVITIES

1. **Crossword Puzzle** Practice your knowledge of the key terms in Chapter 5 by completing the interactive Crossword Puzzle.
2. **Tech News Video Project** Watch the **"Emergency System Restore"** video clip that takes a look at the Windows System Restore option that can restore your system to a previous configuration if a problem occurs with your current settings. After watching the video online, complete the corresponding project.
3. **Student Edition Labs** Reinforce the concepts you have learned in this chapter by working through the interactive **Backing up Your Computer** and **Maintaining a Hard Drive** labs.

TEST YOURSELF

1. **Key Term Matching** Test your knowledge of selected chapter key terms by matching the terms with their definitions.
2. **Self-Quiz** Test your retention of chapter concepts by taking the Self-Quiz.
3. **Exercises** Work these short exercises to review the concepts and terms covered in the chapter.
4. **Practice Test** Test how ready you are for an upcoming exam by completing the online Practice Test.

STUDY TOOLS/ ADDITIONAL RESOURCES

The Understanding Computers Web site has a wide range of additional resources, including an **Online Study Guide** (containing study tips, a chapter outline with room to add your own notes, and a chapter checklist of the activities to complete when the chapter is covered in class and when you are preparing for a test) and an **Online Glossary** for each chapter; **Further Exploration** links; a **Web Guide**, a **Guide to Buying a PC**, and a **Computer History Timeline**; more information about **Numbering Systems**, **Coding Charts**, and **CPU Characteristics**; and much, much more!

CHAPTER

Application Software

OUTLINE

Overview
The Basics of Application Software
- Software Ownership Rights
- Installed vs. Web-Based Software
- Software Suites
- Desktop vs. Mobile Software
- Common Software Commands

Word Processing Concepts
- What Is Word Processing?
- Creating a Word Processing Document
- Tables, Graphics, and Templates
- Word Processing and the Web

Spreadsheet Concepts
- What Is a Spreadsheet?
- Creating a Spreadsheet
- Charts and What-If Analysis
- Spreadsheets and the Web

Database Concepts
- What Is a Database?
- Creating a Database
- Queries and Reports
- Databases and the Web

Presentation Graphics Concepts
- What Is a Presentation Graphic?
- Creating a Presentation
- Finishing a Presentation
- Presentation Graphics and the Web

Graphics and Multimedia Concepts
- Graphics Software
- Audio Editing Software
- Video Editing and DVD Authoring Software
- CD and DVD Burning Software
- Media Players
- Graphics, Multimedia, and the Web

Other Types of Application Software
- Desktop and Personal Publishing Software
- Educational, Entertainment, and Reference Software
- Accounting and Personal Finance Software
- CAD and Other Types of Design Software
- Project Management and Collaboration Software
- Note Taking and Personal Planning Software

LEARNING OBJECTIVES

After completing this chapter, you will be able to:

1. Describe what application software is, the different types of ownership rights, and the difference between installed and Web-based software.
2. Detail some concepts and commands that many software programs have in common.
3. Discuss word processing and explain what kinds of documents are created using this type of program.
4. Explain the purpose of spreadsheet software and the kinds of documents created using this type of program.
5. Identify some of the vocabulary used with database software and discuss the benefits of using this type of program.
6. Describe what presentation graphics and electronic slide shows are and when they might be used.
7. List some types of graphics and multimedia software consumers frequently use.
8. Name other types of application software programs and discuss what functions they perform.

OVERVIEW

As discussed in previous chapters, **application software** consists of programs designed to perform specific tasks or applications. Today, a wide variety of application software is available to meet virtually any user need. Individuals and businesses can buy software to be used to write letters, keep track of their finances, participate in videoconferences, learn a foreign language, entertain themselves or their children, create music CDs or home movie DVDs, manage a business's inventory, create greeting cards and flyers, make business presentations, process orders, prepare payrolls and tax returns, touch up digital photos, teach their kids the ABCs, and hundreds of other applications.

This chapter begins with a look at some characteristics of application software in general. Then we take a look at five of the most widely used types of application software programs: word processing, spreadsheet, database, presentation graphics, and graphics and multimedia software. The chapter concludes with a look at a few other types of application software not discussed in other chapters in this book. ■

THE BASICS OF APPLICATION SOFTWARE

All computer users should be familiar with the basic characteristics and concepts related to application software; for instance, the different possible ownership rights and delivery methods, how software for desktop PCs and handheld PCs differ, and the basic software commands that are common to most types of application software. Although these topics are discussed next in the context of application software, they also apply to other types of software, such as system software (discussed in Chapter 5) and programming languages (discussed in Chapter 13).

Software Ownership Rights

Ownership rights of a software program specify the allowable use of the program. After a software program is developed, the developer holds the ownership rights for that program. Whether or not the program can be sold, shared with others, or otherwise distributed is up to that developer, typically an individual or an organization. When a software program is purchased, the buyer is not actually buying the software. Instead, the buyer is acquiring a **software license** that permits him or her to use the software. This license specifies the conditions under which a buyer can use the software, such as whether or not it may be shared with others and the number of computers on which it may be installed (many software licenses permit the software to be installed on just one PC). In addition to being included in printed form inside the packaging of most software programs, the licensing agreement is usually displayed and must be agreed to by the end user at the beginning of the software installation process (see Figure 6-1).

TIP

Ownership rights for original creative works are referred to as *copyrights* and are discussed in more detail in Chapter 16.

>**Application software.** Programs that enable users to perform specific tasks on a computer, such as writing a letter or playing a game.

>**Software license.** An agreement, either included in a software package or displayed on the screen during installation, that specifies the conditions under which a buyer of the program can use it.

This statement explains that the program will not be installed unless you accept the terms of the license agreement.

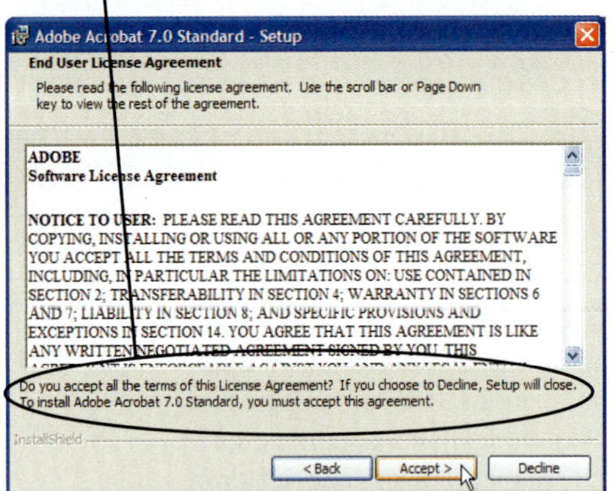

COMMERCIAL SOFTWARE PROGRAM

This statement explains that the program is shareware.

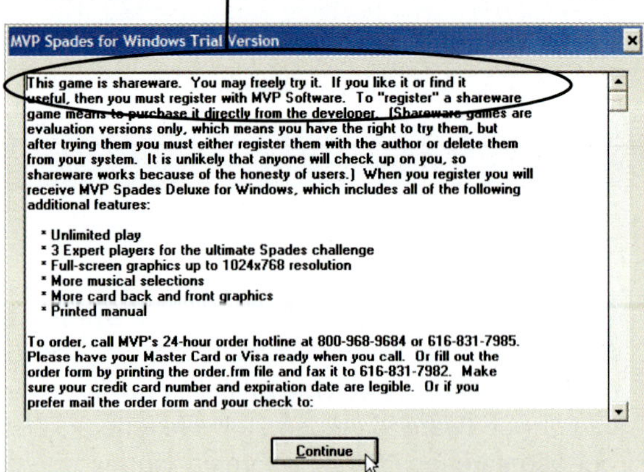

SHAREWARE PROGRAM

FIGURE 6-1
Software licenses.
Most software programs display their licensing agreements at the beginning of the installation process.

There are four basic categories of software: *commercial software*, *shareware*, *freeware*, and *public domain software*. Each of these types of software has different ownership rights, as shown in Figure 6-2 and discussed next. In addition, some software is **open source software**—programs whose source code is available to the general public. Open source programs are copyrighted, but individuals and businesses are allowed to modify the program and redistribute it—the only restriction is that changes must be shared with the open source community, and the original copyright notice must remain intact. For more information about open source software, see the Inside the Industry box.

Commercial Software

Commercial software is software that is developed and sold for a profit. When you buy a commercial software program (such as Microsoft Office, TurboTax, or The Sims), it typically

FIGURE 6-2
Software ownership rights.

TYPE OF SOFTWARE	EXAMPLES	MOST COMMONLY OBTAINED FROM
Commercial software	Microsoft Office (office suite) Norton AntiVirus (antivirus program) Adobe Photoshop (image editing program) Flight Simulator (game)	Manufacturer's Web site, online stores, and physical stores
Shareware	WinZip (file compression program) Media Jukebox (media player and CD ripper) Image Shrinker (image optimizer) Rings of the Maji (game)	Manufacturer/author's Web site and download sites, such as Shareware.com and Tucows.com
Freeware	Internet Explorer (Web browser) Outlook Express (e-mail program) QuickTime Player (media player) Yahoo! Messenger (instant messaging program)	Manufacturer/author's Web site and download sites, such as Shareware.com and Tucows.com
Public domain software	Lynx (text-based Web browser) Pine (e-mail program)	Download, university, and government sites; open source and public domain organizations

>**Open source software.** Software programs whose source code is made available to the general public. >**Commercial software.** Copyrighted software that is developed, usually by a commercial company, for sale to others.

INSIDE THE INDUSTRY

Open Source Software

As discussed in Chapter 5, use of open source software has grown over the past few years, primarily for cost reasons. In addition to the open source operating system Linux, there are low-cost or no-cost alternatives for a wide selection of application programs today. For instance, the free *OpenOffice.org* office suite (see the accompanying screen shot) can be used instead of Microsoft Office; the free *GIMP* (*GNU Image Manipulation Program*) program can be used to retouch photos instead of Adobe Photoshop or another pricey image editing program; and the $495 *MySQL* database program is a much less costly, but viable, alternative to Oracle and other database programs that typically cost between $5,000 and $40,000. In addition to saving you money, these alternative programs typically require less disk space and memory. For instance, installing OpenOffice.org instead of Microsoft Office saves the user about 200 MB of hard drive space and about 128 MB of RAM.

Other benefits of using open source software include increased stability and security, and the ability to modify the application's source code. Perceived risks include lack of support and compatibility issues. However, both Linux and open source application programs are continuing to gain acceptance and their use is growing. For instance, more than 4 million copies of the OpenOffice.org program have been downloaded and there is a proposal in Massachusetts to have all documents in offices run by the state move from proprietary formats (like Word and WordPerfect) to the *OpenDocument* open source file standard. Some insiders feel that the open source movement is finally gathering the momentum that many predicted several years ago.

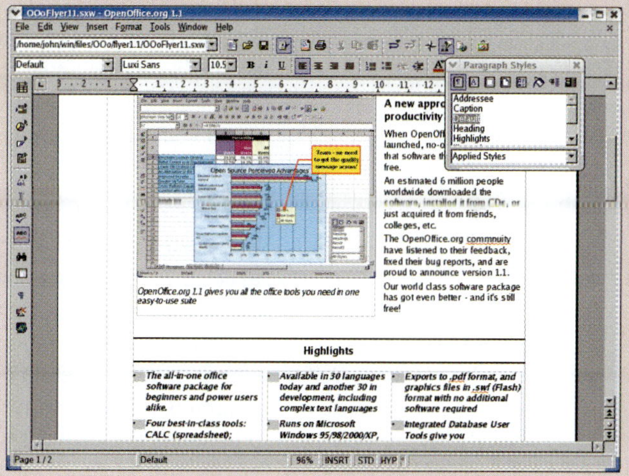

The OpenOffice.org word processing program.

comes with a *single-user license*, which means you cannot legally make copies of the installation CD to give to your friends, and you cannot legally install the software on their computers using your CD. You cannot even install the software on a second PC that you own, unless allowed by the license. For example, some software licenses state that the program can be installed on one desktop PC and one notebook PC; others allow installation on both a home and work PC, as long as the two computers will never be used at the same time. Schools or businesses that need to install software on multiple computers or need to have the software available to multiple users over a network can usually obtain *site licenses* or *network licenses* for the specified number of users. To determine which activities are allowable for a particular commercial software program, refer to the licensing agreement for that program.

In addition to their full versions, some commercial software is available as a *demo* or *trial version*. Typically, these versions can be used free of charge and distributed to others, but often they are missing some key features (such as the ability to save or print a document) or they will not run after the trial period expires. Since these programs are not designed as replacements for the fee-based version, it is ethical to use them only to determine if you would like to buy the full program. If the decision is made against purchasing the product, the demo or trial version should be uninstalled from your PC.

Shareware

Shareware programs are software programs that are distributed on the honor system. Most shareware programs are available to try free of charge, but the author usually requests that you pay a small fee if you intend to use the program regularly (see the shareware license in Figure 6-1). By paying the requested shareware fee, you become a registered user and can use the program for as long as you want to use it. Registered users may also be entitled to product support, documentation, and updates. Shareware programs are widely available from a variety of download sites on the Internet. You can legally and ethically copy shareware programs to pass along to friends and colleagues, but those individuals are expected to pay the shareware fee if they decide to keep the product.

Most shareware programs have a specified trial period, such as one month. Although it is not illegal to use shareware past the specified trial period, it is unethical to do so. Ethical use of shareware dictates either paying for the program or uninstalling it from your PC at the end of the trial period. Shareware is typically much less expensive than commercial versions of similar software because it is often developed by a single programmer and because it uses the shareware marketing system to sell directly to consumers with little or no packaging or advertising expenses. Shareware authors stress that the ethical use of shareware helps to cultivate this type of software distribution. Legally, shareware and demo versions of commercial software are similar, but shareware is typically not missing key features.

Freeware

Freeware programs are software programs that are given away by the author for others to use free of charge. Although freeware is available free of charge and can be shared with others, the author retains the ownership rights to the program, so you cannot do anything with it—such as sell it or modify it—that is not expressly allowed by the author. Freeware programs are frequently developed by students, professional programmers, and amateur programmers either as a programming exercise or as a hobby. Some freeware software programs are released by commercial companies as well, such as Microsoft's Internet Explorer and Netscape's Navigator. Like shareware programs, freeware programs are widely available over the Internet.

Public Domain Software

Public domain software is not copyrighted; instead, the ownership rights to the program have been donated to the public domain. Consequently, it is free and can be used, copied, modified, and distributed to others without restrictions.

Installed vs. Web-Based Software

Software also differs in how it is delivered to the end user. It can either be installed on and run from the end user's PC or delivered to the PC via the Internet.

Installed Software

Installed software—that is, software that is installed on a PC before it is run—is the most common type of software. Installed software programs are either purchased in physical form (such as in a shrink-wrapped box containing a CD, license agreement, and user's manual) or are downloaded from the Internet (see Figure 6-3). Whether or not downloaded software requires a fee depends on whether the program is a commercial program, demo

>**Shareware.** Copyrighted software that is distributed on the honor system; consumers should either pay for it or uninstall it after the trial period. >**Freeware.** Copyrighted software that may be used free of charge. >**Public domain software.** Software that is not copyrighted and may be used without restriction.

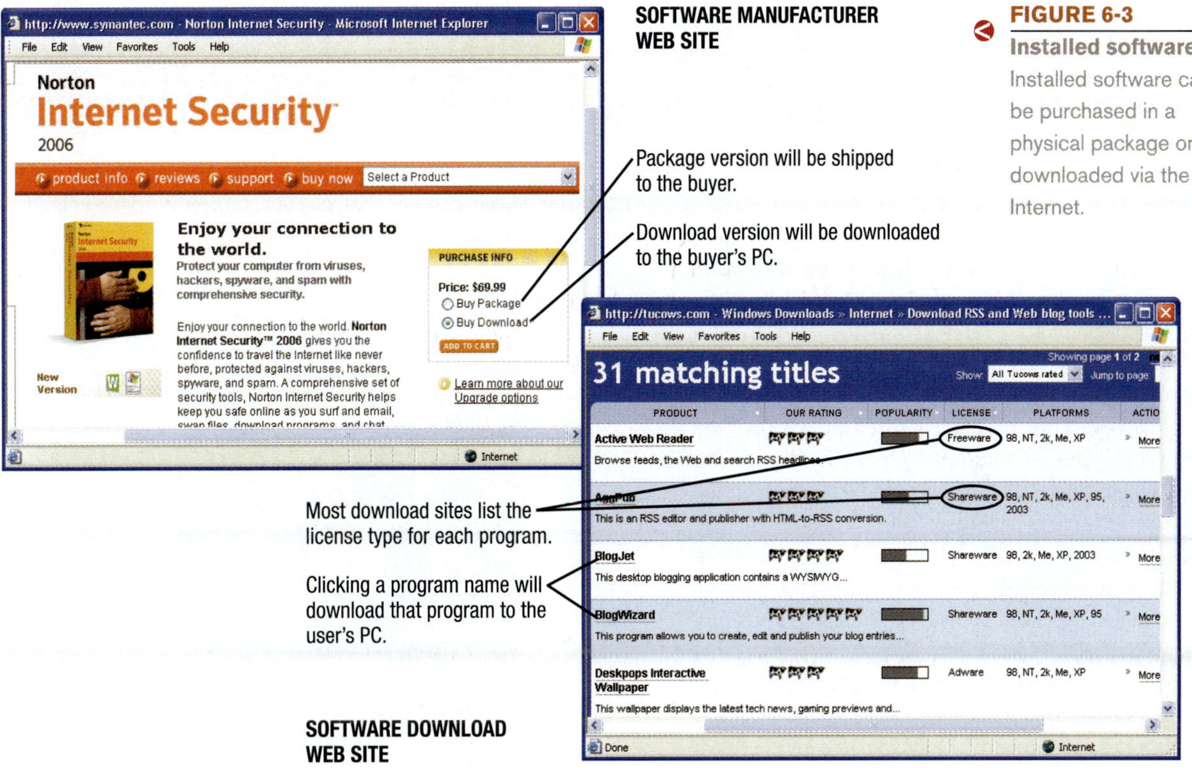

FIGURE 6-3

Installed software. Installed software can be purchased in a physical package or downloaded via the Internet.

program, shareware, freeware, or public domain software. When you purchase software in a downloaded format, you usually place the order, the payment is processed, and then you are provided with a link to download the purchased program. To download free software, you just need to click the appropriate hyperlink (such as on the manufacturer's site or a shareware download site) to download the free program. In either case, downloaded programs typically need to be installed before they can be used. This either occurs automatically after the program is downloaded, or the user needs to launch the downloaded installation program to begin the installation process. With a downloaded program, you do not normally receive a CD containing the program, although some vendors will mail you one for an additional fee, and most allow you to back up the program onto a CD as soon as it is downloaded.

For a look at a new way to purchase software—via *software kiosks*—see the Trend box.

> **TIP**
>
> Some downloaded installation programs don't contain the entire program and so need Internet access during the installation process to download the remaining components. If you are installing a program and receive an error message about the Internet, check your Internet connection to be sure you are still connected and then run the installation program again.

Web-Based Software

Instead of being available in an installed format, some software is run directly from the Internet as *Web-based software*. A Web-based software program can only be accessed via the Internet, and it can be free (such as an interactive game available through a Web site) or fee-based (such as software available from an *application service provider* (*ASP*)—a company that manages and distributes software over the Internet, typically for a monthly or annual fee). There is a wide range of Web-based software available; one example is shown in Figure 6-4. One advantage of Web-based software over installed software is that the programs and your files can be accessed from any PC with an Internet connection regardless of the type of PC or operating system used. Many Web-based programs are available for handheld PCs and mobile devices, in addition to desktop PCs, as shown in Figure 6-4. This makes Web-based software especially appropriate for shared scheduling and other communication or collaboration applications, since documents and other data can be shared regardless of an individual's location or device. Another advantage of Web-based software is that the software may be updated on a regular basis for no additional cost to the

TREND

Software Kiosks

Designed to give customers access to a wider range of software without requiring shelf space, a new kiosk-based software delivery system—called *SoftwareToGo*—is now available in retail stores, such as CompUSA. SoftwareToGo currently offers about 1,500 software titles from nearly 250 publishers. To use the system, the customer selects the program at a consumer kiosk (see the accompanying photo), and an order receipt is printed. The customer brings the order receipt to a salesclerk and pays for the program, and then the salesclerk uses a separate machine to burn the discs and print the labels and documentation. Similar to software programs downloaded from publishers via the Internet, the price is the same as the corresponding shrink-wrapped program and the product is never out of stock, but the user does not have to have an Internet connection or be concerned about viruses or other security risks associated with Internet downloads to obtain the program. The creator of the *SoftwareToGo* system expects the same technology to be used soon to deliver music, movies, audio books, television content, and other digital media products, in addition to software. Starbucks already has a similar system for music delivery that allows customers to download songs and burn customized music CDs.

user. Some potential disadvantages are that the cost may eventually exceed the cost of buying a similar shrink-wrapped package, and you cannot access the program and your data when the server on which they reside goes down.

While Web-based software is typically hosted on a provider's PC (such as a Web server belonging to an ASP or an organization providing Web-based games or other services to the public), some Web-based software is designed to be installed on a company server. Because the software is available via the Web, it can be accessed by company employees and partners, regardless of their current locations. For example, IBM's widely used Lotus Notes product is designed to be installed on a company server and used to facilitate e-mail, calendaring, group scheduling, and collaboration for company employees via the Web. IBM has announced plans to integrate Lotus Notes into Workspace, another of IBM's server-based collaboration products, and to add a productivity suite to Workplace, in order to create a complete suite of private Web-based communication and collaboration tools designed to be delivered to employees and partners via a company network.

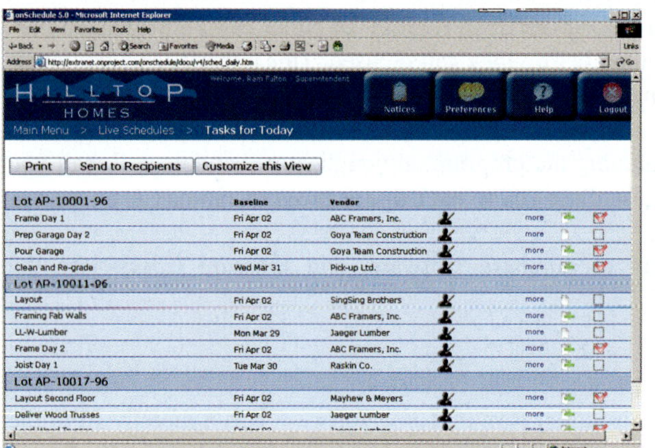

DESKTOP WEB-BASED PROGRAM

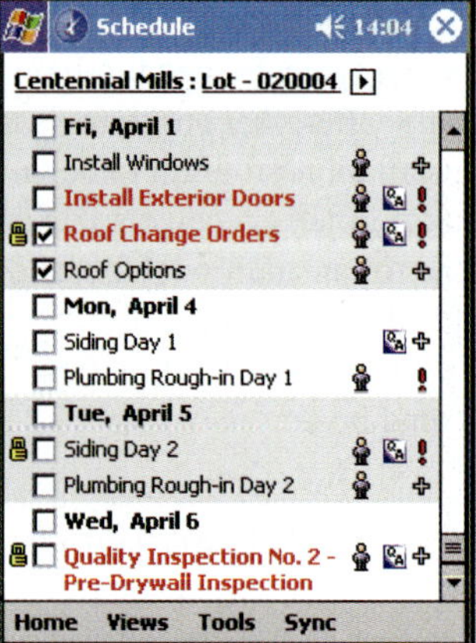

HANDHELD WEB-BASED PROGRAM

FIGURE 6-4

Web-based software. Web based software can be free or (like the programs shown here) fee-based.

Software Suites

Related software programs are sometimes sold bundled together as a **software suite**, such as a group of graphics programs, utility programs, or office-related software. *Office suites*, sometimes called *productivity software suites*, are used by most businesses and many individuals to produce written documents. Typically, office suites contain the programs discussed next; many also contain additional productivity tools—such as a calendar or a messaging program.

- *Word processing software*—allows users to efficiently create, edit, and print the type of documents that would have been created with a typewriter in the past.
- *Spreadsheet software*—provides users with a convenient means of creating documents containing complex mathematical calculations.
- *Database software*—allows users to store and organize vast amounts of data and retrieve specific information when needed.
- *Presentation graphics software*—allows users to create visual presentations to convey information more easily to others.

One of the most widely used office software suites is **Microsoft Office**. The latest versions are *Microsoft Office 2003* (for Windows users) and *Microsoft Office 2004 for Mac* (for Mac OS users); the next version—*Office 12*—is expected to be available sometime in 2006. Similar suites (see Figure 6-5) are available from Corel (*WordPerfect Office*), IBM (*Lotus SmartSuite*), and Sun (*StarOffice*). A free alternative suite similar to *StarOffice* is *OpenOffice.org*, which is available as a free download via the Internet from the OpenOffice.org Web site or on CD for a small fee from various distributors. Many suites are available in different versions, such as a home version containing fewer programs than a professional version. Not all of these suites are available for all operating systems. For example, Microsoft Office is available for both Windows and Mac OS, WordPerfect and SmartSuite are just for Windows users, and StarOffice can be used by Windows, Linux, or Solaris users.

The primary advantages of using a software suite include a total cost that is lower than buying the programs individually and a common interface. Although, as mentioned in an earlier chapter, most programs written for the same operating system (such as Windows or Mac OS) use similar interfaces and commands, a software suite goes one step further. Usually the menu and toolbar structure in the suite is very similar from program to program. This similarity is not just for the basic commands (such as *Save* and *Print*)—all commands

FIGURE 6-5

Office suites. The most common office suites are Microsoft Office, Corel WordPerfect Office, Lotus SmartSuite, and Sun StarOffice.

>Software suite. A collection of software programs bundled together and sold as a single software package. **>Microsoft Office.** One of the most widely used office software suites.

(such as adding borders and shading or inserting a row or column) that appear in more than one program in the suite are performed in the same manner. Once you have experience working with one program in a suite, this cross-program functionality makes it easier to learn another program in that suite.

Although you can often copy content from one program to another even if the two programs are not in the same suite—such as copying a drawing created in the Windows Paint program into a word processing document or copying word processing content into an e-mail message—with a software suite you can sometimes go a step further and *link* documents created within a suite together, such as displaying a spreadsheet document within a word processing document. When two documents are linked, the software will ask if you want to display the most recent version of the linked document (the spreadsheet document in this example) whenever the document containing the link (the word processing document in this example) is opened. If you choose to update the link, the spreadsheet displayed in the word processing document will be refreshed to show the most current version. This process of embedding and linking content from one program to another is called *object linking and embedding* (*OLE*).

Similar to software suites are *integrated software programs*—such as *Microsoft Works* and *AppleWorks*. Integrated software programs are similar to full suites, but contain fewer features and are one integrated program instead of a collection of separate programs. Integrated software programs often come installed on home PCs.

Desktop vs. Mobile Software

Unlike notebook and tablet PCs, which usually run the same application software as desktop PCs, handheld PCs and mobile devices require special application software designed for that type of device, sometimes called *mobile software*. A wide variety of mobile software is available today, such as calendars, e-mail and instant messaging programs, address books, language translators, games, reference software, media players, Web browsers, inventory and pricing programs, synchronization programs, and portable versions of popular productivity programs, like Word, Excel, PowerPoint, and Outlook (see Figure 6-6). Some software typically comes installed on the device when it is purchased; additional software can be purchased or downloaded as needed.

FIGURE 6-6

Mobile software.

There is a wide variety of software available today for handheld PCs and mobile devices.

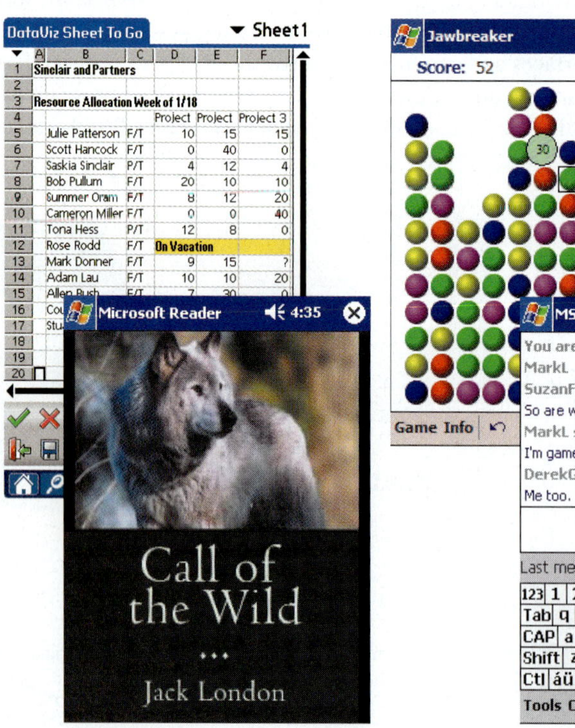

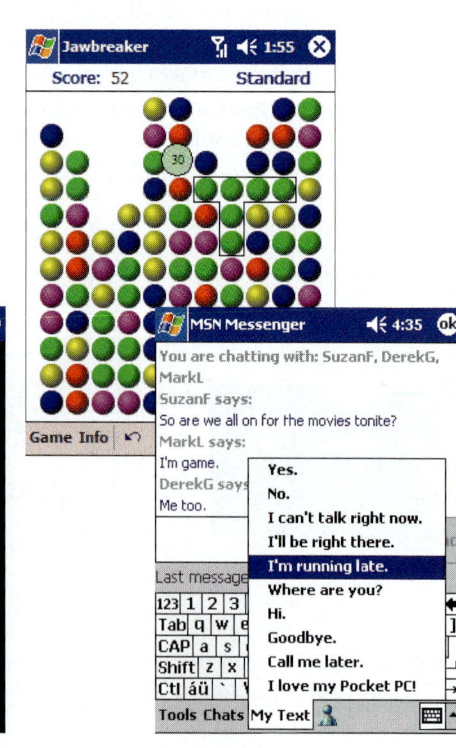

In addition to having a more compact, efficient appearance, many handheld applications include features for easier data input, such as an onscreen keyboard, a phrase list, or handwriting recognition capabilities. Some mobile software programs are designed to be compatible with popular *desktop software* to facilitate sharing documents between the two platforms. For example, both *Documents to Go* (for handheld PCs running Palm OS) and *Pocket Office* (for handheld PCs running Windows Mobile) are compatible with Microsoft Office documents created with a desktop PC. *Synchronization software* can also be used to synchronize the data stored on a desktop PC and a portable PC.

Common Software Commands

Application programs today have a number of concepts and commands in common. For example, many programs allow you to create a new document (such as a letter, drawing, house plan, or greeting card) and then *save* it. To reopen the document at a later time, you use the *open* command, and to print the document, you use the *print* command. One of the greatest advantages of using software instead of paper and pencil to create documents is that you can make changes without erasing or recreating the entire document because the document is created and then saved on a storage medium, instead of it being created directly on paper. Consequently, the document can be retrieved, modified, saved, and printed as many times as needed. Many programs also include tools to help you as you create documents, such as a *spelling and grammar check* feature to help you locate and correct spelling and grammatical errors in your documents, a built-in *thesaurus* to help you enhance the vocabulary used in your documents, a *styles* feature to allow you to apply a common format to a series of documents or a group of similar headings within a single document, and so forth.

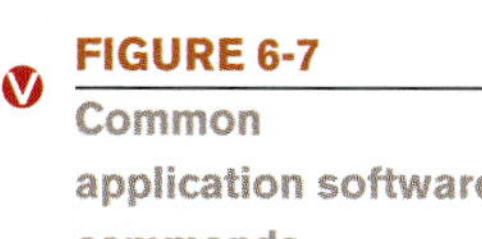

Some of the most common application software commands are described in Figure 6-7, with examples of the toolbar buttons and keyboard shortcuts used to perform these operations in Microsoft Office. Many of these commands would be performed in the same manner in other Windows programs. Some of the most common basic software commands are discussed in more detail next.

FIGURE 6-7
Common application software commands.

COMMAND	TOOLBAR BUTTON	KEYBOARD SHORTCUT	DESCRIPTION
New document		Ctrl+N	Creates a new blank document.
Open		Ctrl+O	Opens a previously saved document from a storage medium, usually for editing or printing.
Save		Ctrl+S	Saves the current version of the document to a storage medium.
Print		Ctrl+P	Prints the current version of the document onto paper.
Spelling and grammar	ABC	F7	Starts the spelling and grammar check for the entire document.
Cut		Ctrl+X	Moves the selected item to the clipboard.
Copy		Ctrl+C	Copies the selected item to the clipboard.
Paste		Ctrl+V	Pastes the contents of the clipboard to the current location.
Undo		Ctrl+Z	Undoes the last change to the document.
Close	X	Alt+F4	Closes the document. Any changes made to the document are lost if the document wasn't saved first.

Editing a Document

Editing a document refers to changing the content of the document, such as adding or deleting text. Most application software programs that allow text editing have an **insertion point** displayed on the screen that usually looks like a blinking vertical line. An insertion point indicates the current location in the document; that is, where the next change will be made to that document. To insert text, just start typing and the text will appear at the insertion point location. To delete text, press the Delete key to delete one character to the right of the insertion point; press the Backspace key to delete one character to the left of the insertion point. If the insertion point is not in the proper location for the edit, it must be moved (by using the arrow keys on the keyboard or by pointing and clicking with the mouse) to the appropriate location in the document. To select an object or block of text, click the object or drag the mouse over the text. Usually, once an object or some text is selected, it can be manipulated, such as moved, deleted, copied, or *formatted*.

TIP

Once an object or block of text is selected, press *Ctrl+C* to copy it or *Ctrl+X* to cut (move) it, and then move the insertion point to the new location and press *Ctrl+V* to paste the object or text there. You can also delete selected objects or text by pressing the Delete key.

Formatting a Document

While editing changes the actual content of a document, *formatting* changes the appearance of the document. Common types of formatting include changing the *font face*, *font size*, *font style*, and *font color* of text; changing the *line spacing* or *margins* of a document; adding *page numbers*; and adding *shading* or *borders*. A font face or *typeface* is a named collection of text characters that share a common design, such as Arial or Times New Roman. The characters in a font face are usually available in a wide variety of font sizes, which are measured in *points*. All the characters in a particular font face and font size are referred to as a *font*; for example, 12-point Times New Roman is a font. *Font style* refers to formatting that adds additional features to the text, such as bold, italic, or underline, and *font color* refers to the color of the text (see Figure 6-8). Default fonts are installed on a PC with the operating system and some application programs; additional fonts also can be purchased and added specifically by the user. Most, but not all, application programs allow you to use any of the fonts installed on your PC.

TIP

When selecting font size in a document, 72 points equals one-inch-tall text.

FIGURE 6-8

Fonts. The face, size, style, and color of text can be specified in many application programs.

SAMPLE FONT FACES

This is 10-point Helvetica
This is 12-point Times New Roman
This is 18-point Lucida Italic
This is 24-point Comic Sans
This Comic Sans text is bold.
This Comic Sans text is italic.
This Comic Sans text is underlined.
This Comic Sans text is red.

SAMPLE FONT SIZES, STYLES, AND COLORS

>**Insertion point.** An onscreen character that indicates the current location in a document, which is where the next change will be made to the document.

Getting Help

Most people run into problems or need some help as they work with a software program. There are various options for getting help when you need it. For instance, most application programs have a built-in help feature, typically available through a *Help* option on the menu bar. The type and amount of built-in help available varies from program to program, but some of the most common configurations are illustrated in Figure 6-9 and listed next. Help may also be available through resources on the Web.

- *Table of Contents*—works similarly to the table of contents in a book with related help topics organized under main topics. With most help systems, selecting a main topic reveals the help topics related to that main topic; selecting a help topic displays related information on the screen.
- *Index*—works similarly to an index in a book with all help topics organized as an alphabetical list. Typically typing the name of a help topic scrolls the index to that help topic if it is contained in the index; selecting a help topic displays the related information on the screen.

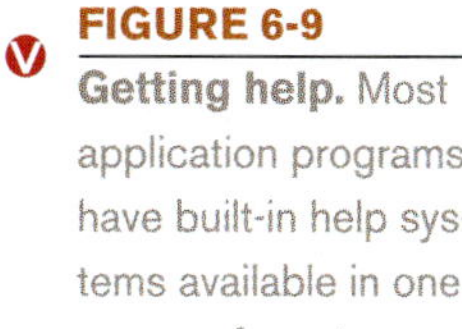

FIGURE 6-9

Getting help. Most application programs have built-in help systems available in one or more formats.

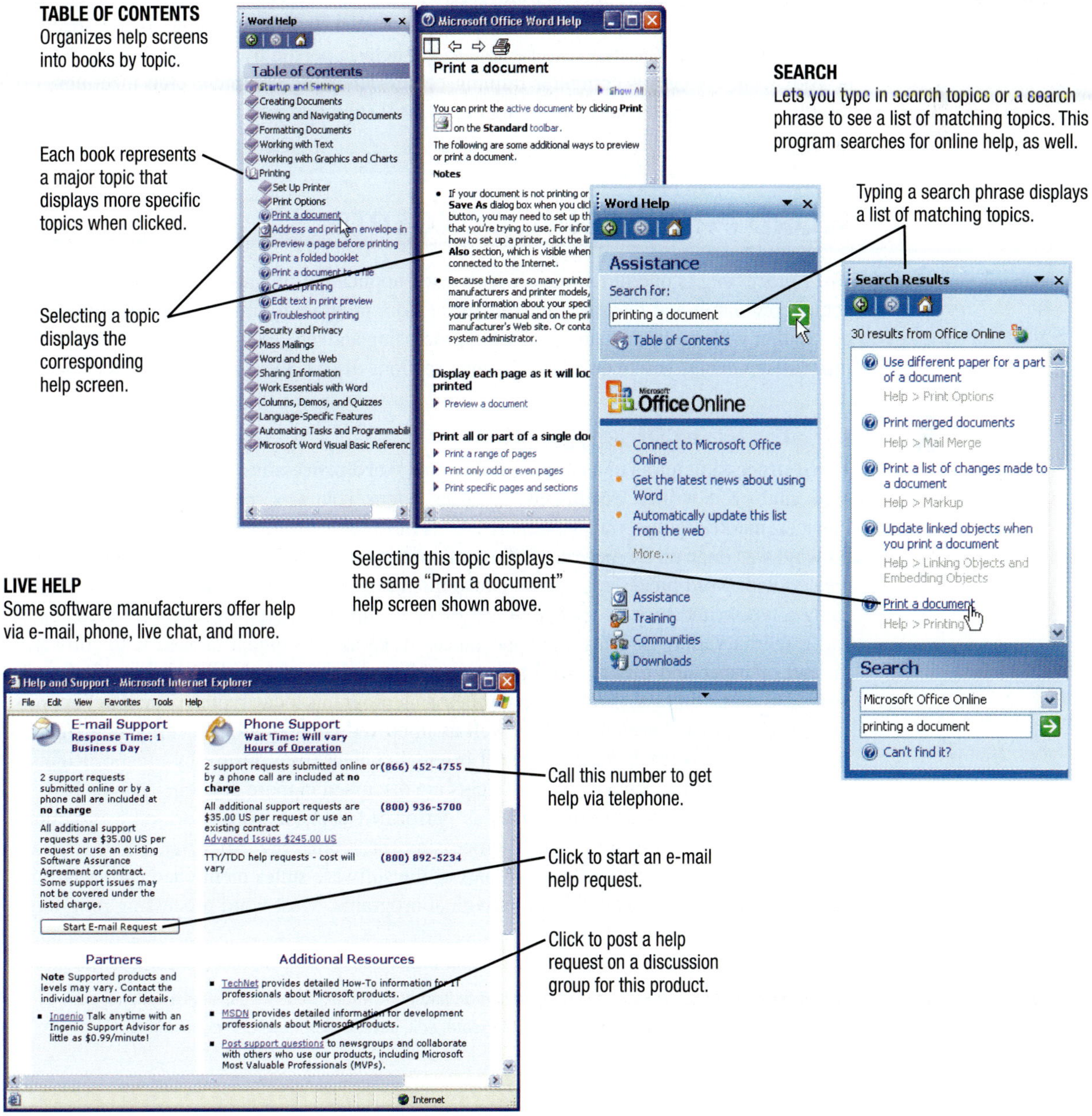

TABLE OF CONTENTS
Organizes help screens into books by topic.

Each book represents a major topic that displays more specific topics when clicked.

Selecting a topic displays the corresponding help screen.

SEARCH
Lets you type in search topics or a search phrase to see a list of matching topics. This program searches for online help, as well.

Typing a search phrase displays a list of matching topics.

Selecting this topic displays the same "Print a document" help screen shown above.

LIVE HELP
Some software manufacturers offer help via e-mail, phone, live chat, and more.

Call this number to get help via telephone.

Click to start an e-mail help request.

Click to post a help request on a discussion group for this product.

SW

- ▶ *Search*—allows you to search for help topics by typing a keyword or phrase (similar to a search site), and then the help system displays a list of possible matching help topics. Because a help search feature usually looks for all help screens containing the search term (not just all help topics containing the search term), a help search generally returns more help screens than searching for the same term using a help index feature.

Some help systems automatically search for online help from the manufacturer's Web site if the program detects an Internet connection. In addition, there is a vast amount of additional information about application software programs available via the Web. For instance, many software manufacturers offer online tutorials and lists of tips and tricks for their programs on their Web sites, as well as free or fee-based support via e-mail, telephone, or discussion group. There are also general-purpose software tutorial sites that provide online tutorials for a variety of programs, as well as sites dedicated to a particular application, such as desktop publishing or digital photo touch-up.

There are also numerous resources for offline help, including periodicals (such as magazines and journals) that often contain articles about how to most effectively use particular software programs, books (both reference books and textbooks) on how to use any number of software programs, and tutorial videos that demonstrate how to use specific software programs. You may also be able to get help in person by taking software classes at your local college or computer training center, attending computer club meetings, or talking with a computer sales professional at a local store that sells the software program in question.

FURTHER EXPLORATION

For links to further information about application software resources, go to www.course.com/uc11/ch06

WORD PROCESSING CONCEPTS

Word processing is one of the most widely used application programs today. Although the actual commands and features vary somewhat from program to program, it is important to be familiar with the basic features of word processing and the general concept of what word processing enables you to do. The following sections discuss these features and concepts.

What Is Word Processing?

Word processing refers to using a computer and **word processing software** to create, edit, save, and print written documents, such as letters, contracts, manuscripts, newsletters, invoices, marketing material, and reports. At its most basic level, word processing is used to do what was done on a typewriter before computers were commonplace. Many documents created with word processing software also include content that was not possible to create using a typewriter, such as photos, drawn objects, clip art images, hyperlinks, video clips, and text in a variety of sizes and appearances. Like any document created with software instead of paper and pencil, word processing documents can be retrieved, modified, and printed as many times as needed. Word processing programs today typically include support for speech and handwritten input, as well as improved collaboration, security, and *rights-management* tools (tools used to protect original content from misuse by others). Rights-management and intellectual property rights are discussed in more detail in Chapter 16.

Virtually all formal writing today is performed using a word processing program. Among today's best-selling word processing programs are *Microsoft Word*, *Corel WordPerfect*, and *Lotus WordPro*—all part of the software suites mentioned earlier in this chapter; some are also available as individual programs. Most word processing programs

>**Word processing.** Using a computer and word processing software to create, edit, save, and print written documents, such as letters, contracts, and manuscripts. >**Word processing software.** Application software used to create, edit, save, and print written documents.

offer hundreds of features, but virtually all support a core group of features used to create, edit, and format documents. Some of these basic features are described in the next few sections, using Microsoft Word as the example.

Creating a Word Processing Document

Every word processor contains an assortment of operations for creating and editing documents, including commands to insert both text and graphics and then move, copy, delete, or otherwise edit the content, as needed. Some features in a typical word processing program are shown in Figure 6-10.

When entering text in a word processing document, it is important to know when to press the Enter key. Word processing programs use a feature called **word wrap**, which means the insertion point automatically moves to the beginning of the next line when the end of the screen line is reached. Consequently, the Enter key should not be pressed until it

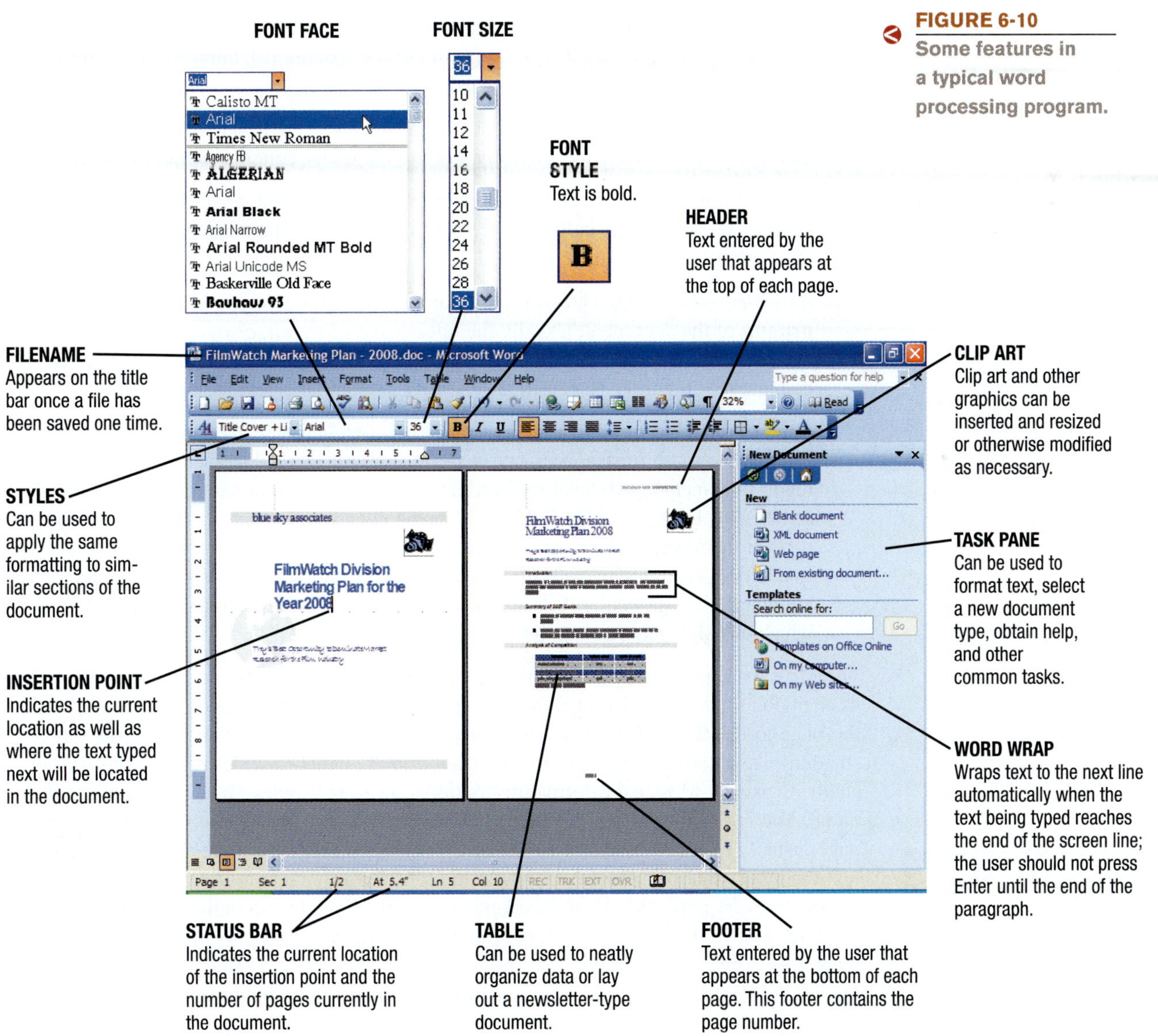

FIGURE 6-10
Some features in a typical word processing program.

SW

>Word wrap. The feature in a word processing program that automatically returns the insertion point to the next line when the end of the screen line is reached.

TIP

When typing text in a word processing program, you should only press Enter after a short line (like a title), at the end of a paragraph, and to leave a blank line between paragraphs.

is time to begin a new paragraph. When changes are made to the document—such as adding, modifying, or deleting text or changing the text size or page margins—the program will automatically adjust the amount of text on each screen line, as long as the Enter key is not pressed at the end of a line.

In most word processing programs, formatting can be applied at the character, paragraph, and document levels. Character *formatting* changes the appearance of individual characters, such as to change the font face, size, style, or color. To format characters, you usually select them with the mouse, and then apply the appropriate format using either toolbar buttons (refer again to Figure 6-10) or the *Font* option on the Format menu.

Paragraph formatting changes an entire paragraph at one time, such as specifying the line spacing for a particular paragraph. To format paragraphs, you usually select the paragraph with the mouse, and then apply the appropriate format using either toolbar buttons or the *Paragraph* option on the Format menu. The most common types of paragraph formatting are listed next.

- *Line spacing*—controls the amount of blank space between lines of text. Usually line spacing is set to single spacing (1) or double spacing (2), although it can be set to fractional spacing—such as 1.5—as well.
- *Left* and *right margins*—indicate how much blank space will be printed on the left and right edges of the paper (usually 1 or 1.5 inches by default).
- *Tabs*—set the location to which the insertion point is moved when the Tab key on the keyboard is pressed. Usually tabs are preset to every half inch across the document, although this setting can be changed by the user.
- *Alignment*—determines how the paragraph is aligned in relation to the left and right margins of the document. Usually the options are *align left*, *center*, *align right*, or *justify* (flush with both the left and right edges of the document). For example, the document in Figure 6-10 is primarily left-aligned and this textbook is justified.
- *Styles*—named format specifications that can be applied on a paragraph-by-paragraph basis to keep a uniform appearance for related sections in a document. For example, a report may include two levels of headings plus a variety of quotations. If a style (such as HEAD1, HEAD2, or QUOTE) is defined and applied to each occurrence of these parts of the report, those sections of the document will have a consistent appearance. In addition, changing the specified format (such as font face, font size, font color, or alignment) of a particular style automatically reformats all text in the document to which that style has been applied.

Most word processing programs also have a variety of *page formatting* options, such as changing the *top* and *bottom margins*, the *paper size* being used, and whether you want the page to use the traditional *portrait orientation* (8½ inches wide by 11 inches tall on standard paper) or the wider *landscape orientation* (11 inches wide by 8½ inches tall on standard paper). Most page formatting options are found under *Page Setup* on the File menu. You can also choose whether to include page numbers at the top or bottom of the page, usually as part of a header or footer (as shown in Figure 6-10, a *header* is specified text or images that print automatically at the top of every page; a *footer* is printed at the bottom of every page). Many of these options can be applied to an individual page as page formatting or to the entire document (called *document formatting*). Other types of document formatting include generating footnotes and end notes, a table of contents, or an index, as well as applying a background or theme to the entire document.

FURTHER EXPLORATION

For links to further information about word processing software, go to www.course.com/uc11/ch06

Tables, Graphics, and Templates

Most word processing programs today have advanced features to help users create documents or add special features to documents. For instance, a *table* feature allows content to be organized in a table consisting of *rows* and *columns*. It can be used for a basic data table, such as the one shown in Figure 6-10; tables can also be used for layout purposes, such as

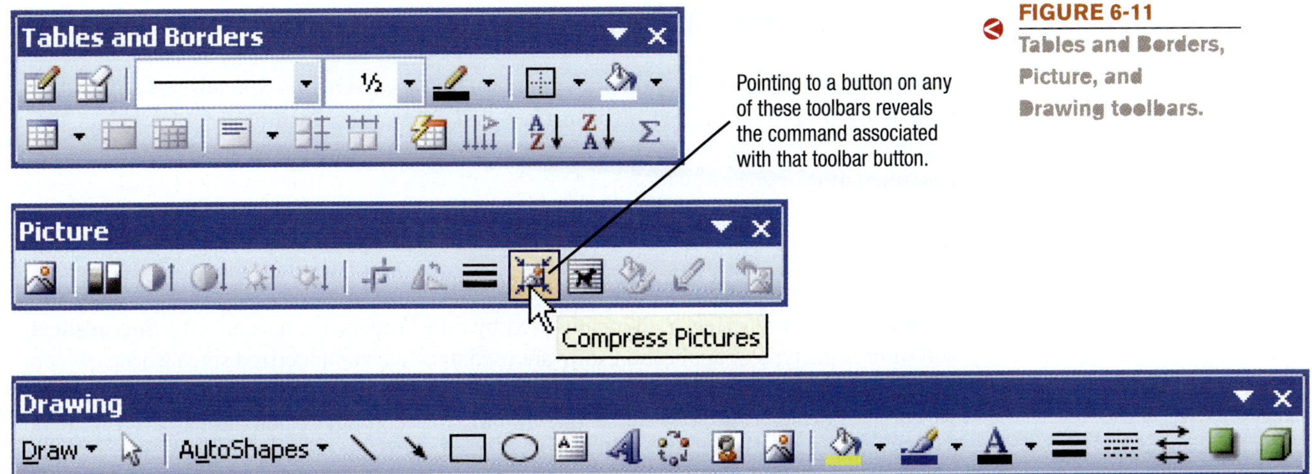

FIGURE 6-11
Tables and Borders, Picture, and Drawing toolbars.

when creating a newsletter or Web page. Once a table has been created, shading, borders, and other formatting can be applied to the table and/or its contents, and rows and columns can be inserted or deleted, as needed. The *Tables and Borders toolbar* available in Word to help users create and modify tables is shown in Figure 6-11.

Graphics or *drawing* features are also commonly found in word processing programs. Virtually all word processing programs allow images (such as a photograph, a drawing from another program, or a *clip art image*, as in Figure 6-10) to be inserted into a document. Once an image is inserted into a document, it can be modified (such as changing the brightness or contrast of a digital photo, cropping an image, converting a color image to grayscale, compressing an image to reduce the file size of the document, or adding borders). The *Picture toolbar* used in Word for these purposes is shown in Figure 6-11 along with the *Drawing Toolbar* that can be used to create new images (such as arrows and other graphical shapes). Once images are inserted into a document, they can be copied, moved, deleted, or otherwise modified, just like any other object in the document.

To help users create new documents quickly, many word processing programs have a variety of *templates* available. A template is a document that is already created and formatted to fit a particular purpose, such as a fax cover sheet, résumé, memo, business card, calendar, business plan, newsletter, or Web page. Usually placeholder text is included for text that can be customized so that all the user needs to do is fill in the blanks on the template document. A similar tool is a *wizard*, which consists of a series of screens that prompt the user for the necessary information and then creates a particular type of document based on the users input. Wizards are typically available for creating documents, such as envelopes, legal pleadings, calendars, and agendas, as well as for tasks, such as sending a fax or publishing a Web page.

TIP

Additional templates are often available for free through software manufacturer Web sites, such as Microsoft's *Office Online* Web site.

Word Processing and the Web

Most word processing programs today include Web-related features, such as the ability to send a document as an e-mail message via the word processing program, the inclusion of Web page hyperlinks in documents, and the ability to create or modify Web pages. Optional file formats for Web pages created in many word processing programs include regular *Hypertext Markup Language* (*HTML*), the more versatile *Extensible Markup Language* (*XML*), and the *single file Web page* or *MHTML* (*MIME Hypertext Markup Language*) format that combines all the elements of a Web site (text, images, sound files, animated items, and other elements) into a single file so it can be more easily published to the Web or sent via e-mail to others.

TIP

When hyperlinks are included in a document, clicking the hyperlink opens the corresponding Web page, as long as the computer being used has an active Internet connection.

SPREADSHEET CONCEPTS

Another widely used application program is *spreadsheet software*. Spreadsheet software is commonly used by a variety of businesses and employees, including CEOs, managers, assistants, analysts, and sales representatives. Basic spreadsheet concepts and features are described next.

What Is a Spreadsheet?

A **spreadsheet** is a group of values and other data organized into rows and columns, similar to the ruled paper worksheets traditionally used by bookkeepers and accountants. **Spreadsheet software** is the type of application software used to create computerized spreadsheets, which typically contain a great deal of numbers and mathematical calculations. Because spreadsheets are designed to be set up with *formulas* that compute calculations based on data entered into the spreadsheet, all formula results are automatically updated whenever any changes are made to the data. Consequently, no manual computations are required, which increases accuracy. In addition, the automatic recalculation of formulas allows individuals to modify spreadsheet data as often as necessary either to create new spreadsheets or to experiment with various possible scenarios to help make business decisions. Spreadsheet software typically also includes the ability to generate charts and perform detailed analysis based on the data in a spreadsheet.

The most widely used spreadsheet programs today are *Microsoft Excel*, *Corel Quattro Pro*, and *Lotus 1-2-3*—again, all part of the software suites mentioned at the beginning of this chapter; some are also available as individual programs. Some of the basic features supported by all spreadsheet programs are described in the next few sections, using Microsoft Excel as the example.

Creating a Spreadsheet

A single spreadsheet document is often called a **worksheet**. Most spreadsheet programs allow multiple worksheets to be saved together in a single spreadsheet file, called a **workbook**. Worksheets are divided into **rows** and **columns**. The intersection of a row and a column is called a **cell**. Each cell is identified by its *cell address*, which consists of the column letter followed by the row number, such as B4 or E22. The *cell pointer* is used to select a cell. The selected cell is called the *active cell* (also called the *current cell*) and has a border around it so it is easy to identify. You can enter content in the active cell, as well as apply formatting to content already in the active cell. The cell pointer can also be used to select more than one cell; if so, the selected cells are called a *range* or *block*. Ranges are always rectangular and are identified by specifying two opposite corners of the range, such as D8 through E9 (usually typed as *D8:E9* or *D8..E9*, depending on the spreadsheet program being used) for the four cells in the range shown in Figure 6-12.

TIP

As with word processing programs, spreadsheet templates are available to help users quickly create common types of business documents, such as balance sheets, income statements, invoices, and purchase orders.

Data is entered directly into worksheet cells by clicking a cell to make it the active cell and then typing the data. Cell content can be erased by pressing the Delete key; typing new content replaces the old content of the active cell with the new content. The data entered into a cell is usually a *label*, a *constant value*, a *formula*, or a *function*. **Labels** are words, column headings, and other nonmathematical data, such as *Profit Statement* and *July* in Figure 6-12. **Constant values** are numbers, such as *105* or *12740.25*, and are entered into a cell without any additional characters, such as a dollar sign or comma. The *numeric format* or *style* applied to a cell (such as *Currency*, *Comma*, or *Percent*) determines how the

TIP

Clip art, graphics, photographs, and other images can also be inserted into a cell–look for a *Picture* option on the Insert menu.

>Spreadsheet. A group of values and other data organized into rows and columns. **>Spreadsheet software.** Application software used to create spreadsheets, which typically contain a great deal of numbers and mathematical computations and are organized into rows and columns. **>Worksheet.** A document in a spreadsheet program. **>Workbook.** A collection of worksheets saved in a single spreadsheet file. **>Row.** In a spreadsheet program, a horizontal group of cells on a worksheet. **>Column.** In a spreadsheet program, a vertical group of cells on a worksheet. **>Cell.** The location at the intersection of a row and column on a worksheet into which data can be typed. **>Label.** A text-based entry in a worksheet cell that identifies data on the worksheet. **>Constant value.** A numerical entry in a worksheet cell.

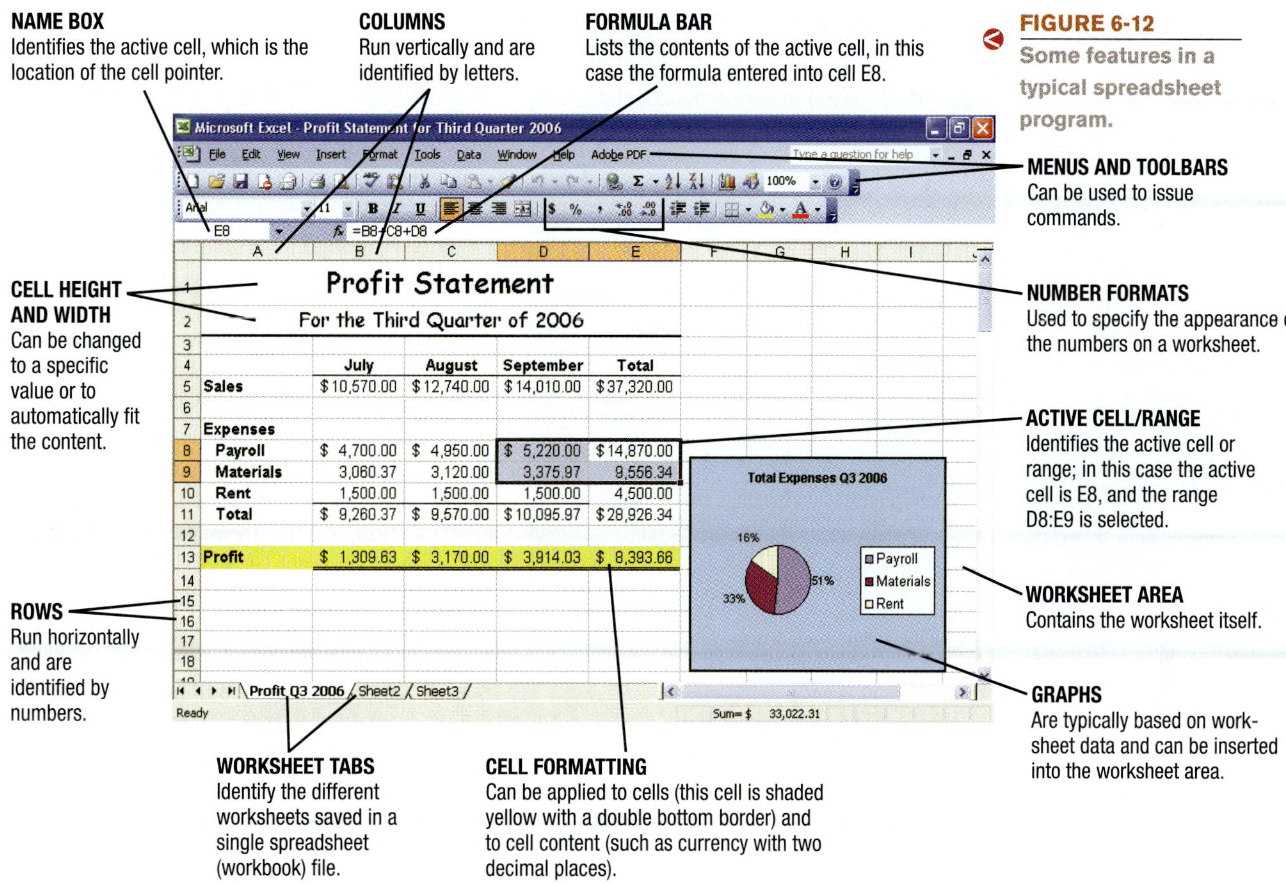

FIGURE 6-12 Some features in a typical spreadsheet program.

numeric content of the cell will display. A **formula** performs mathematical operations on the content of other cells—such as adding or multiplying them—and displays the results in the cell containing the formula. A **function** is a named, programmed formula, such as to compute the average of a group of cells or calculate a mortgage payment amount. Common mathematical operators are listed in Figure 6-13; some commonly used spreadsheet functions are listed in Figure 6-14.

When entering a formula or function into a cell, most spreadsheet programs require that you begin with some type of mathematical symbol, usually the equal sign =. You can then enter the cell addresses and mathematical operators to create the formula, or you can type the appropriate function name and *arguments* (such as a cell or range address). When creating formulas and functions, it is important to always use the cell addresses of *where* the numbers you want to include in the calculation are located (such as =B8+C8+D8 for the formula used to calculate the value displayed in cell E8 in Figure 6-12), rather than the numbers themselves (such as =4700+4950+5220). If the actual numbers are used in the formula instead of the cell addresses, the result of that formula (such as the total in cell E8) will not be correctly updated if one of the numbers (such as July payroll expenses in cell B8) is changed. When a proper formula (using the cell references instead of the actual numbers) is used instead, the formula will be recomputed automatically every time any data in any of the cells used in that formula is changed.

FIGURE 6-13 **Mathematical operators.** These mathematical operators are universal operators used by most application programs that perform calculations, including spreadsheet programs.

SYMBOL	OPERATION
+	Addition
–	Subtraction
*	Multiplication
/	Division
^	Exponentiation

>Formula. An entry in a worksheet cell that performs computations on worksheet data and displays the results. **>Function.** A named formula that can be entered into a worksheet cell to perform some type of calculation or to extract information from other cells in the worksheet.

EXAMPLES OF FUNCTIONS	
= SUM (range)	Calculates the sum of all values in a range.
= MAX (range)	Finds the highest value in a range.
= MIN (range)	Finds the lowest value in a range.
= NOW ( )	Inserts the current date and time.
= COUNT (range)	Counts the number of nonempty cells containing numerical values in a range.
= AVERAGE (range)	Calculates the average of values in a range.
= ABS (cell or expression)	Calculates the absolute value of the cell or expression.
= FV (rate, number of payments, payment amount)	Calculates the future value of an annuity at a specified interest rate.
= PMT (rate, number of payments, loan amount)	Calculates the periodic payment for a loan.
= IF (conditional expression, value if true, value if false)	Supplies the values to be displayed if the conditional expression is true or if it is false

FIGURE 6-14 Common spreadsheet functions.

Because many spreadsheet columns contain similar formulas (such as to add the three columns to the left of the Total column in the spreadsheet shown in Figure 6-12), the copy command can be used to duplicate formulas to help create a spreadsheet much more quickly than typing each formula individually. Although labels and constant values will be copied exactly to the new location, the way formulas behave when they are copied depends on whether they use *relative cell referencing* or *absolute cell referencing*.

Relative cell references are used in most spreadsheet programs by default. With relative cell references, the cell addresses in the copied formula are adjusted to reflect their new location, so the formula performs the same operation (such as adding the two cells to the left of the cell containing the formula) but in the new location. In other words, the formula in the new location does the same *relative* operation as it did in the original location. For example, in the left screen in Figure 6-15, the formula in cell D2, which uses relative cell references to add the two cells to the left of the formula cell, is copied to cells D3 and D4. Because the cell references are all relative, when the formula is copied to the new cells, the cell references are adjusted to continue to add the two cells to the left of the formula cell. For instance, the formula in cell D3 became =B3+C3 and the formula in cell D4 became =B4+C4. Relative cell references are also adjusted accordingly when a row or column is inserted or deleted.

In contrast, when *absolute cell references* are used, formulas are copied exactly as they are written (see the rightmost screens in Figure 6-15). It is appropriate to use an absolute cell reference when you always want to use a specific cell address in all copies of

COPYING WITH RELATIVE CELL REFERENCES
In most formulas, cell addresses are relative and will be adjusted as the formula is copied.

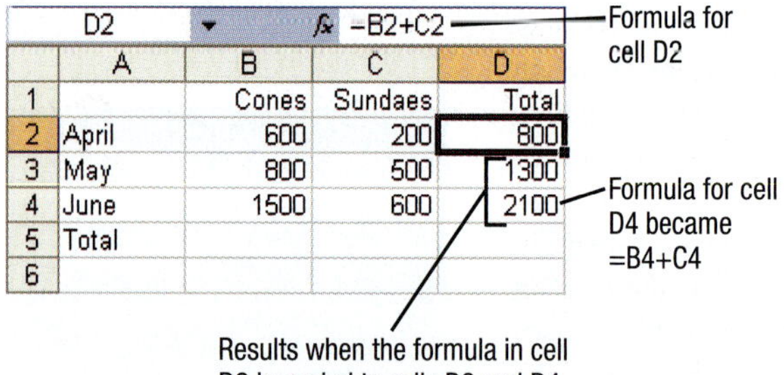

COPYING WITH ABSOLUTE CELL REFERENCES
A dollar ($) sign marks a cell reference as absolute; it will be copied exactly as it appears in the source cell.

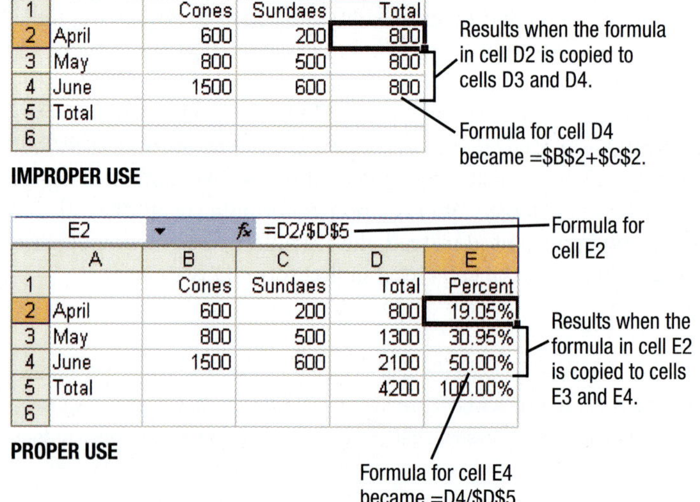

FIGURE 6-15 Relative vs. absolute cell referencing.

the formula—such as always multiplying by a constant value (perhaps a sales tax rate or overtime rate located in a particular cell on the worksheet) or always dividing by a total in order to compute a percentage. In other words, whenever you do not want a cell address to be adjusted when the formula is copied, you must use an absolute cell reference in the formula. To make a cell reference in a formula absolute, a special symbol—usually a dollar sign ($)—is placed before each column letter and row number that should not change. For example, both of the cell references in the formula in cell D2 in the top right screen in Figure 6-15 are absolute, resulting in the formula =$B$2+$C$2 being placed in both cells (D3 and D4) when the formula is copied. Obviously, this is not the correct formula for these cells—the formulas in these cells need to use relative cell references in order to display the proper total. In cells E2 through E4 in the bottom right screen, however, an absolute cell reference is used for cell D5 (written as $D$5) in the formula to compute the percent of total sales by dividing the total sales for each month by the total sales for all three months (located in cell D5). In fact, an absolute reference for cell D5 is necessary if the formula in cell E2 is to be copied to cells E3 and E4, since the denominator in all three cells should be D5.

TIP

Some spreadsheet programs support a shortcut for quickly copying a cell to adjacent cells, such as dragging the bottom right corner of the original cell in Microsoft Excel.

Charts and What-If Analysis

Most spreadsheet programs include some type of *charting* or *graphing* capability. Because the data to be included in many business charts is often already located on a spreadsheet, using that program's charting feature eliminates reentering data. Instead, the cells containing the data to be charted are selected, and then the type of chart—as well as titles and other customizations—can be specified. The finished chart can usually be inserted into a range of cells on an existing worksheet (refer again to Figure 6-12) or placed in a blank worksheet by itself. Types of charts are discussed in more detail later in this chapter.

Because spreadsheet programs automatically recalculate all formulas on a worksheet every time a cell on the worksheet is edited, they are particularly useful for *what-if analysis* (also called *sensitivity analysis*)—a tool frequently used to help make business decisions. For example, suppose you want to know *what* profit would have resulted for July in Figure 6-12 *if* sales had been $15,000 instead of $10,570. You can simply enter the new value (15000) into Cell B5, and the spreadsheet program automatically recalculates all formulas, allowing you to determine (from looking at the new value in cell B13) that the profit would have been $5,739.63. This ability to enter new numbers and immediately see the results allows businesspeople to run through many more possibilities in a shorter period of time before making decisions than in the past when all such calculations had to be performed by hand. Another type of sensitivity analysis (called *goal seeking* in Microsoft Excel) involves having the spreadsheet compute the amount a constant value would need to be in order for the result of a particular formula to become a specified amount (such as the total sales required to obtain a July profit of $5,000 if all of the expenses stayed the same).

FURTHER EXPLORATION

For links to further information about spreadsheet software, go to www.course.com/uc11/ch06

Spreadsheets and the Web

As with word processors, most spreadsheet programs have built-in Web capabilities. Although they are less commonly used to create Web pages, many spreadsheet programs have an option on the File menu to save the current worksheet as a Web page, and hyperlinks can be inserted into worksheet cells. Ranges of cells can also be selected and copied to a Web publishing or word processing program to insert spreadsheet data into a Web page as a table.

DATABASE CONCEPTS

People often need to retrieve large amounts of data rapidly. For example, a customer service representative may need to locate a customer's order status quickly while the customer is on the telephone. The registrar at a university may have to look up a student's grade point average or rapidly determine if the student has any outstanding fees before processing his or her class registration. A clerk in a video store may need to determine if a particular movie is available for rental and, if not, when it is due to be returned. The type of software used for such tasks is a *database management system*. Computer-based database management systems are rapidly replacing the paper-based filing systems that people used in the past to find information. The most common type of database used on PCs today is a *relational database*. The basic features and concepts of PC-based relational database software are discussed next. Other types of database programs are discussed in Chapter 14.

What Is a Database?

A **database** is a collection of related data that is stored on a computer and organized in a manner enabling information to be retrieved as needed (see Figure 6-16). A *database management system* (*DBMS*)—also called **database software**—is the type of program

FIGURE 6-16
Paper-based vs. computerized databases. Data is organized into fields (columns), records (rows), and tables.

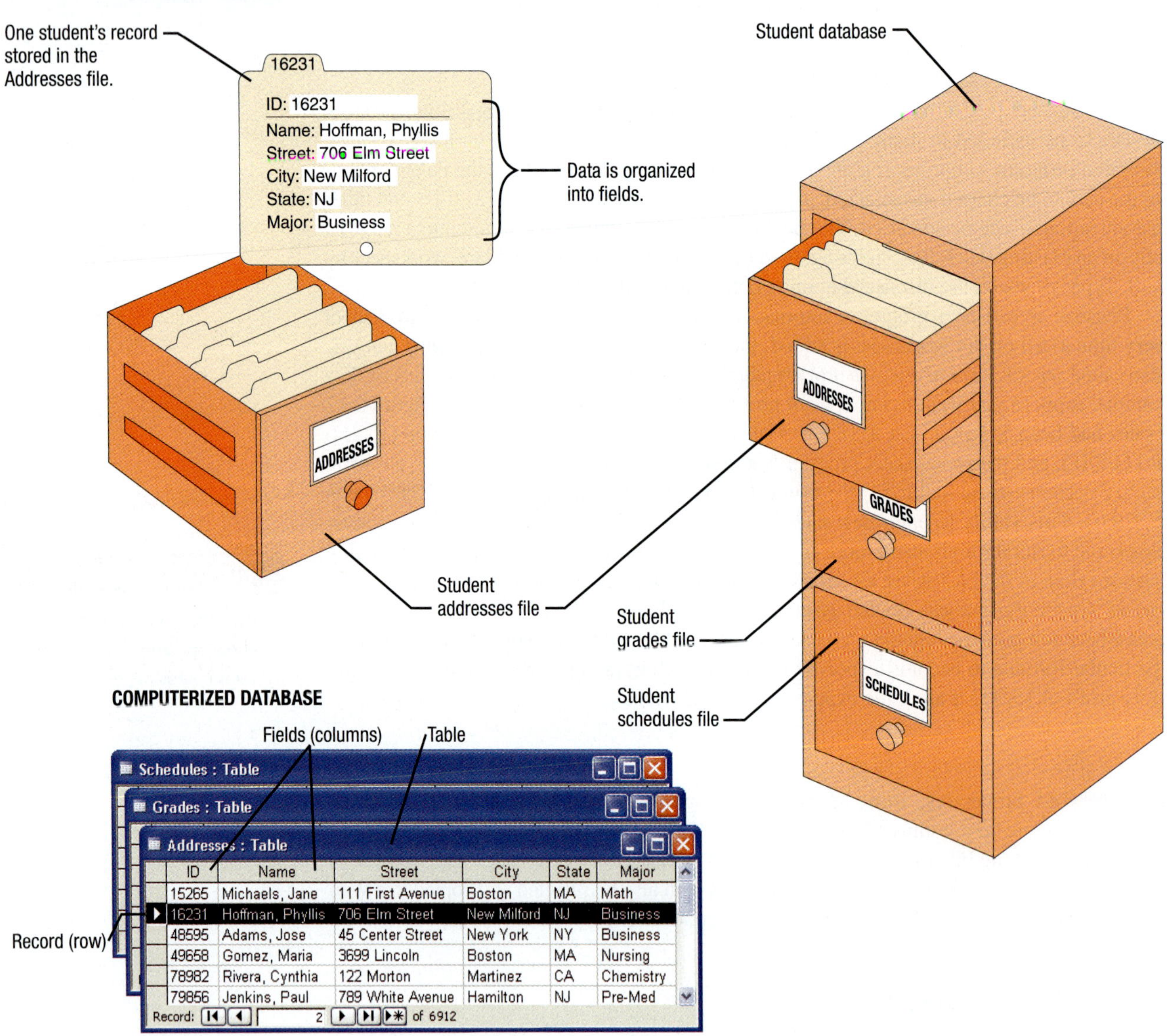

>Database. A collection of related data that is stored in a manner enabling information to be retrieved as needed; in a relational database, a collection of related tables. **>Database software.** Application software that allows the creation and manipulation of an electronic database.

used to create, maintain, and organize data in a database, as well as to retrieve information from it. Although not all databases are organized identically, most are organized into *fields*, *records*, and *files*. A **field** (today more commonly called a **column**) is a single type of data, such as a person's name or a person's telephone number, to be stored in a database. A **record** (today more commonly called a **row**) is a collection of related fields—for example the ID number, name, address, and major of Phyllis Hoffman (refer again to Figure 6-16). A **table** is a collection of related rows (such as all student address data, all student grade data, or all student schedule data). One or more related tables can be stored in a database file.

The most commonly used *relational database management systems* (*RDBMSs*) include *Microsoft Access*, *Corel Paradox*, and *Lotus Approach*—all part of their respective software suites—as well as the stand-alone *Oracle Database* product from Oracle Corporation. Some of the basic features of database programs in general are described in the next few sections, using Microsoft Access as the example.

FURTHER EXPLORATION

For links to further information about database software, go to www.course.com/uc11/ch06

Creating a Database

A database can contain a variety of *objects* (see Figure 6-17). The object that contains the data in a new database is the *table*; other objects (such as *forms*, *queries*, and *reports*, discussed shortly) can be created and used in conjunction with that table when needed. Unlike word processing documents and spreadsheets, you do not see the content of a database table or other object on the screen at all times—only when you request to see it.

To create a database table, the *structure* of the table is specified first. A table's structure includes a list of fields and their properties. As a minimum, each field needs to have a *field name* (an identifying name unique within the table) and a *data type* (the type of data to be contained in the field, for example text, a number, a date, or an object such as a photo) defined. Other possible properties include the *field size* (the maximum number of characters allowed for the content of that field), *default value* (the initial content of the field that remains until it is changed), the format identifying how the field content should be displayed, and whether or not the field is *required* (must contain some content). A table structure is shown in Figure 6-18.

After the table structure has been created, data is entered into the table. This can occur using either the table's *Datasheet view* or a *form* created to enter data into that table (refer again to Figure 6-18). Existing table data can be edited in the same manner. If the structure of the table needs to be changed, such as to change the size or type of a field, the table needs to be opened in *Design view*, which is the same screen used to originally create the table structure.

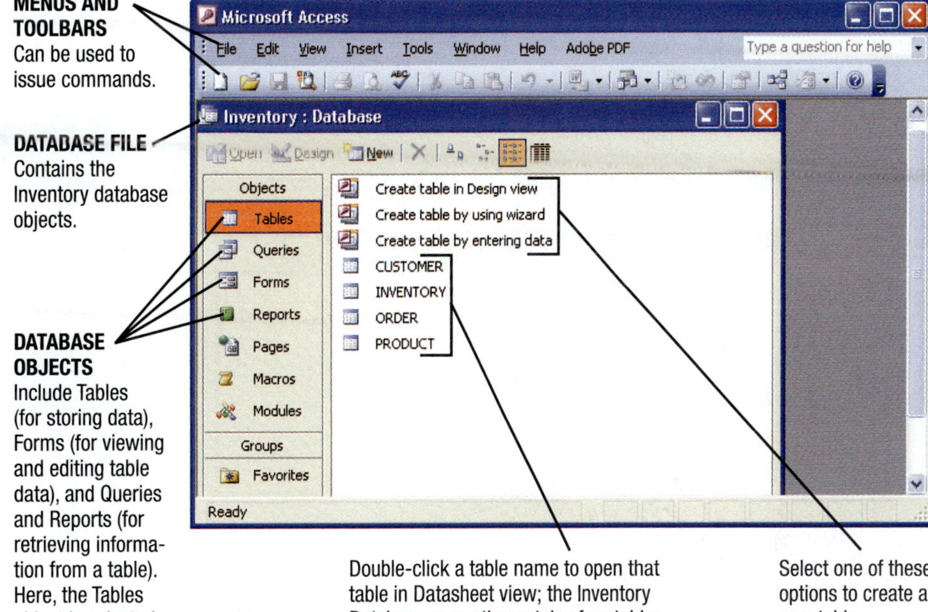

FIGURE 6-17

Typical database objects. Common database objects include tables, forms, queries, and reports. The first object to be created is the table.

>Field. A single category of data to be stored in a database, such as a person's name or telephone number. Also called a column. **>Column.** In a database, a field. **>Record.** A collection of related fields in a database. Also called a row. **>Row.** In a database program, a record. **>Table.** In a relational database, a collection of related records or rows.

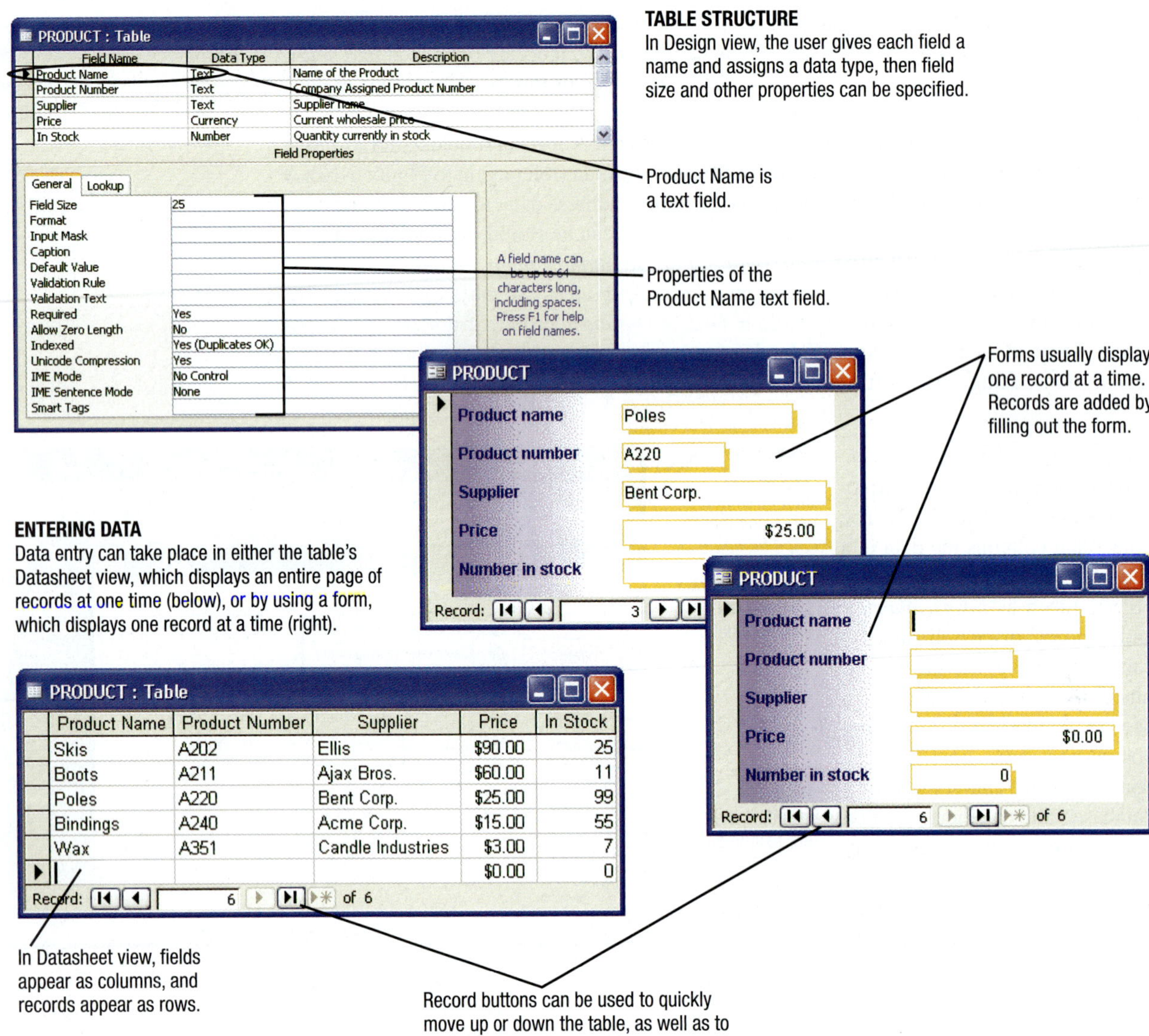

FIGURE 6-18
Creating a database in a typical database program.

Queries and Reports

To retrieve information from a database, *queries* and *reports* are used. A *query* is a question, or, in database terms, a request for specific information from the database. Each query object is created and saved under its own name in the database file. A query object contains *criteria*—specific conditions that must be met in order for a record (row) to be included in the query results—as well as instructions regarding which fields (columns) should appear in the query results. For instance, the criteria for the query shown in Figure 6-19 is all products with prices less than $25 and the query results should display only the Product Name, Product Number, and Price fields. Whenever the query is opened and the results displayed, only the specified three fields for only the records meeting the specified criteria at the time are displayed. Each time the query is opened, the query results will accurately reflect the current data in the database. For instance, the query results shown in Figure 6-19 contain only the two records from the table in Figure 6-18 that contain products with prices less than $25, but if a new product priced less than $25 was added to the database, three records would be displayed when the query was reopened.

TIP

Databases, queries, and reports are discussed in more detail in Chapter 14.

When a more formal output is required, *reports* are used. Report objects are typically created using a wizard and can contain page and column headings, as well as additional formatting and customized output. Whenever a report object is opened, the corresponding table data is displayed in the specified location on the report. Consequently, just as with queries, reports always display the data contained in a table at the time the report is generated. Many database programs allow reports to be created in a variety of styles and can incorporate text formatting, clip art, and other enhancements.

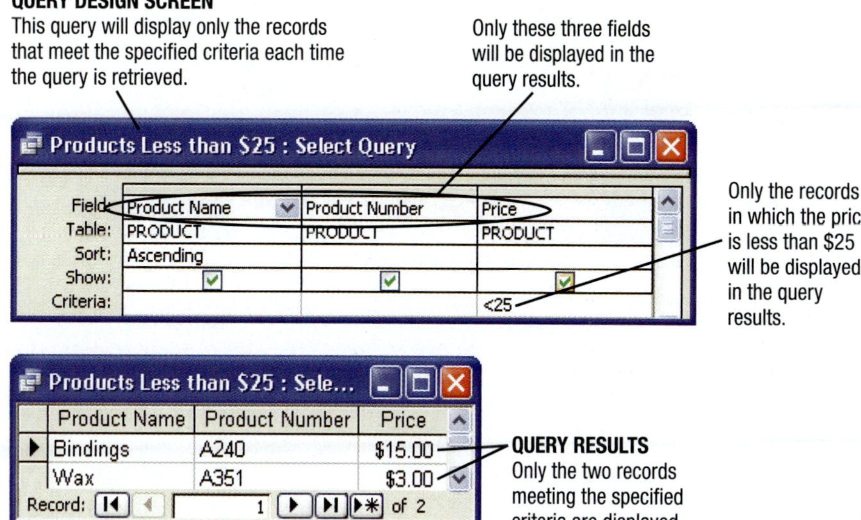

FIGURE 6-19
Creating and using a database query.

Databases and the Web

Databases are used often on the Web. Many Web sites use one or more databases to keep track of inventory; allow searching for people, documents, or other information; place real-time orders; and so forth. For instance, anytime you type keywords in a search site or hunt for a product on a retail store's Web site using its search feature, you are using a Web database. Web databases are explained in more detail in Chapter 14.

PRESENTATION GRAPHICS CONCEPTS

If you try to explain to others what you look like, it may take several minutes. Show them a color photograph, on the other hand, and you can convey the same information within seconds. The saying "a picture is worth a thousand words" is the cornerstone of *presentation graphics*. The basic concepts and features of presentation graphics are discussed in the next few sections.

What Is a Presentation Graphic?

A **presentation graphic** is an image designed to visually enhance a presentation, typically to convey information more easily to people. Presentation graphics can be used in *electronic slide shows*, as well as in printed handouts, overhead transparencies, word processing documents, and Web pages. Some examples of presentation graphics are shown in Figure 6-20.

To create presentation graphics, **presentation graphics software** is used. Some of today's most common presentation graphics programs are *Microsoft PowerPoint*, *Corel Presentations*, and *Lotus Freelance Graphics*. While some presentation graphics programs are designed to create stand-alone graphics, presentation graphics software is more often used to create electronic slide shows; that is, groups of electronic **slides**. Each slide—containing content such as text, images, video clips, or sound clips—is displayed one at a time, typically for a business presentation. Slide shows can be run on individual computers or presented to a large group using a computer projector. The next few sections discuss creating an electronic slide show, using Microsoft PowerPoint as the example.

>**Presentation graphic.** An image, such as a graph or text chart, designed to visually enhance a presentation. >**Presentation graphics software.** Application software used to create presentation graphics and online slide shows. >**Slide.** A one-page presentation graphic that can be displayed in a group with others to form an online slide show.

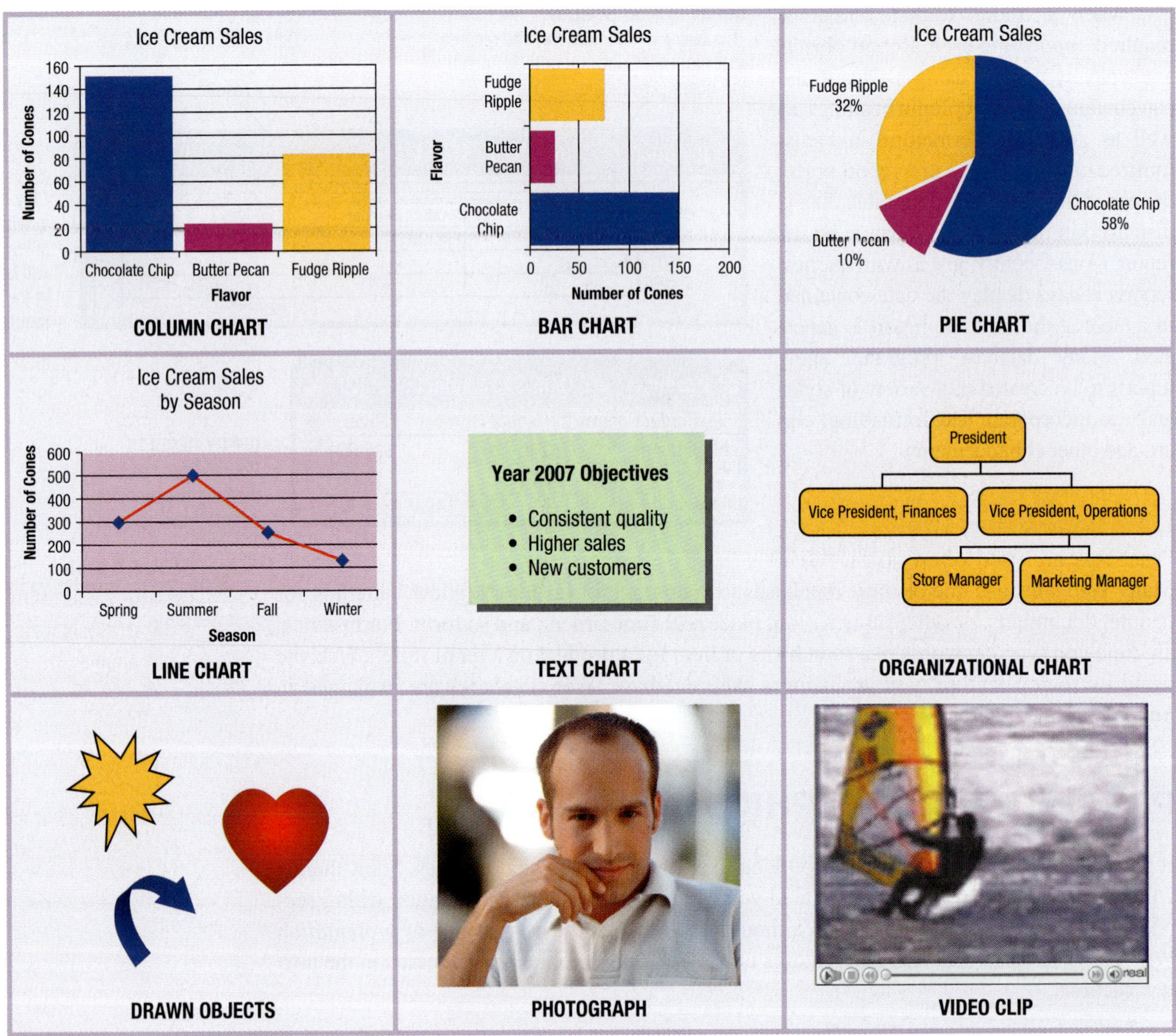

FIGURE 6-20 Examples of presentation graphics. Presentation graphics can include a variety of charts, text, images, video clips, and more.

Creating a Presentation

Presentation graphics programs contain an assortment of tools and operations for creating and editing slides, including preformatted *slide layouts* containing placeholders for the various elements in the slide (such as text, images, or charts) that can be selected to quickly create a basic slide by replacing the placeholders with the proper content. Additional slides can be inserted into the presentation, photos or drawn objects can be added to slides, text can be formatted, and other modifications can be made until the presentation is completed. A typical presentation graphics program is shown in Figure 6-21.

To create more exciting and dynamic presentations, multimedia objects and animated effects can be used. For instance, video and audio clips can be inserted into a slide and set up to play automatically each time the slide containing those elements is displayed, or, alternatively, to play when their placeholders on the slide are clicked. Text or other objects can be *animated* so that a special effect, such as *flying* the text in from the edge of the screen or *dissolving* the text in from a blank slide, will be used to display that text or object each time the slide is viewed. Animation settings can be specified to indicate the sequence in which objects will be displayed (such as to build a bulleted list one item at a time), whether or not a video will loop continuously, and more. In addition, *transitions*—special effects used between slides—can also be applied to specific slides, or random transitions can be selected for the entire slide show.

TIP

Although transitions and other effects can make a presentation more interesting, remember that the most important part of a presentation is the content.

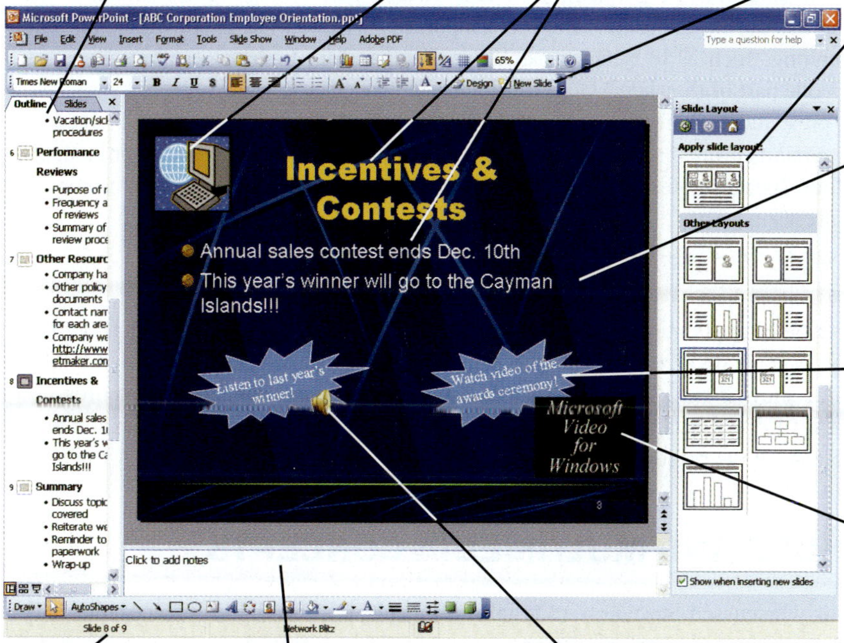

OUTLINE AND SLIDES PANES
Show either slide text (in the Outline pane, as shown here) or thumbnails of the slides in the presentation (in the Slides pane).
CLIP ART AND OTHER GRAPHICS
Can be inserted and resized or otherwise modified.
TEXT
Can be formatted with the toolbar buttons the same as in other Windows programs.
NEW SLIDES
Click to create a new slide.
SLIDE LAYOUT
Select a slide layout to quickly apply that layout to the current slide.
SLIDES
Can contain elements such as text, clip art, photographs, bulleted lists, charts, and video clips. Often a color scheme or design layout is used to apply a universal appearance to all slides.
DRAWN OBJECTS
Can be added, formatted, and resized, include lines, shapes, and more.
VIDEO CLIPS
Can be inserted into slides and set up to play automatically when the slide is loaded or when the video placeholder is clicked.
STATUS BAR
Indicates the current slide number and how many slides are in the presentation.
NOTES
Can be added so they can be seen by the presenter during the slide show or included on printouts.
SOUND CLIPS
Can be inserted into slides and set up to play automatically when the slide is loaded or when the sound placeholder is clicked.
Microsoft PowerPoint - [ABC Corporation Employee Orientation.ppt]
Incentives & Contests
Annual sales contest ends Dec. 10th
This year's winner will go to the Cayman Islands!!!
Listen to last year's winner!
Watch video of the awards ceremony!
Microsoft Video for Windows
Click to add notes
Slide Layout
Apply slide layout:
Other Layouts
Show when inserting new slides
Slide 8 of 9

FIGURE 6-21
Some features in a typical presentation graphics program.

Finishing a Presentation

Once all of the slides in a slide show have been created and the desired animation and transition effects have been applied, the slide show is ready to be run. To preview the slides and rearrange them if needed, presentation graphics programs typically have a special view, such as the *slide sorter view* shown in Figure 6-22. Using this view, slides can easily be rearranged by dragging them with the mouse to their new location in the presentation.

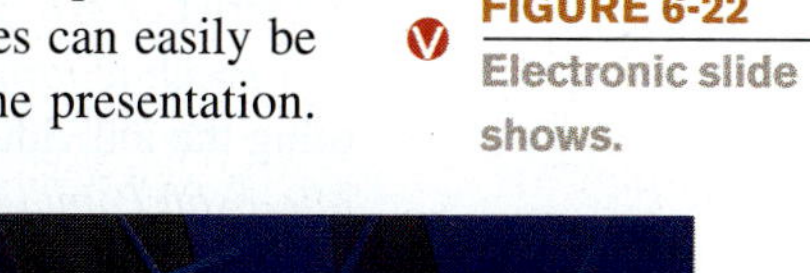

FIGURE 6-22
Electronic slide shows.

ABC Corporation Employee Orientation
Agenda Topics to be Covered
History of the Company
Who's Who
Company Policies
Performance Reviews
Other Resources
Incentives & Contests
Summary

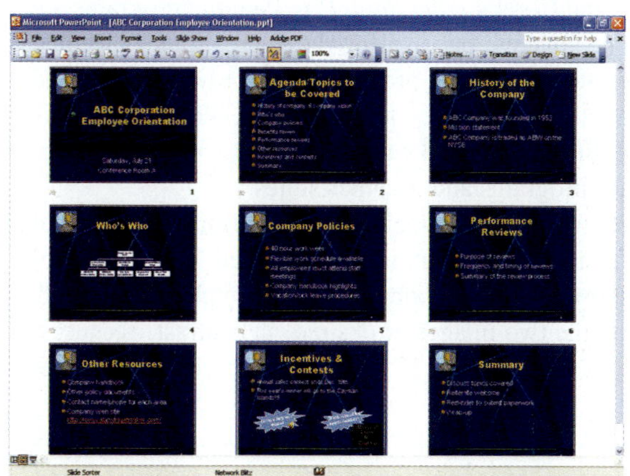

SLIDE SORTER VIEW
This view allows you to preview and rearrange the order that the slides in a presentation will be displayed.

ABC Corporation Employee Orientation
Saturday, July 21
Conference Room A

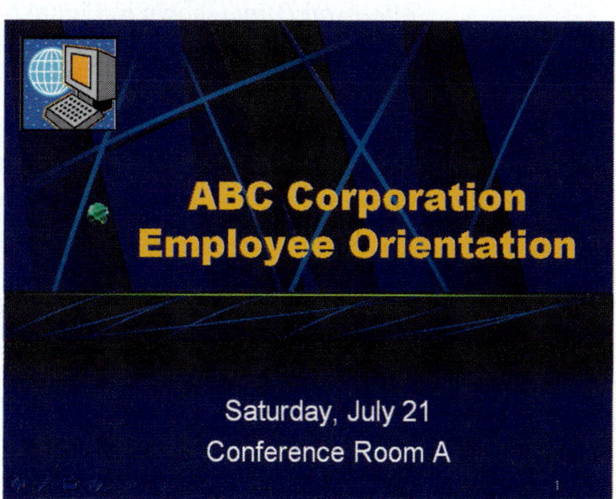

SLIDE SHOW
When a slide show is run, it will usually be displayed full screen. Slides can be advanced at predetermined intervals or by clicking the mouse or pressing the spacebar.

When the slide show is run, the slides are displayed in the designated order. Depending on how the presentation is set up, the slides either automatically advance after a specified period of time, or the speaker (or person viewing the slide show, for a stand-alone presentation) moves to the next slide by pressing the spacebar or clicking anywhere on the screen. Some presentation graphics programs have a pen or highlighter tool that the speaker can use during the presentation to temporarily write on the slides while the slide show is running, such as to circle a particular sentence for emphasis or draw an arrow pointing to one part of the slide.

Most presentation software programs can also print the slides (either full-sized or miniature versions printed several to a page) to create overhead transparencies or an audience handout; speaker notes or the presentation outline can also usually be printed for the speaker's use.

FURTHER EXPLORATION

For links to further information about presentation graphics software, go to www.course.com/uc11/ch06

Presentation Graphics and the Web

As with the other application programs discussed so far, presentation graphics programs can be used to generate Web pages or Web page content, and slides can include hyperlinks. When a slide show is saved as a series of Web pages and displayed using a Web browser, generally forward and backward navigational buttons are displayed on the slides to allow the user to control the presentation.

GRAPHICS AND MULTIMEDIA CONCEPTS

As previously discussed, *graphics* are graphical images, such as digital photographs, clip art, scanned drawings, and original images created using a software program. *Multimedia* typically refers to sound or video. There is a variety of software programs designed to help individuals create or modify graphics, edit digital audio or video, play multimedia files, burn CDs and DVDs, and so forth, as discussed next. Multimedia for Web sites are discussed in Chapter 10.

Graphics Software

Graphics software—also called *digital imaging software*—is used to create or modify images. Graphics programs are commonly distinguished by whether they are primarily oriented toward painting, drawing, or image editing, although these are general categories, not strict classifications.

Painting programs allow you to create *bit-mapped images*, which are created by coloring the individuals pixels in an image. Two of the most common painting programs are *Microsoft Paint* (shown in Figure 6-23) and Corel's *Paint Shop Pro*. Painting programs are often used to create and modify simple images, but use for these programs is limited because the bit-mapped images created using painting programs cannot be enlarged and still maintain their quality, since the pixels in the images just get larger, which makes the edges of the images look jagged. Capabilities associated with painting programs are sometimes included in other types of graphics programs and graphics suites.

Drawing programs typically create images using mathematical formulas, instead of by coloring pixels, so images can be resized and otherwise manipulated without loss of quality. Most drawing programs also allow you to *layer* objects so, if you place one object on top of another, you can later separate the two images, if desired. In contrast, because a painting program colors the actual pixels in an image, if you move one object on top of

>**Graphics software.** Application software used to create or modify images.

PAINTING PROGRAMS
Typically create images pixel by pixel so images cannot be layered or resized.

DRAWING PROGRAMS
Typically create images using mathematical formulas so images can consist of multiple objects that can be layered, and the images can be resized without distortion.

PHOTO EDITING PROGRAMS
Allow users to edit digital photos.

FIGURE 6-23
Graphics software.

SW

another, the pixels are recolored and the objects cannot be separated. Drawing programs are used by individuals and small business owners to create original art, logos, business cards, and more; they are also used by professionals to create corporate images, Web site graphics, and so forth. Some popular drawing programs include *Adobe® Illustrator®* (see Figure 6-23), *Macromedia Freehand*, and *CorelDRAW*.

Image editing or *photo editing programs* are drawing or painting programs specifically designed for touching up or modifying images, such as custom images and digital photos. Editing options include correcting brightness or contrast, eliminating red eye, cropping, resizing, and applying filters or other special effects. Most programs also include options for *optimizing* images to reduce the file size. Optimization techniques include reducing the number of colors used in the image and converting the image to a more appropriate file format. Some of the most widely used consumer photo editing programs are *Adobe PhotoShop Elements*, *Ulead Photo Express*, *Apple iPhoto*, *Nero PhotoShow Elite*, *Nero PhotoSnap* (see Figure 6-23), and *Microsoft Photo Editor*. It is also common for graphics programs today to include photo editing capabilities, even if that is not the program's primary focus.

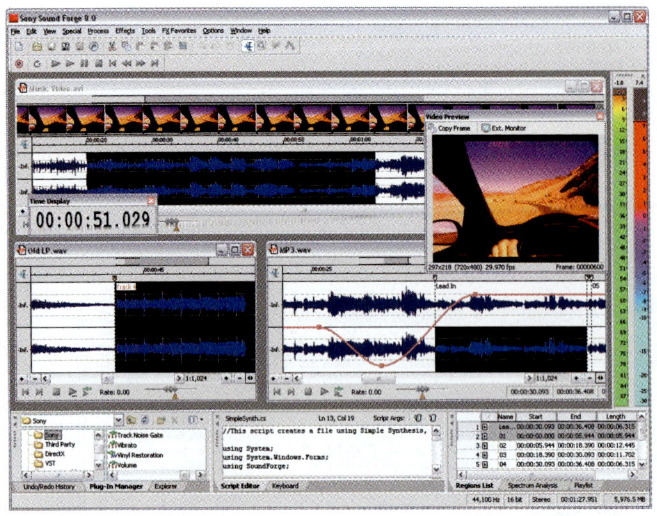

FIGURE 6-24
Audio editing software. Once sound has been captured in digital form, it can be edited as needed.

Audio Editing Software

For creating and editing audio files, *audio editing* software is used. To capture sound, a *sound recorder* can be used to capture input from a microphone or MIDI (musical instrument digital interface) device; to capture sound from a CD, *ripping software* is used. In either case, the audio file can then be modified, as needed. For instance, background noise or pauses may need to be removed, portions of the selection may need to be edited out, multiple segments may need to be spliced together, and special effects such as fade-ins and fade-outs may need to be applied. Some audio editing software is designed to create professional audio for products, Web pages, presentations, and so forth; others are designed for personal use. Common audio editing programs include *Windows Sound Recorder*, *Sony Media Software's Sound Forge® 8* software (shown in Figure 6-24), *Sony Media Software's ACID®* software products, and *Adobe Audition*.

Video Editing and DVD Authoring Software

It is common today for consumers to want to edit home movies and transfer them to DVDs; businesses also often find the need for *video editing*, such as to prepare video clips for presentations and Web sites. Video editing involves modifying existing videos, such as deleting or rearranging scenes or adding voice-overs and other special effects. *DVD authoring* refers to organizing the content to be transferred to DVD, such as importing video clips, creating the desired menu structure, and so forth. Today, these two capabilities are commonly found in a single program, such as *MyDVD Studio 6* (see Figure 6-25), *Adobe Premiere Elements*, *Ulead DVD MovieFactory*, and *Sony Media Software's Vegas® Movie Studio+DVD*. Most DVD authoring programs include *DVD burning* capabilities, as well, in order to transfer the finished DVD content to a DVD disc.

FIGURE 6-25
DVD authoring software. Today, these programs typically include video editing and DVD burning capabilities.

CD and DVD Burning Software

CD and *DVD burning software* is software used to record data on recordable or rewritable CDs and DVDs. CD or DVD burning software typically comes installed on a PC containing a recordable or rewritable drive; other CD or DVD burning software can be added if that software is not capable of everything the user wishes to do. Most programs can burn both CDs and DVDs; some include DVD authoring capabilities and other additional features. Two widely used programs are *Roxio Easy Media Creator* (now owned by Sonic) and *Nero Express*. CD and DVD burning software is widely used by consumers to burn custom music CDs, burn digital photos or movies onto DVDs, back up files, and more. With recordable CDs and DVDs, files cannot be erased later to make room for additional files. With rewritable CDs and DVDs, the files can be erased and new files stored on the disc, just like a floppy disk or hard drive. The How it Works box discusses how digital photos can be transferred to a PC and then backed up using DVD burning software.

Media Players

Media players are programs designed to play audio and video files. They are used to play media available via your PC—such as music CDs or downloaded music or video—as well as online audio and video clips. Some media players, such as the *RealOne Player* shown in Figure 6-26, can also be used to locate and play music from Internet radio stations. Another widely used media player is *Windows Media Player*. Media players typically allow you to arrange your stored music into *playlists*, and many allow you to transfer songs from your music collection to CDs or digital music players. Some also include a *music store* to allow you to select and purchase music files from within the media player program.

It is important when using digital music to adhere to copyright laws, such as only transferring music from CDs that you have purchased and only downloading MP3 files from sites that compensate the artists and record labels. While most music download sites today are legal and charge around $1 per title, illegal *peer-to-peer* (*P2P*) MP3 file exchanges do exist. Copyrights and P2P networks are discussed in more detail in later chapters.

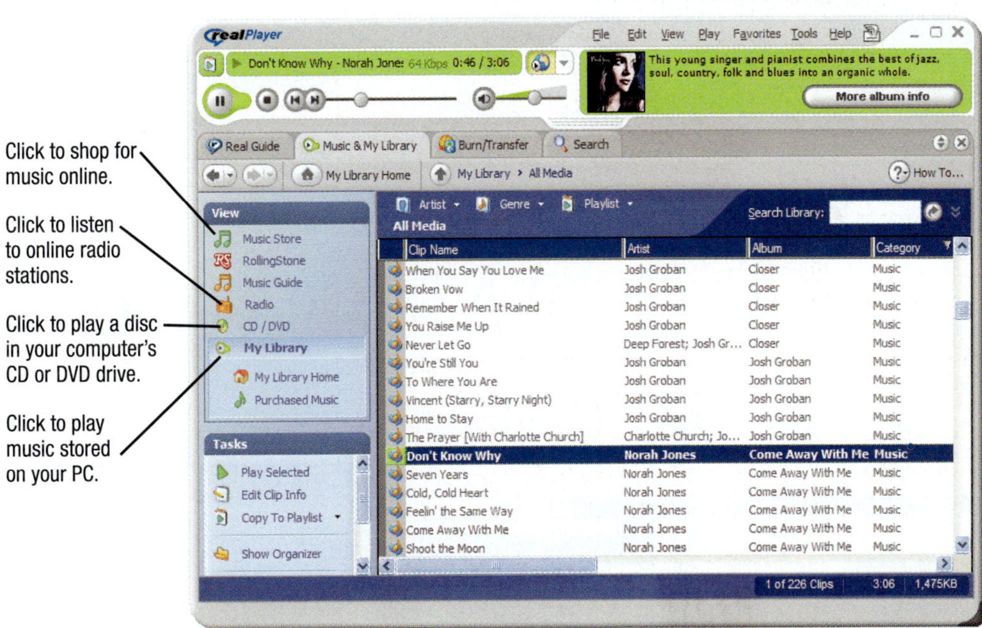

FIGURE 6-26 A typical media player program.

Graphics, Multimedia, and the Web

Graphics and multimedia software is often used by individuals and businesses alike to create Web sites or content to be shared via the Web. In addition, games, tutorials, demonstrations, and other multimedia content available on the Web are often created with multimedia software. Professional graphics and multimedia software, along with creating multimedia Web sites, are the focus of Chapter 10.

FURTHER EXPLORATION

For links to further information about graphics and multimedia software, go to www.course.com/uc11/ch06

HOW IT WORKS

Managing and Archiving Digital Photos

With the proliferation of digital cameras today, it is becoming important to know how to organize a large collection of digital photos, as well as archive the photos for backup purposes. Typically, the first step is transferring the digital photos to your PC. After connecting a digital camera to or inserting a flash memory card into a Windows-based PC, the *Scanner and Camera Wizard* usually starts automatically. As shown in the accompanying figure, this wizard helps you copy the photos to a folder on your PC and assign all of the photos in the group a descriptive name—such as *July 2005* or *Hawaii 2006*—which is used in the filename for each photo (such as *July 2005 001*, *July 2005 002*, and so on). Using group names makes it much easier to locate a desired photo later on.

Once photos have been copied to your PC, you can edit them using photo editing software, move them into other folders to keep them organized or get ready to print them, view them, or archive them on CD or DVD. Burning a DVD +RW disc using the Roxio Easy Media Creator 7.5 Digital Media Suite is shown in the accompanying figure. Because digital photos only exist in digital form (no negatives, for instance), it is extremely important to back them up carefully to ensure you do not lose them if you have computer or hard drive problems.

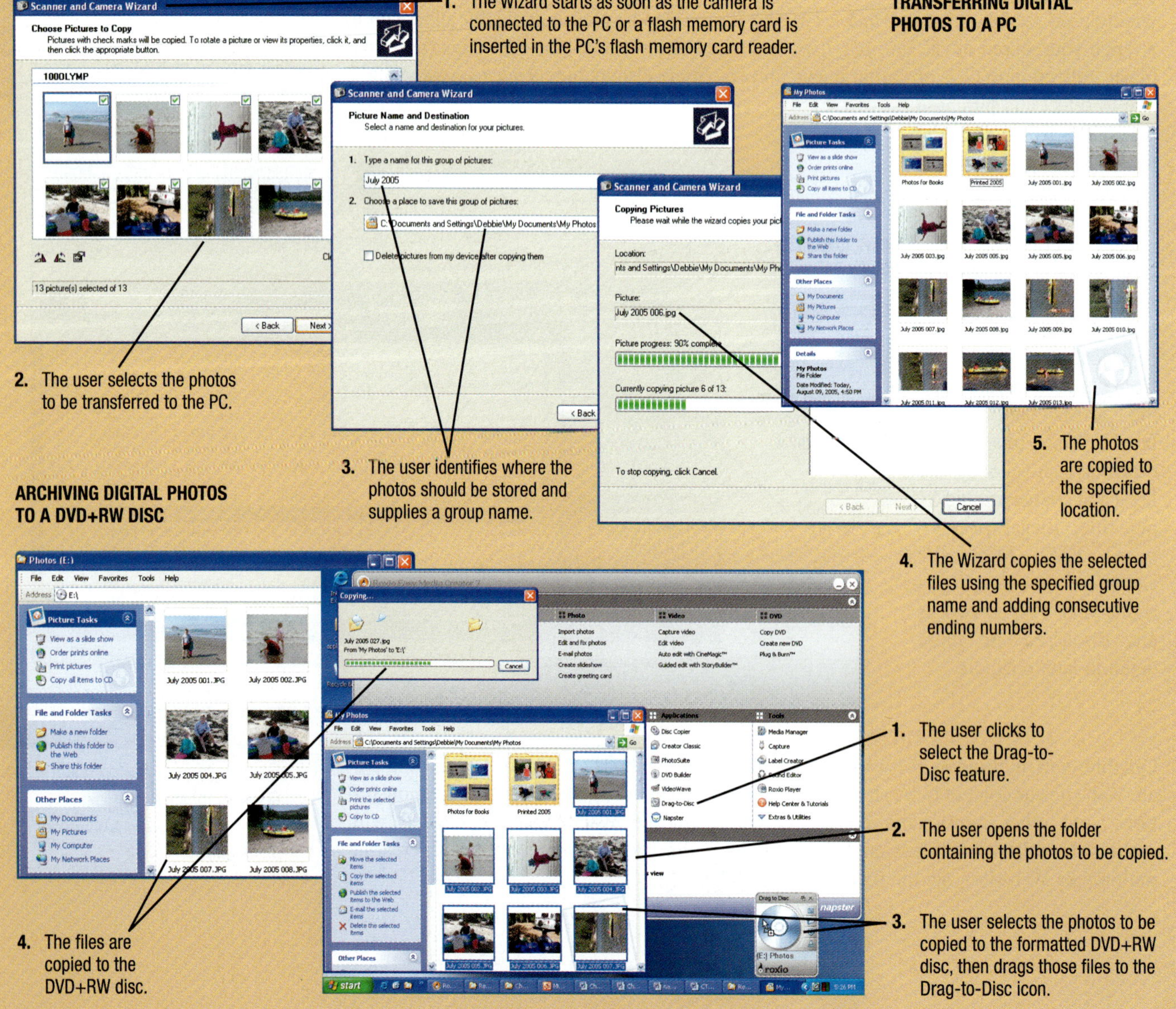

OTHER TYPES OF APPLICATION SOFTWARE

There are many other types of application software available today. Some are geared for business or personal productivity; others are designed for entertainment or educational purposes. Still others are designed specifically for a particular business application, such as accounting or inventory. A few of the most common types of application software not previously covered are discussed next; some are shown in Figure 6-27.

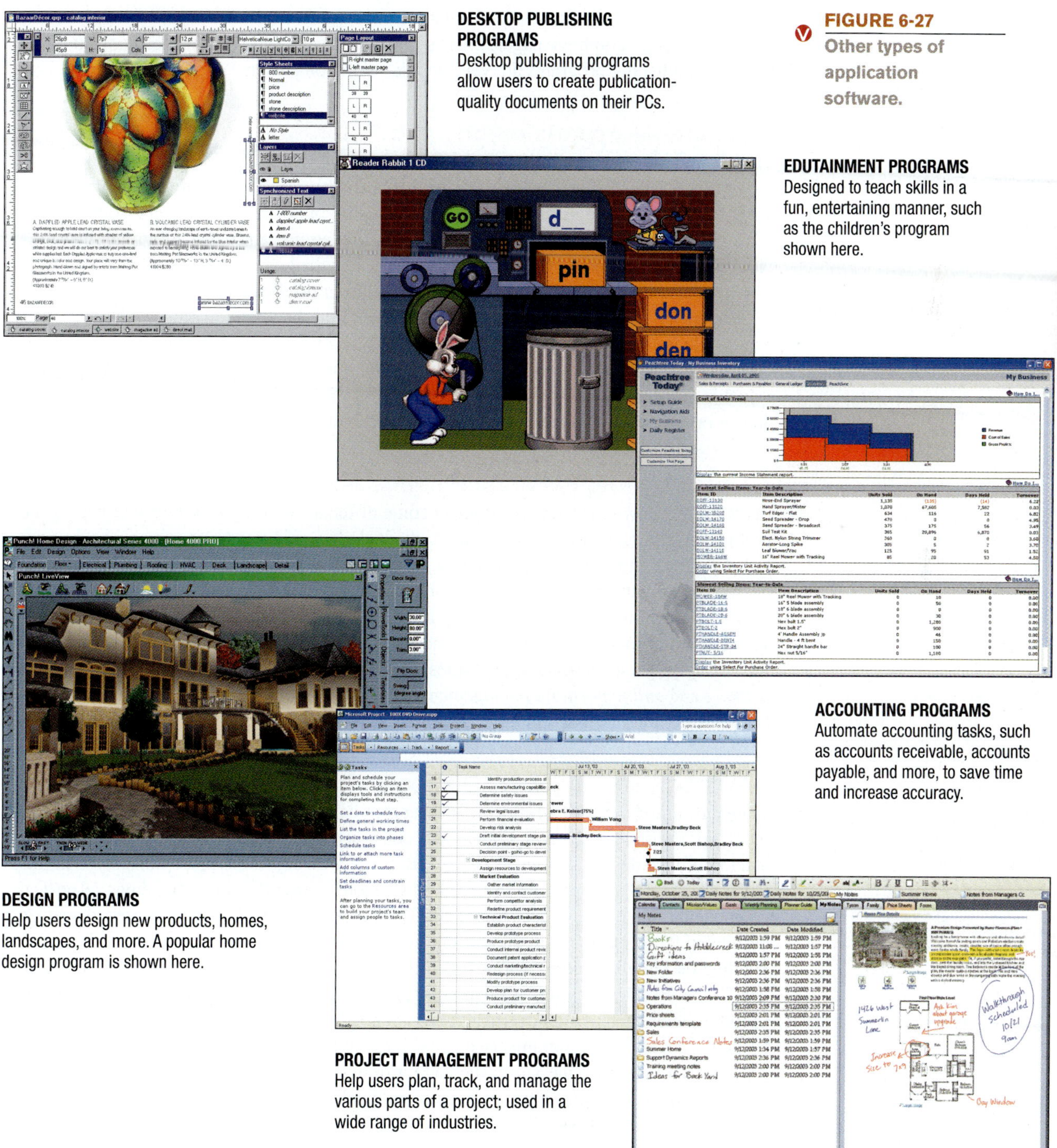

FIGURE 6-27
Other types of application software.

DESKTOP PUBLISHING PROGRAMS
Desktop publishing programs allow users to create publication-quality documents on their PCs.

EDUTAINMENT PROGRAMS
Designed to teach skills in a fun, entertaining manner, such as the children's program shown here.

ACCOUNTING PROGRAMS
Automate accounting tasks, such as accounts receivable, accounts payable, and more, to save time and increase accuracy.

DESIGN PROGRAMS
Help users design new products, homes, landscapes, and more. A popular home design program is shown here.

PROJECT MANAGEMENT PROGRAMS
Help users plan, track, and manage the various parts of a project; used in a wide range of industries.

PERSONAL PRODUCTIVITY PROGRAMS
Allow individuals to access schedules, contacts, notes, and more in one location.

Desktop and Personal Publishing Software

Desktop publishing refers to using a desktop PC to combine and manipulate text and images to create attractive documents that look as if they were created by a professional printer (see Figure 6-27). Although many desktop publishing effects can be produced using a word processing program, users who frequently create publication-style documents usually find a desktop publishing program a more efficient means of creating those types of documents. *Personal publishing* refers to creating desktop-publishing-type documents—such as greeting cards, invitations, flyers, calendars, certificates, and so forth—for personal use. There are also specialized personal publishing programs for particular purposes, such as to create scrapbook pages, cross stitch patterns, CD and DVD labels, and so forth. Personal publishing programs are very popular with home users.

Educational, Entertainment, and Reference Software

There is a wide variety of educational and entertainment application programs available. *Educational software* is designed to teach one or more skills, such as reading, math, spelling, a foreign language, and world geography, or to help prepare for standardized tests. *Entertainment software* includes games, simulations, and other programs that provide amusement. A hybrid of these two categories is called *edutainment*—educational software that also entertains—such as the children's program illustrated in Figure 6-27.

Reference software is another common type of application software. Reference software includes encyclopedias, dictionaries, atlases, ZIP code directories, mapping/travel programs, cookbook programs, legal guides, and any other program designed to provide valuable information. In addition to being available as stand-alone software packages, reference information is widely available on the Internet.

Accounting and Personal Finance Software

Accounting software is used to automate some of the accounting activities that need to be performed on a regular basis. Common tasks include writing and printing checks, recording purchases and payments, managing inventory (refer again to Figure 6-27), creating payroll documents and checks, and preparing financial statements. *Personal finance software* is commonly used at home by individuals to write checks and balance checking accounts, track personal expenses, manage stock portfolios, and prepare income taxes. Increasingly, personal finance activities are becoming Web-based, such as the *online banking* and *online portfolio management* services available through many banks and brokerage firms and discussed in more detail in Chapter 8.

CAD and Other Types of Design Software

Computer-aided design (CAD) software enables designers to design objects on the computer. For example, engineers or architects can create designs of buildings or other objects and modify the design as often as needed. Because drawings are typically displayed in 3D, CAD is especially helpful in designing automobiles, aircraft, ships, buildings, electrical components, and other products. Some CAD programs even include capabilities to analyze designs in terms of how well they meet a number of design criteria, such as testing how a building design will hold up during an earthquake or how a car will perform under certain conditions. Besides playing an important role in the design of finished products, CAD is useful in fields such as art, advertising, law, architecture, and movie production. In addition to the powerful CAD programs used in business, there are also design programs designed for home and small business use, such as for designing new homes (see Figure 6-27), and making remodeling plans, interior designs, and landscape designs.

TECHNOLOGY AND YOU

Taking Digital Classroom Notes

There are several options for digital note taking software, in addition to the standard handwriting software included with a tablet PC. For instance, Microsoft *OneNote* and Agilix Labs *GoBinder* programs (see the accompanying screen shot) are designed specifically to make note taking–and, particularly, retrieving information from the notes–easier. Like a paper notebook, tabbed sections can be created (such as one tab per course) and files, notes, Web links, and any other data are stored under the appropriate tabs. The built-in search tools allow you to find the information that you need quickly and easily. Some programs–such as GoBinder–are set up to integrate with Blackboard Learning System software, for classes using that system. Others–such as OneNote–can store and create links in your notes to audio recordings, such as recorded lectures. Digital note taking programs often include other helpful tools, such as a calendar and address book; some can sync calendars and contact information with the Microsoft Outlook program. As an extra plus, these programs typically save your notes to disk automatically, so you do not have to remember to save the file yourself.

Some examples of classroom note taking software in use include the University of Vermont School of Business Administration (which requires students to have a tablet PC and OneNote software in order to facilitate note taking and collaboration, as well as give students experience using the tools that they will need on the job) and Brigham Young University law school (which uses OneNote software to record audio and video of in-class exercises to help students refine their negotiation and legal counseling skills).

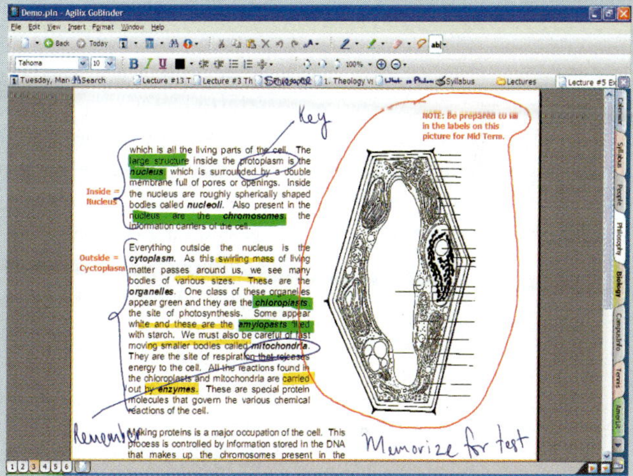

Project Management and Collaboration Software

Project management software, illustrated in Figure 6-27, is used to plan, schedule, track, and analyze the tasks involved in a project, such as the construction of a building or the schedule for preparing a large advertising campaign for a client. This type of software shows how project activities are related and when they must start and finish. Once created, schedules prepared by such software can be shared with others and updated as the project progresses. Project management capabilities are often included in *collaboration software*—software that enables a group of individuals to work together on a project.

Note Taking and Personal Productivity Software

Note taking software is used by both students and businesspeople to take notes during class lectures, meetings, and similar settings. Note taking software today typically supports handwritten input, which can be saved in its handwritten form as an image or converted to typed text. Drawings, typed text, and audio input are usually supported, as well. Some note taking software can even link a student's notes with an instructor's recorded lecture, as discussed in the Technology and You box.

Personal productivity software (sometimes also called *personal organizers* or *personal planners*) today typically also supports handwritten input (see Figure 6-27) and is designed to organize important data, such as appointments, notes, and contact information, in one central location for an individual.

SUMMARY

THE BASICS OF APPLICATION SOFTWARE

Chapter Objective 1:
Describe what application software is, the different types of ownership rights, and the difference between installed and Web-based software.

Application software is software designed to carry out a specific task. Common types of application software include games, Web browsers, word processing programs, multimedia software, utility programs, and more. Many application software programs on the market today are **commercial software** programs that are developed and sold for a profit. When a software program is purchased, individual users receive a **software license** authorizing them to use the software. Some commercial software is available in a *trial version*. Other software is available as **shareware**. Other classes of software are **freeware** and **public domain software**. **Open source software** is the term for programs whose source code is available to the general public. Most software is *installed* on a local PC or network server; other software is *Web-based*. Organizations that provide Web-based software are referred to as *application service providers* (*ASPs*).

Chapter Objective 2:
Detail some concepts and commands that many software programs have in common.

Many office-oriented programs are sold bundled together as a **software suite**. One of the most widely used software suites is **Microsoft Office**. Although different in purpose, most application software programs share some of the same concepts and functions, such as similar document-handling operations and help features. For instance, documents are commonly *opened*, *saved*, *printed*, and *edited* in a similar manner; the **insertion point** typically identifies the current position in a document. Many types of documents can be *formatted* to change their appearance. Handheld PCs require specially designed application software.

WORD PROCESSING CONCEPTS

Chapter Objective 3:
Discuss word processing and explain what kinds of documents are created using this type of program.

Word processing refers to using a PC and **word processing software** to create, manipulate, and print written documents, such as letters, contracts, and so forth. When creating or editing a word processing document, the **word wrap** feature automatically moves the insertion point to the next line when the end of the screen line is reached. Common types of *formatting* include changing the *font face*, *font size*, or *font style* of selected text; adjusting *line spacing*, *margins*, *indentation*, *tabs*, and *alignment*; changing the top and bottom margins, and paper size; and adding *headers* and *footers*. Other enhancements found in most word processing programs include the ability to include graphical images and *tables*, and to use *styles*, *templates*, or *wizards* for more efficient document creation. Documents can also include hyperlinks and be saved as Web pages in many programs. Most word processors also include a spelling and grammar check feature and other useful tools.

SPREADSHEET CONCEPTS

Chapter Objective 4:
Explain the purpose of spreadsheet software and the kinds of documents created using this type of program.

Spreadsheet software is used to create documents (**spreadsheets** or **worksheets**) that typically include a great deal of numbers and mathematical computations; a collection of worksheets stored in the same spreadsheet file is called a **workbook**. A worksheet is divided into **rows** and **columns** that intersect to form **cells**, each of which can be accessed through a *cell address*, such as B3. A rectangular group of cells is referred to as a *range*.

Content is entered into individual cells and may consist of **labels**, **constant values**, **formulas**, or **functions**. Formulas can be typed using *relative cell* or *absolute cell references*, depending on the type of computation required. Once created, the contents of individual cells may be edited and formatted. *Numeric formats* are used to change the appearance of numbers, such as adding a dollar sign or displaying a specific number of decimal places. Spreadsheet programs commonly include a *charting* or *graphing* feature and the ability to perform *what-if analysis*. Some spreadsheet programs allow worksheets to be saved in the form of a Web page and the inclusion of hyperlinks in cells.

DATABASE CONCEPTS

A *database management system* (*DBMS*) or **database software** program enables the creation of a **database**—a collection of related data stored in a manner so that information can be retrieved as needed. In a relational DBMS (the most common type found on PCs), a **field** or **column** is a collection of characters that make up a single piece of data, such as a name or phone number; a **record** or **row** is a collection of related fields; and a **table** is a collection of related records. One or more tables can be stored in a database file.

Chapter Objective 5: Identify some of the vocabulary used with database software and discuss the benefits of using this type of program.

A relational database typically contains a variety of *objects*, such as tables, *forms* to input or view data, *queries* to retrieve specific information, and *reports* to print a formal listing of the data stored in a table or the results of a query. When a table is created, the table fields are specified along with their characteristics, such as *field name*, *field size*, and *data type*. After this *structure* has been created, data can be entered into the table. Both the data in the table and the table structure can be modified. Databases are commonly integrated into the Web, such as to keep track of inventory and to facilitate online ordering.

SW

PRESENTATION GRAPHICS CONCEPTS

Presentation graphics are images used to visually enhance the impact of information communicated to other people. **Presentation graphics software** can be used to create presentation graphics and *online slide shows* consisting of electronic **slides**. Individual slides are created, and then they can be edited and formatted, as can the overall appearance of the slides. Multimedia elements, such as images and video clips, can also be included. After all slides have been created for a presentation, the order of the slides can be rearranged and *transitions* between the slides can be specified. It is becoming increasingly common to find slide-based presentations available through the Web. Web-based slide shows can include multimedia elements, as well as hyperlinks and other navigational buttons.

Chapter Objective 6: Describe what presentation graphics and electronic slide shows are and when they might be used.

GRAPHICS AND MULTIMEDIA CONCEPTS

Graphics are graphical images, such as digital photographs, clip art, and original art. *Multimedia* refers to applications that include more than one type of media, typically text, graphics, animation, and interactivity. To create graphics, **graphics software**—such as a *painting*, *drawing*, or *image editing program*—can be used. *Audio editing*, *video editing*, and *DVD authoring software* are common types of multimedia programs, as are the *media player* programs used to play audio and video files. *CD* and *DVD burning software* can be used to burn songs or other data on a CD or DVD disc.

Chapter Objective 7: List some types of graphics and multimedia software consumers frequently use.

OTHER TYPES OF APPLICATION SOFTWARE

Other types of application software include *desktop publishing* and *personal publishing* programs, *computer-aided design* (*CAD*) and other types of *design software*, *project management software*, *accounting software*, and *personal finance software*. The use of *collaboration*, *note taking*, and *personal productivity software* is growing. *Educational*, *entertainment*, and *reference software* are very popular with home users.

Chapter Objective 8: Name other types of application software programs and discuss what functions they perform.

REVIEW ACTIVITIES

KEY TERMS MATCHING

Instructions: Match each key term on the left with the definition on the right that best describes it.

a. cell
b. database
c. field
d. formula
e. label
f. public domain software
g. record
h. shareware
i. software license
j. workbook

1. ______ A collection of related data that is stored in a manner enabling information to be retrieved as needed; in a relational database, a collection of related tables.

2. ______ A collection of related fields in a database. Also called a row.

3. ______ A collection of worksheets saved in a single spreadsheet file.

4. ______ An agreement, either included in a software package or displayed on the screen during installation, that specifies the conditions under which a buyer of the program can use it.

5. ______ An entry in a worksheet cell that performs computations on worksheet data and displays the results.

6. ______ A single category of data to be stored in a database, such as a person's name or telephone number. Also called a column.

7. ______ A text-based entry in a worksheet cell that identifies data on the worksheet.

8. ______ Copyrighted software that is distributed on the honor system; consumers should either pay for it or uninstall it after the trial period.

9. ______ Software that is not copyrighted and may be used without restriction.

10. ______ The location at the intersection of a row and column on a worksheet into which data can be typed.

SELF-QUIZ

Instructions: Circle **T** if the statement is true, **F** if the statement is false, or write the best answer in the space provided. **Answers to the self-quiz are located in the References and Resources Guide at the end of the book**.

1. **T F** Microsoft Office is one example of a software suite.
2. **T F** Changing the font size in a document is an example of a formatting operation.
3. **T F** In a word processing document, the Enter key is always pressed at the end of each screen line to move down to the next line.
4. **T F** The formula =A2+B2 located in cell C2 would multiply the two cells to the left of cell C2.
5. **T F** One use for a media player program is to play downloaded music files.
6. With a(n) ______ program, the source code for the program is made available to the general public and so can be modified by others.
7. The blinking vertical line displayed onscreen that indicates the current location in a document, such as where the next change will be made to the document in a word processing program, is called the ______.
8. A named formula (such as @SUM) in a spreadsheet program is called a(n) ______.
9. In a relational database, the database object into which the actual data is entered is the ______.

10. Match each application with its type of application program and write the corresponding number in the blank to the left of each application.

a. ______ Creating a home movie DVD.		1. Media player
b. ______ Practicing multiplication tables.		2. Reference software
c. ______ Creating a child's birthday invitation.		3. Educational software
d. ______ Looking up the capital of Brazil.		4. DVD burning software
e. ______ Listening to a music CD.		5. Personal publishing software

EXERCISES

1. List the four main programs included in the Microsoft Office 2003 software suite and identify tasks for which each program is designed.
2. Would rearranging the paragraphs in a document using a word processing program use a cut operation or a copy operation? Explain your answer.
3. Match each spreadsheet element with its term and write the corresponding number in the blank to the left of each term.

a. ______ An absolute cell address	1. =SUM(A1:A2)
b. ______ A constant value	2. =B6*C6
c. ______ A formula	3. $D$4
d. ______ A relative cell address	4. 150
e. ______ A function	5. B6

4. Referring to the database table below, answer the following questions.
   a. How many records are there?
   b. How many fields are there?
   c. How many records would be listed for a query with the criteria State is "CO" and the Balance is less than $10?

CUSTOMER NUMBER	NAME	STREET	CITY	STATE	ZIP	BALANCE
810	John T. Smith	31 Cedarcrest	Boulder	CO	80302	10.00
775	Sally Jones	725 Agua Fria	Santa Fe	NM	87501	0
690	William Holmes	3269 Fast Lane	Boulder	CO	80302	150.35
840	Artis Smith	2332 Alameda	Lakewood	CO	80215	3.50

5. Match each type of presentation graphic with its presentation and write the corresponding number in the blank to the left of each presentation.

a. ______ Adding an arrow to highlight a point located on a slide.	1. Pie chart
b. ______ Conveying the new company privacy policy.	2. Text chart
c. ______ Illustrating the percent of sales coming from each sales territory.	3. Photograph
d. ______ Showing what the latest prototype of an upcoming product looks like.	4. Drawn object

DISCUSSION QUESTION

Open source software is usually reviewed and improved by independent programmers who update the software products at no charge for fun, notoriety, or programming practice. Proponents of open source software believe that if programmers who are not concerned with financial gain work on an open source program, they will produce a more useful and error-free product much faster than the traditional commercial software development process. If open source use continues to grow as expected, it will impact software as we know it today. Will the growth force existing commercial software companies to streamline their development process in order to cut costs to better compete with open source products? Or will they feel the need to produce products that are better and more reliable than open source competitors? Or will commercial software companies simply go out of business? Will commercial software manufacturers be justified in raising their prices to make up for revenue lost to open source competitors? Do you think that strategy would be effective? Do you think open source software will have a positive or negative impact on the quality of software available for use? Would you prefer to use open source software? Why or why not?

PROJECTS

HOT TOPICS

1. **Natural Input** As pen and voice input technologies continue to improve, these types of more natural input methods are increasingly being supported by software programs.

   For this project, research the current state of either pen input or voice input, in conjunction with application software. What are the advantages of your selected method of input? The disadvantages? Select one office application program (such as a word processor or spreadsheet program) and one other application program and find out the extent that your chosen programs can be used with your selected method of input. Would you prefer to use a keyboard and mouse or your selected method of input with these programs? Explain. At the conclusion of your research, prepare a one- to two-page summary of your findings and submit it to your instructor.

SHORT ANSWER/ RESEARCH

2. **Software Search** Just as with toys, movies, and music, the price of a software program can vary tremendously, based on where you buy it, sales, rebates, and more. Although most packages claim a manufacturer's suggested retail price, it is almost always possible to beat that price—sometimes by a huge amount—with careful shopping.

   For this project, select one software program that you might be interested in buying and research it. Either by reading the program specifications in a retail store or on a Web page, determine the minimum hardware and software requirements (such as processor type and speed, amount of free hard drive space, amount of memory, and operating system) for your chosen program. By checking in person, over the phone, or via the Internet, locate a minimum of three price quotes for the program. Be sure to check availability and estimated delivery time, and include any sales tax and shipping charges. If any of the online vendors have the option to download the software, instead of sending a physical package, be sure to record that information, as well. At the conclusion of this task, prepare a one-page summary of your research and submit it to your instructor. Be sure to include a recommendation of where you think it would be best to buy your chosen product and why.

3. **CD Cards** CDs the approximate shape and size of a business card are increasingly being used to replace traditional business cards. Advantages include being able to include a complete multimedia presentation or Web site on the CD, as well as photographs, portfolio materials, and other useful content.

   For this project, research CD business cards. How much data can they contain? Can individuals or businesses create their own CD cards, or do they have to be purchased from a CD business card development agency? How much do the discs cost? Are they widely available? Locate one CD business card development agency (either a local business or an agency with a Web site) and determine what type of content they can supply for a custom card. What are the advantages and disadvantages of using a CD business card? Would you prefer to hand out a multimedia CD card or a traditional business card when meeting new business acquaintances? At the conclusion of your research, prepare a one-page summary of your findings and submit it to your instructor.

HANDS ON

4. **Templates and Wizards** Most word processing, spreadsheet, database, and presentation graphics software programs include a variety of templates, wizards, and other tools to help you create new documents faster and easier.

For this project, select one office suite program that you have access to (select one you will be using in this course, if applicable) and identify three tools included in the program that can be used to create a new document. For each tool, explain how it is accessed and what type of document is created with the tool. Next, pick one of your selected tools and use it to create a new document to evaluate how easy it is to work with and how useful the tool is. At the conclusion of your research, prepare a one-page summary of your findings and submit it to your instructor.

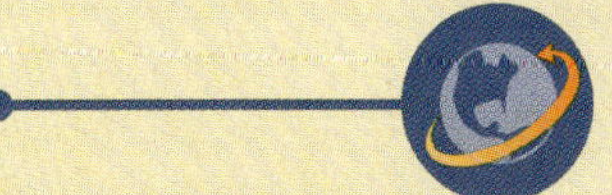

5. **Online Tours** There are many online tours and tutorials for widely used application programs. Some are available through the software company's Web site; others are located on third-party Web sites.

For this project, locate a free online tour or tutorial for a program you are interested in (go to www.course.com/uc11/ch06 for access to the "Application Software Resources" Further Exploration links to tutorials for a variety of application programs) and work your way through one tour or tutorial. Be sure to take notes about those features that are of most interest to you, and evaluate how helpful you think the tutorial is for someone who is just learning how to use the program in question. At the conclusion of this task, prepare a one-page summary of your efforts and submit it to your instructor.

WRITING ABOUT COMPUTERS

SW

6. **Reference Tools** As described in the chapter, reference software includes encyclopedias, dictionaries, atlases, ZIP code directories, mapping/travel programs, and more. Many of these programs are available as commercial software that can be purchased; others are available over the Internet for free or with a paid subscription.

For this project, identify two different types of reference tools that are available via the Internet (use a search site to search for Web sites offering particular reference tools until you find two that interest you). For each of your chosen online reference tools, try out the reference tool (if it is available at no cost) and see how helpful and easy to use it is. If the tool requires a fee or subscription, do not try it out—just make a note of what the service is supposed to consist of and the fee involved. Next, for each of your chosen reference tools, locate a similar offline version of the tool in the form of a hard copy book or an installable software program (visit a local software retailer, local bookstore, or search the Internet to find these non-Web-based alternative reference tools). Evaluate each offline reference tool, noting its capabilities, price, and how this version differs from the online version. At the conclusion of your research, submit this project to your instructor in the form of a short paper, not more than two pages in length. Be sure to include your opinion regarding the availability and usefulness of online versus offline reference tools, which of the tools you evaluated you would prefer to use, and why.

PRESENTATION/ DOCUMENTATION

7. **Compatibility** Files created by an application program are often upward-compatible, but not always downward-compatible. In other words, if you create a file using the most recent version of Microsoft Word and attempt to open the file using Word 95, you may get an error message. However, you would be able to open a Word 95 file in a later version of Word. In addition, you may be able to open a document created in a different program, if the program is of a similar type (such as opening a Word document in WordPerfect). Some application programs feature a "Save As" option to save the file in a format appropriate for an older version of the program, for an entirely different program, or for a more universal file format, such as *.rtf* (*Rich Text Format*), *.html* (*Hypertext Markup Language*), or *.xml* (*Extensible Markup Language*).

For this project, select one widely used software program and determine the file formats in which the program can save documents and which file formats the program can open. If there are older versions of the program, are documents upward-compatible? Downward compatible? If the program can save a document in a plain text (*.txt*) file, is there a downside? In addition, research the *.rtf*, *.html*, and *.xml* formats and determine their purposes, the programs in which documents saved in each of these formats can be opened, and the programs in which documents saved in each of these formats can be edited. What about the *Portable Document Format (.pdf)*? Does your program support it? When might it be useful? Have you ever experienced a compatibility problem with a document? If so, how was the problem resolved? Share your findings with the class in the form of a short presentation. The presentation should not exceed 10 minutes and should make use of one or more presentation aids, such as the chalkboard, handouts, overhead transparencies, or a computer-based slide presentation (your instructor may provide additional requirements). You may also be asked to submit a summary of the presentation to your instructor.

GROUP DISCUSSION

8. **Emotion Recognition Software** An emerging application is *emotion recognition software*, which tries to read people's emotions. Similar to face recognition systems, emotion recognition systems use a camera and software to analyze individuals' faces, but instead of trying to identify the individual, the system attempts to recognize his or her current emotion. The first expected application of such a system is for ATM machines, which already have the necessary hardware (primarily cameras) installed. One expected feature is changing the advertising display to more specifically target each individual, based on the customer's emotional response to displayed advertising. Even more helpful applications would include rephrasing instructions if the customer appeared confused or enlarging the screen text if the customer appeared to be squinting. Emotion recognition applications for the future could include using this type of system to help therapists understand a patient's emotional state. It is not surprising that privacy advocates are concerned about the emotions of citizens being read in public locations without their consent. They also dislike the idea of customer emotions at an ATM machine being connected with their identity. Proponents of the technology argue that it is no different than when human tellers or store clerks interpret customers' emotions and modify their treatment of the customer accordingly. Is this a worthy new technology or just a potential invasion of privacy? What are the pros and cons of such a system from a business point of view, and then from a customer point of view? Are there any safeguards that could be implemented or specific ways of using an emotion-recognition system that would alleviate many of the disadvantages? What other potential uses for such a system might there be besides the ones mentioned in this project? Would you object to using an ATM machine with emotion-recognition capabilities?

   For this project, form an opinion of the use of emotion recognition systems in public locations, as well as in private situations, such as a therapist's office or in the home, and be prepared to discuss your position (in class, via an online class discussion group, or in a class chat room, depending on your instructor's directions). You may also be asked to write a short paper expressing your opinion.

WEB ACTIVITIES

The *Understanding Computers* Web site located at **www.course.com/uc11** features many resources to help reinforce your understanding of the chapter content and help you prepare for exams. Your instructor may also assign specific activities to be completed that will count toward your final grade in the course.

Instructions: Go to **www.course.com/uc11/ch06** to work the following online activities.

Click any link in the navigation bar on the left to access any of the online resources described below.

INTERACTIVE ACTIVITIES

1. **Crossword Puzzle** Practice your knowledge of the key terms in Chapter 6 by completing the interactive Crossword Puzzle.
2. **Tech News Video Project** Watch the **"Software Vending Machines"** video clip that takes a look at purchasing software via consumer kiosks, as an alternative to buying a shrink-wrapped package or downloading the software via the Internet. After watching the video online, complete the corresponding project.
3. **Student Edition Labs** Reinforce the concepts you have learned in this chapter by working through the interactive **Word Processing**, **Spreadsheets**, **Databases**, and **Presentation Software** labs.

TEST YOURSELF

1. **Key Term Matching** Test your knowledge of selected chapter key terms by matching the terms with their definitions.
2. **Self-Quiz** Test your retention of chapter concepts by taking the Self-Quiz.
3. **Exercises** Work these short exercises to review the concepts and terms covered in the chapter.
4. **Practice Test** Test how ready you are for an upcoming exam by completing the online Practice Test.

STUDY TOOLS/ ADDITIONAL RESOURCES

The Understanding Computers Web site has a wide range of additional resources, including an **Online Study Guide** (containing study tips, a chapter outline with room to add your own notes, and a chapter checklist of the activities to complete when the chapter is covered in class and when you are preparing for a test) and an **Online Glossary** for each chapter; **Further Exploration** links; a **Web Guide**, a **Guide to Buying a PC**, and a **Computer History Timeline**; more information about **Numbering Systems**, **Coding Charts**, and **CPU Characteristics**; and much, much more!

EXPERT INSIGHT ON . . .
Software

Novell.

A conversation with AARON WEBER
Product Marketing Manager for Novell Linux Desktop

My Background . . .

I was a Spanish major in college and I only took a computer class to get my math requirement out of the way, but I really enjoyed it, so I took a couple more. The courses pointed out to me what kinds of things could be done with technology. When I graduated, I'd managed to collect some Web development skills, but I wasn't an expert by any means. What I did have going for me was that I knew how to translate geek-speak into every-day English.

I knew a few people who were working at Ximian, and they needed a writer. I had to write Web pages, the business plan, the marketing materials, the instruction manuals, everything. After Novell bought Ximian, I began doing just marketing.

"Eventually, everyone will have terabytes of data and no idea where they put the particular file they're looking for. Applications are going to have to help them find it."

It's Important to Know . . .

About open source software, such as Linux. It does a lot more than people think, and for a lot less than they're used to paying. Open source software allows people more control over what's going on inside their computer, and features are driven by user needs. For instance, people that speak a language that isn't supported by Microsoft Windows can create an open source equivalent interface in their native language. That's what keeps me in this business when I have a bad day at work—knowing that I'm building something that everybody will be able to use, even if they aren't rich and powerful.

About intellectual property and the ways that it's being used and misused. Not just that people are stealing songs via P2P networks, but that the music and movie industry and other rights-holders are trying to control the way that you use your data. I'd like people to ask questions like "Should it be illegal to play a DVD you buy in Europe on a DVD player you buy in the U.S., or print an e-book onto paper, or even read an e-book to a friend?

Who controls your data. Because in a very real sense, whoever controls your data controls you. For example, credit reports control a lot of what you can do, and the quality of that data is not really well regulated. It only takes a few pieces of data to impersonate someone, and then wreck their credit. On a smaller scale, what are you allowed to do with a music file you download? Remix? Copy to a CD? As computers and the data they store and retrieve become more and more central to our lives, individual consumers will need to be sure that they control the way those computers behave—not, say, the manufacturers or the music or movie industry, who are likely to demand that technology behave in ways that benefit industry and not individuals or consumers.

Aaron Weber is currently the Product Marketing Manager for Novell Linux Desktop. He writes materials about the Novell Linux Desktop operating system, does research on competing products to make recommendations about how Novell can best compete with them, and promotes the Novell Linux Desktop to resellers and hardware vendors. Aaron has worked as a technical writer and a Web developer, and has published several articles about Linux and open sources software for O'Reilly, Novell Connection Magazine, and Interex Enterprise Solutions Magazine.

People like the idea of software that doesn't break and is easy to use, but given the choice between that and something with more power and complexity, they almost always go for the power and complexity.

How I Use this Technology . . .

I'm using OpenOffice.org on Novell Linux Desktop right this very minute. I'm also using the Gaim instant messaging client to talk to my friend about news articles we're both reading with the Mozilla Firefox Web browser, and listening to music encoded in the Ogg format.

What the Future Holds . . .

There are two things that are really going to change the industry. One of them is a growing concern with intellectual property—all the Digital Rights Management (DRM) software out there is pretty flawed, but it's reflective of a general attitude that data and ideas have to be guarded. Students can prepare for this by learning as much as possible about fair use, patent restrictions, and copyright restrictions.

The other trend I see is shrinking profits on software. Some software products have huge profit margins that are just not sustainable. As the industry matures, base functionality is going to be available for less and less, and software companies are going to have to prove their worth, or die. That will put pressure on them to cut costs. Students will need to be prepared to learn new skills and apply old skills to new situations.

I also believe that, at some point, people are going to stop noticing the impact that software has on society, because its going to be part of society. We don't talk so much about the impact of, say, the standard-size screw on society these days, but machine screws used to be all different sizes depending on the manufacturer. Now there are a few standard sizes, and it's a lot cheaper to attach things to each other. It'll be that way with software—eventually we'll stop talking about how computers are changing our society, and focus more on using them to get on with our lives and be part of society.

Software in five years will also almost certainly be more complicated. People like the idea of software that doesn't break and is easy to use, but given the choice between that and something with more power and complexity, they almost always go for the power and complexity. And future applications will have to deal with a lot more data. Eventually, everyone will have terabytes of data and no idea where they put the particular file they're looking for. Applications are going to have to help them find it.

My Advice to Students . . .

Encrypt and back up your data. Encryption keeps it from prying eyes, and backing it up means you have a spare in case of disaster. (Don't keep the backup next to the original.)

Discussion Question

Aaron Weber views intellectual property rights as one of the more important issues for the future. He poses an interesting question: "Should it be illegal to print an e-book onto paper or even read an e-book to a friend?" Think about intellectual property rights as they relate to e-books. If you purchase an e-book, what should you be allowed to do with it? Is there any difference to your rights regarding the use of an e-book if you check the e-book out of the library instead of purchasing it? Be prepared to discuss your position (in class, via an online class discussion group, or in a class chat room. depending on your instructor's directions). You may also be asked to write a short paper expressing your opinion.

>For more information on Novell, visit www.novell.com. For general technical information, see www.oreillynet.com. For information about intellectual property rights, visit eff.org.

MODULE

NETWORKS AND THE INTERNET

Computer networks and the Internet play a critical role in our society today. Because of this, it is important for all individuals to be familiar with basic networking concepts and terminology, as well as with the variety of activities that are taking place today via the world's largest network—the Internet. It is also important for all individuals to be aware of the potential problems and dangers these technologies can bring.

Chapter 7 introduces basic networking principles, including networking and communications applications, what a computer network is, and how a computer network works. The Internet and World Wide Web are the topics of Chapter 8. Although they were introduced in Chapter 1, Chapter 8 explains how the Internet and World Wide Web originated, and looks more closely at common Internet activities and how to find information on the Web. Useful strategies, such as how to select an ISP and how to perform Internet searches, are some of the topics included in this chapter. Chapter 9 takes a look at some of the risks related to network and Internet use, as well as measures computer users can take to lessen these risks.

"If you do not understand the threats targeting your network and computing infrastructure, it can be very difficult to determine what types of protection strategies to employ."

For more comments from Guest Expert Jeff Bardin of The Hanover Insurance Group, see the Expert Insight on . . . Networks and the Internet feature at the end of the module.

IN THIS MODULE

Chapter 7 Computer Networks 266
Overview 267
What Is a Network? 267
Networking and Communications Applications 268
Types of Networks 277
How Does Data Travel Over a Network? 281
Communications Protocols 288
Networking Hardware 297

Chapter 8 The Internet and World Wide Web 310
Overview 311
Evolution of the Internet 311
Getting Set Up to Use the Internet 318
Searching the Internet 325
Beyond Browsing and E-Mail 332
Censorship and Privacy Issues 347
The Future of the Internet 353

Chapter 9 Network and Internet Security 362
Overview 363
Why Be Concerned about Network and Internet Security? 363
Unauthorized Access, Unauthorized Use, and Computer Sabotage 364
Protecting Against Unauthorized Access, Unauthorized Use, and Computer Sabotage 372
Online Theft, Fraud, and Other Dot Cons 383
Protecting Against Online Theft, Fraud, and Other Dot Cons 389
Personal Safety Issues 395
Protecting Against Cyberstalking and Other Personal Safety Concerns 396
Network and Internet Security Legislation 396

7 CHAPTER Computer Networks

OUTLINE

- Overview
- What Is a Network?
- Networking and Communications Applications
  - Mobile Phones
  - Paging and Messaging
  - Global Positioning Systems (GPSs)
  - Monitoring Systems
  - Satellite Radio
  - Videoconferencing
  - Collaborative Computing
  - Telecommuting
  - Digital Data Distribution
  - Telemedicine
- Types of Networks
  - Network Topologies
  - Network Architectures
  - LANs, WANs, and Other Types of Networks
- How Does Data Travel Over a Network?
  - Data Transmission Characteristics
  - Wired vs. Wireless Connections
  - Wired Network Transmission Media
  - Wireless Network Transmission Media
- Communications Protocols
  - Ethernet
  - Token Ring
  - Wi-Fi (802.11)
  - Mesh Networks, WiMAX, Mobile-Fi, and xMax
  - Bluetooth and Ultra Wideband (UWB)
  - TCP/IP and Wireless Application Protocol (WAP)
  - Phoneline and Powerline Networks
- Networking Hardware
  - Network Adapters
  - Modems
  - Hubs, Switches, and Other Networking Hardware

LEARNING OBJECTIVES

After completing this chapter, you will be able to:

1. Define a network and its purpose.
2. Describe several uses for communications technology.
3. Understand the various topologies and architectures a computer network might use.
4. Explain the difference between a LAN, a WAN, and a PAN, and between an intranet, an extranet, and a VPN.
5. Understand characteristics about data and how it travels over a network.
6. Name specific types of wired and wireless transmission media and explain how they transmit data.
7. Identify different protocols that can be used to connect the devices on a network.
8. List several types of networking hardware and explain the purpose of each.

OVERVIEW

The term **communications**, when used in a computer context, refers to *telecommunications*; that is, data sent from one device to another using communications media, such as telephone lines, privately owned cables, and the airwaves. Communications usually take place over a private (such as a home or business) network, the Internet, or a telephone network.

In business, communications networks are essential. For instance, business people throughout the world regularly use telephone, e-mail, and messaging systems to communicate with fellow employees, business partners, and customers. Documents can now be sent electronically in mere moments, instead of being physically delivered from person to person. Ordering systems allow ordering to take place in real time via the Internet or telephone, and inventory systems can communicate electronically with supplier ordering systems to facilitate deliveries of the necessary items at the appropriate time. Outside salespeople and traveling executives use portable computers and mobile devices to keep in constant touch with others, as well as to access real-time data located on the company network and Web site. The list of business communications applications is seemingly endless. Communications technology has also had a tremendous impact on our personal lives. It allows us to stay in constant touch with others, work from remote locations, locate useful information, and access services and entertainment.

The purpose of Chapter 7 is to introduce you to the concepts and terminology surrounding a computer network. First, a computer network is defined, followed by a look at some common communications and networking applications. Next, a number of technical issues related to networks are discussed, including the major types of networks, how data is transmitted over a network, and the types of transmission media involved. We then proceed to an explanation of the various ways networked devices communicate with one another, and the chapter closes with a look at the various types of hardware used in conjunction with a computer network. ■

FIGURE 7-1
Common uses for computer networks.

USES FOR NETWORKS
Sharing a printer or an Internet connection among several users.
Sharing application software (with a network license) so it can be purchased less expensively and needs to be installed and updated on only one computer.
Working collaboratively, such as sharing a company database or using collaboration tools to create or review documents.
Exchanging e-mail and files among network users and over the Internet.
Connecting a home computer to the entertainment devices (such as a TV or stereo system) located within a home.

WHAT IS A NETWORK?

A *network*, in general, is a connected system of objects or people. As discussed in Chapter 1, a **computer network** is a collection of computers and other hardware devices connected together so that network users can share hardware, software, and data, as well as electronically communicate with each other. The largest computer network in the world is the Internet. Another type of *communications network* is a *telephone network*. Computer networks and telephone networks are commonly used for a variety of purposes by both individuals and businesses. Some common uses for computer networks are listed in Figure 7-1.

>**Communications.** The transmission of data from one device to another. >**Computer network.** A collection of computers and other hardware devices that are connected together to share hardware, software, and data, as well as to communicate electronically with one another.

One area of recent growth is *home networks*. Today, there are approximately 30 million home networks worldwide, and that number is expected to increase to 71 million by 2007. According to the research firm NPD Group, home network use in the United States grew 20% in 2004, with home networks in over one-third of all households that have computers. Home networks are used to enable computers to share an Internet connection, to share digital photos and other files, and to connect computers and home entertainment devices (such as a television and stereo system) together to facilitate the delivery of downloaded music and movies. In business, networks are used extensively to facilitate communications and file sharing.

NETWORKING AND COMMUNICATIONS APPLICATIONS

Today, a wide variety of important business and personal networking and communications applications take place over some type of communications network, typically a company network, a telephone network, or the Internet. Two of the most widely used Internet applications—accessing Web pages and exchanging e-mail—were discussed in Chapter 1, and additional Internet-based applications are discussed in Chapter 8. The following sections take a look at some other types of networking and communications applications.

Mobile Phones

Mobile phones (also called *wireless phones*) are phones that use a wireless network for communications instead of being connected to the regular telephone network via a conventional telephone jack. The most common type of mobile phone is the *cellular* (*cell*) *phone*. Another, but less common, type of mobile phone is the *satellite phone* (see Figure 7-2). Both types of mobile phones allow people to communicate with other people using mobile phones, as well as with people using conventional *landline* phones. Although their use is similar, the technology driving each type of phone differs, as discussed later in this chapter. While cell phones can only be used in locations within a country where cellular service is available, satellite phone coverage is typically on a country-by-country basis, and some satellite services cover the entire earth. Consequently, satellite phones are most often used by individuals—such as soldiers, journalists, wilderness guides, and researchers—traveling in remote areas, who may not have continuous cellular service.

FIGURE 7-2
Mobile phones.

CELLULAR PHONE

SATELLITE PHONE

Mobile phones today can often be used for exchanging e-mail, text, and video messages; taking and exchanging digital photos; playing games; listening to music; watching TV and videos; and retrieving information from the Web. Mobile phones can even be used to take walking tours of certain cities in the United States and to pay for goods and services, as discussed in the Trend box. Mobile phones are widely used in many countries—there are around 180 million mobile phone users in the United States alone. Many

>**Mobile phone.** A cellular or satellite phone.

TREND

New Mobile Phone Applications: Celebrity Walking Tours and Park-by-Phone

You know you can use your cell phone to make phone calls, send text messages, even download ring tones and games, but many more cell phone applications are available today. From generating maps and driving directions, to allowing you to pay for goods and services, to acting as a personal tour guide, mobile phone applications abound. For instance, if you want to take a walking tour of Washington, D.C., Manhattan, or Boston, let your cell phone be your guide. A new service by Talking Street™ features celebrity tour guides, including Sigourney Weaver, Jerry Stiller, and Steven Tyler. To take a cell phone tour, you follow a map to designated historic locations. At each location, you dial the Talking Street phone number and enter the number of your current location to hear the corresponding narration (see the accompanying photo). You can visit the stops in any order, and can take the tour at your own pace–you can even spread out the tour over several days, if desired, for no additional fees. Tours cost about $5.95 each and take about 30 cell-phone minutes.

Another new cell phone application is Park-by-Phone—a no hassle way to pay for parking. Instead of needing correct change to feed a meter or to buy a parking permit, any individual who has signed up for the Park-by-Phone service can use his or her cell phone to pay for parking at designated parking places. All the Park-by-Phone participant needs to do is to dial the Park-by-Phone telephone number and then enter his or her member number and the parking meter number printed on a bright yellow sticker on the meter (see the accompanying photo). Once the call is completed, the parking fee is charged to his or her Park-by-Phone account.

New cell phone applications include cell phone walking tours (left) and Park-by-Phone (right).

individuals—around 9% of all U.S. adults, according to one estimate—are even dropping their landline telephone service completely in favor of using their mobile phones as their primary telephones. In developing countries and other locations with a poor traditional communications infrastructure, mobile phones may be the only telephone alternative.

An emerging type of cell phone is one designed for young children. These products, such as the Whereifone and Firefly, have limited features and built-in controls, such as to allow children to only call predesignated phone numbers. Some include *GPS* capabilities (discussed shortly) so parents can locate their children at any time via a Web site; others can alert parents by text message if the child carrying the cell phone leaves a prespecified area.

FIGURE 7-3
Pagers. Pagers are commonly used today for notification purposes.

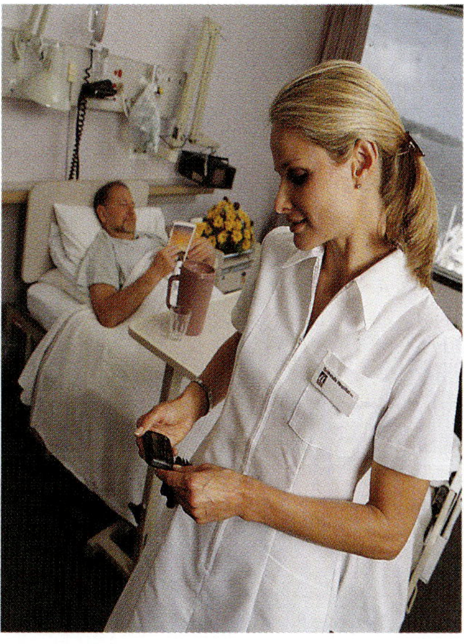

Paging and Messaging

Paging is the term generally used for sending short numeric or text messages to a person's pager from a phone or another pager. With two-way paging, generally referred to as *messaging*, text-based messages can be both sent and received. Messaging today most often takes place via a mobile phone, instead of a stand-alone messaging device. However, stand-alone one-way pagers are still used today, most often for *onsite paging* applications in which workers or patrons are supplied pagers so they can be notified when needed. For instance, one-way pagers are used by restaurants to notify patrons when their tables are ready, by childcare facilities to notify parents if there is an issue with their child, and by hospitals and other healthcare facilities to contact a patient's family members or to contact healthcare workers when they are needed in a particular location (see Figure 7-3).

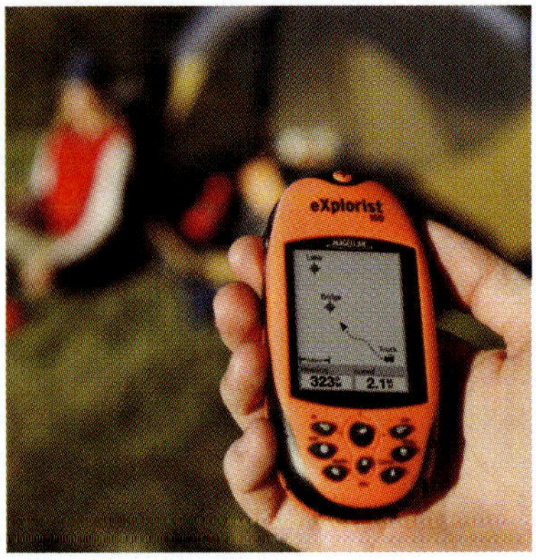

HANDHELD GPS RECEIVER

CAR-MOUNTED GPS RECEIVER

FIGURE 7-4

GPS receivers. Global positioning systems can be used by people who need to know their exact geographical location, usually for safety or navigational purposes.

FURTHER EXPLORATION

For links to further information about GPS, go to www.course.com/uc11/ch07

Global Positioning Systems (GPSs)

A **global positioning system (GPS)** is a satellite-based location and navigation system. It consists of *GPS receivers* (usually handheld or mounted in vehicles or boats) and a group of 24 Department of Defense *GPS satellites*. GPS receivers receive and interpret the data sent via GPS satellites to determine the receiver's exact geographic location, including the latitude, longitude, and altitude.

Although originally used solely by the military, GPS receivers are now widely available for business and personal use. GPS is commonly used by hikers, motorists, surveyors, farmers, fishermen, and other individuals who want or need to know their precise geographical position at specific times. In the past, the government, for national security reasons, required consumer GPS receivers to be less accurate than they were technologically capable of being. This restriction was discontinued in 2000, leading to more accurate GPS receivers, and today's GPS systems are accurate to within 3 meters (less than 10 feet). Handheld GPS receivers are about the size of a mobile phone (see Figure 7-4); wristwatch GPS devices are also available. Some mobile phones and handheld PCs have GPS capabilities built-in or available as an add-on feature. GPS capabilities are also commonly built into cars and can be used in conjunction with some monitoring systems to locate people or objects, as discussed shortly.

In addition to their practical uses, GPS receivers can also be used for entertainment purposes. For example, *geocaching*, in which individuals use GPS receivers to locate secret caches hidden by others, is growing in popularity, particularly among families. To find the secret caches, participants follow the coordinates posted on a geocaching Web site.

Monitoring Systems

There are a number of communications systems available today for monitoring the status of or location of individuals, as well as vehicles or other assets. For instance, electronic *medical monitors* (see Figure 7-5) are available that take the vital signs of an individual (such as weight, blood-sugar readings, or blood pressure) or prompt individuals to answer questions (such as if he or she ate yet that day, took prescribed medication, or feels well). Other medical monitoring systems use pressure pads and motion sensors to track an individual's movement within his or her home, and electronic pill dispensers automatically dispense the proper medication at the proper time. These devices usually transfer readings and the individual's responses to questions to a healthcare provider automatically via the Internet or a telephone network so that potential problems can be detected early. Use of home medical monitoring systems is expected to continue to increase in the United States as the population ages.

Some monitoring systems are designed to locate or track an object, such as a vehicle. These systems typically use GPS satellites to determine the location of the object. Other monitoring systems are designed to monitor how an object is being used. For instance, some car monitoring systems can determine the location of a car if it is stolen; others can

>**Global positioning system (GPS).** A system that uses satellites and a receiver to determine the exact geographic location of the receiver.

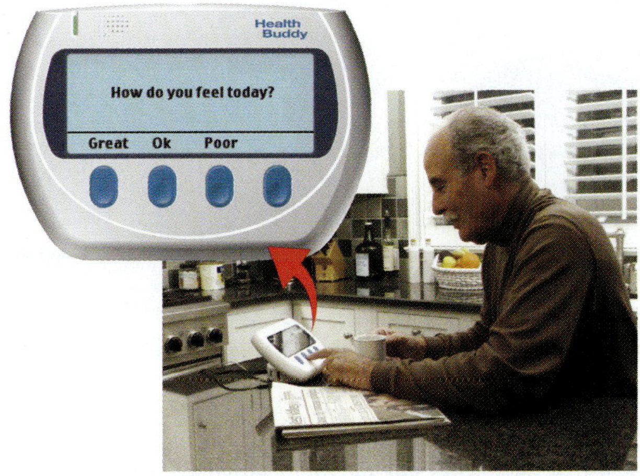

HOME MEDICAL MONITORING
Used to transfer the vital signs of an individual and other health-related information to a medical professional.

REMOTE LOCATION MONITORING
Used to monitor homes and businesses when they are unoccupied in order to detect breaks-in or other problems.

FIGURE 7-5
Examples of electronic monitoring systems.

record data about seat belt usage, speed, and other measures related to safe driving. Some rental car agencies use these latter types of monitoring systems to detect customer speeding and assess a fine accordingly, to both deter reckless driving and to compensate the agency for the cost of the extra wear-and-tear on the rental cars due to the excessive speed used. Progressive Insurance is exploring the use of these monitoring systems to track driver habits and then lower insurance rates for safer drivers. In addition, the data recorded by these types of monitoring systems can be used in accident investigations. Small home models are even available for parents to use to monitor the driving behavior of their children. Other *GPS-based monitoring systems* are used to monitor the location of repair workers and other employees who work outside the office. After the allowable work area for an employee is designated on the employer's computer, the monitoring system sends a notice to that PC if the employee exits that prescribed geographical area.

Some short-range monitoring systems today use *RFID technology*. As discussed in Chapter 4, *radio frequency identification* (*RFID*) is a technology that can store and transmit data located in *RFID tags*. RFID tags contain tiny chips and radio antennas. They can be permanently attached to objects, such as products, vehicles, shipping containers, pets—even people. They can be *passive RFID tags*, which require a reader to "wake them up" so they can broadcast data, or *active RFID tags*, which continually broadcast, allowing their locations to be displayed on a computer monitor in real time. When used in conjunction with a communications network, RFID tags can be used to locate the object the tag is attached to. For instance, hospitals can use their company network to continually monitor the location of equipment or even patients.

Other examples of electronic monitoring systems are those that use sensors or video cameras and the Internet to watch an individual (such as a parent watching his or her child in a daycare center or an individual monitoring the health of an elderly parent) or a location (such as an individual's home or place of business when it is unoccupied, as shown in Figure 7-5). For a look at an emerging type of monitoring system that uses sensors and communications media—*smart dust*—see the Inside the Industry box.

CAR RECEIVER

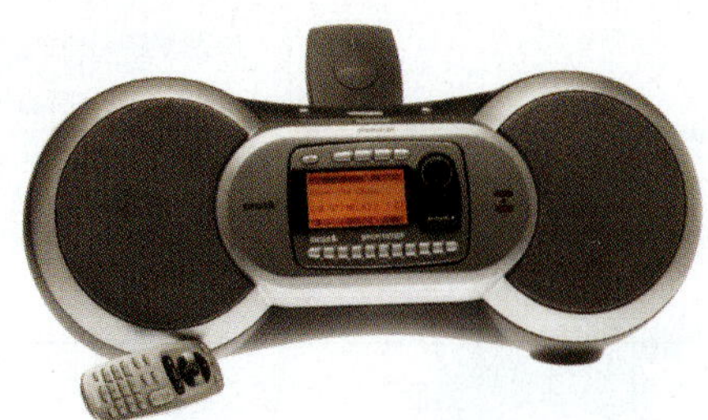

HOME RECEIVER

PERSONAL RECEIVER

FIGURE 7-6
Satellite radio. Satellite radio receivers are available for use in the car, at home, and on the go.

FIGURE 7-7
Videoconferencing. Two of the simplest videoconferencing setups are via a PC or a video phone.

Satellite Radio

Another application that employs the use of satellites is *satellite radio*. Originally designed for the car, satellite radio offers delivery of clear digital music, news, and other radio content across an entire country, instead of just a limited broadcast area as with conventional radio stations. This means that one could drive from coast to coast without ever switching the radio station. And, because it is available on a subscription basis (such as $12.95 per month for about 150 channels), it is typically commercial free. Two popular satellite radio providers are SIRIUS and XM Radio. To receive satellite radio broadcasts, you need a satellite receiver (see Figure 7-6) and an antenna, if one is not built directly into the receiver. Since each satellite provider typically has its own set of two or three broadcast satellites, some satellite radio hardware is not interchangeable and so receivers and antennas need to be compatible with your chosen satellite radio provider. Satellite radio is becoming standard as a new car feature; personal and home receivers are also available to receive radio broadcasts at home or while on the go.

PC VIDEOCONFERENCE
Typically takes place via an Internet connection.

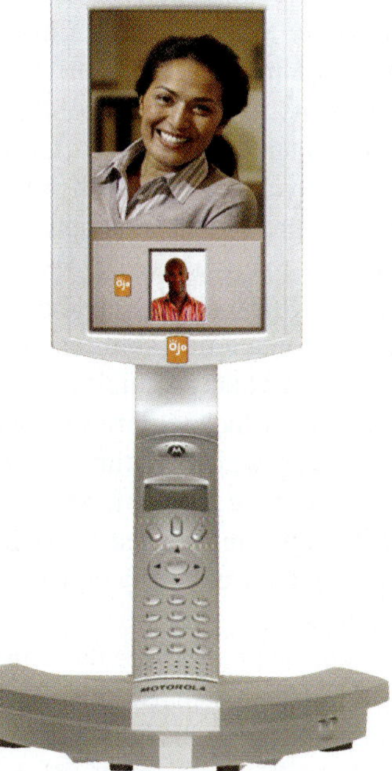

VIDEO PHONE CALLS
Typically take place via standard telephone lines.

Videoconferencing

Videoconferencing is the use of communications technology to conduct real-time, face-to-face meetings between individuals physically located in different places. Videoconferencing can take place via a PC and the Internet (sometimes called *online conferencing* or a *PC video conference*, and illustrated in Figure 7-7) or via a dedicated videoconferencing set up; it is also now available via conventional telephone lines. For example, the *video phone* shown in Figure 7-7 allows two individuals to have

>**Videoconferencing.** A real-time meeting that takes place between people in different locations via computers and communications media.

INSIDE THE INDUSTRY

Smart Dust

Motes—also known as *smart dust*—are tiny computers containing one or more sensors that are powered by a battery and that can communicate with other motes via miniscule radio transmitters. The sensors can perform a variety of measurements, such as assessing temperature, light, sound, position, acceleration, weight, and humidity. Multiple motes can work together to transmit data about their environment. For example, when scattered over a battlefield, motes can be used to detect enemy vehicles in the area and to transmit location information about the vehicles (via GPS coordinates) to neighboring motes, who relay the information to the military commander on an ongoing basis. This information allows the enemy vehicles to be tracked in real time. Currently, the mote circuitry is about the size of a postage stamp—with the necessary batteries, a mote is about the size of a deck of playing cards (see the accompanying figure)—and can run for three to five years on two AA batteries. As battery technologies improve—especially solar technologies for automatic recharging—the size of motes is expected to continue to shrink.

For nonmilitary applications, motes could be embedded into concrete foundations on bridges to take and relay periodic structural and salt readings to detect possible problems with structural damage due to salt or other factors. They could also be attached to power meters and water meters in homes to transmit readings to the utility company on a regular basis, and they could be scattered in vineyards, orange groves, and other agricultural fields to relay temperature and moisture settings to the farmer.

Motes (smart dust) use attached sensors to collect data and an antenna to transmit the data to the other motes on the network.

a video conference using just the video phone connected to their regular telephone lines. Online conferencing typically takes place via an individual's PC using video cameras, microphones, and either videoconferencing software (such as *CUseeMe*), a messaging or chat program that allows voice and video exchange (such as *Microsoft Messenger*, *MSN Messenger*, or *Apple iChat AV*), or the Web site of an *online conferencing service provider* (such as Infinite Conferencing or WebEx). In addition to audio and video, online conferencing typically includes other sharing options, such as a shared electronic whiteboard or workspace so that documents and suggested modifications can be viewed by all participants.

Videoconferencing has grown rapidly since the terrorist attacks on September 11, 2001, due to the initial closure of the airports and the resulting tighter security measures for travel. As businesses continue to discover that videoconferencing is a cost-effective and time-saving alternative for some types of business meetings, many believe that it will continue to grow as a business communications method, as well as for personal use.

Collaborative Computing

Another way of collaborating with others using a computer and communications technology is using collaborative software tools to work together on documents and other project components—often called *workgroup computing* or *collaborative computing*. There are many industries in which collaboration is a very important business tool. For example, engineers and architects commonly collaborate on designs; advertising firms and other businesses need to route proposals and other important documents to several individuals for comments before preparing the final version of a client presentation; and newspaper, magazine, and book editors must read and edit drafts of articles and books before they are published. Instead of these types of collaborations taking place on paper, as in the not-too-distant past, electronic *collaboration tools* are typically used. These tools, such as the revision tools available in Microsoft Office and specialized collaboration software, allow multiple individuals to edit and make comments in a document without destroying the original content. Documents are either stored on and accessed from a network server or routed to individuals via e-mail. When a document has been reviewed by all individuals and is returned to the original author, he or she can read the comments and accept or reject changes that others have made. Other collaboration programs may incorporate shared calendars, project scheduling, and other tools in addition to document sharing. Collaborative computing takes place via both private company networks and the Internet.

Telecommuting

The Internet, e-mail, videoconferencing, mobile phones, and collaborative computing have made **telecommuting** a viable option for some. With telecommuting, individuals work at home and communicate with their place of business and clients via communications technologies. Telecommuting allows the employee to be flexible, such as working nontraditional hours or remaining with the company after a relocation. It also enables a company to save on office and parking space as well as office-related expenses, such as utilities. As an environmental plus, telecommuting helps cut down on the traffic and pollution caused by traditional work commuting.

Digital Data Distribution

With the vast amount of digital data—including digital photos, music, movies, and medical imaging files—that need to be transferred from one location to another, *digital data distribution* is a growing communications application. For instance, the Yankee Group predicts that by 2007 about one in five U.S. households will have a *digital media receiver*—a device used to deliver an individual's digital photos, music, videos, and recorded TV shows from his or her PC to his or her home entertainment devices (such as a TV or stereo system) located anywhere in the house, typically via a wireless network. Digital data distribution can even be used to send television shows and other multimedia content from a user's home TV to his or her portable PC, as discussed in the Technology and You box.

Another digital data distribution application is *digital cinema*. With digital cinema, movies are created, distributed, and projected in digital form. The biggest proponent of digital cinema has been George Lucas, who was not satisfied with the way the digital effects used in his *Stars Wars: Episode 1* movie looked when the movie was transferred to film for distribution. When the movie was released, he set up four digital exhibition sites to show the film in digital format—the first public demonstration of a full-length motion picture from a major studio using digital electronic projectors in movie theatres to replace the normal film projectors—and digital cinema was born. Since then, digital projection equipment has been developed, and movies that are now filmed digitally can remain in digital format from creation through projection—the finished movies are sent to movie theaters in digital form via satellites. Distributing movies digitally saves the Hollywood studios about

>**Telecommuting.** The use of computer and electronic devices to enable an individual to work from his or her home.

TECHNOLOGY AND YOU

Multimedia Place Shifting

The increased use of broadband Internet connections and wireless networks has led to a new communications application—delivering media, such as television shows, music, and movies, from a user's home TV or DVR to the user's computer wherever she or he happens to be at the moment. Similar to the way the VCR allows consumers to *time shift* (watch recorded shows at a more convenient time), these emerging devices and services allow users to *place shift* (watch recorded shows at a more convenient location). One multimedia place-shifting product is Sling Media's *Slingbox* (see the accompanying figure). This product allows the user (via installed software on the PC being used and his or her Slingbox ID code) to remotely control his or her cable box, satellite receiver, or DVR and transfer that content to his or her PC or mobile phone via the Internet. For instance, he or she can watch local news while out of town, watch a recorded TV show while at the beach, or start recording a TV show from the office. In general, place shifting allows users to utilize their cable or satellite services, or access their favorite recorded shows, when they are away from home. Guest passwords can be assigned, such as to allow grandparents to watch home videos of their grandkids remotely; if security cameras are connected to the TV or VCR, home owners can even monitor the security of their home from out of town. It is expected that other uses for multimedia place shifting products will soon be available, such as to stream digital photos, downloaded music, and other multimedia content from a user's home PC to his or her current location.

A Slingbox

The Slingbox (left) allows individuals to placeshift media from their home TVs and DVRs to their portable PCs or mobile devices (right).

$1,500 per film print. It also maintains quality, both for any digital special effects used in the film and for viewing, since the quality drop that occurs with a film print each time it is played is no longer a factor. Although the conversion to digital projection equipment is costly, it also allows movie theaters more flexibility, such as to add additional theaters for a popular film without the additional cost and time delay of ordering a new print. Digital cinema specifications are currently under development by a consortium consisting of the seven major Hollywood studios. Although specifications and security precautions need to be developed to avoid piracy and it is likely that film and digital distribution will coexist for some time (many movies, such as *Star Wars*, *Episode III*, are now distributed in both film format and digital format), it is also expected, that, someday, all movie distribution will be completely digital.

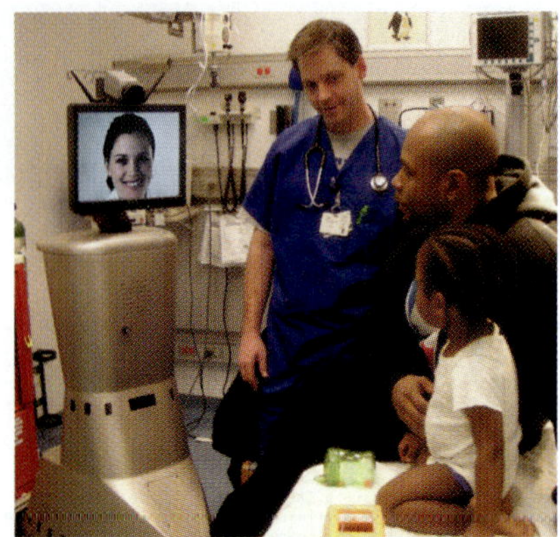

REMOTE CONSULTATIONS
Using remote-controlled teleconferencing robots, physicians can "virtually" consult with patients or other physicians in a different physical location; the robot transmits video images and audio to and from the doctor (via his or her PC) in real time.

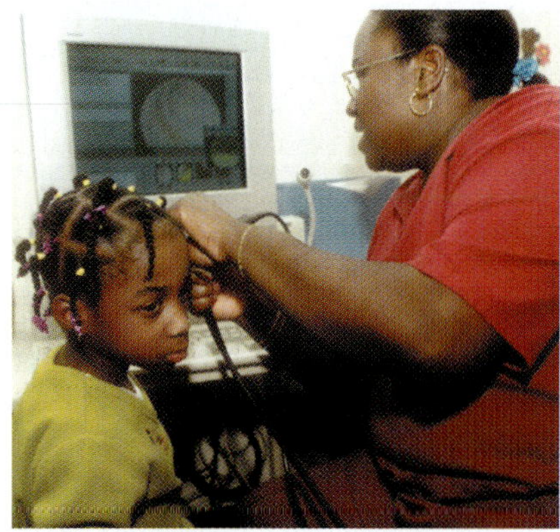

REMOTE DIAGNOSIS
At remote locations, such as the New York childcare center shown here, trained employees provide physicians with the real-time data (sent via the Internet) they need for diagnosis.

TELESURGERY
Using voice or computer commands, surgeons can now perform operations via the Internet; a robotic system uses the surgeon's commands to operate on the patient.

FIGURE 7-8
Examples of telemedicine applications.

Telemedicine

Telemedicine is the use of communications technology to provide medical information and services. In addition to the remote medical monitoring systems already discussed, some physicians offer additional telemedicine services, such as e-mail consultations and Web-based appointment scheduling. Other possibilities include using videoconferencing to communicate with other physicians or with hospitalized patients; to perform remote diagnosis of patients (in which local healthcare workers at rural locations, childcare facilities, and other locations with telemedicine equipment use video cameras, electronic stethoscopes, and other tools to send images and vital statistics of a patient to a physician located at a medical facility); and to perform *telesurgery* (see Figure 7-8).

Telesurgery is a form of *robot-assisted surgery*, in which a robot controlled by a physician operates on the patient. Robot-assisted surgery systems typically use cameras to give the human surgeon an extremely close view of the surgical area. In addition, these systems are typically more precise and make smaller incisions than human surgeons. This allows for less invasive surgery (for example, not having to crack through the rib cage to access the heart), resulting in less pain for the patient, a faster recovery time, and fewer potential complications.

Some robot-assisted surgery takes place with the doctor, patient, and robotic device in the same operating room; with telesurgery, at least one of the surgeons performs the operation by controlling the robot remotely, such as over the Internet. In general, telemedicine has enormous potential for providing quality care to individuals who live in rural or underdeveloped areas and who do not have access to sufficient medical care. Telemedicine will also be necessary for future long-term space explorations—such as a trip to Mars and back that may take three years or more—since astronauts will undoubtedly need medical care while on the journey.

>Telemedicine. The use of communications technology to provide medical information and services. **>Telesurgery.** A form of robot-assisted surgery in which the doctor is in a different physical location from the patient and controls the robot remotely over the Internet or another communications medium.

TYPES OF NETWORKS

Networks can be identified by their *topology*, *architecture*, and size. These topics are described in the next few sections.

Network Topologies

Computer networks vary in physical arrangement or *topology*. Four of the most common topologies are *star*, *bus*, *ring*, and *mesh* (see Figure 7-9).

Star Networks

The **star network**—the oldest topology for computer networks—typically consists of a central device (usually a *hub*, *switch*, or *router*, all of which are discussed later in this chapter) to which all the computers and other devices in the network connect, forming a star shape. The central device contains multiple ports that are used to connect the various network devices (such as a server, PCs, and a printer); all network transmissions are sent through the central device. Star networks are common in traditional mainframe environments, as well as in small office and home networks.

Bus Networks

A **bus network** has no central hub. Instead, it consists of a central cable to which all network devices are attached. For example, the bus network illustrated in Figure 7-9 contains three PCs and a printer attached to a single bus line. In a bus network, all data is transmitted down the bus line from one device to another, and only one device can transmit at a time.

Ring Networks

A less common alternative to the star and bus topologies is the **ring network**. Like a bus network, ring networks do not have a central hub, but the computers and other network devices are connected in a ring formation from one device to the next, without the use of a central cable (see the third illustration in Figure 7-9). In a ring network, data travels from one device to another around the ring in one direction only.

FIGURE 7-9

Basic network topologies. Common topologies are star, bus, ring, and mesh.

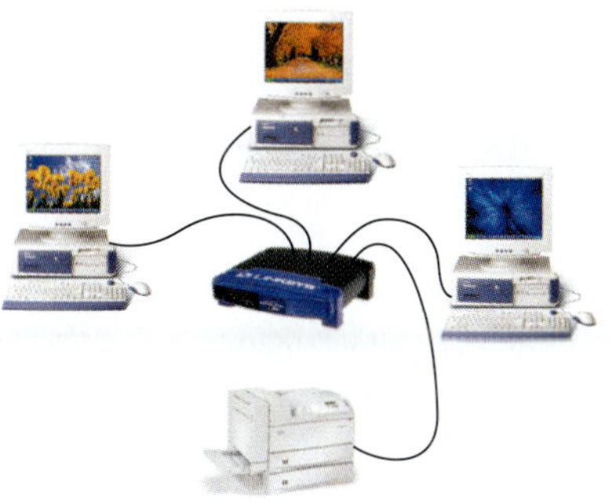

STAR NETWORK
Uses a central hub to connect each device directly to the network.

BUS NETWORK
Uses a single central cable to connect each device in a linear fashion.

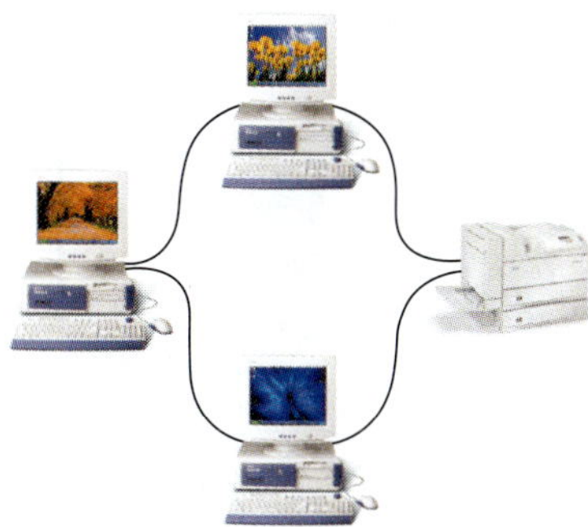

RING NETWORK
Connects computers and other devices one to the next in a loop; there is no central hub or cable.

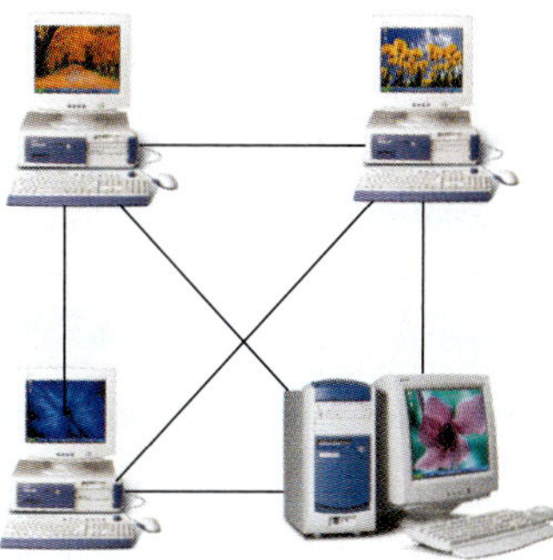

MESH NETWORK
Each computer or device is connected to all other devices.

NET

>**Star network.** A network that uses a host device connected directly to several other devices. >**Bus network.** A network consisting of a central cable to which all network devices are attached. >**Ring network.** A network that connects devices in a closed loop.

Mesh Networks

In a **mesh network**—also called an *ad hoc network*—there are a number of different connections between the devices on the network so that messages can take any of several possible paths from source to destination, instead of having to follow one specific path, as in star, bus, and ring networks. With a *full mesh topology* (such as the one shown in Figure 7-9), each device on the network has a connection to every other device on the network. With a *partial mesh topology*, some devices are connected to all the others, but some are connected only to those other nodes with which they exchange the most data.

Mesh networks are most often used with wireless networks, such as to extend *Wi-Fi networks* or to allow emergency workers within a single agency—such as a city fire department, the highway patrol, or the U.S. Coast Guard—to communicate with workers from other agencies during an emergency, even if they use different radio systems. Wireless networks are discussed in more detail shortly.

Combination Topologies

Some networks, such as the Internet, do not conform to a standard topology. Some networks combine topologies and connect multiple smaller networks, in effect turning several smaller networks into one larger one. For example, two star networks may be joined together using a bus line.

Network Architectures

In addition to topology, networks vary by their *architecture*; that is, the way they are designed to communicate. The two most common network architectures are *client-server* and *peer-to-peer* (*P2P*).

Client-Server Networks

Client-server networks include both *clients* (PCs and other devices on the network that request and utilize network resources) and *servers* (computers that are dedicated to processing client requests). There are a number of different tasks that a server can perform. For example, a *network server* manages network traffic, a *file server* manages shared files, a *print server* handles printing-related activities, and a *mail server* and *Web server* are dedicated to managing e-mail and Web page requests, respectively. Not all networks require all of these server functions, and a single server can perform more than one function. For instance, there is only one server in the network illustrated in Figure 7-10, and it is capable of performing all server tasks for that network.

Network servers are typically powerful computers with lots of memory and a very large hard drive. They can be high-end PCs, midrange servers, or mainframe computers. Regardless of the type of server used, retrieving files from a server

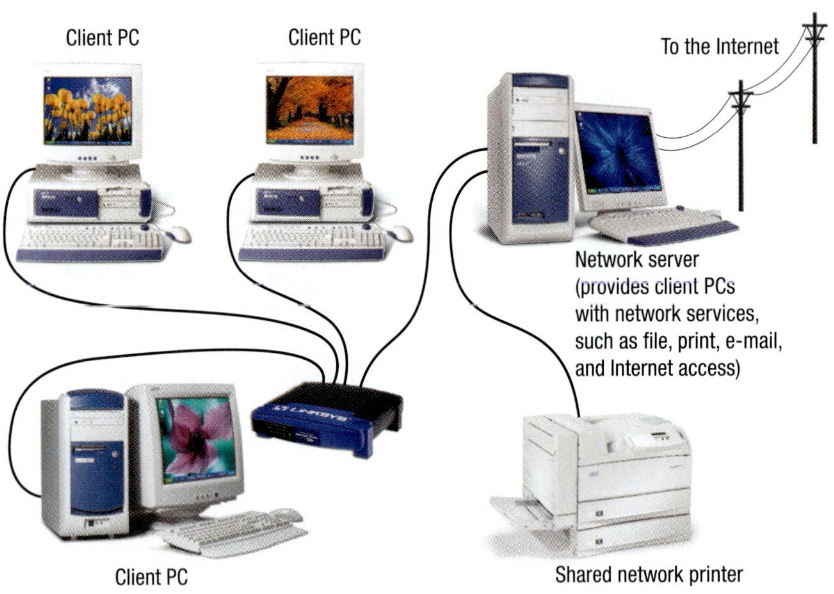

FIGURE 7-10
Client-server networks. With this type of network, client PCs communicate through one or more servers, which provide access to e-mail, the Internet, programs and files stored on the network, network printers, and other network resources.

>**Mesh network.** A network in which there are multiple connections between the devices on the network so that messages can take any of several possible paths.

is called *downloading*; transferring data from a client PC to a server is referred to as *uploading*.

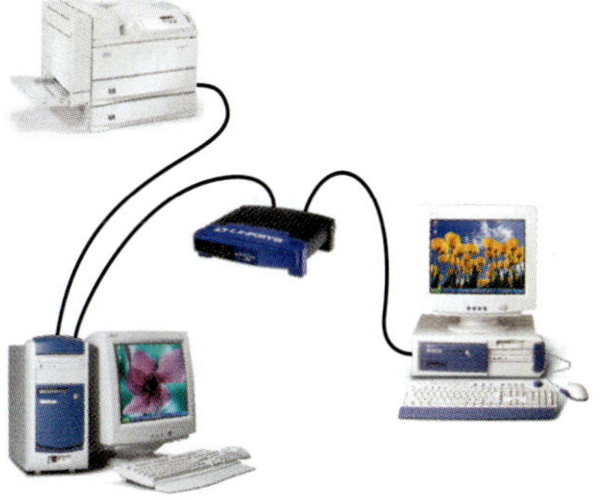

P2P HOME NETWORK
(PCs connect and communicate via network cabling and other networking hardware.)

INTERNET P2P NETWORK
(PCs connect and communicate via the Internet.)

FIGURE 7-11

Peer-to-peer networks. With this type of network, PCs communicate directly with one another, without going through a central server.

Peer-to-Peer Networks

With a *peer-to-peer (P2P) network*, a central server is not used (see Figure 7-11). Instead, all the computers on the network work at the same level, and users have direct access to the other computers and the peripherals attached to the network. For instance, users can access files stored on a peer computer's hard drive and print using a peer computer's printer, provided those devices have been designated as shared devices. Peer-to-peer networks are less expensive and less complicated to implement than client-server networks since there are no dedicated servers, but they may not have the same performance as client-server networks under heavy use. Peer-to-peer capabilities are built into many personal operating systems for small office or home networks.

Another type of peer-to-peer networking—sometimes called *Internet peer-to-peer (P2P) computing*—is performed via the Internet. Instead of placing content on a Web server for others to view via the Internet, content is exchanged over the Internet directly with the other users of the peer-to-peer network. For instance, one user can copy a file from another user's hard drive to his or her own PC via their Internet connections. Internet P2P networking is commonly used for exchanging music files with others over the Internet—an illegal act if the music is copyright-protected and the exchange is unauthorized, although legal Internet P2P networks exist, as discussed more in Chapter 9. Copyright law, ethics, and other topics related to peer-to-peer file exchanges are covered in Chapter 16.

LANs, WANs, and Other Types of Networks

One additional way networks are classified is by their size, which specifies how large an area the network services and what users the network is designed to service. Some of the most common types of networks are listed next.

Local Area Networks (LANs)

A **local area network (LAN)** is a network that covers a relatively small geographical area, such as a home, office building, or school. The devices (sometimes called *nodes*) on the network can be connected with either wired or wireless communications media. The network shown in Figure 7-10 is an example of a LAN.

Wide Area Networks (WANs)

A **wide area network (WAN)** is a network that covers a large geographical area. Typically, a WAN consists of two or more LANs, which could be relatively close to one another (such as in the same city) or far apart. The Internet, by this definition, is the world's largest WAN. WANs may be publicly accessible, like the Internet, or may be privately owned and operated.

NET

>**Local area network (LAN).** A network that connects devices located in a small geographical area, such as within a building. >**Wide area network (WAN).** A network that connects devices located in a large geographical area.

Metropolitan Area Networks (MANs)

A *metropolitan area network* (*MAN*) is a network designed for a metropolitan area, typically a city or county. MANs fall between LANs and WANs on the size continuum and typically consist of multiple LANs. Most MANs are owned and operated by a city or by a network provider who sells access to the MAN to others in that location. Increasingly, wireless MANs are being created to provide free or low-cost Internet access to area residents. According to one estimate, more than 50 cities in the United States have or are in the process of implementing a city-wide wireless network.

FIGURE 7-12

E-clothing. The jacket shown here has compartments to connect the devices in a personal area network (PAN) to each other, as well as to the built-in rechargeable battery pack.

Personal Area Networks (PANs)

A *personal area network* (*PAN*) is a network of personal devices for one individual, such as his or her portable PC, cell phone, and portable printer. The devices in a PAN must be physically located close together and are connected to share data, hardware, and/or an Internet connection. PANs can be either wired or wireless. To facilitate a wired PAN, some *e-clothing* products exist, such as the jacket shown in Figure 7-12 that contains pockets and compartments designed for cell phones, handheld PCs, portable digital music players, and other common devices. In addition to conveniently storing the devices, many e-garments include built-in channels through the lining of the garment to connect the devices easily and without visible wires. The e-jacket in Figure 7-12 even contains built-in solar panels and a corresponding battery pack that can be used to power the devices. In addition to offering convenient hands-free operation, e-garments also allow frequent travelers to speed up the process of going through airport security by allowing them to just remove the e-garment (typically a jacket or vest) to put it through the x-ray machine, instead of having to removing each device separately from the pockets.

Wireless PANs have the convenience of no wires to manage and the ability to use devices (such as a portable printer carried in a briefcase) whenever they are needed without having to physically connect them first. They have the added benefit of enabling a collection of devices to communicate automatically and wirelessly with each other (such as to synchronize portable devices with a desktop PC as soon as the individual returns home or to the office), whenever the devices get within a certain physical distance of each other, even though they are not physically connected.

Intranets and Extranets

An **intranet** is a private network, such as a company LAN, set up by an organization for use by its employees. Intranets are set up like the Internet, with data posted to Web pages that are accessed with a Web browser, so little or no employee training is required, and intranet content can be accessed using a variety of computer types. Intranets today are used for many purposes, such as making company publications available to employees, disseminating forms, and enabling employees to communicate and work together on projects (see Figure 7-13).

>**Intranet.** A private network that is set up similar to the Internet and is accessed via a Web browser.

An intranet that is at least partially accessible to authorized outsiders is called an **extranet**. Extranets are usually accessed via the Internet, and can be used to provide customers and business partners with access to the data they need. Access to intranets and extranets is typically restricted to employees and other authorized users, similar to company networks.

USES FOR INTRANETS

- Facilitating internal e-mail.
- Providing access to company contact information, procedure manuals, and other frequently updated documents.
- Posting and submitting employee forms.
- Posting internal job listings.
- Providing electronic catalogs for ordering supplies.
- Facilitating collaborative computing.
- Scheduling meetings and appointments.
- Posting financial statements and other types of corporate information.
- Maintaining shared calendars, project timelines, and other project documents.
- Providing access to company databases and order systems.

FIGURE 7-13
Uses for intranets.

Virtual Private Networks (VPNs)

A **virtual private network** (**VPN**) is a private, secure path across a public communications network (usually the Internet) that is set up to allow authorized users private, secure access to the company network. For instance, a VPN could allow a traveling employee, business partner, or employee located at a satellite office to connect securely to the company network via the Internet. VPN connections can be temporary or permanent. In either case, the connection between the sender and receiver acts as if it were completely private, even though it takes place over a public network. A process called *tunneling* is used to carry the data over the Internet; special *encryption* technology is used to protect the data, so it cannot be understood if it is intercepted during transit (encryption is explained in Chapter 9). Essentially, VPNs allow an organization to provide secure, remote access to the company network without the cost of extending the physical network.

HOW DOES DATA TRAVEL OVER A NETWORK?

Data transmitted over a network has specific characteristics, and it can travel over a network in various ways. Network devices communicate either through a *wired connection*—via physical cables—or by a *wireless connection*—typically through radio signals. These topics are discussed in the next few sections.

Data Transmission Characteristics

There are a number of characteristics related to data transmission, such as whether the data will be sent in *analog* or *digital* format; the amount of data that can be sent at one time; and the type, direction, and timing used with the transmission.

Analog vs. Digital

One of the most fundamental distinctions in data communications is the difference between analog and digital transmissions. The regular phone system, established many years ago to handle voice traffic, is designed for *analog* signals, which represent data by *continuous* waves over a certain frequency range. Some wireless networks—such as those using *Wi-Fi* or *Bluetooth* technology—as well as some cable TV broadcasts, also use analog signals. Virtually all computing equipment, in contrast, transmit *digital* signals. Some mobile phone networks, television broadcasts (such as HDTV), and cable TV broadcasts are now digital, as well. Digital signals represent data in two *discrete* states: 0s and 1s. Whenever data moves from a digital medium to an analog medium (such as from a computer to a telephone line), an interface (such as a *modem*, discussed shortly) is needed.

Bandwidth

Bandwidth (also called *throughput*) refers to the amount of data that can be transmitted over a communications medium at one time. Text data requires the least amount of bandwidth; video data requires the most. Just as a wide fire hose permits more water to pass

>**Extranet.** An intranet that is at least partially accessible to authorized outsiders. >**Virtual private network (VPN).** A group of secure paths over the Internet that provide authorized users a secure means of accessing a private network via the Internet. >**Bandwidth.** The amount of data that can be transmitted over a communications medium at one time; higher bandwidth media deliver data faster than lower bandwidth media.

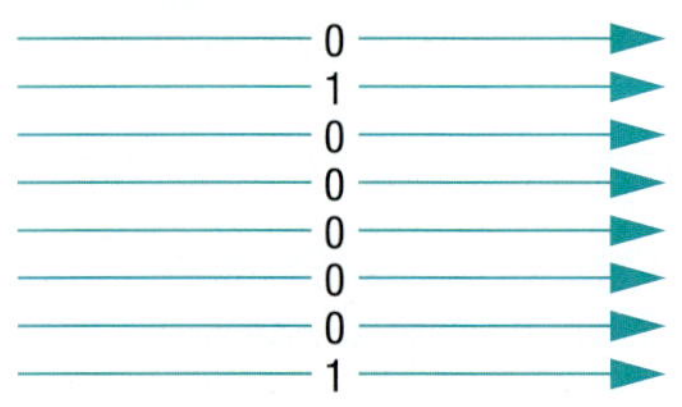

SERIAL TRANSMISSION
All the bits in one byte follow one another over a single path.

PARALLEL TRANSMISSION
The eight bits in each byte are transmitted over separate paths at the same time.

FIGURE 7-14
Serial vs. parallel transmission.

through it per unit of time than a narrow garden hose, a medium with a high bandwidth allows more data to pass through it per unit of time than a medium with a small bandwidth. Bandwidth is usually measured in the number of bits transferred per second, either in *bits per second* (*bps*), *Kbps* (thousands of bits per second), or *Mbps* (millions of bits per second). A medium with a higher bandwidth will deliver data faster than a medium with a lower bandwidth.

Serial vs. Parallel Transmission

Within a computer or over a transmission media, data can travel using *serial transmission* or *parallel transmission*. With **serial transmission**, data is sent one *bit* at a time, one after the other along a single path (see Figure 7-14). If **parallel transmission** is used, the message is sent at least one *byte* at one time with each bit in the byte taking a separate path (refer again to Figure 7-14). While parallel transmission is frequently used within computer components (such as for buses) and for some short-distance applications (such as connecting a printer to a computer, for instance), communications media typically use serial transmission.

Transmission Timing

When data is sent using serial transmission, a technique must be used to separate the bits into groups so that all the bits in one byte can be identified and retrieved together. Three ways of timing serial transmissions are *synchronous*, *asynchronous*, and *isochronous* (see Figure 7-15). Although with all three methods the bits are sent one at a time, the methods vary with how the bits are organized for transfer.

- *Synchronous transmission*—data is organized into groups or blocks of a set number of bits, which are transferred at regular, specified intervals. In other words, the transmissions are synchronized and both devices know when to expect data to be sent and

FIGURE 7-15
Transmission timing. Most network transmissions use synchronous transmission.

SYNCHRONOUS TRANSMISSION
Data is sent in blocks and the blocks are timed so that the receiving device knows that it will be getting them at regular intervals.

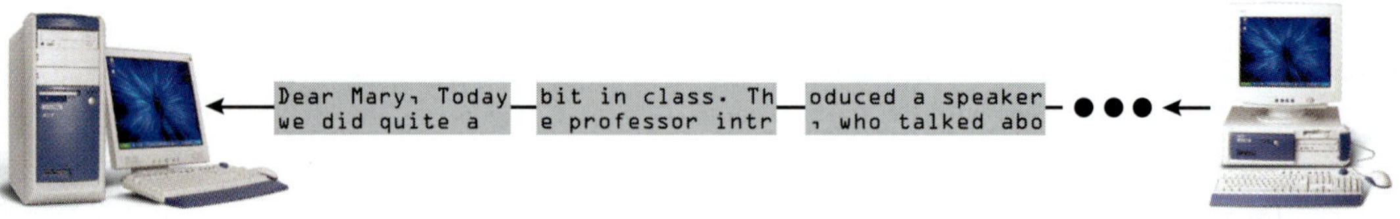

ASYNCHRONOUS TRANSMISSION
Data is sent one character at a time, along with a start and stop bit.

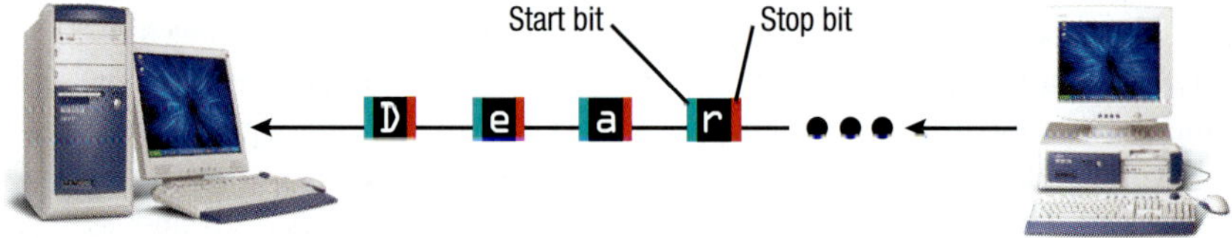

ISOCHRONOUS TRANSMISSION
The entire transmission is sent together after requesting and being assigned the bandwidth necessary for all the data to arrive at the correct time.

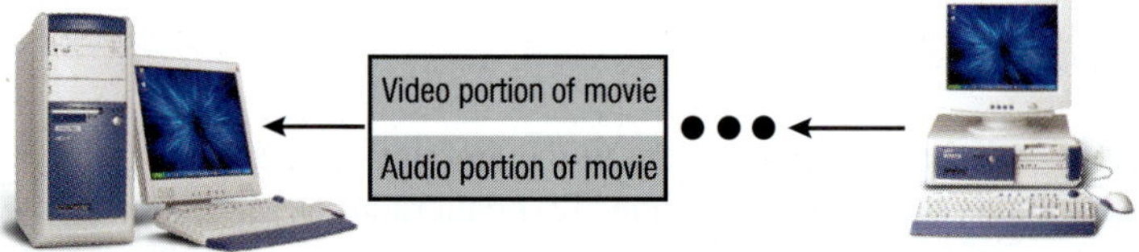

>**Serial transmission.** Data transmission in which the bits in a byte travel down the same path one after the other. >**Parallel transmission.** Data transmission in which bytes of data are transmitted at one time, with the bits in each byte taking a separate path.

when it should arrive. Most communications within a computer are synchronous, as are most network transmissions.

- *Asynchronous transmission*—data is sent when it is ready to be sent, without being synchronized. To identify the bits that belong in each byte, a *start bit* and *stop bit* are used at the beginning and end of the byte, respectively, which makes it less efficient than synchronous transmission. Asynchronous transmission is commonly used for communications between computers and peripheral devices.
- *Isochronous transmission*—data is sent at the same time as other, related, data. For example, when sending multimedia data, the audio data must be received in time to be played with the video data. With isochronous transmission, the entire necessary bandwidth is reserved for that transmission, and no other device can transmit until the transmission is completed, to ensure that the data arrive within the required time period.

Transmission Directions

Another distinction between types of transmissions is the direction in which transmitted data moves (see Figure 7-16).

- *Simplex transmission*—allows data to travel in a single direction only, such as a doorbell. Simplex transmission is relatively uncommon in computer communications since most devices that are usually one-directional, such as a printer, can still transmit error messages and other data back to the PC.
- *Half-duplex transmission*—allows messages to move in either direction, but only in one direction at a time, such as a walkie-talkie in which only one person can talk at a time. Some network transmissions are half-duplex.
- *Full-duplex transmission*—allows data to move in both directions at the same time, like a standard telephone line. Full-duplexing is ideal for hardware devices that need to pass large amounts of data between each other. Many network and most Internet connections are full-duplex.

FIGURE 7-16
Transmission directions. Transmissions can be simplex (one direction only), half-duplex (one direction at a time), or full-duplex (both directions at one time).

NET

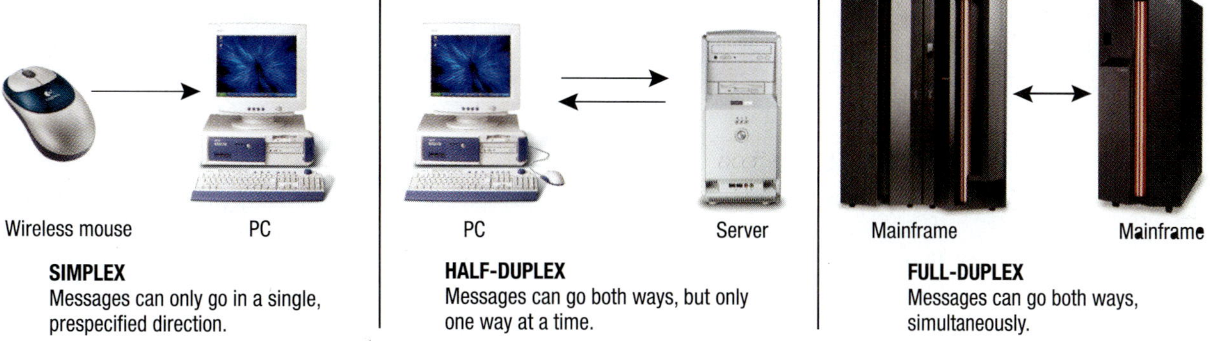

Wired vs. Wireless Connections

With a **wired network** connection, the PC is physically cabled to the network. Wired networks are very common in schools, businesses, and government facilities; they are also found in homes. In general, wired computer networks are less expensive than *wireless*

>**Wired network.** A network in which computers and other devices are connected to the network via physical cables.

networks and are faster. They tend to be easier to secure and are the most efficient way of moving large amounts of data, particularly video and other types of multimedia data, at high speeds. However, they are much more difficult to install in existing structures than *wireless networks*.

Wireless networks typically use radio waves to send data through the air instead of over a physical cable. Consequently, they allow easy connections when physical wiring is impractical or inconvenient (such as inside an existing home or outdoors), as well as give users much more freedom regarding where they can use their PCs. With a wireless network connection, for example, you can surf the Web on your notebook PC from anywhere in your house; access the Internet while traveling just by being close to a public wireless access point in a restaurant, park, or airport; and create a home network without having to run wires between the rooms of your house. Wireless networks are rapidly becoming more popular in both homes and businesses; wireless hotspots are also commonly available in public locations (such as coffee houses, businesses, airports, hotels, and libraries) to allow network access while users are on the road. It is estimated that there were approximately 20,000 public wireless hotspots in the United States at the end of 2004—that number is expected to climb to 150,000 by 2007.

Wired Network Transmission Media

The most common types of wired transmission media are *twisted-pair*, *coaxial*, and *fiber-optic cable*.

Twisted-Pair Cable

Twisted-pair cable (made up of pairs of thin strands of insulated wire twisted together, as illustrated in Figure 7-17) is the least expensive type of networking cable and has been in use the longest. It is the same type of cabling that is found inside the walls of most homes for telephone communications. It is also commonly used for LANs. Twisted-pair cable is rated by category. *Category 3* twisted-pair cabling is regular telephone cable; higher speed cabling—such as *Category 5* and *Category 6*—is frequently used for home or business networks. Twisted-pair wire is twisted together to reduce interference and improve performance. To further improve performance it can be *shielded* with a metal lining. Twisted-pair cable used for networking has a different connector than those used for telephones. Networking connectors are typically *RJ-45* connectors, which are larger than telephone *RJ-11* connectors.

Coaxial Cable

Coaxial cable, the medium pioneered by the cable television industry, was originally developed to carry high-speed, interference-free video transmissions. A coaxial cable (see Figure 7-17) consists of a relatively thick center wire surrounded by insulation and then a grounded shield of braided wire (the shield minimizes electrical and radio frequency interference). Coaxial cable is used today in computer networks, as well as in short-run telephone transmissions outside of the home and for cable television delivery. Although more expensive than twisted-pair cabling, it is much less susceptible to interference and can carry more data more quickly.

>**Wireless network.** A network in which computers and other devices are connected to the network without physical cables; data is typically sent via radio waves. >**Twisted-pair cable.** A communications medium consisting of wire strands twisted in sets of two and bound into a cable. >**Coaxial cable.** A communications medium consisting of a center wire inside a grounded, cylindrical shield, capable of sending data at high speeds.

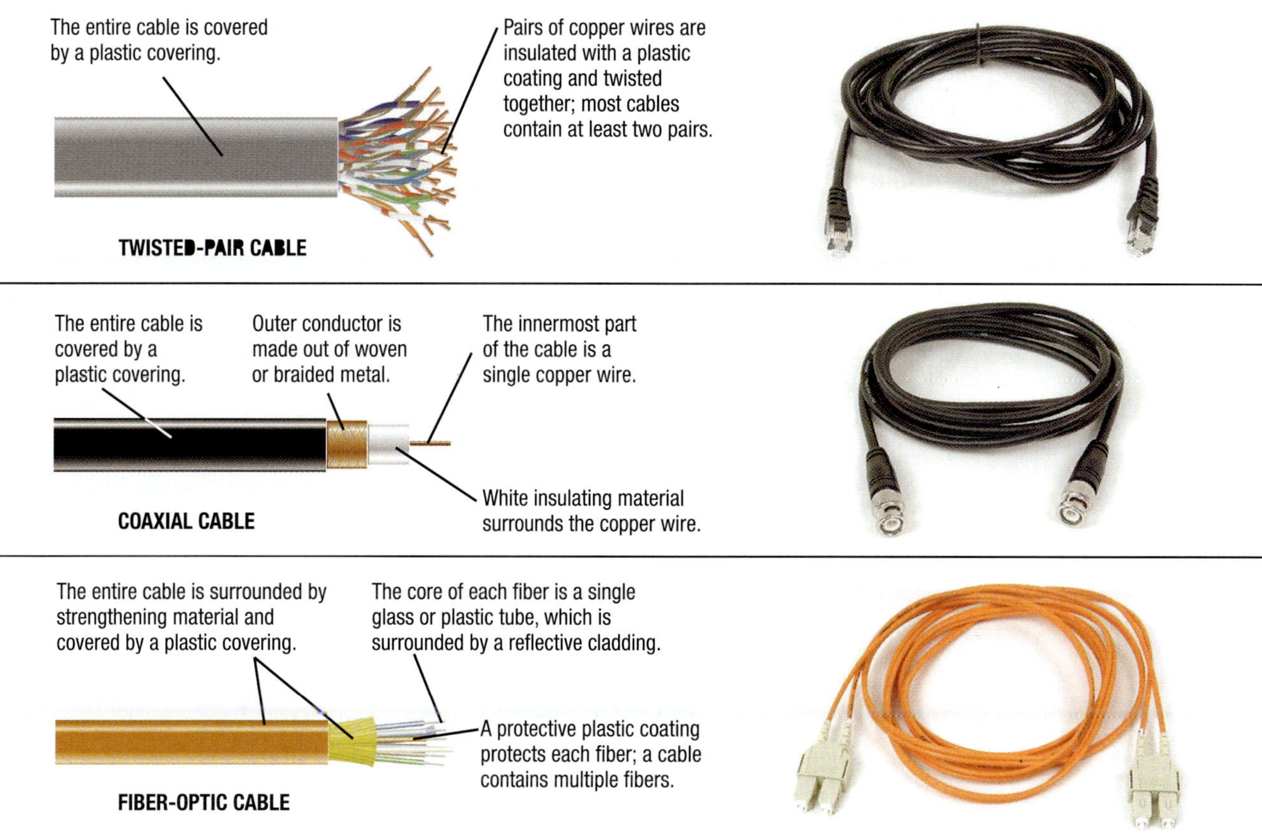

FIGURE 7-17
Wired network transmission media.

Fiber-Optic Cable

Fiber-optic cable is the newest and fastest wired transmission medium. It uses clear glass or plastic fiber strands, each about the thickness of a human hair, to transfer data represented by light pulses (refer again to Figure 7-17). The light pulses are sent through the cable by a laser device at speeds of billions or even trillions of bits per second. Each hair-like fiber has the capacity to carry data for several television stations or thousands of two-way voice conversations. Typically, multiple fibers—sometimes several hundred fibers—are wrapped inside a single fiber-optic cable. Fiber-optic connectors are less standardized than for other types of wired media, so it is important to use cables with the connectors that match the hardware with which the cable will be used. Common connectors include *SC* and *ST*; the SC connector is shown in Figure 7-17.

Fiber-optic cable is commonly used for the high-speed backbone lines of a network, such as to connect networks in separate buildings or for Internet infrastructure. It is also used for telephone backbone lines. The biggest advantage of fiber optic cabling is speed. For example, while it may take a few seconds to transmit a single page of Webster's dictionary over conventional wire cabling, an entire 15-volume set of the *Encyclopedia Britannica* could be transmitted over fiber-optic cable in just a fraction of a second. Another advantage is that data can be transmitted digitally, instead of as analog signals like twisted-pair, coaxial cable, and most wireless media. The main disadvantage of fiber-optic cabling is the initial expense of both the cable and the installation.

NET

>**Fiber-optic cable.** A communications medium that utilizes hundreds of hair-thin, transparent fibers over which lasers transmit data as light.

Wireless Network Transmission Media

Wireless networks use *radio signals*, similar to those used to broadcast radio and television content, to transmit data. The most common types of wireless transmission media are *broadcast radio*, *microwave*, *satellite*, and *cellular radio*.

Broadcast Radio Transmissions

Broadcast radio transmissions (sometimes called *RF*, for *radio frequency*) can be used to send data through the airwaves for a number of different purposes. Short-range radio signals (such as *Bluetooth*) can connect a wireless keyboard or mouse to a PC. Medium-range radio transmissions (such as *Wi-Fi*) are used for wireless LANs and to connect portable PC users to the Internet at public hotspots. (Bluetooth, Wi-Fi, and other networking standards are discussed later in this chapter). Longer-range broadcast radio signals can be used to provide high-speed *fixed wireless Internet access* in some areas.

Because broadcast radio signals can penetrate buildings and other objects, devices connected via a wireless network only have to be within the required range to communicate, not within line of sight with each other. A *transmitter* is needed to send the radio signals through the air; a *receiver* (usually containing some type of antenna) accepts the data at the other end. Sometimes a single piece of hardware functions as both a receiver and transmitter; if so, it is commonly called a *transmitter-receiver* or *transceiver*.

Microwave and Satellite Transmissions

Microwaves are high-frequency, high-speed radio signals. Microwave signals can be sent using *microwave stations* or via *satellites*. Both methods can transmit large quantities of data at high speeds, and so are ideal for television and radio broadcasting, Internet transmissions, and other applications that need to move large amounts of data quickly.

Microwave stations are earth-based stations that can transmit microwave signals directly to each other over distances of up to about 30 miles. Unlike broadcast radio, microwave transmission is line of sight, which means that the microwaves must travel in a straight line from one station to another without encountering any obstacles. To avoid buildings, mountains, and the curvature of the earth obstructing the signal, microwave stations are usually placed on tall buildings, towers, and mountaintops. Microwave stations typically contain both a disc-shaped *microwave antenna* and a transceiver. When one station receives a transmission from another, it amplifies it and passes it on to the next station. Microwave stations can also exchange data transmissions with satellites. Microwave stations designed specifically to communicate with satellites, such as for satellite TV and Internet services, are typically called *satellite dishes*. Satellite dishes are usually installed permanently where they are needed, but can also be mounted on trucks, boats, and other types of transportation devices when portable transmission capabilities are necessary or desirable, such as on military or recreational vehicles.

Communications satellites are space-based devices placed into orbit around the earth to receive and transmit microwave signals to and from earth (see the satellite Internet example in Figure 7-18). Originally used primarily to facilitate microwave transmission when microwave stations were either not economically viable (such as over large, sparsely populated areas) or physically impractical (such as over large bodies of water), satellites can now send and receive transmissions to and from a variety of other devices, such as personal satellite dishes used for television and Internet transmissions, GPS receivers, satellite radio receivers, and satellite phones.

>**Microwave station.** An earth-based device that sends and receives high-frequency, high-speed radio signals. >**Communications satellite.** An earth-orbiting device that relays communications signals over long distances.

4. The ISP's satellite dish receives the data and transfers it to the Internet.

The Internet

5. Data travels over the Internet as usual. Information requested from the Internet takes a reverse route back to the individual.

3. An orbiting satellite receives the data and beams it down to the ISP's satellite dish.

2. Data is sent up to a satellite from the individual's satellite dish.

1. Data is sent from the individual's PC to the satellite dish.

FIGURE 7-18
How satellite Internet works.

Traditional satellites maintain a *geosynchronous* (also called *geostationary*) orbit, 22,300 miles above the earth. Geosynchronous satellites travel at a speed and direction that keeps pace with the earth's rotation, so they appear to remain stationary over a given spot on the globe. Geosynchronous satellites are so far above the surface of the earth that it takes only two of them to blanket the entire planet. Although geosynchronous satellites are excellent for transmitting data, they are so far away that there is a slight delay while the signals travel from the earth, to the satellite, and back to the earth again. This delay—less than a half-second—is very small for the distance involved and does not really interfere with data communications, but it does make geosynchronous satellite transmissions less practical for voice, gaming, and other real-time communications.

Low earth orbit (*LEO*) satellite systems were developed so that telephone communications systems could avoid the delay problem. LEO satellites typically are located about 500 miles above the earth and use between 50 and 60 satellites to cover the earth. LEO satellites are cheaper to build, and, because of their lower orbits, they provide faster message transmission than traditional satellites. *Medium earth orbit* (*MEO*) systems using satellites located about 6,400 miles above the earth are currently being developed for both telephone and Internet service. GPS satellites, which are about 12,000 miles above the earth, are considered MEO satellites, as well.

NET

Cellular Radio Transmissions

Cellular radio is a form of broadcast radio designed for use with cellular telephones. Cellular transmissions take place via *cellular towers*—tall metal poles with antennas on top to receive and transmit cellular radio signals. Cellular service areas are divided into honeycomb-shaped zones called *cells*, each usually measuring between 2 and 10 miles across and containing one cellular tower (see Figure 7-19). When a cell phone user begins to make a call, it is picked up by the cell tower in the cell in which the caller is located. The cell tower then forwards the call to its designated cellular company switching office, and it travels to the recipient via his or her telephone service provider. When a cell phone user moves out of the current cell into a new cell, the call is handed off from the cell tower in the current cell to the cell tower in the cell the user is entering, usually without the user realizing the call has been transferred. To allow multiple conversations to take place at the same time over a single cellular network, different transmission frequencies are used. To avoid interference, towers in adjacent cells always transmit on different frequencies.

Cellular phone use has become incredibly popular for both business and personal use—around 779 million phones were sold worldwide in 2005, according to the research

FURTHER EXPLORATION

For links to further information about wired and wireless communications media, go to www.course.com/uc11/ch07

>**Cellular radio.** A form of broadcast radio that broadcasts using antennas located inside honeycomb-shaped cells.

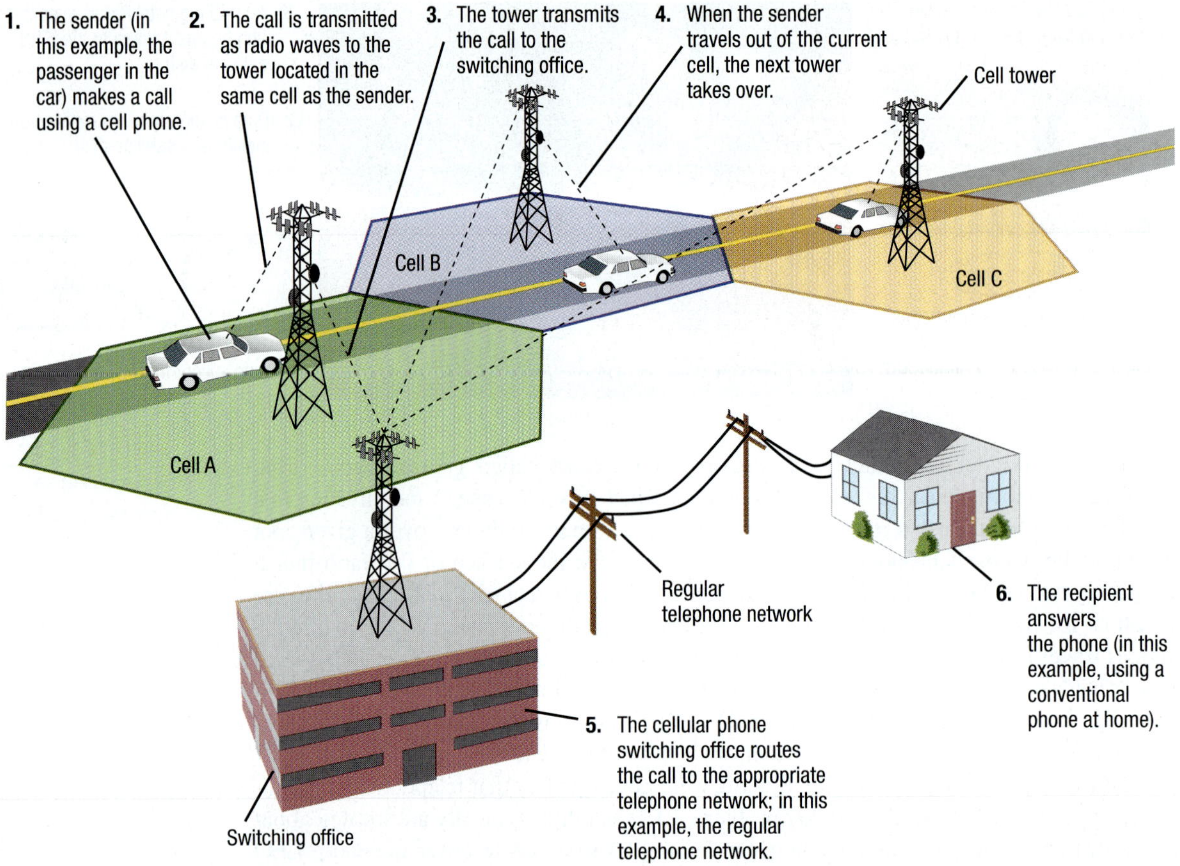

FIGURE 7-19
How cellular transmissions work. Cell phones send and receive calls via cellular radio towers covering a limited geographical area. As the cell phone user moves, the call is transferred from cell tower to cell tower.

group Gartner. That number is expected to exceed 1 billion by 2007, when it is estimated that 2.6 billion people worldwide will actively use a cell phone. Today's cell phones are usually *second-generation (2G)* or *third-generation (3G)* phones. The original *first-generation* phones were analog and designed for voice data only. Newer cell phones, starting with 2G, are digital, support both data and voice, and are faster (2G has a maximum speed of 14.4 Kbps, and 3G phones are designed to transfer data at rates up to 128 Kbps while driving in a car, 384 Kbps in a pedestrian environment, and 2 Mbps in a fixed setup). *Fourth-generation (4G)* cellular services, which are expected to move data at 100 Mbps or more, might arrive as soon as 2006.

COMMUNICATIONS PROTOCOLS

A *communications protocol* is an agreed-upon standard for transmitting data between two devices on a network. Protocols specify how devices physically connect to a network, how data is packaged for transmission, how receiving devices acknowledge signals from sending devices (a process called *handshaking*), how errors are handled, and so forth. Just as people need a common language to communicate effectively, machines need a common set of rules—communications protocols—for this purpose. Two of the most common protocols used to transfer data over a network are *Ethernet* (for wired networks) and *Wi-Fi* (for wireless networks). Other possibilities are *Token Ring* (for wired networks); *Bluetooth* and *Ultra Wideband* (for short-range wireless connections); *TCP/IP* and *WAP* (for Internet communications); *Phoneline* and *Powerline* (for home networks); and the emerging *WiMAX*, *Mobile-Fi*, and *xMax* standards.

Ethernet

Ethernet is one of the most widely used wired networking protocols. It is typically used with LANs that have a bus or star topology and use twisted-pair or coaxial cables. The original Ethernet protocol (called *10Base-T*) was developed in the mid-1970s and supports transmission rates of 10 Mbps. The most common Ethernet standard for LANs today is *Fast Ethernet* (*100Base-T*), which supports data transfer rates of up to 100 Mbps. *Gigabit Ethernet* (*1000Base-T*) is even faster at 1,000 Mbps (1 Gbps) and is most often used for data-intensive business LANs or WANs. The emerging *10-Gigabit Ethernet* standard supports data transfer rates of 10 Gbps.

When transmitting data, an Ethernet network uses a set of procedures collectively called *CSMA/CD*, which stands for *Carrier Sense Multiple Access* and *Collision Detection* (see Figure 7-20). *Carrier sense* means that when a computer on the network is ready to send a message, it first "listens" for other messages on the line. If it senses no messages, it sends one. *Multiple access* means that two computers might try to send a message at exactly the same time, so a *collision* may occur. *Collision detection* means that just after a computer transmits a message, it listens to see if the message collided with a message from another computer (collisions are not noticeable to the user). When a collision takes place,

FIGURE 7-20
How Ethernet networks work.

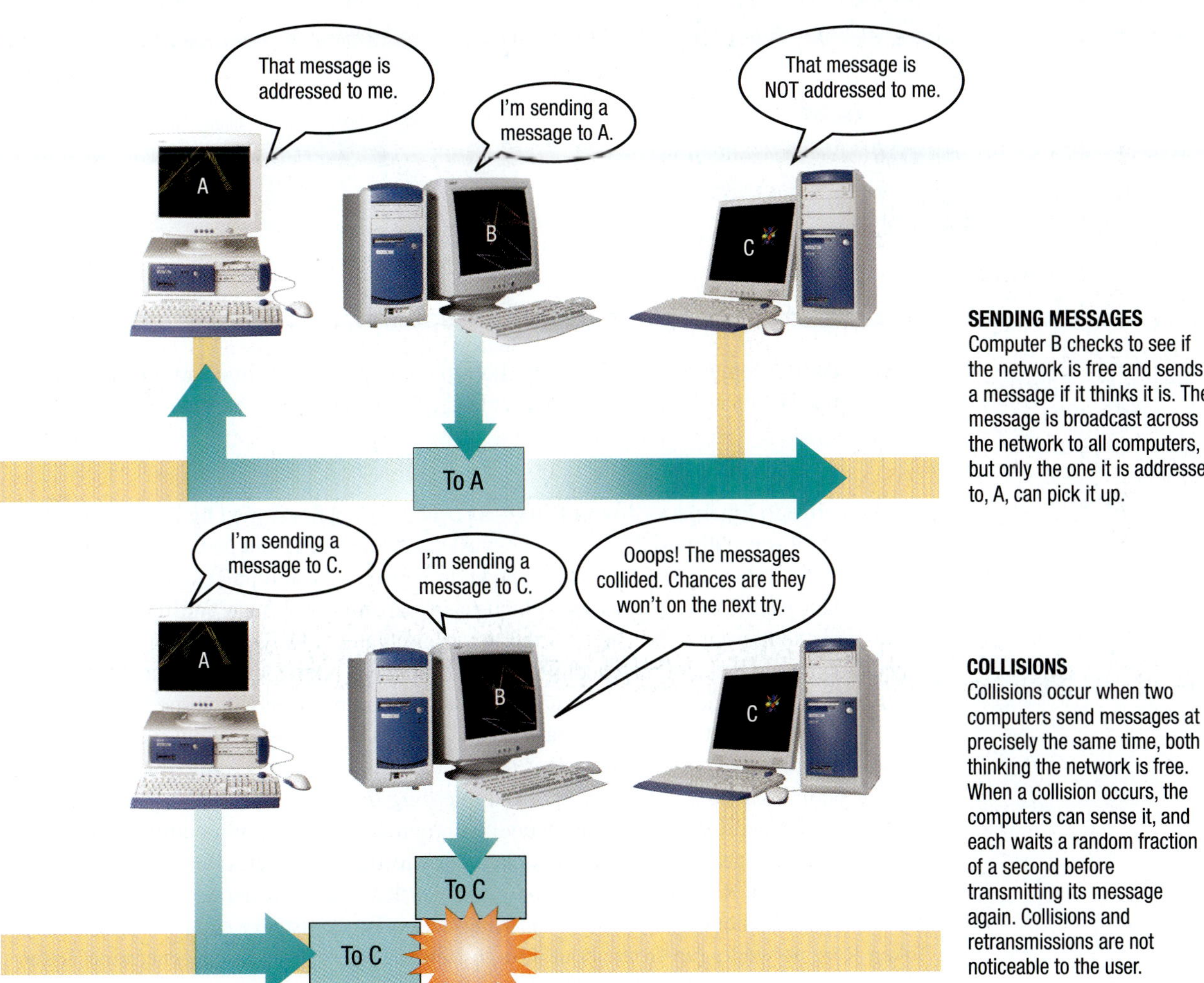

SENDING MESSAGES
Computer B checks to see if the network is free and sends a message if it thinks it is. The message is broadcast across the network to all computers, but only the one it is addressed to, A, can pick it up.

COLLISIONS
Collisions occur when two computers send messages at precisely the same time, both thinking the network is free. When a collision occurs, the computers can sense it, and each waits a random fraction of a second before transmitting its message again. Collisions and retransmissions are not noticeable to the user.

NET

>**Ethernet.** A widely used communications protocol for a LAN.

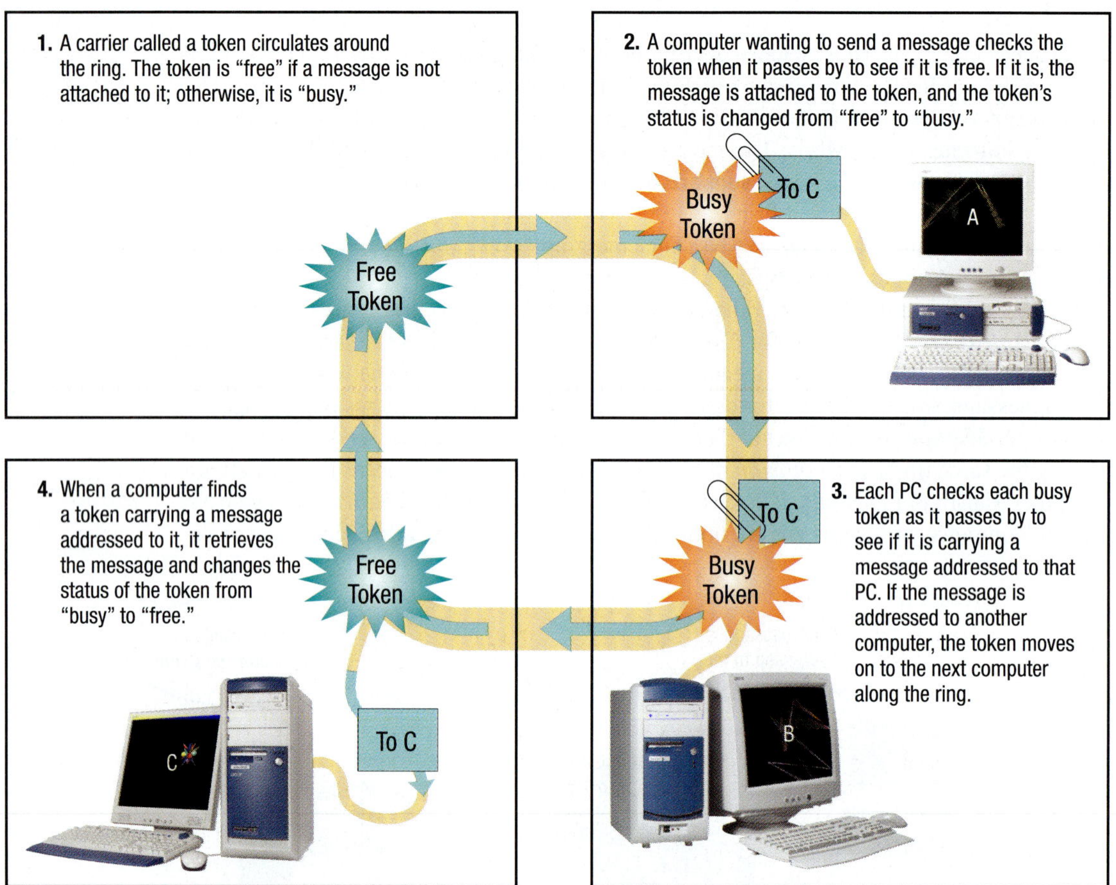

FIGURE 7-21
How Token Ring networks work.
Token Ring networks use token passing to control access.

the two sending computers wait for very short, random periods of time and send their messages again. The chance of the messages colliding a second time is extremely small.

Token Ring

An alternative to Ethernet is **Token Ring**—a LAN protocol developed by IBM. The Token Ring protocol is usually used with ring networks and has a different method of controlling access to the network from Ethernet, as shown in Figure 7-21. With a Token Ring network, a small data packet called a *token*—which has room for a message and the appropriate address—is sent around the ring. As the token circulates (always in a single direction), each computer on the network checks to see if the token is addressed to it; if so, it grabs the token to retrieve the message. A token also contains a control area, which specifies whether the token is free or if it carries a message. When a token is free, any computer can take possession of it to attach a message. It does this by changing the status of the token from free to busy, adding the addressed message, and releasing the token. The message then travels around the ring until it reaches the receiving computer. The receiving computer retrieves the message, changes the status of the token back to free, and then releases the token. In general, the Token Ring protocol maintains more order than the Ethernet protocol because it eliminates collisions. However, Token Ring networks are usually slower. Traditionally, Token Ring networks run from about 4 to 16 Mbps. The newer, second-generation Token Ring architecture can operate at 100 Mbps.

>**Token Ring.** A communications protocol that uses token passing to control the transmission of messages.

Wi-Fi (802.11)

Developed in the late 1990s, **Wi-Fi** (for *wireless fidelity*) is a family of wireless networking standards. Wi-Fi (also known as **802.11** for its official standard number issued by *IEEE*, a nonprofit organization involved with setting standards for computers and communications technology) is the current standard for wireless networks in the home or office, as well as for connecting wirelessly to the Internet via a public hotspot—a geographic area covered by a Wi-Fi *wireless access point*. Wi-Fi can be used to create an entirely wireless network, as well as to add wireless capabilities to an existing wired Ethernet network. For instance, a homeowner may wish to use Wi-Fi to connect a notebook computer to an existing wired home network so the notebook computer can be used anywhere in the house or yard, or a business may wish to add wireless capabilities to the company network to provide Internet and network access in meeting rooms, lobbies, cafeterias, and other common areas. Colleges typically have hotspots on campus to enable students to wirelessly connect to the campus network (see Figure 7-22), and public Wi-Fi hotspots are also becoming increasingly common. Although you cannot get continuous coverage while on the go with Wi-Fi (such as you can with Internet service through a cellular provider, for instance), Wi-Fi is a fast alternative for users who need Internet access while close to an accessible hotspot. Some public hotspots can be accessed for free; others charge by the minute or hour. Numerous cities—such as Spokane and Philadelphia—have set up large wireless networks to provide free or low-cost wireless Internet access for that community. A series of connected hotspots may provide wider, more comprehensive Wi-Fi coverage in the future—such setups are in the experimentation stage.

COLLEGE HOTSPOT
This hotspot is located in the student union in a college in England.

LIBRARY HOTSPOT
This hotspot is located at the New York City Public Library.

FIGURE 7-22
Wireless hotspots.
Wireless hotspots are commonly found on college campuses, public libraries, and other public locations.

Wi-Fi is designed for medium-range data transfers—in theory, no more than 300 feet away indoors or 1,000 feet outdoors, although the maximum distances achieved in real situations are often much less. Factors that affect performance include the distance from the access point, the number of solid objects (such as walls) between the access point and the PC, and possible interference from cordless phones, baby monitors, and other devices that also operate on the same radio frequency (usually 2.4 GHz).

There are a number of different versions of the 802.11 standard; some are new standards, others are improvements to the existing standards. The three most common 802.11 standards are listed in Figure 7-23, along with an emerging standard expected to be finalized in 2007. The *802.11g* standard is the norm today, although it will likely be replaced with one of the improved emerging standards—such as *802.11n*, once it becomes available.

FIGURE 7-23
Wi-Fi standards.

WI-FI STANDARD	DESCRIPTION
802.11b	The original Wi-Fi standard; supports data transfer rates of 11 Mbps.
802.11a (also called *Wi-Fi5*)	About five times faster (up to 54 Mbps) than 802.11b, but it is more expensive and uses a different radio frequency (5 GHz) than 802.11b (2.4 GHz), making the two standards incompatible.
802.11g	The current Wi-Fi standard; supports data transfer rates of 54 Mbps, but it uses the same 2.4 GHz frequency as 802.11b, so their products are compatible.
802.11n	A Wi-Fi standard currently in development that is expected to increase Wi-Fi speeds to more than 100 Mbps; currently uses MIMO technology and is sometimes called *Fast Wi-Fi*.

>**Wi-Fi (802.11).** A widely used communications protocol for wireless networks.

One new application for Wi-Fi is *Voice over Wi-Fi*, which allows users to make telephone calls via a Wi-Fi network. At the present time Voice over Wi-Fi is used mainly by employees who work at large facilities covered by Wi-Fi networks, such as schools, hospitals, and corporate headquarters. As Wi-Fi networks become larger, however, Voice over Wi-Fi could become a viable alternative to conventional or wireless telephone service. Other Wi-Fi applications under development include the *Wi-Fi Positioning System*, which is an alternative to GPS, and large *municipal Wi-Fi networks* (sometimes called *Wi-Fi clouds*), which are very large Wi-Fi hotspots that are designed to provide Internet access to a particular area. For instance, the wireless network being created in the city of Philadelphia, Pennsylvania will cover all 135 square miles of Philadelphia—when completed, this network will be the world's largest Wi-Fi network. To accomplish these large hotspots, *mesh* technology is typically used; mesh and other additional wireless technologies are discussed next.

Mesh Networks, WiMAX, Mobile-Fi, and xMax

A number of wireless networking technologies are currently in development, designed to be used in conjunction with Wi-Fi or instead of Wi-Fi to extend the range of wireless networks. Some of the most promising are discussed next.

Mesh Networks

The phenomenal growth in the number of wireless networks and the use of wireless devices in recent years has created the need to connect these devices and networks. For instance, an individual using Wi-Fi access inside a Starbucks coffeehouse is not able to continue that connection when he or she leaves that immediate area. Instead, the individual needs to locate another hotspot at his or her next location. And, while emergency workers within a single agency—such as a city fire department, the highway patrol, or the U.S. Coast Guard—can communicate with other workers within their agency, they often cannot communicate with other workers from other agencies because they use different radio systems. These problems can be solved by an emerging wireless networking standard known as *wireless mesh*.

FURTHER EXPLORATION

For links to further information about wireless networking protocols, go to www.course.com/uc11/ch07

Developed in the military, wireless mesh networks use a mesh topology, so messages can take any of several possible paths from source to destination. The most common use of mesh technology today is to create MANs. For instance, the city of Medford, Oregon, created Oregon's first wireless mesh network in 2004. This 24-square mile network was implemented to provide high-speed data communications to city workers, including those at law enforcement, fire, rescue, public works, and building inspection agencies. Other mesh MANs are used to provide wireless Internet access to residents in a particular geographic area.

WiMAX

Another emerging wireless standard is **WiMAX** (also known as *802.16*). WiMAX is a series of standards designed to provide wireless Internet access at speeds up to 70 Mbps over a distance of up to 30 miles. In addition to speed and distance, WiMAX does not require line of site and works in areas containing buildings and trees. Similar to Wi-Fi, WiMAX is designed for fixed hotspot locations, but the hotspots are significantly larger. In fact, one of the leaders in WiMAX—Intel—expects it to eventually replace Wi-Fi. A version of WiMAX being developed for mobile use is called *mobile WiMAX* or *802.16e* and is

>**WiMAX.** An emerging wireless networking standard that is faster and has a greater range than Wi-Fi.

expected to be available by the end of 2006. Products for the original WiMAX standards were released at the end of 2005; mobile WiMAX products and services are expected to be available in the United States sometime in 2006.

Mobile-Fi

Mobile-Fi, also known as *802.20* and *Mobile Broadband Wireless Access (MBWA)*, is another standard currently in development for providing high-speed mobile Internet access. Mobile-Fi is designed to be used while in cars or while traveling in other vehicles, such as trains, which are moving at up to 155 miles per hour. Currently a competitor of WiMAX, Mobile-Fi is expected to be compatible with WiMAX. Some experts predict that WiMAX will be used to create large hotspots to provide access to stationary users and users moving around within a limited geographic area, while Mobile-Fi will be used for broader coverage and in high-speed mobile situations, such as to provide Internet access for individuals who commute to work via train. Mobile-Fi products are expected to be available sometime in 2006.

TIP

WiMAX and Mobile-Fi are two of the technologies that mobile carriers are investigating as possible options for delivering *4G* mobile phone services.

xMax

An additional possibility for longer range wireless connections is *xMax*—a technology recently developed by a company called *xG*. xMax is designed to transfer data over the unused portions of radio channels currently used for pagers and TV signals. Because xMax uses very low frequencies, it can transmit over longer distances than other wireless technologies. Consequently, less hardware is required to cover a specific geographic location, making it more feasible for providing wireless Internet to rural areas. Prototype xMax networks are currently being built in Florida.

Bluetooth and Ultra Wideband (UWB)

Bluetooth is another wireless standard that uses radio technology, but it is designed for very short-range (less than 10 meters, approximately 33 feet) communications. It is most appropriate for communications between computers or mobile devices and peripheral devices, such as to connect a wireless keyboard or mouse to a desktop PC, to send print jobs wirelessly from a portable PC to a portable printer, or to connect a smart phone to an earpiece (see Figure 7-24). Since Bluetooth devices automatically recognize each other when they get within transmission range, handheld PCs, desktop PCs, and mobile devices can always be networked wirelessly when they are within range. For instance, Bluetooth can be used to automatically synchronize a handheld PC with a desktop PC on entering the home or office. In addition, some industry experts predict that all major household appliances will be Bluetooth-enabled in the future, resulting in an automatic, always connected, smart home.

FIGURE 7-24

Bluetooth. Bluetooth is designed for short-range wireless communications between PCs or mobile devices and other hardware.

The notebook PC and printer form a piconet when they are within range to communicate with each other.

The desktop PC, keyboard, and mouse form a piconet to communicate with each other.

The headset and cell phone form a piconet when they are within range to communicate with each other.

NET

>**Bluetooth.** A communications standard for very short-range wireless connections; the devices are automatically connected once they get within the allowable range.

Bluetooth works using radio waves in the frequency band of 2.4 GHz, the same as Wi-Fi, and supports data transfer rates of up to 3 Mbps. Once two Bluetooth-enabled devices come within range of each other, their software identifies each other (using their unique identification numbers) and establishes a link. Because there may be many Bluetooth devices within range, up to 10 individual Bluetooth networks (called *piconets*) can be in place within the same physical area at one time (see Figure 7-24). Each piconet can connect up to eight devices, for a maximum of 80 devices within any 10-meter radius. To facilitate this, Bluetooth divides its allocated radio spectrum into multiple channels of 1 MHz each. Each Bluetooth device can use the entire range of frequencies, jumping randomly (in unison with the other devices in that piconet) on a regular basis to minimize interference between piconets, as well as from other devices (such as garage-door openers, Wi-Fi networks, and some cordless phones and baby monitors) that use the same frequencies. Since Bluetooth transmitters change frequencies 1,600 times every second automatically, it is unlikely that any two transmitting devices will be on the same frequencies at the same time. For control, one device in each piconet acts as the *master* device and continually emits requests for other devices to join the network. Any device wishing to network with the master device answers with its identification number and becomes a *slave* device in that piconet.

Another short-range wireless technology used to connect devices is *Ultra Wideband* (*UWB*). UWB was originally developed for the military in the 1960s to locate tanks, enemies, and other objects hidden behind walls or in foliage, but it is now beginning to be used to wirelessly network consumer multimedia devices. UWB can be used to wirelessly deliver multimedia content—such as video, music, and photos—stored on a computer or DVR to other devices that are within range (about 100 feet away or less). The speed of UWB at the present time depends on the distance between the devices being used, but at 100 Mbps at 10 meters (about 33 feet) or 480 Mbps at 2 meters (about 6.5 feet), UWB is significantly faster than Bluetooth and has a greater range. The UWB standard is still evolving and some predict a speed of 1 Gbps by 2007. One of the most recent developments related to UWB is the announcement that new Bluetooth standards may use UWB to speed up connections between Bluetooth devices for transferring larger quantities of data, such as to transfer music or video files from a PC to a mobile phone. Another development is the proposed *wireless USB* standard. Backed by Intel and based on UWB, wireless USB is designed to connect peripheral devices, similar to Bluetooth, and will transfer data at up to 480 Mbps. It is expected that wireless USB will be aimed at PC use, while Bluetooth will continue to be prominent for use with portable PCs and mobile devices.

TCP/IP and Wireless Application Protocol (WAP)

TCP/IP is the protocol used for transferring data over the Internet. It actually consists of two protocols: *Transmission Control Protocol* (*TCP*) and *Internet Protocol* (*IP*). TCP/IP uses a technique called *packet switching* to transmit data over the Internet. With packet switching, messages are separated into small units called *packets*. Packets contain information about the sender and the receiver, the actual data being sent, and information about how to reassemble the packets in order to reconstruct the original message. Packets travel along the network separately, based on their final destination, network traffic, and other network conditions. When the packets reach their destination, they are reassembled in the proper order (see Figure 7-25).

TIP

A related protocol–*Voice over IP (VoIP)*–used to make telephone calls over the Internet using Internet Protocol is discussed in Chapter 8.

>TCP/IP. A communications protocol that uses packet switching to facilitate the transmission of messages; the protocol used with the Internet.

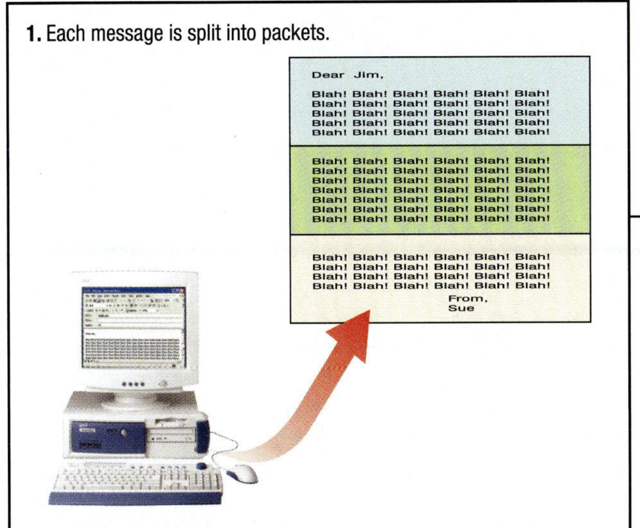

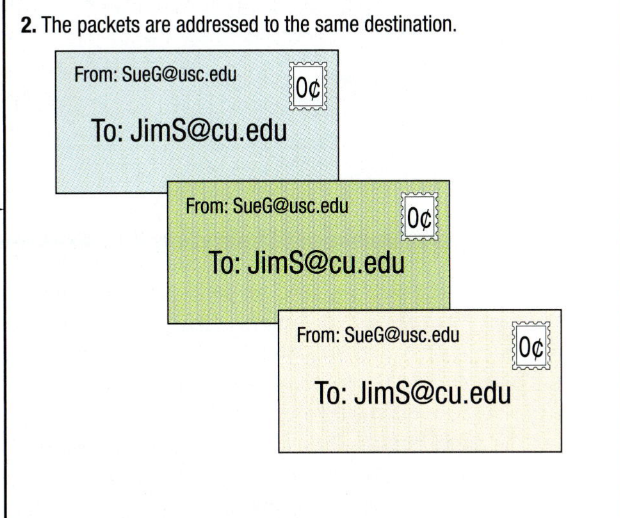

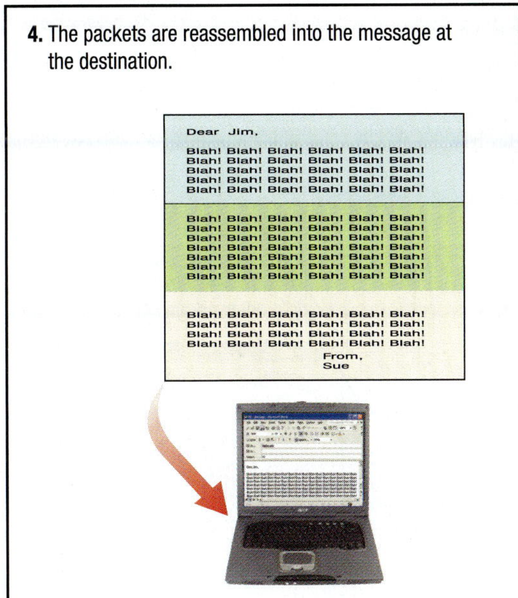

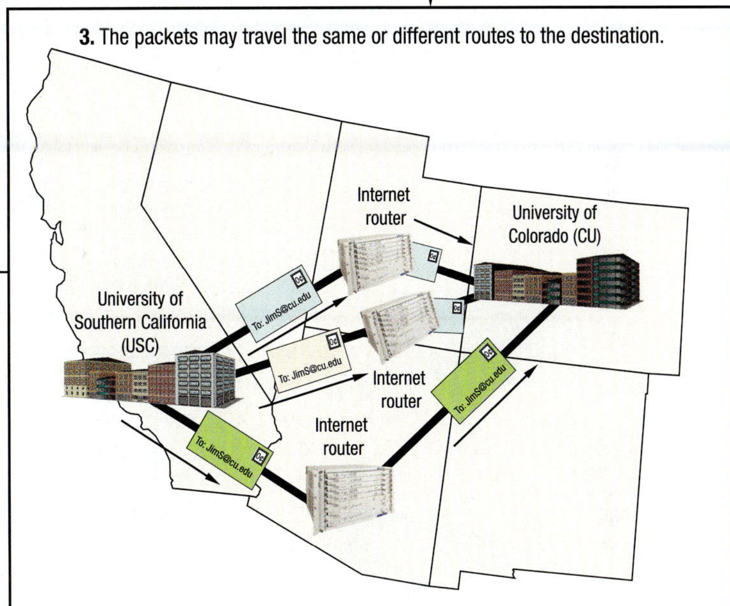

FIGURE 7-25
How TCP/IP networks work. TCP/IP networks (like the Internet) use packet switching.

Support for TCP/IP is built into many operating systems, and IP addresses are commonly used in conjunction with other protocols, such as Ethernet, to identify computers on a LAN. In recent years, packet switching has also begun to be used by telephone companies to provide faster, cheaper transmissions over telephone lines. For a look at how IP addresses are used when setting up an Ethernet home network with Windows PCs, see the How it Works box.

Wireless Application Protocol (**WAP**) is a standard for delivering content to mobile devices, smart phones, pagers, and other wireless communications devices using a cellular telephone network. The content that can be delivered using WAP includes both Web page content and e-mail. To display Web content, a WAP-enabled browser—sometimes called a *microbrowser*—needs to be installed on the device.

>**Wireless Application Protocol (WAP).** A standard for delivering content, such as Web pages, to mobile devices.

HOW IT WORKS

Setting Up a Home Network

The first step in setting up a home network is making sure you have the appropriate hardware and that it is installed correctly. For a wired network, you will need an Ethernet network adapter (usually either an internal card or external USB adapter) for each PC, a hub or switch, and enough Category 5 networking cables with RJ-45 connectors to connect each PC to the hub or switch. (Typically, a modem and a printer are connected to a single PC in the same manner they would be connected to a PC without the network; once connected and once the network is set up, then they are shared through the network.)

Next, you can run the Windows Networking Wizard, or you can change the networking settings manually (as in the accompanying illustration). In either case, you will need to assign a common network name, a unique computer name, and a unique IP address to each PC. The *host* PC connected to the Internet should use an IP address of 192.168.0.1 (IP addresses in the form 192.168.xxx.xxx are reserved for private local area networks and cannot be used as Internet IP addresses); the other PCs on the network can use 192.168.0.xxx, with each PC having a different final extension. You can assign the IP addresses manually, or you can choose to have the IP address assigned automatically. Use the host IP address (192.168.0.1) as the default *gateway* and *DNS server* for all other PCs on the network and use 255.255.255.0 as the *subnet mask*; also use the host IP address as the *proxy server* for the browsers on all other PCs to share the Internet connection. Finally, use Windows Explorer and the *Printers* option in the Control Panel to share drives, folders, and printers as needed, and you are good to go!

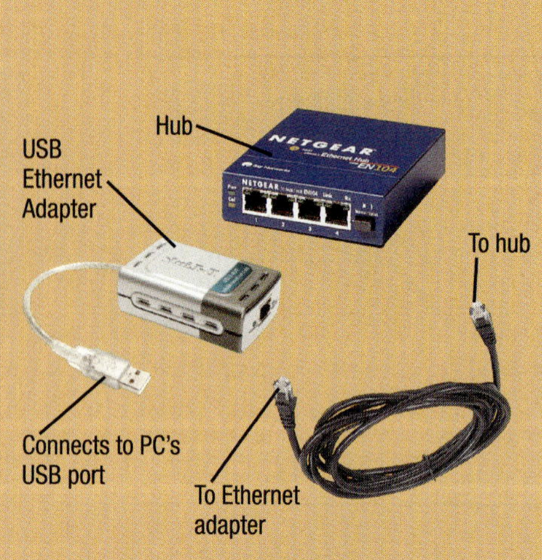

1. Make sure each PC has an Ethernet network adapter, then connect each PC to the hub.

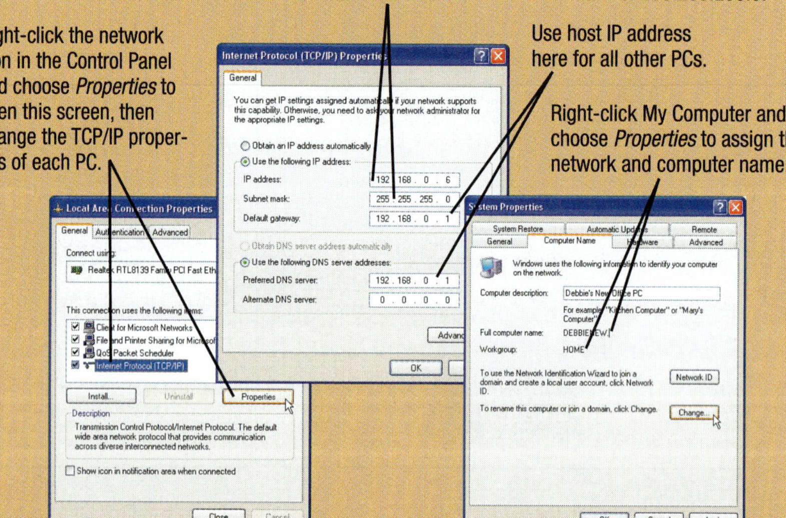

2. Assign an appropriate network name, computer name, and IP address to all PCs on the network. Use the host IP address as the default gateway and DNS server for all other PCs on the network.

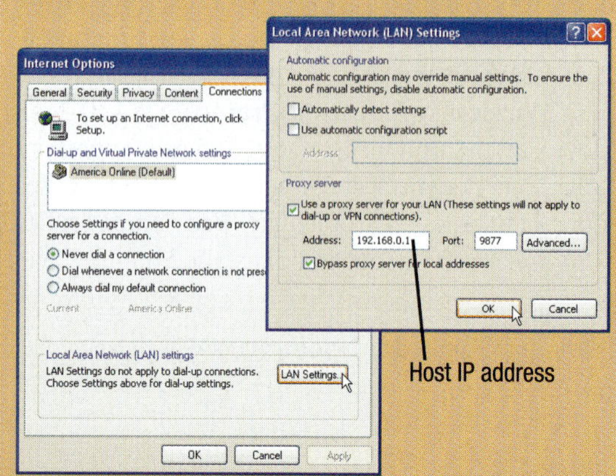

3. Change the settings of each PC's browser to use the host IP address as the proxy server.

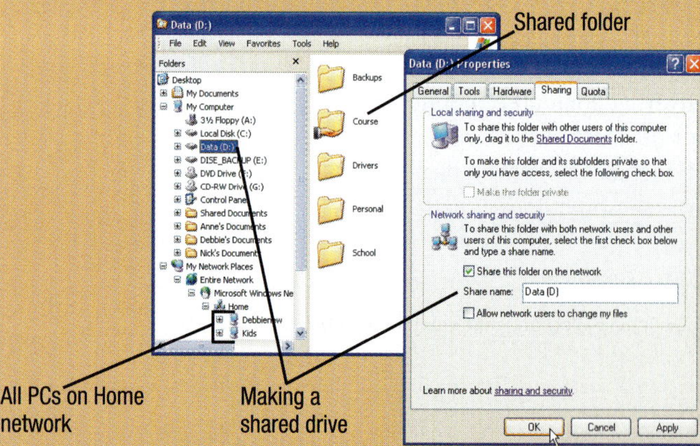

4. Share files, folders, and printers by right-clicking them and choosing the *Sharing* option.

Phoneline and Powerline Networks

The *Phoneline* (more officially called the *Home Phoneline Networking Association* or *Home PNA*) standard allows computers to be networked through ordinary phone wiring and phone jacks, without interfering with voice telephone calls. At its original speeds of 1 Mbps and then 10 Mbps, Phoneline has not been especially fast, but it is geared toward setting up quick and easy home networks, provided that phone jacks already exist at the necessary locations. The newest version of this standard—*HomePNA 3.0*—supports speeds up to 128 Mbps.

The *Powerline* standard allows PCs to be networked over existing power lines using conventional electrical outlets. Similar to Phoneline networks, Powerline networks are quick and easy to set up. In addition, they have the advantage that houses usually have more power outlets than phone outlets. Although relatively slow at roughly 10 Mbps (but a speed increase to 85 Mbps is expected in the near future), the Powerline standard also has great potential for countries in which phone jacks are not as prevalent as they are in the United States. While the original Powerline standard is designed for home computer networks, the upcoming second-generation Powerline standard—named *HomePlug AV*—is designed to network home entertainment devices at speeds of up to 200 Mbps. HomePlug AV will enable a variety of home entertainment devices (such as televisions, DVD players, cable boxes, stereo systems, and DVRs) to connect to each other and to the Internet for access to movies, music, and other forms of digital entertainment.

NETWORKING HARDWARE

Typically, there are a number of pieces of hardware necessary to create a computer network, to connect multiple networks together, or to connect a computer or network to the Internet. Some of the most common types of networking hardware are discussed next.

NET

Network Adapters

A **network adapter**, also called a **network interface card** (**NIC**) when it is in the form of an expansion card, is used to connect a PC to a network. A network adapter connects the PC physically to the network in order to send outgoing data from the PC to the network and to retrieve all incoming data sent via the network to the PC. The type of network adapter used depends on the type of network and communications media being used. For instance, to connect a PC to an Ethernet network using twisted-pair cabling, an Ethernet network adapter with an RJ-45 connector would be used. To connect a PC to a Wi-Fi network, a Wi-Fi network adapter would be used, but no cable is needed since it is a wireless connection. To connect to a Phoneline or Powerline network, a Phoneline or Powerline adapter, respectively, would be required.

In addition, the type of device being used and the available expansion slots and ports need to be considered. For example, network adapters for desktop PCs typically come in either PCI or USB format, and adapters for portable PCs usually connect via USB or a PC Card slot. The version of the networking protocol being used may also affect the type of networking hardware used. For instance, Ethernet hardware is rated for a particular speed. While networking hardware is backward compatible (so an adapter compatible with both the 10 and 100 Mbps standards could be used with either type of network), using a 100 Mbps adapter with a 10 Mbps network would only allow connection speeds of up to 10 Mbps. Some examples of network adapters are shown in Figure 7-26. Increasingly, computers and mobile devices are coming with networking capabilities built in, either via a network adapter or directly integrated into the device.

>**Network adapter.** A network interface, such as an expansion card or external network adapter. >**Network interface card (NIC).** An expansion card through which a computer can connect to a network.

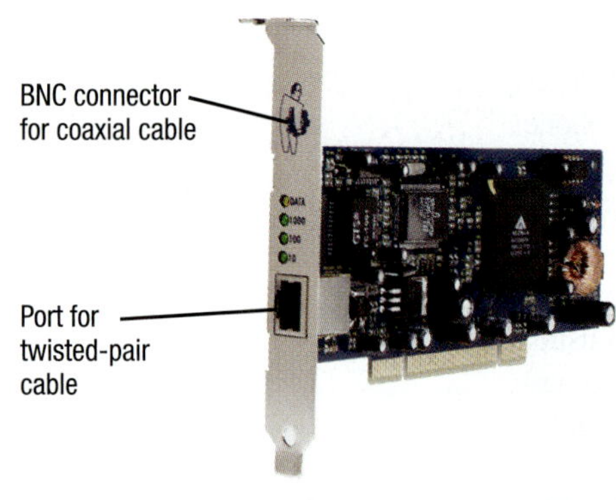

PCI ETHERNET ADAPTER FOR DESKTOP PC

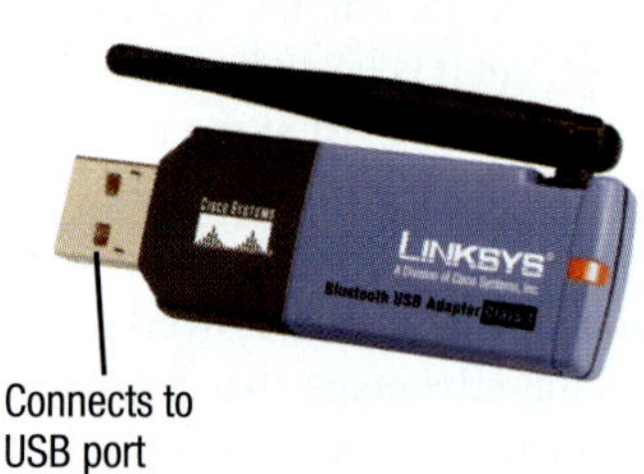

USB BLUETOOTH ADAPTER FOR DESKTOP OR NOTEBOOK PC

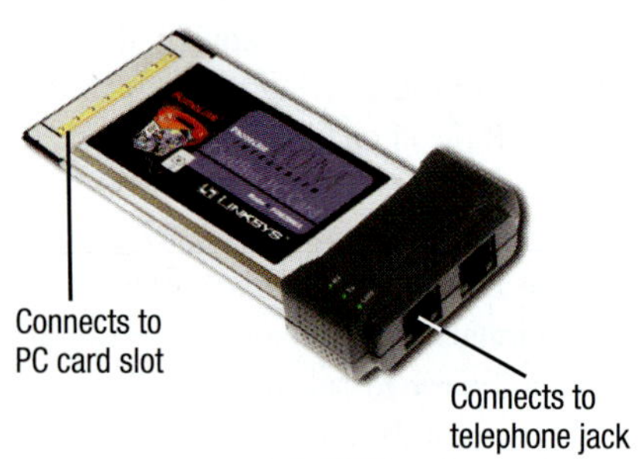

PHONELINE ADAPTER FOR NOTEBOOK PC

USB ETHERNET ADAPTER FOR DESKTOP OR NOTEBOOK PC

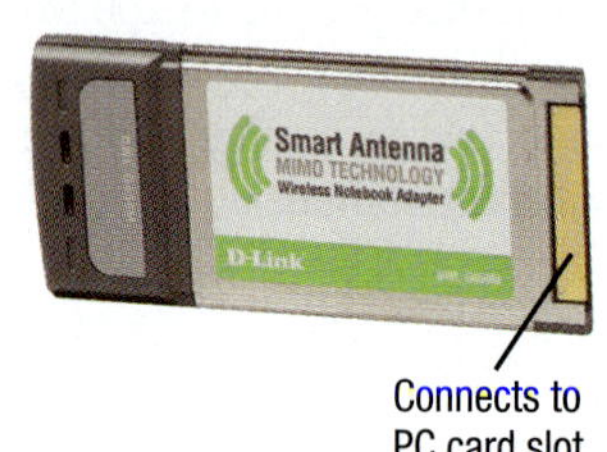

WI-FI ADAPTER FOR NOTEBOOK PC

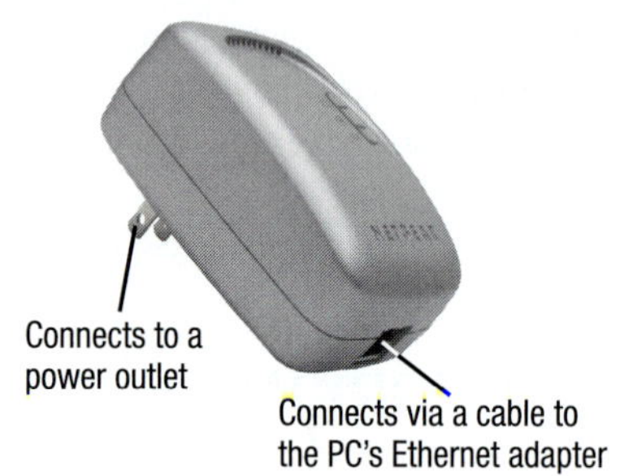

POWERLINE ETHERNET BRIDGE FOR DESKTOP OR NOTEBOOK PC

FIGURE 7-26

Network adapters. Network adapters are available in a variety of configurations.

Some wireless network adapters today conform to a new antenna technology called *MIMO* (for *multiple in, multiple out*), developed to speed up wireless networks or to extend their range. MIMO uses multiple smart antennas to transmit data directly to client devices, instead of transmitting in all directions like older Wi-Fi products. Consequently, data is transmitted faster and further. Network adapters that support the use of MIMO (such as the Wi-Fi adapter for a notebook PC shown in Figure 7-26) are now available. The current version of the emerging 802.11g *Fast Wi-Fi* standard uses MIMO technology.

Modems

Modem is the term used for a device that connects a computer to the Internet. The name comes from the terms *modulation* and *demodulation*. Modulation refers to converting digital signals (such as those from a PC) to analog form so they can be transmitted over analog media (such as conventional telephone lines). Demodulation refers to the translation from analog form back to digital form. There are a number of different types of modems today, each matching a particular type of Internet connection (such as *conventional dial-up*, *cable*, and *DSL*). Although not all of these types of connections require conversion between analog and digital form, the collection of devices used to connect a PC to the Internet are collectively referred to as "modems." Modems are available in a variety of formats—such as PCI, PC card, or external devices that connect via a USB or Ethernet connection (see Figure 7-27)—although not all types of modems may be available in all formats. Some common types of modems are discussed next; the types of Internet services that utilize these modems are discussed in more detail in Chapter 8.

>**Modem.** A communications device that enables digital computers to communicate over analog media, such as connecting to the Internet via telephone lines.

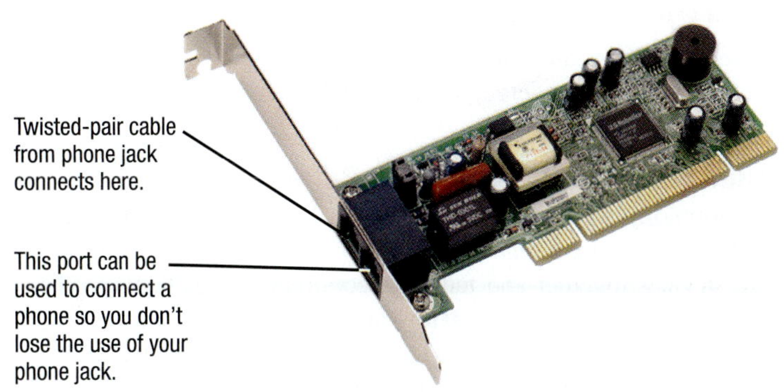

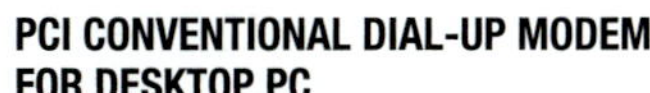

PCI CONVENTIONAL DIAL-UP MODEM FOR DESKTOP PC

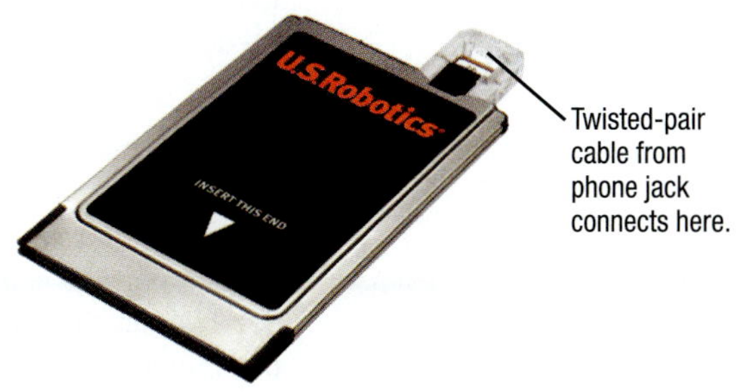

PC CARD CONVENTIONAL DIAL-UP MODEM FOR NOTEBOOK PC

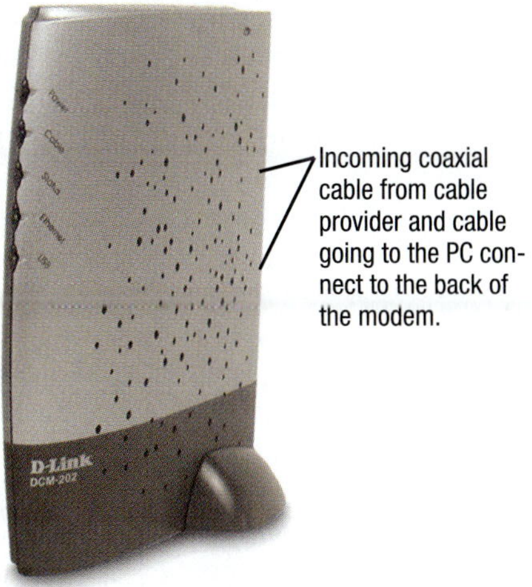

CABLE MODEM

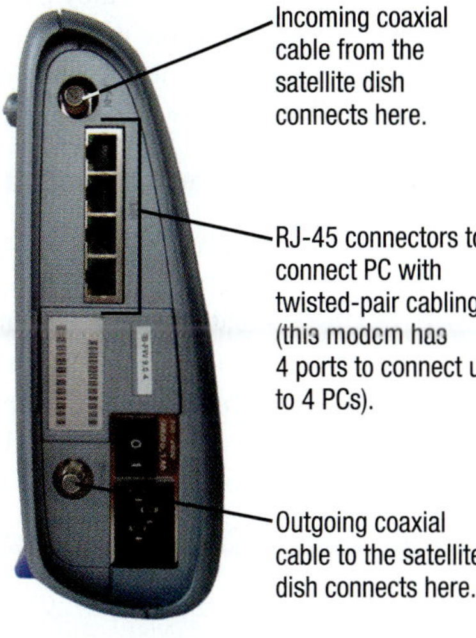

SATELLITE MODEM

FIGURE 7-27
Modems.

- *Conventional dial-up modems*—used to transmit and receive data via regular telephone lines and telephone jacks. The maximum speed for a conventional dial-up modem is 56 Kbps.
- *ISDN (integrated services digital network) modems*—used to transmit and receive data via ordinary telephone lines, similar to conventional dial-up, but by combining (*multiplexing*) signals, ISDN can transmit data faster than a conventional dial-up modem—up to 128 Kbps. To use an ISDN modem, the computer to which you are connecting (such as the one located at your ISP) must support ISDN service.
- *DSL (digital subscriber line) modems*—used to transmit and receive data over standard telephone lines and use a technology that does not tie up your telephone line, so you can use the Internet and make voice calls at the same time; data transmission is faster than via conventional or ISDN modems. DSL can only be used within three miles of a telephone switching station, and the speed degrades as the distance gets closer and closer to the three-mile limit. Consequently, DSL service is not available in all areas.
- *Cable modems*—used to connect a PC to cable Internet service, similar to the way cable boxes are used to obtain cable-TV service. Cable transmissions are similar in speed to DSL—around 1.5 Mbps.
- *Satellite modems*—used to transmit and receive data via a personal satellite dish. Satellite transmissions are a little slower than both DSL and cable transmissions, but they have the advantage of being able to be used in rural areas.

TIP

On a small network, such as a home network, if one PC has a modem and is set up to access the Internet, all PCs on the network can be set up to share that Internet connection without needing additional modems—they connect to the Internet via the network.

Hubs, Switches, and Other Networking Hardware

In addition to network adapters, modems, and cabling, other networking hardware is often needed to tie the components of a network together, or to tie multiple networks together.

Hubs, Switches, Routers, and Wireless Access Points

As already mentioned, star topology networks need a central device to connect all the devices on the network. This device can be a *hub*, *switch*, or *router*. All of these devices contain ports to connect the devices together and facilitate communications between the devices, but they differ in how they transfer data. **Hubs** are the least sophisticated and transmit all data received to all network nodes connected to the hub. Consequently, with a hub, the network capacity is shared among the nodes. In contrast, a **switch** identifies the device for which the data is intended and sends the network data to that node only. This allows each node on the network to use the full capacity of the network. **Routers** are even smarter—they pass data on to the intended recipient only, but they can plan a path through multiple routers to ensure the data reaches its destination in the most efficient manner possible. Routers are used in LANs, WANs, and the Internet. They are also used to extend the range of a wireless network, such as a home or business Wi-Fi network.

A **wireless access point** is a device that functions similarly to a hub, but it is used to connect wireless devices to a wired network. Wireless access points can be used in home networks to connect the devices and share an Internet connection; they can also be used at public hotspots to connect wireless users to a wired Internet connection, such as DSL or cable Internet connections.

Some devices may contain the functions of two or more networking devices. For instance, some cable or satellite modems contain a built-in router to connect multiple PCs to the modem, and some wireless access points have a built-in router to connect a cable or DSL modem plus a built-in switch to connect wired devices to the network. An example of how all the devices discussed in this section, as well as the other networking hardware discussed in the next few sections, might be used in networks is shown in Figure 7-28.

Gateways and Bridges

When one network needs to connect to another network, a gateway or bridge is used.

- A *gateway* is a device that connects two *dissimilar* networks, such as two networks using different networking communications protocols.
- A *bridge* is a device that connects two networks based on *similar* technology—such as a LAN in one city and a similar LAN in another. Bridges can also be used to partition one large LAN into two smaller ones.

Repeaters

Repeaters are devices that amplify signals along a network. They are necessary whenever signals have to travel farther than would otherwise be possible over the networking medium being used.

Multiplexers and Concentrators

High-speed communications lines are expensive and almost always have far greater capacity than a single device can use. Because of this, signals from multiple devices are often combined and sent together to share a single communications medium. A *multiplexer* combines

>**Hub.** A device that is a central location where data arrives and is then transferred in one or more directions. >**Switch.** A device on a network to which data is sent so it can be forwarded to the appropriate network node. >**Router.** A device on a network that sends data via the most efficient route to travel to a specific location. >**Wireless access point.** A device used to connect wireless devices to a wired network.

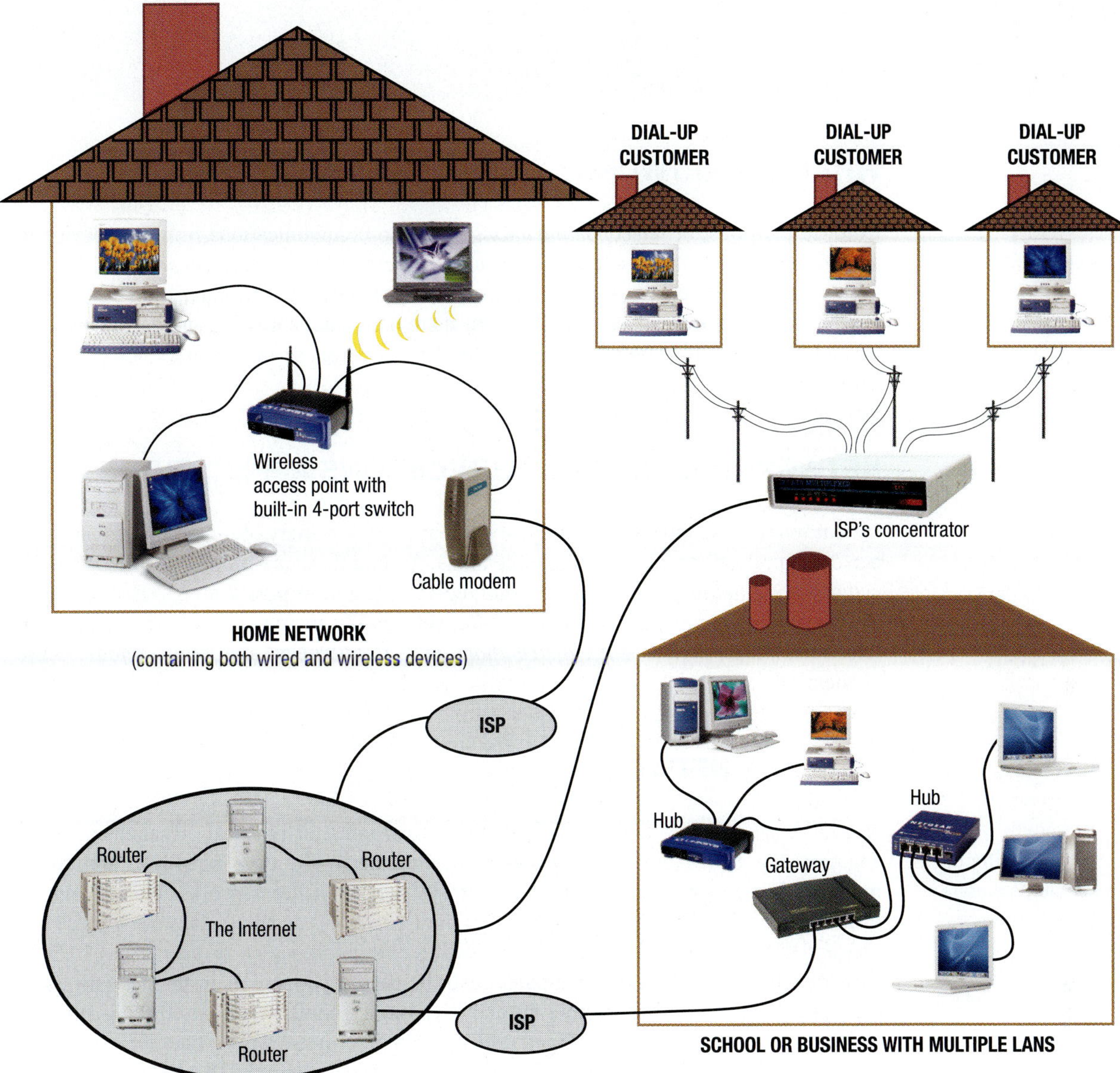

FIGURE 7-28

Networking hardware. As shown in this example, many different types of hardware are needed to connect networking devices.

the transmissions from several different devices and sends them as one message. With *Frequency Division Multiplexing* (*FDM*), each signal is assigned a different frequency over which to travel; with *Wave Division Multiplexing* (*WDM*), each signal is assigned a different wavelength (WDM can be used with fiber-optic cables only). With any type of multiplexing, when the combined signal reaches its destination, the individual messages are separated from one another. Multiplexing is frequently used with fiber-optic cables and other high-capacity media to increase data throughput. For instance, if eight signals are multiplexed together and sent over each fiber in a fiber-optic cable, the throughput of the cable is increased by a factor of eight. Using more wavelengths, such as in *Dense WDM* (*DWDM*), even more data can be transmitted at one time.

A *concentrator* is a type of multiplexer that combines multiple messages and sends them via a single transmission medium in such a way that all the individual messages are simultaneously active, instead of being sent as a single combined message. For example, ISPs often use concentrators to combine the signals from their conventional dial-up modem customers to be sent over faster communications connections to their Internet destinations.

NET

SUMMARY

WHAT IS A NETWORK?

Chapter Objective 1:
Define a network and its purpose.

Communications, or *telecommunications*, refers to communications from one device to another over a distance—such as over long-distance phone lines, via privately owned cables, or by satellite. A **computer network** is a collection of computers and other hardware devices that are connected together to share hardware, software, and data, as well as to facilitate electronic communications. One area of recent growth is in the area of *home networks*.

NETWORKING AND COMMUNICATIONS APPLICATIONS

Chapter Objective 2:
Describe several uses for communications technology.

In addition to basic Internet searching and e-mail, a wide variety of important business and personal applications involve communications. Among these are **mobile phones** (namely, *cellular* and *satellite phones*), *paging* and *messaging*, **global positioning systems (GPS)**, electronic monitoring systems, *satellite radio*, **videoconferencing**, *collaborative computing*, **telecommuting**, *digital data distribution*, and **telesurgery** and other **telemedicine** applications.

TYPES OF NETWORKS

Chapter Objective 3:
Understand the various topologies and architectures a computer network might use.

Chapter Objective 4:
Explain the difference between a LAN, a WAN, and a PAN, and between an intranet, an extranet, and a VPN.

Networks can be classified in terms of their *topologies*, or physical arrangement. Four common topologies are the **star network**, **bus network**, **ring network**, and **mesh network**. Network topologies are often combined when smaller networks are connected to make a larger one. Networks are typically either *client-server* networks, which consist of *server* devices that provide network services to *client* computers, or *peer-to-peer* (*P2P*) networks, in which the users' computers and the shared peripherals in the network communicate directly with one another instead of through a server. With *Internet peer to peer* (*P2P*) *computing*, files are exchanged directly with other peers via the Internet.

Networks can also be classified by size. **Local area networks (LANs)** connect geographically close devices, such as within a single building. **Wide area networks (WANs)** span relatively wide geographical areas. Other possibilities include *metropolitan area networks* (*MANs*) that provide Internet access to cities; *personal area networks* (*PANs*) that connect the devices immediately around an individual; **intranets** (private networks that implement the infrastructure and standards of the Internet and World Wide Web); **extranets** (intranets that are accessible to authorized outsiders); and **virtual private networks (VPNs)** used to transfer private information over a public communications system.

HOW DOES DATA TRAVEL OVER A NETWORK?

Chapter Objective 5:
Understand characteristics about data and how it travels over a network.

Data that travels over a network can be *analog*—that is, sent as continuous waves. Computer hardware, however, are *digital* devices that handle data coded into 0s and 1s. Data transmissions can be characterized by their **bandwidth** (the amount of data that can be transferred over the medium at one time), whether they use **serial transmission** or **parallel transmission**, whether they transmit in *simplex*, *half-duplex*, *or full-duplex* directions, and how the transmissions are timed (namely, *synchronous*, *asynchronous*, or *isochronous transmission*).

Computer networks can be **wired networks** or **wireless networks**, depending on the type of transmission media used. Wired transmission media include **twisted-pair**, **coaxial**, and **fiber-optic cable**. Wireless networks typically send messages through the air in the form of *radio signals*. Wireless networks typically use *broadcast radio*, **microwave stations**, or **communications satellites** (which send and receive data to and from microwave stations and satellites), or **cellular radio** (which sends and receives data via cell towers located within designated areas or *cells*) technology. Wired networks are found in businesses and some homes. Wireless networks are becoming more common in businesses and homes because they do not require physical wiring and they allow the user more mobility. Wireless networks are also commonly used in public locations to provide a wireless connection to a public wireless access point, designed to provide Internet access to the general public.

Chapter Objective 6:
Name specific types of wired and wireless transmission media and explain how they transmit data.

COMMUNICATIONS PROTOCOLS

A *communications protocol* is a collection of procedures to establish, maintain, and terminate transmissions between devices. Because devices transmit data in so many ways, they collectively employ scores of different protocols. Four of the most commonly used networking protocols are **Ethernet**, **Token Ring**, **Wi-Fi (802.11)**, and **TCP/IP**. Wi-Fi is designed for medium-range wireless transmissions, and there are various versions of the standard; the most common today is *802.11g*. Other emerging wireless standards are *wireless mesh* (used to connect wireless devices and networks, as well as to extend the range of wireless networks), **WiMAX** (an emerging wireless standard with a larger range than Wi-Fi), *Mobile-Fi* (a version of WiMAX designed for use while on the go), and *xMax* (which utilizes the unused portions of radio channels used for pagers and TV signals). Wireless networks typically use the 802.11 (Wi-Fi) protocol. For short-range applications (such as wirelessly connecting a keyboard to a PC), **Bluetooth** can be used. *Ultra Wideband* (*UWB*) is a newer standard that can connect devices faster and with a longer range than Bluetooth. **Wireless Application Protocol (WAP)** is a standard for delivering content, such as Web pages, to mobile devices. For home networks, the *Phoneline* or *Powerline* standards may be used instead.

Chapter Objective 7:
Identify different protocols that can be used to connect the devices on a network.

NET

NETWORKING HARDWARE

Computer networks require a variety of hardware. PCs usually connect to a network through either a **network adapter**—called a **network interface card** (**NIC**) when it is in the form of an expansion card—or a **modem**, which converts signals between digital and analog mode as needed. The type of adapter or modem used depends on the type of connection and computer to be used. Possible modems include *conventional dial-up*, *ISDN* (*integrated services digital network*), *DSL* (*digital subscriber line*), *cable*, and *satellite modems*. A **hub** is a device on a network that provides a central location where data arrives and then is transferred on. **Switches** and **routers** can also be used to pass network messages along to their destinations. A **wireless access point** is used to connect wireless devices to a network. Devices on two dissimilar networks can communicate with each other if the networks are connected by a *gateway*. Devices on two similar networks can communicate with each other if they are connected by a *bridge*. *Repeaters*, *multiplexers*, and *concentrators* are most commonly used with larger networks.

Chapter Objective 8:
List several types of networking hardware and explain the purpose of each.

REVIEW ACTIVITIES

KEY TERM MATCHING

Instructions: Match each key term on the left with the definition on the right that best describes it.

a. bandwidth

b. Bluetooth

c. computer network

d. Ethernet

e. global positioning system (GPS)

f. local area network (LAN)

g. mesh network

h. network interface card (NIC)

i. TCP/IP

j. WiMAX

1. ______ A collection of computers and other hardware devices that are connected together to share hardware, software, and data, as well as to communicate electronically with one another.

2. ______ A communications standard for very short-range wireless connections; the devices are automatically connected once they get within the allowable range.

3. ______ A network in which there are multiple connections between the devices on the network so that messages can take any of several possible paths.

4. ______ A network that connects devices located in a small geographical area, such as within a building.

5. ______ An emerging wireless networking standard that is faster and has a greater range than Wi-Fi.

6. ______ An expansion card through which a computer can connect to a network.

7. ______ A system that uses satellites and a receiver to determine the exact geographic location of the receiver.

8. ______ A widely used communications protocol for a LAN.

9. ______ The amount of data that can be transmitted over a communications medium at one time.

10. ______ The communications protocol that uses packet switching to facilitate the transmission of messages; the protocol used with the Internet.

SELF-QUIZ

Instructions: Circle **T** if the statement is true, **F** if the statement is false, or write the best answer in the space provided. **Answers to the self-quiz are located in the References and Resources Guide at the end of the book.**

1. **T F** GPS systems are used only by the government.

2. **T F** With serial transmissions, each bit of data is sent individually.

3. **T F** The Internet is an example of a LAN.

4. **T F** The type of cable used inside most homes for telephone service is twisted-pair wire.

5. **T F** A router is a type of modem.

6. Using communications technology to work from home is called ______.

7. With a(n) ______ network topology, all devices are connected in a line to a central cable.

8. A(n) ______ orbits the earth to send and receive high-frequency, high-speed radio signals.

9. A(n) ______ is a network that transfers private information securely over the Internet or other public network.

10. Match each description to its communications application, and write the corresponding number in the blank to the left of the description.

    a. ________ To diagnose a patient from a distance.
    b. ________ To conduct a meeting between people located at the corporate headquarters in Los Angeles and a Miami-based clothing designer to decide which pieces to include in the final summer swimsuit line.
    c. ________ To work from New York when you live in California.
    d. ________ To drive across the country listening to continuous music.
    e. ________ To receive telephone calls while you are out shopping.
    f. ________ To determine your physical location while hiking in the mountains.

    1. Satellite radio
    2. Telecommuting
    3. GPS
    4. Videoconferencing
    5. Telemedicine
    6. Cellular phone

EXERCISES

1. Answer the following questions about the network to the right.
   a. What topology does the network use? ________
   b. How many nodes are connected to the network? ________
   c. Is this a wired or wireless network? ________
   d. Does this network use a hub? ________
2. For each modem, indicate whether or not it allows for data transmission over ordinary telephone lines.

Type of Modem	Transmits Over Telephone Lines?
a. Cable modem	________
b. Conventional dial-up modem	________
c. DSL modem	________
d. ISDN modem	________
e. Satellite modem	________

3. If you need to download a 350 KB file and have a 56 Kbps conventional dial-up modem, how long should it take to download the file? What real-world conditions might affect this download time?
4. What communications protocol does the Internet use?
5. Explain the difference between Wi-Fi and Bluetooth, including what purposes each protocol is designed for.

NET

DISCUSSION QUESTION

With so many wireless devices available today, interference is happening much more often than in the past. For instance, unlicensed walkie-talkies used on the set of the *Law & Order* television show interfered with real police radios, military radios now using the same frequency as some garage door openers are opening and closing nearby garage doors, and British air traffic control transmissions have been interrupted by transmissions from nearby baby monitors. Although the Federal Communications Commission (FCC) regulates the airwaves in the United States, there are some radio frequencies—such as the popular 2.4 GHz band used by cordless phones and most versions of Wi-Fi—that are unregulated. If commonly used devices interfere with each other, whose fault is it? The individual for buying multiple products that use the same radio frequency? The manufacturers for not developing safeguards for their products to ensure the products switch channels if one is in use? The government for allowing unregulated airwaves? Regulating all airwaves would solve the problem, but then products that normally use unregulated airwaves (Wi-Fi networks, cordless phones, two-way radios, baby monitors, and so forth) would likely not be developed or would be significantly more expensive. In addition, since these products have already found acceptance and wide-spread use among the general public, there would probably be an uproar over such regulation. Is there a solution to this problem? With an increasing number of products going wireless, the problem is likely to get worse before it gets better. Who, if anyone, should be responsible for fixing this problem?

PROJECTS

HOT TOPICS

1. **WiMAX vs. Wi-Fi** As discussed in the chapter, WiMAX and Wi-Fi are both wireless networking standards.

   For this project, research WiMAX and Wi-Fi to determine their current status and the differences between the two standards. Are they designed for the same or different purposes? Explain. Are they both being used today? If not, when are they expected to become available? Do you think the standards will coexist in the future, or will one eventually replace the other? At the conclusion of your research, prepare a one-page summary of your findings and submit it to your instructor.

SHORT ANSWER/ RESEARCH

2. **E-Clothing** As computing and communications devices continue to grow smaller and be carried by many individuals at all times, clothing manufacturers have begun to adapt by creating shorts, pants, jackets, vests, and more with pockets and compartments for cell phones, handheld PCs, portable digital music players, ear buds, and so forth.

   For this project, research e-clothing and identify at least two products that are commercially available. Summarize each product, listing all of the capabilities of the garment, what devices the garment is designed for, and what market the product is designed for. Do any of the products contain features to facilitate a PAN? Be sure to include where the product can be purchased and the suggested retail price. Would you buy either of these garments? Why or why not? Do you think the e-clothing trend will continue to grow, or is it a passing fad? Submit your findings and opinion to your instructor in the format of a one-page paper.

3. **Unwired** As discussed in the chapter, home networks—particularly wireless home networks—are becoming very common today.

   For this project, suppose that you have a home desktop computer and are planning to buy a notebook PC to use at home, as well as on the go. You would like to network the two PCs wirelessly. Determine the hardware you will need to accomplish this. Create a labeled sketch of the network and a list of the hardware you would need to acquire. Next, research the approximate cost of the hardware to determine the overall cost of the network. Does the cost seem reasonable? Would you want to network your home PCs in this manner? If you wanted to also use a printer with both PCs, would you need any additional hardware? At the conclusion of your research, prepare a one-page summary of your findings and submit it to your instructor, along with your sketch and list of hardware.

HANDS ON

4. **Network Topology** As discussed in the chapter, a network's topology refers to the shape in which the computers are connected to the network.

   For this project, investigate a computer lab you have access to on your campus. Draw a sketch of the lab to indicate how the computers are connected, what type of cabling is being used, and what other hardware is included on the network. Indicate the network's topology, as well as whether it is a client-server network or a peer-to-peer network. Finally, log on to a computer in the lab and determine the network resources (such as network hard drives and printers) available to you. At the conclusion of this task, prepare a one-page summary of its findings to submit to your instructor along with the network diagram.

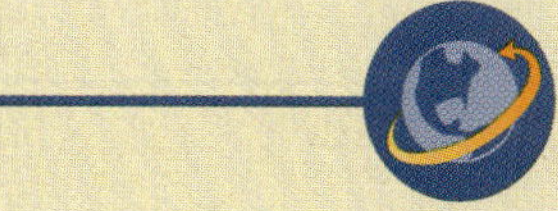

5. **Geocaching** Geocaching is a GPS application that is essentially a form of high-tech hide and seek—someone hides a water-tight container filled with a "treasure" (usually toys or cheap collectors' goodies) and posts the location of the cache (in GPS coordinates) on a geocaching Web site. Other individuals use their GPS equipment to find the cache and then sign a log (if one is included in the cache), take an item from the cache, and put another object into the cache as a replacement. Many caches are stored in scenic locations that individuals and organizations would like others to experience.

   For this project, by searching online or visiting a geocaching Web site, such as geocaching.com, find out how to geocache, including what GPS equipment you would need and any "rules" or courtesies common among geocachers regarding listing or finding a cache, appropriate items for including in a cache, and so forth. Next, use the site to find information about a cache currently hidden close to your city and determine what you would need to do in order to find it. At the conclusion of your research, prepare a one-page summary of your findings and submit it to your instructor.

WRITING ABOUT COMPUTERS

6. **Internet P2P** As discussed in the chapter, peer-to-peer (P2P) networking involves sharing files and other resources directly with other computers, without going through a network server. It is often used for small home networks, as well as via the Internet. Internet P2P computing has been used in the past to illegally exchange copyrighted materials, such as music and movie files. However, it also has legitimate applications.

   For this project, research P2P computing and identify two legal and ethical uses of Internet P2P networking. What are the advantages over using a client-server network for these applications? Are there any disadvantages? How, if at all, should Internet P2P networks be regulated? What if a P2P network set up for legitimate use is used for illegal purposes—should the organization or person who set up the P2P network be responsible? Why or why not? Do you think P2P network use will continue to grow? Would you want to use a P2P network? Submit this project to your instructor in the form of a short paper, not more than two pages in length.

PRESENTATION/ DEMONSTRATION

7. **Wired Home Network** If you have two or more computers at home and want to share files, an Internet connection, or a printer, you will need to set up a home network. Although a wireless network is an option, wired networks still exist and new options for wired networks are emerging.

   For this project, suppose that you want to set up a wired home network. Create a scenario (real or fictitious) that describes the number of PCs and other devices involved, where each item is located, and the tasks for which the network will be used. Select a wired networking option (such as Ethernet, Powerline, or Phoneline) and determine the steps and equipment necessary to implement that network for your scenario. Be sure to include the cost of the necessary hardware and how the network would be physically installed. Share your findings (including a diagram of your proposed network) with your class in the form of a presentation. The presentation should not exceed 10 minutes and should make use of one or more presentation aids, such as the chalkboard, handouts, overhead transparencies, or a computer-based slide presentation (your instructor may provide additional requirements). You may also be asked to submit a summary of the presentation to your instructor.

GROUP DISCUSSION

8. **Regulating Broadband** The year 2005 had a number of interesting rulings and proposed legislation regarding broadband Internet. Two examples are the decision by the Federal Communications Commission (FCC) to free telephone companies from the requirement of sharing their broadband lines with rival ISPs and the ruling by the Supreme Court that freed cable companies from similar requirements. These decisions are expected to impact a number of ISPs who relied on these communications media to provide Internet access—typically DSL Internet access—to their customers. An additional example is the proposed legislation by U.S. House of Representatives member Pete Sessions to prohibit cities from providing any Wi-Fi service that is "substantially similar" to services provided by private companies—essentially banning the free or low-cost Wi-Fi Internet access many cities are currently offering or are planning to offer to their citizens. How much government interference and regulation is needed in the communications industry? If numerous small ISPs are driven out of business by the FCC and U.S. Supreme Court decisions, what impact will that have on ISP selection, services, and price? Does the federal government have the right to ban cities or states from providing Internet access to its residents? Why or why not?

   For this project, form an opinion of the appropriate level of governance needed in the communications industry and be prepared to discuss your position (in class, via an online class discussion group, or in a class chat room, depending on your instructor's directions). You may also be asked to write a short paper expressing your opinion.

WEB ACTIVITIES

The ***Understanding Computers*** Web site located at **www.course.com/uc11** features many resources to help reinforce your understanding of the chapter content and help you prepare for exams. Your instructor may also assign specific activities to be completed that will count toward your final grade in the course.

Instructions: Go to **www.course.com/uc11/ch07** to work the following online activities.

Click any link in the navigation bar on the left to access any of the online resources described below.

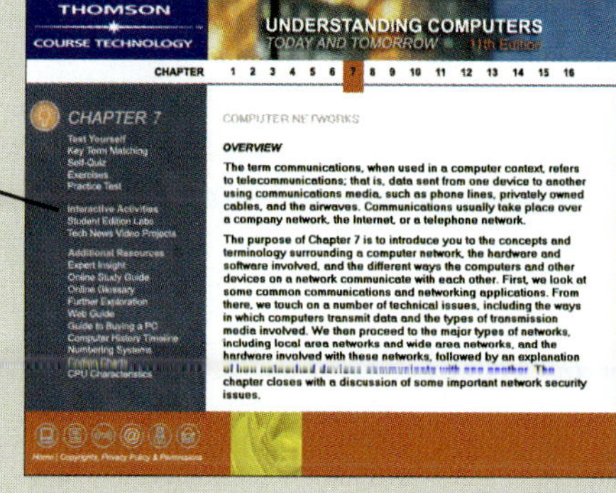

INTERACTIVE ACTIVITIES

1. **Crossword Puzzle** Practice your knowledge of the key terms in Chapter 7 by completing the interactive Crossword Puzzle.
2. **Tech News Video Project** Watch the **"Witness Vehicle Protection System"** video clip that features a vehicle protection system that uses GPS and other communications technology to locate your car, unlock the doors, and perform other tasks at your request. After watching the video online, complete the corresponding project.
3. **Student Edition Labs** Reinforce the concepts you have learned in this chapter by working through the **Networking Basics** and **Wireless Networking** interactive labs.

NET

TEST YOURSELF

1. **Key Term Matching** Test your knowledge of selected chapter key terms by matching the terms with their definitions.
2. **Self-Quiz** Test your retention of chapter concepts by taking the Self-Quiz.
3. **Exercises** Work these short exercises to review the concepts and terms covered in the chapter.
4. **Practice Test** Test how ready you are for an upcoming exam by completing the online Practice Test.

STUDY TOOLS/ ADDITIONAL RESOURCES

The Understanding Computers Web site has a wide range of additional resources, including an **Online Study Guide** (containing study tips, a chapter outline with room to add your own notes, and a chapter checklist of the activities to complete when the chapter is covered in class and when you are preparing for a test) and an **Online Glossary** for each chapter; **Further Exploration** links; a **Web Guide**, a **Guide to Buying a PC**, and a **Computer History Timeline**; more information about **Numbering Systems**, **Coding Charts**, and **CPU Characteristics**; and much, much more!

CHAPTER 8 The Internet and World Wide Web

OUTLINE

Overview
Evolution of the Internet
From ARPANET to Internet2
The Internet Community Today
Myths About the Internet
Getting Set Up to Use the Internet
Type of Device
Type of Connection and Internet Access
Selecting an ISP and Setting Up Your PC
Searching the Internet
Search Sites
Search Strategies
Evaluating Search Results
Citing Internet Resources
Beyond Browsing and E-Mail
Discussion Groups, Instant Messaging, and Other Types of Online Communications
Online Shopping and Investing
Online Entertainment
Peer-to-Peer File Sharing
Online News and Research
Online Education and Writing
Censorship and Privacy Issues
Censorship
Web Browsing Privacy
E-Mail Privacy
The Future of the Internet

LEARNING OBJECTIVES

After completing this chapter, you will be able to:

1. Discuss how the Internet evolved and what it is like today.
2. Identify the various types of individuals, companies, and organizations involved in the Internet community and explain their purposes.
3. Describe device and connection options for connecting to the Internet, as well as some considerations to keep in mind when selecting an ISP.
4. Understand how to effectively search for information on the Internet and how to properly cite Internet resources.
5. List several useful things that can be done using the Internet, in addition to basic Web browsing and e-mail.
6. Discuss censorship and privacy, and how they are related to Internet use.
7. Describe the possible format, structure, and use of the Internet in the future.

OVERVIEW

It is hard to believe that before 1990 few people outside the computer industry and academia had ever heard of the Internet, and even fewer had used it. Why? Because the hardware, software, and communications tools needed to unleash the power of the Internet as we know it today were not available then. In fact, it is only in the last few years that technology has evolved enough to allow multimedia applications—such as downloading music and movies, playing interactive games, and viewing animated presentations—to become an everyday activity. What a difference a few years can make. Today, the Internet and the World Wide Web are household words, and in many ways they have redefined how people think about computers and communications.

Despite the popularity of the Internet, however, many users cannot answer some important basic questions about it. What makes up the Internet? Is it the same thing as the World Wide Web? How did the Internet begin, and where is it heading? What types of tools are available to help people make the optimal use of the Internet? How can the Internet be used to find specific information? This chapter addresses these types of questions.

Chapter 8 begins with a discussion of the evolution of the Internet, from the late 1960s to the present, followed by a look at the many individuals, companies, and organizations that make up the Internet community. Next, the chapter covers the different options for connecting to the Internet, including the types of Internet access devices, Internet connections, and ISPs available today. Then, it is on to one of the most important Internet skills you should acquire—efficient Internet searching. To help you appreciate the wide spectrum of resources and activities available through the Internet, we also take a brief look at some of the most common applications available via the Internet. The final sections of the chapter discuss a few of the important societal issues that apply to Internet use and take a look at the Internet's future. ■

EVOLUTION OF THE INTERNET

The **Internet** is a worldwide collection of separate, but interconnected, networks that are accessed daily by millions of people to obtain information, disseminate information, or communicate with others. Just as the shipping industry has simplified transportation by providing standard containers for carrying all sorts of merchandise via air, rail, highway, and sea, the Internet furnishes a standard way of sending messages and information across virtually any type of computer platform and transmission media. While *Internet* has become a household word only during the past decade, it has actually operated in one form or another for much longer than that.

>**Internet.** The largest and most well-known computer network, linking millions of computers all over the world.

From ARPANET to Internet2

The roots of the Internet began with an experimental project called *ARPANET*. The Internet we know today is the result of the evolution of ARPANET and the creation of the *World Wide Web*.

ARPANET

ARPANET was created in 1969 by the U.S. Department of Defense's *Advanced Research Projects Agency (ARPA)*. One objective of the ARPANET project was to create a computer network that would allow researchers located in different places to communicate with each other. Another objective was to build a computer network capable of sending or receiving data over a variety of paths to ensure that network communications could continue even if part of the network was destroyed, such as in a nuclear attack or by a natural disaster.

Initially, ARPANET connected four supercomputers. As it grew during its first few years, ARPANET enabled researchers at a few dozen academic institutions to communicate with each other and with government agencies on topics of mutual interest. However, with the highly controversial Vietnam War in full swing, ARPANET's e-mail facility began to handle not only legitimate research discussions but also heated debates about United States involvement in Southeast Asia. As students were granted access to ARPANET, other unintended uses—such as playing computer games—also began.

As the experiment grew during the next decade, hundreds of college and university networks were connected to ARPANET. These local area networks consisted of a mixture of DOS-based and Windows-based computers, Apple Macintosh computers, and UNIX workstations. Over the years, *protocols* (standard procedures) were developed for tying this mix of computers and networks together, for transferring data over the network, and for ensuring that data was transferred intact. Other networks soon connected to ARPANET, and this *internet*—or network of networks—eventually evolved into the present day Internet.

The Internet infrastructure today can be used for a variety of purposes, such as exchanging e-mail and instant messages; participating in discussion groups, chat sessions, and videoconferences; downloading software and music; purchasing goods and services; accessing computers remotely; and transferring files between Internet users. One of the most widely used Internet resources is the *World Wide Web*.

The World Wide Web

In its early years, the Internet was used primarily by the government, scientists, and educational institutions. Despite its popularity in academia and with government researchers, the Internet went virtually unnoticed by the general public and the business community for over two decades because it required a computer, and it was hard to use (see the left image in Figure 8-1). As always, however, technology improved and new applications quickly followed. First, communications hardware improved, and then computers gained speed and better graphics capabilities. Then, in 1989, a researcher named Tim Berners-Lee proposed the idea of the **World Wide Web** while working at *CERN* (a physics laboratory in Europe). He envisioned the World Wide Web as a way to organize information in the form of pages linked together through selectable text or images (today's hyperlinks) on the screen. Although the introduction of Web pages did not replace other Internet resources (such as e-mail and collections of downloadable files), it became a popular way for researchers to provide written information to others.

>**ARPANET.** The predecessor of the Internet, named after the Advanced Research Projects Agency (ARPA), which sponsored its development.

>**World Wide Web.** The collection of Web pages available through the Internet.

Things really got rolling with the arrival of the graphical user interface. In 1993, a group of professors and students at the University of Illinois *National Center for Supercomputing Applications* (*NCSA*) released *Mosaic*, the first graphically based Web browser. Mosaic used a graphical user interface and allowed Web pages to include graphical images in addition to text. Soon after, use of the World Wide Web began to increase dramatically because the graphical interface and graphical Web pages made using the World Wide Web both easier and more fun than in the past. Today's Web pages are a true multimedia experience. They can contain text, graphics, animation, sound, video, and three-dimensional virtual reality objects (refer to the right image in Figure 8-1).

EARLY 1990s
Even at the beginning of the 1990s, using the Internet for most people meant learning how to work with a cryptic sequence of commands. Virtually all information was text-based.

TODAY
Today's Web pages organize much of the Internet's content into easy-to-read pages that can contain text graphics, animation, and more. Instead of typing cryptic commands to access information, users click hyperlinks.

FIGURE 8-1
Using the Internet. Back in the "old days" versus now.

Although the Web is only part of the Internet, it is by far one of the most popular and one of the fastest-growing parts. As interest in the Internet snowballed, companies began looking for ways to make it more accessible to customers, to make the user interface more functional, and to make more services available over it. Today, most companies regard their use of the Internet and World Wide Web as an indispensable competitive business tool, and many individuals view the Internet as a vital research and communications medium.

One remarkable characteristic of both the Internet and World Wide Web is that they are not owned by any person or business, and no single person, business, or organization is in charge. Web pages are developed by individuals and organizations and hosted on Web servers owned by an individual; a school, business, or other organization; or a service provider. PCs and other devices used to access the Internet typically belong to individuals, organizations, or public facilities. Each network connected to the Internet is owned and managed individually by that network's administrator, and the main communications media used as the *Internet backbone* are typically owned by telecommunications companies, such as telephone and cable companies. As a whole, the Internet has no owner or network administrator. The closest the Internet has to a governing body is the variety of organizations—such as the *Internet Society* (*ISOC*), *Internet Corporation For Assigned Names and Numbers* (*ICANN*), and the *World Wide Web Consortium* (*W3C*)—committed to overseeing it. These organizations are involved with such issues as establishing the protocols used on the Internet, making recommendations for changes, and encouraging cooperation between and coordinating communications among the networks connected to the Internet.

NET

Internet2

The next significant improvements to the Internet infrastructure might be a result of *Internet2*, a consortium of over 200 universities working together with industry and the government. Internet2 was created to develop and implement advanced Internet applications and technologies, which may lead to improvements for tomorrow's Internet. One of the primary goals of the Internet2 project is to ensure that new network services and applications are quickly applied to the broader Internet community, not just to the Internet2 participants. It is important to realize that Internet2 does not refer to a new physical Internet that will eventually replace the Internet—it is simply a research and development project geared to developing technology to ensure that the Internet in the future can handle tomorrow's applications.

A complementary project is the *Next Generation Internet* (*NGI*). While Internet2 is university sponsored, NGI is a federal government-sponsored, multi-agency research and development program working to develop advanced networking technologies and revolutionary applications that require advanced networking capabilities. Internet2 is working in cooperation with the NGI project, as well as forming partnerships with similar projects in other countries, to ensure a cohesive and interoperable advanced networking infrastructure for the Internet of the future.

The Internet Community Today

The Internet community today consists of individuals, businesses, and a variety of organizations located throughout the world. Virtually anyone with a computer that has communications capabilities can be part of the Internet, either as a user or as a supplier of information or services. Most members of the Internet community fall into one or more of the following groups.

Users

Users are people who use the Internet for activities, such as to look up a telephone number, browse through an online catalog, make an online purchase, download a music file, or send an e-mail message. According to Nielsen/NetRatings, about two-thirds of the population of the United States are Internet users, using the Internet at work, schools, libraries, or homes. Free Internet access at libraries, schools, and other public locations, as well as the availability of low-cost PCs and Internet access in many areas today, has helped Internet use begin to approach the popularity and widespread use of phones and TVs.

FURTHER EXPLORATION

For links to further information about types of Internet access and ISPs, go to www.course.com/uc11/ch08

Internet Service Providers

Internet service providers (ISPs)—often called *service providers* or *access providers*—are businesses or other organizations that provide Internet access to others, typically for a fee. As shown in Figure 8-2, a variety of communications and media companies—such as conventional and wireless telephone companies, as well as cable and satellite TV providers—offer Internet service over their respective media. In addition, a variety of other ISPs provide services over existing communications media. Some, such as America Online and EarthLink, provide service nationwide; others provide service to a more limited geographical area. In either case, ISPs are an onramp to the Internet, providing their subscribers with access to the World Wide Web, e-mail, and other Internet resources. In addition to Internet access, some ISPs provide proprietary online services available only to their subscribers. These ISPs are sometimes referred to as *online service providers*. A later section of this chapter covers ISPs in more detail, including factors to consider when selecting an ISP.

FIGURE 8-2

ISPs today include telephone, cable, and satellite companies, in addition to regional and national ISPs.

TELEPHONE COMPANIES

CABLE AND SATELLITE COMPANIES

REGIONAL AND NATIONAL ISPS

>**Internet service provider (ISP).** A business or other organization that provides Internet access to others, typically for a fee.

Internet Content Providers

Internet content providers supply the information that is available through the Internet. Internet content providers can be commercial businesses, nonprofit organizations, educational institutions, individuals, and more. Some examples of content providers are listed next.

- A photographer who posts samples of her best work on a Web page.
- A political action group that sponsors an online forum for discussions about topics that interest its members.
- An individual who publishes his opinion on various subjects to an online journal or *blog*.
- A software company that creates a Web site to provide product information and software downloads.
- A national newspaper that maintains an online site to provide up-to-the-minute news, feature stories, and video clips.
- A television network that develops a site for its newest reality TV show, including statistics, photographs, and live video feeds.
- A music publisher that creates a site to provide song demos and to sell downloads of its artists' songs and albums.
- A film student who releases her original short movie to be viewed on the Web.

Application Service Providers and Web Services

Application service providers (ASPs) are companies that manage and distribute software-based services to customers over the Internet. Instead of providing access to the Internet like ISPs do, ASPs provide access to software applications via the Internet. In essence, ASPs rent software access to companies or individuals—typically, customers pay a monthly or yearly fee to use the applications. One advantage to using an ASP over buying software outright is less up-front money, which means small businesses might be able to afford the same state-of-the-art applications that larger companies use. Another advantage is that using ASP software may result in a reduction of staffing needs for computer support for the company utilizing the ASP service, since the software is not installed on user PCs. In addition, all users see the most up-to-date software each time they use the application, and free or low-cost technical support and training may be available from the ASP. Leasing applications in this manner also gives customers the flexibility of trying a different application whenever desired (assuming a trial or short-term contract is available), without potentially wasting money purchasing software that might not fit the company's needs. Common ASP applications are office suites, collaboration and communications software, accounting programs, and e-commerce software. Some industry experts—such as the CEOs of Sun Microsystems and Microsoft—predict that within a relatively short period of time, software purchasing as we know it today will not exist. Instead, they believe software will be delivered as a service, and the option to purchase software outright might not exist.

One type of self-contained business application designed to work over the Internet or a company network is a **Web service**. Web services are programs written to strict specifications so that they can work together with other Web services and be used with many different computer systems. Unlike most other applications, Web services themselves do not

>**Internet content provider.** A person or an organization that provides Internet content. >**Application service provider (ASP).** A company that manages and distributes software-based services over the Internet. >**Web service.** A self-contained business application that operates over the Internet.

have a user interface—they are simply a standardized way of allowing different applications and computers to share data and processes via a network. However, a Web service can be added to a Web page or an application program to provide specific functionality to end users. For example, Web services can be used to facilitate communications between suppliers and customers, to provide a service via a Web site that was otherwise not feasible (such as the inclusion of mapping information on a Web site or Web application using Microsoft's MapPoint .NET Web service), or to add functionality to the end user via the Internet (such as a proposed Web service for Microsoft Office users that allows them to print to any Kinko's locations from their program's File menu). A company that provides Web services is sometimes referred to as a *Web services provider*.

Infrastructure Companies

Infrastructure companies are the enterprises that own or operate the paths or "roadways" along which Internet data travels. Examples of infrastructure companies include telephone, satellite, and cable companies.

Hardware and Software Companies

There is a wide variety of hardware and software companies that make and distribute the products used with the Internet and Internet activities. For example, companies that create or sell the software used in conjunction with the Internet (such as Web browsers, e-mail programs, *e-commerce* and *multimedia* software, and Web development tools) fall into this category. So, too, do the companies that make the hardware (modems, cables, routers, servers, PCs, and smart phones, for instance) that are used in conjunction with the Internet.

The Government and Other Organizations

Many other organizations influence the Internet and its uses. Governments have among the most visible impact; their laws can limit both the information made available via Web servers located in a particular country, as well as access to the Internet for individuals residing in that country. For example, in France it is illegal to sell items or post online content related to racist groups or activities and China has imposed tight controls on what information is published on China Web servers and the information its citizens have access to. In the United States, anything illegal offline (illicit drugs, child pornography, and so forth) is illegal online. In addition, rulings—such as the 1968 *Carterfone Decision* (that allowed companies other than AT&T to utilize the AT&T infrastructure), the 1996 *Telecommunications Act* (that deregulated the entire communications industry so that telephone companies, cable-TV and satellite operators, and firms in other segments of the industry were free to enter each other's markets), and the recent ruling by the U.S. Supreme Court that cable companies will not have to share their infrastructure with competing Internet service providers—have had a large impact on the communications industry in general. The ability of the government to block potential mergers between communications companies and to break apart companies based on antitrust law to prevent new monopolies also impacts the Internet and communications industry.

Key Internet organizations are responsible for many aspects of the Internet. For example, the Internet Society (ISOC) provides leadership in addressing issues that confront the future of the Internet and oversees the groups responsible for Internet infrastructure standards, such as which protocols can be used and how Internet addresses are constructed. ICANN (Internet Corporation for Assigned Names and Numbers) is charged with such responsibilities as IP address allocation and domain name management. The World Wide Web Consortium (W3C) is a group of over 450 organizations dedicated to developing new protocols and specifications to promote the evolution of the Web and to ensure its interoperability. In addition, many colleges and universities support Internet research and manage blocks of the Internet's resources.

Myths About the Internet

Because the Internet is so unique in the history of the world—and its content and applications keep evolving—several widespread myths about it have surfaced.

Myth 1: The Internet Is Free

This myth stems from the fact that there has traditionally been no cost associated with online content—such as news and product information—or e-mail exchange, other than what the Internet users pay their ISPs for Internet access. And many people—such as students, employees, and consumers who opt for free Internet service or use free access available at public libraries or other public locations—pay nothing for Internet access. Yet it should also be obvious that someone, somewhere, has to pay to keep the Internet up and running.

Businesses, schools, public libraries, and most home users pay Internet service providers flat monthly fees to connect to the Internet; businesses, schools, libraries, and other larger organizations might also have to lease high-capacity communications lines (such as from a telephone company) to support their high level of Internet traffic. ISPs, phone companies, cable companies, and other organizations who own part of the Internet infrastructure pay to keep their respective physical parts of the Internet running smoothly. ISPs also pay software and hardware companies for the resources they need to support their subscribers. Eventually, most of these costs are passed along to end users through ISP fees. Usually, ISPs that offer free Internet access obtain funds by selling onscreen ads (either ads displayed within the browser interface whenever Web pages or e-mail messages are being viewed or *pop-up* ads that display in new browser windows) or by selling personal or demographic data obtained from subscribers.

Another reason that this is a myth is the growing trend of subscription or per-use fees to access resources—such as journal or newspaper articles, music, and games—via the Internet. Typically, these fees are relatively small, and many companies are working on ways to make the processing of small fees (sometimes called *micropayments*) practical, such as charging a few cents to read each online article and then including all user's micropayments on his or her telephone or credit card bill. In lieu of a mandatory fee, some sites request donations for use of the site (see Figure 8-3). Many experts expect the use of fee-based Internet content to continue to grow at a rapid pace.

FIGURE 8-3

Fee-based Web content. Both required fees and requested donations for accessing Web content are becoming common.

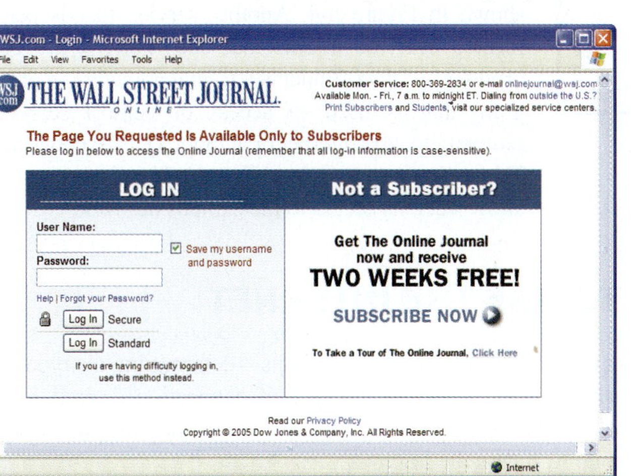

REQUIRED FEE
A subscription is required to view content on this site.

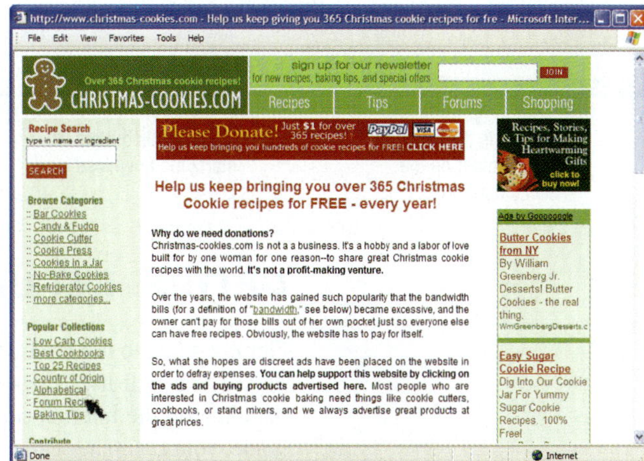

REQUESTED DONATION
A donation is requested for using this site.

Myth 2: Someone Controls the Internet

The popularity of conspiracy theories in past years has contributed to the spread of this myth. In fact, as already discussed, no single group or organization controls the Internet. Governments in each country have the power to regulate the content and use of the Internet within their borders, as allowed by their laws. However, legislators often face serious obstacles getting legislation passed into law—let alone getting it enforced. Making governmental control even harder is the "bombproof" design of the Internet itself. If a government tries to block access to or from a specific country, for example, users can establish links between the two countries through a third country.

FIGURE 8-4

FTP. An FTP program, such as the one shown here, can be used to upload or download files to or from an FTP server.

1. User supplies the proper FTP information to connect to the Microsoft FTP site.
2. The desired folder and file is located and selected.
3. Clicking this button starts the download.
4. The file is downloaded to this folder on the user's hard drive.

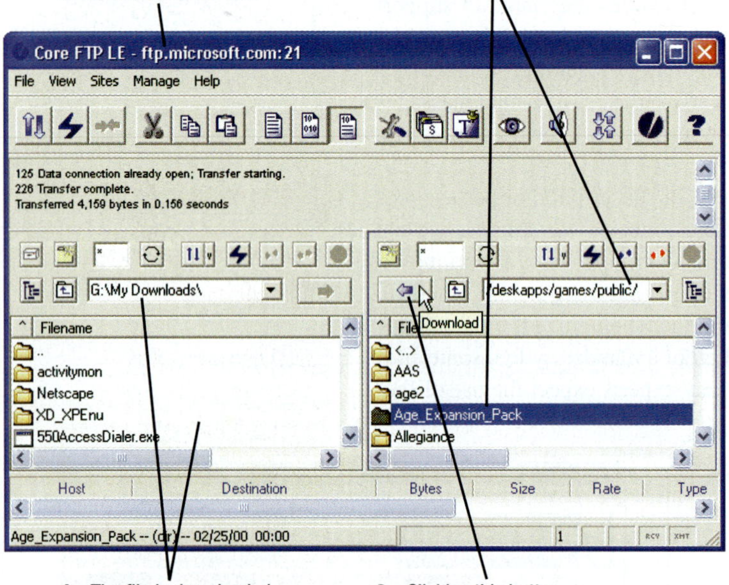

Myth 3: The Internet and World Wide Web Are Identical

Since you can now use a Web browser to access most of the Internet's resources, many people think the Internet and the Web are the same thing. Although in everyday use many people use the terms *Internet* and *Web* interchangeably, they are not the same thing. Technically, the Internet is the physical network, and the Web is the collection of Web pages accessible over the Internet. The majority of Internet activities today take place via Web pages, but there are Internet resources other than the Web. For instance, *FTP* (*File Transfer Protocol*) is a protocol different from the HTTP protocol used to view Web pages. FTP is a common means of uploading files to or downloading files from an *FTP server*—a server set up by a business specifically to host files others might need to access. FTP access can be open to anyone (such as to allow the general public to download software updates or trial programs) or can be password protected (such as to allow only authorized employees or partners access to company files). While FTP can be performed via a Web browser (by using the *ftp://* protocol indicator instead of *http://* followed by the name of the FTP server), it is more often performed using a stand-alone FTP program, such as the one shown in Figure 8-4. Another service that is performed over the Internet but does not use a Web browser is *Telnet*. Telnet is a *terminal emulation* program that is used to access or control servers remotely via the Internet or another TCP/IP network. Telnet is often used in colleges and universities to allow students access to the campus network.

GETTING SET UP TO USE THE INTERNET

Getting set up to use the Internet typically involves three decisions—determining the type of device you will use to access the Internet, selecting the type of connection desired, and deciding on the Internet service provider to be used. Once these determinations have been made, your computer can be set up to access the Internet.

Type of Device

The Internet today can be accessed by a variety of devices. The type of device used depends on a combination of factors, such as the devices available to you, if you need access just at home or while on the go, and what types of Internet content you want to access. Some possible devices are shown in Figure 8-5 and discussed next.

Desktop, Notebook, or Tablet PCs

Most users who have access to a desktop (see Figure 8-5), notebook, or tablet PC at home, work, or school will use it to access the Internet. One advantage of using PCs for Internet access is that they have large screens and can be connected to high-speed Internet connections. They also can be used with virtually any content that can be contained on or accessed from a Web page, such as graphics, animation, music files, games, and video clips. A final advantage is that they usually have a large hard drive and are connected to a printer so Web pages, e-mail messages, and downloaded files can be easily saved and/or printed.

DESKTOP, NOTEBOOK, OR TABLET PC

Internet Appliances

Internet appliances—devices that are designed specifically for accessing the Internet—are most often used in homes that do not have a PC. Also known as *information appliances*, *Internet tablets*, and *Web pads*, these devices are typically very easy to use and can access Web pages, e-mail, or both. Usually, Web page graphics can be displayed, although all multimedia content might not necessarily be accessible. Disadvantages of Internet appliances include little or no local storage space for saving e-mails or downloads (often everything must be stored online), possibly not being able to connect the device to a printer, and not being able to use the device for tasks other than Internet activities. In addition, many of these devices work only with a single specified provider, such as America Online, MSN, or a proprietary service designed just for that type of Internet appliance. Some Internet appliances are designed to be located in a kitchen or other central location (see Figure 8-5); others take the form of a set-top box located on or near a living room TV and can manage television viewing and recording, in addition to Internet access.

INTERNET APPLIANCE

Mobile Devices

Mobile Web use—or *wireless Web*, as it is frequently called—is one of the fastest growing uses of the Internet today. Handheld PCs and mobile phones increasingly have built-in Internet connectivity and can be used to view Web page content, exchange
e-mail and instant messages, and download music and other online content. Some devices, such as the handheld PC shown in Figure 8-5, include a keyboard for easier data entry; others utilize pen input instead.

HANDHELD PC OR SMART PHONE

FIGURE 8-5
A variety of devices can be used to access the Internet.

Type of Connection and Internet Access

In order to use the Internet, your computer needs to be connected to it. Typically, this occurs by connecting your PC to another computer (usually belonging to an ISP, your school, or your employer) that is connected continually to the Internet. As discussed in Chapter 7, there are a variety of wired and wireless ways to connect to another computer. Some Internet connections are *dial-up connections*, meaning your PC dials up and connects to your ISP's computer only when needed. Other Internet connections are *direct* or *always-on connections*, meaning your computer is connected to your ISP whenever your computer is on. Direct Internet connections are typically *broadband* connections; that is, connections that allow more than one signal to be transferred over the transmission medium at one time. Therefore, direct Internet connections are much faster than dial-up connections. In theory, they can be up to 100 times as fast as a dial-up connection, but actual speeds at the present time are closer to 25 to 50 times as fast. This discrepancy is due to outside factors, such as the speed of the device being used, the condition of the transmission media being used, and the amount of traffic currently using the same transmission medium and Web server.

TYPE OF INTERNET CONNECTION	DIAL-UP?	ALWAYS ON?	AVAILABILITY	APPROXIMATE MAXIMUM SPEED *	APPROXIMATE MONTHLY PRICE
Conventional dial-up	Yes	No	Anywhere there is telephone service	56K	Free – $20
Cable	No	Yes	Virtually anywhere cable TV service is available	1.5–3.0 Mbps	$40
DSL	No	Yes	Within 3 miles of a switching station that supports DSL	1.5–3.0 Mbps	$25
Satellite	No	Yes	Anywhere there is a clear view to the southern sky and a satellite dish can be mounted	500 Kbps–1 Mbps	$65 **
Fixed wireless	No	Yes	Mainly urban areas where service is available	500 Kbps–1.5 Mbps	$35
Mobile wireless	No	Yes	Anywhere cellular phone service is available	14.4 Kbps–2 Mbps	Varies greatly

* Many connections have slower upload speeds.

** Also requires expensive hardware, such as a satellite dish or transceiver.

FIGURE 8-6
Internet connection options.

Although dial-up Internet is still common, home broadband use is growing rapidly. More than half of all home Internet connections are now broadband connections, and that percentage is expected to climb to 75% by 2010. Types of Internet connections are discussed next, and the most common types of Internet connections used by individuals are summarized in Figure 8-6.

Dial-Up Connections

Dial-up connections usually work over standard telephone lines. To connect to the Internet, your computer dials its modem and connects to a modem attached to a computer belonging to your ISP. While you are connected to your ISP, your PC can access Internet resources. To end your Internet session, you disconnect from your ISP. One advantage of a dial-up connection is security. Since you are not continually connected to the Internet, it is much less likely that anyone (such as a *hacker*) will gain access to your computer via the Internet, either to access the data located on your PC or, more commonly, to use your computer in some type of illegal or unethical manner.

One disadvantage of using a dial-up connection is the inconvenience of having to instruct your PC to dial up your ISP every time you want to check your e-mail or view a Web page. Also, your telephone line will be tied up while you are accessing the Internet, unless you use a second phone line or an Internet call-waiting or call-forwarding service to notify you about incoming telephone calls while you are connected to the Internet. These services are generally set up to allow the person to leave a short message; some systems give you a short window of time to disconnect from the Internet and pick up the telephone call, if desired. Newer dial-up modems help to facilitate some type of call-waiting service, as well. The two most common forms of dial-up Internet service are *conventional dial-up* and *ISDN*.

TIP

Before using a dial-up access number to connect to the Internet, verify that it is a local telephone number; if it is not, you will incur long-distance charges.

>Dial-up connection. A type of Internet connection in which the PC or other device must dial up and connect to a service provider's computer via telephone lines before being connected to the Internet.

Conventional Dial-Up

Conventional (*standard*) **dial-up Internet access** uses a conventional dial-up modem connected to a standard telephone jack with regular twisted-pair telephone cabling. Conventional dial-up Internet service is commonly used with home PCs and Internet appliances; it can also be used with notebook PCs or other portable devices, provided the device has a conventional dial-up modem. Conventional dial-up Internet access ranges from free to about $20 per month. Advantages include inexpensive hardware, ease of setup and use, and widespread availability. The primary disadvantage, in addition to the disadvantages pertaining to all types of dial-up connections discussed in the previous paragraph, is slow connection speed.

Conventional dial-up connects to the Internet at a maximum of 56 Kbps, although some ISPs offer what they call *high-speed dial-up access*. Although the connection speed is still a maximum of 56 Kbps, high-speed dial-up uses *caching*—saving Web page content on your PC—so the pages that you view often can load faster. Users who visit pages that change frequently or need the pages to load completely from the Web server each time they are viewed (such as pages containing news, stock quotes, and other timely information) may not see much of an increase in speed over conventional dial-up Internet.

ISDN

ISDN (*integrated services digital network*) **Internet access** also transfers data over ordinary telephone lines, but it is faster than conventional dial-up. It typically uses two phone lines to transfer data up to 128 Kbps—over twice as fast as conventional dial-up service—and the telephone calls and the Internet can be used at the same time, although Internet speeds might decline during telephone calls. Fairly pricey for the speed at about $60 per month, ISDN requires a special ISDN modem and is used primarily by businesses.

Direct Connections

Unlike dial-up connections that connect to your ISP only when you need to access the Internet, **direct** (*always-on*) **connections** keep you continually connected to your provider and, therefore, continually connected to the Internet. With a direct connection, Internet access requires only opening a Web browser program, such as Internet Explorer, Netscape Navigator, or Firefox. Direct Internet connections are commonly used in homes and offices. In addition, they are often available at hotels, libraries, and other public locations for use by individuals. Users can connect to direct Internet connections via either wired or wireless media.

Because direct connections keep your computer connected to the Internet at all times (as long as your PC is powered up), it is important to protect your computer from unauthorized access or hackers. Consequently, all home and office PCs with a direct Internet connection should use a *firewall* program. Firewall programs block access to a PC from outside computers and enable each user to specify which programs on his or her PC are allowed to have access to the Internet. Firewalls and other network and Internet security precautions are discussed in more detail in Chapter 9.

The most significant characteristics of the most common types of direct Internet connections are discussed next. Other alternatives—such as the emerging *broadband over power lines* (*BPL*) standard discussed in Chapter 7, which allows people to connect to the Internet through their power outlets—will likely be more available in the future.

T1 Lines

T1 lines are high-speed (about 1.5Mbps) dedicated lines that schools and large businesses often lease from the telephone company or an Internet service provider to provide a fast,

NET

>Conventional dial-up Internet access. Dial-up Internet access via a conventional dial-up modem and standard telephone lines. **>ISDN Internet access.** Dial-up Internet access that is faster than conventional dial-up, but still uses standard telephone lines. **>Direct connection.** An always-on type of Internet connection in which the PC or other device is continually connected to the Internet. **>T1 line.** Fast, direct Internet access via a leased high-speed dedicated line.

direct connection to the Internet for the PCs on their networks. Very large businesses might choose to lease a faster *T3 line* (which transmits data at speeds of up to about 30 Mbps), but these are more commonly used for Internet backbone connections and connections from ISPs to the Internet.

Cable

Cable Internet access is the most widely used type of home broadband connection, with over 50% of the home broadband market. Cable connections are very fast and are available wherever cable TV access is available, provided the local cable provider supports Internet access. Consequently, cable Internet is not widely available in rural areas. Cable Internet service requires a cable modem and costs about $40 per month just for Internet access; cable TV is optional and requires an additional fee.

DSL

As mentioned in Chapter 7, **DSL** (*Digital Subscriber Line*) **Internet access** provides fast transmissions over telephone lines and uses a technology that does not tie up your telephone line. DSL requires a DSL modem and is available only to users who are relatively close (within three miles) to a telephone switching station and who have telephone lines capable of handling DSL. The speed of the connection degrades as the distance between the modem and the switching station gets closer and closer to the three-mile limit, so DSL is typically used in more urban areas. Despite these limitations, DSL Internet access is growing rapidly and has captured over 40% off the home broadband market. Typical monthly fees are around $25 for basic service; some providers offer a premium, faster service for a higher monthly fee.

Satellite

Satellite Internet access is typically a little slower and more expensive than cable or DSL access, but it is often the only broadband option for rural areas. In addition to a satellite modem, it requires a *transceiver* satellite dish mounted outside the home or building to receive and transmit data to and from the satellites being used. Installation requires an unobstructed view of the southern sky (to have a clear line of sight between the transceiver and appropriate satellite), and performance might degrade or stop altogether during very heavy rain or snowstorms. Typical cost is about $65 per month.

Fixed Wireless

Fixed wireless Internet access is similar to satellite Internet in that it requires a modem and sometimes an outside-mounted transceiver, but it uses radio transmission towers instead of satellites. Fixed wireless has traditionally been available only in large metropolitan areas, although a new option is emerging that uses existing cell phone towers to transmit fixed wireless signals, which allows the service to extend to more rural areas. Cost for service is about $35 per month.

Mobile Wireless

Mobile wireless (sometimes called *wireless Web*) **Internet access** is most commonly used with handheld PCs, smart phones, and other mobile devices to keep them connected to the Internet, even as you carry them from place to place. These devices are connected typically through a wireless network and wireless provider using a wireless modem or built-in Internet connectivity. The speed of mobile wireless depends on the standard being used. Common *second-generation (2G) wireless standards* include *GSM (Global System for Mobile Communications)* and *CDMA (Code Division Multiple Access)*, which support speeds up to 14.4 Kbps. *Third-generation (3G) wireless standards*, such as *GPRS (general packet radio service)*, *3GSM*, and *UMTO (Universal Mobile Telecommunications System)* support

---

>**Cable Internet access.** Fast, direct Internet access via cable TV lines. >**DSL Internet access.** Fast, direct Internet access via standard telephone lines. >**Satellite Internet access.** Fast, direct Internet access via the airwaves using a satellite dish and satellite modem. >**Fixed wireless Internet access.** Fast, direct Internet access available in large metropolitan areas via the airwaves and a radio transceiver. >**Mobile wireless Internet access.** Internet access via a wireless communications network, such as the ones used with cellular phones.

faster speeds—from 128 Kbps while traveling in a car to up to 2 Mbps in a fixed setting. There have also been improvements to increase the speed of 2G services, such as *EDGE* (*Enhanced Data Rates for Global Evolution*) and *EV-DO* (*Evolution Data Optimized*)—3G technologies being used by some providers to allow consumers to send and rcccive data at least three times faster than usual. Costs for mobile wireless Internet access vary widely, with some packages including unlimited Internet, some charging by the number of minutes of Internet use, and some charging by the amount of data transferred. A typical cost for unlimited mobile wireless Internet is about $65 per month.

COFFEEHOUSES
Typically fee-based.

HOTELS
Often free for guests.

PUBLIC AREAS
Usually free for residents and visitors, such as at this location in Rome.

CORPORATE MEETING ROOMS
Usually free for employees and visitors.

FIGURE 8-7
Hotspots. Hotspots are used to wirelessly connect to the Internet via the Internet connection belonging to a business, city, school, or other organization.

NET

Hotspots

Both free and fee-based wireless Internet are becoming available at *public hotspots*—public locations with a direct Internet connection that allow users to wirelessly connect to that Internet connection. Examples include the Internet service available at many Starbucks coffee houses and a number of McDonald's restaurants; wireless access points at hotels, airports, and other locations frequented by business travelers; and free hotspots located in the vicinity of some larger metropolitan area libraries, subway stations, parks, and other public locations (see Figure 8-7). Many businesses are also setting up hotspots within the corporate headquarters for use by employees in their offices, as well as employees and guests in conference rooms, waiting rooms, lunchrooms, and other onsite locations. Users typically connect to hotspots via a Wi-Fi connection, although other options—such as the faster WiMAX, discussed in Chapter 7—might soon be an option for some locations.

Selecting an ISP and Setting Up Your PC

Once the type of Internet access to be used is determined, the final steps to getting connected to the Internet are selecting an ISP and setting up your system.

Selecting an ISP

The type of device used (such as a desktop PC or handheld PC), the type of Internet connection and service desired (such as conventional dial-up or cable), and your geographical location will likely limit your ISP choices. The pricing and services available through any two ISPs might differ somewhat. For example, some ISPs simply provide you with an onramp to the Internet; others might include additional content or services, such as instant messaging, music management, Web site hosting, personal online photo galleries, Web site filtering, spam filtering, virus protection, and a personalized starting page. The questions listed in Figure 8-8 can help you understand the factors you need to consider when choosing an ISP.

AREA	QUESTIONS TO ASK
Services	Can I use the browser of my choice?
	Does the e-mail service support attachments, spam filtering, and multiple mailboxes?
	How many e-mail addresses can I have?
	What is the size limit on incoming and outgoing e-mail messages and attachments?
	Do I have a choice between conventional and Web-based e-mail?
	Is there dial-up service that I can use when I'm away from home (for both dial-up and broadband connections)?
	Are there any special member features or benefits?
	Is space available for posting a personal Web site or personal photos?
Speed	How fast are the maximum and usual downstream (ISP to my PC) speeds?
	How fast are the maximum and usual upstream (my PC to ISP) speeds?
	How much does the service slow down under adverse conditions, such as high traffic or poor weather?
	If it's a dial-up connection, how often should I expect to get a busy signal? (A customer-to-modem ratio of about 10:1 or less is optimal.)
Support	Is 24/7 telephone technical support available?
	Is any technical support available through a Web site, such as e-mail support or an online knowledge base?
	What is the response time to answer my phone calls or e-mails when I have a problem?
	Is there ever a charge for technical support?
Cost	What is the monthly cost for the service? Is it lower if I prepay a few months in advance?
	If it's a dial-up connection, is there a local access telephone number to avoid long-distance charges?
	Are there services that can be added or deleted (such as number of e-mail addresses or Web page hosting) to increase or decrease the monthly cost?
	Is there a set-up fee? If so, can it be waived with a 6-month or 12-month agreement?
	What is the cost of any additional hardware needed, such as modem or transceiver? Can the fee be waived with a long-term service agreement?
	Are there any other services (conventional or wireless telephone service, or cable or satellite TV, for instance) available from this provider that I have or want and that can be combined with Internet access for a lower total cost?

FIGURE 8-8
Choosing an ISP. Some questions to ask before making your final selection.

Setting Up Your PC

The specific steps for setting up your PC to use your new Internet connection depend on the type of device, the type of connection, and the ISP you have chosen to use. Once the necessary hardware (your modem and any additional hardware, such as a satellite transceiver or set-top box) has been acquired and is in place, you will usually need to run installation software to set up your system to use the ISP you selected. Typically, the installation process includes downloading and installing any additional required software, setting up your telephone dialing software (for some conventional dial-up connections only), and walking through selecting a username (used to log on to some Internet connections and for your e-mail address), an access telephone number (for dial-up connections), and a payment method. Some ISPs provide the installation program on CD; the installation programs for several common ISPs are also preinstalled on many new PCs. In either case, you need to start the installation program, and then just follow the onscreen instructions to complete the setup process. If you already have an Internet connection and are looking for a new ISP, the necessary installation program can typically be downloaded to your PC from the ISP's Web site and then run on your PC to begin the setup process. If your ISP does not have an installation program, follow its instructions to set up your Web browser and telephone-dialing software (if needed).

Selected screens of the installation process with one provider (America Online) are shown in Figure 8-9; the same general steps occur with most ISP installation programs, although they might occur in a different order.

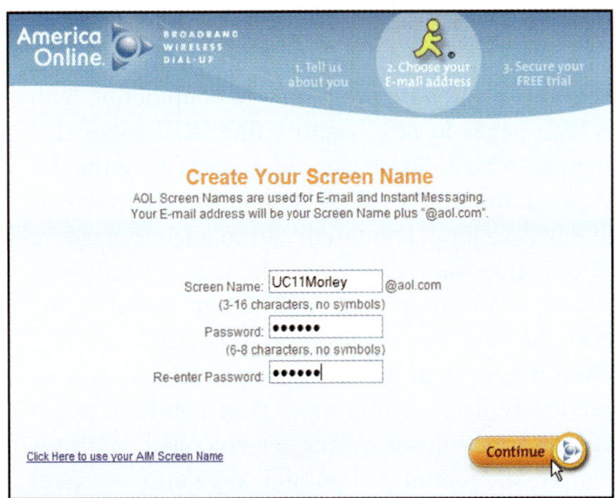

STEP 1: SELECT A SCREEN NAME
The screen name (username) and password you select is typically used for logging on to the Internet, as well as for e-mail.

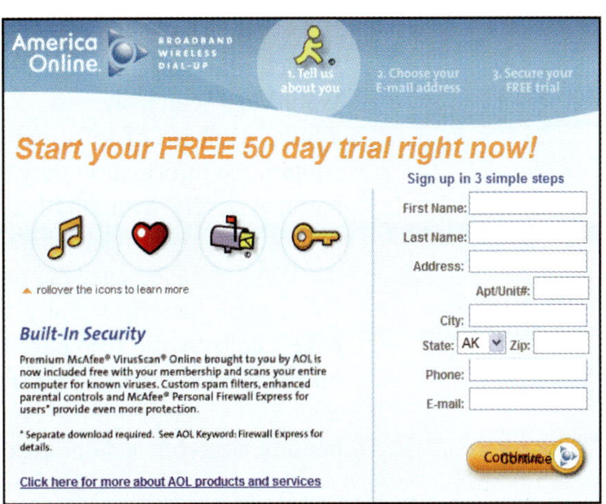

STEP 2: PROVIDE CONTACT AND BILLING INFORMATION
The setup process includes specifying your contact and billing information.

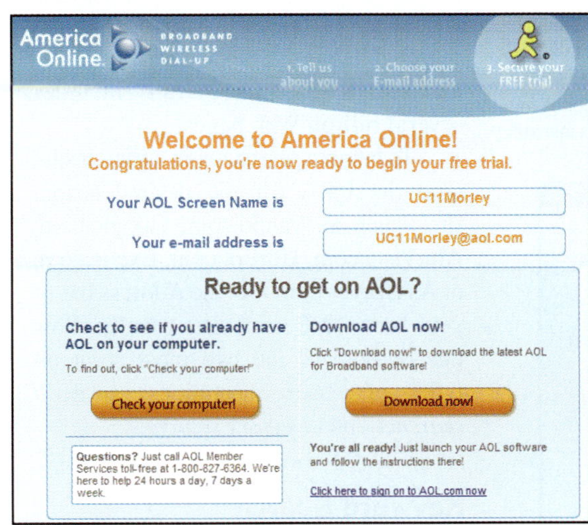

STEP 3: DOWNLOAD SOFTWARE AND SELECT AN ACCESS NUMBER
The necessary software will be downloaded. For dial-up connections, you will then need to select at least one local telephone number for your PC to dial to access the Internet.

STEP 4: LOG ON AND START SURFING
After the browser software is downloaded and installed, you can log on to your new service (with your assigned username and password) and start surfing the Web!

FIGURE 8-9

Setting up a PC for Internet access. Most ISPs have an installation program that walks new subscribers through the setup process.

SEARCHING THE INTERNET

Most people who use the Internet turn to it to find specific information. For instance, you might want to find out the lowest price of the latest Tom Cruise DVD, the flights available from Los Angeles to New York on a particular day, a recipe for clam chowder, the weather forecast for the upcoming weekend, the text of Martin Luther King's "I Had a Dream" speech, or a map of hiking trails in the Grand Tetons. The Internet provides access to a vast amount of interesting and useful information, but that information is useless if you cannot find it when you need it. Consequently, one of the most important skills an Internet user can acquire today is how to successfully search for and locate information on the Internet. Basic Internet searching was introduced in Chapter 1, but understanding the various types of search sites available and how they work, as well as some key searching strategies, can help you save time by performing more successful Internet searches. These topics are discussed next.

Search Sites

Search sites are Web sites designed specifically to help you find information on the Web. Most search sites use a **search engine**—a software program—in conjunction with a huge database of information about Web pages to help visitors find Web pages that contain the information they are seeking. Search site databases are updated on a regular basis, typically with small, automated programs (often called *spiders* or *webcrawlers*) that use the hyperlinks located on Web pages to jump continually from page to page on the Web. At each page, the program records important data about the page—such as its URL, page title, frequently used keywords, and descriptive information added to the page's code by the Web page author when the page was created—into the database. This information is used to find matching Web pages when the search site receives a search request. Spider programs can be tremendously fast, visiting more than 1 million pages per day. Search site databases also obtain information when people who create Web sites submit URLs and keywords to them through an option on the search site, as discussed more in Chapter 11. Some search sites also use human editors to manually classify the Web pages according to content. The size of the search database varies with each particular search site, but typically includes several billion Web pages.

FIGURE 8-10
Using a search site.
Many search sites allow you to search by keyword, directory, or both.

To begin a search using a search site, type the URL for the desired search site—such as Yahoo.com, Google.com, AltaVista.com, HotBot.com, Excite.com, or AskJeeves.com—in the Address bar of your browser. Search sites usually allow one or both of the two most common types of search operations: *keyword searches* and *directory searches*.

Keyword Search

To perform a **keyword search**, enter appropriate **keywords** (one or more key terms) describing what you are looking for in the search box and press Enter. The site's search engine then uses those keywords to return a list of matching pages (called *hits*) that can be viewed by clicking the hyperlinks (see Figure 8-10). Search sites differ in how close a match between the specified search criteria and a Web page has to be before a link to that page is displayed, so the number of hits from one search site to another may vary.

>Search site. A Web site designed to help users search for Web pages that match specified keywords or selected categories. **>Search engine.** A software program used by a search site to retrieve matching Web pages from a search database. **>Keyword search.** A type of Internet search in which keywords are typed in a search box to locate information on the Internet. **>Keyword.** A word typed in a search box on a search site to locate information on the Internet.

To reduce the number of hits displayed, good search strategies (discussed shortly) can be used. Sites also differ regarding the order in which the hits are displayed. Some sites list the most popular sites (usually judged by the number of Web pages that link to it); others list Web pages belonging to organizations that pay a fee to receive a higher rank (typically called *sponsored links*) first.

The keyword search is the most commonly used search type. As shown in Figure 8-11, a keyword search option can be found on many different types of sites. Keyword searches can be found on *metasearch sites* (sites that search multiple search sites and consolidate the results) and *natural language search sites* (sites that are designed to be used with search criteria in full sentence form, instead of just keywords), in addition to conventional search sites. In addition, many Web sites include keyword search capabilities to allow visitors to find information located on the site, such as products in an online catalog.

CONVENTIONAL SEARCH SITE
Allows users to search by both keyword and directory.

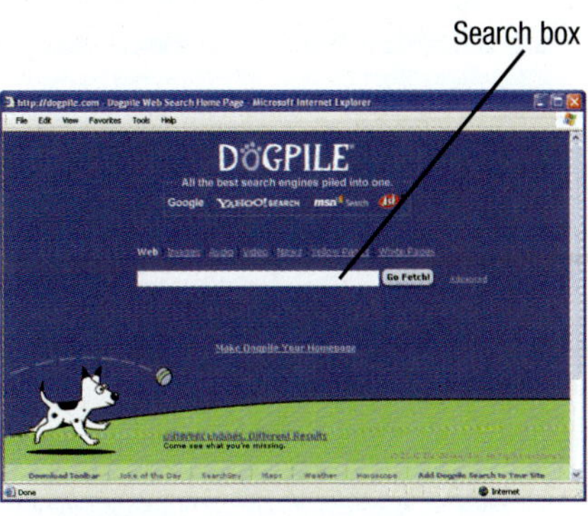

METASEARCH SITE
Allows users to search by keyword and displays hits from several different search sites.

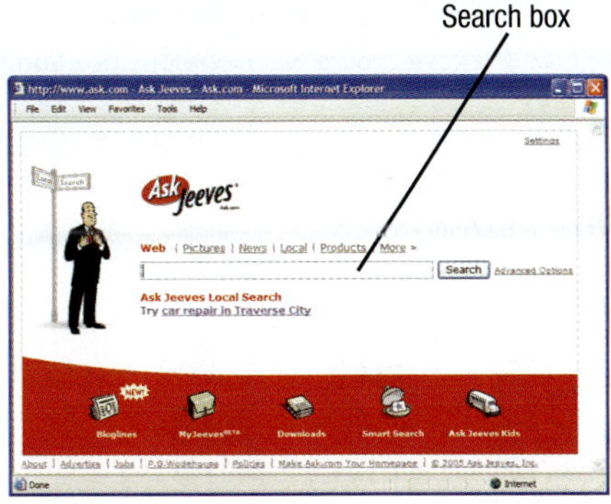

NATURAL LANGUAGE SITE
Allows users to search by using natural language sentences.

E-COMMERCE WEB SITE
Allows users to search the Web site to find products and product information.

FIGURE 8-11
Types of searches. There are many types of searches available through search sites, and many regular Web pages have search capabilities built in.

Directory Search

A **directory search** uses a list of categories displayed on the screen (refer again to Figure 8-11). Directories are usually a good choice if you want information about a particular category but do not have a very specific subject in mind. A directory also uses a database, but one that is typically screened by a human editor, so it is much smaller, although often more accurate. For example, a spider program might classify a Web page about computer chips under the keyword "chips" together with information about potato chips, but a human editor would not categorize those two "chips" concepts together. One of the largest directories—the *Open Directory Project*, located at dmoz.org—has classified over 5 million Web pages using around 70,000 volunteer editors.

To use a directory located on a search site, click the category that best matches what you are looking for. A list of more specific subcategories for the main category that you selected is then displayed, along with a list of matching Web pages. To reach more specific subcategories and matching Web pages, keep selecting categories. Whenever the name of an appropriate Web page appears in the list of matching Web pages, click its hyperlink to display that page.

NET

>**Directory search.** A type of Internet search in which categories are selected to locate information on the Internet.

FUNCTION	EXPLANATION
Calculator	Enter a mathematical expression or a specific conversion to see the result.
Currency converter	Enter an amount and desired currency type to see the corresponding value.
Dictionary	Enter the term "define" followed by a term to view definitions from online sources.
Flight information	Enter an airline and flight number to see status information on that flight.
Number search	Enter a tracking number, area code, UPC code, etc. to view the associated information.
Phonebook	Enter a name and either a city name, area code, or ZIP code to look up that person's address and phone number.
Reverse phonebook	Enter a telephone number to look up the person or business associated with that number.
Site search	Enter the term "site" followed by keywords to search only that site.
Stock quotes	Enter one or more ticker symbols to retrieve stock quotes.
Street maps	Enter an address to find a map to that location.
Weather	Enter the term "weather" followed by a city name or ZIP code to view the weather for that location.
Yellow pages	Enter a type of business and city name or ZIP code to view businesses in that local area.

EXAMPLES:

weather san francisco | Search

Weather for **San Francisco, CA**
75°F
Clear
Wind: N at 7 mph
Humidity: 53%
Thu 78° | 50°
Fri 66° | 54°
Sat 63° | 52°

10 miles in feet | Search

10 miles = 52 800 feet

FIGURE 8-12
Google search tools.

Search Site Tools

Many search sites contain a variety of tools that can be used to search for specific types of information, For instance, some search sites include options for searching for items other than Web pages, such as music files, image files, newsgroups, news articles—even files on your computer. Others allow you to search for maps of locations, search for people or telephone numbers, and other helpful features. Google is one of the most versatile search sites at the present time and is continually adding new search options. Some examples of search tools that can be performed using the Google search box are listed in Figure 8-12.

Search Strategies

There are a variety of strategies that can be employed to help whittle down a list of hits to a more manageable number (some searches can return millions of Web pages). Some search strategies can be employed regardless of the search site being used; others are available only on certain sites. Some of the most useful search strategies are discussed next.

Using Phrases

One of the most straightforward ways to improve the quality of the hits returned is to use *phrase searching*—essentially typing more than one keyword in a keyword search. Most search engines automatically return the hits that include all the keywords typed first, followed by the hits matching most of the keywords, continuing down to the hits that fit only one of the keywords. To force this type of sorting, virtually all search engines allow you to use some type of character—often quotation marks—to indicate that you want to search for all the keywords. Because search options vary from site to site, it is best to look for a search tips link on the search site you are using; the search tips should explain the options available for that particular site. Examples of the results from using various search phrases at different sites to find Web pages about hand signals used with dogs are listed in Figure 8-13.

TIP

When searching, be efficient—if an appropriate Web page is not included among the first page or two of hits, redo the search using more specific criteria or a different search strategy.

SEARCH PHRASE USED	SEARCH SITE	NUMBER OF PAGES FOUND	TITLE OF FIRST TWO NONSPONSORED PAGES FOUND*
dogs	Google	87,300,000	Dogs - Cats - Horses - TerrificPets.com American Kennel Club - akc.org
	Yahoo!	169,000,000	American Kennel Club - akc.org Canine Gallery
hand signals	Google	20,600,000	Cree Hand Signals Soccer Officials' Hand Signals
	Yahoo!	16,300,000	Ann Arbor American H.O.G. Hand Signals HandHealth.net
dog hand signals	Google	6,640,000	Dog Behavior Training, Teach Your Dog Hand Signals! Hand Signals - Obedience Training
	Yahoo!	2,440,000	I-dog Message Board: Hand Signals/Body Language Hand Signals - Obedience Training
"dog hand signals"	Google	378	Command Dog Hand Training Dog Behavior Training, Teach Your Dog Hand Signals!
	Yahoo!	179	Dog Behavior Training, Teach Your Dog Hand Signals! Pedigree.com - Dogknows_Nonverbal

*Highlighted entries indicate Web pages about dog hand signals.

FIGURE 8-13
Examples of phrase searching. Using different search phrases and different search sites can dramatically change the search results.

Using Boolean Operators

To further specify exactly what you want a search engine to find, *Boolean operators*—most commonly AND, OR, and NOT—can often be used in keyword searches. For example, if you want a search engine to find all documents that cover *both* the Intel and AMD microprocessor manufacturers, you can use the search phrase *Intel AND AMD* if the search engine supports Boolean operators. If, instead, you want documents that discuss *either* (or both) of these companies, the search phrase *Intel OR AMD* can be used. On the other hand, if you want documents about microprocessors that are cataloged with no mention of Intel, *microprocessors NOT Intel* can be used. Just as with other operators, the rules for using Boolean operators might vary from search site to search site—check the search tips for the search site that you are using to see if that site supports Boolean operators. Some sites include an *Advanced Search* option using a fill-in form to walk you through using Boolean operators and other advanced search techniques; other sites use the characters + for AND and – for NOT.

Using Multiple Search Sites

Most users have a favorite search site that they are comfortable using. However, as illustrated in Figure 8-13, different search sites can return surprisingly different results. It is important to realize that sometimes a different search site might perform better than the one you use regularly. If you are searching for something and are not making any progress with one search site, then try another search site.

Using Appropriate Keywords, Synonyms, Variant Word Forms, and Wildcards

When choosing the keywords to be used with a search site, it is important to select words that represent the key concept you are searching for. Unless you are using a natural language site, do not include any extraneous words, such as "the," "a," and "in," unless those words are part of a specific phrase you are searching for. For example, if you want to find out about bed and breakfasts located in the town of Leavenworth, Washington, a keyword phrase, such as *Leavenworth Washington bed and breakfast*, should return appropriate results.

If your initial search did not produce the results you were hoping for, you can try *synonyms*—words that have meanings similar to other words. For example, you could replace *bed and breakfast* with *hotel* or *lodging*. To use synonyms in addition to the original keywords, Boolean operators can be used, such as the search phrase *"bed and breakfast" OR "hotel" OR "lodging" AND Leavenworth AND Washington*. *Variant*—or alternate—word forms are another possibility. Try to think of a different spelling or form of your keywords, if your search still does not work as desired. For example, *bed and breakfast* could be replaced or supplemented with the variants *bed & breakfast* and *B&B*, and *hand signal* and *hand signaling* are variant word forms for the *hand signals* keywords used in Figure 8-13. Using alternative spellings is a form of this strategy, as well.

Another strategy that is sometimes used with keywords is the *wildcard* approach. A wildcard is a special symbol that is used in conjunction with a part of a word to specify the pattern of the terms you want to search for. For instance, the asterisk wildcard (*) is used to represent any number of letters at the asterisk location, so on many sites searching for *hand sign** would search for *hand sign*, *hand signal*, *hand signals*, *hand signaling*, and any other keywords that fit this specific pattern.

Using Field Searches

A more advanced search strategy that can be used when basic searching is not producing the desired results is *field searching*—a search limited to a particular search characteristic (or *field*), such as the page title, URL, page text, or domain. When a field search is performed, the keyword text is searched for only in the specified field (see Figure 8-14 for some examples of field searching). Many, but not all, search engines support some type of field searches. Check the search tips for the particular search site you are using to see if it has that option.

FIGURE 8-14

Field searching. Field searches limit search results to just those pages with a specific Web page title, URL, text, or top-level domain.

FIELD TYPE	EXAMPLE	EXPLANATION
Title	title:"tax tips"	Searches for Web pages containing the words "tax tips" in the page title.
URL	url:taxtips	Searches for Web pages containing "taxtips" in the page URL.
Text	text:"tax tips"	Searches for Web pages containing "tax tips" in the text of the page.
Domain	domain:gov	Searches for Web pages located on government Web servers with a domain that ends in .gov.
Combination	title:"tax tips" domain:gov	Searches for Web pages containing "tax tips" in the page title located on government Web servers with a domain that ends in .gov.

Evaluating Search Results

Once a list of Web sites is returned as a result of a search, it is time to evaluate the sites to determine their quality and potential for meeting your needs. Two questions to ask yourself before clicking a link for a matching page are as follows:

- Does the title and listed description sound appropriate for the information you are seeking?
- Is the URL from an appropriate company or organization? For example, if you want technical specifications about a particular product, you might want to start with information on the manufacturer's Web site. If you are looking for government publications, stick with government Web sites.

After an appropriate Web page is found, the evaluation process is still not complete. If you are using the information on the page for something other than idle curiosity, you want to be sure the information can be trusted. Some general guidelines are listed in Figure 8-15.

FURTHER EXPLORATION

For links to further information about citing online references, go to www.course.com/uc11/ch08

GUIDELINE	EXPLANATION
Evaluate the source.	Information from the company or organization in question is generally more reliable than information found on an individual's Web site. Government and educational institutions are usually good sources for historical or research data. If you clicked a link on a Web page to open a document, double-check the URL to make sure you still know what organization the page is from—it may be located on a completely different Web site than the page from which it was accessed.
Evaluate the author.	Does the author have the appropriate qualifications for the information in question? Does he or she have a bias, or is the information supposed to be objective?
Check the timeliness of the information.	Web page content may be updated regularly or posted once and forgotten. Always look for the publication date on online newspaper and magazine articles; check for a "last updated" date on pages containing other types of information you'd like to use.
Verify the information.	When you will be using Web-based information in a report, paper, Web page, or other document in which accuracy is important, try to locate the same information from other reputable Web sources to verify the accuracy of the information you plan to use.

FIGURE 8-15
Evaluating search results. Before using information obtained from a Web page, use the following criteria to evaluate its accuracy and appropriateness.

Citing Internet Resources

According to the online version of the Merriam-Webster dictionary, the term *plagiarize* means "to steal and pass off the ideas or words of another as one's own" or to "use another's production without crediting the source." To avoid plagiarizing Web page content, you need to credit Web pages sources—as well as any other Internet resources—when you use them in papers, on Web pages, or in other documents.

The guidelines for citing Web page content are similar to those for written material. Some guidelines for crediting some Internet-based resources are listed next, based on the guidelines obtained from the American Psychological Association Web site. Figure 8-16 shows some citation examples. If in doubt when preparing a research paper, check with your instructor as to the style manual he or she prefers you to follow and refer to that guide for direction.

- *Web page article (journal, magazine, etc.)*. List the author, date of publication, article title, and periodical information, similar to a print source, and then add a "Retrieved" statement and date with the appropriate URL of the Web page used.
- *Web page content (not an article)*. List the author (if there is one), date of publication (if available; if not, use *n.d.* for "no date"), and Web page title, followed by a "Retrieved" statement and date with the appropriate URL of the Web page used.
- *E-mail correspondence*. List the sender's name followed by a "personal communication" statement and the date received next to the reference in the text. This reference is not included in the references section.

NET

FIGURE 8-16
Citing Web sources. It is important to properly credit your Web sources. These examples follow the American Psychological Association (APA) citation guidelines.

TYPE OF RESOURCE	CITATION EXAMPLE
Web page article (magazine)	Naughton, Keith. (2003, September 29). Chrysler Shifts Gears. *Newsweek*. Retrieved March 13, 2006 from http://www.msnbc.com/news/969677.asp?0dm=s118k.
Web page article (journal)	Mion, L. (2003, May 31). Care Provision for Older Adults: Who Will Provide? *Online Journal of Issues in Nursing*, 8 no. 2. Retrieved March 1, 2006, from http://www.nursingworld.org/ojin/topic21/tpc21_3.htm.
Web page article (not appearing in a periodical)	Sullivan, Bob (2003, September 26). New Arrest in Internet Attacks case. MSNBC. Retrieved February 11, 2006, from http://msnbc.com/news/972467.asp?0dm=C14OT.
Web page content (not an article)	*Biography of Ronald Reagan*. (n.d). Retrieved March 5, 2006 from http://www.whitehouse.gov/history/presidents/rr40.html.
E-mail (cited in text, not reference list)	L.A. Chafez (personal communication, March 28, 2006).

BEYOND BROWSING AND E-MAIL

In addition to basic browsing, searching for specific information, and e-mail, there are a host of other activities that can take place via the Internet. Some of the most common additional Web-based applications are discussed next.

Discussion Groups, Instant Messaging, and Other Types of Online Communications

Many types of online communications methods exist. For example, e-mail and *instant messaging* (*IM*) are extremely popular today, *Voice over IP* (*VoIP*) is emerging, and specialty types of electronic correspondence—such as *electronic invitations* and *electronic greeting cards*—can be sent via *e-vite* or electronic greeting card Web sites. E-mail was discussed in Chapter 1. Some of the most common other types of online communications are discussed next.

Discussion Groups

Discussion groups (also called *message boards*, *newsgroups*, or *online forums*) facilitate written discussions between people on specific subjects, such as TV shows, computers, movies, gardening, music, photography, hobbies, and politics. When a participant posts a message, it is displayed for anyone accessing the message board to read and respond to. Messages are usually organized by topics (called *threads*). Participants can post new messages in response to an existing message and stay within that thread, or they can post discussion group messages that start brand new threads. Many discussion groups can be accessed with just a Web browser, as in Figure 8-17; others require a *newsreader* (a special program for handling newsgroup messages that is often incorporated into e-mail programs). Participants in discussion groups do not have to be online at the same time because messages can be posted and responded to at each participant's convenience.

FIGURE 8-17
Types of online communications.

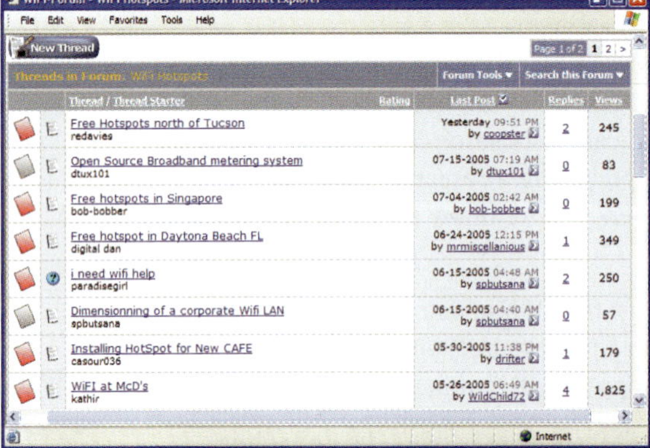

DISCUSSION GROUPS
Allow individuals to carry on written discussions with a variety of people on a specific topic; since messages remain on the site once they are posted, users don't need to be online at the same time to participate.

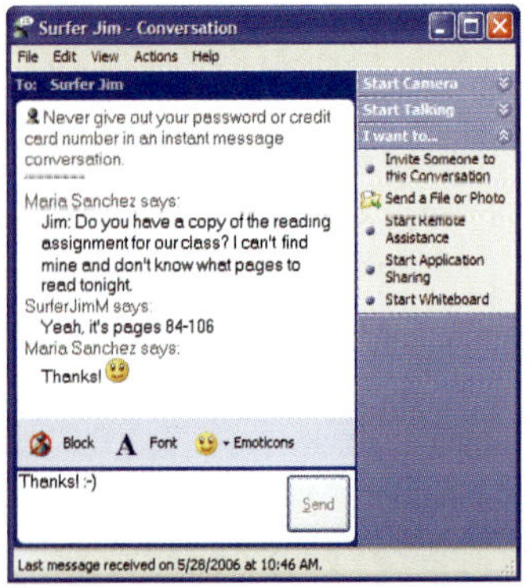

INSTANT MESSAGING
Enables real-time written conversations with friends and other "buddies" who are online at the same time.

VIDEOCONFERENCING
Allows multiple individuals to talk with and see each other during a real-time online meeting. Used both by individuals and businesses.

Chat Rooms

A **chat room** is an Internet service that allows multiple users to *chat* (exchange *real-time* typed messages). Unlike e-mail and discussion groups, chat rooms require participants to be online at the same time. Like discussion groups, chat rooms are typically set up for specific topics. While most chat rooms are open to anyone, an individual can set up a private chat room that is reserved only for users (typically family, friends, or coworkers) who know the proper password.

>**Discussion group.** A type of Internet communications that enables individuals to post messages on a particular topic for others to read and respond to. >**Chat room.** A type of Internet communications that allows multiple users to exchange written messages in real time.

Instant Messaging (IM)

Instant messaging (**IM**) is a form of private chat that allows you to exchange real-time messages easily with people on your *buddy list*—a list of individuals (such as family, friends, and business associates) that you specify. Popular instant messaging services include *AOL Instant Messenger*, *MSN Messenger*, *Windows Messenger*, and *Yahoo! Messenger*. Because there is no single IM standard at the present time, you and your buddies must use the same (or compatible) instant messaging systems in order to exchange instant messages. Whenever one of your buddies is online (that is, connected to the Internet and signed in to the IM program), you can send a short message to that person and it immediately appears on his or her computer (see Figure 8-17). In addition to sending typed messages, IM programs typically include other options, such as sending a photo or file, starting a voice or video conversation, playing an online game, and viewing news headlines or weather forecasts. Originally a popular communications method among friends, IM has also become a valuable business tool. IM frequently takes place on mobile phones, in addition to being used on desktop PCs. According to a late 2004 report by the Pew Internet and American Life Project, about 30% of IM users report using IM at least as much as they use e-mail—a surprising new shift—and use of IM on mobile devices has doubled in the past year, according to AOL.

Videoconferencing

Videoconferencing (also called *teleconferencing* or *Web conferencing*) refers to the use of computers, video cameras, microphones, and other communications technologies to conduct face-to-face meetings among people in different locations over the Internet. Small videoconferences can take place using the participants' PCs, as in Figure 8-17; large group videoconferences might require a more sophisticated setup, such as a dedicated videoconferencing room set up with video cameras, large monitors, microphones, and other hardware. Most videoconferences are two-way, with all users sending and receiving video. Some uses for one-way Internet videoconferencing include locating PC cameras in childcare centers and schools to allow parents to watch live video of their children throughout the day, and setting up surveillance PC cameras in homes and offices to check for intruders and other problems when the location is unoccupied. Videoconferencing can also take place today via smart phones and other mobile devices.

NET

Voice over Internet Protocol (VoIP)

Internet telephony is the original industry term for the process of placing telephone calls over the Internet. In its early stages, Internet telephony took place either from your PC to the recipient's PC (using the PC's speakers and microphones instead of a telephone) or from your PC to the recipient's telephone, depending on the setup. Some free Internet telephony is still available for PC-to-PC phone calls—such as those supported by some IM programs and the popular Skype service, purchased in 2005 by eBay—but the newest Internet telephony applications today involve placing telephone-to-telephone calls over the Internet—called **Voice over Internet Protocol** (**VoIP**). With VoIP, telephone calls are routed over the Internet to and from the user's regular telephone, via his or her Internet connection. VoIP is one of the fastest growing communications applications today and is currently available from a number of telephone, cable, and VoIP companies. *Voice over Wi-Fi*—making telephone calls via a Wi-Fi network—is an emerging related option. For a look at how VoIP works, see the How it Works box.

>**Instant messaging (IM).** A form of private chat set up to allow users to easily and quickly exchange real-time typed messages with the individuals they specify. >**Videoconferencing.** The use of computers, video cameras, microphones, and other communications technologies to conduct face-to-face meetings over the Internet. >**Voice over Internet Protocol (VoIP).** The process of placing telephone calls via the Internet.

HOW IT WORKS

Voice over IP (VoIP)

Voice over Internet Protocol (VoIP) is a technology that allows you to make voice telephone calls using an Internet connection instead of a regular telephone line. A conventional phone call uses *circuit switching*, in which a connection (or *circuit*) is made between the two parties, and that connection is kept open for the duration of the call, but VoIP uses *packet switching*, like the Internet, in which data is divided into small pieces (called *packets*), and each piece is sent independently of each other piece. Because of this, VoIP is much more efficient than the conventional telephone system.

VoIP services are currently available from a number of Internet telephone companies (such as Packet8, Net2Phone, Vonage, and WebPhone), as well as from mainstream communications companies (such as AT&T, Verizon, Comcast, and Time Warner Cable). In fact, the most growth in the VoIP area lately has been from cable companies, which are packaging low-cost VoIP phone service with television and Internet services. VoIP services work via a broadband Internet connection—typically cable, DSL, or a T1 line.

Some VoIP services are designed so that subscribers make calls using a computer microphone and speakers, but most use a standard phone plugged into an adapter box that is connected to a broadband modem, as shown in the accompanying illustration. In either case, you can usually call any telephone number, but the price typically varies from free (for calling a person from your computer to his or her computer, or for calling a person who subscribes to the same VoIP service) to about four cents per minute for domestic calls. Increasingly, VoIP services offer unlimited local and long-distance calls for as little as $20 per month. One of the biggest disadvantages of VoIP at the present time is that it does not function during a power outage or if your Internet connection goes down. In addition, calls to 911 might not be identified with your home address, depending on your VoIP service and how it was set up. To solve this problem, the FCC has ruled that all VoIP phone companies must provide *enhanced 911 (e911)* service by the end of 2005. With e911, consumers must supply their home address to their VoIP provider, and emergency calls are routed directly to a switchboard in the subscriber's area to relay to emergency services.

Although it might take some time to happen, it is likely that circuit-switching telephone networks will eventually be replaced with packet switching technology. Close to 3 million consumers in the United States used VoIP in 2005, and the Probe Group estimates that 27% of phone users worldwide will use VoIP by 2008.

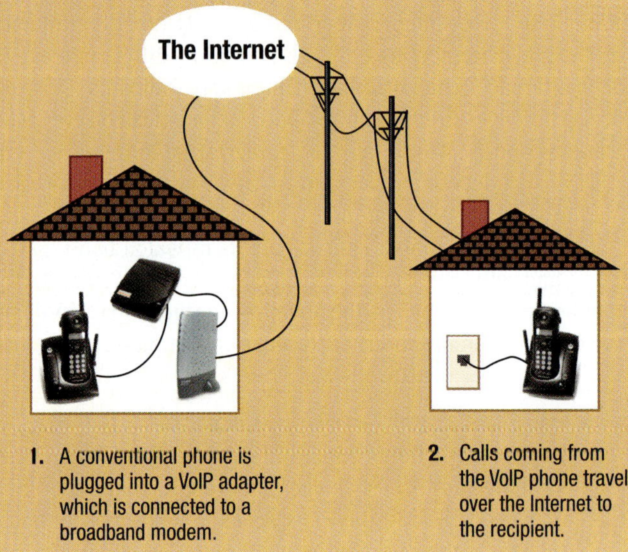

1. A conventional phone is plugged into a VoIP adapter, which is connected to a broadband modem.
2. Calls coming from the VoIP phone travel over the Internet to the recipient.

Online Shopping and Investing

Online shopping and *online investing* are examples of *e-commerce*—online financial transactions. It is very common today for individuals and businesses to order products, buy and sell stock, pay bills, and manage their financial accounts online. In fact, online sales in the United States for 2004 alone were nearly $100 billion, and Forrester research predicts that online sales will reach approximately $331 billion (about 13% of all retail sales) by 2010.

Since *online fraud*, *credit card fraud*, and *identity theft* (a situation in which someone gains enough personal information to pose as another person) are growing problems, it is important to be cautious when participating in online financial activities. To protect yourself, use a credit card whenever possible when purchasing goods or services online so that any fraudulent activities can be disputed, but be sure to enter your credit card number only on a secure Web page. To identify a secure Web page, look for a locked padlock or a complete—unbroken—key at the bottom of your Web browser screen, a URL that begins with *https* instead of *http*, or some other indication that a *secure Web server* is being used.

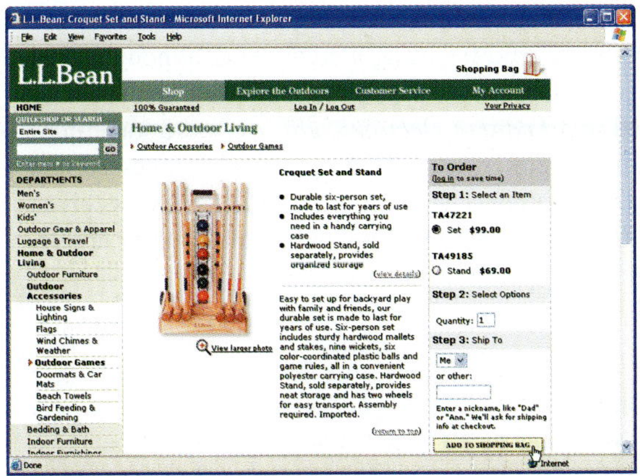

ONLINE SHOPPING
Allows you to purchase goods and services online. As items are selected, they are moved to an online shopping cart or bag.

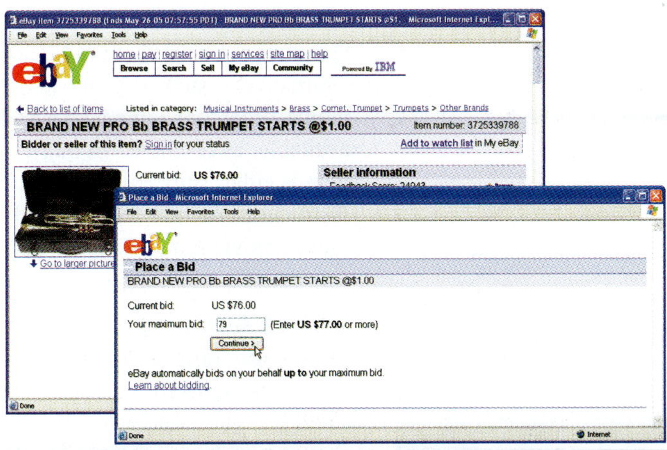

ONLINE AUCTION
Allows you to bid on goods for sale by other individuals; the highest bidder purchases the item.

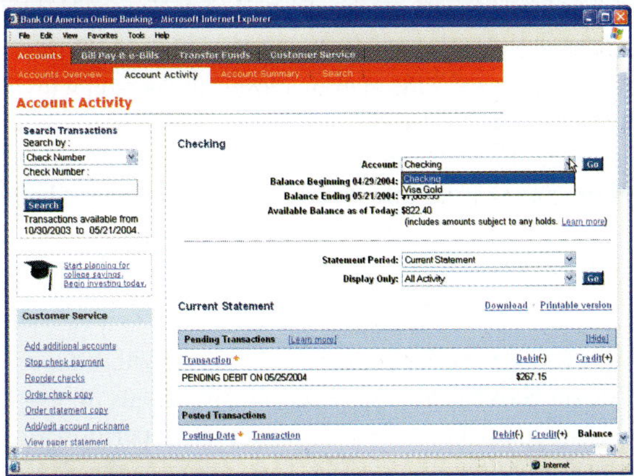

ONLINE BANKING
Allows you to check your account balances, make electronic payments, view your transaction history, and more.

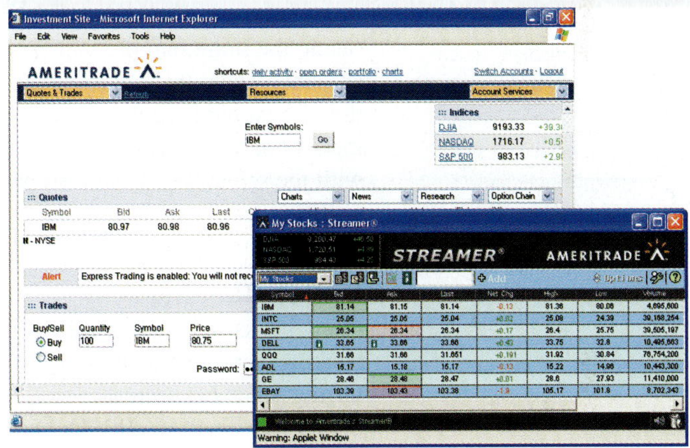

ONLINE INVESTING
Allows you to buy and sell stocks, view your portfolio, get real-time quotes, and more.

FIGURE 8-18
Common e-commerce activities.

NET

Secure Web pages should also be used to enter other types of sensitive information (such as a bank account number or any information that you would not want anyone else to see), and financial accounts should be protected with strong user passwords that are changed frequently. Some of the most common consumer e-commerce activities are illustrated in Figure 8-18 and discussed next. Internet security is discussed in more detail in Chapter 9, and e-commerce is the topic of Chapter 11.

Online Shopping

With **online shopping**, products can be purchased directly from large companies—such as L.L. Bean, Dell Computer, Wal-Mart, Amazon.com, and Macy's—via their Web sites (see Figure 8-18), as well as from a large number of small retailers. Typically, shoppers locate the items they would like to purchase by searching an online retailer site or browsing through the company online catalog, and then adding the items to their online *shopping carts* or *shopping bags*. When shoppers finish shopping, they follow the checkout

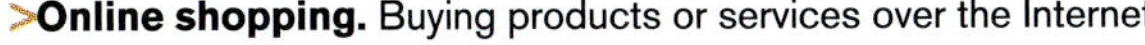

>**Online shopping.** Buying products or services over the Internet.

procedures—including supplying the necessary billing and shipping information—to complete the sale. Most online purchases are paid for using a credit card, although other alternatives—such as using an *online payment account* like *PayPal*, sending in a check or money order, or paying with a preloaded *smart card* or *electronic gift card*—are sometimes available, as discussed in more detail in Chapter 11. After the payment is processed, the item is either shipped to the customer (if it is a physical product), or the customer is given instructions on how to download it (if it is a software program, electronic book or article, music, movie rental, or some other product in electronic form).

Online Auctions

Online auctions are the most common way to buy items online from other individuals. Sellers list items for sale on an auction site (such as eBay or Yahoo! Auctions) by paying a small listing fee and entering a description of the item and a length of time that the auction should run. They can specify a starting bid amount (that bidders see), as well as a minimum selling price (that bidders do not see) that must be met in order for there to be a winning bidder. Individuals can enter bids on auction items (see Figure 8-18) until the end of the auction. For convenience, most auction sites allow bidders to enter a maximum bid amount for a particular auction, and the auction site will automatically bid for that person (using the minimum bid increment for that item) whenever the bidder is outbid, until the amount reaches that bidder's maximum bid. At the time the auction closes, the person with the highest bid is declared the successful bidder (provided the minimum selling price was met, if one was established), who then arranges payment and delivery for the item directly with the seller. The seller also pays a percentage of the sale price as a commission to the auction site.

TIP

The data on Web pages—such as on an online auction page—is typically not updated automatically once it is displayed on your screen. To get updated information—such as the current bid for an auction and auction time remaining—use your browser's Refresh or Reload button to redisplay the page.

Online Banking

Many banks today offer **online banking** as a free service to their customers. With online banking, activities such as reviewing account activity, sending electronic payments, transferring funds between accounts, and looking up credit card balances can all be performed online (see Figure 8-18). Online banking is continually growing—according to the Pew Internet & American Life Project, more than 50 million U.S. adults now bank online.

Online Investing

Buying and selling of stocks, bonds, and other types of securities is referred to as **online investing**. Although it is common to see stock quote capabilities on many search and news sites, trading stocks and other securities usually requires an *online broker*. The biggest advantage to using an online broker is the low transaction fee—often just $7 to $15 per trade, which is generally much less expensive than comparable offline services. Online investing is also much more convenient for those investors who do a lot of trading.

Once an online brokerage account is set up, you can order stock sales and purchases just as you would with an offline broker. Usually the history of your orders can be viewed online, and open orders can be cancelled before they are executed. Many brokerage and financial sites also have convenient access to a variety of performance histories, corporate news, and other useful information for investors. In addition, most online brokers allow you to set up an *online portfolio* that displays the status of the stocks you specify. On some Web sites, stock price data is delayed 20 minutes; on other sites, real-time quotes

>**Online auction.** An online activity for which bids are placed on items, and the highest bidder purchases the item. >**Online banking.** Performing banking activities over the Internet. >**Online investing.** Buying and selling stocks or other types of investments over the Internet.

are available. It is important to realize that Web page data—such as stock price data—is current at the time it is retrieved via a Web page, but it will not be updated (and you will not see current quotes, for instance) until you reload the Web page using your browser's Refresh or Reload toolbar button. An exception to this rule is if the Web page is set up to refresh the content automatically for you on a regular basis. For example, the portfolio shown in Figure 8-18 uses a *Java applet*—a small program built into a Web page—to redisplay updated data continuously.

Online Entertainment

There are an ever-growing number of ways to use the Web for entertainment purposes, such as listening to music, watching videos, and playing online games (see Figure 8-19). Some applications can be accessed with virtually any type of Internet connection; others are only practical with a broadband connection.

Online Music

Online music is perhaps one of the hottest Web-based entertainment activities today. Some of the most widely used possibilities are listening to online radio broadcasts and downloading music singles and albums. Online radio is broadcast from *online radio stations*, also called *Internet radio stations*. To listen to an Internet radio station, you open the radio station's Web page in your browser and click an appropriate hyperlink (see Figure 8-19). A *media player program* usually automatically opens, and you begin to hear the broadcast. Many common media players (such as *Windows Media Player* and *RealOne Player*) are available free of charge and include tools to help you not only listen to radio stations but also organize both your online and offline music.

A number of *online music stores*, such as the iTunes Music Store, RealPlayer Music Store, Napster, Yahoo! Music, and Wal-Mart Music Downloads (see Figure 8-19), are now available to legally download music singles and albums in digital format. Sales of digital music are growing rapidly. The iTunes Music Store exceeded 500 million downloads in mid-2005, and the worldwide online music market is expected to reach $1 billion in sales in 2005, according to the research firm In-Stat. Some online music stores are stand-alone services; others are integrated into a media player program so that songs can be purchased, played, organized, and transferred to a CD or portable music player all from the same program. Still other online music services—such as Real's Rhapsody subscription service—are designed for unlimited access to an enormous collection of online music that can be listened to on demand for a set fee (typically about $10 per month). Music services for cell phones are also available. Consumers are currently spending billions of dollars on ringtones, and cell phones capable of downloading and storing hundreds of songs became available in late 2005. In fact, many expect the cell phone to eventually replace the MP3 player and market research firm Strategy Analytics expects mobile music to be a $9 billion business by 2010.

To avoid copyright violations, all legal downloaded music is available either as free downloads (sometimes found on sites featuring new artists, for example) or for purchase (typically 99 cents per song, part of which is used for royalties owed to the artist or record company for the download). Once downloaded, music files can be played from your PC's hard drive using a media player program installed on your PC. Provided the download agreement did not preclude it, music files can also be copied to a CD to create a custom music CD or transferred to a portable digital music player, such as an iPod.

>**Online music.** Music played or obtained via the Internet.

ONLINE MUSIC
Allows you to listen to live radio stations (left) or download songs (below) to be played later on your PC or digital music player.

Click to listen to this online radio station.

Click to purchase and download this music single.

VIDEO-ON-DEMAND
Allows you to download and watch feature films and other fee-based video content.

Click a movie to download it.

In this game, an *avatar* represents each player; each avatar's movement and speech are controlled by its player.

ONLINE GAMING
Allows you to play games online either alone or with other players, as in this example.

FIGURE 8-19
Common online entertainment activities.

Online TV, Videos, and Video-On-Demand

Additional online entertainment applications include television shows, movies, and video clips. It is common to find news clips, movie trailers, music videos, taped interviews, and similar short, prerecorded videos on Web sites today. Live online TV is fairly limited at the present time, although there are some Web sites that provide live video feeds, such as the interactive Web sites that accompany television shows like *Big Brother*. *Interactive TV (iTV)*—which allows users to perform interactive activities (such as participating in games, ordering merchandise, voting, or looking up related trivia) during a television broadcast—is an emerging option, particularly for cable or satellite TV subscribers. One of the most promising new applications is **video-on-demand (VOD)**.

With VOD, individuals order movies and television shows over the Internet, which are then typically sent via the Internet to their PCs or digital video recorders (DVRs). With VOD, a portion of the movie usually downloads first, and then the movie can be played while the rest of it finishes downloading. This type of delivery—called *streaming media*—is commonly used with both audio and video distributed over the Internet to reduce the time needed to begin to hear or view the selection. One example of a video-on-demand service available today is Movielink (shown in Figure 8-19), which offers downloads of full-length feature films.

>**Video-on-demand (VOD).** The process of downloading movies and televisions shows, on demand, via the Internet.

Downloadable movies are typically "pay-per-view" movies that can only be viewed during a limited time, such as 24 hours after activation; at the end of that time, the downloaded file becomes unusable. For convenience, many VOD services allow users to download pay-per-view downloadable movies up to a month ahead of time, but once the movie has started to play, it only works for a 24-hour period. To watch the movie again after that point requires an additional fee, although the movie does not have to be downloaded again, unless it was deleted from the user's hard drive. Typical fees for video-on-demand movies are comparable with conventional video rental services—about $3 to $5 each—but they provide end users the convenience of not having to leave their houses to pick up or return the movies, and end users get movies faster than services that rent DVDs via regular mail.

In addition to being used with home computers and televisions, VOD is also available for cell phones and other types of mobile devices, as discussed in the Chapter 1 Trend box. For example, in late 2005 Apple introduced an iPod capable of playing video and downloading video and TV shows. Episodes of hit TV shows like *Desperate Housewives* and *Lost* can be downloaded to the iPod the day after they air on television for about $1.99 each.

Online Gaming

Online gaming refers to games played over the Internet. Many sites—especially children's Web sites—include games for visitors to play. There are also sites whose sole purpose is hosting games that can be played online. Some of the games, such as Solitaire, are designed to be played alone. Online *multiplayer* games, such as Hearts, Doom EverQuest, Final Fantasy XI, and City of Heroes (see Figure 8-19), can be played online against other online gamers. Online multiplayer games are especially popular in countries, such as South Korea, that have high levels of both high-speed Internet installations and Internet use in general. As of mid-2004, nearly 80% of the homes in South Korea had broadband Internet access, and one South Korean online gaming network estimates it has about 40 million subscribers for its most popular online game, with an average of 500,000 people playing it at any given time.

Online gaming is also associated quite often with *Internet addiction*—the inability to stop using the Internet or to prevent extensive use of the Internet from interfering with other aspects of one's life. Internet addiction is a growing concern and is discussed in more detail in Chapter 16.

E-Books

E-books—electronic versions of books sometimes also called *online books*—are plentiful. From the entire works of Shakespeare to new best sellers, thousands of books can be read online or downloaded. There are online libraries that host online books (many in HTML format so they can be displayed using a Web browser), and there are online bookstores where e-books can be purchased and downloaded. E-books are most commonly viewed using a handheld PC, but they can be viewed on a variety of other devices, including desktop PCs and special devices designed for reading e-books. Depending on the format, one of several free e-book reader programs (such as *Microsoft Reader*, *Adobe Reader*, or *Palm Reader*) can be used to view e-books.

E-books are also becoming available for checkout via county libraries (see Figure 8-20). After checkout, the books are downloaded to the patron's PC or mobile device and can only be read until the book's

FIGURE 8-20

Library e-books. E-books, that typically only function for a specified check-out time period, can now be downloaded from some public libraries.

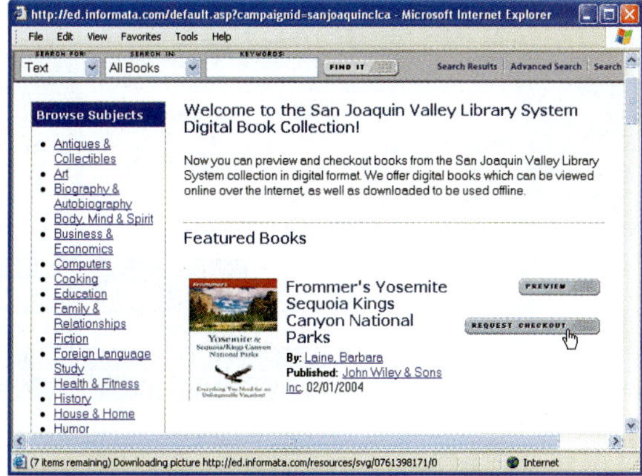

>**Online gaming.** Playing games over the Internet. >**E-book.** A book obtained in electronic format.

due date. The e-books are usually in PDF format and are checked out using the patron's library card number and a PIN number obtained from the local library. When the checkout period expires, the e-book becomes unreadable, and the user simply deletes it from his or her PC. Like books checked out from the local library, there is a limit to the number of copies of each e-book that can be checked out at one time—once the due date is reached, the book is considered "returned," and it becomes available to be digitally checked out by another patron. Unlike conventional library books, e-books never incur overdue charges.

Peer-to-Peer File Sharing

FURTHER EXPLORATION

For links to further information about the Napster controversy and other related peer-to-peer file sharing issues, go to www.course.com/uc11/ch08

One of the earliest widespread applications of **peer-to-peer (P2P) file sharing**—sharing resources directly between users via the Internet—was *Napster*, a P2P music sharing service in place several years ago. Instead of storing music files on the Napster server to facilitate the file sharing, files downloaded using the Napster service were downloaded from one Napster user's PC to another Napster user's PC—from one peer to another. Napster and other P2P sites in place at that time did not have any technology in place to ensure that files were not being shared illegally. As a result, a flood of lawsuits from the music industry eventually shut down Napster and other P2P sites that were being used to exchange copyright-protected content illegally.

Today, peer-to-peer file sharing is still available over the Internet—some legal, and some not. In 2005, the U.S. Supreme Court ruled against one P2P services provider (*Grokster*) and said that companies with the active intent of encouraging copyright infringement should be held liable for their customers' illegal actions. One of the first P2P file sharing services set up to allow legal content distribution between members is Peer Impact, launched in 2005. Peer Impact technology allows music and other digital content to be purchased and shared legally, with artists and record labels being paid appropriately for all music shared via the site. In fact, the Peer Impact service encourages legal file sharing because members who help sell and redistribute authorized content to others earn money for their participation (see Figure 8-21). Other companies have been working to develop technology to allow legal P2P file sharing, but Peer Impact has a distinct head start—by early 2005, all four of the major recording companies agreed to sell their music via the Peer Impact service.

FIGURE 8-21
Legal P2P file sharing. The Peer Impact P2P service shown here reimburses artists and record labels for downloads and also pays participants for facilitating downloads.

With the availability of legal ways to obtain digital content—such as online music stores and legal P2P services, some experts predict that, eventually, these legal alternatives will become the norm for consumers looking for music to use on their PCs, portable music players, home stereos, car stereos, cell phones, and any other device used to play music. But for a look at how illegal file sharing can affect college students in the meantime, see the Technology and You box.

Online News and Research

There is an abundance of news and research information available through the Internet. The following sections discuss a few of these resources. For a look at an alternate way businesses and individuals can keep others up to date—RSS feeds—see the Inside the Industry box.

>**Peer-to-peer (P2P) file sharing.** The process of sharing resources directly between users via the Internet.

INSIDE THE INDUSTRY

RSS Feeds

Really Simple Syndication (*RSS*) is an XML-based format, originally developed by Netscape, which is designed for sharing headlines and other content published to a Web site. A Web site sets up an *RSS feed*—a stream of regularly updated information from the Web site—and then visitors can use an *RSS reader* (usually a stand-alone program, although it might also be built into a Web browser) to retrieve the RSS feed information on a regular basis. Typically, users *subscribe* (add a feed to their RSS readers) to an RSS feed by using a link on a Web page, as shown in the accompanying figure.

Many different types of Web sites today offer RSS feeds, but some of the most common RSS feeds are for national, sports, finance, technical, or entertainment news. As shown in the accompanying figure, many RSS readers—called *RSS aggregators*—can be used to display RSS feeds from multiple Web sites. Clicking the name of a feed displayed within the RSS reader interface usually displays the headlines for that feed somewhere on the screen, and then clicking a headline retrieves that article from the corresponding Web site. Typically, RSS readers are set up to refresh the headlines for all feeds on a regular basis—such as every three hours—but most can be customized to retrieve the headlines more or less frequently.

To help individuals find RSS feeds that match their interests, there are lists of RSS feeds and RSS feed search sites available on the Internet. There are also subscription-based RSS services that provide individuals access to RSS feeds without requiring the individual to manually locate and add each RSS feed to his or her RSS reader. With this type of service, the subscriber selects topics of interest, and then the RSS service provides links to related RSS feeds. These RSS services provide easy access to a large number of RSS feeds—one services claims it has RSS feeds from more than 200,000 Web sites—and cost about $5 to $25 per month, depending on the number of topics and other services selected. Personalized *portal* pages, such as the My Yahoo! Web page available through Yahoo!, are also beginning to incorporate RSS feeds into their members' personalized pages.

There are several versions of RSS (the most widely used is *RSS 2.0*), as well as competing formats—such as the *ATOM* format designed as a universal publishing standard for blogs. Fortunately, most RSS readers today are compatible with most or all of the possible news feed formats. And since virtually all of the feed formats are *XML* (*Extensible Markup Language*)*-based*, they are flexible, so the data contained in a news feed can be delivered to a wide variety of devices. For example, in addition to PC-based RSS readers, RSS feeds today can be delivered to cell phones and other mobile devices. Some companies are even replacing e-mail with RSS for employee and customer notifications—for instance, one Web site uses RSS to alert subscribers to new coupons, and another uses RSS to notify subscribers of new computer virus threats. In the future, expect to see RSS feeds delivered to televisions—perhaps even to watches, refrigerators, and other display devices of the future.

1. Web sites include links to RSS feeds, typically identified with an XML or RSS button. Visitors right-click the link to copy the RSS feed URL.

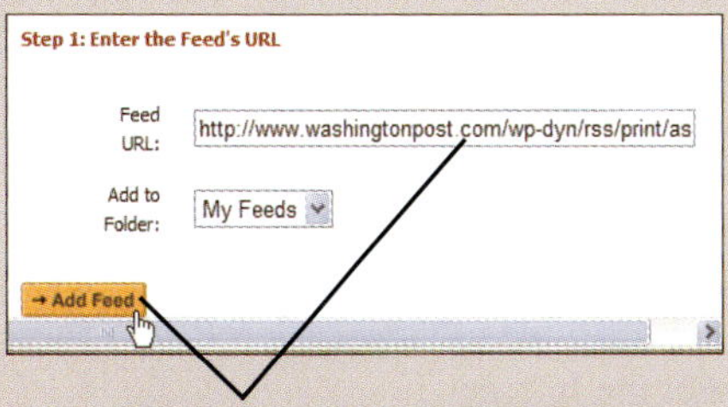

2. The RSS URL is pasted to the appropriate place in the RSS reader program in order to add the RSS feed to the individual's available RSS feeds.

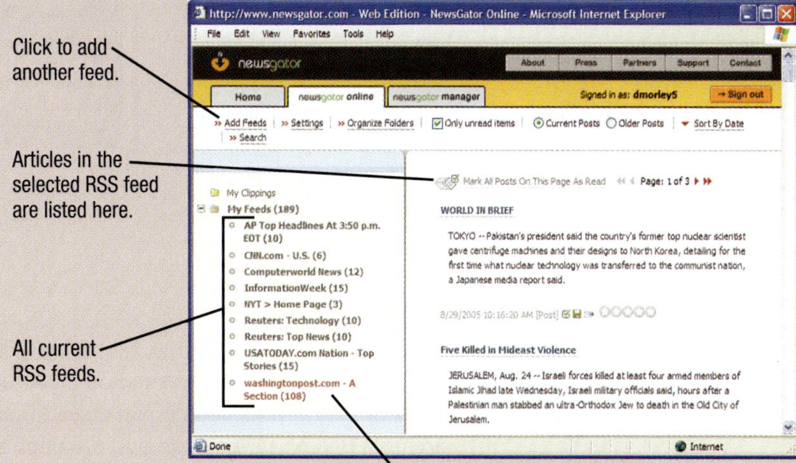

3. The RSS feed is then available in the RSS reader.

TECHNOLOGY AND YOU

P2P Legal Implications for College Students

Since Napster, many individuals—often high school and college students—have been illegally exchanging copyrighted music files via P2P networks. Although Napster and other file sharing services that facilitated the illegal exchange of copyrighted music and movies were eventually shut down, P2P file sharing continues. Since September 2003, recording companies have filed more than 9,000 lawsuits against individuals illegally exchanging music files via P2P services. The most recent focus by the Recording Industry Association of America (RIAA) is on college students. In mid-2005, the RIAA filed more than 400 copyright infringement lawsuits targeted at college students at 18 college campuses who downloaded copyrighted music files for free. The students named in this round of lawsuits were using high-speed networking technologies created in conjunction with the Internet2 project, designed to develop technologies for the next-generation Internet. According to the RIAA, the file sharing was "an emerging epidemic of music theft" and an illegitimate use of Internet2 technology.

Copyright infringement fines are steep—up to $150,000 per instance. In addition to personal liability for students, high amounts of P2P file exchanges also impact colleges—both by making the college vulnerable to industry lawsuits and by slowing down network performance. One solution offered by Dell and the new legal Napster is using Dell servers located on campus to store the entire Napster collection and then legally distributing that music to students for a small fee. Since downloads only need to be transmitted over the college network and not the Internet, student downloads of music files via the Napster service and its local cache of music will have minimal impact on a college's network bandwidth. At most colleges using the Dell/Napster service, a flat fee for the service is passed on to all students–typically around $3 per month instead of the normal $9.95 per month that Napster charges—and then all students have unlimited access to the Napster collection (see the accompanying screen shot of the Napster service).

Despite these efforts, the risk of prosecution, and the risk of accidentally downloading *spyware* (a software program installed without the user's knowledge that secretly gathers information about the user and transmits it through his or her Internet connection, as discussed later in this chapter), a computer virus, or a corrupted file when downloading a file from another person's PC, illegal file sharing continues. For instance, the number of songs downloaded illegally from P2P services in March 2005 totaled nearly 275 million, more than 10 times the number of songs downloaded legally, according to The NPD Group. However, as more peer-to-peer users understand the risks, legal implications, and ethical implications involved with illegal P2P file sharing, they will likely consider it worth their while to pay the roughly $1 per song for music downloads from a legitimate site instead of obtaining the song illegally. And with consumers beginning to want quality, efficiency, and safety, in addition to value, legal digital media distribution is expected to eventually become the norm.

News

News organizations, such as television networks, newspapers, and magazines, typically have Web sites that are updated on a continual basis to post current news and online versions of their offline counterparts (see Figure 8-22). Many news sites also have searchable archives to look for past articles, although some require a fee to view back articles. There are also news radio programs that are broadcast over the Internet.

Product, Corporate, and Government Information

The Web is a very useful tool for locating product and corporate information. Before buying an item online (or in a conventional *brick-and-mortar store*, for that matter), many people research product options online. Manufacturer and retailer Web sites, such as the one in Figure 8-22, often include product specifications, instruction manuals, and other useful information. For investors, a variety of corporate information is available online, both from the corporation directly and from sites, such as Hoover's Online, which contain free company summaries as well as fee-based in-depth corporate information.

Government information is also widely available on the Internet. Most state and federal agencies have Web sites to provide information to citizens, such as government publications, archived documents, forms, and legislative bills. You can also perform tasks, such as downloading tax forms and filing your tax returns online; many cities, counties, and states allow you to pay your car registration, register to vote, view property tax information, or update your driver's license online, as well.

NEWS
News organizations typically update their sites several times per day to provide access to the most current news and information.

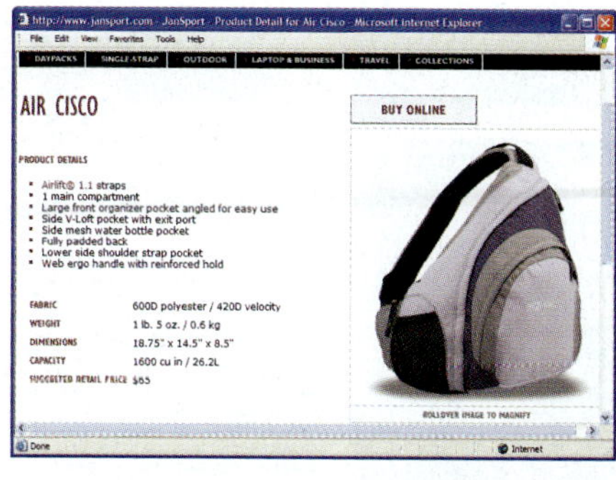

PRODUCT INFORMATION
Businesses use Web sites to provide specifications, instruction manuals, and other types of product information.

GOVERNMENT INFORMATION
Government (local, state, and federal) Web sites provide a variety of information. Some, like this county site, also provide a variety of e-services.

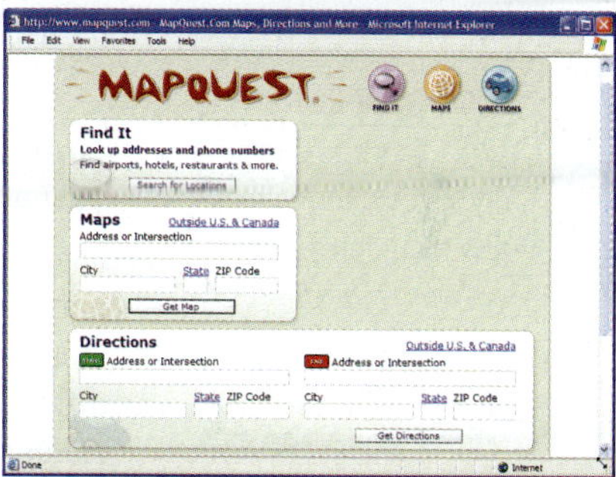

REFERENCE TOOLS
Reference Web sites, such as this site that allows you to generate map and driving directions, provide access to specific types of useful information.

FIGURE 8-22
News and research. Up-to-the minute news, reference tools, product information, and more abound on the Web.

NET

Reference Sites and Portals

There are a number of *reference sites* on the Web, such as those used to generate maps, check the weather forecast, or provide access to encyclopedias, dictionaries, ZIP code directories, and telephone directories. To find an appropriate reference site, type the information you are seeking (such as *ZIP code lookup* or *topographical map*) as keywords in a search site. Some reference sites, such as the MapQuest site shown in Figure 8-22, allow you to send data (such as maps and driving directions) from the Web site to your mobile phone. Additional mobile reference tools are available through some wireless providers.

Portal Web pages are Web pages designed to be selected as a browser's home page and visited on a regular basis. Portal pages typically include reference tools, search capabilities, and other useful content; they also usually allow users to customize the page to display the news of their choice, such as sports, technology, weather, and national or local news. Once the portal page is customized, each time the user visits the portal page, the specified information will be displayed. Popular portals include Yahoo!, AltaVista, MSN, AOL, and Bolt.

>**Portal.** A Web site designed to be designated as a browser home page; typically can be customized to display personalized content.

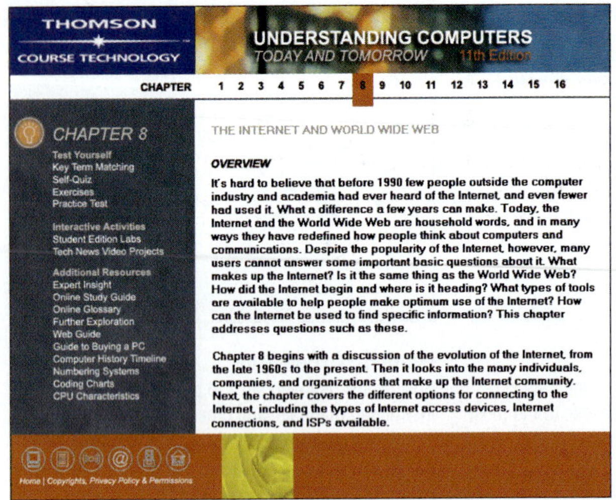

FIGURE 8-23

Web-based learning. The Web site that supplements this book provides Web-based learning opportunities that include online quizzes and other activities, useful Web links, interesting video clips, and more.

Online Education and Writing

Online education—using the Internet to facilitate learning—is a rapidly growing Internet application. The Internet can be used to deliver part or all of any educational class or program, such as through *Web-based training* (*WBT*) and *distance learning*; it can also be used to supplement or support traditional education, such as with *online testing* and *online writing*. In addition, many high school and college courses use Web content—such as online syllabi, schedules, chat rooms, discussion boards, study guides, and tutorials—as required or suggested supplements. For example, the Web site that supplements this book contains an online study guide, online quizzes, online hands-on labs, Web links, and other resources for students taking a course that uses this textbook (see Figure 8-23). The next few sections take a look at some of the most widely used online education applications.

Web-Based Training and Distance Learning

There are more opportunities for online learning today than ever before. Both businesses and schools are utilizing **Web-based training** (**WBT**) for employee training or course materials, and millions of people take classes via **distance learning** each year. With distance learning, students take classes from a location, such as from home or work, which is different from the one where the delivery of instruction takes place. Distance learning (also called *online learning* and *e-learning*) is available through many high schools, colleges, and universities; it is also used for corporate education and training. Distance learning can be used for training employees in just one task or new skill, as well as for an entire college course or degree program. It can enable high school students living in rural areas to take advanced courses not offered at their local schools; young athletes can use distance learning to fit school around their training regimens. Typically the majority of distance learning coursework is completed over the Internet via class Web pages, discussion groups, chat rooms, and e-mail, although schools might require some in-person contact, such as sessions for orientation and testing. Distance learning classes often utilize Web-based training components.

Web-based training and distance learning are typically experienced individually and at the user's own pace. Online content for Web-based training components is frequently customized for each individual user, according to his or her mastery of the material already completed. Online content and activities (such as exercises, exams, and animations) are accessed in real time, just as other Web pages are. Some advantages of Web-based training and distance learning include the following:

- *Self-paced instruction.* Students can usually work at their own pace and at their convenience, at any time of the day or night.
- *Flexible location.* Students do not need to live close to any particular facility to take part in the educational program because Web-based training can be accessed from home, while traveling, or basically anywhere the student has access to a computer with an Internet connection.

>**Web-based training (WBT).** Instruction delivered on an individual basis via the World Wide Web. >**Distance learning.** A learning environment in which the student is physically located away from the instructor and other students; commonly, instruction and communications take place via the Internet.

- *Up-to-date material.* Since all instructional material is hosted on a Web server, it can be updated whenever necessary simply by updating the content on the Web site. Once content is updated, all users will see the newest version of the instructional material the next time they access the Web site.
- *Immediate feedback and customized content.* Web-based training components can be set up to provide immediate feedback from online activities by displaying supplemental material for any problem areas that are identified based on the user's responses. It can also require mastery of material before the student is allowed to move on to the next test or assignment, and it can jump students to more advanced topics as appropriate. This flexibility can result in highly customized content, based on a student's progress and abilities.

While the advantages of Web-based training and distance learning are numerous, potential disadvantages are a concern and include the following:

- *Technology requirements and problems.* In order to participate in Web-based training or distance learning, users must have access to a computer and the Internet. Slow PCs or Internet connections can be frustrating for students as they try to download materials or participate in online discussions. Technological problems—such as a computer crashing or Web server inaccessibility during a test day—can create significant problems for students and instructors.
- *Anonymity.* Because students are in remote locations, it can be difficult to ensure that the student registered for the class is the actual student participating in online discussions and online exams. Some instructors choose to require face-to-face exams at either the school or an authorized testing center in the student's geographical area; newer authentication technology, such as smart cards, fingerprint scanners, and digital signatures, might help to overcome this problem in the future.
- *Lack of face-to-face contact.* Many educators view the interactive exchange of ideas as a very important part of the educational experience. Although interactivity can take place online via chat rooms and discussion groups, the lack of face-to-face contact, which allows students to see, ask questions of, or have discussions with other students and their instructor in person, is cited as a disadvantage by some educators.

NET

Online Testing

In both distance learning and traditional classes, *online testing*—which allows students to take quizzes or tests via the Internet—is a growing trend. Both objective tests (such as those containing multiple choice or true/false questions) and performance-based exams (such as those given in computer classes to test student mastery of software applications) can be administered and taken online. Typically online tests are automatically graded, freeing up instructor time for other activities, as well as providing fast feedback to the students.

Online Writing

Online writing applications used in an educational context today include *blogs*, *wikis*, and *e-portfolios* (*electronic portfolios*). Students might also publish original written material online via personal Web pages. Blogs and wikis are often used for personal and professional commentary, in addition to being used for educational purposes.

A **blog**—also called a *Web log*—is a Web page that contains short, frequently updated entries in chronological order. Basically, a blog is an online personal journal accessible to the

>**Blog.** A Web page that contains short, frequently updated entries in chronological order, typically by just one individual; also called a Web log.

BLOGS
Blogs can be accessed individually or via a blog aggregator. For example, this blog aggregator displays blog entries from all blogs at the University of South Florida.

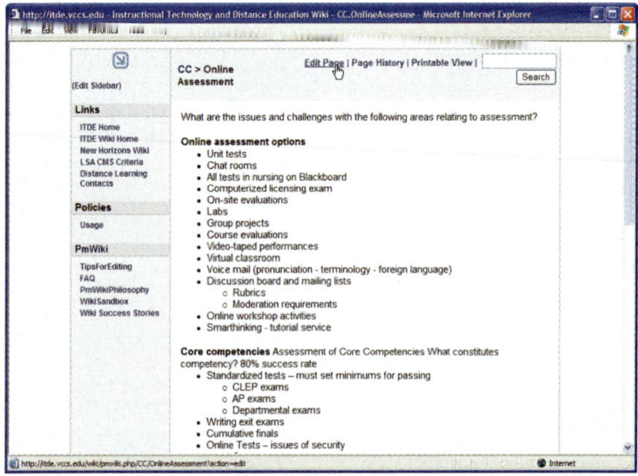

WIKIS
This faculty wiki provides information about distance learning classes at one community college district; the *Edit Page* option at the top of the page is used to edit the page content.

FIGURE 8-24
Blogs and wikis.

public and is typically updated by one individual. Blogs can be used to post personal commentary, research updates, comments on college classes, and more. Blogs can also be set up to have multiple authors, such as a group of employees collaborating on a project or all the students in a particular writing class. *Blog aggregators* collect entries from a variety of blogs—such as all student blogs for a particular university—and post them in a single location (see Figure 8-24). In addition to being published on a school, business, or personal Web site, blogs can also be published to a blogging site, such as Blogger.com. Blogs are usually updated frequently, and entries can be posted via e-mail and mobile devices, in addition to a PC, and entries can contain text, photos, and voice updates stored as MP3 files. For a look at an activity related to blogging—*podcasting*—see the Trend box.

With their increased use and audiences, bloggers and the *blogosphere* (the complete collection of blogs on the Internet) are beginning to have increasing influence on businesses and politicians today. Some popular bloggers have huge audiences, so the impact of blogging is more influential than in the past. As a result of the increasing influence of blogs, there are news services available that monitor blogs—some watch around 100,000 blogs each day—and relay any new blog articles that mention specified company names, brands, people, competitors, or other selected criteria to the subscriber. These services are designed to help businesses and other organizations identify interest in competitor's products or services, potential problems with an existing product or service, and new issues related to their products that they might not be aware of.

Wikis are related to blogs but have a different purpose. From the Hawaiian phrase *wiki wiki* meaning *quick*, a wiki is a way of creating and editing collaborative Web pages quickly and easily. Similar to a blog, the content on a Wiki page can be edited and republished to the Web just by pressing a Save or Submit button, but whereas a blog contribution is added to the existing content (and does not modify the previous blog content), the entire wiki page can be edited to create a new updated page. In a nutshell, blogs are designed for primarily one-way running communications, while wikis are intended to be modified by others. In an educational setting, wikis can be used to create and access a shared workspace easily, such as one used by students or faculty who are collaborating on a group or class project (see Figure 8-24). They can also be used to create and publish Web pages for class projects or presentations easily. To protect the content of a wiki from sabotage, editing privileges can be password protected. One of the largest wikis is *Wikipedia*, a free online encyclopedia that contains over 1.5 million entries in 76 languages. Visitors can read, as well as update, entries.

An **e-portfolio**, also called an *electronic portfolio* or *Webfolio*, is a collection of an individual's work accessible through a Web site. Today's e-portfolios are typically linked to a collection of student-related information, such as résumés, papers, projects, and other original works. Some e-portfolios are used for a single course; others are designed to be used and updated throughout a student's educational career, culminating in a comprehensive collection of information that can be used as a job-hunting tool.

TIP

There are numerous online blog search engines and directories—such as BlogStreet.com—to help you find blogs that meet your interests.

>**Wiki.** A collaborative Web page that is designed to be edited and republished by a variety of individuals. >**E-portfolio.** A collection of an individual's work accessible through a Web site.

TREND

Podcasting

Podcasting is a method of publishing audio broadcasts via the Internet. Podcasts are created by recording audio (typically MP3) files and then making those files available for users to download. The term "podcast" is derived from the iPod digital music player (the first widely used device for playing digital audio files), although podcasts today can be listened to using a desktop or handheld PC, in addition to an iPod or other type of portable digital media player (see the accompanying photograph). With a PC, podcasts can be downloaded manually, or they can be downloaded automatically after subscribing to a particular podcast using *podcatching software*, similar to the way RSS feeds are subscribed to using an RSS reader or aggregator. Downloaded podcasts can be transferred to a digital music player when desired.

Podcasting enables individuals to create self-published, inexpensive Internet radio broadcasts, such as talk shows, to express their opinions on particular subjects, or as a means to share original poems, songs, or short stories with interested individuals. Originally created and distributed by individuals, podcasts are now also being created and distributed by businesses. Some commercial radio stations are making portions of their broadcasts available via podcast, and a growing number of new sites–including ABC News and ESPN–have podcasts. In fact, some view podcasts as the new and improved radio since it is an easy way to listen to your favorite radio broadcasts on your own schedule. The next step? Video podcasting is emerging to deliver both audio and video files.

CENSORSHIP AND PRIVACY ISSUES

There are many important societal issues related to the Internet. One—network and Internet security—will be covered in Chapter 9. Two other important issues—*censorship* and *privacy*—are discussed next, in the context of Internet use. Other societal issues and how they relate to computer use in general are discussed in further detail in Chapters 15 and 16.

Censorship

The First Amendment to the U.S. Constitution guarantees a citizen's right to free speech. This protection allows people to say or show things to others without fear of arrest. People must observe some limits to free speech, of course, such as the prohibition of obscenity over the public airwaves and of child pornography.

But how does the right to free speech relate to alleged patently offensive or indecent materials available over the Internet, where they might be observed by children and the public at large? There have been some attempts at Internet content regulation—what some would view as *censorship*—in recent years, but the courts have had difficulty defining what is "patently offensive" and "indecent" as well as finding a fair balance between protection and censorship. For example, the *Communications Decency Act* was signed into law in 1996 and made it a criminal offense to distribute patently indecent or offensive material online. Although intended to protect children from being exposed to inappropriate Web content, the Supreme Court, in 1997, declared this law unconstitutional on the basis of free speech. The *Children's Online Privacy Protection Act of 1998*, which regulates how Web sites can collect information from minors and provides tax incentives for Web sites and ISPs that protect minors from accessing materials deemed harmful to them, is one example of legislation that has held up under scrutiny.

Internet filtering—blocking access to particular Web pages or types of Web pages—can be used on home computers (for instance, by individuals to protect themselves from material they would view as offensive or by parents to protect their children from material they feel is inappropriate for them). It is also commonly used by employers to keep non-work-related material out of the workplace, by some ISPs and search sites to block access to potentially objectionable materials, and by many schools and libraries. Available through both browser settings (see Figure 8-25) and stand-alone programs, Internet filtering typically restricts access to Web pages that contain specified keywords or that exceed a rating for potentially offensive categories, such as language, nudity, sex, or violence. One limitation with this procedure, however, is that the descriptions of the site and how these categories apply to its content are provided voluntarily by the content provider, not by an independent rating organization. Typically, a password is required to change the filter settings to prevent them from being changed by an unauthorized individual, such as a child or an employee.

An ongoing debate has been whether or not public computers should use Internet filtering. Filtering advocates want to protect children at public locations (such as libraries and schools) from accessing adult material. Individuals and organizations against Internet filtering at libraries and schools believe that filtering violates the patrons' First Amendment rights to free speech. The *Child Internet Protection Act* (*CIPA*) that went into effect in 2001 required public libraries and schools to use Internet filtering to block Internet access to certain materials in order to receive public funds. Although intended to protect children, it was fought strenuously by free speech advocacy groups and some library associations and was ruled unconstitutional by a federal court in 2002. In a 6 to 3 ruling in 2003, however, the Supreme Court reversed the lower court decision and ruled that the law was constitutional because the need for libraries to prevent minors from accessing obscene materials outweighs the free speech rights of library patrons and Web site publishers.

FIGURE 8-25

Internet filtering. Browser settings can be changed to deny access to Web pages with objectionable content.

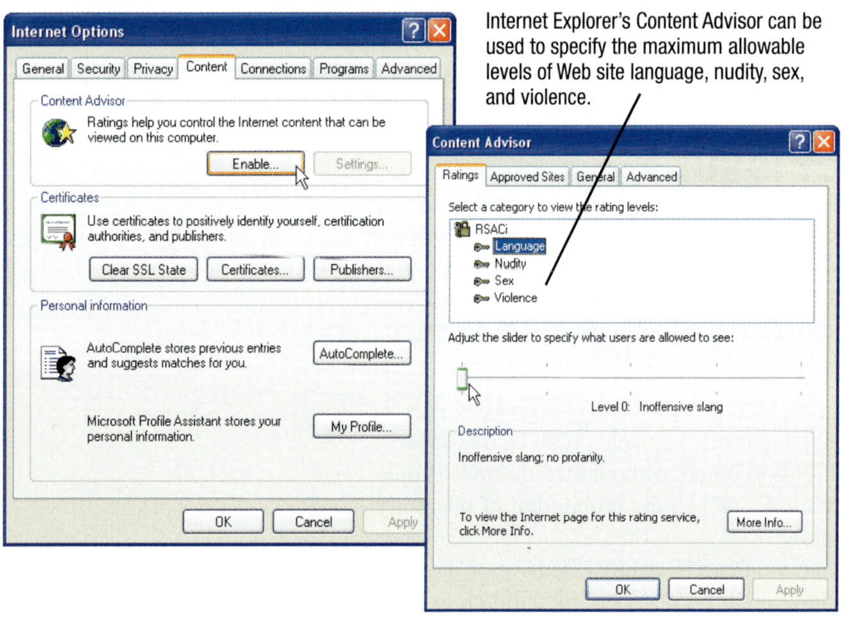

>Internet filtering. Using a software program or browser option to block access to particular Web pages or types of Web pages.

Web Browsing Privacy

Privacy, as it relates to the Internet, encompasses what information about individuals is available, how it is used, and by whom. As more and more transactions and daily activities are being performed online, there is the potential for vast amounts of private information to be collected and distributed without the individual's knowledge or permission. Therefore, it is understandable that public concern regarding privacy and the Internet is on the rise.

One area of concern for many individuals who browse the Web on a regular basis is maintaining the privacy of where they go and what they do at Web sites. You might wonder: Does anyone keep track of which Web sites I visit, what hyperlinks I click on, how long I stay on a Web site, and what things I download and buy? What about the information I provide to a Web site? Can I specify who gets to see it? The answer to each of these questions is "yes" to some extent, but it depends on the specific Web sites visited, the settings on your PC, and what other precautions you have taken to protect your privacy. Although privacy will be discussed in more detail in Chapter 15, a few issues that are of special concern to Internet users regarding Web browsing privacy and e-mail privacy are discussed in the next few sections.

Cookies

Many Web pages today use **cookies**—small text files that are stored on your hard drive by a Web server, typically the one associated with the Web page being viewed—to identify return visitors and their preferences. While some individuals view all cookies as a potentially dangerous invasion of privacy, the use of cookies can provide some benefits to consumers. For example, as shown in Figure 8-26, cookies can enable a Web site to remember preferences for customized Web site content (such as displaying your local weather and your horoscope on your portal page), as well as to retrieve a shopping cart containing items selected during a previous session. Some Web sites use cookies to keep track of which pages on their Web sites each person has visited, in order to recommend products on return visits that match that person's interests.

Cookies are relatively safe from a privacy standpoint. Web sites can read only their own cookie files; they cannot read other cookie files on your PC or any other data on your computer, for that matter. A cookie file might, however, record the pages viewed on the site associated with the cookie, the amount of time spent on pages with similar content, the person's geographic location (which can be determined by his or her PC's IP address, as well as by demographic data supplied while visiting the site), and other factors used to target third-party advertisements. For instance, if you spend a lot of time checking airline prices on a travel site, you might start seeing ads for hotels, rental cars, airfare, and other travel-oriented goods and services displayed on the pages of your travel site—and many of the ads will be from third-party organizations with which the site has an advertising relationship.

The information stored in a cookie file typically includes the name of the cookie, its expiration date, the domain that the cookie belongs to, and either selected personal information that you have entered while visiting the Web site or an ID number assigned by the Web site that allows the Web site's server to retrieve your information from its database. Such a database can contain two types of information: *personally identifiable information* (*PII*) and *non-personally identifiable information* (*Non-PII*). Personally identifiable data is connected with a specific user's identity—such as his or her name, address, and credit card number provided to the site—and is typically given during the process of ordering goods or services. Non-personally identifiable information is anonymous data—such as which product pages were viewed or which advertisements located on the site were clicked—that is not directly associated with the visitor's name or another personally identifiable characteristic.

>**Cookie.** A small file stored on a user's hard drive by a Web server; commonly used to identify personal preferences and settings for that user.

FIGURE 8-26
Cookies. Web site cookies are commonly used to remember customized settings and to facilitate online shopping.

Cookies are typically stored in a Cookies folder on each user's hard drive and can be looked at, if desired—although sometimes deciphering the information contained in a cookie file is difficult. The bottom part of Figure 8-26 shows the content of the cookie file generated by shopping at the BestBuy.com site. Notice that the cookie file contains information about both the shopping cart contents and the signed-in user.

Browser privacy settings can be changed to specify which type of cookies (if any) are allowed to be used, such as permitting the use of regular cookies, but not *third-party cookies* (cookies placed by companies, such as advertising firms who have placed ads on that page) or cookies using personally identifiable information (see Figure 8-27). Turning off cookies entirely might make some features—such as a shopping cart—on some Web sites inoperable. The *Medium High* privacy option in Internet Explorer is a widely used setting since it allows the use of regular cookies but blocks third-party cookies that use personally identifiable information without explicit permission. Both Internet Explorer and Netscape Navigator users who want more control over their cookies can choose to accept or decline cookies as they are encountered. Although this option interrupts your Web surfing frequently, it is interesting to see the cookies generated from each individual Web site. For example, the two cookie prompts shown in the bottom of Figure 8-27 were generated while visiting the BestBuy.com Web site. Although the first cookie request came from the BestBuy.com Web site directly, the second was a third-party cookie from Atlas DMT, an online marketing company. Another alternative for controlling cookies is to delete the cookie files stored on your hard drive periodically, either by using an option available through your Web browser or by finding the Cookie folder located on your hard drive and deleting its contents using your file management program.

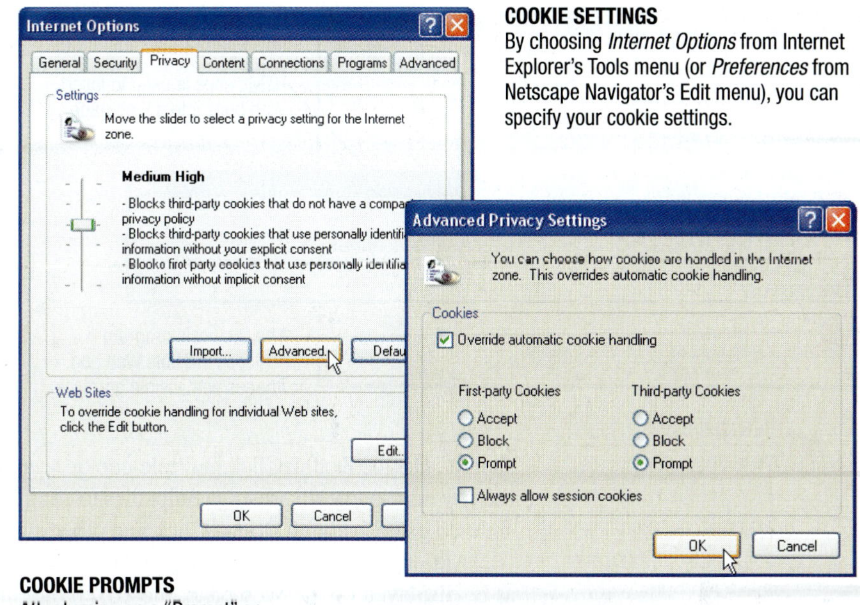

COOKIE SETTINGS
By choosing *Internet Options* from Internet Explorer's Tools menu (or *Preferences* from Netscape Navigator's Edit menu), you can specify your cookie settings.

Although many individuals are slowly becoming more comfortable with the use of cookies, increased use of targeted ads based on e-mail or Web site activities might raise consumer objections, similar to the outrage evoked by the *DoubleClick* fiasco several years ago. DoubleClick, an Internet advertising firm, began the practice of trying to track an individual's Web activity by using multiple cookies. Because DoubleClick had banner ads on literally thousands of different Web sites, that company was in the unique position of being able to place many cookies on a single user's hard drive—one for each site the user visited that contained a DoubleClick ad. DoubleClick then used all of the DoubleClick cookies located on that user's hard drive to get an idea of his or her overall Web activity. Although the data collected was not associated with the person's actual identity, DoubleClick subsequently bought a catalog marketing company and announced plans to merge Web-activity data collected in the future with the consumer data in the newly acquired marketing company database, in order to track customers' Web activity using their identities—and then to sell the information to others. A flood of privacy lawsuits were filed, such as the one by the privacy watchdog group *EPIC* (the *Electronic Privacy Information Center*), which eventually led DoubleClick to agree, in 2002, to obtain permission from consumers before combining any personally identifiable data with Web-surfing history.

COOKIE PROMPTS
After turning on a "Prompt" or "Warn me" cookie feature, you will be prompted to accept or reject cookies as they are encountered.

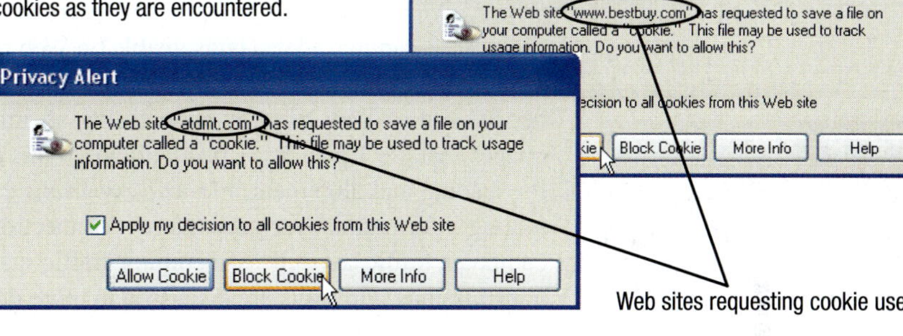

FIGURE 8-27
Browser cookie management. The desired cookies settings can be specified in the browser settings.

In response to the DoubleClick controversy, the advertising industry formed the *Network Advertising Initiative* (*NAI*) and is hoping that voluntary compliance to online marketing standards can be used in lieu of legislation. The NAI works in conjunction with the Federal Trade Commission (FTC) to develop privacy standards for NAI members, which include DoubleClick and several other large Internet advertising companies. These standards detail under what conditions non-personally identifiable information can be merged with personally identifiable information, as well as require that consumers be given the choice to opt out from data collection entirely. However, as consumer concerns about Web privacy continue to grow, legislation is becoming more likely. In late 2003, the European Union adopted privacy regulations on electronic communications, including a ban on all commercial e-mail unless a recipient has asked for it, and set strict rules for the use of cookies. In the United States, there were several bills introduced in Congress in 2005 that addressed the use of personally identifiable information collection on Web sites, and a law in California that went into effect in mid-2004 sets requirements for all Web sites collecting personally identifiable information from California residents.

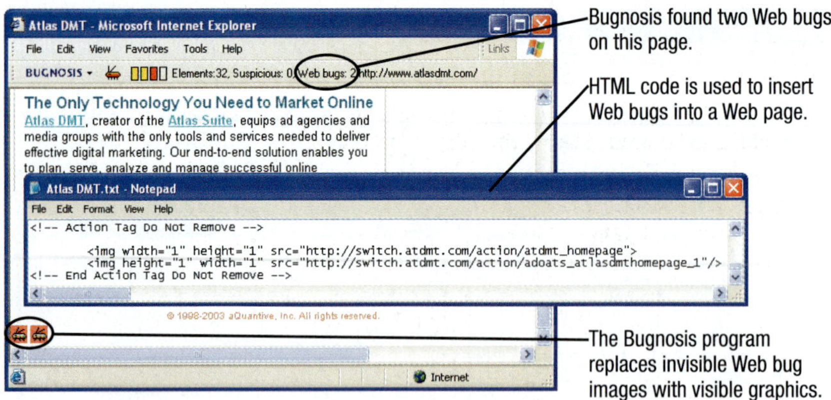

FIGURE 8-28

Web bugs. Some software, such as the Bugnosis program, is available to detect possible Web bugs, although it does not stop their functionality.

Web Bugs

A **Web bug** is usually a very small (often 1 pixel by 1 pixel) image on a Web page that transmits data about a Web page visitor back to the Web page's server. Web bugs are commonly used to gather usage statistics about a Web site, such as the number of visitors to the site, the most visited pages on the site, the time of each visit, and the Web browser used. Web bugs can also be used to retrieve and relay data stored in a cookie file, if the Web bug and cookie are both from the same Web site or advertising company. Consequently, like the DoubleClick multiple-cookie scenario previously discussed, Web bugs can be used by third-party advertising companies to compile data about individuals. In fact, Web bugs are used extensively by DoubleClick and other Internet advertising companies.

Although Web bugs can be normal images that are set up to transfer information, as well as be displayed on the Web page, most Web bug images are tiny and match the color of the Web page's background, so they are invisible. This is perhaps the biggest objection to Web bugs—since they are not visible, users typically are not aware of this potential invasion of privacy. Web bugs are difficult for users to identify, but special programs—such as *Bugnosis*—can make Web bugs visible on Web pages as you surf the Web (see Figure 8-28). Cookie management software can prevent the use of cookies by Web bugs, and some can hinder the use of Web bugs by suppressing all images of a specified dimension, such as all images that are 1 pixel by 1 pixel, although this also suppresses small invisible images used for spacing and alignment. *Firewall programs* can protect against *spyware* programs transmitting information over your Internet connection, since firewalls typically control outgoing computer traffic as well as incoming traffic and will notify the user of any unauthorized transmissions. Firewalls are discussed in more detail in Chapter 9.

FURTHER EXPLORATION

For links to further information about cookies and Web bugs, go to www.course.com/uc11/ch08

Spyware and Adware

Spyware is the term used for any software program that is installed without the user's knowledge and that secretly gathers information about the user and transmits it through his or her Internet connection—typically, to advertisers. Just as with cookies and Web bugs, the information gathered by the spyware software is usually not associated with a person's identity. Instead, it is typically used to provide advertisers with information to be used for marketing purposes, such as to help select advertisements to display on each person's PC. Like Web bugs, people are not normally aware when spyware is being used. Instead of being embedded into a Web page like a Web bug, however, spyware programs are installed—without the user's knowledge—on the user's computer. Spyware programs are usually installed secretly at the same time another program is installed, such as a program downloaded from a Web site or a P2P service. Spyware can also be used by unscrupulous individuals to retrieve personal data stored on your PC and is discussed in more detail in Chapter 9.

A related type of software is *adware*—free or low-cost software that is supported by onscreen advertising. Many free programs that can be downloaded from the Internet, such as the free version of the *NetZero* e-mail program, include some type of adware, which results in onscreen advertising. The difference between spyware and adware is that adware

>**Web bug.** A very small (usually invisible) image on a Web page that transmits data about the Web page visitor to a Web server.

typically does not gather information and relay it to others via the Internet (although it can), and it is not installed without the user's consent. Adware might, however, be installed without the user's direct knowledge, since many users do not read licensing agreements before clicking OK to install a new program. When this occurs with a program that contains adware, the adware components are installed without the user's direct knowledge.

Both spyware and adware can be annoying and use up valuable system resources. In addition, privacy advocates object to spyware because it secretly collects and transmits data about individuals to others, and it can bog down a user's Internet connection without the user's knowledge.

E-Mail Privacy

Many people mistakenly believe that the e-mail they send and receive is private and will never be read by anyone other than the intended recipient. Since it is transmitted over public media, however, only *encrypted* (electronically scrambled) e-mail can be transmitted safely, as discussed in Chapter 9. Although unlikely to happen to your personal e-mail, *nonencrypted* e-mail can be intercepted and read by someone else. Consequently, from a privacy standpoint, a nonencrypted e-mail message should be viewed more like a postcard than a letter (see Figure 8-29).

It is also important to realize that your employer and your ISP have access to the e-mail you send through those organizations, such as to scan incoming e-mail for spam filtering and virus protection, as well as for employee monitoring purposes. Businesses and ISPs typically also *archive* (keep copies of) e-mail messages that travel through their servers and are required to comply with subpoenas from law enforcement agencies for archived e-mail messages.

Chris,

The meeting is Monday at 2 pm. Please bring all related personnel files detailing the anticipated firing of Joe D.

Eve

To: cwilliams@abc.net
From: eve.s@abc.net

REGULAR (NONENCRYPTED E-MAIL) = POSTCARD

ENCRYPTED E-MAIL = SEALED LETTER

FIGURE 8-29
You cannot assume e-mail messages are private, unless they are encrypted.

THE FUTURE OF THE INTERNET

The Internet has changed a great deal since its inception. From only four supercomputers, it has evolved into a vast network connecting virtually every type of computer. The use of the Internet has changed dramatically, as well. As the structure of the Internet evolves and improves, it can support new types of activities. New types of applications also drive the technological improvements necessary to support them.

The exact composition of the Internet of the future is anyone's guess. It will likely be a very high-speed optical network with virtually unlimited bandwidth. It will be accessed by the PC of the day, which will probably be much smaller and less obtrusive than the standard PC today—possibly built directly into desks, refrigerators, and other objects, or carried around on your body or as some type of portable device. The primary interface will likely be the voice, and most network connections will be wireless.

Chances are the Internet will continue to be used for an ever-growing number of day-to-day activities, such as shopping, making voice or video phone calls, controlling home appliances, ordering and downloading TV shows or movies, ordering groceries, paying bills, and telecommuting. It will also continue to be widely used for business purposes, and high bandwidth connections will allow a much higher level of real-time video communications, resulting in even more use of telecommuting, videoconferencing, and home-based offices. A universal payment system for micropayments is likely to facilitate paying small fees for Web content. Ideally, all of an individual's micropayments will be combined into a single monthly bill.

This is an exciting time for the Internet. It is already firmly embedded in our society, and it will be exciting to see what becomes of all the breathtaking new applications and technological improvements on the horizon and how the Internet will continue to evolve.

SUMMARY

EVOLUTION OF THE INTERNET

Chapter Objective 1:
Discuss how the Internet evolved and what it is like today.

The origins of the **Internet**—a worldwide collection of interconnected networks that is accessed by millions of people daily—date back to the late 1960s. At its start and throughout its early years, the Internet was called **ARPANET**. It was not until the development of graphical user interfaces and the **World Wide Web** that public interest in the Internet began to soar. Most companies have Web sites today and consider the Web to be an indispensable business tool. While the Web is a very important and widely used Internet resource, it is not the only one. Over the years *protocols* have been developed to download files, send e-mail messages, and other tasks, in addition to using Web pages. Today, the term *Internet* has become a household word and, in many ways, has redefined how people think about computers and communications. The next significant improvement to the Internet infrastructure may be the result of projects such as *Internet2* and *Next Generation Internet* (*NGI*).

Chapter Objective 2:
Identify the various types of individuals, companies, and organizations involved in the Internet community and explain their purposes.

The Internet community is made up of individual *users*; companies, such as **Internet service providers (ISPs)**, **Internet content providers**, **application service providers (ASPs)**, *infrastructure companies*, and a variety of software and hardware companies; the government; and other organizations. Virtually anyone with a computer with communications capability can be part of the Internet, either as a user or supplier of information or services. **Web services** are self-contained business functions that operate over the Internet.

Because the Internet is so unique in the history of the world—and it remains a relatively new phenomenon—several widespread myths about it have surfaced. Three such myths are that the Internet is free, that it is controlled by some central body, and that it is synonymous with the World Wide Web.

GETTING SET UP TO USE THE INTERNET

Chapter Objective 3:
Describe device and connection options for connecting to the Internet, as well as some considerations to keep in mind when selecting an ISP.

When preparing to become connected to the Internet, you need to decide which type of device (PC, *Internet appliance*, or mobile device) to use, which type of connection—**dial-up connection** (**conventional dial-up** or **ISDN Internet access**) or **direct connection** (through a **T1 line**, **cable**, **DSL**, **satellite**, **fixed wireless**, or **mobile wireless Internet access**, or via a *hotspot*)—to use, and which specific Internet service provider to use. Once all these decisions are made, you can acquire the proper hardware and software and set up your system for Internet access.

SEARCHING THE INTERNET

Chapter Objective 4:
Understand how to effectively search for information on the Internet and how to properly cite Internet resources.

Search sites—Web sites that enable users to search for and find information on the Internet—typically locate pages using a **keyword search** (in which the user specifies **keywords** for the desired information) or a **directory search** (in which the user selects categories corresponding to the desired information). Both types of searches use a *search database* that contains information about pages on the Web and a **search engine** to retrieve the list of matching Web pages from the database. Search site databases are generally maintained by automated *spider* programs; directory databases are typically maintained by human editors. *Metasearch engines* use multiple search engines, some search sites are *natural language* sites, and many search sites use a combination of search options.

There are a variety of search strategies that can be used, including typing phrases instead of single keywords; using *Boolean operators*; trying the search at multiple search sites; and using *synonyms*, *variant word forms*, *wildcards*, and *field searches*. Once a list of links to Web pages matching the search criteria is displayed, the hits need to be evaluated for their relevancy. If the information found on a Web page is used in a paper, report, or other original document, the source should be credited appropriately.

BEYOND BROWSING AND E-MAIL

The Internet can be used for many different types of activities besides basic Web browsing and e-mail exchange. Other common types of online communications tools include **discussion groups** (where people post messages on a particular topic for others to read and respond to), **chat rooms** (online locations where multiple users can carry on real-time typed conversations), **instant messaging (IM)** (a form of private chat in which messages are sent in real time to online "buddies"), **videoconferencing** (real-time meetings taking place online using video cameras and microphones for participants to see and hear each other), and **Voice over Internet Protocol (VoIP)**, which refers to making voice telephone calls over the Internet.

Chapter Objective 5:
List several useful things that can be done using the Internet, in addition to basic Web browsing and e-mail.

Common Web activities for individuals include a variety of consumer *e-commerce* activities, such as **online shopping**, **online auctions**, **online banking**, and **online investing**. When performing any type of financial transaction over the Internet, it is very important to use only *secure* Web pages.

Online entertainment applications include downloading *MP3* files and other types of **online music**, *interactive TV* and **video-on-demand (VOD)**, **online gaming**, and **e-books**. **Peer-to-peer (P2P) file sharing** is also commonly used to exchange entertainment media. A wide variety of news, reference, government, product, and corporate information is available via the Web as well. News, reference, and search tools are commonly found on **portal** Web pages. **Web-based training (WBT)**, **distance learning**, *online testing*, **blogs**, **wikis**, and **e-portfolios** are commonly used *online education* applications.

NET

CENSORSHIP AND PRIVACY ISSUES

Among the most important societal issues relating to the Internet are censorship and *privacy*. Web content is not censored as a whole, but **Internet filtering** can be used by parents, employers, educators, and anyone wishing to prevent access to sites they deem objectionable on computers for which they have control. *Privacy* is a big concern for individuals, particularly as it relates to their Web activity. **Cookies** are typically used by Web sites to save customized settings for that site and can also be used for advertising purposes. Other items of possible concern are **Web bugs** and *spyware*. Unless an e-mail message is *encrypted*, it should not be assumed to be completely private.

Chapter Objective 6:
Discuss censorship and privacy, and how they are related to Internet use.

THE FUTURE OF THE INTERNET

The Internet has evolved remarkably over the past few decades and will, no doubt, evolve in new ways that most people cannot even dream of. The future Internet will likely be high-speed and accessed by wireless devices and appliances. Multimedia applications, such as real-time video communications and TV on demand, will likely be a reality in the near future.

Chapter Objective 7:
Describe the possible format, structure, and use of the Internet in the future.

REVIEW ACTIVITIES

KEY TERM MATCHING

Instructions: Match each key term on the left with the definition on the right that best describes it.

a. cookie

b. dial-up connection

c. direct connection

d. distance learning

e. Internet

f. keyword

g. search engine

h. video-on-demand (VOD)

i. Web bug

j. World Wide Web

1. ______ A learning environment in which the student is physically located away from the instructor and other students; commonly, instruction and communications take place via the Internet.

2. ______ An always-on type of Internet connection in which the PC or other device is continually connected to the Internet.

3. ______ A small file stored on a user's hard drive by a Web server; commonly used to identify personal preferences and settings for that user.

4. ______ A software program used by a search site to retrieve matching Web pages from a search database.

5. ______ A type of Internet connection in which the PC or other device must dial up and connect to a service provider's computer via telephone lines before being connected to the Internet.

6. ______ A very small (usually invisible) image on a Web page that transmits data about the Web page visitor to a Web server.

7. ______ A word typed in a search box on a search site to locate information on the Internet.

8. ______ The collection of Web pages available through the Internet.

9. ______ The largest and most well-known computer network, linking millions of computers all over the world.

10. ______ The process of downloading movies and televisions shows, on demand, via the Internet.

SELF-QUIZ

Instructions: Circle **T** if the statement is true, **F** if the statement is false, or write the best answer in the space provided. **Answers to the self-quiz are located in the References and Resources Guide at the end of the book.**

1. **T F** When the Internet was first developed, it was called Mosaic.

2. **T F** On the Internet, an *access provider* and a *content provider* are essentially the same thing.

3. **T F** With a direct connection, you need only open your browser to start your Internet session.

4. **T F** A locked padlock on the browser's status bar indicates that the Web page currently being viewed is secure.

5. **T F** With peer-to-peer (P2P) file sharing, individuals upload files to a central server, and then others can download them from that server.

6. ______ is a type of always-on broadband Internet service that transmits data over standard telephone lines.

7. With a(n) ______ search, keywords are typed into the search box; with a(n) ______ search, users select categories to find matching Web pages.

8. ______ is a form of private chat set up to allow users to easily and quickly exchange real-time typed messages with the individuals they specify.

9. With a(n) ______, people bid on products over the Internet, and the highest bidder purchases the item.

10. Match each Internet application with its possible situation and write the corresponding number in the blank to the left of each situation.

   a. ________ To communicate with a friend in a different state.
   b. ________ To rent a movie without leaving your home.
   c. ________ To pay only as much as you specify for an item purchased through the Internet.
   d. ________ To pay a bill without writing a check.
   e. ________ To post your original papers, résumé, and other original materials created for school classes.
   f. ________ To find Web pages containing information about growing your own Bonsai trees.

   1. Online banking
   2. E-mail
   3. Online auction
   4. Internet searching
   5. Video-on-demand (VOD)
   6. E-portfolio

EXERCISES

1. Match each type of Internet access with its description and write the corresponding number in the blank to the left of each description.

   a. ________ A fast type of Internet access via standard phone lines; does not tie up your phone.
   b. ________ The most widely used type of home broadband connection; does not use standard phone lines.
   c. ________ Accesses the Internet via standard phone lines and ties up your phone; the maximum speed is 56 Kbps.
   d. ________ Accesses the Internet wirelessly via a handheld PC or mobile device.
   e. ________ Requires a transceiver and a clear view of the southern sky.
   f. ________ Accesses the Internet via standard phone lines and does not tie up your phone; the maximum speed is 128 Kbps.

   1. Conventional dial-up
   2. ISDN
   3. DSL
   4. Cable
   5. Satellite
   6. Mobile wireless

2. What would each of the following searches look for?

   a. hot AND dogs ________________________________
   b. snorkel* ________________________________
   c. text:"Internet privacy" domain:gov ________________________________

3. List three different sets of keywords that could be used to search for information on how to maintain a trumpet.

4. Explain the difference between a blog, a wiki, and a podcast.

5. List one advantage and one disadvantage of the use of Web site cookies.

DISCUSSION QUESTION

Although slow to embrace new technology, courtrooms today are becoming high-tech. For example, videoconferencing systems that allow defendants and witnesses to participate in proceedings from remote locations are becoming more common. Allowing defendants to participate via teleconferencing from the jail facility saves travel time and expense, as well as eliminates any risk of flight. Remote testimony from witnesses can save both time and money. But could having defendants and witnesses participate remotely affect the jury's perspective? If the videoconference takes place via the Internet, can it be assured that proceedings are confidential? Do you think the benefits of these systems outweigh any potential disadvantages? Can you think of other "virtual" courtroom applications or tools that might be a reality in the future? Do you think they should become a reality?

PROJECTS

HOT TOPICS

1. **Blogs** Short for *Web log*, a *blog* is a Web page that serves as a publicly accessible personal journal for an individual. Blogs have been around for several years but could not be implemented on a wide scale because creating and publishing Web pages was fairly complicated; today, *blog tools* make it much simpler to update a blog on a regular basis (many blogs are updated daily). Consequently, there has been a tremendous increase in the use of blogs for personal expression, as well as for work-related collaborations and in writing classes.

   For this project, investigate blogs. By searching a news site (such as MSNBC.com or CNN.com) or by using a search site (such as Google.com), find at least two blogs and review them. What types of information is the user sharing? Why do you think he or she prefers to put this information on the Web instead of in a private written journal? Did the blogs you found belong to a private individual, a well-known person, or an individual representing an organization? Would you want to have your own blog? Why or why not? Do you think blog use will continue to grow? Why or why not? At the conclusion of your research, prepare a one-page summary of your findings and submit it to your instructor.

SHORT ANSWER/ RESEARCH

2. **Auction Pirates** Pirated software being sold via online auctions is reaching epidemic proportions. One estimate by the Software and Information Industry Association was that over 90% of all software sold through online auctions is pirated. Pirated movies are prevalent as well, often available over the Internet before they are released on DVD—sometimes even before they are released worldwide in the theater.

   For this project, consider the following scenario: While on an online auction site, you run across what looks like a great deal on a DVD movie that was just in the movie theater a few months ago. You win the item and, after receiving and cashing your personal check, the seller ships your DVD. When it arrives, the return address is in Thailand, and the text on the cover of the DVD is not English, so you realize that you have bought an Asian import DVD. When you contact the seller, he says that he buys his DVDs in the store in his country, so they cannot be bootleg copies. Next, research the legality of selling DVDs in the United States that are produced in other countries. If a DVD is available for retail sale in a foreign country, does that mean it can be bought there by an individual and then brought into the United States or imported for resale? Is there any way to check whether or not a DVD bought via an online auction is legitimate? Finally, consider the scenario explained above again and determine how this problem might have been avoided in the first place, and what (if anything) could be done after the fact, if you were not happy with your purchase. At the conclusion of your research, submit your findings and opinions to your instructor in the form of a short paper, no more than two pages in length.

3. **Online Travel Planning** Planning and booking travel arrangements online is a very popular Internet activity today. There are a number of sites that claim to give discount rates on airplane tickets, hotel rooms, rental cars, and more. Some sites also offer information about weather, places of interest, and more to help you plan your vacation.

   For this project, review two popular travel sites, such as Expedia.com and Travelocity.com, to see what services they offer and how easy, or difficult, it is to locate the information needed to plan and book a vacation via those sites. Select a destination and use the search facility located on one of the travel sites to obtain a quote for a particular flight on a particular day. Next, go to the Web site for the airline of the flight you were just quoted and use the site to obtain a quote for the same flight. Is there a difference in price or flight availability? Could you make a reservation online through both sites? Would you feel comfortable booking a vacation yourself online, or are there other services that a travel agent could provide that you feel would be beneficial? Do you think these sites are most appropriate for making business travel plans or vacation plans, or are they suited to either? At the conclusion of your research, prepare a one-page summary of your findings and submit it to your instructor.

HANDS ON

4. **Wi-Fi Hotspots** As discussed in the chapter, there are an increasing number of public locations offering Wi-Fi hotspots available for public use.

   For this project, find at least one location in your local area that offers public Wi-Fi access (possibilities include your public library; retail locations such as McDonald's, Starbucks, and Borders; and hotspots set up by parks and other public locations). Once you have identified a public hotspot, either visit the location or call the provider on the phone to find out the following information.

   a. Is there a fee to use the hotspot? If so, do you have to subscribe on a regular basis, or can you pay only when you want to use the hotspot? Where and how is payment made?

   b. Do you need any special software to access the hotspot? Do you need to be assigned a username or WEP (Wired Equivalent Privacy), WPA (Wi-Fi Protected Access), or WPA 2 key before you can use the service?

   At the conclusion of your research, submit your findings to your instructor in the form of a short summary.

NET

5. **Web Searching** As discussed in the chapter, search sites can be used to find Web pages containing specific information, and there are strategies that can be used to make Web searching an efficient and useful experience.

   For this project, perform the following search tasks, answering the questions or printing the information as instructed below. After you have completed all four tasks, submit your results and printouts to your instructor. (Note: Some of the answers will vary from student to student.)

   a. Go to the Google search site located at www.google.com and Search for *rules*. How many pages were found? What is the name of the first page in the list of hits?

   b. Next, search for *backgammon rules*. How many pages were found? Click on the first page and look for a picture of how a backgammon board is initially set up. When you find one, print the page. If you cannot find one on that site, select different pages in the list of hits or perform another search (such as an image search) until you find the proper illustration, and then print the page.

   c. Perform a new search by clicking the link at the top of the Google page to go to the Advanced Search option. Use the form fields to perform a search for pages that contain all the words *hiking trails Sierra*, do not contain the word *horse*, and have the domain *.gov*. After the list of Web pages matching your search criteria is displayed, record the actual search phrase that is now listed in the search box along with the name and URL of the first page displayed in the list of hits.

   d. Use Google to search for a Web site that includes a telephone directory. Go to that site and supply the necessary information to search for yourself in the telephone directory. (If you are not currently listed in the phone book, search for a family member or friend that you know has a listed number.) Print the page displaying the requested information.

   At the conclusion of this task, submit your answers and printed pages to your instructor.

WRITING ABOUT COMPUTERS

6. **Online Job Hunting** There are a number of Web sites dedicated to online career planning, posting and reviewing résumés and job announcements, listing average salary information for various positions, and other useful job-hunting tools.

   For this project, visit at least two career-oriented Web sites (such as Monster.com or CareerBuilder.com) and review the types of information and services available from the perspective of both a job seeker and an employer. Are there fees for any of the services? If you post a résumé, is it available for anyone to see, or are there restrictions on access? When it comes time for you to look for a new job, would you want to use one of these sites? Are the sites useful from an employer's perspective? List any advantages and disadvantages you can think of for using one of these sites to find a new job. Submit your findings and opinions to your instructor in the form of a short paper, not more than two pages in length.

PRESENTATION/ DEMONSTRATION

7. **Free and Low-Cost Internet** There are several free and low-cost ($5 to $10 per month) ISPs. For example, Juno and NetZero (www.juno.com or www.netzero.net) offer users 10 hours of free dial-up access per month, and 550Access.com offers unlimited dial-up service for $5.50 per month.

   For this project, research Juno or NetZero plus one other free or low-cost ISP and investigate their services. Do any of these offer unlimited Internet access for free? Is there still a 10-hour limit with Juno/NetZero? If so, what happens if you go over that limit? Are there any tradeoffs for using these free or low-cost ISPs? If you were looking for a dial-up provider, would you consider using either of your selected ISPs? Why or why not? Would these services be useful for other applications, such as for business travelers or for back up service for broadband subscribers? Share your findings and opinions with the class in the form of a short presentation. The presentation should not exceed 10 minutes and should make use of one or more presentation aids, such as the chalkboard, handouts, overhead transparencies, or a computer-based slide presentation (your instructor may provide additional requirements). You may also be asked to submit a summary of the presentation to your instructor.

GROUP DISCUSSION

8. **Rural Broadband** Citizens who live in rural areas typically have less access to broadband Internet than those in more highly populated areas. Maryland's Speaker of the House Casper R. Taylor views this as the real digital divide. Without broadband, he believes that "our kids are not going to have the advantage of urbanized society going into the future if we're disconnected from the rest of the world...If we don't accomplish this, we are clearly creating a second-class society." There are differing opinions regarding the importance of broadband Internet and whose responsibility it is to provide it. If a region has only 56K dial-up service, does that really put it at a disadvantage? Is the digital divide more about separating those who have access to technology, such as the Internet, and those who do not, or is it about the quality of that technology? What about the government's role—should it provide the necessary infrastructure to ensure an appropriate level of Internet access to all U.S. citizens? If not, how will the digital divide within the United States be eliminated? Will it ever be eliminated?

   For this project, form an opinion of the necessity of broadband Internet and the role of the government (if any) in providing broadband Internet access to its citizens and be prepared to discuss your position (in class, via an online class discussion group, or in a class chat room, depending on your instructor's directions). You may also be asked to write a short paper expressing your opinion.

WEB ACTIVITIES

The *Understanding Computers* Web site located at **www.course.com/uc11** features many resources to help reinforce your understanding of the chapter content and help you prepare for exams. Your instructor may also assign specific activities to be completed that will count toward your final grade in the course.

Instructions: Go to **www.course.com/uc11/ch08** to work the following online activities.

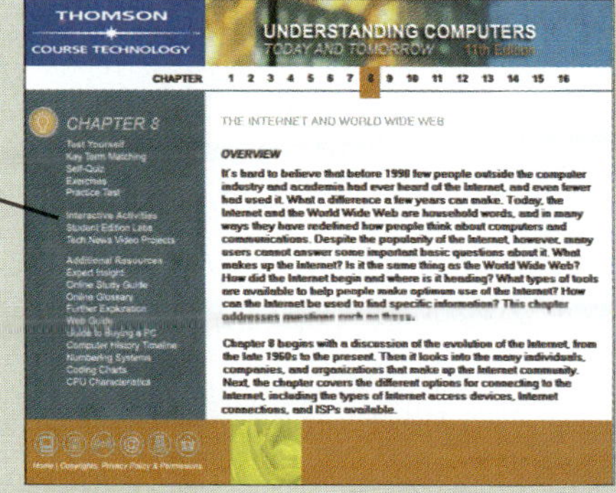

Click any link in the navigation bar on the left to access any of the online resources described below.

INTERACTIVE ACTIVITIES

1. **Crossword Puzzle** Practice your knowledge of the key terms in Chapter 8 by completing the interactive Crossword Puzzle.
2. **Tech News Video Project** Watch the **"Free Wi-Fi Blankets San Francisco"** video clip that takes a look at the "Bay Area Wireless Network"—a network of Wi-Fi access points that provides free Internet access to the surrounding areas. After watching the video online, complete the corresponding project.
3. **Student Edition Labs** Reinforce the concepts you have learned in this chapter by working through the interactive **Connecting to the Internet** and **Getting the Most Out of the Internet** labs.

NET

TEST YOURSELF

1. **Key Term Matching** Test your knowledge of selected chapter key terms by matching the terms with their definitions.
2. **Self-Quiz** Test your retention of chapter concepts by taking the Self-Quiz.
3. **Exercises** Work these short exercises to review the concepts and terms covered in the chapter.
4. **Practice Test** Test how ready you are for an upcoming exam by completing the online Practice Test.

STUDY TOOLS/ ADDITIONAL RESOURCES

The Understanding Computers Web site has a wide range of additional resources, including an **Online Study Guide** (containing study tips, a chapter outline with room to add your own notes, and a chapter checklist of the activities to complete when the chapter is covered in class and when you are preparing for a test) and an **Online Glossary** for each chapter; **Further Exploration** links; a **Web Guide**, a **Guide to Buying a PC**, and a **Computer History Timeline**; more information about **Numbering Systems**, **Coding Charts**, and **CPU Characteristics**; and much, much more!

Network and Internet Security

OUTLINE

Overview
Why Be Concerned about Network and Internet Security?
Unauthorized Access, Unauthorized Use, and Computer Sabotage
Hacking
Interception of Communications
Computer Sabotage
Protecting Against Unauthorized Access, Unauthorized Use, and Computer Sabotage
Access Control Systems
Firewalls and Antivirus Software
Encryption and Other Security Tools
Take Caution with Employees
Online Theft, Fraud, and Other Dot Cons
Theft of Data, Information, and Other Resources
Identity Theft
Online Auction Fraud
Internet Scams, Spoofing, and Phishing
Spyware
Protecting Against Online Theft, Fraud, and Other Dot Cons
Protecting Against Identity Theft
Protecting Against Other Dot Cons
Protecting Against Spyware
Using Digital Signatures and Digital Certificates
Personal Safety Issues
Cyberstalking
Online Pornography
Protecting Against Cyberstalking and Other Personal Safety Concerns
Safety Tips for Adults
Safety Tips for Children
Network and Internet Security Legislation

LEARNING OBJECTIVES

After completing this chapter, you will be able to:

1. Explain why computer users should be concerned about network and Internet security.
2. List several examples of unauthorized access, unauthorized use, and computer sabotage.
3. Explain what risks access control systems, firewalls, antivirus software, and encryption protect against.
4. Discuss online theft, identity theft, Internet scams, spoofing, phishing, and other types of dot cons.
5. Detail steps an individual can take to protect against online theft, identity theft, Internet scams, spoofing, phishing, and other types of dot cons.
6. Identify personal safety risks associated with Internet use.
7. List steps individuals can take when using the Internet to safeguard their personal safety.
8. Name several laws related to network and Internet security.

OVERVIEW

The increased use of networks and the Internet helps users finish many tasks quickly and efficiently and adds convenience to many people's lives. However, there is a downside, as well. As more and more personal and business data is stored on computer networks, the risks and consequences of unauthorized computer access, theft, fraud, and other types of computer crime increase; so do the chances of data loss due to crime or employee misconduct. Some online activities can even put your personal safety at risk, if you are not careful.

This chapter looks at a variety of security concerns stemming from the use of computer networks in our society, including topics such as unauthorized access and use, computer viruses and other types of sabotage, and online theft and fraud. Safeguards for each of these concerns are also covered, with an explanation of precautions that can be taken to reduce the risk of experiencing problems related to these security concerns. Personal safety issues related to the Internet are also discussed, and the chapter closes with a look at legislation related to network and Internet security. ■

WHY BE CONCERNED ABOUT NETWORK AND INTERNET SECURITY?

From a *computer virus* making your PC function abnormally, to a *hacker* using your personal information to make fraudulent purchases, to someone harassing you online in a discussion group, a variety of security concerns related to computer networks and the Internet abound. Many Internet security concerns today can be categorized as **computer crimes**. Computer crime—sometimes referred to as *cybercrime*—includes any illegal act involving a computer. Many computer crimes involve breaking through the security of a network; others include theft of financial assets or information. Still other computer crimes involve manipulating data, such as grades, for personal advantage. Increasingly, computer crimes involve acts of sabotage, such as releasing a computer virus or shutting down a Web server. Regardless of its form, computer crime is an important security concern today.

All computer users should be aware of the security concerns surrounding computer network and Internet use, including the risks and the associated consequences, and they should take appropriate precautions. In some cases, such as when a *spyware program* changes your browser's home page, the consequence may be just an annoyance. In other cases, such as when someone steals your identity and purchases items using your name or credit card number, the consequences are much more serious. The most common types of security concerns related to network and Internet use, along with some precautions users can take to reduce the risks associated with these concerns, are discussed throughout the remainder of this chapter.

>**Computer crime.** Any illegal act involving a computer.

UNAUTHORIZED ACCESS, UNAUTHORIZED USE, AND COMPUTER SABOTAGE

Unauthorized access occurs whenever an individual gains access to a computer, network, file, or other resource without permission. **Unauthorized use** involves using a computer resource for unauthorized activities. Unauthorized use can occur even if the user is authorized to access that computer or network but is not authorized for that particular activity. For instance, while a student may be authorized to access the Internet via a campus computer lab, some use—such as viewing pornography—may be deemed off-limits. If so, viewing that content from a school computer would be considered unauthorized use. For employees of some companies, checking personal e-mail at work might be classified as unauthorized use.

Unauthorized access and many types of unauthorized use are criminal offenses in the United States and other countries and can be committed by both *insiders* (people who work for the company against which the crime occurred) and *outsiders* (people who do not work for that company). In fact, according to the 2005 "Computer Crime and Security Survey" performed by the Computer Security Institute and the FBI, insiders commit computer crimes about as often as outsiders, although companies may be reluctant to press charges against employees fearing bad publicity and loss of public confidence. Whether or not a specific act constitutes unauthorized use or is illegal depends on the circumstances, as well as the specific company or institution involved. To explain acceptable computer use to their employees, students, or other users, many organizations and educational institutions publish guidelines for behavior. These rules are frequently called *codes of conduct* (see Figure 9-1). Codes of conduct typically address prohibited activities, such as installing personal software on the network, violating copyright laws, causing harm to the PC and network, and snooping in other people's files.

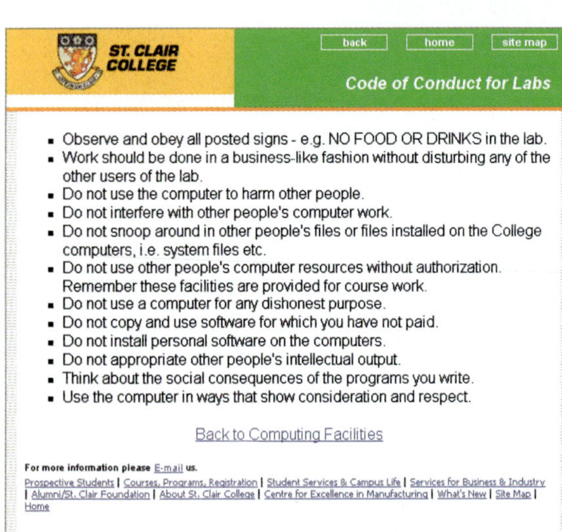

ST. CLAIR COLLEGE

back | home | site map

Code of Conduct for Labs

- Observe and obey all posted signs - e.g. NO FOOD OR DRINKS in the lab.
- Work should be done in a business-like fashion without disturbing any of the other users of the lab.
- Do not use the computer to harm other people.
- Do not interfere with other people's computer work.
- Do not snoop around in other people's files or files installed on the College computers, i.e. system files etc.
- Do not use other people's computer resources without authorization. Remember these facilities are provided for course work.
- Do not use a computer for any dishonest purpose.
- Do not copy and use software for which you have not paid.
- Do not install personal software on the computers.
- Do not appropriate other people's intellectual output.
- Think about the social consequences of the programs you write.
- Use the computer in ways that show consideration and respect.

Back to Computing Facilities

For more information please E-mail us.

Prospective Students | Courses, Programs, Registration | Student Services & Campus Life | Services for Business & Industry | Alumni/St. Clair Foundation | About St. Clair College | Centre for Excellence in Manufacturing | What's New | Site Map | Home

COLLEGE CODE OF CONDUCT
This code, posted on the campus Web site, notifies students of allowable and off-limit actions regarding campus computer lab use.

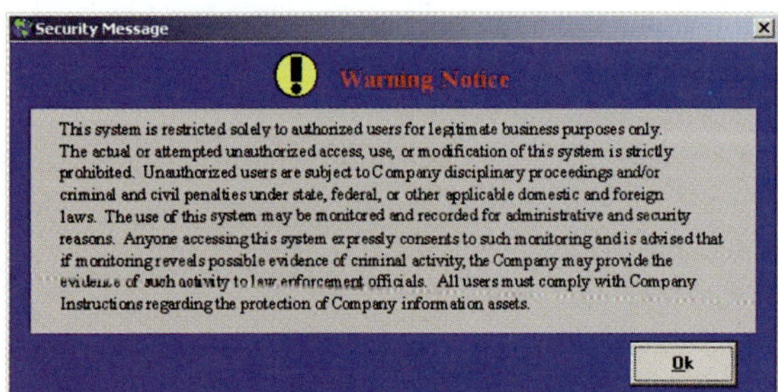

Security Message

Warning Notice

This system is restricted solely to authorized users for legitimate business purposes only. The actual or attempted unauthorized access, use, or modification of this system is strictly prohibited. Unauthorized users are subject to Company disciplinary proceedings and/or criminal and civil penalties under state, federal, or other applicable domestic and foreign laws. The use of this system may be monitored and recorded for administrative and security reasons. Anyone accessing this system expressly consents to such monitoring and is advised that if monitoring reveals possible evidence of criminal activity, the Company may provide the evidence of such activity to law enforcement officials. All users must comply with Company Instructions regarding the protection of Company information assets.

Ok

BUSINESS CODE OF CONDUCT
This code, displayed whenever an employee logs on to the company network, notifies employees that the network can be used for legitimate business purposes only.

FIGURE 9-1
Sample codes of conduct.

Hacking

Hacking refers to the act of breaking into another computer system. The person doing the hacking is called a *hacker*. By definition, hacking involves unauthorized access and is illegal. An exception is authorized hacking, such as *professional hacking* that takes place at the request of an organization to test the security of its system (these individuals are sometimes referred to as *white hat hackers* to differentiate them from *black hat hackers* who break the law) and hacking into computers set up (usually by hacker organizations) specifically to enable hackers to practice their skills legally. Unless authorized, hacking in the United

>**Unauthorized access.** Gaining access to a computer, network, file, or other resource without permission. >**Unauthorized use.** Using a computer resource for unapproved activities. >**Hacking.** Using a computer to break into another computer system.

States and many other countries is a crime and is becoming more vigorously prosecuted. The 2001 *USA Patriot Act* expands the government's authority to prosecute hacking activities and increases the penalties for unauthorized hacks.

Often, the motivation for hacking is to steal information, sabotage a computer system, or perform some other type of illegal act. The recent rash of security breaches of credit card numbers and cardholder information shows that the theft of data is a growing trend. For instance, about 40 million credit card numbers were stolen from the third-party credit card payment processor CardSystems Solutions in 2005—the largest reported data breach to date. Another growing trend is to hack into a PC and "hijack" it for use in an illegal or unethical act, such as generating spam or hosting pornographic Web sites.

Sometimes hackers break into a system just to prove their computer expertise, to expand their knowledge, or to bring attention to a social cause. One example is the collection of attacks in 2002 by two hackers calling themselves the *Deceptive Duo*. These two individuals broke into secured databases (including an airlines database containing flight schedules and passenger manifests, a bank database, and a NASA employee database) and published selected information to Web pages belonging to a variety of government agencies to prove that the databases had been accessed. In their explanation regarding the motivation for the attack, the Deceptive Duo claimed that they hacked into the secure systems in the interest of national security, to bring attention to these systems' vulnerabilities. Both pleaded guilty and were sentenced in 2005—one to four months in prison and three years of probation; the other to two years of probation. They also had to pay restitution—a total of just over $100,000. Regardless of the motivation, unauthorized hacking is illegal.

In addition to the threat toward individuals and businesses, hacking is considered a very serious threat to our nation's security. With the increased number of computers and systems online and with the abilities of hackers continually improving, some experts believe the risk of *cyberterrorism*—in which terrorists launch attacks via the Internet—has increased significantly. In response to this possibility, U.S. White House technology adviser Richard Clarke announced in early 2002 that the United States "reserves the right to respond in any way appropriate" to Internet warfare, including military action against cyberterrorists, and the government released the report "The National Strategy to Secure Cyberspace" in 2003. Current concerns include attacks against the computers controlling such vital systems as the nation's power grids, banks, and water filtration facilities, as well as computers related to national defense. And attacks on Defense Department computers have been steadily increasing. There were almost 75,000 incidents recorded in 2004—almost twice as many as in 2002. The United States continues to show its commitment to protecting government systems against cyberattacks—the budget in 2006 alone for the National Cyber Security Division (NCSD) of the Department of Homeland Security (DHS) is over $70 million.

The general public tends to use the term *hacker* to refer to any type of computer break-in regardless of what activities take place after the security breach. However, many hackers differentiate between types of hacking, and they prefer the term *cracker* when referring to individuals who break into systems to be destructive or for material gain.

NET

Wi-Fi Hacking

While in the past hacking took place primarily via telephone lines or the Internet, it is common today for hackers to also gain access to a computer via a wireless—such as a Wi-Fi (802.11)—network. It is easier to hack into a wireless network than a wired network because it is possible to gain access just by being within about 300 feet of a wireless access point, unless the access point is sufficiently protected. For instance, in 2004 two men allegedly hacked into the Wi-Fi network belonging to a Lowe's Home Improvement store in Michigan and stole several customer credit card numbers. The men were charged with violating the *Computer Fraud and Abuse Act*—the main federal law regarding computer crime—and one has been sentenced to nine years in federal prison.

Although security features are built into Wi-Fi hardware, they are typically not turned on by default. As a result, many wireless networks belonging to businesses and individuals—some estimates put the number as high as 70% of all Wi-Fi networks—are left unsecured. This leaves the transmissions sent by individuals, the company, and customers (such as individuals using a hotspot's Wi-Fi service or hotel guests using the hotel's complementary Wi-Fi Internet access) open to interception. Improvements to the Wi-Fi standards are expected to provide increased security capabilities in the future; one significant improvement recommended by some security experts would be if hardware manufacturers begin enabling security features on Wi-Fi hardware by default so users would have to act to disable the features, instead of the other way around. Despite these potential improvements in the future, however, individuals and businesses with wireless networks should realize that wireless networks are inherently less secure than wired networks since data travels through the air instead of through a physical transmission medium, and they should be especially vigilant in protecting access to those networks.

War Driving

Accessing someone else's Wi-Fi network to gain free access to the Internet is called **war driving**. A form of "bandwidth stealing," war driving is usually accomplished by driving around neighborhoods in a car with a portable computer and appropriate software looking for an unsecured Wi-Fi network to "borrow." While many view war driving as a fun activity, it is a security risk as well as an ethically—if not a legally—questionable act. Possible consequences to the owner of a Wi-Fi network as a result of increased use by outsiders include a slower response time, the introduction of computer viruses (either intentionally or unintentionally), and unauthorized access to the data located on PCs connected to that network. It is also possible that use of an Internet connection by multiple users violates the legitimate user's agreement with his or her ISP and may result in the cancellation of the Internet service. While products are available to help mobile users locate Wi-Fi networks (see Figure 9-2) and some mapping programs (such as *Yahoo! Maps*) have an option to display Wi-Fi hotspot locations on any map, these services are intended to help individuals locate authorized hotspots.

Advocates of war driving state that, unless individuals or businesses protect their access points, they are welcoming others to use them. Critics compare that logic to the case of an unlocked front door—you cannot legally enter a home just because the front door is

FIGURE 9-2
Locating accessible Wi-Fi networks.

WI-FI FINDERS
Indicate the strength of Wi-Fi networks within range.

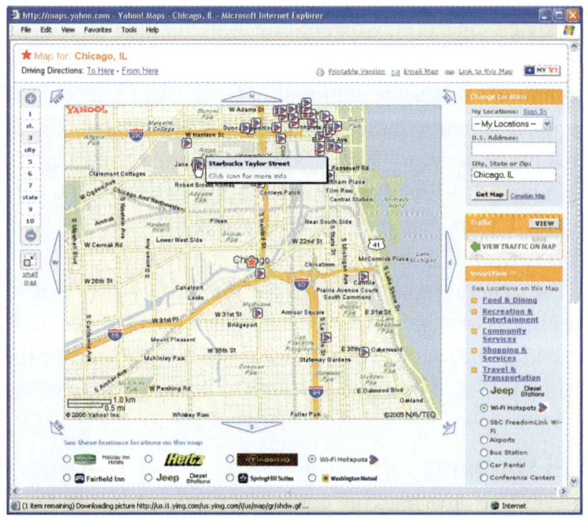

YAHOO! MAPS WI-FI HOTSPOT OPTION
Displays information about public hotspots in the mapped area currently displayed.

>**War driving.** Driving around an area with a Wi-Fi-enabled computer or mobile device to find a Wi-Fi network to access and use without authorization.

unlocked. Although some wireless network owners do leave their access points unsecured on purpose and some communities are creating a collection of wireless access points to provide wireless Internet access to everyone in that community, it is difficult—if not impossible—to tell if an unsecured access point was left that way intentionally or if it is just a private network that has not yet been properly protected (see Figure 9-3). Some feel the ethical distinction of using an unsecured wireless network is determined by the amount of use, believing that it is acceptable to borrow someone's Internet connection to do a quick e-mail check, but that continually using a neighbor's Internet connection to avoid paying for your own is crossing over the line. Others feel that allowing outsiders to share an Internet connection is acceptable use, as long as the owner does not charge the outsider for that access. Still others believe that an Internet connection is intended for use only by the subscriber and that sharing it with others is unfair to the ISP. This issue is beginning to be addressed by the courts, and some answers regarding the legality of war driving and Internet connection sharing will likely be forthcoming in the near future. However, the ethical questions surrounding this issue may take longer to resolve.

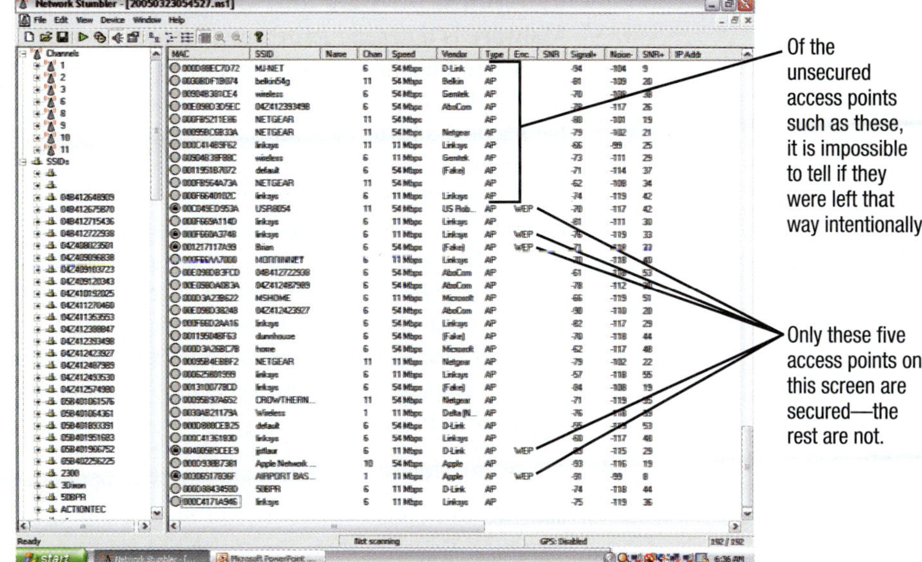

FIGURE 9-3

War driving. On a 20 mile war drive in Massachusetts in 2005, 240 wireless access points were detected and over 77% were unprotected.

Interception of Communications

To gain access to data stored on a particular computer, some criminals attempt to hack directly into that computer—sometimes in person, but more often via the Internet. It is also possible, however, to gain unauthorized access to data, files, e-mail messages, and other content as they are being sent over the Internet. And the increased use of wireless networks and the increased use of wireless connections to transmit data via cell phones, handheld PCs, and other portable devices have opened up new opportunities for data interception. Once intercepted, the content can be read, altered, or otherwise used for unintended purposes. Although it is unlikely that anyone would be interested in intercepting personal e-mail sent to friends and relatives, proprietary corporate information and sensitive personal information (such as credit card, bank account, or brokerage account information) is at risk if it is sent over the Internet—or over a wireless home or corporate network—unsecured.

Computer Sabotage

Computer sabotage—acts of malicious destruction to a computer or computer resource—is another common type of computer crime today. Computer sabotage can take several forms, including launching a *computer virus* or a *denial of service attack*, altering the content of a Web site, or changing data or programs located on a computer. Computer sabotage is illegal in the United States, and acts of sabotage are estimated to cost individuals and organizations billions of dollars per year, primarily for labor costs related to virus removal or other necessary actions, lost productivity, and lost sales.

>**Computer sabotage.** An act of malicious destruction to a computer or computer resource.

Computer Viruses and Other Types of Malware

Malware is a generic term that refers to any type of malicious software. Malware programs are intentionally written to perform destructive acts, although some researchers believe that many young malware creators do not realize the potential consequences of their actions and the huge amount of destruction and expense that can result from releasing a malware program into cyberspace.

One of the most familiar types of malware is the **computer virus**—a small software program that is installed without the permission or knowledge of the computer user, is designed to alter the way a computer operates, and can replicate itself to infect any new media it accesses. Computer viruses are embedded into program or data files and are spread whenever the infected file is downloaded from the Internet or another network, is transferred to a new computer via an infected removable storage medium, or is e-mailed to another computer (see Figure 9-4). Once a copy of the infected file reaches a new computer, it typically embeds itself into program, data, or system files on the new PC and remains there, affecting that PC according to its programmed instructions, until it is discovered and removed. Malware is increasingly being spread through files attached to instant messages, and two cell phone viruses (*Cabir* and *Commwarrior*) have hit mobile phones in many countries. Typically, these viruses spread via Bluetooth connections or text messages. The mobile virus *Sybos/Cardtrap* that was introduced in late 2005 is reportedly the first cell phone virus that tries to move beyond cell phones. It masquerades as pirated software for mobile phones and copies itself to the phone's flash memory card so that any PC into which that flash memory card is later inserted will become infected. According to IBM, more malware directed to cell phones and devices—such as cars—that contain embedded computers is expected in the near future, as those devices continue to incorporate more computer software components and, consequently, become more vulnerable to malware.

FURTHER EXPLORATION

For links to further information about computer viruses and virus detection, go to www.course.com/uc11/ch09

Most malware is designed to harm the computers they are transmitted to—for example, by damaging programs, deleting files, erasing the entire hard drive, or slowing down performance of the PC. This damage can take place immediately after infection, or it can begin when a particular condition is met. A computer virus that activates when it detects a certain condition, such as when a particular keystroke is pressed or an employee's name is deleted from an employee file, is called a *logic bomb*. A logic bomb whose trigger is a particular date or time is called a *time bomb*. In addition to destructive computer viruses, there are so-called "benign" viruses that are not designed to do any permanent damage, but instead they make their presence known by displaying a text or video message, or by playing a musical or audio message. Even though benign viruses may not cause any lasting harm (although some do unintentional damage because of programming errors), they are annoying, can require enormous amounts of time to get rid of, and can disrupt communications for the organizations involved.

Instead of being used to disable computers, malware is increasingly being used to gain access to individuals' PCs—usually to steal identity information, passwords, corporate secrets, and other sensitive data. For instance, many experts believe that the *Sobig* virus released in mid-2003 was created by spammers as a way of gaining access to people's PCs in order to hijack them for spam distribution.

Computer viruses are very expensive because of the labor costs associated with removing the virus and correcting any resulting damage, as well as the cost of lost productivity of employees. In the 2005 "Computer Crime and Security Survey," computer viruses were listed as the most expensive type of computer crime, and a 2005 InfoWorld study revealed that nearly 50% of the respondents cited the increased sophistication of malware as the most serious security challenge their companies will face in the next year.

>**Malware.** Any type of malicious software. >**Computer virus.** A software program installed without the user's knowledge and designed to alter the way a computer operates or to cause harm to the computer system.

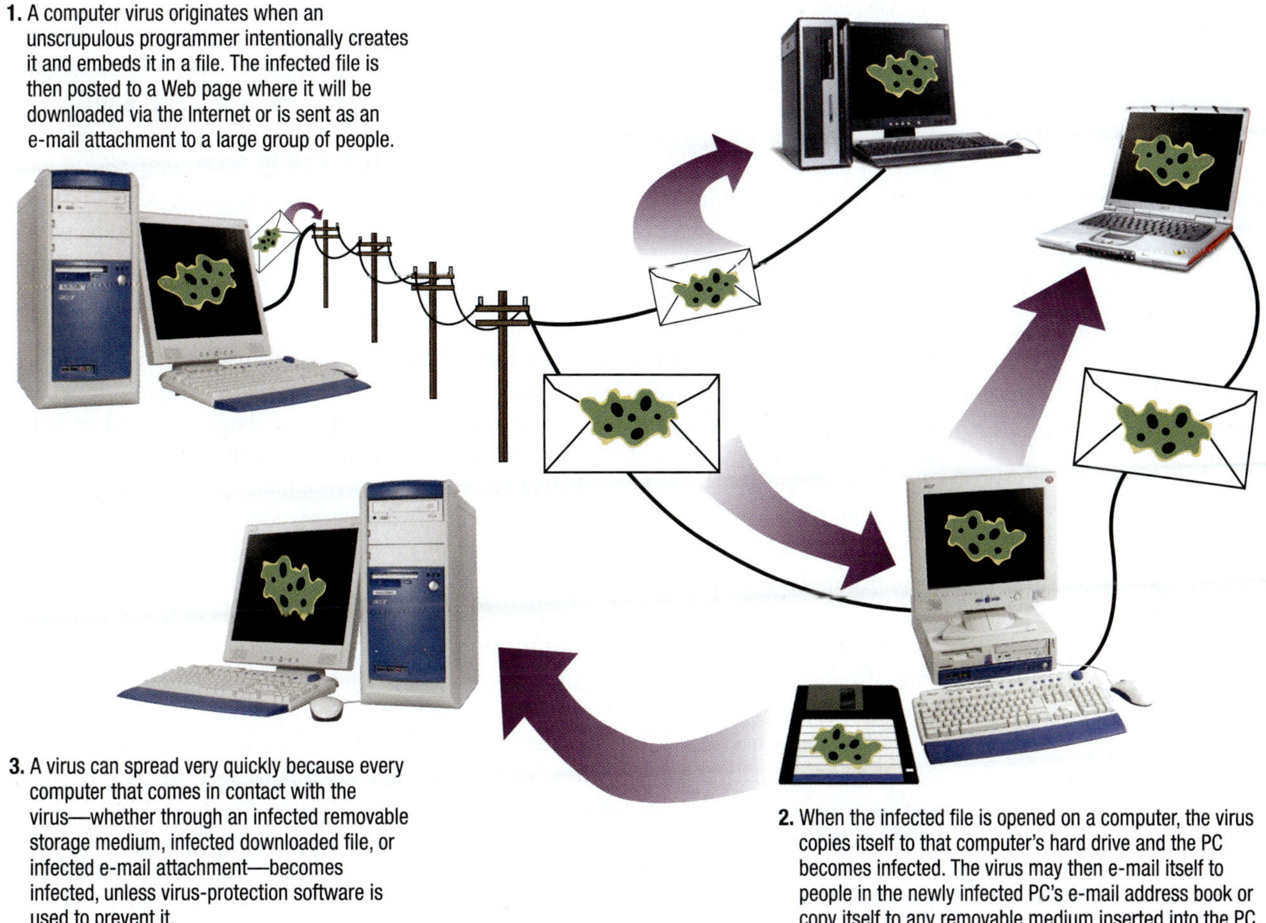

FIGURE 9-4
How a computer virus or other type of malicious software might spread.

Although there are other types of malware in addition to computer viruses, it is common practice for all types of malware to be generically referred to as "viruses," even though some may not technically be true computer viruses. Two other common forms of malware are *computer worms* and *Trojan horses*.

Like a computer virus, a **computer worm** is a malicious program designed to cause damage. Unlike a computer virus, however, a computer worm does not infect other computer files to replicate itself; instead, it spreads by creating copies of itself and sending those copies to other computers via a network. Often, the worm is sent as an e-mail attachment to other computers. After the infected e-mail attachment is opened by an individual, the worm inflicts its damage, and then automatically sends copies of itself to other computers via the Internet or a private network, typically using addresses in the e-mail address book located on the newly infected PC. When those e-mail messages and their attachments are opened, those new computers become infected and the cycle continues. Some newer worms do not require any action by the users (such as opening an e-mail attachment) to infect their PCs. Instead, the worm scans the Internet looking for computers that are vulnerable to that particular worm and sends a copy of itself to those PCs to infect them. Other worms just require the user to view the e-mail message, in order to infect the PC.

>**Computer worm.** A malicious program designed to spread rapidly to a large number of computers by sending copies of itself to other computers.

TIP

Always install update security patches for your operating system and e-mail program as soon as they become available; if you have the option to update automatically, select that option.

Because of its distribution method, a worm can spread very rapidly. For instance, the *Slammer* worm (released in 2003) reached 90% of the Internet within 10 minutes of its release, and the *Mydoom* worm (released in 2004) spread so rapidly that, at one point, one out of every 10 e-mails contained the worm. A disturbing trend is the creation of worms written to take advantage of newly discovered *security holes* (vulnerabilities) in operating systems and e-mail programs. For example, *Blaster* (released in 2003) and *Sasser* and *Plexus* (both released in 2004) were all written to exploit security holes discovered in the Windows operating system. Microsoft made a *security patch* available to correct the problem when it announced the vulnerabilities, but the viruses spread rapidly anyway because many Windows users did not install the patch.

A **Trojan horse** is a malicious program that masquerades as something else—usually as some type of application program. When the seemingly legitimate program (such as what appears to be a game or utility program) is run, the destructive program executes instead. Unlike viruses and worms, Trojan horses cannot replicate themselves and are usually spread by being downloaded from the Internet. A Trojan horse may also be sent as an e-mail attachment, either from the Trojan horse author or from individuals who forward it, not realizing the program is a Trojan horse. Some Trojan horses today are designed to find sensitive information about an individual (such as a Social Security number or a bank account number) or about a company (such as the 2005 *Myfip* Trojan horse that was designed to steal corporate intellectual property—mechanical designs, electronic schematics, and other valuable proprietary information) located on an infected PC and send it to the malware creator. In either case, this information is typically used in illegal activities.

Writing a computer virus or other type of malware or even posting the malware code on the Internet is not illegal, but it is considered highly unethical and irresponsible behavior. Distributing malware, on the other hand, is illegal, and virus writers who release their malware are being vigorously prosecuted. For instance, a man received a two-year prison sentence in Spain in 2004 for creating and releasing the *Cabronator* Trojan horse, which infected over 100,000 computers with the intention of stealing confidential information from them—the first case of a malware author being sentenced to jail in Spain. In the United States, a Minnesota teenager was facing three years in jail and a $250,000 fine for creating and unleashing a variant of the *MSBlaster* worm that infected nearly 50,000 computers and caused over a million dollars worth of damage, according to federal investigators. In 2005, the teenager pled guilty to the crime and was sentenced to 18 months in prison and 225 hours of community service.

Denial of Service Attacks

A **denial of service (DoS) attack** is an act of sabotage that attempts to flood a network server or Web server with so many requests for action that it shuts down or simply cannot handle legitimate requests any longer, causing legitimate users to be denied service. For example, a hacker might set up one or more computers to continually *ping* a server (contact it with a request to send a responding ping back) with a false return address or to continually request nonexistent information. If enough useless traffic is generated, the server has no resources left to deal with legitimate requests (see Figure 9-5).

During the past few years, many leading Web sites have been the victims of DoS attacks. Most of these attacks utilized multiple computers (which is referred to as a *distributed denial of service attack* or *DDoS attack*). To perform DDoS attacks, hackers have begun more frequently to access and take control of unprotected PCs with direct Internet connections (such as those located in schools, businesses, or homes) to use in DDoS attacks. These computers (referred to as *zombies*) participate in the attacks without

>**Trojan horse.** A malicious program that masquerades as something else. >**Denial of service (DoS) attack.** An act of sabotage that attempts to flood a network server or a Web server with so much activity that it is unable to function.

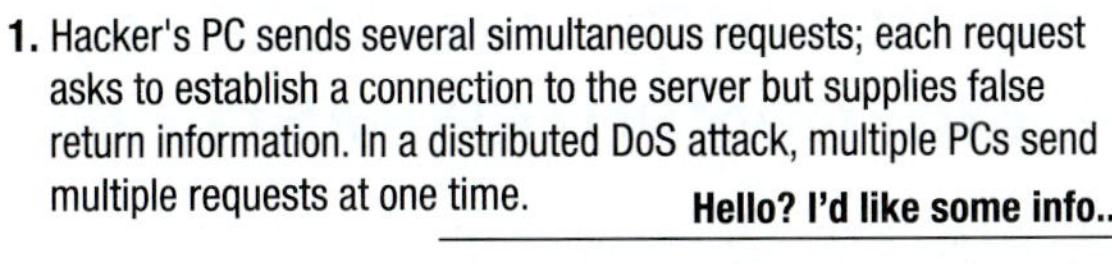

FIGURE 9-5
How a denial of service (DoS) attack might work.

the owners' knowledge. Because home PCs tend to be less protected than school and business PCs, hackers are increasingly targeting home PCs for use as zombie PCs. According to Symantec, up to 2 million computers worldwide are infected with software allowing them to be controlled remotely by a hacker, typically for a DDoS attack or to deliver spam or *phishing* e-mails (phishing is discussed shortly). Another trend is to use malware to launch a DoS attack. For example, the Mydoom worm was programmed to use infected computers as zombies to unleash a DDoS attack on Web sites belonging to Microsoft, the Recording Industry Association of America (RIAA), and SCO Group (a Utah company embroiled in an intellectual property battle regarding the use of Linux). Denial of service attacks can be very costly in terms of business lost (such as when an e-commerce site is shut down), as well as the time and expense required to bring the site back online.

NET

Data or Program Alteration

Another type of computer sabotage occurs when a hacker breaches a computer system in order to delete data, change data, modify programs, or otherwise alter the data and programs located there. For example, students have been caught changing grades in their schools' databases, and disgruntled or former employees have performed vengeful acts, including altering programs so they work incorrectly, deleting customer records or other critical data, or randomly changing data in a company's database. Like other forms of computer sabotage, data and program alteration is illegal.

Web site defacement—defacing or otherwise changing Web sites without permission (see Figure 9-6)—is a type of data alteration that has become more common over the past few years. A form of *cybervandalism*, Web site defacement has become a widely used method for hackers who want to draw attention to themselves or to a specific cause. U.S. Web sites modified by hackers in the last few years include those belonging to the Library of Congress, the FBI, the *New York Times*, CNN, the secretary of defense, Sandia National Laboratories, NASA Jet Propulsion Laboratories, and Stanford University.

FIGURE 9-6
Cybervandalism. Some Web site defacements are politically motivated; many are done just for notoriety.

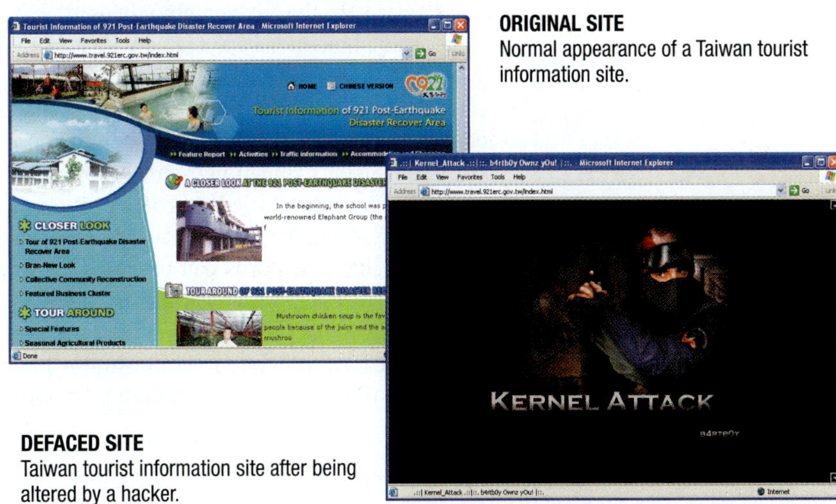

ORIGINAL SITE
Normal appearance of a Taiwan tourist information site.

DEFACED SITE
Taiwan tourist information site after being altered by a hacker.

PROTECTING AGAINST UNAUTHORIZED ACCESS, UNAUTHORIZED USE, AND COMPUTER SABOTAGE

A number of security risks can be reduced by carefully controlling access to an organization's facilities and computer network to ensure that only authorized individuals are granted access, and by using appropriate security software. Reward programs—such as Microsoft's multimillion-dollar reward fund for those individuals who supply information leading to the arrest of virus writers—may also help reduce computer crime by making it riskier for individuals to commit the crime. For example, the Microsoft reward program is credited with identifying and arresting the author of the Sasser worm only one week after it was released. Specific precautions against unauthorized access, unauthorized use, and computer sabotage are discussed in the next few sections.

Access Control Systems

Access control systems are used to control access to facilities, computer networks, and other assets. *Identification systems* can be used to verify that the person trying to access the facility or system is listed as an authorized user, and *authentication systems* can be used to determine whether or not the person attempting access is actually who he or she claims to be. Controlling access to company databases is critical today, considering the vast amount of personal data contained there. And the recent security breaches reveal that many of today's companies need to improve their access systems. Improvements in this area—such as the new *Payment Card Industry* (*PCI*) security standards imposed by major credit card companies on all companies that store, process, or transmit credit cardholder data—are expected to help. The PCI standards include restricting physical access to cardholder data, using a *firewall*, changing default passwords, *encrypting* cardholder data transmissions (encryption and firewalls are discussed shortly), and other security precautions.

The three most common types of access systems are discussed next, followed by a discussion of additional considerations for controlling access to wireless networks.

Possessed Knowledge Access Systems

A **possessed knowledge access system** is an identification system that requires the individual requesting access to provide information that only the authorized user is supposed to know. *Passwords*, *usernames* (typically a variation of the person's first and/or last names), and *PINs* (*personal identification numbers*, such as those used with ATM cards) fall into this category.

Passwords, the most commonly used type of possessed knowledge, are secret words or character combinations associated with an individual. They can be used to restrict access to a facility or, more commonly, to a network or other computing resource. For example, a company or institution might require an authorized user to use one password to access a corporate or school computer system, and then use a different password to access drives, folders, or documents containing sensitive or confidential information on that same network.

It is important to select good passwords and change them frequently. One of the biggest disadvantages of password-only systems is that passwords can be forgotten; another is that passwords can be guessed or deciphered by a hacker's PC easily if good password selection strategies are not applied. For example, it was discovered that the Deceptive Duo hackers were able to access the databases from which they retrieved information because the system administrator passwords for those databases had never been changed—they were still the default passwords (the ones assigned to the programs during

>**Possessed knowledge access system.** An access control system that uses information that only an individual should know to identify that individual. >**Password.** A secret combination of characters used to gain access to a computer, computer network, or other resource.

PASSWORD STRATEGIES
Make the password at least eight characters, if allowed by the application. A four- or five-character password can be cracked by a computer program in less than one minute. A ten-character password, in contrast, has about 3,700 trillion possible character permutations and could take a regular computer decades to crack.
Choose an unusual sequence of characters to create a password that will not be in a dictionary–for instance, mix numbers and special characters with abbreviations or unusual words you will remember. The password should be one that you can remember, yet one that does not conform to a pattern a computer can readily figure out.
To help you remember strong passwords used to protect sensitive data, consider using a *passphrase* that you can remember and using corresponding letters and symbols (such as the first letter of each word) for your password. For instance, the passphrase "My son John is five years older than my daughter Abby" could help you remember the strong password "Msji5yotMd@".
Do not use your name, your kids' or pets' names, your address, your birthdate, or other public information as your password.
Do not keep a written copy of the password in your desk or taped to your monitor. If you need to write down your password, create a password-protected file on your PC to contain all your passwords.
Use a different password for your highly sensitive activities (such as online banking or stock trading) than for Web sites that remember your settings or profile (such as online news, auction, shopping, or bookstore sites). Computers storing passwords used on nonsensitive Web sites are usually easier to break into than those storing passwords used on high-security sites, and if a hacker determines your password on a low-security site, he or she can use it on your accounts containing sensitive data if you use the same password on those accounts.
Change your passwords frequently.

FIGURE 9-7 Strategies for creating secure passwords.

manufacturing) and so were commonly known. As illustrated by this example, any individual possessing the proper password will be granted access to the system because the system recognizes the password, regardless of whether or not the person using the password is the authorized user.

The best passwords are *strong passwords*—at least eight characters long; use a combination of letters, numbers, and symbols; and do not form words found in the dictionary or that match the username. Some additional strategies for selecting secure passwords are listed in Figure 9-7. Passwords, usernames, and PINs are often used in conjunction with each other, as well as with *possessed object access systems* and *biometric access systems*, to add another level of security—called *two-factor authentication*.

Possessed Object Access Systems

Possessed object access systems use physical objects for identification purposes and are frequently used to access facilities and computer systems. Common types of possessed objects are smart cards, encoded badges, and magnetic cards that are similar to credit cards (see Figure 9-8) and that are swiped through or placed close to a reader to be read. Increasingly, *USB security tokens* or *e-tokens*—flash memory drives that are inserted into a PC to grant access to a network, supply Web site passwords, and provide other security features—are being used. For a closer look at how e-tokens are being used to secure computers at one college campus, see the Technology and You box.

One disadvantage of using possessed objects is that the object can be lost or, like passwords, used by an unauthorized individual. This latter disadvantage can be overcome by requiring the user to supply a password or be authenticated by a fingerprint or other type of *biometric* data in order to use the possessed object. For example, some smart card readers and some USB security keys contain *fingerprint readers* used to authenticate that the person using the possessed object is the authorized individual. This type of two-factor authentication is much more secure than security procedures involving only one factor.

FIGURE 9-8 Possessed objects, such as the magnetic card being used here, protect against unauthorized access.

NET

>**Possessed object access system.** An access control system that uses physical objects that an individual has in his or her possession to identify that individual.

FINGERPRINT READER
Typically used to protect access to office PCs, to replace Web site passwords on home PCs, to pay for products or services, and to access resources such as Welfare benefits.

HAND GEOMETRY READER
Typically used to control access to facilities (such as government offices, prisons, and military facilities) and to punch in and out of work.

FACE READER
Typically used to control access to highly secure areas, as well as to identify individuals for law enforcement purposes.

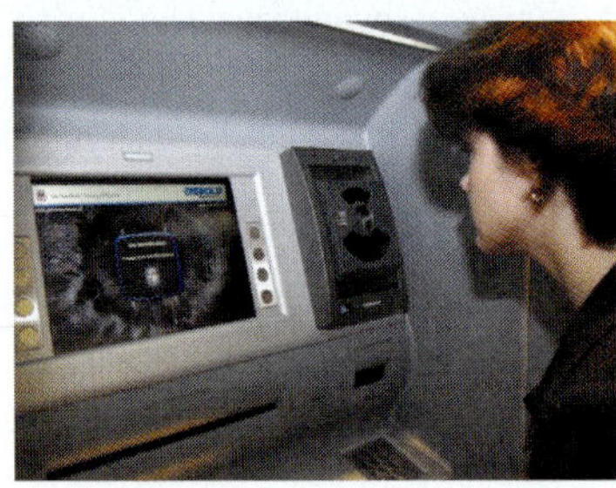

IRIS SCANNER
Typically used to control access to highly secure areas, such as nuclear facilities and prisons; beginning to be used to authenticate users of ATMs and other banking facilities, as shown here.

TYPE OF READER	ADVANTAGES	DISADVANTAGES
Fingerprint	Easy to use; inexpensive.	Sometimes harder to read on older individuals; usually requires contact with scanner; possible negative social image.
Hand	Easy to use.	Usually requires contact with scanner; fairly expensive.
Face	Requires no direct contact with user; can be used without the person's cooperation.	Lighting, disguised appearance, and other factors may affect results; fairly expensive.
Iris	Requires no direct contact with user; easy to use.	Lighting may affect results; expensive.

FIGURE 9-9
Types of biometric devices.

Biometric Access Systems

Biometrics is the study of identifying individuals using measurable biological characteristics. **Biometric access systems** identify users by a particular unique biological characteristic (such as a fingerprint, hand, face, or *iris*—the colored portion of the eye), although a personal trait (such as a voice or signature) can be used in some systems. Because the means of access (usually a part of the body) cannot be lost or forgotten and because it cannot be transferred to another individual or used by anyone other than the authorized individual, biometric access systems can perform both identification and authentication.

Biometric access systems use *biometric readers* (such as *fingerprint*, *hand geometry*, *face*, and *iris readers*) in conjunction with software and a database to match the supplied biometric data with the biometric data previously stored in the database to identify and authenticate an individual. To speed up the process, many access systems require users to identify themselves first (such as with a username, PIN number, magnetic card, or smart card), and then the system uses the identifying information to verify that the supplied biometric data matches that person. In general, biometric access systems are very accurate. According to IrisScan, an industry leader in iris-recognition technology, the odds of two different irises being declared a match are 1 in 10^{78}—even identical twins (who have the same DNA structure) have different fingerprints and irises. Systems based on biological characteristics (such as a person's iris, hand geometry, face, or fingerprint) tend to be more accurate than those based on a personal trait (such as an individual's voice or a written signature) because biological traits do not change, unlike physical traits that might change (such as an individual's voice, which might be affected by a cold, or a written signature, which might be affected by a broken wrist). Some examples of the most commonly used types of biometric devices are shown in Figure 9-9, along with their primary advantages and disadvantages.

>**Biometric access system.** An access control system that uses one unique physical characteristic of an individual (such as a fingerprint, face, or voice) to authenticate that individual.

TECHNOLOGY AND YOU

E-Tokens on Campus

E-tokens have arrived on campus at Dartmouth College in New Hampshire. Instead of just usernames and passwords, sensitive data and applications on the campus network are beginning to be protected by e-tokens—special USB keys that are used to authenticate individuals for network access. The e-tokens contain a digital certificate associated with the individual using the e-token. In addition to being used to identify the individual for access to network resources, the e-token can be used to digitally sign e-mail and other electronic documents and to encrypt documents and data.

To use the e-token (shown in the accompanying photograph), the individual first connects it to his or her PC (via a USB port), and then the individual supplies his or her password. The appropriate applications are then "unlocked" and available to that individual. The two levels of authentication (the actual key and the student's password) provide a more secure way to verify users to network applications than the traditional username/password approach. At Dartmouth, the e-tokens are currently used to gain access to information on the Dartmouth intranet (such as student grades, administrative files, and personal data), as well to education programs, such as Blackboard.

In addition to the conventional academic applications, the Dartmouth computer network is also beginning to host other resources available to students, such as television and telephone service. The goal is to create a ubiquitous campus network that provides both wired and wireless access to network resources anywhere on the entire campus.

Biometric access systems offer a great deal of convenience. Consequently, they are increasingly being used to grant access to secure facilities (such as corporate headquarters and prisons), log users on to computer systems and secure Web sites (by using an external reader or one built into the PC), punch employees in and out of work, and confirm consumers' identities at ATM machines and check-cashing services. Biometric readers are also increasingly being built into notebook PCs, handheld computers, and other devices to protect against unauthorized use and to authenticate online purchases and other financial transactions. Emerging biometric devices identify individuals based on their skin, the veins in their hands, or a combination of biometric features (such as skin, face, and fingerprint)—called *fusion biometrics*.

TIP

Cuts or other changes to a finger may prevent access via a fingerprint reader. To avoid this problem, be sure to enroll more than one finger, if possible, whenever you are being set up in a system that uses a fingerprint reader. Many systems allow the user to enter images for more than one finger and any of the registered fingers may be used for access.

Wireless Network Access Considerations

As already discussed, wireless networks—such as those accessed via a Wi-Fi connection—are less secure, in general, than wired networks. There are Wi-Fi security procedures, however, that can be used to protect against unauthorized use of a wireless network and to encrypt data sent over the network so that it is unreadable if intercepted. The original Wi-Fi security standard—*WEP* (*Wired Equivalent Privacy*)—is in the process of being replaced with the more secure *WPA* (*Wi-Fi Protected Access*) and the even more secure *802.11i* (also known as *WPA2*) standard. However, Wi-Fi security features only work if they are enabled. Most Wi-Fi hardware today is shipped with the security features switched off, and many Wi-Fi home network users never enable them, leaving those networks unsecured. To protect against unauthorized access, Wi-Fi network owners should secure their networks by enabling *encryption*, hiding their networks by not broadcasting the network names, and changing the default network administrator passwords. Once the *key* (essentially a password) is assigned to the network, users who want to connect to that network would need to supply the network identifying information and the appropriate key (see Figure 9-10).

FIGURE 9-10

Wi-Fi security. Wi-Fi networks should be secured to prevent unauthorized access, such as by using WPA keys as shown here.

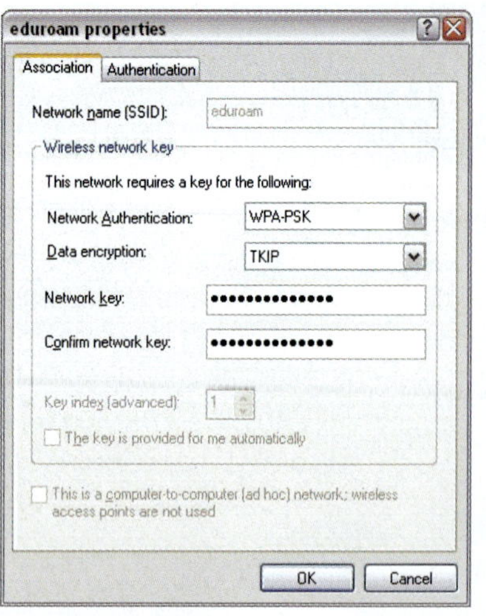

SECURITY SETTINGS
Owners of wireless networks should enable encryption and assign keys to be used by authorized individuals.

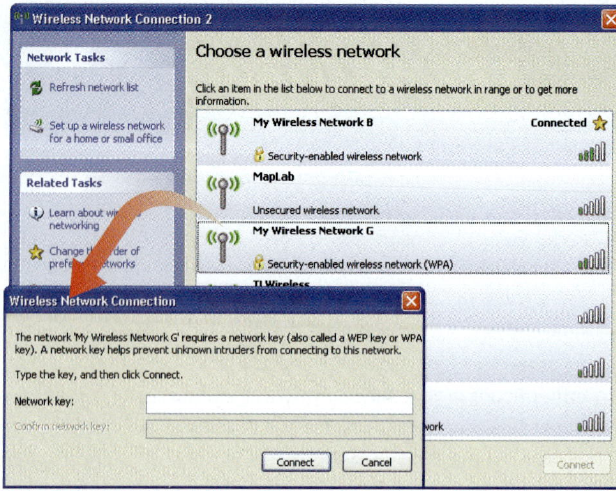

ACCESSING THE NETWORK
To access the network, the appropriate key must be supplied.

Firewalls and Antivirus Software

A **firewall** is a security system that provides a protective boundary between a computer or network and the outside world in order to protect against unauthorized access. *Personal firewalls* are typically software-based systems that are geared toward protecting home PCs from hackers attempting to access those computers through their Internet connections. Hackers who gain access to home PCs can access the information on them (such as passwords stored on the hard drive), as well as use those computers in denial of service attacks and other illegal activities. Consequently, all PCs with direct Internet connections (such as DSL, cable, or satellite Internet access) should use a firewall (PCs using dial-up Internet access are relatively safe from hackers). Firewalls designed to protect business networks may be software-based, hardware-based, or a combination of the two. They can typically be used both to prevent network access by hackers and other outsiders, and to control employee Internet access.

Firewalls work by closing down all external *communications port addresses*—the electronic connections that allow a PC to communicate with other computers—to unauthorized computers and programs for both incoming and outgoing activities. While business firewalls are set up by the network administrator and those settings cannot typically be changed by end users, personal firewalls will usually notify the user when an application program on the PC is trying to access the Internet or another computer on a home network is trying to access the firewall-protected PC. At that point, the user may either grant or deny access (see Figure 9-11). In addition to protecting your

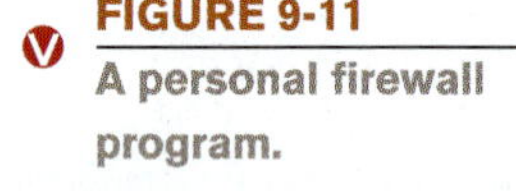

FIGURE 9-11

A personal firewall program.

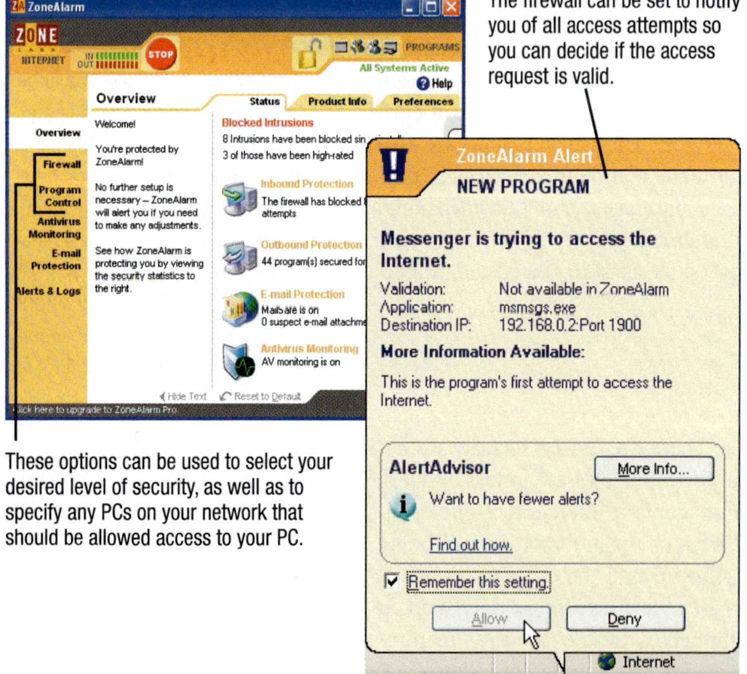

The firewall can be set to notify you of all access attempts so you can decide if the access request is valid.

These options can be used to select your desired level of security, as well as to specify any PCs on your network that should be allowed access to your PC.

>**Firewall.** A collection of hardware and/or software intended to protect a computer or computer network from unauthorized access.

PC from outside access, firewall programs also protect against inside attacks from computer viruses and other malicious programs that may have slipped through your virus protection. If communications port addresses are not blocked by a firewall, malware programs can open the ports and send data from your PC to a hacker at the hacker's request.

To protect against becoming infected with a computer virus or other type of malware, all PCs in both homes and offices should have **antivirus software** installed. To be effective, antivirus software should be set up to run continuously whenever the computer is on to check incoming e-mail messages, instant messages, and downloaded files; it should also be set up to run a complete scan of the entire PC on a regular basis, such as once per week. Antivirus software can protect your PC against getting a virus since it deletes or quarantines any suspicious e-mail attachments or downloaded files on their way in to your PC, and it can detect and remove any viruses or worms that may find their way onto your PC (see Figure 9-12). If a known virus or worm is found, the program will remove it and try to repair any damage it caused.

New viruses and other types of malware are released all the time (according to McAfee Security, a manufacturer of antivirus and security software, there were over 100,000 known viruses in late 2005, with new viruses and other types of malware being introduced at a rate of about 500 per month), so it is vital to keep your antivirus program up to date. Antivirus programs are usually set up to automatically download new virus definitions from its associated Web site on a regular basis—an important precaution. Most

TIP

To ensure you have the latest security updates for your operating system, enable *automatic updates* for your operating system. Windows users should also run the Windows Update program manually at least once per month.

FIGURE 9-12

Antivirus software.

Antivirus programs, such as this one, are used to detect and remove malware infections.

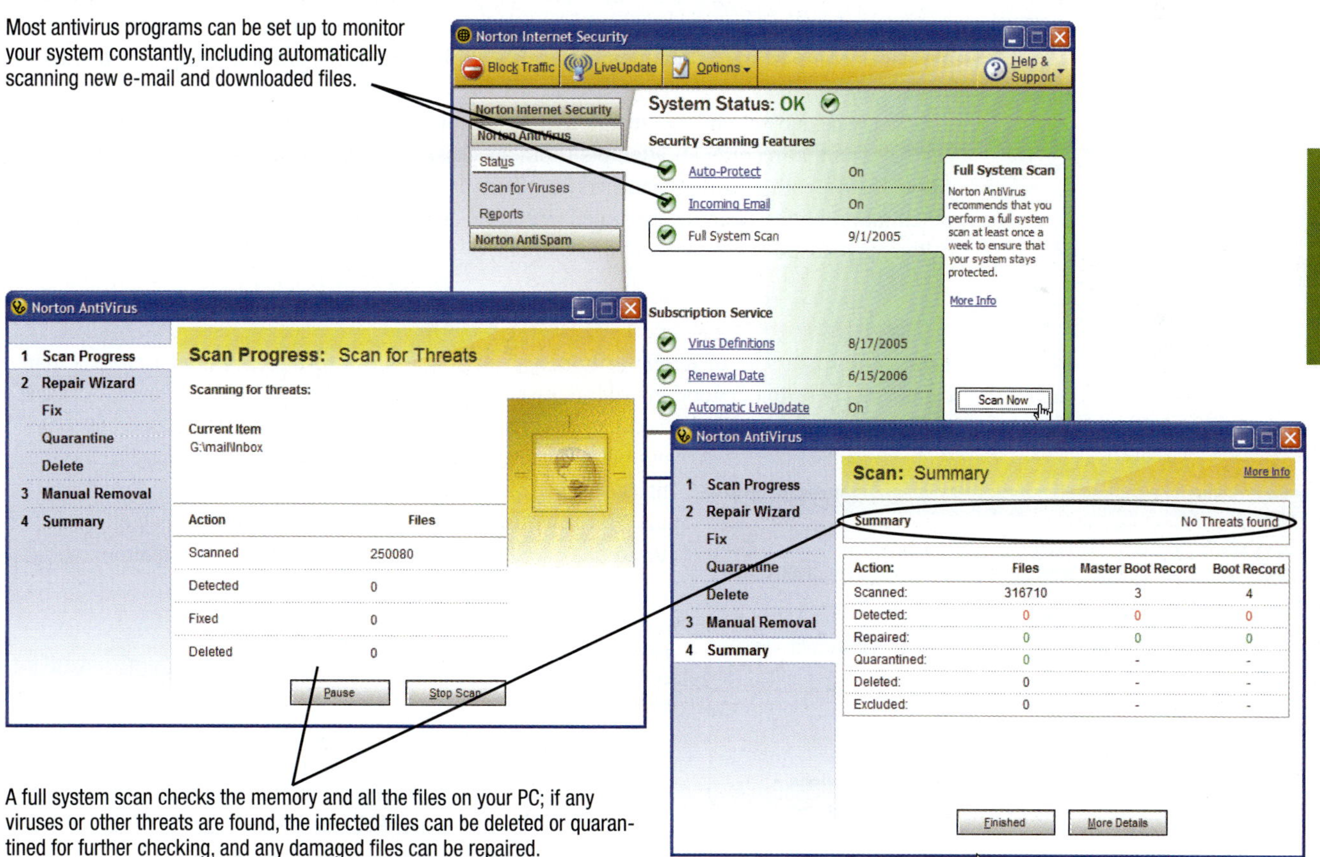

>Antivirus software. Software used to detect and eliminate computer viruses and other types of malware.

VIRUS PREVENTION STRATEGIES
Use antivirus software to check incoming e-mail messages and files, and download updated virus definitions on a regular basis.
Limit the sharing of disks and other removable storage media with others.
Only download files from reputable sites.
Only open e-mail attachments that come from people you know and that do not have an executable file extension (such as *.exe*, *.com*, *.bat*, or *.vbs*); double-check with the sender before opening a seemingly legitimate executable attachment.
Keep the preview window of your e-mail program closed so you will not view messages until you determine that they are safe to view.
Regularly download and install the latest security patches available for your operating sytem, browser, and e-mail program.
Avoid downloading files from P2P sites.

FIGURE 9-13
Sensible precautions can help protect against computer virus infections.

antivirus programs come with a year of access to free updates; users should purchase additional years after that to continue to be protected. Schools and businesses should also ensure that students and employees connecting to the campus or company network with personal PCs are using up-to-date antivirus software so they will not inadvertently infect the network with malware. Some colleges now require new students to go through a quarantine process, in which students are not granted access to the network until they go through a security process that checks their PCs for security threats, updates their operating systems, and installs antivirus software. Some additional virus-prevention strategies are listed in Figure 9-13.

Some antivirus programs also scan for other threats in addition to malware, such as *spyware* and possible *phishing* e-mails (discussed shortly). Many also include a firewall and other security components. In addition to using installed antivirus software, your ISP may offer antivirus protection. Typically, ISP antivirus software scans all incoming e-mail messages at the mail server level to filter out messages containing a virus. If a message containing a virus is detected, typically it is deleted and the recipient is notified that the message contained a virus and was deleted. Another type of program in the works to protect against viruses sent via e-mail is an *e-mail authentication system*—a system designed to tell recipients exactly where e-mail messages come from to help them determine which messages are safe to open and which might contain malware.

Many businesses and organizations also use additional software to monitor network use, such as one that records all attempts (both successful and unsuccessful) to access network resources by both outsiders and insiders. This data is then analyzed to try to identify any potential problems, such as attempted network access by a hacker, access by employees to resources that should not be available to them, or a possible denial of service attack.

FIGURE 9-14
Secure Web pages.
Sensitive information should only be submitted via secure Web pages.

Encryption and Other Security Tools

Encryption is a way of temporarily converting data into a form, known as a *cipher*, that cannot easily be understood in order to protect that data from being viewed by unauthorized people. For instance, Web sites use encryption so that sensitive data (such as credit card numbers) sent via the Web page is protected as it travels over the Internet. Individuals can use encryption to secure e-mail messages or other documents sent over the Internet, as well as data stored on a storage medium. These topics are discussed next.

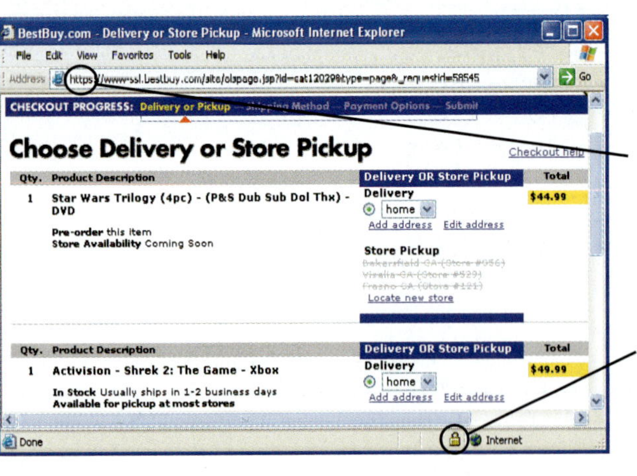

Secure Web Servers

To protect against interception of sensitive information sent via a Web page (such as while shopping, banking, trading stock, or performing some other type of financial transaction online), only *secure Web pages* should be used. A secure Web page (see Figure 9-14) is located on a **secure Web server**, which is protected against unauthorized access and encrypts data

>**Encryption.** A method of scrambling e-mail or files to make them unreadable if they are intercepted by an unauthorized user. >**Secure Web server.** A Web server that uses encryption to protect information transmitted via the Web pages stored on that server.

going to and coming from the server. To indicate a secure Web page, most Web browsers display a locked padlock or a solid (unbroken) key on the status bar at the bottom of the browser window. The most common security protocol used with secure Web pages is *Secure Sockets Layer* (*SSL*). The URL for Web pages using SSL begin with *https:* instead of *http:*.

E-Mail and File Encryption

Although it may not seem likely that the e-mail messages and files you send and receive via the Internet might be intercepted and read by someone else, it is a possibility if they are not secured. To secure e-mail messages or other documents sent over the Internet, encryption techniques are used. An encrypted document is essentially scrambled and as such is unreadable until it is *decrypted*—or unscrambled—correctly. Files, e-mail messages, and instant messages can be encrypted before they are sent over the Internet; individual files can also be encrypted before they are stored on a hard drive so they will be unreadable if opened by an unauthorized person. Encryption is often implemented using a third-party encryption program, such as *Pretty Good Privacy* (*PGP*). How the data is encrypted depends on the *encryption algorithm*—such as *Blowfish* or *Advanced Encryption Standard* (*AES*)—being used. There are also special USB flash memory drives that are designed to encrypt the files on a PC—to access the decrypted versions of those files, the flash memory drive must be inserted in the PC's USB port. *Automatic encryption* (which automatically encrypts all data written to the drive) is beginning to be built into hard drives used in portable PCs so the data will be unreadable if the PC is stolen.

The two most common types of encryption are *private key encryption* and *public key encryption*. **Private key encryption**, also called *symmetric key encryption*, uses a single secret key to both encrypt and decrypt the file or message. It is often used to encrypt files stored on an individual's PC, since the individual who selects the private key is likely the only one who will need to access those files. Private key encryption can also be used to securely send files to others, provided both the sender and recipient agree on the private key (essentially a secret password) that will be used to access the file. For a look at how private key encryption works, see the How it Works box.

Public key encryption, also called *asymmetric key encryption*, utilizes two encryption keys to encrypt and decrypt documents. Specifically, public key encryption uses a pair of keys (a public key and a private key) that has been assigned to a particular individual—each key is a very long number that is mathematically related to the other key. An individual's *public key* is not secret and is available for anyone to use, but a *private key* is used only by the individual to whom it was assigned. Documents or messages encrypted with a public key can only be decrypted with the matching private key.

Public/private key pairs are either generated by the encryption program being used or are obtained through a *Certificate Authority*, such as VeriSign or Thawte (Certificate Authorities are discussed in more detail in a later section). Key pairs obtained from a Certificate Authority need to be installed in your browser, e-mail program, and any third-party encryption program before they can be used, although often this is done automatically for you if your key pairs are downloaded from the Internet. Obtaining a business public/private key pair usually requires a fee, but free key pairs are available for personal use through some Certificate Authorities. Some encryption programs (such as PGP) are also available without charge for personal use.

>**Private key encryption.** A type of encryption that uses a single key to encrypt and decrypt the file or message. >**Public key encryption.** A type of encryption that uses key pairs to encrypt and decrypt the file or message.

HOW IT WORKS

Private Key Encryption

Stand-alone private key encryption programs can be used to encrypt individual files or an entire hard drive. Private key encryption is also incorporated into a variety of programs—such as Microsoft Office, the WinZip file compression program, and Adobe Acrobat (the program used to create PDF files)—to encrypt documents created in those programs so that they can be stored in an encrypted form on a storage medium. As shown in the accompanying illustration of encrypting a Microsoft Word document, once the file is encrypted, the password assigned to that file must be entered to open the original file or any copies of the file, such as those sent via e-mail. A separate password can be issued if you want to control who is able to modify the file; otherwise, anyone with the password to open the file can modify it. To send a privately encrypted file to another individual, the sender uses the agreed-upon private key to encrypt the file, and the recipient uses that same key to decrypt and open the file.

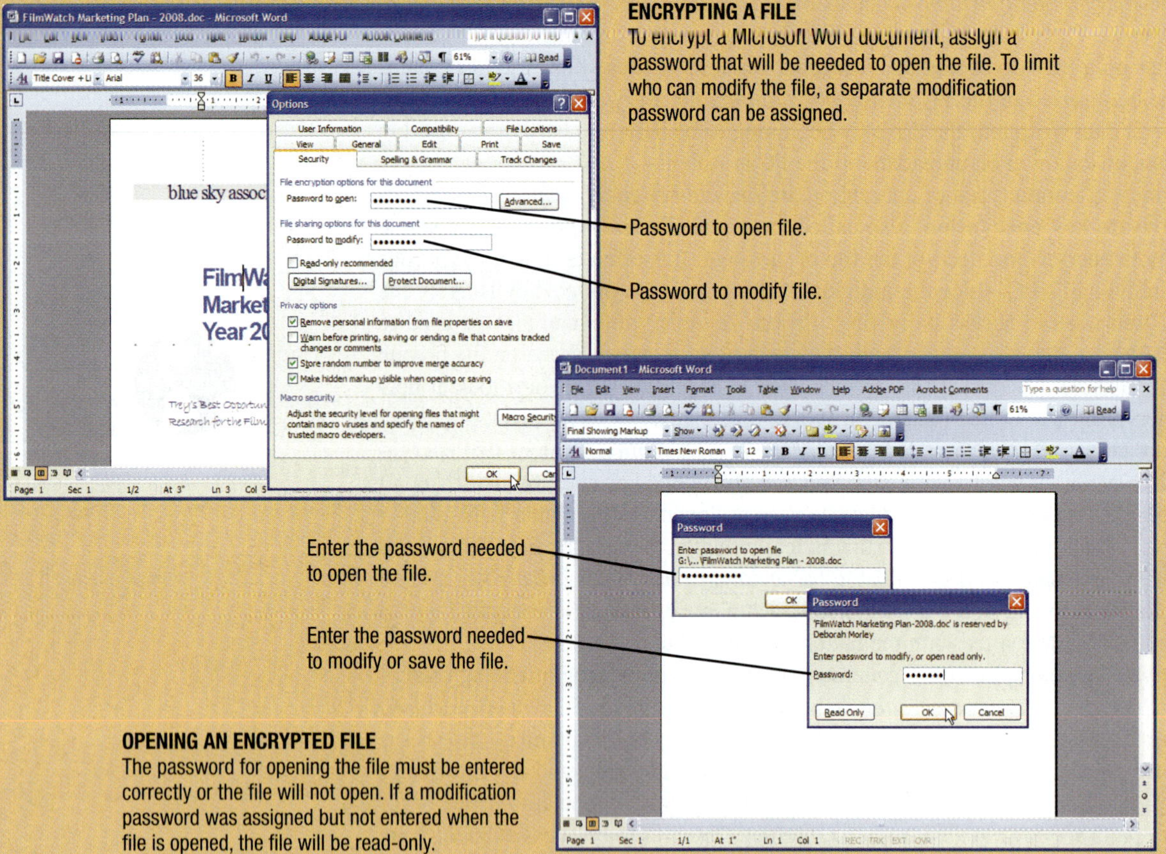

ENCRYPTING A FILE
To encrypt a Microsoft Word document, assign a password that will be needed to open the file. To limit who can modify the file, a separate modification password can be assigned.

OPENING AN ENCRYPTED FILE
The password for opening the file must be entered correctly or the file will not open. If a modification password was assigned but not entered when the file is opened, the file will be read-only.

To send someone an encrypted message using public key encryption, you need his or her public key. If that person has previously sent you his or her public key (such as via an e-mail message), it was likely stored by your e-mail program in your address book or by your encryption program in a special *key ring* feature used by that program. In either case, that public key is available whenever you want to send that person an encrypted document. If you do not already have the public key belonging to the individual to whom you wish to send an encrypted message, you will need to request it from that individual or find it in a *public keyserver*—a database of public keys available through a Web site. Once the recipient's public key has been used to encrypt the file and the message is sent, the recipient uses his or her private key to decrypt the file (see Figure 9-15).

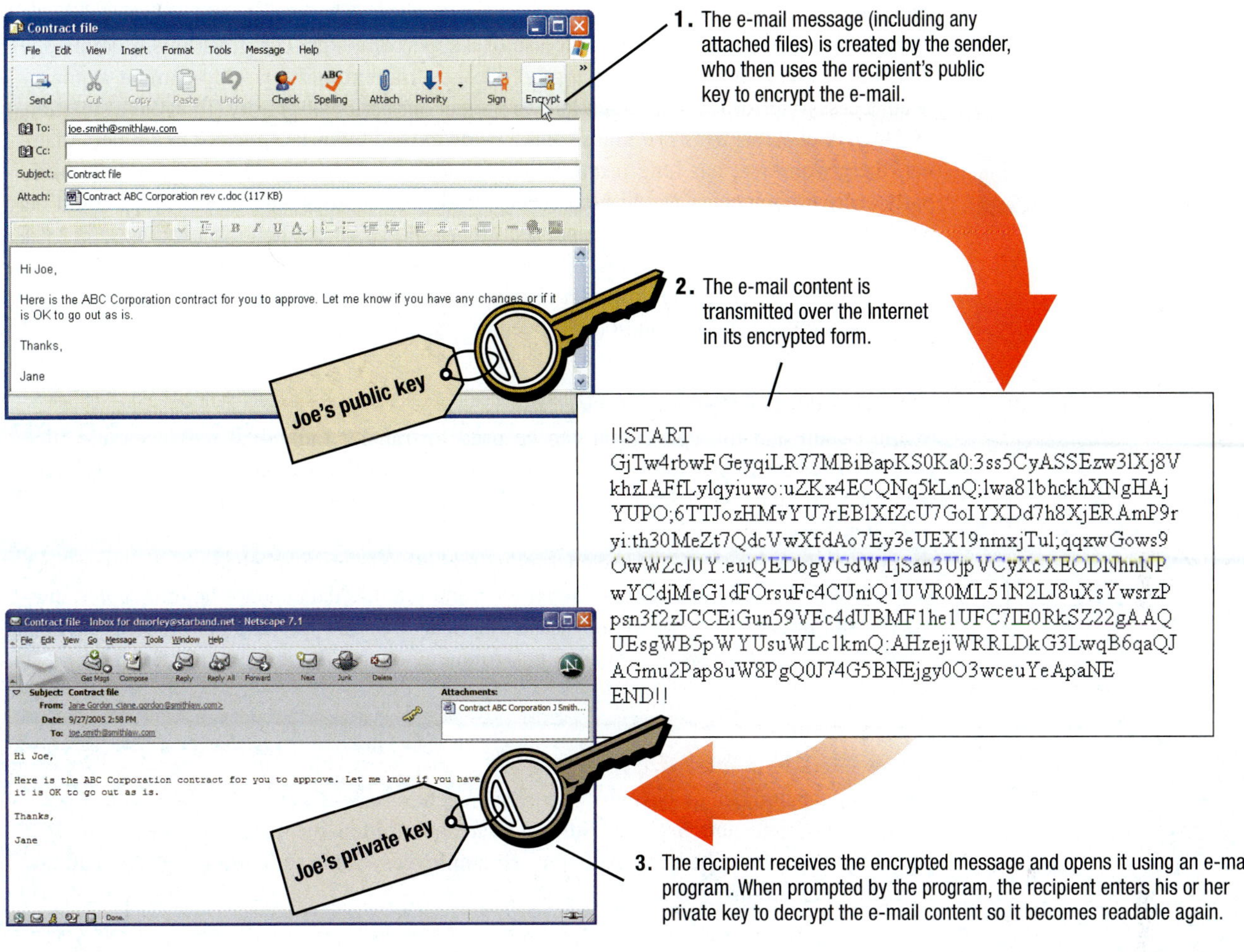

FIGURE 9-15
Using public key encryption to secure an e-mail message.

To avoid the need to obtain the recipient's public key before sending that person an encrypted e-mail, *Web-based encrypted e-mail* can be used. Web-based encrypted e-mail works similarly to regular Web-based e-mail (in which e-mail is composed and viewed on a Web page belonging to the Web-based e-mail service), but Web-based encrypted e-mail systems use secure Web servers to host the Web pages that are used to compose and read e-mail messages. With some Web-based encrypted e-mail systems, the recipient is notified via his or her regular e-mail address that an encrypted e-mail message is waiting, and, using the link included in the e-mail message, the recipient can view the message on a secure Web page. With this type of system, often only the sender is required to have an account through the Web-based encrypted e-mail service. Other Web-based encrypted e-mail systems—such as the popular free *HushMail* service—require both the sender and recipient to have accounts through that system. Since all e-mail sent through the service is automatically encrypted, users just log on to the HushMail Web page and provide their password when requested in order to decrypt and view any encrypted e-mail messages sent to their HushMail e-mail addresses.

There are various strengths of encryption available; the stronger the encryption, the more difficult it is to crack. Older 40-bit encryption (which can only use keys that are 40 bits or 5 characters long) is considered *weak encryption*. Stronger encryption is available today—such as *strong 128-bit encryption* (which uses 16-character keys) and *military-strength 2,048-bit encryption* (which uses 256-character keys)—although not without some objections from law enforcement agencies and the government. According to the government, terrorists routinely use encryption methods to communicate. Current commercial encryption programs are so strong that cracking them can take government agencies days or even weeks and typically requires the use of a supercomputer. The government points out that this is unacceptable because appropriate government and law enforcement agencies need access to terrorist communications to protect our national security. To avoid a situation in which documents from criminals cannot be decrypted by these agencies in a timely manner, the government has long proposed a *key escrow system*, in which independent third-party escrow companies would hold copies of all private keys, and those copies could be used for law enforcement and national security purposes when such use is authorized by a court order. Civil liberties groups, on the other hand, have vowed to fight a key escrow or similar system, calling it an invasion of personal privacy. At the present time, this issue is still being debated and no solution has been reached.

FURTHER EXPLORATION

For links to further information about encryption, go to www.course.com/uc11/ch09

Virtual Private Networks (VPNs)

While e-mail and file encryption can be used to transfer individual messages and files securely over the Internet, a **virtual private network (VPN)** can be used when a business needs a continuous secure channel. A VPN provides a secure private tunnel from the user's computer through the Internet (including all needed servers and wireless access points) to the business's network. VPNs use encryption and other security mechanisms to ensure that only authorized users can access the network and that the data cannot be intercepted during transit. Since it uses a public infrastructure instead of an expensive private physical network, a VPN can provide a secure environment over a large geographical area at a manageable cost.

Take Caution with Employees

A significant number of business security breaches—about half, according to the 2005 "Computer Crime and Security Survey"—are committed by insiders. Consequently, it pays for employers to be cautious with their employees. Some suggestions to avoid attacks by employees are listed next.

Screen Potential New Hires Carefully

Employers should carefully investigate the background of all potential employees. Some people falsify résumés to get jobs. Others may have criminal records or currently be charged with a crime. One embarrassing mistake made by Rutgers University was to hire David Smith, the author of the *Melissa* virus, as a computer technician when he was out on bail following the arrest for that crime.

Watch for Disgruntled Employees and Ex-Employees

The type of employee who is most likely to commit a computer crime is one who has recently been terminated or passed over for a promotion, or one who has some reason to want to "get even" with the organization. Limiting access for each employee to only the resources needed for his or her job and monitoring any attempts to access off-limits resources can help prevent some types of sabotage. According to a 2005 "Insider Threat Study" by the U.S. Secret Service National Threat Assessment Center (NTAC) and the Software Engineering Institute's Computer Emergency Response Team (CERT), 57% of the insiders who sabotaged their companies were perceived as disgruntled employees and, in 92% of the cases, an event or series of events (such as a dispute with another employee or a demotion) triggered the incident. In the majority (nearly 60%) of the cases,

>**Virtual private network (VPN).** A secure path over the Internet that provides authorized users a secure means of accessing a private network via the Internet.

the sabotage took place after the employee left the company and about half of the ex-employees had been fired. Consequently, it is vital that whenever an employee leaves the company for any reason, all access to the system (username, password, e-mail address, and so forth) should be removed immediately—for employees with high levels of system access, simultaneously removing access while the employee is being terminated is even better. Waiting even a few minutes can be too late, since just-fired employees have been known to barricade themselves in their office immediately after being terminated in order to change passwords, sabotage records, and perform other malicious acts. Some wait slightly longer, such as one salesman at a New York staffing company who allegedly accessed the company computer system the evening after being fired and deleted all the e-mail belonging to his boss. He was charged in federal court with one count of unauthorized access to a computer and intentionally causing more than $5,000 in damage. He faces a maximum sentence of 10 years in prison and a fine of $250,000.

Develop Policies and Controls

All companies should develop policies and controls regarding security matters. Employees should be educated about the seriousness and consequences of computer crime, and they should be taught what to do when they suspect a computer crime. Policies such as shredding sensitive documents that are no longer needed, limiting employee access to only needed parts of the network, immediately removing access for any employee who leaves the company, and separating employee functions as much as possible are all wise precautions. Employees should also be instructed about proper computer and e-mail usage policies—such as whether or not downloading and installing software on company PCs is allowed and how to avoid opening attachments containing malware—to avoid accidentally creating a security problem.

Ask Business Partners to Review their Security

In this networked economy, many organizations provide some access to internal resources for business partners. If those companies are lax with their security measures, attacks from business partners' employees are possible. Consequently, businesses should make sure that their business partners maintain adequate security policies and controls. Regulations—such as the *Sarbanes-Oxley Act of 2002*—increasingly require businesses to ensure that adequate controls are in place to preserve the integrity of financial reports. This includes outside companies—such as business partners and *outsourcing companies* (outside vendors for specific business tasks, as discussed in Chapter 12)—if they have access to sensitive corporate data,

ONLINE THEFT, FRAUD, AND OTHER DOT CONS

A booming area of computer crime involves online fraud, theft, scams, and related activities collectively referred to as **dot cons**. The Internet Crime Complaint Center (a joint venture of the FBI and the National White Collar Crime Center, formerly called Internet Fraud Complaint Center) received around 100,000 reports of fraudulent activities taking place over the Internet in 2004. Common types of dot cons include theft of data, information, and other resources; *identity theft*; *online auction fraud*; and *Internet offer scams*, *spoofing*, and *phishing*.

>Dot con. A fraud or scam carried out through the Internet.

NET

Theft of Data, Information, and Other Resources

Data theft or *information theft*—the theft of data or information usually located on a computer—can be committed by stealing an actual PC (as discussed in more detail in Chapter 15); it can also take place over the Internet or a network after a hacker gains unauthorized access to a computer system. Common types of stolen data and information include customer data and proprietary corporate information. Stolen customer data, such as credit card numbers and Social Security numbers, can be used to commit *credit card fraud*, *identity theft*, and other crimes. Recently, there have been numerous examples of personal data stolen via computers, in addition to CardSystems credit card number theft mentioned earlier in this chapter. For instance, 1.4 million credit card numbers were stolen from a DSW Shoe Warehouse database; data about 100,000 alumni, graduate students, and past applicants was compromised when a laptop containing that data was stolen from a U.C. Berkeley office; and around 300,000 records in University of Southern California's online application database were exposed when that database was hacked.

Money is another resource that can be stolen via a computer. Company insiders sometimes steal money by altering company programs to transfer small amounts of money—for example, a few cents' worth of bank account interest—from a very large number of transactions to an account controlled by the thief. This type of crime is sometimes called *salami shaving*. Victims of salami-shaving schemes generally are unaware that their funds have been accessed because the amount taken from each individual is trivial. Another example of monetary theft using computers involves hackers electronically transferring money illegally from online bank accounts, traditional bank accounts, credit card accounts, or accounts at online payment services, such as PayPal. The largest case of Internet fraud to date that has resulted in a conviction involves a California man who stole over $37 million from about 900,000 credit card owners. He signed them up, without their knowledge, for access to his fee-based Web site. He was sentenced in 2004 to more than 11 years in prison and ordered to pay full restitution to his victims.

Identity Theft

Identity theft occurs when someone obtains enough information about a person (such as name, date of birth, Social Security number, address, phone number, and credit card numbers) to be able to masquerade as that person for a variety of activities—usually to buy products or services in that person's name (see Figure 9-16). Typically, identity theft begins with obtaining a person's name and Social Security number, often from a credit application, rental application, or similar form. Once the thief finds that individual's home address (either from the same form or by using a telephone book or an Internet search), he or she usually has enough information to order a copy of the individual's birth certificate over the phone, to obtain a "replacement" driver's license, and to open credit or bank accounts in the victim's name. Assuming the thief requests a change of address for these new accounts after they are opened, it may take quite some time—often until a company or collections agency contacts the victim about overdue bills—for the victim to become aware that his or her identity has been stolen. Although identity theft often takes place via a computer today, information used in identity theft can be gathered from trash dumpsters, mailboxes, and other locations. It can also be obtained by *skimming* (stealing credit card or debit card numbers by attaching a special storage device to ATM machines or credit card readers) or via *social engineering* (pretending to be a bank officer, potential employer, or other trusted individual in order to get the potential victim to offer personal information). In 1998, the federal government passed the *Identity Theft and Assumption Deterrence Act*, which made identity theft a federal crime.

>**Identity theft.** Using someone else's identity to purchase goods or services, obtain new credit cards or bank loans, or otherwise illegally masquerade as that individual.

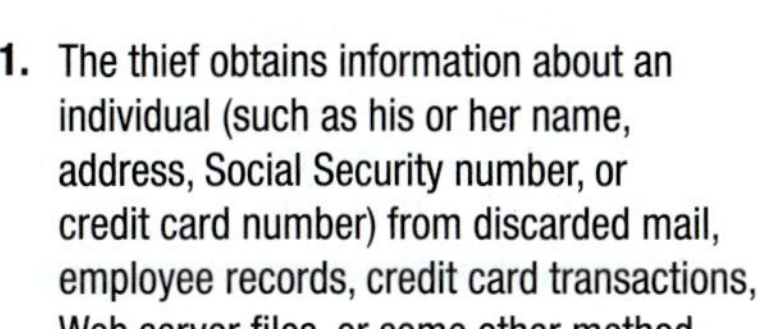

1. The thief obtains information about an individual (such as his or her name, address, Social Security number, or credit card number) from discarded mail, employee records, credit card transactions, Web server files, or some other method.

2. The thief uses the information to make online purchases, open new credit card accounts, sign up for a service, buy or rent property, and more—all in the victim's name. Often, the thief changes the address on the account to delay the victim's discovery of the theft.

3. The victim eventually finds out, usually by being denied credit or by being contacted about overdue bills generated by the thief. Although victims can file reports and complaints, cancel accounts, and dispute unauthorized charges, clearing their names after identity theft is time-consuming and can be very difficult and frustrating.

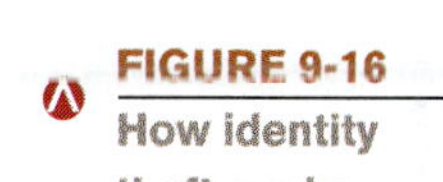

FIGURE 9-16
How identity theft works.

Unfortunately, identity theft is on the rise—it has topped the list of complaints received by the Federal Trade Commission (FTC) for the past five years and represents about 40% of all complaints filed in 2004. Several studies estimate the number of identity theft victims in the United States per year to be close to 10 million individuals, and it is estimated that identity theft cost businesses and consumers more than $52 billion in 2004. The largest identity theft case in U.S. history to date came to light in late 2002 when federal investigators charged three men with running an identity theft ring—based on information obtained from stolen consumer credit reports—that impacted more than 30,000 consumers and cost nearly $3 million in losses.

Identity theft can be extremely distressing for victims, can take years to straighten out, and can be very expensive. According to the Identity Theft Resource Center, identity theft victims spend an average of 600 hours and $1,400 trying to clear their names. Some victims, such as Michelle Brown, believe that they will always be dealing with their "alter reality" to some extent. For a year and a half, an identity thief used Brown's identity to obtain over $50,000 in goods and services, to rent properties—even to engage in drug trafficking. Although the culprit was arrested and convicted eventually for other criminal acts, she continued to use Brown's identity and was even booked into jail using Brown's stolen identity. As a final insult after the culprit was in prison, the real Michelle Brown was detained by U.S. customs agents when returning from a trip to Mexico because of the criminal record of the identity thief. Brown states that she has not traveled out of the country since, fearing an arrest or some other serious problem resulting from the theft of her identity, and estimates she has spent over 500 hours trying to correct all the problems related to the identity theft.

Online Auction Fraud

Online auction fraud (sometimes called *Internet auction fraud*)—which occurs when a buyer pays for merchandise that is never delivered, or it is delivered but is not as represented—is an increasing risk for online auction bidders. According to the Internet Crime Complaint Center, online auction fraud accounted for about 71% of all reported Internet fraud cases in 2004.

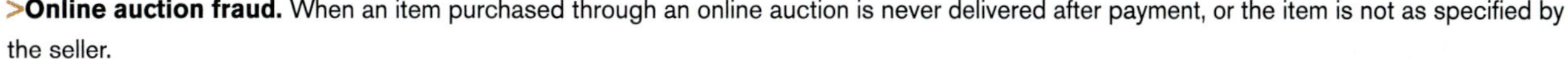

>**Online auction fraud.** When an item purchased through an online auction is never delivered after payment, or the item is not as specified by the seller.

Like other types of fraud, online auction fraud is illegal, but these criminals are often difficult to stop, as well as to identify and prosecute. As is the case in many types of Internet cons, prosecution is difficult because multiple jurisdictions are usually involved. In addition, some online auction fraud victims pay by personal check or money order and know very little about the seller's identity. Although most online auction sites have policies that suspend sellers with a certain number of complaints lodged against them, it is very easy for those sellers to come back using a new e-mail address and identity.

Internet Scams, Spoofing, and Phishing

Internet offer scams include a wide range of scams offered through Web sites or unsolicited e-mails. The anonymity of the Internet makes it very easy for con artists to appear to be almost anyone they want to be, including a charitable organization or a reputable-looking business. Common types of scams include loan scams, work-at-home cons, pyramid schemes, bogus credit card offers and prize promotions, and fraudulent business opportunities and franchises. These offers typically try to sell potential victims nonexistent services or worthless information, or they try to convince potential victims to voluntarily supply their credit card details and other personal information, which are then used for fraudulent purposes.

Some scams involve **spoofing**—making it appear that an e-mail or a Web site originates from somewhere other than its actual source. For instance, con artists create **phishing** (pronounced "fishing") e-mails that appear to be generated by America Online, eBay, PayPal, Citibank, or another well-known organization. They send these e-mails to a wide group of individuals stating that the individual's credit card or account information needs to be updated and requesting that the recipient of the e-mail click the link provided in the e-mail in order to keep the account active (see Figure 9-17). The link actually goes to a Web site belonging to the con artist, although the Web site is usually set up to look as if it belongs to the legitimate organization—an act called *Web site spoofing*.

To accomplish this, the con artist typically uses a copy of the legitimate Web page (sometimes the spoofed Web site even contains live links to selected Web pages of the legitimate site) and a secure connection between the victim and the con artist's server (so the unbroken key or locked padlock on the status bar appears as normal). The con artist can also use JavaScript commands to overwrite the URLs displayed on the browser's status bar and Address bar so that the displayed URLs match the URLs of the legitimate site, which makes a spoofed Web site even more difficult to identify. Because the site looks and responds like the legitimate site, victims often supply the requested information and carry out any additional activities in a seemingly normal fashion, allowing the con artist access to all information—such as account numbers, credit card numbers, and passwords—provided by the victim via the spoofed Web page. To make matters even worse, some phishing e-mail messages now contain a Trojan horse program. After just viewing the phishing e-mail message, the Trojan horse program redirects specific URLs that the user subsequently types (such as the URL for the bank that the phishing e-mail was spoofing) so the

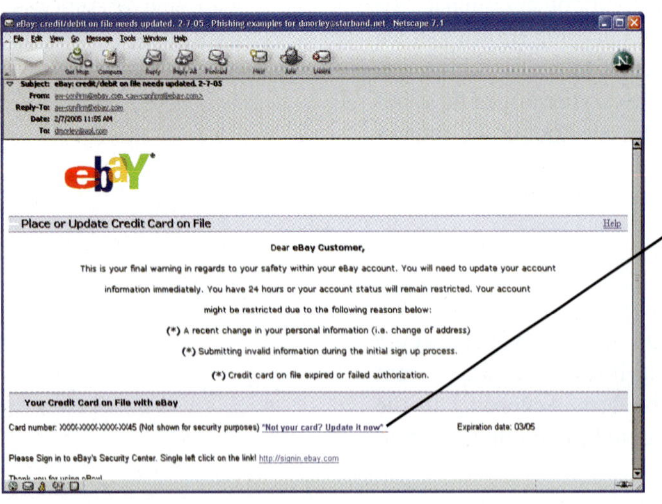

FIGURE 9-17
Phishing. Phishing schemes use legitimate-looking e-mails to trick users into providing private information.

>**Spoofing.** Making it appear that an e-mail or a Web site originates from somewhere other than where it really does; typically used with dot cons.
>**Phishing.** The use of spoofed e-mail messages to gain credit card numbers and other personal data to be used for fraudulent purposes.

TREND

Pharming

As if phishing is not bad enough, now there is *pharming*. Similar to phishing, pharming is used to obtain personal information (such as credit card numbers, account numbers, and passwords) to be used in fraudulent activities, but the technique is a little different, and it is directed at large groups of people at one time, instead of individuals. With pharming, the criminal hacks into a *DNS server*—the computer that translates URLs it receives into the appropriate IP addresses used to display the Web page corresponding to that URL—in order to reroute traffic intended for a commonly used Web site to a phony, usually look-alike, Web site set up by the pharmer. Although pharming can take place at one of the 13 root DNS servers for the Internet, the hacking more often takes place at a company DNS server used to route Web page requests to the appropriate company server. For instance, a company may have several different Web servers set up to process requests received via its Web page URLs, and the company DNS server routes individual requests to an available Web server via that Web server's IP address. After hacking into a DNS server, the pharmer assigns bogus IP addresses to a particular URL (called *DNS poisoning*) so that Web page requests made via that legitimate URL are routed (via the company's poisoned DNS server) to a phony Web site located on the pharmer's Web server. So, even though a user types the proper URL for a Web site in his or her browser, the phony site is displayed instead. Since the phony sites are set up to look like the legitimate sites, the user typically does not notice any difference, and any information sent to the pharmer's server is captured. To avoid suspicion, some pharming sites capture the user's account name and password as it is entered the first time on the phony site, and then display a password error message. The phony site then sends the user back to the legitimate site where he or she is able to log on to the legitimate site, thinking he or she must have just mistyped the password the first time. But, by then, the pharmer has already captured the victim's username and password and can use that information to gain access to the victim's account.

Pharming is much more difficult to recognize than phishing, since it does not require the user to click a hyperlink in an unsolicited e-mail message and the browser and Web pages respond in a legitimate manner to user requests. The best defense against pharming is for businesses to use strong security with their DNS servers, upgrade their DNS server software as needed, and use secure Web servers so that *digital certificates* can be used to verify the site is legitimate. If the name on the digital certificate ever does not match the IP address being used, a warning message will appear (see the accompanying illustration). When this occurs, users should not proceed with the transaction.

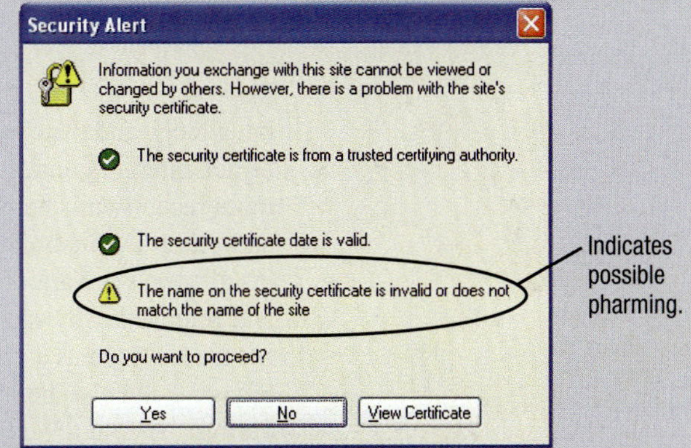

If a message such as this occurs when accessing a secure Web page, it is safer not to proceed.

spoofed site is displayed instead of the legitimate site. Phishing is also now used in conjunction with *spyware*, discussed shortly.

Phishing is growing rapidly. It is estimated that over half of all Americans have received a phishing e-mail and, according to the research firm Gartner, about 1.2 million U.S. consumers suffered phishing-related losses between May 2004 and May 2005, for a total loss of over $900 million. Federal legislation—such as the *Anti-Phishing Act of 2005* that would allow prison time of up to five years and fines of up to $250,000 for people who design fake Web sites for the purposes of stealing money or credit card numbers—has been introduced, but none had passed at the time of this writing, For a look at a new activity related to phishing—*pharming*—see the Trend box.

One ongoing Internet scam is the Nigerian letter fraud scheme, in which an e-mail message appearing to come from the Nigerian government promises the potential victim a share of a substantial amount of money, in exchange for the use of the victim's bank account to supposedly facilitate a wire transfer (but the account is emptied instead) and/or up-front cash to pay for nonexistent fees (that is kept by the con artist with nothing given in return). The theme of these scams (sometimes called *419 scams* after the number of the relevant section of Nigerian criminal law code) sometimes changes to fit current events like the war in Iraq or the Katrina hurricane, but the scams always involve a so-called fortune that is inaccessible to the con artist and individuals lose money when they pay fees or provide bank account information in hopes of sharing in the wealth. Another common scheme involves con artists who solicit donations after disasters and other tragic events, but who keep the donations instead of giving them to any charitable organization. For instance, right after Hurricane Katrina hit the United States in August 2005, a number of fraudulent Web sites appeared that were designed to take advantage of people's sympathy for the hurricane victims by soliciting donations meant for Katrina victims, but these donations were diverted into private accounts instead. In fact, more than 2,500 Katrina- or storm-related domain names were registered—over 450 with the word "Katrina" in them—right after the hurricane. Although some were sites set up to really help victims or solicit legitimate donations, the FBI reports that over 60% of the 2000 sites it has reviewed that claim to offer aid to Katrina victims are registered to people outside the United States and so are likely to be fraudulent.

Another common scam involves setting up a pornographic site that requires a valid credit card, supposedly to prove that the visitor is of the required age (such as over 18), but which is then used for credit card fraud. A new type of scam involves posting fake job listings on job search sites to elicit personal information—such as Social Security numbers—from job seekers. An even more recent twist is to hire individuals through online job sites for seemingly legitimate positions involving money handling (such as bookkeeping or accounting positions), but then use those individuals—often without their knowledge—as legitimate-looking go-betweens to facilitate Internet auction scams and other monetary scams.

Spyware

Spyware is the term used for any software program that is installed without the user's knowledge and that secretly gathers information about the user and transmits it through his or her Internet connection. Traditionally, this information was directed to advertisers, but more recently it is being used in conjunction with phishing schemes to transmit passwords and other sensitive data to the phisher. Typically, clicking a link in the phishing e-mail installs the spyware on the victim's computer, and it will remain there until it is detected and removed. Spyware programs can also be installed secretly at the same time another program—such as a program downloaded from a Web site or a P2P service—is installed. Spyware can also be installed via an instant message, or it can be installed automatically during a visit to a Web site (sometimes called a *drive-by download* because the installation requires no action on the part of the Web site visitor other than visiting the site), if the user's browser security settings do not prevent the installation.

Unfortunately, spyware use is on the rise. A 2004 study by AOL and the National Cyber Security Alliance found that more than 80% of all Internet users have spyware programs installed on their computers, and a 2004 study of two million computers performed by EarthLink and Webroot Software found an average of 26.5 spyware programs installed on each PC. And, according to a 2005 Pew Internet & American Life Project study, nine out of ten Internet users say they have adjusted their online behavior, such as no longer visiting particular Web sites or no longer downloading software, for fear of being infected with spyware. In addition to the potential security risk associated with spyware, these programs can also affect the performance of a PC, such as slowing it down or causing it to work improperly. In 2004, computer manufacturer Dell reported that more than 12% of all technical support calls in its consumer hardware division were due to spyware, and Microsoft claims that half of all computer malfunctions reported by its customers are

>**Spyware.** A software program installed without the user's knowledge that secretly collects information and sends it to an outside party via the user's Internet connection.

caused by spyware. And the problem will likely become worse before it gets any better. Some spyware programs—sometimes referred to as *stealthware*—are getting more aggressive, such as delivering ads regardless of the activity you are doing on your PC, changing your browser home page or otherwise resetting your browser settings (referred to as *browser hijacking*), and performing other annoying actions. The worst spyware programs rewrite your computer's main instructions—such as the *Windows Registry*—to change your browser settings back to the hijacked settings each time you reboot your PC, undoing any changes you may have made to your browser settings.

PROTECTING AGAINST ONLINE THEFT, FRAUD, AND OTHER DOT CONS

Businesses and consumers can both help to prevent some types of online theft—businesses by using good security measures to protect the data stored on their computers, and consumers by only sending sensitive information via secure servers. Various other techniques (as discussed next) can help protect against identity theft, online auction fraud, and other types of dot cons. With any of these cons, it is important to act quickly if you think you have been a victim—work with your local law enforcement agency, credit card companies, and the three major consumer credit bureaus (*Equifax*, *Experian*, and *TransUnion*) to close any accessed or fraudulent accounts, place fraud alerts on your credit report, and take other actions to prevent additional fraudulent activity while the fraud is being investigated.

Arrests and prosecutions by law enforcement agencies may also help cut down on cybercrimes. One successful investigation—called *Operation Web Snare*—has led to the arrests and convictions of over 100 people to date for online theft, online fraud, computer intrusions, and other computer crimes. This cooperative investigation among numerous U.S. attorneys and law enforcement agencies, including the FBI, Secret Service, Postal Inspection Service, and Federal Trade Commission, began in mid-2004 and uncovered more than 870,000 victims with losses topping over $210 million.

NET

Protecting Against Identity Theft

In a nutshell, the best protection against identity theft is to protect your identifying information. Do not give out personal information—especially your Social Security number or mother's maiden name—unless it is absolutely necessary and, before revealing any personal information to a new organization, find out how it will be used and if it will be shared with other organizations. Also, never give out sensitive personal information to anyone who requests it over the phone or by e-mail. Most businesses that need bank account information, passwords, or credit card numbers already have all the information they need and will not call or e-mail a request for more information. If additional information is needed, it will almost always be requested in writing. To prevent someone from using the preapproved credit card offers and other documents containing personal information that frequently arrive in the mail, be sure to tear them up or shred them before throwing them in the trash. To prevent theft of outgoing mail containing sensitive information, do not place it in your mailbox—mail it at the post office or in a USPS drop box.

FURTHER EXPLORATION

For links to further information about how to prevent identity theft and online auction fraud, as well as how to deal with it if it occurs, go to www.course.com/uc11/ch09

To catch instances of credit card fraud or identity theft early, it is a good idea to keep a close eye on your credit card bills and credit history. Make sure your bills come in every month (some thieves will change your mailing address to delay detection), and read credit card statements carefully to look for unauthorized charges. Be sure to follow up on any calls you get from creditors, instead of assuming it is just a mistake. Most security experts also recommend ordering a full credit history on yourself a few times a year to check for accounts listed in your name that you did not open and any other problems. The *Fair and Accurate Credit Transactions Act* (*FACTA*), enacted in December 2003, enables all Americans to get up to three free credit reports per year upon request. For a look at how to get a free credit report online, see the Inside the Industry box. Other legislation related to identity theft—such as one proposed bill that would require businesses to encrypt sensitive data and another that

INSIDE THE INDUSTRY

Getting a Free Online Credit Report

One of the best ways to check for identity theft is to keep a close eye on your credit reports. These reports, such as the ones available through the consumer credit bureaus Equifax, Experian, and TransUnion, contain information about inquiries related to new accounts requested in your name, as well as any delinquent balances or other negative reports. The Fair and Accurate Credit Transactions Act (FACTA), enacted in December 2003, enables all Americans to get a free copy of their credit report, upon request, each year from the three major consumer credit bureaus. Ideally, you will request one every four months to regularly monitor your credit.

One of the easiest ways to get a copy of your credit report is using a Web site, such as the AnnualCreditReport.com site shown in the accompanying illustration. You will first typically be asked your state and then asked to supply identifying information, such as your name, date of birth, and Social Security number. After verifying that the information displayed is your correct information, you will need to correctly answer one or more questions about your credit that only you should know the answer to. After verification, you will be provided with a link to view your report online. Notice that all screens in the process are displayed using a secure Web page.

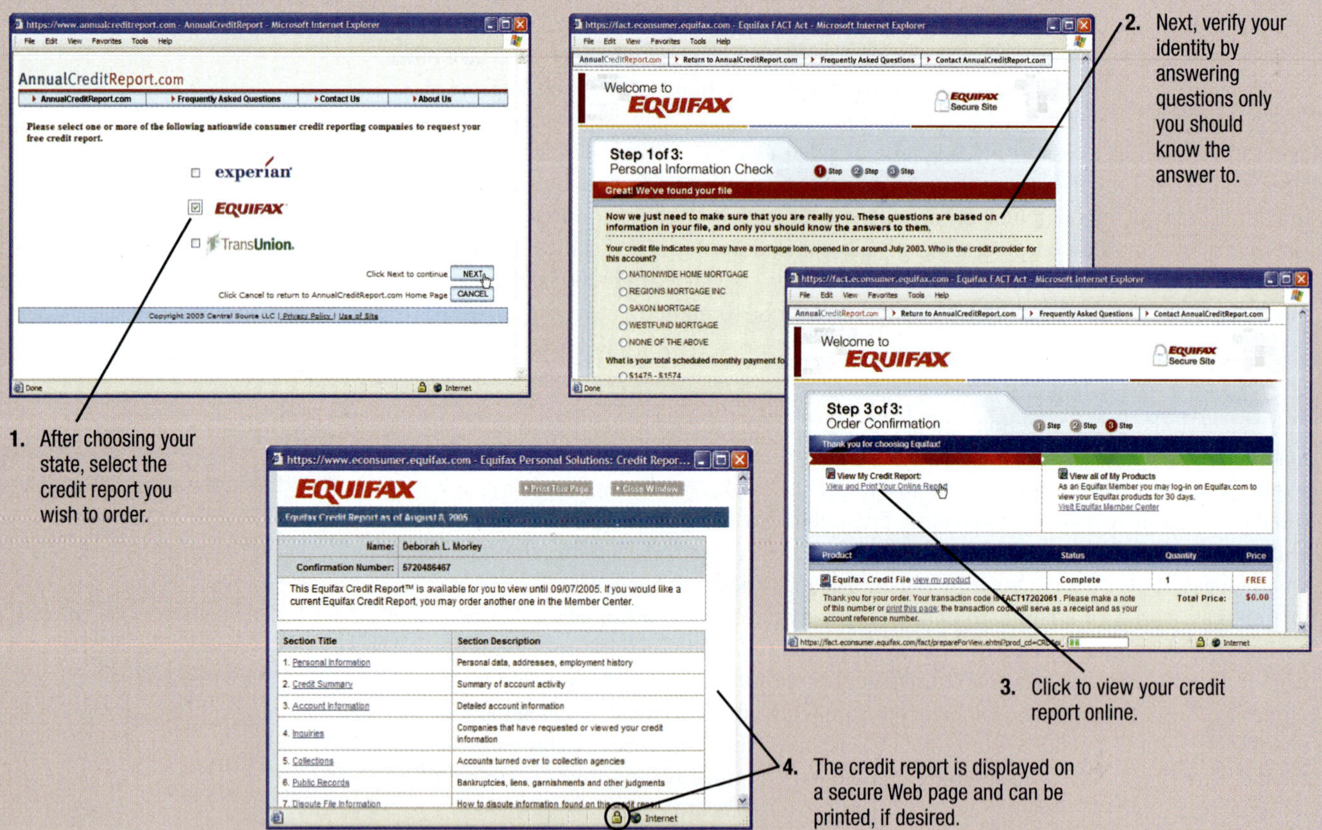

would prohibit businesses from requesting Social Security numbers if another type of identifier could be used instead—is under consideration. Some homeowner's and rental policies include coverage for financial losses resulting from identity theft; stand-alone identity theft insurance is also available.

One emerging possibility for protecting against identity theft is a move by some companies—such as financial institutions and America Online—to offer token-based security systems to protect against unauthorized use of online accounts. Similar to the USB security tokens available to provide access to private networks, these e-tokens are assigned to an individual and used to authenticate that individual when logging on to an account on the Internet. Instead of being physically connected to the PC, the tokens are battery powered and display a different six-digit code every 60 seconds. In order to log on to the financial institution's Web site or an individual's AOL account, the customer must enter his or her username and password, as well as the code displayed on the token (see Figure 9-18). A secure database contains information linking the customer's account to his or her token, as well as the codes generated by the token device.

While two-factor authentication systems such as these are common in other countries, and a few U.S. companies are using two-factor authentication systems to authenticate employees, two-factor authentication systems are not widely used in the United States. But it is expected that more two-factor authentication systems will be introduced in the near future. In fact, one of the recommendations in an FDIC study on identity theft released in 2005 was replacing existing password-based single-factor customer authentication systems with two-factor authentication.

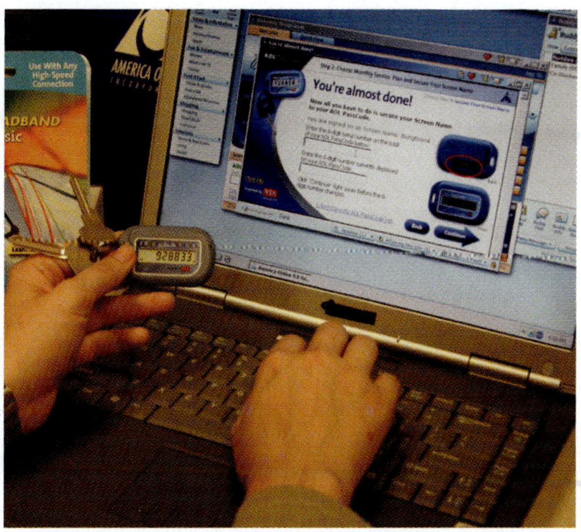

FIGURE 9-18
Token-based authentication. In order to log on to his AOL account, this customer must enter the six-digit code displayed on the token, in addition to his username and password.

Protecting Against Other Dot Cons

The key to protecting against Internet offer scams and other dot cons is common sense. Be extremely cautious of any unsolicited e-mail messages you receive and realize that if an offer sounds too good to be true, it probably is. When dealing with individuals online through auctions and other person-to-person activities, it makes sense to be cautious. Before bidding on an auction item, check out the feedback rating of the seller to see comments written by other auction sellers and buyers (see Figure 9-19). Whenever possible, pay for auctions and other online purchases using a credit card or an online payment service (such as PayPal) that accepts credit card payments so you can dispute the transaction through your credit card company, if needed. Some auction sites offer free buyer protection against

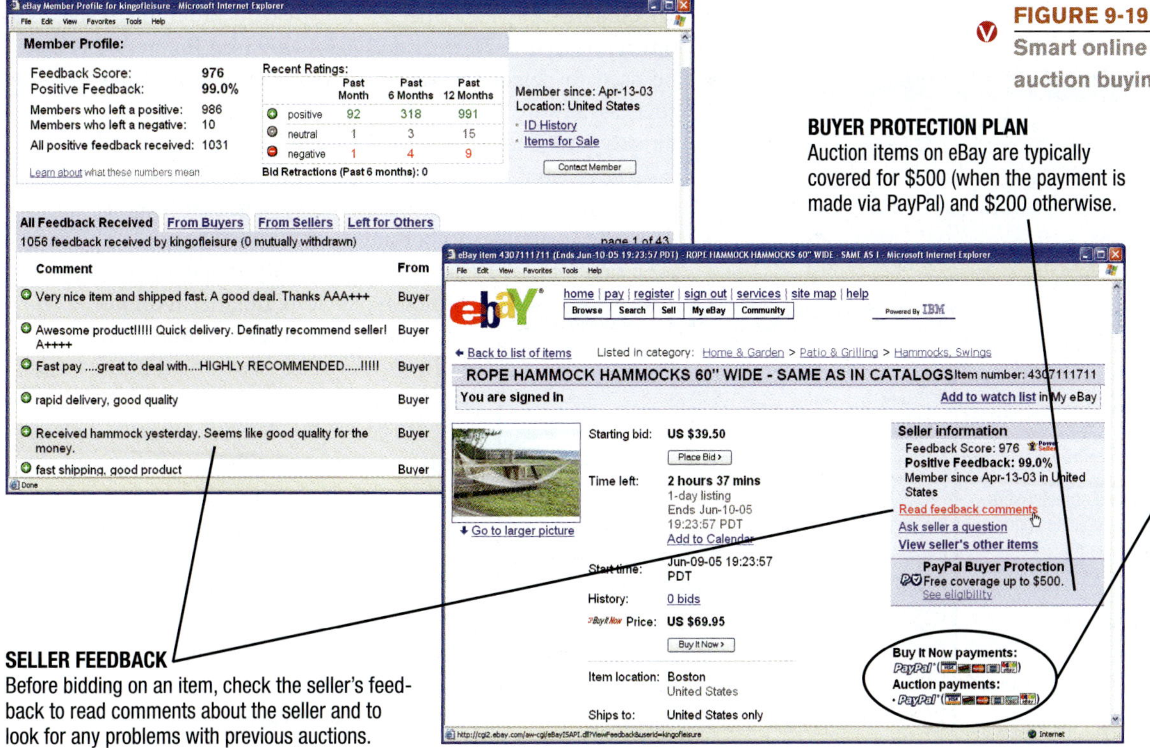

CREDIT CARD PAYMENTS
Look for auctions that allow credit card payments so you can dispute the charge if the item does not arrive or is not as specified.

FIGURE 9-19
Smart online auction buying.

A PHISHING E-MAIL OFTEN . . .

- Tries to scare you into responding by sounding urgent, including a warning that your account will be cancelled if you do not respond, or telling you that you have been a victim of fraud.
- Asks you to provide personal information, such as your bank account number, an account password, credit card number, PIN number, mother's maiden name, or Social Security number.
- Contains links that do not go where the link text says it will go (point to a hyperlink in the e-mail address to view the URL for that link).
- Uses legitimate logos from the company the phisher is posing as.
- Does not include a personalized greeting.
- Appears to be text or text and images but is actually a single image; it has been created that way to avoid being caught in a *spam filter* (a program that sorts e-mail based on legitimate e-mail and suspected spam) since spam filters cannot read text that is part of an image in an e-mail message.
- Contains spelling or grammatical errors.

FIGURE 9-20
Tips for spotting phishing e-mail messages.

undelivered items or auction items that are significantly different from their description provided in the auction information. For instance, eBay offers buyer protection for up to $500 for all items paid for by PayPal and up to $200 for items paid for with other methods. Additional coverage can be purchased, if desired. For expensive items, consider using an *escrow service*, which allows you to ensure that the merchandise is as specified before your payment is released to the seller.

To avoid spoofing and phishing schemes, never respond to e-mail requests for updated credit card information. Some tips for identifying phishing e-mails are shown in Figure 9-20. If you think an e-mail may be legitimate—if, for instance, the credit card you used to automatically pay for your Internet connection or other ongoing service is about to expire—type the URL for the site in your browser to load the legitimate site before updating your account information. *Never* click a link in an e-mail message to update your information. And make sure your operating system and browser are up to date. For instance, Microsoft has released a patch to prevent the installation of the phishing Trojan horse program that redirects URLs, but the patch has to be installed for it to work. Finally, watch your credit card and telephone bills for any erroneous or fraudulent charges.

FIGURE 9-21
Spyware checkers. Spyware removal programs can be used to detect and remove spyware programs.

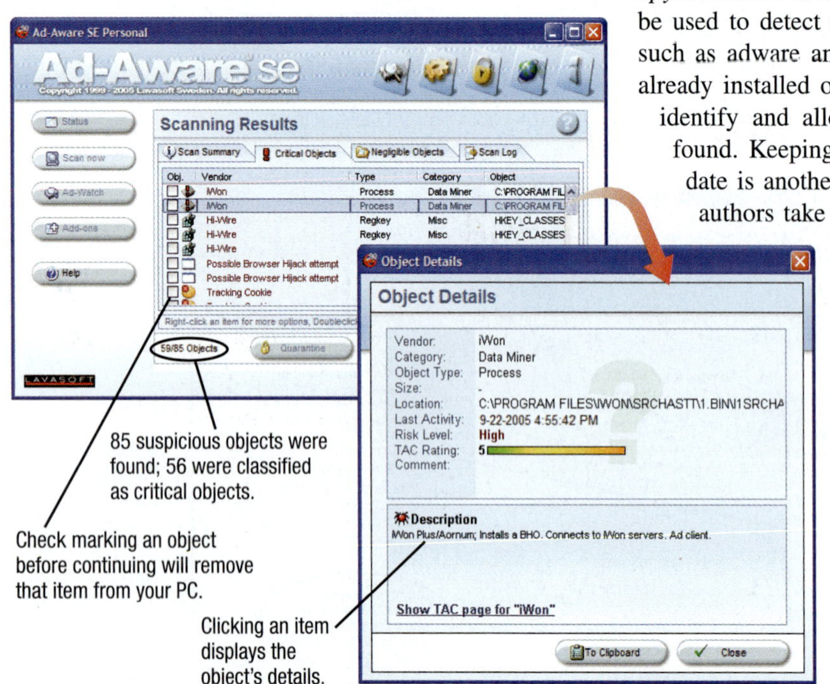

Protecting Against Spyware

To prevent spyware from being installed on your computer, you can check Web sites that list known spyware programs before downloading a program to see if the program is on a list of known programs that contain spyware. Special *antispyware* programs, such as *Spybot Search & Destroy* and *Ad-Aware* (see Figure 9-21) can be used to detect spyware programs (as well as other items, such as adware and cookies, that may involve privacy risks) already installed on your PC. These programs typically both identify and allow you to remove any risky components found. Keeping your operating system and browser up to date is another important precaution since some spyware authors take advantage of security loopholes in popular browsers, such as Internet Explorer. Consequently, using a less common browser—such as Opera or Mozilla's Firefox—can also help to reduce your risk.

A possibility for the future is federal legislation regulating the use of spyware. At the time of this writing, there were at least two bills under consideration by the U.S. Congress. One example is the *Spyblock* (*Software Principles Yielding Better Levels of Consumer Knowledge*) bill that outlaws spyware and adware fr[illegible] users' PCs withou[illegible] sug-gested provisions inclu[illegible]quiring spyware makers to disclose the presence and function of their software more clearly to users (possibly by requiring the users to specifically indicate that they have read and agree with the licensing terms in order for the software to be installed), prohibiting the use of browser hijacking, requiring an uninstall option to be installed along with the program, and giving the FTC responsibility to oversee these new requirements. Successful spyware prosecution may also be a deterrent. For instance, one company was ordered to pay $7.5 million in 2005 for bundling hidden spyware in programs given away for free after it was ruled that the company broke New York state laws prohibiting false advertising and deceptive business practices.

Using Digital Signatures and Digital Certificates

While encryption is used to ensure that a document cannot be intercepted or altered during transmission, the purpose of *digital signatures* and *digital certificates* is to authenticate and guarantee the identity of a person or Web site.

Digital signatures are used to verify the identity of the sender of a document. Digital signatures typically use public key encryption, but the sender's *private* key is used to sign the document instead of his or her public key. The private key and the document being signed are used to generate the actual digital signature (a unique digital code); consequently, the signature is different with each signed document. When a digitally signed document is received, the recipient's PC uses the sender's *public* key to verify the digital signature. Since the document is signed with the sender's private key (that only the sender should know) and the digital signature will be deemed invalid if even one character of the document is changed after it is signed, digital signatures guarantee that the document was sent by a specific individual and that it was not tampered with during transit. Often the digital signature indicator appears as a statement at the bottom of the e-mail or a button that can be clicked to see the identity of the verified sender, as shown in Figure 9-22. Digital signatures can be applied to both encrypted and nonencrypted files and messages.

Since the passing of *The Federal Electronic Signatures in Global and National Commerce Act*, which then-President Clinton signed in 2000 with a digital signature, electronic signatures are as legally binding as handwritten signatures for e-commerce transactions. Designed to facilitate consumer transactions, this law enables people and

FURTHER EXPLORATION

For links to further information about digital signatures and digital certificates, go to www.course.com/uc11/ch09

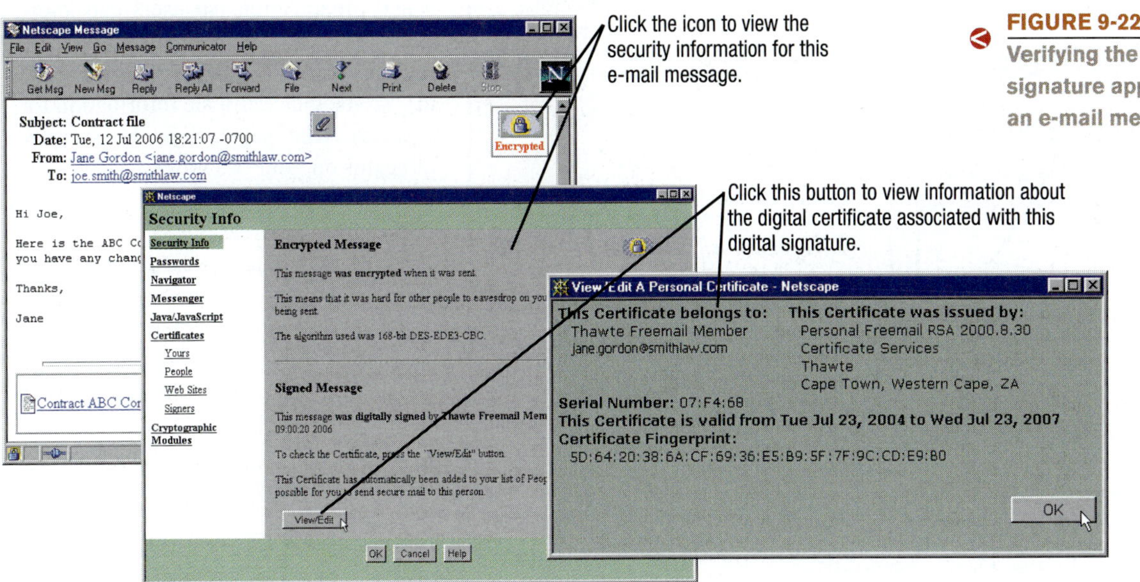

FIGURE 9-22
Verifying the digital signature applied to an e-mail message.

>**Digital signature.** A unique digital code that can be attached to an e-mail message or document to verify the identity of the sender and guarantee the message or file has not been changed since it was signed.

businesses to buy insurance, get a mortgage, open a brokerage account, or finalize other transactions that require a signed authorization, without waiting for physical documents to be mailed back and forth. Although not widely used by individuals, digital signatures are increasingly being used by businesses and the government and are expected to become extremely important as contracts and other legal documents begin to be exchanged more commonly over the Internet. For instance, in 2005, the U.S. Department of Health and Human Services began using digital signatures to approve official correspondence and regulations, and the U.S. Defense Department has already issued more than 5 million smart cards with digital signature capabilities. Experts predict that most federal civilian agencies will begin using digital signatures by 2007. Digital signatures are also used in the *e-mail authentication* systems currently in development by several companies. These systems use digital signatures to authenticate e-mail messages sent from companies, in order to better detect phishing schemes.

In order to add a digital signature to an e-mail message or file, usually a **digital certificate** is needed. Digital certificates are obtained from a *Certificate Authority* and typically contain the name of the person, organization, or Web site being certified along with a certificate serial number, an expiration date, and a pair of keys (one public, one private) that can be used with both digital signatures and encryption. The Certificate Authority guarantees that individuals or organizations granted digital certificates are, in fact, who they claim to be, usually only after verifying their identity with a financial institution or through some other authentication procedure. Certificates issued to businesses and individuals are typically installed in their browser, e-mail program, and any third-party encryption program so that the certificate information is available for use whenever a file or e-mail message needs to be digitally signed or encrypted. Some application programs—such as Microsoft Word—include the option to add a digital signature to documents created in that program, using your digital certificate.

FIGURE 9-23
Verifying the digital signature associated with a secure Web page.

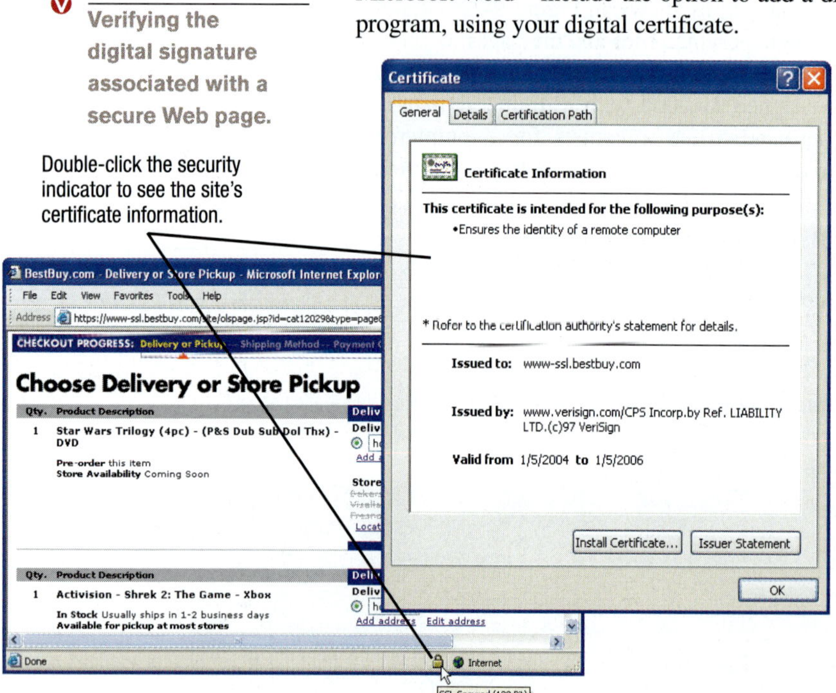

In addition to being used to sign and encrypt files and e-mail messages, digital certificates are also used with secure Web sites to guarantee that the Web site is secure and actually belongs to the stated organization (so users can know for sure who their credit card number or other sensitive data is really being sent to). To see the certificate information for a secure Web page, click the security indicator on your browser's taskbar (see Figure 9-23).

With the increased risk of Internet-related fraud today, it is expected that banks and other financial institutions may soon begin to issue free digital certificates to customers to authenticate both the customer and the bank's Web site each time the customer visits the site, to protect against phishing, identity theft, and other types of dot cons.

>**Digital certificate.** A group of electronic data, such as encryption key pairs and a digital signature, that can be used to verify the identity of a person or organization.

PERSONAL SAFETY ISSUES

Cybercrime can be expensive (as in the case of theft and fraud) and a huge inconvenience (as in the case of identity theft). In addition, it can be physically dangerous. Although most of us may not ordinarily view using the Internet as a potentially dangerous activity, cases of physical harm due to Internet activity do happen. For example, children and teenagers have become the victims of pedophiles who arranged face-to-face meetings by using information gathered via e-mail, discussion groups, or chat rooms. There are also a growing number of *e-bullying* incidents, in which children are getting threatened by classmates via e-mail, Web site posts, or text messages. Adults have fallen for unscrupulous or dangerous individuals who misrepresented themselves online; they have also been victims of *cyberstalking*. In addition, the availability of personal information online has made it more difficult for individuals to hide from people who may want to do them harm, such as abused women trying to hide from their abusive husbands.

Cyberstalking

Cyberstalking can be defined as repeated threats or harassing behavior via e-mail or another Internet communications method. Cyberstalkers often find their victims online—for instance, someone in a chat room who makes a comment or has a screen name that the cyberstalker does not like. There have also been reported cases of employers being stalked online by ex-employees who were fired or otherwise left their position under adverse conditions. Cyberstalking often begins with online harassment, such as sending harassing or threatening e-mail messages or unwanted files to the victim, posting inappropriate messages in chat rooms about the victim or as the victim, signing the victim up for pornographic or otherwise offensive e-mail newsletters, and publicizing the victim's home address and telephone number. Although there is no one exact definition of cyberstalking, the generally accepted definition covers any harassing online activity that would cause a reasonable person to experience fear or some sense of dread or threat. There are as yet no specific federal laws against cyberstalking, but all states have made it illegal, and some federal laws do apply if the online actions include computer fraud or another type of crime, suggest a threat of personal injury, or involve sending obscene e-mail messages.

It has been estimated that about 500,000 people stalk someone online each year. Most cyberstalkers are not caught, however, due in part to the anonymity of the Internet, which assists cyberstalkers in concealing their true identities. Cyberstalking can lead to offline stalking and possibly physical harm—in at least one case, it led to the death of the victim.

Online Pornography

There is a variety of controversial and potentially objectionable material on the Internet. Many parents are concerned about the vast amount of pornography available online. Although there have been attempts to ban this type of material from the Internet, they have not been successful. For example, the *Communications Decency Act*, signed into law in 1996—which made it a criminal offense to distribute patently indecent or offensive material online—was ruled unconstitutional in 1997 by the U.S. Supreme Court. However, like its printed counterpart, online pornography involving minors is illegal. Because of the strong link they believe exists between child pornography and child molestation, many experts are very concerned about the amount of child pornography that can be found and distributed via the Internet. They also believe that the Internet makes it easier for sexual predators to act out, such as by striking up "friendships" with children in chat rooms and convincing them to

>**Cyberstalking.** Repeated threats or harassing behavior via e-mail or another Internet communications method.

meet them in real life. And this can have devastating consequences, as it did for a 13-year-old girl from Connecticut who was strangled to death in 2002 by a 25-year-old man she met in an online chat room, who allegedly confessed to the crime. Although he maintains that the strangling was accidental, the man was sentenced in late 2003 to a total of 40 years in prison for state and federal charges relating to the incident.

PROTECTING AGAINST CYBERSTALKING AND OTHER PERSONAL SAFETY CONCERNS

There is no surefire way to protect against cyberstalking and other online dangers completely, but some common-sense precautions can reduce the chance of becoming involved in serious personal safety problems due to online activities.

Safety Tips for Adults

TIP

Search for yourself using search sites and online telephone books to see what personal information is available about you on the Internet.

It is wise to be cautious and discreet in chat rooms, discussion groups, and other online locations where individuals communicate with strangers. To protect yourself against cyberstalking and other types of online harassment, use gender-neutral, nonprovocative identifying names, such as *jsmith*, instead of *janesmith* or *iamcute*. Do not reveal personal information—such as your real name, address, or telephone number—to people you meet in a chat room. Although they may feel like new friends, they are strangers and you have no idea who they really are or what they are like in real life. In addition, do not respond to any insults or other harassing comments you may receive online. You may also wish to request that your personal information be removed from online directories—especially those associated with your e-mail address or other online identifier.

Safety Tips for Children

Most experts agree that the best way to protect children from online dangers is to stay in close touch with them as they explore the Internet. To be able to check up on their online activities quickly, it is a good idea to have children—including teenagers—use a PC in a family room or other public location, instead of their bedroom, and they should be told which activities are allowed, which types of Web sites are off-limits, and why. In addition, it should be made clear that they are never to reveal personal information about themselves online without a parent's permission. They should also be instructed to tell a parent (or teacher if at school) if an individual ever requests personal information or a personal meeting via an e-mail message, a chat room, an instant message, or other communications medium.

NETWORK AND INTERNET SECURITY LEGISLATION

Although new legislation is passed periodically to address new types of computer crimes, it is difficult for the legal system to keep pace with the rate at which technology changes. In addition, there are both domestic and international jurisdictional issues because many computer crimes affect businesses and individuals located in geographic areas other than the one in which the computer criminal is located, and hackers can make it appear that activity is coming from a different location than it really is. Nevertheless, computer crime legislation continues to be proposed and computer crimes are being prosecuted. In 2005, for instance, a disgruntled Philadelphia Phillies fan charged with 79 counts of computer fraud and identity theft was sentenced to four years in prison. He was found guilty of hacking into individuals' personal computers and using those computer to send hundreds of spam e-mails (using spoofed return addresses so they look liked they came from sports writers for various newspapers) complaining about the

Phillies. Other recent examples include the conviction of a man on 120 counts of unauthorized access of a protected computer, during which he hacked into a marketing database and gained access to over 1 billion consumer records; the sentencing of a former graduate student to 8 months in prison for hacking into computers at several major companies and installing Trojan horse software to capture usernames and passwords in order to gain unauthorized access to other computers; and the conviction and sentencing (to 5 months in prison, 3 years probation, and $60,000 in restitution) of a man charged with 12 counts of wire fraud and seven counts of mail fraud in connection with an eBay Internet auction scam in which he sold items that were never delivered to buyers.

A list of selected federal laws concerning network and Internet security is shown in Figure 9-24. As shown in this figure, the main piece of legislation regarding computers crime—the *Computer Fraud and Abuse Act*—has been regularly amended to better define its scope and to clarify its intent. The law currently outlaws unauthorized access to data stored in federal government computers and federally regulated financial institutions. It also outlaws the deliberate implantation of computer viruses in those computers. The *USA Patriot Act* (*USAPA*), implemented in 2001, grants federal authorities expanded surveillance and intelligence-gathering powers, such as broadening their ability to obtain the real identity of Internet users and to intercept Internet communications. The *Homeland Security Act of 2002* includes a number of provisions that deal with cyberterrorism and powers for obtaining information from computer and ISP sources, such as protecting ISPs against suits from customers for revealing private information to law enforcement agencies, and a variety of acts (such as the Sarbanes-Oxley Act of 2002 and the *Health Insurance Portability and Accountability Act* or *HIPPA*) require increased security for computer networks to project information stored on network servers. The most recent federal computer crime law at the time of this writing was the *Identity Theft Penalty Enhancement Act*, signed into law in mid-2004, which adds extra years to prison sentences for criminals who use identity theft (including the use of stolen credit card numbers) to commit other crimes, including credit card fraud and terrorism. Additional legislation regarding spyware, phishing, and identity theft is under consideration and may become law in the future.

FIGURE 9-24
Computer network and Internet security legislation.

DATE	LAW AND DESCRIPTION
2004	**Identity Theft Penalty Enhancement Act** Adds extra years to prison sentences for criminals who use identity theft (including the use of stolen credit card numbers) to commit other crimes, including credit card fraud and terrorism.
2003	**Fair and Accurate Credit Transactions Act (FACTA)** Amends the Fair Credit Reporting Act (FCRA) to require, among other things, that the three nationwide consumer reporting agencies (Equifax, Experian, and TransUnion) provide to consumers, upon request, a free copy of their credit report once every 12 months.
2003	**PROTECT Act** Includes provisions to prohibit virtual child pornography.
2003	**Heath Insurance Portability and Accountability Act (HIPAA)** Includes a Security Rule that sets minimum security standards to protect health information stored electronically.
2002	**Homeland Security Act** Includes provisions to combat cyberterrorism, including protecting ISPs against lawsuits from customers for revealing private information to law enforcement agencies.
2002	**Sarbanes-Oxley Act** Requires archiving a variety of electronic records and protecting the integrity of corporate financial data.
2001	**USA Patriot Act (USAPA)** Grants federal authorities expanded surveillance and intelligence-gathering powers, such as broadening the ability of federal agents to obtain the real identity of Internet users, intercept e-mail and other types of Internet communications, follow online activity of suspects, expand their wiretapping authority, and more.
1998	**Identity Theft and Assumption Deterrence Act of 1998** Makes it a federal crime to knowingly use someone else's means of identification, such as name, Social Security number, or credit card, to commit any unlawful activity.
1997	**No Electronic Theft (NET) Act** Expands computer piracy laws to include distribution of copyrighted materials over the Internet.
1996	**National Information Infrastructure Protection Act** Amends the Computer Fraud and Abuse Act of 1984 to punish information theft crossing state lines and crack down on network trespassing.
1994	**Computer Abuse Amendments Act** Amends the Computer Fraud and Abuse Act of 1984 to include computer viruses and other harmful code.
1986	**Computer Fraud and Abuse Act of 1986** Amends the 1984 law to include federally regulated financial institutions.
1984	**Computer Fraud and Abuse Act of 1984** Makes it a crime to break into computers owned by the federal government.

SUMMARY

WHY BE CONCERNED ABOUT NETWORK AND INTERNET SECURITY?

Chapter Objective 1: Explain why computer users should be concerned about network and Internet security.

There are a number of important security concerns related to computers and the Internet. Many of these are **computer crimes**. Because computers and networks are so widespread, there is unprecedented opportunity for criminals and other individuals to commit acts that are not in the public interest. All computer users should be aware of the risks of using networks and the Internet so they can take appropriate precautions.

UNAUTHORIZED ACCESS, UNAUTHORIZED USE, AND COMPUTER SABOTAGE

Chapter Objective 2: List several examples of unauthorized access, unauthorized use, and computer sabotage.

Two important risks related to computer networks and the Internet are **unauthorized access** and **unauthorized use**. **Hacking** is the term used for using a computer to break into a computer system. Hacking can take place via the Internet or via a wireless network. **War driving** is the act of looking for unsecured Wi-Fi networks to access without authorization. Data can also be intercepted as it is transmitted over the Internet or a wireless network.

Common types of **computer sabotage** include **malware** (**computer viruses**, **computer worms**, **Trojan horses**, and other programs designed to cause harm to computer systems), **denial of service (DoS) attacks** (attempts to shut down a network or Web server by flooding it with more requests than it can handle), data and program alteration, and *cybervandalism*.

PROTECTING AGAINST UNAUTHORIZED ACCESS, UNAUTHORIZED USE, AND COMPUTER SABOTAGE

Chapter Objective 3: Explain what risks access control systems, firewalls, antivirus software, and encryption protect against.

There are many options for protecting a network against unauthorized access and use. For instance, *access control systems* include **possessed knowledge access systems** that use **passwords** or other types of possessed knowledge; **possessed object access systems** that use physical objects, such as badges and cards; and **biometric access systems** that identify users by a particular unique biological characteristic, such as a fingerprint, hand, face, or iris. To be effective, passwords should be *strong passwords*; *two-factor authentication systems* that use multiple control factors are more effective than single-factor systems.

To protect wireless networks, security features should be enabled. **Firewalls** protect networks and individual computers against unauthorized access; **antivirus software** protects against getting malware, as well as removing it should it ever be installed on your PC. Firewalls and antivirus software can also help prevent against some other types of sabotage, such as your computer being used in a denial of service attack. Keeping your operating system, Web browser, and e-mail programs up to date, such as by installing security patches as soon as they become available, is another good precaution.

Sensitive transactions should be performed only on **secure Web servers**; sensitive files and e-mails should be secured with **encryption** techniques, such as **public key encryption** (in which a private key and matching public key are used) or **private key encryption** (in which only a private key is used). *Web-based encryption* is also available. The strength of an encryption method is measured by the length of its keys, such as *weak* (40-bit) *encryption*, *strong 128-bit*, and *military-strength 2,048-bit encryption* that is very difficult to crack. A **virtual private network (VPN)** can be used to provide a secure remote connection to a company network. Employers should take appropriate precautions to reduce the change of an attack by a current or former employee.

ONLINE THEFT, FRAUD, AND OTHER DOT CONS

There are a variety of types of theft, fraud, and scams related to the Internet—collectively referred to as **dot cons**—that all Internet users should be aware of. Data, information, or money can be stolen from individuals and businesses. Sometimes this occurs in conjunction with **identity theft**, in which an individual poses as another individual. **Online auction fraud**, *Internet offer scams*, **spoofing**, and **phishing** are other common possibilities. **Spyware** programs can also be used to gather sensitive information about individuals, as well as to deliver ads and other possibly annoying content to Internet users.

Chapter Objective 4:
Discuss online theft, identity theft, Internet scams, spoofing, phishing, and other types of dot cons.

PROTECTING AGAINST ONLINE THEFT, FRAUD, AND OTHER DOT CONS

To protect against identity theft, individuals should guard their personal information carefully. To check for identity theft, watch your bills and credit history. When interacting with other individuals online or buying from an online auction, it is wise to be conservative and use a credit card whenever possible. To avoid other types of dot cons, be very wary of responding to unsolicited offers and e-mails, and steer clear of offers that seem too good to be true. Never click a link in an e-mail message to update your personal information. To verify the sender of a document, **digital signatures** can be used. Digital signatures are obtained as part of a **digital certificate** acquired through a *Certification Authority* (*CA*) after the applicant's identity is verified. Digital certificates can also be used to verify the identity of secure Web pages, and the keys included in the certificate can be used for sending encrypted files to others. *Antispyware* programs can help detect and remove spyware installed on your PC.

Chapter Objective 5:
Detail steps an individual can take to protect against online theft, identity theft, Internet scams, spoofing, phishing, and other types of dot cons.

PERSONAL SAFETY ISSUES

There are also personal safety risks for both adults and children stemming from Internet use. **Cyberstalking**—online harassment that frightens or threatens the victim—is more common in recent years, even though most states have passed laws against it. *E-bullying* is a growing risk for children, as is the potential exposure to online pornography and other materials inappropriate for children.

Chapter Objective 6:
Identify personal safety risks associated with Internet use.

PROTECTING AGAINST CYBERSTALKING AND OTHER PERSONAL SAFETY CONCERNS

To protect their personal safety, adults and children should be cautious in online communications. They should be wary of revealing any personal information or meeting online acquaintances in person. To protect children, parents should keep a close watch on their children's online activities, and they should never reveal personal information to others online without a parent's consent.

Chapter Objective 7:
List steps individuals can take when using the Internet to safeguard their personal safety.

NETWORK AND INTERNET SECURITY LEGISLATION

Although the rapid growth of the Internet and jurisdictional issues have contributed to the lack of network and Internet security legislation, some important pieces of legislation are in place, such as the *USA Patriot Act*, *Identity Theft and Assumption Act*, and *Computer Fraud and Abuse Act*.

Chapter Objective 8:
Name several laws related to network and Internet security.

REVIEW ACTIVITIES

KEY TERM MATCHING

Instructions: Match each key term on the left with the definition on the right that best describes it.

a. computer virus
b. denial of service (DoS) attack
c. dot con
d. encryption
e. firewall
f. hacking
g. identity theft
h. password
i. spoofing
j. spyware

1. ______ A collection of hardware and/or software intended to protect a computer or computer network from unauthorized access.

2. ______ A fraud or scam carried out through the Internet.

3. ______ A method of scrambling e-mail or files to make them unreadable if they are intercepted by an unauthorized user.

4. ______ A secret combination of characters used to gain access to a computer, computer network, or other resource.

5. ______ A software program installed without the user's knowledge that secretly collects information and sends it to an outside party via the user's Internet connection.

6. ______ A software program installed without the user's knowledge and designed to alter the way a computer operates or to cause harm to the computer system.

7. ______ An act of sabotage that attempts to flood a network server or a Web server with so much activity that it is unable to function.

8. ______ Making it appear that an e-mail or a Web site originates from somewhere other than where it really does; typically used with dot cons.

9. ______ Using a computer to break into another computer system.

10. ______ Using someone else's identity to purchase goods or services, obtain new credit cards or bank loans, or otherwise illegally masquerade as that individual.

SELF-QUIZ

Instructions: Circle **T** if the statement is true, **F** if the statement is false, or write the best answer in the space provided. **Answers to the self-quiz are located in the References and Resources Guide at the end of the book.**

1. **T F** A computer virus can only be transferred to another computer via a storage medium.
2. **T F** An access system that uses a fingerprint reader is a biometric access system.
3. **T F** Spyware is a malicious program that masquerades as something else.
4. **T F** Secure Web servers use encryption.
5. **T F** Cyberstalking is the use of spoofed e-mail messages to gain credit card numbers and other personal data to be used for fraudulent purposes.
6. A person who drives around looking for a Wi-Fi network to access is said to be ______.
7. A(n) ______ device uses some type of unique physical characteristic of a person to identify or grant access to individuals.
8. A(n) ______ protects a computer or network from unauthorized access by closing down external communications port addresses to unauthorized programs or requests.
9. With ______ encryption, two keys are used—one to encrypt the file or e-mail message and one to decrypt it.

10. Match each type of computer crime with its description and write the corresponding number in the blank to the left of each description.

a. _______ A person working for the Motor Vehicle Division deletes a friend's speeding ticket from a database.

b. _______ An individual attaches a file to an e-mail message that will automatically send itself to the first 10 people on the recipient's e-mail address book when the file is opened.

c. _______ An individual does not like someone's comment in a chat room and begins to send that individual harassing e-mail messages.

d. _______ An individual sells the same item to 10 individuals via an online auction site.

e. _______ A person creates an e-mail message that looks like it belongs to a legitimate company but contains a link to the individual's Web site instead, and sends the e-mail message to numerous individuals.

f. _______ A person accesses a computer belonging to the IRS without authorization.

1. Online auction fraud
2. Hacking
3. Computer sabotage
4. Data or program alteration
5. Phishing
6. Cyberstalking

EXERCISES

1. Write the appropriate letter in the blank to the left of each term to indicate whether it is related to unauthorized access (U), computer sabotage (C), online theft or fraud (O), or personal safety (P).

a. _______ Cyberstalking
b. _______ Phishing
c. _______ Cybervandalism
d. _______ Time bomb
e. _______ War driving
f. _______ Denial of service (DoS) attack
g. _______ Malware
h. _______ Spoofing
i. _______ Hacking

2. Is the password *john1* a good password? Why or why not? If not, suggest a better password.

3. Supply the missing words to complete the following statements.

a. With an encrypted e-mail message, the recipient's _______ key is used to encrypt the message, and the recipient's _______ key is used to decrypt the message.

b. With a digital signature, the sender's _______ key is used to sign the document, and the sender's _______ key is used to validate the signature.

4. To secure files on your PC so they are unreadable to a hacker who might gain access to your PC, what type of encryption (public key or private key) would be the most appropriate. Explain.

5. List two precautions that individuals can take when purchasing items via an online auction to avoid loss due to online auction fraud.

NET

DISCUSSION QUESTION

According to security experts, new variants of several worms released in mid-2004 and 2005 contain more than just the virus code—they contain messages taunting other virus writers and code to remove competing malware from the PCs they infect. For instance, the Netsky worm includes code to remove the Mydoom and Bagle worms from PCs that the Netsky worm infects, and the latest variant of the Bozori worm removes competing worms, like Zotob, from the PCs it infects. The goal seems to be not only to gain control of an increasing number of infected machines—a type of "bot war" to build the biggest network of infected zombie PCs—but also to one-up rivals. Some virus writers may just want to obtain notoriety, but another more alarming possibility is that an increasing percentage of virus writers are interested in gaining control of PCs for monetary gain—such as through identity theft and other fraudulent activities. And the increased use of spam to spread viruses just makes the entire situation worse. If this trend continues, do you think it will affect how hackers and other computer criminals will be viewed? Will they become cult heroes or be viewed as dangerous criminals? Will continuing to increase prosecution of these individuals help or hurt the situation?

PROJECTS

HOT TOPICS

1. **Top Ten Dot Cons** As discussed in the chapter, dot cons are a rapidly growing area for thieves and con artists. In addition to the regular cons that have been around for years, new types of cons—such as Web site spoofing—appear on a regular basis.

   For this project, type the search phrase "FTC top ten dot cons" into the search box of your favorite search site to locate the Federal Trade Commission (FTC) Top Ten Dot Cons Web page. Review the listed cons to determine how many are computer-related. Choose one computer-related dot con and read the information available through the site to figure out how it works and determine what actions a consumer can take to avoid falling prey to this type of dot con. At the conclusion of your research, prepare a one-page summary of your findings and submit it to your instructor.

SHORT ANSWER/ RESEARCH

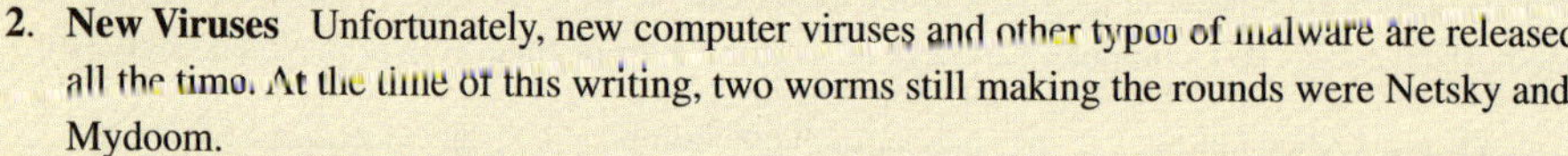

2. **New Viruses** Unfortunately, new computer viruses and other types of malware are released all the time. At the time of this writing, two worms still making the rounds were Netsky and Mydoom.

   For this project, either research one of the worms listed above or research a more recent example of malware (most security companies, such as Symantec and McAfee, list the most recent security threats on their Web sites) and answer the following questions: When was it introduced? What did it do? How was it spread? How many computers were affected? Is there an estimated cost associated with it? Is it still in existence? At the conclusion of your research, prepare a one-page summary of your findings and submit it to your instructor.

3. **Digital Certificates** When you want the capability to both digitally sign and encrypt e-mail messages, a digital certificate is typically your best bet. Although some digital certificates require a fee, free personal certificates are available.

   For this project, locate a Certificate Authority (CA) that provides free digital certificates for personal use. Determine the minimum amount of information needed to obtain one and, if you have Internet access at home, sign up for a free certificate using that process on your home PC. When the digital certificate is sent to you on your home PC, install it for use with your e-mail program, and then send yourself an e-mail that is signed or encrypted. Retrieve the e-mail to make sure it came through in one piece and to see what it looks like on the recipient's end. Does this CA offer a more secure certificate after further authentication? If you were able to send and receive an encrypted e-mail, how easy was the process? Would you want to use it to secure or sign sensitive e-mails in the future? At the conclusion of your research, submit your findings and opinions to your instructor in the form of a short paper, no more than two pages in length.

HANDS ON

4. **Virus Check** There are several Web sites that include a free virus check, as well as other types of diagnostic software.

   For this project, go to the home page for a company that makes antivirus software (such as Symantec at www.symantec.com or McAfee at mcafee.com) and choose the option to run a free virus check (sometimes called a security check). NOTE: The programs may require temporarily downloading a small program or ActiveX component. If you are unable to perform this task on a school PC, ask your instructor for alternate instructions. If the check takes more than 10 minutes and there is an option to limit the check to a particular drive and folder, redo the check just scanning part of the hard drive (such as the My Documents folder) to save time. After the virus scan is completed, print the page displaying the result. Did the program find any viruses or other security threats? At the conclusion of this task, submit your printout with any additional comments about your experience to your instructor.

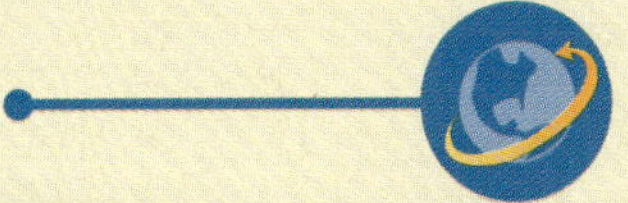

5. **Virus Hoaxes** In addition to the valid reports about new viruses found in the news and on antivirus software Web sites, reports of viruses that turn out to be hoaxes abound on the Internet. In addition to being an annoyance, virus hoaxes waste time and computing resources. In addition, they may eventually lead some users to routinely ignore all virus warning messages, leaving them vulnerable to a genuine, destructive virus.

   For this project, visit at least two Web sites that identify virus hoaxes, such as the Symantec and McAfee antivirus software Web sites and the government Hoaxbusters site, currently found at hoaxbusters.ciac.org. Explore the sites to find information about recent virus hoaxes, as well as general guidelines for identifying virus hoaxes and other types of online hoaxes. At the end of this task, prepare a one-page summary of your findings to submit to your instructor.

WRITING ABOUT COMPUTERS

6. **Hacktivism** *Hacktivism* can be defined as the act of hacking into a computer system for a politically or socially motivated purpose. The individual who performs an act of hacktivism is said to be a *hacktivist*. While some view hacktivists no differently than they view other hackers, hacktivists contend that they break into systems in order to bring attention to political or social causes. Two recent examples of hacktivism include the Web defacements in 2002 by two individuals calling themselves the "Deceptive Duo" and the Web defacements following the death of a Chinese airman when his jet fighter collided with a U.S. surveillance plane in 2001.

   For this project, research one of the two examples of hacktivism mentioned above (or a more recent hacktivism example). Were the hackers identified or found guilty of a crime? What seemed to be the motivation behind the hacks? Form an opinion about hacktivism in general, such as whether or not this is a valid method of bringing attention to specific causes, and whether or not hacktivists should be treated any differently when caught than other types of hackers are treated. Submit this project to your instructor in the form of a short paper, not more than two pages in length.

PRESENTATION/ DEMONSTRATION

7. **Online Rip-Off** Imagine this: You have just been ripped of by an unscrupulous online vendor, and you want to know what you can do about it. The situation surrounding the rip-off was not uncommon. You were surfing the Web about two weeks ago and found this great e-book for sale at one-third the price that you have seen for sale elsewhere, and you decided to use your credit card to purchase it over the Internet. When it was delivered today, the package contained a cardboard version of the e-book consisting of a scrolled piece of paper with two thumb wheels and a cheap pen. You start to panic and one of your friends reminds you of a few organizations that may come to your aid. These organizations are the Internet Fraud Complaint Center, Fraud.org, and the Federal Trade Commission (FTC), as well as your credit card company.

   For this project, consider this scenario and determine what each of these organizations might be able to do to help. In addition, draft a few general guidelines to follow when purchasing products over the Web and give some suggestions for how this rip-off could have been avoided in the first place. Share your findings with the class in the form of a short presentation. The presentation should not exceed 10 minutes and should make use of one or more presentation aids, such as the chalkboard, handouts, overhead transparencies, or a computer-based slide presentation (your instructor may provide additional requirements). You may also be asked to submit a summary of the presentation to your instructor.

GROUP DISCUSSION

8. **Homeless Hacker** Hackers who try to gain access to business and government computers and networks are a growing problem. Some hackers do it for monetary gain; others supposedly to bring attention to system vulnerabilities or other, purportedly more noble, purposes. One example of a business and government network hacker is Adrian Lamo, a young freelance security consultant who regularly tries to hack into computer systems without authorization, looking for their security holes. If hackers like Lamo continue to use real networks and Web servers to practice and improve their hacking skills, what are the implications? Will it expose the data located on those networks to greater danger, or will it result in tightened security and, ultimately, a more secure system? Lamo says that, while he is an intruder, he is guided by a sense of curiosity, and he is helping corporations and consumers understand the limits of Internet security. Should these hackers be treated differently than hackers who break into systems to steal data or other resources? Are there varying degrees of criminal hacking, or is a hack just a hack, regardless of the motivation? Lamo has begun publicizing his successful hacks through the media, instead of contacting the company directly. Does that make his motives more questionable? In 2004, Lamo was indicited and pled guilty to breaking into a database at the New York Times containing employee records for op-ed columnists. He was sentenced to serve two years probation and pay $65,000 in restitution. Does his arrest change your opinion at all about so-called "harmless hacking"?

   For this project, form an opinion of the impact of hackers breaching the security of business and government computers and networks and be prepared to discuss your position (in class, via an online class discussion group, or in a class chat room, depending on your instructor's directions). You may also be asked to write a short paper expressing your opinion.

WEB ACTIVITIES

The ***Understanding Computers*** Web site located at **www.course.com/uc11** features many resources to help reinforce your understanding of the chapter content and help you prepare for exams. Your instructor may also assign specific activities to be completed that will count toward your final grade in the course.

Instructions: Go to **www.course.com/uc11/ch09** to work the following online activities.

Click any link in the navigation bar on the left to access any of the online resources described below.

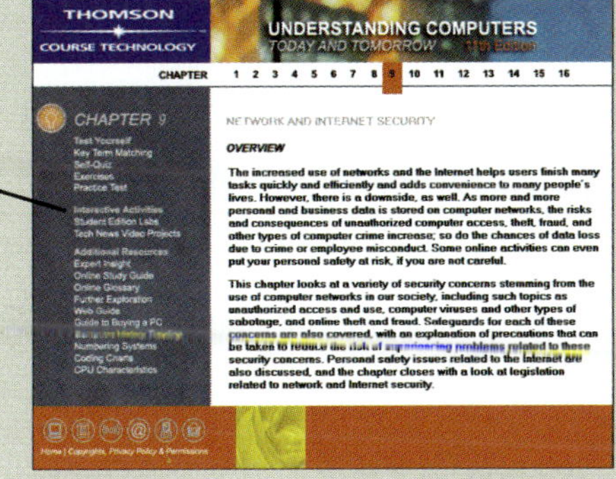

INTERACTIVE ACTIVITIES

1. **Crossword Puzzle** Practice your knowledge of the key terms in Chapter 9 by completing the interactive Crossword Puzzle.
2. **Tech News Video Project** Watch the **"Understanding Spoofing"** video clip that takes a look at how spoofing and personal firewalls work. After watching the video online, complete the corresponding project.
3. **Student Edition Labs** Reinforce the concepts you have learned in this chapter by working through the interactive **Keeping Your Computer Virus Free** lab.

NET

TEST YOURSELF

1. **Key Term Matching** Test your knowledge of selected chapter key terms by matching the terms with their definitions.
2. **Self-Quiz** Test your retention of chapter concepts by taking the Self-Quiz.
3. **Exercises** Work these short exercises to review the concepts and terms covered in the chapter.
4. **Practice Test** Test how ready you are for an upcoming exam by completing the online Practice Test.

STUDY TOOLS/ ADDITIONAL RESOURCES

The Understanding Computers Web site has a wide range of additional resources, including an **Online Study Guide** (containing study tips, a chapter outline with room to add your own notes, and a chapter checklist of the activities to complete when the chapter is covered in class and when you are preparing for a test) and an **Online Glossary** for each chapter; **Further Exploration** links; a **Web Guide**, a **Guide to Buying a PC**, and a **Computer History Timeline**; more information about **Numbering Systems**, **Coding Charts**, and **CPU Characteristics**; and much, much more!

EXPERT INSIGHT ON . . .

Networks and the Internet

A conversation with JEFF BARDIN

Chief Information Security Officer, The Hanover Insurance Group

My Background . . .

I've been working in the Information Technology industry for 20 years. As the Dotcoms started to implode, I saw the need for greater security controls in all the newly created software, hardware, and associated systems and applications. I began more in-depth study into the area, tested for and received several security certifications, and attended classes at Carnegie Mellon University's Software Engineering Institute. My military background and experience in the intelligence field (I held Top Secret clearances while working for the U.S. government breaking codes and ciphers and performing Arabic language translations) provided a necessary level of paranoia that is actually healthy when working in a security position.

As the CISO of The Hanover Insurance Group today, some of my main responsibilities surround developing cost effective information security programs; overseeing the establishment, implementation, and adherence to policies, guidelines, and procedures related to the protection of mission critical assets; conducting risk assessments; interfacing with third-party auditors and state examiners; ensuring proper security controls are in place; managing the security operations team providing perimeter and internal security, including incident handling, investigative support, and forensics activities.

"In a short 20 years we have taken technology that filled two rooms and put the same power into the palm of your hand.

It's Important to Know . . .

Basic networking principles. This ensures a strong foundation upon which to build. Regardless of the industry, establishing a strong educational base is key to understanding additional, more complex concepts.

The possible threats to your devices and information. If you do not understand the threats targeting your network and computing infrastructure, it can be very difficult to determine what types of protection strategies to employ. To secure yourself against the enemy, you have to first know who your enemy is and what tools the enemy has in his arsenal.

Safeguards that can reduce risk. Safeguards reduce risk, but they don't usually eliminate risk completely. Risk left over after the safeguard is applied (residual risk) may be acceptable as long as the risk is kept to a level that fits the sensitivity of the data and criticality of the system. In the risk management model, every risk is analyzed and controlled to an acceptable level by applying safeguards, or countermeasures, to the risk. Once a risk is reduced to an acceptable level, it must be monitored and re-evaluated throughout the systems development lifecycle so that the risk does not rise to an unacceptable level. If it does, new safeguards are selected and applied. The cycle of assessing and managing risk is continuous.

Jeff Bardin is currently the Chief Information Security Officer for The Hanover Insurance Group. He has served in the United States Air Force and the United States Army National Guard, and has worked at the National Security Agency. Jeff is an active security consultant and the author of several articles on information security and IT governance. He has also taught several classes on information security.

We are an "always on" culture where any activity at any time can be filmed, photographed, recorded, and reported. The privacy concerns are huge. The benefits are just as great.

How I Use this Technology . . .

I have often performed war driving to provide examples of the ratio of secured vs. unsecured wireless access points. At home, I have a LAN extended by wireless that is also extended further with high gain, omni-directional antennas. Multiple laptops and desktop computers connect to this 'secure' network as well as a wireless printer. Wireless storage is available as well.

What the Future Holds . . .

The security marketplace is still evolving and immature in several areas. Regulations will only continue to tighten security and privacy. The millions of individual exposures of personally identifiable information we have seen reported (and I stress reported) lately are speeding the regulatory and legislative cycles.

More and more cities will offer wireless access. Commerce will continue to take a larger share of the shopping pie. Biometrics and identity management functions will continue to merge and become the norm. Credit cards will change in form and merge with your cell phone. Television and the Internet will continue their merger as the ability to push this content over wireless channels continues. From health-care diagnosis devices to legal testimony, the Internet will become an essential part of every home, and new homes will be built for the "always on," "always available," "always accessible" world we demand.

The technology has and will continue to have a significant impact on our daily lives. We have become a culture of near real-time communications over various protocols and methods. In a short 20 years we have taken technology that filled two rooms and put the same power into the palm of your hand. We are an "always on" culture where any activity at any time can be filmed, photographed, recorded, and reported. The privacy concerns are huge. The benefits are just as great. In another 20 years, working from home should be expected in several career fields as we look to cut fuel consumption, cease wasted travel time, and squeeze more productivity out of the most productive workforce in the world.

NET

My Advice to Students . . .

Never marry yourself to any one technology because you will die with it through commoditization and obsolescence. Don't be a technology bigot. To prepare for the future, continue to take traditional computer science courses, but also strongly consider a Master's degree that focuses on business management, international organizational management, and technology management. Learning to manage a diverse workforce without borders is critical for success.

Discussion Question

Jeff Bardin views the security and privacy controls in place today as still immature, with room for improvement. Think about the systems that contain personal data about you. How would you feel if those systems were breached and your information was stolen? Does your viewpoint change if the information was monetary (such as credit card information) versus private information (such as grades or health information)? What security precautions, if any, do you think should be imposed by laws? Are organizations that hold your personal data morally responsible for going beyond the minimum requirements? What types of security measures would you implement to protect these systems? Be prepared to discuss your position (in class, via an online class discussion group, or in a class chat room, depending on your instructor's directions). You may also be asked to write a short paper expressing your opinion.

>For more information on network and Internet security, visit www.scmagazine.com, csrc.nist.gov, www.uscert.gov, www.cisecurity.org, www.isc2.org, www.cert.org, and www.ists.dartmouth.edu.

MODULE
WEB APPLICATIONS

In the previous module, we took a look at how the Internet and World Wide Web work and some of the most common online activities. Two applications found on the Web that were not discussed in detail are multimedia and e-commerce. This module introduces you to these two important Web-related topics and their use and significance in today's networked economy.

Chapter 10 delves into multimedia, looking at what it is, advantages and disadvantages of using multimedia, common types of multimedia elements, and how to design and develop a multimedia Web site. The focus of this chapter is on multimedia as an integral part of the World Wide Web. Chapter 11 explains in detail what e-commerce is and how it can be implemented over the Internet.

You will have ubiquitous access to your content, anytime, anyplace, any way you want to consume it, anywhere you want to consume it.

For more comments from Guest Expert Christopher Allen of Yahoo! Music, see the Expert Insight on . . . Web-Based Multimedia and E-Commerce feature at the end of the module.

IN THIS MODULE

Chapter 10 Multimedia and the Web 410

Overview 411

What Is Web-Based Multimedia? 411

Multimedia Elements 414

Multimedia Web Site Design 421

Multimedia Web Site Development 429

The Future of Web-Based Multimedia 438

Chapter 11 E-Commerce 448

Overview 449

What Is E-Commerce? 449

Types of E-Commerce Web Sites 454

E-Commerce Business Models 456

Implementing Web-Based E-Commerce 459

Security Issues 473

10 CHAPTER Multimedia and the Web

OUTLINE

Overview
What Is Web-Based Multimedia?
- Web-Based Multimedia Applications
- Advantages and Disadvantages of Using Web-Based Multimedia

Multimedia Elements
- Text
- Graphics
- Animation
- Audio
- Video

Multimedia Web Site Design
- Basic Design Principles
- Determining the Intended Audience and Objectives
- Using Flowcharts, Page Layouts, and Storyboards
- Navigational Design Considerations
- Access Considerations

Multimedia Web Site Development
- Creating the Multimedia Elements
- Creating the Web Site
- Testing, Publishing, and Maintaining the Site

The Future of Web-Based Multimedia

LEARNING OBJECTIVES

After completing this chapter, you will be able to:

1. Define Web-based multimedia and list some advantages and disadvantages of using multimedia.
2. Describe each of the following multimedia elements—text, graphics, animation, audio, and video—and tell how they differ.
3. Briefly describe the basic steps and principles involved with multimedia Web site design.
4. List the various tasks involved with multimedia Web site development.
5. Explain how markup languages, scripting languages, and other tools are used today to create multimedia Web pages.
6. Discuss the possible format of Web-based multimedia in the future.

OVERVIEW

Multimedia refers to any type of application or presentation that involves more than one type of media, such as text, graphics, video, animation, and sound. Multimedia applications are plentiful both on and off the Web; this chapter focuses on Web-based multimedia—the multimedia found on Web sites. In this chapter, we first take a look at some types of Web-based multimedia applications and some advantages and disadvantages of using multimedia in general. The basic multimedia elements are then discussed. Next, we turn to the fundamental steps and principles involved in designing a multimedia Web site, followed by a discussion of how a multimedia Web site is developed and the software that can be used during this process. The chapter closes with a brief look at the future of Web-based multimedia. ■

WHAT IS WEB-BASED MULTIMEDIA?

Web-based multimedia refers to Web sites containing more than one type of media—typically sound, video, or animation, in addition to text and images. Like other Web pages, multimedia Web pages utilize hyperlinks to display information as requested by the Web page visitor. In addition to this common form of *interactivity*, multimedia Web sites often contain other interactive elements that the user interacts with directly, such as to control the delivery of a sound or video clip, manipulate a 3D object, or play a game.

In the past, Web-based multimedia was very limited because computers and Internet connections were too slow to support it. Today's fast computers and broadband Internet connections, however, make Web-based multimedia much more feasible. The vast majority of Web sites today include multimedia components.

Web-Based Multimedia Applications

There are a vast number of multimedia applications on the Web. Some of the most common Web-based multimedia applications are discussed next.

Information Delivery

Multimedia is commonly used to deliver information on Web sites. For instance, companies use photos of their products to convey information to visitors, company and news Web sites use video clips to share speeches and news clips with visitors, and educational sites often use animation to better illustrate concepts.

E-Commerce

Most e-commerce Web sites include online catalogs so that visitors can find products, see available colors and sizes, and otherwise browse through the items for sale. For multimedia

>**Multimedia.** The integration of a variety of media, such as text, graphics, video, animation, and sound.

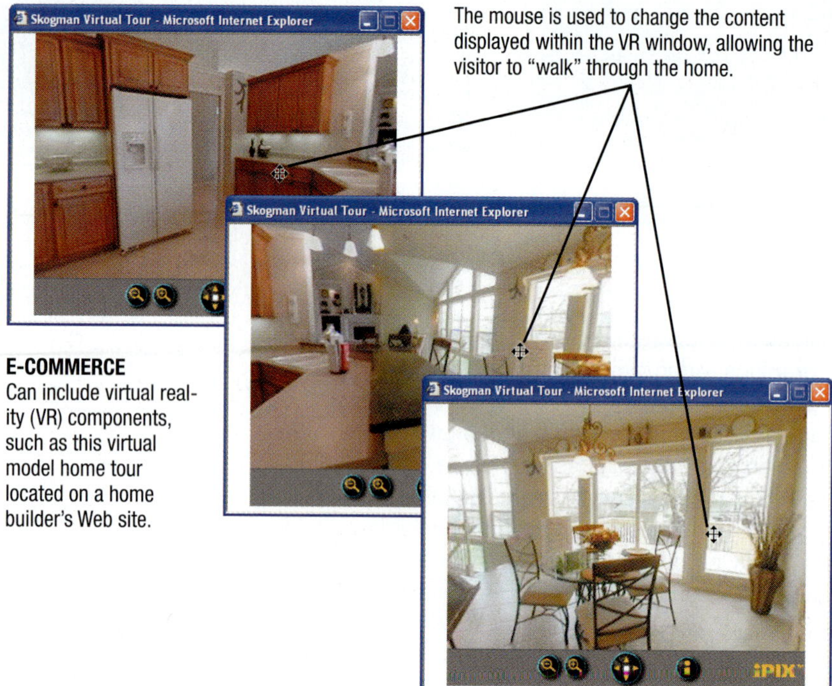

E-COMMERCE
Can include virtual reality (VR) components, such as this virtual model home tour located on a home builder's Web site.

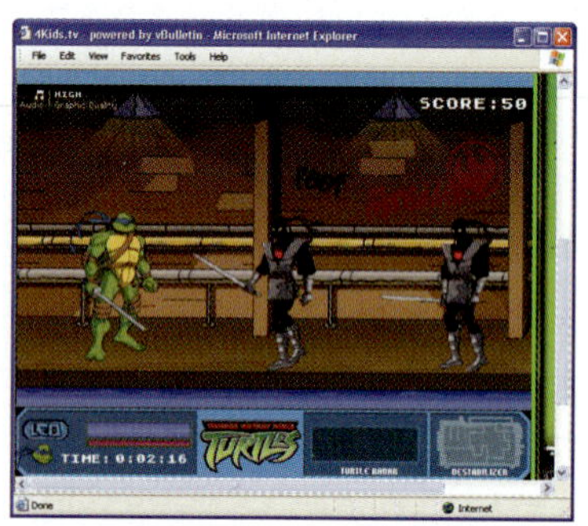

ENTERTAINMENT
Online games for children and adults alike usually include multimedia elements, such as background music, images, animation, and more.

WEB-BASED TRAINING (WBT)
Often includes video clips and animations; online exercises, tutorials, and exams; e-mail links; and other resources.

FIGURE 10-1
Web-based multimedia applications.

products—such as music and movies—multimedia elements are frequently added to the Web page to allow customers to listen to samples of songs or view movie trailers before making a purchase. Some e-commerce Web sites use 3D images of products to better convey product characteristics to potential purchasers; others utilize *virtual reality*. **Virtual reality (VR)** is the use of a computer to create environments that look like they do in the real world. E-commerce Web sites use VR to better show what a selected product (such as a car or home) looks like. For instance the Web-based VR application shown in Figure 10-1 allows potential home buyers to take a virtual tour of model homes, in order to help them select their desired design.

Entertainment

Most entertainment Web sites include multimedia. For instance, online games (such as the one shown in Figure 10-1) typically utilize multimedia. Common multimedia elements included in online games are background music, sound effects, images, animated effects, narration, talking characters, and video clips. In addition, multimedia elements—including video clips, live video feeds, and interactive activities (like instant polls and voting)—are incorporated into a variety of Web sites for entertainment purposes, such as on Web sites associated with popular TV shows like *Big Brother*, *American Idol*, and *Survivor*. For another multimedia entertainment application that you might encounter online—digital worlds—see the You box.

Web-Based Training (WBT)

As discussed in Chapter 8, Web-based training (WBT) is delivering instruction—typically individualized instruction—via the Web. Web-based training is available for a host of subjects, such as test preparation and computer skills, in addition to being used in conjunction with distance learning courses offered by colleges and universities. WBT is also frequently used for employee training and continuing education. An example of one of the Web-based training activities available through this textbook's Web site is shown in Figure 10-1.

>**Virtual reality (VR).** The use of a computer to create three-dimensional environments that look like they do in the real world.

TECHNOLOGY AND YOU

Digital Worlds

Digital communities are online locations where individuals can go to mingle with others—often they are set up to look like virtual cities or other locations. One of the most ambitious digital community projects—*There*—is going a step further by creating a virtual universe. In There world, digital characters or *avatars* are used to represent each actual participant. Like many applications that use avatars, individuals can choose the initial appearance of their avatars; they can also use *Therebucks*—virtual money purchased with actual money—to buy clothing, accessories, and other items for their avatars, as well as pay for activities they want their avatar to participate in, such as parachute rides and hover board races. The avatars can move around There world to explore various locations and can talk with other individuals (via their avatars) as they meet up with one another (see the accompanying screen shot).

Although some There participants have created online businesses, selling clothing and services aimed at the avatars, the main objective for participants is to have fun. There are even online holiday parties, such as for Halloween and Valentine's Day. Participation in There costs about $5 per month.

Advantages and Disadvantages of Using Web-Based Multimedia

Perhaps one of the biggest advantages of using multimedia in general is that it can address a variety of learning styles. Some people are *visual learners* who learn best by seeing; others are *auditory learners* who learn best by hearing. Still others are *kinesthetic learners* who learn best by doing. The use of multimedia elements can help address the needs of all learning styles. While a concept presented using a single medium might be appropriate for some users, other users might be missing out on the full experience simply because the presentation does not match their learning styles. Multimedia has the advantage of presenting the material in multiple learning styles, and studies have shown that when multiple learning styles are used, learning is enhanced. For example, an interactive Web-based exercise that uses printed text, images, spoken narration, and hands-on activities that the user performs covers the three types of learning styles just discussed. The use of multimedia for enhancing retention is applicable to more than just educational Web sites. For instance, a manufacturer could include multimedia elements on its Web site in order to reach the broadest audience with its product message, such as why its product is beneficial or how it is superior over competing products. If a variety of multimedia elements are used, retention will likely be increased for a wide range of visitors.

Another advantage of using multimedia is that it often makes the presented material more interesting and enjoyable. In addition, many ideas are easier to convey in multimedia format than in a single format. For an example, compare listening to the news on the radio to watching the news on TV. The addition of the visual image of the newscaster combined with video clips, photographs, and other graphics typically used on TV news broadcasts likely makes watching the news on TV a more informative experience for most individuals than simply listening to a radio news broadcast. Another example is shown in Figure 10-2. This children's multimedia arts and crafts program includes videos and photos to illustrate how to

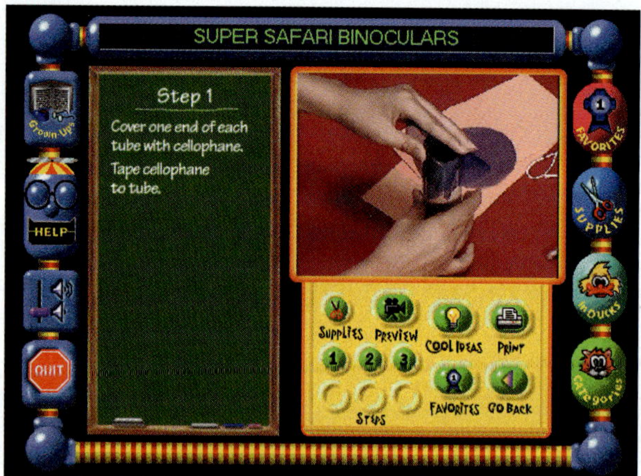

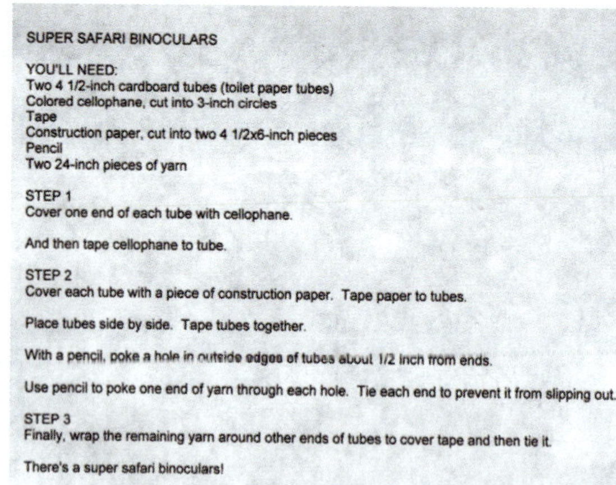
SUPER SAFARI BINOCULARS

YOU'LL NEED:
Two 4 1/2-inch cardboard tubes (toilet paper tubes)
Colored cellophane, cut into 3-inch circles
Tape
Construction paper, cut into two 4 1/2x6-inch pieces
Pencil
Two 24-inch pieces of yarn

STEP 1
Cover one end of each tube with cellophane.

And then tape cellophane to tube.

STEP 2
Cover each tube with a piece of construction paper. Tape paper to tubes.

Place tubes side by side. Tape tubes together.

With a pencil, poke a hole in outside edges of tubes about 1/2 inch from ends.

Use pencil to poke one end of yarn through each hole. Tie each end to prevent it from slipping out.

STEP 3
Finally, wrap the remaining yarn around other ends of tubes to cover tape and then tie it.

There's a super safari binoculars!

FIGURE 10-2
Multimedia-based applications are often more interesting and more effective than their single medium counterparts.

create each craft. Compare that medium to the printed directions shown in the figure—the multimedia version should be much more effective in teaching children how to create the craft than the text-only version.

One disadvantage to using multimedia is development time and cost. Multimedia Web sites are usually much more time-consuming and expensive to create than a simple text-based Web site. Although multimedia elements for a Web site can be created in house (if an employee has the necessary skills and experience with multimedia software), many businesses opt to *outsource* the development of their multimedia Web site to a professional development firm, which tends to add to the expense. Other possible limitations of multimedia include delivery time (delivery of multimedia content is typically slower than text-only content, which may annoy some visitors with slow Internet connections) and compatibility issues (some components may not be compatible with all devices, browsers, and Internet connection speeds used by visitors). These factors need to be considered when a multimedia Web site is designed and created, as discussed in more detail later in this chapter. Improvements in technology and multimedia development products are expected to reduce some of these limitations in the future.

FIGURE 10-3
Typefaces. Typefaces are collections of text characters that share a common design and can be either serif or sans serif.

Serif

ABC DEFGHIJKLM NOPQRSTUV WXYZ 0123456789

Times New Roman

ABC DEFGHIJKLM NOPQRSTUV WXYZ 0123456789

Cooper Black

SERIF TYPEFACES

No serif

ABC DEFGHIJKLM NOPQRSTUV WXYZ 0123456789

Arial

ABC DEFGHIJKLM NOPQRSTUV WXYZ 0123456789

Dom Casual

SANS SERIF TYPEFACES

MULTIMEDIA ELEMENTS

Multimedia Web sites can contain a variety of different multimedia elements. The most common are discussed next.

Text

Text is an important part of most Web sites. It is used to supply basic content, as well as to add text-based menus and hyperlinks. It is also frequently added to buttons, logos, banners, and other Web page graphics. As discussed in Chapter 6, text can be displayed in a variety of font faces, colors, sizes, and appearances; a font face or typeface is a collection of text characters that share a common design, such as the Times New Roman, Cooper Black, Arial, and Dom Casual typefaces illustrated in Figure 10-3. *Serif typefaces*—typefaces (such as Times New Roman) that have small lines called *serifs* on the edges of the letters—tend to be more readable for large bodies of text, and so they are traditionally used for this purpose. *Sans serif typefaces*, such as Arial, do not have serifs and are frequently used for titles,

>**Text.** Alphanumeric characters kept in a text, not graphic, format.

headings, Web page banners, and other text elements that usually are displayed larger than body text or that otherwise need a more distinctive appearance.

There are a wide variety of typefaces available, and one typeface may convey an entirely different feeling than another typeface. For example, Times New Roman is a traditional, business-like typeface, whereas Dom Casual is more whimsical and fun. Consequently, when selecting a typeface to be used on a Web page or in a multimedia element that contains text, it is important to select a typeface that matches the style of the Web site. In addition to selecting an appropriate typeface, it is also important to select the appropriate font size. Normal size is 12-point text—it is not a good idea to use smaller text because it can be difficult to read. Do not make your text too large either because it will take up too much space on the screen. You want to make sure enough information fits on the screen at one time to avoid annoying your users by making them have to scroll needlessly. Also, be sure to watch your color combinations. A high degree of contrast between the text color and the Web page's background color results in the most readable text—do not use dark text on a dark background or light text on a light background. For the same readability reason, do not use a busy image as a background image for a Web page.

When selecting the typeface and size for Web page text, there is one additional important consideration: the computer and Web browser on which the Web page is displayed ultimately determine the typeface and font size used to display the text on a Web page. Only the typefaces installed on a user's computer can be used to display Web page text unless the typeface is sent embedded in the Web page. So it is important to remember that when text is used, there is the chance that it will not be displayed exactly as intended. For these reasons, when a consistent text appearance is required on a Web site—such as for a company logo or navigation buttons—a *graphical image* is used instead. Unlike regular text, text that is incorporated into an image is displayed the same on all computers, regardless of the user's browser settings, because the text is part of the displayed image's file. Images are discussed next.

Graphics

Graphics or *images* refer to digital representations of photographs, drawings, charts, and other visual images. Unlike *animation* or *video* (discussed later in this chapter), graphics are unmoving, static images. Graphics can be created by scanning a photograph or document, taking a picture with a digital camera, or creating or modifying an image in an image editing program. They can also be obtained as *clip art* or *stock photograph* images. **Clip art** consists of predrawn electronic images. Some clip art is typically included with office suite programs and image editing programs; it is also commonly available in collections on CDs, as well as from a variety of Web sites. While most clip art must be purchased, it is usually *royalty-free*, which means it can be freely used in multiple documents (such as in several newsletters and Web pages) without further payment or permission. Some entirely free clip art is also available over the Internet (see Figure 10-4). *Stock photographs* are professional photographs available for use on Web pages and other types of documents; some are royalty-free, others have more restrictive usage requirements. Stock photographs are sold both in collections and individually from stock photograph agencies.

Graphics are available in many formats, such as *TIF*, *BMP*, *GIF*, *JPEG*, and *PNG*. The TIF format is commonly used with scanned images, and the BMP format is used by Windows Paint and similar graphics programs. Web page images are usually saved in the GIF, JPEG, or PNG format. These formats are explained in more detail next.

FURTHER EXPLORATION

For links to further information about clip art sites and other Web page development resources, go to www.course.com/uc11/ch10

>**Graphic.** A digital representation of a photograph, drawing, chart, or other visual image. >**Clip art.** Predrawn electronic images.

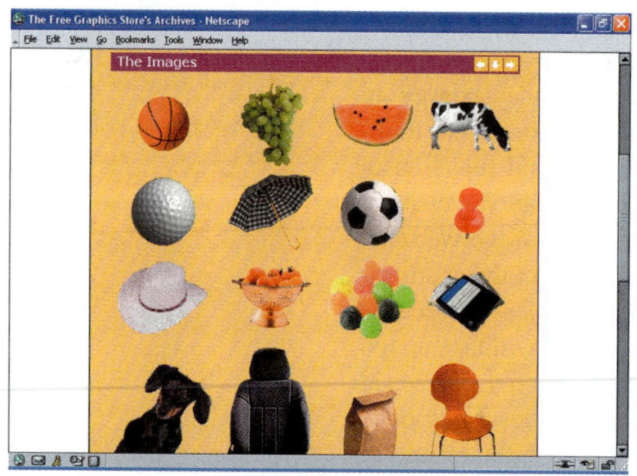

CLIP ART IMAGES
Typically use the GIF format and can be downloaded from a variety of Web sites. The images on this site are free for both personal and commercial use.

STOCK PHOTOGRAPHS
Typically use the JPEG format and are available through stock photograph agencies. The agency shown here has a variety of images organized by topics; all images require a fee for use, but some are royalty free.

FIGURE 10-4
Both clip art and stock photographs are plentiful on the Internet.

GIF

The *Graphics Interchange Format* (usually referred to as **GIF** and saved with the file extension *.gif*) is a standard format for Web page images and is supported by all browsers that display images. It is an efficient, compressed format in which images can contain up to 256 colors; a smaller color palette size can help reduce the file size of the finished image. The GIF format uses *lossless file compression*, so the quality of the image is not decreased when it is saved in the GIF format.

GIF images are always rectangular, but can use a *transparent* background color to make the images appear to be nonrectangular (see Figure 10-5). GIF images can also be *interlaced*, which means that the image is displayed initially at low resolution, and its quality is progressively increased until it is displayed at full quality; noninterlaced GIFs are displayed top to bottom at full quality instead. Even though an interlaced image does not actually load faster, interlacing enables the user to more quickly perceive what the image looks like; therefore, the image appears to load faster. Transparency is usually set by the Web page developer when the image is created; interlacing is typically designated by the Web page developer when the image is inserted into a Web page. The GIF format is used most often with logos and other nonphotographic images.

FIGURE 10-5
Transparent and interlaced GIFs.

TRANSPARENT VS. NONTRANSPARENT GIFS

Nontransparent (image's white background is visible on top of the page's yellow background).

Transparent with white specified as the transparent color (page's yellow background is visible through the transparent areas of the image, so the image appears to be nonrectangular).

INTERLACED VS. NONINTERLACED GIFS

>**GIF.** A graphics format that supports 256 colors and is commonly used for Web page line art images.

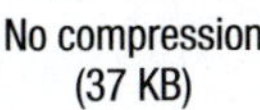

No compression
(37 KB)

40% compression
(13 KB)

80% compression
(7 KB)

100% compression
(3 KB)

FIGURE 10-6
The amount of compression in a JPEG file affects both the file size and the display quality.

JPEG

The *Joint Photographic Experts Group* format (usually referred to as **JPEG** and saved with the file extension *.jpg*) is the standard format for Web page photographs and is supported by all Web browsers that display images. JPEG images are compressed using *lossy file compression*. Consequently, image quality is lost during the compression process. A compression amount from 0% to 100% is selected when the image is saved—the higher the compression, the smaller the file size but the poorer the quality because quality is lost in the compression process, as illustrated in Figure 10-6. JPEGs can be designated as *progressive*, which means that the image is displayed initially in low resolution and the image quality is progressively improved, similar to interlaced GIFs. JPEG images can contain more than 16 million colors (called *true color*), so this format is often used for photographs and other images that may require more than 256 colors.

PNG

The *Portable Network Graphics* format (usually referred to as **PNG** and saved with the file extension *.png*) is a format specifically created for Web page images. It was initially expected to replace the GIF format, but it is still not widely used. The PNG format uses lossless compression, similar to GIF, but it sometimes compresses more efficiently than GIF format for many nonphotographic images, which results in slightly smaller file sizes. PNG images can use a specific color palette of 256 colors or less (like GIF images) or can use true color (like JPEG images). PNG images can also be interlaced and transparent.

Choosing a Graphic Format

When creating an image, it is important to use the most appropriate graphic format. Graphics for multimedia components need to be in a format compatible with the multimedia software being used, and Web page images should use as small a file size as possible (while retaining an acceptable level of quality) to reduce loading time. For Web pages, the GIF format is usually selected for *line art*, such as clip art, logos, navigation buttons, and so forth, although the PNG format could be used, if preferred. The JPEG format is usually used for photographs because JPEG images support true color and the user is able to select the amount of compression used, which often results in a higher-quality image at a smaller file size than if the GIF or PNG formats were used. A line art image and a photograph that were saved with each of these three formats are illustrated in Figure 10-7; for the JPEG images in this figure, varying amounts of compression were used with each file format, and the one that had the smallest file size but that still had acceptable quality was shown in the figure.

FURTHER EXPLORATION

For links to further information about creating graphics for multimedia Web sites, go to www.course.com/uc11/ch10

>**JPEG.** A graphics format that supports true color and is commonly used for photographs inserted in Web pages. >**PNG.** A graphics format designed specifically for use with Web page images.

LINE ART
The GIF or PNG format is usually used for line art images.

GIF format - 3 KB

JPEG format (10% compression) - 5 KB

PNG format - 2 KB

PHOTOGRAPHS
The JPEG format is usually used for photographs.

GIF format - 15 KB

JPEG format (50% compression) - 6 KB

PNG format - 91 KB

FIGURE 10-7
Graphic formats. It is important to select the most appropriate format for each image.

It is also important to realize that the physical size of the image can greatly affect file size. Therefore, images to be used on Web pages should be sized to their appropriate display size and saved as that size before being inserted into a Web page. When a Web page requires a very large image (such as to better show a product, home for sale, or featured piece of art, for instance), a **thumbnail image** can be used to save loading time. Thumbnail images are small versions of images that are linked to a corresponding full-sized image; when a thumbnail image is clicked, the full-sized image is displayed (see Figure 10-8). Because the file size of a thumbnail image is very small, the use of thumbnail images avoids increasing the page loading time for all users, when only some of the users may wish to view the full-sized images.

FIGURE 10-8
Thumbnails. Thumbnail images give users access to the full-sized images, when desired, without slowing down the loading of the Web page for all users.

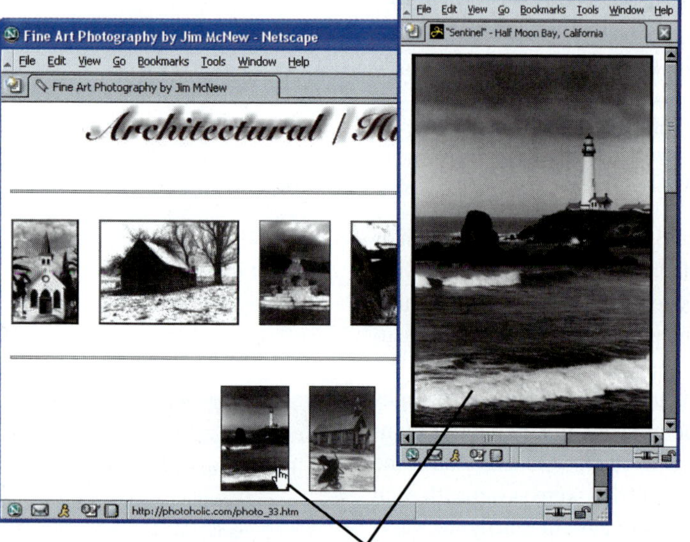

Clicking a thumbnail image displays the full-sized image.

Animation

Animation is the term used to describe a series of graphical images that are displayed one after the other to simulate movement. Cartoons on television are one example of animation; animating objects on Web pages so they move or change their appearance when pointed to is another. Multimedia applications, both on and off the Web, frequently use animation. To add simple animation to a Web page, *Java applets* and *animated GIFs* are frequently used. A **Java applet** is a small program inserted into a Web page that performs a specific task, such as changing the values in a stock portfolio, scrolling text or images across the screen, and so forth. An **animated GIF** is a group of GIF images stored in a special animated GIF file that is inserted in a Web page, similar to any other graphic. The individual images contained in the animated GIF file display one after another to simulate movement (see Figure 10-9). Animated GIFs are frequently used to change the images displayed in an onscreen advertising banner.

>**Thumbnail image.** A small image on a Web page that is linked to a larger, higher-resolution image. >**Animation.** The process by which a series of graphical images are displayed one after the other to simulate movement. >**Java applet.** A small program inserted into a Web page that performs a specific task, such as changing the values in a stock portfolio or scrolling text across the screen. >**Animated GIF.** A group of GIF images saved as an animated GIF file that is inserted in a Web page; the individual images are displayed one after another to simulate movement.

For more complex animations, developers can use *JavaScript* or another scripting language discussed later in this chapter. For instance, a scripting language is commonly used to build interactivity into a Web page, such as having text or an image change as a menu item is pointed to, as in Figure 10-10. *Macromedia Fireworks*, *Macromedia Flash*, *Adobe AfterEffects*, or another *Web animation program* can be used to create animated components—such as games, tutorials, advertisements, and animated introductory pages (called *splash pages*) that are displayed for a short period of time before the home page of a Web site is displayed—to be inserted into a Web page. **Flash** in particular is widely used today. In addition to being used to create individual animated components, Flash is also beginning to be viewed as a viable development tool for overall Web development and is commonly used in place of, or in conjunction with, JavaScript to add interactivity to a Web site.

For more complete stand-alone multimedia applications to be delivered via the Web, *multimedia authoring software*—such as *Macromedia Director MX* or *Adobe Authorware*—can be used. Director MX is an *object-based authoring program*, in which all objects are viewed as part of a movie production, such as cast members, a stage, and a score. Director MX is frequently used to create *Shockwave* content to be incorporated into multimedia Web sites. Authorware is an *icon-based authoring program*. Icons representing the multimedia elements in an application (such as text, graphics, and video) are placed on a *flowline* to indicate the sequence in which the elements should be displayed. Authorware is most often used for multimedia training and educational applications.

Many Web-based animations require a *plug-in* (a free small program that adds additional capabilities to your browser) to be viewed. Some of the most widely used plug-ins are *Macromedia Flash Player* (installed on 98% of PCs used by Internet users, according to one study), *Adobe Acrobat Reader* (87% of Internet PCs), *Java* (86.5%), *Windows Media Player* (84%), and *Macromedia Shockwave Player* (54%). Animation and interactivity can also be achieved using *Dynamic HTML* (*DHTML*) and *programming languages* (DHTML is discussed later in this chapter, and programming languages are discussed in Chapter 13).

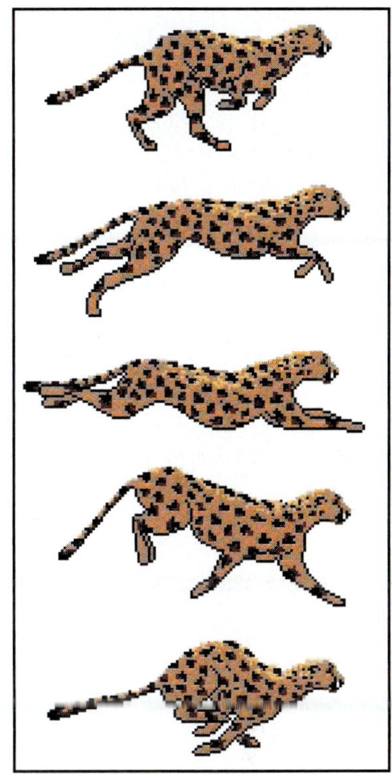

FIGURE 10-9
Animated GIFs.
When the animated GIF containing the images shown above is displayed, it appears that the leopard is running.

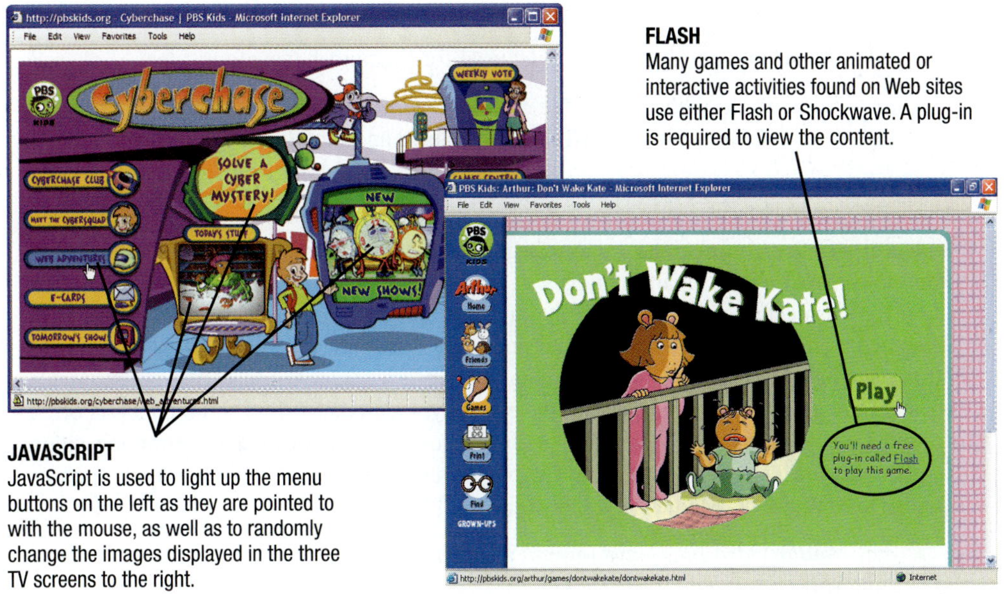

FIGURE 10-10
JavaScript and Flash are commonly used on Web pages.

>**Flash.** A popular Web animation program.

TIP

Professional animation and multimedia authoring programs—such as Flash, Director MX, and Authorware—are very sophisticated and are most often used by multimedia development specialists; individuals new to multimedia should look for products geared to consumer use instead.

Audio

Audio includes all types of sound, such as music, spoken voice, and sound effects. Sound is commonly found on Web sites in the form of background music, downloadable music, and as part of games, tutorials, and other multimedia elements. Audio can be recorded using a microphone or MIDI instrument; it can also be captured from CDs or downloaded from the Internet. Remember that audio files require a great deal of storage space, so compression methods—such as the MP3 format—are frequently used to reduce their file size.

Audio is often played automatically when a particular event occurs, such as background music playing when the home page of a site is first displayed, narration or other audio content starting when a Flash or Shockwave activity is loaded, or a sound effect playing when the mouse points to or clicks a navigation button. Web pages can also contain hyperlinks to audio files so they will not play unless the user clicks that link. Audio files on Web pages are commonly played with plug-ins or player programs, such as *QuickTime*, *Windows Media Player*, or *RealOne Player*.

Audio files on Web pages are often in the form of *streaming audio* to speed up delivery. With a streaming audio file, only a small portion of the audio file is initially downloaded and *buffered* (placed in memory or temporarily stored on the hard drive), and then the audio file can begin playing while the remainder of the file downloads simultaneously. Because it allows the user to see or hear the file's content significantly faster than if the entire file had to be downloaded first, it is recommended to use the streaming approach for all large audio and video files used with Web pages.

Some of the most widely used audio file formats are as follows:

- *.wav—Waveform* format; not compressed, so usually results in large file sizes. Most CD music uses the waveform format.
- *.mp3—Motion Picture Experts Group Audio Layer 3* format; very efficient, high-quality compressed audio. Waveform files can be converted to MP3 format to reduce their file size.
- *.midi—Musical Instrument Digital Interface* format; used for files created with a MIDI device.
- *.aiff—Audio Interchange Format File*; used for Macintosh waveform files.
- *.aac—Advanced Audio Coding*; the *Motion Picture Experts Group Audio Layer 4* format, a newer alternative to MP3 for both fixed and mobile Web applications.

Video

Video differs from animation in that it begins as a continuous stream of visual information that is broken into separate images or *frames* when the video is recorded. When the frames are projected—typically at a rate of 30 frames per second—the effect is a smooth reconstruction of the original continuous stream of information. As you might imagine, at 30 images per second, the amount of data involved in saving a video file can require a substantial amount of storage space. Consequently, video data—like audio data—is often compressed. A variety of compression standards exist. Some of the most common video file formats are listed next; most can be played using a standard media player, such as QuickTime, Windows Media Player, or RealOne Player.

- *.avi—Audio-Video Interleave format*; a standard video file format developed by Microsoft.

>**Audio.** Sound, such as music, spoken voice, and sound effects. >**Video.** A continuous stream of visual information broken into separate images or frames to be displayed one after the other to simulate the original visual event.

- *.mpeg—Motion Picture Experts Group* format; high-quality, compressed video.
- *.mov—QuickTime* format; versatile format developed by Apple and widely used to distribute video over the Web.
- *.rm—Real* format; highly compressed format used for streaming video files.

Video that is to be incorporated into a multimedia Web site can be recorded using a standard (analog) video camera and then converted to digital form as it is input into a computer, but it is more commonly recorded in digital form using a digital video camera. Web page video applications include delivering video clips of television shows, news broadcasts, and corporate speeches; facilitating panoramic video tours of facilities or products; Web cams that display live video feeds from a specific location; and so forth. Similar to audio files, *streaming video* is frequently used on Web pages to speed up delivery; just like streaming audio files, streaming video files begin playing once a portion of the video has been downloaded.

MULTIMEDIA WEB SITE DESIGN

Web site design refers to the process of planning what your Web site will look like and how it will work. Although this chapter focuses on designing and developing multimedia Web sites, the process of designing stand-alone multimedia applications, such as those delivered via a CD or kiosk, and nonmultimedia Web sites are similar in many respects. In all instances, the importance of careful planning cannot be overemphasized. Time spent planning and designing a site on paper before jumping into the development process pays off in the long run. Some of the most important design considerations and guidelines are discussed next.

Basic Design Principles

When designing a multimedia Web site, it is important to keep two basic principles in mind: (1) users like interesting and exciting applications, and (2) users have little patience with slow-to-load or hard-to-use applications.

A site is *interesting* if it provides information of value or interest to its target audience; users find it *exciting* if it rewards them with a stimulating experience. Unfortunately, interest and excitement wear off over time. If visitors see the same information on your site day after day, boredom sets in and they will likely stop visiting. Therefore, it is important to refresh the content of your site regularly with new information.

Web site visitors generally do not have much patience with poorly designed sites—ease of use is a key factor in whether or not individuals will choose to regularly visit a Web site. For example, if they have a hard time figuring out how to navigate a site to get the information they want, or if pages on the site take too long to load, they will often move on to another site and may never return. To facilitate navigation and reduce user frustration, you should design an intuitive site with clear, consistent navigational tools and information presented in a manner that makes sense. Web pages should load quickly and be easy to read—a good rule of thumb is to keep the total file size of a page (the Web page file, plus image files and any other multimedia elements displayed on the page) to around 100 KB to enable the page to load in 30 seconds or less for all users. To accomplish this, you need to select your multimedia elements carefully and modify them as necessary to be as efficient as possible.

Another factor that impacts the design of a Web site is the device that your target audience will use to access the site. Since it can vary from a large screen TV to a 17-inch desktop PC monitor to a handheld PC with a 2-inch screen to a smart phone, obviously a one-size-fits-all Web site is not an acceptable option. At a minimum, you should decide early on whether the site will be targeted for individuals using conventional PCs (with screen sizes ranging from

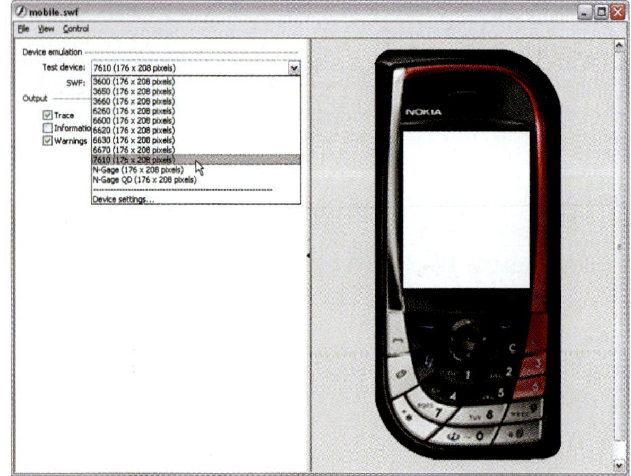

FIGURE 10-11
Testing on multiple platforms. Some multimedia development programs include an emulator to allow you to test your multimedia content on a variety of devices.

about 10 inches and up), whether the site will be designed for handheld or portable device use, or whether content will be optimized for multiple delivery methods. Some development programs—such as Macromedia Flash shown in Figure 10-11—allow you to test your content on a variety of display devices and screen sizes (such as certain PC monitor sizes or specific mobile devices) to see how it will look for visitors using those configurations.

Even if a single delivery method is assumed (such as a conventional PC), there are still many variations of platforms, Web browsers, and settings that can be used by Web page visitors. Because of this, it is important to set up the site so it can be used with as many different configurations as possible. Careful consideration should be given to the following:

- *Features that require a specific browser.* Including snazzy animated effects for Internet Explorer users might be nice for them, but ignores those users with a different browser, such as Netscape, Firefox, and Opera. The capabilities and features of browsers are growing more closely together, but there are still features not supported by all browsers. At the present time, you can choose not to use browser-specific features; choose to use browser-specific features for what should be your target audience's most widely used browser, as long as it does not inhibit the functionality of the application for other users; or choose to identify the browser used by each visitor (called browser sniffing and usually implemented using JavaScript code on the home page of the site) and display a version of your site that matches the visitor's browser.
- *Features that require little used plug-ins.* Although it is annoying to have to download a plug-in before being able to use a Web page feature, most users tolerate downloading a few of the most widely used plug-ins the first time they are needed, if they do not have them already installed. Do not annoy your visitors by requiring unusual plug-ins that they may not have or have no other reason to obtain.
- *The size of the page content.* Keep in mind that different browsers and screen resolutions allow different amounts of room to display Web page content. This affects how wide your images and columns of text should be. To ensure that the content is visible on virtually all PCs with a maximized browser window and a screen resolution of 800 × 600 or higher, without the user having to scroll down unnecessarily, keep *banner images*, *image maps*, and other full-width items to 710 pixels or less. Full-height items (such as an image map) should be less than 420 pixels tall. In general, you should design for screen resolutions of 800 × 600 and 1,024 × 768.
- *High-bandwidth items.* Although broadband Internet use is growing, there is still a very large installed base of dial-up modem users. If the intended audience of your site includes a large number of dial-up users, pay extra close attention to the file size of the images on the site, and use techniques to allow the user to decide whether to take the time to access certain features of the site. For example, instead of automatically downloading and playing a sound or video file, have a link to it (with an estimated download time listed). When large images are needed, use thumbnail images that the user can click to display the full-sized image only when needed. Also, use streaming audio and video files whenever possible. Finally, be sure that all multimedia elements are consistent with the purpose of your site and add something significant. Do not add extra elements—particularly sound and video files—without a good reason. They just slow down your site and annoy your visitors.

TIP

Whenever you include content on a Web page that requires a plug-in (such as Flash Player or a specific media player program), include an obvious link that takes visitors to a Web page where they can download a free version of that plug-in.

TREND

3D Browsers

Similar in purpose to the tabbed browsing available in some Web browsers, *3D browsers* are available that can help users organize and more easily work with a variety of open Web pages at one time. To accomplish this, 3D browsers typically allow users to arrange Web pages in groupings in more than one dimension. For instance, some allow windows to be arranged on cubes representing areas of interest; others use multiple "walls" onto which browser windows can be placed (see the accompanying screen shot) and the user can pan from wall to wall to see the Web pages located there. Using a 3D browser gives the user the ability to use and manipulate many Web pages at one time, but still keep them organized. Similar *3D desktops* are in development (such as *Sun's Project Looking Glass*) that allow all the items on a user's desktop, not just Web browser windows, to be viewed and arranged in 3D—no special glasses required.

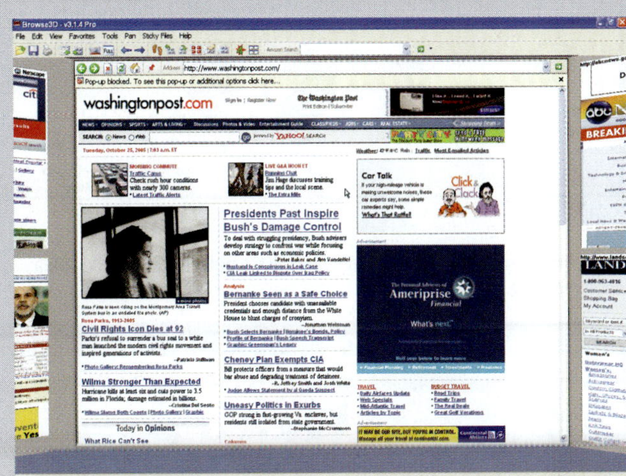

Web sites of the future may also need to plan for the use of *3D browsers*—an emerging option discussed in the Trend box.

Determining the Intended Audience and Objectives

One of the first steps in designing a multimedia application or Web site should be determining the primary objectives of the site and the intended audience. The objectives of the site affect the content of the site because you will want to make sure that the site includes the information needed to meet the site objectives. The intended audience affects the appearance (such as the style, graphics, fonts, and colors) of the site. For example, four sites designed to appeal to distinctly different audiences are shown in Figure 10-12. The intended audience also affects the types of multimedia elements that can be included on a site. If you are designing a site to be accessed through an intranet, for example, you do not have to be as concerned about file size as someone designing a Web site to be accessed by the general public. When determining your target audience, give some thought to how users will access the site and how technologically-savvy they are. Will they be using up-to-date browsers and have a variety of multimedia plug-ins installed? If your answer is "no," that may impact the types of multimedia elements you include on the site.

Once the objectives and audience have been identified, you should have a good idea of the main topics that need to be included in the site. If the needed content is unclear to you, do not go any further into the design process until you understand what the content should be. Rethink your audience and objectives, explore other sites on the Web, and talk to potential users until you determine what the Web site's content should include.

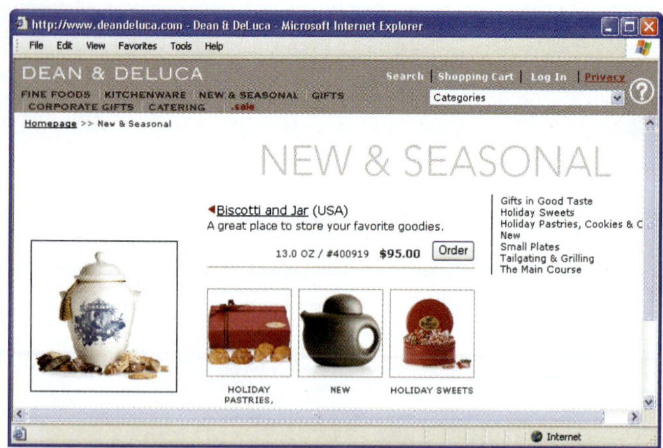

BOLD
Shopping sites often use bold colors and crisp typefaces to give the site a contemporary, but rich, feel.

CONSERVATIVE
Many business sites use a conservative appearance to match their conservative image.

WHIMSICAL
Sites catering to young people often have an especially friendly look, sporting bright graphics and large fanciful typefaces.

BUSY
Sites designed for more technically-savvy users often have a busy appearance with lots of links so that visitors can go directly to the information they are seeking. This style is commonly used with portal pages, as well.

FIGURE 10-12
The intended audience affects the design of a Web site. Shown here are four sites designed for vastly different audiences.

Using Flowcharts, Page Layouts, and Storyboards

After the objectives, intended audience, and basic content to be included in a Web site have been determined, the structure and layout of the site can be designed. To this end, tools, such as *flowcharts*, *page layouts*, and *storyboards*, are often used.

A **flowchart**, when used to design a Web site, describes how the pages in the site relate to one another. The top part of Figure 10-13 shows a flowchart for a bed and breakfast Web site. Essentially a map of the structure of the Web site, a Web site flowchart uses a single box to represent each Web page, and the lines between boxes show the logical organization of the site. Remember, however, that you can link pages in any way you like, and visitors may visit the pages of the site in any order. Although the lines between the flowchart boxes indicate necessary hyperlinks, there would typically be additional links between the pages. For example, it is a good idea to place links to the main pages of the site

---

>**Flowchart.** A tool that can be used during the Web design process to illustrate how the pages in a Web site relate to one another.

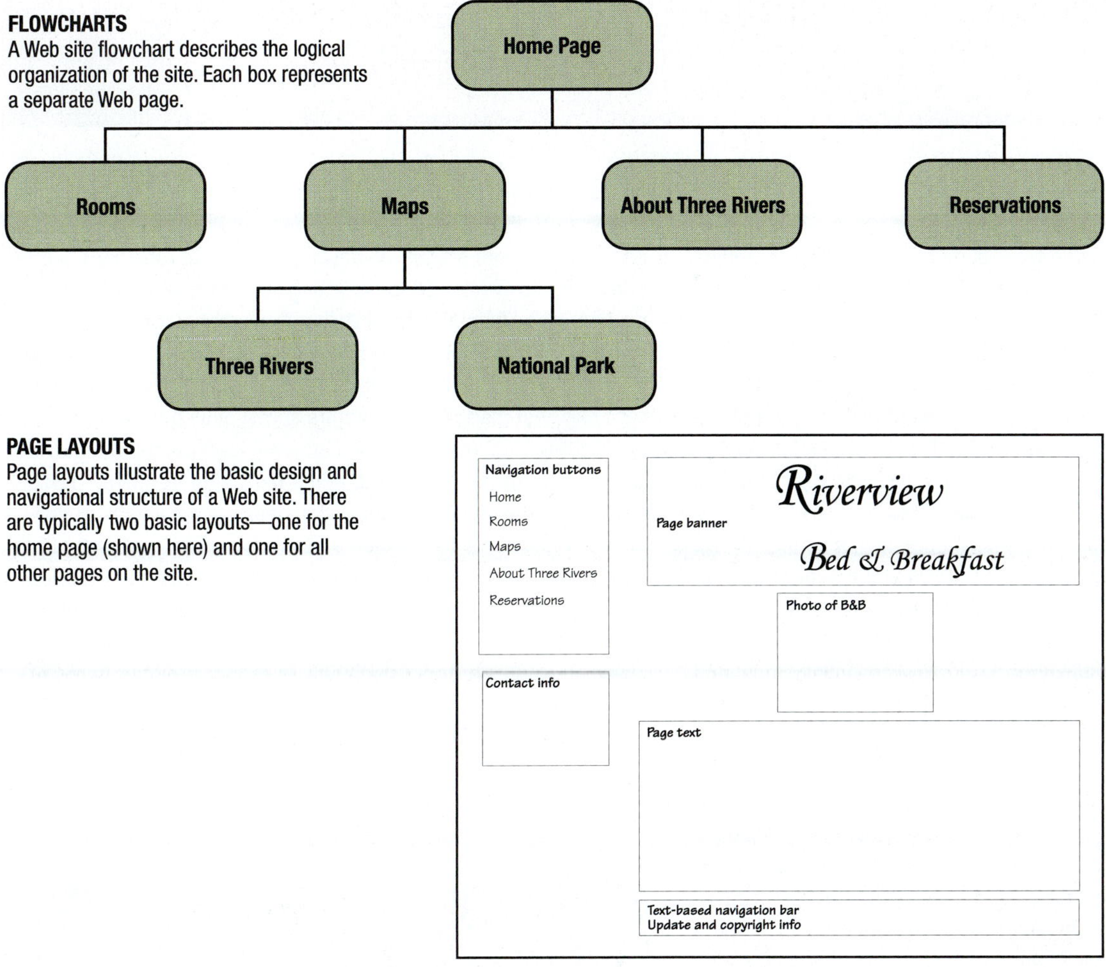

FIGURE 10-13

Web site flowcharts and page layouts. A sample flowchart and page layout for a bed and breakfast Web site are shown here.

(in this example, Home, Rooms, Maps, About Three Rivers, and Reservations) on all pages of the site. More complex flowcharts that illustrate the logical steps and sequence of a multimedia component (similar to the *program flowcharts* used when designing computer programs) can be used when designing multimedia content. Program flowcharts are illustrated and discussed in more detail in Chapter 13.

For designing the layout of a Web page, **page layouts** are typically used; **storyboards** are commonly used instead when designing multimedia components. Both tools are sketches—done by hand or with the help of a computer—that illustrate the layout and navigational structure of the site or multimedia component. For Web sites, typically two page layouts are created: one for the home page (see the bottom screen in Figure 10-13) and one to be used for all other pages on the site. However, if the Web sites use an introductory splash page, it will require its own page layout (or storyboard, if it is animated). Storyboards are ordered series of sketches of each page or screen in a multimedia component, such as a game or product demo. Storyboards are also used in the film industry. For a look at how storyboards and computers are used to create animated feature films, see the Inside the Industry box.

@WEB

FURTHER EXPLORATION

For links to further information about Web site design, go to www.course.com/uc11/ch10

>Page layout. A sketch of a Web page often developed during the Web design process to illustrate the basic layouts of the home page and the rest of the pages on a Web site. **>Storyboard.** An ordered series of sketches that can be developed during the design process of an animated sequence or other multimedia component of a Web site that illustrates what each page or screen in the application will look like.

INSIDE THE INDUSTRY

Creating Animated Films

Multimedia development tools—such as storyboards, graphics software, and animation software—are frequently used in the movie industry. Since Pixar Animation Studios created and produced the first computer-animated feature film, *Toy Story*, released in 1995 under partnership with Disney, computer animated films started reaching a new level of realism. One of the Pixar features released in late 2004, *The Incredibles*, added a new twist—the first Pixar film that used an entire cast of digital humans (see the accompanying illustration).

Like most animated films, the characters and scenes in *The Incredibles* were depicted in storyboards at the early stages. In fact, over 21,000 storyboards were created for the film. Three-dimensional computer models of the characters were then created, and they were assigned *controls*—essentially locations on the model that can be used to move the model—to make the characters move and change their expression. For instance, the Mr. Incredible character required a convincing human musculature, since he is a very strong hero with super strength. The technical team created a skeleton base layer and a separate muscle layer that reacted when certain joints were moved. The team also filmed themselves lifting heaving objects to learn what strength and weight looked like. Next, colors and shading were added to make the characters and other objects into solid forms, and the characters' costumes—all 95 of them—were created. To accomplish this, the technical team hired a tailor for a crash-course in pattern making and created special software to take the character's measurements. Once the patterns were digitally "sewn," they were added to the characters and then run through the simulator to adjust the patterns for a better fit. Next, the digital sets (over 120 for this film) were created and dressed with more than 800 different props. Sounds were also selected and developed to add to the film—for instance, the sound used for the flying vehicles was a combination of the sound from Formula One race cars and knives being sharpened. In the final stages of development, light, shadows, and other effects were added, resulting in a natural and credible environment. To make the human characters look like comic book characters, but still be believable as people, the technical team created a program that used light and an organic translucent skin that made the characters subtly glow from within.

Unlike traditional animation in which each frame of a movie is drawn or painted by hand, computer-generated films utilize animation software to combine and manipulate a variety of digital elements. Once all the elements are in place, rendering software is used to transform that information into the actual frames of the movie. For instance, Pixar uses its RenderMan computer system for this step in the process. It is a very complicated process, requiring about six hours to render a single frame of the movie, which is just 1/24 of a second of actual movie time. Once the film is rendered, final touches, such as the musical score, can be added and the film can be transferred to the appropriate medium for distribution.

Navigational Design Considerations

As already mentioned, careful design of your navigational structure is extremely important. After drawing a preliminary flowchart of a site or application, take a look at the balance of the flowchart. You want enough main topics to keep the information organized, but not so many that users have difficulty finding what they are looking for. For Web sites, users should be able to get to most pages on the site within three mouse clicks. For large sites, navigational tools—such as drop-down menus, *site maps* (table of contents pages that contain links to all main pages on the sites), and search boxes—can help accomplish this. Other navigational options include text-based hyperlinks and navigation bars; image-based navigation bars; *image maps* (single images with separate areas linked to different locations); *frames* (with one frame always displaying the navigation bar and the other

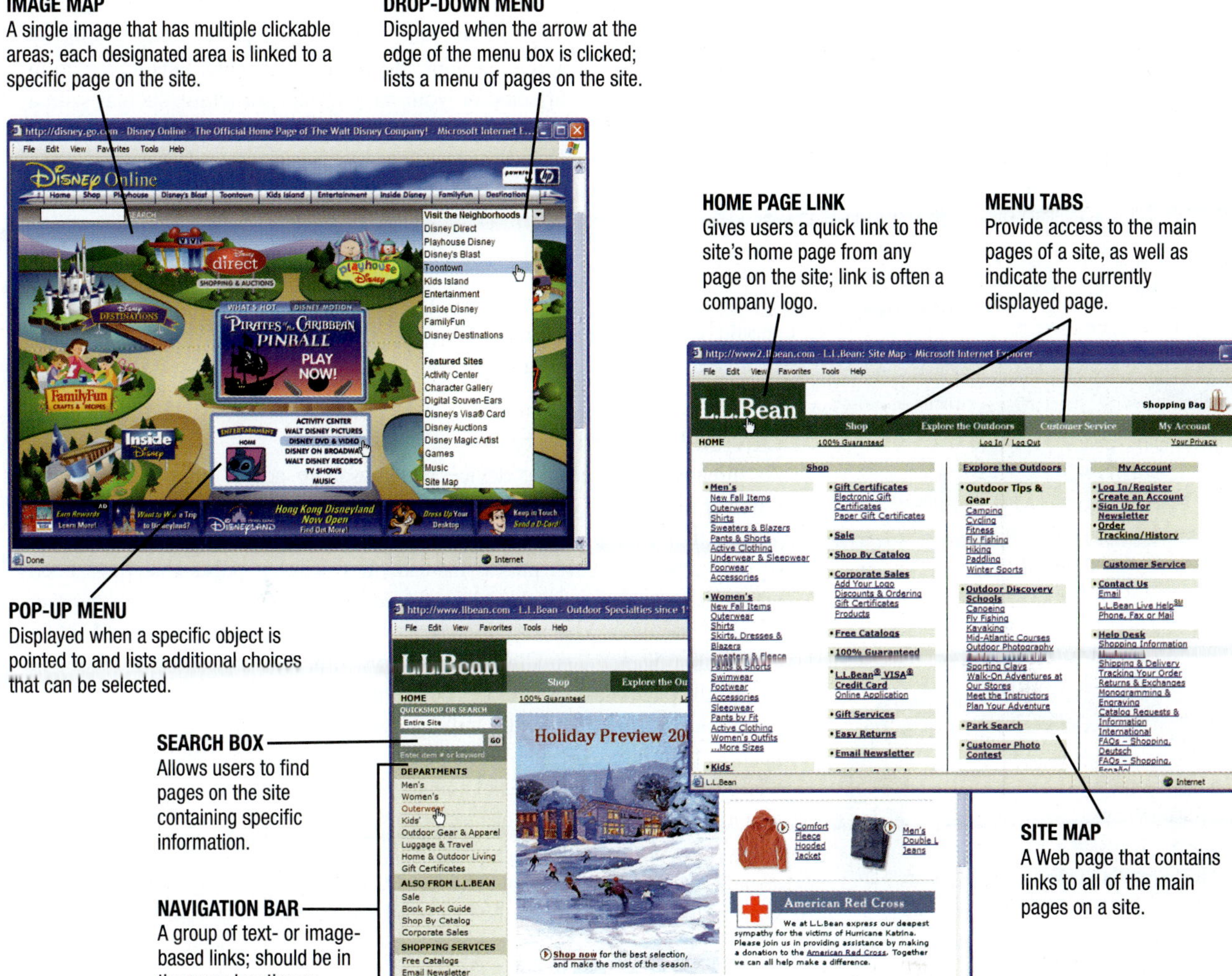

FIGURE 10-14
Navigational tools.
A wide variety of navigational tools exists to help make Web sites easy to use.

frame displaying the site contents as navigational links are clicked); and hyperlinks that display more options or a description of the link when pointed to. Some examples of these navigational elements are shown in Figure 10-14.

When designing your navigational structure, be sure to place the same navigational items in the same location on every page so that users can easily find them. Also be sure that any icons or other graphics are easily understood. When in doubt, add a text name to the image, such as adding the text "Home" to a house icon linked to the site's home page or the "Shopping Bag" text added next to the shopping bag icon on the L.L. Bean page shown in Figure 10-14. In addition, users have come to expect underlined text to be a hyperlink; for that reason, do not underline text that is not a link.

For long Web pages, consider separating the content into several pages to reduce scrolling and loading time; the pages are typically viewed using "Back" and "Next" buttons or with a linked table of contents. When you break a large document apart, consider including a link to view or download the entire document intact either as a Web page or in a common format, such as Word or PDF, so that users can read or print the entire document at one time. For long Web pages that cannot be broken into multiple pages, include a table of contents at the top of the page that allows users to jump to a particular section of the document, and periodically include a link that jumps users back to the top of the page.

TIP

When designing a Web site that will include a company logo on each page, place the logo in the same location on each page and link the logo to the home page of the site to give users a consistent means of displaying the home page from any page on the site.

DESKTOP PC

HANDHELD PC

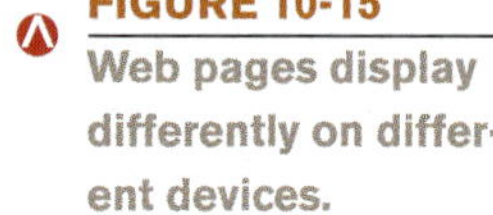

FIGURE 10-15
Web pages display differently on different devices.

One final navigational hint: Be sure to include identifying information on each page of the site to indicate which page is currently displayed because not all users will enter your site at the home page. This information can be text-based or reflected on your navigational structure, such as with a pushed-in navigation button, a different colored tab, or an unlinked or bolded hyperlink on a text-based navigation bar. You should also include the name of the organization and a link to the home page of the site on all pages.

Access Considerations

When designing a multimedia Web site, two types of access considerations should be kept in mind: compatibility with the various types of devices that may be used to access the site and functionality for users with physical disabilities.

Device Compatibility

As already discussed, the device being used to access a Web site affects whether the site will be able to be accessed at all, as well as how functional it will be. For example, many portable devices used to access the Web cannot display regular HTML pages. Instead, they display pages that have been specifically modified for this type of access, typically using *wireless markup language* or *WML* instead of HTML. Other devices can display most HTML content but display a smaller amount at one time than a desktop or notebook PC, so the page must be laid out accordingly (see Figure 10-15). If you anticipate your intended audience will access your site with these devices, you need to plan on modifying the appropriate content into a mobile format. In addition, some browsers are not able to display all of the multimedia elements you may wish to include. Because of this, it is a good idea to include links to sites where users can download any plug-ins that are necessary for your site, as well as the newest version of your recommended browser, for those users who might wish to upgrade their browser before exploring your site.

Assistive Technology

A second access consideration involves the site's ability to be accessed by users of *assistive technology*—hardware and software specially designed for use by individuals with physical disabilities. For example, visually impaired users may use a *Braille keyboard* or voice input system for input and a *screen reader* (software that reads aloud all information displayed on the computer screen) or *Braille display* (which converts all screen output into Braille form on the Braille display device attached to the keyboard) for output. Visitors with physical limitations may utilize alternative devices instead of the keyboard and mouse for input, such as using an onscreen keyboard controlled by breaths of air; a *head-pointing system* or *head mouse*, which controls an onscreen pointer using head movement; or a *foot mouse*, which controls the mouse pointer using foot movement. These and other assistive devices are discussed in more detail in Chapter 16.

Assistive technology affects Web page design because a site that is easy to navigate with as little clicking and scrolling as possible is easier for visitors using assistive input devices to access. In addition, some assistive hardware and software are not compatible with all types of Web content. For example, screen reading software and Braille displays can typically only read text-based data. In order for navigational images or other graphics to be understandable to visitors using these systems, the graphics must be identified with an *alternative text description*. This text can easily be added to a graphical image when the Web page is developed, but it is not always done. In addition to being accessed by screen readers, alternative text descriptions are displayed when the graphic is pointed to with a mouse or other pointing device (see Figure 10-16), as well as in text-only browsers and when graphics are turned off in a regular Web browser. Other features that make a Web page accessible to a broader audience include meaningful text-based hyperlinks—such as *How to Contact Us* instead of *Click Here*—and alternative content for Flash, JavaScript, or other animated components that may be incompatible with assistive technologies used by visitors. When some features included on a Web page make it simply not possible for users with screen readers to understand the content, an alternate text-based page can be made available for those users. Some characteristics of an accessible Web page are shown in Figure 10-16.

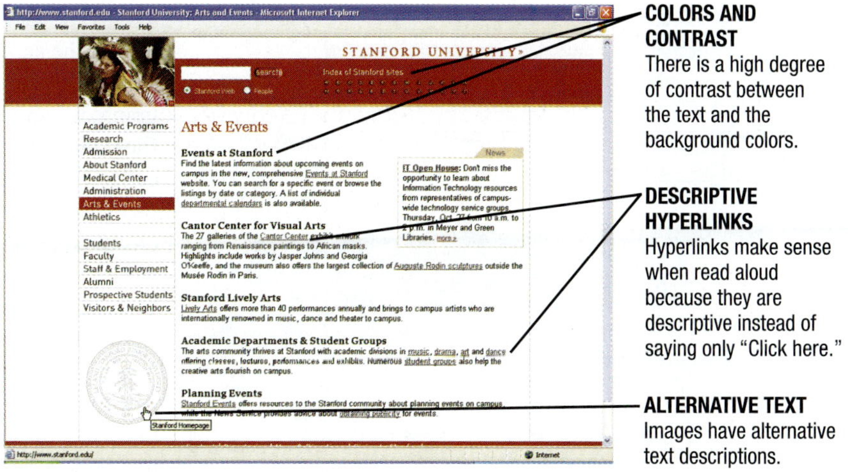

COLORS AND CONTRAST
There is a high degree of contrast between the text and the background colors.

DESCRIPTIVE HYPERLINKS
Hyperlinks make sense when read aloud because they are descriptive instead of saying only "Click here."

ALTERNATIVE TEXT
Images have alternative text descriptions.

FIGURE 10-16
Some Web page characteristics that are compatible with assistive hardware.

In 1998, Congress amended the *Rehabilitation Act* to require federal agencies to make their electronic and information technology accessible to people with disabilities, specifically to make it able to be used as effectively by people with disabilities as by those without. The law—typically referred to as *Section 508*, for the section number in the U.S. Code—applies to all federal agencies and, consequently, all federal Web sites. It was also hoped that passing this requirement would lead other companies to expand their Web content to make it more available to people with disabilities. As Tim Berners-Lee, the inventor of the World Wide Web, once said, "The power of the Web is in its universality. Access by everyone regardless of disability."

Several organizations have released guidelines for creating accessible Web sites, such as the "Web Content Accessibility Guidelines" by the World Wide Web Consortium (W3C). There are also Web sites that can be used to test Web accessibility. For example, the free online *Bobby* service tests Web pages for compliance with both Section 508 and the W3C Web accessibility criteria. Web sites passing the Bobby accessibility tests may display the Bobby Approved icon on their Web pages (see Figure 10-17), if they want to.

One additional accessibility concern for Web sites in the United States is usability by individuals with low literacy levels or whose native language is not English. A study released in late 2003 found that 90 million adult Americans have a low level of literacy, and 25 million primarily speak a non-English language. The study also found that 63% of federal Web sites have a 12th-grade readability level, while the average American reads at or below the eighth-grade level. Consequently, Web site developers should keep readability in mind when they evaluate the accessibility of their Web sites.

FIGURE 10-17
Web sites that pass the Bobby accessibility tests can display the Bobby Approved icon.

@WEB

MULTIMEDIA WEB SITE DEVELOPMENT

Once a Web site has been carefully designed, it is time to create it. This process is called *Web site development*. The development of a Web site can be performed in-house (if employees with the appropriate skills and appropriate software are available), or it can be outsourced to a professional Web developer. In either case, the development process of a multimedia Web site includes three basic steps:

- Creating the multimedia elements.
- Creating the Web site.
- Testing, publishing, and maintaining the site.

These three steps, along with the various types of software that can be used during each step, are discussed next.

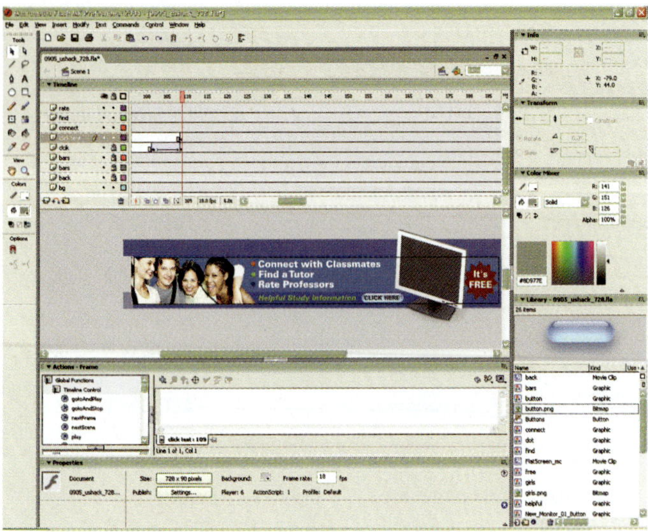

FIGURE 10-18
Macromedia Flash.

Creating the Multimedia Elements

Before the actual Web pages are created, it is a good idea to create all of the individual multimedia elements (such as graphics, animated components, video files, and audio files) that will be used in the site. To accomplish this, typically several different programs are used, such as graphics software to create or modify images, animation software to create animated elements, and audio editing and video editing software to create finished sound and video clips. These programs were discussed in detail in Chapter 6; one example—using Macromedia Flash to create an animated banner—is shown in Figure 10-18. As the elements are finished, they should be saved in the appropriate size, resolution, and file format so that they are ready to be inserted into Web pages or animation sequences.

Creating the Web Site

Most Web pages today are written in a **markup language**—a coding system used to define the structure, layout, and general appearance of the content of a Web page. When a markup language is used, *markup tags* are inserted around the Web page content to identify where elements are to be displayed and how they should look when displayed. JavaScript and other *scripting languages* can be used to add dynamic content to a Web page, and *Web site authoring software* is frequently used to create an entire site, tying together all the marked up Web pages, scripts, and multimedia elements contained within a site.

Hypertext Markup Language (HTML)

The original markup language designed for creating Web pages is **HTML** (**Hypertext Markup Language**). HTML files have the file extension *.htm* or *.html* and use *HTML tags*—text-based codes embedded into a Web page—to indicate where an effect (such as larger text, bolded text, or centering) should begin and where the effect should end. HTML tags are also used to specify where graphical images, hyperlinks, video clips, and so forth are to be located on the page. When a Web page is created—using a word processor, text editor, or Web site authoring program—the HTML tags are inserted in the appropriate locations within the Web page's text. Some tags are used alone; others appear in pairs. Common HTML tags are shown in Figure 10-19. For example, the HTML tag *<b>* turns bolding on for the text that follows the tag until the *</b>* tag is reached, so the HTML statement

<b> This text is bolded. </b>

would produce the following when viewed with most Web browsers

This text is bolded.

FIGURE 10-19
Sample HTML tags.

TAG	PURPOSE
<html> </html>	Marks the beginning and end of an HTML document.
<head> </head>	Marks the head section which contains the page title and meta tags.
<title> </title>	Marks the title of the Web page.
<body> </body>	Defines attributes of an HTML Web document, such as background color, background image, text color, margins, etc.
<h1> </h1> to <h6> </h6>	Formats headings larger or smaller than the regular text in the document; H1 is the largest text.
<img>	Indicates an image file to be inserted; includes attributes for filename, display size, alternative text, border, etc.
<a> </a>	Creates a hyperlink.
<b> </b>	Bolds text.
<i> </i>	Italicizes text.
<center> </center>	Centers text.
<hr>	Inserts a horizontal rule.
 	Inserts a line break (new line within the same paragraph).
<p>	Inserts a paragraph break (starts a new paragraph).

>**Markup language.** A language that uses symbols or tags to describe what a document should look like when it is displayed in a Web browser.
>**HTML (Hypertext Markup Language).** A markup language widely used for creating Web pages.

HTML tags are commonly used to perform tasks such as the following:

- Assigning a title to a page.
- Identifying text as a heading (for example, first-level head, second-level head, and so on).
- Marking the ends of paragraphs.
- Assigning a typeface, *relative size* (smaller or larger than normal-sized text, for instance), or font style (such as italic or bold) to text.
- Making text or images hyperlinks.
- Identifying where elements to be inserted into a Web page (such as graphics, animation, video clips, and sound files) should be displayed.
- Specifying the layout of tables and frames.
- Identifying keywords to be associated with the page (used by search sites).

It is important to realize that with a markup language like HTML, the Web browser, Web browser settings, and computer being used to display the Web page ultimately determine what the Web page will look like. For instance, if you use common fonts—such as Times New Roman and Arial—for your Web page text, those fonts will likely be installed on the user's PC and, if so, will be used to display the text of your Web page. But if you use a font that is not installed on the user's PC, an alternate installed font will be used instead. And, although you can specify font size when developing a Web page, the user can control the size of the text in his or her browser and the size of Web page text varies with the screen resolution used. These factors all contribute to the fact that you cannot be absolutely sure what your Web pages will look like on all users' PCs. A Web page and its corresponding HTML code are shown in Figure 10-20.

TIP

HTML tags are not case sensitive, so it does not matter if they are typed in uppercase or lowercase.

Extensible Markup Language (XML) and Extensible Hypertext Markup Language (XHTML)

XML (**Extensible Markup Language**) is a set of rules for exchanging data over the Web. It is called "extensible" because the data contained in XML documents can be extracted when needed and used in a variety of ways, such as combined to create new documents or used to display a single Web page on a variety of types of PCs or mobile devices. This is possible because XML focuses on identifying the data itself—not the format of that data. To accomplish this, *XML tags* are assigned to pieces of data (such as surrounding the name of a client or employee with the tag pair <name> </name>). There are no standard XML tags—the XML tags to be used in each organization are determined by that organization. Once the data is tagged and the document set up as an XML document, tagged data from a variety of XML documents—such as Web pages, word processing documents, and databases—can be extracted and reused as needed. Unlike other markup languages, XML is not used to control the formatting of a Web page or other document. Instead, the device being used to display the document displays it in a format appropriate for that device. XML is increasingly being used with ordinary business documents and company databases to allow easy retrieval of data by applications and easy updating, since the XML-tagged data can be easily updated without retyping.

XHTML (**Extensible Hypertext Markup Language**) is a newer version of HTML that is based on XML. Like HTML, XHTML is used to create Web pages, but it also supports XML, so XML-tagged data can be easily incorporated into XHTML Web pages.

TIP

Expect to see lots of XML in the near future. For instance, Microsoft has announced that the upcoming Office 12 suite will save documents in XML format by default, instead of the current DOC format.

>**XML (Extensible Markup Language).** A set of rules used for exchanging data over the Web; addresses only the content, not the formatting; the content displays in an appropriate format based on the device being used. >**XHTML (Extensible Hypertext Markup Language).** A newer, stricter version of HTML that is based on XML.

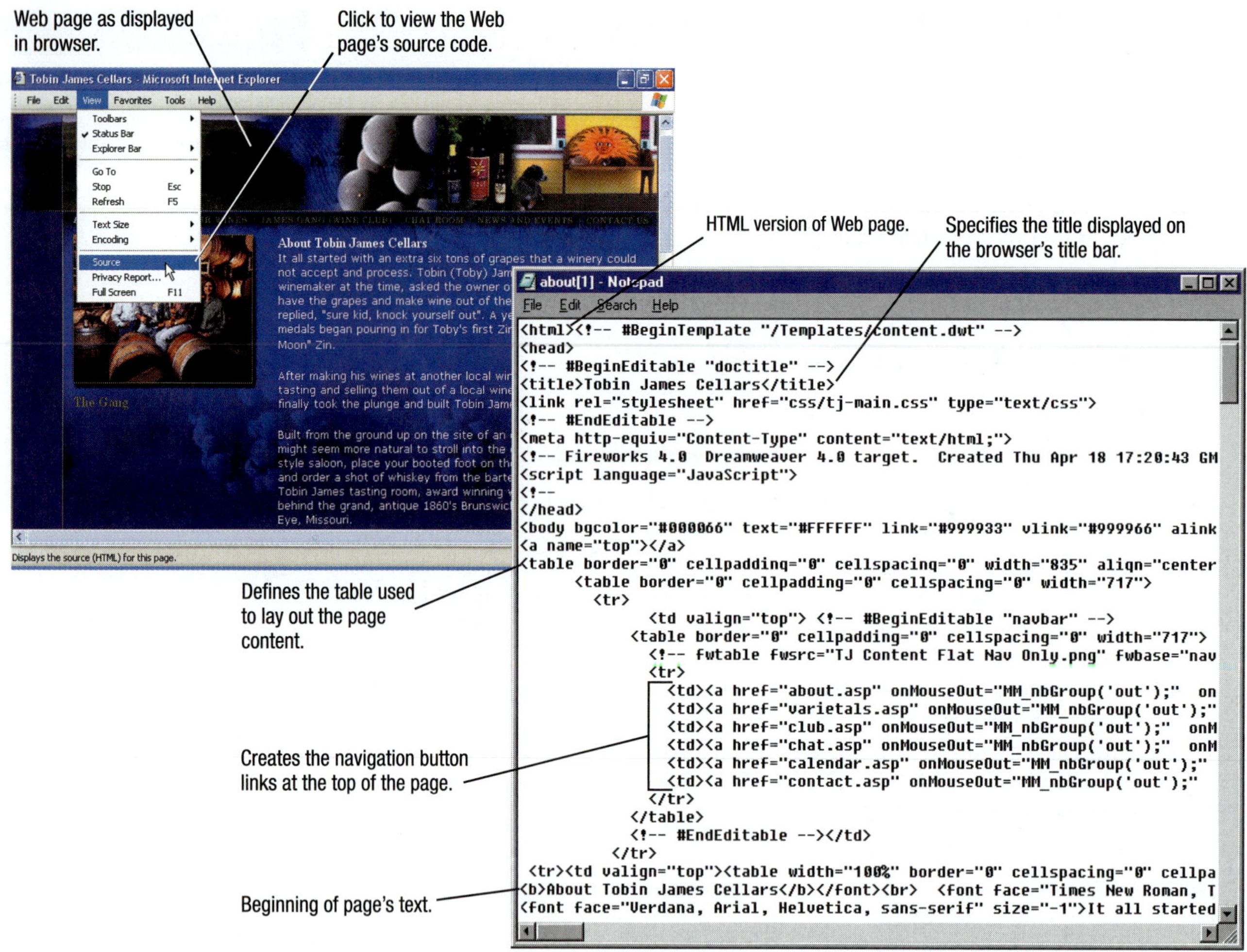

FIGURE 10-20
A sample HTML Web page.

When this occurs, XML controls the content displayed, and XHMTL controls the appearance and format of the Web page. XHTML tags are similar to HTML tags, but there are stricter rules about how the markup tags are written. For instance, all attribute values (such as filenames, numeric values, colors, and so forth) must be enclosed in quotation marks. In addition, all tags are written in lower case (since XHTML is case-sensitive), must be closed (have an ending tag), and must be in the proper order around elements. For example, the statement

<b><i>This text should be bold and italic</i></b>

must be used instead of

<b><i>This text should be bold and italic</b></i>

While this latter sequence would work in HTML, it will not work properly in XHTML. As long as the stricter rules are followed, however, basic HTML tags—such as the ones shown in Figure 10-19—can be used in XHTML Web pages. For instance, to follow the rule regarding closed tags, an open tag (such as <p> to indicate a paragraph break) must have a matching end tag (such as </p>); alternately, you can *self-close* an open tag by including a space and the forward slash in the opening tag (such as <p />), when this format is used, then a closing tag is not used. An example of an XHTML Web page is shown in Figure 10-21.

FURTHER EXPLORATION

For links to further information about XML and XHTML, go to www.course.com/uc11/ch10

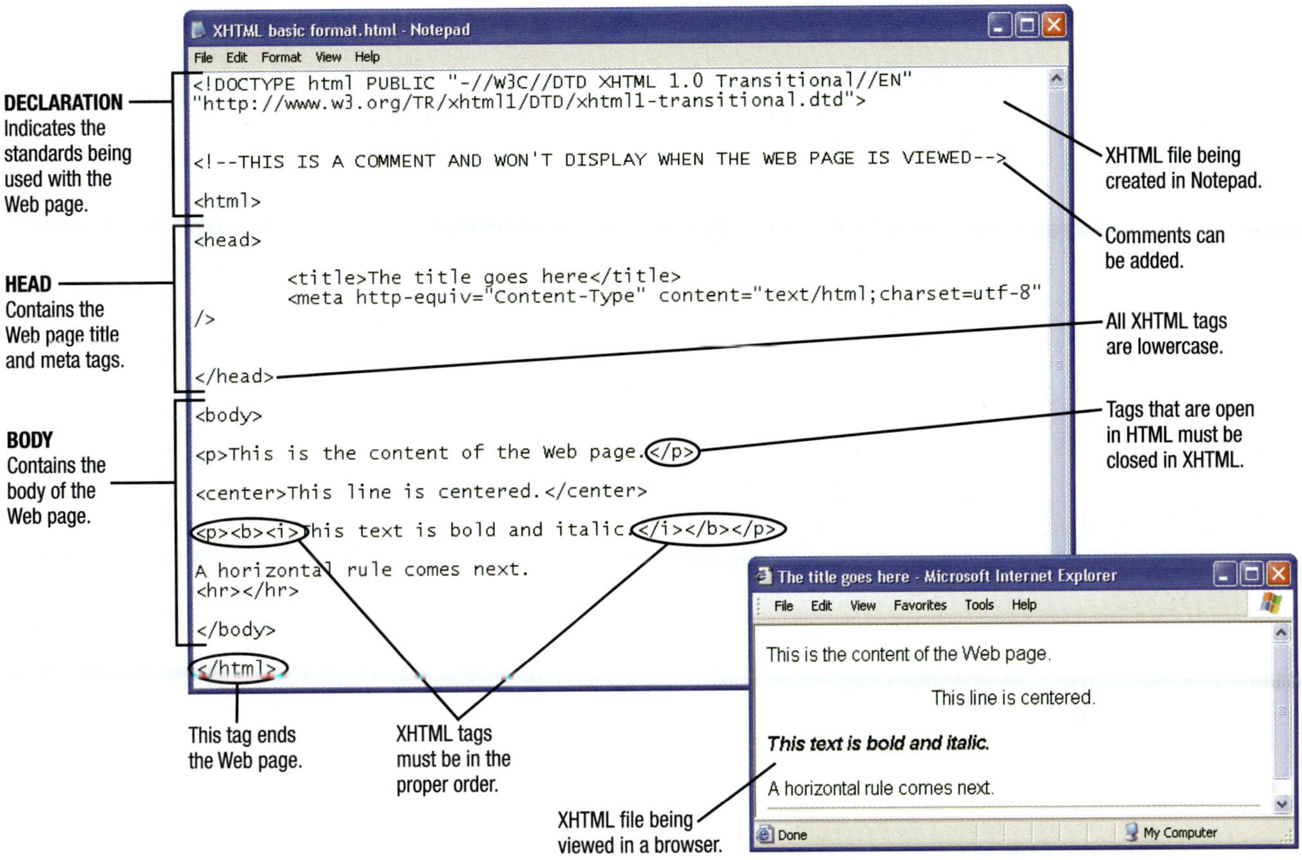

FIGURE 10-21
A sample XHTML Web page.

This example also illustrates the following three main sections of an XHTML Web page:

- A *declaration* statement at the top of the page that indicates the XHTML standard (*Document Type Definition* or *DTD*) being used (the *XHTML transitional* option used in Figure 10-21 supports the older HTML tags, as well as the newer XHTML elements). Notice the <html> tag at the end of the declaration statement is closed at the end of the Web page.
- A *head* statement that contains the title to be displayed on the browser's title bar when the Web page is viewed and any *meta* tags, such as to indicate the character encoding being used with the Web page or keywords to be associated with the Web page.
- The *body* (content) of the Web page.

Dynamic HTML (DHTML)

Dynamic HTML (DHTML) is used to add dynamic capabilities and interactivity to Web pages, such as objects that move, grow, shrink, appear, disappear, or change color based on the user's mouse actions. It enables Web page developers to create pages that change in layout and content without having to continually download new information from the Web server, making the page more exciting but still efficient. Versions 4 and higher of Netscape and Internet Explorer support some forms of DHTML.

WEB

>**Dynamic HTML (DHTML).** A form of HTML used to add dynamic capabilities and interactivity to Web pages.

Wireless Markup Language (WML)

Wireless Markup Language (**WML**) is a language used to create Web pages to be displayed on WAP-enabled wireless devices, such as a smart phones. To display Web content, a WAP-enabled browser—sometimes called a *microbrowser*—is used.

Scalable Vector Graphics (SVG) Format

Scalable Vector Graphics (*SVG*) is a markup language for describing vector-based images that are to be displayed *scalable*; that is, in varying sizes. Instead of displaying a Web page image in the same physical size regardless of the size of the browser window being used, SGV uses XML to adjust the display size of the images to match the size of the browser window in which they are displayed. Images that can be designated as scalable include JPEG and PNG images; images can also be converted to *SVG images* (which have the file extension *.svg*) in many image editing programs. There are also conversion programs available to convert images to the SVG format. Because it is a fairly new specification, all browsers do not support SVG and an *SVG viewer* may be required to view SVG images.

Scripting Languages

For Web pages with a great deal of dynamic content, a *scripting language* is typically used. Such languages enable you to build program instructions, or *scripts*, directly into a Web page's code to add dynamic content or database integration. Scripting languages are typically easy to use. Three of the most popular scripting languages are *JavaScript*, *VBScript*, and *Perl*.

JavaScript

JavaScript was originally developed by Netscape to enable Web authors to implement interactive Web sites (see Figure 10-22). Named JavaScript because it resembled the full *Java* programming language, JavaScript was developed independently from Java. When using JavaScript, it is important to realize that not all JavaScript commands work with all browsers, although it is compatible with both Netscape Navigator and Internet Explorer. Because of this, make sure that the important features you add to your site with JavaScript are not browser specific. JavaScript is commonly used to add interactive content to Web pages, such as pop-up windows, text, or other objects that are displayed when the mouse points to a particular object, button, or menu item on a Web page.

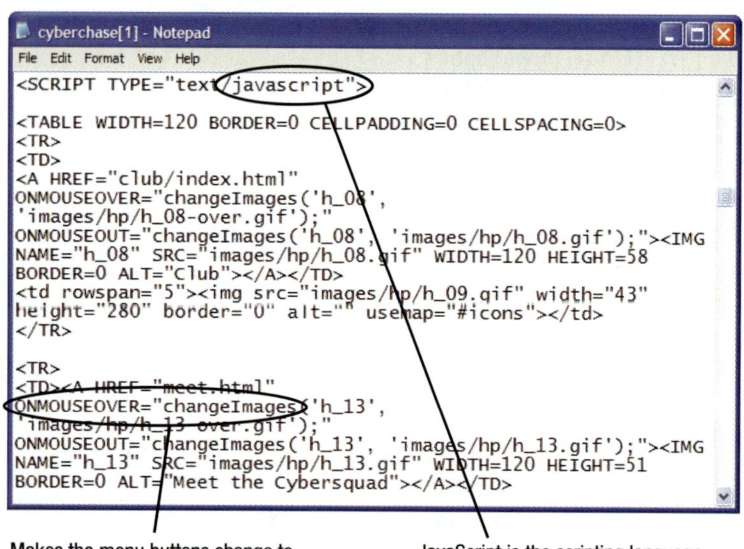

FIGURE 10-22
JavaScript. The JavaScript code here makes the menu images at the left of the Cyberchase Web page shown in Figure 10-10 change color as they are pointed to.

VBScript

Another scripting language in use today is *VBScript* (*Visual Basic Scripting Edition*), a scripting language developed by Microsoft that is based on the *Visual Basic* programming language. VBScript is used for similar purposes as JavaScript—it enables Web developers to include interactive elements, such as pop-up content, on their Web pages viewed with the Internet Explorer browser (VBScript commands are not compatible with Netscape Navigator and some other browsers). Individuals who are already familiar with Visual Basic can easily incorporate VBScript content into their Web pages.

>**Wireless Markup Language (WML).** A language similar to XML that is used with pages to be displayed on WAP-enabled devices.
>**JavaScript.** A scripting language widely used to add dynamic content to Web pages.

Perl

Short for *Practical Extraction and Report Language*, *Perl* was originally developed as a programming language designed for processing text. Because of its strong text-processing abilities, Perl has become one of the most popular languages for writing *CGI scripts*—scripts that are often used to process data entered into Web page forms tied to databases, as discussed in more detail in Chapter 14.

TIP

To avoid possible browser incompatibility problems, consider using browser-sniffing code in your Web pages that contain scripts to check to see which browser is being used and then run either a JavaScript script (for Netscape users) or a VBScript script (for Internet Explorer users).

AJAX

To better handle Web page interactivity, a new set of Web standards—called *Asynchronous JavaScript and XML* or *AJAX*, for short—has been developed. Already in use with a variety of Web sites—including to drive Amazon.com's A9 search feature, Google's Maps and Gmail services, and Netflix's moving ratings—AJAX uses a combination of HTML (or XHTML), JavaScript, and XML to create faster and more efficient interactive Web applications. Traditional interactive Web applications submit data from the user (such as via a form or search box) to a Web server, and then the Web server responds back by displaying a new Web page containing the appropriate information. Because the Web server must provide a new Web page each time user input is received, applications run relatively slowly. AJAX applications, on the other hand, request only new data and refresh the displayed Web page to include that data. To further speed things up, any actions that do not require new data from the server—such as validating user input—are handled within the AJAX application, instead of by the Web server. Consequently, interactive Web pages based on AJAX standards are much faster and more efficient than conventional interactive Web pages.

Other Content Development Tools

Two content development tools not yet discussed are *ActiveX* and *VRML*. These tools are commonly used in multimedia Web environments. Another useful Web development tool is the ability to create a *Web archive* in order to transmit an entire Web site at one time, such as via e-mail. Today, this is usually accomplished with *MHMTL*.

ActiveX

ActiveX, developed by Microsoft Corporation but compatible with most browsers today, is a set of *controls* that can be used to create interactive Web pages. Essentially, ActiveX extends *object linking and embedding* (*OLE*)—also developed by Microsoft and adopted widely as a standard by the software industry—to work on the Web. As discussed in Chapter 6, OLE permits you to integrate content from two or more programs, such as copying and either pasting or linking spreadsheet objects (a chart or group of cells, for instance) from a spreadsheet document to a word processing document. ActiveX, when used to implement OLE on the Web, allows you to view all types of Windows files with your Web browser. For instance, you can add word processing or spreadsheet documents to a Web page, and the appropriate program will be launched from within the Web browser when that page is viewed. It also enables your Web browser to play special content on Web pages; for instance, the Shockwave ActiveX control can play interactive multimedia presentations that are created in the Shockwave format.

ActiveX content can be virtually any type of object, such as a Java applet, a C++ program, an animation, or a PowerPoint presentation. Software that supports ActiveX sets up any such object as an interactive component on the Web page; ActiveX is essentially the "glue" that holds the different page components together. What ActiveX in effect allows Web publishers to do is grab files from their hard drives that are suitable for the Web and drop them directly into Web page documents. Such a capability is especially useful for office intranets, for which a great deal of potential Web page content may already exist in the form of office documents. To view ActiveX content, your browser must either directly support it or have access to an appropriate plug-in.

@WEB

Virtual Reality Modeling Language (VRML) and X3D

Short for *Virtual Reality Modeling Language*, *VRML* is a specification for displaying three-dimensional objects on Web pages. It is essentially the 3D equivalent of HTML. Files written in VRML have the extension *.wrl* (short for "world"). To view VRML files, you need a VRML-compatible browser, such as Internet Explorer with a VRML plug-in. VRML objects—cars, homes, and other photo-realistic 3D objects, for instance—can be rotated as desired, to be viewed from any angle. An example of a VRML application (touring a model home by moving the mouse in the desired direction) was shown in Figure 10-1.

The newest version of VRML is *X3D*. X3D includes support for the latest developments in professional graphics, as well as support for XML and other more recent technologies.

MHTML (MIME HTML)

MHTML (*MIME HTML*) is a format for transmitting all the elements of a Web site (text, graphics, animation, audio, and video) together as a single file. The MHTML file (also referred to as an *encapsulated aggregate HTML document*) uses the *MIME* standard to keep track of the individual elements contained in the file so they can be sent via e-mail. MHTML files use the *.mht* or *.mhtml* file extension. Many application programs today support the MHTML standard.

Web Site Authoring Software

Web pages can be created by typing the page's text, HTML tags, JavaScript code, and other needed content in any word processor or text editor. For instance, the XHTML Web page shown in Figure 10-21 was created in the Notepad program. However, creating complex Web pages (such as those containing tables, frames, animation, or input forms that are linked to a database) in this manner is a very difficult task. **Web site authoring software** (also called *Web site development software*) makes the job of creating Web pages and complete Web sites much easier (see Figure 10-23). Instead of entering the HTML tags by hand, most Web site authoring programs automatically generate the appropriate HTML statements when options are selected from menus, toolbar buttons are clicked, or the developer otherwise specifies what the Web page should contain and look like. Similarly, as menu options are selected, the appropriate JavaScript, DHTML, or other code used to add animation or interactivity is generated. In addition, Web site authoring programs virtually always have the capability to include a wide variety of other multimedia elements, such as Shockwave and Flash animations, animated GIFs, video clips, and audio clips. Some of the most popular Web site authoring programs are *Adobe GoLive*, *Microsoft FrontPage*, and *Macromedia Dreamweaver*.

Another benefit of using a Web site authoring program is that it allows you to create an entire cohesive Web site—not just individual pages. For instance, effects, styles, backgrounds, and navigational tools can be applied to an entire site at one time, saving time and increasing consistency at the same time. In addition, many Web site authoring programs allow you to easily include forms and database connectivity for more dynamic interactions with your visitors, and include other helpful development tools, such as tests for *broken links* (links to nonexistent Web pages) and accessibility tests. Once the entire site is created, the program can be used to quickly publish the entire site onto the appropriate Web server.

>**Web site authoring software.** A type of application program used to create Web pages and complete Web sites.

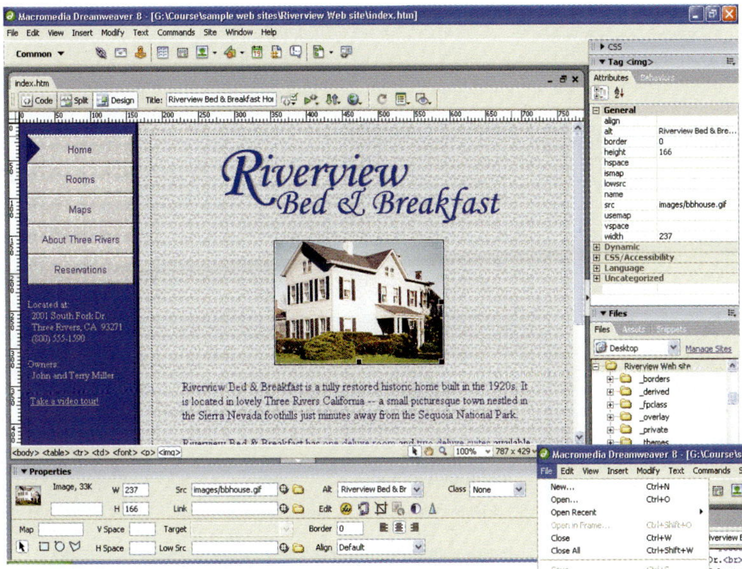

WYSIWYG EDITING

Most Web site authoring programs allow you to create Web pages as you would in a word processing program–inserting graphics, formatting text, and so on using a menu and toolbar buttons. Typically, hyperlinks, tables, forms, and other elements can be easily created, and video clips, animated objects, and other multimedia elements can be easily inserted.

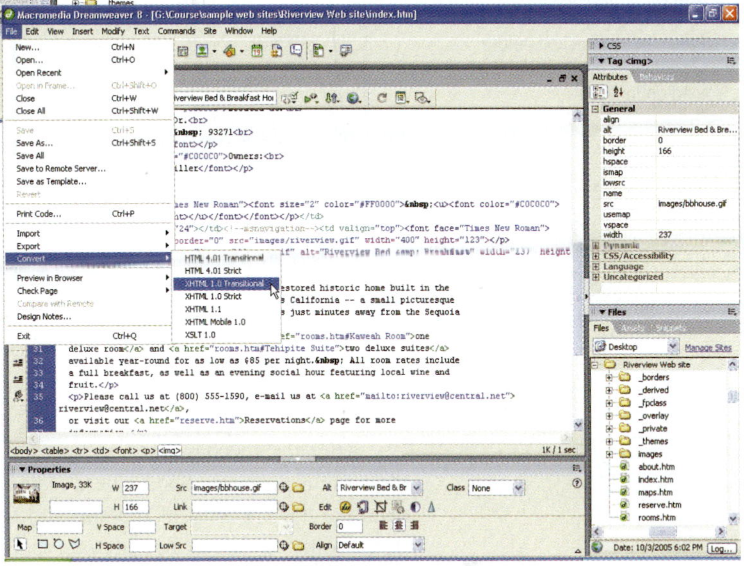

CODE EDITING

Some Web site authoring programs allow you to view the Web page's HTML or XHTML code to edit it, if desired. Web page code can also usually be converted, such as from HTML to XHTML, as shown here.

FIGURE 10-23

Web site authoring software.

Testing, Publishing, and Maintaining the Site

Once a multimedia Web site has been created, it must be thoroughly tested before allowing it to go "live" by publishing it to a Web server. Each and every hyperlink needs to be clicked to ensure it takes the user to the proper location, and every possible action (such as clicking or pointing to) that could take place with an animated element should be tested. Complex animations (such as games and tutorials) should be tested individually before they are inserted into the Web page; after inserting the animation into a Web page, that page should be tested to ensure the animation works correctly. Web page code can be tested in some Web site authoring programs, as well as via some Web page validators, such as the XHTML validator shown in Figure 10-24.

Ideally, Web site testing should take place on a variety of computers using different operating systems, browsers, and screen resolutions, and with a diverse selection of users. The testers should be a variety of ages and have a wide range of computer abilities. If possible, an observer should discretely watch the testers and take note of any point during the testing that users seem confused or end up somewhere they did not intend to go. Finished Web pages should also be checked for spelling and grammatical errors. Your application should appear professional, so be sure to proofread each page or screen carefully. Many Web site authoring programs include spelling and hyperlink checkers to assist you with testing, but these electronic tools should not replace careful proofreading and testing.

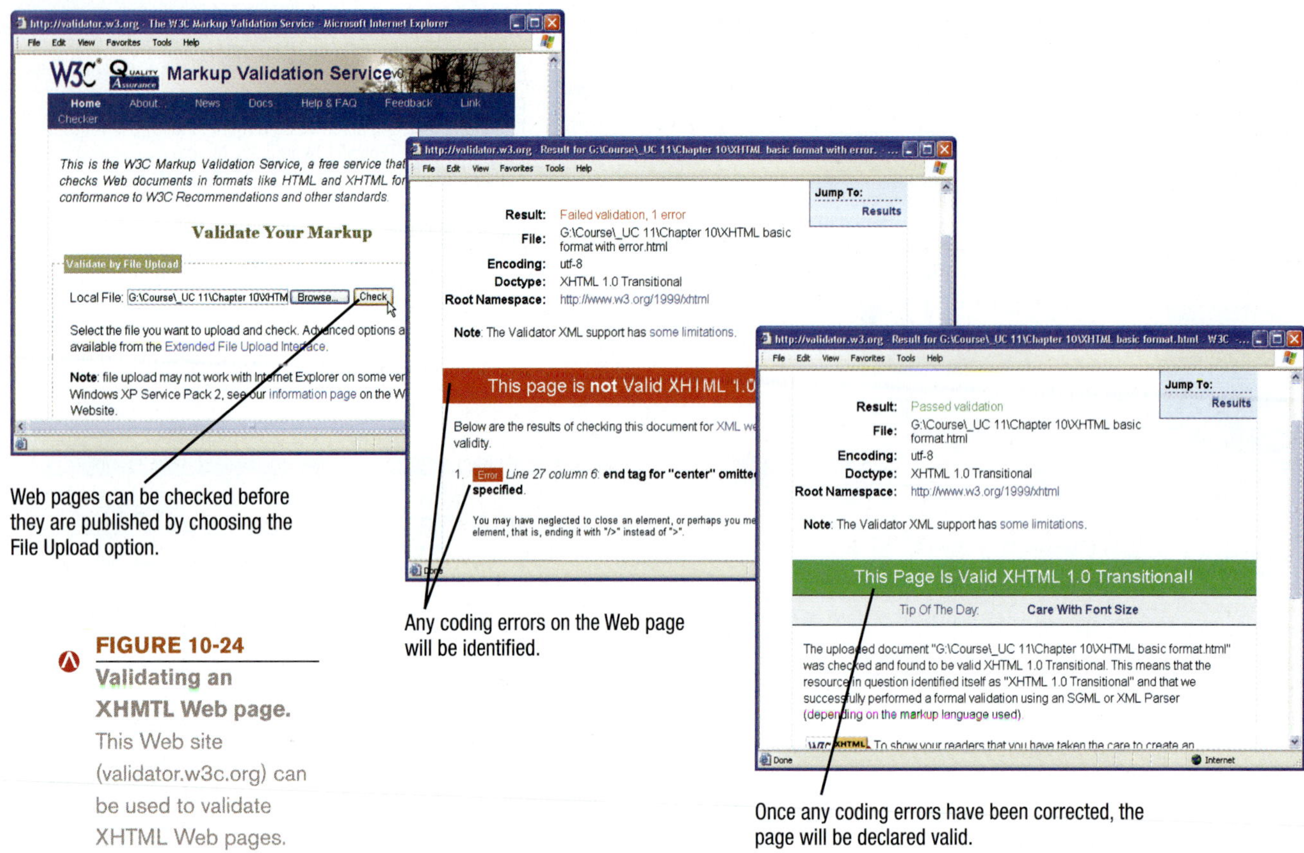

FIGURE 10-24

Validating an XHMTL Web page.

This Web site (validator.w3c.org) can be used to validate XHTML Web pages.

After the mechanics of a Web site are tested, companies should consider subjecting their site to a "stress test." These tests are frequently performed by an outside agency and examine the capacity of the site and how many visitors and orders it can handle at one time. Some stress testing software is also available, and there are also software programs an organization can use to continuously monitor its site for problems and bottlenecks, as well as chart usage (such as which hyperlinks are clicked most often and how long each Web page is viewed).

Once a site is thoroughly tested, it is ready to be *published*; that is uploaded to the appropriate Web server. For a look at how a basic Web site can be published, see the How it Works box. Once a site is up and running, the maintenance phase begins. As mentioned earlier, Web sites should be regularly updated to keep them current and interesting. Web sites should also be evaluated on a regular basis to locate areas needing improvement, new problems that have become apparent, and so forth. Hyperlinks to external Web sites need to be checked on a regular basis because the pages could be moved or become inappropriate for that link. If, at some point, it appears that the site needs a major overhaul, the design and development process should start over from the beginning.

THE FUTURE OF WEB-BASED MULTIMEDIA

Although no one knows exactly what types of multimedia will be available in the future, it is a safe bet that it will be even more exciting and more embedded into everyday events than at present. New types of multimedia will likely be developed to fit our growing need for mobile content and, as Internet users continue to move to broadband, expect to see multimedia Web sites and television merge even more closely together. Game boxes (such as Xbox, Sega Dreamcast 2, and Sony PlayStation 2) already have some built-in Internet and multimedia capabilities, and interactive TV and video-on-demand may soon be the norm on the Web.

HOW IT WORKS

Publishing a Web Site

Once a Web site is completed, it needs to be *published* (a copy uploaded) to a Web server before it can be viewed by others via the Internet. Many organizations have their own Web servers; if that is the case, the organization's Web sites would be published to its Web server. Individuals can often publish Web sites on Web servers belong to their ISPs (often without an additional charge for small personal sites); they can also sign up for free or fee-based Web hosting, such as via the free Web hosting site shown in the accompanying screen shots. Students are sometimes permitted to publish personal Web pages on a school Web server while they are enrolled at the school.

Once the Web server to be used has been identified, all of the content in the Web site (including the HTML files, all image files, any animation files, and so forth) need to be published to the Web server. Depending on the program used to create the Web site and the particular Web server being used, the site may be able to be published from within the Web site authoring program used to create the site, published via *File Transfer Protocol* (*FTP*), or published via online tools located on the host's Web site. The accompanying screen shots illustrate the latter option—the user logs onto the host's Web site, and then uploads all content into his or her folder on the host's Web server.

To view the site once it has been published, the URL associated with the site needs to be typed, including the domain name being used (often the domain name for the host, unless the user has purchased a domain name to use with the site), the proper folder name (if applicable), and the filename of the home page of the site. For instance, to view the home page named XHTMLbasicformat.html stored in the morleyuc11 folder on the FreeWebs.com Web server, the URL http://www.freewebs.com/morleyuc11/XHTMLbasicformat.html would need to be typed in the Address bar of a Web browser. To avoid having to type the home page filename (XHTMLbasicformat.html, in this example) to view that Web page, most Web servers are set up to have a default filename for the home page, such as index.html. If this is the case and the home page is named accordingly, the home page of the site can be viewed by just typing the domain name and folder name (http://www.freewebs.com/morleyuc11), as shown in the final accompanying screenshot.

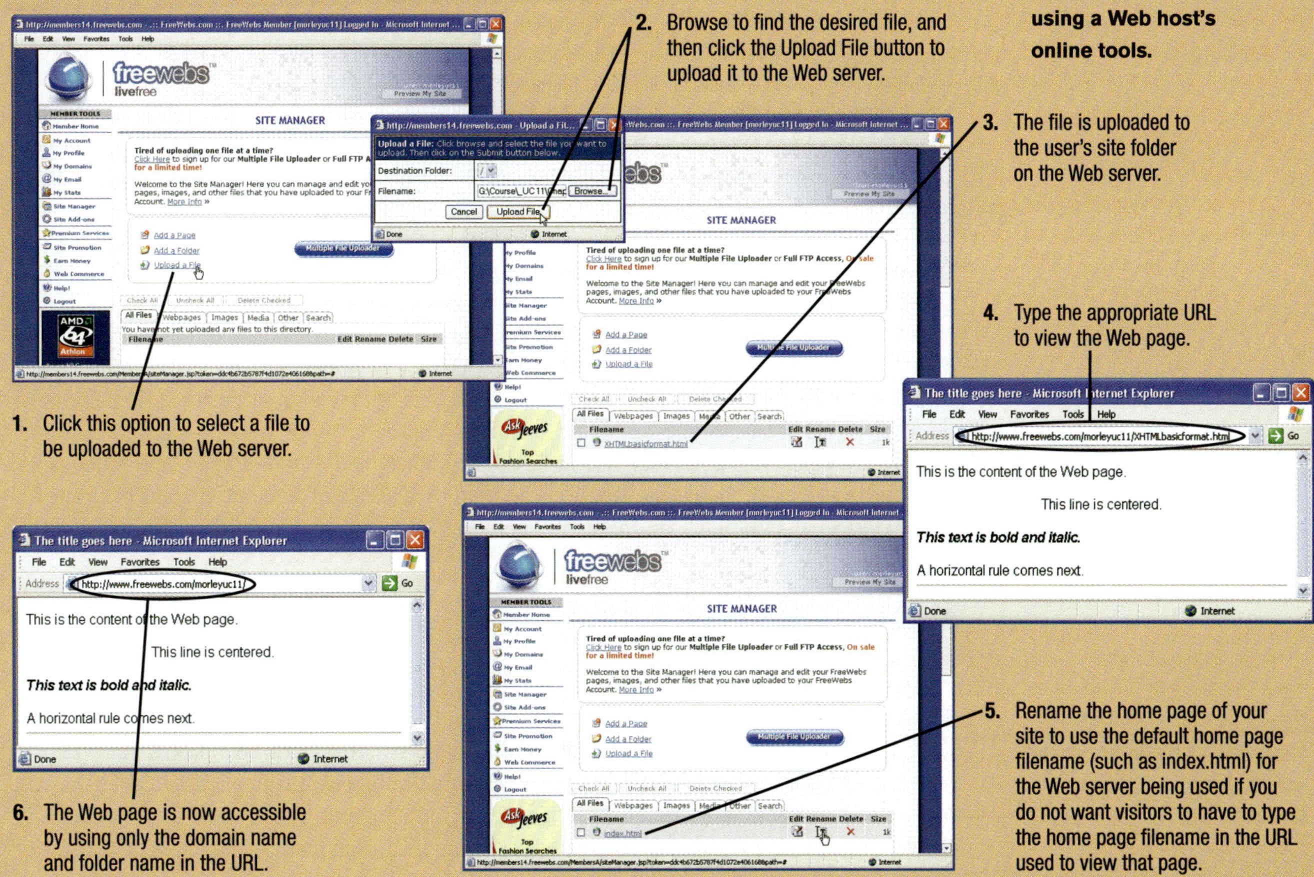

Publishing a Web site using a Web host's online tools.

SUMMARY

WHAT IS WEB-BASED MULTIMEDIA?

Chapter Objective 1: Define Web-based multimedia and list some advantages and disadvantages of using multimedia.

Multimedia is the integrated use of more than one type of media, such as text, graphics, video, animation, and sound. Multimedia applications are usually *interactive*. With today's fast computers and Internet connections, multimedia applications are frequently found on Web pages, such as for information delivery, e-commerce, entertainment, or Web-based training (WBT) purposes. Some Web pages today use **virtual reality (VR)** to create environments that look like they do in the real world.

One major advantage of using multimedia is that it appeals to a wide variety of people and complements different learning styles. Multimedia tends to hold users' interest more than single media applications, and it makes some ideas easier to convey. Disadvantages associated with Web sites that use multimedia are cost and issues related to differing platforms, browsers, and Internet connection speeds.

MULTIMEDIA ELEMENTS

Chapter Objective 2: Describe each of the following multimedia elements—text, graphics, animation, audio, and video—and tell how they differ.

Multimedia applications typically contain **text** in a variety of typefaces and appearances. Text is used to deliver content, as well as for instructions, menus, hyperlinks, and more. *Serif typefaces* are commonly used for large sections of text; *sans serif typefaces* are more frequently used with titles and headings. When a consistent text appearance is important for Web pages, the text is often rendered as a **graphic**, so it will look the same for all users. Other types of graphics include photographs, drawings, charts, and other static images. Already created **clip art** and *stock photographs* are widely available for purchase or for free, and many are available for downloading via the Internet.

Common graphic formats include **GIF** (*Graphics Interchange Format*) and **PNG** (*Portable Network Graphics*) for line art images, and **JPEG** (*Joint Photographic Experts Group*) for photographs. Other possible formats include *TIF* for scanned images and *BMP* for Paint images. When creating images for Web pages, the most appropriate format—as well as the needed physical size and the smallest file size—should be used. For Web pages that include large images, **thumbnail images**—small images that are linked to the full-quality larger images—can be used.

Animation consists of a series of graphical images displayed one after the other to simulate movement. **Java applets**, **animated GIFs**, *Dynamic HTML* (*DHTML*), and *JavaScript* Web applications are examples of animation. **Flash** animations are also common on Web pages today. Some animated elements require a *plug-in* to be viewed. **Audio** includes all types of sound (such as music, spoken voice, and sound effects), and **video** is a continuous stream of visual information captured by a series of separate images or frames. Audio, video, and graphics are frequently compressed to reduce the finished file size.

MULTIMEDIA WEB SITE DESIGN

Chapter Objective 3: Briefly describe the basic steps and principles involved with multimedia Web site design.

When designing a multimedia Web site, careful planning is essential to ensure an interesting and intuitive site that is attractive and easy to use. Web pages should also be efficient and versatile enough to be used with multiple browsers and platform configurations. Early steps in the design process include determining the primary objectives, intended audience, basic layout, and navigational structure for the site or application. Tools, such as **flowcharts**, **page layouts**, and **storyboards**, can be used during the design process. Features that require a specific browser or infrequently used plug-ins should be avoided whenever possible; high-bandwidth items should be used in moderation and should be user-controlled (such as providing a hyperlink for users to click if they wish to view a video file), if possible. There are a number of navigational tools, such as drop-down menus, *site maps*, search boxes, *image maps*, *frames*, and navigation bars, that can be used when creating the navigational structure of the site. In addition, compatibility with the various devices that might be used to access the site, as well as with assistive hardware, should be considered.

MULTIMEDIA WEB SITE DEVELOPMENT

Once a multimedia Web site is designed, the development process can begin. Necessary tasks include creating the multimedia elements to be used in the site, creating the site itself, and testing and publishing the finished product.

Chapter Objective 4:
List the various tasks involved with multimedia Web site development.

To create multimedia elements, graphics software, animation software, and audio and video editing software can be used. Once the individual elements have been created, they can be inserted into Web pages.

Web sites can be created with a **markup language**, such as **HTML** (**Hypertext Markup Language**), which uses *HTML tags* to indicate text characteristics, page layout, hyperlinks, and more. Other markup languages include **XML** (**Extensible Markup Language**), **XHTML** (**Extensible Hypertext Markup Language**), **Dynamic HTML** (**DHTML**), and **Wireless Markup Language** (**WML**). Additional tools for creating Web pages include *scripting languages* such as **JavaScript**, as well as *AJAX*, *ActiveX*, and *VRML*. **Web site authoring software** can also be used to more easily create the site and tie all the site elements together.

Chapter Objective 5:
Explain how markup languages, scripting languages, and other tools are used today to create multimedia Web pages.

After the site has been completed, it must be thoroughly tested to ensure all features and links work, and that it is compatible with as many different types of computers, platforms, operating systems, and browsers as possible. When it is ready to go live, it is *published* on a Web server. The site then needs to be maintained on a regular basis.

THE FUTURE OF WEB-BASED MULTIMEDIA

In the future, multimedia will likely be even more commonplace and integrated into our everyday lives. Trends, such as the convergence of TV and the Internet, will lead us in that direction. How fast this evolves depends, in part, on how soon fast home broadband Internet access becomes the norm.

Chapter Objective 6:
Discuss the possible format of Web-based multimedia in the future.

REVIEW ACTIVITIES

KEY TERM MATCHING

Instructions: Match each key term on the left with the definition on the right that best describes it.

a. animation

b. flowchart

c. GIF

d. JavaScript

e. JPEG

f. markup language

g. multimedia

h. video

i. XHTML (Extensible Hypertext Markup Language)

j. Web site authoring software

1. _______ A continuous stream of visual information broken into separate images or frames to be displayed one after the other to simulate the original visual event.

2. _______ A graphics format that supports 256 colors and is commonly used for Web page line art images.

3. _______ A graphics format that supports true color and is commonly used for photographs inserted in Web pages.

4. _______ A language that uses symbols or tags to describe what a document should look like when it is displayed in a Web browser.

5. _______ A newer, stricter version of HTML that is based on XML.

6. _______ A scripting language widely used to add dynamic content to Web pages.

7. _______ A tool that can be used during the Web design process to illustrate how the pages in a Web site relate to one another.

8. _______ A type of application program used to create Web pages and complete Web sites.

9. _______ The integration of a variety of media, such as text, graphics, video, animation, and sound.

10. _______ The process by which a series of graphical images are displayed one after the other to simulate movement.

SELF-QUIZ

Instructions: Circle **T** if the statement is true, **F** if the statement is false, or write the best answer in the space provided. **Answers to the self-quiz are located in the References and Resources Guide at the end of the book**.

1. **T** **F** One advantage of multimedia Web pages is that they are visual, and this is an advantage because all people are visual learners.

2. **T** **F** Clip art images are predrawn graphics that can be inserted into Web pages.

3. **T** **F** A stock photograph can be used to add animation to a Web page.

4. **T** **F** A flowchart of a Web site illustrates the pages on the site and their relationships to one another.

5. **T** **F** A markup language is typically used to create the animated elements of a Web page.

6. A(n) _______ image can be used to display a full-sized, high-quality image only to the visitors that wish to see it.

7. _______ audio and video files, in which the file begins playing before it has been completely downloaded, are frequently used on Web pages to make their delivery more efficient.

8. One of the first steps in designing a multimedia Web site is to determine the _______ and _______ of the site.

9. _______ software is commonly used to create a multimedia Web site, tying all of the components together into a finished site.

10. Match the acronym or term from the numbered list to its description and write the corresponding number in the blank to the left of each description.

a. ________ A type of animation where a series of images are displayed one after the other to simulate movement, and the entire set of images is saved together in one file.
b. ________ A format commonly used for audio files.
c. ________ A program used in conjunction with a Web browser that enables a multimedia element on the page to work.
d. ________ A scripting language often used to add Web page animation.
e. ________ A markup language for describing scalable vector-based images.
f. ________ A graphics format in which the level of compression can be specified.

1. .mp3 **3.** JPEG **5.** plug-in
2. animated GIF **4.** JavaScript **6.** SVG

EXERCISES

1. Match each acronym to its description and write the corresponding number in the blank to the left of each description.

a. ________ The original markup language used to create Web pages.
b. ________ A markup language that is used with pages to be displayed on mobile devices.
c. ________ The markup language that is similar to HTML but that is newer and has much stricter rules.
d. ________ A set of rules for exchanging data over the Web.

1. WML **2.** XHTML **3.** HTML **4.** XML

2. Suppose that you want to create a Web site to share your favorite short stories with the world. You have decided that the intended audience is anyone interested in reading great fiction, and you would like the site to contain two of your original stories, some personal information about yourself, and a list of your favorite short story Web sites. Draw a possible flowchart for this site.

3. For the site illustrated in the flowchart to the right, sketch one possible page layout for the home page of the site.

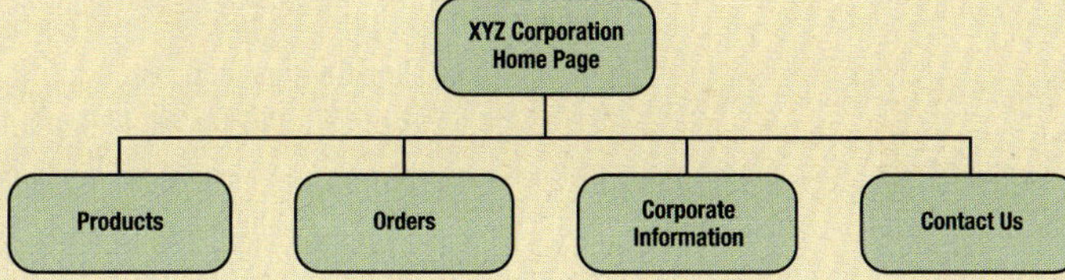

4. List three types of software programs that might be used when creating a Web-based multimedia Web site. Explain what each program would be used for and list one example (program name and publisher) of each.

@ WEB

5. If the Web site authoring program you are using has a tool that checks for broken links (links to nonexistent Web pages), explain why you still need to check the links by hand. Name one situation in which a hyperlink would not be identified as a broken link by a Web site authoring program, but would still be wrong and could only be detected by a human tester.

DISCUSSION QUESTION

Neuromarketing—the study of the brain's responses to advertising—is a somewhat controversial, but growing, new marketing trend. Neuromarketing companies can help businesses analyze their marketing materials by wiring the scalps of volunteers with electrodes and studying their responses as they view commercials, view print ads, experience new products, and so forth. Since neuromarketing data can reveal the feelings and emotions of a volunteer, instead of just the preferences he or she expresses, it can provide valuable information to companies. But neuromarketing is not without its critics. Some organizations have waged a campaign against the practice, fearing the corporate manipulation of consumers. Do you think neuromarketing is a viable business tool? Should there be any regulations governing its use? If a company decided to use this technology to better market a product to you, would you object? What if the government used it to determine the best way to deliver public service messages—would that be any different? How about using it for political purposes?

PROJECTS

HOT TOPICS

1. **RIAA File Sharing Lawsuits** Beginning in 2003, the Recording Industry Association of America (RIAA) began filing hundreds of lawsuits against individuals suspected of "egregiously" swapping copyrighted music via file sharing networks, such as Kazaa and Morpheus. In one of the first cases to be settled, the family of a 12-year-old New York girl agreed to pay $2,000. Other settlements required defendants to pay between $3,000 and $17,000. In the words of the RIAA chief executive, "We're trying to send a strong message that you are not anonymous when you participate in peer-to-peer file sharing and that the illegal distribution of copyrighted music has consequences." As discussed in the chapter, the recent focus of RIAA lawsuits has been college students.

   For this project, research the current status of the RIAA lawsuits. Have most been settled, or are there new suits being introduced on a regular basis? Is there still talk of a "download tax" to be added to the purchase of goods (such as computers, MP3 players, CD-R discs, and related hardware) and services (such as ISP accounts) that will be used to reimburse musicians and copyright holders for music traded and downloaded online? What precautions must a Web site developer take when including music on a Web site to ensure copyright law is not violated? Are there any other related issues a Web developer needs to consider when selecting multimedia content for a Web site? At the conclusion of your research, prepare a one-page summary of your findings and submit it to your instructor.

SHORT ANSWER/ RESEARCH

2. **Section 508** As discussed in the chapter, Section 508 is a section in the U.S. Code that refers to requirements for making electronic and information technology accessible to people with disabilities.

   For this project, research Section 508 and the Rehabilitation Act in general to see how the law applies to Web site design and to whom the law applies. If you were to set up a personal or small business Web site, would you be legally obligated to conform to Section 508 regulations? If not, what would be the advantages and disadvantages of conforming anyway? What types of features or modifications does a Web site need to include to be Section 508 compliant? How would one go about testing to see if a Web site was Section 508 compliant? Prepare a one-page summary of your findings and submit it to your instructor.

3. **Multimedia Plug-Ins** In order to view multimedia over the Web, you may need to download one or more browser plug-in programs, such as a Flash or Shockwave player, the Acrobat Reader program, or a media player program.

   For this project, locate two different Web sites that require plug-ins for multimedia content (you can try news or television network sites for video and audio clips, Internet radio sites, sites that allow you to play songs or view music videos, and sites that feature interactive games, such as the PBSKids.org Web site). Try to access the multimedia content (such as viewing or listening to a clip or playing a multimedia game) to see if you have the proper plug-in installed. If you cannot access the content, make a note of the type of content, what plug-in is required, and whether or not the site contained a link to obtain the proper plug-in. If you are using your own PC, download and install the plug-in and record how easy the installation process was and whether or not the content was available immediately after the plug-in was installed (do not do this on a school PC). If you can access the content, make a note of the type of content, the required plug-in, and whether or not being able to experience that content was beneficial and enhanced your experience of visiting that site. At the conclusion of your research, prepare a one-page summary of your experience and findings and submit it to your instructor.

HANDS ON

4. **Using XHTML** As discussed in the chapter, all that is needed to create a basic Web page is a text editor or word processing program and a basic knowledge of HTML or XHTML coding.

For this project, locate a Windows-based PC (such as one at home, in a campus computer lab, or at your public library) that you are allowed to use and perform the following tasks.

a. Open the Notepad program (usually located under *Accessories* on the Start menu) and type the XHTML code shown to the right to create a basic Web page. Be sure to type all text and XHTML tags exactly as shown, substituting your name for the (*your name*) placeholder.

```
<!DOCTYPE html PUBLIC "-//W3C//DTD XHTML 1.0
Transitional//EN"
"http://www.w3.org/TR/xhtml1/DTD/xhtml1-transitional.dtd">

<html>

<head>
        <title>Sample Web page</title>
        <meta http-equiv="Content-Type"
content="text/html;charset=utf-8" />
</head>

<body>
<center><h1>(your name)'s Sample Web Page</h1></center>
<hr></hr>
<i>This Web page shows some introductory XHMTL tags.</i>
<hr></hr>
My favorite search site is <a
href="http://google.com">Google</a>.
</body>

</html>
```

b. Save your file as *My Web page.html* on a removable storage medium or in a folder on the hard drive or network drive you are allowed to use. Leaving the Notepad program open, use Windows Explorer to locate your saved file, and then double-click the file to open your Web page in your browser.

c. Compare your Web page to the one shown to the right to see if everything looks correct (page title on browser's title bar; size, formatting, and alignment of text; Google hyperlink; and so on) then, if you are connected to the Internet, click on the Google hyperlink to make sure it works. If you find any errors, return to Notepad, make the corrections, save the file again, and refresh the display in your browser window to display the new page.

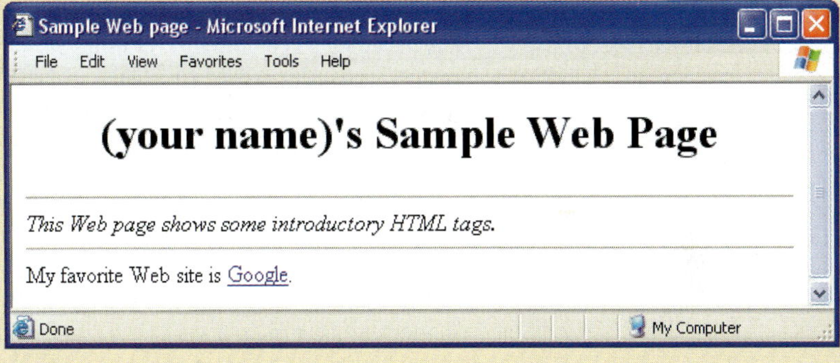

d. Once your Web page is correct, return to Notepad and edit the code to change the second sentence in the Web page ("This Web page...") to be centered and bold, in addition to being italic (refer to the table of sample HTML tags in Figure 10-19, if needed). Save the file again and refresh the display in your browser window to display the revised page.

e. Print your finished Web page to turn in to your instructor.

@ WEB

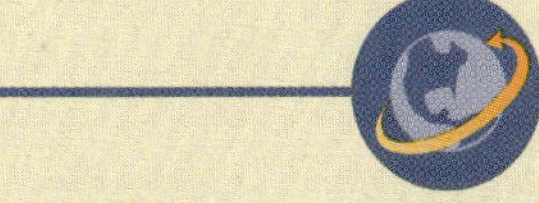

5. **Free Images** Many Web sites have free clip art or animated GIF images available for download.

For this project, use a search site to find a Web site (such as Clip-Art.com or The Free Graphics Store Archives) that offers free images. Select one clip art image and one animated GIF and download them to a removable storage medium or a folder on the hard drive or network drive you are allowed to use. How did you download the file? After downloading, open the two images by clicking them one at a time in Windows Explorer. In which program did each image open? Was it the same program for both images? Was the GIF animated? At the conclusion of this task, prepare a short summary including the site used, images downloaded, and answers to the questions listed above, and then submit it to your instructor.

WRITING ABOUT COMPUTERS

6. **Online News** Many news sites today are continually updated throughout the day and contain an abundance of audio and video clips, in addition to images, Webcasts, animations, and other mutimedia components.

For this project, visit at least two news Web sites (such as MSNBC.com, CNN.com, or CBSNews.com), investigate the types of multimedia features they offer, and evaluate their usefulness. Do the components work smoothly and add value to your experience? What are the advantages to using an online news site, as opposed to radio or television news broadcasts? Are there any disadvantages? If you wanted to find out about a national news item, would you turn to your local newspaper, a radio or TV news broadcast, or an online news site? Why? Do you think online news coverage is more balanced, less balanced, or the same as offline news counterparts? Submit your opinion on this issue to your instructor in the form of a short paper, not more than two pages in length.

PRESENTATION/ DEMONSTRATION

7. **Web Hosts** Once you have created a Web site, it needs to be published to a Web server in order to be available via the Internet. Web-hosting options include using a free Web-hosting service, publishing the site on your ISP's Web server, or paying to post a site on a Web server.

For this project, suppose you are starting your own business and have created a small Web site. Investigate your Web-hosting options, identifying one ISP that offers Web hosting, one free Web-hosting service, and one fee-based Web-hosting service. For all three possibilities, determine the cost, if any, and if there is a limit on the size of the site, amount of traffic generated, or other restrictions. For the selected ISP, determine whether or not free Web hosting is included in the monthly fee and, if so, is it just for personal sites, or can subscribers post a business site? Share your findings and opinions with the class in the form of a short presentation, including a demonstration of using one of the Web-hosting services, if possible. The presentation should not exceed 10 minutes and should make use of one or more presentation aids, such as the chalkboard, handouts, overhead transparencies, or a computer-based slide presentation (your instructor may provide additional requirements). You may also be asked to submit a summary of the presentation to your instructor.

GROUP DISCUSSION

8. **Digitally Altered Photos** Using a computer and graphics software, manipulation of images is much easier today than in the past. Artistic examples include recent photographs of New York that include some hint of the World Trade Center Twin Towers added to them; beneficial uses include aging the photo of a runaway or kidnap victim for easier identification. Less noble examples include putting a celebrity's head on another person's nude body and altering prisoner photographs before posting them on a pen pal site so the convicts do not look like they are in prison.

For this project, look through magazines, newspapers, Web sites, or other media to locate two examples of digitally altered photographs. You may need to compare two photographs of the same person or location to notice subtle alterations, such as changing an individual's eye color, removing wrinkles, or erasing an offending tree or building from a photograph. Make a photocopy of each example and indicate on each copy what manipulation you believe was performed. For each example, decide if you think the manipulation is ethical or unethical and why you think it was done. Was the photograph altered to mislead the public? For artistic purposes? To make a statement? To entertain us? Form an opinion of using a computer to digitally alter photographs and be prepared to discuss your position (in class, via an online class discussion group, or in a class chat room, depending on your instructor's directions). You may also be asked to write a short paper expressing your opinion.

WEB ACTIVITIES

The ***Understanding Computers*** Web site located at **www.course.com/uc11** features many resources to help reinforce your understanding of the chapter content and help you prepare for exams. Your instructor may also assign specific activities to be completed that will count toward your final grade in the course.

Instructions: Go to **www.course.com/uc11/ch10** to work the following online activities.

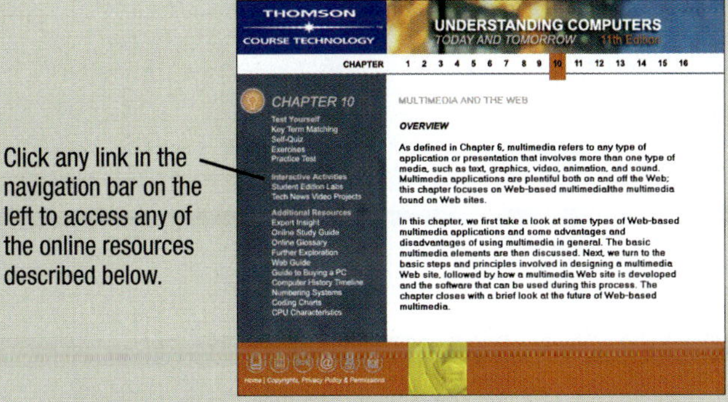

INTERACTIVE ACTIVITIES

1. **Crossword Puzzle** Practice your knowledge of the key terms in Chapter 10 by completing the interactive Crossword Puzzle.
2. **Tech News Video Project** Watch the **"The Army's Virtual World"** video clip that takes a look at the U.S. Army's latest training simulator—a Web-based virtual Baghdad that soldiers can use to become familiar with the area before deployment to Iraq, as well as to train for various wartime scenarios (such as a terrorist bombing or a surprise attack at a checkpoint). Each soldier is represented by an avatar and interacts with other avatars, manned by real people located throughout the world. After watching the video online, complete the corresponding project.
3. **Student Edition Labs** Reinforce the concepts you have learned in this chapter by working through the interactive **Working with Graphics**, **Working with Audio**, and **Working with Video** labs.

Student Edition Labs

@WEB

TEST YOURSELF

1. **Key Term Matching** Test your knowledge of selected chapter key terms by matching the terms with their definitions.
2. **Self-Quiz** Test your retention of chapter concepts by taking the Self-Quiz.
3. **Exercises** Work these short exercises to review the concepts and terms covered in the chapter.
4. **Practice Test** Test how ready you are for an upcoming exam by completing the online Practice Test.

STUDY TOOLS/ ADDITIONAL RESOURCES

The Understanding Computers Web site has a wide range of additional resources, including an **Online Study Guide** (containing study tips, a chapter outline with room to add your own notes, and a chapter checklist of the activities to complete when the chapter is covered in class and when you are preparing for a test) and an **Online Glossary** for each chapter; **Further Exploration** links; a **Web Guide**, a **Guide to Buying a PC**, and a **Computer History Timeline**; more information about **Numbering Systems**, **Coding Charts**, and **CPU Characteristics**; and much, much more!

CHAPTER 11 E-Commerce

OUTLINE

Overview
What is E-Commerce?
- Advantages of E-Commerce
- Disadvantages of E-Commerce

Types of E-Commerce Web Sites
- Manufacturer and E-Tailer Web Sites
- Brokerage Sites

E-Commerce Business Models
- Business to Consumer (B2C)
- Business to Business (B2B)
- Consumer to Consumer (C2C)
- Business to Government (B2G)
- Intermediary Hubs

Implementing Web-Based E-Commerce
- Step 1: Select Appropriate Business Models and Types of Web Sites
- Step 2: Select the Desired E-Commerce Applications
- Step 3: Develop Procedures for Handling Electronic Financial Transactions
- Step 4: Design and Develop an Effective Web Site
- Step 5: Implement Appropriate Sales and Marketing Strategies

Security Issues

LEARNING OBJECTIVES

After completing this chapter, you will be able to:

1. Explain what e-commerce is and describe some of the advantages and disadvantages involved with implementing e-commerce.
2. Discuss the types of Web sites that can be used to implement e-commerce.
3. Identify a variety of e-commerce business models and discuss their differences.
4. List several strategies for implementing e-commerce using the Web, including some of the decisions that need to be made, the options available for accepting payments, and the process of designing and developing an effective Web site.
5. Outline some sales and marketing strategies that can be used in conjunction with an e-commerce Web site.
6. Discuss some security issues related to e-commerce transactions.

OVERVIEW

The Internet and World Wide Web have greatly affected the way most of us live and do business. Frequently named as the fastest-growing sector of the Internet economy, Web-based e-commerce (electronic commerce)—the act of doing business transactions over the Internet—is redefining the way businesses operate and compete in the 21st century. It has been estimated that over 50,000 U.S. companies make some or all of their money online, and it is predicted that Internet-based revenue in the United States alone will exceed one trillion dollars annually by 2012. In addition, the Web influences offline sales, such as the scores of consumers who use the Web to research purchases they eventually make offline.

This chapter initially examines some of the potential advantages and disadvantages of e-commerce, to both businesses and consumers. It also covers the various types of e-commerce Web sites and e-commerce business models. Among other things, you learn the meaning of Internet buzzwords, such as "B2B" and "e-tailer." Then, we turn to the issues a business needs to consider if it plans to implement Web-based e-commerce. These issues include the type of business model and Web site to be used, how to handle the financial transactions generated via the Web site, and how to design and develop an effective e-commerce Web site. The chapter closes with a look at sales and marketing strategies for e-commerce Web sites and a discussion of e-commerce security issues. ■

WHAT IS E-COMMERCE?

E-commerce is the term used to describe conducting business transactions—generally financial transactions—via communications technology. Although the term *e-commerce* is most often used today in conjunction with the Internet, large corporations have been conducting e-commerce for decades using private networks. For example, the banking industry has carried out *electronic funds transfers (EFT)* for many years. The collection of hardware, software, people, policies, and strategies used to perform and support e-commerce is referred to as an *e-commerce system.*

The past few years, e-commerce in the United States has continued to grow at a steady pace. According to the U.S. Census Bureau, online sales grew 26% from 2004 to 2005 and total about 2.2% of all retail sales. Many expect this trend to continue, such as comScore Networks vice president Michelle David Adams, who recently stated, "E-commerce will continue to outgrow traditional retail, as the Internet appeals to growing numbers of consumers in search of the best deals, convenience, and breadth of offerings." Forrester Research predicts that e-commerce will make up about 13% of all retail sales by 2010 and, according to Leadpile, e-commerce sales have the potential to make up 25% of all sales in the United States by 2012. *M-commerce—mobile commerce*, such as using a cell phone or mobile

>**E-commerce.** The act of doing business transactions over the Internet or similar technology.

ADVANTAGES	DISADVANTAGES
To businesses	*To businesses*
• Reduced costs • Increased customer satisfaction • More effective management tools • Potentially higher sales	• Must have an effective, always-working Web site • Lost business, since some people will never perform online transactions • High rate of fraudulent transactions • Recurrent threat of new competitors offering lower prices
To customers	*To customers*
• Convenience • Easier comparison shopping • Higher degree of selection • Potential cost savings	• Potential for fraud • Buying goods without seeing them in person • Possible expensive returns

FIGURE 11-1
Potential advantages and disadvantages of e-commerce.

device to pay for goods or services—is also growing. In the United States, m-commerce reached $13 billion in 2005 and is expected to grow to nearly $60 billion by 2007. A new *u-commerce* (*universal commerce*) trend being strongly supported by Visa is also on the rise. For more information about m-commerce and u-commerce, see the Technology and You box.

There are many advantages and some disadvantages involved with implementing an e-commerce system. Some of the more prominent are listed in Figure 11-1 and discussed in the next few sections.

Advantages of E-Commerce

There are many advantages to both a business and that business's customers for implementing an e-commerce strategy. Most of these advantages center on convenience and efficiency. A few of the most significant advantages are listed next.

To Businesses

The primary advantages to businesses include reduced costs, increased customer satisfaction, more effective management tools, and potentially higher sales.

The primary cost reductions are due to smaller facilities and lower staffing requirements. *Internet-only stores* particularly benefit from these cost reductions because they do not have the expenditure of maintaining a physical storefront, like conventional **brick-and-mortar stores** do. Internet-only stores are often called **dot-coms** because they typically have a *.com* top-level domain in the URL used to access their Web site. Even though dot-com stores need a company headquarters and possibly one or more inventory warehouses, these types of facilities are much less expensive to operate than retail stores that may need to have a physical presence in multiple prime locations in order to reach potential customers. Many businesses have both brick-and-mortar stores and an online store. These businesses are sometimes referred to as *click-and-mortar stores*. Other potential areas of cost reductions associated with e-commerce include eliminating middlemen and selling directly to customers, using electronic means (such as e-mail announcements and Web site ads) instead of mailed materials for marketing activities to save on postage costs, and increased accuracy in order processing and pricing.

Increased customer satisfaction is another potential advantage to businesses for using e-commerce. Convenience is a big factor in determining whether or not a customer is satisfied—with a properly set up e-commerce Web site, the customer should find the process of shopping and obtaining information very convenient. Online stores are open *24/7/365* (24 hours a day/7 days a week/365 days a year) so customers can shop at their convenience. They also do not have to drive to a physical location to pick up their purchases since purchases are typically shipped directly to the customers' homes or businesses. Gifts can also often be shipped directly to the recipient—an added convenience for the buyer.

Another possibility for increased customer satisfaction is the ability to send customers personalized information, such as notices of specials on products they might be interested in, notification when an out-of-stock product becomes available, and regularly updated

>**Brick-and-mortar store.** A conventional store with a physical presence. >**Dot-com.** An Internet-only store with no physical presence.

TECHNOLOGY AND YOU

M-Commerce and U-Commerce: Steps Towards a Cashless Society

Imagine your parking meter calling you on your cell phone to ask if you want to add another hour to it while you are shopping. Or you may have seen the television commercial in which a young lady presses a button on her cell phone to get a Coke from the vending machine. Surprising? Perhaps, but the technology is in place for cashless transactions for small purchases, such as from *smart vending machines*. For instance, with the "Dial-a-Coke" vending machine shown in the accompanying photo, sodas can be purchased with a compatible cell phone and the charge is added to the user's cell phone bill. These types of purchases are referred to as *m-commerce* (*mobile commerce*), and proponents predict it will lead us toward a cashless society. Although debit, credit, and check cards have helped to move us in this direction, until recently it was difficult to buy a soda or pay for parking without cash. With m-commerce, consumers can use their mobile phone (or other wireless device, such as a handheld computer) to pay for goods and services, from buying a soda or movie ticket with a cell phone to using a pocket PC to pay for groceries or a fast-food order.

Another m-commerce tool is the *wallet phone*—a cell phone that stores *digital wallet* data, including a cash balance that can be used to pay for goods and services instead of charging each m-commerce transaction to your cell phone bill. While wallet phones are slow to reach the United States, their use is growing in other countries. For instance, the Japanese mobile provider NTT DoCoMo launched a new mobile wallet service called *FeliCa* in late 2004 that allows subscribers to use their mobile phones as credit cards, ID cards, train passes, and door keys. DoCoMo has sold over 5 million of these wallet phones, and about 20,000 stores so far have installed the equipment to allow customers to make payments using their phones. SK Telecom, South Korea's top mobile operator, offers a similar *Moneta* wallet phone service—subscribers can use their cell phones to facilitate credit card transactions, transportation fee payments, cash withdrawals, and stock trading. For added convenience, payment capabilities are becoming integrated into other consumer products, such as wristwatches. For instance, tests of the *Offica Watch*—a wristwatch that contains employee ID, access control, and electronic payment functions—began in Japan in 2004. It is designed to be used within a corporate campus to access facilities and charge purchases at the company cafeteria. A commercial product based on this technology is expected to be released in the near future. In Spain, implanted RFID *VeriChips* are being used for the first time for electronic payments—regular patrons at a nightclub in Barcelona, Spain, can use an implanted VeriChip to charge their purchases to their house accounts.

Examples of types of m-commerce that are currently available in the United States include the *Speedpass* and *ExpressPay* systems (in which a small keychain-sized RFID wand is waved at a gas pump, a grocery store register, or a fast food register to automatically pay for purchases) and electronic toll collection (in which drivers can drive the legal speed limit past an electronic toll booth and the toll is automatically deducted from the cash balance associated with their cars' smart tags). Most major credit card companies are in the process of introducing credit cards with embedded RFID chips so that small purchases—typically less than $25—can be charged to the credit card by just waving the credit card close to a special RFID-enabled credit card reader.

A step beyond m-commerce that is expected to help move us even closer to a cashless society is *u-commerce*. U-commerce (*universal commerce*)—thought by many to be the next natural progression for e-commerce and m-commerce—continues to move these activities from the "point of sale" to "point of convenience"—wherever and whenever a financial transaction needs to occur. With u-commerce, transferring funds electronically via your PC, PDA, smart phone, or other electronic device is expected to continue to get easier and easier. It is predicted that this convenience will facilitate activities such as instructing your PC to automatically pay a bill on its due date, transferring funds to your secretary for your share of an office gift, ordering lunch and paying the taxi fare during the cab ride to a restaurant, or buying a movie or lottery ticket from a public kiosk at the mall. With u-commerce, these types of transactions can take place seamlessly regardless of the time of day, physical location, or currency and payment device being used.

online order information. These types of *customer relationship management* (*CRM*) activities are discussed later in this chapter and in more detail in Chapter 12. Because e-commerce transactions are performed electronically, another benefit to businesses is the possibility of capturing a wide variety of customer data via Web site activities. This data can be used in conjunction with an organization's information systems to give immediate feedback on sales and performance measures, as well as to identify trends and patterns, as discussed in more detail later in the chapter.

There is also enormous potential for increased sales with e-commerce since there are no geographical boundaries for a customer base. Instead of serving a specific geographical area, businesses can now offer their goods or services worldwide. There are fewer physical restraints to growth, as well. When increased business strains the organization's sales department, e-commerce businesses can just add more electronic facilities (such as a more powerful server) and as many new internal employees as necessary to handle the resulting transactions, instead of having to build new physical stores or other expensive, time-consuming solutions.

To Customers

Advantages to customers include convenience, easier comparison shopping, a higher degree of selection, and potential cost savings.

As already mentioned, e-commerce is a tremendous convenience for those customers who take advantage of it. They can shop from their homes or offices at any time of the day or night and have the products delivered to the appropriate locations, usually within just a few days. If the appropriate online customer service tools are in place, they can also check on the status of their orders, track the delivery shipment, obtain reports of their past purchases, and so forth. E-commerce is especially convenient when individuals are ill or otherwise would prefer not to go to a retail establishment, such as during inclement weather or busy shopping times.

Many customers like to comparison shop before purchasing products or signing up for certain services. With a brick-and-mortar business, this requires physically going to the store to look at the selections available, or at least calling and gathering information over the telephone. With e-commerce sites, however, information on a wide variety of products and services through a wide variety of vendors is available over the Internet. The increased number of merchants to choose from and the ability to comparison shop mean that online shoppers often save money, although not all products available over the Internet are less expensive than those in their brick-and-mortar counterparts. Many comparison shopping Web sites—sometimes called *shopping bots*—are available to gather prices, shipping, and delivery information from multiple sites for a particular product and summarize the results to help locate the best buys from potential vendors. Some portal pages offer this service; others sites, such as MySimon.com and PriceGrabber.com (see Figure 11-2), are dedicated to this purpose. In addition to being able to compare prices from a variety of online retailers, online shoppers have the opportunity to choose from a much wider selection of products than can be provided by brick-and-mortar stores. Because of the enormous number of products and services available via the World Wide Web, chances are that at least one online store will carry the item of interest, and it usually does not matter where that store is physically located. Another potential cost savings is the lack of sales tax on some online purchases, although that may change in the future if a mandatory Internet sales tax is implemented.

Disadvantages of E-Commerce

E-commerce is not without disadvantages and risks, for businesses or consumers. Despite the disadvantages and risks to businesses or consumers, e-commerce is expected to continue to become an integral part of our society. A few of the most significant disadvantages and risks are listed next.

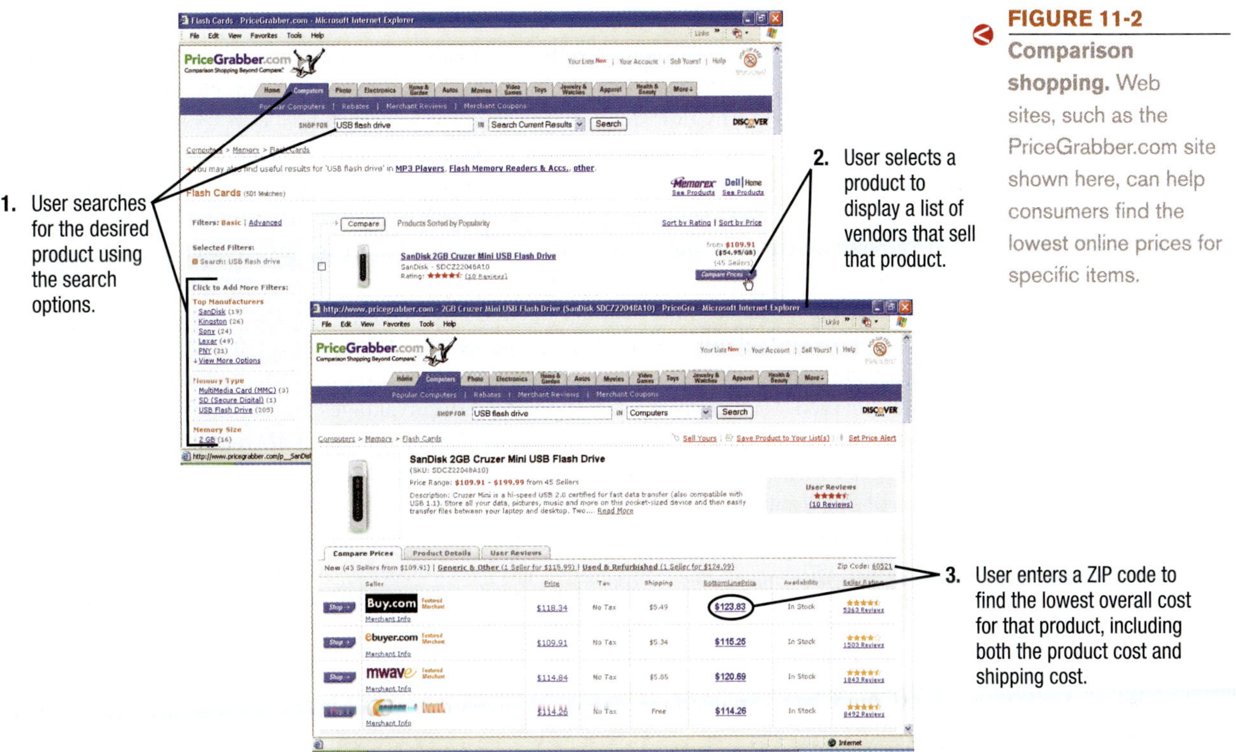

FIGURE 11-2
Comparison shopping. Web sites, such as the PriceGrabber.com site shown here, can help consumers find the lowest online prices for specific items.

To Businesses

One disadvantage of doing a significant amount of your business through an online presence is that sales can only take place when your Web site is up and running. The "always open" nature of e-commerce puts enormous pressure on online businesses to have solid, well-designed, and reliable Web sites and Web hosting setups. A Web site that is offline, is not working properly, or that is simply too slow or disorganized can drive potential customers away in a hurry. Another disadvantage is the possibility of lost business since some individuals will choose to never perform financial transactions over the Internet. Without a brick-and-mortar store or some other acceptable alternative, those individuals' business can never be obtained. A third disadvantage is the risk of fraudulent credit card transactions. One study found that Internet credit card transactions were 1,200% more likely to be fraudulent than conventional credit card transactions. Improvements in credit cards—such as adding smart card capabilities to better authorize transactions or more secure credit cards—will likely help to reduce fraudulent charges. The secure credit card prototype shown in Figure 11-3 is being developed by IBM and contains a tiny numerical keypad located on the card. Each time the card is to be used, the user enters his or her PIN number, and then the card generates and displays a one-time-only transaction code. Because each transaction code can only be used once and the credit card cannot be used without a transaction code, the credit card is more secure than a conventional credit card and might help to prevent identity theft and credit card fraud.

FIGURE 11-3
Secure credit cards. This card, which generates a unique one-time transaction code each time it is used, is currently in development by IBM.

Another disadvantage for e-commerce companies is the ease of entry into the marketplace for competitors. While large brick-and-mortar businesses may not be threatened by a new "mom and pop" business opening in the area, small online businesses with low overheads may open up a storefront relatively inexpensively and attract business away from other organizations by undercutting their prices. If the new business has a professional-looking, well-designed Web site, consumers may never realize how small or new the company is. Of course, from the perspective of the new business, this is an opportunity, not a risk.

@WEB

To Customers

Perhaps the biggest disadvantage from a customer standpoint is the risk of fraud and other potential security problems. From placing an order with a nonexistent company, to having your credit card information stolen from a legitimate company's Web server, the opportunity for fraud exists when transactions take place online or through a company that stores purchase information on a computer that is potentially accessible to a hacker. In addition to the actual risk of fraud and other problems, the fear of a problem resulting from an e-commerce transaction may put a damper on the online shopping experience for some consumers. Improvements, such as *buyer protection programs*, will likely reassure online shoppers. For instance, many online auction sites today offer free buyer protection for items up to a certain dollar amount if the items do not arrive or are not as advertised, and most credit card companies today offer 100% protection against fraudulent online purchases charged to a credit card. Other potential disadvantages include not being able to see and touch goods in person before purchasing them—emerging *3D online shopping* capabilities in which customers can view products in three-dimensions may help to overcome some of this limitation. Another possible risk is the expense of returning merchandise the consumer finds unacceptable. Some click-and-mortars, such as Old Navy, Circuit City, Best Buy, and Barnes & Noble, eliminate this concern by allowing consumers to return merchandise they ordered online to a local store in order to avoid return shipping charges.

TYPES OF E-COMMERCE WEB SITES

A variety of Web site types are used for e-commerce activities. Some of the most widely used are manufacturer and *e-tailer* Web sites and brokerage sites.

Manufacturer and E-Tailer Web Sites

Both manufacturers and online retailers—often called **e-tailers** or *e-retailers*—can sell directly to customers via their Web sites (see Figure 11-4). The customers may be consumers, businesses, or the government. Web sites that sell goods online are sometimes referred to as *electronic storefronts*. Most often, these sites feature an online catalog from which items are selected, and orders can be placed directly at the site. Items are then either shipped to the buyer (for physical goods), the buyer is allowed to download the product (for electronic products, such as software, music, and e-books), or the service is activated. Some manufacturers are leaning toward not selling products directly on their sites because of the conflict of interest with retail partners. To avoid this problem, those manufacturer's Web sites typically focus on product information and customer service, leaving the actual selling of their products to their online and offline retailers.

TIP

To monitor the status of several online auctions at one time, use the online auction site's *watching* feature, if one is available. By logging into the online auction site and displaying your personalized page, you can see the current status of the items you are watching and bidding on.

Brokerage Sites

Brokerage sites bring buyers and sellers together to facilitate transactions between the two parties. Instead of selling products or services directly to an individual or business, brokerage sites earn revenue in the form of commissions on sales made via the site. Three examples of brokerage sites are discussed next.

Online Auctions

Consumer-oriented **online auction sites**, such as eBay and Yahoo! Auctions, provide individuals with a structured medium for selling goods and services to other individuals. These

>**E-tailer.** An online retailer. >**Brokerage site.** A type of Web site used to bring buyers and sellers together to facilitate transactions, such as online stock trading and exchanging goods, services, and commodities. >**Online auction site.** A Web site where potential buyers bid on an item and, at the end of a set time period, the highest bidder buys the item as long as all bidding criteria, such as minimum selling price, have been met.

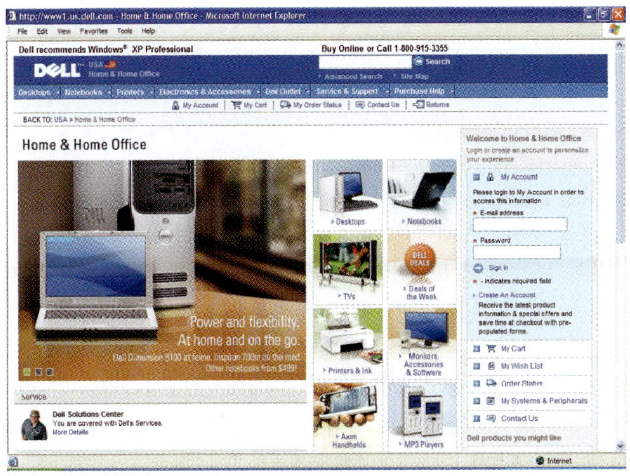

MANUFACTURER WEB SITES
Sell their own products directly to customers.

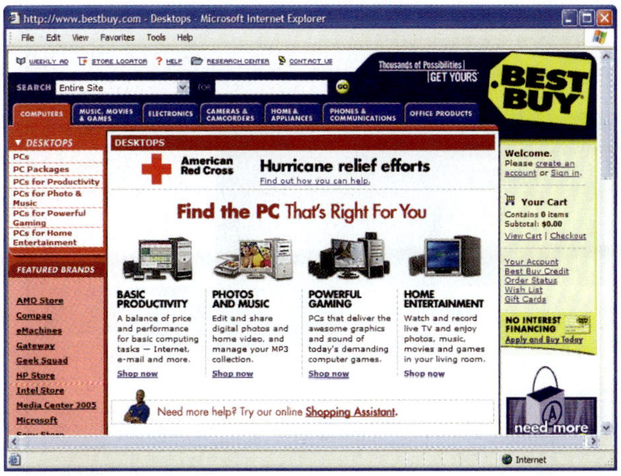

E-TAILER WEB SITES
Sell products from a variety of manufacturers to customers.

FIGURE 11-4
Both manufacturers and online retailers (e-tailers) can sell products and services via their Web sites.

sites provide standardized rules so that all bidders are treated equally. Many online auction sites also collect comments about buyers and sellers from individuals to help others decide whether or not they want to do business with a particular buyer or seller. When items are put up for auction, the seller provides information about the item, such as a detailed description and a photo. Potential buyers find items on the site that they would like to bid on, and then place their desired bids. If outbid, a bidder can place a higher bid. To facilitate this, some online auction sites (such as eBay featured in Figure 11-5) allow a bidder to specify a maximum bid, and the online auction site automatically keeps bidding (using the minimum bid increment, such as $1) whenever the bidder is outbid until his or her specified bid limit is reached. Once the online auction closes, the highest bidder arranges payment and delivery directly with the seller.

An online auction site usually obtains revenue when the items are initially listed for sale, as well as when the successful bidder purchases the item. For example, at the time of this writing, the fee for listing an item on eBay was 25 cents to $4.80, depending on the opening bid; special features, such as specifying the minimum bid amount and adding more than one photo, incurred additional charges. When the online auction closes, the seller also pays the online auction site a percent of the final selling price (from 5.25% on up, depending on the final sale price).

Although many online auction sites are designed for transactions between consumers, some small businesses also sell their products at *consumer auction sites* (such as eBay), either in addition to, or instead of, maintaining an e-commerce Web site. There are also *business auction sites* designed for business purchases. A type of site related to online auctions is the *dynamic pricing site*. Instead of a formal auction with a specific ending time and an automatic winner, these sites—such as Priceline.com—allow buyers to bid on

FIGURE 11-5
How online auctions work.

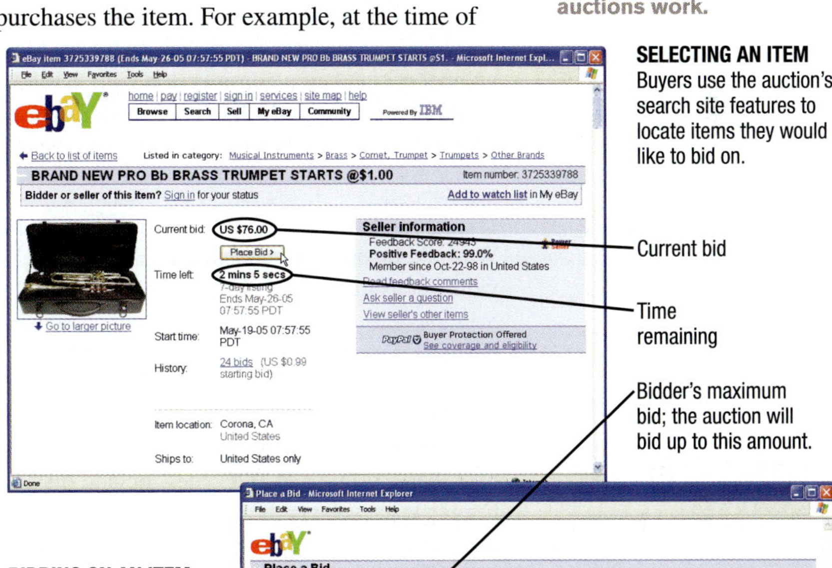

SELECTING AN ITEM
Buyers use the auction's search site features to locate items they would like to bid on.

Current bid

Time remaining

Bidder's maximum bid; the auction will bid up to this amount.

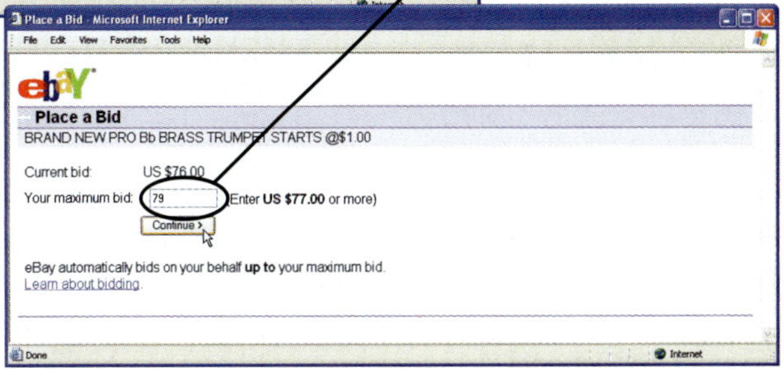

BIDDING ON AN ITEM
Buyers place and confirm their bids; the highest bidder at the time the auction closes buys the item, provided the winning bid meets the seller's minimum bid.

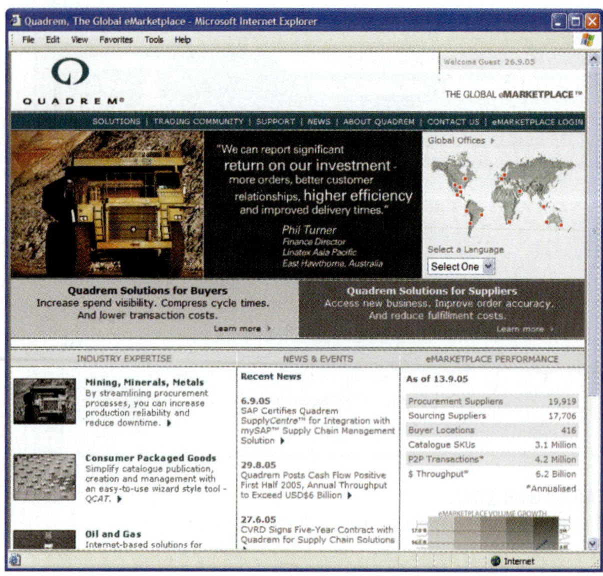

FIGURE 11-6

Exchange sites.

Exchange sites (e-marketplaces) specialize in matching buyers and sellers for goods and services.

items or services listed for sale, and then the seller decides whether or not to accept each offer on an individual basis.

Financial Brokerages

Online investing (illustrated in Figure 8-18 in Chapter 8) is one example of a *financial brokerage site*. Other activities include buying and selling bonds, futures, and options. Financial brokerage sites generate revenue by charging commissions or transactions fees for each transaction.

Market and Commodity Exchanges

With a *market exchange* site, organizations with goods or services to sell list those resources on the exchange site, which assists in matching up potential buyers and sellers. Similar to an online auction site, a market exchange site—sometimes referred to as *e-marketplace* or *intermediary hub*—acts only as an *intermediary* between the buyer and seller, creating a community in which buyers and supplies can easily find one another and do business (see Figure 11-6). Products sold via a market exchange site can range from computers to office supplies to specialty equipment and more. When commodities, such as natural resources and raw goods, are being sold, the terms *commodity exchange* or *commodity broker* are sometimes used. Common commodities sold in this manner include energy, cattle, chemicals, and metals. Like a financial brokerage site, a market exchange site earns a fee for each transaction it facilitates.

E-COMMERCE BUSINESS MODELS

A company's policies, operations, and technology define its **business model**. In essence, a company's business model describes how the company generates revenue. There are a number of standard **e-commerce business models**, including *business to consumer (B2C)*, *business to business (B2B)*, *consumer to consumer (C2C)*, and *business to government (B2G)*. Some of the most commonly used models are discussed next.

Business to Consumer (B2C)

With the **business-to-consumer (B2C) model**, businesses sell goods or services to individual consumers. The B2C model was one of the first major types of e-commerce business models to be defined and implemented using the Web. Some examples of B2C businesses include Amazon.com, Walmart.com, Overstock.com, and BestBuy.com (shown in Figure 11-4). These businesses can be Internet-only stores (dot-coms) or click-and-mortar stores with both online and traditional storefronts.

Essentially, any business that sells goods or services online to consumers is a B2C business. Service-oriented B2C sites include distance learning programs, online banking, and insurance agencies; product-oriented B2C sites sell a wide variety of goods, such as clothing, electronics, medicine, airline tickets, flowers, books, sports equipment, toys, movies, and office supplies. Selling multimedia products online—such as video-on-demand movie

>**Business model.** A description of how a company does business, such as its policies, operations, and technology. >**E-commerce business model.** A description of the types of buyers and sellers involved in an e-commerce company, such B2B, B2G, and so forth. >**Business-to-consumer (B2C) model.** An e-commerce model in which a business provides goods or services to consumers.

HOW IT WORKS

Music Downloads

There are a number of online music stores—such as iTunes Music Store, Yahoo! Music, RealPlayer Music Store, Napster 2, Wal-Mart Music Downloads, and Peer Impact—that enable consumers to download songs legally and ethically. Similar to other e-commerce sites, most of these music stores allow you to add products (such as music singles or entire albums) to your shopping cart and, after the purchase is finalized, download the songs to your PC (see the accompanying illustration). Once music is downloaded to your PC, your media player program can be used to organize your music library, play songs from your PC, burn songs to CDs, or transfer music to a portable music player. At around 99 cents per song, online music stores today are a bargain.

The Peer Impact online music service shown in the accompanying illustration adds an interesting twist to the online music store model. Instead of downloading songs from a central server, the songs are downloaded from other individuals. Exchanges via this P2P service are legal, however, since the service charges for downloads and pays the appropriate royalties to the artist and record company. For allowing songs to be uploaded from their PCs to other users, Peer Impact members earn *Peer Cash* that they can use to pay for additional songs they want to download. In addition to music, other multimedia content—such as PC-based video games—can be downloaded; music videos, audio books, movies, and television shows are expected to be available for P2P distribution via the Peer Impact service in late 2006.

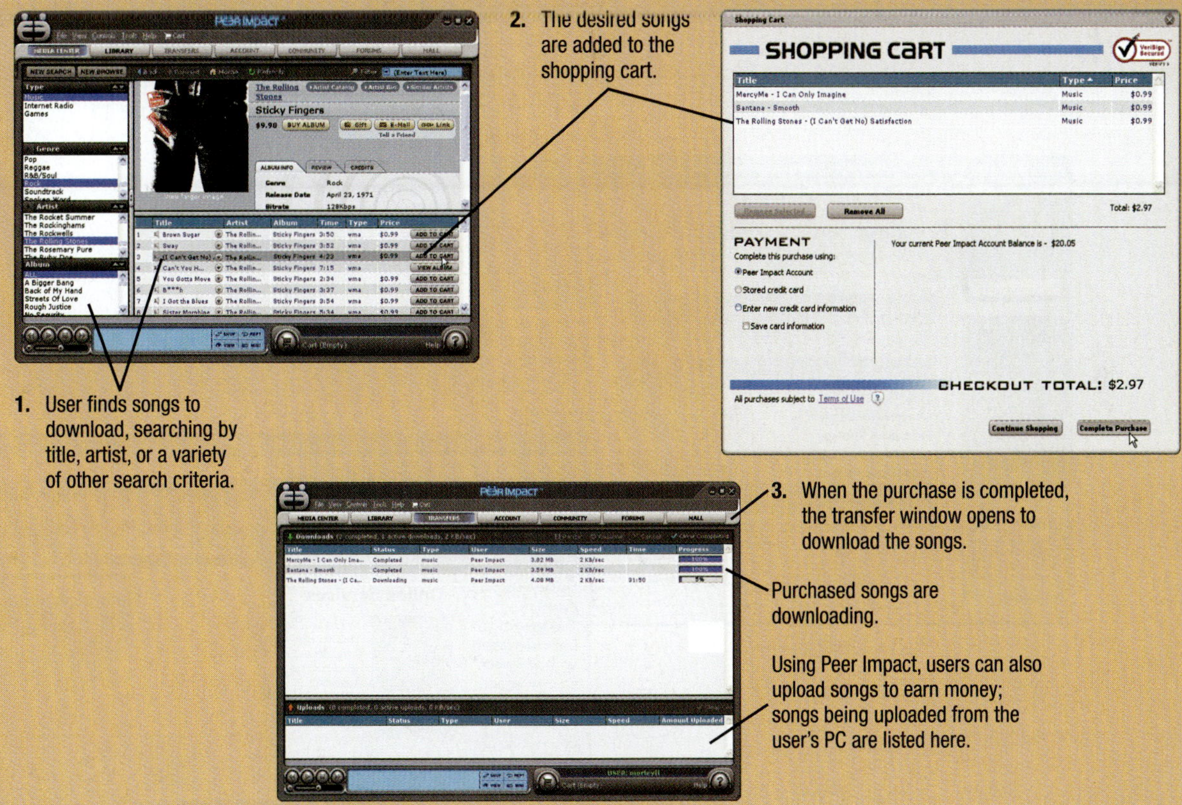

rentals and music downloads—is another big B2C application today, and it is continuing to grow as traditional entertainment applications transition to being online. For a look at how downloaded music works, see the How it Works box.

> **TIP**
>
> Some online auction sites offer escrow services, essentially acting as a middleman in the payment/delivery process so that the seller does not get paid until the buyer receives and accepts the merchandise. Although too expensive for smaller transactions, escrow services are a useful precaution for expensive merchandise purchased through an online auction site or another *consumer-to-consumer* medium.

Business to Business (B2B)

The **business-to-business (B2B) model** includes any type of e-commerce transaction taking place between two businesses. Possibilities include buying goods and services needed for business operations, as well as purchasing manufacturing supplies and raw goods. Although B2C was initially expected to be the most prominent type of e-commerce business model, revenues from the B2B model are now expected to far surpass the B2C marketplace. Forester Research predicts that B2B revenues in the United States alone will surpass $250 billion annually by 2008.

Consumer to Consumer (C2C)

The **consumer-to-consumer (C2C)**—sometimes referred to as the *person-to-person* or *P2P*—**model** almost solely consists of online consumer auctions in which consumers sell products to other consumers. With millions of products up for auction at any time, and online auction sites located in many different countries (bidders can bid on sites outside of their own countries), eBay (shown in Figure 11-5) is one of the largest C2C e-commerce businesses today.

Business to Government (B2G)

With U.S. government spending exceeding $500 billion per year and showing no signs of slowing, the **business-to-government (B2G) model** is becoming more prominent. B2G businesses sell products and services to local, state, and federal government buyers. In general, the government sector has been slower to embrace e-commerce than the private sector. This is slowly changing, however, as a result of recent *e-government* initiatives geared toward moving government procurement and other activities online. There are Web sites dedicated to facilitating B2G transactions, such as the one shown in Figure 11-7.

FIGURE 11-7
Business to government (B2G) and consumer to government (C2G) Web sites.

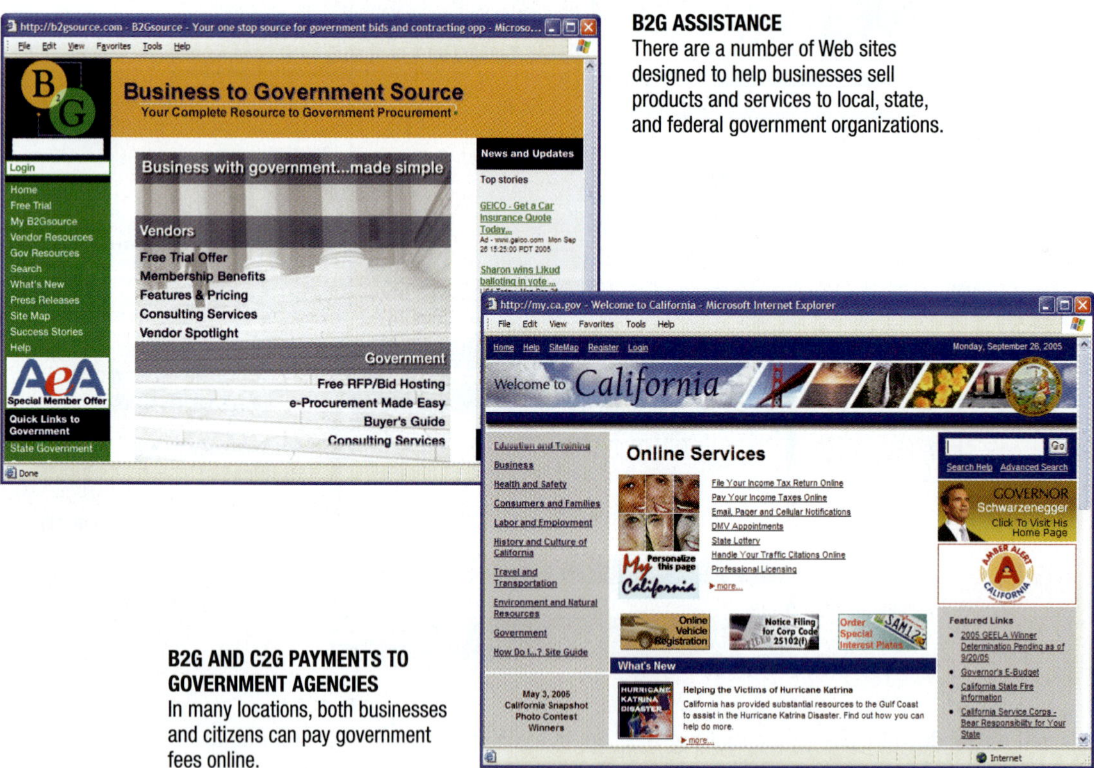

B2G ASSISTANCE
There are a number of Web sites designed to help businesses sell products and services to local, state, and federal government organizations.

B2G AND C2G PAYMENTS TO GOVERNMENT AGENCIES
In many locations, both businesses and citizens can pay government fees online.

>**Business-to-business (B2B) model.** An e-commerce model in which a business provides goods or services to other businesses.
>**Consumer-to-consumer (C2C) model.** An e-commerce model in which a consumer provides goods or services to other consumers.
>**Business-to-government (B2G) model.** An e-commerce model in which a business provides goods and services to government organizations.

Related B2G activities include some states allowing businesses and citizens to make payments online, such as vehicle and boat registration; state, property, and income taxes; and parking fees (see Figure 11-7). Sites that facilitate these types of *consumer-to-government* transactions are sometimes referred to as *C2G* sites.

Intermediary Hubs

Companies that follow the **intermediary hub model**—also called the *brokerage model*—do not sell goods or services directly to others, but instead bring buyers and sellers (usually both businesses) together within a specific industry or business process. The Internet has greatly eliminated the need for traditional intermediaries or middlemen—a trend called *disintermediation*. For example, individuals and businesses can now bypass a travel agent and purchase airline tickets directly from an airline online. New types of intermediaries are emerging as e-commerce evolves, however, such as travel sites that help consumers find the lowest prices on airline tickets and make reservations. This trend is called *reintermediation*. The use of these new types of intermediaries can help businesses and individuals save time and money.

Some intermediaries bring an individual buyer and seller together, such as B2B auction sites and market exchanges. Others combine a number of individual buyers so they can buy as a group and receive volume pricing to better compete with larger organizations. In either case, intermediary hubs usually receive a transaction fee from the seller, frequently based on the dollar amount of the sale, although some intermediaries charge a monthly or an annual fee to use their service. Intermediaries that provide additional services, such as payment settlement or order-fulfillment services, are sometimes referred to as *metamediaries*. Two specific types of intermediary hubs are *vertical hubs* and *horizontal hubs*.

- *Vertical hubs* match buyers and sellers within a specific industry. Some vertical hubs offer more information and services than just facilitating purchases or exchanges; these sites are becoming known as *vertical portals* or *vortals*. Vortals typically provide news, research and statistics, discussion forums, newsletters, online tools, and other industry-specific services.
- *Horizontal hubs*, sometimes called *functional hubs*, focus on providing the same type of products or services or automating the same business process across different industries—a site that specializes in used office equipment or energy management, for example.

Some intermediaries match buyers and sellers within a specific industry and a specific product or service—essentially functioning as both a vertical and horizontal hub.

FIGURE 11-8
Implementing Web-based e-commerce.

TYPICAL STEPS

1. Select appropriate business models and types of Web sites.
2. Select the desired e-commerce applications.
3. Develop procedures for handling electronic financial transactions.
4. Design and develop an effective Web site.
5. Implement appropriate sales and marketing strategies.

IMPLEMENTING WEB-BASED E-COMMERCE

Several factors should be considered when an organization decides to use Web-based e-commerce. These include the type of Web site and software to be used and the means of handling financial transactions. Strategies for sales and marketing, as well as security issues, should also be considered. These issues are discussed in the remainder of this chapter.

Five basic steps are typically followed when implementing a Web-based e-commerce system. These steps are listed in Figure 11-8 and discussed next. Some companies perform some or all of these steps themselves; others hire a firm specializing in e-commerce implementation to carry out these tasks for them. Because the fine

>**Intermediary hub model.** An e-commerce model in which a business brings buyers and sellers together, instead of directly selling goods or services.

details involved with developing a Web-based e-commerce system are beyond the scope of this book, this discussion focuses on the general tasks involved in this process.

Step 1: Select Appropriate Business Models and Types of Web Sites

The first step for a company planning on implementing a Web-based e-commerce system is to evaluate its business plan and determine which business models are currently being used and which models it would like to use with the new e-commerce system. These business models (B2C, B2B, intermediary hub, and so on) are not necessarily mutually exclusive. For example, one business could sell both to consumers and to businesses.

Next, the company should decide which type of Web site it would like to have (such as an e-tailer, an online auction site, or an exchange site). Just as with business models, some companies can choose to implement more than one type of site, although often multiple site models are phased in slowly. For example, Amazon.com was an e-tailer site long before it added its online auction capabilities. When selecting business and Web site models, it is important to realize that some e-commerce business model features are protected by trademark law. For example, the buyer-driven commerce concept and functionality of Priceline.com and the one-click ordering method of Amazon.com are legally protected and cannot be used without permission.

Step 2: Select the Desired E-Commerce Applications

In addition to determining the desired business models and types of Web sites to be used, a company should decide which e-commerce applications will be performed. Although most will likely involve online selling or buying, other activities can be implemented, as well. For instance, many e-commerce sites include *electronic customer relationship management (eCRM)*—activities used to support customers and increase their satisfaction and loyalty. Common eCRM activities include providing online order status information, links for tracking delivery shipments, online product manuals, and online technical support, such as via e-mail or live chat (see Figure 11-9). Other important factors to be decided include whether an ordering system will be linked in real time to an inventory database, as well as what type of order fulfillment system will be used. Once the applications to be included in the Web site have been determined, the necessary software to implement those applications can be determined. Common vendors for business software include SAP, PeopleSoft, IBM, i2, and Oracle.

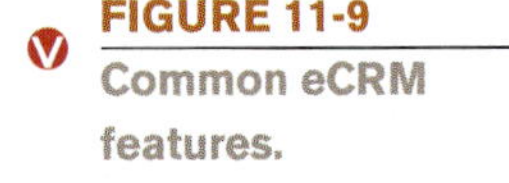

FIGURE 11-9

Common eCRM features.

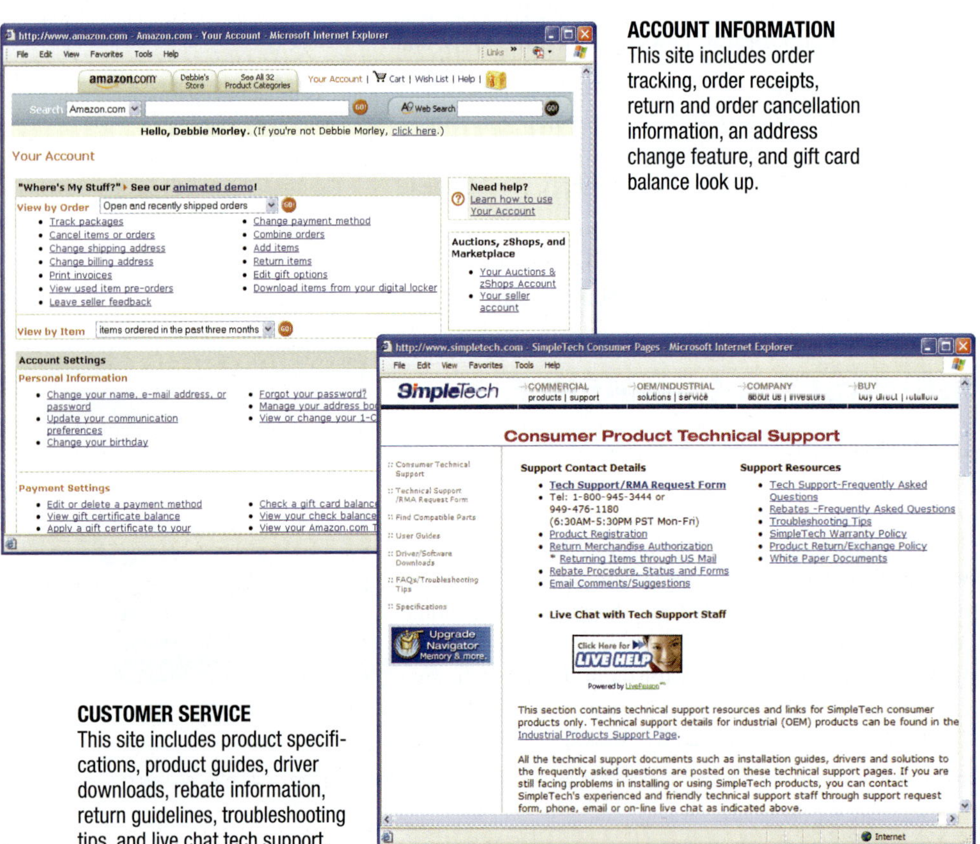

ACCOUNT INFORMATION

This site includes order tracking, order receipts, return and order cancellation information, an address change feature, and gift card balance look up.

CUSTOMER SERVICE

This site includes product specifications, product guides, driver downloads, rebate information, return guidelines, troubleshooting tips, and live chat tech support.

Step 3: Develop Procedures for Handling Electronic Financial Transactions

Successfully performing electronic financial transactions is the cornerstone of any e-commerce site. Therefore, a business should give careful thought as to which payment options it will offer, based on the type of site and the type of customers involved. The options range from standard credit cards and debit cards, to electronic checks, to online payment accounts, to digital wallets, to smart cards (see Figure 11-10). Some of the most common ways of implementing electronic funds transfers for payment processing are discussed next. Typically, an e-commerce site employs more than one of the following options.

Credit and Debit Card Processing

Credit card processing is the first thing that comes to mind when considering online payments. Although some people are hesitant to send their credit card information over the Internet, it is by far the most common payment method used for online purchases. And, though it is possible to run an online business without accepting credit cards, for most B2C e-commerce sites, it is essential.

In order to accept credit cards, a business typically opens an *e-commerce merchant account*, also called an *Internet merchant account*. The bank that issues this account handles all the credit and debit transactions. Each time an online credit card transaction is made, the bank obtains the money from the issuing credit card company and transfers it to the merchant account. When an online purchase is made using a debit card, the bank immediately deducts the amount from the buyer's checking account and transfers it to the merchant account. For providing these services, the bank usually is paid a monthly fee, plus a transaction fee or commission for each credit card or debit card sale.

If a business is set up to accept credit or debit cards online, its order form will include a place to enter the appropriate information. As discussed in earlier chapters, order forms should always be set up as secure Web pages; it is also good practice for the business to include a statement about its security and privacy policies to reassure customers, as shown on the Walmart.com checkout page in Figure 11-10. Once the order form is completed and submitted, the transaction is processed in a manner similar to an offline transaction.

To avoid losing business to customers who do not feel comfortable sending credit card or debit card information over the

FIGURE 11-10

E-commerce payment options. Each e-commerce site must decide the payment options to be supported.

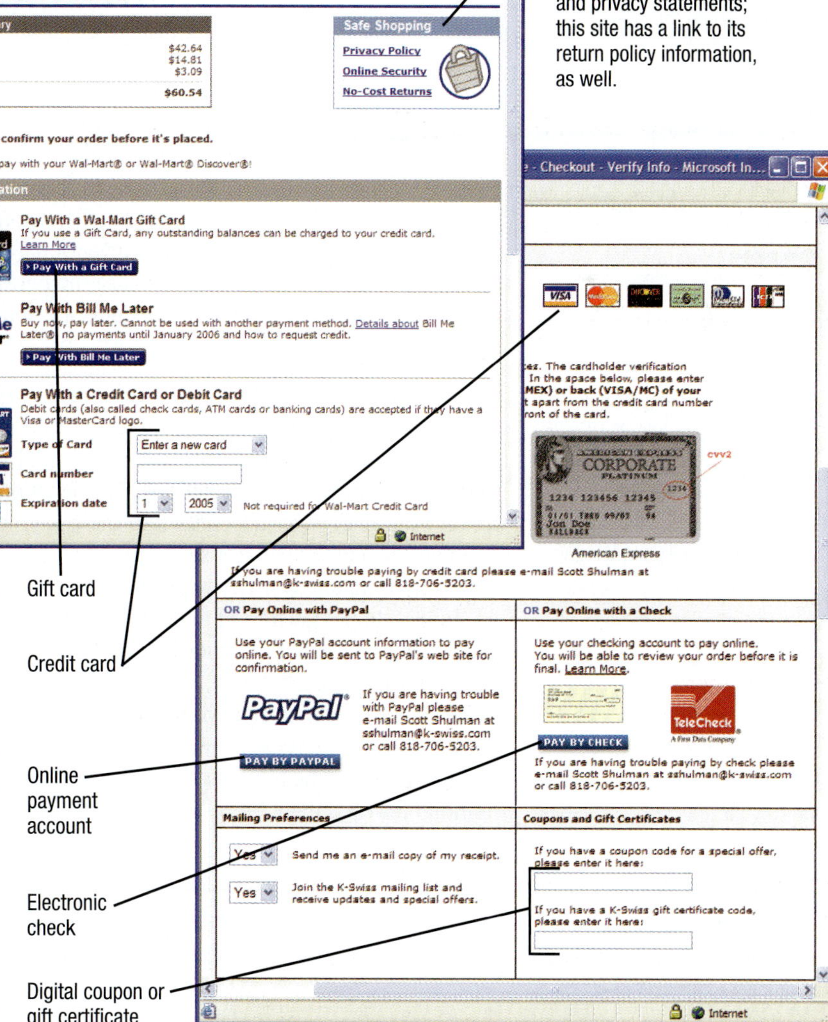

FURTHER EXPLORATION

For links to further information about online shopping precautions, go to www.course.com/uc11/ch11

Internet, many businesses include a toll-free number that can be used to place orders or a mailing address to which conventional checks and money orders can be sent, if the customer prefers. To help increase consumer confidence and to encourage skeptical shoppers to use a credit card for e-commerce transactions, most credit card companies offer $0 liability for online purchases instead of the standard $50 liability. In addition, it is becoming increasingly common for credit card companies to offer cardholders *virtual account numbers*—essentially disposable credit card numbers that can be used to buy goods and services that will be charged to the customer's regular credit card. Because they can be used only one time, the numbers are useless if they are intercepted during transmission or stolen from a Web server's database.

Electronic Checks, Online Payment Accounts, and Other Types of Digital Cash

Payment methods that electronically transfer money from a buyer to the seller have become increasingly popular—especially for online auction payments. These options are sometimes referred to as *digital cash*. Common types of digital cash include *electronic checks*, *online payment accounts*, and *electronic gift certificates*, *gift cards*, and *coupons*.

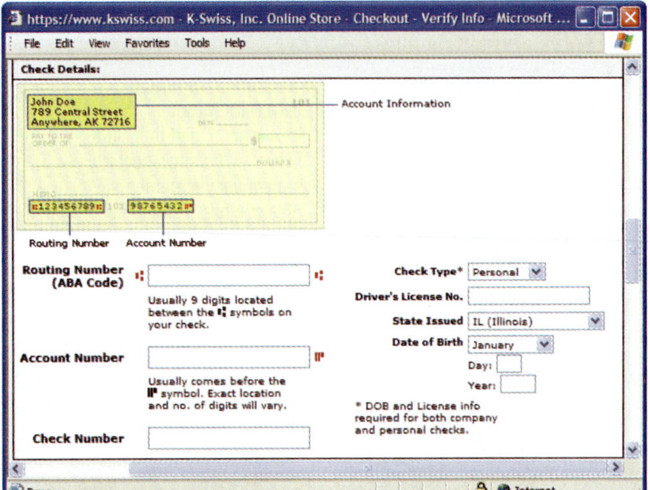

FIGURE 11-11

Electronic checks. To create an electronic check–such as to pay for goods on the site shown here–the checking account information is entered into the appropriate locations on the Web page form.

Electronic Checks

An **electronic check** (sometimes called an *online check*) works as a paper check does, except that the check is created on a Web page, and the appropriate bank account and routing information is supplied, along with the payee and payer information (see Figure 11-11). Electronic checks transfer money directly from one checking account to another checking account. Electronic checks are significantly faster than conventional checks because they are sent and received immediately, instead of having to wait for the check to be physically received through the mail and cashed. Consequently, using an electronic check instead of a conventional check speeds up the delivery process because the period of time between the purchase and when the funds are actually transferred to the seller is reduced.

Online Payment Accounts

Online payment accounts allow individuals to easily transfer money from one person to another. They are commonly used with online auctions sites and small business e-commerce Web sites as a means to enable individuals and small businesses to accept credit card payments for e-commerce transactions. To use an online payment account, individuals deposit funds from their bank accounts into their payment accounts, set up the account to charge payments to a credit card, or set up the account to have funds automatically transferred from a bank account to cover payments as they are made. Once the online payment account is set up, funds can be transferred to another individual or to a business to pay for purchases, and funds can be received by other individuals, typically via their e-mail addresses. If the payment recipient does not have an online payment account, he or she will usually be asked to create one in order to receive the money. For security purposes, a password procedure is used to authorize payments made from the online payment account. While there are usually no fees for either the buyer or the seller on personal transactions, online stores usually pay a nominal fee (less than 2% of the sale up to a maximum of $10, for instance) for each online

>**Electronic check.** A check written and submitted electronically via the Internet. >**Online payment account.** A type of payment account accessed via the Internet and used to make electronic payments to others, either from funds deposited into the account or by charging the appropriate amount to a credit card.

FIGURE 11-12
How online payment accounts work.

@WEB

sale. This fee is typically less than most credit card transaction fees. Individuals can add money to or remove money from their online payment account at any time, transferring it between their online payment account and checking account, or requesting a check, as needed.

One of the leading online payment companies is *PayPal*, shown in Figure 11-12. Services such as PayPal (now owned by eBay) are extremely popular with online auction sellers because they offer a fast, secure way to finalize auction payments. Many online payment accounts can be used to send funds to anyone for any reason, not just to settle an online purchase. Funds can be sent in a variety of currencies, such as U.S. Dollars, Canadian Dollars, Euros, Pounds Sterling, and Yen.

TIP

When deciding on deposit amounts for online payment companies like PayPal, keep in mind that they are not banks, and so they are not FDIC insured.

Electronic Gift Certificates, Gift Cards, and Coupons

Electronic gift certificates and *gift cards* are convenient methods of allowing a gift recipient to select his or her own gift. They work similarly to conventional gift certificates and

TREND

Cell Phone Coupons

For years we have had coupons in the Sunday newspaper, and then electronic coupons became available via the Internet. The newest trend in coupon distribution is delivery to your cell phone.

Although common in Asia and Europe for several years, electronic coupons delivered to cell phones is new to the United States. But as businesses and consumers alike continue to view the mobile phone as more than just a voice communications device, cell phone coupon use is expected to grow. Some companies experimenting with cell phone coupons in the United States include McDonald's and Dunkin' Donuts. Dunkin' Donuts, for instance, did a mobile promotion for its latte among Boston-area high-school and college students; after opting in to receive the digital coupons on their cell phones, an astounding 17% of the students receiving a coupon (see the accompanying photo) redeemed them.

What is the next step expected to be for electronic coupons? One likely possibility is sending electronic coupons to a cell phone based on an individual's location. For instance, an individual that walks by a Starbucks might get an electronic coupon via his or her cell phone for 50 cents off a mocha Frappuccino. Now that's effective impulse marketing!

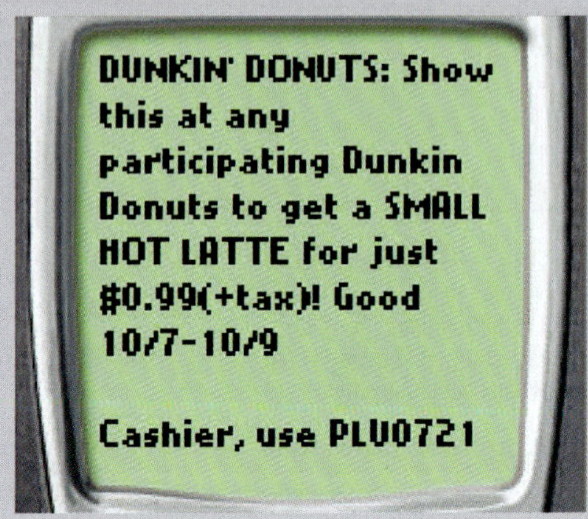

gift cards, but a serial number or other identifying number is entered during the checkout procedure at an online store to use and verify the certificate or card. Some gift certificates and gift cards that are redeemed electronically are purchased in physical form; others are entirely electronic. *Electronic coupons* are comprised of codes—typically called *coupon codes*—that are entered into the appropriate location on a checkout page to deduct the coupon amount from a purchase total. Many sites specialize in gathering and summarizing coupon codes for a variety of online merchants. If an invalid coupon code is entered, or if a coupon code has expired, the coupon discount will not be applied. Electronic coupons are even beginning to arrive on cell phones, as discussed in the Trend box.

FIGURE 11-13

Smart cards. Smart cards are one alternative for buying goods and services online.

Smart Cards

Another type of electronic funds transfer method is the **smart card**, discussed in earlier chapters. While it is expected that the initial main use for e-commerce smart cards will be with point-of-sale card readers installed on vending machines, inside taxis, and other locations where small cash transactions take place, smart cards can also be used for online purchases. As discussed in Chapter 4, smart cards have an embedded computer chip that holds more information than the magnetic stripe on the back of a credit card. Unlike a magnetic stripe, the information in the chip can be updated when appropriate. For e-commerce purposes, the smart card stores an amount of prepaid money and is read by a smart card reader attached to the buyer's PC as an external device (see Figure 11-13) or built

>**Smart card.** A credit card-sized piece of plastic containing a chip and other circuitry into which data can be stored.

into a keyboard or pointing device. Advantages to consumers for using smart cards include a limited amount of liability if the card is lost or stolen since the card contains a limited amount of money and the security provided by password protection that can be used with some smart cards. Advantages to merchants include a low charge-back rate for fraudulent charges as compared to credit cards and lower transaction fees. Smart cards can also contain *digital signatures* for use with transactions that require one, as well as biometric characteristics to be used to authenticate the smart card holder, when needed.

Digital Wallets

Digital wallets (sometimes referred to as *e-wallets*) offer customers a convenient way of storing purchasing information that is needed on a regular basis, such as an online payment account number, smart card information, Web site passwords, a digital signature, and shipping and billing information. There are third-party digital wallets, such as the Illium Software *eWallet* program shown in Figure 11-14, that hold credit card information and site passwords, in addition to a number of other important types of personal data. Typically, an individual opens his or her digital wallet and copies the information from the wallet to online forms as needed, although e-commerce Web sites that support the *Electronic Commerce Modeling Language (ECML)* format can transfer billing, shipping, and payment information directly from a digital wallet with the click of a button. Digital wallet programs and services are available for handheld PCs and smart phones, in addition to desktop PCs. Digital wallets today can hold information, cash values, or both.

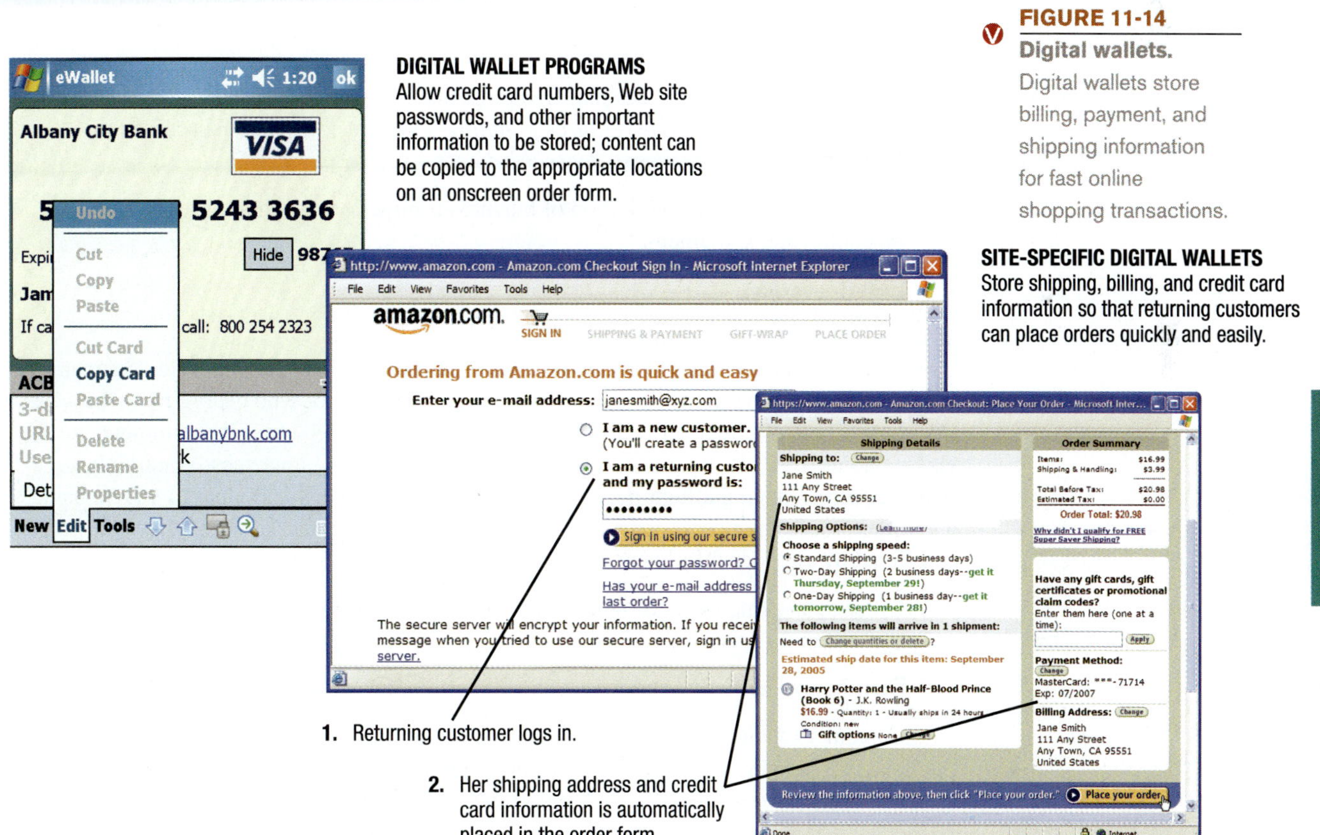

FIGURE 11-14
Digital wallets.
Digital wallets store billing, payment, and shipping information for fast online shopping transactions.

@ WEB

>**Digital wallet.** An encrypted electronic file that holds information, such as electronic payment, billing, and shipping information, that can speed up online purchase transactions.

FURTHER EXPLORATION

For links to further information about e-commerce payment options, go to www.course.com/uc11/ch11

Most third-party digital wallets can be used with a variety of Web sites; some automatically supply the customers' shipping and billing information when the checkout page of an online store is reached. E-commerce sites wanting to offer their customers digital wallet services need to decide whether to support one or more existing third-party digital wallet programs or whether to offer a custom digital wallet service just for their particular sites. For instance, many e-commerce Web sites use password-protected customer accounts—essentially *site-specific digital wallets*—to store shipping, billing, and credit card data to facilitate return purchases (see the Amazon.com site in Figure 11-14).

Special Considerations for B2B Financial Transactions

Although some of the payment methods already discussed can be used with B2B financial transactions, the size of B2B purchases often requires other considerations.

B2B Transaction Processing

Larger B2B businesses may benefit from using an electronic payment company specializing in *business-to-business transaction processing*. These companies—a type of horizontal intermediary hub—usually allow merchants to customize their payment-processing plans to fit their needs. They commonly offer many of the following services:

- Credit card, debit card, check, and digital cash settlement.
- Credit checking for new customers.
- Online expense tracking.
- Electronic billing.
- Payment settlement services that are compatible with other widely used systems (such as *ERP—enterprise resource planning*—systems, which are discussed in Chapter 12).
- Consolidation and reconciliation of business transactions, such as order processing, invoicing, and settlement.
- Escrow services.

Order-Fulfillment Companies

Order-fulfillment companies (sometimes also called *e-fulfillment companies*) are companies that provide a distribution network for merchants who cannot or who choose not to process their own orders. While order-fulfillment companies can be used with all e-commerce models, including B2C, B2B, and B2G transactions, these services are most commonly used with businesses having a high transaction volume that do not already have a warehousing and order processing operation in place to meet their needs. Some of the services that may be offered by an order-fulfillment company include the following:

- Order management—real-time online ordering, ideally integrated with purchasing and inventory services.
- Distribution services—services such as shipping, inventory, and returns processing.
- Customer relationship management services—a professional customer response system that is integrated with the distribution process to provide services, such as order tracking, and designed to help build effective customer relations.
- Marketing tools—reports and other tools to assist in planning for the future.
- E-fulfillment strategic planning—consulting and development services for areas, such as a business's supply chain, database, and e-commerce Web site.
- Integration with existing systems—seamless integration of a business's e-commerce site with its other system, such as *ERP*.

Step 4: Design and Develop an Effective Web Site

As discussed in Chapter 10, *Web site design* refers to the process of planning what a Web site will look like and how it will work, and *Web site development* refers to the actual creation of the Web site, including creating all of the components to be used on the Web site, creating the actual Web pages, testing the site, and publishing the site. Ideally, the e-commerce site will be created and tested for a variety of computer platforms and be usable by visitors with a wide range of computer skills. In addition, any Web pages that collect credit card data or other sensitive data must be located on a secure Web server, the Web site must be diligently maintained, and the security of the Web site and any collected sensitive data should be evaluated on a continual basis. E-commerce Web sites can be designed and developed in-house, although it is common for a business to *outsource* these tasks to a professional Web development company.

It is extremely important that an e-commerce site be attractive, fast loading, easy to use, and secure. Some basic guidelines for Web site design, as well as the steps involved in developing a Web site, were covered in Chapter 10. One additional topic related to e-commerce sites—*storefront software*—is discussed next.

Storefront software is special e-commerce software that allows the creation of an online store (see Figure 11-15). Storefront software varies widely in capabilities and is

FIGURE 11-15
Storefront software can be used to quickly and easily create an e-commerce site.

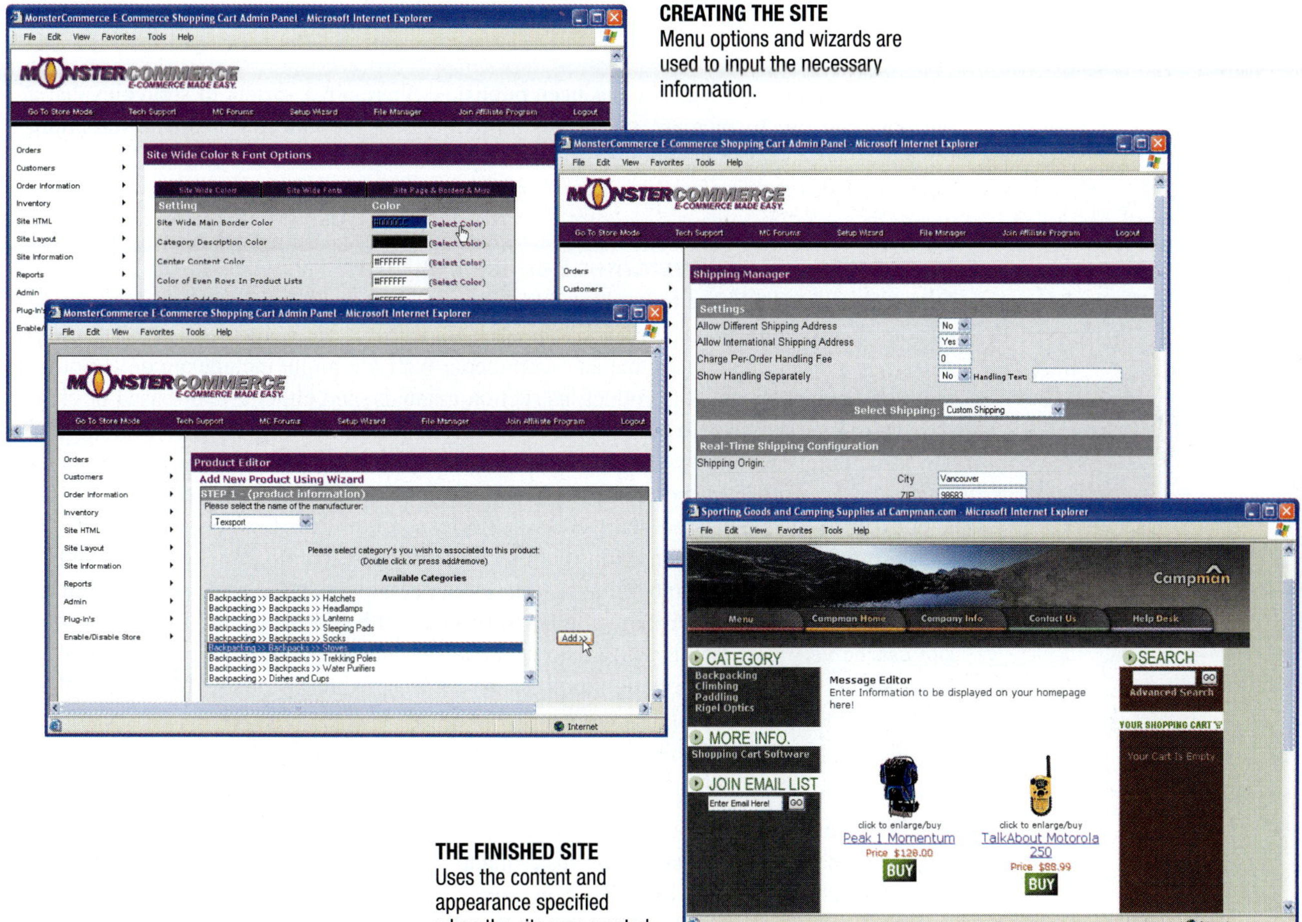

>**Storefront software.** E-commerce software that facilitates the creation of an online store.

available in both packaged and Web-based versions. Some programs have multiple versions available, suitable for any type of e-commerce business—from a small business owner wanting to begin selling a limited number of products online to a large business that requires real-time inventory, multiple pricing structures, the ability for salespeople to place orders from the field, and other more complex features. Virtually all storefront software programs support credit card sales and secure order forms; some have wizards and other tools to help create the storefront quickly and easily.

Some programs are designed to create the entire Web site; others—sometimes called *shopping cart software*—are designed to add only ordering capabilities to an existing Web site. Web hosting services often offer free shopping cart software to Web sites hosted on their servers, and some storefront software companies offer Web-hosting as an optional service. Other possibilities for creating an e-commerce Web site include using a Web-based storefront service (that typically walks you through the creation of the site that is created directly on the server so it is ready to use as soon as it is finished) and using a storefront development firm (that creates and maintains the site for you). E-commerce sites created with storefront software can usually be published to the company Web server, to the storefront software service's Web server, or to a third-party Web hosting service, depending on the preference of the business.

Step 5: Implement Appropriate Sales and Marketing Strategies

Once the e-commerce Web site has been published, there are a variety of strategies that a business can use to increase sales and the use of its e-commerce site. One important topic—designing and developing an effective Web site—has already been discussed. A few other strategies are discussed next.

Include Adequate Customer Service Features

Every e-commerce Web site should include adequate customer service features to increase customer satisfaction and begin to build new customer loyalty. Good *customer relationship management* (*CRM*) services that an e-commerce Web site might include are online order tracking, online versions of product instruction manuals, and either e-mail-based or chat-based customer service. To be successful, e-mail support must use a very short turnaround time—definitely within 24 hours. Studies have shown, however, that businesses are lacking in this area of CRM. For instance, one 2005 study by BenchmarkPortal revealed that about half of the businesses surveyed failed to respond to e-mail inquiries by customers and, of those who did respond, four out of five responded with inaccurate or incomplete information. A toll-free number that customers can call to place orders or ask questions is also an important feature. Automating CRM services with eCRM features added to a Web site can be very cost effective. If customers can find the information they need (such as order status, warranty information, products specs, or product manuals) themselves, they do not have to e-mail or call the company, which can be very expensive—one cost estimate for a customer speaking with a live customer service agent is $6.85 to $15 per call.

Collect Taxes from Customers Only If Required by Law

Similar to mail order purchases, purchases made via the Internet have not been universally subject to sales tax, thanks to a 1992 Supreme Court decision that said states can only collect sales tax on online and catalog sales when the buyer lives in the same state where the merchant maintains a physical presence, such as a brick-and-mortar store or distribution center. With more and more sales tax revenue being lost due to online shopping, however, many state and local governments want that law to change, and a national online sales tax plan—called the *Streamlined Sales Tax Project* (*SSTP*)—has been in development since 2000. With over 7,500 taxing jurisdictions in the United States—each of which may use different tax rates, definitions, and procedures—a uniform, feasible, taxation plan is necessary before an online sales tax can be considered. Nearly all of the states in the SSTP have passed legislation or their governors have issued executive orders to adopt the streamlined tax rules, in order to prepare for online sales tax collection. In late 2005, software vendors contracted by SSTP began providing free tax collection and remittance software and services to online merchants who voluntarily agree to collect taxes on all online sales on behalf of the 13 states that currently comply with SSTP sales tax standards. Other states will be added as their tax codes are brought into full compliance. If the SSTP proves to be successful, it is expected that an increasing number of e-tailers will feel pressured to participate and, as more states participate, it could possibly lead to new legislation or rulings that would make Internet sales tax collection mandatory. Until the time a mandatory online sales tax is in effect, however, collecting sales taxes only when you are required to can be a draw for your Web site.

Display a Privacy Policy and Security Statement

Many online consumers are very concerned about their online privacy and security when purchasing items over the Internet. To reassure these customers, all e-commerce sites should develop and display a privacy policy stating how collected information will be used. One of the most recognized privacy certification organizations is *TRUSTe*. Web sites displaying the TRUSTe trustmark (shown in Figure 11-16) must adhere to established privacy principles and agree to comply with ongoing TRUSTe oversight and consumer resolution procedures.

FIGURE 11-16
TRUSTe. Web sites displaying the TRUSTe trustmark must follow TRUSTe guidelines for setting and adhering to privacy policies.

As mentioned earlier in this chapter, all exchanges of financial information should take place on a secure Web page. A security statement or a link to a security policy (such as the one on the Walmart.com checkout screen in Figure 11-10) should be used to reassure customers that their transactions are secure and their information cannot be intercepted by a third party when it is transferred over the Internet.

Use an Appropriate Domain Name and URL

Because many customers will type the URL of an e-commerce site to shop or to return for customer service, it is important that the URL is easy to remember and easy to type. Try to register an intuitive domain name (such as your business's name or the name of your key product) and use your Web server's default home page name for the home page of your site (as discussed in the Chapter 10 How It Works box) so that customers do not need to type anything other than the domain name and the appropriate top-level domain such as ".com" or ".biz" to access the home page of your e-commerce Web site. For instance, the home page for Wal-Mart uses the URL *walmart.com*—visitors do not need to type a Web page name or a folder path in addition to the domain name (such as walmart.com/index.html) to view the home page of that site.

As discussed in Chapter 1, domain names are unique and are registered with an official domain name registrar. You can visit a domain name registrar Web site, such as NetworkSolutions.com or Register.com, to see if a domain name that matches your business's name is available. If not, you can try variations of the name—many registration sites automatically help by displaying available names that are similar to the one typed if the name you originally requested is unavailable. Keep in mind, however, that if you own the trademark to your business name, the *Anticybersquatting Consumer Protection Act of 1999* protects your trademark in cyberspace. According to the law, domain names similar to a trademarked name cannot be registered, unless the person has a legitimate claim to that name (for example, the domain name is the same as his or her last name) or if the domain name was registered prior to the use of the registered trademark. Registering a domain name to cause confusion, to dilute the established trademark, or with the intent of reselling the trademark (called *cybersquatting*) has been ruled illegal.

FIGURE 11-17

Keyword meta tags. Keywords added to a Web page by the Web page author are used by search sites when classifying that page in their search databases.

Promote Your Web Site Sufficiently

Promotion of your site—that is, advertising its existence, purpose, and URL—is critical to ensure that customers are aware of your site and can find it when they want to shop online. One of the best ways to promote your site is by getting it listed with as many search sites—such as Google, Yahoo!, Excite, AltaVista, AskJeeves, and Lycos—as fast and accurately as you can. Usually this process involves two steps. First, add appropriate *meta tags* to the pages of your site. Meta tags are special HTML codes that provide information about a Web page and are inserted into a Web page's HTML code by the person creating the Web page. The meta tag *keywords* is used to specify keywords that should be associated with that page (see Figure 11-17); that is, the search terms you expect people to enter when searching for your Web page. For example, if you have developed a Web site for a fishing-tackle-and-outfitter business in Boise, Idaho, possible keywords are *fish*, *fishing*, *trout*, *tackle*, *hobby*, *outfitter*, *recreation*, *Boise*, and *Idaho*, in addition to the actual name of the company; these keywords should be included in the site's home page HTML code. Meta tags are also used by search engines to classify Web pages when they are added to a search database. Since it may take some time until your Web page is classified automatically by a spider program traveling the Web, the second step is to submit your site directly to search sites. Some search sites may not take submissions and others may only take suggestions for additions to their search databases—check each site for an appropriate link for more information about that site's policy. When you do submit a site to a search site, typically a form is filled out specifying the title, URL, description, keywords, and other information needed to appropriately classify the page.

As an alternative to submitting your Web pages to search sites directly, there are *site submission services* that allow you to fill out one form that the service then submits to several search sites at one time, usually for a fee of about \$200 or less. Most businesses find that using a submission service is the most efficient means of promoting a new site. In addition to submitting your site to the general-purpose search sites, be sure to submit your site to any specialty search sites that exist for your industry.

In addition to just adding your site to a search site's database, you can consider paid search listings, in which you are listed as a *sponsored link* or *sponsored listing* for a specific search term. To obtain a sponsored keyword or phrase, you bid against any other companies interested in that keyword or phrase by specifying the maximum amount you are willing to pay each time someone clicks on the sponsored link. Often, the search site will allow more than one Web site to be associated with a keyword or phrase—the company paying the highest amount per click (called the *cost per click* or *CPC*) is listed first in the sponsored link list. Some search sites use the amount of traffic using the sponsored link (called the *click through rate* or *CTR*) to determine placement, and some search sites allow companies to specify a maximum budget per billing period—after that amount is reached, the Web site will not be a sponsored link until the next billing period begins. Typical CTRs are between a few cents and \$15 per click, depending on the term.

FURTHER EXPLORATION

For links to further information about Web site promotion, go to www.course.com/uc11/ch11

Other promotional options should also be considered. For instance, Internet advertising—typically through the use of *banner ads*—is growing. It is estimated that $22 billion was spent worldwide on Internet advertising in 2005. Banner ads can appear in a wide variety of shapes and sizes (see Figure 11-18) and are found on many Web pages. Banner ads almost always are linked to the advertised company's Web site. In addition to static banner ads, it is becoming more common to use dynamic banner ads that play a short video or animation sequence when the page hosting the banner ad is displayed. Use of these types of ads—called *rich media ads*—is growing. They accounted for about 8% of total online advertising dollars in 2004 and are expected to grow to about 25% by 2008, according to the EMarketer research company. For a look at another Internet advertising trend—*behavioral targeting*—see the Inside the Industry box. In addition to paid placement, free banner ad placement is available via banner ad exchanges. Using this method, you display banner ads for other sites on your Web site in return for your banner ad being displayed on other sites—this is a good alternative for small businesses with a limited advertising budget. You can also hire a Web promotion firm to publicize your site for you. A definite must is using your site's URL on all offline advertising and print material, such as letterhead, business cards, and television, radio, and print ads.

STATIC BANNER ADS
These ads are linked to the appropriate Web site, but they are not animated.

RICH MEDIA BANNER ADS
These banners contain animated components that play when the ad is viewed on a Web page; the ads are also linked to the appropriate Web site.

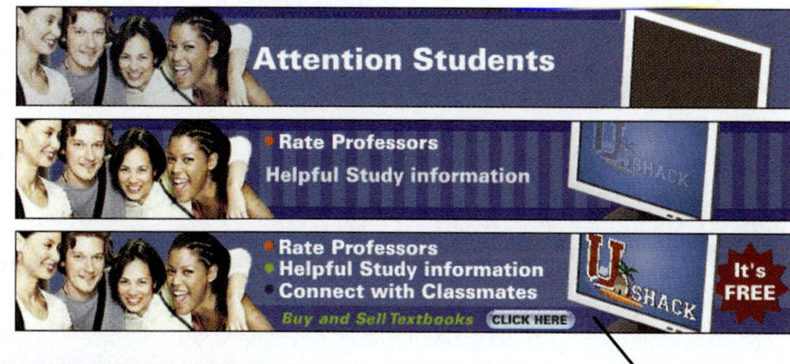

The text and images in this ad build slowly until the completed ad (bottom image) is displayed.

This text changes. A video plays here. This text changes.

FIGURE 11-18
Banner ads. Banner ads, in a variety of shapes and sizes, are used on Web sites for marketing purposes. Typically, a banner ad is linked to the corresponding Web site.

A final important promotional strategy is regularly updating your site with new content. Visitors will come back to your Web site on a regular basis if you consistently refresh it with interesting or exciting information or with offers to win freebies. Sweepstakes and contests are especially popular. If you require an e-mail address to register for a prize, contest, or other special service, these promotional strategies can help you build your customer database to target promotions and marketing materials to your customers, as discussed in the next section.

Data Warehousing and Mining

Two marketing concepts that all businesses should be aware of are *data warehousing* and *data mining*. A **data warehouse** is a comprehensive collection of data about a company and its customers. In a data warehouse, data from transaction processing and other operations are reorganized and put into a form that is optimized for queries. For e-commerce businesses, data about customers' activities on the company Web site (sometimes called *clickstream* data) may be included as well.

>**Data warehouse.** A comprehensive collection of data about a company and its customers.

INSIDE THE INDUSTRY

Banner Ads and Behavioral Targeting

Behavioral targeting—targeting ads to individuals based on their individual preferences, buying habits, or interests—began online in the 1990s with the DoubleClick cookie fiasco. It was not successful then because users had fears about their online habits being tracked and then matched to their personal identity. Today, behavioral targeting (also called *contextual advertising*) is hot again, but marketers are being careful to protect the privacy of individuals. For instance, most targeted ads today are based on the individual's interest (based on the Web pages visited), but are not linked to their personal identity. Google's keyword ads, known as *AdWords*, are one of the first successes of behavioral targeting and partly the reason for its resurgence. With Google's keyword ads, banner ads are displayed on the search results page based on the keywords that the user entered into the search box. A similar service by Tacoda displays banner ads related to an individual's interest whenever the individual views a Web page belonging to a business in the Tacoda advertising network. The relevance is determined by the user's surfing habits—individuals are placed into categories based on what they seem to be interested in. For instance, if a visitor to one site reads an article on new cars, he or she might be labeled a potential car buyer and be presented with ads for new cars when viewing other Web pages in the Tacoda network. Similar to the DoubleClick program, cookies are used to track the user's surfing habits, but no personal information about the user is recorded.

Behavorial targeting can also be used to generate additional revenue within a single site. For instance, Amazon.com lists product recommendations for signed-in customers that are based on products purchased in the past from Amazon.com, as well as products recently viewed on that Web site. Another form of behavioral targeting is *permission-based advertising*. These services, such as the *Direct Messaging* service offered by the advertising company Dotomi—provide real-time targeted ads to consumers who opt in to the service. After selecting the brands to be used in targeted ads directed to them, consumers see targeted banner ads (see the accompanying illustration) on a regular basis as they surf the Web. These types of ads have a high click-through rate, which is getting advertisers' attention.

In a nutshell, the goal of behavioral targeting is to find out what products or services individuals are looking for or are likely to buy and deliver ads accordingly. Consequently, it can be beneficial to both the business and the individual, if done properly. The use of behavioral targeted ads is on the rise—according to a study by iMedia Communications, behavioral targeting advertising is expected to increase 65% in 2006, for a total of over 20% of all online ads.

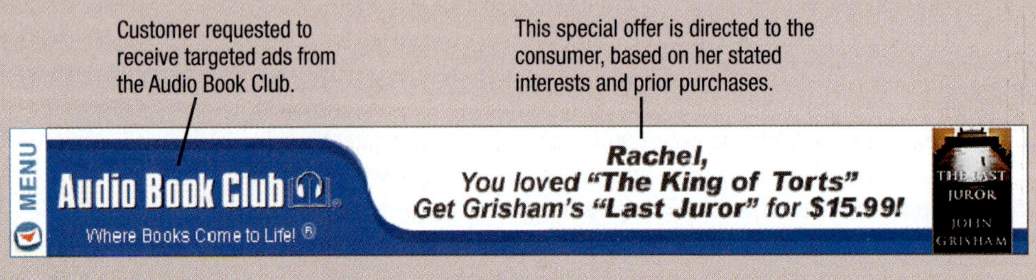

This custom banner ad is displayed on Web pages viewed by a customer who opted into the Dotomi Direct Messaging service.

Data mining makes use of a data warehouse by applying intelligent software to scan its contents for subtle patterns that may not be evident to management (see Figure 11-19). Put another way, data mining identifies patterns and relationships between data—some of which may be fairly obvious; others of which may be more subtle patterns and relationships that are difficult to ascertain without data mining software. Data mining can be a

>**Data mining.** The process of using intelligent software to analyze data warehouses for patterns and relationships.

useful sales and marketing tool to help retail companies match customers with products that they would be likely to purchase—a type of customer *profiling*. Wal-Mart is one company that uses extensive data mining and targets specific types of merchandise in their local stores, based on the characteristics of the people that live in that geographical area.

Both data warehousing and data mining are widely used in most large enterprises. The amount of data that can be collected via a Web site, however, makes these activities an exciting opportunity for e-commerce businesses. E-commerce sites can use data to entice customers to return to the Web site by offering free shipping to return customers or by notifying customers of new products or specials on products in which they might be interested. It can also be used to encourage customers to buy products by using personalized content, such as by displaying banner ads that match the customer's interest or recommending an additional related product when the customer moves an item into his or her shopping cart. Personalized shopping experiences are a powerful way to satisfy customers and keep them coming back to a Web site. Data mining used in conjunction with Web site data is sometimes referred to as *Web mining*.

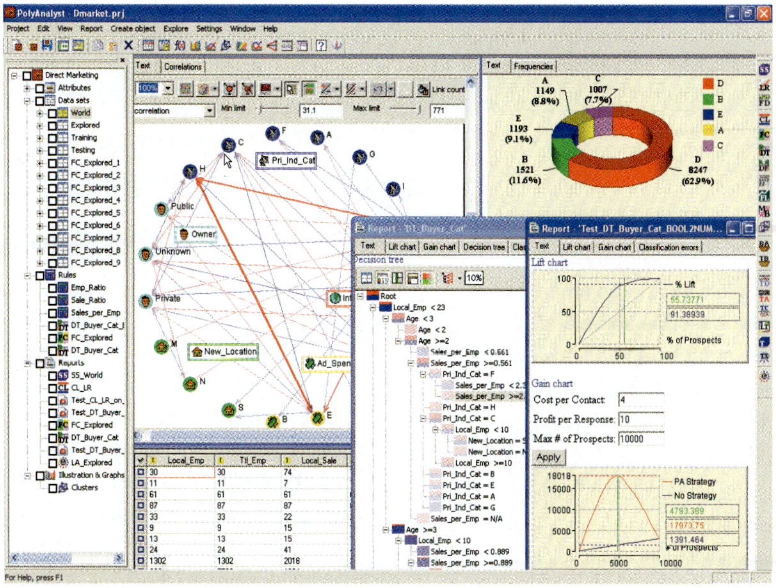

FIGURE 11-19

Data mining. The goal of these tools is to find patterns and relationships in data.

As you may have already guessed, the amount of data in a data warehouse can be enormous. For instance, Wal-Mart recently expanded its data warehouse to hold over 200 terabytes. If that data was printed out on regular 8½ × 11 sheets of paper and laid end to end, it would reach to the moon and back 38 times. Some experts predict that the first petabyte data warehouse will emerge in the near future. With the amount of data being stored by businesses growing at such a rapid pace, it is becoming clear that managing this vast amount of data and retrieving useful information to increase sales and improve customer relations will continue to be one of a business's greatest challenges.

SECURITY ISSUES

Security issues are covered in more detail in other chapters, but it is such an important topic for e-commerce that some of the key points are emphasized here. An e-commerce Web site must provide the following:

- *Secure financial transactions*—All financial transactions should take place on a secure Web server. As mentioned in Chapter 9, secure Web sites use encryption to safely transfer sensitive data over the Internet.
- *Secure sensitive documents and files*—Sensitive business documents should also be encrypted when sent. They can then be decrypted when received by the authorized party.
- *Authenticate online business partners*—As discussed in Chapter 9, tools such as *digital certificates* and *digital signatures* can be used to verify and authenticate the validity of each party involved in an Internet transaction. This is especially important when contracts and other important documents are signed and exchanged electronically.

@WEB

SUMMARY

WHAT IS E-COMMERCE?

Chapter Objective 1:
Explain what e-commerce is and describe some of the advantages and disadvantages involved with implementing e-commerce.

The term **e-commerce** is used to describe the process of performing financial transactions online. Although implemented today most commonly via the Internet, e-commerce has been performed for years via private networks, such as *electronic funds transfers* (*EFT*) by banks. E-commerce is growing at a rapid pace. Related activities are *m-commerce* (*mobile commerce*) and *u-commerce* (*universal commerce*).

A **brick-and-mortar store** is a traditional store with a physical presence; online stores that also have a physical presence are sometimes called *click-and-mortar stores*. Internet-only stores are sometimes referred to as **dot-coms**.

The benefits of e-commerce to businesses include reduced cost, increased customer satisfaction, more effective management tools, and potentially higher sales. For consumers, the benefits include convenience, easier comparison-shopping, a higher degree of selection, and possibly, lower cost. The risks of conducting e-commerce for businesses include losing sales when its Web site is down, as well as potentially reducing the customer base because some customers are not comfortable performing transactions online. Risks to consumers include potential security and privacy problems with e-commerce activity. An additional disadvantage for consumers is not being able to see and touch items before purchasing them.

TYPES OF E-COMMERCE WEB SITES

Chapter Objective 2:
Discuss the types of Web sites that can be used to implement e-commerce.

A variety of Web site types can be used for e-commerce activities. Some of the most common are manufacturer sites and **e-tailer** (online retail) Web sites, as well as **brokerage sites**. **Online auction sites** are brokerage sites that allow individuals and companies or individuals to bid on merchandise. Other brokerage sites that facilitate transactions in addition to the auction site include *financial brokerages* and *market exchanges*. Brokerage sites typically obtain revenue by charging commissions or fees for each brokered transaction.

E-COMMERCE BUSINESS MODELS

Chapter Objective 3:
Identify a variety of e-commerce business models and discuss their differences.

A company's **business model** defines its policies, operations, and technology in generating revenue. **E-commerce business models** typically define the types of buyers and sellers involved. Some of the most common e-commerce business models include the **business-to-consumer (B2C)**, **business-to-business (B2B)**, **consumer-to-consumer (C2C)**, and **business-to-government (B2G)** models. With B2C, businesses sell products and services directly to consumers; with B2B, businesses sell products and services to other businesses; C2C transactions are between consumers; and B2G transactions are between businesses and the government. The **intermediary hub model** is used by companies that bring buyers and sellers together within a specific industry (*vertical hub*) or business process (*horizontal hub*) but do not sell products or services directly to their customers.

IMPLEMENTING WEB-BASED E-COMMERCE

When implementing Web-based e-commerce, five basic steps are usually followed. First, the types of business models and Web sites to be used are selected (a site may select one or more than one of each). Then, the desired e-commerce and e-business applications are determined. The business must also decide how to handle the electronic financial transactions that occur via the site. Most B2C sites accept credit card payments. Other possibilities include accepting debit cards, **electronic checks**, **online payment account** transfers (such as via *PayPal*), *electronic gift certificates* or *gift cards*, and **smart cards**. Some customers may want to use a **digital wallet** to supply shipping and billing information; e-commerce sites can also choose to implement a *site-specific digital wallet* to remember this information for return customers. In general, each online business must decide which payment possibility it wants to support. B2B sites may want to consider using a *B2B transaction processing service* or *order-fulfillment company* to assist with their transactions. These businesses can help with payment processing, billing, customer relationship services, escrow services, and other services.

Chapter Objective 4:
List several strategies for implementing e-commerce using the Web, including some of the decisions that need to be made, the options available for accepting payments, and the process of designing and developing an effective Web site.

The design and development of the e-commerce Web site are extremely important. An intuitive, easy-to-use site is a must. In addition, the site must be secure so that potential customers feel confident performing financial transactions online. **Storefront software** is commonly used to create an e-commerce site or add shopping cart capabilities to an existing Web site. Storefront software is available both in packaged form and as a Web-based service.

After an e-commerce site has been completed, some of the strategies the site can use to increase traffic and sales include adequate customer service features, collecting sales tax only if required by law, displaying privacy and security statements prominently on the site, using an appropriate domain name and URL, and promoting the Web site sufficiently. Using appropriate *meta tags*, submitting the site to search sites, and using *banner ads* on other sites are all ways of promoting the site. Two growing online marketing trends are *rich media ads* and *behavioral targeting*. In addition, data warehousing and data mining can be used. A **data warehouse** is a comprehensive collection of data about a company and its customers. **Data mining** consists of intelligent software that can analyze data warehouses for patterns and relationships—sometimes discovering patterns and relationships that management may not even realize exist.

Chapter Objective 5:
Outline some sales and marketing strategies that can be used in conjunction with an e-commerce Web site.

SECURITY ISSUES

Some of the key security issues that all businesses conducting e-commerce activity should consider are using a secure Web server for all financial transactions, encrypting sensitive documents and files sent over the Internet, and authenticating online business partners.

Chapter Objective 6:
Discuss some security issues related to e-commerce transactions.

REVIEW ACTIVITIES

KEY TERM MATCHING

Instructions: Match each key term on the left with the definition on the right that best describes it.

a. brick-and-mortar store
b. business-to-business (B2B) model
c. business-to-consumer (B2C) model
d. data mining
e. digital wallet
f. e-commerce
g. e-tailer
h. online payment account
i. smart card
j. storefront software

1. ______ A conventional store with a physical presence.
2. ______ A credit card-sized piece of plastic containing a chip and other circuitry into which data can be stored.
3. ______ A type of payment account accessed via the Internet and used to make electronic payments to others, either from funds deposited into the account or by charging the appropriate amount to a credit card.
4. ______ An e-commerce model in which a business provides goods or services to other businesses.
5. ______ An e-commerce model in which a business provides goods or services to consumers.
6. ______ An encrypted electronic file that holds information, such as electronic payment, billing, and shipping information, that can speed up online purchase transactions.
7. ______ An online retailer.
8. ______ E-commerce software that facilitates the creation of an online store.
9. ______ The process of using intelligent software to analyze data warehouses for patterns and relationships.
10. ______ The act of doing business transactions over the Internet or similar technology.

SELF-QUIZ

Instructions: Circle **T** if the statement is true, **F** if the statement is false, or write the best answer in the space provided. **Answers to the self-quiz are located in the References and Resources Guide at the end of the book**.

1. **T F** E-commerce typically takes place via the Internet.
2. **T F** Because most users shop online during the daytime, e-commerce sites can shut down for maintenance during the middle of the night without losing sales.
3. **T F** A company's business model describes how the company does business, such as its policies, operations, and technology.
4. **T F** A business can use more than one type of e-commerce business model.
5. **T F** With an electronic check, the user typically writes a check, scans it, and e-mails the image of the check to the e-tailer.

6. A company selling parts to NASA is using the ______ e-commerce business model.
7. With a(n) ______, such as PayPal, funds can be transferred from one individual to another using just the recipient's e-mail address.
8. A(n) ______ can help speed up online purchases by storing a buyer's payment, shipping, and billing information so it can be supplied electronically.
9. A(n) ______ is a small, usually image-based, advertisement placed on one site that is linked to the advertised site; can be static or dynamic.

10. Match each e-commerce business model with it description and write the corresponding number in the blank to the left of each description.

a. ______	Online bookstore, such as BarnesandNoble.com.	**1.** B2C
b. ______	Consumer auction site, such as eBay.	**2.** B2B
c. ______	State government site enabling businesses to electronically pay the sales tax they collect.	**3.** C2C
d. ______	Office supply storefront selling primarily to businesses.	**4.** B2G

EXERCISES

1. List two potential advantages of e-commerce to a business.

2. List two potential disadvantages of e-commerce to a business.

3. Answer the following questions regarding e-commerce Web site marketing strategies.

a. Which of the following three URLs would be the best to use for the home page of an online store called "Johnson Music Supply" that sells sheet music, instrument supplies, and so forth? Explain your answer.

www.johnson.com
www.johnson.net
www.johnsonmusic.com

b. For the Johnson Music Supply online store described in the previous question, list five possible keywords that should be included in the site's home page keywords meta tag.

4. Match each description with its best payment method and write the corresponding number in the blank to the left of each description.

a. ______	A person purchasing an expensive painting from an individual at an online auction site who wants to ensure the painting arrives and is as advertised before releasing the payment.	**1.** Credit card
b. ______	A person buying a book from Amazon.com who does not have an online payment account.	**2.** Online payment account
c. ______	A person who wants to type in a code found on a Web site to reduce the cost of a purchase.	**3.** Online escrow service
d. ______	A person purchasing an inexpensive item from an individual via an online auction.	**4.** Electronic coupon

5. Describe the difference between data warehousing and data mining.

@ WEB

DISCUSSION QUESTION

As discussed in the chapter, purchases made via the Internet have not been subject to sales tax in the United States, unless the buyer lives in the same state where the merchant maintains a physical presence, such as a store or distribution center. An increasing amount of state sales tax revenue is being lost due to online shopping; as a result, many states want that law to change. Already, several popular e-commerce Web sites have been sued for failing to collect sales taxes. In response to these lawsuits, many of the nation's largest retailers—such as Wal-Mart, Toys-R-Us, and Target—began charging taxes in 2003 on all of their online sales, and, as discussed in the chapter, plans are underway for a national online sales tax plan that would apply a simplified, standardized sales tax on all online, mail-order, and telephone purchases. Do you think an online sales tax plan should be enacted? If so, do you think online sales will decline? If you do not think online sales should be taxed, will other taxes need to be increased if state tax revenues continue to decline as more and more purchases are made online? What is the best solution to this issue?

PROJECTS

HOT TOPICS

1. **M-Commerce** As discussed in the chapter, mobile commerce (m-commerce) is slowly becoming available in several countries.

   For this project, research the current status of m-commerce in the United States. Are there any cell phone providers offering m-commerce services to enable subscribers to pay for goods or services using only their cell phones? If so, determine how the system works and what types of transactions are supported. Also investigate RFID-based systems, such as Speedpass. Are there any locations in your area in which you could purchase goods or services using an RFID payment method such as this one? At the conclusion of your research, prepare a one-page summary of your findings and submit it to your instructor.

SHORT ANSWER/ RESEARCH

2. **Click Fraud** As discussed in the chapter, companies that have sponsored links at a search site pay a fee each time that link is clicked. *Click fraud* occurs when sponsored links are clicked—such as by using a software program, low-cost workers, or employees of rival companies—with the goal of costing the sponsor money.

   For this project, research click fraud and determine how big the problem is and the form it most commonly takes today. What are search sites doing to detect or prevent click fraud? What actions can a company take if it believes it is a victim of click fraud? Is click fraud illegal? At the conclusion of your research, prepare a one-page summary of your findings and submit it to your instructor.

3. **Privacy Breaches** In the course of doing business, companies collect data about their customers that is generally considered personal information. Customers are usually willing to provide this information in return for such benefits as receiving personalized service, special promotions, free information, and so forth. The problem arises when businesses, which are always looking for additional ways to increase revenue, decide to sell this information to an *infomediary*. These infomediaries can then sell the information to just about anyone, which can constitute a breach of privacy. This whole issue might best be summed up with the following, now famous, quote from Sun Microsystems CEO Scott McNealy: "You have no privacy. Get over it."

   For this project, research the legal restrictions, if any, for the information that customers provide to e-commerce companies located in the United States. If the privacy policy of an e-commerce Web site states that personal information may be shared with others, do consumers generally have any recourse? Do they have to be provided with a procedure to opt out of having their information shared? What if a privacy policy initially stated that personal information would not be shared, but then the company decides to change the policy to allow it—do they have to notify customers before sharing any of the previously collected information? At the conclusion of your research, prepare a one-page summary of your findings and submit it to your instructor.

HANDS ON

4. **Storefront Options** As discussed in the chapter, there are several options for adding storefront capabilities to an existing Web site.

   For this project, suppose you have a small business and you already have a basic Web site, but now you want to add the necessary components to allow customers to place orders via your Web site. Select one of the options discussed next and investigate it thoroughly to determine the steps and costs involved.

a. Web developer option: Contact one possible firm, explain your hypothetical situation, and request a rough quotation in both cost and time to get the storefront up and running. In addition, find out how ongoing maintenance will work. Will the storefront be tied into a database that you will update? How will items be added and deleted from the storefront as your business evolves? Is there a maximum number of items the system will handle?

b. Software option: Locate and choose one particular product and find out more about it. Try to locate a review of the product to form an opinion about the software and how easy it is to use. Determine the approximate pricing of the product and with what types of Web sites it is compatible. In addition, determine how ongoing maintenance will work. Will the storefront be tied into a database that you will update? How will items be added and deleted from the storefront as your business evolves? Is there a maximum number of items the system will handle? Can the software be used in conjunction with a Web development program, such as Dreamweaver?

c. Web host option: Contact one possible firm, explain your hypothetical situation, and request a rough quotation in both cost and time to get the storefront up and running. In addition, find out how ongoing maintenance will work. Will the storefront be tied into a database that you will update? How will items be added and deleted from the storefront as your business evolves? Is there a maximum number of different items the system will handle? Is the software compatible with any types of Web sites or are there restrictions?

At the conclusion of your research, submit a short summary of your findings to your instructor.

5. **Safe and Effective Online Shopping** There are a wide variety of online stores where everyday items (such as books, clothes, CDs, and DVDs) can be purchased.

For this project, select a specific product that you might want to buy and find two places where you could buy it online, such as by visiting Web sites for a retail store directly or by searching for the product using a comparison shopping service or search site. Once you have located the item on two e-commerce Web sites, perform the following steps at each site.

a. Make a note of the price of the item and add the item to your shopping cart.

b. Begin the checkout procedure to try to determine any sales tax and shipping charges that will be added to your order (but DO NOT actually purchase the item—stop at the point the site requires you to enter a credit card number or other payment information). Does the checkout page use a secure Web server (look for a locked padlock or a nonbroken key on your browser's status bar or *https:* in the URL in the Address or Location bar at the top of your browser's window)? If not, is there a security or privacy statement on the site that states that it uses a secure server later in the checkout process?

c. Delete the item from your shopping cart, then look for a return policy on the site to see if you can return the product if you are dissatisfied with it.

d. Form an opinion about how easy or difficult the shopping experience was on the site. If you were asked to make any recommendations for improvement, what would they be?

At the conclusion of your research, prepare a one-page summary of the information you gathered. Be sure to include which of the two stores (if any) you would want to buy the item from and why, as well as your recommendations for improvement for each site.

WRITING ABOUT COMPUTERS

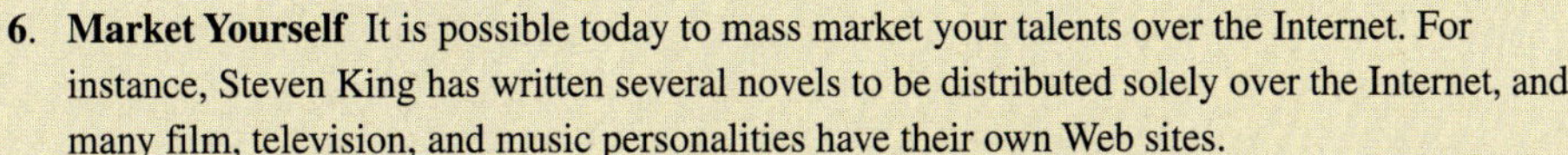

6. **Market Yourself** It is possible today to mass market your talents over the Internet. For instance, Steven King has written several novels to be distributed solely over the Internet, and many film, television, and music personalities have their own Web sites.

For this project, investigate how authors, musicians, actors, and other individuals can market themselves online. Visit at least two Web sites belonging to these types of individuals and evaluate how effective you think they are. Do you have a talent or skill that can be marketed over the Internet? If so, do you think a Web site would be an effective marketing tool? Submit this project to your instructor in the form of a short paper, not more than two pages in length.

PRESENTATION/ DEMONSTRATION

7. **Your Domain** As mentioned in the chapter, e-commerce Web sites should select domain names that are easy for customers to remember.

   For this project, investigate how domain name registration works. First, select a domain name you would like to use for your fictitious e-commerce site. Next, visit at least two domain name registration Web sites (such as NetworkSolutions.com or Register.com) to determine what information you would need to provide to register your domain name and how much it would cost. Which top-level domains (such as *.com*, *.net*, *.org*, *.info*, *.name*, *.biz*, and *.us*) would you be able to use for your Web site? Determine any requirements—such as length and allowable characters—for domain names using those top-level domains. Think of an appropriate domain name for your site and use a lookup feature available on a registration site to see if that domain name is available. If not, keep trying variations of that name until you find an appropriate available domain name. Would the available name be easy for customers to remember? Share your findings with the class in the form of a short presentation. The presentation should not exceed 10 minutes and should make use of one or more presentation aids, such as the chalkboard, handouts, overhead transparencies, or a computer-based slide presentation (your instructor may provide additional requirements). You may also be asked to submit a summary of the presentation to your instructor.

GROUP DISCUSSION

8. **Internet Access: Luxury or Necessity?** A luxury can be defined as something that is an indulgence, rather than a necessity. Most people in the world would view such items as food, shelter, and water as necessities. In the United States, many would likely add electricity, indoor plumbing, and, possibly, telephone service to that list. But about 2.5 billion people in the world have no access to electricity, let alone indoor plumbing or telephone service. This opens up an interesting question: How can one item—such as electricity—be a luxury for some and a necessity for others? The answer may lie in the fact that what we view as a necessity tends to evolve over time as access to that item improves. For example, think of telephone use in the United States. A century ago, it was rare to have a telephone. Fifty years ago, many people had party lines. A decade or two ago it was uncommon to meet someone who did not have a telephone. Now it is quite rare. Today, many individuals are beginning to view cell phones, pagers, and Internet connections as necessities, rather than luxuries. For e-commerce businesses to continue to thrive, viewing Internet access as a necessity is a good trend. But is it really a necessity—that is, essential for existence? For instance, are there activities that must be performed online? If so, what about the other half of the population that does not have Internet access? How does this lack of Internet access affect them? There will likely always be some individuals who will never use a computer or the Internet, just as there are some individuals in this country who choose to live without electricity or indoor plumbing. How does the reality that some individuals live without a product or service viewed as a necessity affect that product's or service's necessity status? Can it still be viewed as a necessity, even if everyone does not seem to need it? Why or why not? Do you think Internet access is a necessity?

   For this project, form an opinion regarding whether Internet access is a necessity or luxury and how that viewpoint may affect the growth of e-commerce. Be prepared to discuss your position (in class, via an online class discussion group, or in a class chat room, depending on your instructor's directions). You may also be asked to write a short paper expressing your opinion.

WEB ACTIVITIES

The *Understanding Computers* Web site located at **www.course.com/uc11** features many resources to help reinforce your understanding of the chapter content and help you prepare for exams. Your instructor may also assign specific activities to be completed that will count toward your final grade in the course.

Instructions: Go to **www.course.com/uc11/ch11** to work the following online activities.

Click any link in the navigation bar on the left to access any of the online resources described below.

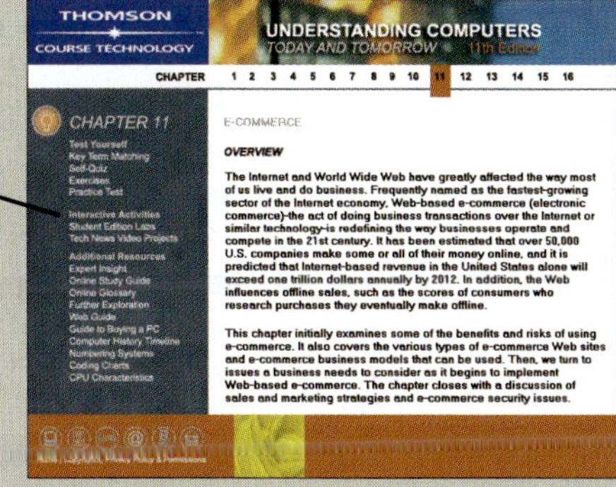

INTERACTIVE ACTIVITIES

1. **Crossword Puzzle** Practice your knowledge of the key terms in Chapter 11 by completing the interactive Crossword Puzzle.
2. **Tech News Video Project** Watch the **"Telesurgery"** video clip that features Dr. Louis Kavoussi of Johns Hopkins Bayview Medical Center, who performs surgery on patients all over the world from his home office instead of in a hospital operating room. He uses his PC to control robotic surgical tools and cameras, as well as to give surgeons written and verbal instructions. After watching the video online, complete the corresponding project.
3. **Student Edition Labs** Reinforce the concepts you have learned in this chapter by working through the interactive **E-Commerce**, **Web Design Principles**, and **Creating Web Pages** labs.

TEST YOURSELF

1. **Key Term Matching** Test your knowledge of selected chapter key terms by matching the terms with their definitions.
2. **Self-Quiz** Test your retention of chapter concepts by taking the Self-Quiz.
3. **Exercises** Work these short exercises to review the concepts and terms covered in the chapter.
4. **Practice Test** Test how ready you are for an upcoming exam by completing the online Practice Test.

STUDY TOOLS/ ADDITIONAL RESOURCES

The Understanding Computers Web site has a wide range of additional resources, including an **Online Study Guide** (containing study tips, a chapter outline with room to add your own notes, and a chapter checklist of the activities to complete when the chapter is covered in class and when you are preparing for a test) and an **Online Glossary** for each chapter; **Further Exploration** links; a **Web Guide**, a **Guide to Buying a PC**, and a **Computer History Timeline**; more information about **Numbering Systems**, **Coding Charts**, and **CPU Characteristics**; and much, much more!

EXPERT INSIGHT ON . . .

Web-Based Multimedia and E-Commerce

A conversation with **CHRISTOPHER ALLEN**

Head of Product Strategy, Yahoo! Music

My Background . . .

I have always loved technology and the ability of technology to empower consumers to consume the media that they want, when they want it, how they want to, and where they want it. I got involved in online multimedia after spending more than 10 years in product management at AT&T and NCR working on data warehouse decision support, CRM, and business intelligence initiatives. An early adopter of digital music, I converted my CD collection to digital files in 1998 using Musicmatch Jukebox and was one of the first purchasers and users of the original Creative Nomad portable digital music player.

Professionally, my first online multimedia endeavor was co-founding Kablink, an online photo service company. I joined Musicmatch in 2000, and then moved to Yahoo! Music when Musicmatch was acquired by Yahoo! in 2004. At Yahoo! Music, I am responsible for driving the global product vision and managing the strategic product and service roadmap, as well as analyzing future trends related to integrating digital music services into emerging technologies and devices. Specifically, my team and I are responsible for the product and service vision, merchandising, e-commerce, and product marketing activities for Yahoo! Music, as well as customer acquisition and retention strategies for Yahoo! Music's subscription services. Over the years I've found that a relentless and passionate focus on the customer is always relevant in any endeavor.

“. . . successful online enterprises will make it very easy for consumers to discover, sample, buy, and consume content.”

It's Important to Know . . .

Multimedia and e-commerce will continue to grow online. Online music is already having a significant impact on the $40 billion global media market and the $30 billion global music market as we transition to an all-digital, online world.

Web sites should design for superior usability, performances, and reliability. The engagement and retention of consumers interacting with your products and services will increasingly be determined by their overall user experience.

Web sites should make it easy to buy and easy to repeat purchases. Both from a usability and merchandising (personalization) perspective, successful online enterprises will make it very easy for consumers to discover, sample, buy, and consume content.

Christopher Allen is currently the Head of Product Strategy for Yahoo! Music and has over 10 years of product and marketing experience. Christopher oversees worldwide product planning and marketing activities for Yahoo! Music; holds multiple degrees in Electrical and Computer Engineering, and an MBA; is a frequent speaker at digital media and music conferences; and is often interviewed for newspapers, magazines, and industry journals.

. . . personalization will be increasingly important as the sheer amount of information, media, and content across the Web continues to grow substantially.

How I Use this Technology . . .

I consume quite a bit of digital content—from Weblogs, to digital photo albums, to a LOT of digital music. I subscribe to Musicmatch On Demand and Yahoo! Music Unlimited since I can access and play over 1 million tracks with these music services. I subscribe to an online DVD rental service, and I also purchase most of my electronic, computer, and media gear, books, and other products exclusively via the Web.

What the Future Holds . . .

Broadband will become increasingly ubiquitous, including the emergence of wireless (Wi-Fi) hotspots making access to, and the consumption of, digital content and media commonplace. With an estimated 700 million cell phone handsets sold worldwide in 2005, the cellular/mobile opportunity is also enormous. In many countries outside of the United States, the mobile platform is already larger than the PC-based platform for the delivery of products and services.

The Web of the future (sometimes referred to as Web 2.0) will evolve from a publication medium to more of a platform for distributed services. Content will be personalized just for you and relevant. This personalization will be increasingly important as the amount of information, media, and content across the Web continues to grow substantially. We already see households that don't watch TV or listen to radio anymore in a conventional sense, since those activities have been replaced with user-controlled, on-demand experiences personalized for the customer. Personalization helps give users what they want, but don't know it yet—helping them to find relevant media and information in a vast sea of content.

In addition, e-commerce activities will be more seamless and secure, with more subscriptions to access a vast array of digital content. You will have ubiquitous access to your content, anytime, anyplace, any way you want to consume it, anywhere you want to consume it.

My Advice to Students . . .

There is likely no area of commerce, communication, entertainment, finance, etc. that will not be fundamentally impacted or transformed by the Internet. Understanding the fundamental consumer shift to online media consumption, the innovative multimedia technologies, and the need to help consumers discover, share, and create meaningful content will be paramount to this transformation.

@WEB

Discussion Question

Christopher Allen views the Web as the multimedia delivery platform of the future. Think about the multimedia activities and purchases you make today, such as watching TV, listening to music, purchasing music, renting movies, and so forth. Which of those activities do you currently perform via the Internet? Which do you expect to perform via the Internet within the next two years? Are there some you don't ever expect to take place online? If so, which ones and why? Christopher also foresees a future where personalization will help deliver just the information and Web content you desire—how will such personalization affect your life? Do you view such personalization as a helpful tool or do you have privacy concerns? How could your privacy concerns be addressed? Be prepared to discuss your position (in class, via an online class discussion group, or in a class chat room, depending on your instructor's directions). You may also be asked to write a short paper expressing your opinion.

>For more information about Yahoo! Music and Musicmatch.com, visit music.yahoo.com/unlimited or www.musicmatch.com/download/ondemand_intro.htm.

MODULE SYSTEMS

This module integrates many of the concepts discussed in earlier chapters. It brings hardware, software, data, people, and procedures together to form complete systems.

Chapter 12 looks at the information systems found in organizations, including the principal types of systems used in an organization, followed by a look at the activities performed during the system development process. Chapter 13 covers the program development process—one important step in the system development process—and the various programming languages developers may choose from when creating a new program. Database management systems are the subject of Chapter 14. This chapter discusses database concepts in much more detail than previous chapters, including more specific database vocabulary, wider coverage of possible database models, and how databases are used in conjunction with the World Wide Web.

"Collecting, storing, and mining data to derive meaningful information will continue to impact the way we live . . . "

For more comments from Guest Expert Anthony Briggs of Best Buy, see the Expert Insight on . . . Systems feature at the end of the module.

IN THIS MODULE

Chapter 12 Information Systems and System Development 486

Overview 487

What Is an Information System? 487

Who Uses Information Systems? 488

Types of Information Systems 489

Responsibility for System Development 508

The System Development Life Cycle (SDLC) 511

Approaches to System Development 520

Chapter 13 Program Development and Programming Languages 530

Overview 531

Approaches to Program Design and Development 531

The Program Development Life Cycle (PDLC) 534

Tools for Facilitating Program Development 551

Programming Languages 553

Chapter 14 Databases and Database Management Systems 574

Overview 575

What Is a Database? 575

Data Concepts and Characteristics 581

Database Classifications 589

Database Models 591

Databases and the Web 601

CHAPTER 12 Information Systems and System Development

OUTLINE

Overview
What Is an Information System?
Who Uses Information Systems?
- Executive Management
- Middle Management
- Operational Management
- Nonmanagement Workers

Types of Information Systems
- Office Systems
- Transaction Processing Systems
- Management Information Systems (MISs)
- Decision Support Systems (DSSs)
- Geographic Information Systems (GISs)
- Enterprise-Wide and Inter-Enterprise Systems
- Design and Manufacturing Systems
- Artificial Intelligence Systems

Responsibility for System Development
- The Information Systems Department
- Outsourcing Companies

The System Development Life Cycle (SDLC)
- Preliminary Investigation
- System Analysis
- System Design
- System Acquisition
- System Implementation
- System Maintenance

Approaches to System Development
- The Traditional Approach
- Prototyping
- End-User Development

LEARNING OBJECTIVES

After completing this chapter, you will be able to:

1. Understand what information systems are.
2. Explain who uses information systems in a typical organization.
3. Identify several types of information systems commonly found in organizations and describe their purpose.
4. Explain the people involved with system development.
5. Identify and describe the different steps of the system development life cycle (SDLC).
6. Discuss several approaches used to develop systems.

OVERVIEW

In previous chapters of this textbook we have looked at different types of hardware and software. Here we turn to the process of putting these elements together to form complete systems.

Systems are found in all organizations. For example, systems facilitate accounting activities, such as sending out bills and processing payrolls; they provide information to help managers make decisions; they help run factories efficiently; and they enable workers to exchange information and collaborate on projects. Such systems require considerable effort to design, build, and maintain. Unfortunately, since no two situations are exactly alike, there is no single, surefire formula for successful system development. A procedure that works well in one situation may fail in another. These facts notwithstanding, there is a set of general principles that, if understood, will enhance the likelihood of a system's success. Those principles are the subject of this chapter.

The chapter opens with a discussion of information systems—systems that support the information needs of companies—and how they are used by different levels of employees in an organization. Next, we cover the most common types of information systems. From there we turn to the process of system development, beginning with the computer professionals who develop systems and their primary responsibilities. We then look at the system development life cycle—the set of activities that is at the heart of every serious systems-building effort. The chapter concludes with a discussion of the major approaches to system development. ■

WHAT IS AN INFORMATION SYSTEM?

A **system** is a collection of elements and procedures that interact to accomplish a goal. A football game, for example, is played according to a system. It consists of a collection of *elements* (two teams, a playing field, referees) and *procedures* (the rules of the game) that interact to determine which team is the winner. A transit system is a collection of people, buses or trains, work rules, fares, and schedules designed to get people from one place to another. Similarly, an **information system** is a collection of people, hardware, software, data, and procedures that interact to generate information to support users in an organization. Sometimes also referred to as "a collection of people, processes, and technology," information systems manage and process data from its generation (such as data resulting from orders, documents, and other business transactions) through its conversion into information; the resulting information is often used to support decision making. Although most information systems within organizations serve employees, increasingly information systems are expanding to support the needs of customers and suppliers, as well.

The function of many systems, whether manual or computerized, is to keep an organization well managed and running smoothly. Systems are created and modified in response

>**System.** A collection of elements and procedures that interact to accomplish a goal. >**Information system.** A system used to generate information to support users in an organization.

to changing needs within an organization and shifting conditions in its surrounding environment. When problems arise in an existing system or when a new system is needed, *system development* comes into play. **System development** is the process of analyzing a work environment, designing a new system or making modifications to the current system to fit the needs of the work environment, acquiring any needed hardware and software, training users, and getting the new or modified system to work.

System development may be required for many reasons. New laws may call for the collection of data that was not collected in the past. For example, the government may require new data on personnel or require additional reports regarding financial data, internal controls, and procedures, like those required by the *Sarbanes-Oxley Act* signed into law in 2002. Or the government may require new security or privacy procedures to be used with collected data, such as the procedures regulated by *the Health Insurance Portability and Accountability Act (HIPAA) Privacy Rule* or the proposed *Personal Data Privacy and Security Act of 2005*. The introduction of new technology, especially new computer technology, may also prompt the revision of a system. For instance, it is common today for a company to convert certain applications to work with other applications via the corporate network or to modify an information system to enable customers and suppliers to access it via the Internet. These and other kinds of requirements prompted by new regulations or the need to stay abreast of the competition often bring about major changes in an organization's systems.

In the early days of commercial computing, businesses purchased computers almost exclusively to perform routine processing tasks related to business transactions, such as processing orders and payments. Used in this manner, the computers cut clerical expenses considerably. As time passed, however, it became apparent that the computer could do much more than just *transaction processing*—it could also provide information to assist managers in their decision making role. As data analysis tools and information systems continue to improve—such as the data mining tools discussed in Chapter 11 and the powerful *business analytics* tools discussed in this chapter—they are becoming an increasingly important and valuable business component.

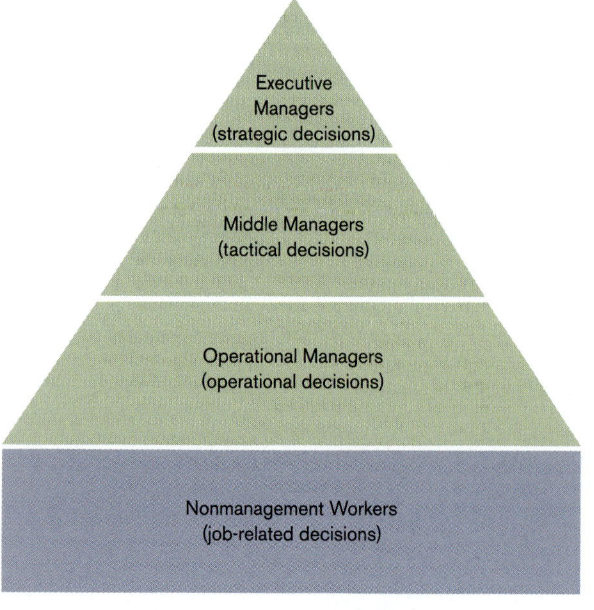

FIGURE 12-1
The management pyramid. Management positions are generally classified as executive, middle, or operational.

WHO USES INFORMATION SYSTEMS?

Since information systems are often used to generate information for organizational decisions, much of the time they are used by decision makers, such as managers. By using information systems, managers spend less time gathering facts but have access to more information when making their decisions. As a result, managers have more time to do the things they do best—thinking creatively and interacting with people.

Managers are usually classified into three categories: *executive*, *middle*, and *operational*. These positions are often pictured as a pyramid to illustrate their usual ratio and hierarchical ranking (see Figure 12-1) with executive managers fewer in number and at the top of the pyramid and operational managers greater in number and at the bottom of the pyramid, immediately above nonmanagement employees. Middle managers usually fall between the other two types of managers, although with the increased use of information systems and

>**System development.** The process of designing and implementing a new or modified system.

other technological advances the middle-management level is becoming less essential and has begun to disappear in some organizations. This trend is referred to as the *flattening* of the organizational structure.

Managers most often manage the employees one level below them on the pyramid. For example, executive managers are typically in charge of middle managers, and operational managers supervise nonmanagement workers. Management jobs are classified into one of these categories based on the job functions performed and the types of decisions made by the manager. The most common types of information systems used by each level of management are discussed next.

Executive Management

Executive managers, also called *senior managers* or *top-level managers*, are the highest management positions in an organization. They include the president, vice-president, chief executive officer (CEO), chief information officer (CIO), and so forth. Executive managers spend a great deal of time on long-range planning and use information systems to make *strategic decisions*, although their decision making process tends to be fairly unstructured. That is, unlike lower-level managers who make more structured decisions on a regular basis (such as whether to give a specific employee a raise or when to reorder inventory items), executive managers focus on long-term, strategic decisions that shape the focus and direction of a company.

Middle Management

Middle managers use information systems to make *tactical decisions* that affect the organization's activities approximately one to five years in the future. Some examples of middle-management positions are human resources and purchasing managers. The decisions made by middle management are moderately structured.

Operational Management

Operational managers supervise nonmanagement workers. They include various types of supervisors, foremen, office managers, and so forth. Operational managers use information systems to make *operational decisions* geared toward meeting *short-term objectives*, usually within the current fiscal year. These decisions tend to be highly structured.

Nonmanagement Workers

Nonmanagement workers, such as office workers, accountants, or engineers, use information systems when needed to make the *on-the-job decisions* necessary to perform their jobs. Nonmanagement workers today have more information available to them than in previous decades, and consequently, they make more on-the-job decisions than in the past.

TYPES OF INFORMATION SYSTEMS

Undoubtedly, you have already encountered many types of systems in organizations. When you go into the supermarket, for instance, you generally see the electronic cash registers and barcode readers that are part of the supermarket's inventory and pricing system. Or when you have registered for college classes, perhaps you have observed someone at a PC checking to see whether a certain class you want to take is still open and whether you have any outstanding school fees—these actions are all part of the school's registration system.

While hundreds of specific types of information systems are in existence today, many fall into one of eight categories: *office*, *transaction processing*, *management information*, *decision support*, *geographic information*, *enterprise-wide/inter-enterprise*, *design and manufacturing*, and *artificial intelligence systems*. These systems are summarized in Figure 12-2 and discussed next. For a look at how information systems are used in some everyday situations, see the Technology and You box.

TECHNOLOGY AND YOU

Laundry Room and Roller Coaster Information Systems

Information systems are usually associated with organizations, but they can also be associated with objects. For example, would you suspect that laundry rooms and roller coasters have something in common? Well, new smart laundry rooms and roller coasters do—they both use information systems.

To avoid the problem of college students hauling laundry down to the campus laundry room only to find no machines are available, some college laundry rooms today are going high-tech. The new *eSuds* online laundry system is installed in over 130 colleges and universities in the United States. With the eSuds system, students can go online from their dorm rooms to see which machines are available, or they can request to be notified via an e-mail or a text message sent to a PC or cell phone when the machine they requested is free. The system also notifies the student when his or her laundry is done, and it allows the company to remotely monitor the machines for service needs.

The Top Thrill Dragster (see the accompanying photo), a roller coaster in the Cedar Point Amusement Park in Ohio, is another example of an object that has its own information system. In an attempt to create a consistently perfect roller coaster ride, a complex information system—consisting of cabling, sensors, computers, and software—is used. The Dragster is wired with 560,000 feet of copper cable to carry back performance data from 300 redundant pairs of sensors located throughout the track and engine room. In addition to taking readings for safety purposes, the sensors measure the movement of roller coaster cars over the track, wind speed, outside temperature, and passenger weight load. The collected data is analyzed by proprietary software developed just for this roller coaster. After every three rides, the system makes corrections as needed to make sure each roller coaster ride clears the top of the 420-foot tower (about the height of a 42-story building), but it slows down enough at the top to ensure the maximum ride experience for customers.

FIGURE 12-2
Types of information systems.

TYPE OF SYSTEM	DESCRIPTION
Office system	Facilitates communications and enhanced productivity in office tasks.
Transaction processing system	Processes and records business transactions.
Management information system (MIS)	Provides routine information to decision makers.
Decision support system (DSS)	Helps decision makers organize and analyze information to support decision making.
Geographic information system (GIS)	Organizes a variety of data by geographic location to support decision making.
Enterprise-wide/inter-enterprise system	Integrates activities through an entire enterprise/ links multiple enterprises.
Design and manufacturing system	Helps with the decision and/or manufacturing of products.
Artificial intelligence system	Performs actions that are characteristic of human intelligence.

Office Systems

In recent years, computer technology has been used widely to increase productivity in the office. The term **office automation** (**OA**) describes this phenomenon. Office automation can be achieved through a variety of technologies and processing techniques, as described in this section. The combination of hardware, software, and other resources used to facilitate communications and enhance productivity is collectively referred to as an **office system**. Office systems are used by all levels of management and by nonmanagement employees.

Document Processing Systems

The cornerstone of most organizations is the document—memos, letters, reports, manuals, forms, invoices, and so forth. Consequently, a major focus of office automation relates to the creation, distribution, and storage of documents. Sometimes the phrase *document processing* is used to collectively refer to such office technologies as word processing, desktop publishing, and other types of electronic document handling. The predicted *paperless office* has yet to materialize, and some in the industry are not sure it will anytime soon—as information systems continue to improve and become capable of generating more detailed analyses and reports, individuals tend to want them. And, since many individuals prefer working with printed copies of documents instead of electronic copies, this growing trend may actually increase the use of paper documents in the office. Nevertheless, *electronic document management* is common today and there are a growing number of electronic document management software programs available to help store, organize, and retrieve documents once they have been created in or converted to electronic form.

In addition to normal office documents like letters, reports, spreadsheets, and databases, a variety of other types of documents are increasingly becoming electronic. For instance, a growing number of medical records are kept electronically today, digital x-rays are becoming the norm, and the U.S. Navy is in the process of replacing paper-based nautical maps with digital version on all ships by 2009. The conversion to digital documents has many advantages, including increased efficiency, better service, and a reduction of errors. For instance, hospital information systems can enable physicians to access patient records and X-rays via portable PCs so they can make diagnoses and issue orders from wherever they happen to be at the moment. In addition, hospital information systems allow prescription medicines to be administered correctly and efficiently, because nurses have real-time access to prescription information and they can scan the medication bottle and the patient wristband to confirm the drug, as well as the dosage, is correct before administering it. One hospital network that recently implemented a drug-dispensing system estimates the system cuts the time required to dispense medication to patients in half, while at the same time avoiding 20,000 potential dispensing errors in one year alone.

As the volume of data and information in electronic format grows, so does the challenge of preserving that data and information for the future. Both the government and private companies have an enormous amount of electronic records that need to be preserved and made accessible for future generations, such as for historic, educational, or legal reasons. For example, the National Archives and Records Administration (NARA) estimates that there are 36.5 billion e-mail messages received each year by the federal government, plus there are an additional billion or so military intelligence documents, more than 50 million electronic court case files, and about 600 million pages of information from the 2000 census alone—all this is information that needs to be archived. The challenge is developing an archival system that can be implemented on a wide-scale basis and be compatible with future technology.

>Office automation (OA). Computer-based office-oriented technologies, such as word processing, e-mail, workgroup computing, and the like.

>Office system. A type of system in which office automation hardware, software, and other resources are used to facilitate communications and enhance productivity.

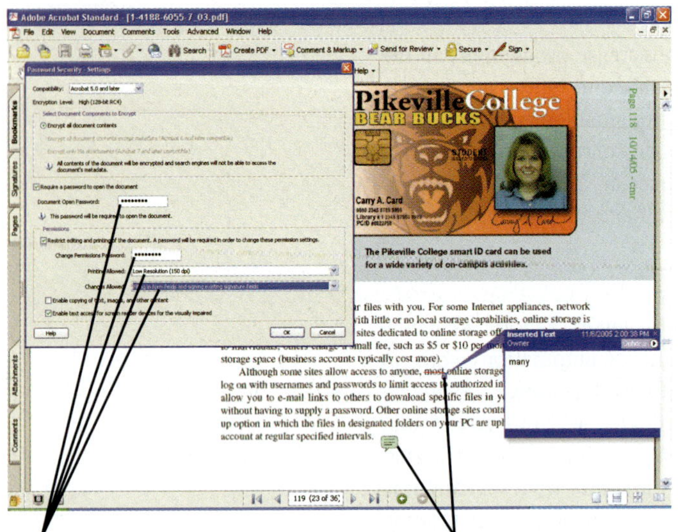

FIGURE 12-3
Adobe Acrobat. The Adobe Acrobat program is used to create and modify PDF documents and includes a variety of reviewing and security features.

One of the leaders in this area is Adobe with its *Adobe®Acrobat®* products used to create *PDF* (*Portable Document Format*) documents. The PDF format is designed to create electronic documents that retain their appearance regardless of the device being used to view them, so a press release, budget, or other document will look the same when it is viewed by anyone (the free *Adobe Reader* program is used to view PDF files). Any document that can be printed can be converted into a PDF document, using the Adobe Acrobat program. Once converted into a PDF document, the fonts, images, graphics, and layout of the original document are preserved. In addition, the Acrobat program (see Figure 12-3) allows others to make comments in the document (such as on sticky notes) and allows the creator of the PDF document to apply restrictions regarding printing and modification access. A version of PDF called *PDF-Archive* (*PDF-A*) is emerging as a standard for archiving documents so the contents of documents can be preserved over an extended period of time and can be retrieved in the future with consistent and predictable results.

TIP

If you have the Adobe Acrobat program installed on your PC, you can create PDF files by choosing the *Print* command from the File menu and then selecting *Adobe PDF* as your printer.

Communications Systems

The various types of *communications systems* in place in many organizations include e-mail, messaging, online conferencing, collaborative (workgroup) computing, and telecommuting. These systems, discussed in detail in Chapter 7, allow employees to communicate with each other, as well as with business partners and customers.

Transaction Processing Systems

Virtually every organization carries out a number of routine, structured accounting operations, most of which involve some form of tedious recordkeeping. These operations, such as payroll and accounts receivable, inspired some of the earliest commercial applications for computers and are still among the most widely used. Because these systems involve processing business transactions—paying employees and recording customer purchases and payments, for instance—they are called **transaction processing systems**.

Transaction processing systems are typically used to process transactions and then provide information to operational managers. Some of the most common types of transaction processing systems are discussed in the following paragraphs. In addition to these normal business transaction processing systems, there are also specialty transaction processing systems used by law enforcement, the military, and other organizations. For instance, city, state, and federal governments need to have systems in place to process tax payments, fines, and other transactions, and law enforcement and judicial organizations need systems to issue citations and judgments. Like other transaction processing systems, these systems are increasingly being automated. For example, *electronic citation systems* are being implemented in some states. With these systems, officers can quickly and easily fill out moving violations via a computer, using the barcodes on driver's license to automatically add the driver information. Citations can be issued much more quickly than by hand and are entered into the system automatically so that data is available to other electronic systems when needed without reentering the data.

>**Transaction processing system.** A type of information system that processes and records data created by an organization's business transactions.

TREND

Fingerprint Payment Systems

Biometric devices are increasingly being used for consumer applications, such as granting access to a gym or college dormitory or authenticating that the person using some type of access card (such as an ATM card, student ID card, or corporate ID card) is really the authorized individual. One of the newest consumer applications is the *fingerprint payment system*—the use of fingerprint readers to buy goods and services at restaurants, grocery stores, video stores, warehouse stores, and other types of retail establishments. One of the leading fingerprint payment services is *Pay By Touch*, which uses a standard point-of-sale credit card reader with a small fingerprint reader attached (see the accompanying photo). Pay By Touch systems are currently available in a number of stores—such as Piggly Wiggly, Albertsons, Cub Foods, Farm Fresh, Thriftway, and Pick 'n Save—in ten states in the United States. A consumer who would like the option of paying with this method simply enrolls in the program at any location offering the service. To enroll, an individual touches the fingerprint reader to scan in his or her fingerprint characteristics and then enters appropriate contact and payment information (such as credit card or checking account information). To pay for goods and services using the service from that point on, the customer only needs to place one finger on the reader located at any retail establishment using that fingerprint payment service and enter a search number (often the customer's telephone number) to enable the system to quickly retrieve his or her personal payment information. The customer then selects the desired payment method from the list. The transaction is then processed normally as if a credit card or check had been presented (similar to credit card processing, the merchant pays any transaction fees).

Although fingerprint payment systems are convenient for consumers, reduce fraudulent transactions, and move customers through check-out lines faster, there are skeptics. Some individuals, worried about privacy and security, will likely never permit their fingerprint images to be entered into a payment database. In addition, although information entered into one type of system (such as Pay By Touch or a competitive system) is available at any retailer using that same system, it is not available at retailers using a different system. Until one standard or clear winner in this market emerges, incompatibility between rival systems may become a frustration for consumers. However, consumer reaction so far seems to be positive. In a recent two-year Pay By Touch pilot test, 82% of the participants were not concerned about giving a fingerprint reading in order to be able to use the service.

To alleviate privacy and security concerns, Pay By Touch has a stringent privacy policy that states that a customer's personal information will never be provided to outside companies for marketing or advertising purposes. In addition, they stress that the system captures data points of the finger image that are used to uniquely identify an individual, but that those data points cannot be used to reconstruct and duplicate the individual's fingerprint. Whether consumers will trust fingerprint payment systems when they are widely introduced remains to be seen, but the outlook appears very promising.

Order Entry Systems

Many organizations handle some type of order processing on a daily basis. Customers submit orders by phone, by mail, via the Internet, or in person. The systems that record the data generated from these transactions and help staff members manage them are called **order entry systems**. Two specific types of order entry systems are *e-commerce systems* (used for financial transactions performed over the Internet) and *point-of-sale (POS) systems* (used to record purchases at the point where the customer physically purchases a product or service, such as at a checkout counter). For a look at one emerging way to pay for products and services at some POS systems—*fingerprint payment systems*—see the Trend box.

>**Order entry system.** A type of transaction system that records and manages order processing.

FIGURE 12-4

Electronic checks. To facilitate the Check 21 system, many ATMs now capture check images electronically as they are deposited.

Check Processing Systems

Financial institutions need to process checks in an accurate, timely manner. A new check processing system—*Check Clearing for the 21st Century Act* or *Check 21*—was implemented in late 2004. The Check 21 system is designed to make it easier for banks to process checks electronically without having to wait for paper checks to be physically exchanged. Under the new rules, electronic images of checks instead of the physical checks are sent to other banks to clear. This new system allows checks to be processed in hours, instead of days. Printed copies of the processed electronic checks—called *substitute checks*—can be obtained from the bank and are legal equivalents of original processed checks. To further speed up check processing, new ATMs have been introduced that are designed for checks to be deposited without an envelope (see Figure 12-4) so that the check image can be captured when the check is deposited in the ATM machine. With these new machines, the amount of the check is automatically determined, and the check and amount is displayed on the screen for customer verification. After the transaction is completed, the electronic check image is transmitted to the bank's server to be stored and sent to the appropriate bank for further processing, and the check image is printed on the ATM receipt for the customer's records.

Payroll Systems

Payroll systems accept input about employee pay rates or salaries, hours worked, and deduction amounts, and then compute deductions, subtract them from gross earnings, and issue paychecks to employees for their net pay. These systems also contain programs that prepare reports for management and for tax purposes for federal, state, and local governments.

Accounting Systems

Accounting systems refer to the variety of systems in place to record the details of financial transactions, such as payments and purchases. A few specific types of accounting systems are as follows:

FIGURE 12-5

Transaction processing systems. The programs in a transaction processing system typically tie into a general ledger system, which keeps track of all financial transactions.

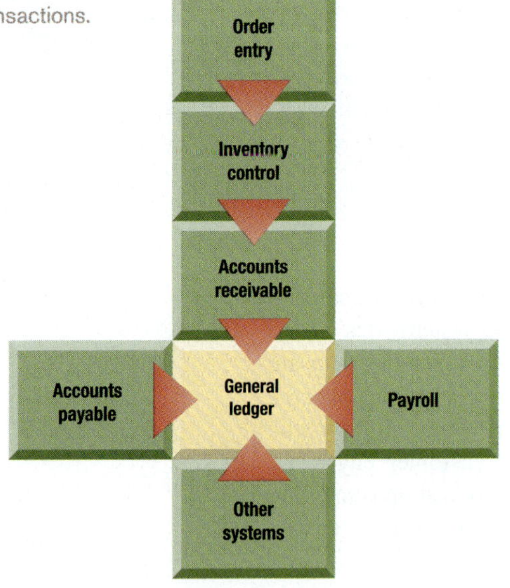

- *Accounts receivable systems*—keep track of customers' purchases, payments, and account balances. They also produce invoices and monthly account statements and provide information to management, such as sales analyses and past-due account reports.
- *Accounts payable systems*—keep track of bills to be paid and often generate checks to pay them. They record who gets paid and when, handle cash disbursements, and may advise managers about whether they should accept discounts offered by vendors in return for early payment.
- *General ledger systems*—keep track of all financial summaries, including those originating from payroll, accounts receivable, accounts payable, and other sources (see Figure 12-5). They also ensure that a company's books balance. A general ledger system typically produces income statements, balance sheets, and other accounting documents.

>**Payroll system.** A type of transaction system that generates employee payroll amounts and reports. >**Accounting system.** A type of transaction system that deals with the financial transactions and financial recordkeeping for an organization.

Management Information Systems (MISs)

Management information systems (**MISs**)—sometimes called *information reporting systems*—evolved from transaction processing systems. They provide decision makers with preselected information, usually in the form of computer-generated reports. The types of information produced from an MIS are usually preplanned, just like the information you see on your monthly checking account statements. The individual *values* on your statements (such as check numbers, check amounts, deposit and withdrawal amounts, and so forth) change from month to month, but the *types* of information you receive (checks cashed and deposits and withdrawals made, for instance) remain the same. Every other person receiving a checking account statement from your bank receives virtually the same type of information.

The goal of an MIS is to provide managers and other decision makers with the information they need to perform their jobs. Much of the time, this information is generated from the data obtained from transaction processing. For example, a manager in the accounts receivable department might regularly receive a report listing overdue accounts, a sales manager would likely receive regular sales reports, and an inventory supervisor would receive reports on the current status of the inventory and which items need reordering. The information generated from an MIS is most frequently used to make moderately structured, middle-management decisions.

Decision Support Systems (DSSs)

A **decision support system** (**DSS**) helps people organize and analyze the information they need to consider when making decisions. It is useful to anyone whose requirements for information are unpredictable and unstructured. Instead of the more structured transaction processing and management information systems, decision support systems provide information on demand whenever a decision making situation arises. DSSs may incorporate data from internal (within the company) and external (outside of the company) sources. External data used in a DSS might include interest rates, consumer confidence index numbers, and other economic indicators.

Decision support systems are usually tailored around the needs of an individual or group and are designed to help with specific types of decisions. For instance, a *Sales Support DSS* is aimed at the special decision making needs of sales or marketing personnel, and a *Transportation DSS* provides the information needed to route trucks, planes, and other transportation vehicles. Figure 12-6 shows a Web-based DSS that can be used to help a rancher evaluate if it is necessary to remove a cow from the herd. Decision support systems are typically used by middle and upper managers for unstructured, on-demand information needed for decisions. A special type of DSS specifically targeted to upper management is called an *executive information system* (*EIS*).

FIGURE 12-6

Decision support systems (DSSs). This DSS can help a rancher make decisions regarding the cows in his or her herd.

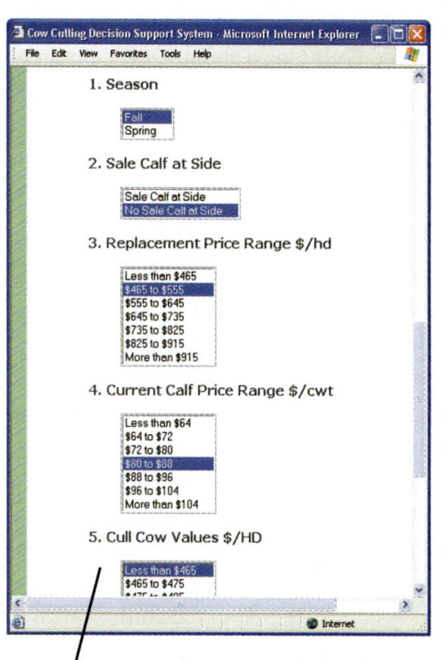

1. The rancher answers questions to provide information to the DSS.

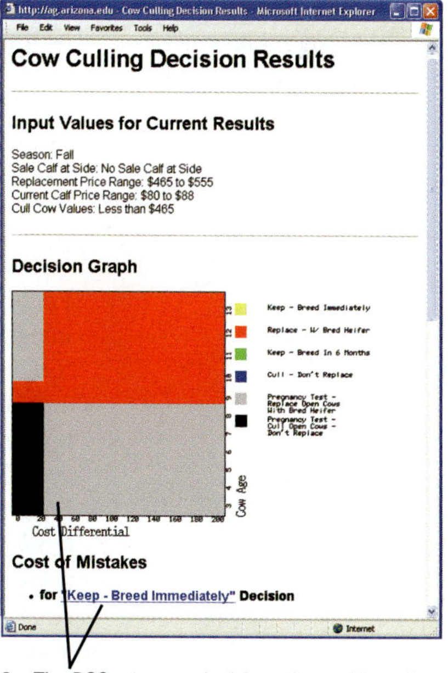

2. The DSS returns a decision, along with cost estimates for wrong decisions.

>**Management information system (MIS).** A type of information system that provides decision makers with preselected information that can be used to make middle-management decisions. >**Decision support system (DSS).** A type of information system typically used by upper management that provides people with the tools and capabilities to organize and analyze their decision making information.

As many executives see it, the business world today is so competitive and fast-paced that they need instant access to the most current information. These systems typically demand powerful computers to run the appropriate software and handle the extremely large databases that must be accessed, such as the data warehouses discussed in Chapter 11. In fact, a growing trend is the use of supercomputers to support executive decision making.

Geographic Information Systems (GISs)

Although they have been around for quite some time, there has been increased use lately of **geographic information systems (GISs)**. A GIS is an information system that combines geographic information with other types of data (such as information about customers, sales, population, income, and so forth) in order to provide a better understanding of the relationships between the data. It can allow decision makers to see relationships, patterns, or trends that are not possible to see with traditional charts, graphs, and spreadsheets. GISs allow decision makers to model scenarios to test various hypotheses and see outcomes visually to help determine the best scenario. They are commonly used to make decisions that involve locations, such as finding the best location for a new store, analyzing flood or tornado risk, or detecting geographical patterns in crime. For example, visualizing the potential locations for a new store on a map along with data representing other factors—such as traffic, population, weather, housing prices, household income, and possible environmental concerns like wetlands or protected species that might hamper construction—can help a manager select the optimal location (see Figure 12-7).

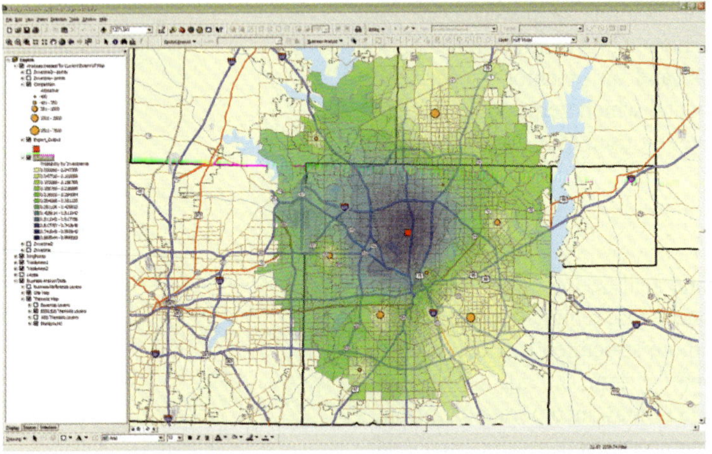

FIGURE 12-7
Geographic information systems (GISs). The GIS shown here shows the probability of shoppers visiting particular store locations in Dallas, Texas.

GISs are also essential parts of disaster-relief systems used by emergency workers. For instance, in the first two weeks after Hurricane Katrina hit the Gulf Coast in late 2005, about 60 volunteer GIS experts were assembled to use GIS to assist in the rescue and disaster-relief efforts. For instance, they used GIS to build search maps to be used by rescue workers; to create maps illustrating various issues, such as where electrical power had been restored; and to translate street addresses of survivors requiring helicopter rescues into map coordinates for the helicopter pilots.

Enterprise-Wide and Inter-Enterprise Systems

Large businesses are sometimes referred to as *enterprises*. Consequently, a system that integrates an entire company or enterprise is referred to as an **enterprise-wide system**. Systems that link multiple enterprises—such as a business and its customers, suppliers, and partners—are often called **inter-enterprise systems**. Enterprise-wide systems are typically implemented via a corporate network, although some parts of an enterprise-wide system also may be accessible via the Internet. Inter-enterprise systems are typically implemented via the Internet, supported by technologies such as Web services and XML (Extensible Markup Language). RFID systems were explained in Chapter 4 and GPS systems were included in Chapter 7; some other specific types of enterprise-wide and inter-enterprise systems are discussed in the following sections. Many of these are considered to be *business intelligence (BI) systems*.

>**Geographic information system (GIS).** An information system that combines geographic information with other types of data (such as information about your customers, sales, and so forth) in order to provide a better understanding of the relationships among the data. >**Enterprise-wide system.** A system that integrates activities throughout an entire enterprise. >**Inter-enterprise system.** A system that links multiple enterprises, such as a business and its customers, suppliers, and partners.

Electronic Data Interchange (EDI)

Short for **electronic data interchange**, **EDI** refers to the transfer of data between different companies using networks, such as the Internet. EDI is used to strategically link one organization's computers to the computers of key customers or suppliers. EDI facilitates the exchange of standard business documents—such as purchase orders and invoices—from one company's computer system to the system of another company. In order to exchange information using EDI, documents must be translated into a format that complies with an EDI standard. Then they are sent to the recipient and translated into a format usable by that company's systems.

Many large companies today order sizable percentages of their supplies or raw materials through EDI. The company doing the purchasing often uses EDI to electronically track the progress of its orders on the seller's computer system; the system can even be set up to continually replenish inventory as needed using selected real-time inventory information systems. For example, materials are automatically ordered, shipped, and the corresponding electronic invoices sent when the stocks of those materials have reached the designated reorder point.

In addition to traditional EDI activities, new types are expected as electronic document submission and electronic signatures become more acceptable business practices.

Enterprise Resource Planning (ERP) and Enterprise Application Integration (EAI)

Enterprise resource planning (**ERP**) is a special type of large, integrated system that ties together all types of a business's activities, such as planning, manufacturing, sales, marketing, distribution, customer service, and finance. Instead of each department having its own computer system, as in the past, an ERP system combines them into a single, integrated application so the various departments can more easily share information and communicate with each other. For example, when an order is placed, the employee who takes the order from a customer has all the information necessary to complete the order (such as the customer's credit information and history, the company's inventory levels, and the shipping schedule). Throughout the order fulfillment and billing process, everyone in the company who deals with the order in some manner has access to the same information regarding the customer's order, without having to reenter the necessary data. When one department finishes with the order, the ERP system may automatically route it to the next department. At any point in the process, the order status can be determined by anyone in the company.

Today's ERP applications are commonly put on the Web so users both inside and outside of the company can get easy access to ERP-generated data. When information from an ERP or other type of internal system is exchanged between different applications within an organization or between organizations, it is called **enterprise application integration** (**EAI**). EAI tools can respond to and initiate events from multiple third-party applications and act as a common integration point for all of an organization's critical business processes. EAI is beginning to be viewed as a critical business tool because it allows an organization to quickly extend any and all of its administrative systems to customers, suppliers, and other business partners over the Internet.

Customer Relationship Management (CRM)

All of a company's customer service programs together make up its **customer relationship management** (**CRM**) system. The goal of a CRM system is to build relationships with

>Electronic data interchange (EDI). The transfer of data between different companies using the Internet or another network. **>Enterprise resource planning (ERP).** A large integrated system that ties together all of a business's activities. **>Enterprise application integration (EAI).** Exchanging information from an ERP or other internal system among different applications and organizations. **>Customer relationship management (CRM).** The process of building and managing good relationships with customers.

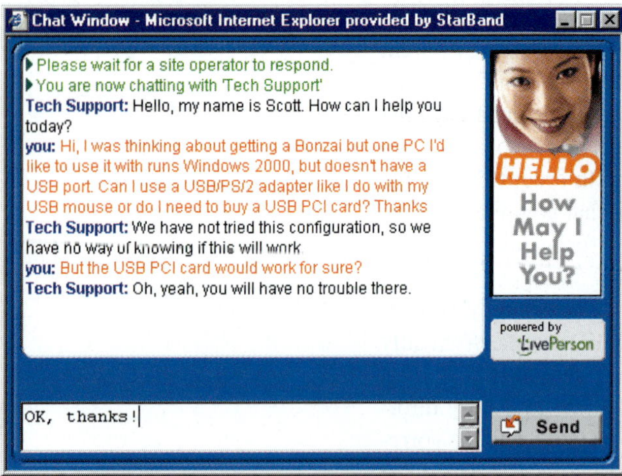

FIGURE 12-8

eCRM. Customer service or technical support live chat accessible through the company Web site is becoming more widely used as an eCRM tool.

customers in order to increase customer satisfaction and loyalty, which, in turn, will lead to increased profits. CRM is an essential component of most businesses today and is frequently delivered, at least in part, via the Web. Common Web-based CRM—sometimes referred to as *eCRM*—activities include data mining based on data collected from Web site visitors, tracking Web site activity to identify customers and their needs, providing product information and technical assistance via a Web site, providing order tracking, and notifying customers by e-mail about product upgrades, specials, service reminders, and so forth. New eCRM tools, such as those that add an *e-community* to the company Web site for customers to use, are becoming more prevalent. These tools allow customers to exchange ideas, ask questions, and provide feedback on products, as well as chat online live with technical support who provide instant answers to questions (see Figure 12-8). Research firm Jupiter predicts that CRM spending in the United States will continue to grow at a steady pace, and it expects CRM spending to surpass $16 billion by 2006.

In general, a CRM system can do the following:

- Provide an organization's marketing department with quality leads for its sales teams.
- Assist an organization in improving sales and sales management.
- Allow the formation of individualized relationships with customers, with the aim of improving customer satisfaction and maximizing profits.

TIP

If you have a question about a product you bought online or offline, go to the manufacturer's Web site and see what types of eCRM features—such as online manuals, online chat, or e-mail tech support—is offered that might be of help to you.

Supply Chain Management (SCM)

Supply chain management (SCM) is the oversight of materials, information, and finances as they move from the original supplier to the consumer. The goal of SCM is to deliver the right product to the right place, at the right time, and at the right price. An effective supply chain management system shares information upstream to the organization's suppliers and downstream to the organization's customers, reduces inventory, and increases profits.

Three items typically flow through an organization's supply chain management system. The *product flow* includes the movement of goods from the supplier to the customer or from the customer back to the supplier in the form of returned items. The *information flow* involves processing orders and updating the order/delivery status. The *financial flow* consists of credit and payment information. Most supply chain management software ties in with a company's ERP system. Increasingly, SCM systems use RFID technology (as discussed in Chapter 4) to track inventory. Specific types of SCM systems include *value chain management systems*, *just-in-time (JIT) systems*, and *inventory management systems*.

The *value chain* concept views a business or a network of businesses as a chain of business activities that add value to the resulting products or services. **Value chain management** is the process of maximizing the flow of products, services, and information from raw materials to the final consumer through a value-added network of suppliers. Each organization adds value to the product or service as it passes through the supply chain. Value chain management software can help companies find better ways to manufacture and distribute products by integrating the different activities of the value chain.

>**Supply chain management (SCM).** The oversight of materials, information, and finances as they move from the original supplier to the consumer. >**Value chain management.** The process of maximizing the flow of products, goods, services, and information through a value-added network of suppliers.

Just-in-time (JIT) systems are used in manufacturing to eliminate waste. With a JIT system, inventory, production resources, and finished products are limited to the right number at the right time as required to fill orders. By bringing production rates in line with market demand, JIT increases productivity and work performance and saves inventory and facility costs. Disadvantages include potential lost sales or delayed shipments if materials are unavailable (due to supplier problems, defective materials, or materials ruined during manufacturing, for instance) because no extra materials are kept in inventory. The JIT concept is not new—it was introduced in Japan decades ago. The recent integration of the Internet with manufacturing and supply systems, however, has allowed JIT systems to be implemented on a much wider scale.

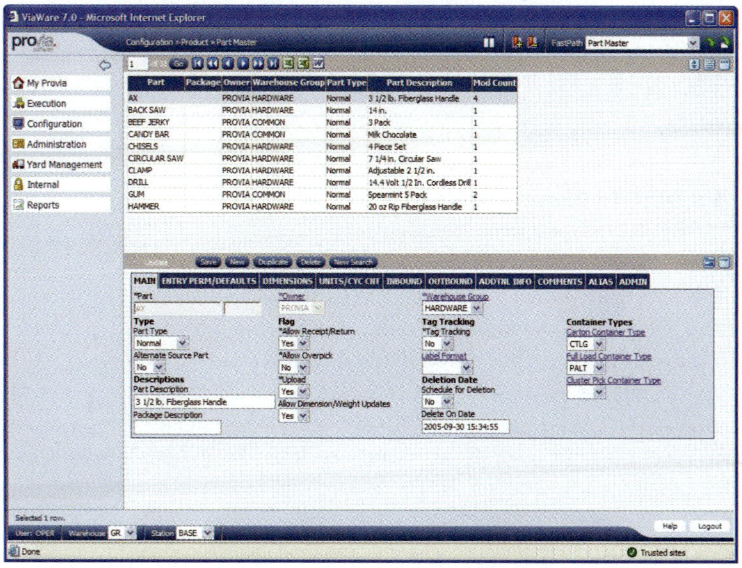

Inventory management systems (sometimes called *inventory control systems*) are systems used specifically to track and manage inventory. They can help organizations make decisions to optimize supply chain performance and reduce costs, such as by optimizing quantities and decreasing transportation costs. One specific type of inventory management system—a *warehouse management system (WMS)*—is shown in Figure 12-9. For a look at a new UPS information system to track and manage the delivery of packages, see the How it Works box.

FIGURE 12-9
Warehouse management system (WMS) software.

Product Lifecycle Management (PLM) and Price Optimization Systems

The goal of *product lifecycle management (PLM)* is to organize and correlate all information about a product (such as specifications, quality history, customer feedback, research and testing results, and sales history) to help companies improve products, more efficiently create and manage the production of products, and better track costs and profits. *PLM software*—often available as a Web-based application—links all facets and members of a project team electronically, regardless of the team members' locations, making new information available to the entire team as it becomes known. According to a recent survey by AMR Research, managers selected PLM as one of their most needed new software applications.

PLM can dramatically reduce the amount of time needed to implement design changes and get products to market. For instance, Cannondale Bicycle credits PLM for enabling its first-ever ATV product to be released on time, after just 14 months of development. Cannondale Bicycle estimates its motorsport group spends 40% less time on communications, and old problems—such as delayed production due to out-of-date schematics and wasted days test-driving prototypes containing outdated components—have virtually been eliminated.

Price optimization is the practice of maximizing revenues and profits by determining the optimal price to maximize product profitability. Price optimization uses *price optimization software* to analyze sales data and determine the optimal price of a product and its competing products to maximize a retailer's overall profit. Until recently, the complex calculations required for this type of analysis demanded sophisticated computers that

SYS

>**Just-in-time (JIT) system.** An inventory system in which inventory, other production resources, and finished products are limited to the right number at the right time as required to fill orders. >**Inventory management system.** A system used to track and manage inventory.

HOW IT WORKS

UPS DIAD IV Delivery System

DIAD (*Delivery Information Acquisition Device*) *IV* is a new UPS package delivery system that began implementation in 2005 and is expected to be fully deployed by the end of 2007. This new system includes new software, hardware, and procedures to improve customer service, such as the ability to handle unique or unusual delivery instructions, offer more customized time commitments, and allow customers to make in-transit changes to package deliveries. The heart of the new system is the new DIAD IV wireless computer used by UPS drivers and shown in the accompanying illustration. The DIAD IV is designed to be used in conjunction with smart labels and wireless scanners, but it also has a number of additional built-in technologies to ensure that the device can perform whatever communications tasks become necessary. For instance, each DIAD IV can communicate via a cell phone network, a dial-up modem, a Wi-Fi connection, a Bluetooth connection, and an infrared port. It also contains GPS capabilities to allow drivers to easily verify customer locations for package pickup or delivery. The new color screens offer the advantage of easier readability, as well as color-coding messages to the driver by importance, such as red for the most urgent messages.

With the new system, smart labels placed on the packages before they are picked up contain information—both in printed and barcode form—about the sender and the recipient. The information contained in the label helps to facilitate sorting, shipping, and loading processes. In addition, the new software used with this system automates delivery route planning, instead of drivers having to plan their own routes, as in the current system. This feature alone is expected to reduce the distance driven by UPS delivery trucks by more than 77,000 miles per day, saving millions of gallons of fuel each year. At the time the package is delivered, the label is scanned again and the customer's signature recorded. This information is relayed to the central system automatically, without the driver having to walk back to the truck and connect the device to a wireless WAN hookup, as in the current system.

The new system requires a substantial investment by UPS—the software alone costs about $30 million and UPS drivers use about 90,000 DIADs every day—but the increased efficiency and improved customer service is considered essential to provide UPS with its desired competitive advantage.

1. Customers or UPS-authorized shipping centers print smart labels to be affixed to packages before delivery.

2. The smart labels are scanned using Bluetooth-enabled portable scanners, and the information is relayed to the UPS system where it is used for sorting, shipping, and loading the packages onto the proper trucks.

3. On the trucks, the software uses the information contained in the smart labels to generate automated route plans for the drivers.

4. The DIAD IV is used to verify and record package deliveries. It also contains many other communications capabilities, such as being able to use GPS to find delivery addresses, to exchange data with other computers, and to wirelessly communicate with a printer.

were out of the price range of many businesses. With today's cheaper and more powerful computers, price optimization is now a powerful business tool available to many. If a product is still unsold toward the end of its life cycle, *markdown optimization software* can be used to maximize revenue by timing markdowns of products. Forrester Research estimates that the move from "gut instinct" pricing to a price optimization software system will increase a company's gross margin anywhere from 2% to 10% in the first three months. To eliminate the problems of employees mismarking shelf prices, some retailers are turning toward *electronic shelf labels* (*ESLs*), such as the one shown in Figure 12-10. ESLs use radio technology to communicate wirelessly with the store's pricing computer so that shelf prices always match the optimized price. Similar ESLs that can attach to products, such as shoes and clothing items, are also available.

FIGURE 12-10
Electronic shelf labels (ESLs).

Enterprise Architecture

A growing trend in the area of enterprise systems is the concept of **enterprise architecture**. The goal of enterprise architecture is to provide a detailed picture of an organization, its functions, its systems, and the relationships between them. In essence, enterprise architecture is a map of an organization's business functions and systems. Enterprise architecture has existed in theory for some time, but only recently have businesses focused on applying these principles on a practical level. With the complexity of today's systems, enterprise architecture allows managers to better organize and maximize the use of IT resources, as well as make informed decisions with fewer mistakes. Experts agree that developing an enterprise architecture is not easy and requires a great deal of time and effort. The first step is usually to examine the existing systems and functions to identify gaps, overlaps, and other possible issues with the existing setup. Enterprise architecture development is usually viewed as a long-term process, but, after it is in place, it is a valuable decision support tool. A variety of software tools can be used to assist in the process, such as to model processes and tasks and to create explanatory reports and diagrams.

Design and Manufacturing Systems

Computers are widely used in systems to improve productivity at the product design stage—through *computer-aided design* (*CAD*)—and at the manufacturing stage—through *computer-aided manufacturing* (*CAM*).

Computer-Aided Design (CAD)

As discussed in Chapter 6, **computer-aided design** (**CAD**) is used by designers to reduce the time they spend developing products. CAD software, such as *AutoCAD*, is available to help design buildings, bridges, and other structures; design new end products; design mechanical and electrical systems; create landscape and interior designs; and so forth (see Figure 12-11).

FIGURE 12-11
Computer-aided design (CAD). The AutoCAD program shown here can be used for a wide variety of design applications.

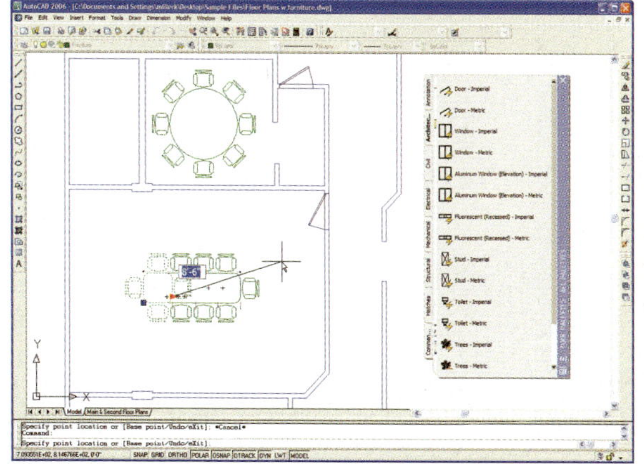

Computer-Aided Manufacturing (CAM)

Computer-aided manufacturing (**CAM**) refers to the use of computers to help manage manufacturing operations and control machinery used in those processes. One example is a system that observes production in an oil refinery, performs calculations, and

>**Enterprise architecture.** A comprehensive framework used to describe and manage an organization's business functions and systems. >**Computer-aided design (CAD).** A general term applied to the use of computer technology to automate design functions. >**Computer-aided manufacturing (CAM).** A general term applied to the use of computer technology to automate manufacturing functions.

INSIDE THE INDUSTRY

The Turing Test and Loebner Prize

According to John McCarthy, who coined the term in 1956 and is considered by many to be one of the fathers of artificial intelligence (AI), AI is "the science and engineering of making intelligent machines." In other words, AI researchers are working to create intelligent devices controlled by intelligent software programs; that is, machines that think and act like people. In 1950, Alan Turing—one of the first AI researchers—argued that if a machine could successfully appear to be human to a knowledgeable observer, then it should be considered intelligent. To illustrate this idea, Turing developed a test—later called the *Turing Test* in which one observer interacts electronically with both a computer and a person. During the test, the observer submits written questions electronically to both the computer and the person, evaluates the typed responses, and tries to identify which answers came from the computer and which came from the person. Turing argued that if the computer could repeatedly fool the observer into thinking it was human, then it should be viewed as intelligent.

Many Turing Test contests have been held over the years, and in 1990, Dr. Hugh Loebner initiated the Loebner Prize, pledging a grand prize of $100,000 and a solid gold medal (see the accompanying photo) for the first computer whose responses to a Turing Test were indistinguishable from that of a human's responses. A contest is held every year, awarding a prize of $2,000 and a bronze medal to the most human computer, but so far the gold medal has not been awarded.

The Loebner Prize gold medal.

opens and shuts appropriate valves accordingly. Another system that is commonly used in the steel industry works from preprogrammed specifications to shape and assemble steel parts automatically. Increasingly, *robots* (discussed shortly) are used to carry out manufacturing processes that were once performed by humans. CAM is also widely used to build cars and ships, monitor power plants, manufacture food and chemicals, and perform a number of other functions.

Artificial Intelligence Systems

Computers are continually becoming faster and smarter. Although they cannot yet think completely on their own, computers and software programs have become more sophisticated, and computers are being programmed to act in an increasingly intelligent manner. When computer systems perform in ways that would be considered intelligent if observed in humans, it is commonly referred to as *artificial intelligence* (*AI*). In other words, AI is concerned with creating intelligent devices controlled by intelligent software programs—machines that think and act like humans. Researchers have been working in the field of artificial intelligence for decades. One of the first researchers, English mathematician Alan Turing, gave a lecture on it in 1947. For a look at two activities related to AI—the *Turing Test* and the *Loebner Prize*—see the Inside the Industry box.

Some of the initial advances in AI were made in the area of game playing—namely, chess. Early chess-playing programs were easily defeated by amateur chess players. But, eventually, as computers became more powerful and AI software became more sophisticated, chess-playing programs improved. In 1996, IBM's Deep Blue computer won two of six games in a chess match against world chess champion Garry Kasparov. A landmark moment in AI history occurred in 1997 when Deep Blue beat Kasparov in a rematch (see Figure 12-12), winning the match 3½ to 2½ (three of the six games ended in a draw). In late 2003, Kasparov played a chess match against a 3D chess program called *X3D Fritz*. The match was played on a virtual chessboard and ended in a draw of 2 to 2. Kasparov believes that it is still possible for a person to win a series of games against a top chess-playing program, but he also believes that the window is rapidly closing. As Kasparov has discovered, one disadvantage of playing against a computer is that once the human player makes a mistake, there is no hope (as there would be with a human opponent) that the computer opponent will make its own mistake at a later time, to level the playing field in that game.

KASPAROV VS. DEEP BLUE
In 1997, IBM's Deep Blue computer (operated here by research scientist Murray Campbell, right) beat chess master Garry Kasparov in a chess match.

KASPAROV VS. X3D FRITZ
In 2003, the 3D chess match between Kasparov and X3D Fritz ended in a draw. The games were played on a virtual chessboard.

FIGURE 12-12
AI and chess playing.

Today's AI applications contain some aspect of artificial intelligence, although they tend to mimic human intelligence rather than display pure intelligence. Technological advances will undoubtedly help AI applications continue to evolve and become more intelligent and sophisticated in the future. While many welcome the idea of more intelligent computers to help people, some foresee a future in which people and computers may eventually merge. Not surprisingly, others find that scenario frightening and objectionable. Just as the debate about what constitutes intelligence in nonhumans continues, so will the debate about how far we as a society should go into the area of artificial intelligence.

Systems that use artificial intelligence are called **artificial intelligence (AI) systems**. AI systems that exist in some form today include *intelligent agents*, *expert systems*, *neural networks*, and *robotics*.

Intelligent Agents

Intelligent agents are programs that perform specific tasks to help to make a user's work environment more efficient or entertaining. Put another way, intelligent agents are *virtual assistants*. Typically, intelligent agents can modify their behavior based on the user's actions, and they are used extensively on the Web in addition to being built into operating systems, e-mail programs, Web browsers, application programs, and other products. Some specific types of intelligent agents include the following:

- *Application assistants*—provide help or assistance for a particular application program.
- *Search agents*—search for specified information on the Web, such as regularly gathering news articles and other information on specified subjects.
- *Shopping bots*—search through online stores to find the best overall prices for the products that you specify.
- *Entertainment bots*—provide entertainment, such as a virtual pet that you care for online, or an animated character that plays a game with you.

SYS

>**Artificial intelligence (AI) system.** A system in which a computer performs actions that are characteristic of human intelligence.
>**Intelligent agent.** A program that performs specific tasks to help to make a user's work environment more efficient or entertaining and that typically modifies its behavior based on the user's actions.

FIGURE 12-13
A Web page chatterbot.

- *Chatterbots*—carry on written "conversations" with people in a *natural language* (such as English, Spanish, French, or Japanese), are often represented by an animated character, and typically respond both verbally and with appropriate physical gestures to create the illusion that the exchange is taking place between two thinking, living entities (see Figure 12-13).

Expert Systems

Expert systems are software programs that perform tasks that would otherwise be performed by a human expert. For example, there are expert systems that can diagnose illnesses, make financial forecasts, schedule routes for delivery vehicles, diagnose mechanical problems, and perform credit authorizations. Figure 12-14 is a simplified example of how an expert system might work.

Some expert systems are designed to take the place of human experts, while others are designed to assist them. For instance, medical expert systems, which incorporate the knowledge and decision making guidelines of some of the world's best physicians, are used to assist physicians with patient diagnoses. To use such a system, the symptoms exhibited by a patient are entered into the expert system. The program then asks the attending healthcare provider questions and compares the provided data to a large database of successfully diagnosed cases, in order to suggest one or more possible diagnoses. Because the expert system has access to a wide base of knowledge, the expert system may include additional possible diagnoses other than the ones offered by the attending physician.

Expert systems consist of two main components: a *knowledge base* and an *inference engine*. The *knowledge base* is a database that contains facts provided by a human expert and rules that the expert system should use to make decisions based on those facts. For instance, an expert system used to authorize credit for credit card customers would have in its knowledge base facts about customers, as well as rules, such as "Do not automatically authorize purchase if the customer has exceeded his or her credit limit." The *inference engine* is a software program that applies the rules to the data stored in the knowledge base, in order to reach decisions.

FIGURE 12-14
An expert system at work.

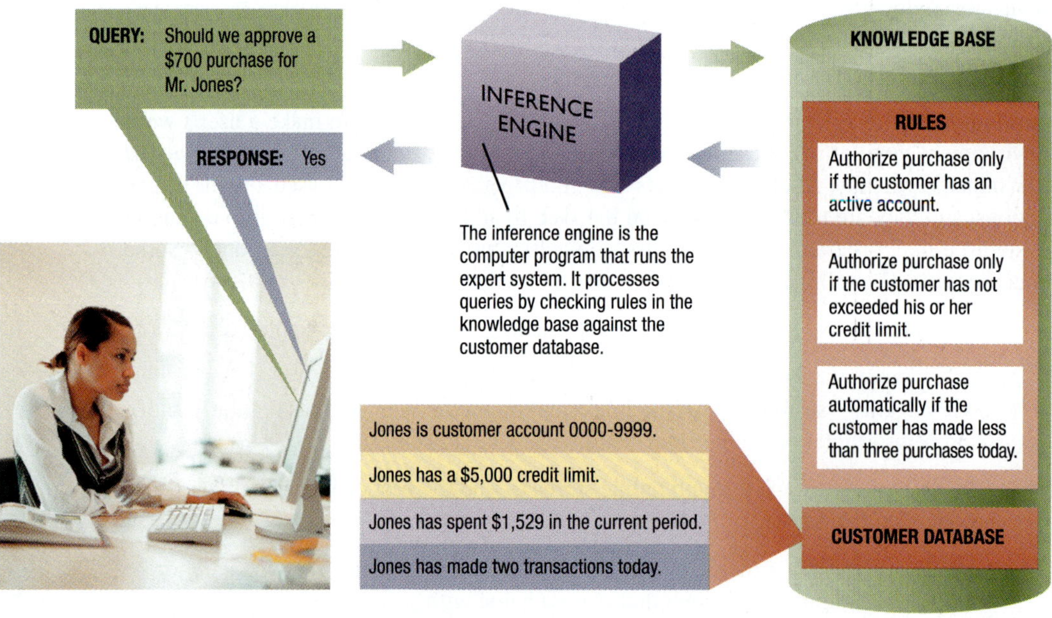

>**Expert system.** A computer system that provides the type of advice that would be expected from a human expert.

Expert systems can be built from scratch or by using an *expert system shell*—a skeletal system that needs to be supplied with the expert knowledge and rules to be used in the system. Regardless of how an expert system is created, it is important to realize that the conclusions of an expert system are based on the data and rules stored in its knowledge base, as well as the information provided by the users. If the expert knowledge is correct, the inference engine program is written correctly, and the user supplies honest, correct information in response to the questions posed by the expert system, the system will draw correct conclusions; if the knowledge base is wrong, the inference engine is faulty, or the user provides incorrect input, the system will not work correctly.

Neural Networks

Artificial intelligence systems that attempt to imitate the way a human brain works are called **neural networks**. Neural networks (also called *neural nets*) are networks of processors that are connected together in a manner similar to the way neurons in a human brain are connected. Neural networks can learn by observation, as well as by trial and error. They are designed to emulate the brain's pattern-recognition process in order to recognize patterns in data and make much more progressive leaps in associations and predictions than conventional computer systems. Neural networks are used in areas such as handwriting, speech, and image recognition; geographical mapping; medical imaging; crime analysis; and biometric identification (see Figure 12-15). They are also increasingly being used in *vision systems*, in which cameras are used in conjunction with a neural network to inspect objects and make determinations—for example, the systems that check products for defects at manufacturing plants or that recognize stamps during postal processing.

FIGURE 12-15
Neural network systems. Neural networks are often used in biometric identification systems, such as analyzing fingerprints in the fingerprint identification system shown here.

Robotics

Robotics is the field devoted to the study of **robots**—devices, controlled by a person or a computer, that can move and react to sensory input. Robots are currently used in factories to perform high-precision but monotonous jobs, such as welding, riveting, and painting. They are used for *robot-assisted surgery* (illustrated in Figure 7-8 in Chapter 7) because their precision allows the surgeon to operate using much smaller incisions and greater dexterity than are possible without the robot assistance. They are also used in situations that are dangerous or impossible for people, such as mining coal, defusing bombs, exploring the bottom of the ocean, repairing oil rigs, locating land mines, locating survivors in collapsed mines and buildings, and photographing the surface of Mars. For instance, the iRobot *PackBot Mobile Tactical Robot* shown in Figure 12-16 is used by the U.S. military to investigate caves, buildings, trails, and other locations before soldiers enter them to make sure the locations are safe. Larger unmanned robotic vehicles are becoming available; some are already deployed in Iraq.

An emerging military robotic application is the *exoskeleton suit*, whose name is derived from the term "exoskeleton," which refers to a hard protective or supportive outer structure. Currently being researched and developed by several organizations under grants from the Defense Advanced Research Projects Agency (DARPA), exoskeleton suits are wearable robotic systems designed to give an individual additional physical capabilities and protection (see Figure 12-16). For instance, an exoskeleton suit can give a soldier the ability to run faster and carry heavier items than he or she could without the suit. The exoskeleton suits that will eventually be used by the military will likely be made of light, protective material that will be bulletproof and be able to solidify on demand to form a

>**Neural network.** An expert system in which the human brain's pattern-recognition process is emulated by the computer system. >**Robotics.** The study of robot technology. >**Robot.** A device, controlled by a human operator or a computer, that can move and react to sensory input.

BATTLEFIELD ROBOTIC SYSTEM
This robot, PackBot, designed to check out caves and other areas to ensure they are safe before soldiers enter them, is shown here entering a cave on its first mission in Kandahar, Afghanistan.

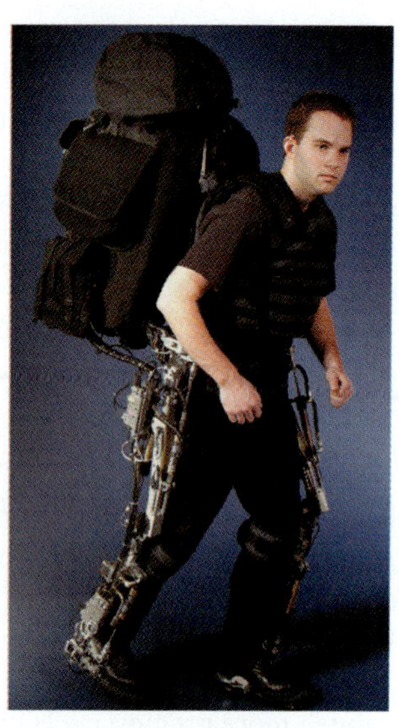

EXOSKELETON SYSTEM
Designed to enable soldiers to carry large loads safely; using the lower extremity prototype shown here, a 70-pound load feels like 5 pounds.

SECURITY ROBOT SYSTEM
This robot, OFRO+detect, transmits video as it patrols facilities; its sensors can also detect nuclear, biological, or chemical hazards.

FIGURE 12-16
Military and business robotic systems.

shield or turn into a medical cast if a soldier is injured. Other possible features include changing its color automatically for camouflage purposes; relaying information via sensors about a soldier's health, injuries, and location to field headquarters; and administering painkillers or applying pressure to a wound when directed by a physician. Although they hope to deliver some usable exoskeleton components within the next five years, most researchers project that a true exoskeleton suit is many years from reality. In addition to the military possibilities, exoskeleton suits may eventually lead to stronger and safer search and rescue workers, be used to give the elderly back their youthful physical abilities, or provide paralyzed people with a means of mobility. One exoskeleton suit currently in development is designed to help nurses lift patients without risking injuries to their backs.

Business robots can be used to perform business-oriented tasks, such as monitoring facilities for security purposes or facilitating videoconferencing by sitting in for a participant—the robot relays video and audio images to and from the participant, who is at a remote location, during the meeting. The security robot shown in Figure 12-16 is an example of a robot used by businesses to patrol facilities looking for intruders, gas leaks, and other hazards.

Personal robots are also available. Most robots today use sensors, cameras, and microphones to input data about their current surroundings; some personal robots are also designed to remember faces and personal details to make small talk with people, as well as to deliver messages. One of the first personal robots is Sony's robot dog *AIBO*, shown in Figure 12-17. AIBO can recognize up to 180 voice commands, sing and dance, take pictures, and change its behavior based on its treatment and training. AIBO can be controlled remotely via e-mail commands, deliver prerecorded messages to family members, read aloud text-based e-mail messages and text-based Web pages, and transmit digital images of what it sees to a remote computer or mobile device, which, for example, allows parents while at work or on a trip to view their homes or children. One version even has an LED face panel to provide a means for the robot to express its feelings, emotions, and current conditions. The *humanoid robot ASIMO* (shown in Figure 12-17) can recognize faces, follow spoken and hand commands, avoid obstacles, and navigate stairs. In 2005, Disneyland introduced a new exhibit in Tomorrowland featuring ASIMO using all of its unique technological capabilities—such as walking forward and backward, climbing and descending a flight of stairs, and taking direction from a person—in a modern home environment. The demonstration is designed to offer visitors a glimpse into a not-too-distant future when humanoid robots, like ASIMO, will assist humans in their homes. Additional humanoid personal robots are becoming available, such as the *Wakamaru* personal robot that became available in late 2005 and is being advertised as the world's first communicative home-use robot. Wakamaru—a 40-inch tall, bright yellow childlike robot (see Figure 12-17)—can wake you up, and then recite the day's headlines and weather. It can recognize up to 10 people and 10,000 words, instant message or e-mail you when you are late, alert family and friends if you do not respond, and pass on telephone and e-mail message when you return home. It can also be accessed remotely through the Internet so you can view images of your home while you are away, and it can be set up to e-mail a particular e-mail address if it senses movement in the house while you are not home. Other personal robots with similar functions, such as a small man-shaped robot named *Nuvo* that began being mass-produced for home use in Japan, are becoming available. But they are not cheap—for example, Wakamaru costs about $14,000.

While current humanoid personal robots, such as Wakamaru and Nuvo, are not designed to perform household chores at the present time, there are specialized robots designed to do some common everyday chores. For example, robotic lawn mowers are available that automatically mow within a predesignated area, and robotic floor cleaning systems (such as the iRobot *Scooba FloorWashing Robot* shown in Figure 12-17) can be set to clean a specified room size and then left unattended so it can complete the job. These robots typically cost between $150 and $1,500 each. A robotic wheelchair —the *iBOT Mobility System* designed by Dean Kamen—is controlled with a joystick and uses sensors and gyroscopes to enable users to climb stairs, roll through sand, and adjust the seat height to have eye-level conversations with others or reach high shelves in the supermarket.

AIBO
Can follow voice commands, sing and dance, take photos, deliver recorded messages, read aloud e-mail messages, and perform other personal tasks.

ASIMO
Can recognize faces, follow voice commands, and navigate its environment, including climbing stairs.

WAKAMARU
Can recognize faces, follow voice commands, wake you up, read aloud the weather forecast and headlines, relay phone and e-mail messages, and perform other personal tasks.

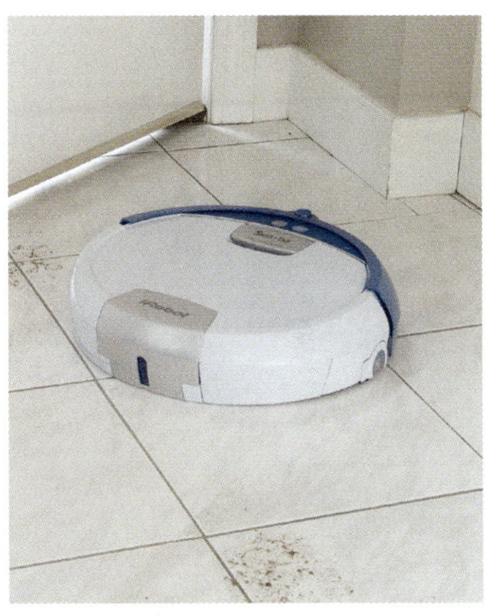

SCOOBA
Can prep, wash, scrub, and dry hard floors in a single pass.

FIGURE 12-17
Personal robots.

As new robotic applications are developed, and as the prices come down, robots are expected to be used increasingly in both homes and businesses. Newer robots will likely have improved vision and sensor systems, which will allow for better navigation and more accurate assessments of the hardness and temperature of objects. Artificial intelligence and facial emotions will make humanoid robots appear even more lifelike, and their communications systems will continue to improve. Many would agree that the use of robots has many benefits to society—such as adding convenience to our lives, replacing people in dangerous situations, and, potentially, monitoring and assisting the disabled and the elderly. But some individuals are concerned that, as true artificial intelligence becomes closer to reality, a class of robots with the potential for great harm could be created. The issue of the role robots should take in our society is likely to continue to be debated for quite some time.

FURTHER EXPLORATION

For links to further information about robots, go to www.course.com/uc11/ch12

RESPONSIBILITY FOR SYSTEM DEVELOPMENT

As mentioned earlier, the process that includes planning, building, and maintaining systems is called *system development*. Systems can be developed in-house or *outsourced* to external companies. Organizations with thousands of employees and thousands of details to keep track of use hundreds of systems, ranging from small systems that involve only a few people to enterprise-wide systems that encompass an entire company. Deciding which systems best support the direction of the organization and how much attention to give each one is where the job of system development begins. A variety of individuals are responsible for one or more parts of the system development process, as discussed next.

A company's *chief information officer* (*CIO*) has primary responsibility for system development. Usually this position is a vice president or a similar management position. One of a CIO's duties is to develop a strategy that defines the role of information technology within the organization. Another duty is to develop a plan that maps out which systems are to be studied and possibly built or revamped now and over the next several years. Because information technology plays such a pervasive role within most companies, *steering committees* comprised of top-level executives normally approve information technology plans and set broad guidelines for performing computer-related activities. These committees do not involve themselves with technical details or administer particular projects. Such functions are the responsibility of the organization's *information systems department*.

The Information Systems Department

The *information systems* (*IS*) *department*—sometimes called the *information technology* (*IT*) *department*—varies in structure from one company to another, but includes most, if not all, of the computer and networking personnel for that organization. For instance, an IS department may include the people who design and implement enterprise-wide systems, people who provide support services to PC users, and people who build and manage networks and databases. Although some studies predict that the size of IT departments in large and midsize companies will shrink by nearly two-thirds by 2010, there is still a high demand for quality computer professionals. Figure 12-18 describes a number of typical jobs available to the computer professional. According to the Bureau of Labor Statistics, four of the projected fastest growing top-ten fields in the United States through 2012 are IT jobs. The job classified as "network systems and communications analyst" is number 1, with a projected growth of 57% between 2002 and 2012; the other computer-related jobs in the top ten are software engineers, database administrators, and systems analysts.

FURTHER EXPLORATION

For links to further information about computer careers and computer certification programs, go to www.course.com/uc11/ch12

The pillar of most information systems departments is *data processing*—the primary function of data processing is to keep the critical transaction processing systems within the company running smoothly. These systems, by and large, control the money coming into and going out of the organization. Data processing predates all other functions within the information systems department and is still considered by many to be the most important. After all, if their computers stopped processing the high volumes of business transactions that take place every day at many companies, most large organizations would have to shut down.

The person most involved with system development is the **systems analyst**. Generally speaking, the systems analyst's job is to plan, build, implement, and modify the large systems that use the computers the organization has or will acquire. When a new system or system modification is needed, the systems analyst manages the necessary activities involved with designing and implementing the new or modified system. The systems analyst

>**Systems analyst.** A person who studies systems in an organization in order to determine what work needs to be done and how this work may best be achieved.

generally is involved in all stages of the development process, from beginning to end. Another individual critical to systems development is the *business analyst*. A business analyst is responsible for identifying and understanding the business needs of a system, as well as helping the systems analyst and system designers ensure those requirements are integrated into the final system. Essentially, the business analyst makes sure that new systems meet the business requirements of the organization. Other key individuals include members of the *system analysis and design group* (who analyze, design, and implement new software and hardware systems), the *programmers* (who code computer programs from design specifications), and the *operations personnel* (who manage day-to-day processing once a system has become operational).

Most large system development projects use a team of people. A systems analyst is often appointed as a *project manager* to head up the team. Other people on the team might include users, programmers, an outside consultant, a cost accountant, and an auditor. Current and potential users are especially vital to any system development team because they can provide insight into the practical side of the application; that is, the nuts and bolts of how the system should work on a day-to-day basis.

Application programmer Codes application software.	**Network analyst/engineer** Manages the networks in an organization and determines what changes, if any, are needed to the current infrastructure.
Business analyst Identifies the business needs of a system and makes sure systems meet those needs.	**Network operator/troubleshooter** Responsible for overseeing the day-to-day activities for a network, such as troubleshooting problems, documenting network events, and performing necessary duties to keep the network operating smoothly.
Computer operations manager Oversees the computer operations staff and facility in an organization.	**Network technician** Installs, maintains, and upgrades networking hardware and software.
Computer operator Responsible for the operation of mainframe computers and their support.	**Programmer/analyst** Performs both application programming and systems analysis and design.
Database administrator Responsible for setting up and managing large databases within an organization.	**Security specialist** Responsible for seeing that an organization's hardware, software, and data are protected from hackers, malware, natural disasters, accidents, and the like. Also known as the chief security officer (CSO).
Database analyst Responsible for designing and developing an organization's data flow models and database architecture.	**Software engineer** Designs and builds complex software applications.
Data communications analyst Installs, maintains, and troubleshoots data communications networks and assists with connectivity.	**System administrator** Responsible for maintaining a large, multiuser system.
Data entry operator Responsible for keying data into a computer system.	**Systems analyst** Studies systems in an organization to determine what work needs to be done and how this work may best be achieved.
Data processing director In charge of developing and/or implementing the overall plan for transaction processing in an organization and for overseeing the activities of programmers, systems analysts, and operations personnel.	**System programmer** Codes system software, fine-tunes operating system performance, and performs other system-software-related tasks.
Help desk technician Assists users in solving software and hardware problems.	**Trainer** Provides education to users about a particular program, system, or technology.
Information systems manager Manages an organization's overall IT architecture.	**Vice president of information systems** Oversees routing transaction processing and information systems activities, as well as other computer-related areas. Also known as the chief information officer (CIO).
Knowledge engineer Responsible for setting up and maintaining the base of expert knowledge used in expert system applications.	**Webmaster** Responsible for establishing and maintaining an organization's Web site.
Multimedia developer Develops the multimedia content needed for Web sites and other applications.	**Web page designer/developer** Designs and develops Web pages or an entire Web site.
Network administrator Responsible for planning and implementing networks within an organization.	**Web programmer** Writes the program code necessary for a Web site, such as to provide animation and database connectivity.

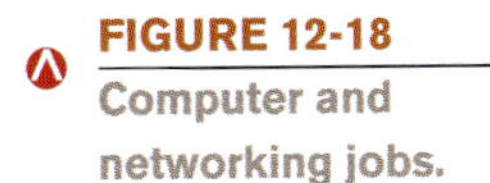

FIGURE 12-18
Computer and networking jobs.

Outsourcing Companies

When an organization lacks the staff to build or operate a system it needs, it often chooses to *outsource* the system development process. **Outsourcing** involves turning over certain tasks to an outside vendor—usually one that specializes in outsourcing. For instance, many smaller banks outsource check-processing and customer-statement operations to companies that are skilled at this type of high-volume processing. It is also common for a business to outsource the development of its ERP or e-commerce system, Web site, and its technical support.

The primary reason companies outsource is cost. For instance, a small firm might find it too expensive to keep specialized personnel or equipment on hand, or a large company might not have the capacity or capital to expand its operations in-house, so it may outsource some of them temporarily. In general, firms typically turn to an outsourcer when they think that the outsourcer can do the job better or at a lower cost than they can. Much of outsourcing today is *offshore*; that is, outsourced to another country. In the United States, for example, technical support, programming, credit card processing, payroll accounting, and other business tasks are often sent to India and the Caribbean. In fact, at an annual revenue of about $8 billion per year, outsourcing is one of India's biggest industries. One innovative call center in India is even recruiting and hiring young Europeans to work at the India-based call center. Although the individuals (often recent college graduates) work for Indian wages (about $5,000 to $8,000 per year), they receive free housing, a housekeeper, and a chance to experience a new culture.

Another innovative outsourcing idea in the works is placing outsourcing workers on ships at sea. For instance, one company—called *SeaCode*—has announced plans to buy an old cruise ship, place programmers on it, and park it just inside international waters off the coast of California. Because it will be located outside of the United States, the company will not have to pay U.S. payroll taxes, and it intends to employ programmers from Russia and India to work in shifts around the clock. Because of these factors, the company expects to be competitive with outsourcing companies based in India while at the same time being able to offer higher wages, good living conditions, and travel opportunities in the United States during off time.

The cost savings for offshore outsourcing can be enormous. For instance, according to the research firm PayScale, Inc., a computer programmer in New York with five year's experience would earn an average salary of $57,000—in Delhi, India that individual would earn just under $14,000 in U.S. dollars. Market research firm Gartner predicts that the money spent on outsourcing enterprise applications will reach nearly $50 billion by the end of 2007.

Outsourcing is not without drawbacks, however. Some firms simply hand over their work to an outsourcer and then expect miracles. This is not effective because leadership needs to come from the client firm, not from the outsourcer. Also, when in-house personnel have to mix with the outsourcer's personnel, conflicts can arise. The in-house personnel may feel their jobs are threatened by the outsourcer's personnel, or they may disagree about who is in charge. When tasks are outsourced to other countries, there may be communications problems; cultural differences need to be taken into consideration, as well. Finally, the matters of control and security need to be considered. Although an outsourcer provides some assistance in these areas, a company achieves the most control over its information processing and the best security when it keeps its work in house. When work goes outside, anything can happen. Some outsourcing companies utilize very strict security measures—such as employee searches, no ability for employees to copy files, no outside telephone access, and so forth—to reassure customers. At other outsourcing companies, however, security measures are lax. And when a

>**Outsourcing.** Turning over specific business tasks to an outside vendor; increasingly, the vendor is located in a different country with lower labor costs.

problem—such as data or proprietary information being stolen—occurs, prosecution and data recovery is much more complicated since it must be pursued via law enforcement agencies in the outsourcing company's country.

Businesses that outsource need to ensure that appropriate security and privacy controls are in place since security and privacy breaches do occur. For instance, at the time of this writing, British police were working with Interpol to investigate an incident that occurred in mid-2005 when an undercover newspaper reporter was able to purchase personal data (including addresses, telephones, and bank account, credit card, passport, and drivers' license numbers) on 1,000 British citizens from an Indian call center employee. And employees at another call center in India used their customer support positions for Citibank to trick four U.S. Citibank customers into revealing their PIN numbers. The employees then used that information to steal $350,000 from the customers' accounts. In addition to the concern about overall security and privacy breaches when data is sent out of house, as more and more programming is outsourced offshore, there is a growing concern about the possibility of offshore outsourcing being used to sabotage software or otherwise launch a cyberattack on the United States or U.S. companies. Despite the potential drawbacks, outsourcing appears to be an unstoppable trend.

As an alternative to offshore outsourcing, some companies are creating *captive offshoring sites* in less expensive countries; that is, organizing their own facilities and hiring employees in a foreign country instead of using a third-party outsourcing company. Although more expensive than conventional outsourcing since company staff must maintain the facilities, train employees, and oversee the facility, captive offshoring does give the company much more control. Captive offshoring is a rapidly growing trend, accounting for 30% of outsourcing employment today, according to the research firm A.T. Kearney.

THE SYSTEM DEVELOPMENT LIFE CYCLE (SDLC)

There are many specific tasks involved with system development. Although the arrangement and order of these tasks may vary from organization to organization, a system development project typically contains six steps or phases.

- Phase 1: Preliminary investigation
- Phase 2: System analysis
- Phase 3: System design
- Phase 4: System acquisition
- Phase 5: System implementation
- Phase 6: System maintenance

Collectively, these phases make up the **system development life cycle** (**SDLC**). As illustrated in Figure 12-19, the SDLC describes the development of a system from the time it is first studied until the time it is it updated or replaced. When a new business pressure necessitates a system change, the steps of the cycle begin anew.

The six steps of the SDLC define in principle the process for building systems for multimillion-dollar information systems used in large corporations, as well as for information systems developed for a home office PC. As shown in Figure 12-19, each step results in some type of *documentation* that carries forward to the next step in the cycle. The activities that may occur during each step of the SDLC are discussed shortly.

SYS

>**System development life cycle (SDLC).** The process consisting of the six phases of system development: preliminary investigation, system analysis, system design, system acquisition, system implementation, and system maintenance.

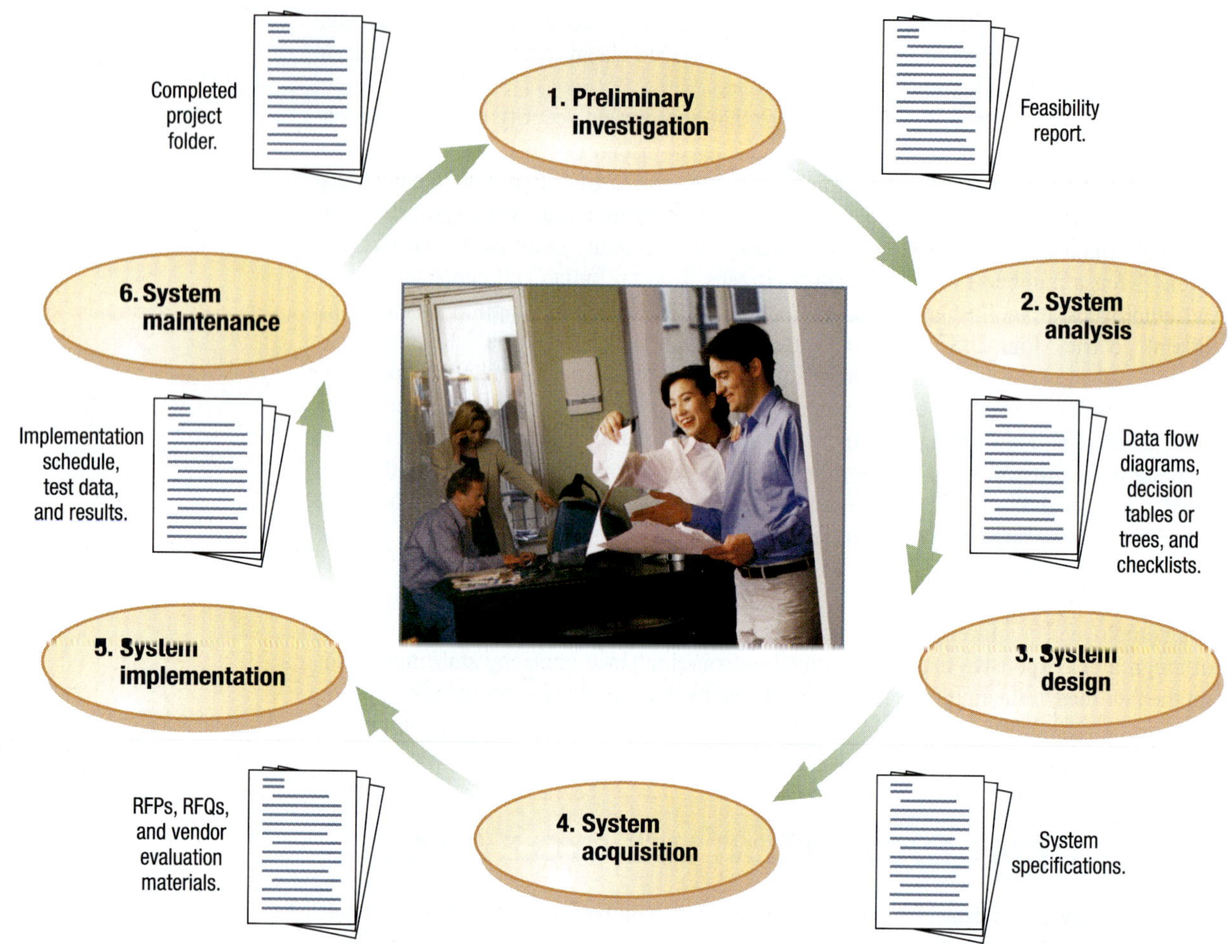

FIGURE 12-19

The system development life cycle (SDLC). Each phase of the system development life cycle produces some type of documentation to pass on to the next phase.

Before taking a look at each of the steps in the SDLC, it is important to realize that these six steps may not always follow one another in a strict sequence. For example, analysis and design are frequently interwoven. Compare this process with an example from everyday life—vacation planning. People do not always design their entire vacation plan as the first step and then execute it, without modification, as the second step. They might design a plan ahead of time, but when the first day of the vacation is over, they might use that day's experiences as a basis for modifying the plan for the second day. Many systems are designed this way as well. Smaller systems in smaller companies may also follow a less formal process of development, skipping or condensing some activities. The role of the systems analyst during each step of the SDLC is illustrated in Figure 12-20 and the phases are discussed next.

Preliminary Investigation

When a proposal for a new system or system modification is submitted, one of the first steps is to conduct a **preliminary investigation**, also called a *feasibility study*. The purpose of this investigation is to define and evaluate the problem area at hand relatively quickly, to see if it is worthy of further study, and to suggest possible courses of action. Accordingly, the investigation examines such issues as the nature of the problem, the scope of the work involved to solve it, possible solutions, and the approximate costs and benefits of each proposed solution.

>Preliminary investigation. The phase of the system development life cycle in which a brief feasibility study is performed to assess whether or not a full-scale project should be undertaken.

Documentation: Feasibility Report

The main output of the preliminary investigation is the *feasibility report*, which includes the systems analyst's findings on the status of the existing system, as well as the benefits and feasibility of changing to a new system. Feasibility is commonly measured using a few different perspectives, such as whether the organization has, or can acquire, the hardware, software, and personnel needed to implement the new system; whether the new system would fit well with the other systems in the organization; whether the estimated benefits of the new system outweigh the estimated costs; and so forth. The feasibility report also contains the systems analyst's recommendations about whether or not the project should move on to the next stage in the SDLC: *system analysis*.

System Analysis

System analysis is the phase of system development in which the problem area is studied in depth and the needs of system users are assessed. The main activities conducted during system analysis are *data collection* and *data analysis*.

Data Collection

The objective of *data collection* is to gather information about the system under study to try to ascertain what resources users need to better perform their jobs. Later in this phase, the data collected should suggest some possible solutions. Which data is collected depends largely on the problem being studied. Some data-gathering tools that can be used include reviewing documents that show how the system is supposed to work, sending questionnaires to users, observing current activities, and interviewing those who use the system or the information produced by it.

An *organizational chart* that covers the functions being studied and the people in charge of those functions can also be a useful document. An organizational chart gives an overview of the decision making chain and how areas of responsibility are organized. Because people often do not do exactly what their job descriptions say they do, however, the only way a systems analyst can really determine if a system operates the way it is supposed to is by going to where people work and observing what they do.

Data Analysis

As information about the system is gathered, it must be analyzed so the requirements for a new system can be determined. Three useful tools for performing *data analysis* are diagrams, tables, and checklists.

One of the diagrams commonly used during data analysis is the *data flow diagram*. A data flow diagram shows the relationships among activities that are part of a system as well as the data or information flowing into and out of each activity. In essence, it provides a visual representation of data movement in an organization. Figure 12-21 shows a data flow diagram for the order entry operation of a mail-order firm.

Decision tables are useful for identifying procedures and summarizing the decision making process for one step of a system. For example, the decision table in Figure 12-21 summarizes the decisions involved with the "Verify order is valid" process on the data flow diagram in that same figure. By using the table, the system can unequivocally determine which action to take during this process. For instance, according to the information in the first column in the decision table shown in Figure 12-21, a new customer without complete information would result in an invalid order. The process of creating the table helps to

DUTIES OF THE SYSTEMS ANALYST

Preliminary investigation During this phase the systems analyst studies a problem briefly and suggests solutions to management.

System analysis If management decides that further development is warranted, the systems analyst studies the situation in depth.

System design The systems analyst develops a model of the new system and prepares a detailed list of benefits and costs.

System acquisition Upon management approval of the design, the systems analyst decides which vendors to use in order to meet software, hardware, and servicing needs.

System implementation After system components have been acquired, the systems analyst supervises the lengthy process of training users, converting data, and the like.

System maintenance The systems analyst evaluates the system on an ongoing basis to determine any corrections or modifications that should be considered.

FIGURE 12-20
The role of the systems analyst in the six phases of system development.

SYS

>System analysis. The phase of the system development life cycle in which a problem area is thoroughly examined to determine what should be done.

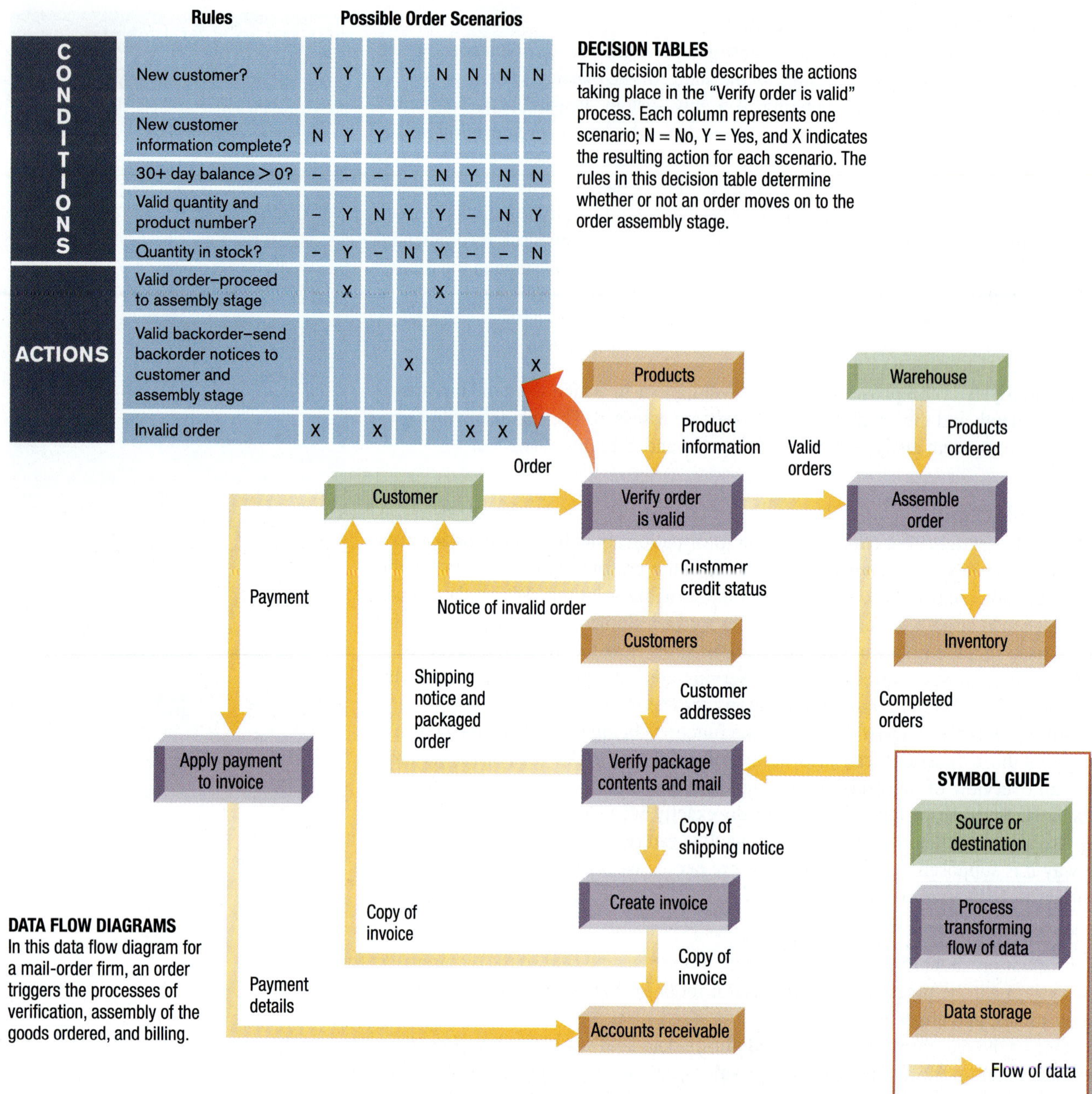

	Rules	Possible Order Scenarios							
CONDITIONS	New customer?	Y	Y	Y	Y	N	N	N	N
	New customer information complete?	N	Y	Y	Y	–	–	–	–
	30+ day balance > 0?	–	–	–	–	N	Y	N	N
	Valid quantity and product number?	–	Y	N	Y	Y	–	N	Y
	Quantity in stock?	–	Y	–	N	Y	–	–	N
ACTIONS	Valid order–proceed to assembly stage		X			X			
	Valid backorder–send backorder notices to customer and assembly stage				X				X
	Invalid order	X		X			X	X	

FIGURE 12-21

Data flow diagrams and decision tables. These tools are frequently used to analyze a system during the system analysis phase of the system development life cycle.

ensure that all possible conditions have been considered. When the data in a decision table is expressed in a tree format, it is called a *decision tree*.

Checklists are often developed for important matters, such as the goals of the system and the information needs of key people in the system. An accounts receivable system, for example, should have such goals as getting bills out quickly, informing customers about late payments, and cutting losses due to bad debts—these goals can be summarized in a checklist.

The type of tool (diagram, table, or checklist) used depends on which tool is most appropriate for the situation at hand. The principal purpose of these tools is to help the systems analyst organize his or her thoughts so that he or she may draw conclusions about what the system under study should do.

Documentation: Data Flow Diagrams, Decision Tables, Decision Trees, and Checklists

The documentation resulting from the system analysis phase includes any instruments (such as questionnaires or interview questions) used in the data gathering stage, as well as the resulting diagrams, tables, trees, checklists, and other tools used to summarize and analyze the gathered data.

System Design

System design focuses on specifying what the new system will look like and how it will work. The system design phase primarily consists of developing a model of the new system and performing a detailed analysis of the expected benefits and costs.

Developing a Model of the New System

Once the systems analyst understands the nature of the problem or situation under study, it is helpful to draw a number of diagrams of the new system. For example, the data flow diagrams discussed in the last phase show how data flows using the existing system; new data flow diagrams would be necessary to show how data would flow using the new system.

When designing a system, the systems analyst must take into account input requirements; output requirements; data access, organization, and storage; processing power and speed; system controls, including security and privacy requirements; and personnel and procedure specifications. Figure 12-22 covers some of the issues that should be addressed during the design stage.

Some of the tools a systems analyst can use to model the new system are *system flowcharts*, *input/output designs*, and a *data dictionary*. System flowcharts illustrate operations that occur throughout the system—similar to a data flow diagram but much more specific regarding each individual process. Input and output (I/O) designs show in what form input

FIGURE 12-22

System design issues. System design ultimately addresses all major elements of a computer system: hardware, software, data, people, and procedures.

INPUT CONSIDERATIONS	STORAGE CONSIDERATIONS
• What data needs to be input into the system, and how will that occur? • How often does data need to be input? • What format will the input take? Will input take place via desktop PCs, handheld PCs, portable input devices?	• How will data be accessed and organized? • What storage capacity is required? • How fast must data be accessed? • What storage devices are appropriate?
PROCESSING CONSIDERATIONS	**SYSTEM CONTROLS**
• What types of processing is required? • What type of processing power is required? A mainframe? A midrange server? A PC? • Will the system need to be accessible via a network or the Internet? Does it need to tie into a database or other existing system?	• What measures must be taken to ensure that data is secure from unauthorized use, theft, and natural disasters? • What measures must be taken to ensure the accuracy and integrity of data going in and information going out? • What measures must be taken to ensure the privacy of individuals represented by the data?
OUTPUT CONSIDERATIONS	**PERSONNEL AND PROCEDURES**
• Who are the system users, and what types of information do they need? • How often is this information needed? Annually? Monthly? Daily? On demand? • What output devices and storage media are necessary to provide the required information? • How should output be formatted or arranged so that it can easily be understood by users?	• What personnel are needed to run the system? • What procedures should be followed on the job? • How much training will be required for employees using the new system?

SYS

>**System design.** The phase of the system development life cycle in which a model of the new system and how it will work is formally established.

and output will appear—for example, designs for input screens, output screens, and printed reports. Flowcharts and related design tools are discussed in more detail in Chapter 13.

A *data dictionary* is used to describe the characteristics of data used in a database or other type of computer system. It includes such information as the name and description of each piece of data, the files in which the data will be found, what type and size of data is allowed, any restrictions on the format of input (such as having to be within a certain range of numbers or allowing only certain letters of the alphabet), and who has the authority to update that data. Data dictionaries are discussed in more detail in Chapter 14.

Cost/Benefit Analysis

Most organizations are acutely sensitive to costs, including computer system costs. The cost of a new computer system includes the initial investment in hardware, software, and training, as well as ongoing expenses, such as for personnel and maintenance. Some benefits can be computed easily by calculating the amount of labor the new system will save, the reduction in paperwork it will allow, and so on. These gains are called *tangible benefits* because they represent quantifiable dollar amounts.

Other benefits, such as improvements in customer service or better information supplied to decision makers, are significantly more difficult to express as dollar amounts. These gains are called *intangible benefits*. Clearly, the existence of intangible benefits complicates management efforts to make cost/benefit decisions. Yet some of the most important systems projects undertaken in a company involve strategic opportunities that are difficult to quantify. On a project with a large number of intangible benefits, management must ask questions such as "Are the new services that we can offer to customers worth the $3 million they will cost us?"

Documentation: System Specifications

The system specifications developed during the system analysis phase consist of all the documentation necessary to illustrate the new system. This documentation includes data flow diagrams, system flowcharts, input and output designs, a data dictionary, and so forth.

System Acquisition

Once a system has been designed and the required types of software and hardware have been specified, the systems analyst must decide where to obtain the necessary components. This decision lies at the heart of the **system acquisition** phase. While hardware is usually purchased from outside vendors, software can be developed either in-house or obtained from an outside vendor, depending on the needs of the company. This decision is referred to as the *make-or-buy decision*.

The Make-or-Buy Decision

One of the first steps in the system acquisition phase is to determine whether the programs needed for the new system should be created in-house or acquired from a software vendor. Since it is not always possible to find application software that exactly meets an organization's specific needs, a custom program developed by an outside software development company or in-house personnel may be needed.

>**System acquisition.** The phase of the system development life cycle in which hardware, software, and other necessary system components are acquired.

The "Make" Alternative

If an organization decides to develop its own custom application software, it moves into the *program development* process. As will be described in Chapter 13, this process has a life cycle that begins with the *problem analysis stage*—the stage that looks at the system specifications generated by the system design phase in the SDLC—and continues through writing, testing, and maintenance of the program. Once the *program development life cycle* has been completed, the system development life cycle continues, just as it would if the software had been purchased, as discussed next.

The "Buy" Alternative

A choice often made by organizations is to select products that require virtually no in-house programming. During the past couple of decades, prewritten application programs for such tasks as payroll, accounting, financial planning, project management, and scores of others have become more widely available from software publishers. Because they provide immediate results at a cost far lower than that of developing similar software from scratch, application packages are quite popular for some systems—either for the complete system (such as a transaction processing system) or for some individual components of a system (such as payroll, or order entry). However, even third-party application programs often need some custom work in order to integrate them with existing systems.

RFPs and RFQs

Once it has been determined that specific types of hardware or software (either packaged programs or custom software) must be acquired for the new system, some organizations may go directly to a strategic partner to purchase the necessary items. Other organizations choose to or may be required to (as is the case with items over a particular dollar amount that will be purchased with public funds) prepare a *request for proposal* (*RFP*). This document contains a list of technical specifications for equipment, software, and services determined during the system design phase and requests that vendors propose products that meet those specifications. If the organization already knows exactly which hardware, software, and services it needs from vendors and is interested only in a quote on that specific list of items, a *request for quotation* (*RFQ*)—which names the desired items and asks only for a quote—may be used instead. In either case, the RFP or RFQ document is made available to potential vendors (such as by being mailed to a list of vendors who have participated in the past or by being advertised in a posted document or newspaper notice). Each interested vendor then sends a response (called a *bid*) back to the initiating organization, indicating its recommended solution and price (for an RFP) or just the price (for an RFQ).

Evaluating Bids

Once vendors have submitted their bids in response to an RFP or RFQ, the acquiring organization must decide which one to accept. Two useful tools for making this choice are *vendor rating systems* and *benchmark tests*.

In a *vendor rating system*, important criteria for selecting computer system resources are identified and each is given a weight. For example, if the weights of 60 and 30 are given for hardware and documentation, respectively, it may be loosely interpreted to mean that the organization considers hardware twice as important as documentation. Each vendor that submits a bid is rated on each criterion (such as from 0 to 60 for its hardware). The buyer then totals the scores and, all other things being equal, chooses the vendor with the highest total. Although such a rating tool does not guarantee that the best vendor will always have the highest point total, it has the advantage of being simple to apply and relatively objective. If several people are involved in the selection decision, individual biases tend to average out.

After tentatively selecting a vendor, some organizations make their decision contingent on the successful completion of a **benchmark test**. Such a test normally consists of trying to simulate running a pilot version of the new system using the hardware and software that is to be purchased from the vendor under consideration. To do this, the acquiring organization can visit the vendor's testing center and try out the proposed hardware and/or software to determine how well the chosen hardware/software configuration will work. Custom benchmark tests, however, are expensive and far from foolproof. It is quite possible that the pilot system will perform admirably at the benchmark site, but the real system, when installed, will not. If the hardware to be used in the new system is already in place, another alternative is installing a demo or trial version of the proposed software to see how the software performs on the organization's hardware. Benchmark test results for some existing products are also often available through independent testing organizations and trade magazines to compare and rate specific pieces of hardware and/or software, such as to evaluate a selection of 64-bit PCs or a particular software program. The results of these tests can be helpful when evaluating bids for existing (noncustom) products.

Documentation: RFPs, RFQs, and Vendor Evaluation Materials

The RFP or RFQ sent to potential vendors, the proposals received, and any documentation produced during the evaluation of the bids (such as vendor rankings and benchmark test results) comprise the documentation gathered during the system acquisition stage.

System Implementation

Once arrangements for the delivery of any new hardware and software have been made, the **system implementation** phase begins. This phase includes the tasks necessary to make the system operational. Implementation consists of converting programs and data files from the old system to the new one, preparing any existing equipment to work in the new system's environment, testing the system, and training personnel.

Converting to a new system can take place using one or more strategies (see Figure 12-23). With a *direct conversion*, the old system is completely deactivated and the new system is immediately implemented—a fast, but extremely risky, strategy. With a *parallel conversion*, both systems are operated in tandem until it is determined that the new system is working correctly, and then the old system is deactivated. With a *phased conversion*, the system is implemented by module, with each module being implemented with either a direct or a parallel conversion. With a *pilot conversion*, the new system is used at only one location within the organization. After it is determined that the new system is working correctly, it is installed at the other locations. It is not unusual for an organization to implement a new system using some combination of these conversion options.

During system conversion, the system needs to be thoroughly tested to ensure it is working properly. Test data should be selected to run through the system, and then the results should be examined to see if the proper actions were taken by the system. To ensure the test data is realistic, it is best to use copies of actual data for validity tests; the system should also be tested with incorrect data to ensure that errors are generated when they should be. After the system has passed the testing phase, the data used in the testing process and the results

---

>**Benchmark test.** A test used to measure computer system performance under typical use of conditions prior to purchase. >**System implementation.** The phase of the system development life cycle that encompasses activities related to making the system operational.

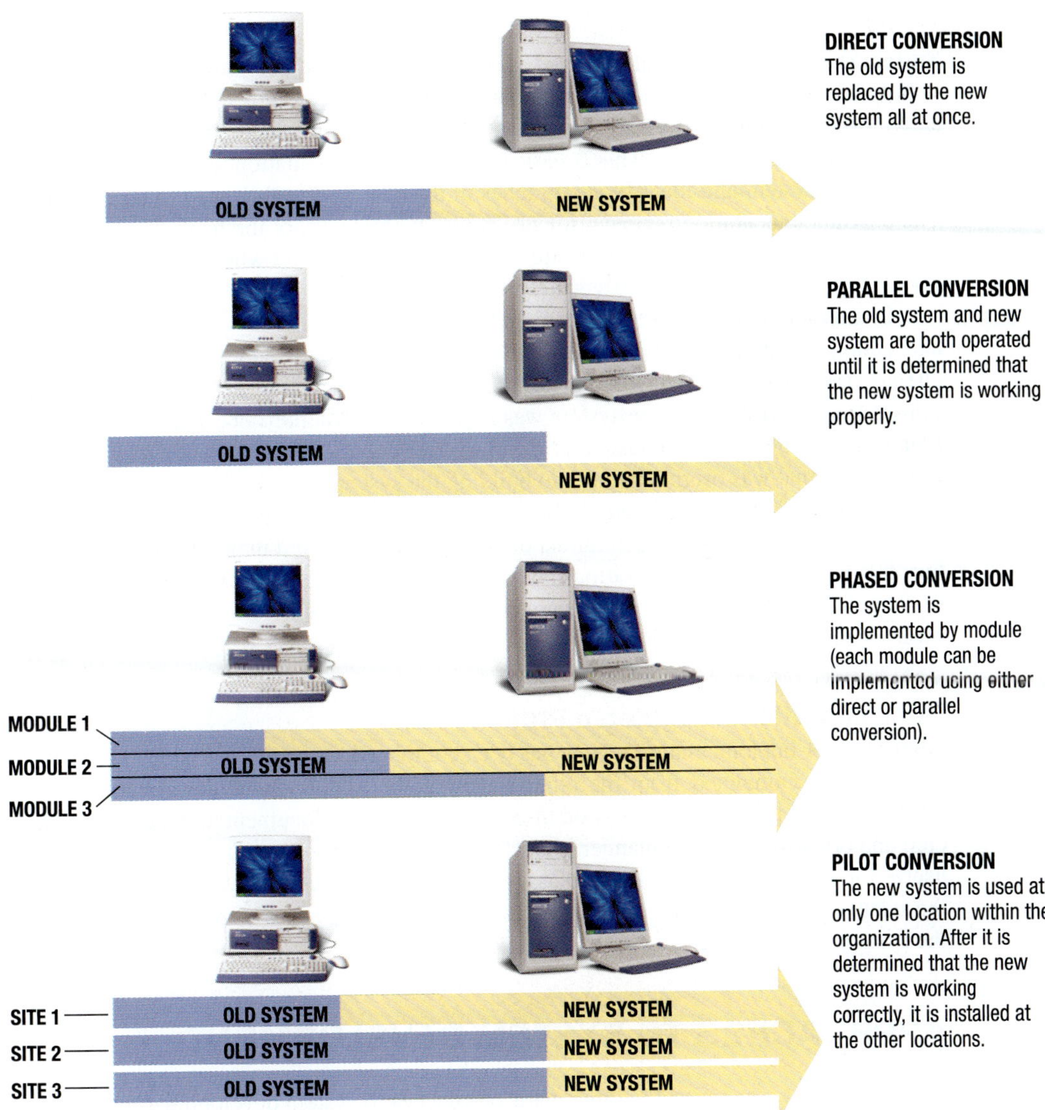

FIGURE 12-23

System conversion. Converting from an old system to the new one often follows one of these four approaches.

obtained are usually saved in case they are needed at a later time. For instance, the test data can be used to retest the system in the future, if modifications are made to the system. The data and corresponding results are also useful for determining if problems that become evident at a later time were tested for during this phase. That determination can indicate if the new problem is a result of a situation that was not taken into consideration during the system design process, or if there is another reason for the problem.

To ensure that the system will be working by a certain date, the systems analyst usually prepares a timetable. One tool for helping with this task is *project management software* (illustrated in Chapter 6 in Figure 6-27), which shows how certain implementation activities are related and when they must start and finish. The schedule should include adequate time for installing the new system as well as testing it to make certain it is working properly. Once created, schedules prepared by such software can often be shared over a company network or the Internet and fine-tuned through feedback, as necessary.

After the system is working properly, end users need to be trained. Ideally, the training will take place on the actual system with a variety of realistic sample data so that users will be exposed to the various situations they will encounter once the system is fully implemented.

Documentation: Implementation Schedule, Test Data, and Results

The schedule and any documentation regarding the type of implementation used, as well as the test data and results, should all be saved for future reference.

System Maintenance

System maintenance is usually viewed as an ongoing process, beginning when the system is fully implemented and continuing on until the end of the system's life. One of the first activities that often takes place after the system has been implemented is some type of *post-implementation review*. This is basically a follow-up evaluation that is used to evaluate the new system and identify any glitches in the new system that need to be corrected. The post-implementation review also checks into whether or not the new system is meeting its intended goals, whether costs are within expectations, and whether users are adapting favorably to the new system's environment.

Common ongoing system maintenance activities include modifying existing software and adding additional software and hardware to the system, either to update what is already in place or to add new features. It also includes correcting any problems or situations that have arisen since the system was implemented. Maintenance can be costly to an organization, and it is not unusual to spend several dollars in maintenance over time for every dollar that was originally put into building the system.

A well-designed system should be flexible enough to accommodate changes over a reasonable period of time with minimal disruption. However, if a major change eventually becomes necessary, the organization should consider developing another system to replace the current one. At this point, the system development life cycle—beginning with the preliminary investigation—begins again.

Documentation: Completed Project Folder

After the post-implementation review has been completed, its results are added to the documentation accumulated from the other stages of the SDLC. Since the system is fully implemented at this point, it is a good time to ensure that all documentation has been gathered and organized in some manner, such as inside a *project folder*. This documentation is useful for auditors who may need to assess that proper procedures were followed during the system development process, as well as for systems analysts who may need to modify the system in the future.

APPROACHES TO SYSTEM DEVELOPMENT

In this section, we examine the three main approaches to system development: *traditional system development*, *prototyping*, and *end-user development*.

The Traditional Approach

In **traditional system development**, the phases of system development are carried out in a preset order: (1) preliminary investigation, (2) analysis, (3) design, (4) acquisition, (5) implementation, and (6) maintenance. Each phase begins only when the one before it has been completed. Often, the traditional system development approach is reserved for the development of large transaction processing systems. Because the traditional system development approach is usually expensive and time-consuming, knowledgeable professionals—typically systems analysts—normally carry it out.

With traditional system development, the entire system is planned and built before anyone gets to test it or use it. As each phase of development is completed, users "sign off" on the recommendations presented to them by the systems analyst, indicating their acceptance.

>**System maintenance.** The phase of the system development life cycle in which minor adjustments are made to the finished system to keep it operational until the end of the system's life or until the time that the system needs to be redesigned. >**Traditional system development.** An approach to system development whereby the six phases of the system development life cycle are carried out in a predetermined sequence.

Although this approach allows the system development process to proceed in a logical order, it often is viewed as taking too long. For instance, by the time the new system finally begins operating, important new needs that were not part of the original plan may have already surfaced. Also, the system developed may turn out to be the wrong one. Some managers and other users of information systems have difficulty expressing their information needs, and it is not until they begin to use a system that they discover what they really need, which, at the end of a traditional system development process, would be too late.

These problems notwithstanding, the traditional system development approach is useful when the system being developed is one with which there is a great deal of experience, where user requirements are easy to determine in advance, and where management wants the system completely spelled out before giving its approval.

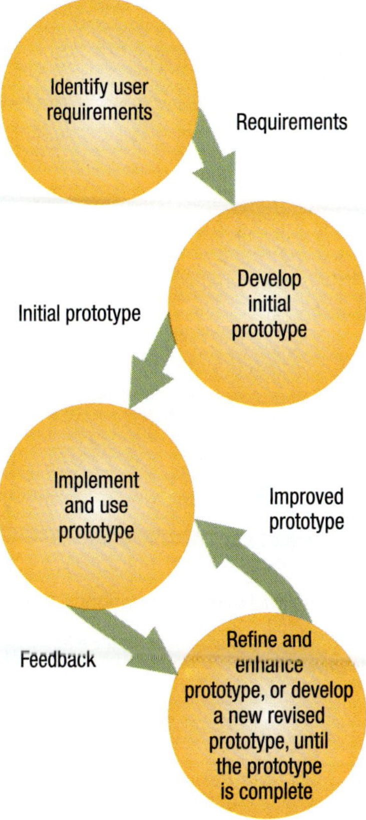

FIGURE 12-24

Prototyping.

Prototyping is an interactive process. After each prototype is built, the user and analyst try it out together and attempt to improve it.

Prototyping

To avoid the potential problem of a system being incompatible with the system user, many systems analysts have advocated prototyping. In **prototyping**, the focus is on initially developing a small model, or *prototype*, of the overall system instead of developing the entire system before users can try it out. With prototyping, users are able to work with the prototype and suggest modifications, and then the prototype can be modified or entirely redesigned, if needed. As soon as a prototype is refined to the point where management feels confident that a larger version of the system will succeed, either the prototype can be expanded into the final system, or the organization can move ahead with the remaining steps of the system development process, using the prototype as a model.

In prototyping, analysis and design generally proceed together in small steps that finally result in a completed system (see Figure 12-24). Prototyping is highly applicable in situations where user needs are difficult to precisely define, the system must be developed quickly, and some experimentation is necessary to avoid building the wrong system.

Prototyping and the traditional system development approach sometimes are combined when building new systems—for instance, by following the traditional approach but using prototyping during the analysis and design phases to clarify user needs.

End-User Development

End-user development is a system development effort in which the user is primarily responsible for the development of the system. This is in contrast to the other types of development discussed here, in which a qualified computer professional, such as a systems analyst, takes charge of the system development process.

Although end-user development can take place with any size system, it is most feasible when the system being developed is relatively small and inexpensive. For instance, an end user might develop a small marketing system to merge a mailing list with form letters. In developing the system, the user might follow a prototyping approach or a condensed version of the traditional system development approach. While end-user development is performed primarily by the end user, his or her manager would also typically be involved to some extent in the process to ensure that the system is compatible with existing systems and that no new problems are introduced. For instance, possible problems that might occur are proper security measures not being incorporated into the new system, the new system interfering with other systems within the organization, and the new system not being able to be effectively supported. Nonetheless, when computer professionals within an organization are too overloaded to build small important systems to help users, end-user development may be the only alternative.

>Prototyping. A system development alternative whereby a small model, or prototype, of the system is built before the full-scale systems development effort is undertaken.

SUMMARY

WHAT IS AN INFORMATION SYSTEM?

Chapter Objective 1:
Understand what information systems are.

A **system** is a collection of elements and procedures that interact to accomplish a goal. An **information system** is a system used to generate information to support users in an organization. **System development** is the process that consists of all activities needed to put a new system into place. System development may be required for many reasons—for example, changes in government regulations, the availability of new computer technology, or a new feature that the company wants to offer customers.

WHO USES INFORMATION SYSTEMS?

Chapter Objective 2:
Explain who uses information systems in a typical organization.

Information systems are used by decision makers—most commonly by managers. Managers typically manage the employees one level below them on the management pyramid. *Operational managers* typically manage *nonmanagement workers*. *Executive managers* generally use information systems to help them make relatively unstructured *strategic decisions*; *middle managers* typically use them to make relatively structured *tactical decisions*; and operational managers use them to help make *operational decisions*. Nonmanagement workers may access information systems to make *on-the-job decisions*.

TYPES OF INFORMATION SYSTEMS

Chapter Objective 3:
Identify several types of information systems commonly found in organizations and describe their purpose.

Many types of information systems are used by businesses and other organizations. **Office automation (OA)** refers to computer-based office-oriented technologies, such as **office systems**. **Transaction processing systems** perform tasks that generally involve the tedious record keeping that organizations handle regularly. Among these are **payroll**, **order entry**, and **accounting systems**. These types of systems are most commonly used by operational managers.

Management information systems (MISs) provide decision makers—primarily middle managers—with preselected types of information. A **decision support system (DSS)** helps middle and executive managers organize and analyze their own decision making information. *Executive information systems* (*EISs*) are decision support systems customized to meet the special needs of executive managers. A **geographic information system (GIS)** is an information system that combines geographic information with other types of data (such as information about an organization's customers, sales, and so forth) in order to provide a better understanding of the relationships among the data.

A number of **enterprise-wide systems** can be found in businesses today, including **electronic data interchange (EDI)**, **enterprise resource planning (ERP)**, **enterprise application integration (EAI)**, **customer relationship management (CRM)**, **supply chain management (SCM)**, **just-in-time (JIT)**, **value chain management**, and **inventory management systems**. Any system that links multiple enterprises, such as a business and its customers, suppliers, and partners, can be referred to as an **inter-enterprise system**. A comprehensive framework used to describe and manage an organization's business functions and systems is called **enterprise architecture**.

Computers are widely used in industry to improve productivity at both the design stage—through **computer-aided design (CAD)**—and the manufacturing stage—via **computer-aided manufacturing (CAM)**. The ability of some computer systems to perform in ways that would be considered intelligent if observed in humans is referred to as *artificial intelligence* (*AI*). Currently, the four main types of **artificial intelligence (AI) systems** are **intelligent agents**, **expert systems**, **neural networks**, and **robotics**—the study of **robot** technology. Robots for the military, business, and personal use are available today.

RESPONSIBILITY FOR SYSTEM DEVELOPMENT

The *chief information officer* (*CIO*) typically holds primary responsibility for the overall direction of system development. **Systems analysts** are the people involved most closely with the development of systems from beginning to end. When a company lacks the in-house expertise, time, or money to do its own system development, it often turns to an **outsourcing** company to provide system services.

Chapter Objective 4:
Explain the people involved with system development.

THE SYSTEM DEVELOPMENT LIFE CYCLE (SDLC)

System development usually proceeds through six phases, which are often collectively referred to as the **system development life cycle (SDLC)**. The first step is to conduct a **preliminary investigation**, or *feasibility study*. This investigation addresses the nature of the problem under study, the potential scope of the system development effort, the possible solutions, and the costs and benefits of these solutions. By the end of this phase, a *feasibility report* discussing the findings of the feasibility study is prepared.

Chapter Objective 5:
Identify and describe the different steps of the system development life cycle (SDLC).

During the **system analysis** phase, the main objectives are to study the application in depth to assess the needs of users and to prepare a list of specific requirements that the new system must meet. These objectives are accomplished through *data collection* and *data analysis*. A number of tools can help with analysis, including *data flow diagrams*, *decision tables*, *decision trees*, and *checklists*.

The **system design** phase consists of developing a model of the new system and performing a detailed analysis of benefits and costs. Various tools, such as *system flowcharts*, *input/output diagrams*, and a *data dictionary* can be helpful during this phase. Once a system has been designed and the required types of software and hardware have been specified, the **system acquisition** phase begins. The *make-or-buy decision* determines whether the necessary components will be purchased or developed in-house. Many organizations that elect to buy system components use a *request for proposal* (*RFP*) or a *request for quotation* (*RFQ*) to obtain input and *bids* from vendors. Vendors submitting bids are commonly evaluated through a *vendor rating system* and then, possibly, a **benchmark test**.

Once arrangements have been made with one or more vendors for delivery of the necessary hardware and software, the **system implementation** phase begins. This phase includes all the remaining tasks that are necessary to make the system successfully operational, including conversion of data, preparing any equipment to work in the new systems environment, and training. **System maintenance** is an ongoing process that begins when the system is fully implemented and continues until the end of the system's life.

APPROACHES TO SYSTEM DEVELOPMENT

In **traditional system development**, the phases of the SDLC are carried out in the traditional order. The focus in **prototyping** is on developing small models, or *prototypes*, of the target system. *End-user development* is a system development approach in which the user is primarily responsible for building the system. This is in contrast to other types of development, in which a qualified computer professional, such as a systems analyst, takes charge of the system development process.

Chapter Objective 6:
Discuss several approaches used to develop systems.

REVIEW ACTIVITIES

KEY TERM MATCHING

Instructions: Match each key term on the left with the definition on the right that best describes it.

a. benchmark test

b. computer-aided design (CAD)

c. customer relationship management (CRM)

d. management information system (MIS)

e. neural network

f. robot

g. supply chain management (SCM)

h. system development life cycle (SDLC)

i. systems analyst

j. transaction processing system

1. ______ A device, controlled by a human operator or a computer, that can move and react to sensory input.

2. ______ A general term applied to the use of computer technology to automate design functions.

3. ______ An expert system in which the human brain's pattern-recognition process is emulated by the computer system.

4. ______ A person who studies systems in an organization in order to determine what work needs to be done and how this work may best be achieved.

5. ______ A test used to measure computer system performance under typical use of conditions prior to purchase.

6. ______ A type of information system that processes and records data created by an organization's business transactions.

7. ______ A type of information system that provides decision makers with preselected information that can be used to make middle-management decisions.

8. ______ The oversight of materials, information, and finances as they move from the original supplier to the consumer.

9. ______ The process consisting of the six phases of system development: preliminary investigation, system analysis, system design, system acquisition, system implementation, and system maintenance.

10. ______ The process of building and managing good relationships with customers.

SELF-QUIZ

Instructions: Circle **T** if the statement is true, **F** if the statement is false, or write the best answer in the space provided. **Answers to the self-quiz are located in the References and Resources Guide at the end of the book.**

1. **T F** Executive managers tend to make highly unstructured decisions.

2. **T F** A decision support system would most likely be used by a nonmanagement worker.

3. **T F** An expert system is an example of an office system.

4. **T F** Assigning business tasks to an external company is referred to as outsourcing.

5. **T F** Users are only involved in the system development life cycle if the end-user approach is being used.

6. The software program used in an expert system in conjunction with the knowledge base to reach decisions is called the ______.

7. A(n) ______ is the computer professional who holds primary responsibility for system development within an organization.

8. Benefits that are easy to quantify in dollars are called ______ benefits.

9. A(n) ______ is a model of a system that is built before the full-scale systems development effort is undertaken.

10. Match each term with its description and write the corresponding number in the blank to the left of each description.

a. ________ An inventory system in which only the right amount of materials and finished products are kept on hand at any given time.

b. ________ A large integrated system that ties together all of a business's activities, such as planning, manufacturing, sales, marketing, and finance.

c. ________ An organization's customer service solution.

d. ________ A system that oversees materials, information, and finances as they move from the original supplier to the consumer.

1. SCM
2. ERP
3. JIT
4. CRM

EXERCISES

1. Match each SDLC phase with its description and write the corresponding number in the blank to the left of each description.

a. ________ The final phase of the SDLC.
b. ________ The phase of the SDLC that involves studying the system in depth.
c. ________ The phase of the SDLC in which the old system is converted to the new system.
d. ________ The phase of the SDLC that involves RFP or RFQ preparation, vendor rating systems, and benchmark tests.
e. ________ The phase of the SDLC in which a feasibility study is performed.
f. ________ The phase of the SDLC which generates system specifications and a list of costs and benefits for the new system.

1. design
2. implementation
3. preliminary investigation
4. analysis
5. maintenance
6. acquisition

2. For the following descriptions, indicate to which of the following information system categories the activity best belongs by writing the appropriate letters—O (office system), T (transaction processing system), M (management information system), D (decision support system), DM (design and manufacturing systems), or AI (artificial intelligence systems)—in the space provided. Note that categories may be used more than once and not all categories may be used.

Activity	Type of Information System
a. An employee creating a budget using a spreadsheet program.	________
b. A manager receiving the same type of report every month.	________
c. A person buying a software package on the World Wide Web.	________
d. An architect using a computer system to plan the layout of an office building.	________

3. Indicate what type of employees operational managers typically manage and what type of information systems those employees would most commonly use.

4. Explain the difference between a request for proposal (RFP) and a request for quotation (RFQ).

5. Assume that a company is ready to install a new system at a single location. If they have a reasonable amount of time in which to implement the new system, select the two most appropriate conversion methods for the company to consider and explain under what circumstances they may wish to select one method over the other.

DISCUSSION QUESTION

As discussed in the chapter, many objects today that would not normally be associated with a computer or information system now, in fact, are. The chapter discussed campus laundry rooms and roller coasters. It also mentioned an expected growth in the use of robotic devices in the home, such as for personal service. There must be substantial benefits in order for manufacturers to add information systems or robotic components to products, but is there a downside as well? For instance, would you feel more or less comfortable riding on a roller coaster that was computer controlled? What are the benefits? What are the potential risks? Do the benefits outweigh the risks, in your opinion? Movies, such as *iRobot*, show conflicting views of increased robotic assistants. What is your opinion? Would you want a personal robot? Is there any difference between trusting your e-mail and phone messages to a robot instead of a conventional computer or answering machine? Which would you prefer?

PROJECTS

HOT TOPICS

1. **Today's Robots** As discussed in the chapter, robots can be used today for a variety of activities in businesses and the military, as well as in the home.

   For this project, select one type of robotic device available on the market today—for instance, a robotic toy, vacuum cleaner, or lawn mower; a security or manufacturing robot; a robot used by the military or NASA; a robotic wheelchair; or a robotic personal assistant—and research it. Find out what the product does, what types of hardware it contains, how it is powered, how it is controlled, if it can be reprogrammed, what it costs, and more. What advantages does the robotics part of the product add? Do you think this is a worthwhile or beneficial product? At the conclusion of your research, prepare a one- to two-page summary of your findings and submit it to your instructor.

SHORT ANSWER/ RESEARCH

2. **Computer Certification** There are a number of certification programs available for computer professionals in a variety of areas, such as application software, computer networking, programming, and system security. Four of the companies or organizations offering the most respected and widely used certification programs are Microsoft, Novell, Cisco Systems, and the Institute for Certification of Computing Professionals (ICCP).

   For this project, select one of the companies or organizations listed in the previous paragraph and research the computer certification programs they currently offer. Find out the certification programs available, and then select one specific program and research it more thoroughly. Who is the certificate targeted to? To earn a certificate, what type of training or testing is required? Do you have to have on-the-job work experience in the computer field to qualify? What fees and other additional requirements are necessary? Where can you participate in the program? Is it an onsite program, or can you participate through a local college or training center or complete the program online? At the conclusion of your research, prepare a one-page summary of your findings and submit it to your instructor. Be sure to include your opinion regarding whether or not you think the certificate program you researched is worthwhile and why.

3. **Exoskeleton Suits** As discussed in the chapter, *exoskeleton suits* are currently being researched and developed by several organizations. While much of the focus is on the military, other applications—such as being used with construction workers to give them additional capabilities and being used with disabled individuals—are possible.

   For this project, investigate the current status of exoskeleton suits. Have any been implemented yet? What features do the ones currently under development expect to contain? What is the expected timeline of exoskeleton components being used by the military? Of a full exoskeleton suit? Are any current or future projects being targeted for nonmilitary applications? Try to locate a photo or drawing of one possible exoskeleton suit and discuss its pros and cons. At the conclusion of your research, prepare a one- to two-page summary of its findings to submit to your instructor.

HANDS ON

4. **Your Decision** The construction of a decision table can be beneficial during the system development process. This tool can be used during the analysis phase to document how a decision is currently being made, during the design phase to document how the decision will be made in the new system, and during the actual coding of the new programs to assist the programmer in determining what actions to take, based on the identified rules and conditions. The utility of this tool is not limited to the analysis, design, and coding of information systems, however. It can just as easily be used to clarify and add structure to a decision about your future career plans. In this case, the analysis involved in identifying the rules and conditions that lead to the alternative actions may prove to be as productive and meaningful as the resulting table.

   For this project, select a particular job you may want to pursue upon graduation and construct a "Career Options" decision table that includes various conditions and rules and that could be used to determine if you have completed the necessary actions to obtain that job. On the table, mark your current status for each specified condition and the decision that results in at the bottom of the table. Prepare a short summary of what conditions in your table you have already accomplished and which ones are still to come, and submit your summary to your instructor along with your marked-up decision table.

5. **Chatterbots** As discussed in the chapter, a *chatterbot* is a program that attempts to simulate the "chat" of another human. These programs have been available since the early 1960s and have recently begun to appear on Web sites. The Cybelle chatterbot from Agentland.com was shown in Figure 12-13.

   For this project, find a chatterbot on a Web page (either Cybelle on the Agentland.com Web site or another you find using a search site) and have a conversation with the chatterbot. Form an opinion about how humanlike the exchange was. Do you think the chatterbot responded to your comments in a humanlike fashion? Was it able to answer your questions? If not, what did it do when it could not answer a question? Was the experience enjoyable? Why or why not? Do you think chatterbots can be a worthwhile addition to a Web site? Would you prefer to chat in real time with a customer service chatterbot if it could answer your questions correctly, or would you rather wait for an e-mail reply or telephone call from a human customer service representative? Explain. At the conclusion of your research, prepare a one-page summary of your experience and submit it to your instructor.

WRITING ABOUT COMPUTERS

6. **Outsourcing** As discussed in the chapter, outsourcing is becoming more widely used as businesses find themselves without the necessary skilled employees for a particular task or find the cost of certain processes performed in-house prohibitive.

   For this project, develop an order fulfillment system for a fictitious very small company just going into business. Assume that the company is being started by a single individual who will work full time in the business, but no other employees have yet been hired. The company will sell handmade gift baskets via a Web site and anticipates fulfilling between 5 and 50 orders per day during the first year in business, depending on the season. List the duties involved with order fulfillment for this company and design one possible system. Be sure to consider all aspects of the system, including the actual order processing, basket creation, shipping, billing, inventory management, and so forth. Did you choose to outsource any parts of the system? Why or why not? How many (if any) new employees does your system require and what are their duties? Which duties did you assign to the owner and why? Submit your system design to your instructor in the form of a short paper, not more than two pages in length.

PRESENTATION/ DEMONSTRATION

7. **Employee Perks** As quality specialized employees—such as computer professionals—become increasingly harder to find and even harder to keep, and companies face increasing economic challenges, employers are increasingly turning toward nonmonetary perks. For instance, on-site childcare, gyms, and other facilities, as well as on-site services, such as massages, dry-cleaning drop off and pickup, and farmer's markets, are becoming more common. Sometimes the cost of providing these services are paid for by the company; other times, employees pay the cost or receive the services in lieu of a pay raise or other benefit.

   For this project, investigate these types of "soft" benefits being used today. Find one company that provides at least one of these types of benefits to its employees and determine the services available and the cost to both the employer and the employee. What are the advantages and disadvantages to both employers and employees of these types of employee benefits? Would they make you more or less inclined to work at that company? Share your findings and opinions with the class in the form of a short presentation. The presentation should not exceed 10 minutes and should make use of one or more presentation aids, such as the chalkboard, handouts, overhead transparencies, or a computer-based slide presentation (your instructor may provide additional requirements). You may also be asked to submit a summary of the presentation to your instructor.

GROUP DISCUSSION

8. **NASA Robot Crews** Robotics research is continuing to make smarter and more capable robots. For instance, NASA researchers have developed a way to make a crew of robots work together to grasp, lift, and move heavy loads across rough, varied terrain. These robot crews are expected to eventually be used to set up a base camp on Mars before human colonists arrive. One difference between the new NASA robot crews and other robots is special software that allows the robots to "share a brain" so that each robot knows what the rest are doing and can compensate or react accordingly. This technology enables the robots to work together to develop plans, such as how to maneuver around a rock or other obstacle the crew may encounter. Some might worry that this technology also provides the potential for a "super robot" in the future, such as the Borg enemy portrayed in the *Star Trek: The Next Generation* television show. Can robots get too smart? What steps should our society take to ensure that robots cannot become physically dangerous? What is the potential implication of replacing human laborers with robots? Currently robots are used mainly for monotonous or dangerous tasks, but what if the range of jobs given to robots continues to expand? Will it adversely affect our economy, or will human workers automatically be able to evolve to more advanced positions? Would you feel comfortable being in physical proximity to a group of robots capable of working together on tasks?

   For this project, form an opinion about the potential impact of continuing to make smarter and more capable robots and be prepared to discuss your position (in class, via an online class discussion group, or in a class chat room, depending on your instructor's directions). You may also be asked to write a short paper expressing your opinion.

WEB ACTIVITIES

The *Understanding Computers* Web site located at **www.course.com/uc11** features many resources to help reinforce your understanding of the chapter content and help you prepare for exams. Your instructor may also assign specific activities to be completed that will count toward your final grade in the course.

Instructions: Go to **www.course.com/uc11/ch12** to work the following online activities.

Click any link in the navigation bar on the left to access any of the online resources described below.

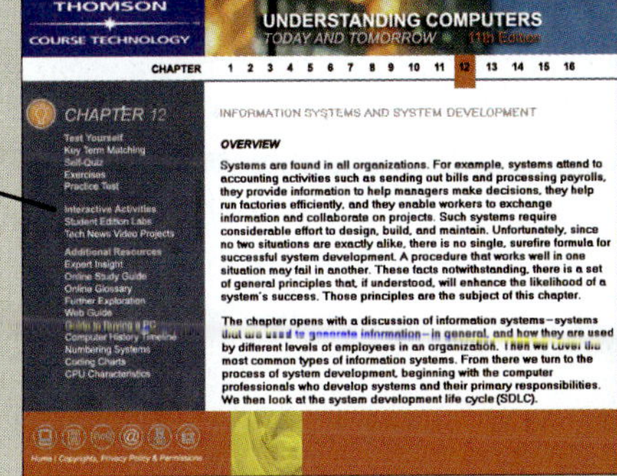

INTERACTIVE ACTIVITIES

1. **Crossword Puzzle** Practice your knowledge of the key terms in Chapter 12 by completing the interactive Crossword Puzzle.
2. **Tech News Video Project** Watch the **"Online Project Management Tools"** video clip that takes a look at online project management tools that can be used to manage projects, such as system, program, or Web development projects. After watching the video online, complete the corresponding project.
3. **Student Edition Labs** Reinforce the concepts you have learned in this chapter by working through the interactive **Project Management** lab.

TEST YOURSELF

1. **Key Term Matching** Test your knowledge of selected chapter key terms by matching the terms with their definitions.
2. **Self-Quiz** Test your retention of chapter concepts by taking the Self-Quiz.
3. **Exercises** Work these short exercises to review the concepts and terms covered in the chapter.
4. **Practice Test** Test how ready you are for an upcoming exam by completing the online Practice Test.

STUDY TOOLS/ ADDITIONAL RESOURCES

The Understanding Computers Web site has a wide range of additional resources, including an **Online Study Guide** (containing study tips, a chapter outline with room to add your own notes, and a chapter checklist of the activities to complete when the chapter is covered in class and when you are preparing for a test) and an **Online Glossary** for each chapter; **Further Exploration** links; a **Web Guide**, a **Guide to Buying a PC**, and a **Computer History Timeline**; more information about **Numbering Systems**, **Coding Charts**, and **CPU Characteristics**; and much, much more!

Program Development and Programming Languages

OUTLINE

Overview
Approaches to Program Design and Development
- Structured Programming
- Object-Oriented Programming (OOP)
- Aspect-Oriented Programming (AOP)

The Program Development Life Cycle (PDLC)
- Problem Analysis
- Program Design
- Program Coding
- Program Debugging and Testing
- Program Implementation and Maintenance

Tools for Facilitating Program Development
- Application Lifecycle Management (ALM) Tools
- Application Generators
- Software-Asset Management Tools
- Device Software Development Tools

Programming Languages
- What Is a Programming Language?
- Categories of Programming Languages
- Popular Programming Languages

LEARNING OBJECTIVES

After completing this chapter, you will be able to:

1. Understand the differences between structured programming, object-oriented programming (OOP), and aspect-oriented programming (AOP).
2. Identify and describe the activities involved in the program development life cycle (PDLC).
3. Understand what constitutes good program design and list several tools that can be used by computer professionals when designing a program.
4. Explain the three basic control structures and how they can be used to control program flow during execution.
5. Discuss some of the activities involved with coding, debugging, maintaining, documenting, and ensuring the quality of programs.
6. List some tools that can be used to speed up or otherwise facilitate the program development process.
7. Describe several programming languages in use today.

OVERVIEW

If you wanted to build a house, you would probably begin with some research and planning. You might speak to people about home design, draw up some floor plans, estimate the cost of materials, and so on. In other words, you would not start digging a hole and pouring concrete on the first day. Creating successful application programs for a computer system also requires considerable planning.

When computer professionals need to develop new applications, they use a *programming language*—a set of rules used to write computer programs. In Chapter 12 we discussed developing complete systems. In this chapter we look specifically at practices and tools for developing the application programs used within these systems.

The chapter opens with a discussion of the three most common approaches to program design and development, followed by a look at the program development life cycle; that is, the steps that occur when a new program needs to be created or an existing program needs to be modified. This process includes problem analysis, program design, coding, debugging, testing, and maintenance. In this section, topics—such as tools that can be used to design a program, good program design techniques, and types of program errors—are discussed. Next, we turn our attention to tools that can facilitate program development, and the definition and categories of programming languages. The chapter closes with a look at some of the most popular programming languages. ■

APPROACHES TO PROGRAM DESIGN AND DEVELOPMENT

There have been various approaches to programming over the years. Two of the most significant approaches are *structured programming* and *object-oriented programming*. An emerging approach is *aspect-oriented programming*.

Structured Programming

Beginning in the 1960s, a number of researchers began to stress program planning and design and the merits of separating the design process from the actual program coding. Such a division of labor is a natural one. For example, architects design buildings and construction crews work from those specifications to build them. Many of the proposed ideas of the researchers caught on, and techniques evolved that made program design more systematic and the program code easier to understand and maintain. These techniques are usually grouped together under the term **structured programming**.

>**Structured programming.** An approach to program design in which a program is separated into smaller subprograms, and step-by-step instructions are executed one after the other, accessing the subprograms when needed.

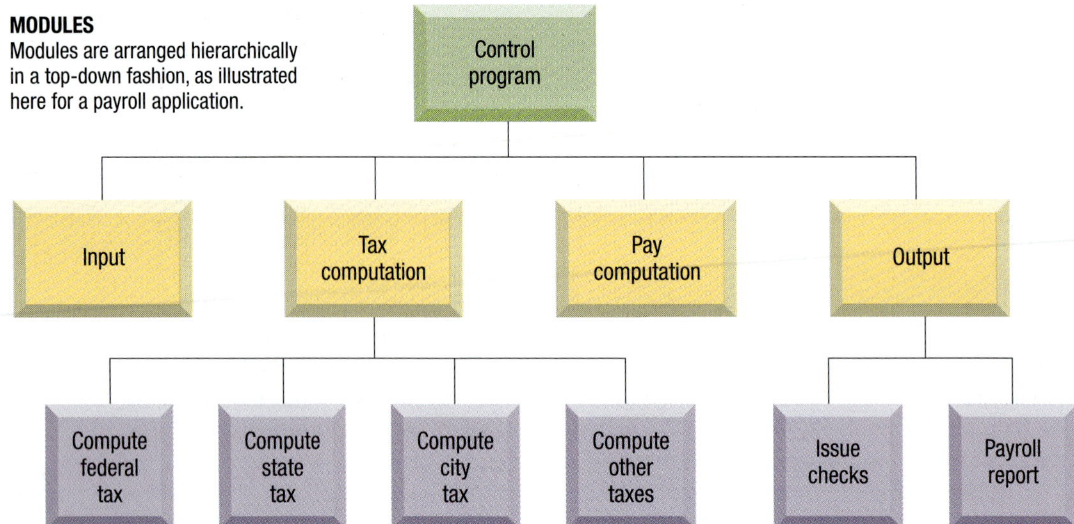

FIGURE 13-1
Structured programming. A structured program is divided into individual modules; each module represents a specific processing task.

In structured programming, specific logical sections of the program are written as separate, smaller programs called *modules* or *subprograms* (see Figure 13-1). Prior to structured programming, programs were written as one large set of instructions containing statements that sent control to different parts of the programs. These programs used statements that jumped from one part of the program to another, such as the "GOTO 100" statement that sends program control to line 100 of the code to execute commands from that point in the program code on, until another GOTO statement is reached. This jumping around continued until the program ended. Code like this is sometimes referred to as "spaghetti code" because it is a disorganized, intertwined, jumble of statements, which makes following the logic of the program as difficult as tracing the path of a single strand of spaghetti in a plate of spaghetti. Structured programming eliminates this disorganization problem and GOTO statements by sending control out to a module that performs a specific task whenever it is necessary to perform that task. The module performs the task, and then program control returns to the main program. The module can be used as often as needed, in any part of the control program (or another module, for that matter) that needs that task to be performed.

Object-Oriented Programming (OOP)

A newer approach to program design is called **object-oriented programming** (**OOP**). OOP focuses on an application's data and the *methods* or instructions that can be used to manipulate that data. In an *object-oriented program* (also abbreviated as *OOP*), objects—such as GUI objects like buttons and windows, as well as real-world objects such as products and employees—are modeled using software *objects*. Although this type of modeling can be done with conventional programming languages, *object-oriented programming languages* provide direct support for objects, making it significantly easier to do. An object contains *variables* (data about the state of the object) and related methods that can be used to control the current behavior of the object. For example, a button object displayed on the screen might include one variable to hold the coordinates for the size and location of the button's display rectangle and one variable to hold the color of the button (see Figure 13-2). The button object would also include methods for any actions that may be taken, such as to display, hide, or dim the button; each method contains the specific actions that will be taken

>**Object-oriented programming (OOP).** An approach to program design in which a program consists of a collection of objects that contain data and methods to be used with that data.

when a message is passed to the object to invoke that method. The same message can be sent to different objects; when an object receives a message, it invokes the method associated with that message and performs the actions appropriate for that object. For instance, a message invoking the *Display* method for a button object might result in the button being displayed on the screen, whereas the same message invoking the Display method for an employee object might cause the employee's information (name, address, and photo, for instance) to be displayed on the screen. How each object reacts to each message is determined by the corresponding method (*Display* method, in this example) stored in the object. The ability to create multiple methods with the same name that act differently and appropriately with different types of objects is an important OOP principle called *polymorphism.* The bundling of an object's variables and methods into a single package so that the details are hidden from the user's view is called *information hiding* or *encapsulation.*

The data contained within an object can be in a variety of formats, such as numeric, text, image, video, audio, and so forth. This characteristic, combined with the ability to manipulate different types of objects with the same methods, leads to new applications that were difficult, or impossible, to create with traditional programming languages. For example, the statement

$$c = a + b$$

is a typical statement in most programming languages. It would generally be used to combine (add) two numbers. In an OOP language, however, the same statement could be used to combine two strings of data to display a first and last name next to each other. It could also be used to combine two audio clips, or one video clip and one soundtrack, in order to play them at the same time. In an object-oriented program, there is no limit to the complexity of an object.

Objects in an OOP are organized into classes. A *class* defines the unique characteristics common to all objects of a certain kind. For example, a button class would describe the characteristics that buttons have in common. There may also be *subclasses* below a class, such as one subclass for round buttons and one subclass for polygon buttons. In addition to the characteristics of the subclass, all objects in a subclass automatically possess—or *inherit*—all characteristics of the class from which it was derived. Classes and objects are discussed and illustrated a little later in this chapter.

One advantage of OOP is that objects can be accessed by multiple programs. The program being used to access an object determines which of the object's methods are available. Therefore, objects can be reused without having to alter the code contained in each object, which shortens program development time.

Button color
Display coordinates
Display
Hide
Dim

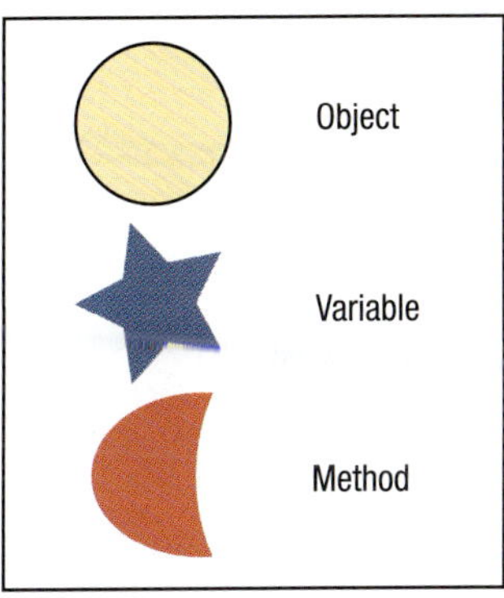

FIGURE 13-2

Objects. The Button object shown here contains two variables to hold data about the current state of the button and three methods (sets of instructions) to be used to react to messages the object receives.

Aspect-Oriented Programming (AOP)

Aspect-oriented programming (AOP) is an emerging software development approach that is based on more than a decade of research at IBM, Xerox's PARC, Boston's Northeastern University, and the Netherlands's University of Twente. AOP continues the programming trend of making software programs smaller and more manageable by sharing and reusing more code across their parts. Specifically, AOP more clearly separates different functions so that program components can be developed and modified individually from one another and the components can be easily reused with separate, nonrelated objects. Although both structured programming and object-oriented programming focus on separating components (such as by using modules and classes), some common tasks or *programming policies* cannot easily be separated using structured programming or

>**Aspect-oriented programming (AOP).** An approach to program design in which different functions are clearly separated so program components can be developed and modified individually from one another, and the components can be easily reused with separate, nonrelated objects.

OOP. Because of this, important programming policies—such as running a security check, performing error-handling procedures, and opening a database connection—may end up being located in hundreds or thousands of places scattered throughout a program's code, making it very difficult to update them when needed. AOP can encapsulate these policies or functions into *aspects*—code segments that can be used as needed without having to repeat the code throughout the program. This ability to cut across the typical divisions of responsibility in a program—such as across multiple classes in an object-oriented program—is called *crosscutting* and helps to avoid this redundancy problem, improving software quality and lowering IT development and maintenance costs at the same time. According to IBM, AOP has yielded significant benefits in the quality of the code and the speed with which programmers can write programs. AOP and OOP are currently considered to be complementary, not competing, technologies, although some AOP advocates view AOP as the next logical step after object-oriented programming. And John Seely Brown, director emeritus of Xerox PARC, views AOP as "the next generation of software engineering."

THE PROGRAM DEVELOPMENT LIFE CYCLE (PDLC)

Creating application programs is referred to as *application software development* or **program development**. Program development traditionally begins with the system specifications that are developed during the analysis and design phases of the system development life cycle (SDLC), which was discussed in Chapter 12. The steps involved in program development (see Figure 13-3) are referred to as the **program development life cycle** (**PDLC**) and consist of the following:

- Step 1: Problem analysis
- Step 2: Program design
- Step 3: Program coding
- Step 4: Program debugging and testing
- Step 5: Program implementation and maintenance

The activities that take place during each step of the program development life cycle are discussed in the next few sections. As each critical development activity is taking place, documentation is generated. The types of documentation generated, which consists of details about what the program does and how it works, is summarized in Figure 13-3.

Problem Analysis

As discussed in detail in Chapter 12, the systems analyst develops a set of specifications during the first few steps of the system development life cycle indicating exactly what the new system should do and how it will work. These specifications (data flow diagrams, system flowcharts, input and output designs, data dictionary, and so forth) are used during **problem analysis**—the first step of the PDLC. During this step, these specifications are reviewed by the systems analyst and the **programmer**—the person who will use a programming language to code the software program to these specifications. The systems analyst and programmer may also meet with the users of the new system to fully understand what functions the software program they are creating for the new system must perform.

>**Program development.** The process of creating application programs. >**Program development life cycle (PDLC).** The process containing the five steps of program development: analyzing, designing, coding, debugging and testing, and maintaining application software. >**Problem analysis.** The step in the program development life cycle in which the problem is carefully considered and the program specifications are developed. >**Programmer.** A person whose job it is to write, test, and maintain computer programs.

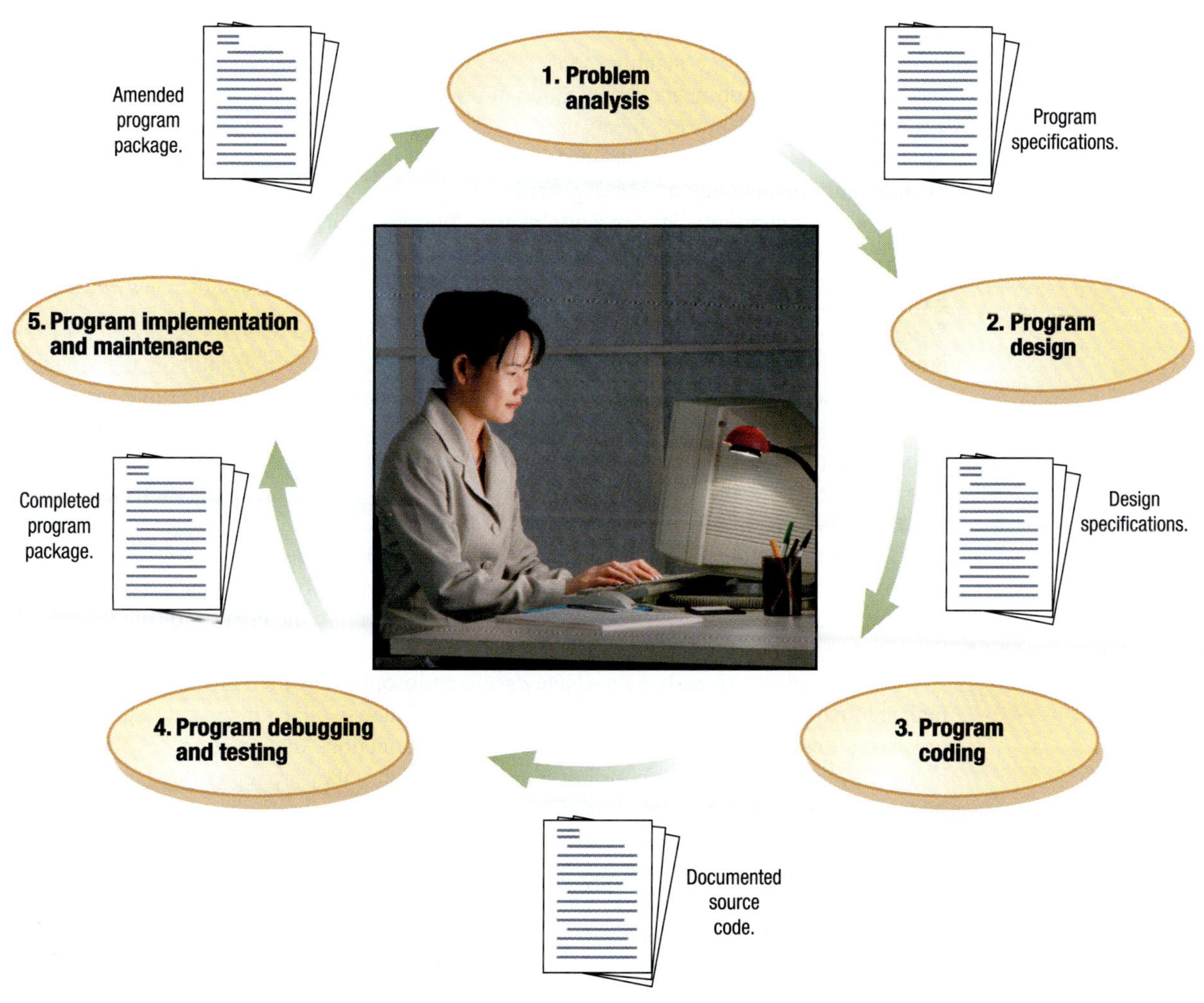

FIGURE 13-3
The program development life cycle (PDLC). Each step of the program development life cycle produces some type of documentation to pass on to the next step.

Documentation: Program Specifications

The end result of this first step in the PDLC is a set of program specifications outlining what the program must do, the timetable for completing the program, which programming language will be used, how the program will be tested, and what documentation is required.

Program Design

In the **program design** step of the PDLC, the specifications developed during the problem analysis step are used to develop an *algorithm* for the program; that is, the set of steps that are needed in order for the program to perform all the tasks that it is supposed to do. Only when the program design is complete does the next step—the actual program coding—begin.

Good program design helps the development process go more smoothly and makes revisions to the software program easier to do when changes to the program are needed in the future. Just as with Web site design (discussed in Chapter 10), careful planning and design of a computer program are extremely important and pay off in the end. Some program design tools and considerations are discussed next.

SYS

>**Program design.** The step in the program development life cycle in which the program specifications are expanded into a complete design of the new program.

Program Design Tools

Program design tools are planning tools. They consist of diagrams, charts, tables, models, and other tools that outline the organization of program tasks, the steps the program will follow, or the characteristics of objects used by the program. Once a program has been coded and implemented, the program designs generated by program design tools can also be useful program documentation. Three program design tools widely used—particularly with structured programming—are *structure charts*, *flowcharts*, and *pseudocode*. A fourth tool sometimes used with OOP design is *data modeling*. Each of these tools is discussed next.

Structure Charts

Structure charts (sometimes called *hierarchy charts*) depict the overall organization of a program. They show how program segments, or modules, are defined and how they relate to one another. Figure 13-1 at the beginning of this chapter contains a structure chart for a payroll application. As shown in this figure, a typical structure chart, with its several rows of boxes connected by lines, resembles a corporate organization chart. Each box on the chart represents a program module; that is, a set of logically related operations that perform a well-defined task. The modules in the upper rows invoke the modules under them whenever the specific processing functions contained in the modules in the lower boxes are needed. These latter modules do the majority of the program work and may be further broken down into *submodules*, if necessary. The lines connecting the boxes indicate the relationship between higher-level and lower-level modules.

Structure charts embody a *top-down design* philosophy, in which modules are conceptualized first at the highest levels of the hierarchy and then depicted in greater detail at progressively lower levels. Put another way, the broad functions that are first defined at the highest levels are broken down further, level by level, until they are represented by the specific tasks that need to be carried out. This top-down design is similar to what happens in a corporate organization chart—departments (such as marketing, production, human resources, and information systems) are listed at higher levels on the chart than the specific areas associated with those departments. For example, the information systems department might list operations, programming, and systems analysis/design under it; programming might be further broken down into application programming, system programming, and Web programming.

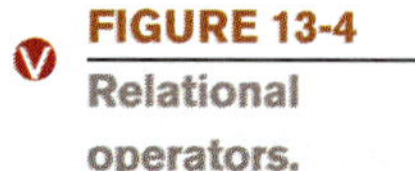

FIGURE 13-4
Relational operators.

OPERATOR	MEANING
<	Less than
<= ≤	Less than or equal to
>	Greater than
>= ≥	Greater than or equal to
=	Equal to
≠ <> ><	Not equal to

Program Flowcharts

Once the organization of a program has been determined, program **flowcharts** can be used to illustrate the step-by-step logic that is to take place within each module. Program flowcharts use geometric symbols and *relational operators*, such as < for "less than" and = for "equal to" (see Figure 13-4), to graphically portray the sequence of steps involved in a program. The steps in a flowchart are arranged in the same logical sequence that their corresponding program statements will appear in the program.

To help you understand what the symbols and operators used in a flowchart mean and how they are used, consider an example. Suppose a company's human resources department wants a printed list of all employees who meet a certain set of criteria, such as having computer experience and at least five years of company service. A flowchart that shows how to accomplish this task and also totals the number of employees who meet these criteria is shown in Figure 13-5, along with an explanation of the symbols used in that flowchart. These symbols—start/stop, processing, input/output, decision, and connector—are some of the most common flowchart symbols.

Every flowchart begins and ends with an oval-shaped *start/stop symbol*. The first of these symbols in the program contains the word *Start*, and the last contains the word *Stop*.

>Flowchart. A program design tool that shows graphically step-by-step how a computer program will process data.

FLOWCHART LOGIC

This flowchart represents reading an entire personnel file to determine all people who have computer experience and at least five years of company service. When those individuals are located, their names are printed. When the end of the personnel file is reached, the running count of the number of people matching the criteria is printed to complete the printed report.

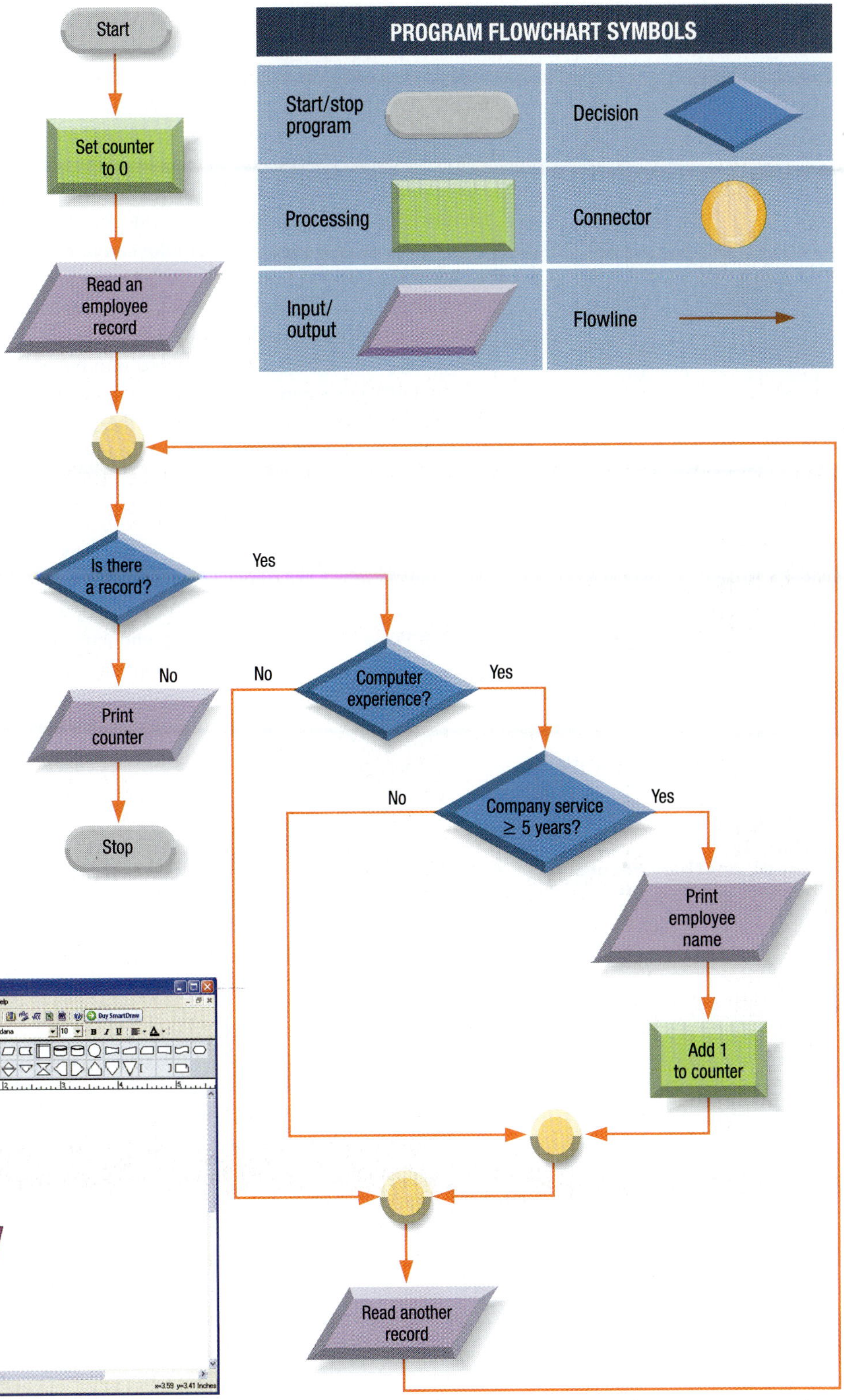

PROGRAM FLOWCHART SYMBOLS

Start/stop program	Decision
Processing	Connector
Input/ output	Flowline

Start
Set counter to 0
Read an employee record
Is there a record?
Yes
No
Print counter
Stop
Computer experience?
No
Yes
Company service ≥ 5 years?
No
Yes
Print employee name
Add 1 to counter
Read another record

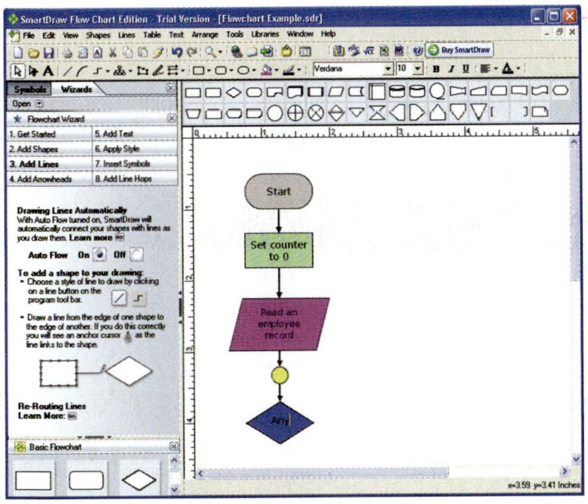

FLOWCHART SOFTWARE

Can be used to create and modify flowcharts.

FIGURE 13-5

A flowchart example.

SYS

The diamond-shaped *decision symbol* indicates a question, generally with only two possible answers—yes or no (true or false). Decision symbols always have one *flowline* (a line with arrows that link the symbols on a flowchart and indicate the flow of logic) entering and at least two flowlines (representing each of the possible outcomes) exiting. The rectangular *processing symbol* contains an action to be taken—for example, "Set counter to 0" and "Add 1 to counter." The *connector symbol* provides a meeting point for several flowlines. The *input/output symbol* indicates the point where data will be either input or output.

The flowchart in Figure 13-5 also includes a *looping* operation. The program reads an employee record and, if there is an employee record in the file (that is, the end of the file was not reached), the program inspects the record and takes an action; then the program reads another record, inspects that record, and takes action. This looping process continues until the end of the file is reached. When the computer reads a record, as indicated by the input/output symbol, it retrieves the record into memory. If the record meets both search criteria, the employee's name is printed, and a counter is incremented by 1. After the last record is read and processed, the value of the counter is printed to complete the printed report, and then the program ends. To facilitate flowchart development and modification, flowcharting software (also shown in Figure 13-5) can be used.

Pseudocode

An alternative to the flowchart is **pseudocode**. Pseudocode also expresses the steps in a program, but uses English-like statements in place of the flowchart's graphic symbols. As shown in Figure 13-6, pseudocode looks more like a program coded in a programming language than a flowchart. Flowcharts, however, are sometimes better than pseudocode for designing logically-complex problems since they are more visual, and they are usually faster to create.

No formal set of standard rules exists for writing pseudocode; however, Figure 13-6 follows some commonly used conventions. Note that all words relating to a control structure (to be discussed shortly) are capitalized and the processing steps contained within those structures are indented. Indentation can also be used to enhance the readability of the pseudocode. The keywords *Start* and *Stop* are often used to begin and end pseudocode.

```
Start
Counter = 0
Read a record
DO WHILE there are records to process
   IF computer experience
      IF company service ≥ 5 years
         Print employee name
         Increment Counter
      ELSE
         Next statement
      END IF
   ELSE
      Next statement
   END IF
   Read another record
END DO
Print Counter
Stop
```

FIGURE 13-6

Pseudocode. This pseudocode corresponds to the example illustrated in the flowchart in Figure 13-5.

Data Modeling

Data modeling is a tool to illustrate the data in an application and is often used when designing an object-oriented program. In a data model, each object in the program is identified along with its corresponding class, class properties, and variables. For example, Figure 13-7 contains a data model for *Bicycle* objects; the model shows the data that might be used in an OOP program to model bicycles controlled by users in a program such as a simulation or game. As shown in the figure, the Bicycles class specifies the *properties* that all Bicycle objects have in common. Each individual object (called an *instance*) in the Bicycles class contains *variables* to indicate the current value for the number of gears, and the current gear, speed (in mph), and pedal cadence (in rpm) for that Bicycle object. There are also methods that are used with the Bicycle objects, such as for braking, changing the pedal cadence, and changing gears, but those methods are not illustrated in this diagram. Note that while each instance (specific object in a class) inherits the properties of the class and has the same variables, the values for the variables may or

>**Pseudocode.** A program design tool that uses English-like statements to outline the logic of a program.

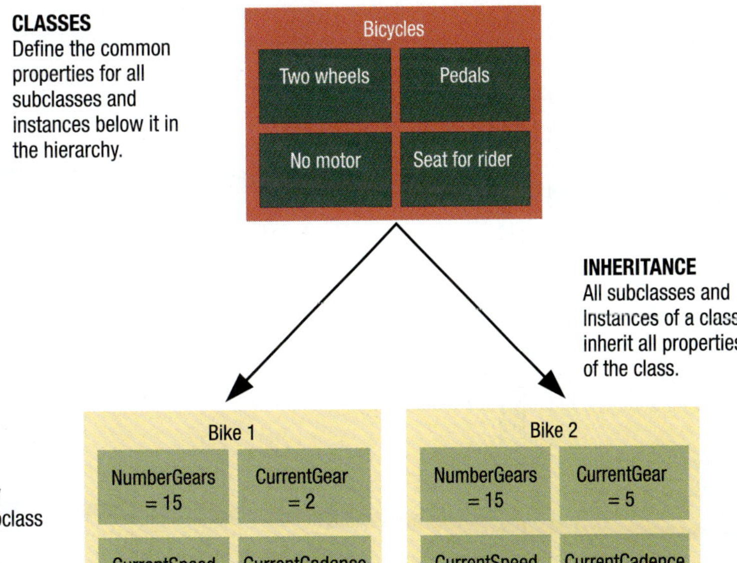

FIGURE 13-7

Data model for one class of objects in an object-oriented program.

may not be the same for all instances in that class. For instance, while both bikes modeled in Figure 13-7 have the same value (15) for the *NumberGears* variable, the values for the other three variables are different. It is also important to note that, when appropriate, a single class can be broken into subclasses. For example, the single Bicycles class in Figure 13-7 could be broken down into racing, mountain, and regular bikes, if appropriate for the application.

Control Structures

A **control structure** is a pattern that controls when and how the instructions in a computer program are performed. The three fundamental control structures: *sequence*, *selection*, and *repetition* are illustrated in Figure 13-8 and discussed next.

The Sequence Control Structure

A *sequence control structure* is simply a series of procedures that follow one another. After the first procedure has been carried out completely, the program control moves to the next procedure.

The Selection Control Structure

With a *selection control structure*, the direction that the program control takes depends on a certain condition. The basic selection control structure is the *if-then-else structure* shown in Figure 13-8, in which the condition can only result in two possibilities—true or false (yes or no). *If* a certain condition is true, *then* the program follows one procedure; else, if false, the program follows a different procedure.

An alternate selection control structure can be used when there are more than two possibilities. This structure—known as the *case control structure* and shown in Figure 13-8—allows for as many possible results of the specified condition as needed. For example, the flowchart in Figure 13-5 uses two *nested* if-then-else statements (one statement located inside another) to test for the two conditions "Computer experience?" and "Company

>**Control structure.** A pattern for controlling the flow of logic in a computer program.

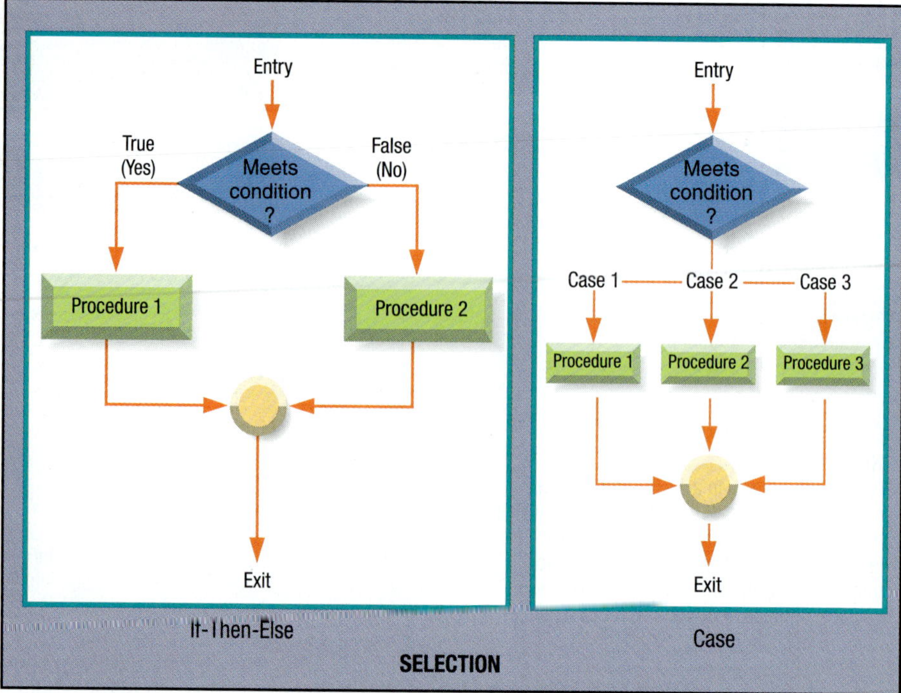

FIGURE 13-8

Examples of the three fundamental control structures of structured programming. Note that each structure has only one entry point and only one exit point.

service ≥ 5 years?" Since the second condition is only tested if the first condition is true, these two conditions together result in the following three possibilities, or *cases*:

- Case 1: No computer experience
- Case 2: Computer experience, company service < 5 years
- Case 3: Computer experience, company service ≥ 5 years

The case control structure with these three choices could be used in the flowchart in Figure 13-5 instead of the two nested if-then-else statements. The actions of printing the employee's name and incrementing the counter would be listed under Case 3 (the other cases would result in no action being taken), and the next statement after exiting the case structure would be to read another record.

The Repetition Control Structure

The *repetition control structure* (also called the *iteration control structure*) is used when one or more instructions are to be repeated in a loop until a particular condition is reached. This control structure can take one of two forms: the basic *do while structure* or the alternate *do until structure*.

With the *do while structure*, the instructions in the loop are repeated as long as a certain condition is true ("do *while* true"). Therefore, if the condition is not true to begin with, the instructions within the loop are never executed (notice that the decision appears before the procedure at the top of the do while structure in Figure 13-8). With the *do until structure*, the instructions in the loop are repeated as long as a certain condition is false ("do *until* true"). With do until, the procedure in the loop is always executed at least once, because the procedure appears before any test is made about whether or not to exit the loop (see Figure 13-8).

Good Program Design

Good program design is essential. If a program is not well planned before the coding process begins, it usually results in a more time-consuming and, potentially, lower-quality result than if the design process had been carried out properly. In general, time spent planning is time well spent. A few principles that should be kept in mind to help facilitate good program design are discussed next.

Be Specific

When illustrating the instructions that a computer will follow, *all* things that the computer must do or consider must be specified. Although the instruction "Please make me a piece of toast" would be a clear enough request for another person to follow, it is not specific enough for a computer to follow. To properly instruct a computer, every step the computer must perform and every decision the computer must make has to be stated precisely. For example, the instructions that would be needed in order to instruct a computer to make a piece of toast are listed in Figure 13-9.

FIGURE 13-9

Writing instructions for a computer versus a person. A computer requires step-by-step instructions.

One-Entry-Point/One-Exit-Point Rule

An extremely important characteristic of the control structures just discussed is that each permits only one entry point into and one exit point out of any structure. This property is

DIRECTIONS FOR HUMAN	DIRECTIONS FOR COMPUTER
1. Please make me a piece of toast.	1. Take one slice of bread out of the bag of bread. 2. Put the bread into the slot on the toaster, narrow edge first with the widest part of the bread fitting into the widest part of the slot. 3. Push the start lever on the toaster down. 4. When the toast pops up, remove the toast from the toaster. 5. Place the toast onto a plate. 6. Open the silverware drawer, take out a knife, then close the silverware drawer. 7. Open the refrigerator, remove the margarine, and shut the refrigerator. 8. Take the lid off the margarine. 9. Scoop out one teaspoon of margarine with the knife. 10. Spread the margarine on the top side of the toast, evenly covering that surface of the toast. 11. Place the lid back on the margarine. 12. Open the refrigerator, replace the margerine, and shut the refrigerator.

sometimes called the *one-entry-point/one-exit-point rule*. Observe the marked entry and exit points in the control structures in Figure 13-8. The one-entry-point/one-exit-point convention makes programs much more readable and easier to maintain.

No Infinite Loops or Logic Errors

An *infinite loop* is a set of instructions that repeats forever. An infinite loop occurs when a do while condition never becomes false or a do until condition never becomes true. This can happen when the statement to increment a counter is forgotten, when the wrong operators are used—such as less than (<) instead of greater than (>)—or when a similar error in logic is made. To test for infinite loops and other logic errors, it is a good idea to trace through the steps of your finished flowchart, keeping track of the values of any loop counters and other variables to ensure the program does what you intended. Examples of testing a flowchart and recording the tracing results (for one correct flowchart and one flowchart containing an error) are shown in Figure 13-10.

FURTHER EXPLORATION

For links to further information about program design, go to www.course.com/uc11/ch13

Documentation: Design Specifications

The documentation resulting from the design step of the program development life cycle is a set of design specifications illustrating the set of steps needed to solve the problem in question. These specifications can be expressed using one or more design tools, such as flowcharts, pseudocode, structure charts, and data models.

Program Coding

Once the program design is complete, the program is *coded*. **Coding** is the process of writing the actual program steps in the proper format for a particular programming language. During the coding process, computer professionals often use techniques to help them produce code rapidly while, at the same time, creating programs that are both easy to maintain and as error-free as possible. Some techniques that are useful in this regard are selecting the most appropriate programming language and using consistent *coding standards*, *reusable code*, and *data dictionaries*. These coding techniques are discussed in the next few sections.

Choosing a Programming Language

There are a number of different programming languages to choose from when coding a program. These languages are discussed in detail later in this chapter, but several factors that may affect the program language used are listed next.

- *Suitability*. Probably the most important selection criterion is the suitability of the language for the application under consideration. For instance, Java is a natural choice for creating programs to be used on the Web.
- *Integration*. If the application is going to mesh with others that are already coded in a certain programming language, it should probably be coded in the same language. This is why *COBOL* programs are still in existence, even though many people consider it old-fashioned. New trends in programming—such as Microsoft's *.NET framework*, which is a platform designed for building integrated, service-oriented applications from reusable chunks of code that can communicate and share data over the Internet, regardless of the operating system or programming language being used—are helping to bridge different platforms and programming languages.

>**Coding.** The process of writing the programming language statements to create a computer program.

TRACING RESULTS FOR CORRECT FLOWCHART

Flowchart Stage	Counter	Decision Test Results (Counter < 2)	Number	Sum
Initialization	0	–	–	0
First decision test	0	T (enters loop)	–	0
After first loop	1	–	6	6
Second decision test	1	T (enters loop)	6	6
After second loop	2	–	3	9
Third decision test	2	F (exits loop)	3	9
Printed Results: Sum = 9				

TRACING RESULTS FOR INCORRECT FLOWCHART

Flowchart Stage	Counter	Decision Test Results (Counter < 2)	Number	Sum
Initialization	1	–	–	0
First decision test	1	T (enters loop)	–	0
After first loop	2	–	6	6
Second decision test	2	F (exits loop)	6	6
Printed Results: Sum = 6				

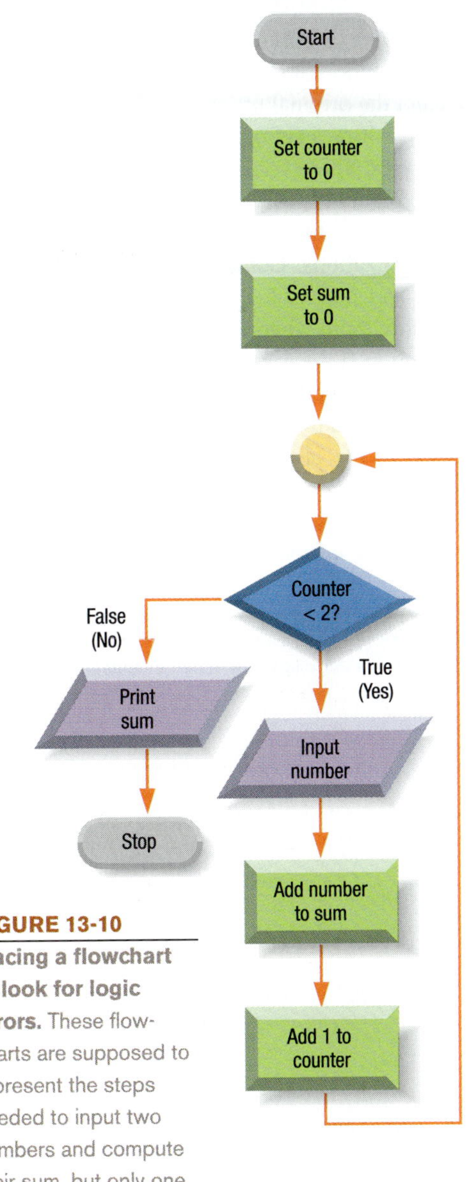

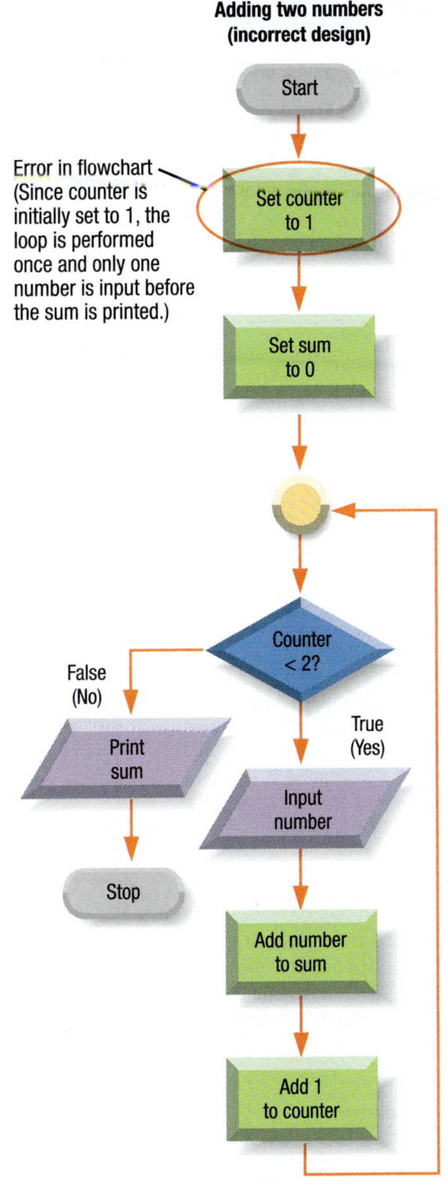

FIGURE 13-10

Tracing a flowchart to look for logic errors. These flowcharts are supposed to represent the steps needed to input two numbers and compute their sum, but only one flowchart is correct.

- *Standards.* Many information systems departments have standards that dictate using a specific language in a given application environment—such as COBOL for transaction processing and Java for Web programming.
- *Programmer availability.* Both the availability of in-house programmers fluent in the programming language and the market for new programmers need to be considered. Choosing a widely used language means programmers can be hired more easily.
- *Portability.* If the application is to run on different computers or operating systems—such as Windows, Macintosh, and Linux computers—the ability of those platforms to collectively handle the programming language becomes a key factor.
- *Development speed.* The faster an application is coded, the sooner it can be put into use to generate benefits. Programs that reuse large chunks of code already in existence, or that use a programming language that is easier to code and test (as discussed later in this chapter), can be developed faster.

TIP

It is easier to write comments—particularly comments explaining the logic of a program—at the time the program is coded, instead of trying to add those comments at the end of the project.

Coding Standards

In the early days of computers, programmers were largely left to code programs in their own styles. The result was often a confusing collection of statements that, while producing correct results, were difficult for anyone except the original programmer to understand. To avoid this problem, many organizations today follow a set of *coding standards*—a list of rules designed to standardize programming styles. These coding standards help make programs more universally readable and easier to maintain.

The proper use of *comments* or *remarks* is one of the most important, but often one of the least adhered to, coding standards in organizations. Comments are notes within the actual program code that identify key features and steps of the program but that are written in such a way that the computer knows to ignore them when the program is executed (see Figure 13-11). Usually there is a comment section at the top of the program that identifies the author, the date the program was written or last modified, and the names and descriptions of the *variables*—the named entities that contain values during a program, such as Counter, Sum, First_name, and so on—used in the program. Comments also typically appear at the beginning of each main step of the program to describe the function of that section, such as "Initialize variables," "Compute taxes," "Calculate net amount due," and so forth. Comments are also called *internal documentation*.

FIGURE 13-11

Comments. Comments (programming notes) in a program make a program more easily understood; this is especially important when the program needs to be revised at a later time.

COMMENTS

Comments are usually marked by a specific symbol (such as *, C, ', or //) in the first column; the symbol used depends on the programming language being used. Anything else in a comment line is ignored by the computer.

Comments at the top of a program should identify the name and author of the program, date written and last modified, purpose of the program, and variables used in the program.

Comments in the main part of a program should indicate what each section of the program is doing. Blank comment lines can also be used to space out the lines of code, as needed for readability.

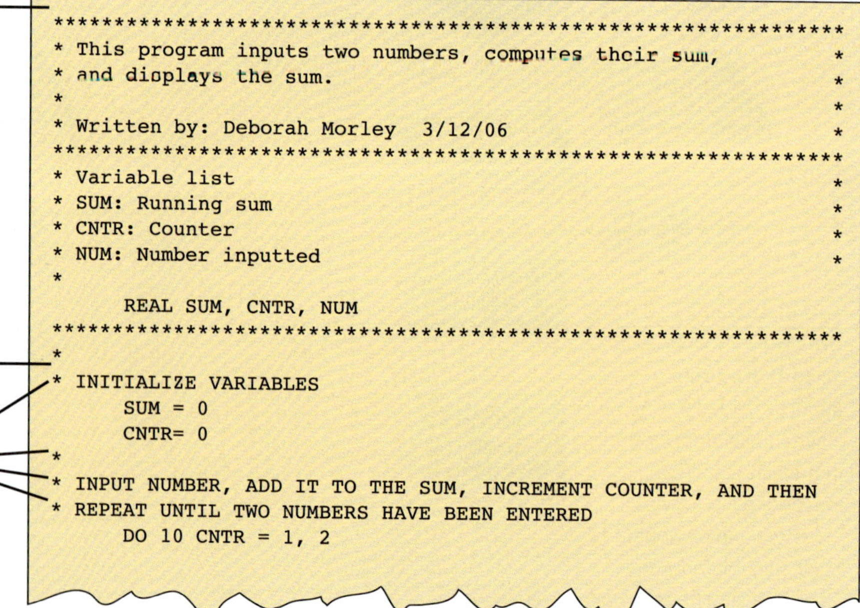

```
*******************************************************************
* This program inputs two numbers, computes their sum,            *
* and displays the sum.                                           *
*                                                                 *
* Written by: Deborah Morley  3/12/06                             *
*******************************************************************
* Variable list                                                   *
* SUM: Running sum                                                *
* CNTR: Counter                                                   *
* NUM: Number inputted                                            *
*
      REAL SUM, CNTR, NUM
*******************************************************************
*
* INITIALIZE VARIABLES
      SUM = 0
      CNTR= 0
*
* INPUT NUMBER, ADD IT TO THE SUM, INCREMENT COUNTER, AND THEN
* REPEAT UNTIL TWO NUMBERS HAVE BEEN ENTERED
      DO 10 CNTR = 1, 2
```

Reusable Code

Different programs often use some of the same blocks of code. For example, a company may have a dozen or more programs that do the same routine tasks, such as computing sales tax or displaying product or employee information. Rather than having programmers code each program or program piece from scratch, most organizations maintain libraries of reusable code. *Reusable code*, as you might guess, refers to generic code segments that can be used over and over again with minor modifications. Reusable code enables portions of new programs to be created by copying and pasting pretested, error-free code segments from existing programs, which greatly reduces development time.

Data Dictionaries

A *data dictionary* contains information about the data used in a program, such as the names, descriptions, and rules of usage for every variable and data item used in the program. Many data dictionaries are *active*, meaning they are online and connected to the applications that they support. If, for example, a programmer attempts to use a variable improperly or inconsistently, the active data dictionary immediately warns the programmer and prohibits the usage from being part of the finished program. Once a data dictionary is created for an application, it is modified as needed to keep it up to date. If applicable, data dictionaries can be shared between applications. Data dictionaries used in conjunction with databases are discussed in Chapter 14.

Documentation: Documented Source Code

The program coding phase results in finished source code, written in the desired programming language. The source code should implement the logic illustrated by the program design specifications and include enough internal documentation (comments) to make the source code understandable and easy to update.

Program Debugging and Testing

Debugging is the process of ensuring that a program is free of errors, or *bugs* (for a look at the origin of the term *bug*, see the Inside the Industry box). Debugging is usually a lengthy process, sometimes amounting to more than 50% of a program's development time. The more careful one is in designing a program, testing the logic of a program's design, and writing the actual code, the less time one needs for debugging.

Translating Coded Programs into Executable Code

Before a program can be run—and, therefore, before it can be debugged—it needs to be translated from the code a programmer writes to the code a computer can execute. The collection of program statements that a person writes using a programming language is referred to as the **source code** or *source module*. Source code is the only type of code easily read by humans. To run a program on a computer, however, source code needs to be converted into the bits and bytes the computer can understand. This binary or *machine language* version of the program is called the **object code** or *object module*. Code is converted from source code to object code using a *language translator*.

A **language translator** is a software program that converts the programmer's coded program into machine language. Three common types of language translators are *compilers*, *interpreters*, and *assemblers*. Each one performs translations in its own way.

SYS

>**Debugging.** The process of ensuring a program is free of errors. >**Source code.** A computer program before it is compiled. >**Object code.** The machine language version of a computer program generated after the program's source code is compiled. >**Language translator.** A software program that converts program code to machine language.

INSIDE THE INDUSTRY

The Original Program "Bug"

A program *bug* is an error that causes a program to malfunction. The first official recorded use of the word *bug* in the context of computing is associated with the temporary failure of the Mark II computer, which was in service at the Naval Weapons Center in Dahlgren, Virginia, on September 9, 1945. The problem was traced to a short circuit caused by a moth caught between two contacts in one of the computer's relays. The offending moth was taped into the log book with the notation, "First actual case of a bug being found" (see the accompanying photograph).

Legend has it that *Grace Hopper*, a naval officer and mathematician who is often referred to as the mother of computing, actually discovered the moth. Hopper led the committee that invented COBOL, is credited with developing the first compiler, and became the first woman to achieve the rank of rear admiral in the United States Navy.

Although some say the wording implies that the term *bug* was already in existence at the time and that this was the first instance of an actual bug being found in a computer, many prefer to believe that this was the origin of the term. Regardless, it is certainly the most widely known "bug" story, and it will likely be repeated for decades to come.

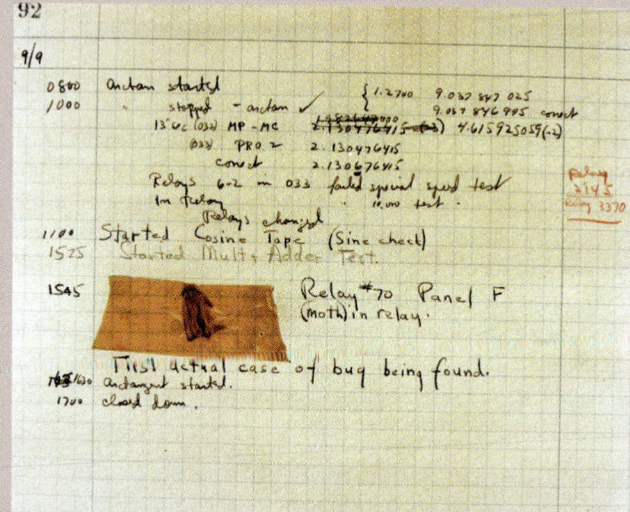

The dead moth that caused the temporary failure of the Mark II computer in 1945, thought to be the origin for the computer term *bug*, was taped into the actual log book for that computer.

Compilers

A **compiler** is designed for a specific programming language and translates programs written in that language into machine language so it can be executed. For instance, a program written in the *COBOL* programming language needs a COBOL compiler; COBOL source code cannot be converted into object code using a *BASIC* compiler.

Normally, before the object code actually begins execution, it is combined with other object modules (either previously written by the programmer or stored in a common library) that the CPU needs to process the program. For example, most computers cannot compute square roots directly. Instead, they rely on small object modules stored in the system library. If a program calls for a square root calculation, the operating system temporarily binds the object module of the program together with a copy of the object module for the square root routine. The binding process is referred to as *linkage editing*, or the *link-edit stage*; this activity produces an executable program called a *load module*. System software includes a special program called a *linkage editor* that automatically carries out this binding.

When the computer is ready to execute or run the load module, it has reached the *Go (execution) stage*. Figure 13-12 shows the process from compiling, to linkage editing, to execution. The executable load module can be saved for later use to avoid repeating the

>**Compiler.** A language translator that converts an entire program into machine language before executing it.

compilation and linkage editing every time the program executes. Filenames for object and load modules often carry the extensions *.obj* and *.exe*, respectively.

Interpreters

Interpreters are also language-specific, but they translate source code differently than compilers. Rather than creating a complete object module for a program, an interpreter reads, translates, and executes the source program one line at a time. It performs the translation into machine language at the same time the program is run, every time the program is run.

Using an interpreter instead of a compiler has its advantages and disadvantages. Two major advantages associated with interpreters are (1) they are easier to use, and (2) they help programmers discover program errors more easily because the execution usually stops at the point where an error is encountered. The interpreter program itself requires relatively little storage space, and because it does not generate an object module, the required storage space is reduced even more. For these reasons, interpreters provide ideal tools for beginning programmers and nonprogrammers.

The major disadvantage associated with interpreters is that they work less efficiently than compilers do, so interpreted programs run more slowly. Because an interpreter must translate each program statement into machine language just before executing it, a lot of time is wasted. This is especially true when the program must repeatedly execute the same statements thousands of times, reinterpreting each one every time. In contrast, a compiler translates each program statement only once—when the object module is created. Compiled programs need to be recompiled only when the source code is modified.

Some programming languages include both an interpreter and a compiler, giving the programmer the best of both worlds. He or she can work with the interpreter to discover and correct any program errors and then compile the finished error-free program, saving the object module to run whenever it is needed.

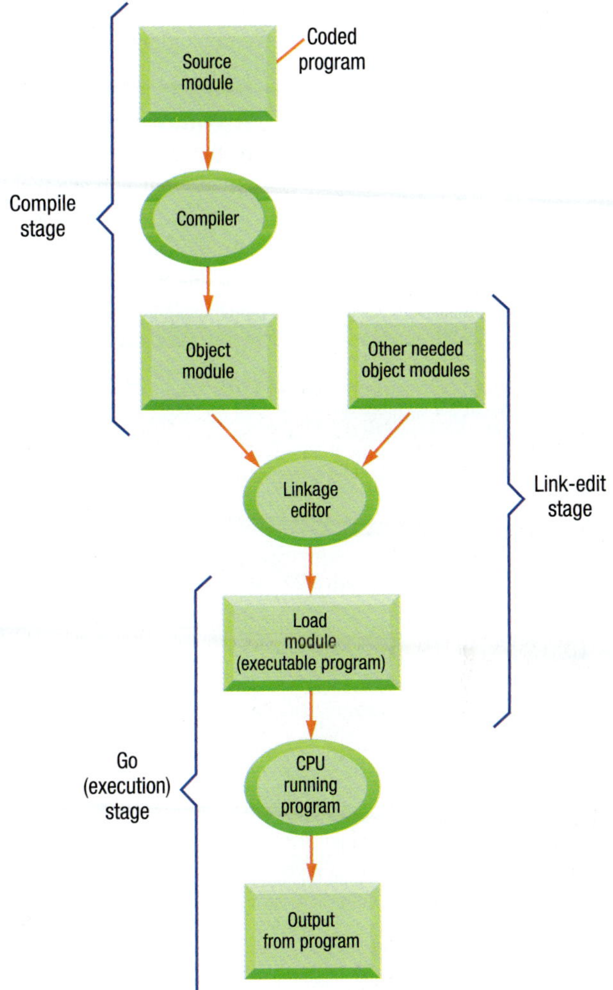

FIGURE 13-12
Compiler and linkage editor. A compiler and a linkage editor convert a source module into a load module for processing by the CPU.

Assemblers

The third type of language translator, an *assembler*, converts *assembly language* statements into machine language. Assembly language, discussed later in this chapter, is used almost exclusively by professional programmers to write efficient code. An assembler works like a compiler, producing a stored object module, but it is used with a specific type of assembly language and, consequently, with a specific computer architecture, such as specific Windows PCs, specific Macintosh computers, a particular type of mainframe, a specific supercomputer, and so forth.

SYS

Preliminary Debugging

The debugging process begins after the source code is complete and it is ready to be compiled or interpreted. With most programs, compiling or interpreting a program will result in errors—the debugging process consists of locating and correcting these errors. The first

>**Interpreter.** A language translator that converts program statements line-by-line into machine language, immediately executing each one.

goal is to eliminate *syntax errors* so that the program is executable; then, any *logic errors* can be identified and corrected. These two main types of errors are discussed next.

Syntax Errors

A **syntax error** occurs when the programmer has not followed the proper *syntax* (rules) of the programming language being used. For example, a computer is not able to understand what you are trying to do if you misspell PRINT as PRNT, if you type END OF IF STATEMENT instead of the correct phrase END IF, or if you put a required comma or semicolon in the wrong place. As shown in Figure 13-13, when a syntax error is reached

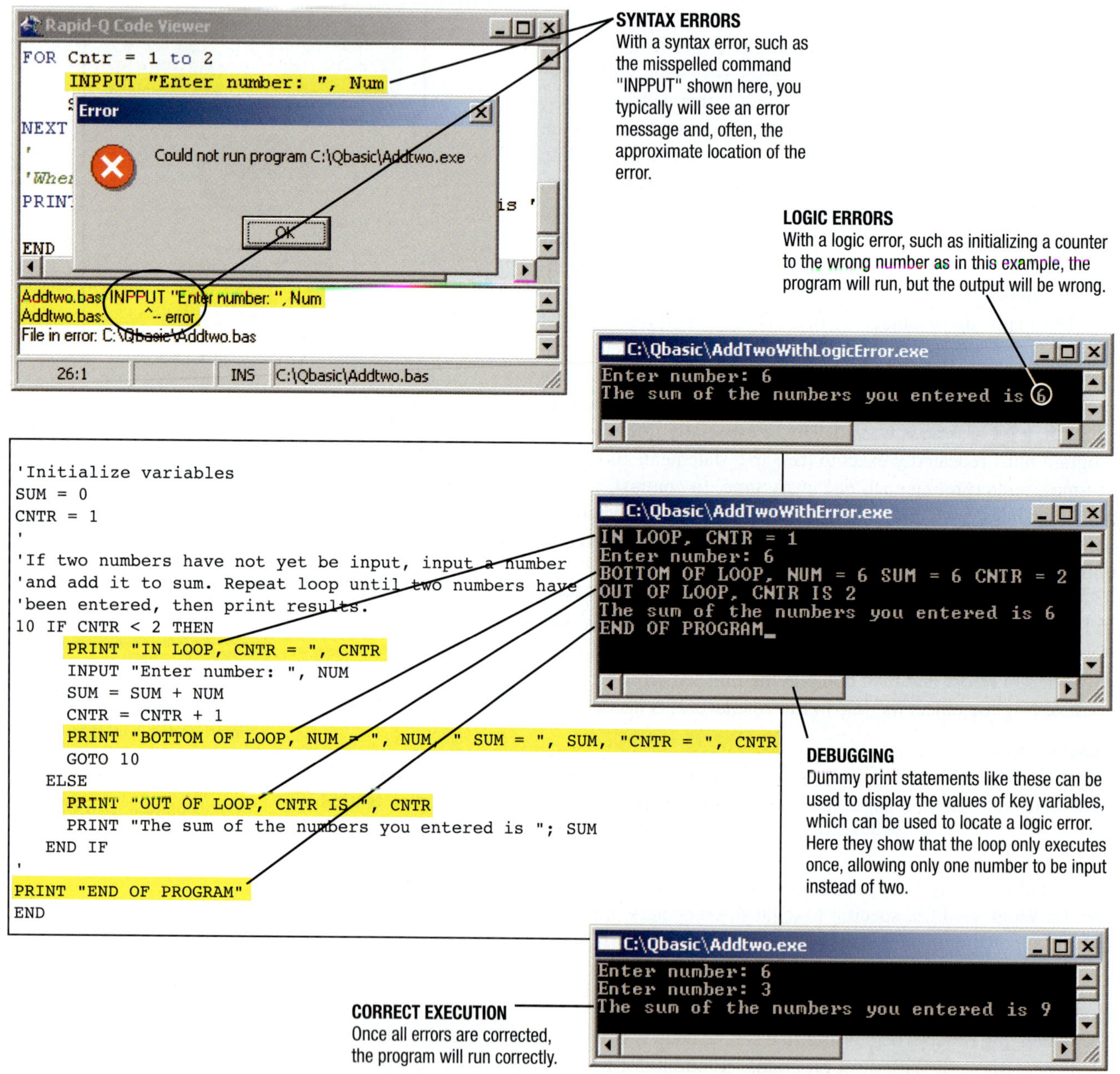

FIGURE 13-13

Syntax and logic errors. Syntax errors occur when the syntax (grammar rules) for a program is not followed precisely; logic errors are more difficult to identify.

>**Syntax error.** A programming error that occurs when the programmer has not followed the rules of the programming language.

in a program, the interpreter or compiler being used typically displays an error message indicating the approximate location of the syntax error.

Logic Errors

Logic errors, or *execution-time errors*, stem from a logic problem in the program's design and are often difficult to detect. Such an error results when the command syntax is correct but the program produces incorrect results. This may happen if you have written a formula incorrectly, if you have made a mistake on a decision condition (such as using the wrong relational operator or initializing a counter variable to the wrong value), or if you have wrongly defined the problem. Knowing the values of certain key variables and where the program control branched can often help identify a logic error. Consequently, programmers often use temporary *dummy print statements*—print statements that are temporarily inserted into the code—to help locate a logic error. Dummy print statements can be inserted at various locations to show how a program is branching (such as *"Inside loop, counter is ", COUNTER* which prints the identifying text "Inside loop, counter is " followed by the current value of the counter) and to output the values of key variables at specific places in the program.

For example, running a program to add two numbers based on the logic in the incorrect flowchart in Figure 13-10 would result in an incorrect sum, as shown in the first logic error screen in Figure 13-13. As shown in the second logic error screen and the program code in Figure 13-13, dummy print statements (used to show the program control and the values of the counter and sum variables at specific locations in the program) reveal that only one number is being input because the counter is initialized to 1, instead of 0. Once the error is corrected, the program runs correctly (see the bottom screen in Figure 13-13). If a logic error is serious enough, it may involve going back to the program design step—a costly mistake that emphasizes the importance of good program design.

To more easily help programmers locate logic errors, most compilers today include built-in debugging tools. Debuggers typically color-code comments, command statements, and variables to assist readability, and these tools allow the programmer to choose between line-by-line execution and full-speed execution, among other features. These tools help programmers more quickly identify and correct errors. After finding and locating all identified errors and making the necessary corrections, the programmer recompiles and re-executes the program to see if all errors have been removed. This "execute, check, and correct" process is repeated until the program is free of bugs.

TIP

When using dummy print statements to identify a logic error, be sure to label each statement with the variable name and the location in the program (such as "Just before loop, counter is ", COUNTER") so you can tell which printed values belong to which variables and when those values change during the program.

FURTHER EXPLORATION

For links to further information about program debugging and testing, go to www.course.com/uc11/ch13

Testing

At the end of the preliminary debugging process, the program will appear to be correct. At this time, the original programmer—or, preferably, someone else—runs the program with extensive *test data* to try to find any additional errors remaining in the program. Good test data should be the same type of data generated by the system's users to subject the program to the conditions it will encounter when it is finally implemented. Ideally, the test data would be actual data, but to protect the privacy of personal information during testing, test data is usually created that has the same structure as actual data, but does not contain any personally identifiable data. The test data should also check for likely sources of coding omissions. For example, will the program issue a check or a bill in the amount of $0.00? Does the program provide for leap years when dating reports? Will it allow a product quantity of less than 0? Although rigorous testing significantly decreases the chance of a program malfunction when the program is implemented, there is no foolproof guarantee that the completed program will be bug-free. However, proper debugging and testing is vital,

SYS

>**Logic error.** A programming error that occurs when running a program produces incorrect results.

> **TIP**
>
> If you participate in a beta test for a program, you might be given a free copy of the finished program or some other small token of appreciation, in addition to having been given the opportunity to help improve the program.

because an error that costs only a few dollars to fix at this stage in the development process may cost many thousands of dollars to correct after the program is implemented.

Programs created for mass distribution often have two stages of testing: an internal on-site test (sometimes called an *alpha test*) and one or more rounds of outside tests (called *beta tests*). For instance, new versions of commercial software programs, such as Microsoft Office, enlist a large number of beta testers to test the version for bugs and compatibility problems, as well as to provide suggestions for improvement, while the program is in development. *Beta versions* of freeware and open source software are also often subjected to beta tests. Beta testing allows the programs to be tested by a wide variety of individuals and on a wide variety of hardware—a much more thorough test for programs that are to be distributed out of house than just alpha testing. However, beta testing is not usually performed for programs that are being developed only for one particular company.

Documentation: Completed Program Package

When the program debugging and testing step is finished, a copy of the test data, results, finished program code, and other documentation generated during this step should be added to the program package. The test data is useful for future program modifications, as well as to see in which situations the program was tested if a problem develops in the future.

So far, virtually all the documents in the collected program documentation could be referred to as *developer documentation*—tools that may be useful when a programmer needs to look at or modify the program code in the future. To finish the *program package*, the necessary *user documentation* should be developed. User documentation normally consists of a user's manual containing such information as instructions for running the program, a description of software commands, and a troubleshooting guide to help with difficulties. Since users may have widely differing levels of computer expertise, user documentation should be written in such a manner that it is comprehensible to all users. User documentation can be in paper format, electronic format, or both.

Program Implementation and Maintenance

Once a program has finished the debugging and testing step, it is ready to be implemented as part of the SDLC, as discussed in Chapter 12. Once the system containing the program is up and running, the *implementation process* is complete. However, virtually every program, if it is to last a significant amount of time, requires ongoing maintenance. *Program maintenance* is the process of updating software so it continues to be useful. For instance, if new types of data are added to a company database, program maintenance is necessary so that existing programs can use the new data. Software revisions, new equipment announcements, new legislative mandates, and changes in the way business is conducted also commonly trigger program maintenance.

Program maintenance is costly to organizations. It has been estimated that many organizations spend well over half—some estimates put it closer to 80%—of their programming time maintaining existing application programs. A major reason tools such as coding standards, object-oriented programming, reusable code, and data dictionaries are so popular is because they can result in lower maintenance costs.

Documentation: Amended Program Package

As program maintenance takes place, the program package should be updated to reflect what new problems or issues occurred and what changes to the program were necessary because of them. If a problem is too serious for routine program maintenance, the program development cycle should begin again.

TOOLS FOR FACILITATING PROGRAM DEVELOPMENT

If you ask most IT managers when they need programs in development to be finished, you will usually get an answer like "yesterday." The sad truth in business today is that developers are typically under tremendous time pressure to get finished work out the door. In extreme cases, getting product into the user's hands is not just a priority—it is *the* priority.

To help developers create quality systems and programs in a timely manner, many types of *program development tools* are available, as discussed next. The tools can be used in traditional program development as well as with *rapid application development (RAD)*—a software development process designed to create programs very quickly. With RAD, sections of a program are typically coded and finalized as the design for that section is completed, instead of waiting for the entire design to be completed. RAD typically also uses prebuilt components (such as for user interface components) and reusable code. The RAD method was developed as a result of applications that took so long to build that requirements had changed before the system was complete, which often resulted in unusable systems that needed to be immediately modified.

Application Lifecycle Management (ALM) Tools

Application Lifecycle Management (ALM) is a broad term to describe creating and managing an application throughout its entire lifecycle—from design through testing. ALM programs typically have several integrated components that work together. For instance, the program shown in Figure 13-14 has one component to develop the model of the overall system and needed programs—including data flow diagrams, structure charts, and other tools

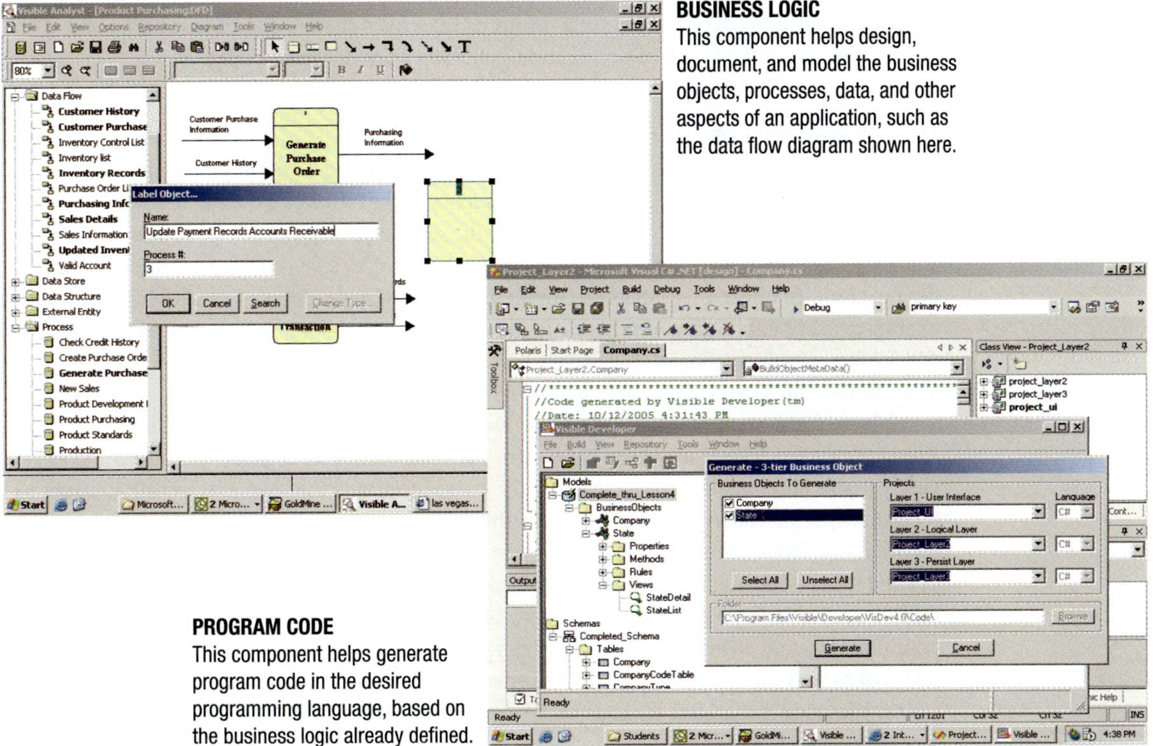

FIGURE 13-14
Application Lifecycle Management programs can help to more easily create both the business logic and the program code for an application.

SYS

>**Application Lifecycle Management (ALM).** A broad term to describe complete systems that can be used to create and manage an application throughout its entire lifecycle–from design through testing.

discussed earlier in this chapter and in Chapter 12—and another component that generates the program code for the application in whatever language is required—such as for *Visual Basic*, C#, and .NET applications. In other words, one component is used to develop the *business logic*, and the other generates the actual program code needed to implement the business logic. Advantages to using an ALM system is that it helps developers define a solid model of a program first, and then that model can be implemented in whatever programming language—and in as many programming languages—as needed with no additional effort since the ALM program's *code generator* generates much of the code automatically upon demand. Consequently, this can greatly reduce the time needed to convert a program design to actual code. For instance, the program shown in Figure 13-14 can generate at least 90% of a program's code. This saves programming time, as well as makes it possible for companies without a large programming staff to develop applications in-house without having to outsource the coding portion of the program development process.

Some programs used for ALM are referred to as *CASE* (*computer-aided software engineering*) tools or *business modeling tools*. In general, all types of ALM programs are designed to automate, manage, and simplify the program development process. One of the principal advantages of ALM is the increased application development speed; another is its ability to maintain consistency throughout the entire development process, while at the same time separating the business logic from the actual program code.

Application Generators

An *application generator* is a software product that enables programmers, as well as end users, to code new applications quickly. One type of application generator already discussed is a code generator, used to generate program code from pseudocode, a program model, or some other form. Another simple example is a wizard program. Wizards, which commonly appear in word processors, spreadsheets, and other application programs, allow you to quickly and easily create such things as fax cover sheets, database reports, and Web pages. Some specific types of application generators are described next.

Macro Recorders

Many application programs—particularly word processing and spreadsheet programs—allow you to create macros. A *macro* is a sequence of keystrokes saved in a special file that can be replayed whenever you wish within the application program in which it was created. These simple programs can be created by the user or may come prewritten as part of the program. In either case, macros can be used to automate repeated or difficult tasks. For example, users could create a macro to type a standard closing to a letter whenever they press a key combination, such as Ctrl+Y, or use the Date macro built into a specific program to type the current date whenever Ctrl+D is pressed.

Macros are written in a *macro programming language* (such as *Visual Basic for Applications* for Microsoft Word macros or for Microsoft Excel macros) and can be difficult to write and understand. Consequently, most programs that use macros allow users to record them instead of having to write them. *Macro recorders* work similarly to tape recorders or video cameras in that you start the macro recorder and then you perform the desired tasks—the macro recorder records all of the keystrokes and mouse clicks you make until the recorder is turned off. The macro is then saved and assigned a name or keystroke combination, and then each time the macro is run, the computer performs the recorded keystrokes and mouse clicks in the recorded order. After a macro has been recorded and saved, the code generated by the macro recorder can typically be edited to make minor modifications, as needed.

Report and Form Generators

A *report generator* is a *GUI tool* that enables individuals to prepare reports quickly and easily. Report generators packaged with database management systems allow reports to be created simply by declaring which data fields are to be represented as report columns and how the data should be sorted; once defined, a report can be edited as needed, and then generated on demand. *Form generators* create the forms or screens used to input data into a program or database. Most database programs contain some type of form generator; similar to report generators, once the basic format of the form is defined, the form can be modified as needed, such as to add a company logo, change the screen title or text, and so forth (see Figure 13-15). Database forms and reports are discussed in more detail in Chapter 14. Other types of GUI tools—such as *screen painters*—can be used to create other types of user interfaces needed for the application.

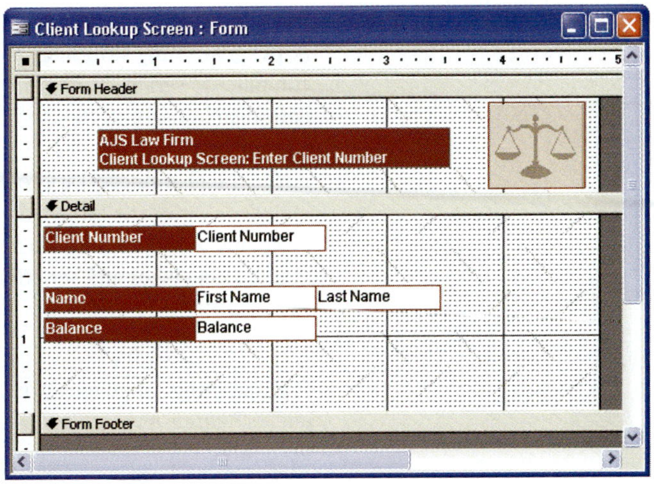

FIGURE 13-15
Form generators.
This database form generator shown here is used to create input screens for a database application.

Software-Asset Management Tools

Software-asset management tools are designed to help facilitate reusable code. They act as a central repository of tested software components, such as a company's Java and .NET components and Web services, which can be reused in new applications quickly and effectively. Software-asset management can take place anywhere from an individual project level to an enterprise level because search features allow easy retrieval of appropriate assets. The goal in using software-asset management tools is to build new applications and support new business processes more quickly and reliably.

FIGURE 13-16
Device development software.

Device Software Development Tools

Program development tools, which are used to assist in the planning, development, and deployment of new programs and systems, have been available for quite some time. However, they have not typically been used to help write programs for devices that use embedded software, such as cars, ATM machines, and other consumer devices. Recently, programs have become available to assist with embedded software development. For instance, in December 2004, Wind River Systems—the developer of the embedded operating system that was installed on the Mars Exploration Rover "Spirit"—released a *device software development suite* called *Wind River Workbench*. The programs in this suite are designed to optimize the entire development and support life cycle of device software development, from the concept stage, through the coding and debugging process (see Figure 13-16 for a look at the most recent version of this program), to the finished product.

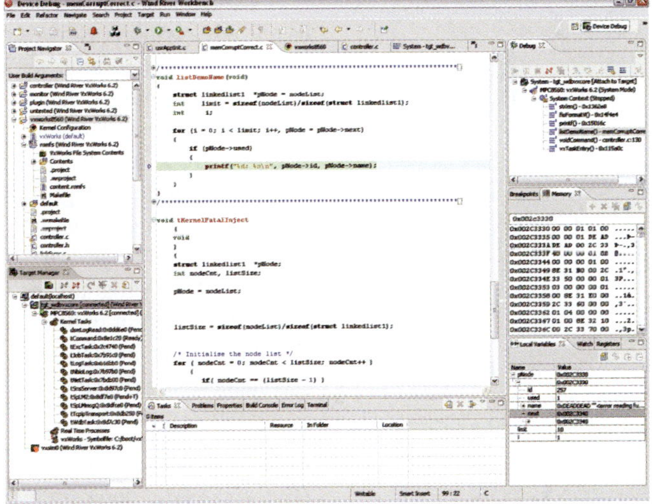

PROGRAMMING LANGUAGES

As discussed earlier, deciding which programming language will be used is an important program development decision. There are several general categories of programming languages and many widely used programming languages from which to choose. These topics are discussed in the remainder of this chapter.

What Is a Programming Language?

A **programming language** is a set of rules used to write computer programs. To write a computer program, a *programming software package*—a program whose principal purpose is to enable users to develop computer programs in a specific programming language—is used. The programming software allows the user to code the program and contains the language translator necessary to convert the finished source code into object code; it may also include a variety of tools that make it easier to develop, debug, edit, maintain, and manage programs. Programming languages are discussed in detail next. Related languages—namely markup languages and scripting languages—were discussed in Chapter 10.

Categories of Programming Languages

Programming languages are commonly divided into three classes: *low-level*, *high-level*, and *very-high-level (fourth-generation) languages*. They can also be *natural* or *visual* programming languages.

Low-Level Languages

The earliest programming languages—*machine language* and *assembly language*—are referred to as **low-level languages**. They are so named because the programmers who code in them must write instructions at the lowest level (such as just using 0s and 1s) so the computer's hardware can easily and quickly understand them. In both machine languages and assembly languages, each line of code corresponds to a single action of the computer system. Both types of languages are *machine dependent*, which means that they are usually not transportable between different computer architectures. For example, an assembly-language program written for a particular mainframe at one organization cannot be used on one of the organization's PCs, and a machine language program designed for one type of CPU and operating system will not be able to be used on a PC that is not compatible with that architecture. Machine languages and assembly languages were developed during the first- and second-generations of computing.

Virtually no one writes programs in **machine language**, which consists of strings of 0s and 1s, anymore. Nonetheless, all programs must be converted into machine language by a language translator before they can be executed, as discussed earlier in this chapter. **Assembly languages** were developed to replace some of the 0s and 1s of machine language with names and other symbols that are easier to understand and remember. The big advantage of assembly language programs today is executional efficiency. They are fast and require little storage compared with their higher-level counterparts. Unfortunately, assembly language programs take longer to write and maintain than programs written in higher-level languages, and they are not transportable to other types of computers. An example of the program for adding two numbers (the program illustrated by the correct flowchart shown in Figure 13-10) written in assembly language for one type of computer system is shown in Figure 13-17. Also illustrated in that figure are some machine language statements that correspond to the assembly language statements in the program.

High-Level Languages

High-level languages differ from their low-level predecessors in that they are closer to natural languages and make programs easier to write. High-level languages are also typically machine independent, which makes programs written in these languages much more flexible. Although a program will normally be designed to run using a specific operating system, the programmer does not need to know the specific details about the hardware that

>Programming language. A set of rules, words, symbols, and codes used to write computer programs. **>Low-level language.** A class of programming languages that is highly detailed and machine-dependent. **>Machine language.** A low-level programming language in which the program code consists of 0s and 1s. **>Assembly language.** A low-level programming language that uses names and other symbols to replace some of the 0s and 1s in machine language. **>High-level language.** A class of programming languages that is closer to natural language and easier to work with than a low-level language.

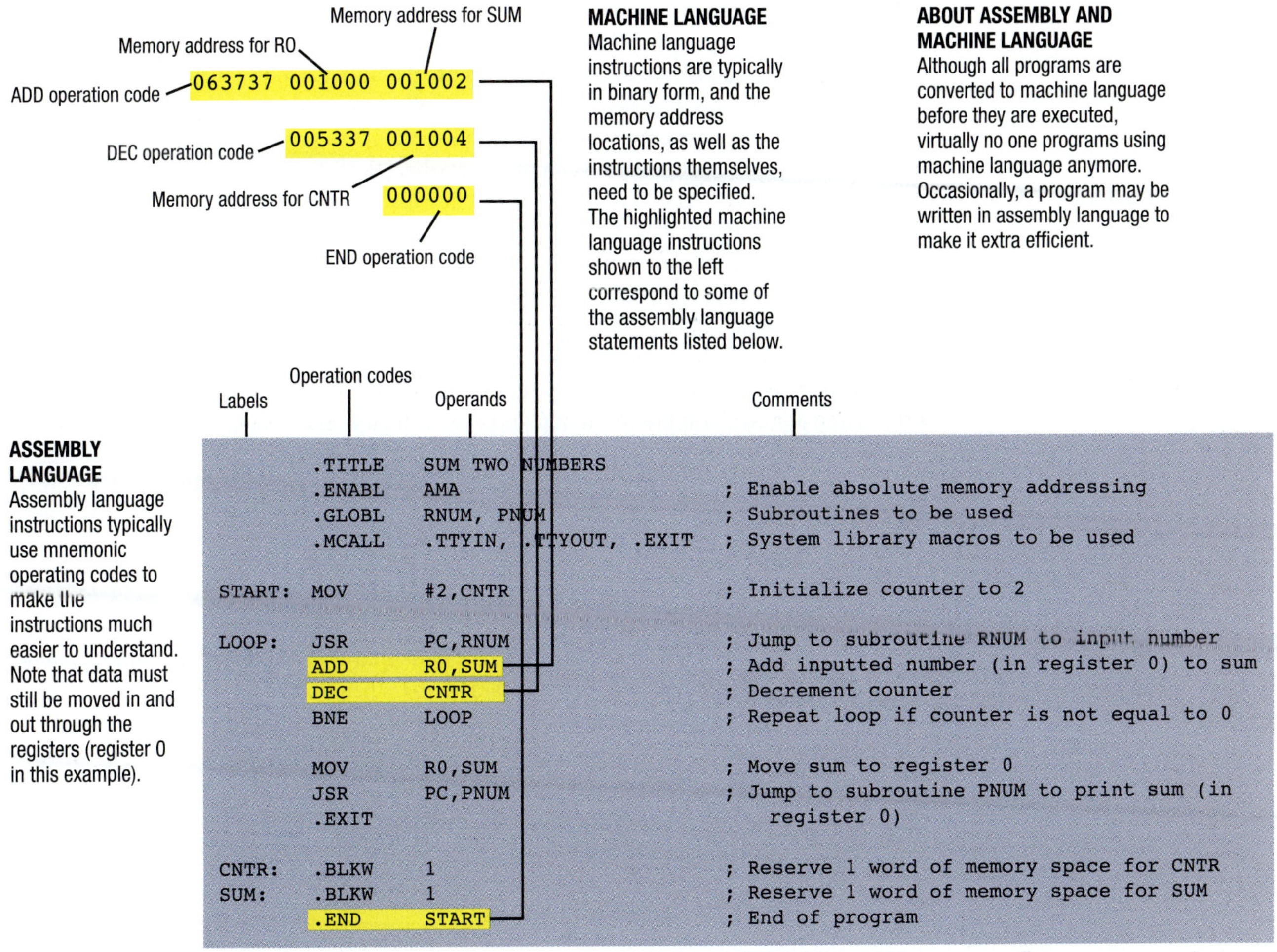

MACHINE LANGUAGE
Machine language instructions are typically in binary form, and the memory address locations, as well as the instructions themselves, need to be specified. The highlighted machine language instructions shown to the left correspond to some of the assembly language statements listed below.

ABOUT ASSEMBLY AND MACHINE LANGUAGE
Although all programs are converted to machine language before they are executed, virtually no one programs using machine language anymore. Occasionally, a program may be written in assembly language to make it extra efficient.

ASSEMBLY LANGUAGE
Assembly language instructions typically use mnemonic operating codes to make the instructions much easier to understand. Note that data must still be moved in and out through the registers (register 0 in this example).

```
        .TITLE   SUM TWO NUMBERS
        .ENABL   AMA                      ; Enable absolute memory addressing
        .GLOBL   RNUM, PNUM               ; Subroutines to be used
        .MCALL   .TTYIN, .TTYOUT, .EXIT   ; System library macros to be used

START:  MOV      #2,CNTR                  ; Initialize counter to 2

LOOP:   JSR      PC,RNUM                  ; Jump to subroutine RNUM to input number
        ADD      R0,SUM                   ; Add inputted number (in register 0) to sum
        DEC      CNTR                     ; Decrement counter
        BNE      LOOP                     ; Repeat loop if counter is not equal to 0

        MOV      R0,SUM                   ; Move sum to register 0
        JSR      PC,PNUM                  ; Jump to subroutine PNUM to print sum (in
        .EXIT                               register 0)

CNTR:   .BLKW    1                        ; Reserve 1 word of memory space for CNTR
SUM:    .BLKW    1                        ; Reserve 1 word of memory space for SUM
        .END     START                    ; End of program
```

FIGURE 13-17
Assembly language and machine language.

will be used to run the program. Included in this class of languages are what have come to be known as *third-generation programming languages* (*3GLs*), such as *BASIC*, *COBOL*, *Pascal*, *C*, and *FORTRAN*. These types of programming languages are sometimes referred to as *procedural programming languages* and are typically used for structured programs. Newer high-level languages that are most often used for object-oriented programs include *C++*, *C#*, and *Java*. Ultimately, programs written in a high-level language must be translated into machine language by a compiler or interpreter before they can be executed.

Fourth-Generation Languages (4GLs)

Fourth-generation languages (**4GLs**) are also sometimes called *very-high-level languages*. Although there is no precise definition of a 4GL, many people agree that they are closer to natural language than third-generation languages and are much easier to use. Because 4GLs often allow programmers to create programs while writing very little code, if any, using 4GLs also results in increased productivity. A disadvantage to using 4GLs is that they can result in a greater number of program statements and less efficient object code when they are compiled into machine language. Because they use more storage space and execute more slowly, professional programmers may choose to use a third-generation or assembly language instead of a fourth-generation language in some instances.

>**Fourth-generation language (4GL).** A class of programming languages that is closer to natural language and easier to work with than a high-level language.

Fourth-generation languages are commonly used to access databases. For example, *structured query language* (*SQL*) is a 4GL commonly used to write *queries* to retrieve information from a database, as discussed in more detail in Chapter 14. Other examples of 4GLs are *decision support system tools*, which provide computing capabilities to help people make decisions. Application generators and some of the programs discussed earlier as tools to help facilitate program development are also usually considered fourth-generation languages. The newer versions of Visual Basic are also often considered 4GLs.

The property that makes 4GLs easier to use is that they are *declarative*, rather than *procedural*, as the third-generation languages are. This means that you tell the computer *what* to do without telling it *how* to do it. For instance, to draw a bar chart in a procedural programming language, you must tell the computer pixel by pixel how to draw the bars and where to place them. In a *declarative programming language*, you point to the data you want graphed, select a graph type, and supply some titles to get the same results as a chart coded using a procedural programming language. Much of the coding in a declarative language consists of mouse clicks to select instructions and issue commands to the program. However, if you want a highly customized program to do something well beyond the ordinary, you will probably need a procedural language. To provide more flexibility, some software packages have both declarative and procedural components.

Natural and Visual Programming Languages

Some recent programming languages can also be classified as *natural* or *visual programming languages*. Programs with either of these characteristics help to make programming easier.

Natural Programming Languages

Software that uses a *natural-language interface* enables humans to communicate with the computer system in their native language, such as English, Spanish, Japanese, or French. The user of a natural-language interface does not have to learn the rules, or syntax, of a particular computer language. Instead, the user enters requests using a keyboard or voice commands that the computer can understand. Natural programming languages are still in the infancy stage. Fourth-generation languages are currently the closest languages we have to natural programming languages. Some believe that *fifth-generation* programming languages will be pure natural languages.

Visual Programming Languages

A *visual programming language* is one that uses a graphical programming environment for developing graphical user interfaces. Instead of worrying about syntax details, programmers using a visual environment can create a substantial amount of code simply by dragging and dropping an object and then defining its appearance and behavior. Visual languages are also sometimes referred to as *event-driven* languages since the program continually checks for and reacts to messages or events, like a click on a button or an icon. The first programming language that used a visual environment was Visual Basic. Since then, visual environments have been created for many programming languages, including C++, Pascal, and Java. These programming languages are all described in the next section.

Popular Programming Languages

There have been a number of programming languages developed over the years. Some, such as *Logo* (which is designed to teach children how to program), *PL/1* (a structured programming language used for business and scientific applications), *Prolog* and *LISP* (used for artificial intelligence applications), and *SmallTalk* (one of the first object-oriented programming languages) are not widely used today. Others, such as COBOL, are in the process of being phased out in many organizations. Some of the most significant programming languages still in use today are discussed and illustrated next.

FORTRAN

FORTRAN (*FORmula TRANslator*), which dates back to 1954, was designed by scientists and is oriented toward manipulating formulas for scientific, mathematical, and engineering problem solving applications. Because of the numerous computations and frequent looping that characterize such applications, execution speed is a primary concern. Consequently, FORTRAN was designed to be a very efficient language for math and scientific applications.

A FORTRAN program to add two numbers (as illustrated in the flowchart in Figure 13-10) appears in Figure 13-18. Note the short comments above each main section in the program.

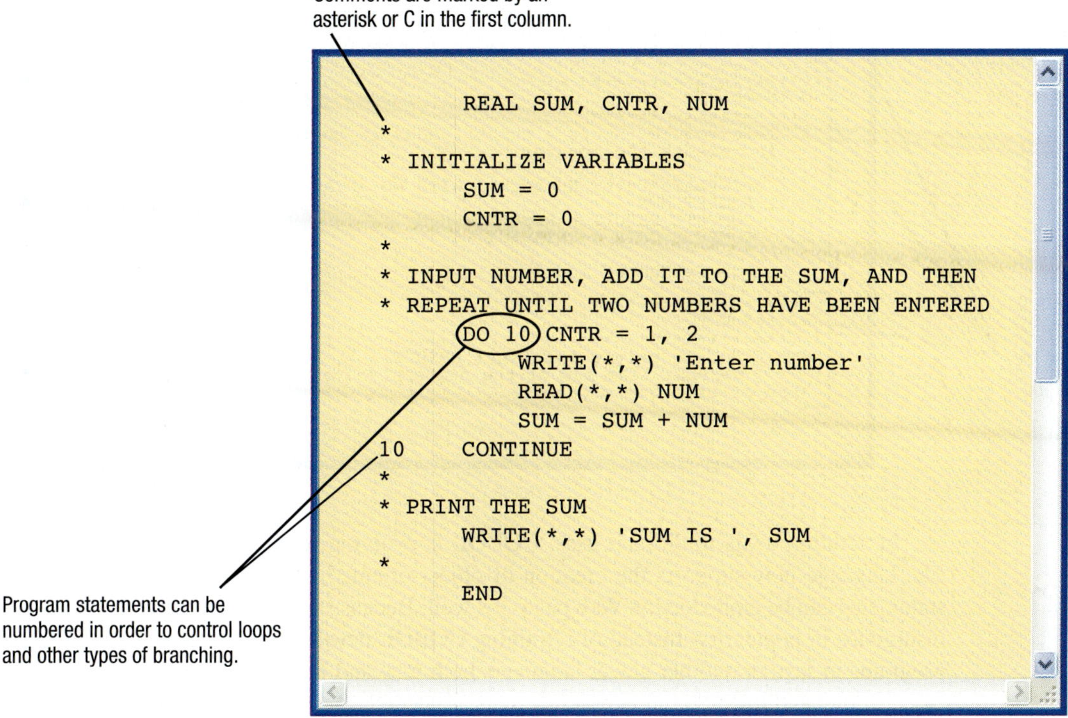


```
      REAL SUM, CNTR, NUM
*
* INITIALIZE VARIABLES
      SUM = 0
      CNTR = 0
*
* INPUT NUMBER, ADD IT TO THE SUM, AND THEN
* REPEAT UNTIL TWO NUMBERS HAVE BEEN ENTERED
      DO 10 CNTR = 1, 2
          WRITE(*,*) 'Enter number'
          READ(*,*) NUM
          SUM = SUM + NUM
10    CONTINUE
*
* PRINT THE SUM
      WRITE(*,*) 'SUM IS ', SUM
*
      END
```

FIGURE 13-18
The adding-two-numbers program written in FORTRAN.

COBOL

COBOL (*COmmon Business-Oriented Language*) is a structured programming language designed for business transaction processing. COBOL makes extensive use of *modules* and *submodules*; that is, most COBOL programs are made up of smaller subprograms, each of which is itself a structured program (see Figure 13-19). This modular building-block approach makes it easier to develop large programs.

Many mainframe transaction processing applications in large organizations are coded in COBOL. COBOL programs are lengthy and take a long time to write and maintain. Some complain that COBOL is old-fashioned and cumbersome, but with billions of dollars invested in COBOL programs and thousands of programmers versed in COBOL use, the language will likely endure for some time yet.

SYS

>**FORTRAN.** A high-level programming language used for mathematical, scientific, and engineering applications. >**COBOL.** A high-level programming language developed for transaction processing applications.

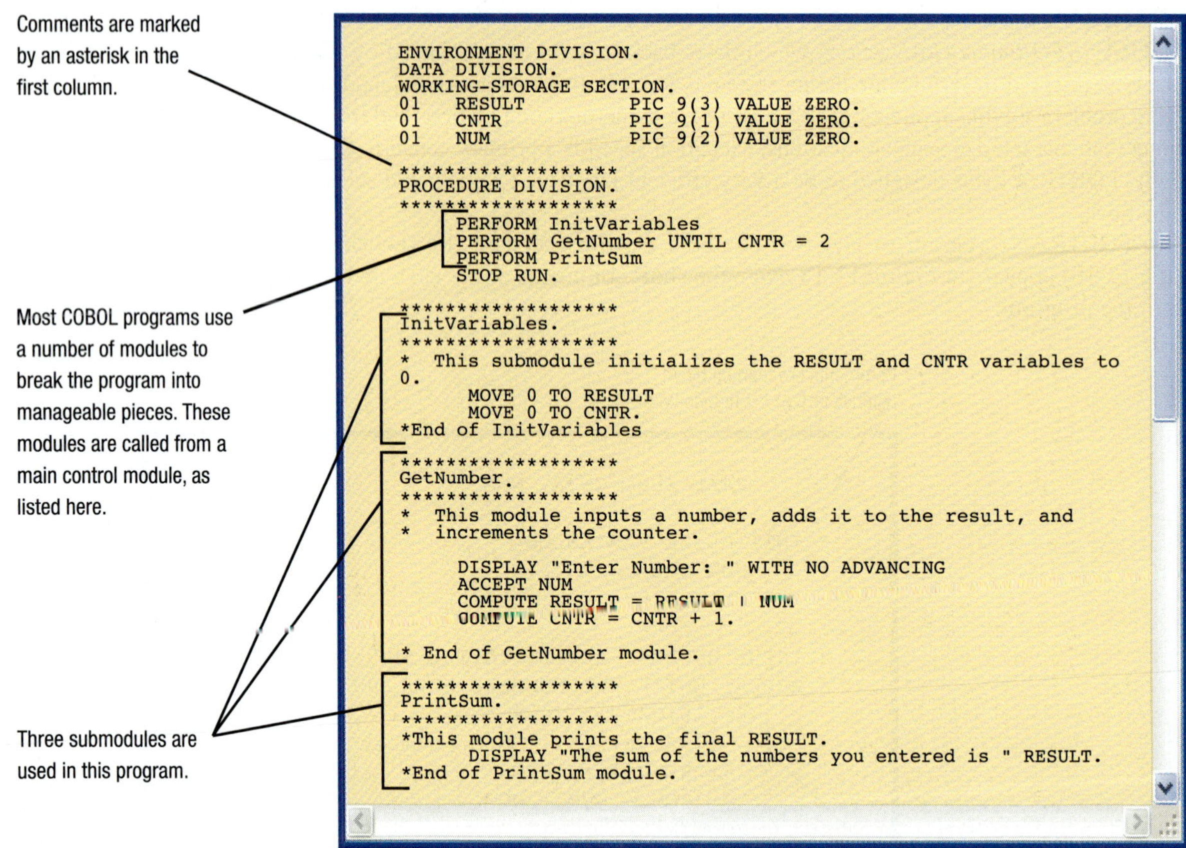


```
ENVIRONMENT DIVISION.
DATA DIVISION.
WORKING-STORAGE SECTION.
01    RESULT          PIC 9(3) VALUE ZERO.
01    CNTR            PIC 9(1) VALUE ZERO.
01    NUM             PIC 9(2) VALUE ZERO.

*******************
PROCEDURE DIVISION.
*******************
     PERFORM InitVariables
     PERFORM GetNumber UNTIL CNTR = 2
     PERFORM PrintSum
     STOP RUN.

*******************
InitVariables.
*******************
*  This submodule initializes the RESULT and CNTR variables to
0.
      MOVE 0 TO RESULT
      MOVE 0 TO CNTR.
*End of InitVariables
*******************
GetNumber.
*******************
*  This module inputs a number, adds it to the result, and
*  increments the counter.

     DISPLAY "Enter Number: " WITH NO ADVANCING
     ACCEPT NUM
     COMPUTE RESULT = RESULT + NUM
     COMPUTE CNTR = CNTR + 1.

* End of GetNumber module.
*******************
PrintSum.
*******************
*This module prints the final RESULT.
      DISPLAY "The sum of the numbers you entered is " RESULT.
*End of PrintSum module.
```

FIGURE 13-19
The adding-two-numbers program written in COBOL.

In addition to its traditional uses, COBOL is evolving to support new applications. The language now supports the creation of object-oriented COBOL programs; COBOL statements can be embedded in Web pages, as well. Because of this, COBOL is enjoying a resurgence in popularity. Instead of retraining COBOL developers and rewriting COBOL programs in Java or another newer language, both new and legacy COBOL programs can be converted and restructured in other formats as needed, such as the ActiveX controls discussed in Chapter 10, or *Java bytecode* (which is discussed later in this chapter).

The adding-two-numbers problem implemented as a COBOL program is shown in Figure 13-19.

Pascal

Pascal, named after the mathematician Blaise Pascal, was created to fill the need for a teaching tool to encourage structured programming. Most versions of Pascal contain a rich variety of control structures that are used to manipulate program modules in a systematic fashion. Pascal also supports an abundance of data types and is especially appropriate for math and science applications. Figure 13-20 shows the adding-two-numbers program written in Pascal.

>**Pascal.** A structured, high-level programming language often used to teach structured programming, especially appropriate for use in math and science applications.

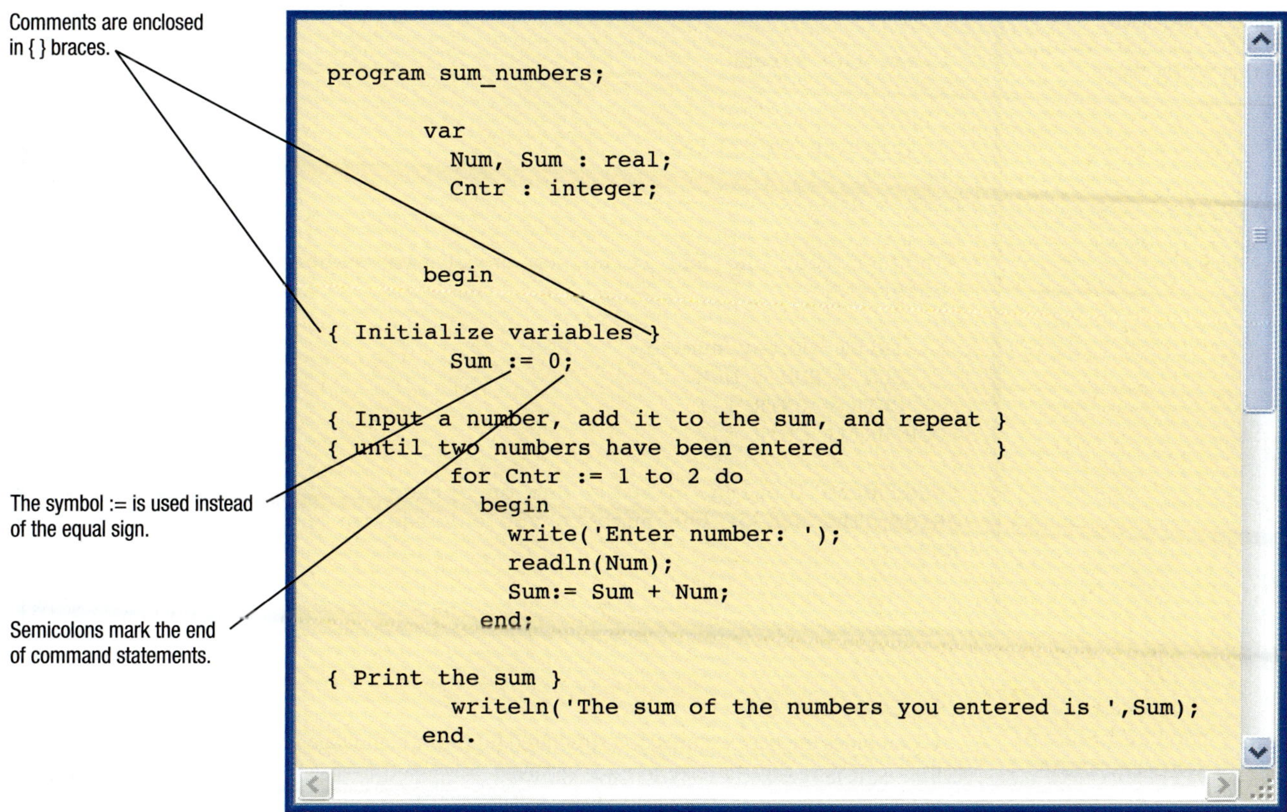

FIGURE 13-20
The adding-two-numbers program written in Pascal.

BASIC and Visual Basic

BASIC (*Beginner's All-purpose Symbolic Instruction Code*) was designed as an easy-to-learn beginner's language that would work in a friendly, nonfrustrating programming environment. Because it is easy to learn and use, and because the storage requirements for its language translator are small, BASIC works well on almost all PCs and is one of the most widely used instructional languages for beginners.

BASIC is often used for interactive programs, enabling programmers to write instructions that pause a program so that the user can take a specific action. When such an instruction is encountered during program execution, the program expects an event—such as the user making a selection or typing some input—to take place before it proceeds. Figure 13-21 shows the BASIC version of the adding-two-numbers program.

Visual Basic is an object-oriented, fourth-generation version of BASIC designed to create sophisticated applications that run under the Microsoft Windows operating system. On the front end, Visual Basic has drag-and-drop tools that enable a programmer to develop screens for graphical user interfaces quickly; on the back end, it has a code generator that can supply the underlying programming code. Code can also be entered manually by the programmer, as needed. Visual Basic has become widely used in recent years—the most recent version is *Visual Basic 2005*. For a look at how Visual Basic can be used to create a program, see the How It Works box.

SYS

>BASIC. An easy-to-learn, high-level programming language that was developed to be used by beginning programmers. **>Visual Basic.** An object-oriented, fourth-generation version of the BASIC programming language.

Comments are marked by a single quotation mark in the first column.

```
'Clear the screen
CLS
'
'Initialize variables
SUM = 0
CNTR = 0
'
'Input number and add it to sum until two numbers have been
'entered.
DO
    INPUT "Enter number: ", NUM
    SUM = SUM + NUM
    CNTR = CNTR + 1
LOOP UNTIL CNTR = 2
'
'When done looping, display Sum on screen
PRINT "The sum of the numbers you entered is "; SUM
END
```

FIGURE 13-21
The adding-two-numbers program written in BASIC.

C, C++, and C#

C combines the best features of a structured high-level language and an assembly language—that is, it is relatively easy to code (at least compared to assembly language), and it uses computer resources efficiently. Although originally designed as a system programming language (in fact, the first major program written in C was the UNIX operating system), C has proven to be a powerful and flexible language that can be used for a variety of applications. It is used mostly by computer professionals to create software products. Although it is technically a high-level language, C is closer to an assembly language than are most other high-level languages. This allows C programmers to write very efficient code, but it can also make programming in C more difficult.

A newer object-oriented version of C is called **C++** (see Figure 13-22). C++ includes the basic features of C, making all C++ programs understandable to C compilers, but it has additional features for objects, classes, and other components of an OOP. There are also visual versions of the C++ language, such as *Microsoft Visual C++*. C++ is one of the most popular programming languages for graphical applications. For a look at an emerging C++ application—*game programming*—see the Trend box.

The newest version of C is **C#** (pronounced "C sharp"). A hybrid of C and C++, C# is Microsoft's newest programming language developed to compete directly with Sun Microsystems' Java language, discussed next. C# is an object-oriented programming language designed to improve productivity in the development of Web applications. In essence, C# is a simplified and more modern version of C++ designed to make the development of the next generations of applications much easier.

>**C.** A high-level structured programming language that has the executional efficiency of an assembly language. >**C++.** A newer, object-oriented version of the C programming language. >**C#.** The newest, object-oriented version of the C programming language.

HOW IT WORKS

Visual Basic

Programming in Visual Basic begins in much the same way as programming with any other language begins. First, you need to define and understand the problem, and then you can develop the solution and logic. Design tools, such as flowcharts and pseudocode, can be used to represent logical sections of the program. In addition, the interface (such as the red box with the buttons and text boxes in the accompanying illustration) should be designed.

Programs in Visual Basic are referred to as *projects*; a project folder contains all of the files that make up the application. Once the design has been completed, the first task using the Visual Basic program is to build the user interface, if one will be used. When a new project is started, a blank form (called "Form1") is displayed that can be used for the user interface. The form can be resized and text and images can be added to the form; text boxes for input and various user controls, such as command buttons, can be added as well. These items are added using the toolbox shown on the left edge of the screen, and then their properties can be adjusted as needed using the Properties window at the right edge of the screen. For instance, properties for a form include the form's name, color, and so forth, as shown in the first screen of the accompanying illustration. Common property changes for a text box include changing the box's name (to be used when referring to that box in the program code), color, the text (if any) that should be displayed in the box, and the font and border to be used with that text box.

To specify what should happen when the user performs a specific action (called an *event*), such as clicking a command button, the appropriate code needs to be associated with that event. Double-clicking any item located on the form opens the appropriate section of the code for that item so it can be edited by the user as needed. Once all events have been specified, the *Build* option tests the code for syntax errors and then the *Debug* option runs the program so the logic can be tested. Once all errors have been corrected, the program can be run, as shown in the final screens in the accompanying illustration.

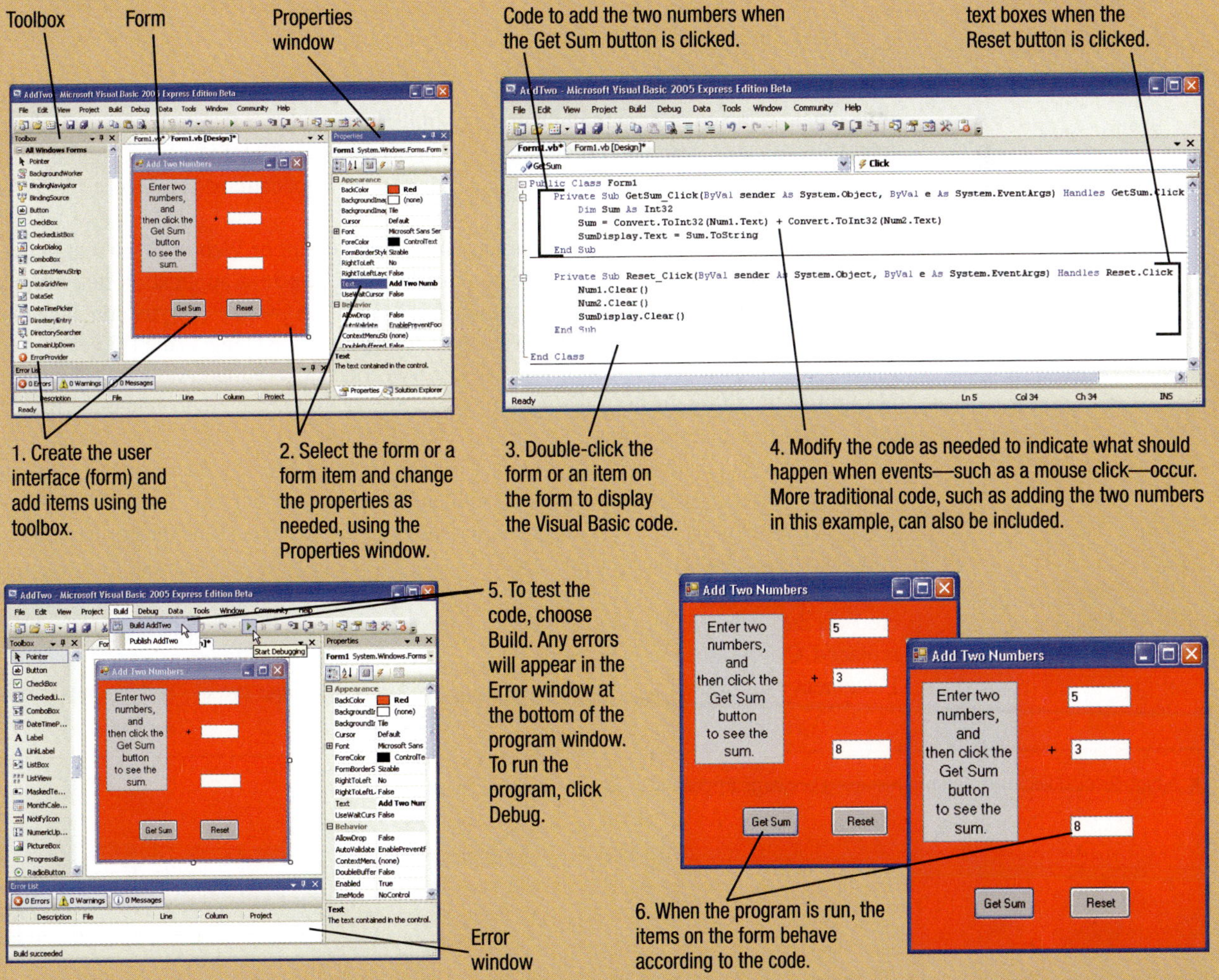

Comments are preceded by two slashes //.

The instructions in a function or loop are enclosed in { } braces.

```
#include <iostream.h>

void main ()
{

// Declare and initialize variables
      float fSum = 0;
      float fNum;
      int iCntr = 0;

// Input a number, add it to the sum, and repeat
// until two numbers have been entered
      do
         {
         cout << "Enter number: "; // Prompt for input
         cin >> fNum;
         fSum = fSum + fNum;
         iCntr = iCntr + 1;
         }
      while(iCntr < 2);

// Print the sum
      cout << "The sum of the numbers you entered is " << fSum;
}
```

FIGURE 13-22
The adding-two-numbers program written in C++.

Java

Java is a high-level programming language developed by Sun Microsystems in 1995. Java is an object-oriented programming language similar to C++, but it is simplified to eliminate features that cause common programming errors. Java is a general purpose programming language that can be used to write complete stand-alone applications (see Figure 13-23) or smaller programs called *Java applets*.

Java applications can be run using any operating system or Web browser that understands *Java bytecode*. Bytecode is the compiled format of a Java application that usually has the *.class* extension. Once a Java application has been converted to bytecode, it can be run on any platform—such as Windows, UNIX, or Mac OS—as long as the PC being used includes the *Java Virtual Machine* (*Java VM*). Bytecode's operating system independence is significantly different from the operating system-specific object code generated by traditional programming languages.

Platform independence is one of Java's biggest advantages. Because of it, programs can be written once and then run on any number of computer configurations, without special accommodations. This unique characteristic has led Java to become the cornerstone of applications that run over the Internet. Consequently, some expect the use of Java programming to explode as more and more applications are written specifically to be delivered via the Web. It is currently one of the most popular programming languages and has replaced C++ as the programming language used for the computer science Advanced Placement exam taken by high school students to earn college credit. Today, Java is the

>**Java.** A high-level, object-oriented programming language frequently used for Web-based applications.

TREND

DVD GAME PROGRAMMING

Multimedia programming—such as for Web sites, video games, and computer animated movies—has grown by leaps and bounds in recent years and has led to an increase in the need for video game programmers. The solid base of DVD players in homes today has also led to a related trend—developing games specifically for DVD players. One leader in this area is Imagination Entertainment, an Australian company that creates DVD games based on board games, television shows, and movies, such as *Family Feud* and *SpongeBob SquarePants*™ (see the accompanying screen shot). Imagination Entertainment has already sold over six million copies of its twelve DVD game titles and expects sales to double over the holiday season because of its distribution deals with Wal-Mart, Toys R Us, Kmart, and Target. Imagination Entertainment currently employs three programmers who are members of a production team of 15 to 20 people. The games are written using C++, as well as proprietary programs. In addition to programmers, game publishers also typically employ quality-assurance testers—gamers who play through every conceivable game scenario, looking for bugs and other problems before the game is released. One video game publisher, Incredible Technologies, estimates that a single undetected bug in a new program could cost as much as $100,000 to fix the problem and send out an update. Consequently, with the increasing sophistication of video games and the increasing number of things that can go wrong with the programming, game testers are of increasing importance.

DVD game programming. A new gaming trend is to create games specifically for DVD players.

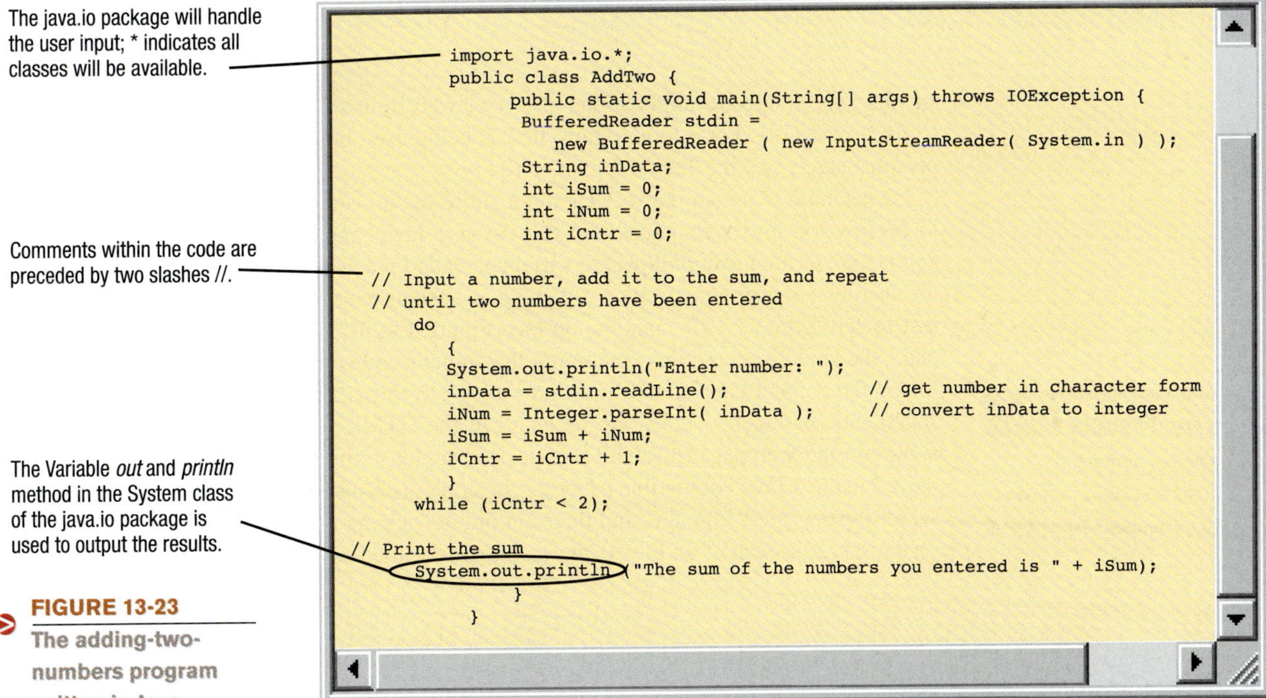

The java.io package will handle the user input; * indicates all classes will be available.

Comments within the code are preceded by two slashes //.

The Variable *out* and *println* method in the System class of the java.io package is used to output the results.

```
import java.io.*;
public class AddTwo {
      public static void main(String[] args) throws IOException {
       BufferedReader stdin =
          new BufferedReader ( new InputStreamReader( System.in ) );
       String inData;
       int iSum = 0;
       int iNum = 0;
       int iCntr = 0;
// Input a number, add it to the sum, and repeat
// until two numbers have been entered
   do
     {
     System.out.println("Enter number: ");
     inData = stdin.readLine();              // get number in character form
     iNum = Integer.parseInt( inData );      // convert inData to integer
     iSum = iSum + iNum;
     iCntr = iCntr + 1;
     }
   while (iCntr < 2);
// Print the sum
   System.out.println("The sum of the numbers you entered is " + iSum);
         }
     }
```

FIGURE 13-23
The adding-two-numbers program written in Java.

TECHNOLOGY AND YOU

Java-Based Systems for Personal Safety

As the use of Java-based application grows, some Java-based systems are being developed to help secure your personal safety. For instance, in late 2005, the U.S. Justice Department officials began distributing a free Java-based software program to police departments as part of a new crime prevention system. The program allows regional law enforcement agencies to store crime-mapping data—including areas of past criminal activity and the locations of known domestic violence criminals, as well as gangs and prostitution rings—in a central database that can be accessed by officers on patrol. In addition, the system—called the *Geospatial Repository for Analysis and Safety Planning* (*GRASP*)—can also assist police during a disaster, such as to map out search and rescue efforts. To ensure the system can be accessed with a variety of types of computers and devices, Java was used as the programming language, in conjunction with XML (Extensible Markup Language) and SVG (Scalable Vector Graphics).

Another safety-oriented Java-based system has been developed by the National Oceanic and Atmospheric Administration (NOAA). This system allows public- and private-sector organizations to better browse and view radar data archived at the agency's National Climatic Data Center (NCDC) Web site. Via its interactive viewer and data exporter applications, this system enables federal agencies, scientific and academic communities, and emergency management officials to quickly analyze more information from the Next Generation Weather Radar (Nexrad) system. For example, officials can overlay Nexrad data (data from about 140 Doppler radars operating nationwide) with Census Bureau data to analyze who and what was affected by a hurricane or other natural disaster, including the numbers, ages, and racial distributions of affected individuals. This information can be used by emergency officials to aid in disaster response and recovery efforts (see the accompanying screenshot for a look at population data overlayed over Hurricane Katrina data, during that hurricane in 2005).

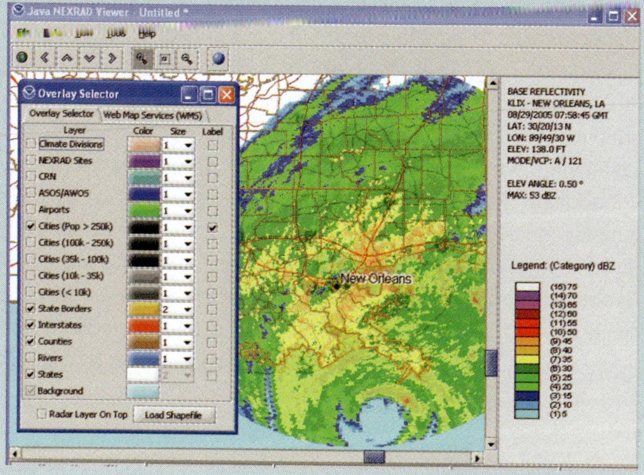

standard for enterprise applications and is viewed by many as the replacement for both COBOL and C++. For a look at how Java is being used in systems that may impact your personal safety, see the Technology and You box.

Java applets are similar to Java applications but are small programs that are designed to be inserted into Web pages and run using a Java-enabled Web browser. Many Java applets are written using allowable variables (called *parameters*) that enable the applet to be customized when it is used on a Web page, such as to specify the colors to be used, the text to scroll, the text size, and so on (see Figure 13-24). To use a Java applet on a Web page, the applet's .class files containing the applet's code must be stored in the Web site's folder. The applet can then be inserted into the Web page using the appropriate HTML statements; parameter values are included in the HTML statements used to display the applet on the Web page to specify the desired applet settings. When the Web page is displayed using a Java-compatible browser, the applet is typically downloaded from the Web server hosting the Web page, and then run on the viewing computer. Java applets that run on the server instead of on the client computer are called *servlets*.

FURTHER EXPLORATION

For links to further information about programming languages, go to www.course.com/uc11/ch13

APPLETS
Are inserted on Web pages using HTML and are run when the Web page is loaded.

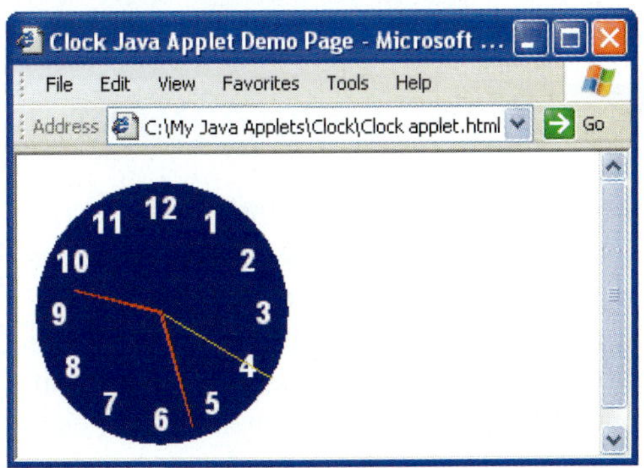

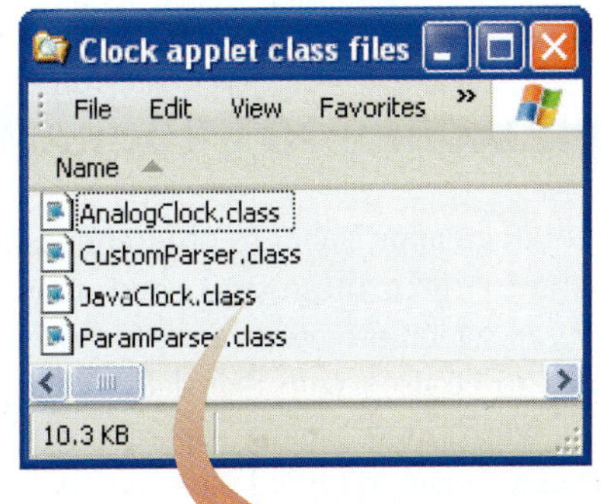

CLASS FILES
Java applets use one or more class files that are written in the Java programming language. The Clock applet requires four different class files. These files must be located in the same folder as the Web page file and other Web page content.

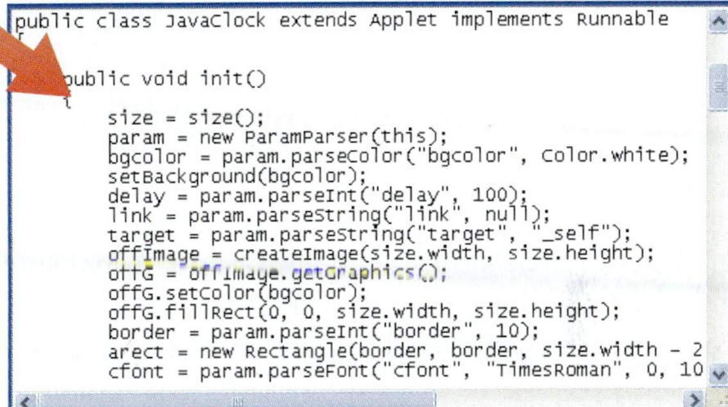

APPLET DOCUMENTATION
The parameters and allowable values should be included in the applet's documentation.

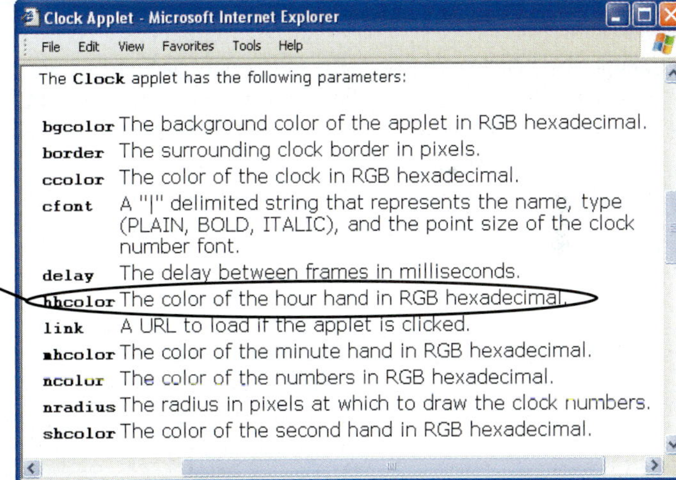

Description and allowable values for the hhcolor (hour hand color) parameter.

This statement identifies the location of the class files.

This parameter specifies that the hour hand display color is red (hexadecimal value ff0000).

Clock applet.html - Notepad

File Edit Format View Help

```
<title>Clock Java Applet Demo Page</title>
</head>

<body>
<applet  codebase="Clock applet class files" code="JavaClock.class"
width="150" height="150" >
<param  name="bgcolor"  value="ffffff">
<param  name="border"  value="0">
<param  name="ccolor"  value="000080">
<param  name="cfont"  value="Arial|BOLD|18">
<param  name="delay"  value="100">
<param  name="hhcolor"  value="ff0000">
<param  name="mhcolor"  value="ff0000">
<param  name="ncolor"  value="ffffff">
<param  name="shcolor"  value="ffff00">
</applet>
```

PARAMETERS
Are used to specify colors and other variables used with the applet. The desired values are entered into each parameter line in the HTML statements used in the Web page file to insert the applet into the Web page.

FIGURE 13-24
Java applets. Java applets are displayed on Web pages and typically add some type of animation, such as the Clock applet featured here.

SYS

SUMMARY

APPROACHES TO PROGRAM DESIGN AND DEVELOPMENT

Chapter Objective 1:
Understand the differences between structured programming, object-oriented programming (OOP), and aspect-oriented programming (AOP).

Two common approaches to program design are **structured programming**, in which programs are written in an organized, modular form, and **object-oriented programming (OOP)**, in which programs are comprised of a collection of *objects* that contain data and *methods* to be used with that data. A newer approach is **aspect-oriented programming (AOP),** which more clearly separates different functions so that program components can be developed and modified individually from one another, and the components can be easily reused with separate, nonrelated objects.

THE PROGRAM DEVELOPMENT LIFE CYCLE (PDLC)

Chapter Objective 2:
Identify and describe the activities involved in the program development life cycle (PDLC).

Creating application programs is referred to as **program development**. The steps involved with program development are called the **program development life cycle (PDLC)**. These steps begin with **problem analysis**, in which the system specifications are reviewed by the systems analyst and **programmer** to understand what the proposed system—and corresponding new program—must do. In the next step—**program design**—the program specifications from step one are refined and expanded into a complete set of design specifications.

Chapter Objective 3:
Understand what constitutes good program design and list several tools that can be used by computer professionals when designing a program.

Good program design is essential. Some key design principles include being very specific, using only one *entry point* into and one *exit point* out of any structure, and ensuring that there are no *infinite loops* in your programs. Many *program design tools* are available to help programmers as they design programs, including *structure charts*, *flowcharts*, and *pseudocode*.

Structure charts depict the overall hierarchical organization of program modules. *Top-down design* indicates that modules are defined first at the highest levels of the hierarchy and then at successively lower levels. Program **flowcharts** use geometric symbols and relational operators to provide a graphic display of the sequence of steps involved in a program. The steps in a flowchart are presented in the same logical sequence as their corresponding statements will be listed in a program. **Pseudocode** is a structured technique that uses English-like statements in place of the graphic symbols of the flowchart. *Data modeling* is a technique used in designing an application to be developed using object-oriented programming. A data model identifies the *classes* and *subclasses* in an application, as well as their unique characteristics.

Chapter Objective 4:
Explain the three basic control structures and how they can be used to control program flow during execution.

There are three fundamental **control structures**—*sequence*, *selection*, and *repetition*—typically found in programs. A *sequence control structure* is simply a series of procedures that follow one another. The *selection* (or *if-then-else*) *control structure* involves a choice: *If* a certain condition is true, *then* follow one procedure; *else*, if false, follow another. When more than two conditions are used, the resulting structure is known as the *case control structure*. A *repetition control structure* repeats the statements in a loop until a certain condition is met. A loop can take one of two forms: *do while* or *do until*.

Chapter Objective 5:
Discuss some of the activities involved with coding, debugging, maintaining, documenting, and ensuring the quality of programs.

Once the program design for an application is finished, the next stage is to code the program. **Coding**, which is the job of programmers, is the process of writing a program in a particular *programming language* based on a set of design specifications. Among the techniques that have been developed to increase programmer productivity are coding standards, *reusable code*, and *data dictionaries*.

Debugging, part of the fourth step in the program development life cycle, is the process of making sure that a program is free of errors, or "bugs." Debugging can be a lengthy process, sometimes amounting to significantly more than half of the total development time for an in-house program. Before a program can be run—and, therefore, before it can be debugged—it needs to be translated from the code a programmer writes to the code a computer can execute. A **language translator** converts the application program's **source code** into *machine language* or **object code**. A **compiler** translates the entire program into machine language before executing it. An **interpreter** translates and executes program statements one line at a time. An *assembler* is used to convert an assembly language program into machine language.

Most bugs can be classified as being either **syntax errors** or **logic errors**. While programs with syntax errors will not run, programs with logic errors will run but with erroneous results. Once preliminary debugging is complete, programs will also have to be thoroughly *tested*. Good test data will subject the program to all the conditions it might conceivably encounter when finally implemented. Mass-distributed commercial programs are also *beta tested*.

Program implementation and maintenance, the final step in the program development life cycle, involves first getting the program up and running in the new system, and then updating the software, as needed, so that it continues to be useful. Program maintenance can be costly.

TOOLS FOR FACILITATING PROGRAM DEVELOPMENT

Program development tools can be used to facilitate the program development process—referred to as *rapid application development* (*RAD*). **Application Lifecycle Management (ALM)** tools can be used to create and manage an application throughout its entire lifecycle—from design through testing; many include *code generators* to help programmers by generating code based on the design already created with another component of the program. *Application generators*, such as *macros* and *report generators*, enable programmers and end users to code new applications quickly. *Software-asset management tools* can help manage reusable code and other programming resources. *Device software development* tools are used to optimize the entire development and support life cycle of device software development.

Chapter Objective 6:
List some tools that can be used to speed up or otherwise facilitate the program development process.

PROGRAMMING LANGUAGES

An important decision that must be made during the design phase is the selection of a **programming language**. Programming languages are **low-level languages**, such as **machine** and **assembly languages**; **high-level languages**, such as **FORTRAN**, **COBOL**, **Pascal**, **BASIC**, **C**, **C++**, **C#**, or **Java**; or *very-high-level languages*, which are also called **fourth-generation languages (4GLs)**. 4GLs are predominantly *declarative languages*, whereas 3GLs are mostly *procedural languages*. Programming languages can also use a *natural-language interface*, as well as be a *visual language*, such as **Visual Basic**. Different programming languages are designed for different purposes. For instance, FORTRAN and Pascal are designed for math and science applications; COBOL is best suited for business transaction processing; C# and Java are designed for Web applications, and Visual Basic is designed to help programmers create sophisticated applications with user interfaces quickly and easily. Java, which can be used to write complete stand-alone applications, as well as *Java applets*, is one of the most popular programming languages today. Java programs can be run under any operating system or Web browser that understands *Java bytecode*.

Chapter Objective 7:
Describe several programming languages in use today.

REVIEW ACTIVITIES

KEY TERM MATCHING

Instructions: Match each key term on the left with the definition on the right that best describes it.

a. coding
b. compiler
c. debugging
d. flowchart
e. logic error
f. object code
g. object-oriented programming (OOP)
h. source code
i. structured programming
j. syntax error

1. _____ A computer program before it is compiled.
2. _____ A language translator that converts an entire program into machine language before executing it.
3. _____ An approach to program design in which a program consists of a collection of objects that contain data and methods to be used with that data.
4. _____ An approach to program design in which a program is separated into smaller subprograms, and step-by-step instructions are executed one after the other, accessing the subprograms when needed.
5. _____ A programming error that occurs when running a program produces incorrect results.
6. _____ A programming error that occurs when the programmer has not followed the rules of the programming language.
7. _____ A program design tool that shows graphically step-by-step how a computer program will process data.
8. _____ The machine language version of a computer program generated after the program's source code is compiled.
9. _____ The process of ensuring a program is free of errors.
10. _____ The process of writing the programming language statements to create a computer program.

SELF-QUIZ

Instructions: Circle **T** if the statement is true, **F** if the statement is false, or write the best answer in the space provided. **Answers to the self-quiz are located in the References and Resources Guide at the end of the book.**

1. **T F** A systems analyst is an individual who writes the code for a computer program.
2. **T F** The terms *class* and *inheritance* are associated with the object-oriented programming approach.
3. **T F** With a do until structure, the program statements in the loop are always executed at least once.
4. **T F** Pascal is an example of a fourth-generation language.
5. **T F** Visual Basic is a version of the C programming language.
6. Program flowcharts and pseudocode would most likely be developed during the _____ step of the program development life cycle.
7. A(n) _____ converts the source code of an application program into executable object code (machine language) one line at a time.
8. Using an incorrect formula is an example of a(n) _____ error.
9. A(n) _____ programming language uses a graphical programming environment, allowing programmers to create code by dragging and dropping items with the mouse instead of actually typing code.

10. Match each phase of the program development life cycle (PDLC) with it description and write the corresponding number in the blank to the left of each description.

    a. ______ The step of the PDLC that generates the program's source code.
    b. ______ The step of the PDLC that continues until the program is retired or needs redesigning.
    c. ______ The step of the PDLC in which a beta test may take place.
    d. ______ The step of the PDLC in which system specifications are reviewed and program specifications are developed.
    e. ______ The step of the PDLC in which a flowchart might be developed.

1. problem analysis	**3.** program coding	**5.** program implementation and maintenance
2. program design	**4.** program debugging and testing	

EXERCISES

1. List at least three types of information that should be included in a program's internal documentation (comments).
2. Select the most appropriate language from the numbered list below that best matches each of the following descriptions and write the corresponding number in the blank to the left of each description. Note that all languages will not be used.

    a. ______ A programming language used to write applets for use with Web pages.
    b. ______ A low-level programming language.
    c. ______ A high-level programming language developed to teach structured programming and used most often for math and science applications.
    d. ______ A very-high-level visual programming language.
    e. ______ A high-level programming language designed for business transaction processing applications.

1. assembly language	**3.** Java	**5.** C++	**7.** C
2. Visual Basic	**4.** COBOL	**6.** Pascal	**8.** BASIC

3. Draw a flowchart for the following situation: Input a person's age. If the person is less than 21 years old, the message "You are under 21" should be displayed. For individuals 21 or older, display the message "You are 21 or older." Be sure to test your flowchart to make sure it illustrates the proper logic.
4. Write pseudocode for the problem described in Exercise #3 above.
5. Trace through the accompanying flowchart illustrating the logic of a program that computes the sum of two numbers, creating a tracing table as you go, to see if the flowchart does what is intended (use any numbers for your input). If it does not do what it is supposed to do, identify the problem and state how it could be corrected.

FLOWCHART TO COMPUTE THE SUM OF TWO NUMBERS

Start
Set counter to 0
Set sum to 0
Counter < 2?
False (No)
Print sum
Stop
True (Yes)
Input number
Subtract 1 from counter
Add number to sum

DISCUSSION QUESTION

There is a trend in programming languages and program development tools to make the coding more and more transparent to the user. In fact, some experts predict that in the near future, much coding will be done automatically for programmers. Some welcome this trend—after all, who would want to code in 1s and 0s anymore like early programmers?—but others are concerned about programmers of the future missing out on the fundamentals of programming, if programming is no longer required. For instance, without understanding how looping and variable initializations work, how easily could an individual find a logic error in a looping process? Do you think programmers of the future should still learn programming fundamentals, even if coding is no longer required? Or will programming languages evolve to the point where that is no longer necessary? If you have ever written a computer program, were basic programming fundamentals necessary?

PROJECTS

HOT TOPICS

1. **Open Source Programming** The use of open source software (programs in which the source code is available free of charge to the public to be used and modified) is growing by leaps and bounds and some believe the software industry of the future will be based on open source code. One of the benefits of open source software is that improvements to the program are shared with the open source community. Open source projects provide opportunities for individuals to work on open source programs, and they are often open to anyone who wants to participate. Some organizations—such as Google with their "Summer of Code" program—sponsor programming students who agree to participate in open source projects.

   For this project, find and investigate at least two open source projects and determine who is able to participate and how participants share their improvements with others. Would you be interested in participating in an open source project? What are some advantages for programming students? Any disadvantages? At the conclusion of your research, prepare a one-page summary of your findings and submit it to your instructor.

SHORT ANSWER/ RESEARCH

2. **A Cup of Oak?** The story behind the Java platform dates back to 1990 and is filled with several aspiring software engineers, a few top executives at Sun Microsystems, a sudden realization that the Internet was the future software medium, and a strong desire to beat Hewlett Packard, IBM, and Microsoft to the punch.

   For this project, research the history of the Java (originally named "Oak") programming language from its inception through the present. Be sure to include the reason the language was developed and the major events, people, and challenges that were faced by Sun Microsystems during the development of Java. Is the use of Java today consistent with what Sun had in mind when they developed the language? If not, how has Java evolved? At the conclusion of your research, prepare a one-page summary of your findings and submit it to your instructor.

3. **The Other Interface** Computers have at least two notable interfaces. The one most commonly referred to is the interface between the user and the computer, called the graphical user interface (GUI). Although this interface usually receives most of the press, the second interface is perhaps the more important of the two, at least from the programmer's point of view. The second interface is called the *application program interface* (*API*) and is only seen by the programmer in the process of writing the source code. This interface allows the application programs to talk with each other and the operating system in the course of processing. It has been suggested that the evolution of APIs actually drives the computer industry and defines the limits of the application software.

   For this project, investigate the evolution of APIs and determine what their impact has been on the computer industry. What are some common APIs in use today? What are they used for? Do you believe that APIs drive the computer industry? Do you think that APIs will drive the computer industry in the future? At the conclusion of your research, prepare a one-page summary of your findings and submit it to your instructor.

4. **Pass or Fail** As described in the text, a program flowchart is a graphical representation of the sequence of steps involved in a program.

   For this project, draw a flowchart that depicts the sequence of steps involved in passing the course for which you are using this textbook. To simplify the diagram, you may assume that you will either pass or fail this class (no grade will be issued) and that there are only three graded components (midterm, final, and homework). The flowchart should print the names of all students on the instructor's roster who have passed the course by achieving a score of at least 70% on all graded components. In addition, you should print the total number of students on the roster, as well as the number that passed the class. Be sure to trace the flowchart to verify your logic, then write a pseudocode version of this situation. When you have completed this task, submit a copy of the flowchart and pseudocode to your instructor.

5. **Java Applets** The *Applets* section on Sun Microsystems's Java Web site contains a variety of applets that individuals can try out and download.

   For this project, go to the Applets Web site at java.sun.com/applets and click on the link to go to the "Freebie Applets" page. Select a basic applet, such as Clock or Banner, and click on its name to get more information. Determine what the applet does and what types of parameters you could set if you choose to include that applet on your Web page. Also determine which pair of HTML tags must surround the Java applet code when that code is inserted into a Web page file. At the conclusion of your research, prepare a short summary of what you learned and submit it to your instructor.

WRITING ABOUT COMPUTERS

6. **Who's to Blame?** When humans and computers are both involved in accomplishing a task and something goes wrong, we tend to blame the computer program. There is little question about the existence of software bugs or glitches, but can all errors we read about in the newspapers or see on the television be attributed to the software program?

   For this project, investigate at least two publicized problems in which a computer was involved (such as erroneous bank transactions, military training incident, privacy breach, or delayed paychecks) and determine if the fault of the incident rests with a human, the computer program, or both. Be sure to summarize the events and provide some basis for your conclusion. Do you think it is more likely that a computer or a human being would be responsible for a serious system problem? Why? Submit this project to your instructor in the form of a short paper, not more than two pages in length.

PRESENTATION/ DEMONSTRATION

7. **Bug Hunters** Many security freelance programmers in the software industry (sometimes referred to as *bug hunters*) like to search for security flaws in their spare time and make this information public. The goal is to make unsuspecting users aware of the possible security problem and encourage the producer of the software to write a security patch. Unfortunately, some of these bug hunters like to go public with the security flaw immediately in order to get public recognition for their efforts and end up compromising the security of more users than if they had not found the flaw in the first place.

For this project, research two recent major security flaws discovered in a widely used software program and present a summary about who found them, how the information was made public, what the security problem was, and how the problem was resolved (or is being resolved). Share your findings and opinions with the class in the form of a short presentation. The presentation should not exceed 10 minutes and should make use of one or more presentation aids, such as the chalkboard, handouts, overhead transparencies, or a computer-based slide presentation (your instructor may provide additional requirements). You may also be asked to submit a summary of the presentation to your instructor.

GROUP DISCUSSION

8. **Consumer Hacks** There have been many instances where individuals have hacked into consumer products—such as toys, game consoles, DVRs, and more—to alter their functionality and then share their experiences with others. For instance, one individual figured out how to alter the software that controls Sony's AIBO robotic dog and posted techniques that could be used to alter the software that controls AIBO's actions or personality on his Web site. According to several published reports, Sony sent a cease-and-desist letter to the individual based on the Digital Millennium Copyright Act, which prohibits breaking technological controls placed on any copyrighted work. The owner of the Web site acknowledged that he did need to break Sony's encryption to be able to create his software, but states that users of his programs and instructions do not have to break through Sony's copy protection to use them. Do you think the AIBO hack violated the Digital Millennium Copyright Act? Why or why not? Should the hacker be prosecuted? What about individuals who used the hacked program with their AIBO robotic dogs but who did not break Sony's encryption to use the program? Should the law apply to those individuals who break through a copy protection scheme for their own use, or only to those individuals who share the circumvention process with others? What about those individuals who try to break a copyright or security technology just to prove it can be done? Should they be prosecuted, sued, or congratulated for uncovering a weakness in the existing technology?

   For this project, form an opinion of the ethical and legal ramifications of consumer hacks and be prepared to discuss your position (in class, via an online class discussion group, or in a class chat room, depending on your instructor's directions). You may also be asked to write a short paper expressing your opinion.

WEB ACTIVITIES

The ***Understanding Computers*** Web site located at **www.course.com/uc11** features many resources to help reinforce your understanding of the chapter content and help you prepare for exams. Your instructor may also assign specific activities to be completed that will count toward your final grade in the course.

Instructions: Go to **www.course.com/uc11/ch13** to work the following online activities.

Click any link in the navigation bar on the left to access any of the online resources described below.

INTERACTIVE ACTIVITIES

1. **Crossword Puzzle** Practice your knowledge of the key terms in Chapter 13 by completing the interactive Crossword Puzzle.
2. **Tech News Video Project** Watch the **"Game Programming"** video clip that features a teen programmer and his recommendations for learning video game programming with an easier language—a form of BASIC called BlitzBasic. After watching the video online, complete the corresponding project.
3. **Student Edition Labs** Reinforce the concepts you have learned in this chapter by working through the interactive **Visual Programming** and **Advanced Spreadsheets** labs.

TEST YOURSELF

1. **Key Term Matching** Test your knowledge of selected chapter key terms by matching the terms with their definitions.
2. **Self-Quiz** Test your retention of chapter concepts by taking the Self-Quiz.
3. **Exercises** Work these short exercises to review the concepts and terms covered in the chapter.
4. **Practice Test** Test how ready you are for an upcoming exam by completing the online Practice Test.

STUDY TOOLS/ ADDITIONAL RESOURCES

The Understanding Computers Web site has a wide range of additional resources, including an **Online Study Guide** (containing study tips, a chapter outline with room to add your own notes, and a chapter checklist of the activities to complete when the chapter is covered in class and when you are preparing for a test) and an **Online Glossary** for each chapter; **Further Exploration** links; a **Web Guide**, a **Guide to Buying a PC**, and a **Computer History Timeline**; more information about **Numbering Systems**, **Coding Charts**, and **CPU Characteristics**; and much, much more!

CHAPTER 14 Databases and Database Management Systems

OUTLINE

Overview
What Is a Database?
- Relational Databases: A Simple Example
- Individuals Involved with a Database Management System
- The Evolution of Databases
- Advantages and Disadvantages of the Database Approach

Data Concepts and Characteristics
- Data Hierarchy
- Entity Relationships
- Data Definition
- The Data Dictionary
- Data Integrity, Security, and Privacy
- Data Organization

Database Classifications
- Single-User vs. Multiuser Database Systems
- Client-Server Database Systems
- N-Tier Database Systems
- Centralized vs. Distributed Database Systems
- In-Memory Databases

Database Models
- The Hierarchical and Network Database Models
- The Relational Database Model
- The Object-Oriented Database Model
- Multidimensional Databases

Databases and the Web
- Examples of Web Databases in Use
- How Web Databases Work

LEARNING OBJECTIVES

After completing this chapter, you will be able to:

1. Explain what a database is, including common database terminology, and list some of the advantages and disadvantages of using databases.
2. Discuss some basic concepts and characteristics of data, such as data hierarchy, entity relationships, data definition, and organization.
3. Describe the importance of data integrity, security, and privacy and how it affects database design.
4. Identify some basic database classifications and discuss their differences.
5. List the most common database models and discuss how they are used today.
6. Understand how a relational database is designed, created, used, and maintained.
7. Describe some ways databases are used on the Web.

OVERVIEW

People often need to sort through a large amount of data rapidly to retrieve one piece of information. One of the easiest and most widely used methods of organizing data is in a *database*. Databases range from a small address book created and used by an individual, to a companywide database consisting of product and customer data used by company employees, to a search engine database consisting of data about millions of Web pages accessed by individuals around the entire world.

In this chapter, we cover database management systems—the type of software used to create, maintain, and use electronic databases. The chapter opens with a look at what a database is and some important database concepts and vocabulary. We then turn to key characteristics about the data in a database. A brief discussion of how databases evolved comes next, followed by an explanation of database classifications and models, with an extended discussion of the most widely used database model: the relational database. The chapter closes with a discussion of how databases are used on the Web. ■

WHAT IS A DATABASE?

As discussed in Chapter 6, a **database** is a collection of related data that is stored and organized in a manner enabling information to be retrieved from the database as needed. *Database software*—more formally called a **database management system** (**DBMS**)—is used to create, maintain, and access databases. A DBMS also controls the organization of the data and protects the *integrity* and *security* of the data, so it is accurate and protected against both intentional and accidental damage. The key component of a DBMS is the *database engine*—the part of the program that actually stores and retrieves data. Widely used database engines include *Microsoft Jet*, *Microsoft Database Engine* (*MSDE*), and the *Oracle* database engine.

In addition to a database engine, most DBMSs come bundled with a set of tools to perform a variety of necessary tasks, such as building *user interfaces*, creating *forms* and *reports*, and interfacing with *query languages* and programming languages for complex applications. Programming languages typically used with databases today include Visual Basic, Java, and C++, although many older *legacy* database systems still use COBOL.

Databases are used in both *batch processing*, in which a set (or *batch*) of transactions are collected over a period of time and then processed all together (such as each evening), and *real-time processing*, in which transactions are processed as they occur in real time. With real-time processing—sometimes called *interactive processing*—the user and computer interact during processing; with batch processing, there is no interaction with the user while the processing is taking place. Real-time processing is by far more common today.

A database typically consists of interrelated **tables** consisting of *fields* and *records*. As discussed in Chapter 6, a **field** (also called a **column**) is a single type of data to be

SYS

>**Database.** A collection of related data that is stored in a manner enabling information to be retrieved as needed; in a relational database, a collection of related tables. >**Database management system (DBMS).** A type of software program used to create, maintain, and access databases. >**Table.** In a relational database, a collection of related records (rows). >**Field.** A single category of data to be stored in a database, such as a person's name or telephone number. Also called a *column*. >**Column.** A field in a database.

stored in a database, such as a person's name or a person's telephone number. A **record** (also called a **row**) is a collection of related fields. The technical difference between the terms *row* and *record* in database terminology is that a row is contained within a single database table; a record is a collection of fields, either a specific row from a single table or a collection of related fields from multiple tables, as in the results of the Order Request screen shown in Figure 14-1. However, in this chapter, as in common usage, the two terms are used interchangeably.

To illustrate these important concepts, we will take a look at a simplified example of a possible *relational database*—the type of database most widely used at the present time and the type of database used as the focus in this chapter.

Relational Databases: A Simple Example

Some of the fields, records, and tables used in an inventory system for a ski equipment retailer are illustrated in Figure 14-1. As shown in this figure, there are three tables in this database that contain data related to products: Product table (for product descriptions and selling price), Inventory table (for current stock levels of products), and Uncommitted Order table (for future shipments of products that have been ordered from suppliers but that have not yet been promised to customers). Each table consists of several records (rows). The Product table, for example, contains five records—one each for Skis, Boots, Poles, Bindings, and Wax. Each record consists of distinct fields (which appear as columns). The Product table stores four fields for each record—Product Number, Product Name, Supplier, and Price. The Inventory table contains five records and three fields, and the Uncommitted Order table contains six records and three fields. The database example shown in Figure 14-1 is a simplified one, and as such it does not show any of the tables related to customers and their orders. Real-world databases often consist of many more tables than in this example, each containing thousands of records.

For this example, imagine that you are the sales manager of this company and a customer calls on the phone and wants to order 160 pairs of ski boots. You first need to find out if the order can be filled from stock in inventory. If it cannot, you need to know how long it will be before enough stock is available. You have an impatient customer on the phone who wants an immediate response.

Not a problem. Using your PC, you execute the appropriate command to display an Order Request screen and enter the product description, "Boots," and the order size, "160." The DBMS responds with a screen that shows the current level of uncommitted stock in inventory as well as information about stock arriving soon from suppliers that has not yet been committed to other customers. It also provides an estimate as to when the order can be filled: January 12. Within seconds, right in front of you, you have the information you need to respond to the customer's request and close the order.

In a relational database, data from several tables is tied together (*related*) using a field that the tables have in common so that information can be extracted from multiple tables, if needed, to fulfill a user request. For instance, in Figure 14-1, data from all three tables was pulled together through a common Product Number field (the green shaded columns) to complete the Order Request screen shown in that figure. Specifically, the Product table was first accessed to print the product number, then the Inventory table was used to print the number of stock on hand, and then the Uncommitted Order table was used to print the quantities and delivery dates for as many incoming shipments as needed to get a total of at least 160 boots. The end user, however, is typically not aware of the multiple tables are being used and the relationships between the tables; instead the user knows only that the information is "somewhere in the database system."

TIP

Primary keys can be a combination of two key fields (called *composite primary keys*), but single primary keys are more typical in simple databases; only single primary keys are used in the examples in this chapter.

>Record. A collection of related fields in a database. Also called a *row*. **>Row.** A collection of related fields located in a single table in a database.

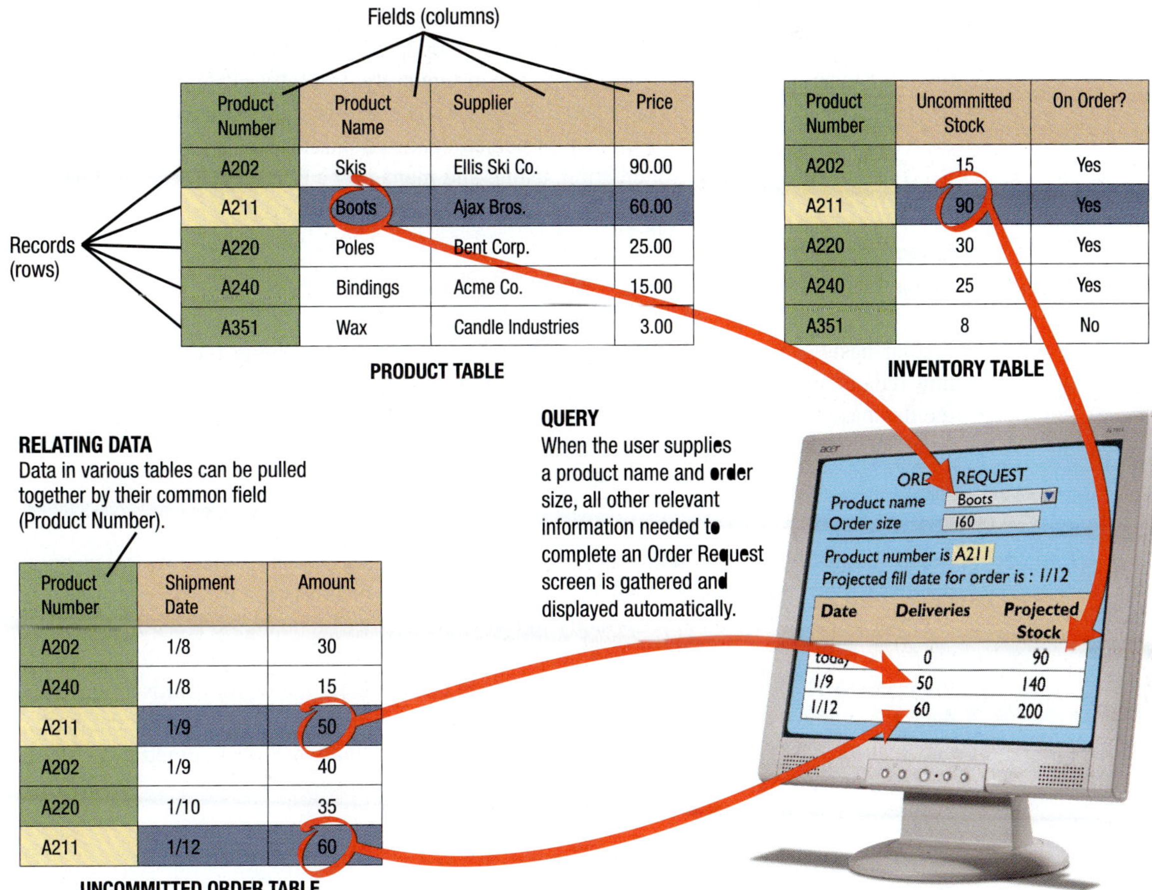

Product Number	Product Name	Supplier	Price
A202	Skis	Ellis Ski Co.	90.00
A211	Boots	Ajax Bros.	60.00
A220	Poles	Bent Corp.	25.00
A240	Bindings	Acme Co.	15.00
A351	Wax	Candle Industries	3.00

Product Number	Uncommitted Stock	On Order?
A202	15	Yes
A211	90	Yes
A220	30	Yes
A240	25	Yes
A351	8	No

Product Number	Shipment Date	Amount
A202	1/8	30
A240	1/8	15
A211	1/9	50
A202	1/9	40
A220	1/10	35
A211	1/12	60

FIGURE 14-1
Using a relational database in an inventory system.

The specific field in a table that is used to identify the records in that table and relate that table to other tables is called the **primary key**. A primary key must uniquely identify each record in that table, so no two records in that table can have the same value in the primary key field. To ensure the uniqueness of the primary key, it usually consists of an identifying number, such as a Social Security number, customer number, or product number. For example, in Figure 14-1, the Product Number field is the primary key field for the Product table. When selecting a primary key field, it is important to pick a field that is unique and is not likely to change. Consequently, fields containing names, telephone numbers, and addresses are poor choices for a primary key (see Figure 14-2). Although telephone numbers and complete addresses are unique, they may change and will not necessarily always be associated with the original individual.

While most complex database systems will have multiple interrelated tables, you can choose not to interrelate tables, or you can choose to have only a single table in a database file when using a DBMS. DBMSs available for use on PCs include *Microsoft Access*, *Corel Paradox*, and *Lotus Approach*. Of these, Access is the most widely used. For more comprehensive enterprise databases, *Oracle*, *IBM DB2*, or another more robust DBMS may be used instead.

FIGURE 14-2
Primary key fields. A key field must contain unique data so it can be used to identify each record in the table.

The yellow fields will always contain unique data and so would be good primary keys.

The blue fields will not always contain unique data and so would not be good primary keys.

Product Number	Product Name	Supplier	Price
Student ID Number	Student Name	Address	Phone
Customer Number	Address	Phone	Balance

SYS

>**Primary key.** A specific field in a database table that uniquely identifies the records in that table.

Individuals Involved with a Database Management System

To be effective, data in a DBMS must be entered, updated as necessary to stay current, and then retrieved in the form of information. Consequently, virtually all DBMSs include a *user interface* for easy data input and data access. There must also be a way for the database to be maintained, backed up, and protected against unauthorized access. The individuals most often involved with creating, using, and managing a DBMS are described next.

Users

The *users* in a database system are the ones who enter data, update data, and pull information out of the database when necessary; that is, the individuals who use the database on a regular basis. Typically, users have no knowledge of the underlying database structure, how data is organized, or the manner in which data is retrieved. Instead, they interact with the database via a user interface consisting of menus, buttons, and fill-in-the-blank forms (such as the Order Request screen shown in Figure 14-1).

Database Designers

As the name suggests, a *database designer* is the individual responsible for designing a database. Because data and databases are so critical in business today, it is essential for databases to be designed appropriately to fulfill the needs of a business. Database designers work with systems analysts and other individuals involved in the system development life cycle (SDLC) to identify the types of data to be collected, the relationships among the data, the types of output required, and other factors that affect the design of the database, and then design the database accordingly. These individuals are also sometimes called *database architects*, *database engineers*, and *database analysts*.

Database Developers and Programmers

Database developers actually create the database, based on the design generated by the database designer, and get it ready for data entry. This includes setting up the database structure, as well as creating the user interface, typically using the tools included with the DBMS. In addition to the database itself, most databases require additional programs that are used to access the database or to tie the database to other applications, such as to a Web site. Creating these programs, when needed, is the job of the *database programmer*. Sometimes the user interface is also built using a programming language when very specific requirements exist. In some organizations, one individual may be both the database developer and database programmer; he or she may function as the database designer, as well.

Database Administrators

Database administrators (DBAs) are the people responsible for managing the large databases within an organization. They perform regular maintenance, assign and monitor user access to the database, monitor the performance of the database system, perform backups, and carry out other necessary maintenance and security duties. Database administrators also work closely with database designers, developers, and programmers to ensure the integrity and security of the data will remain intact when a new system is designed or changes are made to an existing system. The DBA also periodically runs reports and checks the data in the database to confirm that the structural integrity of the data is intact.

The Evolution of Databases

Databases have evolved significantly since the early 1960s. This evolution has occurred in response to our increased reliance on information systems, advances in programming languages, and the need to store and retrieve a variety of complex data, such as multimedia objects (digital images, video files, audio files, and so forth). The significant advances in

MODEL	FLAT FILES	HIERARCHICAL	NETWORK	RELATIONAL	OBJECT-ORIENTED	MULTI-DIMENSIONAL
YEAR BEGAN	1940s	1960s	1960s	1970s	1980s	1990s
DATA ORGANIZATION	Flat files	Trees	Trees	Tables and relations	Objects	Data cubes, tables and relations, or a combination
DATA ACCESS	Low-level access	Low-level access with a standard navigational language	Low-level access with a standard navigational language	High-level, nonprocedural languages	High-level, nonprocedural, object-oriented languages	OLAP tools or programming languages
SKILL LEVEL REQUIRED TO ACCESS DATA	Programmer	Programmer	Programmer	User	User	User
ENTITY RELATIONSHIPS SUPPORTED	One-to-one	One-to-one, one-to-many	One-to-one, one-to-many, many-to-many	One-to-one, one-to-many, many-to-many	One-to-one, one-to-many, many-to-many	One-to-one, one-to-many, many-to-many
DATA AND PROGRAM INDEPENDENCE	No	No	No	Yes	Yes	Yes

FIGURE 14-3
The evolution of databases.
Databases have evolved over the years, becoming more flexible, more capable, and easier to use.

databases can be summarized primarily in terms of their organization of data and access to data. The organization of data has evolved from a collection of independent *flat files* with tree or branching structures and high levels of data redundancy, to a collection of tables and objects that support interrelated multimedia objects with a minimum of data redundancy, to databases that can be viewed from a variety of perspectives or *dimensions*. (For a look at the file management systems used to create flat files, see the Inside the Industry box.) A summary of this evolution is shown in Figure 14-3; the models and relationships listed in the figure will be discussed in more detail later in this chapter.

Advantages and Disadvantages of the Database Approach

Some of the major advantages of using a DBMS are as follows:

- *Better information.* Because data is integrated in a database environment, information that otherwise might be difficult or impossible to compile can be collected.
- *Faster response time.* Because data is integrated into a single database, complex requests can be handled much more quickly.
- *Lower operating costs.* Because response time is faster, users can do more work in less time.
- *Lower storage requirements.* Integration means the same data does not need to appear over and over again in separate tables, thereby saving valuable storage space.
- *Improved data integrity.* The lower level of redundancy means that data updates need to be made in only one place to be reflected throughout the system automatically. This avoids the errors that can easily occur when the same update (such as an address change for a customer) has to be made manually in multiple tables.
- *Better data management.* Central storage in a single database gives a DBMS better control over the *data dictionary* (discussed shortly), security, and standards.

The database approach also has a downside that companies and individuals using databases should be aware of. Some of the major disadvantages are listed next.

INSIDE THE INDUSTRY

File Management Systems

A *file management system* is a program that allows the creation of individual database tables (often referred to as *flat files*), each of which is stored in its own physical file and is not related to any other file. Consequently, file management systems can work with only one table at a time, and each table has to contain all the data that may need to be accessed or retrieved at one time. As a result, file management systems have a much higher level of redundancy than database management systems (for example, in the accompanying illustration, the Product Name, Supplier, and Price data must be entered and stored in all three tables). This redundancy can lead to data entry errors in the database, as well as storage issues since the files contain more data than they would if a DBMS was used. It also requires additional work. For example, the task illustrated in Figure 14-1 would require the sales manager to perform the following steps:

1. Access the Product table to get the product number.
2. Check the Inventory table for that product number to see if the company can fill the order from current stock.
3. If current stock is inadequate, check the Uncommitted Order table to see when enough stock will be available to fill the order.

In addition, the date on which the order could be filled would have to be hand calculated. Because this file management method would be much slower than if the tables were integrated, both service to clients and efficiency would suffer.

Because of these limitations, file management systems are rarely used today. They are useful, however, in appreciating the advantages of a DBMS and some of the advances the industry has made over the years.

Since file management systems cannot retrieve data from more than one table at a time, there is a much higher level of redundancy.

PRODUCT NUMBER	SHIPMENT DATE	PRODUCT NAME	SUPPLIER	PRICE	AMOUNT
A202	1/8	Skis	Ellis Ski Co.	90.00	30
A240	1/8	Bindings	Acme Co.	15.00	15
A211	1/9	Boots	Ajax Bros.	60.00	50
A202	1/9	Skis	Ellis Ski Co.	90.00	40
A220	1/10	Poles	Bent Corp.	25.00	35
A211	1/12	Boots	Ajax Bros.	60.00	60

UNCOMMITTED ORDER TABLE

REDUNDANT FIELDS
Instead of just having one field duplicated like in a DBMS (green shaded columns), file management systems require many more fields to be duplicated (green and blue shaded columns). Notice that the blue shaded columns shown here appear only in the Product table in Figure 14-1; when using a DBMS, these fields are deleted from the Uncommitted Order and Inventory tables.

PRODUCT NUMBER	PRODUCT NAME	SUPPLIER	PRICE
A202	Skis	Ellis Ski Co.	90.00
A211	Boots	Ajax Bros.	60.00
A220	Poles	Bent Corp.	25.00
A240	Bindings	Acme Co.	15.00
A351	Wax	Candle Industries	3.00

PRODUCT TABLE

PRODUCT NUMBER	PRODUCT NAME	SUPPLIER	PRICE	UNCOMMITTED STOCK	ON ORDER?
A202	Skis	Ellis Ski Co.	90.00	15	Yes
A211	Boots	Ajax Bros.	60.00	90	Yes
A220	Poles	Bent Corp.	25.00	30	Yes
A240	Bindings	Acme Co.	15.00	25	Yes
A351	Wax	Candle Industries	3.00	8	No

INVENTORY TABLE

- *Higher software cost.* Relative to other types of file management software, a DBMS is expensive. Database packages designed for use on large computer systems can cost several thousand dollars. However, some free or low-cost enterprise database software programs—such as the open source *MySQL* program—are available.
- *Increased vulnerability.* Database processing can increase a system's vulnerability to failure. Because the data in the database is highly integrated, a problem with one element might render the whole system inactive, and the potential for data loss is much greater. Also, the limited redundancy can create problems if records in one table are deleted accidentally or the table becomes unusable. Consequently, backup procedures are an extremely important part of using a DBMS.

DATA CONCEPTS AND CHARACTERISTICS

Data is frequently considered to be one of an organization's most valuable assets. Without it, businesses would find it impossible to perform some of their most basic activities. Data is also the heart of a database. Consequently, its concepts and characteristics need to be understood in order to successfully design, create, and use a database. Some of the most important concepts and characteristics are discussed in the following sections.

Data Hierarchy

Data in a database has a definite hierarchy. At the lowest level, *characters* are entered into database *fields/columns* (refer again to Figure 14-1), which hold single pieces of data in the database, such as product names or quantities. Next are *records/rows*—groups of related fields (such as all the fields for a particular product). Then come *tables*, which are made up of related records. At the top of the hierarchy is the *database*, which consists of a group of related tables.

Entity Relationships

An **entity** in a database system is something (such as a person, object, or event) of importance to the organization. If an entity is something that the organization wants to store data about, it typically becomes a database table. Characteristics of entities are called **attributes**. For instance, if a company collects data about a customer, then Customer is an entity. Possible Customer attributes are name, phone number, address, and so forth. Attributes typically become fields in the entity's database table.

A *relationship* describes an association between two or more entities. The three basic entity relationships are discussed next.

One-to-One Entity Relationships

One-to-one (1:1) entity relationships exist when one entity is related to only one other entity of a particular type, so knowing one of the two entities is enough information to determine the second entity. For example, if a business had multiple store locations and each store had a single manager, the relationship between Store and Manager would be a 1:1 relationship. For each store location, you would be able to determine the appropriate manager, and for each manager, you could identify his or her store. In this type of relationship, each record in the table belonging to the first entity can have only one matching record in the table belonging to the second entity. This type of relationship is not common, however, because all the information would typically be located in a single table instead of creating a table (such as one for store and one for manager, in this example) for each entity.

>**Entity.** Something in a database system (such as a person, object, or event) that is of importance to the organization. >**Attribute.** A characteristic of an entity.

One-to-Many Entity Relationships

One-to-many (O:M) entity relationships are the most common and exist when one entity can be related to more than one other entity. Knowing one of the "many" entities is enough information to determine the "one" entity, but not vice versa. For example, an individual supplier would have only one entry in a Supplier table, but the supplier would appear multiple times in the Product table if the supplier supplied more than one product to the company. If a specific product number is known, its supplier can be unequivocally determined, but if a supplier is known, a single product number cannot be identified (assuming that supplier provided more than one product).

Many-to-Many Entity Relationships

Many-to-many (M:M) entity relationships exist when one entity can be related to more than one other entity, and those entities can be related to multiple entities of the same type as the original entity. With this type of relationship, knowing one of the many entities is not enough information to determine a single corresponding entity. For example, there is a many-to-many relationship between orders and products; that is, one order can contain multiple products, and one product can appear on many orders. As a result, knowing an order number is not enough information to determine a single corresponding product number, and knowing a product number is not enough information to identify a single corresponding order. This type of relationship requires a third table—such as an Order Details table—to tie the two tables together.

TIP

For numeric database fields, be sure to first select the appropriate type of field (such as *Number* or *Currency*) and then select the appropriate field size (such as *Integer*, *Long Integer*, or *Decimal* for Number fields) based on the data that will be contained in the field.

Data Definition

Data definition involves describing the properties of the data that go into each database table, specifically the fields or columns that make up the database. During the data definition process, the following are supplied for each field:

- *Name* (must be unique within the table).
- *Data type* (such as *Text*, *Number*, *Currency*, *Date*, and so forth); indicates the type of data that will be entered into the field (see Figure 14-4).
- *Properties* (such as the *field size* and format of the field, any allowable range or required format for the data to be entered into the field, whether or not the field is required, and any initial value to appear in the field of all new records).

FIGURE 14-4
Common data types. Each field in a table must be assigned a specific data type.

DATA TYPE	DESCRIPTION
Text	Text (character) fields store data that is not manipulated arithmetically, such as Johnson or 123-45-6789. You can sort, index, or compare text fields.
Number	Numeric (Number) fields store data to be arithmetically manipulated; usually subcategories, such as integer and decimal, are available.
Currency	A special field type for numeric data that is to be output in a currency format, with dollar signs, decimal points, and commas.
Yes/No	Yes/No (Logical) fields can contain only one of two values–for instance, a "Y" (for "yes") or an "N" (for "no").
Date/Time	Date/time fields store dates and times as values; usually they can be sorted, added, or otherwise manipulated. Several formats, such as short date (e.g., 12/13/06) and medium time (e.g., 3:34 PM), are available.
Memo	Memo fields store large blocks of text; they cannot be arithmetically manipulated or compared, but they can be edited and output.
Hyperlink	Hyperlink fields store hyperlinks to Web pages, e-mail addresses, or files.

The properties that can be set for a field depend on the data type being used for that field. For instance, for fields using the Text data type, the field size indicates the number of characters that will be entered for that field. For Number fields, the field size typically indicates how much storage space (in bytes) can be used for each entry and if decimal places are allowed. For instance, the

>**Data definition.** The process of describing the characteristics of data that is to be included in a database table.

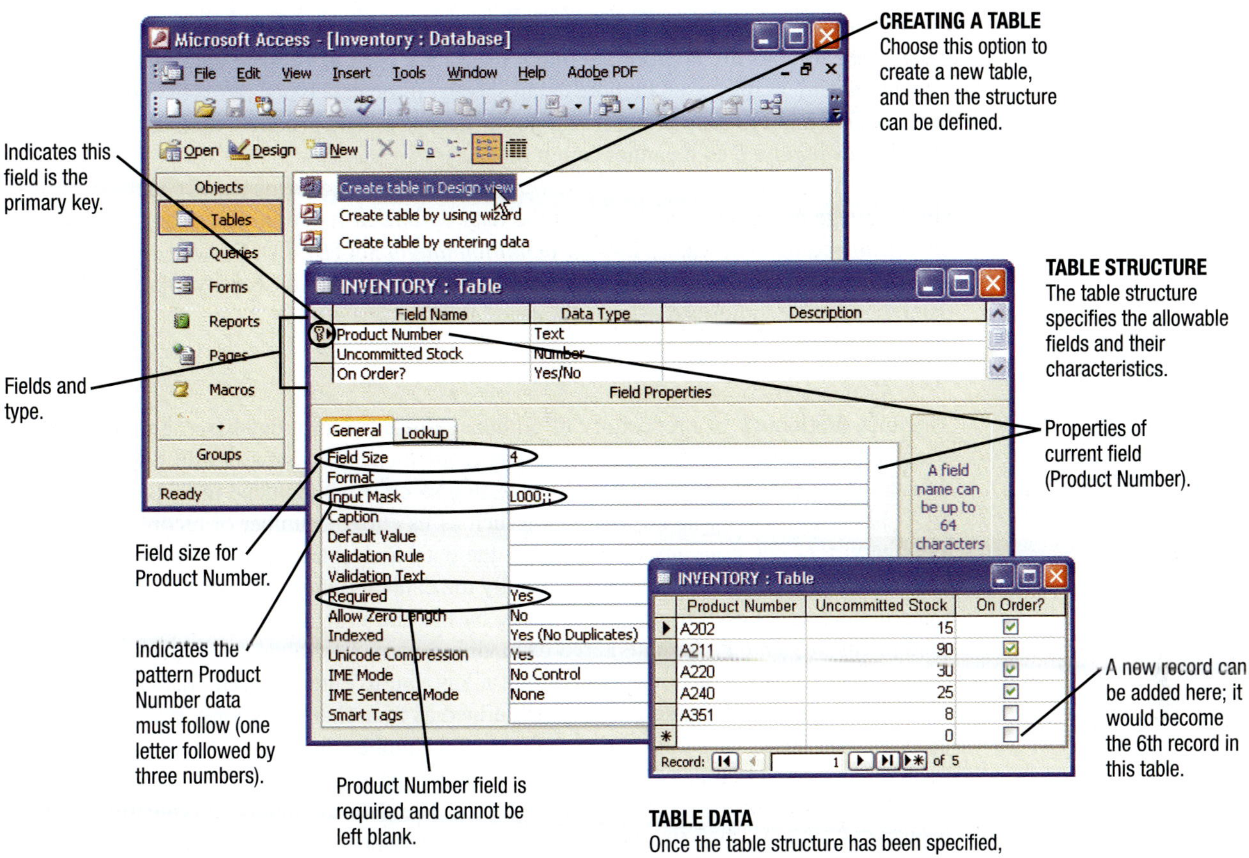

FIGURE 14-5
Data definition. Before data can be entered into a database table, the table must be created by defining the fields to be contained in that table and then saving the table.

field size *Integer* for Number fields in Microsoft Access allocates 2 bytes of storage space and can hold any number from -32,768 to 32,767; the *Long Integer* field size can be used for Number fields that will store longer integers. If a field needs to store decimal places, the *Decimal* field size can be used instead.

The finished specifications for a table (the fields and the properties for those fields) are commonly referred to as the *table structure*. For example, the structure of the Inventory table from Figure 14-1, shown in Figure 14-5, consists of three fields: *Product Number*, *Uncommitted Stock*, and *On Order?* The Product Number field will contain text (character-based) data so the Text field type is assigned to the Product Number field. A field size of 4 is specified in this field's properties because product numbers in this application consist of four characters. The Uncommitted Stock field will contain numeric data that requires no decimal places (data entered into this field will all be integers because stock is counted in product units and so cannot contain decimal places), so the Number data type and the Integer field size are assigned to the Uncommitted Stock field. The On Order? field in this table is specified as a *Yes/No* (sometimes called a *logical*) field. Fields using this data type contain either the value *T* for *true* (sometimes represented instead by a *Y* for *yes*, or a checked box), or *F* for *false* (sometimes represented instead by an *N* for *no*, or an unchecked box). In the Inventory table, a product that is on order is given the value *true*; a product not on order has the value *false*.

In addition to the field size, other properties for the Product Number field in the Inventory table are displayed in the middle screen in Figure 14-5. For instance, an *input mask*—a required format for input—has been specified as L000;; which means one letter followed by three numbers. Because the Product Number field has been assigned this input mask, every product number must be entered as one letter followed by three numbers; no other input will be accepted in the Product Number field. Other less cryptic input masks include

TIP

Some database programs—such as Microsoft Access—allow you to create a table by just entering data, and then the program will create the table structure based on the data entered. The field properties can then be edited, if needed.

(___)___-____ for telephone numbers and __:__ for times specified in hours and minutes, when those formats are appropriate. Input masks are used to validate data as it is entered into the system, as discussed in more detail shortly. If the data typed into a field does not fit the specified input mask pattern, it will not be accepted. The Product Number field is also specified as *required*, so it cannot be left blank.

DBMS packages designed for use with large computer systems usually include a special language component dedicated to the data definition function. Such languages have generically come to be known as *data definition languages* (*DDLs*). Besides simply defining data, a major function of the DDL in these large packages is security—protecting the database from unauthorized use, as discussed shortly.

The Data Dictionary

The **data dictionary** is a repository of all data definitions for a database, including table structures, security information (such as passwords needed to view or edit a table), relationships between the tables in the database, and so on. Also included in the data dictionary is basic information about each table, such as its current number of records. The data dictionary does not store any of the data *in* the database tables, only data *about* the database tables (what is called *metadata*). Usually the data dictionary file is hidden from users since it is accessed only by the DBMS (not by the end user) when the database is being used to ensure that data being entered or modified does not violate any specified criteria. For example, the data dictionary would not allow you to enter a seven-character product number in a Product Number field that is defined as four characters long, it would not let you type text-based data into a field defined as a Number field, and it would not let you leave a required field blank. And without the proper password, the data dictionary would not allow you to view password-protected data. The data dictionary is typically created automatically by the DBMS as the structure of each database table is defined.

Data Integrity, Security, and Privacy

Because data is so essential to organizations, *data integrity* and *security* are very important issues. Although data integrity and security have always been high-priority database issues, there has been increased attention paid to these issues due to the recent terrorist attacks and threats. The total destruction of the computer housing a crucial database, as well as the threat of unauthorized access and data alteration of a vital system, is being viewed as a much more real possibility than just a few years ago. Consequently, many businesses and government organizations are evaluating their data integrity and security methods and improving them, if needed. Database privacy is also of increasing concern to many individuals.

Data Integrity

Data integrity refers to the accuracy of data. The longstanding computer saying "garbage in, garbage out" or "GIGO" is very appropriate for database systems. The quality of the information generated from a database is only as good as the accuracy of the data contained in the database. Although it is possible to generate poor information from quality data by making poor assumptions or using poor data analysis, it is virtually impossible to generate quality information from inaccurate data. Because so many important decisions are made based on information generated by information systems (which almost always

>**Data dictionary.** The repository of all data definitions in a database. >**Data integrity.** The accuracy of data.

use some type of database), data integrity is a vital concern for organizations. Responsible, reliable employees at the data entry level, teamed with good *data validation* methods, can increase the accuracy of the data in a database.

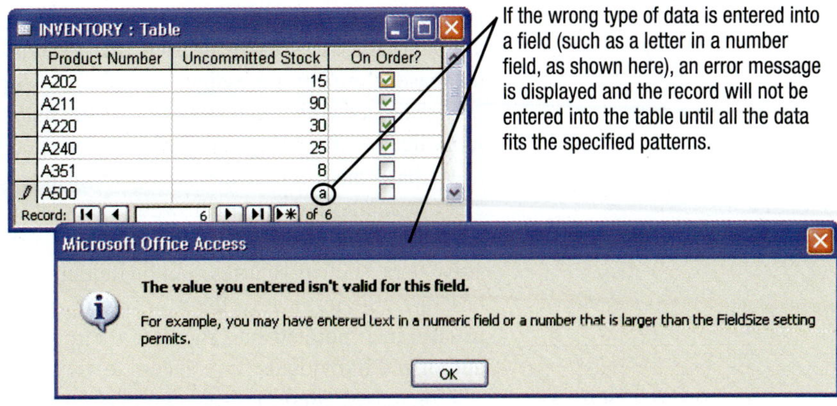

FIGURE 14-6
Data validation.

Data validation refers to the process of ensuring that the data entered into a database matches the specified type, format, and allowable value. As previously discussed, the data dictionary is responsible for comparing all data entered into a table with these requirements and only allows data to be entered into the database table if it follows the specified rules. If invalid data is supplied, a message may be displayed on the screen (see Figure 14-6), and the record is not entered into the database table until all fields are deemed valid. In some systems, data integrity is enforced on a *per transaction* basis. This means that if invalid data is supplied and not corrected at some point during the steps necessary to enter a complete transaction into the system, then the entire transaction will fail, not just that one step of the transaction. This ensures that a complete transaction is always entered into the system at one time and that the database is never left with just a piece of a transaction completed. Even if multiple tables will be affected by the transaction, users will not be able to see the changes until they are *committed*; that is, all steps in the transaction are deemed valid and the appropriate changes are made to all the affected tables. Once a transaction has been committed, all the changes pertaining to the transaction become visible in all corresponding tables at the same time.

Because different users and applications may be trying to change the same data at the same time, it is important that the database be able to temporarily "lock" data that is being accessed so that no other changes can be made to the data until the first user or application is finished. For example, going back to the inventory database scenario shown in Figure 14-1, assume that while the sales manager is working on the order for the 160 boots, using information pulled from the Inventory and Uncommitted Order tables, another person in the sales department gets a request for 75 of the same boots. If the database does not lock the pertinent tables while they are being accessed, both of these employees could sell the same 75 in-stock boots to different customers at the same time. This potential problem can be avoided if *database locking* is used. Databases often support various types of locking, such as *row-level locking* (in which an entire table row is locked when any part of that record is being modified), and *column-level locking* (in which the table column involved in the changes is locked until the changes to that field have been completed).

Data Security

Because large DBMSs are typically used by numerous people, its databases are particularly vulnerable to security problems. For example, unscrupulous employees may attempt to alter payroll data, access privileged salary or financial account data, or even steal or erase data. **Data security** refers to protecting data against destruction and misuse—both intentionally and accidental. It involves protecting database access by users and protecting

SYS

>**Data validation.** The process of ensuring that data entered into a database matches the data definition. >**Data security.** Protecting data in a database against destruction and misuse.

against data loss. Usually access to a database is protected by usernames and passwords, although access cards or a biometric system can be used instead, when warranted. The database administrator assigns specific access privileges (such as whether the user can just read data, can add data, can modify data, and so forth) to specific individuals or groups of individuals—this access can typically be specified down to the individual column level of a database table. For example, in an airline's passenger reservation database, a regular clerk or agent may not be allowed to rebook a special-rate passenger on an alternate flight, but a high-level supervisor who knows the proper password is able to do so. Similarly, sensitive data, such as salaries, can be hidden from view so that only certain users of the database are able to retrieve them or modify them. As mentioned earlier, these privileges are usually incorporated into the data dictionary and enforced by the DBMS to ensure only authorized individuals have access to view and change data.

Increased attention has been given to external security (such as firewalls and network access control) lately, but significant database breaches are still occurring, such as the 40 million credit card numbers that were stolen from the database of a third-party credit card payment processor in 2005. Although external security has been improved in recent years, many information technology industry experts agree that the problem today is that databases are not adequately protected at the application level. In fact, according to the technology research firm Gartner, about 75% of attacks are now occurring at the application level after hackers—sometimes outsiders, but also possibly insiders (such as employees, partners, or contractors)—gain access to the system. As a result, businesses today are looking toward stronger security measures for the database itself, often utilizing security firms specializing in database security. Security measures can include a variety of software programs and tools, such as network-based vulnerability assessment scanners for databases (see Figure 14-7), real-time database intrusion detection and auditing tools, and tools that allow column-level database encryption.

FIGURE 14-7
Database security tools. This program is designed to scan for possible database vulnerabilities.

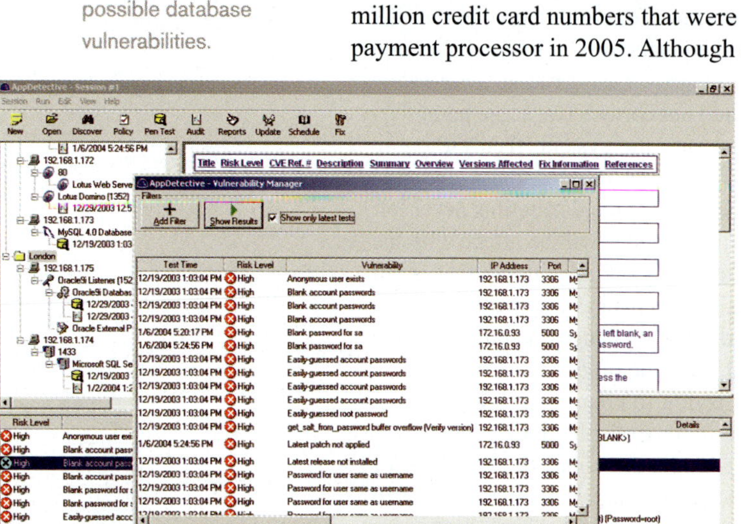

To prevent against data loss, stringent backup and *disaster-recovery* procedures should be implemented. To protect against disasters, such as hard drive failure or the total destruction of the computer, possible precautions include keeping a redundant copy of the database on a mirrored drive, backing up the data at very frequent intervals, and having a comprehensive *disaster-recovery plan.* As part of its disaster-recovery plan, some firms maintain a *hot site*—an alternate location equipped with identical hardware and software that can be used (along with the most current data backup) to resume operations quickly in case of a major disaster. Backup procedures were discussed in Chapter 5; disaster-recovery plans are discussed in more detail in Chapter 15. For a look at some of the security concerns surrounding databases linked to college portals, see the Technology and You box.

Data Privacy

A company that stores data about individuals is responsible for protecting the privacy of that data. *Data privacy* is a growing concern because of the vast amounts of personal data stored in databases today and the many data privacy breaches that have occurred in the recent past. To protect the privacy of collected data, companies need to ensure that the data they are collecting and storing is, in fact, necessary, and then they need to evaluate their data security measures to ensure that the data is adequately protected. Additional privacy issues related to computer use are discussed in Chapter 15.

TECHNOLOGY AND YOU

Databases and College Portals

The word *portal* means an entrance; in computer context, it is used to refer to a Web page that is designed as an entrance—or starting point—to the Internet or other network resources. A growing trend on college campuses today is the *college portal*—a gateway to a vast collection of resources for students, faculty, alumni, and other members of the campus community. One of the most complete and innovative college portals is Gettysburg College's *CNAV* (for College Navigation) system (see the accompanying illustration).

Created in 1995, CNAV evolved over the years from a simple collection of Web pages to a powerful information system capable of distributing a wide variety of highly customized, college-related information to many different groups and individuals. For example, students regularly use the CNAV system to get information about campus events, view the course catalog and their grades, access and update their personal information, access personal information about other students, communicate with students and faculty, schedule appointments, and access course materials. Faculty members, alumni, parents, and community members can also use the system to view information appropriate for their use.

Because many college portals are tied into databases containing sensitive information about students and the college, their implementation can raise a host of privacy and security questions. For instance, if outsiders are allowed access to the system, is there a higher risk of security and privacy breaches? How do you protect confidential records? Who should decide what personal information about individuals should be available to others?

Since CNAV's development began, privacy and security have been very important considerations for Gettysburg College. To protect the system from misuse, several levels of security are in place. For example, the system resides on a secure server, and access to CNAV is restricted to account holders only. Student accounts are automatically created, but parents, alumni, and other outsiders need to apply for their accounts and have their IDs verified before an account can be opened. In addition, students need to approve their parents' accounts before an account will be issued.

To further protect student privacy, each student has complete control regarding what personal information (photo, campus address, campus phone, home address, class schedule, and so on) is available through the system and which users are authorized to view each piece of information. For example, one student may grant all students access to his or her photo and e-mail address, deny outsiders access to any personal information, and give his or her parents access to all information including transcripts. Another student may allow everyone access to all personal information, but deny his or her parents access to grades and transcripts. For a further level of control, the college can globally turn on and off access to a particular piece of information as needed.

Giving the students control of who can access their personal information and having a highly secure system resolves many of the privacy concerns associated with a college portal, but other problems can emerge as the system grows and needs change. For these reasons, the potential impact of adding a new feature should be carefully evaluated prior to its implementation. For example, before adding the ability to post and retrieve grades online, colleges should consider when that information should be available. Even though the system may be capable of allowing students access to their grades as soon as they are posted, whether or not that is the best thing to do needs to be considered. For instance, will knowing their final grades in one course affect the students' ability to concentrate on final exams not yet taken? Will students who get their grades back earlier than others tie up instructor time that might be better spent helping students who still have to take their final exams? Also, if students have the ability to correct their contact information or upload a more current photo, are there controls in place to prevent erroneous or inappropriate updates from being made?

With proper planning and a great deal of input from all possible users of a college portal, the vast majority of potential problems and controversies involving such a system can be avoided or greatly eliminated as any concerns are dealt with before the system is implemented. Provided that adequate security and privacy controls remain in place as both technology and hackers' abilities improve, college portals, such as CNAV, should remain useful tools for the college community. They can save students and faculty time, increase the enjoyment of the campus experience, and provide an information bridge to parents, alumni, and prospective students.

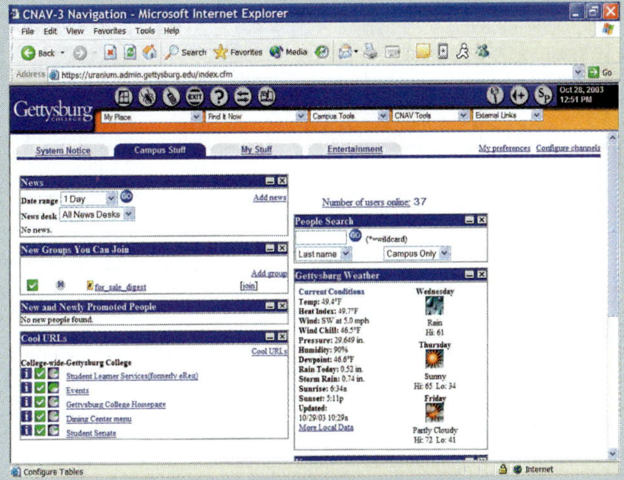

Data Organization

Virtually all databases are organized in some manner to facilitate the retrieval of information. Arranging data for efficient retrieval is called *data organization*. Most methods of data organization use a primary key to identify the location of records so they can be retrieved when needed. New database records are typically added to the bottom of the database table, and tables are not often physically resorted because their content changes frequently and sorting is very time-consuming. The use of a primary key and data organization method allows a specific record to be efficiently located, regardless of the physical order of the records in the table. The two most common types of data organization used today—*indexed* and *direct*—are discussed next. Both are frequently used with real-time transaction processing, in which records are accessed and updated as transactions occur. An older type of data organization is *sequenced organization,* in which the order of the records is physically based on the contents of the key field. Sequenced organization is designed for use with batch processing using a sequential access medium (such as magnetic tape) and so is not frequently used today.

Indexed Organization

With **indexed organization**, an **index** is used to keep track of where data is stored. An index is a small table consisting only of a list of the primary key field for each record in a table along with location information for that record (see Figure 14-8). For example, the Customer

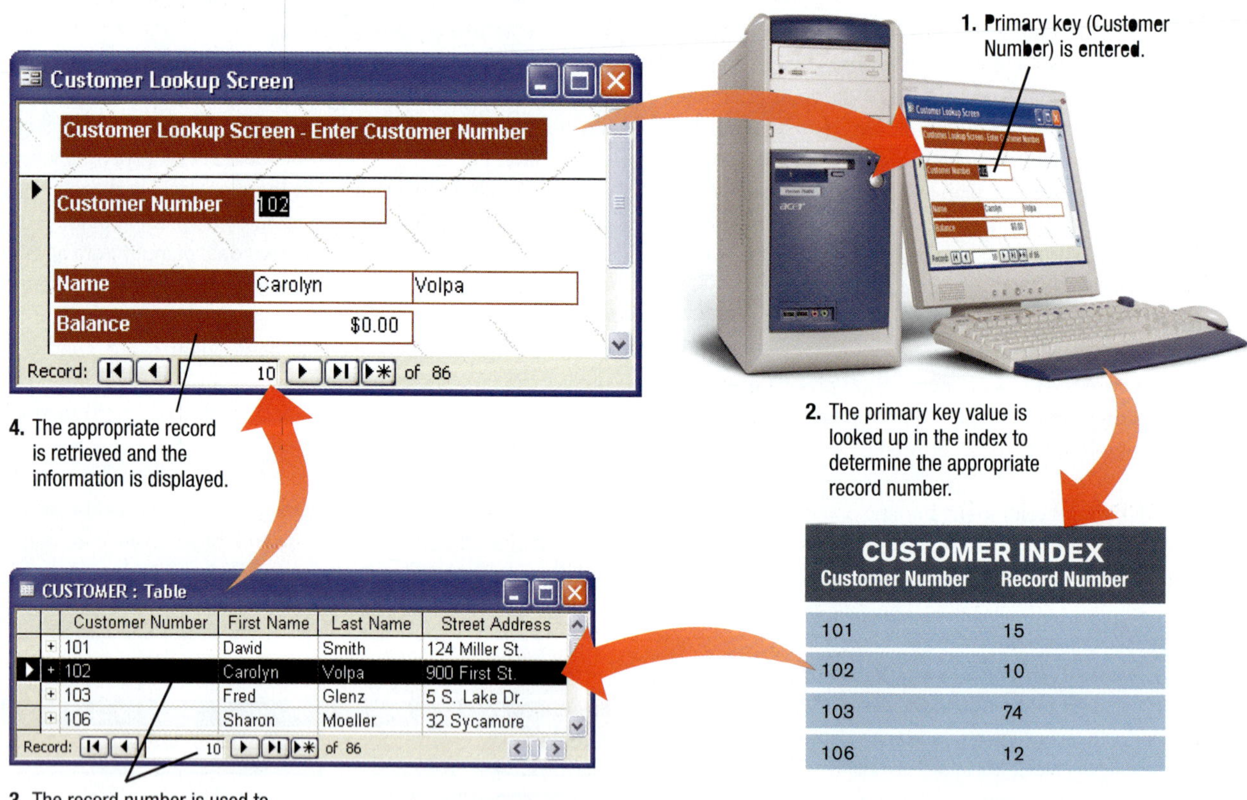

FIGURE 14-8
Indexed organization is often used for real-time transaction processing.

>**Indexed organization.** A method for organizing data on a storage medium or in a database that uses an index to specify the exact storage location. >**Index.** A small table containing a primary key and the location of the record belonging to that key; used to locate records in a database.

table shown in Figure 14-8 uses the Customer Number field as the primary key, so the Customer index shown in that figure includes the Customer Number field plus the current record number for each record in the Customer table. As shown in the figure, indexes are sorted in order by the primary key field to allow records to be looked up in the index and their location determined very quickly. In addition to a record number index, as in Figure 14-8, there can also be indexes to determine the physical location of the record on a storage medium, such as track or cylinder number. Indexes are usually viewed only by the program, not the user.

Direct Organization

Although indexed files are suitable for many applications, finding information through index searches is potentially more time-consuming than is appropriate for some real-time applications. **Direct organization** was developed to provide faster access.

Direct organization uses each record's primary key field to determine a unique address identifying where the record will be physically stored in the database file. The computer does this by applying mathematical formulas called *hashing algorithms*. Several hashing algorithms have been developed. One of the simplest involves dividing the primary key field by a particular prime number. The prime number is determined by the number of records to be stored or the number of storage areas to be used. The *remainder* of this division procedure (see Figure 14-9) becomes the address at which the record will be physically stored.

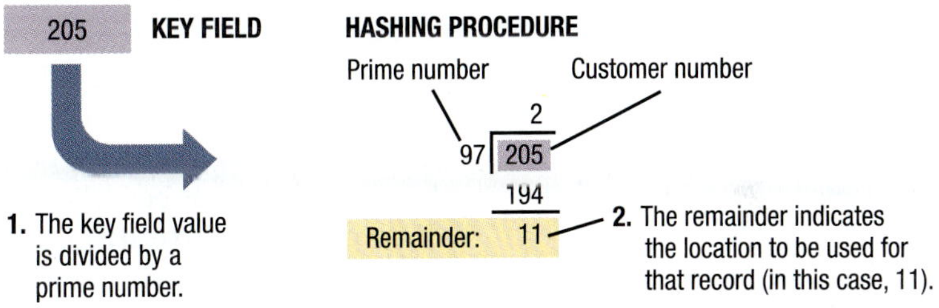

FIGURE 14-9
Direct organization is frequently used for faster real-time processing.

Hashing procedures are difficult to develop, and they pose certain problems. For example, hashing procedures usually result in two or more records being assigned the same storage address, an event known as a *collision*. When this occurs, one record is placed in the computed address location and assigned a "pointer" that chains it to the other record. Then the other record typically goes into an available location closest to the hashed address. Good hashing procedures result in an appropriate number of collisions for the table size used—usually a larger table requires the possibility of a larger number of collisions in order to have sufficient speed.

Some systems use a combination of both indexed and direct organization—the key field indicates where the record is located within the table, and a hashing procedure is used to determine where the record will be physically stored on the storage medium.

DATABASE CLASSIFICATIONS

Database systems can be classified in a variety of manners. Three of the most common classifications are discussed next.

Single-User vs. Multiuser Database Systems

Single-user databases are located on a PC and are designed to be accessed by one user. *Single-user database systems* are widely used for personal applications and very small businesses. Most business database systems today are designed for multiple users, and the database is accessed via a network. Because two or more users in a *multiuser database system* may try to access and modify the same data at the same time, some type of database locking must be used to prevent users from making conflicting changes to the same data at the same time.

SYS

>**Direct organization.** A method of arranging data on a storage medium that uses hashing to specify the exact storage location.

FIGURE 14-10
Client-server database systems. A typical client-server arrangement consists of front-end client PCs that input transactions and a back-end server—with the database—that processes transactions.

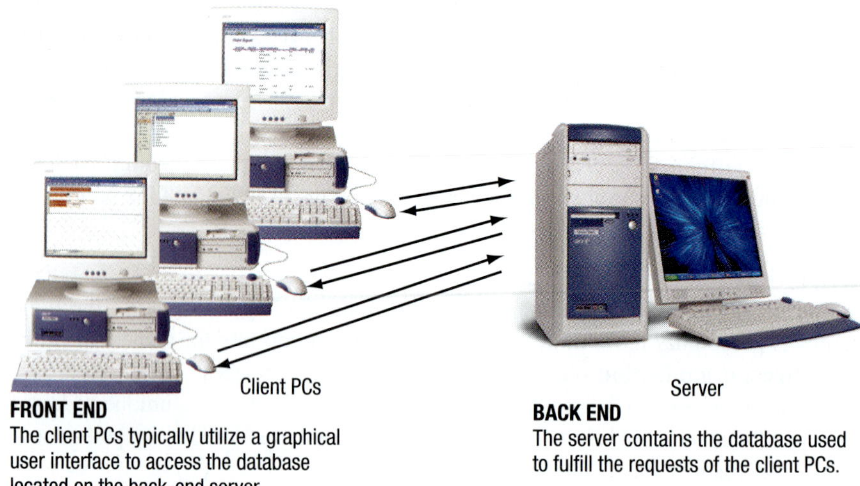

FRONT END
The client PCs typically utilize a graphical user interface to access the database located on the back-end server.

BACK END
The server contains the database used to fulfill the requests of the client PCs.

Client-Server Database Systems

As discussed in Chapter 7, *client-server networks* consist of servers that supply resources to PCs, which function as client devices. Similarly, a *client-server database system* is a database system that has both clients and at least one server.

In a typical client-server database application, the client is called the *front end*; the database server is called the *back end*. The back end server contains the database itself, as well as a DBMS, and it processes the commands coming from the front-end client PCs. A typical client-server database system scenario is illustrated in Figure 14-10.

Client-server database systems have many compelling benefits, perhaps the most important of which are lower hardware costs and scalability to meet future needs. PCs are easier to use and much less expensive than larger computers, which reduces hardware costs for client computers. Also, when you need extra capacity, you can add a new server or add more power to an existing one. The client-server database system is the most commonly implemented type of database system.

N-Tier Database Systems

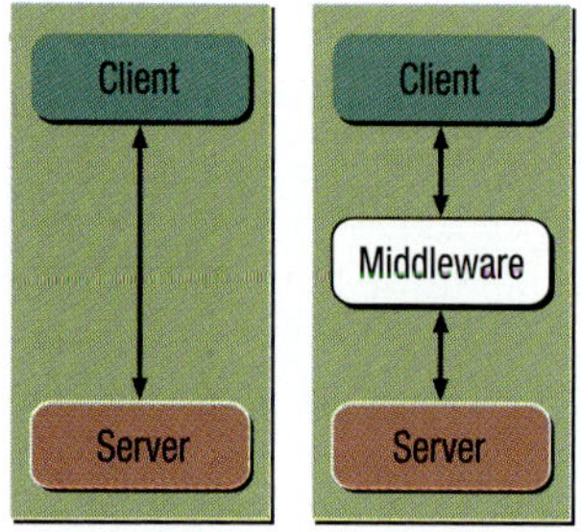

2-TIER MODEL (has just a client and a server)

N-TIER MODEL (middleware includes additional programs used to connect the client and server)

FIGURE 14-11
A 2-tier vs. an n-tier database model.

A growing trend is to use an *n-tier database system*, in which there is at least one middle piece of software—referred to as *middleware*—between the client and the server, instead of just having two components (the client and the server) as in the typical *two-tier* client-server database system (see Figure 14-11). The additional tiers—such as the middle tier in a *three-tier database system*—typically include the programs used with the database and the programs needed to connect the client and server components of the database system, as discussed later in this chapter. Middleware may be stored on a single computer or spread across multiple computers in a network.

One advantage of the n-tier architecture is that it allows the program code used to access the database to be separate from the database, and the code can be divided into any number of logical components. The programming for the programs contained in each tier in an n-tier database system can be written in programming languages different from the programming languages used in other tiers, the tiers can use different platforms, and tiers can be changed or relocated without affecting the other tiers. Consequently, n-tier database systems provide a great deal of flexibility and scalability, allowing the system to be modified as new needs and opportunities arise. N-tier database systems are most commonly found in e-commerce database applications.

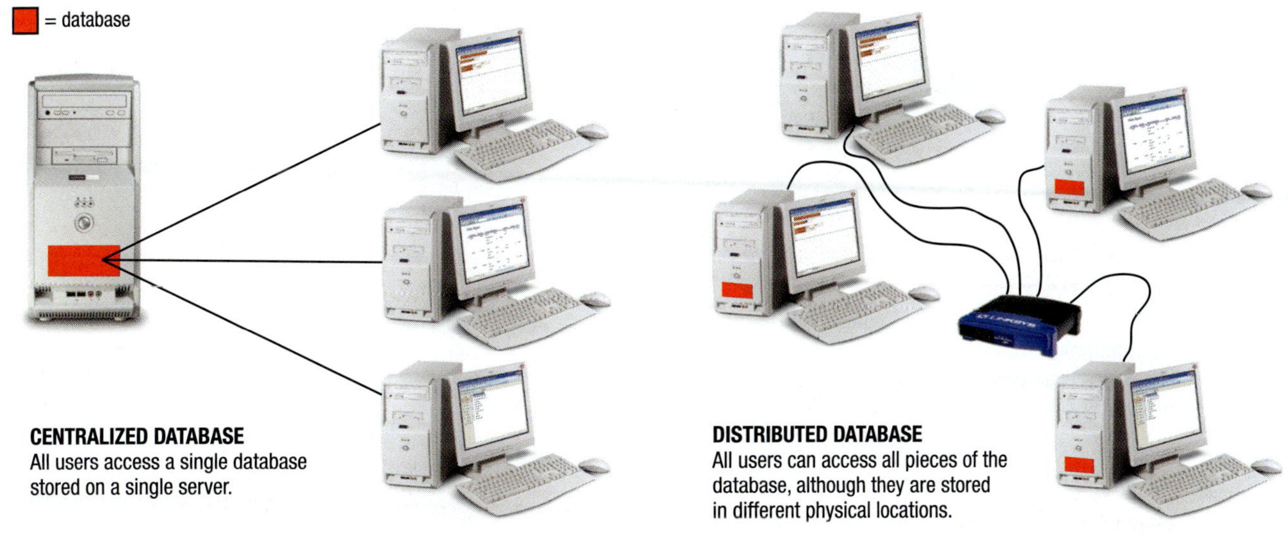

FIGURE 14-12
Centralized vs. distributed databases.

Centralized vs. Distributed Database Systems

With a *centralized database system*, a database is located in its entirety on a single computer, such as a server or mainframe computer. With a *distributed database system*, the data is divided among several computers connected via a network (see Figure 14-12). With a distributed database system, the data is logically set up as belonging to a single database and appears that way to the user. Consequently, it can be accessed by any authorized user through the network, regardless of the computer on which the requested data is physically stored. For example, customer addresses may be stored at the corporate headquarters while customer credit histories may be stored in the credit department located in another office across town, but employees in the credit department can access the customer-address information seamlessly without knowing where the data is stored.

In determining the location where specific data is to be stored in a distributed DBMS, factors such as communications cost, response time, storage cost, and security are key considerations. In addition, data is often placed at the sites at which they are needed most frequently and best managed. When the user requests information from a distributed DBMS, the DBMS displays the data and the user is typically not aware of the steps performed by the DBMS to display the requested information.

In-Memory Databases

While most databases are stored on hard drives, the use of *in-memory databases (IMDBs)*—databases that are designed to hold all data in the main memory of the computer, rather than on disk—is growing because of the lower cost of RAM today and the need for faster processing. In-memory databases can perform dramatically faster than disk-based databases; however, backing up data or otherwise periodically storing the data on a nonvolatile medium is extremely important since data in RAM is lost if the computer goes down or power goes out. IMDBs are beginning to be used both in high-end systems where performance is crucial (such as in e-commerce applications) and in small-footprint, embedded applications (such as set-top boxes and other smart consumer electronic devices).

SYS

DATABASE MODELS

As discussed earlier in this chapter and illustrated in Figure 14-3, databases have evolved significantly since the early 1960s. Two older models are the *hierarchical* and *network models*; the models more commonly used today include the *relational*, *object-oriented*, and *multidimensional models*.

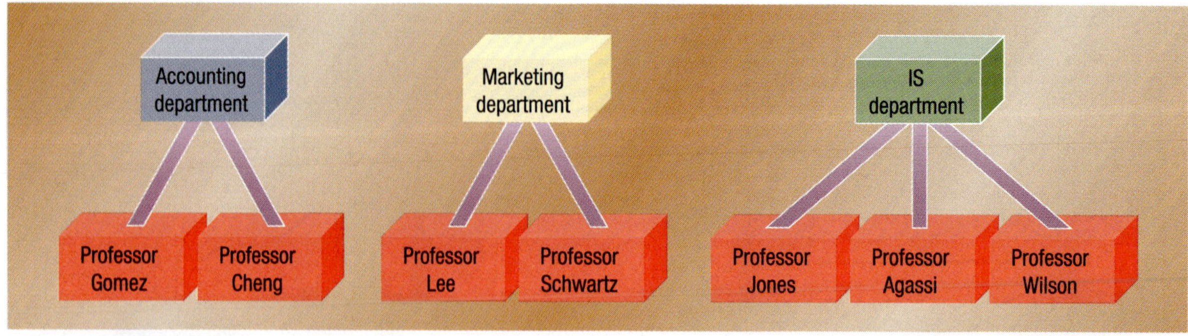

HIERARCHICAL
Hierarchical databases are in the form of a tree, with one-to-many relationships between entities.

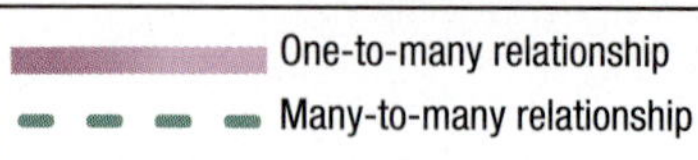

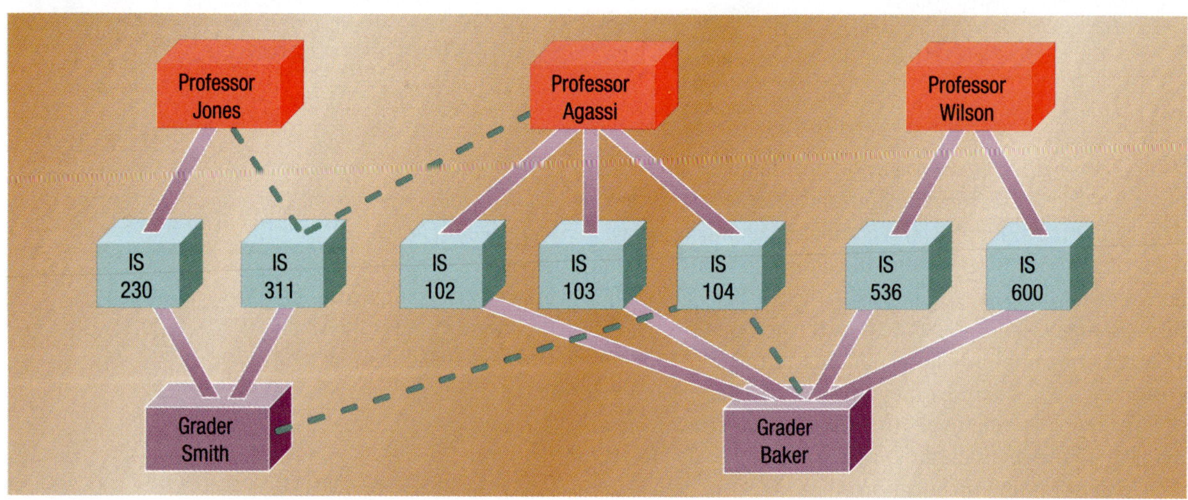

NETWORK
Network databases also use a tree format and can have both one-to-many and many-to-many entity relationships.

Professor table

Course	Professor
IS 230	Jones
IS 311	Jones
IS 311	Agassi
IS 102	Agassi
IS 103	Agassi
IS 104	Agassi
IS 536	Wilson
IS 600	Wilson

Grader table

Course	Grader
IS 230	Smith
IS 311	Smith
IS 102	Baker
IS 103	Baker
IS 104	Baker
IS 104	Smith
IS 536	Baker
IS 600	Baker

Department table

Professor	Department
Jones	IS
Agassi	IS
Wilson	IS

RELATIONAL
Relational databases organize data into tables with little redundancy.

FIGURE 14-13
The hierarchical, network, and relational database models.

The Hierarchical and Network Database Models

The relational database model, discussed earlier in this chapter, is particularly useful in managerial (decision support) retrieval situations in which users are free to pose almost any query to the database. For example, a user might first ask for the price of an item, then request a sales total on a group of items, then see how many units of another item are in stock. In this situation, the database must be designed to be flexible. In other situations, however, the types of queries that users make are highly predictable and limited. For example, in banking, tellers usually only need such facts as current customer account balances, deposits, and withdrawals. In such transaction processing environments, *hierarchical* and *network database models*—which are designed more for speed and security than flexibility—are sometimes used instead of the relational model. However, most databases created today do not use the hierarchical or network models; these models are generally used with *legacy* systems that are still operational and must be maintained. The hierarchical and network models are briefly explained next and illustrated in Figure 14-13.

FURTHER EXPLORATION

For links to further information about database classifications and models, go to www.course.com/uc11/ch14

Hierarchical Databases

A *hierarchical database management system* stores data in the form of a tree, with typically a one-to-many relationship between data entities. For example, each professor in the top part of Figure 14-13 is assigned to one and only one department. If Professor Schwartz was a member of two departments—such as marketing and information systems (IS)—she would have to be represented twice in the database to maintain the hierarchical structure, once under marketing and once under IS. So, when using a hierarchical database model, the DBMS would treat Professor Schwartz as two distinct individuals. She might even get two separate graduation invitations. Such inefficiency can be tolerated, however, if it is relatively rare.

Network Databases

In a *network database management system*, the relationship between data elements is usually either one-to-many or many-to-many. The solid lines in Figure 14-13 depict one-to-many relationships; for example, one professor and one grader can each handle many courses. The dotted lines, on the other hand, represent many-to-many relationships, such as classes that are co-taught by two or more professors or have multiple graders. Network databases with many-to-many relationships are harder to model, but they can always be converted into simple networks consisting of only one-to-many relationships. Sometimes this is done when, as in the earlier case of Professor Schwartz, some minor duplication can be tolerated.

The Relational Database Model

The **relational database management system** (**RDBMS**) is the most widely used database model today. As discussed earlier in this chapter and illustrated in Figure 14-13, relational databases organize data using tables. Tables are independent, but data can be retrieved from related tables using primary key fields whenever necessary to respond to a user's request for information.

Before a relational database can be created, it should be properly designed and the table structure created. Then the process of adding data into the database or otherwise using the database in some hands-on fashion—called *data manipulation*—can be carried out. These topics are discussed next.

>**Relational database management system (RDBMS).** A type of database system in which data is stored in tables related by common fields; the most widely used database model today.

BASIC DATABASE DESIGN PROCEDURES

1. Identify the purpose of the database.
2. Determine the tables and fields to include in the database.
3. Assign the fields to the appropriate table and restructure as needed to minimize redundancy (normalization).
4. Finalize the structure of each table, listing each field's name, type, size, and so on and selecting a primary key (data definition).

FIGURE 14-14
Database design steps.

TIP

When you are beginning to design a new database, sketching a diagram of the reports and other desired database output can be helpful in identifying the necessary fields to be contained in the database.

TIP

For most databases, you will want to stop at 3NF. Although some very specialized applications may require 4NF or 5NF, higher normal forms typically result in slower performance–finding the best balance that results in acceptable performance and the lowest level of redundancy is the optimal goal.

Designing a Relational Database

The steps involved with designing a relational database are summarized in Figure 14-14. As shown in this figure, the first step in designing a relational database is to identify the purpose of the database. Then the data (fields) that need to be included in the database can be determined and the fields can be organized into tables, grouping fields that logically belong together into one table, grouping other fields that belong together into a second table, and so on. Next, primary keys can be determined. Before continuing, it is important to evaluate the proposed table structure to ensure that it is the most appropriate for the data to be collected. At this point, the tables can be restructured, if necessary, to minimize the redundancy of the data. To keep redundancy to a minimum, fields should only be repeated in a table as needed in order to relate the table with other tables. Another consideration when designing and evaluating the basic structure of each table is to ensure the fields are constructed in a manner consistent with the type of information that will need to be extracted from the database. For example, if you want to be able to generate a listing of people by just their last name, two separate fields (such as *Last Name* and *First Name*) should be used instead of just a single field called *Name*.

This process of evaluating and correcting the structures of the tables in a database to minimize data redundancy is called *normalization*. Normalization is usually viewed as a multistep process, from *zero normal form (ZNF)* to usually *third normal form (3NF)*, although procedures exist to reach *fifth normal form (5NF)*. During normalization, one of the most important things to do is ensure that redundant fields from table to table are kept to a minimum. The first three normal forms can be summarized as follows:

- First normal form (1NF)—the table has unique fields (no *repeating groups*—groups of related entries that belong to one unique person or thing, such as a customer, an order, and so forth) and all fields are dependent on the primary key. Any repeating groups have been placed in a second table and related to the original table via a key field (such as customer number or order number).
- Second normal form (2NF)—the table is in 1NF with no *partial dependencies*; that is, fields in a table that are dependent on part of the primary key (if, at this point, the table has a composite primary key), and all fields are dependent on a single primary key or on all fields in a composite primary key. Any partial dependencies have been removed and these dependent fields (such as those containing product information in an order table) are placed in a separate table and related to the original table via a key field, for instance by moving product information to a new table and relating product and order information via a product number field occurring in both tables.
- Third normal form (3NF)—the table is in 2NF with no *transitive dependencies*; that is, two fields that are not primary keys and are dependent on one another, such as the supplier name and supplier number fields in a product table. These dependent fields are placed in a separate table and related to the original table via a key field, for instance by moving the supplier information to a new table and relating the supplier and product information via a supplier number field occurring in both tables.

Once the tables and the data to be stored in each table have been determined, the structure of each table should be developed. As discussed in the Data Definition section earlier in this chapter, the structure includes a unique field name for each field, as well as the data type to be used and the necessary properties (such as field size, any restrictions on input format, and whether or not a field is required) for that field.

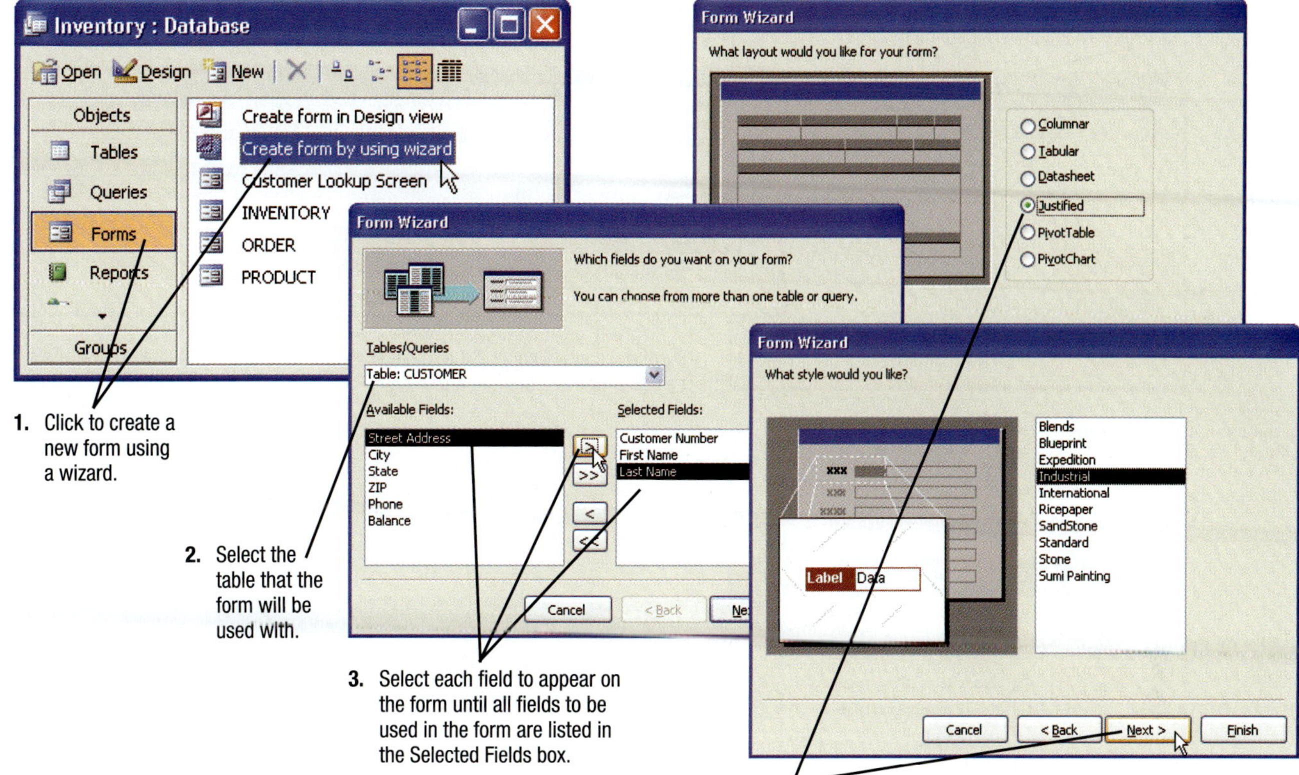

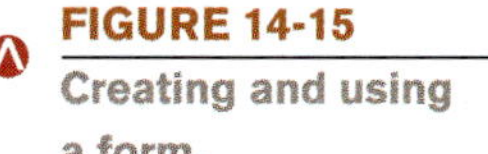
FIGURE 14-15
Creating and using a form.

Creating a Relational Database

To create a relational database, first the structure of each individual table is created (based on the design already determined), and then the actual data can be entered into each table in the database, as illustrated earlier in the chapter in Figure 14-5. If desired, a form can be created and then used to input and edit data (see Figure 14-15). If a wizard is used to create the form (as in Figure 14-15), a basic form will be created based on the input supplied by the user, such as the fields to be included in the form and the overall appearance. Completed forms can then be modified using the Design view for that form, such as to add a title to the form, if desired, or rearrange the input boxes, if needed.

Once a database table has been created, it can be opened using a form or the Datasheet view (see Figure 14-16) and then data can be input and edited, as needed. In either case, the data in the table is being edited. So if a new record is added using a form, for example, the new record will be visible when the table is viewed using Datasheet view, and if an address is edited in Datasheet view, the new address will be visible when the record is viewed using a form.

If a new database is to be used with existing data, the data needs to be transferred from its existing form into the new system—a process called *migration*. Once data has been either entered into a table or migrated to a table and the primary key designated, that table can be *related* to other tables via the primary key so that the primary key can be used to extract data from other tables as needed. The process of relating tables, specifically four tables (Customer, Order, Product, and Inventory) in the Inventory database, is shown in Figure 14-17. This figure also illustrates how, once the tables are related, the related data located in other tables can be viewed from inside one table.

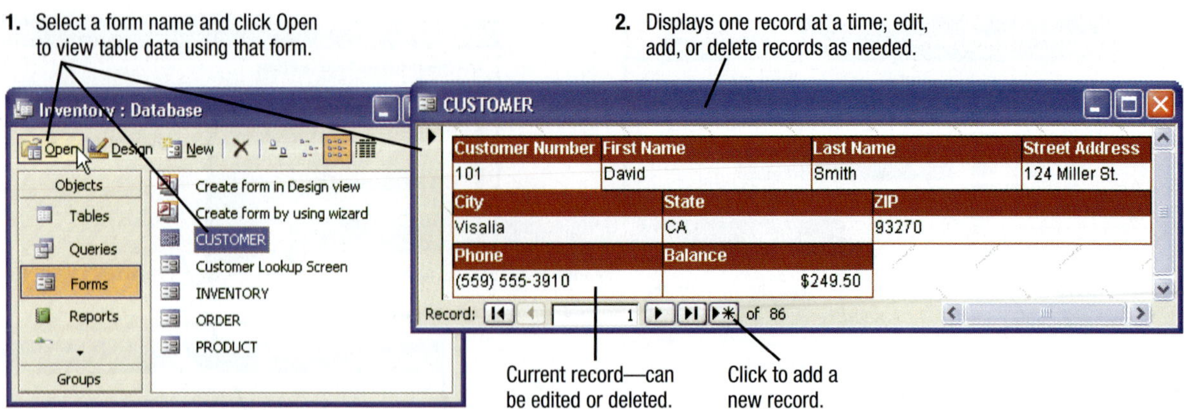

USING A FORM

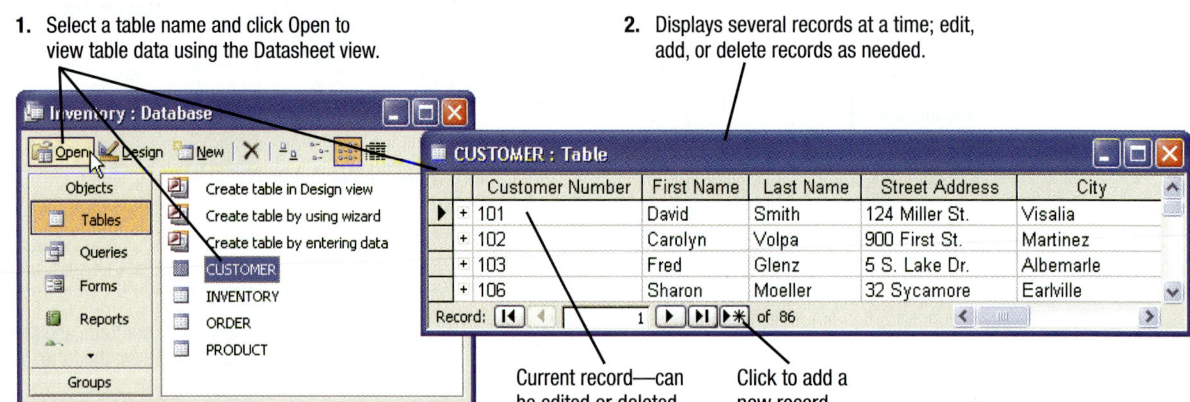

USING THE DATASHEET VIEW

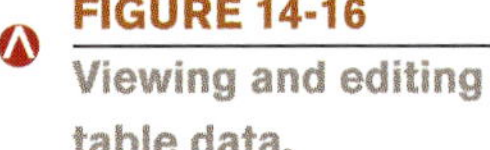

FIGURE 14-16
Viewing and editing table data.

Retrieving Information from a Relational Database

Information retrieval usually takes the form of a *query* or a *report*. A **query** extracts specific information from a database by specifying particular conditions (called *criteria*) about the data you would like to retrieve, such as retrieving all names of customers who live in Tennessee, or all products whose inventory level is below 100 units. Every DBMS provides its own tools through which users query the database for information. One such tool is a *query language*. The query example shown in Figure 14-18 is based on **structured query language** (**SQL**), which is recognized as today's de facto standard for information retrieval in relational databases. When an instruction or other necessary feature cannot be performed using SQL and the other tools available through the DBMS, *database programming* is typically used to write more specific instructions.

The design of the queries to be used with a database system is very important. Queries need to be designed to extract the needed information in as efficient a manner as possible. Poorly written queries can impact the overall performance of the system, especially if they are executed frequently—in some systems, queries may be enacted several times per second. In frequently used queries, even a marginal improvement in performance can significantly improve the overall performance of the system. Consequently, it is the job of the database administrator to identify queries that need improvement and to suggest ways in which to make them perform better. Common techniques include alterations to the query itself to improve its

>**Query.** A request to see information from a database that matches specific criteria. >**Structured query language (SQL).** A popular query language standard for information retrieval in relational databases.

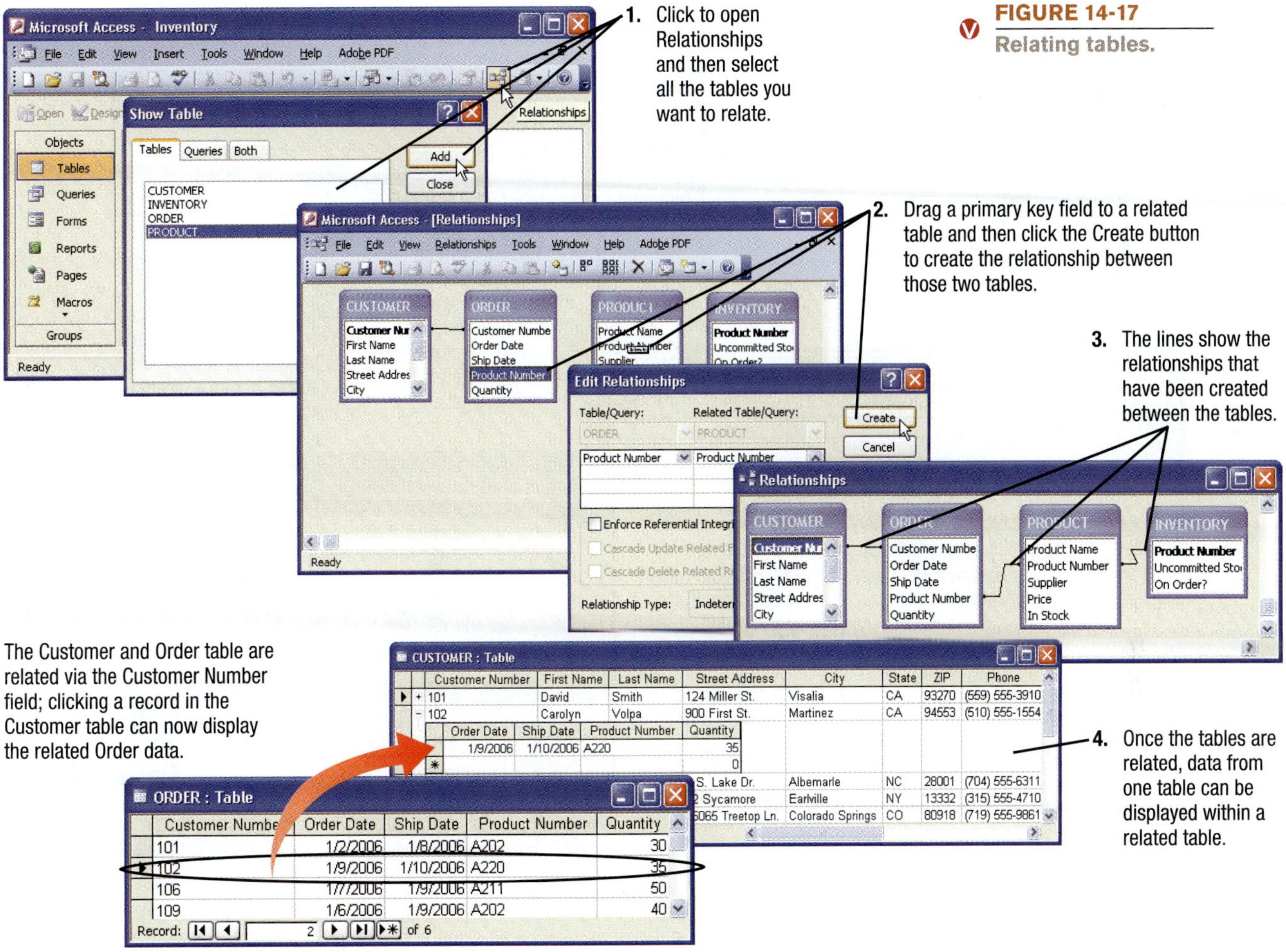

1. Click to open Relationships and then select all the tables you want to relate.
2. Drag a primary key field to a related table and then click the Create button to create the relationship between those two tables.
3. The lines show the relationships that have been created between the tables.
The Customer and Order table are related via the Customer Number field; clicking a record in the Customer table can now display the related Order data.
4. Once the tables are related, data from one table can be displayed within a related table.

FIGURE 14-17
Relating tables.

performance, adding "hints" to the query to tell the database which tables should be accessed first to speed up performance, and adding additional indexes to heavily used tables.

In order to allow individuals to create queries without knowledge of a query language, most DBMSs include wizards or other graphical tools that can be used to create queries quickly and easily. An example of creating a query in this manner is shown in Figure 14-19. Queries can pull information from more than one table at a time, if the tables are related.

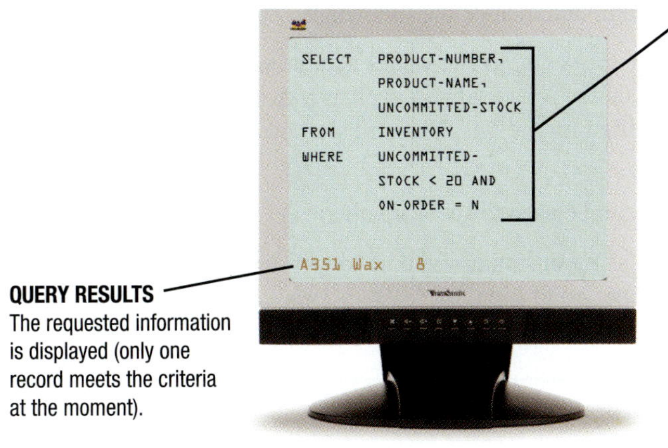

SELECT PRODUCT-NUMBER, PRODUCT-NAME, UNCOMMITTED-STOCK
FROM INVENTORY
WHERE UNCOMMITTED-STOCK < 20 AND ON-ORDER = N
A351 Wax 8
SQL COMMAND
This command selects all records in the Inventory file that have an uncommitted stock level of less than 20 and that are not on order; it outputs the Product Number, Product Name, and Uncommitted Stock field values for each matching record.
QUERY RESULTS
The requested information is displayed (only one record meets the criteria at the moment).

FIGURE 14-18
Querying a database using structured query language (SQL). This example pulls information from the database illustrated in Figure 14-1.

SYS

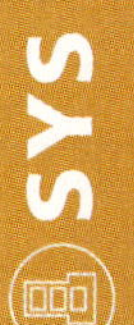

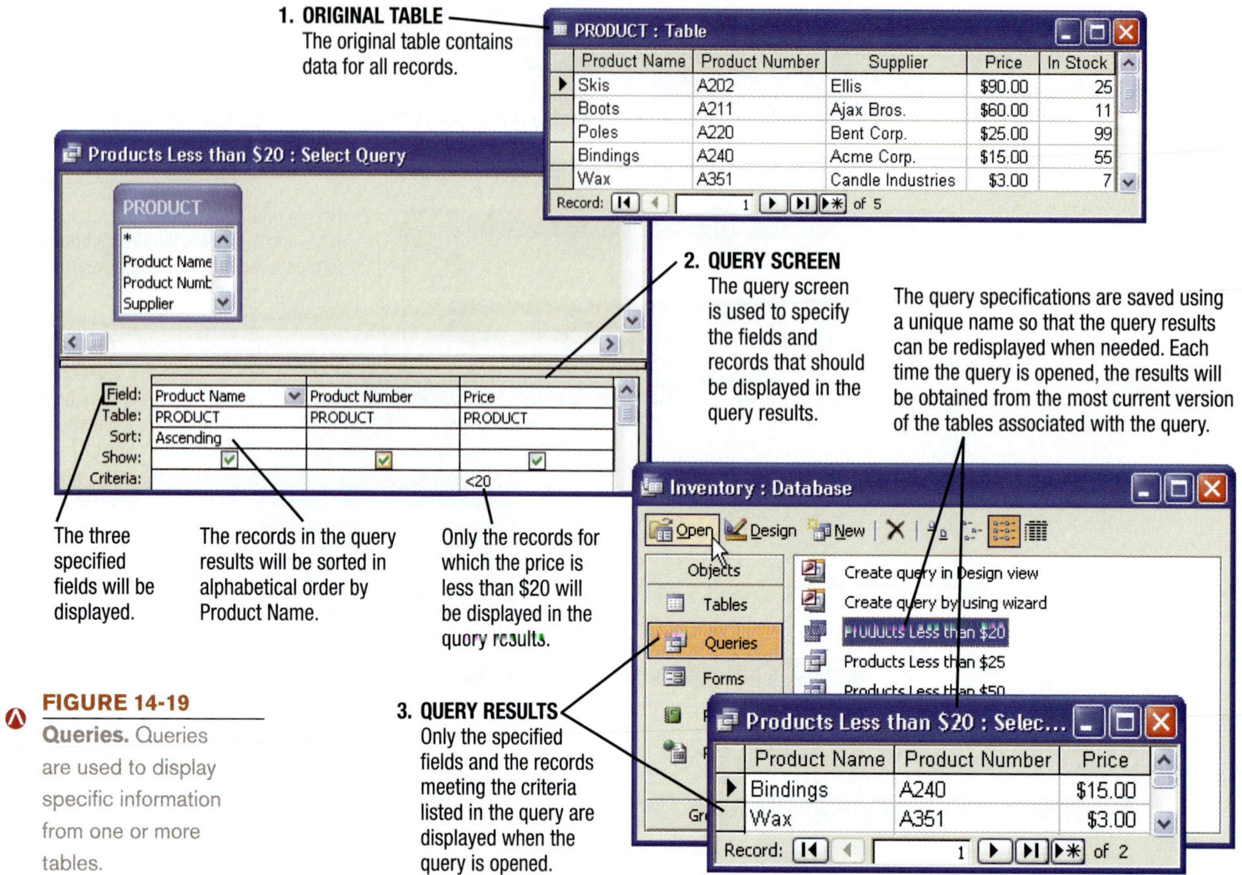

FIGURE 14-19
Queries. Queries are used to display specific information from one or more tables.

DBMS programs also usually include wizards for creating **reports**. In essence, a report is a more formal, formatted way of looking at the data contained in a database. A report can be designed to include all the data from one or more tables, or it can be designed to include just the records retrieved by a query. Just as with queries, reports can pull information from more than one table at a time, if the tables are related. An example of a report is shown in Figure 14-20.

Maintaining a Relational Database

Although small, personal databases may need little or no maintenance, large enterprise databases frequently require regular maintenance. Maintenance activities are usually performed by the database administrator and include the following:

- Modifying the table structure to accommodate values that turned out to be different than anticipated when the database was designed, such as a customer last name that is longer then field size specified for the Last Name field or adding the extra 4 digits to a 5-digit ZIP code field.
- Adding new indexes, which can be used to speed up queries.
- Deleting obsolete data, such as for customers who no longer exist or who have not placed orders for a specified period of time.

>**Report.** A formatted means of looking at a database table or the results of a query.

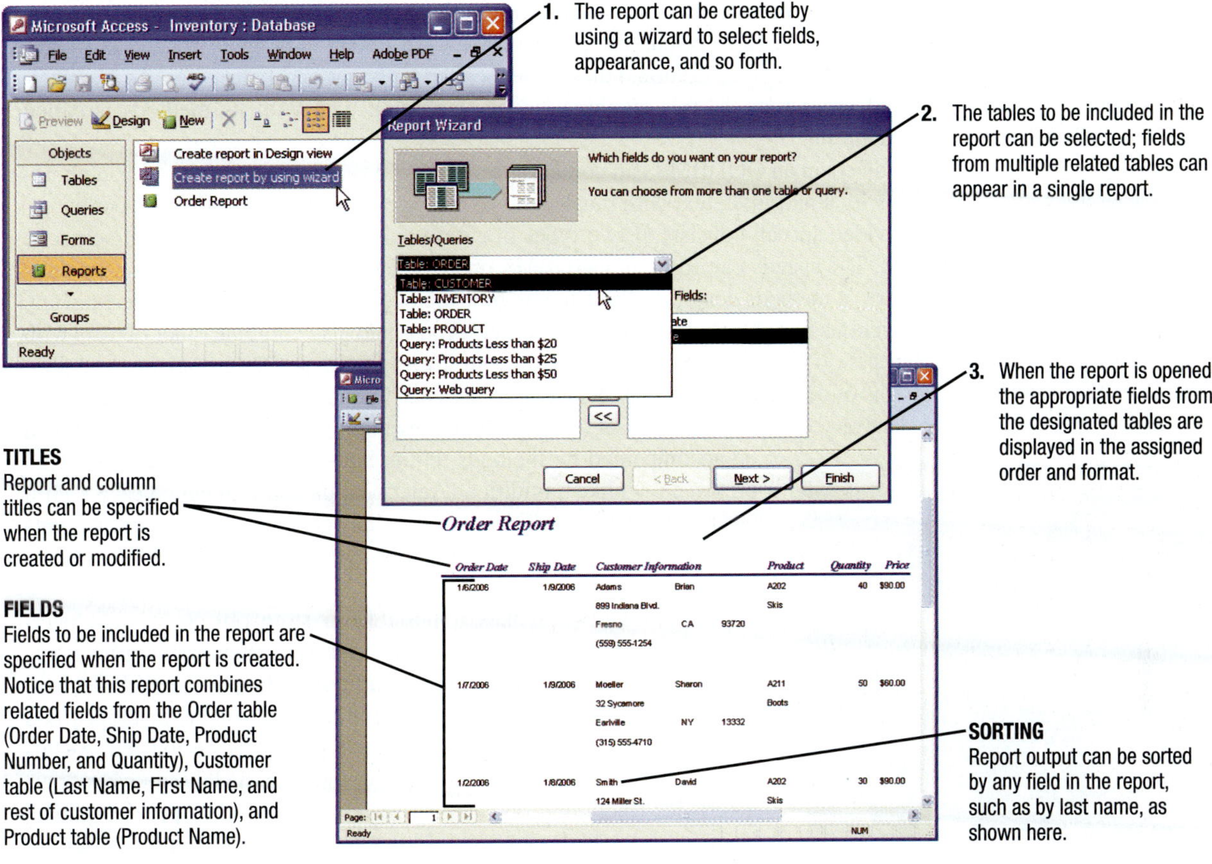

FIGURE 14-20

Reports. Reports display table information with a more formal, businesslike appearance.

- Upgrading the database software and installing patches as needed.
- Repairing or restoring data that has become corrupt, perhaps as the result of a disk error or computer virus.
- Continuing to evaluate and improve the security measured used with the database.

The Object-Oriented Database Model

Traditionally, data management software has dealt with *structured* types of data, that is, primarily text-based data that can be organized neatly into columns (fields) and rows (records). Structured data is the type you have mostly been reading about in this chapter and probably the type you have been working with on your PC. However, user needs and technologies have led to a new type of data that has changed the traditional approach to data management. In addition to handling conventional record data (such as text, numbers, and dates), computer databases are now being used to store documents, diagrams, still photographs, video, animation, and sound. The growing use of databases in conjunction with Web pages and the rising number of computer users who desire a wide variety of data to be presented in a natural-looking way that resembles experiences from real life have been big factors in pushing database developers to cater to these new data types. The growing interest in other data types and the need to include them in a database format that accommodates multimedia have given rise to the **object-oriented database management system (OODBMS)**.

SYS

>Object-oriented database management system (OODBMS). A type of database system in which multiple types of data are stored as objects along with their related code.

FIGURE 14-21

Object-oriented databases. The database shown here contains images and information from the Sloan Digital Sky Survey, an astronomical survey that is in the process of mapping one-quarter of the entire sky in detail, including more than 100 million celestial objects.

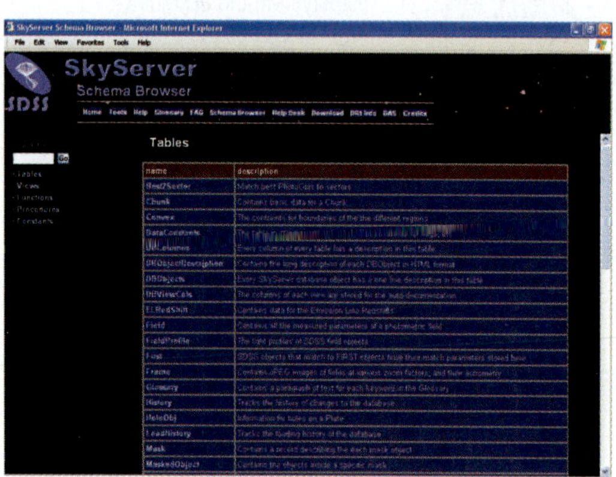

VIEWING THE SCHEMA

This Web page is used to view the various tables, views, functions, procedures, and constants used with this database; currently the tables are listed.

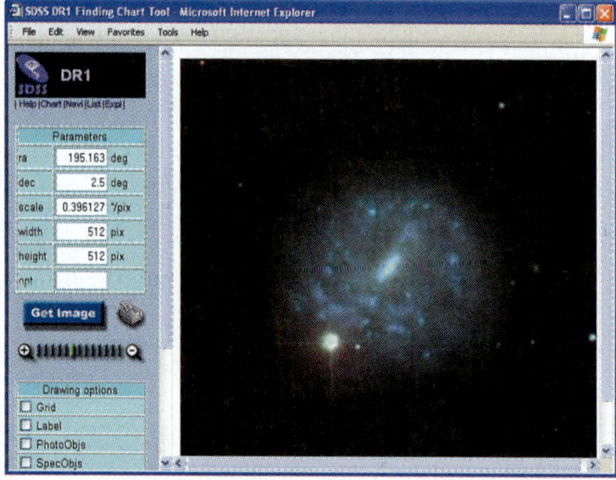

USING THE DATABASE

By entering location parameters using one of the provided forms or by typing an SQL query, images can be retrieved from the database.

Objects in an OODBMS are similar in concept to the objects in an object-oriented programming application, discussed in Chapter 13. An object is a set of related attributes along with the *methods* (actions) that are associated with that set of attributes. As in object-oriented programming, this combination of combining data with its methods is called *encapsulation*.

Objects in an OODBMS can contain virtually any type of data—a video clip, a photograph with a narrative, text with music, and so on—along with its related code. For example, a video speech consists of two types of data: voice and a moving image of someone talking. The speech can form an OODBMS object made up of voice, moving-image data, and a set of methods describing how to combine the two when the speech is played and any other actions that should occur with that object. You could also combine other objects with the speech. If the speech is on the environment, for example, pollution statistics and photographs of defoliated areas may be useful to include. These, too, would exist as objects in the database, each with its own set of methods. For example, the pollution statistics would be accompanied by methods telling how the data should be displayed on screen. Unlike a traditional relational database in which each record has a similar format, little similarity may exist among the data elements that form the objects. An example of a Web-based OODBMS is shown in Figure 14-21.

An OODBMS makes it possible to store objects in an object-oriented database, as well as to copy and paste them into applications, where people can access them and manipulate them as needed. Because all stored objects are reusable, new applications can be developed in a fraction of the time it took before this type of DBMS existed. At this time there is not one single standard for the OODBMS, but its key characteristics (including objects, methods, encapsulation, polymorphism, classes, and inheritance) are similar to the object-oriented programming principles discussed in Chapter 13. Object-oriented databases are generally accessed using an object-oriented programming language, such as Java or C++, or an *object query language* (*OQL*), essentially an object-oriented version of SQL. The ability to directly manipulate data stored in an object-oriented database using an object-oriented programming language is called *transparent persistence*.

Although it is not expected that object-oriented databases will replace relational databases any time soon, the use of object-oriented database fundamentals is expected to grow in popularity as existing traditional databases need to include more complex, nontraditional content, such as multimedia elements. An OODBMS is faster, more efficient, and more appropriate for some applications than other database models—especially for very large volumes of data. OODBMSs are becoming more common on Java servers and databases accessed via the Internet.

A new type of relational DBMS is the *object-relational database management system* (*ORDBMS*). These hybrid systems, such as recent versions of the Oracle program, are DBMSs that combine object and relational technology. Some industry observers speculate that object-relational databases will eventually replace relational databases as the standard for desktop PCs.

Multidimensional Databases

The growth and importance of data warehousing today has led to another type of database model—the **multidimensional database** (**MDDB**). Whereas relational databases are good for transactional applications in which data is retrieved or updated typically by rows and object-oriented databases are appropriate when a variety of types of objects need to be stored and retrieved, multidimensional databases are designed to store a collection of summarized data for quick and easy data analysis. The data is typically collected from a variety of enterprise-wide activities and is then summarized and restructured so that it can be viewed from multiple perspectives—called *dimensions*. For example, sales for a company could be viewed in the dimension of product model, geography, time, or salesperson, or viewed as a combination of dimensions, such as sales by a particular product model in the southwest United States for Quarter 2 in 2006. The dimensions for each application are predefined, based on what are viewed to be meaningful for that particular application, and the summarized data values are automatically calculated. Multidimensional databases are frequently created and updated using data input from existing relational databases.

One of the most common types of software used in conjunction with a multidimensional database is *Online Analytical Processing* (*OLAP*). According to SAS, a leader in business intelligence and analytics, OLAP is typically implemented in one of three ways. With *MOLAP* (*Multidimensional OLAP*), data is stored in single multidimensional database structures (sometimes called *data cubes*). With *ROLAP* (*Relational OLAP*), the multidimensional information is stored in an existing relational database using tables to store the summary information. With *HOLAP* (*Hybrid OLAP*), a combination of MOLAP and ROLAP technologies are used.

DATABASES AND THE WEB

Databases are extremely common on the Web. Virtually all companies that offer product information, online ordering, research resources, or similar activities via a Web site use a database. The most common applications involve a three-tier structure, in which the browser passes the request to a Web server, which passes it on to the database.

Examples of Web Databases in Use

There are scores of examples of how databases can be used on the Web. Databases facilitate information retrieval and processing, as well as allow more interactive, dynamic content. A few specific examples that provide the context in which Web-enabled databases may be encountered are covered next. Following these sections is a discussion and example of how a Web database might work and a brief look at issues related to Web databases. For a look at emerging search-related Web-based database applications, see the Trend box.

Information Retrieval

By their very nature, databases lend themselves to Web-based information retrieval—the Web is, in essence, a huge storehouse of data waiting to be retrieved. Data to be accessed and displayed via a Web page is typically stored in a database, and Web site visitors can request and view information upon demand, as shown in Figure 14-22. The information retrieved and displayed can be product information, press releases, maps, photographs, documents, Web page hits, and so forth. Information retrieved from organizations, as well as search sites and reference sites, fits into this category.

>**Multidimensional database (MDDB).** A type of database in which data can be viewed from multiple dimensions; commonly used with data warehousing.

TREND

Innovative New Search Possibilities

As many search site users already know, search sites and databases are interrelated. In order to return a list of matching Web pages without searching the Web in real time, a search database containing data about Web pages is used. But emerging search options go beyond keyword searches. They are moving toward providing an increasing amount of information to a variety of devices, and the information is becoming more and more tailored to the individual. As discussed in Chapter 8, one of the most popular search sites—Google—is continually adding new search features, such as package tracking, conversions and calculations, address searches, mapping, and more. Yahoo! Maps allows you to add points of interest—such as Wi-Fi hotspots, hotels, schools, restaurants, post offices, grocery stores, and ATM machines—to maps displayed with its service. One new related application is the use by some Web sites of Google's mapping database in combination with data in other databases in order to offer visual information not previously available. For instance, the Housingmaps.com Web site shown in the accompanying screen shot uses Google's mapping data in conjunction with a Craigslist database about homes for sale or rent to allow individuals to display only those homes for sale or rent in a particular area and particular price range. Other sites use Google maps and other databases to display maps of other items of interest, including maps of the cheapest gas in a particular area and the locations of registered sexual predators.

As individuals perform more and more searching via their smart phones, new search capabilities are expected to be developed to increasingly offer personalized information based on an individual's location. Other search databases are including more data on images, sounds, and video. For instance, one site uses speech-recognition technology to turn the audio tracks of movies into searchable text. According to one engineer at Microsoft, searches in the future will be as good as having 1,000 human experts who know your tastes scanning billions of documents within a split second. Now that's a personalized search.

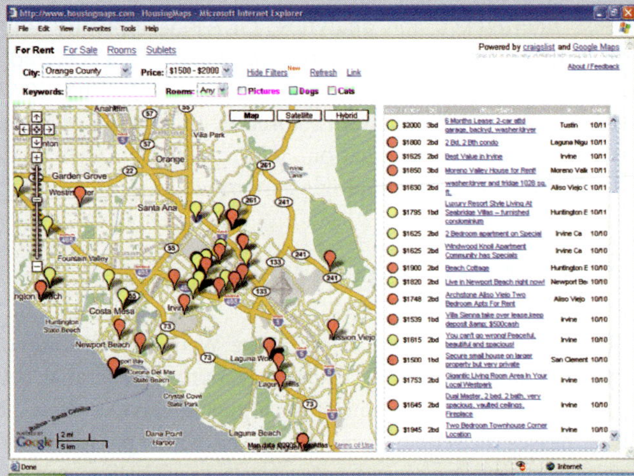

Housingmaps.com

FIGURE 14-22
Database use on the Web.

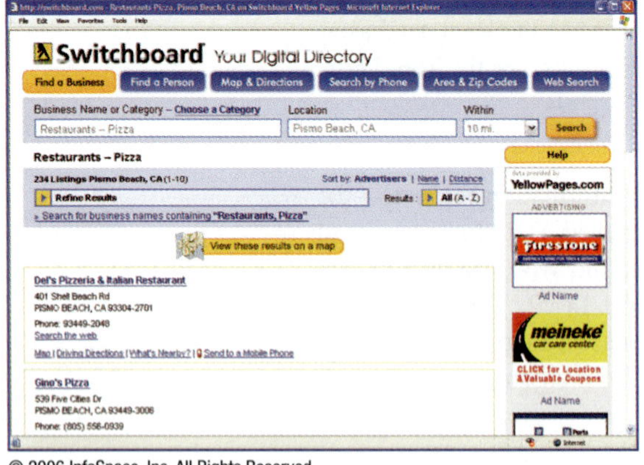

REFERENCE SITE
This site stores address information for individuals and businesses in the United States. After the user enters a name or category and location (in this case, pizza parlors in Pismo Beach, California), the matching information is retrieved from the database.

DYNAMIC SITE
This site retrieves information from its database to create a personalized page for signed-in viewers, such as recently viewed products, recommendations based on viewed and purchased products, and so forth.

Dynamic Web Pages

Static Web pages display the same information for everyone, each time the page is displayed, until the Web page file is modified. In contrast, the appearance and content of *dynamic* Web pages change based on a user's input. This input can be based on selections specified on a form located on the page or controlled by some other aspect, such as a cookie, Java applet, ActiveX control, or the activities that the user has already performed on the site, such as specifying personal settings or clicking a product's hyperlink. Most dynamic Web pages utilize databases.

Used in conjunction with a database, a dynamic Web page can feature more customized content. One example of a dynamic Web page—a personal portal page displaying the user's specified content—was shown in Figure 8-26 in Chapter 8. Another example is shown in Figure 14-22. As shown in this figure, the Amazon.com Web site displays personalized data for signed-in visitors, including a list of recently viewed products and suggestions for products the user might be interested in, based on the products viewed or purchased in the past. Although dynamic Web pages are almost always slower than static ones, they result in a more engaging experience for the user.

E-Commerce

Another widely used database application on the Web is to support and facilitate e-commerce. Catalog information, pricing, customer information, shopping cart contents, and more can be stored in a database to be retrieved on demand using an appropriate script or program to link the database with the Web site (as illustrated in Figure 14-23). A growing customer service trend is to enable customers to track the status of their order or shipment, as discussed in the How it Works box.

FIGURE 14-23
A Web database in action.

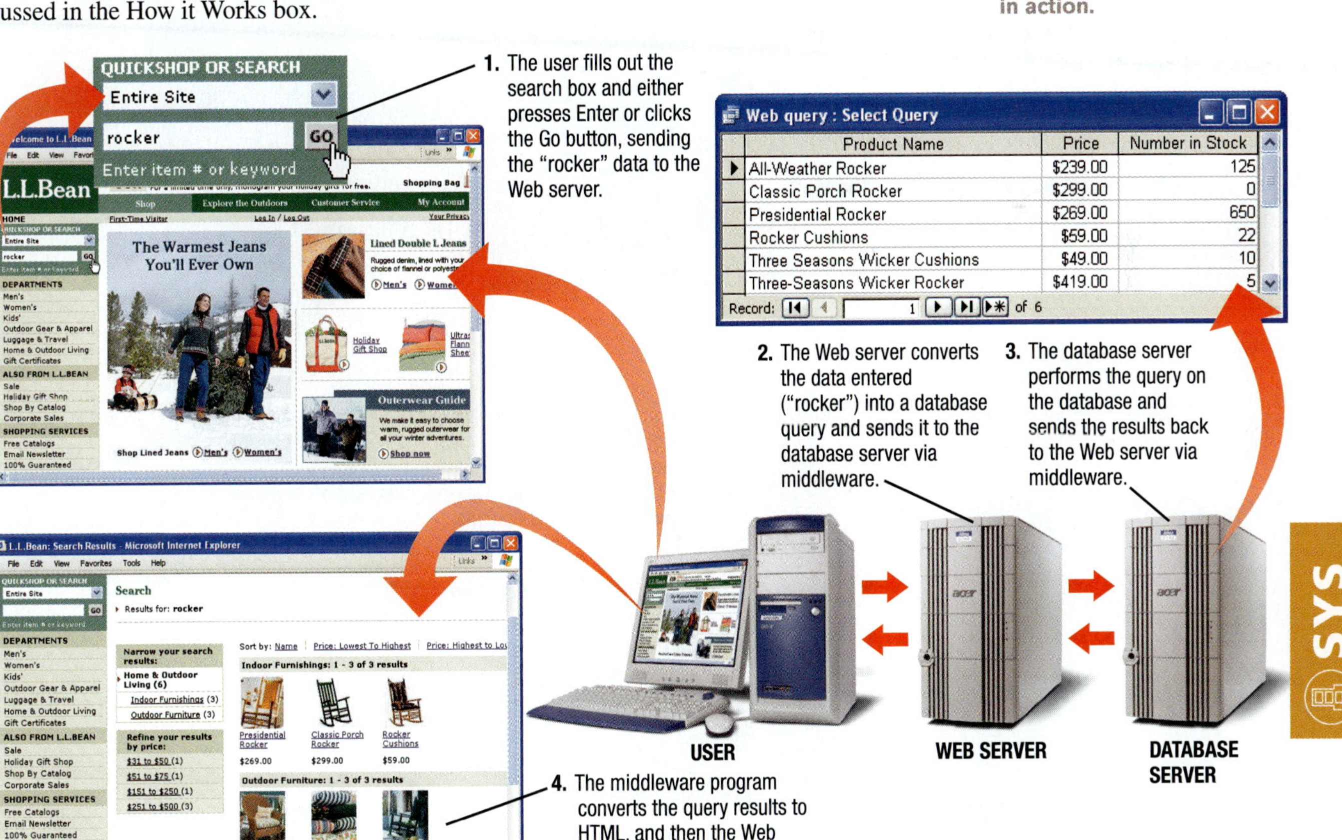

SYS

HOW IT WORKS

Web-Based Customer Service and Package Tracking

As discussed in earlier chapters, Web-based customer service (eCRM) is a rapidly growing trend. Either to supplement or to replace telephone-based customer support, many organizations are offering customers information through the company's Web site. Many eCRM services require the use of a database. After a customer places an order, for example, he or she can use the company's Web site to check the status of the order, to see when the order was shipped, and to use the shipper's package tracking system to find out when it will be delivered (see the accompanying illustration). All of these applications require databases.

Package shipment companies, such as FedEx and UPS, as well as the U.S. Postal Service have online tracking services. Data about all shipments are recorded periodically during the shipping process, such as when packages enter or leave a facility or vehicle. By entering a tracking number into the shipper's Web site or by using a tracking link located on an order status page or e-mail receipt, the status of the shipment can be retrieved from the corresponding database. The tracking information indicates where the package has been scanned, so its approximate location can be estimated. Once the package has arrived, the delivery date and time are also recorded in the database. Some shippers also include delivery signatures in their databases, which can be viewed via the tracking number, in addition to the other shipping information.

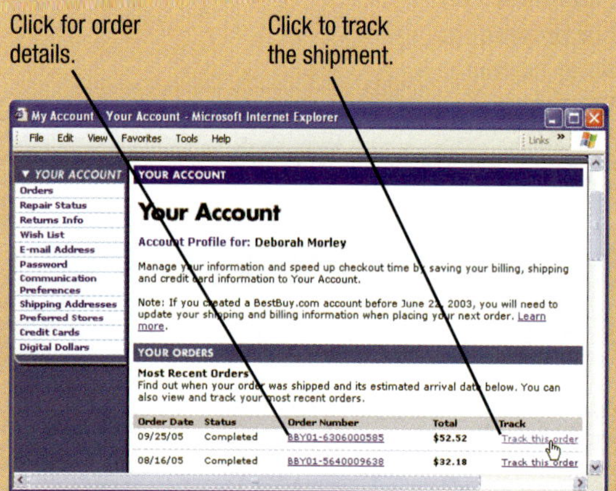

1. With many e-commerce sites, customers can log on to their account to view the status of their orders. Once the order has shipped, it can be tracked through a link on the Web site or e-mail receipt, through the shipper's Web site, or through a Google search.

2. When the package is shipped, it is given a number that is used to track the package throughout the shipping process. As the package travels from location to location, it is scanned to record its arrival and departure from that location, and the tracking information is updated.

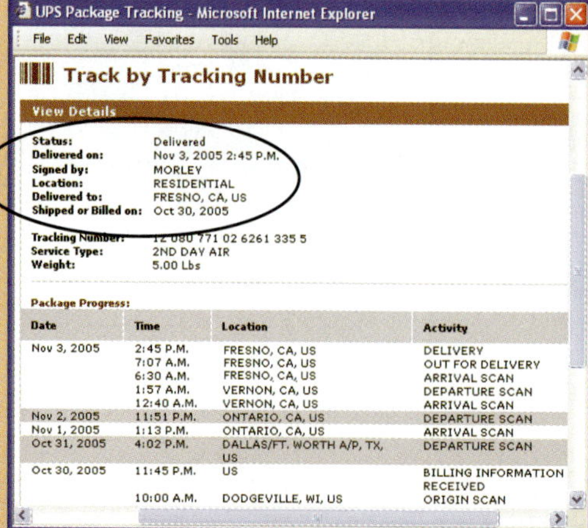

Date	Time	Location	Activity
Nov 3, 2005	2:45 P.M.	FRESNO, CA, US	DELIVERY
	7:07 A.M.	FRESNO, CA, US	OUT FOR DELIVERY
	6:30 A.M.	FRESNO, CA, US	ARRIVAL SCAN
	1:57 A.M.	VERNON, CA, US	DEPARTURE SCAN
	12:40 A.M.	VERNON, CA, US	ARRIVAL SCAN
Nov 2, 2005	11:51 P.M.	ONTARIO, CA, US	DEPARTURE SCAN
Nov 1, 2005	1:13 P.M.	ONTARIO, CA, US	ARRIVAL SCAN
Oct 31, 2005	4:02 P.M.	DALLAS/FT. WORTH A/P, TX, US	DEPARTURE SCAN
Oct 30, 2005	11:45 P.M.	US	BILLING INFORMATION RECEIVED
	10:00 A.M.	DODGEVILLE, WI, US	ORIGIN SCAN

3. Any time during the shipping process when the customer tracks the package, he or she will see its current location. When the package arrives at its destination, the delivery is recorded and noted on the tracking page. Delivery signatures (captured in digital form) are also entered into the database so they can be displayed upon request.

How Web Databases Work

The following example further illustrates how databases and the Web can work together.

Web Databases: A Simple Example

The request to retrieve information from or store data in a Web database is typically initiated by the Web site visitor. Filling out a Web page form or selecting an option from a displayed menu are common ways Web-based database requests are made. The request is received by the Web server, which then converts the request into a database query and passes it on to the database server with the help of intermediary software called *middleware*, discussed in the next section. The database server retrieves the appropriate information and returns it to the Web server (again, via middleware) where it is displayed on the visitor's screen in the form of a Web page (refer again to Figure 14-23).

FURTHER EXPLORATION

For links to further information about Web-based databases, go to www.course.com/uc11/ch14

Middleware

Software that connects two otherwise separate applications—such as a Web server and a DBMS, as in Figure 14-23—is referred to as **middleware**. Middleware for Web database applications is commonly written as *scripts*—short sections of code written in a programming or scripting language that are executed by another program. Two of the most commonly used are *CGI* and *API*. A newer scripting language becoming increasingly more popular is *PHP*. As an alternative to writing scripts from scratch, many Web site authoring programs include capabilities to generate the appropriate scripts for dynamic Web pages when the developer selects the appropriate menu options and supplies the needed information. This capability allows even novice Web developers to easily include input forms on their sites, as well as connect their site and a database, without having to write any scripts directly.

CGI

A *CGI* (*common gateway interface*) *script* is a set of instructions written in a programming language (such as C++, Perl, Java, or Visual Basic) that is designed to accept data from and return data to a Web page visitor. CGI scripts usually reside on the Web server and handle tasks, such as processing input forms and information requests. On very busy sites, CGI can slow down server response time significantly because it processes each request individually.

API

To alleviate the inefficiency problems that result from using CGI on busy Web sites, the server's *API* (*application program interface*) can be used. An API is an interface designed for a particular operating system or application program and can be used to make requests of that operating system or program. Common APIs used with Web databases include *ISAPI* (*Internet Server Application Program Interface*) for Windows-based Web servers and *NSAPI* (*Netscape Server API*) for Netscape Web servers. On the Web, API applications are increasingly being used instead of CGI scripts because they run faster.

PHP

PHP (*PHP Hypertext Preprocessor*) is a scripting language that is increasingly being used to create dynamic Web pages. It uses code similar to Perl or C that is inserted into the HTML code of a Web page using special *PHP tags*. This allows Web page authors to jump between HTML and PHP when they are creating the page. PHP is a server-side script, so the client PC cannot view the PHP code. PHP is typically used to perform tasks similar to CGI and API, but it has the advantage of high compatibility with many types of databases. It is also an open-source program, available free to all users.

SYS

>**Middleware.** Software used to connect two otherwise separate applications, such as a Web server and a database management system.

SUMMARY

WHAT IS A DATABASE?

Chapter Objective 1:
Explain what a database is, including common database terminology, and list some of the advantages and disadvantages of using databases.

A **database** is a collection of related data that is stored and organized in a manner that allows information to be retrieved as needed. Most databases consist of one or more **tables**; each table contains a collection of related **records** (**rows**), each of which, in turn, is a collection of related **fields** (**columns**).

A **database management system** (**DBMS**) is a software program used to create database applications and information to be stored in or retrieved from more than one table at a time. A *relational database* is the most common type of computerized database. This type of database relates data in various database tables by using a **primary key**—a field in each table that contains unique data that is unlikely to change.

The individuals involved with a DBMS include *users*, *database designers*, *database developers*, *database programmers*, and *database administrators*. Over the years, databases have evolved from *flat files* to collections of tables and objects that support interrelated multimedia content with a minimum of data redundancy.

A DBMS can offer several advantages. Among these advantages are better information, faster response time, lower operating costs, lower data storage requirements, improved data integrity, and better data management. The biggest potential disadvantages are cost and a greater vulnerability to failure.

DATA CONCEPTS AND CHARACTERISTICS

Chapter Objective 2:
Discuss some basic concepts and characteristics of data, such as data hierarchy, entity relationships, data definition, and data organization.

Data in a database has a definite hierarchy. Data is entered as characters into fields in the database. Related fields form records, related records form tables, and a group of related tables forms the database.

One task performed by anyone setting up a database is **data definition**—the process of describing data to the DBMS prior to entering it. The descriptions of the data are used to create a *table structure* for each table. This structure contains a description of the data to be entered into the table (field name, data type, and other properties) and a **data dictionary**, which contains information about all data in the application (*metadata*). Different types of databases may relate their **entities** differently. Common types of entity relationships include *one-to-one*, *one-to-many*, and *many-to-many*. A characteristic of an entity is called an **attribute**. Entities typically become database tables; attributes typically become table fields.

Chapter Objective 3:
Describe the importance of data integrity, security, and privacy and how it affects database design.

Because data is so vital to an organization, **data integrity**, **data validation**, and **data security** must be maintained to ensure the quality of information retrieved from the database and the safety of the database. Good data validation techniques (such as specifying an allowable range of values or a mandatory format) enforced on a *per transaction* basis coupled with data locking when data is being modified can help ensure data integrity and data validation. Good access control methods can help increase data security.

Databases typically use **indexes** to more easily locate data when it is requested. In conjunction with or as an alternative to **indexed organization**, **direct organization** can be used. Direct organization uses hashing to provide for rapid direct access. Both indexed and direct organization can be used for *real-time* transaction processing.

DATABASE CLASSIFICATIONS

Database systems can be classified as *single-user* or *multiuser database systems*, depending on how many users need to access the database. In addition, *client-server database systems* are accessed by client computers at the *front end*; the database resides on server computers at the *back end*. In an *n-tier database system*, at least one piece of *middleware* exists between the client and the server.

Chapter Objective 4: Identify some basic database classifications and discuss their differences.

Many applications are set up on *distributed databases*. Instead of a single *central database system* existing on a large centralized mainframe—the most widespread practice for storing database data in large companies—the database is divided among several smaller computers that are connected and accessed via a network. *In-memory databases* (*IMDBs*) hold all data in the main memory of the computer.

DATABASE MODELS

Database models have evolved over time. Traditionally, database systems have conformed to one of three common types: hierarchical, network, and relational, although only the relational model is widely used today. A *hierarchical database management system* stores data in the form of a tree, in which the relationship between data elements is usually one-to-many. In a *network database management system* the relationship between data elements is typically either one-to-many or many-to-many. The **relational database management system** (**RDBMS**) stores data in tables related by primary keys and is the most widely used database model today. The growing interest in other data types and the need to combine them into multimedia formats for applications have given rise to the **object-oriented database management system** (**OODBMS**). These databases combine disparate data types into storable entities called *objects*. An object contains both data and relevant code; data can be virtually any type, such as a video clip, photograph, text, or music. Applications such as data warehousing have led to a fifth type of data model—the **multidimensional database** (**MDDB**).

Chapter Objective 5: List the most common database models and discuss how they are used today.

To create a relational database, the structure of the database is designed based on the purpose of the database, the fields that need to be included, and the relationships between them. The tables are evaluated and modified as needed to minimize redundancy—a process called *normalization*. *Third-normal form* (*3NF*) is common for business applications. Next, the structure of each table is created, and then data can be entered into the database. Information is usually retrieved using **queries** and **reports**. Queries most often use **structured query language** (**SQL**). Once a database has been designed and created, regular maintenance activities are needed.

Chapter Objective 6: Understand how a relational database is designed, created, used, and maintained.

DATABASES AND THE WEB

Database applications are plentiful on the Web. When information is retrieved via an input form or other interactive element on a Web page, a database is used. In addition to information retrieval, e-commerce and *dynamic* Web pages are database oriented.

Chapter Objective 7: Describe some ways databases are used on the Web.

When a request for information is transferred from a Web page to a database, it is converted—using **middleware** software—to a request the database can process. The retrieved information is then passed back to the Web server and displayed in the form of a Web page.

REVIEW ACTIVITIES

KEY TERM MATCHING

a. database

b. data dictionary

c. data validation

d. index

e. middleware

f. primary key

g. query

h. record

i. relational database management system (RDBMS)

j. table

Instructions: Match each key term on the left with the definition on the right that best describes it.

1. _______ A collection of related data that is stored in a manner enabling information to be retrieved as needed.
2. _______ A collection of related fields in a database. Also called a row.
3. _______ A request to see information from a database that matches specific criteria.
4. _______ A small table containing a primary key and the location of the record belonging to that key; used to locate records in a database.
5. _______ A specific field in a database table that uniquely identifies the records in that table.
6. _______ A type of database system in which data is stored in tables related by common fields; the most widely used database model today.
7. _______ In a relational database, a collection of related records (rows).
8. _______ Software used to connect two otherwise separate applications, such as a Web server and a database management system.
9. _______ The process of ensuring that data entered into a database matches the data definition.
10. _______ The repository of all data definitions in a database.

SELF-QUIZ

Instructions: Circle **T** if the statement is true, **F** if the statement is false, or write the best answer in the space provided. **Answers to the self-quiz are located in the References and Resources Guide at the end of the book**.

1. T F In a relational database, more than one table can be included in a database.
2. T F Metadata is stored in the data dictionary.
3. T F Using usernames and passwords is a data validation technique.
4. T F The network database model is the most widely used model today.
5. T F Databases are commonly used to implement dynamic Web pages.
6. In a student information database, *Name* would be considered a(n) _______ in the table, while all of Jennifer Mitchell's information would be called a(n) _______.
7. Data _______ refers to the accuracy of data.
8. When direct organization is used, a(n) _______ procedure determines where data is stored.
9. The terms *front end* and *back end* refer to _______ database systems.
10. Match each term with its example and write the corresponding number in the blank to the left of the example.

    a. _______ When the database does not allow a user to enter a letter in a phone number field.
    b. _______ Requiring users to log on to a database system via a thumbprint scanner.
    c. _______ Assigning a field the property of "required."
    d. _______ Contains data about the data in a database.

    1. Data dictionary **2.** Data definition **3.** Data integrity **4.** Data security

EXERCISES

1. Would the data type Text, Number, or Yes/No be the most appropriate for a telephone number field that needs to store data in the format (123)555-7890? Explain your answer.
2. Of the following fields, which would be the most appropriate for the primary key in a customer information table? Explain your answer.

   a. Customer Name **b.** Customer Number **c.** Phone Number **d.** Customer Address
3. Refer to the two relational database tables below and answer the following questions:

   a. Which employees work in the Accounting department and make at least $60,000 per year?

   b. Which employees have Hurt as their manager?

   c. In which of the preceding questions did you have to relate data in both tables to get an answer? Through what field(s) did you relate the tables?

Employee table

NAME	LOCATION	DEPARTMENT	SALARY
Doney	Phoenix	Accounting	$58,000
James	Cleveland	Sales	$44,000
Giles	San Diego	Accounting	$62,000
Smith	Miami	Accounting	$73,000
Fink	San Diego	Sales	$64,000

Office table

LOCATION	MANAGER
San Diego	Hurt
Cleveland	Holmes
Miami	Jonas
Phoenix	Alexis

4. Suppose that you need to create a two-table database to record information for a video rental store. The following information needs to be recorded:

   - For all movies: Movie number, title, category, rental rate, and whether or not it is available for rent
   - For all customers: Customer number, name, address, city, state, zip, and telephone number
   - For all rented movies: Customer who rented it and due date

Fill in the field names in the two tables below to design a possible two-table database for this scenario, locating the fields in the most appropriate tables and having a minimum of redundancy.

Movie table							
Customer table							

5. For exercise #4 above, is there a field in common in both tables that is appropriate to use as a primary key to relate the two tables? If so, which field? If not, redo Exercise 4 to include an appropriate primary key.

DISCUSSION QUESTION

There are numerous databases that contain personal information about individuals. For instance, information about purchases made via a credit card are contained in the credit card company database; information about births, marriages, home purchases, court judgments, and other public transactions are contained in government databases; address and telephone information are contained in telephone book databases; and so forth. Although in the past, it was difficult to access the data in databases—for instance, you would have to go to the county recorder's office to look up property or marriage records for that county—today much of this data is available online. How do you feel about your personal information being contained in databases that other individuals can access or that might be breached via the Internet? Do you mind that anyone with an Internet connection might be able to find out how much you paid for your house, if you are married, where you live, and other personal information? As more and more personal data is contained in databases, how important is it to you to have those databases protected from unauthorized access?

PROJECTS

HOT TOPICS

1. **Terrorist Databases** There are a number of databases—such as the FBI's *Combined DNA Index Systems* (*CODIS*) and *Integrated Automated Fingerprint Identification System* (*IAFIS*), the military's *Biometrics Automated Toolset* (*BAT*), and Homeland Security Department's *Automated Biometric Identification System* (*IDENT*)—in use today for national security purposes.

   For this project, select one database (either one of the ones listed in the previous paragraph or an alternate database) currently being used for national security purposes. Determine the purpose of the database, who has access to it, and if it has been useful in identifying criminals or terrorists or helpful in other ways. Has there been any movement toward a national database for citizen identification? At the conclusion of your research, prepare a one-page summary of your findings and submit it to your instructor.

SHORT ANSWER/ RESEARCH

2. **ERIC** The world's largest collection of educational information is organized and available through a database called the *Educational Resources Information Center* (*ERIC*). The database was established in 1966 and is supported by the U.S. Department of Education, the Office of Educational Research and Improvement, and the National Library of Education.

   For this project, research ERIC and determine what types of information are available in the ERIC database, and what the terms *digest*, *component*, and *clearinghouse* mean as they relate to ERIC. How can you access ERIC resources? Are they available online? In the library? Where would you go to access ERIC articles? At the conclusion of your research, prepare a one-page summary of your findings and submit it to your instructor.

3. **Normalization** The process of normalizing the data for a database was first proposed by Dr. E. F. Codd in 1972, when President Nixon was in the process of normalizing relations with China (the process was so-named because of Nixon's efforts). The overall objective of normalization is to reduce the redundancy of data in a database and to ensure that update errors do not occur.

   For this project, research the normalization process and determine the name and steps usually involved with the first five normal forms. At what normal form are database designers usually satisfied? Can a database be fully normalized, or is this impractical? What is the difference between unnormalized data, normalized data, and denormalized data? Some say there is a sixth normal form. Try to find out what they are referring to and if, indeed, you believe it is an additional normal form. At the conclusion of your research, prepare a one-page summary of your findings and submit it to your instructor.

HANDS ON

4. **Designing a Database** While designing a database system for a large enterprise is a highly complex task, designing a small relational database can be a fairly straightforward process.

   For this project, design a relational database to contain data about the students, instructors, and class offerings at your school. The database should consist of three tables (one each for students, classes, and instructors), and each table should have at least four fields. Be sure to select an appropriate primary key for each table and determine which of the tables will be related together. On paper, you should design one input screen, one query screen, and one report that might be used with this system, and then you should annotate each of the three designs with the table and field names for each piece of information to be included. Did any of your three designs utilize data from more than one table? If so, make sure that it is possible to do that, based on your table design and stated relationships. Be sure to include at least one sample record for each table in your design documentation. At the conclusion of this project, submit the completed database design to your instructor.

5. **Web Databases** As discussed in the chapter, many Web pages today utilize databases to display information requested by visitors, for customized Web pages, and other dynamic applications.

For this project, visit one Web site that utilizes a database (such as Switchboard.com, the Internet Movie Database Web site located at imdb.com, Google Maps, or Amazon.com) and request some information from the database. Were you satisfied with the results? Did the database return the correct results in a timely manner? Do you have any suggestions to improve the user interface, such as different directions, additional options, and so forth? At the conclusion of this project, submit a summary of your experience and your recommendations to your instructor.

WRITING ABOUT COMPUTERS

6. **Database Protocols** In order for an application program to access a specific database without the programmer having to write code that is unique to that database, the programmer could use an application programming interface (API), as discussed in the chapter. A few of these interfaces are ODBC, DAO, ADO, OLE-DB, and JDBC.

For this project, select two of the APIs listed above (or select alternate APIs) and research them. Determine what the acronyms stand for, who created the APIs, when they are useful, and how they are used. Are there other APIs that can be used for this same purpose as the two you selected? Are the two APIs you selected interchangeable? Submit this project to your instructor in the form of a short paper, not more than two pages in length.

PRESENTATION/ DEMONSTRATION

7. **Certifications** Companies that make database software often establish standards to measure an individual's competence in using that software. In order to accomplish this, the software companies generally develop and offer certification exams in one or more core competencies for each of their database products. The larger database companies, such as Oracle and Sybase, offer several certification exams. Aside from the proprietary database programs, you can also get certified in SQL by a number of different organizations, including IBM.

For this project, research three database certification programs. Find out the organization offering them, how long it takes to complete them, how much the programs and exams cost, and what the employment prospects look like after passing each exam. Try to find jobs that prefer one of your selected database certifications. What positions did you find, and what is the starting salary? Do the jobs require experience as well? A college degree? Would you be interested in taking one of these certification programs? Share your findings with the class in the form of a short presentation. The presentation should not exceed 10 minutes and should make use of one or more presentation aids, such as the chalkboard, handouts, overhead transparencies, or a computer-based slide presentation (your instructor may provide additional requirements). You may also be asked to submit a summary of the presentation to your instructor.

GROUP DISCUSSION

8. **Biometric Access** It is becoming increasingly common for biometric devices to be used to grant or deny access to corporate and government facilities. They are also beginning to be used to identify consumers for financial transactions, such as making ATM withdrawals or cashing checks. Biometric systems can use *one-to-one matching* (where the system authenticates that a person is who he or she claims to be), as well as *one-to-many matching* (where the system tries to identify a person by matching him or her to a photo in a database, such as when facial recognition is used to see if a person photographed at an airport is someone in a database containing known criminals or terrorists). With one-to-one matching, the system needs to be provided with the identity of the person to be authenticated, usually by the individual entering a PIN number or swiping an ID card. The system then obtains the appropriate biometric data (via a hand scanner or iris reader, for example) and checks whether or not that data matches the data stored for the specified individual. With one-to-one matching, the stored biometric data can be located either in a database on the computer or contained only on an ID card or other type of possessed object supplied by the user. Different individuals may have differing opinions as to which type of system is more preferable if they had to use it. For instance, from a convenience standpoint, is one method preferable? What about from a privacy standpoint? What about from a system resource standpoint? In what situations might one system be preferred over the other? If your school or company was going to implement a biometrics system to grant access to facilities, which method would you prefer? Why?

   For this project, form an opinion about one-to-one versus one-to-many matching systems for biometric databases used for access purposes and be prepared to discuss your position (in class, via an online class discussion group, or in a class chat room, depending on your instructor's directions). You may also be asked to write a short paper expressing your opinion.

WEB ACTIVITIES

The *Understanding Computers* Web site located at **www.course.com/uc11** features many resources to help reinforce your understanding of the chapter content and help you prepare for exams. Your instructor may also assign specific activities to be completed that will count toward your final grade in the course.

Instructions: Go to **www.course.com/uc11/ch14** to work the following online activities.

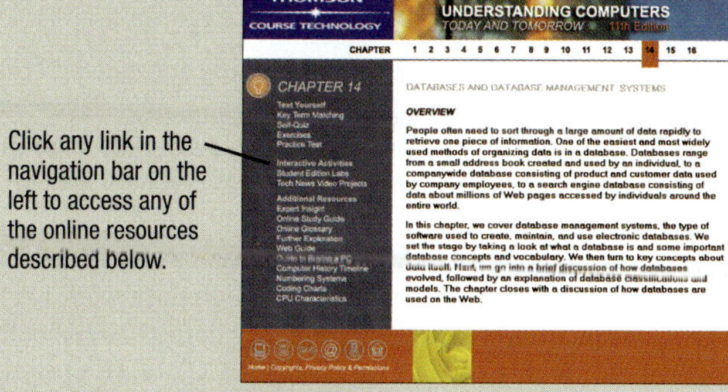

INTERACTIVE ACTIVITIES

1. **Crossword Puzzle** Practice your knowledge of the key terms in Chapter 14 by completing the interactive Crossword Puzzle.
2. **Tech News Video Project** Watch the **"Google Maps Meets Craigslist"** video clip that takes a look at how databases can be integrated with the data in the Google Maps system to display additional information—in this case, housing information from Craigslist—on a Google map. After watching the video online, complete the corresponding project.
3. **Student Edition Labs** Reinforce the concepts you have learned in this chapter by working through the interactive **Advanced Databases** lab.

TEST YOURSELF

1. **Key Term Matching** Test your knowledge of selected chapter key terms by matching the terms with their definitions.
2. **Self-Quiz** Test your retention of chapter concepts by taking the Self-Quiz.
3. **Exercises** Work these short exercises to review the concepts and terms covered in the chapter.
4. **Practice Test** Test how ready you are for an upcoming exam by completing the online Practice Test.

STUDY TOOLS/ ADDITIONAL RESOURCES

The Understanding Computers Web site has a wide range of additional resources, including an **Online Study Guide** (containing study tips, a chapter outline with room to add your own notes, and a chapter checklist of the activities to complete when the chapter is covered in class and when you are preparing for a test) and an **Online Glossary** for each chapter; **Further Exploration** links; a **Web Guide**, a **Guide to Buying a PC**, and a **Computer History Timeline**; more information about **Numbering Systems**, **Coding Charts**, and **CPU Characteristics**; and much, much more!

EXPERT INSIGHT ON . . .

Systems

A conversation with ANTHONY BRIGGS

Business Information Officer for Best Buy

> "Remember that technology is a rapidly growing field...keep learning, because knowledge, and more specifically its application, is power."

My Background . . .

Before college, I took a few programming classes and did some basic programming and data processing for a restaurant chain's corporate office. At West Point, I took additional programming classes and I wrote a number of programs and created databases for a variety of applications during my time in the military. I received an award for one of the database applications I developed—this certainly encouraged me to continue doing IT work and develop my skills.

After the military, I worked as an independent consultant, an MIS Director, and a college instructor teaching classes in programming, databases, and other business applications. I currently work for Best Buy, overseeing information systems for HR, Finance and IT Infrastructure. My duties include delivering and evaluating IT projects, driving down the Total Cost of Ownership (TCO) of IT operations, assessing and implementing future technology solutions, ensuring continual operational readiness, and ensuring compliance with Sarbanes-Oxley and data privacy laws.

Over the years, I've found that a good combination of education and practical experience is important. In addition to my education, my leadership, management and programming experience have been critical success factors in my career.

It's Important to Know . . .

The systems development life cycle (SDLC) and information reporting systems. The SDLC is important because all systems have a development lifecycle, and to successfully manage systems, anyone in IT must have a very good understanding of this lifecycle approach. Information reporting systems are extremely important to users because they are used to make decisions on the job. Because information systems provide decision support, they are critical to running businesses.

The product development life cycle (PDLC). The PDLC is related specifically to methodologies for managing projects and programs. This set of skills is paramount for project and program managers, but certainly important for everyone involved in delivering system capabilities.

Database concepts and characteristics. Fundamentally, nearly all applications access, manipulate, store, or report data. Basic concepts of databases, as well as their classifications, models, and use on the Web impact nearly everyone involved with creating, supporting, or using systems. A good basic understanding of these principles is useful to anyone in an IT field.

Anthony Briggs is currently a Business Information Officer for Best Buy. He is the executive responsible for overseeing Best Buy's information systems in support of Finance, Human Resources, Legal, and IT infrastructure/security. As a U.S. Army officer, he served in the Infantry, as well as planned and executed logistics and movement control for overseas military deployments. Anthony holds a degree in General Engineering with a minor in German, has taken and taught programming classes, and has written several college textbooks on databases and programming.

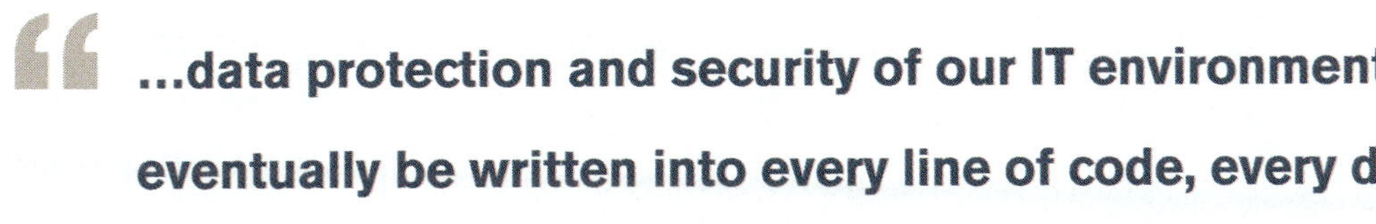

How I Use this Technology . . .

Our society is an information society, so nearly everything we do relies on the use of systems, including banking and finance, medical care, automobiles, law enforcement, military, education, and so on. In addition, I do use systems personally to an extent. For instance, I set up my own databases to keep track of friends, pay bills, do budgeting, and even catalog various collections, such as my books. I have my own home network that ties my television and computers together, and this, of course, is a type of system.

What the Future Holds . . .

Data management will be more important than ever. Databases will continue to house data that can be interpreted and linked to other data components to create very useful information. Collecting, storing, and mining data to derive meaningful information will continue to impact the way we live, where we live, how we shop, what we watch on television, how we work, and how we enjoy our leisure activities.

However, understanding what data is important and how to protect sensitive data will be paramount. Protection of data is often an afterthought, but data protection and security of our IT environments must eventually be written into every line of code, every database design, every data transfer, and every systemic interaction. We can no longer tolerate systems that are not inherently secure. Anyone designing, programming, interfacing, or even using systems must be aware of these risks and how to mitigate them to acceptable levels. Software providers must write these capabilities inherently into their software.

As our systems evolve, they will likely be built more efficiently. For example, programming can now be done far more quickly and cost effectively today, thanks to better tools. And if other types of computing—such as quantum computing—ever become mainstream, programming will need to change, since these computers work and calculate in a completely different way than computers do today. But no matter what form systems and programming take in the future, one thing will remain constant—they will have life cycles.

My Advice to Students . . .

Always keep learning. Never assume you know all you need to know about technology. Keep taking classes, read books or periodicals, and always be a student of your field.

Remember that technology is a rapidly growing field in the extreme. Technology has enhanced our lives in many ways, and is moving faster than we can comprehend it. Don't fall behind—keep learning, because knowledge, and more specifically its application, is power. When you empower yourself in this way, you can accomplish your dreams and goals.

Discussion Question

Anthony Briggs views data management as continuing to impact our lives in the future. Think about the databases you currently use on a regular basis, such as an online or offline telephone directory, television guide, and product catalogs, as well as the databases that are used on your behalf. Do you expect databases to be used even more in the future? How might computers, the Internet, and other technologies need to evolve to accommodate this? What protections would you want for the databases of the future that contain your personal information? How can this best be accomplished? Be prepared to discuss your position (in class, via an online class discussion group, or in a class chat room, depending on your instructor's directions). You may also be asked to write a short paper expressing your opinion.

>For more information on Best Buy, visit www.bestbuy.com. For more information about systems, SDLC, and PDLC, visit www.pmi.org/info/default.asp. For more information about retail in general, visit www.retail-leaders.org/new/index, www.chainstoreage.com, or www.retailsystems.com.

MODULE
COMPUTERS AND SOCIETY

No study of computers is complete without a look at the growing impact of computers and related technologies on society and our daily lives. As the use of computers at school, on the job, and in our personal lives continues to grow, so do the associated risks, such as hackers accessing your personal information, computer viruses affecting the performance of your PC, or other potential security or privacy problems. Our networked society also impacts ethical, access, and environmental issues; our physical and mental health; and the ways intellectual property are used and need to be protected.

Security risks related to network and Internet use were discussed in Chapter 9. Chapter 15 takes a look at some of the additional security and privacy issues surrounding us today, including a discussion of possible concerns and corresponding safeguards that we can take. Chapter 16 addresses issues related to intellectual property rights, ethics, health, access, and the environment.

"The impact of security and privacy technology on society is huge, but it is not yet well understood."

For more comments from Guest Expert Frank Molsberry of Dell Inc., see the Expert Insight on . . . Computers and Society feature at the end of the module.

IN THIS MODULE

Chapter 15 Computer Security and Privacy 618

Overview 619

Why Be Concerned About Computer Security? 619

Hardware Loss, Damage, and System Failure 620

Software Piracy and Digital Counterfeiting 627

Why Be Concerned About Information Privacy? 630

Databases, Electronic Profiling, Spam, and Other Marketing Activities 631

Electronic Surveillance and Monitoring 640

Computer Security and Privacy Legislation 648

Chapter 16 Intellectual Property Rights, Ethics, Health, Access, and the Environment 658

Overview 659

Intellectual Property Rights 659

Ethics 663

Computers and Health 675

Access to Technology 682

Environmental Concerns 689

Related Legislation 693

15 CHAPTER Computer Security and Privacy

OUTLINE

Overview
Why Be Concerned About Computer Security?
Hardware Loss, Damage, and System Failure
  Hardware Loss
  Hardware Damage
  System Failure and Other Disasters
  Protecting Against Hardware Loss, Damage, and System Failure
Software Piracy and Digital Counterfeiting
  Software Piracy
  Digital Counterfeiting
  Protecting Against Software Piracy and Digital Counterfeiting
Why Be Concerned About Information Privacy?
Databases, Electronic Profiling, Spam, and Other Marketing Activities
  Databases and Electronic Profiling
  Spam and Other Marketing Activities
  Protecting the Privacy of Personal Information
Electronic Surveillance and Monitoring
  Computer Monitoring Software
  Video Surveillance
  Employee Monitoring
  Presence Technology
  Protecting Personal and Workplace Privacy
Computer Security and Privacy Legislation

LEARNING OBJECTIVES

After completing this chapter, you will be able to:

1. Explain why all computer users should be concerned about computer security.
2. List some risks associated with hardware loss, damage, and system failure, and understand ways to safeguard a PC against these risks.
3. Define software piracy and digital counterfeiting and explain how they may be prevented.
4. Explain what information privacy is and why computer users should be concerned about it.
5. Describe some privacy concerns regarding databases, electronic profiling, spam, and telemarketing, and identify ways individuals can protect their privacy.
6. Discuss several types of electronic surveillance and monitoring and list ways individuals can protect their privacy.
7. Discuss the status of computer security and privacy legislation.

OVERVIEW

The increasing use of and dependence on computers in our society today has many advantages. It also, however, opens up new possibilities for problems (such as data loss due to a system malfunction or a disaster), as well as new opportunities for computer crime (such as hardware theft, software piracy, and digital counterfeiting). In addition, our networked society has raised a number of privacy concerns. Although we can appreciate that sometimes selected people or organizations have a legitimate need for some types of personal information, whenever information is provided to others, there is always the danger that the information will be misused. Facts may be taken out of context and used to draw distorted conclusions. Private information may end up being distributed without one's consent or knowledge. Erroneous facts may cause individuals to be denied services that they are entitled to or to be accused of actions they did not perform. Particularly with the vast amount of information that is contained in databases accessible via the Internet, privacy is becoming a growing societal concern.

Chapter 9 discussed security risks related to network and Internet use. This chapter takes a look at some of the other computer-related security concerns, as well as the most pressing computer-related privacy concerns facing us today. First, we explore security concerns, including hardware loss and damage, and the safeguards that can be used to reduce the risk of a problem occurring due to hardware loss or damage. Then, software piracy and digital counterfeiting are discussed, along with the steps that can be taken to reduce the occurrence of these computer crimes. Privacy topics come next, including possible risks for personal privacy violations, followed by some precautions that can be taken to safeguard one's privacy. The chapter closes with a discussion of legislation related to computer security and privacy. ■

WHY BE CONCERNED ABOUT COMPUTER SECURITY?

From having your PC stolen, to losing a term paper because the storage medium on which your paper was stored became unreadable, to running the risk of buying pirated or digitally counterfeited products via an online auction, there are a number of security concerns related to computers that all computer users should be aware of since they can cost you time and money, as well as be an inconvenience. The most common network and Internet security risks and computer crimes were discussed in Chapter 9. The remaining common computer security concerns, along with some precautions that users can take to reduce the risk of a problem occurring due to that security concern, are discussed in the next few sections.

HARDWARE LOSS, DAMAGE, AND SYSTEM FAILURE

Hardware loss can occur due to the theft of a computer or other hardware, as well as the owner losing the hardware item. Additional hardware security issues include hardware damage (both intentional and accidental) and *system failure*.

Hardware Loss

One of the most obvious types of hardware loss is **hardware theft**—when hardware is stolen, such as from a school, business, home, or individual. Desktop PCs, printers, and other larger items can be stolen during break-ins; notebooks and other portable PCs are also frequently stolen from homes, airports, hotels, and cars. Although security experts stress that the vast majority of hardware theft is done for the value of the hardware itself, executives of some companies and employees of some government agencies may be targeted for computer theft for the information contained on their PCs. And even if the data on a PC is not the primary reason for a theft, any sensitive data stored on that PC is at risk of being exposed or used for fraudulent purposes. In 2005, for instance, a number of portable computers containing personal data were stolen from schools, banks, businesses—even the military. According to the 2005 "Computer Crime and Security Survey" performed by the Computer Security Institute and the FBI, laptop theft was listed as the sixth most expensive computer crime, with losses for the year totaling over $4 million.

In addition to hardware theft, hardware loss can occur when an individual misplaces or otherwise loses a piece of hardware. It can also occur when hardware is being transported in luggage or in a package that is lost by an airline or shipping company. With the vast amount of portable hardware devices that individuals carry with them today, this type of hardware loss is a growing concern. Even if data lost due to hardware theft or misplacement is not used in a fraudulent manner and the stolen or misplaced hardware is covered by insurance, having to replace the hardware and restore the data—or, worse yet, losing the data entirely if it was not backed up—is still a huge inconvenience.

Hardware Damage

PCs consist of sensitive electronic devices and delicate components that are damaged easily. Power fluctuations, heat, dust, and static can all damage computer hardware. Dropping a computer or a piece of hardware will often break it; spilling a drink on a keyboard or other hardware component will also likely cause some damage. In addition to accidental damage, burglars, vandals, disgruntled employees, and other individuals sometimes intentionally damage the computers and other hardware they have access to.

System Failure and Other Disasters

Although many of us may prefer not to think about it, **system failure**—the complete malfunction of a computer system—and other types of computer-related disasters do happen. From accidentally deleting a file to having your computer just stop working, computer problems can be a huge inconvenience, as well as cost you a great deal of time and money. When the system contains your personal documents and data, it is a problem; when it contains the only copy of your company records or controls a vital system—such as a nuclear power plant—it can be a disaster.

>**Hardware theft.** The theft of computer hardware. >**System failure.** The complete malfunction of a computer system.

System failure can occur because of a hardware problem, software problem, or a computer virus. It can also occur because of a natural disaster (such as a tornado, fire, flood, or hurricane), sabotage, or terrorist attack. The terrorist attack on the New York City World Trade Center Twin Towers on September 11, 2001, illustrated this all too clearly. When the Twin Towers collapsed, nearly 3,000 people were killed and hundreds of offices—over 13 million square feet of office space—were completely destroyed; another 7 million square feet of office space was damaged (see Figure 15-1). In addition to the terrible human loss, the offices located in the WTC lost their computer systems—including all the equipment, records, and data stored at that location. The ramifications of these system failures and the corresponding data loss were felt around the world by all the businesses and people connected directly or indirectly to these organizations.

FIGURE 15-1
System destruction. The 9/11 attacks killed nearly 3,000 people and destroyed hundreds of business offices, including critical cables located in this Verizon office adjacent to Ground Zero.

For a look at other systems that need to be carefully protected against system failure and data loss—*e-voting systems*—see the Technology and You box.

Protecting Against Hardware Loss, Damage, and System Failure

To protect against hardware loss, damage, and system failure, a number of precautions can be taken, as discussed next.

Door and Computer Equipment Locks

Simple deterrents, such as locked doors and equipment, can go a long way in preventing computer theft. In addition to securing facilities with door locks, alarm systems, and other access control methods (such as the biometric access systems discussed in Chapter 9), cable locks (see Figure 15-2) are often used to secure desktop PCs and other semipermanent equipment in most schools and many businesses. Cable locks can also be used to secure portable PCs, external hard drives, and other portable pieces of hardware to a table or other object.

FIGURE 15-2
Securing PCs with cable locks.

DESKTOP PC

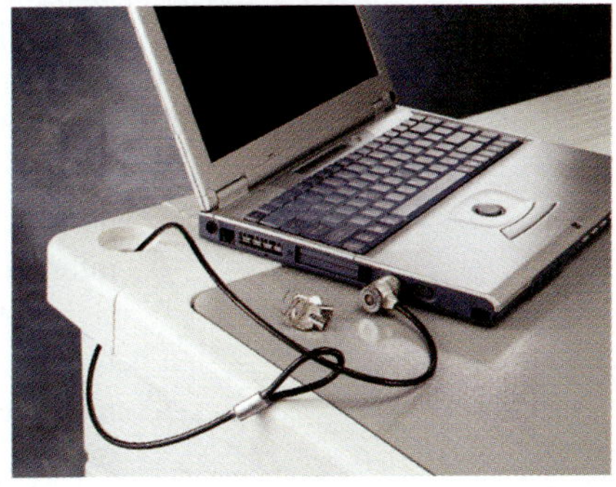

NOTEBOOK PC

While on the go, the best antitheft measure is common sense; for example, you should never leave a portable PC unattended in a public location, and you should either take your PC with you or lock it in the hotel safe when you leave your hotel room for the day. To ensure sensitive data on a portable PC cannot be read by others if the device is stolen, the data should be encrypted. Portable PCs can also be password protected or protected with a biometric feature (such as a built-in fingerprint reader) so they cannot be used if they are stolen. Some external storage devices—such as USB flash memory drives and external hard drives—can also be protected in this manner. Labeling your portable PC (and other portable hardware that you take with you on the go) with your contact information in case a lost or stolen item is recovered is another sensible precaution.

In addition to securing computers, schools and businesses should consider securing expensive supplies (such as blank hard disk cartridges, spare flash memory drives, and replacement toner cartridges) in a locked cabinet. To safeguard against theft by employees, only a limited number of employees should have access to the keys used to secure computers and storage cabinets. For highly secure facilities, it is also extremely important that employees always follow security protocols (such as signing in and out portable hard drives and other storage media), as underscored by the reports in recent years of misplaced Zip disks and portable hard drives containing classified data at Los Alamos National Laboratory.

TECHNOLOGY AND YOU

E-Voting

Many people view the 2000 U.S. presidential election as a complete breakdown of the voting process. The outcome of the election was delayed for over a month by voting discrepancies, forced recounts, and court battles over the ballots used in Florida. The Florida controversy centered primarily on punch card ballots with holes that were not completely punched through, which resulted in hanging "chads"—the small pieces of paper that are supposed to be separated from the ballots when the holes are punched. Depending on whether or not a chad was blocking a punched opening when a ballot was read by the tabulation machine, the vote might or might not have been tallied correctly.

The 2000 election problems shifted attention to alternative voting systems, with the primary emphasis on replacing paper ballots with electronic voting systems. Two possibilities are *e-voting machines* and *online voting.*

Most *electronic voting (e-voting)* devices are *direct recording electronic (DRE) devices.* A DRE system enables the voter to enter his or her choices directly into a computer, typically using a touch screen (see the accompanying photo). For security purposes, the machines cannot be used until the voter inserts a smart card or other special storage medium containing information needed to activate the ballot. The voter can then select the language of choice, indicate his or her desired vote choices, and then review the vote choices before submitting his or her vote. DRE machines can also be equipped with headphones and a Braille keyboard for visually impaired voters. The voter's choices are typically stored in the DRE device while the polls are open, and then sent to the main election computer system after the polls close.

While there has been a big push to implement touch-screen voting systems as soon as possible, there are security and privacy concerns, such as those related to election fraud, software tampering, the accuracy of the machines, and the ability to audit or recount votes. For security purposes, e-voting machines are typically not connected to a wired network, a wireless network, or any telephone lines. They also typically use redundant storage media in case of media failure and generate a printed record of each vote so that votes can be manually recounted or audited, as needed. For instance, the DRE device shown in the accompanying photo prints an audit log under a locked window (shown attached to the left side of the DRE in the photo) so that voters can confirm as they make selections that their votes are being cast correctly. There are several groups working to develop e-voting standards to be used in all states to ensure that all e-voting machines are secure and accurate. One, the Commission of Federal Election Reform, released 87 recommendations in 2005, including the following: Congress should pass a law to require all e-voting machines to have a voter-verified paper audit trail, states should develop unambiguous procedures to reconcile differences between paper and electronic tallies, independent testing authorities should certify the security of the source code used in e-voting machines, and the source code should be stored in escrow in case it needs to be reviewed by experts in the future. In mid-2005, the National Science Foundation

Computer Tracking Software and Antitheft Tools

Some software tools are not designed to prevent hardware from being stolen; instead, they are designed to aid in its recovery. This can be beneficial, since, according to FBI statistics, the recovery rate of a stolen or lost PC is about 2% or 3%. One software tool that can be used to help increase the chance of a stolen or lost PC being recovered is *computer tracking software*. Computer tracking software—sometimes called *stealth tracking software*—sends identifying information (such as ownership information and the IP address or telephone number currently being used) whenever the PC is connected to the Internet. Once a computer is reported as stolen or lost, the computer tracking software company can provide this information to law enforcement agencies to help them recover the computer. Because any sign that the software is running on the PC or is sending information (typically via e-mail) is hidden from the user, the thief is usually not aware that a computer tracking system is installed on the PC. These systems (the software and the support from the computer tracking software company) cost between $30 and $50 per year.

Other software tools are designed to prevent the data on a stolen PC from being compromised. For instance, encryption software, discussed in Chapter 9, can be used to ensure created a new, $7.5 million national research center that includes researchers from five universities to focus on improving the reliability of e-voting systems.

Also under consideration is *online voting*—casting votes via the Internet. In actuality, online voting already exists, although not on a widespread basis. In March 2000, Arizona's Democratic Party held the first binding U.S. election in which voters could cast their ballots online. For security purposes, PIN identification numbers and an assortment of personal questions were used to verify the identity of voters casting their ballots from remote (nonpolling place) locations. Nearly half of the ballots cast in that election were cast online. In 2004, Michigan's Democratic primaries were held online, and Switzerland had its first legally-binding Internet vote in 2003. In 2005, Estonia became the first country in the world to hold an election allowing voters nationwide to cast ballots via the Internet.

Online voting has several advantages, the most obvious of which is convenience. With more than half of all U.S. households having Internet access, online voting could increase voter turnout significantly. For individuals with limited mobility, it would be a tremendous convenience. Another consideration is the citizens in rural areas who now need to travel great distances to reach a polling place. Kelsey Begaye, President of the Navajo Nation, states that typically only about 40% of the people in his Navajo chapter can make it to the polls to cast their votes and he believes that "Internet voting will open up underrepresented minority sectors of the population to active participation in the voting process." Many believe that online voting will also entice younger citizens to participate in the elections process, due to the convenience factor and their high level of computer and Internet use.

Potential disadvantages for online voting typically center on security and privacy concerns. How will the system prevent someone from posing as someone else and voting as that person? Can the system be adequately protected against hackers and computer viruses? Can an accurate recount be performed? These and other security concerns led the Pentagon to cancel plans to allow e-voting in the 2004 election for soldiers and U.S. citizens stationed overseas. Possible solutions for voter authentication include using voter PIN numbers (as in the Arizona primary), as well as smart cards, fingerprint readers, and other emerging security technologies.

In some voting precincts, you can cast your vote via a touch screen.

the data on a stolen or lost PC cannot be read by an unauthorized individual. Instead of encrypting each file individually, however, encryption software designed to protect an entire PC typically encrypts all data stored on the computer automatically, so it is continually protected—a username and password or biometric characteristic is needed in order to access the data on the PC. Encryption can also be used with removable media, such as flash memory cards and USB flash memory drives (see Figure 15-3).

FIGURE 15-3
Encrypted media.
The data on this encrypted USB flash memory drive cannot be accessed until the user is authenticated via a quick fingerprint scan.

Another antitheft tool is the use of *tamper evident labels* on hardware and other expensive assets. These labels usually identity the owner of the asset and are designed to be permanently attached to the asset. If someone (typically a thief) tries to remove the label, they are designed to change their appearance to indicate that they have been tampered with. For instance, some labels change the text printed on the label and others have a printed message hidden underneath the label that is exposed when the label is removed. Both of these features are designed to bring attention to the fact that the item the original label was attached to is likely stolen.

SEMIRUGGED NOTEBOOK PC

FULLY RUGGED NOTEBOOK PC

FULLY RUGGED TABLET PC

FIGURE 15-4

Ruggedized PCs. Semirugged PCs are designed to withstand more abuse than conventional PCs; fully rugged PCs are even more durable.

Proper Hardware Care

Proper care of hardware can help to prevent serious damage to a computer system, including the data that is stored on it. The most obvious precaution is not to physically harm your hardware, such as by dropping a portable PC, knocking a piece of hardware off a desk, or jostling a system unit. For users that need a more durable system, *ruggedized PCs* are available (see Figure 15-4). These computers—typically portable PCs—are designed to withstand much more physical abuse than a conventional PC and range from *semirugged* to *ultrarugged PCs*. For instance, semirugged PCs typically have a more durable case and are spill-resistant. Rugged and ultrarugged PCs go a few steps further—they are designed to withstand drops of three feet or more onto concrete, extreme temperature ranges, wet conditions, and use while being bounced around over rough terrain in a vehicle. Ruggedized PCs are most often used by individuals who work out of the office, such as field workers, construction workers, outdoor technicians, military personnel, and so forth.

To protect hardware from damage due to power fluctuations, it is important for all users to use a **surge suppressor** with a PC whenever it is plugged into a power outlet. When electrical power spikes occur, the surge suppressor prevents them from harming your system. For desktop PCs, surge suppressors should be used with all of the powered components in the computer system (such as the system unit, monitor, printer, and scanner). A typical consumer surge suppressor is shown in Figure 15-5; there are also industrial models, some of which can even protect a system against a power surge caused by a lightning hit to a power line.

FIGURE 15-5

Surge suppressors and uninterruptible power supplies (UPSs).

SURGE SUPPRESSOR FOR PERSONAL PC

UPS FOR BUSINESS PC

UPS FOR SERVER

>**Surge suppressor.** A device that protects a computer system from damage due to electrical fluctuations.

For users who cannot afford to have the power to their systems go out without warning, **uninterruptible power supply (UPS)** units are available (see Figure 15-5). A UPS is a device containing a built-in battery that provides continuous power to a PC and other connected components when the electricity goes out. UPSs designed for use by individuals usually provide power for a few minutes to allow the user to save open documents and shut down the PC properly. Industrial-level UPSs typically run for a significantly longer amount of time. Most UPS devices have built-in surge suppression; if not, a separate surge suppressor should be used.

Dust, heat, static, and moisture can also be dangerous to a PC. Do not place your PC equipment in direct sunlight or in a dusty area. Small handheld vacuums made for electrical equipment can be used periodically to remove the dust from the keyboard and from inside the system unit. Also, be sure the system unit has plenty of ventilation, especially around the fan vents. To prevent static electricity from damaging the inside of your PC when installing a new expansion card or other internal device, turn off the power to the PC and unplug the power cord from the PC before removing the cover from the system unit. You should also discharge the static electricity from your fingertips by touching the outside of the power supply module inside the system unit before touching any other components. Unless your PC is ruggedized, do not use it in the rain (see Figure 15-6) or in other adverse conditions.

FIGURE 15-6
Proper hardware care. Unless your PC is ruggedized, keep it out of the heat, cold, rain, and other adverse conditions.

Both internal and external hard drives also need to be protected against jostling or other excess motion that can result in a *head crash*, which occurs when a hard drive's read/write head actually touches the surface of a hard disk. In addition, storage media, such as floppy disks, hard disks, CDs, and DVDs, are all extremely sensitive storage media that work well over time, as long as appropriate care is used. Floppy disks should be kept out of extremely hot or cold temperatures; CDs and DVDs should be kept in their protective *jewel cases* and handled carefully to prevent fingerprints and scratches on the data sides of the discs (usually the bottom, unprinted side on a single-sided disc).

For more tips on how to protect your PC, see the How it Works box.

Backups and Disaster Preparedness

As discussed and illustrated in Chapter 5, creating a *backup* means making a duplicate copy of important files so that when a problem occurs, you can restore those files using the backup copy. Businesses should make backups of at least all new data on a regular basis (such as once per day); individuals should make backups of important documents as they are created and consider making backups of all data periodically. For an even higher level of security, emerging software products feature *continuous data protection* (*CDP*), which is a technology that enables data backups to be made on a continual basis so that data can be recovered from any point in time, even just a few minutes ago, when needed. Although expensive, it is one of the best ways to ensure that company data is protected. Businesses with remote offices should have backup procedures for each physical location.

TIP

Backup procedures, such as making copies of important documents and storing them in a safe location, also apply to important nonelectronic documents in your life, such as birth certificates, tax returns, passports, and so forth.

Backup media needs to be secured so that it will be intact when it is needed. If stored in-house, backup media should be placed in a fire-resistant safe. Even better is to store backup media in a different physical location. For instance, many companies today use third-party *data storage companies* to store that media at a secure remote location; the backups can be returned to the company whenever they are needed. To secure the data on the backup media during transit and storage, the data should be encrypted. This lesson was learned by Time Warner in mid-2005 when 40 backup tapes containing information about 600,000 current and former employees were lost during transit to the data storage company.

>**Uninterruptible power supply (UPS).** A device containing a built-in battery that provides continuous power to a PC and other connected components when the electricity goes out.

HOW IT WORKS

Protecting Your PC

All computer users should take specific actions to protect their PCs. In this world of viruses, worms, hackers, spyware, and "buggy" (error-prone) software, it pays to be somewhat cautious. Although safeguards have been covered in detail throughout this book, some specific precautionary steps all computer users should follow are summarized in this box.

Step 1: Protect your hardware.
Be sure to plug all components of your computer system (such as the system unit, monitor, printer, scanner, and powered subwoofer) into a surge suppressor. Be careful not to bump or move the computer when it is on. Do not spill food or drink onto the keyboard or any other piece of hardware. Store your disks and CDs properly. If you ever need to work inside the system unit, turn off the PC, unplug it, and ground yourself by touching the power supply before touching any other component inside the system unit. When taking a portable PC on the road, do not ever leave it unattended, and be careful not to drop or lose it.

Step 2: Install and use an antivirus program, personal firewall, and antispyware program.
Install a good antivirus program and set it up to scan all files and e-mail messages before they are downloaded to your PC, as well as to perform a full-system scan periodically, such as every Friday night. To detect the newest viruses and types of malware, keep your antivirus program up-to-date and use a personal firewall program to protect your PC from unauthorized access via the Internet, as well as to detect any attempts by spyware to send data from your PC to another party. For additional protection if you have a home network, enable file sharing only for files and folders that really need to be accessed by other users. To turn file sharing on or off in the Windows environment, right-click on the file or folder and select the *Sharing* or *Sharing and Security* option. Run an antispyware program—such as *Ad-Aware* or *Spy Sweeper*—on a regular basis to detect and remove spyware.

Step 3: Back up regularly.
Once you have your new PC set up with all your programs installed and the menus and other settings the way you like them, create a full backup so the PC can be restored to that configuration in case of a major problem with your computer or hard drive. Be sure also to back up your data files on a regular basis. Depending on how important your documents are, you may want to back up all your data every night, or copy each document to a removable storage medium after each major revision. To facilitate data backup, keep all your data organized in folders (such as all in a main folder called "Data"). For an even higher level of security, install a second hard drive just for data. That way, if your main hard drive ever becomes unstable and needs to be reformatted, your data drive will remain untouched. Backups should be stored in a different location than your PC, such as in a different building or in a fire-resistant safe. An easy way to accomplish this is to use an online backup service or upload your backup files to an online storage service.

Step 4: Update your operating system, browser, and e-mail program regularly.
Most companies that produce operating systems, Web browsers, or e-mail programs regularly post updates and *patches*—small programs that take care of software-specific problems, or *bugs*, such as security holes—on their Web sites. Some programs include an option within the program to check online for updates; for other programs, you will need to go to each manufacturer's Web site directly to check for any critical or recommended updates. For any programs—such as Windows and most antivirus and firewall programs—that have the option to check for updates automatically, enable that option.

Step 5: Test your system for vulnerabilities.
There are several free tests available through Web sites to see if your PC's ports are accessible to hackers or if your PC is infected with a virus or spyware. These tests, such as the one on the Symantec Web site shown in the accompanying figure, should be run to check for any remaining vulnerabilities once you believe your antivirus software, firewall, and any other protective components you are using are set up correctly.

Free online security checks can help identify your PC's vulnerabilities.

After the incident, Time Warner announced that it would begin encrypting data stored on backup media.

To supplement backup procedures, businesses and other organizations should have a **disaster-recovery plan**—a plan that spells out what the organization will do to prepare for and recover from a disruptive event. Disaster-recovery plans should include information such as who will be in charge immediately after the disaster has occurred, what alternate facilities and equipment can be used, where backup media is located, the priority of getting each operation back online, disaster insurance coverage information, and so forth. If *hot sites*—alternate locations equipped with the computers, cabling, desks, and other equipment necessary to keep the business's operations going—are to be used following a major disaster, they should be set up ahead of time, and information about the sites should be included in the disaster-recovery plan. Businesses that cannot afford to be without e-mail should also consider using an *emergency mail system provider* that can act as a temporary mail server if the company mail server is unavailable. Copies of a disaster-recovery plan should be located off-site, such as at an appropriate employee's house or at the office of an associated organization located in a different city.

The importance of a good disaster-recovery plan was made obvious following the collapse of the World Trade Center Twin Towers in 2001. Minutes after the first airplane hit the towers, corporate executives, disaster-recovery firms, and backup storage companies began arranging for employees and backup data to be moved to prearranged hot sites. Employees at the data storage company Recall Corporation spent the day of the attack gathering backup tapes belonging to clients located in and near the attacks, using barcode scanners to locate the needed 30,000 tapes out of the 2 million in their secure storage facility. Bond trader Cantor Fitzgerald, which lost 700 employees and all the equipment and data located in its WTC offices, relocated to a prearranged hot site where employees received backup tapes the day after the attack, and it was able to begin trading the next morning. Although Cantor Fitzgerald—like the other organizations and businesses located in the WTC—suffered enormous human loss, good disaster-recovery planning enabled Cantor Fitzgerald to completely restore the records containing client accounts and portfolios.

TIP

For an extra level of security for data that you want to archive for a long period of time, use at least two common file formats (such as JPEG and TIF for image files and Word's DOC format and HTML or XML for text files) for the best chance that one of the formats will still be usable with PCs in the future. Also, be sure to make multiple copies of each backup medium.

SOFTWARE PIRACY AND DIGITAL COUNTERFEITING

Instead of stealing an existing computer program, object, or other valuable that belongs to someone else, *software piracy* and *digital counterfeiting* involve creating duplicates of these items, and then selling them or using them as authentic items.

Software Piracy

Software piracy, the unauthorized copying of a computer program, is illegal in the United States and many other—but not all—countries. Because of the ease with which computers can create exact copies of a software program, software piracy is a widespread problem. According to a 2005 report from the *Business Software Alliance* (*BSA*)—an organization formed by a number of the world's leading software developers that has antipiracy programs in 65 countries worldwide—approximately 35% of all business application software globally (and about 22% of all business application software in the United States) is installed illegally. In more than half the countries studied, the software piracy rate exceeded 60%; in 24 countries, it was over 75%. The report estimates that the monetary loss due to software piracy during 2004 was approximately $31 billion worldwide, and research firm IDC predicts that nearly $200 billion worth of software will be pirated in the next five years.

>**Disaster-recovery plan.** A written plan that describes the steps a company will take following the occurrence of a disaster.
>**Software piracy.** The unauthorized copying of a computer program.

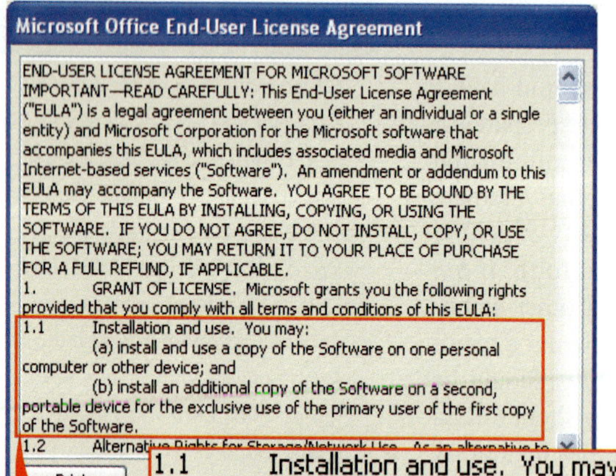

Microsoft Office End-User License Agreement

END-USER LICENSE AGREEMENT FOR MICROSOFT SOFTWARE
IMPORTANT—READ CAREFULLY: This End-User License Agreement ("EULA") is a legal agreement between you (either an individual or a single entity) and Microsoft Corporation for the Microsoft software that accompanies this EULA, which includes associated media and Microsoft Internet-based services ("Software"). An amendment or addendum to this EULA may accompany the Software. YOU AGREE TO BE BOUND BY THE TERMS OF THIS EULA BY INSTALLING, COPYING, OR USING THE SOFTWARE. IF YOU DO NOT AGREE, DO NOT INSTALL, COPY, OR USE THE SOFTWARE; YOU MAY RETURN IT TO YOUR PLACE OF PURCHASE FOR A FULL REFUND, IF APPLICABLE.
1. GRANT OF LICENSE. Microsoft grants you the following rights provided that you comply with all terms and conditions of this EULA:
1.1 Installation and use. You may:
(a) install and use a copy of the Software on one personal computer or other device; and
(b) install an additional copy of the Software on a second, portable device for the exclusive use of the primary user of the first copy of the Software.
1.2 Alternative Rights for Storage/Network Use. As an alternative to

Print

1.1 Installation and use. You may:
(a) install and use a copy of the Software on one personal computer or other device; and
(b) install an additional copy of the Software on a second, portable device for the exclusive use of the primary user of the first copy of the Software.

FIGURE 15-7

An end-user license agreement (EULA). An EULA specifies the number of PCs on which the software can be installed and other restrictions for use.

Software piracy can take many forms, including individuals making illegal copies of programs to give to friends, businesses installing software on more computers than permitted in the program's *end-user license agreement* (see Figure 15-7), PC sellers installing unlicensed copies of software on PCs sold to consumers, and large-scale operations in which the software and its packaging are illegally duplicated and then sold as supposedly legitimate products. Pirated software—as well as pirated music CDs and movie DVDs—are commonly offered for sale at online auctions. They can also be downloaded from some Web sites and peer-to-peer file sharing services. Creating and distributing pirated copies of any type of *intellectual property* (such as software, music, and movies) is illegal. Intellectual property is discussed in more detail in Chapter 16.

Digital Counterfeiting

The availability of high-quality, full-color imaging products (such as scanners, color printers, and color copiers) has made **digital counterfeiting**—creating counterfeit copies of items, typically currency and other printed resources, using computers and other types of digital equipment—more viable and prevalent. According to the U.S. Secret Service, many of today's counterfeiters have moved from the traditional method of offset printing to digital counterfeiting. The U.S. Secret Service estimates that about 40% of all counterfeit money today is produced digitally—up from 0.005% in 1995.

With digital counterfeiting, the bill (or other item to be counterfeited) is scanned into a computer and then printed, or it is color-copied. In addition to counterfeiting currency, some criminals choose to create fake business checks or printed collectibles, such as baseball cards, celebrity autographs, even T-shirts. For instance, it has been estimated that, in the first three months following NASCAR racer Dale Earnhardt's death in 2001, over $20 million worth of counterfeit Earnhardt products and collectibles were sold. Other common digital counterfeiting activities include creating fake identification papers, such as corporate IDs, driver's licenses, passports, and visas (see Figure 15-8).

FIGURE 15-8

Digital counterfeiting. Documents commonly counterfeited include currency, credit cards, driver's licenses, passports, and checks.

Counterfeiting is illegal in the United States and is taken very seriously. For creating or knowingly circulating counterfeit currency, for instance, offenders can face up to 15 years in prison for each offense. Counterfeiting of U.S. currency and other documents is a growing problem both in the United States and in other countries; in fact, over half of the counterfeit U.S. currency passed in the United States originates from other countries. Although the majority of counterfeit currency is produced by serious criminals—such as organized crimes, gangs, and terrorist organizations—the Secret Service has seen a dramatic increase in counterfeiting among high school and college students. This is attributed primarily to the ease of creating counterfeit bills—although not necessarily high-quality counterfeit bills—with digital technology. Because the paper used with real U.S. currency is very expensive and cannot legally be made by paper mills and because bills contain a

>**Digital counterfeiting.** The use of computers or other types of digital equipment to make illegal copies of currency, checks, collectibles, and other items.

number of other characteristics that are difficult to reproduce accurately, the majority of the counterfeit money made by amateurs is easily detectable.

Protecting Against Software Piracy and Digital Counterfeiting

Software piracy and digital counterfeiting affect more than just big businesses and the government. Because software pirates cost software developers a great deal of money, these companies have to charge higher prices and have less money available for research and development, which hurts law-abiding consumers. Some tools currently being used to curb software piracy and digital counterfeiting are discussed next.

Education, Holograms, and Other Antipiracy Tools

One noteworthy tool the software industry is using in an attempt to prevent software piracy is education. By educating businesses and consumers about the legal use of software and the possible negative consequences associated with breaking antipiracy laws, the industry hopes to reduce the known use of illegal software significantly. Paired with this, the industry is continually working on strengthening antipiracy laws and adapting them to fit new technology, such as broadband Internet and rewritable DVDs. The industry is also working to find more convenient ways to deliver content quickly—such as over the Internet—to give consumers a legal option that is as fast as downloading a pirated version.

To make it more difficult for criminals to create pirated copies of software, *holograms*—printed text or images that change their appearance when the item containing the hologram is tilted or looked at from a different angle—are commonly used on CDs, DVDs, and stickers located on new PCs containing preinstalled software. Because holograms are difficult to duplicate, end users can feel confident that the software package they are buying or was installed on the PC they received is authentic if the hologram works correctly. Requiring a unique activation code—such as during a mandatory online product registration—before the software can be used or before certain key features of the program are unlocked is another antipiracy tool. Some software manufacturers have launched extensive campaigns—such as including information on their Web sites, in product information, and in advertisements—to inform consumers of how these precautions work and why they are needed.

Other antipiracy techniques used by software companies include watching online auction sites and requesting the removal of suspicious items, and buying pirated copies of software via Web sites and then filing lawsuits against the sellers. The increase in prosecution of consumers for illegally selling or sharing software, music, and movies may also help reduce some types of piracy and encourage individuals to obtain legal copies of these products. As countries with high levels of pirated software become more willing to curb piracy within their borders, the amount of global software piracy should drop as well. For instance, in a 2005 meeting with Microsoft's Bill Gates, the Vietnamese Prime Minister promised to crack down on piracy in his country. With 92% of the software in Vietnam pirated, reducing the piracy rate in that country alone would have a significant impact on the total amount of global software piracy.

Digital Counterfeiting Prevention

To prevent the counterfeiting of U.S. currency, the Treasury Department releases new currency designs every 7 to 10 years. These new designs (such as the $50 design introduced in late 2004 and shown in Figure 15-9) contain features that make the new currency more difficult to duplicate than older currency. In addition, digital imaging equipment (such as color copiers and scanners) is equipped with technologies that can be used to track currency and other counterfeit items created with those devices. For example, many color copiers print invisible codes on copied documents, making counterfeit money copied on those machines traceable. This type of technology is also thought to be incorporated into many scanners. In fact, printer and scanner manufacturer Canon has revealed that it has been incorporating anticounterfeiting technologies into its products since 1992, but the

FIGURE 15-9
Anticounterfeiting measures used with U.S. currency.

company is prohibited by the government from disclosing any information about those technologies. In 2004, researchers at HP Labs and experts from HP's printing and imaging business met with U.S. and international officials to discuss ideas regarding ways to prevent counterfeit U.S. currency from being produced on home imaging equipment. One of the goals of the group was to ensure that whatever technology is used will not affect the quality or the print speed of the equipment. Their recommendations are also secret but may be incorporated into currency and digital imaging equipment in the future.

Prevention measures against the counterfeiting of other types of documents—such as checks and identification cards—include using holograms, *digital watermarks*, and other difficult-to-reproduce content. As discussed in more detail in Chapter 16, a digital watermark is a subtle alteration that is not noticeable when the work is viewed or played, but that can be read using special software to authenticate the item. Finally, educating consumers about how the appearance of fake products differs from that of authentic products is a vital step in the ongoing battle against counterfeiting.

WHY BE CONCERNED ABOUT INFORMATION PRIVACY?

Privacy is usually defined as the state of being concealed or free from unauthorized intrusion. The term **information privacy** refers to the rights of individuals and companies to control how information about them is collected and used. The problem of how to protect personal privacy—that is, how to keep personal information private—existed long before computers entered the picture. For example, sealing wax and unique signet rings were used centuries ago to seal letters, wills, and other personal documents to guard against their content being revealed to unauthorized individuals, as well as to alert the recipient if such an intrusion occurred while the document was in transit. But today's computers, with their ability to store and manipulate unprecedented quantities of data in a very short amount of time, combined with the fact that databases containing our personal information can be accessed and shared via the Internet, have added a new twist to the issue of personal privacy.

As discussed in Chapter 8, one concern of many individuals is the privacy of their Web site activities and e-mail messages. *Cookies*, *Web bugs*, and *spyware* are all possible privacy risks. In addition, e-mail can be read if intercepted by another individual during

>**Privacy.** The state of being concealed or free from unauthorized intrusion. >**Information privacy.** The rights of individuals and companies to control how information about them is collected and used.

transit unless it is encrypted (as discussed in Chapter 9). For businesses and employees, there is the additional issue of whether or not Web activities, e-mail, and instant messages sent through a company network are private, and businesses need to make sure they comply with privacy laws regarding the protection of the security of private information they store on their servers.

In addition, all individuals today should be familiar with privacy issues related to databases, *spam*, and other marketing activities, as well as those related to *electronic surveillance* and *electronic monitoring*. These issues, along with precautions that can be taken to safeguard information privacy, are discussed throughout the remainder of this chapter.

DATABASES, ELECTRONIC PROFILING, SPAM, AND OTHER MARKETING ACTIVITIES

There are marketing activities that can be considered privacy risks or, at least, an invasion of privacy. These include *databases*, *electronic profiling*, and *spam*.

Databases and Electronic Profiling

Information about individuals can be located in many different databases. For example, most educational institutions maintain databases containing student information, most organizations have an employee database for employee information, and most physicians and health insurance providers maintain databases containing individuals' medical information. From a privacy standpoint, these databases, provided they are adequately protected from hackers and other unauthorized individuals, are not of significant concern to consumers because the information can rarely be shared without the individuals' permission. On the other hand, *marketing databases* and *government databases* are associated with a higher risk of personal privacy violations.

Marketing databases contain data about people, such as where they live and what products they buy. This information is used for marketing purposes, such as sending advertisements that fit each individual's interests (via regular mail or e-mail) or trying to sign people up over the phone for some type of service. Virtually anytime you provide information about yourself online or offline—for example, when you subscribe to a magazine, fill out a sweepstakes entry or product registration card, or buy a product or service using a credit card—there is a good chance that information will find its way into a marketing database. Information about individuals is also available in **government databases**. Some information, such as Social Security earnings and income tax returns, is confidential and should only be seen by authorized individuals. Other information—such as birth records, marriage certificates, divorce information, and property purchases, assessments, liens, and tax values—is available to the public, including to the marketing companies that specialize in creating marketing databases. For a look at how databases are beginning to be used to store *digital health records*—see the Trend box.

In the past, the data about any one individual was stored in a variety of separate locations, such as at different government agencies, individual stores, the person's bank and credit card companies, and so forth. Because it would be extremely time-consuming to locate all the information about one person from all these different places, there was a fairly high level of information privacy. Today, however, most of an individual's data is stored on computers that can communicate with each other via the Internet, which means accessing personal information about someone is much easier than it used to be. For example, a variety of

>**Marketing database.** A collection of data about people that is stored in a large database and used for marketing purposes.

>**Government database.** A collection of data about people that is collected and maintained by the government.

TREND

Digital Health Records

In 2004, President Bush set a national goal for most Americans to have *electronic health records* (*EHRs*) by 2014. Since then, there has been movement in that direction. For instance, many private physicians use digital patient records (see the accompanying photo), the Veteran's Administration uses electronic health records in all 1,300 VA medical facilities, and Kaiser Permanente is in the process of converting to an electronic medical records system. Most electronic health records systems provide access to the system in examining rooms, X-ray rooms, labs, and other locations throughout the medical care facility so that patient information is available to any physician or technician who needs it and information can be updated in real time. Some systems tie into electronic prescription systems so that e-prescriptions can be double-checked with patient records for allergies or drug interactions. Prescription instructions and any other information that the patient needs can also be quickly printed right in the examination room and handed to the patient. In addition, some electronic health systems are tied into an *e-health network* so that medical records can be accessed outside the medical care facility—such as by an emergency room doctor when the patient needs medical care when he or she is out of town.

Although some privacy advocates are concerned about the security and privacy of digital health records, the public is supportive. For instance, a 2005 study by the IT consulting firm Accenture found that 93% of Americans believe digital health records improve quality of care, 92% think digital health records reduce treatment errors in hospitals, 75% say the systems reduce overall health costs, and 78% believe they help shorten waiting times in doctor offices and hospitals. Provided adequate backup systems are in place, digital health records also ensure that a patient's medical records will not be destroyed in a fire or other disaster. For instance, Hurricane Katrina in 2005 destroyed or left inaccessible the medical records of untold numbers of people and focused new attention on the need for digital health records that can follow patients, even if their doctors' offices no longer exist. In the future, many electronic health records are expected to be available to patients via the Internet; it is also possible that we will carry our own personal electronic health records with us on a USB flash memory drive, smart card, or other storage medium. Wherever the information is stored, virtually everyone will agree that for privacy purposes the computers and storage media containing electronic health records will need to be protected against unauthorized access. In fact, in the United States, companies storing health information electronically must comply with the minimum security standards in the *Health Insurance Portability and Accountability Act* (*HIPAA*) *Privacy Rule*. In addition, electronic health records systems must only allow necessary information to be viewed, depending on who is accessing a patient's record. For instance, an assistant scheduling the patient's doctor's appointment should only be able to view information needed for that task, while the patient's physician should be able to access all of the patient's records. Digital health record systems are in place or being implemented in several countries, including the United States, Canada, and Australia. In the United States, there is proposed legislation—such as the *Wired for Health Care Quality Act of 2005*—that will provide financial assistance to healthcare providers to develop electronic health record systems, and a model for a nationwide electronic health system is being set up through the cooperative efforts of two foundations.

information about individuals is available for free through the Internet; there are also paid services that perform online database searches (see Figure 15-10). Although often this ability to search online databases is an advantage—such as checking the background of potential employees or looking up a misplaced phone number—it does raise privacy concerns. In response to the increased occurrence of identity theft, some local governments have removed birth and death information from their available online records.

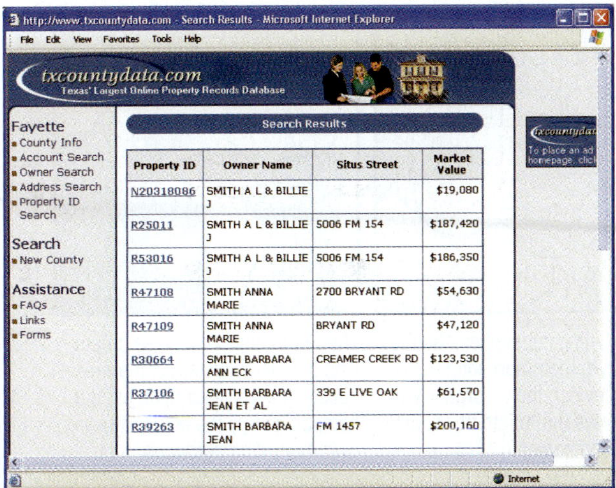

PROPERTY VALUE SEARCH
Some states permit searches for property located in that state, such as the Texas database shown here that allows searches by address or owner name and displays the owner's name, address, and property value.

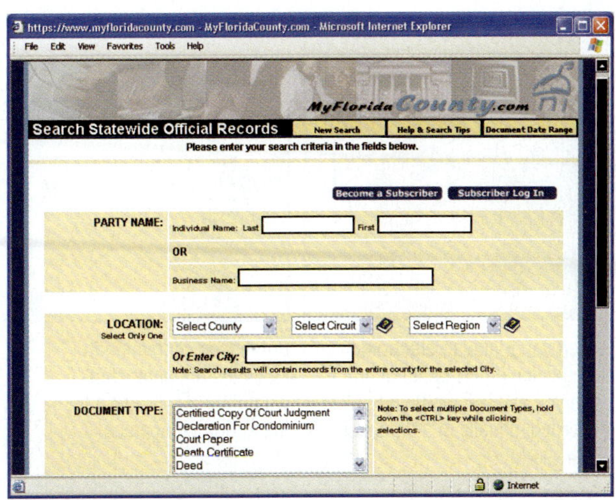

VITAL RECORDS SEARCH
Some counties and states allow searches for documents related to marriages, divorces, births, legal judgments, deeds, liens, powers of attorney, and so forth.

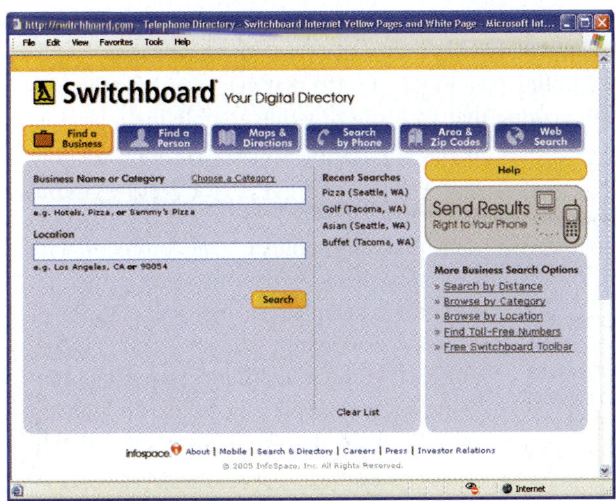

ADDRESS NUMBER AND PHONE NUMBER SEARCH
Any information listed in a U.S. telephone book can be found using this site. You can search either by name or telephone number to view the available information.

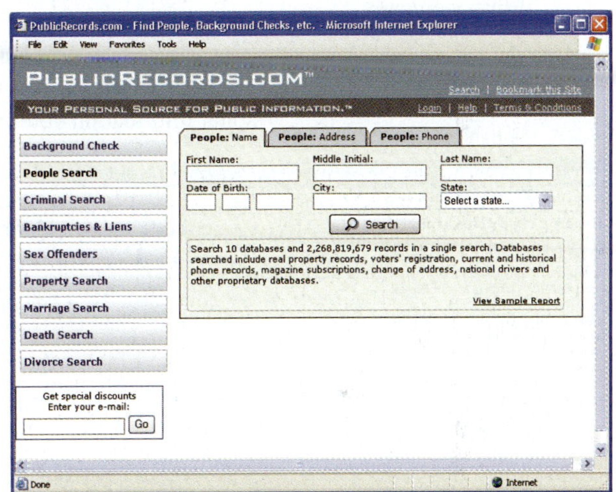

PAID PUBLIC RECORDS SEARCH
A number of sites offer a variety of public records searches, such as for criminal records or court records, to the public for a fee.

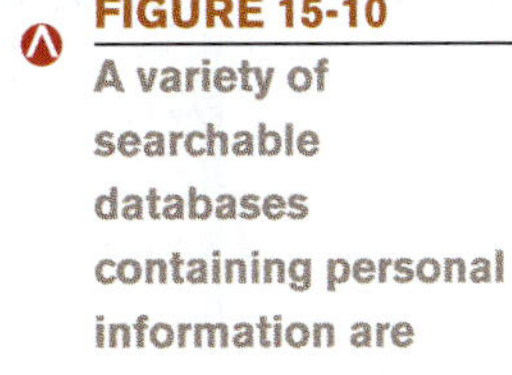
FIGURE 15-10
A variety of searchable databases containing personal information are available via the Internet.

Collecting in-depth information about an individual is known as **electronic profiling**. Marketing companies use data acquired from a variety of sources—such as from product and service purchases that are personally identifiable, as well as from public information, such as property values, vehicle registrations, births, marriages, and deaths—to create electronic profiles of individuals. Electronic profiles generally provide specific information and can include an individual's name, current and previous addresses, telephone number, marital status, number and age of children, spending habits, and product preferences. The information contained in electronic profiles is then sold to companies upon request to

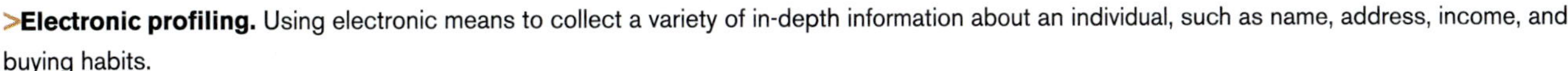
>**Electronic profiling.** Using electronic means to collect a variety of in-depth information about an individual, such as name, address, income, and buying habits.

When you make an electronic transaction, information about who you are and what you buy is recorded, usually in a database.

Databases containing the identities of people and what they buy are sold to marketing companies.

The marketing companies add the new data to their marketing databases; they can then reorganize the data in ways that might be valuable to other companies.

The marketing companies create lists of individuals matching the specific needs of companies; the companies buy the lists for their own marketing purposes.

FIGURE 15-11

How electronic profiling might work.

FIGURE 15-12

Privacy policies. Web site privacy policies explain how your personal information might be used.

be used for marketing purposes (see Figure 15-11). For example, one company might request a list of all individuals in a particular state whose street addresses are considered to be in an affluent area and who buy baby products. Another company might request a list of all SUV owners in a particular city who have not purchased a car in five years. Still another company may want a list of business travelers who frequently fly to the East Coast.

Many Web sites have a **privacy policy** (see Figure 15-12) that discloses how the personal information you provide while visiting that Web site or while completing a product registration will be used. As long as their actions do not violate their privacy policy, it is legal for businesses to sell the personal data that they collect. One problem with privacy policies is that they are sometimes difficult to decipher; in addition, many businesses periodically change their privacy policies without warning, requiring consumers to reread privacy policies frequently or risk their personal information being used in a manner that they did not agree to when the information was initially provided. Some companies notify customers by e-mail when their privacy policies change but, more commonly, they expect customers to check the current policy periodically and notify the business if any new actions are objectionable.

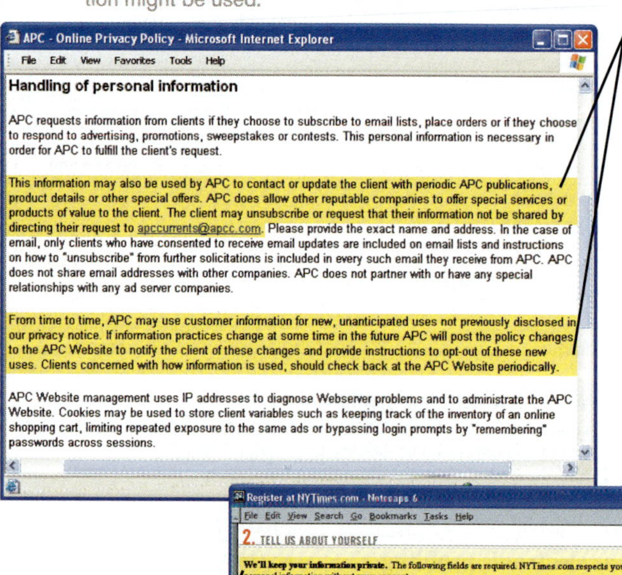

APC - Online Privacy Policy - Microsoft Internet Explorer

File Edit View Favorites Tools Help

Handling of personal information

APC requests information from clients if they choose to subscribe to email lists, place orders or if they choose to respond to advertising, promotions, sweepstakes or contests. This personal information is necessary in order for APC to fulfill the client's request.

This information may also be used by APC to contact or update the client with periodic APC publications, product details or other special offers. APC does allow other reputable companies to offer special services or products of value to the client. The client may unsubscribe or request that their information not be shared by directing their request to apccurrents@apcc.com. Please provide the exact name and address. In the case of email, only clients who have consented to receive email updates are included on email lists and instructions on how to "unsubscribe" from further solicitations is included in every such email they receive from APC. APC does not share email addresses with other companies. APC does not partner with or have any special relationships with any ad server companies.

From time to time, APC may use customer information for new, unanticipated uses not previously disclosed in our privacy notice. If information practices change at some time in the future APC will post the policy changes to the APC Website to notify the client of these changes and provide instructions to opt-out of these new uses. Clients concerned with how information is used, should check back at the APC Website periodically.

APC Website management uses IP addresses to diagnose Webserver problems and to administrate the APC Website. Cookies may be used to store client variables such as keeping track of the inventory of an online shopping cart, limiting repeated exposure to the same ads or bypassing login prompts by "remembering" passwords across sessions.

The privacy policy displayed on this Web site indicates that your personal information may be disclosed to third parties unless you specifically opt out. It also reserves the right to change the policy at a later time, so it suggests that you check back periodically.

Register at NYTimes.com - Netscape 6

File Edit View Search Go Bookmarks Tasks Help

2. TELL US ABOUT YOURSELF

We'll keep your information private. The following fields are required. NYTimes.com respects your privacy, so we will never share any personal information without your consent.

Gender: Male Female

Year of Birth: 19 (Click here if you are under 13)

Zip Code (U.S. Residents Only):

Country of Residence: ——Select One——

Household Income Range: ——Select One——

Industry in which you work: ——Select One——

Job Title: ——Select One——

Job Function: ——Select One——

Please select your usage of *The New York Times* newspaper: ——Select One——

According to this privacy statement, information provided during online registration will not be shared with others without your consent.

Spam and Other Marketing Activities

Spam refers to unsolicited e-mail sent to a large group of individuals at one time. The electronic equivalent of junk mail (see Figure 15-13), spam is most often used to

>**Privacy policy.** A policy, commonly posted on a company's Web site, that explains how personal information provided to that company will be used. >**Spam.** Unsolicited, bulk e-mail sent over the Internet.

sell products or services to individuals. Spam is also used in phishing schemes, as discussed in Chapter 9. A great deal of spam involves health-related products (such as medicine or weight loss systems), pornography, and new—and sometimes fraudulent—business opportunities. Spam can also be generated by individuals forwarding e-mail messages they receive (such as jokes, recipes, or new possible virus alerts or health concerns) to everyone in their address books. In addition to spam, most individuals receive marketing e-mails either from companies they supplied their e-mail addresses to or from other companies that acquired their e-mail addresses from a third-party, such as via a purchased mailing list. While these latter types of marketing e-mail messages do not technically fit the definition of spam since they were permission-based, many individuals consider them to be spam. Spam is also beginning to appear in instant messages (called *spim*), on cell phones, and on fax machines.

The sheer volume of spam is significant today. For instance, America Online alone blocks more than 1.4 billion spam messages each day, and MessageLabs reports that nearly 75% of the e-mail sent to the customers of its e-mail filtering service is spam. At best, large volumes of spam are an annoyance to recipients and can slow down a mail server's delivery of important messages. At worst, spam can disable a mail network completely, or it can cause recipients to miss or lose important e-mail messages because those messages have been caught in a spam filter or accidentally deleted by the recipient while he or she is deleting a large number of spam e-mail messages. And spim is on the rise, as well. According to the Radicati Group, spim instant messages totaled 1.2 billion in 2004, and the average IM user can expect to be interrupted 27 times per day with spim by 2008.

Most Internet users spend at least 10 minutes per day dealing with spam, spim, and unsolicited e-mails, making these communications very expensive for businesses in terms of lost productivity, consumption of communication bandwidth, and drain of technical support. The Radicati Group estimates spam will cost companies nearly $200 billion by 2007. Two reasons for the increase in spam, spim, and other unsolicited e-mails are low implementation cost (one marketing resource offers 15 million e-mail addresses for about $100) and a decent success rate (one spammer reports that the typical response rate is 4% to 5%).

SPAM
Users should be wary about responding to offers, like the one shown here, that they receive via unsolicited e-mail messages.

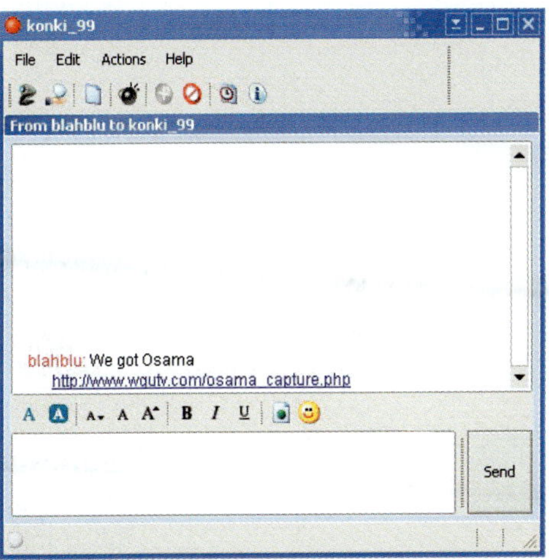

SPIM
This unsolicited instant message is more than just annoying—it installs a worm on the user's PC if the link is clicked.

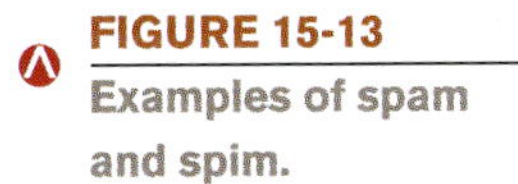
FIGURE 15-13
Examples of spam and spim.

One of the most common ways of getting on a spam mailing list is by having your e-mail address entered into a marketing database, which can happen when you sign up for a free online service or use your e-mail address to register a product, place an order, or respond to an online or e-mail offer. Spammers also use software to gather e-mail addresses from Web pages and discussion group posts. Many individuals view spam as an invasion of privacy because it arrives on computers without permission and costs them time and other resources (bandwidth, mailbox space, and hard drive space, for instance). With spam beginning to arrive on smart phones, pagers, and other wireless devices—which often charge on a per message or bandwidth basis—spam is rapidly becoming an expensive annoyance for individuals and businesses that use these types of devices. And the disturbing new trend of using computer viruses and other malware to hijack home PCs to be used—without the owner's knowledge or consent, similar to the zombie PCs used for the distributed denial of service (DDOS) attacks discussed in Chapter 9—to distribute spam makes spam a security risk now, as well.

Other unsolicited marketing activities that can be viewed as privacy violations because of their intrusion factor include *pop-up ads*, *pop-under ads*, and *telemarketing*. Pop-up and pop-under ads are Web-based advertisements that show up in a separate browser window when you are surfing the Web, typically generated by viewing a particular Web page. As their names suggest, pop-up ads initially appear on top of all other browser windows, and pop-under ads appear beneath all other browser windows (and so may not be noticed until a later time). *Telemarketing*—a marketing activity that most individuals encounter on a regular basis—consists of unsolicited offers made via the telephone. Unlike pop-up and

TIP

To protect against spim, set your IM program to accept messages only from people on your buddy list; to prevent pop-up ads from disturbing your Internet sessions, use a *pop-up blocker*–such as the one built-into the *Google toolbar* or the ones that can be enabled through many Web browsers.

TIP

Reducing spam can save you money if you are an employer. Assuming employees work 230 days per year, are paid $25 per hour, receive 50 spam e-mails per day, and spend on average 5 seconds reviewing and deleting spam messages, it costs the company 25 hours or $399 in lost productivity per year for each employee.

pop-under ads, which are typically displayed in response to a Web page just displayed, most telemarketing targets individuals based on the data contained in a marketing database, compiled from both offline and online activities.

Most types of spam are legal, but that is beginning to change. For example, the *CAN-SPAM Act of 2003* enacted some requirements (such as using truthful subject lines and honoring remove requests) for spammers and other bulk e-mailers, and those who break the law can be prosecuted. In 2004, for instance, one individual was sentenced to seven years in jail and fined $16 million for sending 850 million junk e-mails through accounts he opened with stolen identities. In addition, large settlements are beginning to be awarded in spam cases. In 2005, for example, legal settlements cost spammers $13 million in one case involving AOL and $7 million in another case involving Microsoft. The CAN-SPAM Act also applies to spim, and the first federal charge of spimming took place in 2005 against an 18-year old man who allegedly sent more than 1.5 million automated spim instant messages advertising pornography and mortgages. In addition to the CAN-SPAM Act violations, the man is being charged with intending to extort and cause damage to the IM hosting service, and he faces up to 18 years in federal prison if convicted.

Protecting the Privacy of Personal Information

There are a number of precautions that can be taken to protect the privacy of personal information. Safeguarding your e-mail address and other personal information is a good start. You can also surf anonymously, *opt out* of some marketing activities, and use filters and other tools to limit your exposure to spam and onscreen ads. Businesses need to take adequate measures to protect the privacy of information stored on their servers and storage media.

Safeguard Your E-Mail Address

Protecting your e-mail address is one of the best ways to avoid spam. One way to accomplish this is to use one private e-mail address for family, friends, colleagues, and other trusted sources. For online shopping, signing up for free offers, discussion groups, product registration, and other activities that typically lead to junk e-mail, use a *disposable* or **throw-away e-mail address**—such as a second address obtained from your ISP or a free e-mail address from Yahoo! or Hotmail. Although you will want to check your alternate e-mail address periodically (to check for online shopping receipts or shipping notifications, for instance), this method can prevent a great deal of spam from getting to your regular e-mail account. Another advantage of using a throw-away e-mail address for only noncritical applications is that you can quit using it and get a new one if spam begins to get overwhelming or too annoying.

FURTHER EXPLORATION

For links to further information about protecting your privacy online, go to www.course.com/uc11/ch15

To comply with truth-in-advertising laws, an *unsubscribe* e-mail address included in an unsolicited e-mail must be a working address. If you receive a marketing e-mail from a reputable source, you may be able to unsubscribe by clicking the supplied link or otherwise following the unsubscribe instructions. Since spam from less-legitimate sources often has unsubscribe links that do not work or that are present only to verify that your e-mail address is genuine—a very valuable piece of information for future use—many privacy experts recommend never replying to or trying to unsubscribe from any spam.

Be Cautious of Revealing Personal Information

In addition to protecting your real e-mail address, protecting your personal information is a critical step to safeguarding your privacy. Consequently, it makes sense to be cautious

>**Throw-away e-mail address.** An e-mail address used only for nonessential purposes and activities that may result in spam; the address can be disposed and replaced if spam becomes a problem.

about revealing your private information to anyone. Privacy tips for safeguarding personal information include the following:

- Read a Web site's privacy policy (if one exists) before providing any personal information. Look for a phrase saying that the company will not share your information with other companies under any circumstances. If the Web site reserves the right to share your information if the company is sold or unless you specifically notify them otherwise, it is best to assume that any information you provide will eventually be shared with others.
- Consider using privacy software, such as the free *Privacy Bird* program, created by AT&T. This program works in conjunction with your browser to notify you (by changing the appearance of its icon on the browser's title bar, as shown in Figure 15-14) if the Web sites you view meet your specified privacy criteria (such as how your health, financial, purchasing, contact, or other types of personal information will be used). The program makes its determination by comparing your specified criteria with the site's privacy information, which is based on the *Platform for Privacy Preferences* (*P3P*)—a set of privacy policy standards developed by the World Wide Web Consortium (W3C).
- Do not supply personal information online to people you meet in chat rooms. Although they may seem like close friends, it is important to realize that you do not know for sure who they are or what they are like in real life.
- Avoid putting too many personal details about yourself on your Web site. If you would like to post photographs or other personal documents on a Web site for far-away friends and family members to see, consider using a password-protected service (such as *PictureTrail*, *Yahoo! Photos*, or *Fotki*).
- Beware of Web sites offering prizes or the chance to earn free merchandise in exchange for your personal information. Chances are good that the information will be sold to direct marketers, which will likely result in additional spam. If you choose to sign up for services from these Web sites, use your throw-away e-mail address.
- Consider using an *anonymous Web browsing* service, such as Anonymizer. These services work in conjunction with a Web browser to hide personal information as the user browses the Web so that information is not revealed, and the user's activities cannot be tracked. All requests for Web pages go through the anonymous Web browsing service so that the service's IP address and identifying information are revealed instead of the user's information. Essentially, these services act as *cloaking services* and cost around $30 per year. Anonymous e-mail services are also available.
- Just because a Web site or registration form asks for personal information, that does not mean you have to give it (see Figure 15-15). Supply only the required information (these fields are often marked with an asterisk or colored differently than nonrequired fields—if not, you can try leaving fields blank and seeing if the form will still be accepted). If you are asked for more personal information than you are comfortable providing, look for an alternate product or Web site. Either way, do not provide an e-mail address (or else use a throw-away address) if you do not want to receive offers or other e-mail from that company.

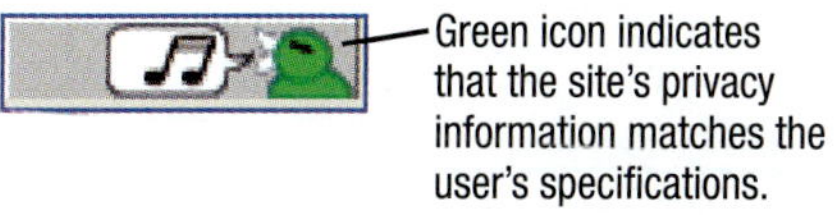

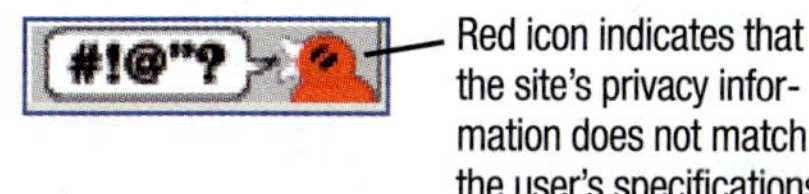

FIGURE 15-14

Privacy Bird icons. The Privacy Bird icon is displayed on the browser's title bar and changes its appearance to notify the user if the Web site being viewed matches his or her privacy specifications.

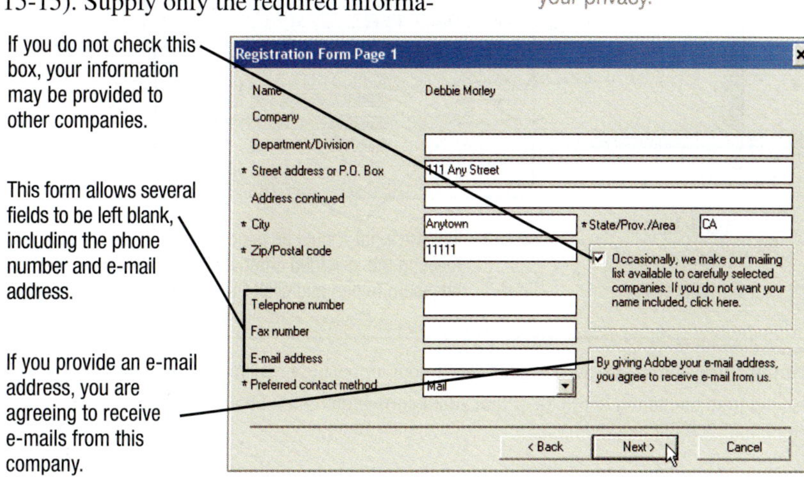

FIGURE 15-15

Forms and privacy. Completing only the required information on both online and offline forms can help protect your privacy.

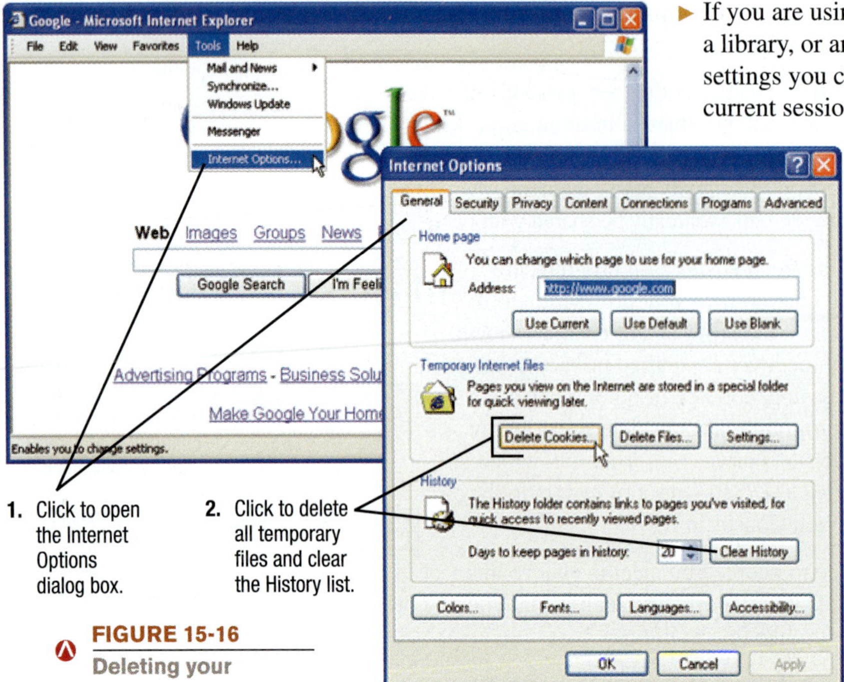

FIGURE 15-16
Deleting your browsing history.

- If you are using a public computer (such as at a school, a library, or an Internet café, be sure to reset any e-mail settings you changed in the e-mail program during the current session in order to remove any of your personal settings. Also, be sure to clear the browser's *cache* (copies of frequently visited Web pages that are stored on your hard drive to speed up browsing), cookies, and any other temporary Internet files that might contain information about you or your Web activity (see Figure 15-16).

Use Filters and Opt Out

Keeping your personal information—particularly e-mail address, mailing address, and telephone number—as private as possible can help to reduce spam and other direct marketing activities. One common way to deal with spam that makes it to your PC is to use an **e-mail filter**—a tool for automatically sorting your incoming e-mail messages. Businesses can set up filters in-house, but they are increasingly turning to dedicated *antispam appliances* to filter out spam without increasing the load on the companye-mail server. Some ISPs automatically block all e-mail messages originating from known or suspected spammers; many flag suspicious e-mail messages as possible spam, based on their content or subject line. To customize spam filtering, individuals can create their own e-mail filters in their e-mail program or using third-party filtering software.

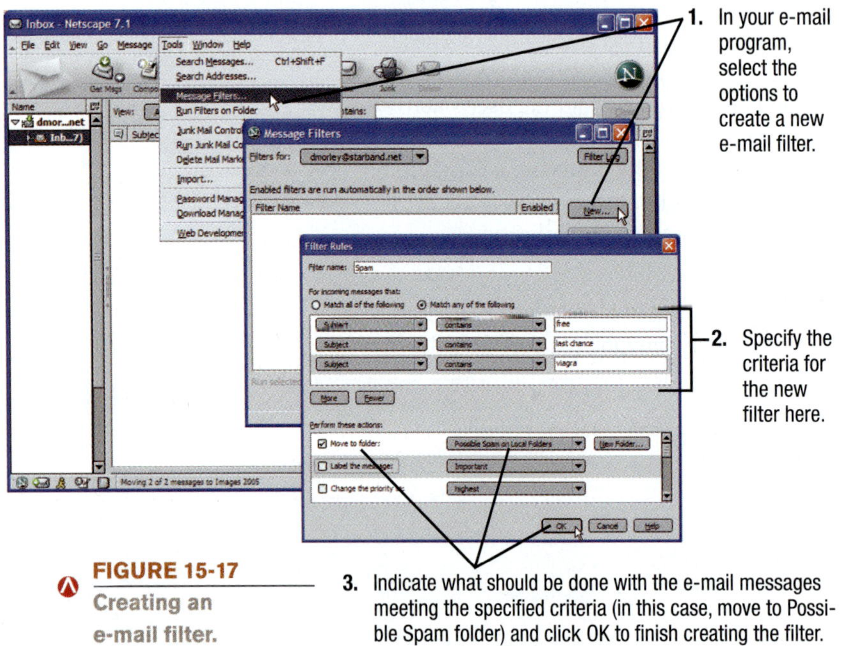

FIGURE 15-17
Creating an e-mail filter.

E-mail filters typically route messages automatically into particular folders based on stated criteria (see Figure 15-17). For example, you could specify that e-mail messages with keywords frequently used in spam subject lines, such as *free, porn, opportunity, last chance, weight, pharmacy*, and similar terms, be routed into a folder named Possible Spam, and you could specify that all e-mail messages from your boss's e-mail address be routed into an Urgent folder. Filtering can help you find important messages in your Inbox by preventing it from becoming cluttered with spam, but remember, you need to check the Possible Spam folder periodically to locate any e-mail messages mistakenly filed there before you permanently delete those messages.

You can also choose to **opt out** as a way to reduce the amount of spam you

>**E-mail filter.** A tool that automatically sorts your incoming e-mail messages based on specific criteria. >**Opt out.** To request that you be removed from marketing activities or that your information not be shared with other companies.

receive and other direct marketing activities you encounter. *Opting out* refers to following a predesignated procedure to remove yourself from marketing lists, or otherwise prevent your personal information from being obtained by or shared with others. By opting out, you instruct companies you do business with (such as your bank, insurance company, investment company, or online store) that they cannot share your personal data with third parties. You can also opt out of being contacted by direct and online marketing companies.

To opt out from a particular company or direct marketing association, you can contact them directly—many organizations include opt-out instructions in their privacy policies. For Web sites that use registered accounts for repeat visitors, opt-out options are sometimes included in your personal settings and can be activated by modifying your personal settings at that site. Opt-out instructions for financial institutions and credit card companies are often included in the disclosure statements that are periodically mailed to customers; they can also often be found on a company's Web site.

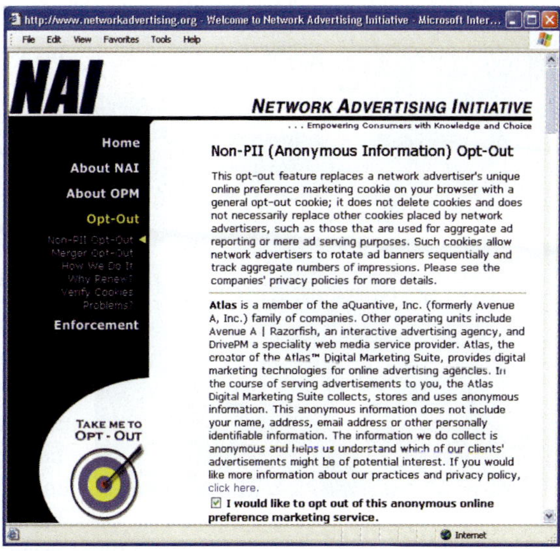

FIGURE 15-18

Opting out. Web sites, such as the NAI site shown here, can help you opt out of marketing activities.

To assist consumers with the opt-out process, there are a number of Web sites, such as the Center for Democracy and Technology and the PrivacyRightsNow! Web sites, which provide opt-out tools for consumers. For example, some sites help visitors create opt-out letters that can be sent to the companies in order to opt out. For online marketing activities, organizations—such as the *Network Advertising Initiative* (*NAI*)—have options on their Web sites to help consumers opt out of online targeted ads (see Figure 15-18). Typically, this process replaces an advertiser's marketing cookie with an *opt-out cookie*. The opt-out cookie prevents any more marketing cookies belonging to that particular advertiser from being placed on the user's hard drive as long as the opt-out cookie is present (usually until the user deletes the opt-out cookie file).

At the present time, opting-out procedures are confusing and time-consuming, and they do not always work well. Consequently, some privacy groups are pushing to change to an *opt-in* process, in which companies would need to obtain an individual's consent before collecting or sharing any personal data (as is the case in the European Union). Until there is a change in legislation in the United States, however, the general practice in the U.S. business community is to use your information as allowed for by their privacy policy unless you specifically opt out.

One of the biggest advancement in consumer privacy in the United States is the implementation of the *National Do-Not-Call Registry* in October 2003. Within three months of adding your telephone numbers (including home, business, and cell phones) to the registry via the Internet or telephone, telemarketers can no longer call you, unless you have an established business relationship with them. The Do-Not-Call Registry also covers unsolicited calls—including spam—sent to mobile phones. Similar legislation for PC-based spam is in the works on the federal level. For instance, the CAN-SPAM Act of 2003 laid the groundwork for the creation of a federal *Do-Not-E-Mail Registry*, although many insiders view such a registry as impractical and see *e-mail authentication systems* (systems that mark e-mail from authenticated senders as legitimate, as opposed to spam filters that mark suspected spam) as a better alternative.

FURTHER EXPLORATION

For links to further information about opting out, go to www.course.com/uc11/ch15

Secure Servers Containing Personal Information

Any business that stores personal information about employees, customers, or other individuals must take adequate security measures to protect the privacy of that information. There are some privacy laws already in place, and, in response to the number of privacy breaches occurring lately, additional legislation is under consideration, such as to require that businesses notify all individuals whose private information may have been exposed. As discussed in Chapter 9, secure servers and encryption can protect the data stored on a server; firewalls and access systems can prevent against unauthorized access. To prevent personal information from intentionally or inadvertently being sent via e-mail, organizations can use

FIGURE 15-19

Media disposal. When disposing of CDs, DVDs, and other storage media, the media should be shredded to ensure the information on the media is destroyed.

e-mail encryption systems that automatically encrypt e-mail messages containing certain key words. For instance, some hospitals use encryption systems that scan all outgoing e-mail messages and attachments and then automatically encrypt all messages that appear to contain patient-identifiable information, such as a Social Security number, medical record number, patient name, or medical terms like "cancer". Recipients of these encrypted e-mail messages receive a link to a Web site set up to deliver the hospital's encrypted e-mail messages. After being authenticated, they can view their e-mail messages. Similar systems are used by banks and other businesses.

Properly Dispose of Hardware

A final consideration for protecting the privacy of personal information is protecting the information located on hardware to be disposed of, such as old backup media, used CDs, obsolete PCs, and so forth. CDs, DVDs, and other media containing sensitive data should be shredded (see Figure 15-19), and the hard drives of computers to be disposed of should be *wiped* clean—overwritten several times using special *disk-wiping* or *disk-erasing* software. Unlike the data on a drive that has merely been erased or even reformatted (which can still be recovered), data on a wiped drive is unrecoverable.

ELECTRONIC SURVEILLANCE AND MONITORING

There are many ways electronic tools can be used to watch individuals, listen in on their conversations, or monitor their activities. Some of these tools—such as devices used by individuals to eavesdrop on wireless telephone conversations—are not legal. Other products and technologies, such as the GPS devices that are built into some cars so they can be located if they are stolen or the monitoring ankle bracelets used for offenders sentenced to house arrest, are used solely for law enforcement purposes. Still other electronic tools, such as *computer monitoring software* and *video surveillance* equipment, can be used legally by individuals, businesses, and law enforcement agencies, as discussed next.

Computer Monitoring Software

Computer monitoring software is used specifically for the purpose of recording keystrokes or otherwise monitoring someone's computer activity (see Figure 15-20). These programs are typically marketed towards parents (to check on their children's online activities), spouses (to determine if a spouse is having an affair, viewing pornography, or participating in other activities that are unacceptable to the other spouse), employers (to ensure employees are using company computers and time only for work-related or otherwise approved activities), or law enforcement agencies (to collect evidence against suspected criminals). Computer monitoring programs can be set up to keep a log of all computer keystrokes, to record activity predesignated as questionable (such as visiting certain Web sites), or to take screen shots at specified intervals. Some computer monitoring software also includes the ability to block access to certain Web sites or Internet activities (such as instant messaging). It can also be used to block access to the Internet in general for specific individuals or during specific time periods (such as a parent blocking all Internet access on workdays until a predesignated time or an employer blocking access to certain popular non-work-related Web sites, except during the lunch hour).

>Computer monitoring software. Software that can be used to record an individual's computer usage, typically either by capturing images of the screen or by recording the actual keystrokes used.

Although it is legal to use computer monitoring software on your own computer or on the computers of your employees, installing it on other PCs without the owners' knowledge to monitor their computer activity is usually illegal. For example, in 2001, a Michigan man installed monitoring software on the computer of his estranged wife, who was living in a separate residence at the time. The software recorded all of her computer activity, including all e-mail messages sent and received and all Web pages visited, and sent that information to the man's e-mail account. After he mentioned information that he should not have known to a friend of his wife, the matter was investigated, and the man was charged with four felony counts (installing an eavesdropping device, eavesdropping, using a computer to commit a crime, and having unauthorized computer access). Faced with up to five years in prison and fines of up to $19,000, the man pled guilty in 2002 to two of the charges and was sentenced to two years' probation plus court costs and fees.

Screen shot of program being used.

Date and time program was accessed.

Program name and URL for Web pages visited.

Keystrokes typed in any program.

A growing illegal use of computer monitoring software is for a hacker to use a *keystroke-logging program*—a computer monitoring program that records all keystrokes performed on the PC—to capture usernames, passwords, and other sensitive data entered into the PC via the keyboard. The software can be installed on an individual's PC via malware, or it can be installed on public computers in person, if the proper precautions are not taken. For instance, in 2003, a New York man admitted that he installed keystroke-logging software on computers located at Kinko's stores throughout Manhattan to collect computer usernames and passwords of Kinko's customers. In 2005, he was sentenced to 27 months in prison, three years probation, and over $200,000 in restitution for this and four other charges related to computer fraud and software piracy.

FIGURE 15-20

Computer monitoring software. Most programs keeps a log of the programs used and Web sites visited, as shown here.

In addition to monitoring products designed for consumers, there are also computer monitoring programs available for use only by law enforcement and other government agencies. Like wiretapping, electronic monitoring of computer activity requires a court order or similar authorization to be lawful (although the *USA Patriot Act* does allow the FBI to conduct a limited form of Internet surveillance first, such as to capture e-mail addresses or IP addresses used on traffic going into or coming from a suspect's PC). Several years ago, before computer monitoring software was widely available, the FBI developed a special monitoring program called *Carnivore* to intercept e-mail and Web activity from individuals suspected of criminal activity. In 2005, the Carnivore program was official retired and replaced with commercial computer monitoring software. With proper authorization and cooperation from a suspect's ISP, law enforcement agencies can use computer monitoring software to intercept files and e-mail messages sent to or from the suspect's PC. If the documents are encrypted, keystroke-logging software can be used to record e-mail messages and documents before they are encrypted, as well as to record the encryption keys used with messages and files.

Video Surveillance

The idea of **video surveillance** is nothing new. For years now, closed-circuit security cameras have been monitoring activities in retail stores, banks, office buildings, and other facilities open to the public. What is new, however, is the increased use of video cameras in public locations for law enforcement purposes.

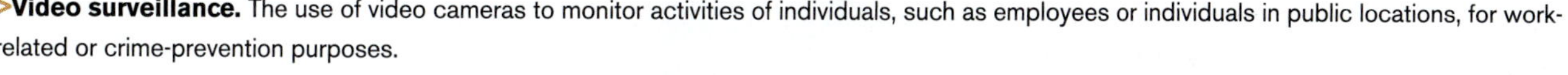

>**Video surveillance.** The use of video cameras to monitor activities of individuals, such as employees or individuals in public locations, for work-related or crime-prevention purposes.

SOC

Often used in conjunction with face recognition technology, video cameras are now being used in sporting arenas, airports, public parks, and high-crime areas in hopes of identifying known terrorists and other criminals and preventing crimes. Although one of the first public trials of this technology (at the 2001 Super Bowl—nicknamed the "Snooper Bowl" by some) resulted in a huge public outcry, public opinion since 9/11 has become more tolerant of video surveillance. In a September 2001 Harris poll, an astounding 86% of the Americans polled approved of the use of face recognition technology to scan for suspected terrorists at various public locations and events. This poll shows a clear shift in some Americans' priorities from personal privacy to personal safety. A follow-up poll in 2004 reported that 80% of Americans continue to approve of the use of face recognition technology for these purposes, and 61% continue to support expanded camera surveillance on streets and in public places.

The focus of public video camera installations in the United States immediately after the terrorist attacks of 9/11 was in New York and Washington, D.C. Since then, however, the use of public video cameras has been growing all over the United States and in other countries. Worldwide, Britain is the leader in video surveillance usage, with over four million video surveillance cameras installed in public locations—it is estimated that the average Briton can expect to be caught on camera up to 300 times a day. Video surveillance data is proving to be valuable to police for catching terrorists and other types of criminals. For instance, video from some of the London subway's 6,000 video cameras was used to identify four suicide bombers who killed at least 55 people in the 2005 London subway bombings. New video surveillance installations in the United States include Baltimore, where a $2 million network of more than 90 surveillance cameras in tourist areas and high-crime neighborhoods is being installed; Chicago, where an additional 250 cameras are being installed in high-crime areas that will be linked to 2,000 other cameras that monitor public locations (such as public housing, the transit system, and public buildings) so their feeds can all be watched at the city's emergency operations center; and Los Angeles, where video cameras are being installed in three neighborhoods to detect and prevent street sales of bootleg DVDs.

In many cases, public video surveillance cameras are outside and hidden from view or disguised, such as inside lamp fixtures (see Figure 15-21). Other installations, such as the cameras set up for face recognition screening in airports, are more obvious. Schools in the United States and other countries are also installing video cameras in classrooms to enable administrators to monitor both teacher and student activities and to have a record of incidents as they occur. A snapshot of a live video feed from a camera installed inside a campus building at the University of Helsinki is shown in Figure 15-21.

Privacy advocates object to the use of video surveillance and face recognition technology in public locations, primarily based on concerns regarding how the video captured by these systems will be used and doubt about the usefulness of these systems in protecting against terrorism. They also object to the fact that, unlike private security video which is typically only viewed after a crime has occurred, the images from many public video cameras are watched all the time. In addition, networks of police video cameras that feed into a central operations point allow the observation of innocent people and activities

FIGURE 15-21
Examples of public video surveillance.

OUTDOOR SURVEILLANCE
Many cameras placed in public locations are designed to blend into their surroundings to be less intrusive, such as the camera inside this light fixture on a Washington, D.C. street.

INDOOR SURVEILLANCE
Many cameras are placed inside businesses, schools, and other locations, such as the ones that broadcast live video from several indoor locations at the University of Helsinki; a snapshot from one of the video cameras is shown here.

on a massive scale. However, law enforcement agencies contend that face recognition systems and public video surveillance are no different than the many private video surveillance systems in place today in a wide variety of public locations, such as in retail stores and banks. They view this technology as just one more tool to be used to protect the public, similar to scanning luggage at the airport. Privacy advocates fear being under perpetual police surveillance and the eventual expansion of these security surveillance systems, such as using them to look for "deadbeat dads" or for other applications not vital for national security. How accepting the public will be about being in a perpetual digital lineup—while at the grocery store, pumping gas, or playing in a park, for instance—remains to be seen. However, the 2004 Harris poll found that the overwhelming majority of Americans continue to support law enforcement surveillance measures—including public video surveillance cameras and face recognition technology. For a look at another high-tech law enforcement application that concerns some privacy advocates—border control—see the Inside the Industry box.

A related privacy concern is the inclusion of digital camera capabilities in many cell phones today—approximately 500 million camera phones were purchased in 2005, according to the research firm Future Image, Inc., and that number is expected to reach 900 million units by 2009. Although camera functions are included for personal enjoyment and convenience and are increasingly being used to help law enforcement (such as being used by citizens to take photos of crimes as they are being committed), some fear that the ubiquitous nature of cell phones, combined with the inability to easily tell that a cell phone is being used to take a photo, will lead to increased privacy violations. In fact, some athletic clubs have banned cell phones entirely to protect the privacy of their members while working out and in the dressing rooms. Many YMCAs, city parks and recreation departments, and other recreational facilities have banned camera phone use in locker rooms and restrooms to protect the privacy of both children and adults. Camera phones are also being banned by some schools to prevent cheating, by many courthouses to prevent witness or jury intimidation, and by many research and production facilities to prevent corporate espionage. Legally speaking, people typically have few rights to privacy in public places, but many believe that new technology—such as camera phones—will require the law to reconsider and redefine what is considered to be a public place and where citizens can expect to retain particular aspects of personal privacy.

Employee Monitoring

Employee monitoring refers to companies recording or observing the actions of employees while on the job. With today's technology, employee monitoring is very easy to perform, and much of it can be done through the use of computers. Common employee monitoring activities include screening telephone calls, reviewing e-mail, and tracking computer and Internet usage. Although many employees feel that being watched at work is an invasion of their personal privacy, it is legal and very common. According to the American Management Association (AMA), the vast majority (nearly 78%) of all U.S. companies uses some type of electronic surveillance with their employees, 65% of the companies had disciplined employees for misuse of e-mail or the Internet at work, and 27% had fired an employee for that reason. Typically, the main reason is to monitor Internet usage, since misuse of the Internet among employees has become a major concern. According to IDC Research, 30% to 40% of Internet use in the workplace is not related to business. In fact, a

>**Employee monitoring.** Observing or reviewing employees' actions while they are on the job.

INSIDE THE INDUSTRY

High-Tech Border Control

In addition to the face recognition systems used in conjunction with video surveillance systems at airports, other high-tech border control systems are in place. For instance, there are biometric systems in place that are used to authenticate frequent travelers in order to speed up security checks at airports and border crossings. These systems—most often using hand geometry readers, fingerprint scanners, or iris scanners—enroll individuals by capturing their biometric data and verifying their identities using a credit card or other means. Once enrolled, these travelers can bypass the complex security checks required of other individuals. For example, the U.S. Transportation Security Administration (TSA) completed pilot testing of its *Registered Traveler* program at several airports around the country in 2005. This program allows frequent travelers—those who fly at least once per week—to use special security checkpoints set up to verify the travelers' identities using registered biometric data. The main benefits of the system include convenience for the traveler and freeing up more time for security personnel to concentrate on unverified individuals. It has yet to be determined if the system will be implemented nationwide.

Countries with a high level of border activity have also found that technology can tremendously speed up border checks. For example, a border-security program called *US-VISIT* that was introduced in the United States in 2004 can approve individuals for entry to the United States in less than 15 seconds. The system uses *laser visas* containing digital fingerprint data and a digital photograph in conjunction with a laser visa reader and fingerprint scanner (see the accompanying figure) to verify the identity of foreign visitors entering the United States. To identify an individual whose identity is suspect, the new system can use a digital fingerprint scan of all 10 fingers to search both the Homeland Security Department's *Automated Biometric Identification System* (*IDENT*), which contains identities of individuals who have illegally entered the United States, and the FBI's *Integrated Automated Fingerprint Identification System* (*IAFIS*) database, which contains about 47 million criminal records, histories of individuals, and outstanding arrest warrants. The search takes an average of 10 minutes—a significant improvement over the old system, which required between 8 hours and 3 months for fingerprints to be faxed or mailed to the FBI and then identified. US-VISIT is currently being used for entry procedures in the United States at 115 of the country's busiest airports, 15 seaports, and 50 land borders, and it is used for exit procedures at 12 airports and two seaports. The system is scheduled to be expanded to all land ports of entry by the end of 2005. A related system in place at Ben Gurion Airport in Tel Aviv, Israel, uses a combination of hand geometry and face recognition, and it processes tens of thousands of travelers each month at a pace of less than 20 seconds each. To process the 40,000 Palestinian workers entering Israel each day from Gaza, an automated hand geometry system in place at that border allows or rejects people entering or exiting Israel in less than two seconds—replacing a manual system requiring hundreds of security personnel.

Biometrics are also beginning to be implemented in other U.S. identification documents, such as passports, driver's licenses, and personal identification cards. For instance, the *Real ID Act* of 2005 requires state governments to implement minimum security standards, including biometric data, into driver's licenses and personal ID cards within three years. And several other countries have or are implementing biometric ID or border control programs. For instance, the British government is planning a national ID card that will contain biometric data, as well as a national identity registry that will contain biometric data and be used to track foreign visitors, similar to the US-VISIT program.

The US-VISIT border control system, installed at many ports of entry, uses laser visas to verify the identity of each visitor entering the United States.

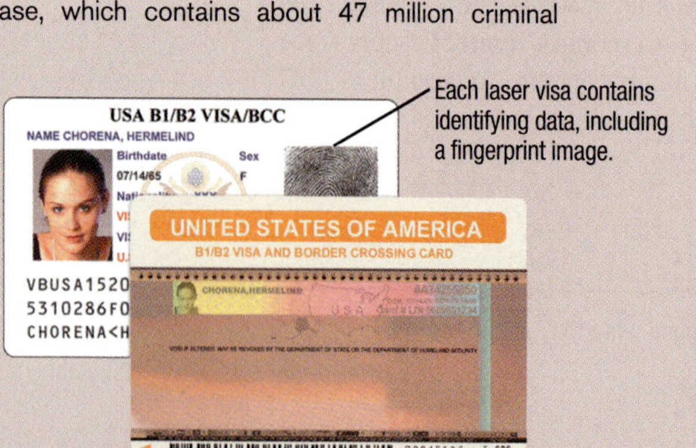

U.S. LASER VISA

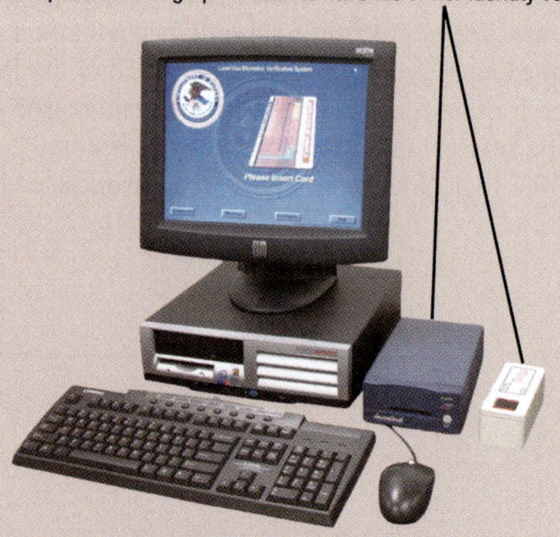

U.S. BORDER CONTROL STATION

2005 study by Salary.com and America Online revealed that the average American employee admits to wasting two hours each workday (over an hour more than human resources specialists expect), and the bulk of that time is spent on personal Internet use. Typically, computer and Internet usage is monitored using computer monitoring software, discussed in a previous section.

For monitoring the physical locations of employees, video cameras can be used, but another possibility is the use of **proximity cards**. A proximity card is similar to the magnetic stripe ID cards frequently used to grant access to facilities or computer systems, but it has built-in smart card capabilities (see Figure 15-22) to give it additional functionality. For monitoring purposes, proximity cards can identify, on a continual basis, the location of each employee wearing one—an application that some privacy advocates feel crosses the line between valid employee monitoring and an invasion of privacy. Other less controversial uses for proximity cards include regular access capabilities (like conventional access cards), automatically locking an employee's PC when he or she gets a certain distance away from it (to eliminate the problem of nosy coworkers), and automatically unlocking the PC when the employee returns (to eliminate the need for passwords). Other types of employee monitoring systems designed for tracking an employee's location are GPS-based systems, such as those systems that track an employee via his or her cell phone, or those that notify the employer if the employee's company vehicle exits a prescribed work area. These types of GPS monitoring systems were discussed in Chapter 8.

FIGURE 15-22
Proximity cards. Proximity cards with smart card capabilities can be used for facility access, PC access, and employee monitoring.

Although some employees may view workplace monitoring as an invasion of their personal privacy, employers have several valid reasons for monitoring employee activities, such as security concerns, productivity measurement, legal compliance, and legal liability. For example, management has a responsibility to the company (and to its stockholders, for publicly held corporations) to make sure employees do the job that they are being paid to do. If any employees are spending too much time away from their desks chatting with other employees, answering their personal e-mail, or placing bids at online auctions, the company has the right to know and the responsibility to stop that misuse of company time and resources. For instance, there are many instances of employees viewing pornography, downloading pirated movies or music, watching live sports video feeds—even running their own businesses—on company time and computers. In addition, the company needs to protect itself against lost business (due to employee incompetence or poor client skills, for example) and lawsuits (such as from employees, if offensive e-mail messages are circulated within the office or if inappropriate Web sites are displayed on someone's PC). In addition, government regulations—such as the *Sarbanes-Oxley Act*, which requires publicly traded companies to keep track of which employees look at sensitive documents—may require it.

Even though employee monitoring systems can be expensive—from $20,000 for small companies to hundreds of thousands of dollars for larger firms, according to some estimates—many companies view the cost as insignificant compared to the risk of a potential multimillion-dollar lawsuit. It is becoming increasingly common for U.S. firms to face sexual harassment and/or racial discrimination claims stemming from employee e-mail and Internet use. A 2004 AMA study found that 21% of employers have had employee e-mail and instant messages subpoenaed in the course of a lawsuit or regulatory investigation. And lawsuits can be costly—Chevron was once ordered to pay female employees $2.2 million to settle a sexual harassment lawsuit stemming from inappropriate e-mail sent by male employees.

>**Proximity card.** An identification card with built-in smart card capabilities; used for access purposes, as well as for location monitoring.

Case law strongly supports employee monitoring since the equipment and network the employee uses belong to the employer; even e-mail messages sent or received at work have been ruled to be the employer's property. There have been several cases where employees have learned this fact the hard way, such as in December 1999 when 23 *New York Times* employees were fired for sending inappropriate e-mail messages to one another over the company's network. A trend very worrisome for employers is the high occurrence of e-mail or Web activity involving pornography or other potentially offensive content that leaves the employer liable for lawsuits. One AMA study found that 46% of the companies surveyed initiated disciplinary action against employees for sending sexually suggestive or explicit material via office e-mail (25% have fired an employee for violating the company e-mail policy), and 36% have disciplined employees for downloading, uploading, or viewing pornography.

To reduce cost and objections from employees, some businesses have found employee training and education to be an effective and cost-efficient alternative to continuous monitoring. Others use statistical-analysis software to detect unusual patterns in data collected about employee computer usage and just investigate the employees and situations that may indicate a problem. Regardless of the techniques used, it is wise for businesses to inform employees about their monitoring practices (including what activities may be monitored and how long records of that monitoring will be archived), although they are not required by law, at the current time, to do so. However, bills have been introduced in several states in the United States that would prohibit employee monitoring without employee notification.

Presence Technology

Presence technology refers to the ability of one computing device (such as a desktop PC, handheld computer, or smart phone) on a network (such as the Internet) to locate and identify another device on the same network and determine its status. In theory, it can be used to tell when someone on the network is using his or her computer or wireless phone, as well as where that device is physically located at any given time. For example, when an employee at a company using presence technology (sometimes called *presence management* in a business context) has a question that needs answering, he or she can check the directory displayed on his or her PC or cell phone to see which team members are available, regardless of where those team members are physically located (see Figure 15-23). The employee can then call a team member or send an instant message. Presence technology is also expected to be used on regular Web pages so that visitors—usually potential or current customers—can see which salespeople, service representatives, or other contacts are currently available. Another possible application is including dynamic presence buttons in e-mail messages—the presence button would display one message (such as "I'm online") if the sender is online at the time the e-mail message is read, and a different message (such as "I'm offline") if the sender is not online at that time. Support for online presence information is included in the latest version of Microsoft Office and is expected to be integrated in the upcoming Microsoft Windows Vista operating system. In addition, some U.S. states are beginning to test using presence technology to track cars in certain areas (via any cell phones in the cars that are on) to monitor traffic and help transportation agencies spot congestion and possibly divert drivers by issuing alerts on the radio or electronic road signs. Similar systems are already in place in some other countries, but privacy advocates object to cell phones being used to track individuals' movements without their consent.

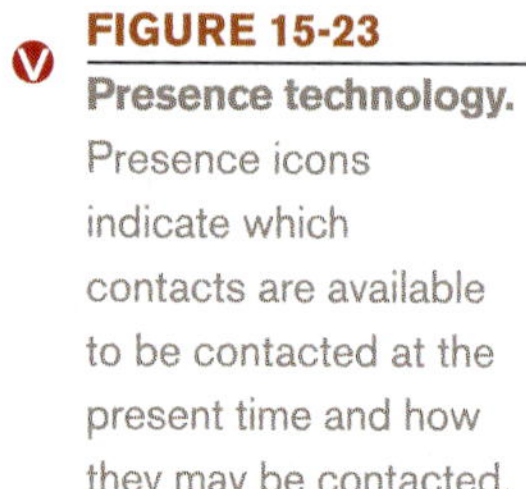

FIGURE 15-23
Presence technology. Presence icons indicate which contacts are available to be contacted at the present time and how they may be contacted.

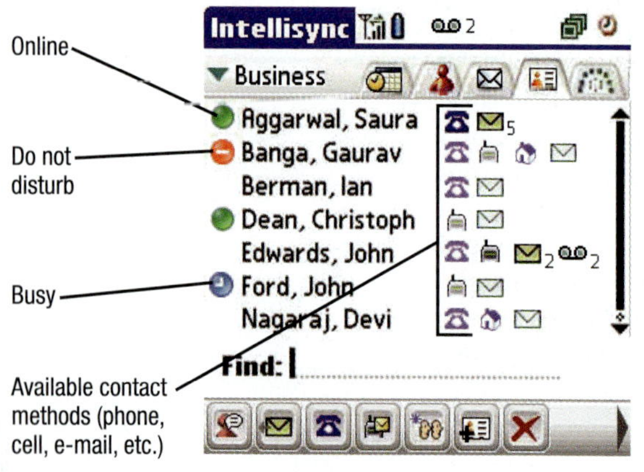

>**Presence technology.** Technology that enables one computing device (such as a desktop PC, handheld computer, or smart phone) to locate and identify the current status of another device on the same network.

Although presence technology is currently in the early stages, it has been in the works since 1996 in the form of the FCC *enhanced 911* (*e911*) mandate for wireless phones. The e911 mandate was prompted by the tremendous increase in 911 calls made from cell phones (now estimated to be one wireless call to 911 in the United States every four seconds) paired with the fact that 911 operators are unable to locate the position of wireless callers using older telephones, unlike callers using a land-based telephone. The e911 mandate specifies that new cell phones must have built-in GPS capabilities to enable emergency services personnel to pinpoint the location of people calling 911 using that phone. Phase I requires only the location of the nearest cell tower; phase II, which began in October 2001 and is scheduled to be fully implemented by the end of 2005, requires more precise location information. The e911 mandate has also been expanded to require Voice over IP (VoIP) companies to meet e911 requirements by the end of 2005. To accomplish this, VoIP customers must supply their home addresses to their VoIP providers; when those customers make emergency calls to 911 using VoIP, their calls are routed directly to a switchboard in the subscriber's area to relay the necessary information to emergency services.

Although these location services were designed to assist in emergencies, phone vendors and advertising agencies are expected to develop other uses for them, such as targeting ads and information to individuals based on their current physical location (such as close to a particular restaurant at lunchtime). Some aspects of presence technology are useful and intriguing, such as being able to tell that a loved one's flight arrived safely when you notice that his or her cell phone is on again, or knowing if a friend or colleague is available for a telephone call before dialing the number. However, privacy advocates are pushing for legislation and standards to ensure that presence technology providers protect users' security and privacy. A bill was introduced in the House of Representatives requiring informed customer consent for the use of wireless presence information, but the bill was still in committee at the time of this writing.

Protecting Personal and Workplace Privacy

There are not many options for protecting yourself against computer monitoring by your employer or the government or against video surveillance systems, but *antispy software* programs (see Figure 15-24) can be used to determine if your activities are being monitored by a hacker or other unauthorized individual. Because computer monitoring software can be attached to a file—such as an electronic greeting card, game, or other file that you might choose to download or open—it is possible that someone may install monitoring software on your PC without your knowledge. A hacker might do this in an attempt to record account numbers, passwords, and other sensitive data that could be used in identity theft or other fraudulent activities. If an antispy program detects such an intrusion, it will remove the offending program for you.

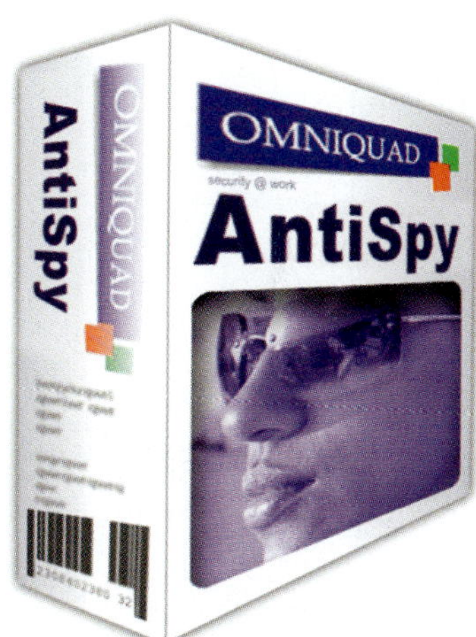

FIGURE 15-24
Antispy software.
Antispy software can detect and remove illegally installed computer monitoring software.

The Employer's Responsibilities

To protect the personal privacy of their employees and customers, businesses and organizations have a responsibility to keep private information about their employees, the company, and their customers safe. Strong security measures, such as firewalls and access-prevention methods for both computer data and facilities, can help to protect against unauthorized access by hackers. Businesses and organizations should take precautions against both intentional and accidental breaches of privacy by employees. Finally, businesses and organizations have the responsibility to monitor their employees' activities to ensure workers are productive. In general, businesses must maintain a safe and productive workplace environment and protect the privacy of their customers and employees, while at the same time avoid leaving the company vulnerable to lawsuits.

To inform employees of what personal activities (if any) are allowed during company time or on company equipment, as well as what employee activities (such as Web surfing, e-mail, telephone calls, and downloading files to an office PC) may be monitored, all businesses should have an *employee policy*. Employee policies are usually included in an employee handbook or posted on the company intranet.

The Employee's Responsibilities

Employees have the responsibility to read a company's employee policy when initially hired and to review it periodically to ensure that they understand the policy and do not violate any company rules while working for that organization. In addition, since at-work activities may legally be monitored by an employer, it is wise—from a privacy standpoint—to avoid personal activities at work entirely. From reading your organization's employee policy, you can determine if any personal activities are allowed at all (such as checking your personal e-mail on your lunch hour), but it is safer to perform personal activities at home, regardless. Be especially careful with any activity, such as sending a joke via e-mail to a coworker, that might be interpreted as harassment. For personal phone calls, use your cell phone or a pay phone outside during your lunch hour or rest break.

COMPUTER SECURITY AND PRIVACY LEGISLATION

The high level of concern regarding computer security and personal privacy has led state and federal legislators to pass a variety of laws since the 1970s (see Figure 15-25), including the *Computer Fraud and Abuse Act* and the USA Patriot Act. However, it is difficult for the legal system to keep pace with the rate that technology changes. In addition, there are jurisdictional issues domestically and internationally, since many computer crimes affect businesses and individuals located in geographic areas other than the one in which the computer criminal is located. Internet privacy is viewed as one of the top policy issues facing Congress today, and numerous bills have been proposed in the last several years regarding spam, telemarketing, spyware, online profiling, and other very important privacy issues, but new legislation has been slow in coming. One of the reasons is the struggle to balance freedom of speech with the right to privacy. Another issue is weighing legislation versus voluntary methods. For instance, the *Children's Online Protection Act* (*COPA*) has been highly controversial since it was passed in 1998, and, in fact, it has never been implemented. This legislation prohibited making pornography or any other content deemed harmful to minors available to minors via the Internet and carried a $50,000 fine. In mid-2004, the issue reached the U.S. Supreme Court for the third time, and the court ruled that a lower court was correct to block the law from taking effect because it likely violates the First Amendment. The case was sent back to a lower court for a trial to determine if Internet filtering and other related technologies provide sufficient protection for minors (that is, are they effective at keeping the material in question out of the hands of children) while allowing adults to view and buy material that is legal for them.

As discussed in the chapter, the Do-Not-Call Implementation Act (which implemented the National Do-Not-Call Registry) was enacted in late 2003 and the CAN-SPAM Act of 2003 enacted some requirements for spammers. Although the frequency with which users change e-mail addresses (compared to telephone numbers) and the varying opinions as to what constitutes spam makes many experts believe that it will be difficult, if not impossible, to develop fair and effective antispam legislation, a federal *Do-Not-E-Mail Registry* is in the works. The FTC is also proposing the use of "bounties"—a percentage of whatever civil penalty the FTC collects based on the provided information—to be given to individuals reporting spammers performing illegal activities, such as hijacking another person's PC to distribute spam. In response to the number of data security breaches in 2005, several pieces of legislation have been introduced—such as the proposed *Personal Data Privacy and Security Act of 2005*—to help consumers better protect the privacy of their personal information. Another law related to privacy is the *Health Insurance Portability and Accountability Act (HIPAA)*, which includes a Security Rule that sets minimum security standards to protect health information stored electronically.

FURTHER EXPLORATION

For links to further information about computer security and privacy legislation, go to www.course.com/uc11/ch15

DATE	LAW AND DESCRIPTION
2005	**Junk Fax Prevention Act** Requires unsolicited faxes to have a highly-visible opt-out notice.
2003	**CAN-Spam Act** Implements regulations for unsolicited e-mail messages and lays the groundwork for a federal Do-Not-E-Mail Registry.
2003	**Do-Not-Call Implementation Act** Amends the Telephone Consumer Protection Act to implement the National Do-Not-Call Registry.
2003	**Health Insurance Portability and Accountability Act (HIPAA)** Includes a Security Rule that sets minimum security standards to protect health information stored electronically.
2002	**Sarbanes-Oxley Act** Requires archiving a variety of electronic records and protecting the integrity of corporate financial data.
2001	**USA Patriot Act (USAPA)** Grants federal authorities expanded surveillance and intelligence-gathering powers, such as broadening the ability of federal agents to obtain the real identity of Internet users, intercept e-mail and other types of Internet communications, follow online activity of suspects, expand their wiretapping authority, and more.
1999	**Financial Modernization (Gramm-Leach-Bliley) Act** Extends the ability of banks, securities firms and insurance companies to share consumers' non-public personal information, but requires them to notify consumers and give them the opportunity to opt-out before disclosing any information.
1998	**Children's Online Privacy Protection Act (COPPA)** Regulates how Web sites can collect information from minors and communicate with them. Also provides an exception from Internet tax moratoriums for Web sites providing material that is harmful to minors (unless access to such material is restricted to those 18 or over), and for ISPs (unless they offer screening software that allows customers to limit access to Internet material that is deemed harmful to minors).
1998	**Telephone Anti-Spamming Amendments Act** Applies restrictions to unsolicited, bulk commercial e-mail.
1996	**National Information Infrastructure Protection Act** Amends the Computer Fraud and Abuse Act of 1984 to punish information theft crossing state lines and crack down on network trespassing.
1992	**Cable Act** Extends the Cable Communications Policy Act to include companies that sell wireless services.
1991	**Telephone Consumer Protection Act** Requires telemarketing companies to respect the rights of people who do not want to be called and significantly restricts the use of recorded messages.
1988	**Computer Matching Privacy Act** Limits the use of government data in determining federal-benefit recipients.
1988	**Video Privacy Protection Act** Limits disclosure of customer information by video-rental companies.
1986	**Computer Fraud and Abuse Act of 1986** Amends the 1984 law to include federally regulated financial institutions.
1986	**Electronic Communications Privacy Act** Extends traditional privacy protections governing postal delivery and telephone services to include e-mail, cellular phones, and voice mail.
1984	**Cable Communications Policy Act** Limits disclosure of customer records by cable TV companies.
1984	**Computer Fraud and Abuse Act of 1984** Makes it a crime to break into computers owned by the federal government.
1978	**Right to Financial Privacy Act** Provides guidelines that federal agencies must follow when inspecting an individual's bank records.
1974	**Education Privacy Act** Stipulates that, in both public and private schools that receive any federal funding, individuals have the right to keep the schools from releasing such information as grades and evaluations of behavior.
1974	**Privacy Act** Stipulates that the collection of data by federal agencies must have a legitimate purpose.
1970	**Fair Credit Reporting Act** Prevents private organizations from unfairly denying credit to individuals and provides individuals the right to inspect their credit records for truthfulness.
1970	**Freedom of Information Act** Gives individuals the right to inspect data concerning them that are stored by the federal government.

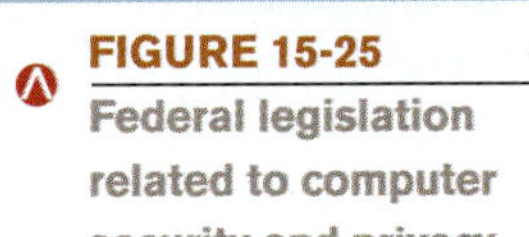

FIGURE 15-25
Federal legislation related to computer security and privacy.

SUMMARY

WHY BE CONCERNED ABOUT COMPUTER SECURITY?

Chapter Objective 1:
Explain why all computer users should be concerned about computer security.

There are a number of important security concerns related to computers, such as having your PC stolen, losing data, and running the risk of buying pirated or digitally counterfeited products via an online auction. All computer users should be aware of the possible security risks and know some safeguards to prevent against security problems since these problems can cost you time and money, as well as be an inconvenience.

HARDWARE LOSS, DAMAGE, AND SYSTEM FAILURE

Chapter Objective 2:
List some risks associated with hardware loss, damage, and system failure, and understand ways to safeguard a PC against these risks.

Hardware loss (perhaps as a result of **hardware theft** or misplaced hardware), damage (both intentional and unintentional), and **system failure** are important concerns about which all users need to be aware. System failure can occur because of a hardware problem, as well as result from a natural or man-made disaster. To protect against hardware theft, door and equipment locks can be used. To protect against accidental hardware damage, **surge suppressors**, **uninterruptible power supplies** (**UPSs**), proper storage media care, and precautions against excess dust, heat, and static are important. To be prepared for data loss, backups are essential for both individuals and businesses—most businesses should also develop a **disaster-recovery plan** for natural and man-made disasters.

SOFTWARE PIRACY AND DIGITAL COUNTERFEITING

Chapter Objective 3:
Define software piracy and digital counterfeiting and explain how they may be prevented.

Software piracy (the unauthorized copying of a computer program) and **digital counterfeiting** (creating fake copies of currency and other resources) are illegal in the United States. They cost manufacturers billions of dollars each year, and some of these costs are passed on to law-abiding consumers. Various tools, such as consumer education and holograms, can be used to prevent software piracy. Many businesses are also aggressively pursuing pirates in court in an attempt to reduce piracy. The government has various methods in place to prevent digital counterfeiting of currency, such as using difficult-to-reproduce materials and features.

WHY BE CONCERNED ABOUT INFORMATION PRIVACY?

Chapter Objective 4:
Explain what information privacy is and why computer users should be concerned about it.

There are a number of important **privacy** concerns related to computers and the Internet. For instance, **information privacy** refers to the rights of individuals and companies to control how information about them is collected and used. Privacy issues affect the lives of everyone.

DATABASES, ELECTRONIC PROFILING, SPAM, AND OTHER MARKETING ACTIVITIES

Chapter Objective 5:
Describe some privacy concerns regarding databases, electronic profiling, spam, and telemarketing, and identify ways individuals can protect their privacy.

The extensive use of **marketing databases** and **government databases** brings concern to both privacy organizations and individuals. Information in marketing databases is frequently sold to companies and other organizations; information in some government databases is available to the public. Some database information can be retrieved via the Web. **Electronic profiling** is the collection of diverse information about an individual, such as information collected from these databases. An organization's **privacy policy** addresses how any personal information submitted to that company will be used. Other privacy issues concerning individuals include the vast amounts of **spam** (unsolicited bulk e-mail) that occur today.

Protecting your e-mail address is one of the best ways to avoid spam. A **throw-away e-mail address** can be used for any activities that may result in spam; then your permanent personal e-mail address can be used only for those communications that should not result in spam. Before providing any personal information on a Web page, it is a good idea to review the Web site's privacy policy to see if the information will be shared with other organizations. Consider whether or not the Web site is requesting too much personal information, and only provide the required data. Do not provide personal details in chat rooms and personal Web sites. Unless you do not mind spam or are using a throw-away e-mail address, avoid completing online forms to enter sweepstakes, win free merchandise, or take part in other marketing activities.

E-mail filters can be used to manage an individual's e-mail, including spam. To reduce the amount of spam, junk mail, online ads, and telemarketing calls received, an individual can **opt out**. Typically, this requires contacting each company directly, although some Web sites provide links to online opt-out forms or create form letters that can be printed and mailed to the appropriate companies. Users should be cautious when disposing of old hardware, such as hard drives and CDs, that contain sensitive data. Hard drives should be *wiped* clean, and CDs and other media should be shredded.

ELECTRONIC SURVEILLANCE AND MONITORING

Chapter Objective 6:
Discuss several types of electronic surveillance and monitoring and list ways individuals can protect their privacy.

Computer monitoring software that can record an individual's computer use can be viewed as a privacy violation by some, as can the increased use of **video surveillance** in public locations. Although it is allowed by law, some employees view **employee monitoring** (such as monitoring computer use, telephone calls, and an individual's location using **proximity cards** or video surveillance) as an invasion of their privacy. **Presence technology**—the ability of one computer on a network to know the status and location of another computer on that network—was originally developed in response to an *enhanced 911* (*e911*) mandate that required 911 operators to be able to identify the location of callers using a mobile phone. Although in the early stages, presence technology is expected eventually to allow users of computers, mobile phones, and other devices used for communication to be able to determine the availability of other individuals before contacting them.

To protect the privacy of employees and customers, businesses have a responsibility to keep private information about their employees, the company, and their customers safe. Firewalls, password-protected files, and encryption can help secure this information. Businesses also have the responsibility to monitor employee activities to ensure that employees are performing the jobs they are being paid to do, not causing lost business, and not leaving the company open to lawsuits. To inform employees of allowable activities, an *employee policy* or code of conduct should be developed and distributed to employees. For the highest level of privacy while at the workplace, employees should perform only work-related activities on the job.

COMPUTER SECURITY AND PRIVACY LEGISLATION

Chapter Objective 7:
Discuss the status of computer security and privacy legislation.

Although computer security and privacy are viewed as extremely important issues, legislation is difficult due to ongoing changes in technology, jurisdictional issues, and varying opinions. Legislation related to computer security includes the *Computer Fraud and Abuse Act* and the *USA Patriot Act*. Privacy legislation includes the *Do-Not-Call Implementation Act*, *CAN-Spam Act*, and *Health Insurance Portability and Accountability Act (HIPAA)*.

REVIEW ACTIVITIES

KEY TERM MATCHING

Instructions: Match each key term on the left with the definition on the right that best describes it.

a. digital counterfeiting

b. disaster-recovery plan

c. hardware theft

d. information privacy

e. presence technology

f. proximity card

g. software piracy

h. surge suppressor

i. system failure

j. uninterruptible power supply (UPS)

1. ______ A device containing a built-in battery that provides continuous power to a PC and other connected components when the electricity goes out.

2. ______ A device that protects a computer system from damage due to electrical fluctuations.

3. ______ A written plan that describes the steps a company will take following the occurrence of a disaster.

4. ______ An identification card with built-in smart card capabilities; used for access purposes, as well as for location monitoring.

5. ______ Technology that enables one computing device (such as a desktop PC, handheld computer, or smart phone) to locate and identify the current status of another device on the same network.

6. ______ The complete malfunction of a computer system.

7. ______ The rights of individuals and companies to control how information about them is collected and used.

8. ______ The theft of computer hardware.

9. ______ The unauthorized copying of a computer program.

10. ______ The use of computers or other types of digital equipment to make illegal copies of currency, checks, collectibles, and other items.

SELF-QUIZ

Instructions: Circle **T** if the statement is true, **F** if the statement is false, or write the best answer in the space provided. **Answers to the self-quiz are located in the References and Resources Guide at the end of the book.**

1. **T** **F** As long as a business owns one legal copy of a software program, it can install that program on as many computers as desired without fear of retribution.

2. **T** **F** Electronic profiling is the act of using electronic means to collect a variety of in-depth information about an individual, such as name, address, income, and buying habits.

3. **T** **F** Encryption can be used for privacy purposes in addition to security purposes.

4. **T** **F** One way of safeguarding your e-mail address is to use a single e-mail address for all Internet activity, such as personal communications, online shopping, and completing online surveys.

5. **T** **F** Very few major U.S. companies monitor the online activities of their employees.

6. A(n) ______ plan can help a business get operational again following a fire, act of sabotage, or similar disaster.

7. Color copying money is an example of ______.

8. An e-mail ______ can be used to route suspected spam automatically into a separate e-mail folder.

9. If you ______, you are requesting that you be removed from marketing activities or that your information not be shared with other companies.

10. Match each precaution with the security risk it is designed to protect against and write the corresponding number in the blank to the left of each security risk.

a. ________ Digital counterfeiting		**1.** Hologram
b. ________ Hardware theft		**2.** Encryption
c. ________ Privacy breach		**3.** Surge suppressor
d. ________ System damage		**4.** Microprinting
e. ________ Software piracy		**5.** Cable lock

EXERCISES

1. Match each privacy risk with its related term and write the corresponding number in the blank to the left of each term.

a. ________ Throw-away e-mail address	**1.** Employee monitoring
b. ________ Do-Not-Call Registry	**2.** Video surveillance
c. ________ Proximity card	**3.** Telemarketing
d. ________ Riding public transportation	**4.** Spam

2. Match each employee monitoring tool with its description and write the corresponding number in the blank to the left of each description.

   a. ________ Used to create a visual record of the actions an employee takes in a particular location.
   b. ________ Used to locate and identify the current status of an employee via a network.
   c. ________ Used to record the activities an employee performs on his or her computer.
   d. ________ Used to determine the current physical location of the employee.

1. Computer monitoring software	**3.** Proximity card
2. Presence technology	**4.** Video surveillance

3. List two precautions that can be taken while traveling with a portable PC to guard against its theft.

4. Explain the purpose of an uninterruptible power supply (UPS) and how it differs in function from a surge suppressor.

5. Think of one computer-related security or privacy risk you have encountered recently. Describe the risk and list at least one precaution that could be taken to minimize that risk.

DISCUSSION QUESTION

According to a study by the Missouri School of Journalism at Columbia's University of Missouri, many Internet users are willing to accept spam in return for a discount on their ISP bill, and the study found that the users paying the highest rates for Internet access were more willing to trade spam for monetary savings. With the amount of spam-blocking taking place at the ISP level and the proliferation of third-party software to block spam, pop-up ads, and other forms of onscreen marketing, it makes one wonder what the long-term effect will be on online advertising and the Web in general. If these types of marketing techniques eventually become unprofitable, will free Web content begin to disappear? Is paying Internet users to receive spam a viable option? Would you be willing to pay higher rates for Internet access or pay for an increasing amount of Web content if you were guaranteed an ad-free and spam-free environment? Just as with television, some amount of advertising is typically necessary in order to support free content. What do you think is the optimal balance for the Web?

PROJECTS

HOT TOPICS

1. **Electronic Health Records** As discussed in the Trend box, the use of electronic health records (EHRs) is growing rapidly. Proponents view EHRs as a means to deliver better care more efficiently. Some privacy advocates are concerned about the possible security breaches of servers containing digital private medical information.

   For this project, research the current use of EHRs. What are the benefits? Are EHRs widely used? Have you personally filled out a digital patient information form or other medical document via a computer? If so, share your experience and how easy or difficult the system was to use. Do you have any privacy concerns about your medical history being stored on a computer that, potentially, could be accessed by a hacker or other unauthorized individual? Do you think the risk of a privacy breach is higher with EHRs as compared with the records contained in conventional paper file folders? Do the benefits of EHRs outweigh the potential risks? At the conclusion of your research, prepare a one-page summary of your findings and submit it to your instructor.

SHORT ANSWER/ RESEARCH

2. **E-Voting** The chapter Technology and You box takes a look at e-voting. Consider the concerns raised in that box. For example: Are e-voting machines secure and accurate? With online voting, how will the system prevent someone voting as another individual? Can an online voting system be adequately protected against hackers and viruses? With either method, can an accurate recount be performed?

   For this project, research the current status of e-voting. Have universal standards been developed for all e-voting machines used in the United States or is that decision made on a state-by-state basis? Has online voting been allowed recently? Also, form an opinion about the use of e-voting machines and online voting. Would you be comfortable casting your vote via a DRE machine? How about online? What types of authentication methods would you want in place to verify your identify before submitting an online ballot? At some point, do you think online voting will become the norm? If so, how would you suggest handling individuals who have no Internet access available to them on Election Day? At the conclusion of your research, submit your findings and opinions to your instructor in the form of a short paper, no more than two pages in length.

3. **Spam** Despite antispam legislation and tools, many Internet users today are flooded with unsolicited e-mail messages. Typically, the more often you share your e-mail address with companies, the more spam you will receive.

   For this project, research the current status of spam and spam-related legislation. How many spam messages do you receive daily? Does it interfere with your life? Have you ever had the experience of signing up for something at a Web site or clicking a particular Web page ad and shortly thereafter receiving spam related to that action? Do you typically just delete spam messages, or do you try to unsubscribe? If you have ever tried to unsubscribe, does it seem to work? Find out what federal antispam legislation has been implemented, how it works, and if it seems to be effective. Is there any additional federal legislation in the works? At the conclusion of your research, submit your findings and opinions to your instructor in the form of a short paper, no more than two pages in length.

HANDS ON

4. **Employee Monitoring** As mentioned in the chapter, it is not unusual for organizations to monitor their employees' activities, including telephone calls, e-mail, Web activity, and Internet downloads.

   For this project, research the employee monitoring activities of an organization in your community (such as your school, place of business, or another business or organization). Find out if employee monitoring is used at your chosen organization (you will likely need to contact the human resources department of that organization to obtain the needed information). Determine the activities that the organization monitors, how frequently monitoring takes place, and how the employees to be monitored are selected. Is there a written employee policy regarding this? If not, are employees notified that monitoring may take place? At the conclusion of your research, submit your findings to your instructor in the form of a short summary. Be sure to include an opinion of whether or not the employee monitoring practices at this organization would influence whether or not you would like to work there.

5. **Browser Privacy Settings** There are a variety of settings in a Web browser that pertain to privacy, such as cookie, cache, history, and e-mail settings.

   For this project, find a public computer (such as in a computer lab at your school or at your local public library) on which you are permitted to make changes to the e-mail settings and delete the cookie files, cache, and history information (ask permission first if you are not sure if these actions are allowed) and perform the following tasks.

   a. Open the available browser and check the current browser settings (in Internet Explorer, select *Internet Options* from the Tools menu and look at the General and Privacy tabs; in Netscape Navigator, select *Preferences* from the Edit menu and look under the Navigator and Advanced options). Find the appropriate options to clear the cache (temporary files), history list, and cookie files. Also, open the associated e-mail program and delete any current e-mail settings (in Outlook Express, select *Accounts* from the Tools menu and click the Mail tab; in Netscape Mail, select *Mail/News Account Settings* from the Edit menu).

   b. Return to the browser and visit at least five different Web sites to build a history and cookie list. You may want to go to a shopping Web site and add items to your shopping cart (but do not complete the checkout process) or personalize a portal page, such as specifying your ZIP code at MSNBC.com.

   c. Find the appropriate menu option or toolbar button to display your history list. Are the Web sites you visited listed there? Display the browser settings again and find the option to view the cookie files. Were new cookies added during your browser session? If so, are all of them from the Web sites you visited, or are any of them third-party advertising cookies?

   d. Delete all temporary Internet files (cache, cookie files, and the history list), then close the browser window. Prepare a short summary of your work to submit to your instructor.

WRITING ABOUT COMPUTERS

6. **Fourth Amendment** The Fourth Amendment to the U.S. Constitution is frequently mentioned in the privacy debate.

   For this project, locate the text of the Fourth Amendment and analyze it. Does it address personal privacy? If you think so, which part of the amendment applies to personal privacy? If you do not think it addresses privacy, why do you think this amendment is quoted so often in proprivacy arguments? Next, find at least two articles (either in print or online) in which the Fourth Amendment is mentioned in relation to personal privacy. In what context is the Fourth Amendment used in the articles? Do you agree with the stated opinions? Why or why not? Do you believe the Fourth Amendment guarantees all Americans privacy? Submit your findings and opinions to your instructor in the form of a short paper, not more than two pages in length.

PRESENTATION/ DEMONSTRATION

7. **Privacy Policy Flip-Flops** Although a company's privacy policy may look acceptable when you read it before submitting personal information to that company, there is no guarantee that the policy will not be changed.

For this project, locate three different privacy policies on Web sites, analyze them, and compare them. Do the policies specify what personal information might be shared and with whom? Do any of the organizations reserve the right to change their policy at a later time without notice? If so, will they try to notify consumers? Do any of the policies allow for any sharing of data to third-party organizations? If so, is the data personally identifiable, and can customers opt out? Can you find any additional clauses in the policies that might be of concern to users? Also, determine if there are any recent examples of companies changing or violating their privacy policies and any new or impending related legislation. Form an opinion regarding a company's right to change its privacy policy and the impact such a change may have on customer loyalty. Share your findings with the class in the form of a short presentation. The presentation should not exceed 10 minutes and should make use of one or more presentation aids, such as the chalkboard, handouts, overhead transparencies, or a computer-based slide presentation (your instructor may provide additional requirements). You may also be asked to submit a summary of the presentation to your instructor.

GROUP DISCUSSION

8. **Washington, D.C. Security Camera Network** Live surveillance cameras are being used at an increasing number of public locations. Washington, D.C. is going one step further than using individual cameras at a specific location—it is building what will be the nation's biggest network of surveillance cameras. The system includes hundreds of cameras to watch over mass transit stations, public schools, traffic intersections, shopping malls, national monuments, and more. There are varying opinions about this type of live public video surveillance. Some view it as a valid crime prevention tool; others think it is an invasion of privacy. With this network, the cameras do not record activities unless there is a reason for it. Should that alleviate some critics' objections, or do you think they object to potentially being watched in public, regardless of whether or not their activities are recorded? At the present time, the system does not have face recognition capabilities. If adding that feature might help to capture terrorists and other criminals, should the government install it? Does the government have the responsibility to use every means possible to protect the country and its citizens? Or do citizens have the right not to be watched in public? One objection stated about this system is "It's not the same as a cop on the corner. This is a cop on every corner." What if it were a live police officer at each video camera location instead of a camera? Would that be more acceptable from a privacy standpoint? If people do not plan to commit criminal acts in public, should they be concerned that law enforcement personnel may see them?

For this project, form an opinion about the impact of public video surveillance on our society and who should have the final say regarding how (or if) it will be used. Be prepared to discuss your position (in class, via an online class discussion group, or in a class chat room, depending on your instructor's directions). You may also be asked to write a short paper expressing your opinion.

WEB ACTIVITIES

The ***Understanding Computers*** Web site located at **www.course.com/uc11** features many resources to help reinforce your understanding of the chapter content and help you prepare for exams. Your instructor may also assign specific activities to be completed that will count toward your final grade in the course.

Instructions: Go to **www.course.com/uc11/ch15** to work the following online activities.

Click any link in the navigation bar on the left to access any of the online resources described below.

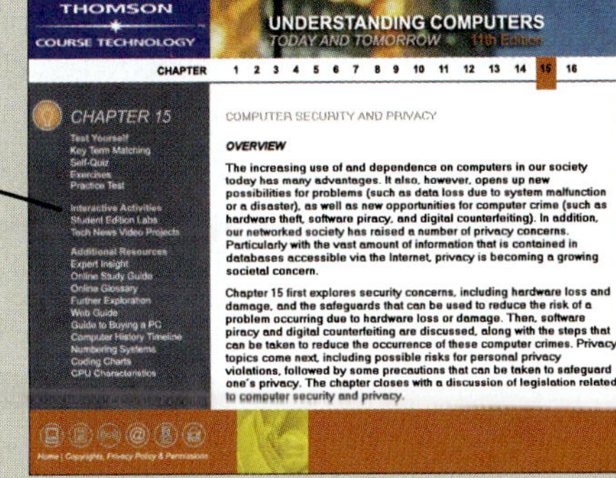

INTERACTIVE ACTIVITIES

1. **Crossword Puzzle** Practice your knowledge of the key terms in Chapter 15 by completing the interactive Crossword Puzzle.
2. **Tech News Video Project** Watch the **"Gmail Privacy"** video clip that takes a look at Google's Gmail Web-based mail service and some of the privacy concerns the targeted ads have raised. After watching the video online, complete the corresponding project.
3. **Student Edition Labs** Reinforce the concepts you have learned in this chapter by working through the interactive **Protecting Your Privacy Online** lab.

TEST YOURSELF

1. **Key Term Matching** Test your knowledge of selected chapter key terms by matching the terms with their definitions.
2. **Self-Quiz** Test your retention of chapter concepts by taking the Self-Quiz.
3. **Exercises** Work these short exercises to review the concepts and terms covered in the chapter.
4. **Practice Test** Test how ready you are for an upcoming exam by completing the online Practice Test.

STUDY TOOLS/ ADDITIONAL RESOURCES

The Understanding Computers Web site has a wide range of additional resources, including an **Online Study Guide** (containing study tips, a chapter outline with room to add your own notes, and a chapter checklist of the activities to complete when the chapter is covered in class and when you are preparing for a test) and an **Online Glossary** for each chapter; **Further Exploration** links; a **Web Guide**, a **Guide to Buying a PC**, and a **Computer History Timeline**; more information about **Numbering Systems**, **Coding Charts**, and **CPU Characteristics**; and much, much more!

Intellectual Property Rights, Ethics, Health, Access, and the Environment

OUTLINE

Overview
Intellectual Property Rights
- Copyrights
- Trademarks
- Patents

Ethics
- Ethical Use of Copyrighted Material
- Ethical Use of Resources and Information
- Computer Hoaxes and Digital Manipulation
- Ethical Business Practices and Decision Making

Computers and Health
- Physical Health
- Emotional Health

Access to Technology
- The Digital Divide
- Assistive Technology

Environmental Concerns
- Green Computing
- Recycling and Disposal of Computing Equipment

Related Legislation

LEARNING OBJECTIVES

After completing this chapter, you will be able to:

1. Understand the concept of intellectual property rights and how they relate to computer use.
2. Explain what is meant by ethics and provide several examples of unethical behavior in computer-related matters.
3. Describe some possible physical and emotional health risks associated with the use of computers.
4. Discuss the impact that factors such as nationality, income, race, education, and physical disabilities may have on computer access and use.
5. Suggest some ways computer users can practice "green computing" and properly dispose of obsolete computer equipment.
6. Discuss the current status of legislation related to intellectual property rights, ethics, access, and the environment in relation to computers.

OVERVIEW

Like any fast-paced revolution, the computer revolution has impacted our society in more ways than could have been imagined when it first began. Computers often make daily tasks easier, but they also can make it easier to perform some types of illegal or unethical acts, can cause serious health and emotional problems, and can have a negative impact on the environment. In addition, although computer use is becoming almost mandatory in our society, many believe that access to computers is not equally available to all individuals. This chapter continues where Chapter 15 left off—exploring computer-related societal issues beyond computer security and privacy.

The chapter begins with a look at a legal issue that all computer users should be aware of—intellectual property rights. The different types of intellectual property rights are discussed along with what types of property each one protects. Next is a discussion of ethics, including what they are and a variety of ethical issues surrounding computer use by individuals and businesses. Topics include the ethical use of copyrighted material, ethical uses of resources and information, unethical use of computer hoaxes and digital manipulation, and ethical business practices and decision making. The chapter continues with a look at health-oriented concerns, including the impact computers may have on a user's physical and emotional health, as well as strategies individuals can use to lessen those risks. Next, we turn to the issue of equal access, including a discussion of the digital divide and how other factors—such as gender, age, and physical disabilities—may affect computer access and use. Following a look at the potential impact of computers on our environment, the chapter closes with a look at legislation related to the issues discussed in this chapter. ■

INTELLECTUAL PROPERTY RIGHTS

Intellectual property rights are the legal rights to which the creators of *intellectual property*—original creative works—are entitled. Intellectual property rights indicate who has the right to use, perform, or display the creative work; how long the creator retains rights to the property; and other related restrictions. Examples of intellectual property include original music compositions; paintings, computer graphics, and other works of art; poetry, books, and other types of written work; movies and video clips; architectural drawings; symbols, names, and designs used in conjunction with a business; and inventions. The three main types of intellectual property rights are *copyrights*, *trademarks*, and *patents*.

FURTHER EXPLORATION

For links to further information about intellectual property rights, go to www.course.com/ uc11/ch16

Copyrights

A **copyright** is a form of protection available to the creator of an original artistic or literary work, such as a book, movie, software program, musical composition, or painting. It gives the copyright holder the exclusive right to publish, reproduce, distribute, perform, or display

>**Intellectual property rights.** The rights to which creators of original creative works (such as artistic or literary works, inventions, corporate logos, and more) are entitled. >**Copyright.** The legal right to sell, publish, or distribute an original artistic or literary work; is held by the creator of a work as soon as it exists in physical form.

HOW IT WORKS

Digital Rights Management

As more and more intellectual property (such as movies, music, and photos) is distributed in electronic form via the Internet, the need for *digital rights management (DRM)*—techniques for managing or protecting the rights of digital creative works—has grown. Digital rights management tools can be used to identify the copyright holder of a creative work (via a *digital watermark*), as well as to control the use of a creative work (via *digital rights management software*). These options are discussed next.

A digital watermark is a subtle alteration of digital content that is not noticeable when the work is viewed or played but that identifies the copyright holder. Digital watermarks are designed to be completely invisible or, in the case of audio clips, inaudible. For example, the digital watermark for an image might consist of slight changes to the brightness of a specific pattern of pixels. Digital watermarks are incorporated into works using software, and they are designed to remain intact as the work is copied, compressed, or otherwise used in a normal fashion. The digital watermark can be retrieved at any time using software; for instance, the digital watermark for the photo shown in the accompanying figure can be viewed using a compatible image editing program (as shown in the figure) or using a Web browser with a special plug-in (the watermark shows up as an icon displayed on the photo that can be clicked to view the information contained in the watermark). The information in digital watermarks is being used to trace pirated movies and music back to the original source, such as to identify the theater in which a pirated movie was videotaped illegally.

While digital watermarks can be used to inform potential users of the identity of the copyright holder, and they can be used in copyright-infringement lawsuits to prove that the work was copyright-protected, they are not designed to control how the work can be used. Instead, DRM software can be used to assign usage rights (such as granting the ability to view, copy, or edit) to a creative work and to specify an expiration date after which time the content becomes inaccessible (such as assigning expiration dates for video-on-demand rentals); it may also determine what types of devices can be used to access the work (such as playing downloaded music files only on digital music players that are compatible with the DRM software used with the music files). For example, the music files available via most Web-based music services (such as *iTunes Music Store* and *Wal-Mart Music Downloads*) use a special file format (such as *AAC* for iTunes songs and *WMA* for Wal-Mart songs) that includes DRM coding, which impacts both the digital music players these music files can be played on and the use of the song. For instance, it is common for downloaded songs to have a limit for the number of times the song can be burned to a CD disc. Once the user has reached the allowable limit—typically ten CDs—the DRM software displays a message informing the user that the song cannot be transferred to any more CDs, unless the user purchases an additional download of that song. In addition, the DRM software used with most subscription-based music services that allow you to download an unlimited number of songs will allow those songs to be played only on a PC or a portable digital music player (you cannot burn them to CDs) and you can play the songs only as long as you are a subscriber. Once you cancel your monthly subscription, you can no longer play songs downloaded via the subscription service, unless you paid the necessary fee to purchase a burnable version of those songs. If you purchased a burnable version of a song, it can be transferred to a digital music player, burned to a CD, or so forth, the same as a conventional downloaded song. DRM software is also frequently included on purchased CDs to control the use of the songs on the CD.

While the current incompatibility of music download services is an inconvenience for users (for instance, they have to make sure they have a digital music player device compatible with their selected music service or they will not be able to transfer songs to that device), privacy and personal freedom advocates are more concerned with the overall loss of functionality related to digital music in general. For instance, they believe that consumers are getting less for their money now that they cannot do everything they may want to do with a purchased song. In addition, some DRM software used with purchased CDs makes CDs less reliable (for instance, they may play only on some CD players). The DRM software used on some Sony CDs released in late 2005 was even classified as malware because it installed hidden files which were nearly impossible to remove. These files also left the PC vulnerable to other malware that had been written to take advantage of the file-hiding capabilities of the DRM software; since the malware was hidden by the DRM, it could not be detected by antivirus programs.

The watermark embedded in this image is not visible.

The information contained in the watermark can be viewed using an image-editing program.

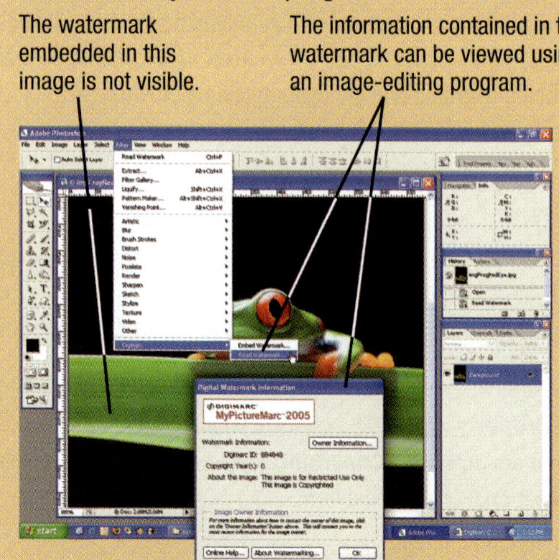

the work. A major revision to U.S. copyright legislation was the *1976 Copyright Act*. This act extended copyright protection to nonpublished works, so, immediately after creating a work in some type of material form (such as on paper, film, videotape, disk, CD, or DVD), the creator automatically owns the copyright of that work. Consequently, the creator is entitled to copyright protection of that work and has the right to make a statement, such as "Copyright © 2006 by John Smith. All rights reserved." Although works created in the United States after March 1, 1989, are not required to display a copyright notice to retain their copyright protection, it is wise to display this type of copyright statement on a published work (see Figure 16-1) to remind others that the work is protected by copyright law and that any use must comply with copyright law. Only the creator of a work (or his or her employer if the work is created as a *work for hire*—that is, within the scope of employment) can rightfully claim copyright. Copyrights can be registered with the U.S. Copyright Office. Although registration is not required for copyright protection, it does offer an advantage if the need to prove ownership of a copyright ever arises, such as during a copyright-infringement lawsuit.

COPYRIGHT © 2007 Course Technology, a division of Thomson Learning, Inc. Thomson Learning™ is a trademark used herein under license.

BOOK COPYRIGHT NOTICE

Fine Art Photography by Jim McNew
© 1997 - 2005 J R McNew
All Rights Reserved
Fine Art Photography by Jim McNew is the exclusive property of Golden J Studios -- Fresno, California

WEB SITE COPYRIGHT NOTICE

FIGURE 16-1
Copyright statements.
Statements such as these are often included on books, Web sites, and other original copyrighted works.

Anyone wishing to use copyrighted materials must first obtain permission from the copyright holder and pay any required fee. One exception is the legal concept of *fair use*, which permits limited duplication and use of a portion of copyrighted material for certain purposes, such as criticism, commentary, news reporting, teaching, and research. For example, a teacher may legally read a copyrighted poem for discussion in a poetry class, and a news photographer may take a photograph of a newly installed sculpture to show on the evening news. Copyrights apply to both published and unpublished work and last until 70 years after the creator's death. Copyrights for works registered by an organization or as anonymous works last 95 years from the date of publication or 120 years from the date of creation, whichever is shorter.

It is important to realize that purchasing a copyrighted item—such as a book, painting, or movie—does not change the copyright protection afforded to the creator of that item. Although you have purchased the right to use the item, you cannot legally duplicate it or portray it as your own creation. Some of the most widely publicized copyright-infringement issues today center around individuals illegally distributing copyright-protected music and movies via the Internet, as discussed later in this chapter.

To protect their rights, some creators of digital content—such as art, music, photographs, and movies—incorporate **digital watermarks** containing copyright information into their works or use **digital rights management (DRM) software** to control the use of the work. For a closer look at how these tools can be used, see the How it Works box.

FIGURE 16-2
Examples of trademarked logos.

Trademarks

A **trademark** is a word, phrase, symbol, or design (or a combination of words, phrases, symbols, or designs) that identifies and distinguishes one product or service from another. Trademark rights prevent others from using a confusingly similar mark, but they do not prevent others from making or selling the same goods or services under a clearly different mark. Trademarks that are claimed but not registered with the U.S. Patent and Trademark Office can use the mark ™; registered trademarks can use the symbol ®. Trademarked words and phrases—such as Windows® XP and BLOCKBUSTER®—are common; so are trademarked logos (see Figure 16-2). Trademark law also protects domain names that match a company's trademark, such as Amazon.com and Lego.com.

>**Digital watermark.** A subtle alteration of digital content that is not noticeable under normal use, but that identifies the copyright holder. >**Digital rights management (DRM) software.** Software used to protect and manage the rights of creators of digital content, such as art, music, photographs, and movies. >**Trademark.** A word, phrase, symbol, or design that identifies goods or services.

There have been a number of claims of online trademark infringement in recent years, particularly involving domain names that contain, or are similar to, a trademark. For instance, several celebrities—such as Madonna—have fought to be given the exclusive right to use what they consider their rightful domain names (Madonna.com, in this example). Other examples include Microsoft's complaint against another organization using the domain name *microsof.com* and Radio Shack's objection to a private individual using *shack.com* for the Web site of his business called DesignShack.

Typically, disputes such as these are brought to the registry service that registered the name or, ultimately, to the Arbitration and Mediation Center of the *World Intellectual Property Organization (WIPO)*, which has the power to award the disputed domain name to the most appropriate party. If the domain appears to have been acquired by someone other than the holder of the trademark for the purpose of harming the trademark holder or selling the domain name at an inflated price—an act referred to as *cybersquatting*—the trademark holder generally prevails. If the current domain name holder has a legitimate reason for using that name and does not appear to be a cybersquatter, WIPO may allow the holder to continue to use that domain name. For instance, WIPO ruled that microsof.com was confusingly similar to the trademark already owned by Microsoft and that its owner had no legitimate interest in that domain name, so WIPO transferred the disputed domain name to Microsoft Corporation. However, the owner of DesignShack (whose nickname is "Shack") was allowed to keep the shack.com domain name because it was ruled that he had a legitimate interest in that name.

The *U.S. Anticybersquatting Act*—also called the *Trademark Cyberpiracy Prevention Act*—passed in 1999 made cybersquatting illegal and allows for penalties up to $300,000 for each willful registration of a domain name that infringes on a trademark. Sometimes, determining whether or not a domain name was registered in bad faith is a difficult judgment call. For example, a British individual registered the domain name *iTunes.co.uk* in November, 2000, two months before Apple announced its iTunes service. In November, 2004, Apple offered to buy the name, but the two parties could not agree on a price (Apple reportedly offered $5,000, but the individual suggested $94,000). Apple filed a formal complaint with Nominet, the British registry for Internet names, and was awarded the domain name in 2005. The reason? The individual offered to sell the domain name to Napster in late 2004 so, even though he may have registered the domain name without being aware of the iTunes service and without any cybersquatting intent, it was ruled that his offer to Napster showed "abusive intent," and the domain name was awarded to Apple.

Patents

Unlike copyrights (which protect artistic and literary works) and trademarks (which protect a company's logo and brand names), a **patent** protects inventions by granting exclusive rights of an invention to its inventor for a period of 20 years. A patented invention is typically a unique product, but it can also be a process or procedure that provides a new way of doing something or that offers a new technical solution to a problem. Like trademarks, U.S patents are issued by the U.S. Patent and Trademark Office; a recent patent issued for the StorCard smart card discussed in Chapter 4 is shown in Figure 16-3. Patent procedures vary widely from country to country; global patents are an issue for any company wishing to produce products or services on a global scale.

The number of patent applications—particularly for computer- or Internet-related products—has skyrocketed in recent years. Also growing is the number of patents requested for business methods and models, such as CoolSavings.com's Internet coupon

>**Patent.** A form of protection that can be granted by the government for an invention; gives exclusive rights of an invention to its inventor for 20 years.

distribution method, Amazon.com's one-click purchase procedure, and Priceline.com's name-your-own-price business model. When a product or business model is patented, no other organization can duplicate it without paying a royalty to the patent holder or risking prolonged patent litigation. Patents can be difficult, expensive, and time-consuming to obtain. However, patents can also be very lucrative. For instance, IBM—which has been the top patenting company for 12 consecutive years, was issued over 3,200 patents in 2004, and has over 25,000 active patents—earns an estimated $2 billion per year from its patents.

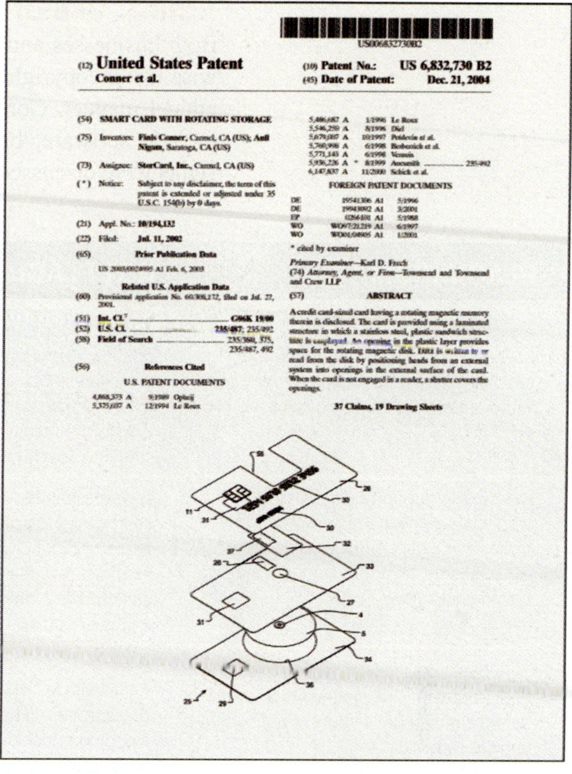

(12) **United States Patent**
Conner et al.

(10) **Patent No.: US 6,832,730 B2**
(45) **Date of Patent: Dec. 21, 2004**

(54) **SMART CARD WITH ROTATING STORAGE**

(75) Inventors: **Finis Conner**, Carmel, CA (US); **Anil Nigam**, Saratoga, CA (US)

(73) Assignee: **StarCard, Inc.**, Carmel, CA (US)

(*) Notice: Subject to any disclaimer, the term of this patent is extended or adjusted under 35 U.S.C. 154(b) by 0 days.

(21) Appl. No.: **10/194,132**

(22) Filed: **Jul. 11, 2002**

(65) **Prior Publication Data**

(51) **Int. Cl.**[7] **G06K 19/00**

(52) **U.S. Cl.** **235/487**; 235/492

(58) **Field of Search** 235/380, 375, 235/487, 492

(56) **References Cited**

U.S. PATENT DOCUMENTS

FOREIGN PATENT DOCUMENTS

* cited by examiner

Primary Examiner—Karl D. Frech

(74) *Attorney, Agent, or Firm*—Townsend and Townsend and Crew LLP

(57) **ABSTRACT**

A credit card-sized card having a rotating magnetic memory therein is disclosed. The card is provided using a laminated structure in which a stainless steel, plastic sandwich structure is employed. An opening in the plastic layer provides space for the rotating magnetic disk. Data is written to or read from the disk by positioning heads from an external system into openings in the external surface of the card. When the card is not engaged in a reader, a shutter covers the openings.

37 Claims, 19 Drawing Sheets

FIGURE 16-3

Patents. The patent shown here is for a smart card with a thin embedded magnetic disk.

ETHICS

The term **ethics** refers to standards of moral conduct. For example, telling the truth is a matter of ethics. An unethical act is not always illegal, although it might be, but illegal acts would be viewed as unethical by most people. For example, purposely lying to a friend is unethical but usually not illegal, while perjuring oneself in a courtroom as a witness is both illegal and unethical. Whether or not criminal behavior is involved, ethics guide our behavior and play an integral role in our lives.

Much more ambiguous than the law, ethical beliefs can vary widely from one individual to another. Ethical beliefs may also vary based on one's religion, country, race, or culture. In addition, different ethical standards can apply to different areas of one's life. For example, *personal ethics* guide an individual's personal behavior; *business* or *professional ethics* guide an individual's or business's workplace behavior. Ethics with respect to the use of computers are referred to as **computer ethics**.

Computer ethics have taken on more significance in recent years because the proliferation of computers in the home and the workplace provides more opportunities for unethical acts than in the past. The Internet also makes it easy to distribute information that some would view as unethical. For example, the young virus writer from Belgium known as "Gigabyte" does not release the viruses she writes, but she has been known to post the codes for her viruses on her Web site, where others who are so inclined can access and release them. When asked about someone else taking her viruses and releasing them on the Internet, Gigabyte has responded that it is certainly not her fault. Undoubtedly, many people would disagree and would view making viruses easily available for other individuals to release as a highly unethical act.

Whether at home, at work, or at school, individuals encounter ethical issues every day. For example, you may need to make such ethical decisions as whether or not to accept a relative's offer of a free copy of a CD or movie, have a friend help you take an online exam, print your child's birthday party invitations on the office color printer, or forward the most recent e-mail warning about a new computer virus to everyone in your address book. Businesses also deal with a variety of ethical issues in the course of normal business activities—from determining how many computers on which a particular software program should be installed, to identifying how customer and employee information should be used, to deciding business practices. **Business ethics** are the standards of conduct that guide a business's policies, decisions, and actions.

>Ethics. Overall standards of moral conduct. **>Computer ethics.** Standards of moral conduct as they relate to computer use. **>Business ethics.** Standards of moral conduct that guide a business's policies, decisions, and actions.

Ethical Use of Copyrighted Material

Both businesses and individuals should be very careful when copying, sharing, or otherwise using copyrighted material to ensure that the material is used in both a legal and an ethical manner. Common types of copyrighted material encountered on a regular basis include software, books, Web-based articles, music, and movies. Software ownership rights were discussed in Chapter 6; the remainder of these topics are covered next.

Books and Web-Based Articles

Print-based books, e-books, Web-based articles, and other types of literary material are all protected by copyright law. Consequently, they cannot be reproduced, presented as one's own original material, or otherwise used in an unauthorized manner. Students, researchers, authors, and other writers need to be especially careful when using literary material as a resource for papers, articles, books, and so forth, to ensure the material is properly credited to the original author. To present someone else's work as your own is **plagiarism**, which is both a violation of copyright law and an unethical act. It can also get you fired, as some reporters—such as Jason Blair, who was fired from the *New York Times* in 2003, and Nada Behziz, who was fired from the *Bakerfield Californian* in 2005—found out the hard way. Both individuals were fired for faking quotes and plagiarizing content from other newspapers. Some examples of what constitutes and what does not constitute a plagiaristic act are shown in Figure 16-4.

PLAGIARISM	NOT PLAGIARISM
A student copying or retyping a few sentences or a few paragraphs written by another author to include in his term paper without crediting the original author.	A student copying or retyping a few sentences or a few paragraphs written by another author to include in his term paper, either indenting the quotation or placing it inside quotation marks, and crediting the original author with a citation in the text or with a footnote or endnote.
A newspaper reporter changing a few words in a sentence or paragraph written by another author and including the revised text in an article without crediting the original author.	A newspaper reporter paraphrasing a few sentences or paragraphs written by another author without changing the meaning of the text, including the revised text in an article, and crediting the original author with a proper citation.
A student copying and pasting information from various online documents to create her research paper without crediting the original authors.	A student copying and pasting information from various online documents and using those quotes in her research paper either indented or enclosed in quotation marks with the proper citations for each author.
A teacher sharing a poem with a class, leading the class to believe the poem was his original work.	A teacher sharing a poem with a class, clearly identifying the poet.

FIGURE 16-4
Examples of what is and what is not normally considered plagiarism.

With the increased availability of online articles and fee-based online term paper services, some students might be tempted to create their papers by copying and pasting excerpts of online content into their documents. But these students should realize that this is plagiarism, and instructors can usually tell when a paper is created in this manner. There are also online sources instructors can use to test the originality of student papers; the results of one such test are shown in Figure 16-5. Many colleges and universities have strict consequences for plagiarism, such as automatically failing the assignment or course, or being expelled from the institution.

TIP

For a review of how to cite online material properly, refer to Figure 8-16 in Chapter 8.

Music

There have been several issues regarding the legal and ethical use of music over the past few years, fueled primarily by the emergence and widespread use of Napster and other P2P file sharing sites, recordable and rewritable CD and DVD drives, and portable digital music players. For instance, downloading a music file from a P2P site without compensating the artist and record label is a violation of copyright laws and an unethical act; so is transferring legally obtained songs to a storage medium to sell or give to others. Partly as a result of the Napster controversy, there are many options for legally downloading music, as discussed in

>**Plagiarism.** Presenting someone else's work as your own.

detail in Chapter 8. And once an MP3 file or audio CD has been obtained legally, most experts agree that it falls within the fair use concept for an individual to transfer those songs to a CD-R disc, PC, or portable digital music player, as long as it is for personal, noncommercial use and does not violate a user agreement. However, as discussed in the How it Works box, digital rights management (DRM) software is increasingly limiting the legal actions individuals can take with downloaded music and purchased CDs.

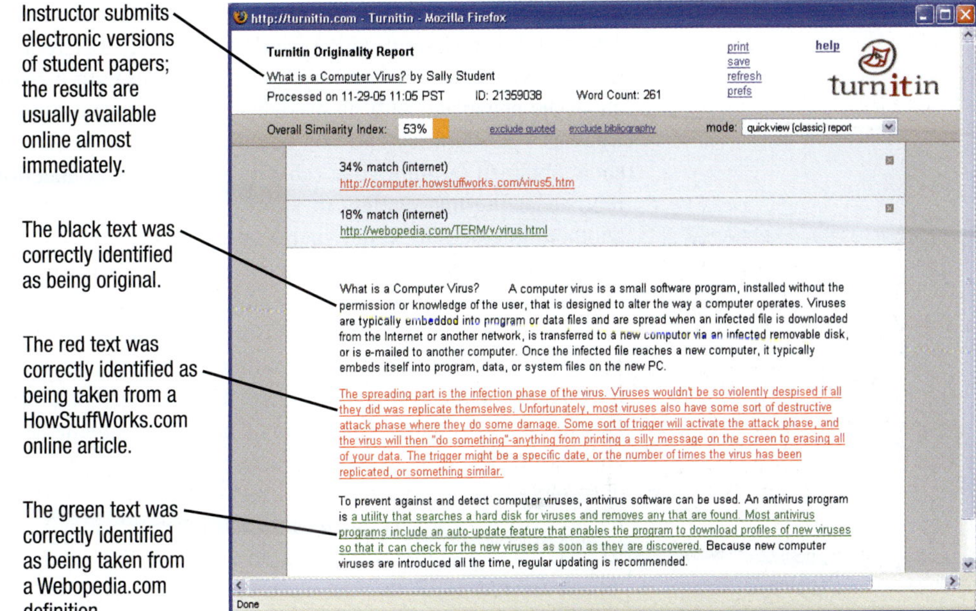

FIGURE 16-5
Results of an online originality test on an essay that contained plagiarized content.

Movies

Since 1984, when Disney and Universal sued Sony to stop production of the *Betamax* (the first personal VCR to come on the market), concern about movie piracy has increased dramatically. Obviously, the lawsuit was eventually decided in Sony's favor—the Supreme Court upheld the consumers' rights to record shows for convenience (called *time shifting*), as long as it was for personal use. As a result of this Supreme Court decision, VCR use became commonplace. Interestingly, in direct contrast to the views held by the entertainment industry in 1984, videos have been credited with boosting Hollywood's revenues tremendously in past years. Nevertheless, the entertainment industry continues to be concerned about the ability of consumers to make copies of movies—especially today, since digital copies of movies can be duplicated an unlimited number of times without losing quality. The Motion Picture Association of America (MPAA) estimates that losses due to offline movie piracy alone exceed over $3.5 billion per year. In addition, the MPAA estimates that movies are downloaded illegally from the Internet 400,000 to 600,000 times every day, adding to its losses.

To prevent individuals from making unauthorized copies of VHS, DVD, and pay-per-view movies, copy protection and other forms of DRM have been built into many of those items. Movie pirates, however, can often circumvent copy protection with software and other tools to create illegal copies. Pirated copies of movies are also often created today by videotaping them with a camcorder during a prerelease screening or on the opening day of a movie; this practice has resulted in a vast number of movies becoming illegally available on DVDs and via the Internet at about the same time they arrive in theaters. As a result, Congress passed the *Family Entertainment and Copyright Act of 2005* (*FECA*) which makes transmitting or recording a movie during a performance at a movie theater illegal. To help identify and prosecute a "cammer," some movie studios now embed invisible digital codes in each print released to a theater. These codes can be used to identify the location where the movie was recorded once a bootleg copy of a movie is discovered. In 2005, several Hollywood movie studios created *Motion Picture Laboratories Inc.* (also called *MovieLabs*)—an organization to develop technologies that will prevent illegal copying and distribution of movies over the Internet.

The access to both authorized and unauthorized copies of movies via the Internet and the widespread use of digital video recorders (DVRs) creates new legal and ethical dilemmas for individuals today. If one individual records a television show and then shares it with a friend via the Internet, does that go beyond the concept of fair use? If you run across a location from which you can download a copy of a movie not yet out on video or DVD, are you legally at risk if you make the download? What if you watch the movie once and then delete it—are you still in the wrong? What if you download a video-on-demand movie and then share it with a friend? Is that any different, legally or ethically, from sharing a movie rented from a physical video store with a friend before you return it? What about the new place shifting products on the market, such as the Slingbox discussed in the Chapter 7 Technology and You box? If you use such a product to transfer a movie or TV show obtained through your cable or satellite TV connection to another location, are you rebroadcasting that content or simply place shifting it? What if you send the content to another individual to watch via his or her PC—is that legal?

While the answers to these questions have yet to be unequivocally decided, and some of these scenarios may be impacted by the impending *broadcast flag* (a DRM tool that the FCC would like to see embedded in all digital broadcast signals to manage the digital rights of those broadcasts, distributing bootleg copies of movies via the Internet is both illegal and unethical. In mid-2005, the U.S. Justice Department announced "Operation Site Down", a coordinated international law enforcement action targeting online piracy of copyrighted software, movies, music, and games. It has resulted in several convictions to date, including the first conviction under the Family Entertainment and Copyright Act for using a camcorder to make illegal copies of movies. The convicted individual—a teenager—pled guilty to making an unauthorized recording of "Bewitched" in a movie theater in mid-2005, as well as to copyright infringement (for distributing "Bewitched" and one other movie via the Internet). He faces up to three years in prison for making the unauthorized recording and up to five years in prison for each act of copyright infringement. Another first in 2005 was Sweden's first Internet piracy conviction in which a man was found guilty and fined approximately $2,000 U.S. for distributing a movie online. And a Hong Kong man was convicted in 2005 for distributing three Hollywood movies via a P2P service—the country's first successful action against peer-to-peer file sharing. The man is awaiting sentencing and faces a maximum penalty of four years in prison and a hefty fine.

The MPAA also recently began pursuing civil litigation against movie pirates. The organization is concentrating mainly on those who create illegal DVDs, but prosecution of those who upload movies to be shared via the Internet is also occurring. To catch people who are sharing movies illegally on the Internet, the MPAA uses special software that monitors file sharing networks to find copyrighted movies and then identifies the responsible individual by using the IP address of the computer being used to share the movie. The movie industry also hires special firms, such as BayTSP, that specialize in monitoring P2P networks to identify copyrighted material (such as documents, graphics, music, or movie files) being misused on the Internet. These companies typically use automated programs to scan P2P networks in order to find intellectual property that the company is charged with protecting. When it finds a file that is being illegally shared, the company can identify the IP address of the user who originally uploaded the file, as well as all individuals who have downloaded the file. At the request of the copyright holder, an infringement notice can be sent to the violator via his or her ISP, and the necessary data can be collected in case the copyright holder decides to pursue legal action.

To prevent the sharing of legally downloaded movies (such as movies obtained through Movielink or another video-on-demand service), many downloaded movies include DRM controls that allow the movie to be used only for a 24-hour period beginning when the movie first starts to play.

Ethical Use of Resources and Information

There are a variety of resources and types of information that can be used in an unethical manner, such as school computers, company computers and equipment, and customer or employee information. For example, some employees use company computers for personal use, some students perform dishonest acts while completing assignments or taking exams, and some job applicants provide erroneous or misleading information during the application or interview process.

Ethical Use of School or Company Resources

What is considered proper and ethical use of school or company resources may vary from school to school or company to company. To explain what is allowed, many schools and businesses have policies that specify which activities are allowed and which are forbidden. Often, these policies are available as a written document—frequently called a **code of conduct**—included in a student or employee handbook; they are also often available online via an organization's intranet or Web site (two codes of conduct were shown in Figure 9-1 in Chapter 9). Policies can vary from organization to organization—for example, one school may allow the use of school PCs to download software programs and another school may not, and one business may allow limited use of the office photocopier or printer for personal use while another may forbid that activity. As a result, all students and employees should make it a point to find out what is considered ethical use of resources at their school or place of business, including what types of computer and Internet activities are considered acceptable, and what personal use (if any) of resources, such as PCs, printers, photocopiers, telephones, and fax machines, is allowed. To enforce its policies, businesses may use employee monitoring techniques, such as those discussed in Chapter 15.

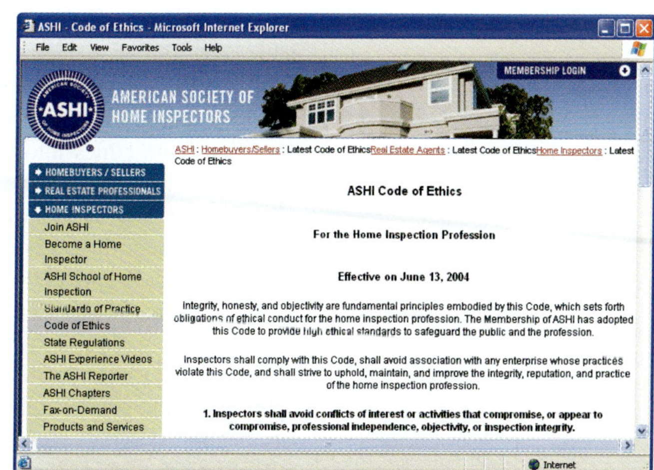

FIGURE 16-6
A sample code of ethics.

Another common type of code widely used by various industries and organizations is a **code of ethics**. Codes of ethics, such as the one shown in Figure 16-6, summarize the moral guidelines adopted by a particular organization (frequently a professional society) and typically address such issues as honesty, integrity, fairness, responsibility to others, proper use of intellectual property, confidentiality, and accountability. So, while codes of conduct usually address specific activities that can and cannot be performed, codes of ethics cover broader ethical standards of conduct.

Although employees are typically forbidden from revealing confidential or proprietary information to outsiders, a dilemma exists when that information is related to an illegal, unethical, or dangerous activity involving the business. Employees who reveal wrongdoing within an organization to the public or to authorities are referred to as *whistle-blowers*. These individuals have varying degrees of protection from retaliation, such as being fired, for whistle-blowing. The type and extent of protection depends on the kind of wrongdoing and the organization involved, as well as the state in which the company and employee are located. The *Sarbanes-Oxley Act* (also called the *Corporate Responsibility Act* and signed into law in mid-2002) provides federal protection for whistle-blowers who provide information to a federal regulatory or law enforcement agency, a member of Congress or a Congressional committee, or a person with supervisory authority over the employee. At the time of this writing, federal whistle-blowing legislation was being proposed to protect whistle-blowers further.

TIP

For a review of *netiquette*—generally-accepted rules for online behavior—see Figure 1-31 in Chapter 1.

FURTHER EXPLORATION

For links to further information about codes of ethics for a variety of industries, go to www.course.com/uc11/ch16

Ethical Use of Employee and Customer Information

While a business may be legally bound by such restrictions as employee confidentiality laws, union contracts, and its customer privacy policy, there are gray areas inside which ethical decisions need to be made. For example, even if it is legal for a business to share or sell customer information, should it do so? This is a decision that many businesses have struggled with, especially in challenging economic times when a quick source of revenue gained from selling customer data is tempting. Although some businesses have succumbed

>**Code of conduct.** A policy, often for a school or business, that specifies allowable use of resources such as computers and other equipment.

>**Code of ethics.** A policy, often for an organization or industry, that specifies overall moral guidelines adopted by that organization or industry.

to this temptation and have sold their customer lists, others believe that any short-term gains achieved through ethically questionable acts will adversely affect customer loyalty and will ultimately hurt the business in the long run.

To prepare future employees for these types of decisions, most business schools incorporate business ethics into their curriculum. However, the startling number of corporate scandals in the past few years and the perceived degrading moral climate today have caused some schools to reevaluate their curriculum to see if it is sufficient. According to George Brenkert, director of the Business Ethics Institute at Georgetown University, business schools have spread the message of maximizing profit at nearly any cost for too long. He believes that businesses have to derive a profit and a return on their investments, but that they have to do it in the broader context of ethical considerations and social responsibility. Future business curriculum for many schools will likely incorporate this new philosophy, at least to some extent. Corporate philosophies and employee training programs are also beginning to move in this direction. In fact, in a 2005 National Business Ethics Survey (NBES) by the Ethics Resource Center, 69% of the employees reported that their organizations have implemented ethics training, up 14% from the 2003 NBES survey.

Cheating and Falsifying Information

Just as computers and the Internet make it easier for individuals to plagiarize documents, computers and the Internet can also make it easier for individuals to cheat on assignments or online exams, or perform other similar unethical acts.

Unfortunately, cheating by students at both the high school level and the college level is rampant today. According to recent studies by Donald L. McCabe of Rutgers University, about 70% of students on most campuses admit to some cheating. In his 2005 study of over 12,000 students, nearly 40% of the students admitted to Internet plagiarism (such as cutting and pasting content from Internet sources without crediting the source), and 77% believe it is not a serious issue. About 25% of the students surveyed admitted to serious cheating on exams; half admitted serious cheating on written assignments. Although cheating can occur with noncomputerized assignments and exams, the editing ability of a PC makes it faster and easier to cheat on assignments created on a computer, and taking online exams offsite makes it easier to cheat on those exams. To prevent this possibility, some colleges and universities require online exams to be taken in person (instead of via the Internet) so that the identity of the exam-taker can be verified. Most of the time, the in-person exams are taken at the campus through which the course is offered, although some colleges allow exams to be taken at authorized testing centers for distance learning students who are not located close to the campus.

FIGURE 16-7
Academic honor codes. The honor code at the University of Denver is signed by virtually all incoming students.

In addition to cheating themselves of an education, students who choose to cheat are being unfair to honest students by possibly altering the grading curve or even lessening the overall value of a diploma. Widespread cheating can also have a negative impact on society, such as underprepared employees entering the workforce.

To explain to students what behavior is expected of them, many schools are developing *academic honor codes*. These codes are usually published in the student handbook and on the school Web site; they may also be included in course syllabi. Research has shown that having an academic honor code effectively reduces cheating. For example, the McCabe studies have found that cheating on tests on campuses with honor codes is typically one-third to one-half less than on campuses that do not have honor codes, and the level of cheating on written assignments is one-quarter to one-third lower. To bring attention to their honor codes, some schools encourage incoming students to sign their honor codes upon admission. For instance, all incoming University of Denver students are asked to sign the school's honor code publicly (see Figure 16-7). Regardless of whether or not students choose to sign the honor code, they are required to abide by it. To remind students of this responsibility at the University of Denver, the honor code pledge "I affirm my commitment to the University of Denver Honor Code" appears on every exam blue book purchased through the university bookstore.

Like academic cheating, lying on a job application or résumé is more common than most of us may think it is. The practice of providing false information in an attempt to look more qualified for a job, sometimes referred to as *résumé padding*, is both dishonest and unethical. And it is also widespread. Recent research conducted by the *New York Times* advertising department found that almost half of hiring managers and 84% of job seekers believe that résumé padding is done by a significant number of candidates. In addition to being unethical, providing false information to a potential employer can have grave consequences. The majority of the companies surveyed in the *New York Times* study have a policy that lists termination as the appropriate action for employees who were hired based on falsified résumés or applications. Being blacklisted from an industry or being sued for breach of contract are also possibilities. Résumé writers should remember that background checks are easily available on the Web, so credentials are easy to check and verify. Regardless of whether or not they think they may get caught, applicants should not embellish their résumés or job applications to any extent because it is an unethical thing to do.

In addition to employment documents, there are other occasions that tempt some individuals to provide inaccurate personal information, such as when writing personal advertisements, when participating in chat rooms, and when individuals may wish to appear differently from who they really are. There are differing opinions about how ethical these actions are—some individuals believe that it is a person's right to portray himself or herself in any way desired; others feel that any type of dishonesty is unethical.

TIP

When looking for a distance learning program, be sure to check the school's accreditation since some human resources departments view college degrees from online diploma mills or other nonaccredited organizations as another form of résumé padding.

Computer Hoaxes and Digital Manipulation

Most people realize that information in print media can, at times, be misleading and that photos can be manipulated. Information found on the Internet may also be inaccurate, misleading, or biased. Some of this information is published on Web pages; other information is passed on via e-mail. Two types of computer-oriented misinformation include computer hoaxes and digital manipulation.

Computer Hoaxes

A **computer hoax** is an inaccurate statement or story—such as the "fact" that flesh-eating bacteria have been found in banana shipments or that antiperspirant use causes cancer—spread through the use of computers. These hoaxes are sometimes published on Web pages, but they are more commonly spread via e-mail, as discussed in the Technology and You box. Common computer hoax subjects include nonexistent computer viruses, serious health risks of a particular product, impending terrorist attacks, chain letters, and free prizes or giveaways. Because hoaxes are so common, it is a good idea to double-check any warning you receive by e-mail or read on a Web site before passing that warning on to another person, regardless of how realistic or frightening the information appears to be. One reliable source to use is the government's Hoaxbusters site shown in Figure 16-8 and found at hoaxbusters.ciac.org.

Digital Manipulation

Computers make it very easy to copy or modify text, images, photographs, music, and other digital content. In addition to being a copyright concern, **digital manipulation** (digitally altering digital content) can be used to misquote individuals, repeat comments out of context, retouch photographs—even create false or misleading photographs. While there are some beneficial, ethical, noncontroversial applications of digital manipulation—such

>**Computer hoax.** An inaccurate statement or story spread through the use of computers. >**Digital manipulation.** The alteration of digital content, usually text or photographs.

FIGURE 16-8
The Hoaxbusters Web site.

as aging photos of missing children to show what they may look like at the present time, or altering photos of wanted criminals or suspects to show possible appearances for law enforcement purposes—the matter of altering photos to be published is the subject of debate. Some publications and photographers see no harm in altering photographs to remove an offending item (such as a telephone pole behind someone's head), to make someone look a little more attractive, to illustrate a point, or to increase circulation; others view any change in content as unethical and a great disservice to both the public and our history. For example, fifty years from now, will anyone know that a staged or altered photograph of a historical event was not an actual depiction of the event?

Although manipulation of photographs has occurred for quite some time in tabloids and other publications not known as being reputable news sources, there have been several incidents of more reputable news publications using digitally altered photographs in recent years. Most of these became known because the unaltered photograph was used in another publication at about the same time. One of the most widely publicized cases occurred in 1994, just following the arrest of O. J. Simpson. While *Newsweek* ran Simpson's mug shot unaltered, *TIME* magazine darkened the photograph, creating a more sinister look and making Simpson's skin color appear darker than it actually is. This photo drew harsh criticism from Simpson supporters who felt the photograph made him appear guilty, the African-American community who viewed the alteration as an act of racial insensitivity, and news photographers who felt that the action damaged the credibility not only of that particular magazine, but also of all journalists.

A more recent example occurred during the 2005 New Jersey governor's race. The Web site of one of the candidates, Bret Schundler, displayed a photo showing Schundler in the foreground with a group of college students in the background (see Figure 16-9). The problem? The photo of Shundler (a Rebulican) was superimposed onto a photo taken at a rally for Howard Dean (a Democrat) the year before. The digital manipulation came to light when one of the college students who had attended the Dean rally recognized herself in the Schundler photo, which had been digitally altered to show her wearing a Shundler hat and holding a Shundler sign (refer again to Figure 16-9). The Shundler campaign admitted it was aware that Schundler's photo was superimposed onto a political rally photo, but they did not know it was taken at a Dean event. The photo was removed from the Web site after the issue came to light.

FIGURE 16-9
Digital manipulation. The Schundler photo (right) is a digital manipulation of the Dean photo (left).

Student's hat was altered.

Sign was altered.

Perhaps the most disturbing thing about known alterations such as these is that some may never have been noticed, and may consequently have been accepted as true representations. Adding to the problem of unethical digital manipulation is the use of digital cameras today, which virtually eliminates any concrete evidence—namely, negatives—that can show what photographs actually looked like at the time they were taken. Although some publications allow the use of "photo illustrations," others have strict rules about digital manipulation—especially for news photojournalists. For instance, the *LA Times* fired a staff photographer covering the war in Iraq when he combined two of his photographs into one to better convey a point.

TECHNOLOGY AND YOU

E-Mail Hoaxes

E-mail hoaxes—hoaxes spread via e-mail—are all too common today. Some e-mail hoaxes that just do not seem to go away are the $250 Neiman Marcus cookie recipe, the notice of a free trip given away by Disney for forwarding an e-mail to a certain number of people, and the Applebee's giveaway hoax (see the accompanying screen shot that is displayed to all visitors to the Applebee's Web site to show Applebee's response to the e-mail hoax).

E-mail hoaxes are written with the purpose of being circulated to as many people as possible. Some are started as experiments to see how fast and how far information can travel via the Internet; others originate from a joke or the desire to frighten people. You can often use common sense to identify some hoaxes. For example, for e-mail messages that state you will receive some sort of free prize or other reward from a known company (such as Disney or Applebee's) for forwarding an e-mail message on to others, you should ask yourself: How could the company possibly know who I am and if I forwarded the message? Since the company needs that information in order to send you a reward, common sense tells you that the message must be a hoax. Some hoaxes include a message stating that a company is testing some sort of e-mail tracking program that can tell if you forward the message, but that statement is false—there is no such type of program.

In addition to being annoying and wasting people's time reading and checking into these false stories, e-mail hoaxes bog down e-mail systems and clog users' Inboxes. An additional problem is the embarrassment factor—do you really want all those people to whom you forwarded an email hoax to think you are that gullible? A good rule of thumb is "better safe than sorry"—check out potential hoaxes before hitting the Forward button.

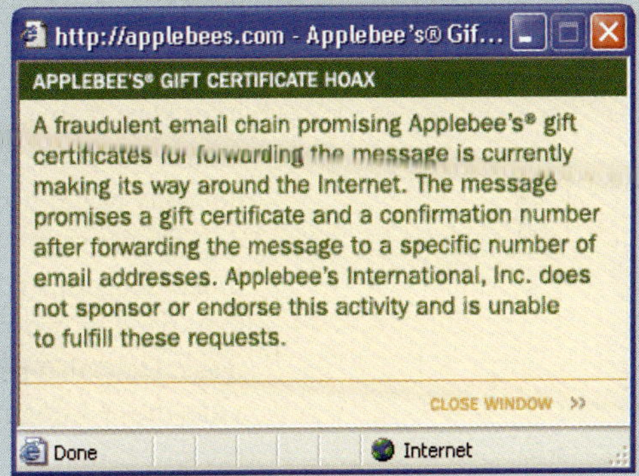

Ethical Business Practices and Decision Making

Companies must make ethics-related business decisions, such as whether or not to sell a product or service that some may find offensive or objectionable, whether or not to install monitoring cameras in the workplace, whether or not to release potentially misleading information, and whether or not to perform controversial research. In addition, corporate integrity, in terms of accounting practices and proper disclosure, is a business ethics topic that has come to the forefront, as a result of the many recent incidents involving corporate scandals and bankruptcies.

Fraudulent Reporting and Other Scandalous Activities

Following the large number of corporate scandals occurring since 2002, business ethics have never been quite so much in the public eye. The scandals, such as the ones surrounding executives at Enron, Tyco International, and WorldCom, involved lies, fraud, deception, and other illegal and unethical behavior. This behavior forced both Enron and WorldCom into bankruptcy proceedings. When asked to comment on the scandals, 3Com Chief Executive Officer Bruce Claflin said on CNBC, "I would argue we do not have an accounting problem—we have an ethics problem."

As a result of these scandals, the public's attention has become more focused on corporate integrity, as well as on the responsibility of executives to make sure illegal and fraudulent activity does not take place within the company. Before these scandals became public, a survey done for the Pew Research Center found that 66% of the public rated the heads of major companies as "low or very low" in terms of honesty and ethical standards. Since then, public confidence in corporate America has apparently eroded even further. After these scandals became public, a Gallup poll revealed that only about 18% of Americans believe that business executives have high or very high ethics, and the public perception of the honesty and ethics of business executives and stockbrokers is slightly lower than it was before the wave of business scandals in recent years.

In reaction to the scandals, Congress passed the Sarbanes-Oxley Act of 2002, which includes provisions to improve the quality of financial reporting, independent audits, and accounting services for public companies; to increase penalties for corporate wrongdoing; to protect the objectivity and independence of securities analysts; and to require CEOs and CFOs to personally vouch for the truth and fairness of their company's disclosures.

Ethically Questionable Products or Services

One ethical issue a business may run into is whether or not to sell products or services that some people find objectionable. For example, the eBay Web site states that it will not allow auction listings for items that promote hate, violence, or racial intolerance. Consequently, it bans items that bear symbols of the Nazis or the Ku Klux Klan (KKK), crime scene and morgue photographs, and letters and belongings of notorious criminals, even though sellers may legally be able to sell such items elsewhere. Policies within a particular industry may vary from company to company. For instance, pornographic movies and other adult-oriented materials are not permitted to be sold via Yahoo! Auctions, but they are permitted on eBay at the time of this writing.

Businesses that offer products or services that are inappropriate for children need to make decisions regarding access; for example, how many and what types of safeguards do they need to provide to ensure that children do not have access to these products and services? They also need to consider if the company is required legally, or just ethically, to provide these safeguards. This is especially significant for businesses with an e-commerce presence. In a conventional store, individuals can be asked to show an ID to prove they are of the required age before they are allowed to buy tobacco products, alcohol, pornographic materials, and other products that cannot legally be sold to minors. But, during an online transaction, it is much more difficult to verify that a buyer is the required age. According to government officials, most online tobacco sales are illegal because the merchants do not sufficiently comply with age verification practices or register sales with government agencies to insure the collection of the appropriate state taxes. Because of this, several major credit card companies—including Visa, MasterCard, and American Express—no longer accept payment for tobacco products bought online, making it even more difficult for companies who wish to sell tobacco products online.

FIGURE 16-10

Ethical e-commerce. Businesses selling products or services that are inappropriate or illegal for minors should require proof of age at delivery.

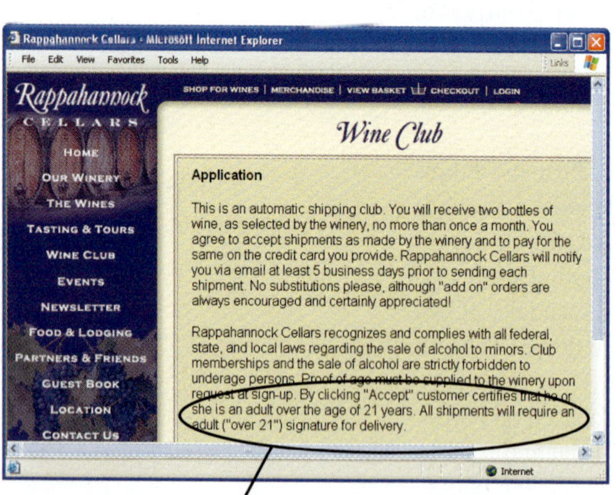

This wine club requires proof of age at sign-up and an adult signature at the time of delivery.

To protect themselves from potential litigation, some Web sites selling adult products and services require visitors to click a statement declaring they are the required age or to enter a valid credit card number before accessing or purchasing adult-only content or products. However, these precautions can be easily overcome. For example, a 2003 study from the University of North Carolina at Chapel Hill found that children were able to buy cigarettes online 92% of the time and, in an online alcohol sales sting performed in 2004 by the Alcohol Beverages Control (ABC) Commission, underage college students were able to order dozens of bottles of liquor from online retailers. Although some of the Web sites required the buyers to check a box verifying they were at least 21, others did not ask for any verification of legal age. Requiring proof of age at delivery (see Figure 16-10) is a safer precaution and is required by law in some states for certain types of shipments. However, in the 2004 ABC sting, some of the deliveries that were supposed to require proof of age did not ask for it, and some deliveries were just left on the buyers' doorsteps.

The decisions about which products or services to offer online and offline are important—and sometimes difficult—ethical decisions for businesses to make. Typically, these decisions are based on the company's overall corporate mission and desired public image. Consequently, some businesses may choose not to sell adult-only content at all. Others may decide not to sell it via the Internet until the age of online buyers can be proven beyond a doubt, or to sell those products or services online but require an adult to sign for the items when they are delivered. Still other businesses may feel that a warning statement or similar precaution on their Web sites is all that is needed, and that it is the parents' responsibility to make sure their children do not purchase illegal or inappropriate items or view adult-only content via the Internet.

FIGURE 16-11

Ethical Web site considerations. Two individuals created this Web site as a means to coerce visitors to send them money to prevent them from eating their pet rabbit, Toby.

Individuals also need to consider the ethics of actions they participate in via the Internet. One example of an ethically questionable act by two individuals is the 2005 "Save Toby" incident. Two college students started the Save Toby Web site (see Figure 16-11) to persuade individuals to send them money. The Web site contains photos of a rabbit, allegedly their pet rabbit Toby, along with recipes for cooking rabbit and the threat that they will butcher and eat the rabbit if they do not raise enough money—the original deadline was in 2005 for a minimum total donation of $50,000. After a siege of complaints by animal lovers, PayPal shut down the Save Toby donation link. However, the individuals have now published a *Save Toby!* book and extended the deadline to November, 2006. The new deadline states that a minimum of 100,000 copies of the book must be sold in order to save the rabbit's life. Although some believe the Web site is a hoax and there is no pet rabbit, the ethics surrounding such a site—real threats or not—are a topic for considerable debate.

Vaporware

Vaporware is a term sometimes used to designate software and hardware products that have been announced and advertised, but are not yet—and may never be—available. Sometimes a premature announcement is not intentional, such as when a delay in production or other last-minute problem results in a late introduction. At other times, it may be an intentional act, designed to convince customers to wait for the company's upcoming product instead of buying an existing competitive product—an act some consumers are likely to view as an unethical business practice.

Workplace Monitoring

As discussed in Chapter 15, the majority of businesses monitor employees to some extent. Although businesses have the right and responsibility to ensure that employees are productive and that company resources are not being abused, many believe that businesses also have an ethical responsibility to inform employees of any monitoring that takes place.

Cultural Considerations

With today's global economy, businesses need to be sensitive to the ethical differences that may exist between different businesses located in the same country, as well as between businesses located in different countries. Ethics are fundamentally based on values, so when beliefs, laws, customs, and traditions vary among businesses, the ethics associated with those businesses will likely differ as well. One example is the concept of *human cloning*. There are widely differing beliefs within the United States about the ethics of human cloning—some disabled Americans look to cloning as a means of finding a medical cure to their disabilities, while other citizens and groups oppose cloning for religious or ethical reasons.

Ethical decisions also need to be made whenever a business practice or product is legal or socially acceptable in one country, but not another. One example is copyright law. While the United States and many other countries have copyright laws, some countries do

TIP

When purchasing goods from another country, remember that the laws regarding the sale of products, as well as the laws regarding the privacy of personal information supplied to a vendor during a transaction, vary from one country to another.

FIGURE 16-12
Cultural considerations. In some countries, bootleg copies of music CDs and movie DVDs are sold openly, such as by this street vendor in Peru.

not. Although an individual may be able to purchase a bootleg copy of a software program, music CD, or movie in such a country (see Figure 16-12), import restrictions prevent these items from coming into the United States to be sold. With the Internet, however, U.S. citizens now have the capability of buying unauthorized copies of copyrighted materials from countries in which those copies are legal or copyright law is laxly enforced. This raises the question of ethical responsibility. Is it the individual's responsibility not to make these types of unethical purchases, even if technology makes it possible? What role should the government play in preventing citizens from buying products from other countries that are illegal in its country? What legal and ethical responsibility do businesses have to ensure that customers do not have access to products or services that are illegal in their particular location?

One incident that brought these issues into the forefront is the November 2000 French court ruling ordering the Yahoo! Auction Web site to prevent people located in France from accessing pages on the U.S. auction site containing Nazi books, daggers, uniforms, badges, and other items for sale that are illegal under French law. Although the Yahoo! France auction site did not list those items for sale, the French court order required Yahoo! to block access to these pages on its U.S. auction site from French Web surfers. Yahoo! appealed in a U.S. court on the grounds that this order was not technologically possible without completely removing all Nazi materials from its U.S. auction site, which would violate its First Amendment rights. In a decision that may set an important precedent regarding how far foreign jurisdictions can go to impose regulations against Internet content originating within the United States, a U.S. District Court in California ruled in May 2002 that the French order could not be enforced against Yahoo! in the United States.

In addition to legal issues, organizations conducting business in other countries should also take into consideration the ethical standards prevalent in the countries with which they do business. Factors such as gender roles, religious beliefs, and cultural customs should be considered and respected when corresponding, negotiating, and otherwise interacting with businesses located in other countries. For example, some cultures may require a handshake or other ritual that is impossible to carry out online in order to close a deal. In this case, while the terms of the deal may be carried out online, the deal itself would need to be closed in person. Some cultures also move at a different pace than others, such as in India where a strong sense of hierarchy often means that immediate answers via e-mail are not possible. And, while private e-mail messages in the United States are often respected as private and not forwarded to others, group-focused cultures may feel obligated to share personal e-mails with the entire team—a potential embarrassment for individuals working with businesses in those countries, if they are not aware of that custom. Businesses should also be careful not to offend the other countries with which they do business. Some straightforward questions acceptable in the United States—such as a request to verify certain numbers or double-check a source—may be viewed as an insult in some cultures. Several instances of poor judgment and cultural insensitivity on the part of Microsoft that cost the company millions of dollars and a great deal of foreign goodwill came to light in 2004. In one instance, Microsoft colored the disputed Kashmiri territory on a map of India in a software program a different color than that of the rest of India, implying that area was non-Indian. India promptly banned the program and required Microsoft to recall all 200,000 copies of that program sold in that country. In another case, Microsoft used chanting of the Koran in a soundtrack for a computer game, which greatly offended the Saudi Arabian government. And a poor English-to-Spanish translation of the Windows XP operating system resulted in the use of an offensive term for "female" in a prompt for which users are asked to select their gender.

TIP

With business e-mail—especially when exchanging e-mail with individuals in other countries—avoid trying to add humor to your messages. Humor can be difficult to translate to other languages and cultures, and it can be misinterpreted if read at a later time, such as during an audit or legal proceeding.

To properly prepare students to succeed in our global economy, some business schools include diversity and cross-cultural training in their curriculum; some international organizations arrange for their employees to have such training prior to traveling out of the country, in order to avoid offending their international business partners or clients. For instance, Microsoft has implemented geography training for its employees who need to have that knowledge, in order to avoid some of the mishaps of the past. Other companies are modifying products and services to appeal to a more global customer base. For instance, at least two cell phone models today are geared toward Muslims and include Muslim-oriented features, such as reminder alarms at prayer hours and built-in compasses that point to Mecca.

COMPUTERS AND HEALTH

Despite their many benefits, computers can pose a threat to a user's physical and mental well-being. *Repetitive stress injuries* and other injuries related to the workplace environment are estimated to account for one-third of all serious workplace injuries and to cost employees, employers, and insurance companies over $50 billion each year in lost wages, health care expenses, legal costs, and worker's compensation claims. *Stress*, *burnout*, *computer/Internet addiction*, and other emotional health problems are more difficult to quantify, although many experts believe computer-related emotional health problems are on the rise. Researchers are continuing to investigate the physical and emotional risks of computer use and are working to develop strategies for minimizing those risks. In the meantime, all computer users should be aware of the possible effects of computers on their health and what they can do today to stay healthy while using a computer at home and on the job.

Physical Health

Common physical conditions caused by computer use include eyestrain, blurred vision, fatigue, headaches, and backaches. A condition known as **carpal tunnel syndrome (CTS)**—a painful and crippling condition affecting the hands and wrists—has been linked to the repetitive finger movements made when using a keyboard, although it can be caused by non-computer-related activities, as well. CTS is an example of a **repetitive stress injury (RSI)**, in which hand, wrist, shoulder, or neck pain is caused by performing the same physical movements over and over again. Extensive mouse use has also been associated with RSIs. Another physical condition is *computer vision syndrome* (*CVS*)—a collection of eye and vision problems associated with computer use. The most common symptoms are eyestrain or eye fatigue, dry eyes, burning eyes, light sensitivity, blurred vision, headaches, and pain in the shoulders, neck, or back.

A proper work environment and good habits—a concept known as *ergonomics*—can prevent many physical problems caused by computer use and is important for anyone who works on a computer, including employees using a computer on the job, individuals using a PC at home, and children doing computer activities at home or at school.

FURTHER EXPLORATION

For links to further information about computer use injuries and how they can be prevented, go to www.course.com/uc11/ch16

What Is Ergonomics?

Ergonomics is the science of fitting a work environment to the people who work there. It typically focuses on making products and workspaces more comfortable and safe to use. With respect to computer use, it involves designing a safe and effective workspace, which includes properly adjusting furniture and hardware and using *ergonomic hardware* when needed. But there is more to ergonomics than just physical equipment—good user habits and procedures are important, too. These topics are discussed in the next few sections.

Workspace Design

The design of a safe and effective computer workspace—whether it is located at work, home, or school—includes the placement and adjustment of all the furniture and equipment

>**Carpel tunnel syndrome (CTS).** A painful and crippling condition affecting the hands and wrist that can be caused by computer use. >**Repetitive stress injury (RSI).** A type of injury, such as carpal tunnel syndrome, that is caused by performing the same physical movements over and over again. >**Ergonomics.** The science of fitting a work environment to the people who work there.

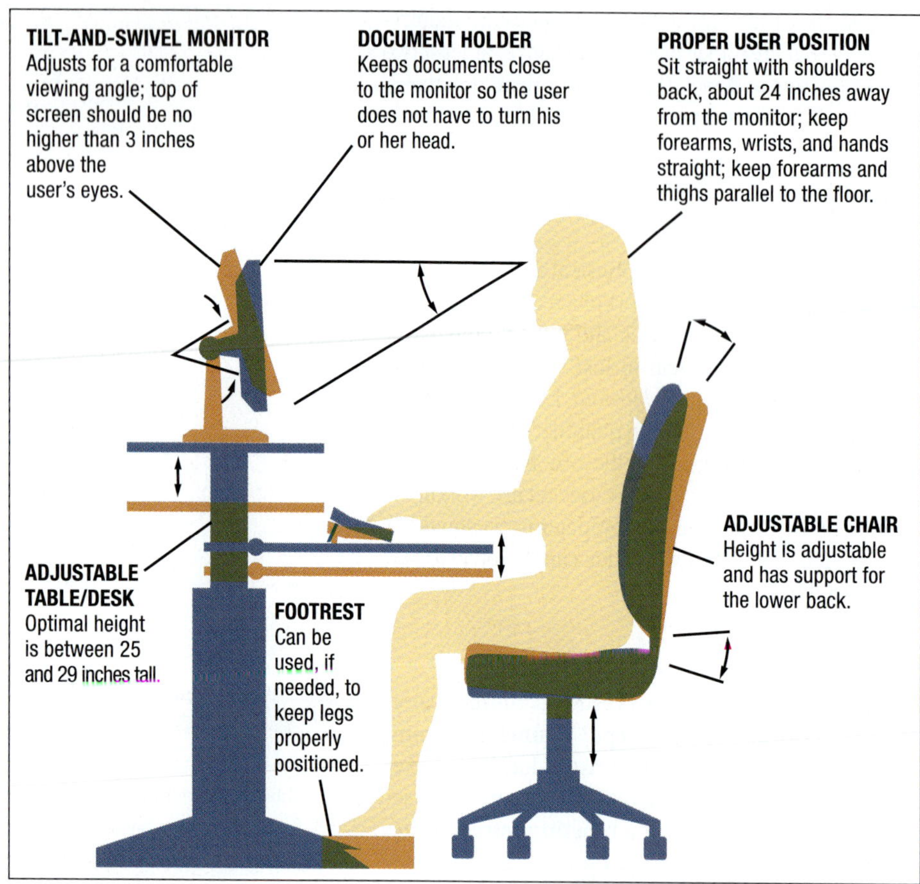

FIGURE 16-13

Workspace design. Shown here are some guidelines for designing an ergonomic workspace.

involved, such as the user's desk, chair, keyboard, and monitor. Workspace lighting or glare from the sun also needs to be taken into consideration. Proper workspace design can result in fewer injuries, headaches, and general aches and pains for computer users. Businesses can reap economic benefits from proper workspace design, such as fewer absences taken by employees, higher productivity, and lower insurance costs. For example, when one government department in New Jersey installed ergonomically correct workstations in their offices, computer-related health complaints fell by 40% and doctor visits dropped by 25% in less than one year.

Proper placement and adjustment of furniture is a good place to start when evaluating a workspace from an ergonomic perspective (see Figure 16-13). The desk should be placed where the sun and other sources of light cannot shine directly onto the screen or into the user's eyes. The monitor should be placed directly in front of the user about an arm's length away, and the top of the screen should be no more than 3 inches above the user's eyes once the user's chair is adjusted. The desk chair should be adjusted so that the keyboard is at, or slightly below, the height at which the user's forearms are horizontal to the floor. A footrest should be used, if needed, to keep the user's feet flat on the floor once the chair height has been set. The monitor settings should be adjusted to make the screen brightness match the brightness of the room and to have a high amount of contrast. The screen should also be periodically wiped clean of dust.

When designing or evaluating a computer workspace, the type of computer work to be performed should be considered. For example, people who refer to written documents while working on their PCs should use *document holders* to keep their documents close to their monitors to avoid the repetitive motion of looking between the document and the monitor—an action that can create or aggravate neck problems. These users should also place their keyboards directly in front of them for easy access. On the other hand, for Web surfing or other computer activities (such as computer-aided design or graphics design) that require a great deal of mouse work, placement of the mouse for comfortable access should be given high priority.

The workspace design principles just discussed and illustrated in Figure 16-13 apply to users of both desktop and portable PCs. However, an ergonomic workspace is more difficult to obtain when using a portable PC because the keyboards and monitors cannot normally be positioned and adjusted separately. To create a safer and more comfortable work environment, notebook and tablet PC users can attach peripheral devices—such as a keyboard and mouse—to use with their PCs both at home and while traveling (special *travel mice* and *travel keyboards* are smaller and lighter than conventional models to make them more portable). If there is a location where a notebook or tablet PC will be used on a regular basis, a *docking station* or a *notebook stand* can be used.

OCCASIONAL USERS	FULL-TIME USERS
Sit with the notebook on a table and position it for comfortable wrist posture.	Sit with the notebook on a desk or table and position it for comfortable wrist posture.
Adjust the screen to a comfortable position, so you can see the screen as straight on as possible.	Elevate the notebook so the screen is at the proper height, or connect the PC to a stand-alone monitor instead of using the notebook's built-in monitor; consider using a docking station or notebook stand.
Consider bringing a travel keyboard and mouse to use with the notebook PC, when possible.	Use a separate keyboard and mouse, either attached directly to the PC or to a docking station.
When purchasing a notebook, pay close attention to the total weight of the system (PC, batteries, power supply, additional drives, etc.); purchase a lightweight system to avoid neck and shoulder injuries when carrying the notebook from one location to another.	When purchasing a notebook, pay close attention to the size and clarity of the monitor, unless you will be using a separate stand-alone monitor, and pay close attention to the keyboard design, unless you will be using a separate keyboard.

FIGURE 16-14
Ergonomic tips for notebook users.
These tips are organized by type of user.

A **docking station** (shown in Figure 1-17 in Chapter 1) contains a connector to attach a portable PC, plus ports to connect conventional desktop PC peripherals, such as a keyboard, mouse, monitor, and printer. The docking station connects the portable PC and the peripheral devices so those devices (which are always connected to the docking station) can be used with the portable PC whenever the PC is connected to the docking station.

A *notebook stand* (see Figure 16-14) is an alternative to a docking station designed primarily to elevate the display screen of a notebook or tablet PC so it can be used instead of an external monitor. Although some notebook stands have a built-in USB hub to connect USB peripheral devices to the portable PC, most peripheral devices—such as a keyboard and mouse—used with the portable PC while it is inserted into a notebook stand are connected directly to the portable PC, not to the notebook stand. Consequently, unlike a docking station, the notebook stand requires the peripheral devices to be connected to the portable PC each time it is inserted into the notebook stand, in order to be used. Some additional ergonomic tips for notebook users are included in Figure 16-14.

TIP

Since all programs and data are accessed from and stored on the portable PC's storage hardware, a docking station or notebook stand lets you use the same PC at home and on the road, while still having a comfortable work environment at home.

Ergonomic Hardware

To help users avoid physical problems due to extensive PC use or to help alleviate the discomfort associated with an already existing condition, various types of **ergonomic hardware** are available (see Figure 16-15).

- *Ergonomic keyboards* use a shape and key arrangement designed to lessen the strain on the hands and wrists. To fit a child's hand size better, a child's keyboard—which is smaller than a regular keyboard—can be used.
- *Ergonomic mice* typically look more like joysticks than mice and are designed for more comfortable use by extensive mouse users. Child-sized mice are also available. Some users find other types of pointing devices (such as a trackball) more comfortable than a mouse when extensive mouse use is required.
- *Keyboard drawers* lower the keyboard, enabling the user to keep his or her forearms parallel to the floor more easily.

>Docking station. A device that connects a portable PC to conventional hardware, such as a keyboard, mouse, monitor, and printer.

>Ergonomic hardware. Hardware, typically input and output devices, that is designed to be more ergonomically correct than its nonergonomic counterparts.

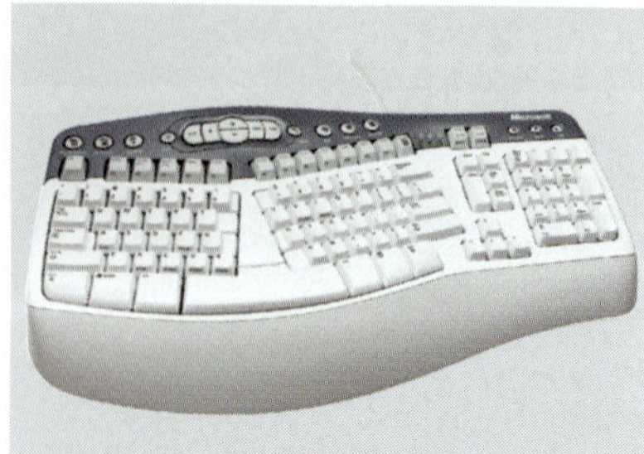
ERGONOMIC KEYBOARD

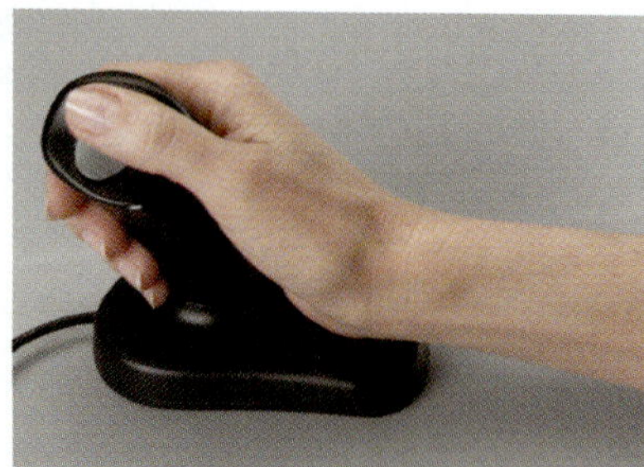
ERGONOMIC MOUSE

KEYBOARD DRAWER

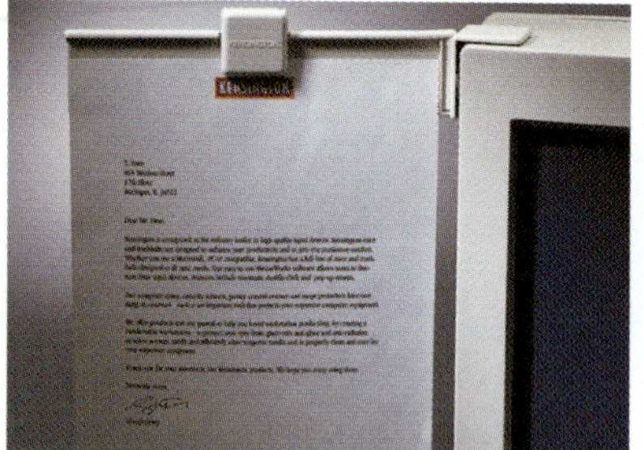
DOCUMENT HOLDER

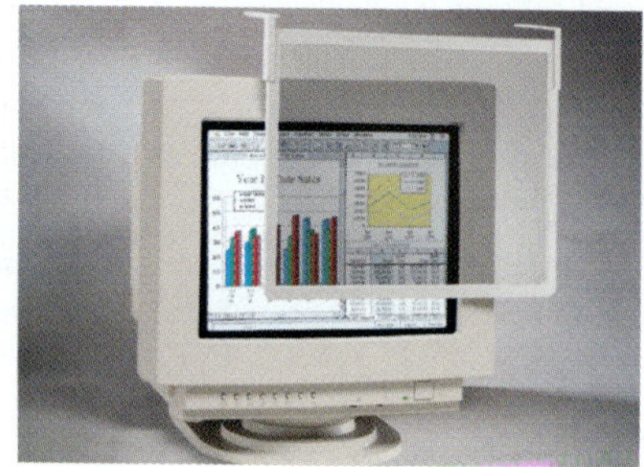
ANTIGLARE SCREEN

WRIST REST

FIGURE 16-15
Ergonomic devices.

- *Document holders*—sometimes called *copy holders*—can be used to keep documents close to the monitor, enabling the user to see both the document and the monitor without turning his or her head. Document holders are available for both desktop and portable PCs.
- *Antiglare screens* or *antiglare shields* that cover the monitor screen can be used to lessen glare and resulting eyestrain. Some manufacturers claim antiglare screens reduce the amount of radiation emitted from a monitor, although many experts believe that today's monitors—particularly those that adhere to the *MPR II* or *TCO 92* standards of acceptable levels of radiation—are not a significant health hazard. Some antiglare screens double as privacy screens, preventing others sitting next to you (such as on an airplane) from reading what is displayed on your notebook screen.
- *Wrist rests* designed to be placed next to the mouse or keyboard can be used to help keep wrists straight while those devices are being used, as well as to provide support for the wrists and forearms when the devices are not being used.

FIGURE 16-16
Good user habits.

CONDITION	PREVENTION
Wrist/arm soreness and injury	▪ Use a light touch on the keyboard. ▪ Rest and gently stretch your fingers and arms every 15 minutes or so. ▪ Keep your wrists and arms relaxed and parallel to the floor when using the keyboard.
Eyestrain	▪ Cover windows or adjust lighting to eliminate glare. ▪ Concentrate on blinking your eyes more often. ▪ Rest your eyes every 15 minutes or so by focusing on an object in the distance (at least 20 feet away) for one minute and then closing your eyes for an additional minute. ▪ Make sure your monitor's brightness and contrast settings are at an appropriate level. ▪ Use a larger text size or lower screen resolution, if needed (you should be able to read what is displayed on your monitor from three times the distance at which you normally sit).
Sore or stiff neck	▪ Use good posture. ▪ Place the monitor and any documents you need to refer to while using your PC directly in front of you. ▪ Adjust your monitor to a comfortable viewing angle with the top of the screen no higher than 3 inches above your eyes. ▪ Use a telephone headset if you spend a significant amount of time each day on the telephone.
Backache; general fatigue	▪ Use good posture and adjust your chair to support your lower back. ▪ Use a footrest, if needed, to keep your feet flat on the floor. ▪ Walk around or stretch briefly at least once every hour. ▪ Alternate activities frequently.

Good User Habits and Precautions

Computer users can follow a number of preventive measures while working at their PCs (see Figure 16-16), in addition to establishing an ergonomic workspace. Finger and wrist exercises and frequent breaks in typing are good precautions for helping to prevent repetitive hand and finger stress injuries. Using good posture and periodically taking a break to relax or stretch the body can help reduce or prevent back and neck strain. Rotating tasks—such as alternating between computer work, telephone work, and paperwork every 15 minutes or so—is also a good idea. For locations where some glare from a nearby window is unavoidable at certain times of the day, closing the curtains or blinds can help to prevent eyestrain. Eyeglass wearers should discuss any eye fatigue or blurriness during computer use with their eye doctors—sometimes a different lens prescription or special *computer glasses* can be used to reduce eyestrain while working on a PC.

Emotional Health

The extensive use of computers and related technology in the home and office in recent years has raised new concerns about emotional health. Factors such as financial worries, feelings of being overworked, being unable to relax, and information overload often produce emotional stress. Decades of research have linked stress to a variety of health concerns, such as heart attacks, stroke, diabetes, and weakened immune system. Workers who report feeling stressed incur more healthcare costs—an average of $600 more per person, according to one study—than nonstressed workers. Consequently, workplace stress is expensive. According to the American Institute of Stress, it costs U.S. employers more than $300 billion each year in healthcare, missed work, and stress-reduction services provided to employees.

For many individuals, computer use or computer-related events are the cause of, or at least partially contribute to, the stress that they experience. Another emotional health concern related to computer use is *computer/Internet addiction*.

Stress of Ever-Changing Technology

When computers were first introduced into the workplace, workers needed to learn the appropriate computer skills if their jobs required computer use. Airline agents, for example, had to learn to use computer databases. Secretaries and other office employees needed to learn to use word processing and other office-related software. Today, many people entering the workforce are aware of the computer skills they will need to perform the tasks associated with their chosen professions. However, as computers have become continually more integrated into our society, jobs that did not require the use of a computer in the recent past may very well require it today (see Figure 16-17). And, at the rapid pace that technology keeps changing, many workers must regularly learn new skills to keep up to date. For example, they may need to upgrade to a new version of a software program, learn how to use a new software program, or learn how to use a new piece of hardware. Although some find this exciting, the ongoing battle to stay current with changing technology creates stress for many individuals.

FIGURE 16-17

Computer-related jobs. Many jobs that did not require computer use in the past require computer use today.

UTILITY WORKER

AIRPLANE TECHNICIAN

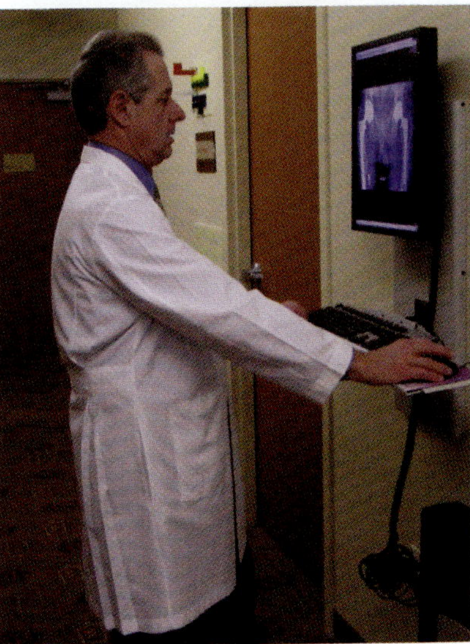
PHYSICIAN

HYDROGEOLOGIST

SOC

A related problem is the tenuous nature of many technology- and Internet-related companies at the present time. Since the technology bubble burst in 2000, a large number of dot-coms have gone out of business, and many of the companies that survived are tightening their belts. Outsourcing work to lower-paid workers in countries such as India, China, and Eastern Europe, is also becoming increasingly common for clerical work, technical support, and software development. The market research firm Gartner predicts that U.S. companies will outsource nearly $50 billion in software development alone by the end of 2007. These factors and the risk of more layoffs and losses are an added stress for people—such as workers, management, and investors—who are associated with companies in the technology sector.

FIGURE 16-18

Our 24/7 society. With mobile phones, pagers, and portable PCs, many individuals are available 24/7.

Impact of Our 24/7 Society

One benefit of our communications-oriented society is that one never has to be out of touch. With the use of personal cell phones and pagers, as well as the ability to access e-mail and company networks from virtually anywhere, individuals can be available around the clock, if needed (see Figure 16-18). Although the ability to be in touch constantly is an advantage for some people under certain conditions, it can also be a source of great stress. For example, employees who feel that they are "on call" 24/7 and cannot ever get away from work may find it difficult to relax during their downtime. Others who are used to being in touch constantly may not be able to relax when they are on vacation and supposed to be unavailable because they are afraid of missing something important that may affect their careers. In either case, these individuals may lose the distinction between personal time and work time, and so they may end up being always on the job. This can affect their personal lives, emotional health, and overall well-being. Finding a balance between work time and personal time is important for good emotional health.

Information Overload

Although the amount of information available through the Internet is a great asset, it can also be overwhelming at times. When you combine TV and radio news broadcasts; newspaper, journal, and magazine articles; and telephone calls, voice mail messages, and faxes, some Americans are practically drowning in information. The amount of e-mail received each day by some individuals and organizations is almost unfathomable. For example, the U.S. Senate receives millions of e-mail messages each day, and it is estimated that workers in the United States spend an average of two hours per day dealing with e-mail messages. Several strategies can be used to avoid becoming completely overwhelmed by information overload.

TIP

For a review of how to perform efficient and effective Internet searches, refer again to Chapter 9.

For efficiently extracting the information you need from the vast amount of information available over the Internet, good search techniques are essential. Perhaps the most important thing to keep in mind when dealing with information overload is that you cannot possibly read everything ever written on a particular subject. At some point in time when performing Internet research, the value of additional information decreases and, eventually, it is not worth your time to continue the search. Knowing when to quit a search or when to try another research approach is an important skill in avoiding information overload.

RSS feeds (discussed in the Chapter 8 Inside the Industry box) can be used to deliver only the Web site content you specify on a regular basis, which helps reduce information overload. *Intelligent agents*—software programs that do specified jobs based on your instructions—can also gather information for you on a regular basis, as well as perform other helpful tasks, such as notifying you when a particular Web page has been updated or a certain stock hits a specified price. Other programs can suppress those annoying pop-up ads or otherwise help you have a more efficient and pleasant Internet experience.

Efficiently managing your incoming e-mail is another way to avoid information overload. Tools for managing e-mail can help alleviate the stress of an overflowing Inbox, as well as cut down the amount of time you spend dealing with your online correspondence.

As discussed in Chapter 15, e-mail filters can be used to route messages automatically into specific folders (such as suspected spam), based on criteria you set. This allows you to concentrate on the messages most important to you first and leave the others—such as the possible spam—to be sorted through and dealt with at your convenience. Some productivity training companies advise treating e-mail like physical mail and opening e-mail only a limited number of times per day. According to these companies, avoiding continually jumping back and forth between e-mail and other activities can both increase productivity and decrease stress significantly.

TIP

View your Inbox as a temporary location only; after reading an e-mail message, immediately delete it or file it in an e-mail folder to keep your Inbox clean.

Burnout

Our heavy use of computers, combined with information overload and 24/7 accessibility via technology, can lead to **burnout**—a state of fatigue or frustration brought about by overwork. Burnout is often born from good intentions—when, for example, hardworking people try to reach goals that, for one reason or another, become unrealistic. Early signs of burnout include a feeling of emotional and physical exhaustion, no longer caring about a project that used to be interesting or exciting, irritability, feelings of resentment about the amount of work that needs to be done, and feeling pulled in many directions at once.

When you begin to notice the symptoms of burnout, experts recommend reevaluating your schedule, priorities, and lifestyle. Sometimes, just admitting that you are feeling overwhelmed is a good start to solving the problem. Taking a break or getting away for a day can help put the situation in perspective. Saying no to additional commitments and making sure that you eat properly, exercise regularly, and otherwise take good care of yourself are also important strategies for coping with and alleviating both stress and burnout.

Computer/Internet Addiction

When an individual overuses, or is unable to stop using, a computer or the Internet, it becomes a problem and is referred to as **computer/Internet addiction**—also called *computer addiction disorder* (*CAD*) or *Internet addiction disorder* (*IAD*). According to Maressa Hecht Orzack, a Harvard Medical School assistant clinical professor and the director of the Computer Addiction Study Center at McLean Hospital in Massachusetts, computer addiction is "an emerging disorder suffered by people who find the virtual reality on computer screens more attractive than everyday reality." She estimates that between 5% and 10% of all Internet users suffer some sort of Internet dependency and the level of addiction for individuals who play online role playing games is much higher—up to 40%. In addition, as technologies improve and *massive multiplayer online role-playing games* (*MMORPG*) become even more sophisticated and exciting, the level of Internet addiction may continue to increase. Addiction to online gambling is another growing concern.

Computer/Internet addiction can affect people of any age and can take a variety of forms. Some individuals become addicted to e-mailing or instant messaging. Others become compulsive online shoppers or become addicted to chat room activities. Still others cannot stop playing online or offline games. Currently, the most common forms of addictive behaviors include instant messaging, online chatting, online pornography, and massive multiplayer online role-playing games. One example is that of a 17-year-old high school student who was addicted to instant messaging. This young woman would come home from school and immediately go online. During summer vacation, she stayed online all day. When people did not respond immediately to her messages, she took it personally and became depressed and, eventually, suicidal. After breaking her addiction cold turkey with counseling and antidepressants, she now has a healthy balance between the Internet

>**Burnout.** A state of fatigue or frustration usually brought on by overwork. >**Computer/Internet addiction.** The problem of overusing, or being unable to stop using, a computer and/or the Internet.

MPUTER/INTERNET ADDICTION
...puter in order to experience pleasure, excitement, or relief.
... when not on the computer, becoming anxious, angry, or depressed.
... overwhelming thoughts about the computer before you power it up, while it is on, and after you have turned it off.
...ou crave the newest hardware or software, and you are never satisfied with what you have.
You need to spend increasing amounts of time or money on computer activities in order to get the same effect.
You lie to everybody about the amount of time spent on the computer and where you are spending that time.
You risk the loss of relationships with your family and friends because of your compulsive computer use.
You face financial ruin because of excessive computer use.
You repeatedly fail at efforts to stop your compulsive computer use.
Your physical health suffers because you miss meals, do not exercise, and neglect personal hygiene.
You experience repetitive stress injuries, backaches, dry eyes, migraines, and changes in sleep patterns as a result of excessive computer use.

FIGURE 16-19
Symptoms of computer addiction. You may be addicted to or dependent on your computer if you experience at least five of these symptoms.

and other activities. Another case of IAD is that of the divorced mother who, because of her habit of spending 10 hours or more online each day and neglecting her children, lost custody of her children. An additional incident involved one manager who was fired from two different computer companies because he could not stop visiting pornographic Web sites at work. IAD can even result in death, such as in the case of one 28-year old man in South Korean who collapsed in an Internet café in 2005 after playing online games nearly 50 hours straight; he died shortly after being taken to a hospital.

Like other addictions, computer/Internet addiction may result in many losses, such as loss of relationships, job loss, academic failure, obesity, repetitive stress injuries, and suicide, and may be the result of either a mood disorder or an anxiety disorder. These behaviors may result in increasing amounts of time and money spent on computers and other problems. Many experts believe computer/Internet addiction is a growing problem—some studies indicate that over 6% of Internet users suffer from computer/Internet addiction to some degree (see Figure 16-19 for Dr. Orzack's list of computer/Internet addiction symptoms). Computer/Internet addiction is also a global ailment. Countries with a high level of broadband Internet access—such as South Korea—are reporting high levels of Internet addiction. It is estimated that 3% of Germany's population is addicted to the Internet, and the country has a summer camp for children suspected of being computer addicts. China opened its first officially licensed clinic for Internet addiction in 2005, and the clinic's director estimates that up to 2.5 million Chinese suffer from Internet addiction. And Finland is temporarily dismissing an increasing number of young people from their compulsory military responsibilities due to Internet addiction—reportedly, they are physically too weak and are mentally unprepared to deal with people directly and not through the Internet, and, consequently, cannot adjust to boot camp routines. Many experts believe that computer/Internet addiction is a growing problem, but it can be treated, similar to other addictions, with such methods as therapy, support groups, and medication.

ACCESS TO TECHNOLOGY

For many, a major concern about the increased integration of computers and technology into our society is whether or not technology is accessible to all individuals. Some believe there is a distinct line dividing those who have access and those who do not. Factors such as age, gender, race, income, education, and physical abilities can all impact one's access to technology and how one uses it.

The Digital Divide

The term **digital divide** refers to the gap between those who have access to information and communications technology and those who do not—often referred to as the "haves" and "have nots." Typically, the digital divide is thought to be based on physical access to computers and other types of related technology. Some individuals, however, believe that the definition of digital divide goes deeper than just access. For example, they classify those individuals who have physical access to technology but who do not understand how to use it or are discouraged from using it in the "have not" category. Groups and individuals trying to eliminate the digital divide are working toward providing real access to technology (including access to up-to-date hardware, software, and training) so that it can be used to improve people's lives.

The digital divide can refer to the differences between individuals within a particular country, as well as to the differences between countries. Within a country, use of computers and related technology can vary based on such factors as age, race, education, and income.

The U.S. Digital Divide

Although there is disagreement among experts about the current status of the digital divide within the United States, there is an indication that it has begun to shrink in the last few years. The digital divide involves more than just Internet use—it involves the use of any type of technology necessary to succeed in our society—but the increased Internet use noted in the past few years is an encouraging sign. According to Nielsen/NetRatings, about two-thirds of the population of the United States is now online, using the Internet at work, schools, libraries, or home. Low-priced computers and free and low-cost dial-up Internet access have made computers and Internet access more feasible for low-income families today than in the past. In general, however, according to a 2005 report by the Pew Internet & American Life Project, individuals with a higher level of education are more likely to go online, younger individuals are more likely to be online than older Americans, and households with children under age 18 are more likely to be online than households without children. Some overall demographic data about Internet use in the United States is shown in Figure 16-20.

In addition to access differences based on factors such as income, age, education, and race, some believe a new divide is being created related to broadband Internet use. Over 60% of Internet users in the United States have high-speed connections at home, according to Nielsen/Netratings, but an October 2005 report by the Pew Internet & American Life Project revealed that U.S. Internet users with less education, with lower household incomes, and who are age 65 and older are less likely to have broadband Internet. The report suggests the population of the United States can be divided into three tiers with respect to Internet use: broadband users (33%), dial-up and intermittent users (40%), and those who do not use the Internet at all (22%).

Because the United States is such a technologically advanced society, reducing—and trying to eliminate—the digital divide is extremely important to ensure that all citizens have an equal chance to be successful in this country. Although there has been lots of progress in that direction, more work still remains. Because of the significant promise of broadband Internet, President Bush has established a national goal for "universal, affordable access for broadband technology by the year 2007." However, it is important to realize that not all individuals want to use computers or go online. Just as some people choose not to have televisions, cell phones, or other technologies, some people—rich or poor—choose not to have a PC. Sometimes this is a religious decision; at other times, it is simply a lifestyle choice.

>**Digital divide.** The gap between those who have access to technology and those who do not.

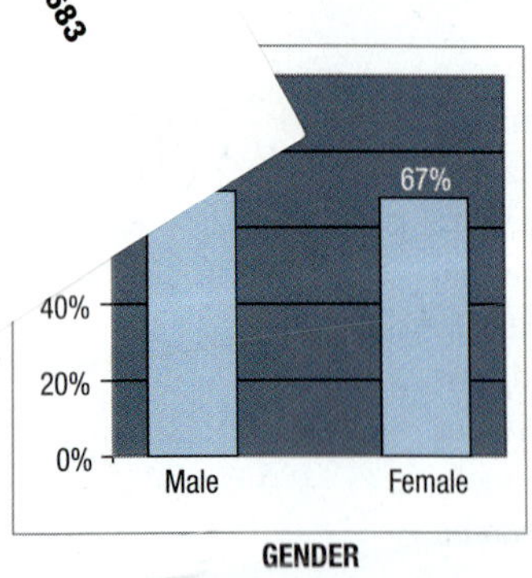

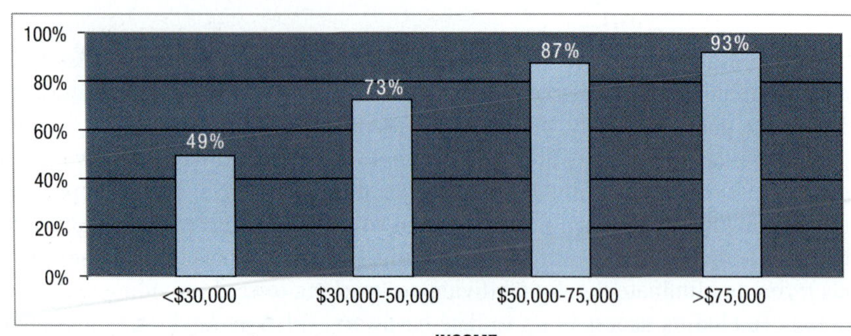

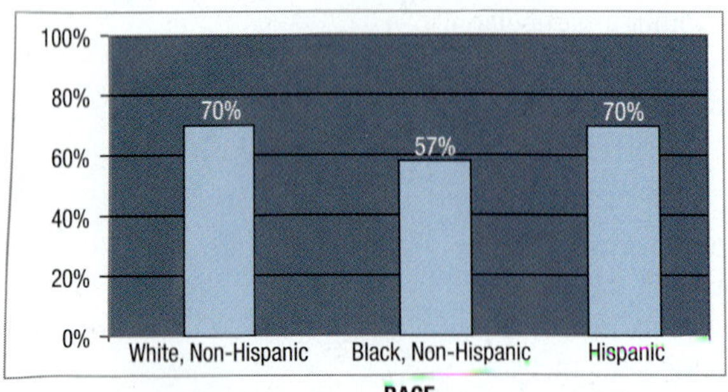

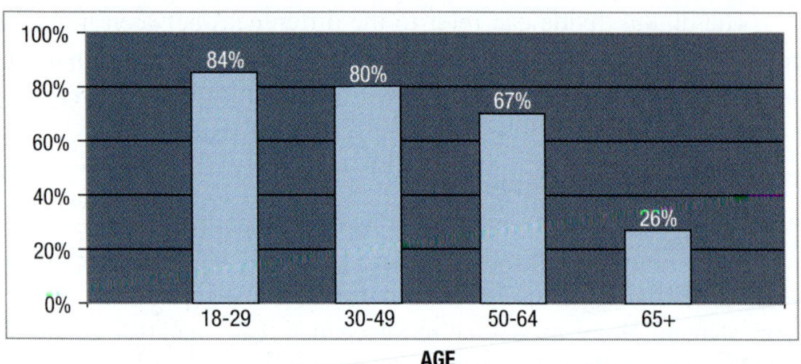

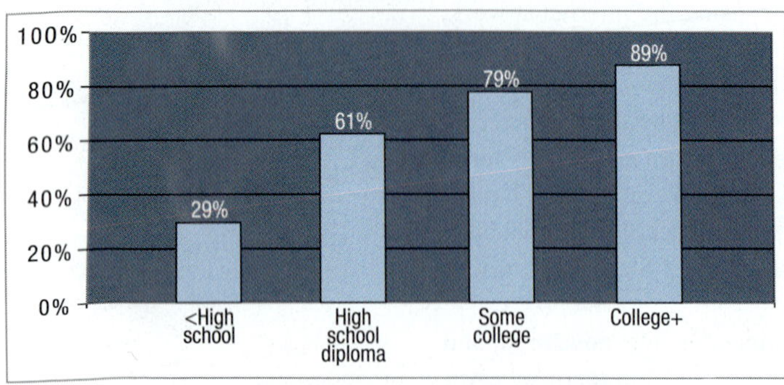

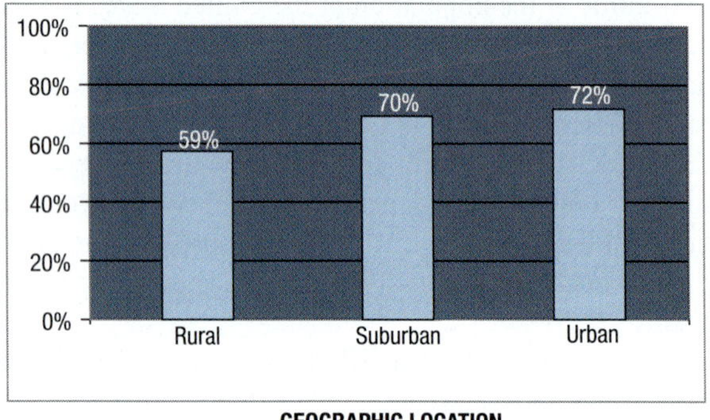

Source: Pew Internet & American Life Project, May–June 2005

FIGURE 16-20

Key U.S. Internet use statistics. Shows the percent of individuals in each category who use the Internet.

The Global Digital Divide

While the digital divide within a country is about some individuals within a country having access to technology and others not, the global digital divide is about some countries having access to technology and others not. It is becoming increasingly important for all countries to have access to information and communications technology in order to be able to compete successfully in our global economy.

The global digital divide is perhaps more dramatic than the U.S. digital divide. It is estimated that nearly one billion people are online globally—only about 15% of the world's population. The United States has about 22% of the world's Internet users, according to July 2005 figures from InternetWorldStats.com. Partly, this can be attributed to the use of technology in general and the sophisticated technological infrastructure that exists and is continually being upgraded in the United States. Another factor is income versus cost. For example, research indicates that the typical U.S. consumer spends just 1% to 2% of his or her average monthly income on Internet access, compared to the 191% of monthly income that the average citizen in Bangladesh would need to spend in order to have Internet access. But some countries are beginning to catch up to and even surpass the United States in overall Internet usage in respect to population. For instance, according to the InternetWorldStats.com data, the United States is now fourth in overall Internet penetration—73.6% of the people in Sweden, 70.7% of the people in Hong Kong, and 68.7% of the people in Denmark are online, compared with 68.5% of U.S. residents.

For some, it is difficult to imagine how computers and the Internet would benefit the world's hungry or the 2 billion people without access to reliable electricity. Others view technology as a means to bridge the global digital divide. Some technological applications already in place in developing countries include mobile phones with solar-rechargeable batteries and computers to be used for telemedicine and distance learning. For instance, a telemedicine project in Siliguri, India, a remote town in the foothills of the eastern Himalayas, provides specialized medical care via computers to local residents. Without telemedicine, residents would have to travel overnight to Calcutta to see a specialist; with telemedicine, residents are diagnosed and treated without leaving their village. And one specialist—a cardiologist—estimates that his care via telemedicine, primarily analyzing patient data and advising local physicians, has brought down the mortality rate after heart attacks in Siliguri from 50% to about 5%.

For personal computer use, new products are emerging that could help alleviate the global digital divide. For example, the *Simputer* (see Figure 16-21) was developed to bring low-cost computer use first to India, and then to other countries—particularly third-world countries. Developed by a Bangalore-based group of seven professors and engineers, the Simputer uses a simple user interface based on sight, touch, and audio. The Simputer accepts input via voice, in addition to electronic pen and onscreen keyboard, and includes text-to-speech capabilities to read screen output to users, allowing the device to be used by individuals who cannot read or write—a giant step toward bridging the digital divide in third-world countries. Designed to be shared by members in a community, the Simputer is sometimes referred to as a *community digital assistant* or *CDA*. It is possible to share a Simputer because each villager stores personal information and settings on his or her inexpensive rewritable smart card. When a user wants to use a Simputer, he or she inserts this card into any Simputer, and then the individual's information and personal settings specified on the smart card are available for use. Data can be read from and written to the card, until the card is removed. A USB flash memory stick can be used for a larger amount of personal storage, such as for written documents, photos, and e-mail messages. Current features of the Simputer include an electronic notepad in which to take notes in either English or one of several Indian languages, an MP3 player, an address book, and a calculator. Web browsing and e-mail is possible via a dial-up Internet connection or by connecting the Simputer to a wired or Wi-Fi network.

Simputers are currently being used in several villages in India and cost between about $200 U.S. and $400 U.S., depending on configuration. If a unit is available in the village to rent or to borrow—such as through the local school or a village shop—villagers only need to buy a smart card to be able to use a Simputer. The Simputer can be used today by farmers to check the latest crop prices, fishermen to get accurate weather reports, village accountants to collect and transmit crop data on location, and schoolchildren to access educational lessons. Expected future applications include using the Simputer to facilitate long-distance medical diagnostics, basic literacy training, banking and commodity trading, communications, voting, and GPS navigation. AMD has also developed a low-cost computer—the *Personal Internet Communicator* (*PIC*) designed for use in Latin and Indian nations. Featuring a 366 MHz AMD processor, 128 MB RAM, a 10 GB drive, and Windows CE operating system, the PIC is expected to sell for $250 with monitor and $185 without when it becomes available for purchase.

FIGURE 16-21
Low-cost computing devices.

SIMPUTER
Designed to bring low-cost computing to third-world countries; can be shared by members in a village.

$100 LAPTOP
Designed to bring low-cost computing to schoolchildren in third-world countries; intended to have one laptop per child.

Another low-cost computer designed for use in third-world countries is under development by the Massachusetts Institute of Technology Media Labs on behalf of the *One Laptop Per Child* (*OLPC*) independent, nonprofit association. This laptop computer is expected to cost only $100 each and is capable of performing all necessary tasks except storing large quantities of data. It will be encased in rubber and use flash memory instead of a hard drive to make it more durable, use Linux and a 500 MHz processor to keep the cost down, and connect to peripheral devices and the Internet via USB ports and Wi-Fi connections. It also includes a hand crank that can be used to power the laptop when no power supply is available. The laptops will not be sold commercially. Instead, they are designed to be purchased by governments to be distributed to schools; governments must commit to buying one million units at $100 each in order to participate in the program. Initial countries currently discussing this type of distribution with OLPC include Brazil, China, Egypt, Thailand, and South Africa. In the United States, Massachusetts governor Mitt Romney has announced an interest in buying the $100 laptops for all middle and high school students in the state as soon as they become available. The units are expected to begin shipping in late 2006 or early 2007.

Assistive Technology

Research has found that people with disabilities tend to use computers and the Internet at rates below the average for a given population. Part of the reason may be that some physical conditions—such as visual impairment or limited dexterity—make it difficult to use a conventional computer system. That is where **assistive technology**—hardware and software specially designed for use by individuals with physical disabilities—fits in. There has been much improvement in the area of assistive hardware and software in recent years. This may be due in part to the *Americans with Disabilities Act* (*ADA*), which requires companies with 15 or more employees to make reasonable accommodations for known physical or mental limitations of otherwise qualified individuals, unless doing so results in undue hardship for the company. Consequently, assistive input and output devices—such as *Braille keyboards*, specialized mice, large monitors, and *screen readers*—and wheelchair-compatible workspaces have become more commonplace in businesses, as well as in homes and schools.

Assistive Input Systems

Assistive input devices allow for input in a nontraditional manner (see Figure 16-22). For example, *Braille keyboards*, large-key keyboards, or conventional keyboards with Braille or large-print key overlays are available for visually impaired computer users. *Keyguards*—metal or plastic plates that fit over conventional keyboards—enable users with limited hand mobility to press the keys on a keyboard, using his or her fingers or a special device, without accidentally pressing other keys. *One-handed keyboards* are available for users who have the use of only one hand, and *voice input systems* (also called *voice recognition systems* and *speech recognition systems*) use special software and a microphone to input data and give commands to the PC hands-free. *Switches*—hardware devices that can be activated with hand, foot, finger, or face movement or with sips and puffs of air—can be used in conjunction with a keyboard, mouse, or other input device to perform a preprogrammed set of actions, such as opening the Windows Start menu or performing a left mouse click. Some conventional input devices can also be used for assistive purposes, such as scanners, which—if they have optical character recognition (OCR) capabilities—can input printed documents into the computer as editable text.

>**Assistive technology.** Hardware and software specifically designed for use by individuals with physical disabilities.

For mouse alternatives, there are assistive pointing devices that can be used—sometimes in conjunction with a switch—to move and select items with an onscreen pointer; used in conjunction with an onscreen keyboard, they can also be used to enter text-based data. There are also *feet mice*, which are controlled by the feet, and *head pointing systems* or *head mice*, which control the onscreen pointer using head movement. For example, the head pointing systems shown in Figure 16-22 use a reflective dot placed on the forehead or eyeglasses in conjunction with a tracking camera to move an onscreen pointer based on the user's head movement.

In addition to its use by disabled computer users, assistive hardware can also be used by the general population. For example, one-handed keyboards are sometimes used by people who wish to keep one hand on the mouse and one hand on the keyboard at all times; voice input systems are used by individuals who would prefer to speak input instead of type it; and head pointing systems are available for gaming and virtual reality (VR) applications.

For a look at an emerging alternative—*brain-to-computer interfacing*—and other types of digital implants, see the Trend box.

BRAILLE KEYBOARD
The keys on this keyboard contain Braille overlays.

ONE-HANDED KEYBOARD
All keys can be reached with either the left or right hand, depending on which version of the keyboard is being used (right-handed is shown here).

HEAD-POINTING SYSTEM WITH PUFF SWITCH
With this system, head movement controls the pointer movement, and puffs of air into the tube are used to "click" objects.

HEAD-POINTING SYSTEM WITHOUT A SWITCH
With this system, head movement (tracked via the reflective dot on her glasses) controls the pointer movement, and pointing to an object for a specified period of time "clicks" that object.

FIGURE 16-22
Assistive input devices.

Assistive Output Systems

Once data has been input into the computer, a variety of *assistive output devices* (see Figure 16-23) can be used. For blind and other visually impaired individuals, *screen readers* (software that reads aloud all information displayed on the computer screen, such

FIGURE 16-23
Assistive output devices.

SCREEN READER SOFTWARE

BRAILLE DISPLAY

BRAILLE PRINTER

TREND

Digital Implants

Brain-to-computer interfacing (*BCI*) is essentially just what it sounds like—the process of connecting the brain with a computer, such as implanting electrodes directly into the brain to restore lost functionality to or facilitate the communications of severely disabled individuals. For instance, it has been shown that a severely paralyzed individual implanted with such a device can, after training, move a mouse, click it to type text, and perform other computer-related tasks using only his or her thoughts. And in BCI experiments conducted with monkeys, the monkeys were able to control both a cursor and a robotic arm with their thoughts—raising the possibility that paralyzed individuals will someday be able to control robot assistants with their thoughts. Despite the potential benefits of brain implants, there is the concern that this technology could be misused. Medical ethicists are currently working on setting up standards and criteria to ensure that brain implant devices allow, according to medical ethicist Joseph Fins of Cornell University, "...patients to have control, not be under control." Currently, the focus of brain implants and thought-controlled computers is bringing communications capabilities to the severely disabled. Some researchers, however, foresee the technology someday becoming mainstream—viewing brainwave input as the next step in the evolution of the human-computer input interface.

Another somewhat controversial type of digital implant is the *VeriChip*—a tiny RFID chip about the size of a grain of rice (see the accompanying photo) that is implanted under a person's skin (usually on the hand or arm) and is used for identification purposes. Like the chips used to identify pets and to track the migration habits of animals, each VeriChip contains a unique verification number that can be read when a proprietary scanner is passed over the implanted chip. Although the VeriChip itself does not contain any personal data, it is designed to be used in conjunction with a database to access personal data, as needed. Applications in development include access control to government installations, nuclear power plants, and other highly secure facilities; identity verification for airport security purposes and financial transactions; emergency record retrieval, such as to provide hospital emergency room personnel with health information about an unconscious patient; and access control for personal computers, cars, homes, and other personal security applications. Electronic payments are another possibility—the VeriChip is already being used by some regular patrons at a nightclub in Barcelona, Spain, to charge their purchases to their house accounts. Versions of the VeriChip with GPS capabilities could also be used to find missing individuals, such as kidnap victims and lost Alzheimer's patients, like the clip-on and wristwatch monitoring systems available today that allow location information to be broadcast continuously to a proprietary receiver. Although privacy-rights advocates worry that a chip like the VeriChip could someday be used by the government to track citizens, others view it as no different from a medical ID bracelet and are not concerned because it is available on a purely voluntary basis.

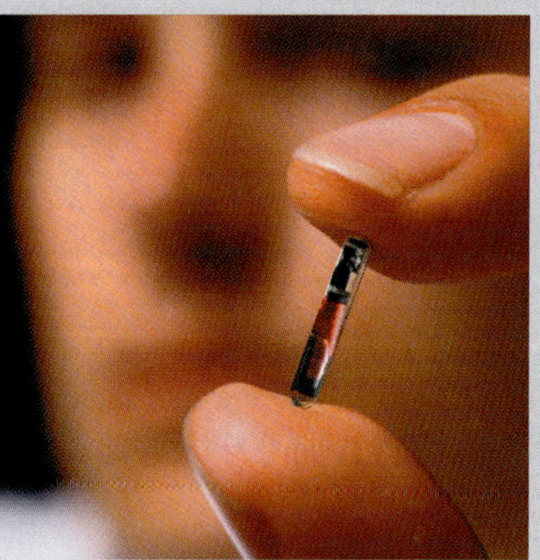

A VeriChip is about the size of a grain of rice.

as instructions, menu options, documents, and Web pages), *Braille displays* (which continuously convert screen output into Braille form on the Braille display device attached to the keyboard), and *Braille printers* (which print embossed output in Braille format on paper) are available. Some operating systems—such as Windows—also have settings that can be used to magnify the screen, change text size and color, convert audio cues into written text, and otherwise make the computer more accessible.

ENVIRONMENTAL CONCERNS

The increasing use of computers in our society has caused a variety of environmental concerns. The amount of energy used to power PCs and other computer components, as well as the heat generated by computing equipment, is one concern. Another is our extensive use of paper and how much of it ends up as trash in landfills. The hazardous materials contained in computer equipment or generated by the production of computers and related technology, as well as the disposal of used computing products, are additional concerns.

FIGURE 16-24
Eco-labels.

Green Computing

The term **green computing** refers to the use of computers in an environmentally friendly manner. Minimizing the use of natural resources, such as energy and paper, is one aspect of green computing. To encourage the development of energy-saving devices, the U.S. Department of Energy and the Environmental Protection Agency (EPA) developed the **ENERGY STAR** program. Hardware that is ENERGY STAR compliant exceeds the minimum federal standards for reduced energy consumption and can display the ENERGY STAR label shown in Figure 16-24. This figure also shows some **eco-labels**—environmental performance certifications—used in other countries.

Computer and CPU manufacturers are continually working to develop ways to make computers more energy-efficient. Some energy-saving features found on computer equipment today include hardware (such as computers and printers) that can go into low-power sleep mode when not in use, low-power-consumptive chips and boards, flat-panel displays, and CPUs that power up and down on demand. Low-power alternatives are important from an environmental perspective because a typical desktop PC with a 19-inch CRT monitor consumes approximately 300 watts per hour and can raise the temperature of the room at least 5 degrees. Saving energy also saves money—just switching from a conventional CRT monitor to a flat-panel display saves about $60 per year in electricity costs. Green computing products currently in development include more energy-efficient hardware, as well as notebooks that run on *fuel cells*, and portable PCs and cell phones that use other types of alternate power.

Solar power is a growing alternative to power electronic devices, including cell phones and portable computers (see Figure 16-25). With solar power, *solar panels* convert sunlight into direct current (DC) electricity, which is then stored in a battery. The intensity of the sun reaching the solar panels, as well as the size and number of the panels being used, affects the amount of time needed to recharge a battery. If your computer's solar system is powerful enough to charge the battery in your PC or other device being used at the same rate as you use it, your battery will never run down. However, even if the computer's solar system is not powerful enough to keep up with the rate of battery consumption, it can still greatly extend the amount of time your device can operate without recharging its batteries. PCs and other devices can also be charged via solar power when they are not being used to prepare them for the next use. As solar technology improves, solar panels will likely become integrated into a wider variety of products. Already solar panels are being designed to be built into

FIGURE 16-25
Alternate power chargers. Hand-powered and solar-powered chargers can be used to power cell phones, digital music players, GPS devices, or portable PCs.

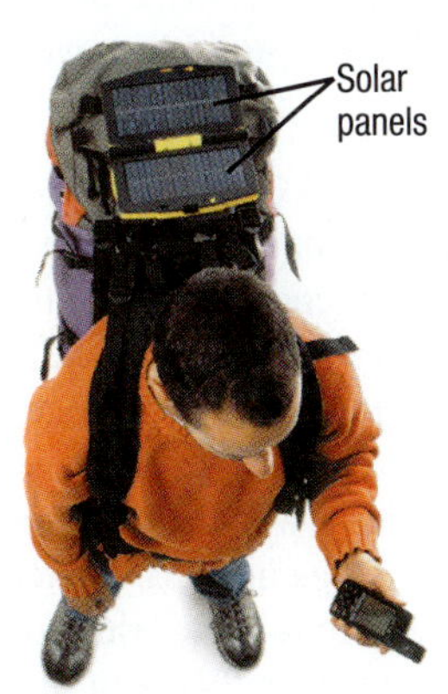

SOLAR-POWERED CHARGER

HAND-POWERED CHARGER

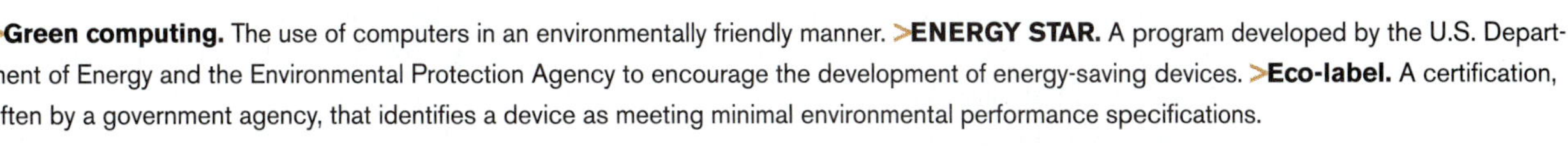
>**Green computing.** The use of computers in an environmentally friendly manner. >**ENERGY STAR.** A program developed by the U.S. Department of Energy and the Environmental Protection Agency to encourage the development of energy-saving devices. >**Eco-label.** A certification, often by a government agency, that identifies a device as meeting minimal environmental performance specifications.

the covers of notebook computers and they are integrated into some e-clothing garments, such as the e-clothing jacket shown in Figure 7-12 in Chapter 7. Both solar-powered and hand-powered chargers (refer again to Figure 16-25) are available for use with portable PCs, cell phones, and other small portable devices. These devices can be used wherever dependable electricity is not available, such as in developing countries and while outdoors. Some countries also offer kiosks that can be used to recharge cell phones and mobile devices. For instance, China has an estimated 65,000 *cell phone gas stations* that are equipped with a variety of plugs to accommodate the most popular devices and can power up a cell phone for eight hours of talk time in just 10 minutes for about 12 cents.

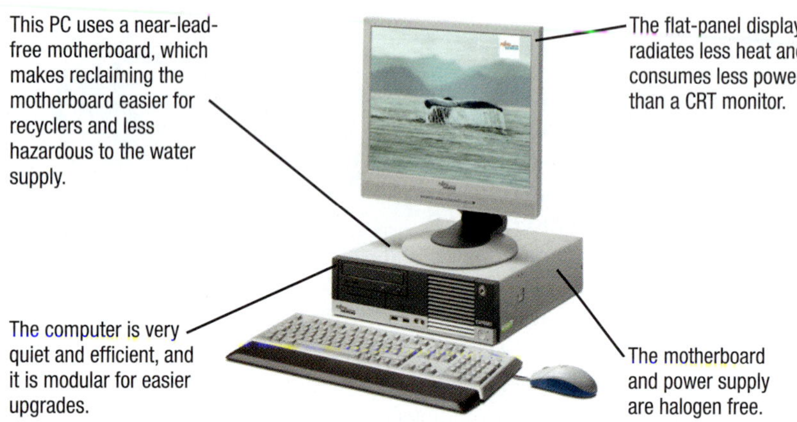

FIGURE 16-26
An environmentally friendly PC.

In addition to being more energy-efficient, computers today are being built to run quieter and cooler, and they are using more recyclable hardware. Many PC manufacturers are also reducing the amount of toxic chemicals being used in PCs. For instance, Dell bars the use of some hazardous chemicals, such as cadmium and mercury, and has reduced the amount of lead used in several desktop computers. It plans to meet the European Union's July 2006 deadline requiring all electronics shipped to the EU to be completely lead-free. All professional PCs made by Fujitsu Siemens computers will also comply with the EU requirements. For instance, the ESPRIMO E computer shown in Figure 16-26 has only one gram of lead in the motherboard, and the motherboard and power supply are halogen free. It is very quiet and efficient, and it is modular for easier upgrades.

Another environmental concern stemming from the use of computers and computing equipment is paper use and paper waste. It now appears that the so-called *paperless office* that many visionaries predicted would arrive is largely a myth. Instead, research indicates that global paper use has grown more than sixfold since 1950, and one-fifth of all wood harvested in the world today ends up as paper. According to a Gartner study, Web users alone print an average of 28 pages per day. The estimated number of pages generated by computer printers worldwide is almost one-half billion a year—an amount that would stack more than 25,000 miles high. One possible solution for the future—electronic paper—was discussed in the Inside the Industry box in Chapter 4. For a look at another electronic imaging application—*digitally republishing*—see this chapter's Inside the Industry box.

Recycling and Disposal of Computing Equipment

Another environmental concern is the amount of trash—and sometimes toxic trash—generated by computer use. In addition to paper-based trash, computing refuse includes used toner cartridges, obsolete or broken hardware, as well as discarded CDs, DVDs, and other storage media. Cell phones that are discarded when individuals switch providers—as well as new disposable consumer products, such as cell phones, digital cameras, and rental DVD movies—will likely increase the amount of electronic trash—also called *e-trash* or *e-waste*. A surge in discarded televisions is also expected as TV signals continue to switch from analog to digital, prices of plasma TVs continue to decrease, and many consumers replace their older TVs with flat-screen models and TVs that support HDTV.

Compounding the problem of the amount of e-trash generated today is the fact that conventional PCs, cell phones, and related hardware contain a variety of toxic and hazardous materials. For instance, the average CRT monitor alone contains about eight pounds of lead, and a single computer may contain up to 700 different chemical elements and compounds, many of which (such as arsenic, lead, mercury, and cadmium) are hazardous and expensive to dispose of properly. A 2004 study revealed that other electronic

INSIDE THE INDUSTRY

Digital Republishing

The term "digital republishing" refers to republishing a printed work in digital (electronic) form. One of the most common digital republishing applications today is converting printed books to electronic form so they are available through the Internet. Some individual libraries are working on converting material on an ongoing basis, such as the Stanford University Library which is digitizing millions of books, journals, and magazines through the use of a robotic scanner (see the accompanying photograph) that can turn and scan pages at a rate of over 1,000 pages per hour. Other sites feature electronic versions of dictionaries and other reference materials.

One large digital republishing project is Project Gutenberg, which began in 1971 as the brainchild of Michael Hart. The goal was to make famous and important texts freely available to everyone in the world. Project Gutenberg was based on the premise that anything that can be entered into a computer can be reproduced indefinitely. Consequently, once a book or any other item is converted to electronic form, then any number of copies can and will be available to anyone in the world with a computer. In late 2005, Project Gutenberg had over 17,000 titles available for free via the Internet, either books that reside in the public domain or books for which the copyright holder gave permission to distribute the book in this manner.

Another digital publishing application is Amazon.com's "Search Inside the Book" feature, introduced in 2003. This feature allows visitors to search the content of books for sale, not just the title or description. Although visitors cannot read the entire book online, this feature allows searchers to retrieve and view specific pages that match their search conditions (plus a few surrounding pages) to help them find the books they would like to purchase. To make this feature possible, publishers submit physical copies of the books they would like to be included in the Search Inside the Book feature, and the books are scanned into a database.

When reproducing printed media in electronic form, obviously copyright laws need to be taken into consideration. That is why Amazon.com customers cannot print previewed pages and why most digital libraries concentrate on older materials that are out of copyright. Although focusing on older books eliminates recent bestsellers, it does leave in classic books from the start of this century and previous centuries, from authors such as Shakespeare, Poe, Dante, Sir Arthur Conan Doyle, Lewis Carroll, and thousands of others.

Some believe the digitizing trend will continue to make an increasing number of types of information easily archivable and searchable. This is becoming more important as the volume of information created on print, film, disk, and other media continues to grow at a record pace. One recent study estimated that this information has doubled in the past three years and is expected to grow even faster in the future.

The automatic book digitizing system shown here is being used to create the Stanford University digital library.

equipment—such as PCs, cell phones, computer mice, and keyboards—released enough lead in laboratory tests to be classified as hazardous waste under federal Environmental Protection Agency (EPA) regulations. Conventional computers may also be constructed out of material that is difficult to recycle.

A global concern regarding e-trash is where it all eventually ends up. The majority of all discarded computer equipment ends up in landfills (see Figure 16-27). A study by the Silicon Valley Toxics Coalition and the Basel Action Network revealed that up to 80% of America's technology trash that is sent for recycling ends up as trash in other countries, such as China, India, and Pakistan. Much of the e-trash exported to these countries is simply dumped into fields and other informal dumping areas. Unaware of the potential danger

SOC

FIGURE 16-27

E-trash. The vast majority of the 40 million or so computers that become obsolete each year end up as e-trash in landfills.

of these components, rural villagers often sort through and dismantle discarded electronics parts looking for precious metals and other sources of revenue—potentially endangering their health as well as polluting nearby rivers, ponds, and other water sources. Compounding the problem, the remaining waste is often burned, generating huge clouds of potentially toxic smoke. Activists believe unchecked dumping by the United States and other countries—such as England, Japan, Australia, and Singapore—has been going on for at least 10 years. The primary reason for exporting e-trash is expense—proper disposal of a computer in the United States normally costs between $5 and $10, compared to $1 or less in third-world countries. Another reason is that some states in the United States are beginning to ban the most dangerous computing equipment—such as CRT monitors—from landfills.

While it is difficult—or, perhaps, impossible—to correct the damage that has already occurred from e-waste, many organizations are working on ways to protect people and the environment from future contamination. For instance, the *National Electronics Product Stewardship Initiative*—a coalition of computer companies, government agencies, and recycling centers—is developing a plan that would accept old computers and other electronic products, recycle what is possible, and safely dispose of the rest. The initiative is based on the concept of *product stewardship*, in which all parties who have a role in producing, selling, or using a product also have a role in managing it at the end of its useful life. The plan is expected to be financed through a fee added to the selling price of participating products. In the meantime, some states—such as California—are implementing mandatory fees of $6 to $10 on all TV and computer monitor purchases, to be used to recycle and properly dispose of the discarded TVs and monitors currently in existence. In the United States, PC manufacturers are beginning to produce more environmentally friendly components, such as system units made from recyclable plastic, nontoxic flame-retardant coatings, and lead-free solder on the motherboard.

Even though recycling computer equipment is difficult because of the materials currently being used, proper disposal is essential to avoid pollution and health hazards. Some recycling centers will accept computer equipment, but many charge a fee for this service. Many computer manufacturers have recycling programs that will accept obsolete or broken computer equipment from consumers, typically for a fee of about $15 to $30 per unit. Expired toner cartridges and ink cartridges can sometimes be returned to the manufacturer (using the supplied shipping label included with some cartridges) or exchanged when ordering new cartridges; the cartridges are then *recharged* (refilled) and resold. Cartridges that cannot be refilled can be sent to a recycling facility. In addition to helping to reduce e-trash in landfills, using recharged printer cartridges saves the consumer money since they are less expensive than new cartridges. Other computer components—such as CDs, DVDs, and computer disks—can also be recycled through some organizations, such as the Green Disk group that accepts shipments of these items free of charge and then uses the components to make new disks and other products. There are also a number of recycling programs for discarded cell phones. These programs typically refurbish and sell the phones; many organizations donate a portion of the proceeds to nonprofit organizations.

FURTHER EXPLORATION

For links to further information about green computing, go to www.course.com/uc11/ch16

In lieu of recycling, older equipment that is still functioning can be donated to schools and nonprofit groups. Some organizations accept and repair donated equipment and then distribute it to disadvantaged groups. For example, the organization Computers for Africa (see Figure 16-28) refurbishes used computers, networks them, and then ships ready-to-set-up labs to nonprofit organizations in Africa. In the United States, Operation Homelink refurbishes donated PCs and sends them free of charge to families of U.S. military personnel deployed overseas, who use the PCs to communicate with the soldiers via e-mail (refer again to Figure 16-28).

For security and privacy purposes, data stored on all computing equipment should be completely removed before disposing of that equipment so the data cannot be recovered by someone else. Hard drives should be wiped clean (not just erased) using special software that overwrites the data on the drive several times to ensure it is completely destroyed; storage media that cannot be wiped (such as DVD+R discs) should be shredded.

Consumers and companies alike are recognizing the need for green computing. A growing number of computing equipment manufacturers are announcing that they are committed to environmental responsibility. Support for a nationwide recycling program, such as the National Electronics Product Stewardship Initiative, is growing. New classifications from the EPA are expected to encourage recycling of an even greater number of computer components. So, even though computer manufacturing and recycling have a long way to go before computing equipment stops being an environmental and health hazard, it is encouraging that the trend is moving toward creating a safer and less wasteful environment.

COMPUTERS FOR AFRICA
Sends computer labs consisting of refurbished, donated PCs to nonprofit organizations in Africa.

RELATED LEGISLATION

There have been several new laws over the past few years attempting to revise intellectual property laws to reflect digital content and the Internet. For instance, the *Family Entertainment and Copyright Act of 2005* (*FECA*) makes it illegal to transmit or record a movie being shown at a movie theater. Other recent laws related to intellectual property include the *Copyright Term Extension Act*, which added 20 years to the existing copyright term, so the current copyright term is now 70 years after the creator's death or 95 years after creation for corporate works; the *U.S. Anticybersquatting Act*, which makes domain name cybersquatting illegal; and the *Digital Millennium Copyright Act* (*DMCA*), which makes it illegal to circumvent antipiracy measures built into digital media and devices. Several other laws, such as one to increase the penalties for illegally sharing music and movies via the Internet, were under consideration at the time of this writing.

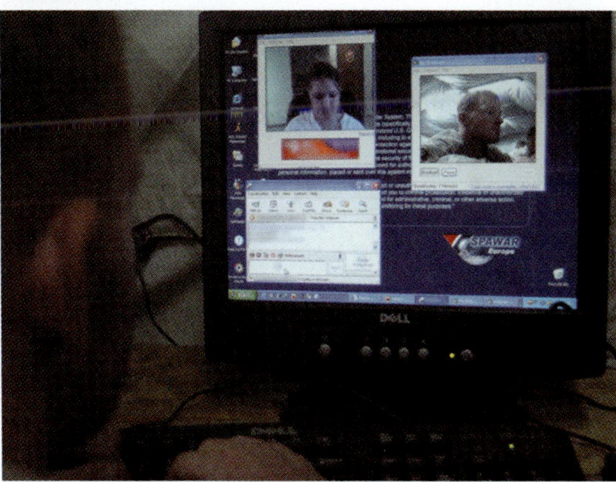

OPERATION HOMELINE
Sends donated PCs to families of soldiers stationed overseas so they can communicate with their loved ones, such as with this soldier in Iraq.

FIGURE 16-28
Donating PCs. You can donate computer equipment to nonprofit organizations so it can be given to others who can use it.

Legislation regarding ethics has been difficult to pass—or to keep as law once it has passed. For example, the *Communications Decency Act*, which was signed into law in 1996, made it a criminal offense to distribute patently indecent or offensive material online. Although the law was intended to protect children from being exposed to inappropriate Web content, the U.S. Supreme Court in 1997 declared this law unconstitutional on the basis of free speech. The courts so far have had difficulty defining what is "patently offensive" and "indecent" as well as finding a fair balance between protection and censorship. Consequently, very few ethically oriented laws have been passed in recent years. Some exceptions are the *Children's Online Privacy Protection Act of 1998*, which regulates how Web sites can collect information from minors and provides tax incentives for Web sites and ISPs that facilitate protecting minors from accessing materials deemed harmful to them; the *Sarbanes-Oxley Act of 2002* (*Corporate Responsibility Act*), which includes provisions to improve the quality of financial reporting and increase penalties for corporate wrongdoing; and the *Child Internet Protection Act* (*CIPA*), which requires public libraries and schools to use filtering software to block Internet access to certain materials in order to receive public funding. The most significant recent legislation regarding accessibility has been the 1998 amendment to the *Rehabilitation Act* requiring federal agencies to make their electronic and information technology accessible to people with disabilities. This act applies to all federal Web sites, as well, creating a trend of Web sites that are Section 508 compliant.

SUMMARY

INTELLECTUAL PROPERTY RIGHTS

Chapter Objective 1:
Understand the concept of intellectual property rights and how they relate to computer use.

Intellectual property rights specify how *intellectual property*, such as original music compositions, drawings, essays, software programs, symbols, and designs, may be lawfully used. **Copyrights** protect the creators of original artistic or literary works and are granted automatically once a work exists in a physical medium. The copyright can be registered, which provides additional protection should infringement occur. The copyright symbol © can be used to remind others that content is copyrighted; **digital watermarks** can be incorporated into digital content so that the copyright information can be viewed, even if the work is altered. **Digital rights management (DRM) software** can be used to protect the rights of creators and manage digital content, such as art, music, photographs, and movies. **Trademarks** are words, phrases, symbols, or designs that identify an organization's goods or services and can be either claimed ™ or registered ®. **Patents** grant an exclusive right to an invention for 20 years. In addition to products, processes and procedures may be patented as well.

ETHICS

Chapter Objective 2:
Explain what is meant by ethics and provide several examples of unethical behavior in computer-related matters.

Ethics are standards of moral conduct. *Personal ethics* guide one's personal life; **business ethics** provide the standards of conduct guiding business decisions, and **computer ethics** provide the standards of conduct in respect to computers and computer use. Computer ethics have taken on more significance in recent years because the increased use of computers in the home, in the workplace, and at school provides more opportunities for unethical behavior than in the past.

Today one of the most important ethical concerns regarding computers is using someone else's property in an improper way. Books, music, movies, and other types of intellectual property are protected by copyright law. Presenting someone else's work as your own is referred to as **plagiarism** and is illegal and unethical. It is becoming increasingly common for businesses and schools to establish **codes of conduct** to address what behavior is considered ethical and unethical at that particular organization. Some organizations and industries publish **codes of ethics** listing overall standards of conduct, such as honesty, fairness, confidentiality, and more.

A **computer hoax** is an inaccurate statement or story spread through the use of computers, often by e-mail. It is a good idea to check questionable information as a possible computer hoax before passing the information on to others. **Digital manipulation** is the use of computers to modify something in digital form, usually text or a photograph. Ethics are highly intertwined with determining business practices and making business decisions. Decisions, such as which financial information to publicize, which products or services to provide, which safeguards (if any) to establish with products or services that are illegal for minors or objectionable to some individuals, and whether or not to promote potential *vaporware* products, all require ethical consideration. Because ethics are fundamentally based on values, different types of businesses may have different ethics. Ethics and moral standards may vary from country to country and from culture to culture. In addition to legal considerations, businesses with global connections should consider the prevailing ethical standards of all countries involved when making business decisions.

COMPUTERS AND HEALTH

Since the entry of computers into the workplace and their increased use in our society, they have been blamed for a variety of physical ailments. **Carpal tunnel syndrome (CTS)** and other types of **repetitive stress injuries** (**RSI**), *computer vision syndrome* (*CVS*), eyestrain, fatigue, backaches, and headaches are all possible physical risks related to computer use.

Chapter Objective 3: Describe some possible physical and emotional health risks associated with the use of computers.

Ergonomics is the science of how to make the computer workspace, hardware, and environment fit the individual using it. In addition to using **ergonomic hardware** and an ergonomically correct workspace, users should use good posture, take rest breaks, alternate tasks, and take other common-sense precautions. For portable PCs, **docking stations** can be used to allow easy connections to more ergonomically correct hardware.

The *stress* of keeping up with ever-changing technology, layoffs, always being in touch, fear of being out of touch, information overload, **burnout**, and **computer/Internet addiction** are all possible emotional problems related to computer use.

ACCESS TO TECHNOLOGY

The **digital divide** refers to the gap between those who have access to computers and communications technology and those who do not. There can be a digital divide within a country or between countries. Globally, the digital divide separates countries with access to technology from those without access to technology.

Chapter Objective 4: Discuss the impact that factors such as nationality, income, race, education, and physical disabilities may have on computer access and use.

Research suggests that people with disabilities tend to use computers and the Internet at rates less than the average population. Part of the reason may be because some types of conventional hardware—such as keyboards and monitors—are difficult to use with some types of physical conditions. **Assistive technology** includes hardware and software that makes conventional PC systems easier for users with disabilities to use, such as *Braille keyboards*, *Braille displays*, *Braille printers*, *screen readers*, and *voice input systems*.

ENVIRONMENTAL CONCERNS

Green computing refers to using computers in an environmentally friendly manner. It can include using hardware approved by an **eco-label** system, such as **ENERGY STAR** in the United States. Environmentally friendly computers are just starting to come on the market, and alternate-powered hardware is expected to be introduced sometime in the future.

Chapter Objective 5: Suggest some ways computer users can practice "green computing" and properly dispose of obsolete computer equipment.

In addition to practicing green computing when buying and using computer equipment, discarded equipment should be reused whenever possible. Computer equipment that is still functioning may be able to be donated and refurbished for additional use, and toner and ink cartridges can often be refilled and reused. Hardware that cannot be reused should be recycled if possible, or properly disposed of if not recyclable, so it does not end up as hazardous *e-trash* in landfills in this or another country.

RELATED LEGISLATION

There are numerous laws in place to protect intellectual property. Because moral and ethical standards are more difficult to agree on, ethical legislation is slower in coming. The most significant legislation regarding accessibility is the 1998 amendment to the *Rehabilitation Act* requiring federal agencies to make their electronic and information technology accessible to people with disabilities.

Chapter Objective 6: Discuss the current status of legislation related to intellectual property rights, ethics, access, and the environment in relation to computers.

REVIEW ACTIVITIES

KEY TERM MATCHING

Instructions: Match each key term on the left with the definition on the right that best describes it.

a. assistive technology
b. computer ethics
c. computer/Internet addiction
d. copyright
e. digital divide
f. ergonomic hardware
g. intellectual property rights
h. patent
i. plagiarism
j. trademark

1. ______ A form of protection that can be granted by the government for an invention; gives exclusive rights of an invention to its inventor for 20 years.
2. ______ A word, phrase, symbol, or design that identifies goods or services.
3. ______ Hardware and software specifically designed for use by individuals with physical disabilities.
4. ______ Hardware, typically input and output devices, that is designed to be more ergonomically correct than its nonergonomic counterparts.
5. ______ Presenting someone else's work as your own.
6. ______ Standards of moral conduct as they relate to computer use.
7. ______ The gap between those who have access to technology and those who do not.
8. ______ The legal right to sell, publish, or distribute an original artistic or literary work; is held by the creator of a work as soon as it exists in physical form.
9. ______ The problem of overusing, or being unable to stop using, the Internet.
10. ______ The rights to which creators of original creative works (such as artistic or literary works, inventions, corporate logos, and more) are entitled.

SELF-QUIZ

Instructions: Circle **T** if the statement is true, **F** if the statement is false, or write the best answer in the space provided. **Answers to the self-quiz are located in the References and Resources Guide at the end of the book.**

1. **T F** All unethical acts are illegal.
2. **T F** Changing the background behind a television newscaster to make it appear that he or she is reporting on location instead of from inside the television studio would be an example of digital manipulation.
3. **T F** Carpal tunnel syndrome can be caused by using a computer keyboard.
4. **T F** As computer use has become more common, the potential for stress related to computer use has decreased.
5. **T F** Assistive technology is hardware and software designed to help all beginning computer users learn how to use a computer.
6. A software program would be protected by ______ law, while a corporate logo would be protected by ______ law.
7. Turning in a copy of a poem you found on a Web site as an original composition for a poetry class assignment is an example of ______.
8. Craving more and more time at the computer can be an indicator of ______.
9. The ______ can be used to describe discrepancies in access to technology by individuals within a country, as well as to compare access from country to country.

10. Match each term to its description or example and write the corresponding number in the blank to the left of each description or example.

a. ________ What the symbol © stands for.
b. ________ Can vary from another's depending on his or her values, culture, and so forth.
c. ________ A warning about a nonexistent virus spread via e-mail.
d. ________ Darkening of O.J. Simpson's photograph in the 1994 *TIME* magazine cover.
e. ________ Creating a more comfortable and healthy work environment.
f. ________ A subtle alteration of digital content that identifies the copyright holder.

1. Computer hoax
2. Copyright
3. Digital manipulation
4. Digital watermark
5. Ergonomics
6. Ethics

EXERCISES

1. For each of the following situations, write the appropriate letter—I (illegal), U (legal, but unethical), or N (neither)—in the blank to the right of the situation to indicate whether the act is illegal, legal, or neither.

Situation	Type of Situation
a. A teenager rips a new CD she just bought and e-mails the MP3 files to all her friends.	________
b. An employee finds a coworker's résumé and shows it to other workers.	________
c. A photographer combines two of his photographs to create a new composite artistic piece.	________
d. A physician incorporates another doctor's research into her journal article submission, including the researcher's name and article in her submission.	________

2. Assume that you have created a Web site to display your favorite original photographs. Explain whether or not the site you created would be protected by copyright law. What about the photographs? If they would not be protected, explain what steps, if any, you could take to ensure they were protected.

3. List three possible negative physical effects that can result from computer use and describe one way to lessen each effect.

4. List three possible negative effects on the environment that can result from computer use and describe one way to lessen each effect.

5. Select the image from the numbered list on the right that best matches each of the following names and write the corresponding number in the blank to the left of each name.

a. ________ Document holder
b. ________ Braille keyboard
c. ________ Braille display
d. ________ Ergonomic mouse
e. ________ Eco-label
f. ________ Wrist rest

1. **2.** **3.** **4.**

5. **6.**

DISCUSSION QUESTION

Unarguably, the Web contains a vast amount of extremely useful information. Some content, however, is more debatable and, in fact, may be extremely harmful. For example, suicide Web sites that explain in detail how to kill oneself and Web sites broadcasting the beheadings by terrorists have received increased attention lately. And what about Web sites that explain how to build bombs and other types of weapons? If a Web site instructs visitors how to perform an illegal act, should the site's creators be criminally liable if a visitor carries out those instructions? Who, if anyone, is responsible for preventing potentially harmful information from being shared via the Web? Is there any Internet content that you believe a government has the right or obligation to censor? If so, what? Where do we draw the line between freedom of speech and national or personal safety?

PROJECTS

HOT TOPICS

1. **Warchalking** An emerging activity related to the war driving discussed in Chapter 9 is *warchalking*. Warchalking is the practice of marking symbols on sidewalks and walls with chalk to indicate the locations of wireless access points so that others can more easily find them. The term *warchalking* comes from the practice of hobos using chalk marks to indicate which homes were the most friendly and generous during the Great Depression. Common warchalking symbols include)(to indicate an unprotected node and O to indicate a secure node requiring a password. Warchalkers claim that what they are doing is not illegal or unethical—instead they are providing a helpful service to assist people in finding something they need (an Internet connection). Since they are not actually taking anything from the person or business, they do not see any harm in this activity.

   For this project, form an opinion about warchalking. Do you agree with the reasoning above that it should not be viewed as unethical since the targeted person can still use his or her wireless Internet connection? What if enough wardrivers used one connection so that the owner's Internet service slowed down or, worse yet, was discontinued by his or her ISP for inappropriate use? Would that change your opinion? Do you think there is a difference between using a network marked as unprotected versus one marked as secure? Would you mind if you had a Wi-Fi connection and walked outside to find you had been warchalked? Submit your opinions to your instructor in the form of a short paper, no more than one page in length.

SHORT ANSWER/ RESEARCH

2. **Copyright Registration** Think of a paper or poem that you have written, a photograph or other piece of art you have created, a song or play you have written, or another original creation to which you believe you are entitled copyright protection. As you know from reading the chapter, copyright protection begins as soon as the creation exists on some type of physical medium, but assume that you would like to register a copyright for your creation.

   For this project, research how you would obtain a copyright for your chosen creation. Visit the U.S. Copyright Office Web site (search for it using your favorite search site) and determine the necessary procedure for registration, the required paperwork, and the necessary fee. Use the information located on the site to make sure your creation is entitled to copyright protection, then find the appropriate online registration form (if one is available online). If possible, open and print just one page of the form. From the site, also determine what notice you will receive once your copyright claim has been recorded and how long it will take to receive it. Prepare a short summary of your findings to submit to your instructor, stapled to the single page of the appropriate application if you were able to print it.

3. **Ergonomic Workspaces** Some aspects of an ergonomic workspace, such as a comfortable chair and nonglaring light, may feel good right from the beginning. Others, such as using an ergonomic keyboard or wrist rest, may take a little getting used to.

   For this project, find at least one local store that has some type of ergonomic equipment—such as adjustable office chairs, desks with keyboard drawers, or ergonomic keyboards—on display that you can try out. Test each piece adjusting it as needed, and evaluate how comfortable it seems. Next, evaluate your usual computer workspace. Do you notice any difference between the ergonomic equipment and your usual equipment? Are there any adjustments you should make or any new equipment you would need to acquire to make your workspace setup more comfortable? Make a note of any changes you could make for free, as well as a list of items you would need to purchase and the estimated cost. Prepare a short summary of your findings to submit to your instructor. If you made any adjustments to your regular workspace during this project, be sure to include a comment regarding whether or not you think it increased your comfort.

HANDS ON

4. **Green Computing** There are several easy things any computer user can do to practice green computing. For instance, most operating systems have energy-saving options that can be enabled, such as turning off the monitor and hard drive when the PC has been idle for a specified period of time. To save paper, many programs have a print preview option that can be used before printing to make sure the document is ready to print.

   For this project, find a Windows computer that you can use to explore power-saving features and perform the following tasks.

   a. Open the Control Panel using the Start menu and look for a Power Management option. Select that option to find the option that allows you to specify when the monitor and hard drive will be turned off and record the current settings.

   b. Next, open any word processing program (such as Word, WordPerfect, or WordPad) available on your PC. Either open an existing document that is at least two pages long or enter enough text to fill up two pages (the text does not have to make sense). Find the *Print Preview* option (usually located on the File menu) to see what the document will look like when printed. Are there any changes you would make to the document before printing, such as changing the margins or adjusting where a page breaks? How might previewing documents before printing on a regular basis help the environment?

   c. Close your word processing program (do not save your file) and open your Web browser. Go to a news site (such as CNN.com or MSNBC.com) and click a hyperlink for a news story. Use your browser's File menu to see if it has a *Print Preview* feature. If so, preview the document to see if all the pages would need to be printed or if the page looks strange. Close the preview screen and select *Print* from your browser's File menu (do not use the Print toolbar button). If the Web page will print on more than one page, find the appropriate option on the Print dialog box to print only the specified pages of the document. If the page was divided into frames, see if the Print dialog box has an option to print only the current frame or the entire page as it appears on the screen (if not, you will need to close the Print dialog box, click in the desired frame, and then return to the Print dialog box before continuing). Use the Print dialog box to print only the first page of the Web page.

   d. Prepare a short summary of your work to submit to your instructor along with the first page of the news article you printed, describing what you discovered and which, if any, of these techniques you plan to use on a regular basis.

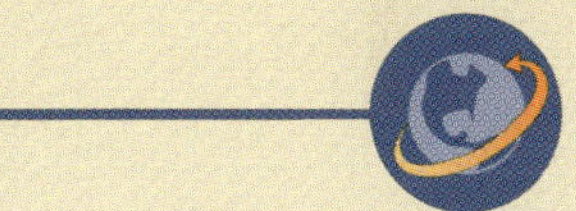

5. **Virtual Reality Vacations** While it is easy to make a case that computer use can harm the environment, it is also possible that PCs can help. For instance, shopping online instead of in person saves energy and does not add to the smog problem. Building on that idea is the *virtual vacation*—exploring vacation destinations from your PC instead of traveling there in person. Many Web sites feature virtual reality panoramas to enable visitors to move around a particular location (such as a historical monument or a museum) to explore the location. To view these programs, many of them require a plug-in, such as QuickTime.

   For this project, visit any Web site containing a VR tour (refer to the list of possible sites below) and see if the browser you are using is capable of viewing the VR component. If the feature is not available and you are using a school computer, ask your instructor for additional directions. If you are missing the required plug-in and you are working on your home PC, follow the instructions on the Web site to download and install the necessary plug-in.

   - *Virtual Visitor* (virtualvisitor.com)—includes VR tours of towns, restaurants, universities, resorts, ball parks, boats, museums, and more.
   - *Desert USA* (www.desertusa.com)—clicking the QuickTime VR link in the directory on this Web page provides a list of links to VR tours of national parks.
   - *VR Seattle* (www.vrseattle.com)—includes VR tours of a variety of Washington State locations, such as the Space Needle, parks, zoos, museums, colleges, churches, and restaurants.

   If you are able to view the VR component on a Web page, follow the directions on the site to navigate through the virtual tour (usually you will place your cursor at an edge of the VR window to move the display in that direction). Feel free to try more than one site or VR tour until you find one that you are interested in. At the end of your exploration, prepare a one-page summary of your experience to turn in to your instructor. Be sure to include the steps you had to take in order to take a tour, how easy or difficult you found the experience, and whether you would like to take more VR tours in the future. Would you consider taking a VR tour of a vacation destination instead of going there in person?

WRITING ABOUT COMPUTERS

6. **Codes of Ethics** As discussed in the chapter, many industries and organizations publish codes of ethics to convey general ethical or moral standards expected to be followed by members. For instance, one well-known code of ethics in the computer industry is the Association of Computing Machinists (ACM) Code of Ethics and Professional Standards.

   For this project, locate and review at least one code of ethics issued by an organization and prepare a short summary of the document. Assuming you were a professional in this industry, do you agree with the principles involved? Do you think other professionals in this industry would agree with the ethics and principles contained in the code? Submit your findings and opinions to your instructor in the form of a short paper, no more than two pages in length.

PRESENTATION/ DEMONSTRATION

7. **Recycle or Trash?** As mentioned in the chapter, most obsolete computer equipment eventually ends up in a landfill, although there may be alternative actions that could be taken instead.

   For this project, research what options would be available to discard the following: (1) a 10-year-old computer that is no longer functioning, (2) a 4-year-old computer that still works but is too slow for your needs, and (3) a used-up toner cartridge for a laser printer. Check with your local schools and charitable organizations to see if they would accept any of these items. Contact your trash disposal company or local dump to see what their regulations are for accepting computer equipment. In addition, check with at least two computer manufacturers to see if they have a trade-in or recycling program, as well as with vendors selling recharged toner cartridges to see if they buy old cartridges or require a trade-in with an order. Share your findings with the class in the form of a short presentation. Be sure to include any costs associated with the disposal options you found, as well as your recommendation for each disposal situation. The presentation should not exceed 10 minutes and should make use of one or more presentation aids, such as the chalkboard, handouts, overhead transparencies, or a computer-based slide presentation (your instructor may provide additional requirements). You may also be asked to submit a summary of the presentation to your instructor.

GROUP DISCUSSION

8. **Toxic PCs** PC hardware contains a variety of toxic and hazardous materials. It has been estimated that about 40 million computers become obsolete each year, and most of them end up in landfills threatening the environment. Whose responsibility is it to correct this problem? Is the United States at fault for allowing the exportation of our e-waste? A computer may contain up to 700 different chemical compounds—such as arsenic, lead, mercury, and cadmium—many of which are hazardous. Should manufacturers be allowed to continue to use those materials, or should they be forced to find alternatives? What if a restriction on these compounds severely limited the types of computer equipment that could be manufactured? Or are landfills full of discarded equipment just the price we pay for being a technological society? What efforts should be made to recycle discarded PCs? Who should bear the cost of the recycling—the manufacturers, the consumers, or the government?

   For this project, form an opinion about the impact of e-waste on our society and who (if anyone) is responsible for reducing the amount of e-waste being generated. Be prepared to discuss your position (in class, via an online class discussion group, or in a class chat room, depending on your instructor's directions). You may also be asked to write a short paper expressing your opinion.

WEB ACTIVITIES

The ***Understanding Computers*** Web site located at **www.course.com/uc11** features many resources to help reinforce your understanding of the chapter content and help you prepare for exams. Your instructor may also assign specific activities to be completed that will count toward your final grade in the course.

Instructions: Go to **www.course.com/uc11/ch16** to work the following online activities.

Click any link in the navigation bar on the left to access any of the online resources described below.

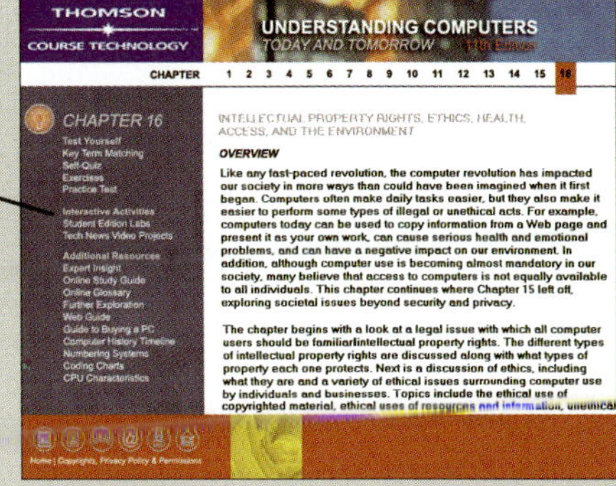

INTERACTIVE ACTIVITIES

1. **Crossword Puzzle** Practice your knowledge of the key terms in Chapter 16 by completing the interactive Crossword Puzzle.
2. **Tech News Video Project** Watch the **"Digital Bouncers"** video clip that takes a look at a database being used by some bars in Canada to record data about patrons, in order to block troublemakers from the establishments, and some of the privacy and ethical issues surrounding the system. After watching the video online, complete the corresponding project.
3. **Student Edition Labs** Reinforce the concepts you have learned in this chapter by working through the interactive **Installing and Uninstalling Software** lab.

TEST YOURSELF

1. **Key Term Matching** Test your knowledge of selected chapter key terms by matching the terms with their definitions.
2. **Self-Quiz** Test your retention of chapter concepts by taking the Self-Quiz.
3. **Exercises** Work these short exercises to review the concepts and terms covered in the chapter.
4. **Practice Test** Test how ready you are for an upcoming exam by completing the online Practice Test.

STUDY TOOLS/ ADDITIONAL RESOURCES

The Understanding Computers Web site has a wide range of additional resources, including an **Online Study Guide** (containing study tips, a chapter outline with room to add your own notes, and a chapter checklist of the activities to complete when the chapter is covered in class and when you are preparing for a test) and an **Online Glossary** for each chapter; **Further Exploration** links; a **Web Guide**, a **Guide to Buying a PC**, and a **Computer History Timeline**; more information about **Numbering Systems**, **Coding Charts**, and **CPU Characteristics**; and much, much more!

EXPERT INSIGHT ON . . .
Computers and Society

A conversation with **FRANK MOLSBERRY**
Technologist for Dell Inc.

My Background . . .

I've been in the field of computer software and hardware development for over 20 years. I joined Dell in 1998 after working at IBM for 15 years. I am currently a Technologist in the Office of the CTO. My focus area is on Security Architecture and Technology. In that role I support the current engineering efforts for incorporating security hardware and software into Dell products, work with the various security technology companies to evaluate and influence current and planned offerings, and participate with standards organizations such as the Trusted Computing Group (TCG) in the definition of future security standards.

In many cases the subjects we focus on now (such as security) are not about stand-alone systems anymore, but instead involve an entire ecosystem of hardware devices, software applications, and the infrastructure connecting them. Because this can entail a great deal of breadth and depth of knowledge, I've found that it is important to have a "big-picture" vision and the ability to rapidly drill into the details as needed, but only to the level needed to answer the questions in front of you.

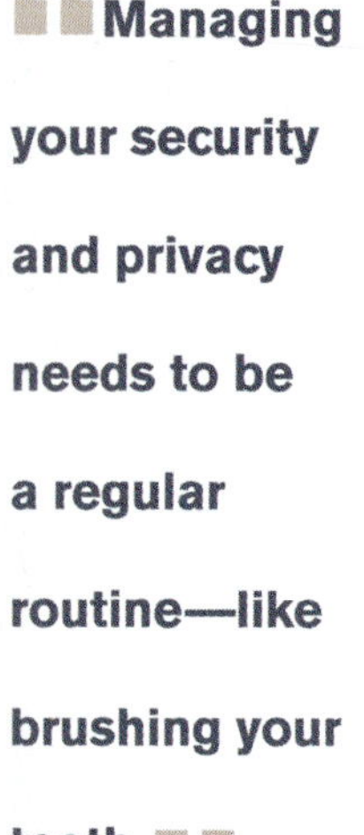

It's Important to Know . . .

The recommendations presented in these chapters are not one time things. Managing your security and privacy needs to be a regular routine—like brushing your teeth.

Technology is a double-edged sword and can always have a dark side. As you develop new and innovative hardware or software applications, you must always look at the threats that can be brought against it and, more importantly, how the technology could be misused beyond its intended purpose. By stepping back and identifying these issues up front, the developers and users of the technology can be better prepared to combat it.

We now have a global economy. The products you develop and the services you provide must consider a global culture and have the flexibility to satisfy the varying customs, rules, and requirements of a global economy.

How I Use this Technology . . .

I use all the standard precautions on my personal computer—such as antivirus software, antispyware software, and backing up my data—to avoid data loss. I keep my systems on a UPS/surge protector and have most of the power management features configured. When traveling, I use a privacy screen to prevent others from viewing my work and I carry a portable cable lock to secure my notebook when I am away from it.

Frank Molsberry is a Technologist in Dell's Office of the CTO. Prior to his current position, he helped found Dell's Workstation Architecture and Development team and, more recently, the Enterprise Architecture and Technology Group. In all, he has over 20 years of management and engineering experience in advanced system software development and PC system architectures. Frank has a Bachelor's degree in Computer Science and has several patents in the area of computer security. He does regular customer briefings on emerging technology trends.

It is important not to just focus on the "coolness" of something new, but the problem it is trying to solve, the user experience, and the barriers to adoption.

What the Future Holds . . .

The next big thing is not usually a revolution as much as it is a continued progression that, when looked at over a long window of a time, shows up as a major change in technology or use model. So the trends of faster, smaller, cheaper will continue for the next decade.

The impact of security and privacy technology on society is huge, but it is not yet well understood. One of the biggest issues is identity theft and the tremendous effort it takes to recover from it. Tasks like shredding papers and monitoring your credit report activity can help prevent identity theft or alert you to suspicious activity. Patent reform is also getting significant attention right now, as many individuals feel that the focus on patent quantity over quality has increased litigation and decreased innovation in the industry. This is a global problem as patent rules can vary significantly from country to country.

For the impact of technology on health and the environment, the activities in place already will continue and expand. Major manufactures such as Dell have already implemented initiatives to reduce or eliminate things like lead from their systems. There are now major programs for system recycling and even for returning consumables such as printer cartridges. Another development is the trend to move toward more modular architectures in the future, allowing the average user to easily change or upgrade the capabilities of a computer, TV, or printer without having to purchase an entirely new system.

In terms of the digital divide, it's important to realize that the digital divide is not new. It has always existed when each new method of information communication was developed, such as with the introduction of radio and television. We focus on it more now because of the volume of information available via the Internet and the bidirectional nature of electronic communications. The continued decreases in the cost of computing and the increases in wireless connectivity will continue the closing of this divide, but there may be new digital divides in the future. For this divide, we must not lose sight of where information communication fits in the hierarchy of needs. For those populations where the basic needs of food, clothing, and shelter are not being met, free access to computing resources may not be the most important thing to focus on. Another key is connectivity. It does little good to have a PC today without Internet access. Advancements in broad reach wireless communication like WiMAX are crucial.

My Advice to Students . . .

Computers and the ever changing technology they are based on are just tools. It is important not to just focus on the "coolness" of something new, but the problem it is trying to solve, the user experience, and the barriers to adoption.

Discussion Question

Frank Molsberry views technology as a double-edge sword and believes that hardware and software developers must look at how new products could be misused beyond their intended purposes. Think about a few recent new technologies or products. Have they been used in an illegal or unethical manner? If so, did the manufacturer build in controls to prevent this misuse? If not, should they have? What responsibility, if any, does a developer have if their product or service is used inappropriately? Be prepared to discuss your position (in class, via an online class discussion group, or in a class chat room, depending on your instructor's directions). You may also be asked to write a short paper expressing your opinion.

>For more information on Dell, visit www.dell.com and www.dell.com/innovation. For security information, visit www.trustedcomputing.org and searchsecurity.techtarget.com. For a summary of many online tech news sites, visit www.dailyrotation.com.

2007 UPDATE

OUTLINE

Chapter 1 Introduction to the World of Computers
Chapter 2 The System Unit: Processing and Memory
Chapter 3 Storage
Chapter 4 Input and Output
Chapter 5 System Software: Operating Systems and Utilities
Chapter 6 Application Software
Chapter 7 Computer Networks
Chapter 8 The Internet and World Wide Web
Chapter 9 Network and Internet Security
Chapter 10 Multimedia and the Web
Chapter 11 E-Commerce
Chapter 12 Information Systems and System Development
Chapter 13 Program Development and Programming Languages
Chapter 14 Databases and Database Management Systems
Chapter 15 Computer Security and Privacy
Chapter 16 Intellectual Property Rights, Ethics, Health, Access, and the Environment
Expert Insight on Windows Vista
Windows Vista and You
Tech News Video Projects

INTRODUCTION

The world of computers is continually changing and evolving. Although the computer concepts covered in the *Understanding Computers, 11th Edition* text are still applicable today, there have been some improvements in technology, and some new products have become available, since the *Understanding Computers, 11th Edition* was published. Bringing you up to date on the latest advances in these areas is the purpose of this update.

Update 2007 has three sections. First, a two-page spread for each chapter covers new developments related to the topics discussed in the *Understanding Computers, 11th Edition* text, followed by a look at new and emerging trends not included in that edition. Each two-page spread is designed to be covered immediately after its corresponding *Understanding Computers, 11th Edition* chapter.

The next part of Update 2007 is related to the release of the newest version of the Windows operating system: *Windows Vista*. A new "Expert Insight" feature shares insights about Vista and other new technologies from a member of the Microsoft Windows Vista Group, including their impact on the world now and predictions for the future. A special "Windows Vista and You" feature then takes a look at this new operating system and how it impacts us as computer users.

The final part of Update 2007 contains new Tech News Video Projects not included in *Understanding Computers, 11th Edition.* These projects are structured around CNET TV video clips, which are available through the Online Companion Web site. As directed by your instructor, you will watch the video clip and then express your opinion on the issue detailed in the video either in class, via an online discussion group or class chat room, or in a written paper.

"One of the biggest impacts on society that Windows Vista will have is enhanced security for users."

For more comments from Guest Expert Graham Watson of Microsoft Corporation, see the Expert Insight on . . . Windows Vista feature at the end of the Update.

Chapter 1–Introduction to the World of Computers

UPDATE

The capabilities of personal computers and mobile devices have continued to grow and converge. This year also brought a new release of the Internet Explorer browser.

FIGURE U-1
New mobile devices and handheld computers.

NOKIA MULTIMEDIA COMPUTER
Can be used as a phone, digital camera, Web browsing tool, and media player.

SONY ULTRAPORTABLE COMPUTER
This fully functioning PC weighs just over one pound.

Update on Personal Computers and Mobile Devices

Both PCs and mobile devices have grown more powerful during the past year. They have also continued to converge with each other and with other digital devices, such as digital cameras, GPS devices, and digital music players. For instance, the first device shown in Figure U-1 can be used as a phone but also supports e-mail, messaging, Web browsing, and a variety of multimedia capabilities, such as being able to take and display high-quality digital photos and video, download and play digital music and movie files, and edit digital photos and video. It can connect to other devices via Wi-Fi, Bluetooth, and USB connections, and stores up to two gigabytes of data. Because of its increased capabilities, Nokia considers it a multimedia computer instead of a mobile phone.

Other mobile devices are adding features to allow them to be used more easily as handheld computers. For instance, some smart phones today include a full keyboard and the ability to view and edit Microsoft Office documents. And the use of smart phones is on the rise—according to a Gartner study, global shipments of smart phones grew by more than 75 percent in the first six months of 2006 compared to the same time period in 2005. Notebook and tablet PCs are increasingly being used as desktop replacements for both business and personal use, and *ultraportable computers*—fully functioning handheld computers, such as the second device shown in Figure U-1—are becoming more common.

Web Browser Update

The most commonly used Web browser is still Microsoft Internet Explorer, although its market share has dropped to about 86%, according to the Web analytics firm OneStat.com. Mozilla Firefox is the second most widely used Web browser, with a market share of over 11%. In late 2006, Microsoft released *Internet Explorer 7*, the first major upgrade to Internet Explorer in several years. This version (see Figure U-2) features tabbed browsing, RSS support, integrated searching, improved display and printing options, and the ability to create a favorite for a group of tabbed windows in order to open all of those windows again at a later time with a single mouse click using the Favorites list. Internet Explorer 7 also includes new security features (such as not allowing the Address bar of any browser window to be hidden and a new *Security Status bar*, located next to the Address bar, that is used for security notifications) to help protect users from malicious software attacks and phishing scams.

FIGURE U-2
Internet Explorer 7.

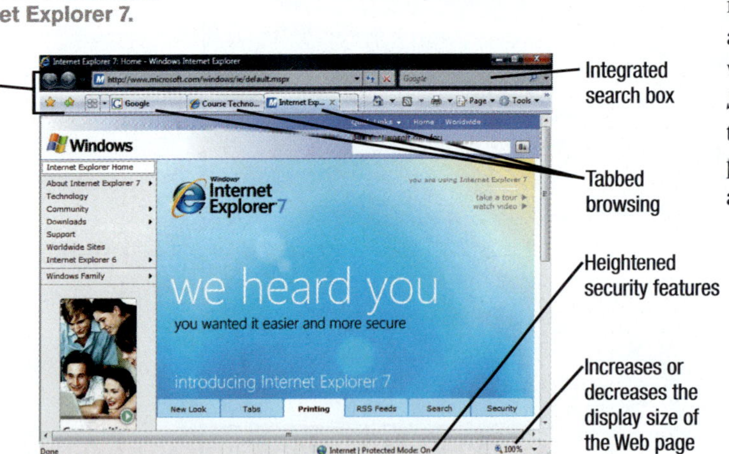

NEW AND EMERGING TRENDS

One new and emerging computing trend is *virtualization*. For a look at how iPods and other devices are being used as workout tools, see the Technology and You box.

TECHNOLOGY AND YOU

High-Tech Workouts

Got an iPod? You now have a personal trainer. Training podcasts–available this year in both audio and video versions (see the accompanying photo)–are on track to replace the workout video. Numerous trainers have a variety of workouts–from body sculpting to aerobics to meditation to boxing and more–available for download on their Web sites. Costs range from 99 cents to about $20 a workout, depending on the format (audio or video) and the length of the workout. Cheaper than a personal trainer, these podcasts allow individuals to more easily work out at home or on the road.

A new high-tech workout aid available from Nike and designed for runners contains a sensor that goes inside your running shoe and a receiver that plugs into your iPod. The sensor transmits data about your run–such as time, distance, calories burned, etc.–to your iPod as you work out. A related mobile phone application uses the GPS capabilities of your cell phone to collect data about your workout. Both of these applications allow you to upload data to a Web site to create an online running logbook; the GPS application can even map your route on a Google satellite map.

Server and Desktop Virtualization

In general, the term "virtualization" refers to creating an environment whose appearance to end users is different from its physical structure. For instance, if an individual uses a computer to access an operating system and application software located on a server, but it appears to the user that he or she is working directly on his or her computer, that is virtualization. Typically, virtualization is used to create separate environments on a computer that, although physically located on the same PC, do not interact with each other. Virtualization was originally used on mainframe computers in the 1970s, but today's extensive computing demands have led to renewed interest in virtualization and it is currently a hot computing trend.

Today, virtualization is most often used with servers to divide one physical server into multiple isolated virtual environments—this is called *server virtualization*. The primary reason companies are turning towards server virtualization is efficiency. Traditionally, individual servers are often allocated to particular applications or groups of users and are not used to full capacity—one estimate is a utilization of only about 10% compared with the 90% utilization common with mainframe computers. With virtualization, all applications for an organization are installed in virtual environments on one or more physical servers, enabling companies to fulfill their computing needs with fewer servers. This translates into reduced costs as well as a server architecture that is easier to manage. Each virtual environment is self-contained and can be backed up individually, as well as moved to another physical server as needed.

While widespread *desktop virtualization* is a little further down the road, it is expected to enable servers to host an entire desktop environment for each user. When the user boots up (typically using a thin client or other access device), he or she sees his or her own personal desktop, even though the processing hardware, operating system, and application programs are located on the shared server. The virtual desktops can be displayed wherever the user happens to be at the moment—such as in the office, at home, or on the road. In addition to servers and desktops, the concepts of virtualization are also beginning to be applied to other computing areas, such as networking and storage.

Chapter 2–The System Unit: Processing and Memory

UPDATE

Some of the most significant changes in the area of processing over the past year involved improvements in CPUs and the increasing use of nanotechnology in technology components.

Update on CPUs

As expected, recent CPUs support 64-bit processing and have a least two cores. Multi-core CPUs allow computers to work efficiently on more than one task at a time. They also use less power and experience fewer heat problems than single-core CPUs because each core typically runs slower than a single-core CPU, although the total processing power of the multi-core CPU is greater. Dual-core CPUs are available from both AMD and Intel and are used with desktop and portable PCs for both IBM-compatible and Apple computers. *Quad-core* CPUs have four computing cores in a single processor package (see Figure U-3) and became available at the end of 2006; *octo-core* CPUs (with eight cores) are in the prototype stage. According to Jerry Bautista, director of technology management at Intel's Microprocessor Technology Lab, "Thousands of cores are possible. The trick is finding what's practical."

FIGURE U-3
Illustration of a quad-core CPU.

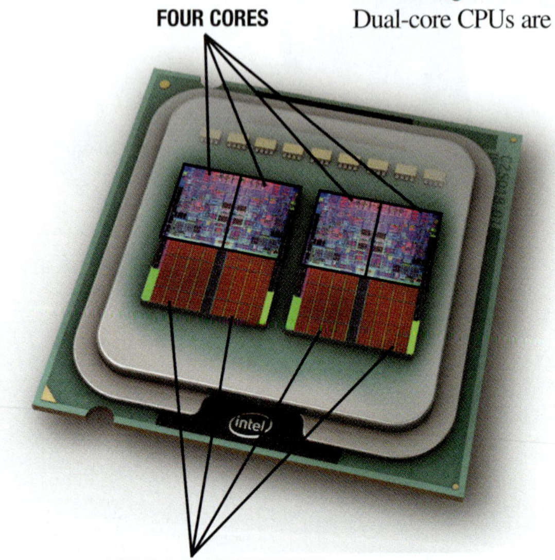

One of the limitations of multi-core CPUs at the present time is software since programs need to be written to take advantage of the parallel processing and multithreading capabilities of these CPUs. Another limitation is the rest of the system architecture. Today's multi-core CPUs typically utilize the same buses that were designed for single-core CPUs, and these buses tend to be the bottlenecks in single-core systems. Although CPU manufacturers are working on ways to speed up the rest of the system—such as increasing the speed and number of buses and encouraging peripheral manufacturers to connect to faster expansion buses (such as AMD's HyperTransport bus and Intel's PCI Express bus)—bus bottlenecks are viewed as a serious limitation to increasing the number of cores in a CPU.

CPUs are also increasingly including additional technology to meet new needs, such as support for virtualization (discussed in the Chapter 1 Update section). Increased 3D graphics processing is expected to begin to be integrated into CPUs once *Windows Vista*—the newest version of the Windows operating system—is in widespread use. And AMD has converted a graphics processor into a dedicated *stream processor* designed to perform floating-point calculations for high-performance workstations and servers. Many business, scientific, and animation applications extensively use floating-point calculations, and using a dedicated stream processor can increase the computing power of a computer system tremendously—ten-fold or better for some applications.

FIGURE U-4
Carbon nanotubes make this bike frame very strong, but light.

Nanotechnology Update

The interest in nanotechnology has continued and expanded this past year. Governments around the world are investing in nanotechnology research—the United States alone is budgeting $1.3 billion for nanotechnology research in 2007. And products that use carbon nanotubes are growing. For instance, lithium ion batteries that use nanotubes are currently on the market, Samsung has created a 15-inch prototype LCD screen that uses carbon nanotubes to illuminate images on the screen, and *NRAM*—a new type of fast, nonvolatile nanotube-based memory developed by Nantero, Inc.—is scheduled to begin shipping in late 2007.

Because of their strength and lightness for their size, carbon nanotubes are also being integrated into noncomputing products, such as automobile panels and racing bikes. In fact, the frame of the bike that Floyd Landis rode in the 2006 Tour de France is built with carbon nanotubes (see Figure U-4)—the entire bike frame weighs less than one kilogram (2.2 pounds). In another nanotechnology development, researchers at the University of Arizona discovered this year how to turn single molecules into working transistors and created transistors as small as a single nanometer. While still in the experimental stage, this discovery may singificantly impact computing technologies in the future.

NEW AND EMERGING TRENDS

Two emerging trends in the area of processing include *silicon photonics* and *terascale computing*.

Silicon Photonics

Silicon photonics refers to the process of making optical devices using silicon manufacturing techniques—essentially converging *photonics* (the control and manipulation of light) and electronics. The past year has brought several developments in this area. For example, researchers from Intel Corporation and the University of California, Santa Barbara, developed the world's first electrically powered *hybrid silicon laser*. Located on a silicon chip (see Figure U-5), the laser combines the light-emitting properties of Indium Phosphide with the light-routing capabilities of silicon. When voltage is applied to the chip, a continuous laser beam is generated. This development overcomes one of the last remaining obstacles of integrated silicon photonics—developing a low-cost light source on silicon. Researchers believe that silicon photonic chips containing dozens or even hundreds of hybrid silicon lasers could someday be built using standard high-volume, low-cost silicon manufacturing techniques. Silicon photonics technology has great potential in the area of transferring large amounts of data very quickly, such as for creating very fast connections between chips inside computers, between PCs, and to and from servers.

FIGURE U-5
Hybrid silicon laser.

Terascale Computing

As demand by consumers and businesses for online software, services, and media-rich experiences continues to increase, some experts predict that *terascale computing*—the ability of computers to process one trillion floating-point operations per second (teraflops)—will eventually be needed. Terascale research is currently focusing on multi-core processors used in conjunction with multithreaded hardware and software to increase the number of tasks that can be processed at the same time. It also includes working to develop higher-speed communications between computers, such as between Web servers and high-performance mobile devices or PCs. Intel, one of the leaders in terascale research, has created a teraflop processor that contains 80 cores to test strategies for rapidly moving terabytes of data from core to core and between cores and memory. It has also developed a 20-megabyte SRAM memory chip that is attached directly to the processor in order to speed up communication between processors and memory. This design allows thousands of interconnections to enable data to travel at more than one *terabyte per second* (*TBps*) between memory and the processor cores. Products based on current terascale research are likely many years away and may not resemble what today's researchers have in mind. However, according to Intel's Chief Technology Officer, today's terascale research will "definitely affect the way products look later in the decade and early into the next."

UPDATE

Not surprisingly, improvements in storage over the past year center on hard drives, optical discs, and flash memory media.

FIGURE U-6
A hard drive smart phone.

Hard Drive Update

The capacity of hard drives has continued to increase—internal hard drives that hold 750 GB are widely available—and new technologies are being used to increase capacity without increasing physical size. For instance, *perpendicular recording* is now being used by several hard drive manufacturers. Instead of aligning the magnetic particles horizontally, as in conventional hard drives, perpendicular recording flips the bits upright to place them more closely together than is possible with a horizontal layout. Currently, 2.5-inch drives that hold 160 GB using perpendicular recording are available for notebook computers, and that capacity is expected to increase in the near future. For instance, hard drive manufacturer Seagate has demonstrated a recording density of 245 gigabits per square inch (Gbpsi) with perpendicular recording and believes 500 Gbpsi is possible, which translates into 2 TB of storage for a 3.5-inch desktop internal disk drive, 500 GB for a 2.5-inch notebook internal disk drive, and 50 GB for a 1-inch drive like those used with digital music players and other mobile devices.

Auto-encrypting hard drives are becoming more common, and hard drives are beginning to be built into smart phones, such as the Samsung phone shown in Figure U-6. This phone has a built-in 8-GB hard drive to allow users to more easily store digital photos, music, and videos. It can also be used to store and transfer files to and from a PC via a USB port.

Optical Disc Update

Although discs and players for both HD-DVD and Blue-ray Discs are available and are becoming more common in the United States, the war over these two competing standards is still raging. One possible solution in the near future: high-definition hybrid drives that read all types of optical discs, including HD-DVDs, Blu-ray Discs, CDs, and DVDs. In late 2006, several companies announced new technology that will enable these hybrid drives to be developed. Hybrid players are expected to beome available sometime in 2007.

An additional promising development in the area of optical discs is a discovery by a Harvard research team that dramatically narrows the width of a laser beam. This is significant because the narrower the beam, the more data that can be stored on a disc. Instead of using a lens to focus the laser light (which results in a laser beam width of 405 billionths of a meter when recording DVDs), the researchers used two tiny gold rods as antennas at the end of a laser and were able to narrow the laser beam width to just 40 billionths of a meter. Although products based on this technology may be 10 years away, researchers predict that this new technique could eventually result in regular-size optical discs that hold 3 TB—roughly 600 times more than a standard DVD. To improve optical disc longevity, at least one company has developed a scratch-proof disc that uses bumpers around the edges and a clear polymer coating to protect the playing surface of the disc.

FIGURE U-7
Wristband USB flash memory drive.

Flash Memory Update

For handheld PCs, digital cameras, smart phones, and other types of mobile devices, flash memory cards are still the most common storage media. A number of new, smaller formats have been developed, such as *mini SD*, which is about one-half the size of a standard SD card; *micro SD*, which is about one-quarter the size of a standard SD card; and *RS-MMC* (*Reduced-Size MultiMediaCard*), which is about one-half the size of a standard MMC card. Typically, these cards are used in mobile phones and other devices with the appropriate sized built-in flash memory card reader; they can also be used in some conventional flash media card readers.

TREND

Baseball, Hot Dogs, and iPods?

One growing use of external storage devices is their use by professional sports teams to store digital video of practices and games for archival and training purposes. Compared to analog video, which is cumbersome and time-consuming to edit and scan through, digital video is much easier to work with. If game footage is captured in digital format, coaches can view plays during breaks in the game, and then make adjustments to their game plans. Footage can also be viewed by individual players to study their performance between games, as well as to study players on opposing teams. Often, team videos are stored on external hard drives, although the Colorado Rockies Major League Baseball team uses another tool—the iPod (see the accompanying photograph). An iPod with an 80-GB hard drive can store about a 100 hours of video, enabling players to carry with them a large collection of footage of themselves and opponents to study on demand to help them refine their swings and pitches. According to Brian Jones, assistant video coordinator for the Rockies, "Hard drives are vital to everything we do. The technology is a major part of the game now."

Todd Helton was the first Rockies player to use the iPod to study footage of opponents before games.

USB flash memory drive use has grown widely, and using these devices to transport files from one computer to another and to back up important files is commonplace. Flash memory drives are available in a wide range of sizes, colors, and appearances to appeal to a wide variety of users, including drives with clips to attach to a backpack and drives with a built-in wristband (see Figure U-7).

NEW AND EMERGING TRENDS

One new and emerging trend is the use of flash memory drives in conjunction with the *ReadyBoost* and *ReadyDrive* features of Windows Vista. For a look at an interesting storage application used by professional baseball players, see the Trend box.

Microsoft Windows Vista ReadyBoost and ReadyDrive

Two new features of the Windows Vista operating system are related to flash memory drives. Windows *ReadyBoost* allows users to use removable flash memory media—typically a USB flash memory drive—as additional memory for the PC to increase performance. Windows *ReadyDrive* involves *hybrid hard drives*, which contain both traditional hard drive and flash memory components. Although hybrid hard drives have been in development for the past year or so, they became more widely available this year and will likely see increased demand with the release of Windows Vista in early 2007. Hybrid hard drives in general are faster and consume less power than conventional hard drives. Windows ReadyDrive utilizes the flash memory contained in a hybrid hard drive as disk cache to enable PCs to boot faster, come out of hibernatation in less time, and preserve battery power. ReadyDrive-capable hybrid hard drives from a number of manufacturers are scheduled to be released in early 2007.

UPDATE

Input and output devices have continued to improve over the past year, and the use of *radio frequency identification* (*RFID*) has continued to grow.

FIGURE U-8
Concept touch screen mobile phone.

Changes in Input Devices

This past year has brought several new features to keyboards and mice to add increased functionality. For instance, Logitech's new MX Revolution wireless mouse includes a super fast scroll wheel that spins freely for up to seven seconds with a flick of the finger, a *One-Touch* search button that can be used to perform an Internet search on any word or phrase that is selected with the mouse, and a built-in zoom button. Microsoft's new wireless keyboard designed for Windows Vista users includes backlighting that adjusts to the amount of light in the room for more visible keys, as well as special buttons to launch the Vista Start menu, Windows Media Center, Windows *Gadgets* (a variety of mini-applications and tools), *Windows Live Messenger* (the new version of MSN Messenger), and more.

While an increasing number of mobile devices include full keyboard capabilities, the recent announcement by Apple of the upcoming *iPhone* (a device that can be used as an iPod, mobile phone, and Internet device and that uses a touch screen interface) and a concept phone by Nokia (see Figure U-8) suggest the touch screen may be the interface of the future for cell phones and other mobile devices.

Update on RFID

While retail RFID use has not grown significantly this past year, costs of RFID tags have come down, and the technology is being used with a wider range of applications—from a bookstore in the Netherlands that attaches RFID tags to each book to significantly reduce inventory time and cost, to numerous hospitals and other organizations that attach RFID tags to assets for tracking purposes. This year also marked the deadline for U.S passports to begin including built-in RFID tags, sparking numerous debates and proposed legislation from states hoping to control the use of RFID tags. Wisconsin, for instance, passed proactive legislation this year to prohibit the implantation of an RFID chip into a person's body without his or her consent. The RFID tag built into the new *e-passports* contains a duplicate copy of the passport photograph and data and is used to identify forged passports since the data in the RFID tag cannot be changed. To ease privacy concerns, the e-passport covers are shielded to prevent the tags from being read when the passports are closed, and the tags can only be read from a distance of about four inches.

FIGURE U-9
E-paper technology is used for the capacity indicator on this USB flash drive.

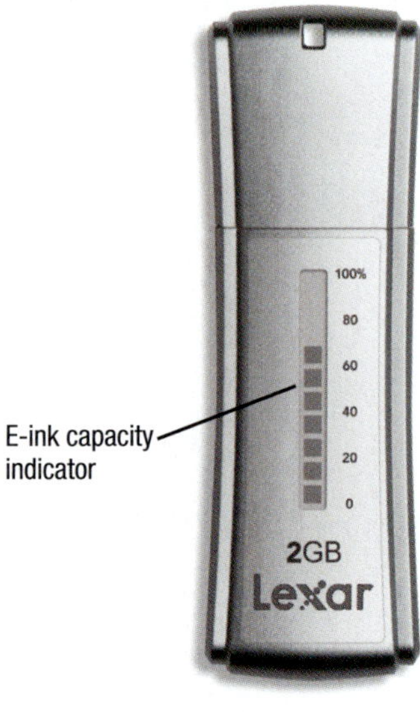

Changes in Output Devices

This year, larger flat-panel monitors (such as LCD monitors from 21 to 55 inches in diameter) are becoming more common as prices fall and features improve. Today, many of these large monitors feature picture-in-picture and picture-by-picture technologies to create a secondary screen within the original screen. They are also increasingly adding more connectivity options, such as built-in USB hubs and flash card readers. And e-paper and e-ink applications are on the rise. In addition to use with e-signs and electronic shelf labels, e-paper technology is beginning to become incorporated into a number of everyday devices. For instance, this year's firsts include e-paper mobile destinatation displays on trains in Germany, animated e-paper e-signs, e-paper wristwatches, e-paper-based e-book readers, and the first USB flash drive with an e-paper capacity display (see Figure U-9).

TREND

Soldier Sensor Systems

To collect a variety of data that may be useful in evaluating military operations and planning future operations, the Defense Advanced Research Projects Agency (DARPA) is exploring the use of soldier-worn sensors and recorders. The sensors can be used to record and store video and still images; the sound of acceleration and deceleration of vehicles, speech, and weapons fire; and other data. Sensor data, along with time and location data (gathered via GPS), is stored locally on the soldier, although the ability to transmit data when needed (such as sending the last 10 seconds of recorded video when the solider encounters an enemy contact situation) is a possibility for the future. Software used in conjunction with the sensor system is expected to assign keywords to each piece of data and create an indexed representation of the data collected so that information can be easily retrieved. The sensor systems currently being developed and tested (see the National Institute of Standards and Technology (NIST) prototype in the accompanying photograph) are part of the *Advanced Soldier Sensor Information System and Technology* (*ASSIST*) project, a project charged with developing sophisticated data collection systems to augment the soldier's recall and reporting capability. According to Craig Schlenoff, NIST's ASSIST project coordinator, "Soldiers endure tremendous physical and psychological stresses which can make it difficult to remember details about what they experienced over prolonged missions. We hope that ASSIST will keep our soldiers safer and increase the probability of mission success." Future capabilities may include language translation capabilities and other communications technology.

Future combat gear may include wearable sensors to input a variety of data.

NEW AND EMERGING TRENDS

A number of new trends in display technology are emerging. For a look at a new soldier sensor system being used to input a variety of data during military operations, see the Trend box.

New Display Technologies

While the OLED technologies discussed in the chapter are still being developed, uses for conventional *LEDs* (*light emitting diodes*) are growing. LEDs are now appearing in digital camera flashes, Christmas lights, television sets, car headlights—even clothing. For instance, the LED vest shown in Figure U-10 contains embedded LEDs that light up the appropriate images or messages, powered by a small detachable battery pack. LED fabrics are washable and are expected to be commercially available in the near future.

One new display technology in development is *interferometric modulator* (*iMoD*) *displays*. Designed initially for cell phones and other portable devices, an iMoD screen is essentially a complex mirror that uses external light—such as from the sun or artificial light inside a building—to display images. Because iMoD displays are utilizing light instead of fighting it the way LCD displays do, images are bright and clear even in direct sunlight. And because backlighting isn't used, power consumption is much less than LCD displays. A display technology in development for high-definition displays is *Surface-conduction Electron-emitter Display* or *SED*. SED, being developed by Toshiba and Canon, uses millions of tiny electron guns to power its pixels and is brighter and has less flicker than LCD and plasma screens. Televisions based on SED technology are expected to reach the market sometime in 2007.

FIGURE U-10
LED clothing.

Chapter 5–System Software: Operating Systems and Utilities

UPDATE

The biggest operating systems news this year is the release of *Microsoft Windows Vista* in late 2006. This past year also brought a preview of the new Mac OS operating system expected in 2007—*Mac OS X Leopard.*

FIGURE U-11
Windows Vista.

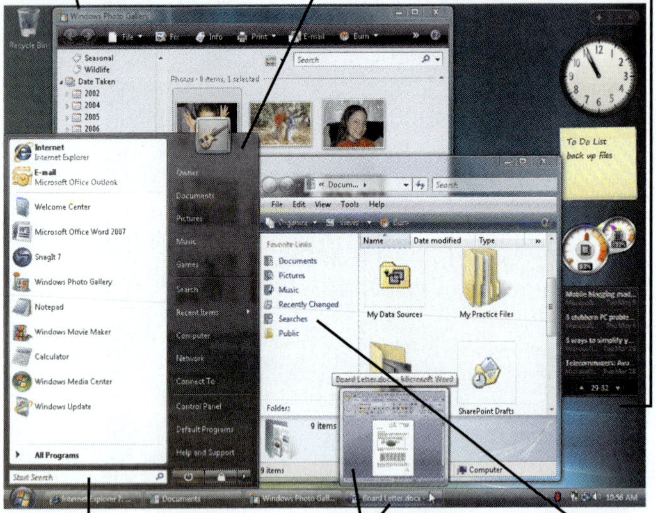

NEW PROGRAMS
Include multimedia, security, and collaboration programs.

AERO INTERFACE
Features translucent, glass-like windows and 3D effects.

SIDEBAR
Contains the user's selected gadgets.

START MENU
Includes a search box to search for documents, programs, and Web sites.

LIVE THUMBNAILS
Show the contents of a window when its taskbar button is pointed to.

SEARCHES
Can be saved for later use.

Windows Vista

Windows Vista, the latest release of Microsoft Windows, was a long time coming—more than five years after the release of Windows XP. In general, Windows Vista is designed to make the user experience more exciting, enjoyable, efficient, secure, and productive. The overall appearance of Windows Vista is shown in Figure U-11; some of the primary features include:

- *Aero user interface*—a new user experience available to users running a *Home Premium*, *Business*, or *Ultimate* edition of Windows Vista on a PC with compatible hardware. Features include translucent, glass-like windows to better display window content, thumbnails of taskbar items and open windows, and the ability to flip through open windows in 3D.
- New *Desktop Search* capabilities—a search box is now located at the bottom of the Start menu to allow you to easily search for programs and data files stored on your PC, as well as for Web sites. Searches can be saved in the *Searches* folder so that updated search results can be viewed at any time by just opening the appropriate saved search.
- *Windows Sidebar* and *gadgets*—*gadgets* are mini applications, such as calculators, clocks, weather indicators, and news headlines. *Windows Sidebar* is a customizable pane on the side of the Windows Vista desktop that organizes gadgets and makes them easy to access.
- *Windows Speech Recognition*—allows users to interact with their computers using their voice; users can control the operating system, dictate documents, and fill out Web-based forms.
- Improved multimedia capabilites—include *Windows Photo Gallery*, *Windows DVD Maker*, and *Windows Media Center*.
- Improved sharing and collaboration tools—include *Windows Meeting Space* for group meetings, a *Sharing Wizard* to more easily share files with other users, and *Windows Vista Sync Center* for managing data synchronization among multiple PCs.
- Improved security—includes *Windows Vista Firewall* to help protect against hackers, viruses, and worms attempting access via the Internet, and *Windows Defender* to help protect against spyware.

TIP

For a closer look at Windows Vista, see the "Windows Vista and You" feature at the end of the 2007 Update.

Mac OS X Leopard

The newest update to Apple's OS X operating system is *OS X 10.5*, named *Leopard* and due out in Spring 2007. New features include *Time Machine* (a new automatic backup and restore system); a new *Mail* program that includes stationery templates and a media browser to quickly create multimedia e-mail messages, as well as the ability to add *Notes* and *To-Do* lists to your e-mail folder to view anytime you view your e-mail; a *Spaces* feature that allows you to organize groups of applications and windows into Spaces that can be displayed or hidden as desired to help you work more efficiently and unclutter your

TECHNOLOGY AND YOU

Smart Notebook Covers

Ever want to change the cover of your PC to reflect your mood or check your e-mail when your notebook PC is powered down? Well, the solution is just about here. Because of the progress being made in the area of flexible electronics, experts predict that soon a variety of images and information will be able to be displayed on the cover of portable PCs, even if the PC is turned off. Possibilities include displaying images for decorative purposes, as well as usable content from the PC. While this feature has yet to materialize on the entire notebook cover, Windows Vista does include support for a secondary display device located on a portable PC. The new technology, called SideShow, allows users to access content–such as e-mail messages, schedules, maps, flight information, address books, Wi-Fi connectivity information, digital music, and more–located on the portable primary PC and display that information on the secondary display (see the accompanying photo). This display, technically a tiny computer, can be left on continually since it uses minimal power, and it can access information on the portable PC even if that PC is powered down. SideShow technology also allows hardware manufacturers to build auxiliary displays into peripheral devices (such as keyboards, LCD monitors, remote controls, and cell phones, for instance), which can then display information received from a Windows Vista-based PC. SideShow-compatible hardware is expected to reach the market sometime in 2007.

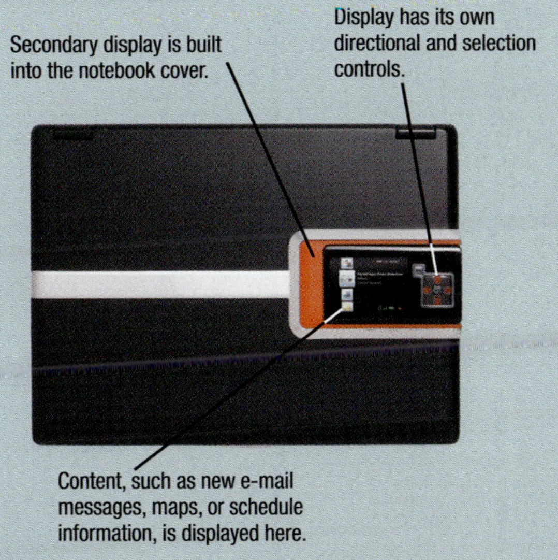

Windows SideShow enables notebook PCs to display information on a secondary screen, even if the PC is off.

desktop; and more parental controls that allow parents to control the programs and Web sites visited by their children—even the times of day the computer can be used.

NEW AND EMERGING TRENDS

One new and emerging trend is increased cooperation among operating system manufacturers. For a look at how you can view information from a portable PC using a secondary display built into the notebook cover, see the Technology and You box.

Operating System Cooperation

A somewhat surprising trend is the growing cooperation among operating system companies. For instance, this year Microsoft and Novell announced plans to make SUSE Linux and Windows work better together, including Microsoft offering sales support for SUSE Linux and working with Novell to increase document compatibility between Microsoft Office and the Novell Edition of OpenOffice, as well as making it easier for users to run both SUSE Linux and Windows on their computers. On a similar note, Apple released their *Boot Camp* program this year; this program allows users to install Windows XP on an Intel-based Mac so that either Mac OS X or Windows XP can be run on the computer. According to Apple, the company has no desire or plan to sell or support Windows, but they are responding to customer requests to run Windows on Apple hardware now that it uses Intel processors. Boot Camp will be included in Mac OS X Leopard, and that version is expected to support Windows Vista. This year also marked the beginning of the use of Windows Mobile software on some Palm PCs instead of the Palm OS operating system. PalmSource, now owned by ACCESS, CO., is also in the process of developing the *ACCESS Linux Platform* (*ALP*) designed for Linux-based smart phones and mobile devices.

UPDATE

Changes in application software over the past year include a new version of Microsoft Office and new software licensing options.

Microsoft Office 2007

The latest version of Microsoft Office—called *Microsoft Office 2007*—was released to manufacturers in late 2006 and to consumers in early 2007. Office 2007 uses a redesigned interface intended to make it easier for users to find and use all the features included in the Office suite of programs. One of the biggest changes is the replacement of menus and toolbars with a new *Ribbon* feature (see Figure U-12). The Ribbon organizes commands into a set of tabs related to the most common and relevant tasks for the program being used. For instance, Microsoft Word and Excel both contain *Insert* and *Page Layout* tabs, but Word also includes *References* and *Mailing* tabs while Excel has *Formula* and *Data* tabs. Most programs also have a *Home* tab that contains the most frequently used commands for that program. Each tab contains groups of command buttons related to that tab. Clicking a command button either carries out that command or displays a *gallery* of choices from which the user can select the desired action, such as a list of bulleted list styles, font sizes, margin settings, paper sizes, and so forth.

FIGURE U-12
Microsoft Office 2007.

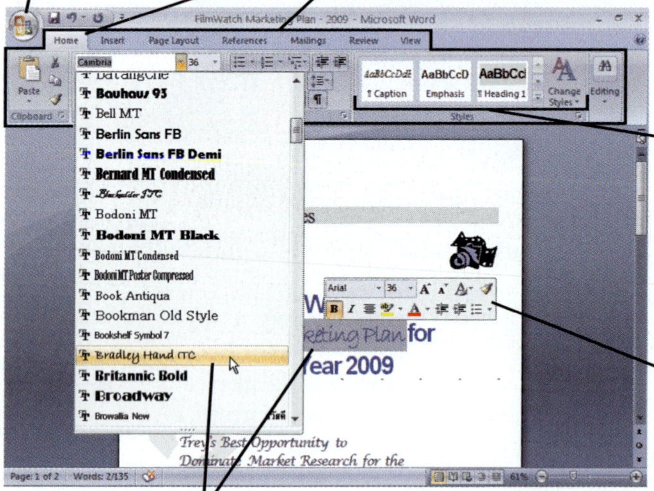

OFFICE BUTTON
Replaces the File menu.

RIBBON
Contains tabs of commands; the Home tab is selected here.

GROUPS
Commands on the Ribbon are organized into related groups.

MINI TOOLBAR
Appears whenever text is selected with the mouse.

LIVE PREVIEW
Changes the appearance of selected items when a formatting command is pointed to.

Another new feature is *Live Preview*, which allows the user to see the results of many formatting commands before they are applied, such as watching selected text change as the user scrolls through a list of font faces or sizes. To further speed up issuing commands, *contextual tabs*—new tabs that appear on the Ribbon only when certain items (such as a photo) are selected and contain the commands needed for that item—and the *Mini toolbar*—a floating toolbar containing common text-editing tools that appears whenever text is selected—have been added. Replacing the File menu is the *Office Button*, which contains commands commonly used with documents, such as to open, save, print, send, and publish them. Files now default to a new XML-based file format (such as *.docx* for Word files and *.xlsx* for Excel files). Office 2007 is available in eight editions, each containing a different combination of Office 2007 programs. Most editions of Office 2007 contain a number of Web and collaboration tools and are integrated with the *Office Live* product designed to help small businesses develop an online presence.

TIP

The Microsoft Office Home and Student 2007 edition contains the 2007 versions of Word, Excel, PowerPoint, and OneNote.

While the new design and interface are expected to be well received by users once they become accustomed to them, many businesses are concerned about employee retraining time and initial reduced productivity, as well as the initial cost of the software upgrade. According to Forrester Research, many enterprises don't expect to move to Office 2007 before 2009, although they view eventual migration to Office 2007 as inevitable.

Software Licensing Update

Recent trends in computing—such as the multi-core processors and virtualization discussed in the Chapter 1 and 2 Update sections, for instance—are leading to new software licensing models. For example, some software companies have decided to require a single license for a computer with a dual-core processor, but charge extra for computers with more cores. The reasoning is that computers using these new processors can do substantially more with the software than single-core systems, so fewer copies of the software may be required. On the other hand, many users prefer the more conventional per processor or per user pricing models

TREND

Up Next: A 3D Virtual World

It started with Web sites like Yahoo! Maps and MapQuest. The ability to display an address on a map via the Internet was revolutionary for business and personal travelers. Next came the ability to plot a variety of data on the maps, plus Web sites–such as Craigslist and Zillow–that utilize online maps to create other applications. Up next? A 3D virtual earth.

Google Earth was one of the first satellite mapping applications and now displays 3D illustrations of buildings and terrain in about 38 U.S. cities. The *Microsoft Virtual Earth 3D* interface, introduced in late 2006, goes one step further by using photorealistic images of buildings for a growing number of cities in applications such as Microsoft's Live Search (see the accompanying screen shot). The 3D interface gives you a bird's eye view of locations and allows you to zoom in and out and move from place to place dynamically. You can view the locations of businesses, current traffic conditions–even virtual billboards that are linked to advertiser sites. And Microsoft has opened up the Virtual Earth 3D interface to third-party developers to create even more applications. Both of these products point to the trend of creating 3D realistic tools to explore the real world online. According to Bill Gates, chairman of Microsoft, "The immersive 3D experience provides a more powerful and engaging interface that delivers better experiences not only for consumers, but also for developers and advertisers."

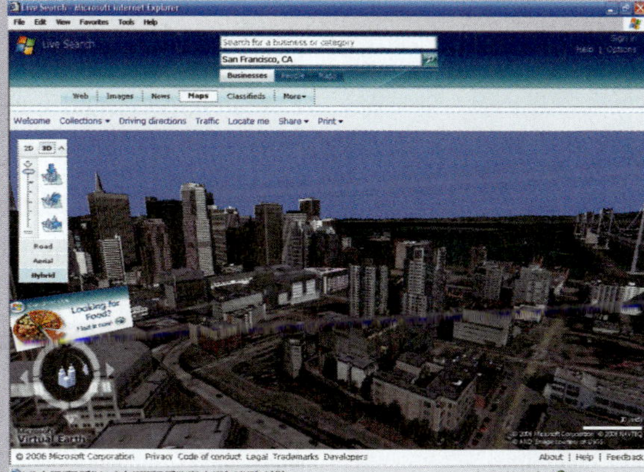

Virtual Earth 3D recreates cities in three dimensions.

to reduce costs. Virtualization adds yet another wrinkle to the problem since a single software program may be included in many more virtual environments than are ever actually used at one time. To address this, some software companies—like Microsoft—are charging on a *per running instance* basis; that is, the number of software instances (installed or virtual) being used at any given time. Software vendors are expected to develop and implement new licensing models that more specifically address virtualization in the near future.

Another option is *Software as a Service* (*SaaS*), where software is delivered on demand via the Web to wherever the user is at the moment, provided he or she has an Internet connection. Typically, SaaS uses a subscription (often per user, per month) pricing scheme, which is growing as a user preference as compared to conventional software licenses because of the decreased initial cost and implementation time and the increased flexibility. In fact, research firm Gartner predicts that 25% of new business software will be delivered as services by 2011, up from 5% of new software puchases for last year.

NEW AND EMERGING TRENDS

One new and emerging trend is *Web 2.0 applications*. For a look at one new 3D Web application—*Microsoft Visual Earth 3D*—see the Trend box.

Web 2.0 Productivity Applications

Although it lacks a precise definition, *Web 2.0* generally refers to Web-based applications and services that let people collaborate and share information online. These applications are taking off and include SaaS, photo sharing sites, online calendars, social networking sites, blogs, wikis, podcasts, RSS feeds, and *browser-based personal productivity software*. This year, a number of browser-based office suites became available, such as from Google and Zoho (see Figure U-13). Typically, browser-based productivity suites include at least a word processor and a spreadsheet and allow you to create new documents, as well as import documents from Microsoft Office and other installed office suites. Although these suites aren't typically as feature-rich as installed applications, many are currently free and have adequate features for many users.

FIGURE U-13
Online office suites are available from a variety of companies.

UPDATE

This year has brought continued improvements in wireless networking technologies and videoconferencing.

Cellular, Wi-Fi, and WiMAX Update

Not surprisingly, cell phone use has continued to soar—over half of all Americans now own mobile phones. Although hampered by slow connection speeds until recently, 3G services are now widely available and offer downloads speeds of around 400 to 700 Kbps. And the first WiMAX-based fourth-generation (4G) services, with speeds of 2 to 4 Mbps, are expected to become available by the end of 2007.

FIGURE U-14
The Zune digital media player.

For home networks, business networks, and stationary access to the Internet in public locations, Wi-Fi is becoming the norm. Wi-Fi hardware is built into just about every notebook PC sold today, and hotspots are still multiplying at a rapid pace. According to ABI Research, retail and hospitality establishments are the drivers behind the growth—even 17% of all McDonald's restaurants are Wi-Fi-enabled. And Wi-Fi capabilities are becoming increasingly integrated in everyday products, such as printers and gaming devices. In fact, all three of the consumer gaming consoles released in 2006 (*Xbox 360*, *Playstation 3*, and *Nintendo Wii*) and Microsoft's new *Zune* digital media player (see Figure U-14) all contain built-in Wi-Fi networking capabilities.

The most current Wi-Fi standard is still 802.11g, although some *Draft-N* hardware (hardware based on the draft standards of 802.11n) is now available. Because the 802.11n standard will likely not be finalized and ratified until late 2007 or early 2008, Draft-N hardware may not be completely compatible with the final standard. However, using MIMO and other draft technology, the routers and network interfaces available this year boast of speeds up to 12 times 802.11g hardware, with up to four times the range. Applications that require even longer distance will likely soon use WiMAX, once it becomes available. WiMAX technology is due to be embedded in notebooks and other hardware beginning in 2007.

Wireless networking technology (such as Bluetooth and the emerging wireless USB standard) is also being increasingly used to connect hardware together, such as to connect headsets to mobile phones and digital media players, as well as to connect conventional hardware to both desktop and notebook PCs. For home entertainment devices like high-definition TVs, cable boxes, gaming consoles, DVD players, and so forth, a new *WirelessHD* format is in development. Backed by seven major electronics companies, WirelessHD is designed to transfer full-quality high-definition video within a single room and is expected to hit the market in 2008 capabilities.

FIGURE U-15
Videoconferencing.

Life-size video images of remote participants appear on the display screen.

Videoconferencing Update

Videoconferencing technology is continuing to improve to more closely mimic a real-time meeting environment, as well as to apply to new applications. For instance, one new videoconferencing product allows participants in different physical locations to see high-quality life-sized video images of each other in real-time (see Figure U-15); the corresponding audio even appears to be coming from the appropriate individual. Available in setups as small as two participants at each location, this new technology allows videoconferences to more closely resemble face-to-face meetings. In hospitals, videoconferencing has been expanded to include language interpreting. Because they are unable to provide translators for the wide variety of non-English speaking patients that are treated today, hospitals are turning to videoconferencing to share a staff of interpreters with a network of hospitals. Unlike telephone interpreting services, which require handing the phone back and forth and are not compatible with nonverbal languages, such as American Sign Language, videoconferencing interpreting systems allow patients to more easily and effectively communicate with their health care providers.

TECHNOLOGY AND YOU

New Mobile Phone Parking Applications

We've already seen parking meters that can be paid via a mobile phone. Now your cell phone can help you find a parking place in the first place. For instance, a service started in Paris in late 2006 allows drivers to use their mobile phone or GPS device to find out which of the 120 participating parking garages have spaces available. A collaboration of eight technology companies, this free service connects the parking garages to a central server via the Internet, and when the status of the garage changes–such as it becomes full or vacancies become available–that information is made available to users of the service. To find the closest garage, users can either enter an address or let the service use cell tower location information to determine the closest garage with available spaces. Next year, the service is expected to use the GPS capabilities of cell phones to guide the driver to the nearest available garage much more precisely. It is also scheduled to be implemented in Germany in 2007.

A related service in the United States is *SpotScout*. SpotScout is working to create a virtual marketplace for parking spaces in high-demand areas, beginning with Boston, New York, and San Francisco. With this system, users can find and reserve open parking spaces (see the accompanying photograph) based on location, cost, and other criteria (such as user rating or handicapped access, for instance). The parking facilities available through this service are private (such as private parking garages and private driveways), and the owners set the prices. SpotScout manages the reservations and financial transactions and collects a small transaction fee. The system is also set up to allow individuals parked in public parking spaces on the street to sell their departure time to someone interested in being there when the spot becomes available. The system is scheduled to go live in early 2007.

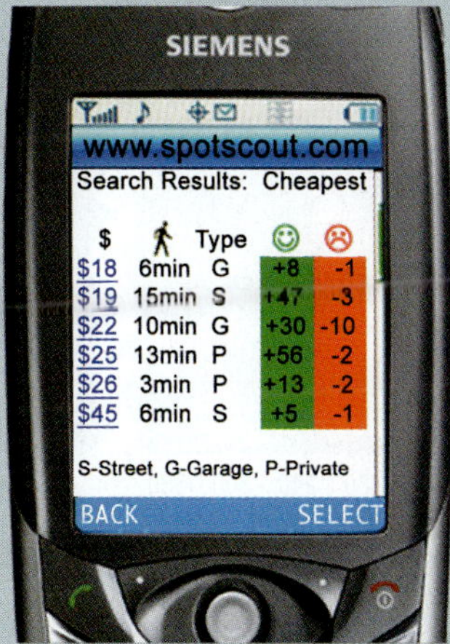

SpotScout can help you find parking spots in some U. S. cities.

NEW AND EMERGING TRENDS

One new and emerging trend is *cellular and Wi-Fi convergence*. For a look at new cell phone parking applications, see the Technology and You box.

Cellular and Wi-Fi Convergence

One of the most interesting developments in wireless technology today is the convergence of cellular and Wi-Fi technologies. Using *dual-mode handsets* (such as the Motorola handset shown in Figure U-16), users can make and receive calls and messages, as well as check e-mail and perform other normal tasks, over either their cellulur or Wi-Fi networks. Typically, this capability is facilitated by *Unlicensed Mobile Access* (*UMA*) technology, which allows phones to seamlessly switch between the two networks as the user moves in and out of range of the Wi-Fi network. Research firm In-Stat predicts that there will be more than 132 million dual-mode handsets in use by 2010. An alternative emerging standard to UMA is *IP Multimedia Subsystem* (*IMS*).

FIGURE U-16
Dual-mode handsets can place and receive phone calls over both cellular and Wi-Fi networks.

Chapter 8–The Internet and World Wide Web

UPDATE

Over the past year, Internet access continued to improve for many Americans. One Internet application that is really taking off is Voice over IP (VoIP).

Internet Access Update

This year, the number of consumers with broadband Internet connections continued to increase (now about 55% of U.S. homes have high-speed Internet), and both cable and DSL connections got faster and cheaper. Download speeds of 6 Mbps for cable are common, and faster speeds are available in some areas. DSL averages about half the speed of cable but is usually much less expensive—specials of $12 or so per month for one year for new DSL subscribers are not uncommon.

FIGURE U-17
Length of time to download a 1.5 MB movie using different home Internet options.

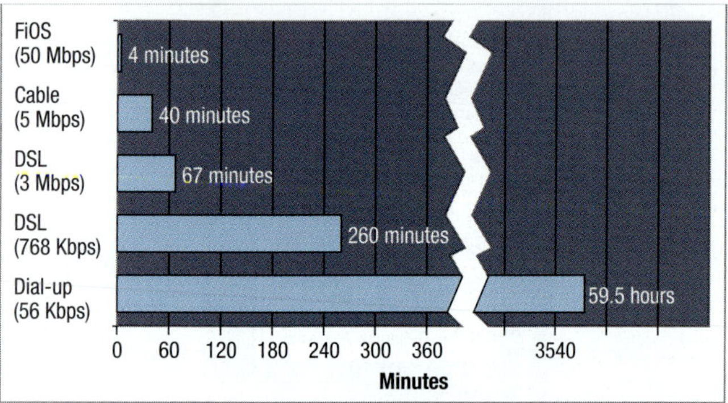

One new option this year in areas where the telephone company has replaced conventional communications infrastructure with fiber optics is *fiber optic service* (*FiOS*)—sometimes called *broadband over fiber* (*BOF*). Where available, download speeds for FiOS service can be as fast as around 50 Mbps (typically several packages are available with different speeds and pricing with the fastest speeds being relatively expensive), and 100 Mbps may not be far off. What to do with all that bandwidth? Certainly Web browsing and e-mail will continue to be popular Internet activities, but applications requiring high-speed connections are growing in popularity as Internet speeds continue to improve. For instance, high-definition television, video-on-demand (VOD), and other multimedia applications all benefit from fast broadband connections (see Figure U-17).

Voice over IP (VoIP) Update

With VoIP now available from communication giants (such as AT&T, Sprint, and Earthlink), as well as the original Skype and Vonage VoIP companies, VoIP has hit mainstream. Skype alone has over 100 million registered users. While problems—such as dropped or poor quality calls, telephone number transfer problems, and hidden fees—are common complaints with some VoIP providers, VoIP shows no signs of slowing down. In fact, new products are becoming available to make it easier to use and more seamless with other technology. For instance, *Voice over Wi-Fi phones* allow users to place VoIP phone calls over Wi-Fi networks without using a computer, and Vonage's *V-Phone* USB flash memory device (see Figure U-18) includes all of the information (phone number, contact list, call history, voice mail, on-screen dialer, etc.) to enable users to easily make Vonage phone calls from any PC with a broadband connection, without installing any software.

In addition to phone calls, VoIP technology is leading towards other voice content delivered via the Web. For instance, voice is now an option for most instant messaging (IM) programs, and it is beginning to become embedded in some Internet applications, such as online gaming, dating services, and online voice and video chat services (such as *Paltalk*). Several companies are introducing *pay-per-call* advertising links that show up on search site and online phone directory search results—the company collects a fee whenever someone calls the displayed phone number—and Google started testing a free *click-to-call* service this year that enables users to click links on Google Local and Google Maps results to have Google connect your phone to the business listed. In addition, Skype links can now be added to eBay auction listings to generate Skype calls for buyer questions.

FIGURE U-18
The Vonage V-Phone.

TREND

Social Networking Sites

Social networking sites can be loosely defined as sites that create communities of individuals with common interests linked together. Along with video-sharing sites like *YouTube* (now owned by Google) and photo-sharing sites like *Flickr* (now owned by Yahoo!), both of which became immensely popular this year, social networking sites are hot. According to the Pew Internet & American Life Project, more than one in ten adult Internet users in the United States have visited a social networking site. Some sites, such as *MySpace* and *FaceBook*, allow users to post information about themselves for others to read. The new *Ning* site (see the accompanying screen shot) goes one step further by allowing users to create social Web sites without having to write any code. The free service includes templates for creating a group site, as well as sites to share music, photos, and videos. Sites can be public or private and can be customized as much as desired by the users. For a collaborative news community, *Digg* (which allows members to submit and vote on news articles, and the articles with the most "diggs" get promoted to the home page of the site) is the current leader. For saving and sharing bookmarks of favorite sites, newcomer *del.icio.us*–a self-proclaimed *social bookmarking site* that allows users to create bookmarks, as well as search and view bookmarks made by other member–is widely used.

Both adults and children should be cautious about revealing too much personal information on social networking sites, both for personal safety reasons and to prevent against the information being used in personalized, targeted *spear phishing attacks*, discussed in the Chapter 9 Update. And adults should also take a close look at their online posts and photos and remove anything that might be potentially embarrassing if viewed by current or future employers, a future mate, or other people important to the individual.

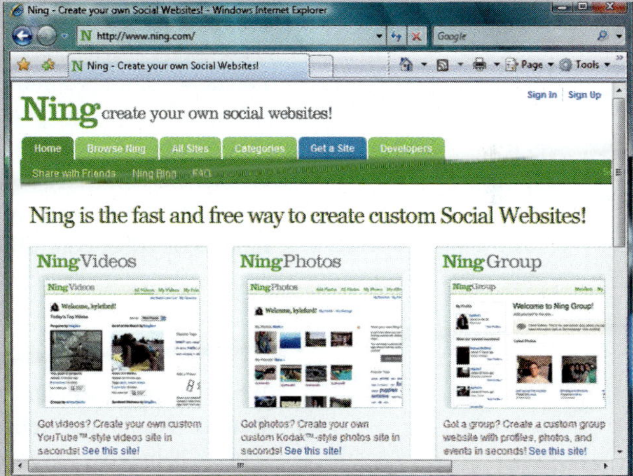

Ning allows users to create their own social Web sites.

NEW AND EMERGING TRENDS

One new controversial issue relating to the Internet is the debate over *Net neutrality*. For a look at some of the social networking sites that became available this year, see the Trend box.

The Debate over Net Neutrality

The term "Net neutrality" refers to the equality of data as it is transferred over the Internet. That is, whether it is a podcast, Web page, or phone call, and whether it is coming from your house or Microsoft headquarters, the data is treated the same. This type of exchange allows a level playing field for all individuals and businesses that have content on the Web—everyone has the same potential audience as everyone else. The concept isn't new—it's the way the Internet and World Wide Web were developed—but what is new is that some telecommunications and cable companies have indicated that they want to provide higher speeds over their infrastructure for large companies that can afford to pay premium prices for that privilege. Since telecomm and cable companies provide the vast majority of high-speed Internet to consumers, it would essentially separate the Internet into two pieces: a free lane and an express, premium lane.

Critics argue that startups like *YouTube* would never have gotten the audiences they have today if their content—in the case of YouTube, videos—ran slower than competitors, and allowing Net neutrality to end would be the end of the Internet innovation that we see now. They also fear that it would lead to telecomm and cable companies blocking selected traffic from certain companies—such as to block competing VoIP or video services. Proponents argue that network operators need a reasonable opportunity to recoup the cost of their infrastructure. Legislation has been proposed to preserve Net neutrality, but some experts believe that legislating against something that hasn't happened yet isn't necessary.

Chapter 9–Network and Internet Security

UPDATE

Over the past year, viruses, identity theft, and other security risks continued to grow, and some new precautions were developed.

Security Risk Update

Unfortunately, malware attacks are still an everyday security risk, and phishing is still on the rise. According to a report by Gartner, nearly 110 million U.S. adults received phishing e-mails in 2006—nearly double the number in 2004—and the average amount lost by phishing victims grew from $257 to $1,244. Phishers are increasingly targeting higher-income individuals who tend to perform more transactions on the Web, and the attacks are becoming increasingly sophisticated. For instance, one recent phishing e-mail warned customers about phishing and asked them to update their information to ensure that they would be protected from phishers. To assure wary users, the legitimate 800 phone number of the company being spoofed was included in the e-mail message. In addition to e-mail, phishing attempts also occur today via IM, fake messages from eBay or MySpace members—even by phone (called *voice phishing* or *vishing*). In a vishing attempt, the potential victim is either called directly or receives a phishing e-mail that directs the recipient to call a specific phone number to verify personal or account information.

Another tool being increasingly used in attacks are *botnets*—collections of broadband-enabled PCs that have been hijacked and are now under control of the attacker. According to Symantec, an average of 57,000 active bots were observed per day during the first six months of 2006, controlling 4.7 million distinct computers to distribute spam, launch DoS attacks, install malware, or log keystrokes to gather personal data to be used in identity theft.

Security Precaution Update

While Internet users are becoming more knowledgable about malware, phishing, and other security risks, more sophisticated attacks mean that fraudulent activities are more difficult to spot. To help protect Web site visitors against phishing schemes, a number of browser tools are available. Some display a warning when a known phishing site is displayed; others try to analyze the site's address to see if it's misleading, such as if the URL contains the term "ebay" but it is not located on the ebay.com domain. The antiphishing toolbar shown in Figure U-19 displays a variety of information about the site and who it is registed to, along with a risk rating.

While phishing sites are becoming more difficult to recognize, common sense precautions—such as never clicking a link in an e-mail message (type the URL instead) and guarding your personal data (don't include your Social Security numbers on an online résumé posted on a job site, for instance, and be careful with the information you post on MySpace and other social networking sites)—can help. One program designed to notify users if too much personal information is available online is *Identity Angel*, developed at Carnegie Mellon University. The Identity Angel software program searches the Internet to locate Social Security numbers and dates of birth that match up with a name and address—considered to be the "holy trinity" of identity theft. If it finds an individual's holy trinity (about 5,000 were discovered in the first week alone), the program will notify the individual if an e-mail address is available.

FIGURE U-19
The Netcraft antiphishing toolbar.

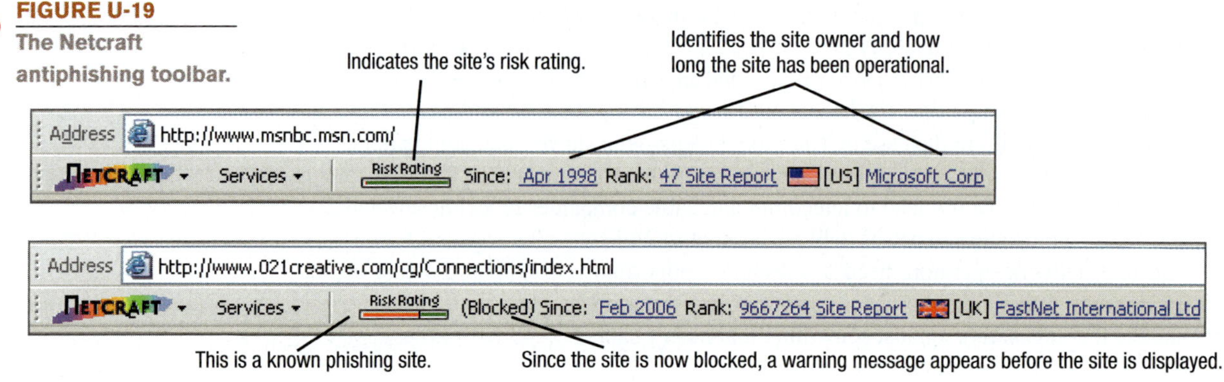

TREND

Spear Phishing

Going along with the trend of more sophisticated attacks is the emergence of a new type of phishing attack referred to as *spear phishing*. Essentially a more targeted, personalized phishing scheme, spear phishing attacks are directed to individuals. Spear phishing e-mails typically appear to come from an organization or person that the target has an association with and include personalized information (such as the potential victim's name) to make them seem even more legitimate. Several spear phishing attacks were targeted at users of social networking sites like MySpace this year since the personal information (name, age, hobbies, friends list, favorite music, and so forth) typically included on these sites makes them a good resource for spear phishers. Some attacks (see the MySpace Messages spear phishing example in the accompanying figure) were geared towards obtaining an individual's log-on information. Since many individuals use the same password for a variety of sites, once a scammer has a valid user name/password combination, he or she can try it on a variety of sites and buy products, send money via PayPal, and perform other types of financial transactions if he or she is able to log on as the victim. Another attack aimed at MySpace users this past year brought potential victims to a fake music download site, in hopes of capturing credit card information.

Spear phishers also target employees of selected organizations by posing as someone within the company, such as a human resources or technical support employee. These spear phishing e-mails typically either request confidential information, such as log-in IDs and passwords, or direct the employee to click a link to reset his or her password. The goal for corporate spear phishing attacks is usually to steal intellectual property, such as software source code, design documents, or schematics. Both phishing and spear phishing e-mail messages and Web sites are now more professional-looking than in the past, and the response rate has increased accordingly–current estimates are a 3 to 5% response rate for conventional phishing schemes and close to 20% for spear phishing schemes.

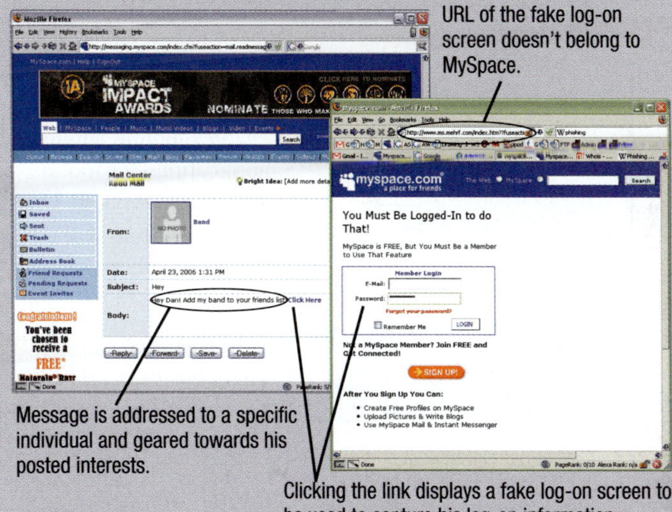

A spear phishing example.

NEW AND EMERGING TRENDS

One new and emerging trend is malware on cell phones and other devices besides PCs. For a look at a new type of phishing—*spear phishing*—see the Trend box.

Mobile Malware

With the increase of data being sent to and from devices other than PCs, malware writers and hackers are now targeting those devices as well. For instance, viruses have hit mobile phones and digital media players—in fact, some video iPods shipped this past year had a worm already installed on them. Mobile phones with Bluetooth capabilities in particular are vulnearable since they can be infected via a Bluetooth connection by just being within the vicinity (about 30 feet) of a carrier. Some viruses are designed to crash the phone's operating system; others are designed to be a nuisance by changing icons or otherwise making the device more difficult to use. And some are money-oriented, such as one Trojan horse currently infecting Russian phones that sends text messages to certain phone numbers that charge the sender a fee. For some tips to keeping your mobile phone virus-free, see Figure U-20.

CELL PHONE SECURITY PRECAUTIONS
Install and use a mobile antivirus program.
Disable open Bluetooth ports when they are not needed.
Don't download or launch unknown programs.
Watch the itemized portion of your cell phone bill to identify unauthorized charges.
Businesses should only allow preapproved software to run on company phones, encrypt data that is stored or transmitted via a company phone, and ensure that the phone can be locked or the data can be erased if the phone is lost or stolen.

FIGURE U-20
Security tips for mobile phone users.

UPDATE

Over the past year, the use of tools to create interactive multimedia Web sites has increased, and the use of online video has taken off.

Interactive Multimedia Tools Update

Last year, we saw the beginning of the use of AJAX in Web site development. This past year, use of AJAX has taken off, due in part because of the growing demand for interactive and customized Web sites and Web services. AJAX is used in the new *Windows Live Mail* application (the replacement for Hotmail), as well as on Google Maps, Gmail, FlickR, and numerous other popular Web applications. Sites built with AJAX run faster and have the responsiveness users associate with desktop applications. And, if done correctly, AJAX applications require less bandwidth than conventional Web applications since page layout and structure data is downloaded only once, and then only the data on the page that needs updating is downloaded as needed. To more easily implement AJAX, a variety of *AJAX toolkits*—AJAX application development programs—are now available.

Flash is another multimedia development tool whose use is continuing to grow. In addition to being used with multimedia Web applications for desktop computers, Flash is also now being used for mobile applications. A new version of Flash—*Flash Lite*—enables mobile application developers and designers to create rich, engaging content and applications for mobile phones and consumer electronic devices (see Figure U-21). Verizon Wireless is one company using Flash Lite for mobile applications and is hoping that the use of Flash will allow existing Web content written in Flash to be more easily adapted for mobile phone delivery, as well as make obtaining new content easier.

FIGURE U-21
Flash Lite is used to deliver rich content to mobile phones.

Online Video Update

There has been a huge increase this past year in the amount of video available on demand via the Web—particularly TV shows. Many popular TV shows (including Survivor, Desperate Housewives, Grey's Anatomy, LOST, The Office, The Class, and more) are available online—some episodes can be viewed for free via the network's Web sites; others can be viewed on a mobile phone via a mobile TV service. Still others can be downloaded for a small fee via iTunes or another online store to be viewed on a PC or digital media player (see Figure U-22). While many individuals turn to online video for convenience—such as to catch a missed episode of a favorite TV show—others prefer online viewing to television viewing because of the increased user control. A growing number of original and Hollywood movies are also available online. Downloaded movies can be viewed via a PC, mobile phone, or other device, and an increasing number of products are becoming available to help move online video and other downloaded multimedia content into the living room. For instance, a new product announced by Apple that is expected to become available sometime in 2007 is code-named *iTV*. A small settop box for the living room, iTV is a Wi-Fi-enabled device that takes all the digital content on your PC and the Internet—photos, movies, TV shows, music, and more—and easily delivers it to your TV set.

FIGURE U-22
TV shows delivered to PCs, mobile phones, and digital media devices are plentiful today.

NEW AND EMERGING TRENDS

One new and emerging trend is the use of virtual reality for posttrauamtic stress disorder. For a look at a Web site development trend—the use of *mashup tools*—see the Trend box.

TREND

Mashup Sites

A *mashup site* is a Web site that combines content from more than one source. While technically a mashup can be any sort of composite Web application (and mashups are beginning to be used by businesses to create enterprise applications), one of the most common sources for mashup sites today is Google Maps. Hundreds of mashup sites overlay customized data on top of the Google Maps interface, such as homes for sale or rent in a particular area, the distance for a specified walking route, the best fishing areas, New York subway routes, and more. This is possible since Google Maps has released its *Maps API* (*application programming interface*)—the published specifications that describe to developers how they can access the Google Maps service (see the accompanying illustration). With the API, developers can use JavaScript commands to display maps of specified locations and then overlay customized information on top of them. Other popular sources for mashup sites include FlickR, Amazon, VirtualEarth, YouTube, and eBay.

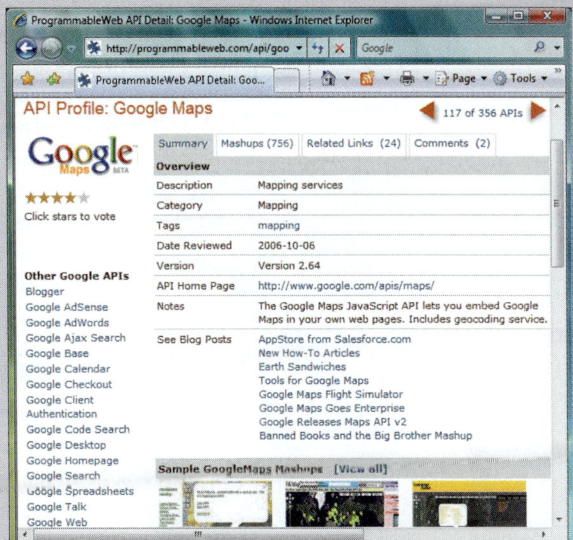

APIs, available via numerous Web sites, make mashups possible.

Virtual Reality (VR) as a Therapy Tool

Virtual reality has been used for entertainment and e-commerce applications for several years. It now has a new purpose—a therapy tool. This year, VR has been used to help treat posttraumatic stress disorder (PTSD) for both 9/11 survivors and war veterans. Called *virtual-reality exposure therapy*, these VR simulators allow patients to relive traumatic events—the goal is to allow patients to confront their fears and relive them in order to become desensitized to them. For the 9/11 survivors, researchers built a simulator that recreates events inside the Twin Towers. Patients sit on a vibrating platform wearing VR goggles and see 3D images, hear recorded sounds, and even experience burning smells. The therapy typically takes weeks of sessions as patients move through the environment at an individualized pace, gradually increasing the amount of trauma as the patient is ready. During the experience, a clinician controls the virtual environment in real time to better match the memories the patient is recounting, as well as to modulate the patient's anxiety level.

Similarly, a number of VR systems are being developed to treat PTSD in military personnel returning from Iraq and Afghansitan. The simulators allow soliders to revisit locations and experiences in Iraq and Afghanistan, such as moving through military compounds and marketplaces, going on patrols through Iraqi homes, and participating in conflicts. Similar to the 9/11 simulators, most systems include sight, sounds, smells, and movement for a more realistic experience, and the environment is monitored and controlled in real time by a clinician (see Figure U-23).

FIGURE U-23

Virtual reality exposure therapy. The system shown being tested here simulates activities in Iraq to help treat soldiers with PTSD.

UPDATE

This past year, there has been a surge of m-commerce applications in the United States, as well as growth in the number of customized products available online.

M-Commerce Update

Although m-commerce has been around for several years, it has been slow to take off in the United States, due primarily to a lack of standards and compatible devices. But many think the time for m-commerce has arrived, and several new options are becoming available. For instance, *Billmycell* allows users to pay for services, such as cab rides, food deliveries, and concert tickets, via their mobile phones, and *MobiRelay* is testing a *Mobile Box Office* system that allows moviegoers to buy tickets for movies at specific theaters using their mobile phone, and the tickets appear as a barcode that can be displayed on the screen when needed for admittance. Many m-commerce services today are via text messaging; an alternative is *Near Field Communication* (*NFC*) technology, which uses RFID to facilitate communication between devices, including payments between terminals and mobile phones (see Figure U-24). NFC phones and terminals are beginning to come on the market (research firm In-Stat predicts as many as 25 million NFC-enabled phones will be in use in the United States by 2011), which is expected to increase the number of merchants supporting m-commerce payments.

FIGURE U-24
Near Field Communication (NFC) facilitates m-commerce transactions.

Other new m-commerce services are designed for exchanging money between individuals. With an estimated $103 billion of "social money" exchanged each year for splitting dinner checks or cab fares or reimbursing friends for purchases made, the market for this type of service is huge. And, since more people now carry a mobile phone than not, the mobile phone is a logical medium for these transactions. Both existing companies and new companies have new person-to-person mobile payment systems available this year. For instance, PayPal launched *PayPal Mobile*, a free service that lets PayPal users send money to individuals via text message.

Buying Customized Products Online

Over the past few years, digital cameras have made customized products—such as photo mugs, T-shirts, calendars, and more—more common. FedEx Kinkos has offered photo products in the store and online for several years, and Snapfish is a popular source for online photo gifts. As more and more content is in digital form, and people are growing more accustomed to personalized online experiences, the market for customized products is growing. Today, individuals can order professional-looking, customized products online one at a time, such as from *Zazzle*. Via the Zazzle Web site (see Figure U-25), customers create custom products (such as T-shirts, postage, and posters) based on their own photos, licensed popular images, or historical images, and then add text as desired. There is no minumim order or setup fee, and most items ship within 24 hours. If the business at Zazzle is any indication—the company ships tens of thousands of customized products each day—the demand for fast and affordable custom products will only increase in the future.

FIGURE U-25
Zazzle. Sites like this one allow customers to create customized merchandise online quickly and easily.

TREND

Gold Rush: Reality Shows Hit the Web

Did you follow the new *Gold Rush* show to see who won the $1 million prize? If you did, it wasn't using your TV–Gold Rush is on the Internet. A creation by Mark Burnett, the man behind such hit reality shows as Survivor and The Apprentice, Gold Rush is the first online reality show. Introduced in late 2006, contestants complete puzzles and answer pop-culture questions to advance to the next level. Each week, the three contestants with the fastest correct answers compete for a $100,000 prize. Those winners advance to the semi-finals and then the finals, where they perform both physical and mental challenges in order to win the grand prize of $1 million in gold bars.

In addition to breaking new ground in online entertainment and bringing new traffic and revenue to the game's host site, AOL.com, Gold Rush features several interesting new promotional strategies. For instance, answers to clues for the weekly challenges are located on the AOL.com Web site, as well as in magazines belonging to AOL's magazine partners and CBS TV shows like Survivor, The Amazing Race, and The Class. Contestants can look up information on the Gold Rush Web site (see the accompanying screen shot), watch video clips of the TV shows, and perform other online activities to find the answers to the clues. As a result, visitors to the Gold Rush Web site stay there much longer than is typical–an average of 17 to 20 minutes, according to one estimate–and more than half are new to AOL. In addition, products from corporate sponsors (such as Best Buy, Coke, Chevrolet, and T-Mobile) are highly integrated into the show. For instance, one challenge displays questions on a T-Mobile device with T-Mobile references (like tie-ins to "Fave Five" periodically included in the questions); another is built around songs that had the word "Chevy" in the lyrics. Not your typical banner ad.

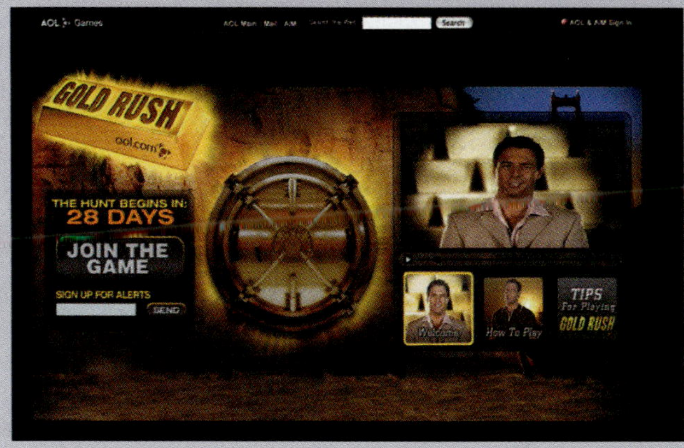

NEW AND EMERGING TRENDS

One new controversial topic related to e-commerce is *click fraud*. For a look at the first online interactive reality game, which gave away $1 million and earned millions in advertising revenue, see the Trend box.

Click Fraud

Click fraud occurs when sponsored links—such as on a search site results page—are clicked when there is no interest in the target of the link. The links could be clicked by a person or an automated clicking program (sometimes referred to as a *clickbot*). The motive is almost always financial. For instance, although viewed as unethical in the business world, a company might click on a competitor's sponsored links in order to deplete that company's advertising budget. And since sponsored ads on Google, Yahoo!, and other search sites are often placed on other Web sites, click fraud is also being performed by some companies or individuals that create Web pages consisting primarily of sponsored links, since the Web site hosting the page containing the link receives a fee each time that link is clicked.

This year, click fraud has become the subject of some controversy and increasing litigation. For instance, Google agreed to pay $90 million in response to an Arkansas lawsuit alleging that the search site was charging them for clicks not generated by legitimate users. While not denying that click fraud exists, search site companies maintain that losses are very small—approximately 1%. Other parties, however, believe the problem is much greater. For instance, the Internet auditing firm ClickFacts found during a test of one Web site's clicks that 35% of the site's sponsored link clicks in Google could be attributed to fraud. Both Google and Yahoo! try to identify clicks due to click fraud and credit the advertiser's account accordingly, but many advertisers feel that the search sites could do a better job combating click fraud. And the problem is compounded by the fact that as search sites improve their ability to detect click fraud, the fraudsters continue to develop ways to disguise the origins of fraudulent clicks. Pay-per-click advertising is currently one of the fastest-growing types of advertising, but some fear that click fraud may inhibit further growth of Internet advertising unless a solution is reached.

Chapter 12–Information Systems and System Development

UPDATE

The past year brought new trends in IS staffing, as well as new interest in *service-oriented architecture* (*SOA*).

Update on IS Jobs and Outsourcing

While IS jobs in past years have been a little harder to find and often required long hours, that seems to be changing. Demand for skilled workers in hot areas—such as network engineering, Web services, mobile applications, and business intelligence—is growing, and many IS professionals are demanding more of a balance between their work and personal lives than they have in the past. To that end, an increasing number of companies are allowing flexible work schedules and other incentives to retain skilled employees. Two emerging trends in IS staffing are *homeshoring* and *micro-multinational companies*.

FIGURE U-26
Homeshoring is a growing trend.

Homeshoring—outsourcing work, typically customer service and tech support call centers, to home-based workers (see Figure U-26)—is a rapidly growing area. Homeshoring workers are often located in the United States, Mexico, and India and typically work for outsourcing companies, who are then hired by businesses. Advantages for the worker include convenience and no commuting time or expense; employers benefit since they may be able to get more experienced and qualified workers (such as experienced retired workers or educated stay-at-home moms). For instance, the average age of employees at one homesourcing firm is 38, and 80% have at least some college education, whereas the typically call-center employee is in their early 20s with very little college education.

Similar to homesourcing, *micro-multinational companies* use communications technology to allow qualified individuals to work from wherever they happen to live. These small, multinational companies are often startup companies, and they select business locations and recruit skilled workers wherever it makes sense to do so.

With any type of remote workers, security is still an important issue. Studies show that while the majority of remote workers are aware of security issues, they don't necessarily use good judgement or behave appropriately. For instance, in one study conducted for Cisco, while 68% of the U.S. workers interviewed stated they had been warned about risky laptop behavior, 30% said they still use their company-issued computers for personal tasks, 24% still open e-mail messages from unknown senders, 19% allow others to use their work computers, and 12% connect to unfamiliar wireless networks.

Service-Oriented Architecture (SOA)

Although not a new concept, *service-oriented architecture* (*SOA*) has become a hot systems topic this year. Essentially, SOA is a collection of *services* (well-defined, self-contained functions that don't depend on the state of other services) that communicate with each other. While the integration of software applications has been possible for many years, it has typically required costly and complex middleware. SOA uses common standards for message exchange, so exchanges between services are much less expensive and much more efficient. And, via the Web, SOA allows services to work together regardless of the physical location or the type of computer being used with the service.

SOA has the potential to add flexibility to business processes by breaking them down into smaller functional elements that can then be assembled, as needed, into composite applications. Any process useful to a business can be a service, such as verifying a credit card transaction, calculating interest rates, or processing a purchase order. Because each service is small, specific, reusable, and shared within a company, making changes to a system is much easier and cleaner and has to be performed only once. And services can be added, changed, or deleted from the system without altering the underlying architecture, making the entire system very flexible. In essense, the point of SOA is to create an architecture that supports a set of streamlined, flexible, business processes.

INSIDE THE INDUSTRY

High-Tech Ice Cream

One interesting new high-tech system that became available this year is a computer-controlled on-demand ice cream vending machine. Developed by *MooBella*, this complex system makes ice cream on demand from room temperature ingredients, flash freezing it to deliver a custom ice cream serving in 45 seconds. The machine contains 12 flavor mixes in both premium and low-carb versions and the option of adding one of three dry-ingredient mix-ins (such as cookies, candies, and nuts), for a total of 96 possible varieties. While it might not seem that ice cream and technology are related, the MooBella ice cream system is high-tech. It runs the Linux operating system, has a touch screen for input, and accesses multiple databases, such as for recipes, machine components, sales, and machine errors. It also includes wireless communication systems that are used by the temperature sensors and to remotely access the machine to check inventory and the status of the machine. Currently installed in two locations in Boston, the company plans to expand first to food service environments, such as hospital and university cafeterias, and then move on to locations where it would not otherwise be possible to experience high quality ice cream, such as airports and sports stadiums. According to the company, MooBella is where taste meets technology. Sweet.

The MooBella ice cream system.

One new and emerging trend in the area of systems management is *identity management* (*IDM*). For a look at a new ice cream vending system, see the Inside the Industry box.

NEW AND EMERGING TRENDS

Identity Management (IDM)

With many companies having multiple systems that require employees to provide user names and passwords to access, as well as the heightened concerns regarding security and privacy today, *identity management* (*IDM*) is a hot topic. In an IS context, IDM usually applies to identifying users and managing access to enterprise systems. One solution to having multiple user names and passwords for the various systems he or she needs to access during the course of the work day is *single sign-on* (*SSO*)—a single ID and password to grant each individual the appropriate rights to all of the systems in the company that he or she is allowed to access. SSO vastly reduces the number of password resets a company has to perform due to forgotten passwords since users have to remember only a single user name and password; for better security, two-factor authentication (such as requiring both a password and a smart card, as in Figure U-27, or requiring a password in conjunction with some type of biometric authentication) and periodic required password resets can be used. Another aspect of IDM is *automated user provisioning*. Automated user provisioning immensely reduces the amount of time required and work involved in managing user accounts as employees are hired, transferred, promoted, and leave the company. IDM also supports a company's ability to comply with federal regulations, such as the Sarbanes-Oxley Act (SOX) and the Healthcare Information Portability and Accountability Act (HIPAA). The goal of developing and implementing an IDM strategy is to improve efficiencies through automation, while improving security and limiting privacy liabilities.

FIGURE U-27
This identity management system uses two-factor authentication.

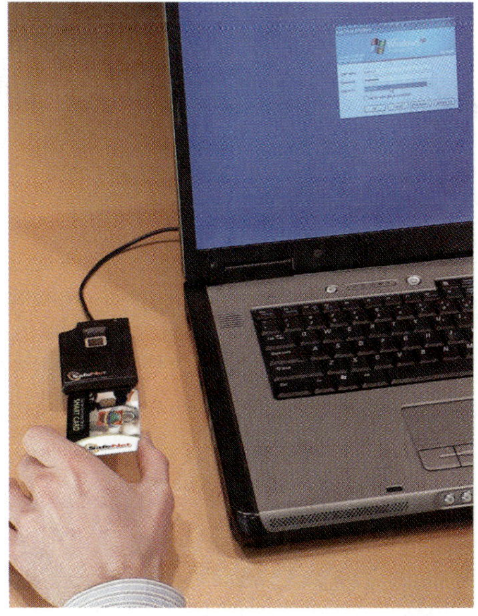

Chapter 13–Program Development and Programming Languages

UPDATE

New program development tools are emerging that help automate and manage application requirements. Over the past year, programming has continued to evolve to meet current needs, but traditional programming languages—such as COBOL—are still in use.

Program Development Update

One trouble spot in the program development process in many organizations is documenting and updating application requirements as they are defined and then modified through the program development process. With a manual requirements management process, Word documents or spreadsheets are typically used to record program requirements and update changes throughout the development process. Since often these documents are hundreds of pages long and need to be shared and updated by numerous individuals, making sure all comments are written down and developers are always working with the most recent version is a struggle at best. According to a recent report by Forrester Research, defects in requirements are the source of the majority of problems identified during testing. Poorly written or inconsistent requirements can lead to costly reworks or even failure of a project. *Requirements definition software* and *requirements management software*, both Application Lifecycle Management (ALM) tools, automate the requirements process.

TIP

Download the Express Editions of Visual Basic, Visual C#, and more for free from the Microsoft Visual Studio Express Web site to try out these languages and practice programming fundamentals.

Requirements definition software is used at the beginning of a project to ensure that software requirements are defined accurately and completely. With requirements definition, collaboration and communication is essential. Consequently, requirements definition software typically allows real-time collaboration between project members and includes visual tools to help better convey the requirements scenario to all project members to avoid communication problems as well as to promote additional discussions and questions. Once the requirements are defined, *requirements management software* is used throughout the development process to manage the requirements as they evolve throughout the project. Since the requirements often change during development—due to technological improvements, competitive pressures, or budget changes, for instance—requirements management software facilitates real-time collaboration between the individuals working on a project to ensure that everyone sees and works with the same version of the current requirements. The goal of requirements management software is to ensure that the delivered solution actually meets the needs of the business. Requirements management software is also increasingly integrated with other software, such as development and testing tools.

Programming Languages Update

Java, Visual Basic, C, C++, and C# are still among the most popular modern programming languages today. The .NET version of Visual Basic (*Visual Basic .NET* or *VB.NET*) is moving up in popularity; according to a recent Computerworld survey of IT managers, VB.NET (see Figure U-28) is the fifth most widely used programming language.

Because COBOL is procedural and not object-oriented, it is not well suited to developing interactive applications or Web-based applications. Instead, its strength lies in batch processing and its stability—reasons why so many COBOL programs exist. In fact, COBOL ranked second in use in the Computerworld survey. However, while 62% of the companies stated they still use COBOL, 36% said they plan to gradually migrate from it. The main reason for not doing it already? The cost of rewriting all those lines of code plus concerns about changing the programs that were written over the course of many years by programmers who may no longer be with the company. It is possible that business processes embedded in the code that no one implicitly knows about will be lost or altered after translation, or the source code for some of the code may no longer exist. To avoid this problem, some companies are leaving most of their back-end software in COBOL and just moving front-end and new applications to other languages. Others are converting existing COBOL applications to COBOL.NET so they can better integrate with other .NET applications.

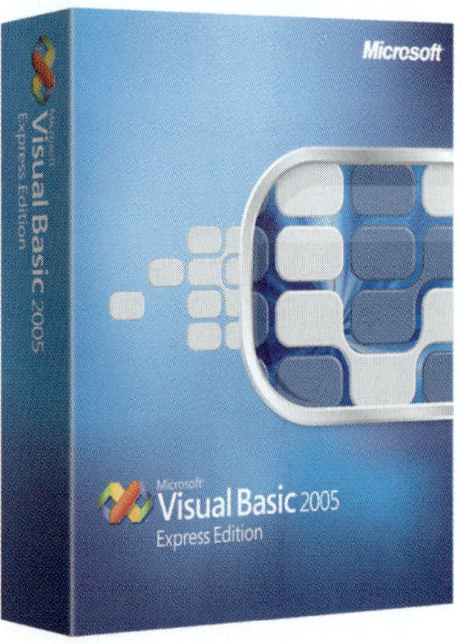

FIGURE U-28
Visual Basic .NET is a popular programming language today.

TECHNOLOGY AND YOU

Programming Contests

Think you're an awesome programmer? There are a number of contests available in which programmers can show their stuff. One of the most widely known is the *Google Global Code Jam*. In this contest, coders compete for bragging rights and a $10,000 prize, and Google gets a firsthand look at the best and the brightest–potential future Googlers. The contest begins with a timed online qualification round in which contestants have 60 minutes to code solutions for two problems. Solutions must be original and can be coded in Java, C++, C#, VB.NET, or Python. The submitted solutions are tested, and then the individuals with the highest scores move on through two more online rounds. The top 100 scorers from Round 2 advance to the Championship Round, which took place this year at Google's New York City offices. This year's contest attracted a record number of contestants–over 21,000–from all over the world, and the winner was a 21-year old student at Moscow State University (shown competing in the accompanying photograph). The annual Google Global Code Jam is produced in conjunction with TopCoder, a leader in programming competitions. At any given time, TopCoder offers online competitions in software design, development, assembly, and testing, including some contests specifically for high-school students. While winning a programming contest is good for your reputation and résumé, it can also net you some pretty big bucks. All 100 finalists in the Google contest receive a minimum prize of $750 and an all expenses paid trip to New York.

This Moscow State University student won the 2006 Google Global Code Jam, as well as two TopCoder championships back-to-back.

Another factor affecting programming today is the proliferation of multi-core processors. This new computing direction is creating the need for programmers with multithreading skills who can write safe and efficient code that takes advantage of the multi-core CPUs.

NEW AND EMERGING TRENDS

One emerging programming language is *Python*. For a look at the programming contests available for both professional and amateur coders alike, see the Technology and You box.

Python

Python (see Figure U-29) is a dynamic object-oriented programming language. It can be used to develop a variety of applications, including games and desktop, scientific, database, and Web applications. Python programs run on computers using the Windows, Linux, Unix, Mac OS X, or OS/2 operating systems, as well as on Palm and Nokia mobile devices. Although the language was originally developed in the early 1990s, it is just recently gaining a large following. Python is now widely used by many large organizations, including NASA, Google, Honeywell, and the New York Stock Exchange, and some colleges—such as MIT—are replacing other languages with Python for some programming courses.

FIGURE U-29

The Python programming language.

Comments are marked by a pound symbol in the first column.

```
# Initialize variable
total = 0.0

# Input a number, add it to the total, and repeat
# until two numbers have been entered
for iteration in range(2):
    text = raw_input("Enter number: ")
    total = total + float(text)

# Print the sum
print "The sum of the numbers you entered is", total
```

The indented statements in this For statement will be executed two times.

Chapter 14—Databases and Database Management Systems

UPDATE

The past year has brought a new *hybrid XML/relational database management program*, as well as continued concerns about database security.

Hybrid XML/Relational Databases

This year, IBM released *DB2 9* (previously code-named *Viper*), the most recent version of IBM's DB2 relational database management system. One new feature that sets this program apart is that is a *hybrid XML/relational database server*. Several vendors have implemented XML data management capabilities into their relational database management systems, but DB2 9's *pureXMLTM* feature goes one step further by allowing XML data to be entered into a database while preserving its structure (the XML record itself and all its properties). This means that nonrelational business data (such as Excel spreadsheets or word processing documents) can be easily and efficiently combined with traditional relational data in the same database. Keeping the XML data structure intact allows queries and other data operations to be much more efficient—IBM claims a performance increase of between two and seven times over Microsoft and Oracle competing products. Both the relational and XML data stored in the database can be accessed via queries and otherwise manipulated, and can work together in a single application as needed (see Figure U-30).

FIGURE U-30
Hybrid XML/relational databases.

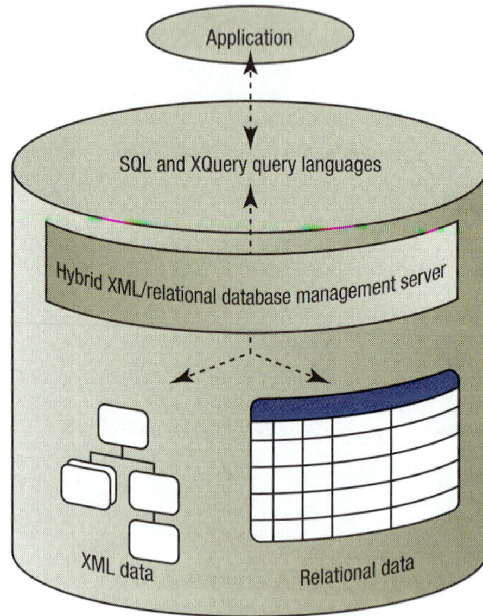

Database Security Update

Unfortunately, database hacking is on the rise. For example, managed security provider SecureWorks reports as many as 8,000 attacks per day on databases owned by its clients, up from an average of 100 to 200 attacks per day just a few months earlier. Hackers from a number of countries are also using more sophisticated attacks to try to access personal and financial data stored on company servers. To better ward off the increased attacks, the Payment Card Industry (PCI) data security standards, released in 2005, were recently updated. The new rules are aimed at protecting credit card data from emerging Web application security threats (such as requiring antivirus software to also check for spyware and other types of malicious software) and also require companies to ensure that any third parties that they deal with (such as Web hosting providers) have proper controls in place for securing credit card data. Merchants who fail to comply with the new rules can face fines or be excluded from processing credit cards.

To help businesses secure their data, an increasing number of database vulnerability accessment tools are available to detect intrusions, compare access data with termination reports to prevent access from newly-terminated employees, search for weak passwords, and more. New *database activity monitoring programs* (see Figure U-31) monitor the database continually for threats in real time and update their knowledge base of known database security threats automatically to protect against new threats as they become known. To avoid security problems at the application level, some companies are using scanning tools during software development to locate and plug security holes in application software while it is being developed instead of after it has been deployed. Stronger database encryption tools are also becoming available.

FIGURE U-31
Alerts displayed in a database activity monitoring program.

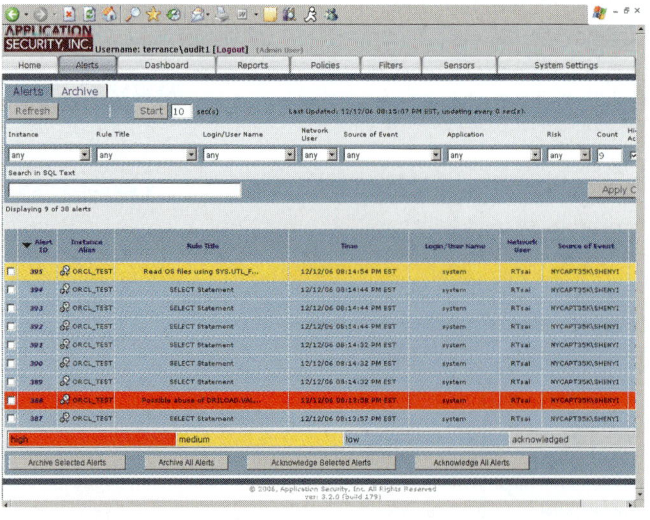

NEW AND EMERGING TRENDS

One new and emerging database trend is the increased use of databases in politics. For a look at a new database to track sex offenders, see the Trend box.

TREND

Law Enforcement Databases

Databases are widely used in law enforcement, from fingerprint databases, to databases containing complaint and arrest records, to evidence databases. One new database—the Sex *Offender Registry and Identification System* (*SORIS*)—is a national biometric database designed specifically to track sex offenders (see the accompanying illustration).

SORIS, the first U.S. sex offender database to use iris biometric technology, stores high resolution digital photographs of the eye. To enter a convicted sex offender into the system, a special camera captures the iris image and creates a unique code to be entered into the registry along with the iris image and information about the sex offender. The database can be accessed by law enforcement officers in any participating county to quickly determine (via an iris scan of a suspect) if that individual is a registered sex offender. The main goal of the system is to identify the tens of thousands of sex offenders nationally who fail to register in the county in which they reside, as required by law. With the typical child sex offender molesting an average of 117 children, according to the National Institute of Mental Health, SORIS is viewed by law enforcement as a tool for protecting children by quickly identifying registered sex offenders in the community.

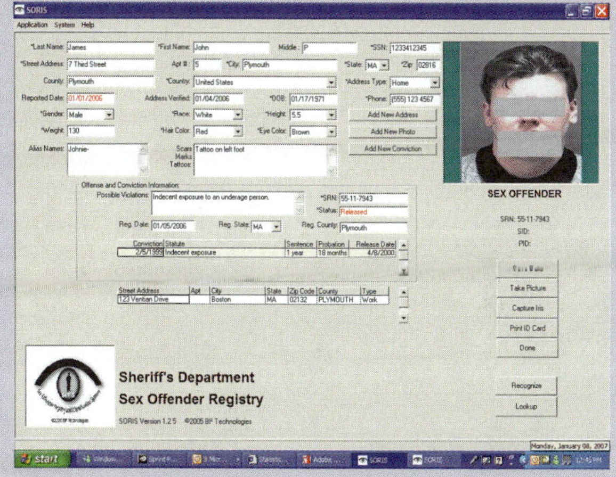

The SORIS database.

New Political Database Applications

There is an increased use of databases in the United States for a variety of political applications. In addition to the new statewide voter registration databases enacted this year to comply with the *2002 Help America Vote Act* (*HAVA*), both the Democratic and Republican parties in the United States have new or improved voter database applications. The Democratic National Committee alone has spent $8 million since the 2004 presidential election to overhaul its core voter database to correct data quality problems found during that election. For example, the Colorado voter database contained more names than the total population of the state, and some Fort Lauderdale, Florida voters were listed as living in the city "Fort" and the state "Lauderdale." The party's database was rebuilt from scratch and now is used in conjunction with data mining and data modeling tools as part of an effort to erase data-quality problems.

One tool used extensively by both parties is *microtargeting*. Microtargeting uses public consumer data, demographics, voting histories, and poll results in conjunction with modeling tools to identify patterns that can be used to identify groups of voters throughout a state who are likely to vote a certain way or feel a particular way about certain issues. The individuals are then targeted for campaining, either in person, on the phone, or via mail, focusing on the issues that are important to those individuals. In the 2006 election, for instance, Republican volunteers campaigned door-to-door in Detroit for the first time since 1962 because microtargeting identified 44,000 traditionally Democratic voters likely to side with Republicans on social issues. Before microtargeting, it wasn't feasible for that party to campaign in areas of the state where less than 50% of the people voted Republican. With microtargeting, parties can literally identify campaign targets household by household.

Another new interesting political database application is available via the *MAPLight.org* Web site. This site links together data about how California state legislators voted on specific bills and sources of campaign donations. Web site visitors can search by bill number, subject, legislator, or interest group to view how a legislator voted on a particular bill and who the top contributors are for that legislator, or how often legislators voted to support bills their top contributors supported.

Chapter 15–Computer Security and Privacy

UPDATE

This past year has brought new security and privacy concerns, as well as new antipiracy tools.

Security and Privacy Update

This year, there were an unprecedented number of high-profile data breaches. In fact, according to the Privacy Rights Clearinghouse, more than 300 incidents of lost or stolen personal data involving more than 67 million records containing personal data were compromised in 2006 alone. Some of the losses were due to hacking or hardware theft; others were losses due to carelessness with papers or storage media containing Social Security numbers or other sensitive data. For instance, computers and storage media were sold or lost; CDs and papers were found in recycling containers, trash cans, and other locations; backup tapes and documents were lost during transit; and documents containing sensitive information were posted online with that information intact, or were faxed or e-mailed to the wrong recipient. In addition to the loss of hardware, a damaged reputation, and the expense and trouble of notifying customers of a data breach (required by law in over half the states in the United States), businesses with data breaches also need to be concerned about legal ramifications.

FIGURE U-32
Common sense precautions for portable PC and mobile device users.

PRECAUTIONS AGAINST DATA LOSS
Install and use encryption, antivirus, antispyware, and firewall software.
Use only secure Wi-Fi connections and disable Wi-Fi and Bluetooth when they are not needed.
Never leave user names, passwords, or other data attached to your PC or inside its carrying case.
Use a plain carrying case to make a portable PC less conspicuous.
Keep an eye on your devices at all times, especially when going through airport security.
Avoid setting your devices on the floor or leaving them in your hotel room.
Back up the data stored on the device regularly.
Consider installing tracking or kill switch software.

In response to this growing problem, businesses and the government are working to improve security procedures.To protect against data leaks via devices plugged into the USB port of a company PC—sometimes referred to as *podslurping*—some businesses are removing those ports entirely. Another option is installing software that controls which devices can be connected to a PC and what those devices are allowed to do, or that records the filenames of or duplicates the contents of all files copied via a USB port. Software can also be used to monitor outgoing e-mail messages to block messages that contain sensitive data in the e-mail message or in a file attachment.

A new alternative for protecting the data on a portable computer if it is stolen is a *kill switch*—software installed on a PC that begins overwriting preselected files multiple times, rendering them unreadable, once the PC is reported as stolen and connects to the Internet. This can be used instead of computer tracking software when a business is less concerned about recovering the hardware than ensuring the data located on the PC is not compromised. Many businesses are also using encryption on all desktop PCs, portable PCs, and smart phones issued to employees. While using encryption with mobile phones hasn't been as much of an issue in the past, with the increased amount of data located on mobile phones today, it is now an important consideration. Figure U-32 lists some common sense precautions for keeping portable PCs and mobile devices safe while on the road. One additional possiblity: using a thin client portable PC that has no hard drive, such as the new *SafeBook* PC that looks like an ordinary notebook PC. Since all programs and data are stored on the company server and accessed via the Internet through a Wi-Fi, Ethernet, or 3G wireless connection, no data is lost and the PC cannot be used if it is stolen.

Antipiracy Update

One somewhat controversial discussion regarding piracy surrounds Windows Vista's new authentication program to ensure that all installations are legal installations. The new system gives users who install Vista 30 days to activate their installation, either online or by phone using the product key that comes with the product (PCs purchased with Vista installed come already activated). If Vista isn't activated within that time period, the system changes to "reduced functionality mode." In this mode, the user is able to use a Web browser for one hour only until being logged off. The user may log in again, but can use only one browser window and will continue to be logged off each hour until the user obtains and registers a legitimate product key. The goal is to make pirated software unusable enough so that individuals who illegally install a copy of Vista on their PC will buy a license. An even more controversial limitation announced by Microsoft was the ability to reinstall Windows Vista on a new computer only one time, unlike earlier versions that could be moved to as many PCs as needed, as long as they were uninstalled from the previous computers. Following a huge outcry by computer enthusiasts who frequently change their PCs, Microsoft announced in late 2006 that the new license terms would not go into effect.

TECHNOLOGY AND YOU

Data Dots: A High-Tech ID System

Would you like a cheap, easy way to identify your PC, iPod, bike, and other expensive personal items? Well, *DataDots* might be the answer.

Based on the concept of hiding secret codes in tiny elements of a document or image, DataDots are pieces of film about the size of a grain of sand with text etched onto them using a sophisticated laser process. The text can be vehicle identification numbers (VINs) for DataDots placed on cars, or unique PIN numbers for DataDots to be placed on personal or business assets (see the accompanying illustration). DataDots are applied using a special adhesive that shows up under any UV black-light. Once a DataDot is located, the data contained inside can be read using a magnifying reader, and law enforcement agents can look up PIN numbers in the DataDot database to determine the owner of an object. Because they are so small, DataDots can be applied to numerous locations on an object—both obvious and hidden—to make it very difficult for a thief to locate and remove every DataDot on an object. In fact, when used in new car production, up to 10,000 DataDots are sprayed on the chassis and other parts of the car.

At less than $25 for 500 DataDots, DataDots can provide relatively cheap peace of mind to individuals who own a variety of expensive electronic devices.

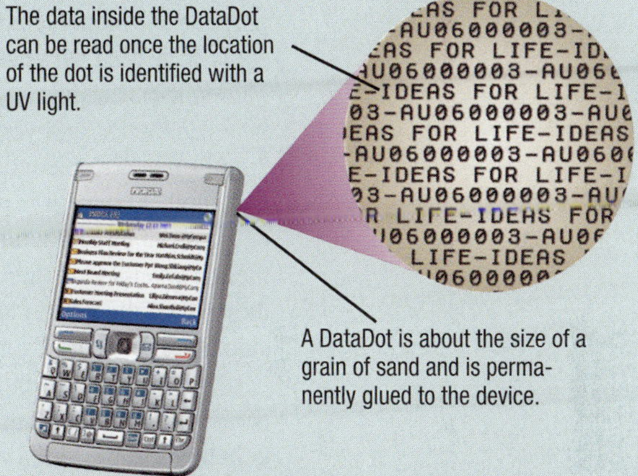

DataDots can be used to identify PCs and other electronic devices.

One new and emerging security safeguard is the locking mobile phone. For a look at a new way of identifying PCs, mobile phones, and other electronic devices, see the Technology and You box.

NEW AND EMERGING TRENDS

Locking Mobile Phones

With an increasing amount of personal data being stored on mobile phones today, as well as the ability of some mobile phones to be used to make purchases and unlock doors, security features that guard against the unauthorized use of a mobile phone are growing increasingly more important. A new security feature now available on some Japanese mobile phones is designed to only allow the phone to be used by its owner. The NTT DoCoMo phone shown in Figure U-33 comes with a security key—a small black card about the size of a movie-ticket stub. The card connects wirelessly to the phone and locks the phone if the card moves too far away (the distance is specified by the user, but can be 26, 66, or 130 feet away). The idea is for the user to keep the security key in his or her bag or pocket, and if the phone is lost or stolen, it can't be used (if the owner loses the security key, he or she can enter a password to unlock the phone). To protect the data on the phone from unauthorized access, the phone also comes with a face recognition option. After initially taking a variety of photos of himself or herself with the phone's camera, the user takes another photo with the phone's camera to unlock the phone, assuming the new photo matches the stored one. To protect against someone trying to access data on a phone using a photograph of the owner, the face recognition software is designed to recognize whether or not the eyes are blinking. One additional useful feature is built-in GPS tracking software that allows the owner to locate its position via a Web site if the phone is lost or stolen.

FIGURE U-33
Locking mobile phones.

Chapter 16–Intellectual Property Rights, Ethics, Health, Access, and the Environment

UPDATE

This past year has brought more concerns about health risks from the use of technology, as well as new concerns about energy conservation.

Health Risk Update

A number of health and safety concerns related to the use of technology came into the forefront this past year. For instance, some notebook computers are now hot enough to burn a person's lap, and some notebook batteries caught on fire due to a manufacturing defect. Many portable PC manufacturers now warn against letting any part of the PC touch your body (one study measured the peak temperature on the underside of a typical notebook PC at over 139° Fahrenheit), and a variety of *laptops desks* (see Figure U-34) are now available to place between the PC and your lap for those occasions when a better work surface is not available. And Dell and Apple recalled the nearly 6 million Sony batteries at risk for catching on fire.

Another concern is noise-induced hearing loss due to headset use. Today's portable digital devices can be turned up high without distortion, and the earbud headsets typically used with them deliver sound directly into the ear. In addition, people often listen to these devices while they are on the go and have a tendency to increase the volume in an attempt to drown out outside noise, further posing a risk to their hearing. To protect against hearing loss, experts suggest a 60/60 rule—using earbuds for only about 60 minutes per day with the volume less than 60% of the device's maximum volume. For extended use, *noise reduction headphones* that help block out external noise to allow listeners to hear music better at lower volumes can help.

Another new danger that came into the forefront this year is text messaging while driving. There were many cases of texting-related car accidents, including several fatalities. A survey by the the national "Drive for Life" safety initiative found that six percent of all Americans (and 32% of all drivers 16 to 20 years old) said they have read or sent a text message while driving, and one study in Great Britain found that almost 60% of people under 30 text message while they drive. This year, several states in the United States made talking on the phone using a handheld mobile phone illegal while driving. To comply with the law, drivers must place calls using hands-free devices, such as via a Bluetooth headset or a speakerphone setup (refer again to Figure U-34). While most of these laws do not specifically include text messaging, that is expected to soon change.

FIGURE U-34
Personal safety devices.

LAPTOP DESKS
Help avoid getting burned from a hot notebook PC.

BLUETOOTH HEADSETS
Allow drivers to place mobile phone calls more safely while driving.

Green Computing Update

With the increased cost of electricity today, power consumption and heat generation by computers is a key concern for businesses today. Today's faster and more powerful computers tend to use more energy in the first place plus run hotter, which leads to greater cooling costs. Servers, in particular, are power-hungry, using approximately 135 watts per processor today compared to 30 watts per processor five years ago. In response to this growing problem, manufacturers are working to develop more energy efficient PCs, microprocessors, surge suppressors, and other computer components. Virtualization also helps by reducing the overall number of servers required.

Because computer systems still draw quite a bit of power when they are in standby mode with a screen saver on, business and schools are also increasingly using software to

TREND

Nano Fans: The Fan of the Future?

Computers are running hotter than ever. Devices are getting smaller, and processors are working at increasingly faster speeds in smaller spaces, generating even more heat than in the past. To compensate, researchers are working to develop new cooling techniques. For instance, researchers from the University of Washington are designing a tiny silicon-based cooling device that uses ionized air and an electric field to cool the surface. The device has no moving parts and uses minimal energy consumption. To cool a CPU or other component the device is located by, an electrode tip is set to a high voltage, creating a high electric field that strips electrons from molecules of oxygen and nitrogen in the air, ionizing them. These positively charged ions then flow from the electrode tip to a negatively charged collector electrode. As the ions move towards the collector electrode, they drag the surrounding air with them, creating a net flow of air to cool the area beneath the collector electrode (see the accompanying illustration). The voltage being applied to the electrode tip can be modified to cool the area to different temperatures, and since the device is made of silicon, it could eventually be integrated into CPUs and other computer components during manufacturing. While just in the prototype stage at the moment, researchers estimate that a commercial product based on this technology may reach the market by 2010.

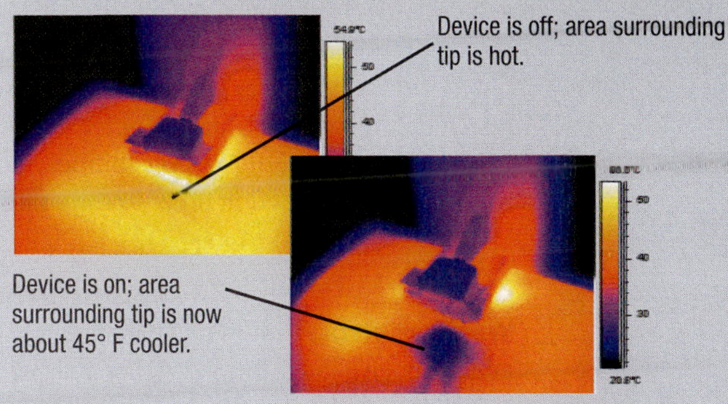

Nano fan in use.

automatically shut down computers when they are not in use. For instance, Seminole Community College in Florida is currently installing automated shutdown software on 3,500 PCs and estimates that the technology may save up to $65,000 per year in electricity costs. And mobile phone manufacturers are joining together to reduce the environmental impact of their products, including displaying reminders on mobile phones to unplug them from their chargers when they are fully charged since chargers can draw up to five watts per hour even if nothing is plugged into them. For alternate power, UPSs that are powered by *flywheels*, hydrogen fuel cell battery chargers, and an increasing number of solar panel devices (see the backpack notebook case with a built-in solar charging system in Figure U-35) are becoming available.

FIGURE U-35
Solar backpacks can be used to both carry and charge electronic gear.

NEW AND EMERGING TRENDS

One new and emerging trend in the area of access to technology is the growing number of cities implementing free or low-cost Wi-Fi. For a look at a possiblity for cooling PCs in the future, see the Trend box.

Free Wi-Fi

Free or low-cost city-wide Wi-Fi networks are continuing to appear. Cities across the United States are developing wireless mesh networks and funding hot spots to provide Internet access to their citizens. In addition to being a civic gesture, some cities are using the incentive of free Wi-Fi to attract people to downtown areas, and some use a special city home page displayed when users first connect to the network that contains links to services available in the city—essentially free advertising for the city and local businesses. Now, in addition to local governments, two big players have jumped on the free Wi-Fi bandwagon. This year, Google launched a free Wi-Fi network for the city of Mountain View, California, and is in the process of creating one for San Francisco, and Microsoft announced that it will develop a free Wi-Fi network for Portland, Oregon.

EXPERT INSIGHT ON . . .

Windows Vista

Microsoft

A conversation with **GRAHAM WATSON**

Senior Product Manager, Vista Group, Microsoft

My Background . . .

I actually got started with computers at school when I discovered I could either take a lesson where I played with a computer terminal or one involving cross-country running in winter! I quickly worked out that the computer was more fun! I'm now part of the Windows Client Product Marketing Group at Microsoft. My specific responsibilities include making sure that the IT professional has the tools and information they need in order to fully understand and be able to deploy and support Windows Vista.

"One of the biggest impacts on society that Windows Vista will have is enhanced security for users."

The Most Important Developments this Past Year . . .

Windows Vista. Windows is the operating system used by over 90% of the world's personal computers, and it's been a long time since there has been a major update. Windows Vista is a major step forward and offers hundreds of useful improvements over older versions of Windows.

The Internet. This isn't really something that occurred just during 2006 obviously, but the functionality, usage, and reach of the Internet continues to grow in leaps and bounds each year. Things such as music downloads, blogs, RSS feeds, instant messaging, Voice over IP, and more continue to extend the usefulness of the Internet far beyond the initial concept of linked documents.

Search. One issue with the Internet (and storage technologies) is the difficulty in finding what you need. Search technologies have improved tremendously over the last year, and now make it much easier to find the right information without having to enter complex queries. Extending search to encompass files on your own machine and on local network resources has helped even more.

The Impact of Windows Vista . . .

One of the biggest impacts on society that Windows Vista will have is enhanced security for users. One problem with the connectivity that computers provide is that it can also provide thieves and other miscreants with access to you. Windows Vista is the most secure mass market operating system, and its introduction will improve resilience against the most common forms of attack.

One of the biggest impacts on users' lives will be the improved user interface—not just the new visual effects, but other things, such as the enhanced help facilities, built-in search, simpler task flows, and many other improvements.

Graham Watson is a Senior Product Manager in the Windows Client Product Marketing Group at Microsoft. He has worked for Microsoft for 13 years, initially as an enterprise infrastructure consultant. Prior to his current position, he worked as a computer operator and a support engineer. In all, he has over 30 years of experience working with computer systems, networks, and other computer-related areas. Graham has a Bachelor of Arts degree in Computer Studies and, along with his client, had the honor of sending the first ever production e-mail from Microsoft Exchange.

Students should also know that there are many features of Windows Vista which would be of real help to a student . . .

What a Student Should Know about Windows Vista Before Upgrading . . .

The most important things to know before you upgrade your computer to Windows Vista are if the hardware is capable of running the operating system and if any of your applications won't work. Students should also know that there are many features of Windows Vista which would be of real help to a student, including improved security, search, usability, and digital media management.

How I Use this Technology . . .

There are two main areas where computers and Windows Vista in particular affect me personally. The first one is the most obvious—it provides me with highly enjoyable employment! The second one is the same as for many people—my family and friends are all connected, and I often communicate with my wife and children via e-mail or IM. I also do most of my shopping via the Internet—I think I got most of my Christmas shopping done without leaving my desk. It's hard to imagine how I would live my life without Windows Vista!

What the Future Holds . . .

Connectivity is probably the biggest thing—not just between people, but also between parts of computer applications. Web services will continue to grow in importance, and Windows Vista, together with .NET 3.0, will further enable the ability to quickly develop applications by "stitching together" services obtained from a variety of companies and building on them to fulfill specific needs. Mobility is another interesting area—as computers become smaller, more powerful, and more connected, additional opportunities open up. On one hand, we are finding some devices becoming more general purpose (for example, your cell phone may also take pictures and play music), but at the same time there is an opposite movement towards more dedicated devices which work together better. Some people just want a simple-to-use cell phone.

I expect that the software we know today will continue to evolve and get more sophisticated but simpler to use—for example, Microsoft Office continues to improve on its ability to very easily create very professional documents. There will probably be at least one "left field" innovation—something that will be obvious once it's taken off, but almost unnoticed until that time. Examples of this from the last few years include digital video recorders, such as TiVo (or Windows Media Center Edition), and Voice over IP. Possibilities for the future include intelligent search (imagine being able to ask your computer almost any question in the same way you would ask a friend, and get a single, correct answer) and improved connectivity between computers and devices (imagine phoning a friend and arranging to meet them, and then automatically getting directions given to you by your car, meetings set up and moved, flights booked, etc.).

My Advice to Students . . .

Make sure you REALLY know what you want to do with your career. Are you interested purely in the technology, or in its application? For people involved in the computer industry to any degree in the future, hybrid skills will be important—for example, being an expert in astronomy, medical research, or financial investments *together with* IT skills. And two key things I'd look for would be enthusiasm and confidence—backed up by practical experience.

>For more information on Microsoft, visit www.microsoft.com. For interesting IT-related information, visit www.technet.com and www.msdn.com. To set up a personalized browser home page, visit www.live.com. To check if your PC is Vista ready, go to www.microsoft.com/windowsvista/getready.

Windows Vista and You

The long-awaited upgrade to Windows XP is here! But do you want to upgrade your current computer to Windows Vista? *Can* you run Windows Vista on your computer? Which edition of Vista should you get if you are buying a new PC? The purpose of this guide is to give you a closer look at Windows Vista and provide you with answers to these and other Vista-related questions.

Look and Features

One of the most obvious initial changes in Windows Vista is the interface. Assuming that your edition of Vista and your hardware allow it, you have the option of using the new *Aero* interface. Aero is a more graphical interface that uses glass-like transparency, vibrant colors, and dynamic elements to make the Vista experience more enjoyable (see Figure U-36). For instance, placing your mouse over a button on the taskbar shows a *live thumbnail* of the contents of that window, and pressing Alt+Tab invokes *Windows Flip*—a thumbnail display of all open windows. *Flip 3D* (invoked by pressing Windows+Tab) lets you flip through your open windows like playing cards. Windows Vista also includes a new *Sidebar* that contains *gadgets*—integrated and add-on small applications that perform a variety of tasks, such as displaying RSS feeds, stock tickers, weather information, clocks, calendars, notepads, news headlines, and more. The Start menu is more streamlined and contains an *Instant Search* feature that allows you to quickly find any document or program located on your PC. Vista also contains several built-in security features, such as the *Windows Defender* and *Windows Firewall* programs, and much improved networking, collaboration, and syncronization tools. The primary multimedia improvements are the integration of *Windows Media Center* into some editions of Vista, an improved *Windows Movie Maker* program, a new *Windows Photo Gallery* for organizing, printing, and editing digital photographs, and a new *Windows DVD Maker* for built-in DVD-burning support.

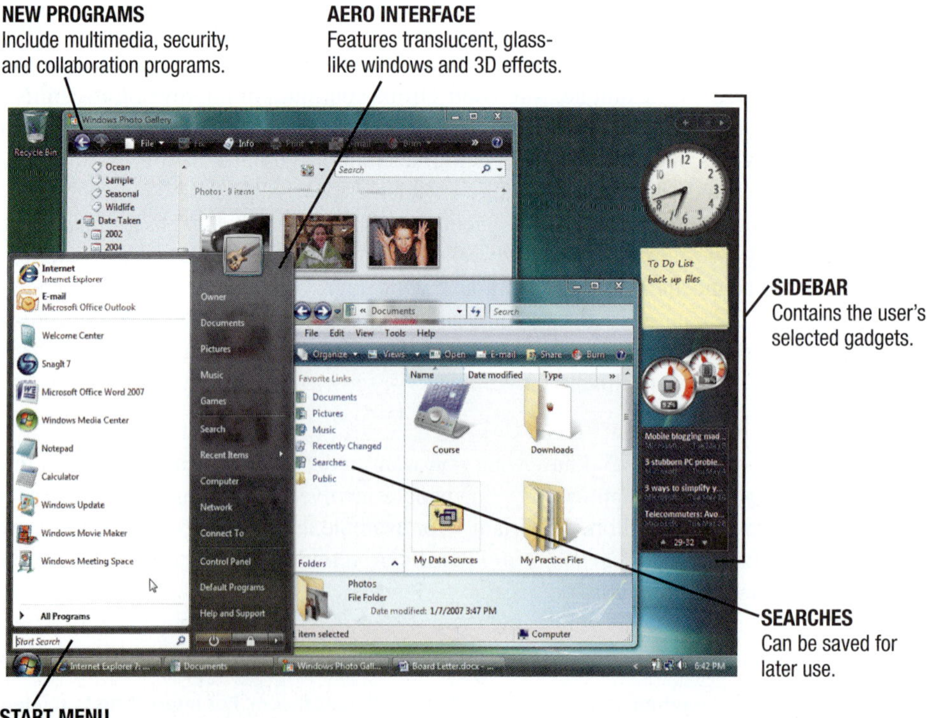

FIGURE U-36
Windows Vista.

FEATURES	MICROSOFT VISTA EDITION			
	HOME BASIC	HOME PREMIUM	BUSINESS	ULTIMATE
Enhanced security (Windows Defender and Firewall)	✓	✓	✓	✓
Search and browsing (Instant Search and (Internet Explorer 7)	✓	✓	✓	✓
Vista experience (Aero and Flip 3D)*		✓	✓	✓
Portable PCs (Windows Mobility and Tablet PC support)		✓	✓	✓
Collaboration (Windows Meeting Space)		✓	✓	✓
Home entertainment (Windows Media Center)		✓		✓
Business backup, networking, and remote desktop support			✓	✓
Data protection (BitLocker Drive Encryption)				✓
Suggested full price:	$199	$239	$299	$399
Suggested upgrade price:	$100	$159	$199	$259
Can upgrade from:	XP Home	XP Home or Media Center	XP Home, Tablet PC, or Professional	XP Home, Media Center, Tablet PC, or Professional

* Requires a Windows Vista Premium Ready PC

FIGURE U-37
Windows Vista features by edition.

Editions

So, which edition of Windows Vista should you get? Vista has four basic editions: *Home Basic*, *Home Premium*, *Business*, and *Ultimate*. As shown in Figure U-37, Home Basic edition users cannot run the Aero interface or many other of the new Vista features. Consquently, the Home Premium edition will likely be the most popular choice for home users who have the hardware necessary to run Aero and the other graphical features, as discussed shortly. Business users will typically select the Business or Ultimate editions. Individuals with 64-bit PCs can also choose between a 32-bit and 64-bit version of the program. Individuals with computers running Windows 2000 or Windows XP can buy an *upgrade copy* of Windows Vista instead of a full version, though a *clean install* (where you have to reinstall your applications and data after Vista is installed on your PC) is required for some upgrade paths, as shown in Figure U-37.

Hardware Requirements and Upgrades

Beginning in January 2007, Windows Vista will be available installed on new computers. Users who bought Windows XP PCs in late 2006 should have a coupon to upgrade to Vista for free. Individuals with older PCs will need to decide if they want to upgrade their current operating system to Vista. One important consideration for all computer users considering Vista in any form is the increased hardware requirements. In addition to requiring a fairly fast CPU and a decent amount of memory, Vista also has specific graphics requirements in order to be able to use the Aero interface. Individuals purchasing new computers should pay attention to whether the PC is classified as *Windows Vista Capable* or *Windows Vista Premium Ready*. The minimum specifications for each classification are listed in the

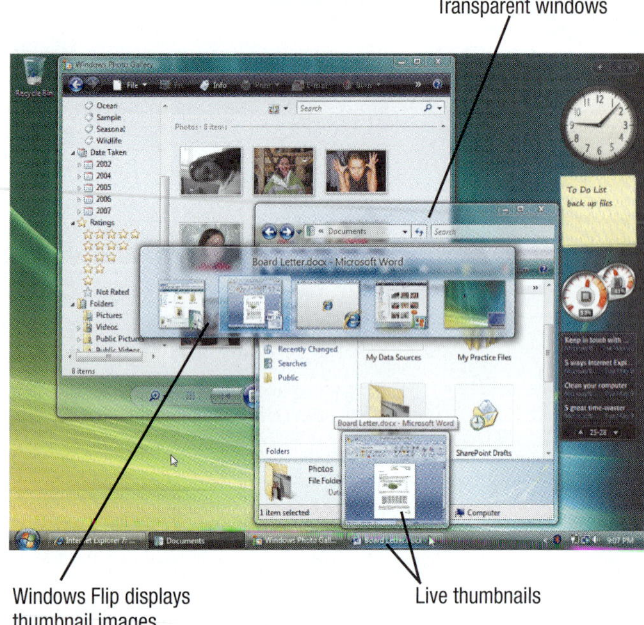

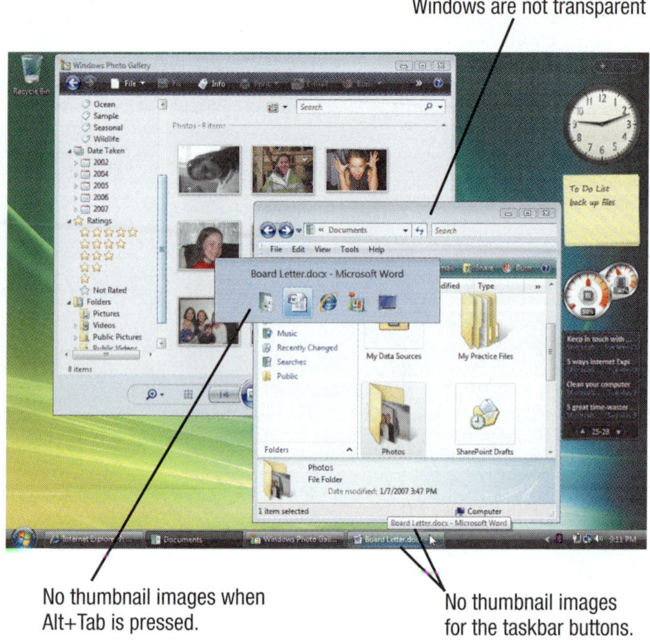

FIGURE U-38
Windows Vista Aero feature.

Technology and You box. It is important for computer buyers to realize that computers meeting only the Windows Vista Capable specifications can run the core Vista features, but not the Aero interface or the other more graphical features. Anyone wanting these additional features will need to buy a Windows Vista Premium Ready computer or upgrade their existing PC to meet (or, ideally, surpass) the Windows Vista Premium Ready specifications. Figure U-38 shows the same desktop with and without the Aero experience enabled.

Because some of the specifications (such as for the graphics card) are difficult for many users to evaluate on a PC they may wish to upgrade to Vista, Microsoft has a *Windows Vista Upgrade Advisor* tool available via its Web site to help users decide if they can upgrade to Vista. After the Upgrade Advisor software is downloaded and installed, it scans your system and prepares a report of any problems (such as insufficient RAM or disk space) and informs you of which edition of Vista best fits your PC (see Figure U-39). It also checks for known compatibility issues with your PC's hardware and any attached peripherals. Individuals upgrading to Windows Vista should back up their data located on their computers before installing Vista and then visit Windows Update to download any new patches, drivers, and other software that is now available. If desired, individuals can choose a clean install instead of an upgrade; a clean install installs Vista and overwrites all files (including software and data files) on the PC.

FIGURE U-39
The Upgrade Advisor helps users determine if their existing PC can run Vista.

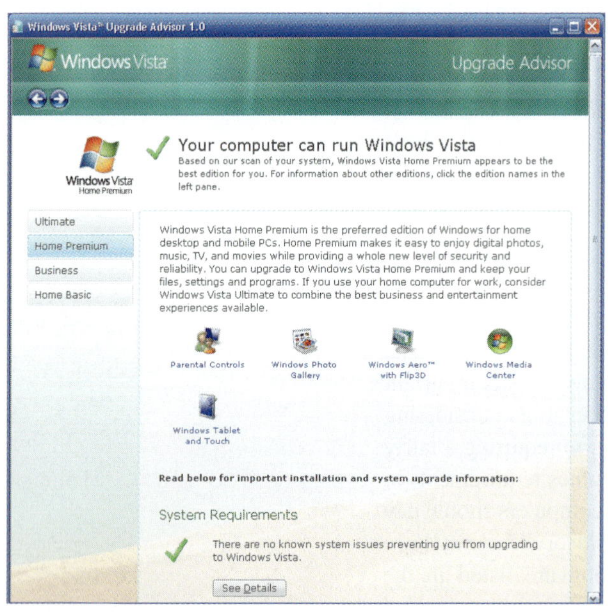

TECHNOLOGY AND YOU

Can My PC Run Vista?

If you want to install Windows Vista on your existing PC, it's crucial to ensure that you have the appropriate hardware to use the features of Vista that you want to use. For instance, if you have only 512 MB of RAM or a video card that doesn't meet Vista's requirements, you may be able to run Vista but you won't be able to use the Aero interface. The accompanying table lists the minimum specifications to run the basic features of Vista (Windows Vista Capable PC) or to run Vista with the Aero interface and the other graphical features of Vista (Windows Vista Premium Ready PC). One way to evaluate an existing PC is to run the Windows Vista Upgrade Advisor tool (see Figure U-39) available through the Microsoft Web site. But perhaps the most important thing to realize about Vista's minimum specifications is that they are *minimum specifications*. For optimal performance, a good rule of thumb is to double the minimum RAM requirement. For Windows Vista, this equates to 1 GB of RAM for basic features and 2 GB for the full Aero experience.

WINDOWS VISTA CAPABLE PC	WINDOWS VISTA PREMIUM READY PC
800 MHz 32-bit or 64-bit processor	1 GHz 32-bit or 64-bit processor
512 MB of RAM	1 GB of RAM
DirectX 9 capable graphics processor	DirectX 9 graphics processor that has 128 MB of graphics memory (if it is not shared memory) and supports Windows Display Driver Module (WDDM), Pixel Shader 2.0, and 32 bits per pixel
	40 GB of hard drive capacity with at least 15 GB free space
	DVD drive
	Audio output capability
	Internet access

Windows Vista minimum hardware requirements.

TECH NEWS VIDEO PROJECTS

These two new Tech News Video Projects are designed to be used in conjunction with selected CNET TV video clips (accessible through the Online Companion site at www.course.com/uc11). These projects may be assigned at any time during the course—check with your instructor if you are not clear about when you are expected to complete these projects.

Instructions: First watch the project's video either individually or as a class, according to your instructor's directions, and then form an opinion on the issue detailed in the video and the project. Be prepared to discuss your position on this issue (in class, via an online class discussion group, or in a class chat room) or write a short paper stating and supporting your opinion, depending on your instructor's directions. Use the video clip and the questions asked in the project instructions as the foundation for your response; you might also be asked to do research and provide additional resources to support your opinion.

1. iPods and Hearing Loss The extensive use of headphones with digital media devices today has led to concerns about the possible long-term effects on people's hearing. The accompanying video clip discusses the possible dangers of listening to an iPod and what you can do to protect your hearing.

TECH NEWS VIDEO PROJECT

To view the "iPods and Hearing Loss" video clip, go to www.course.com/uc11

After watching the video, think about the impact of technology on your personal health. When you listen to your iPod or use your computer, do you consider the possible health affects? Have you ever accidentally turned up the volume on your iPod and potentially hurt your ears? Do you find that you need to increase the volume when you are in noisy surroundings? Have you ever developed a headache or backache when working on your PC? Would you ever considering purchasing ergonomic hardware or safer headphones to protect yourself? According to the video, using an iPod for too long or with the volumne turned up too high can permanently damage your hearing. Should it be up to the consumer or hardware manufacturers to ensure that computers and other digital devices don't endanger the health of consumers?

Form an opinion: Assuming that the use of computers and other digital devices can permanently affect your health, whose responsibility is it to ensure your health is protected? You? Hardware manufacturers? The government?

2. Picking Secure Passwords With so many activities on the Web requiring passwords today, good passwords techniques are essential. The accompanying video clip discusses how to select a secure password and ways you can manage the various passwords that you use.

TECH NEWS VIDEO PROJECT

To view the "Picking Secure Passwords" video clip, go to www.course.com/uc11

After watching the video, think about the Web site passwords you use. According to the criteria listed in the video, are they secure? Do you change them frequently? Do you use the same password for all Web sites? Have you ever been concerned about someone being able to crack your passwords and access your online accounts? Do you think it's feasible for computer users today to follow good password techniques? Do the benefits of secure passwords outweigh the inconvience? The video discusses the option of using password managers or biometric system to help users remember their passwords—are these tools the answer?

Form an opinion: How important is it today for users to follow secure password techniques? Should Web sites require the use of secure passwords and require users to change them at regular intervals?

CREDITS

Throughout the 2007 Update: Screen shots of Microsoft Word and Windows reprinted with permission from Microsoft Corporation. Internet Interface: Copyright Microsoft Explorer reprinted with permission from Microsoft Corporation.
Figure U-1a, Photo courtesy of Nokia. Copyright © 2006 Nokia. All rights reserved. Nokia and Nokia Connecting People are registered trademarks of Nokia Corporation.; **Figure U-1b**, Courtesy of Sony; **Figure Chapter 1 Trend**, Courtesy of www.PumpOne.com; **Figure U-3**, Courtesy of Intel Corporation; **Figure U-4**, Courtesy of BMC Cycling; **Figure U-5**, Courtesy of Intel Corporation; **Figure U-6**, Courtesy of Samsung; **Figure U-7**, Courtesy of Imation; **Figure Chapter 3 Trend**, © AP Wide World Photos; **Figure U-8**, Photo courtesy of Nokia. Copyright © 2006 Nokia. All rights reserved. Nokia and Nokia Connecting People are registered trademarks of Nokia Corporation.; **Figure U-9**, Courtesy of Lexar Media, Inc.; **Figure U-10**, Courtesy of Philips Research; **Figure Chapter 4 Trend**, Courtesy of NIST; **Figure Chapter 5 You**, Courtesy of PortalPlayer; **Figure U-13a**, Courtesy of Zoho.; **Figure U-13b**, Google screenshot © Google Inc. and is used with permission. Courtesy of Google; **Figure U-14**, Courtesy of Microsoft Corporation; **Figure U-15**, Courtesy of Cisco Systems, Inc.; **Figure U-16**, Courtesy of Motorola, Inc.; **Figure Chapter 7 You**, Courtesy of SpotScout, Inc.; **Figure U-18**, Courtesy of Vonage; **Figure Chapter 8 You**, Courtesy of Ning, Inc.; **Figure U-19**, Courtesy of Netcraft; **Figure Chapter 9 Trend**, Courtesy of Dan Leveille (www.dan-lev.com); **Figure U-21**, Extreme Hangman ™ & © 2006 SkyZone Entertainment, Inc. All rights reserved. Used with permission.; **Figure U-22**, Photo courtesy of Nokia. Copyright © 2006 Nokia. All rights reserved. Nokia and Nokia Connecting People are registered trademarks of Nokia Corporation.; **Figure U-23**, Courtesy USC Institute for Creative Technologies; **Figure U-24**, Courtesy of Philips Research; **Figure U-25**, Courtesy of Zazzle; **Figure Chapter 11 Trend**, Courtesy of *JAMCAM PRODUCTIONS INC.* AOL and the triangle logo are registered trademarks of AOL LLC. Used with Permission. Gold Rush and the Gold Rush logos are courtesy of Mark Burnett Productions. TM and © 2006 JMBP, Inc. All Rights Reserved.; **Figure U-26**, Courtesy of Bluetooth SIG; **Figure U-27**, Courtesy of SafeNet Inc.; **Figure Chapter 12 Inside**, Courtesy of Moobella; **Figure U-28**, Courtesy of Microsoft Corporation; **Figure Chapter 13 You**, Courtesy of Topcoder; **Figure U-31**, Courtesy of Application Security, Inc.; **Figure Chapter 14 Trend**, Courtesy of BI2 Technologies; **Figure U-33**, Courtesy of NTT DoCoMo; **Figure Chapter 15 You a**, Photo courtesy of Nokia. Copyright © 2006 Nokia. All rights reserved. Nokia and Nokia Connecting People are registered trademarks of Nokia Corporation.; **Figure Chapter 15 You b**, Courtesy of DataDotsDNA; **Figure U-34a**, Courtesy of LapWorks Inc., home of the Laptop Desk protective platform for lap or desk use.; **Figure U-34b**, Courtesy of Parrot; **Figure U-35**, Courtesy of Innovus Designs, Inc.; **Figure Chapter 16 Trend**, Courtesy of Kronos Air Technologies and the University of Washington; **Expert Insight**, Courtesy of Microsoft Corporation.

REFERENCES AND RESOURCES GUIDE

INTRODUCTION

When working on a PC, you often need to look up information related to computers. For instance, you may need to find out when the IBM PC was first invented, you may want tips about what to consider when buying a PC, or you may want to learn how to send an e-mail message. To help you with the tasks just mentioned and more, this References and Resources Guide brings together in one convenient location a collection of computer-related references and resources. Some of the resources are located in this handy section; these resources plus additional resources (such as information on numbering systems, characteristics of past and current CPUs, and URLs for useful Web resources) are located on the Web site that accompanies this textbook, which is located at www.course.com/uc11.

OUTLINE

Computer History Timeline R-2

Coding Charts R-8

Guide to Buying a PC R-10

E-Mail Fundamentals R-15

Answers to Self-Quiz R-17

COMPUTER HISTORY TIMELINE

The earliest recorded calculating device, the abacus, is believed to have been invented by the Babylonians sometime between 500 B.C. and 100 B.C. It and similar types of counting boards were used solely for counting.

500 B.C.

1621

The slide rule, a precursor to the electronic calculator, was invented. Used primarily to perform multiplication, division, square roots, and the calculation of logarithms, its wide-spread use continued until the 1970's.

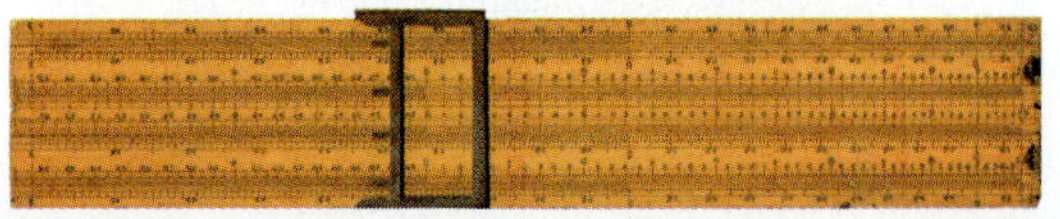

Blaise Pascal invented the first mechanical calculator, called the Pascaline Arithmetic Machine. It had the capacity for eight digits and could add and subtract.

1642

1804

French silk weaver Joseph-Marie Jacquard built a loom that read holes punched on a series of small sheets of hardwood to control the pattern weaved. This automated machine introduced the use of punch cards and showed that they could be used to convey a series of instructions.

Dr. John V. Atanasoff and Clifford Berry designed and built ABC (for Atanasoff-Berry Computer), the world's first electronic computer.

1937

1944

The Mark I, considered to be the first digital computer, was introduced by IBM. It was developed in cooperation with Harvard University, was more than 50 feet long, weighed almost five tons, and used electromechanical relays to solve addition problems in less than a second; multiplication and division took about six and twelve seconds, respectively.

Precomputers and Early Computers

Precomputers and Early Computers (before approximately 1945)

Most precomputers and early computers were mechanical machines that worked with gears and levers. Electromechanical devices (using both electricity and gears and levers) were developed toward the end of this era.

First Generation (approximately 1946–1957)

Powered by vacuum tubes, these computers were faster than electromechanical machines, but they were large and bulky, generated excessive heat, and had to be physically wired and reset to run programs. Input was primarily on punch cards; output was on punch cards or paper. Machine and assembly languages were used to program these computers.

The UNIVAC 1, the first computer to be mass produced for general use, was introduced by Remington Rand. In 1952, it was used to analyze votes in the U.S. presidential election and correctly predicted that Dwight D. Eisenhower would be the victor only 45 minutes after the polls closed, though the results were not aired immediately because they weren't trusted.

1951

The COBOL programming language was developed by a committee headed by Dr. Grace Hopper.

1960

The first floppy disk (8 inches in diameter) was introduced.

1967

UNIX was developed at AT&T's Bell Laboratories; Advanced Micro Devices (AMD) was formed; and ARPANET (the predecessor of today's Internet) was established.

IBM unbundled some of its hardware and software and began selling them separately, allowing other software companies to emerge.

1969

First Generation | Second Generation | Third Generation

1947

John Bardeen, Walter Brattain, and William Shockley invented the transistor, which had the same capabilities as a vacuum tube but was faster, broke less often, used less power, and created less heat. They won a Nobel Prize for their invention in 1956 and computers began to be built with transistors shortly afterwards.

1957

The FORTRAN programming language was introduced.

1964

The first mouse was invented by Doug Engelbart.

The IBM System/360 computer was introduced. Unlike previous computers, System/360 contained a full line of compatible computers, making upgrading easier.

1968

Robert Noyce and Gordon Moore founded the Intel Corporation.

Second Generation (approximately 1958–1963)

Second-generation computers used transistors instead of vacuum tubes. They allowed the computer to be physically smaller, more powerful, more reliable, and faster than before. Input was primarily on punch cards and magnetic tape; output was on punch cards and paper; and magnetic tape and disks were used for storage. High-level programming languages were used with these computers.

Third Generation (approximately 1964–1970)

The third generation of computers evolved when integrated circuits (IC)—computer chips—began being used instead of conventional transistors. Computers became even smaller and more reliable. Keyboards and monitors were introduced for input and output; magnetic disks were used for storage. The emergence of the operating system meant that operators no longer had to manually reset relays and wiring.

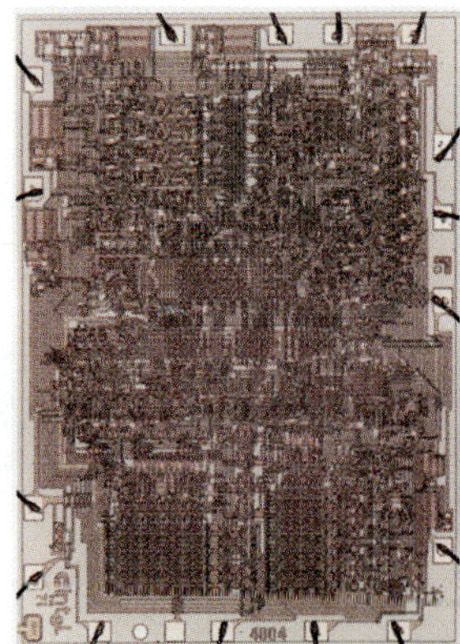

The first microprocessor, the Intel 4004, was designed by Ted Hoff. The single processor contained 2,250 transistors and could execute 60,000 operations per second.

Bill Gates and Paul Allen wrote a version of BASIC for the Altair, the first computer programming language designed for a personal computer. Bill Gates dropped out of Harvard to form Microsoft with Paul Allen.

Hailed as the first "personal computer," the Altair—allegedly named for a destination of the Starship Enterprise from a Star Trek TV episode—began to be sold as a kit for $395. Within months, tens of thousands were ordered.

Software Arts Inc.'s VisiCalc, the first electronic spreadsheet and business program for PCs, was released. This program is seen as one of the reasons PCs first became widely accepted in the business world.

1971

1975

1979

Fourth Generation

1972

The C programming language was developed by Dennis Ritchie at Bell Labs.

Seymor Cray, called the "father of supercomputing," founded Cray Research, which would go on to build some of the fastest computers in the world.

1976

Steve Wozniak and Steve Jobs founded Apple computer and released the Apple I (a single-board computer), followed by the Apple II (a complete PC that became an instant success in 1977). They originally ran the company out of Job's garage.

1980

Sony Electronics introduced the 3.5-inch floppy disk and drive.

Seagate Technologies announced the first Winchester 5.25-inch hard disk drive, revolutionizing PC storage.

IBM chose Microsoft to develop the operating system for its upcoming PC. That operating system was PC-DOS.

Fourth Generation (approximately 1971–present)

The fourth generation of computers began with large-scale integration (LSI), which resulted in chips that could contain thousands of transistors. Very large-scale integration (VLSI) resulted in the microprocessor and the resulting microcomputers. The keyboard and mouse are predominant input devices, though many other types of input devices are now available; monitors and printers provide output; storage is obtained with magnetic disks, optical discs, and memory chips.

IBM introduced the IBM PC. This DOS-based PC used a 4.77 MHz 8088 CPU with 64 KB of RAM and quickly became the standard for business PCs.

Compaq Corporation released the first IBM-compatible PC that ran the same software as the IBM PC, marking the beginning of the huge PC-compatible industry.

The first general-interest CD-ROM product (*Grolier's Electronic Encyclopedia*) was released, and computer and electronics companies worked together to develop a universal CD-ROM standard.

Intel introduced the Intel386 CPU.

Quantum Computer Services was founded; this company became AOL.

Tim Berners-Lee of CERN created the World Wide Web.

Intel introduced the Intel486 chip, the world's first million transistor CPU.

REF

1981

1983

1985

1989

1982

Intel introduced the 80286 CPU.

TIME magazine named the computer its "Machine of the Year" for 1982, emphasizing the importance the computer had already reached in our society at that time.

1984

The first version of Microsoft Windows, a graphical enviro-ment, was released.

The Apple Macintosh debuted. It featured a simple, graphical user interface, used an 8 MHz, 32-bit Motorola 68000 CPU, and had a built-in 9-inch black and white screen.

1986

Microsoft was listed on the New York Stock Exchange and began to sell shares to the public; Bill Gates became one of the world's youngest billionaires.

Apple's Steve Jobs founded Pixar.

1993

Marc Andreessen and James H. Clark founded Netscape Communications and released Netscape Navigator, a graphical Web browser based on the Mosaic browser Andreessen had created the previous year.

Intel introduced the Pentium CPU.

1994

Linus Torvalds created Linux, which launched the open source revolution. The penguin logo/mascot soon followed.

1997

The first DVD players used for playing movies stored on DVD discs were sold.

After winning 2 of 6 games in their first contest in 1996, the IBM computer Deep Blue beat chess master Garry Kasparov in a chess match.

The Intel Pentium II was introduced.

1999

Shawn Fanning, 19, wrote the software to drive his Napster P2P service and began the debate about P2P filesharing and online music.

Palm released the Palm VII, its first handheld PC with wireless Internet access.

The Intel Pentium III CPU was introduced.

1995

Windows 95 was released and sold more than one million copies in four days.

Both eBay and Amazon.com were founded.

Sun Microsystems released Java, which is still one of the most popular Web programming languages.

1998

Microsoft shipped Windows 98.

Apple released the iMac, a modernized version of the Macintosh computer. Its futuristic design helped to make this computer immensely popular.

2000

Intel introduced its Pentium 4 CPU chip. A popular advertising campaign, launched in 2001, featured the Blue Man Group.

The first USB flash memory drives were released.

Microsoft released the Windows 2000 Professional Server business operating systems and Windows ME for home users.

E-commerce skyrocketed, but unprofitable dot-com companies began going out of business at a record pace.

Intel's first 64-bit CPU, the Itanium, was introduced.

Microsoft released its XP line of products, including Windows XP and Office XP.

2001

The Internet and wireless networks enabled people to work and communicate with others wherever they go.

Spyware became a major problem; some studies indicated that over 80% of computers had spyware installed.

Wal-Mart and other major retailers announced requirements for suppliers to begin using RFID tags on shipments.

2004

Broadband Internet access approached the norm and improvements to wireless networking (such as WiMAX) continued to be developed.

Use of the Internet for online shopping, as well as downloads of music, movies, games, and television shows continued to grow.

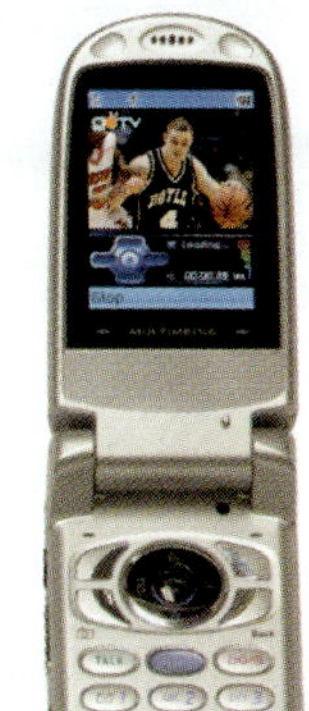

Delivery of TV shows and other media to cell phones became more common.

2006

2003

Digital camera sales in the United States exceeded 14 million, surpassing film camera sales for the first time.

Microsoft shipped the Office 2003 editions of its Microsoft Office System.

AMD released the 64-bit Opteron server microprocessor and the Athlon 64, the first 64-bit CPU designed for desktop PC use.

2005

Portable media players, such as the iPod, were common; digital music capabilities were built into a growing number of objects and devices, such as the OAKLEY THUMP sunglasses shown here.

Intel and AMD both released their first dual-core CPUs.

Phishing and identity theft became household words as an increasing number of individuals fell victim to these Internet scams.

The capabilities of mobile devices continued to grow; Palm's LifeDrive comes with a 4 GB hard drive and built-in Wi-Fi and Bluetooth support.

CODING CHARTS

As discussed in Chapter 2 of this text, coding systems for text-based data include ASCII, EBCDIC, and Unicode. ■

ASCII and EBCDIC

Figure R-1 provides a chart listing the ASCII and EBCDIC representations (in binary) for most of the symbols found on a typical keyboard.

FIGURE R-1
ASCII and EBCDIC binary codes for typical keyboard symbols.

SYMBOL	ASCII	EBCDIC
A	0100 0001	1100 0001
B	0100 0010	1100 0010
C	0100 0011	1100 0011
D	0100 0100	1100 0100
E	0100 0101	1100 0101
F	0100 0110	1100 0110
G	0100 0111	1100 0111
H	0100 1000	1100 1000
I	0100 1001	1100 1001
J	0100 1010	1101 0001
K	0100 1011	1101 0010
L	0100 1100	1101 0011
M	0100 1101	1101 0100
N	0100 1110	1101 0101
O	0100 1111	1101 0110
P	0101 0000	1101 0111
Q	0101 0001	1101 1000
R	0101 0010	1101 1001
S	0101 0011	1110 0010
T	0101 0100	1110 0011
U	0101 0101	1110 0100
V	0101 0110	1110 0101
W	0101 0111	1110 0110
X	0101 1000	1110 0111
Y	0101 1001	1110 1000
Z	0101 1010	1110 1001
a	0110 0001	1000 0001
b	0110 0010	1000 0010
c	0110 0011	1000 0011
d	0110 0100	1000 0100

SYMBOL	ASCII	EBCDIC
e	0110 0101	1000 0101
f	0110 0110	1000 0110
g	0110 0111	1000 0111
h	0110 1000	1000 1000
i	0110 1001	1000 1001
j	0110 1010	1001 0001
k	0110 1011	1001 0010
l	0110 1100	1001 0011
m	0110 1101	1001 0100
n	0110 1110	1001 0101
o	0110 1111	1001 0110
p	0111 0000	1001 0111
q	0111 0001	1001 1000
r	0111 0010	1001 1001
s	0111 0011	1010 0010
t	0111 0100	1010 0011
u	0111 0101	1010 0100
v	0111 0110	1010 0101
w	0111 0111	1010 0110
x	0111 1000	1010 0111
y	0111 1001	1010 1000
z	0111 1010	1010 1001
0	0011 0000	1111 0000
1	0011 0001	1111 0001
2	0011 0010	1111 0010
3	0011 0011	1111 0011
4	0011 0100	1111 0100
5	0011 0101	1111 0101
6	0011 0110	1111 0110
7	0011 0111	1111 0111

<table>
<tr><th>SYMBOL</th><th>ASCII</th><th>EBCDIC</th></tr>
<tr><td>8</td><td>0011 1000</td><td>1111 1000</td></tr>
<tr><td>9</td><td>0011 1001</td><td>1111 1001</td></tr>
<tr><td>(</td><td>0010 1000</td><td>0100 1101</td></tr>
<tr><td>)</td><td>0010 1001</td><td>0101 1101</td></tr>
<tr><td>/</td><td>0010 1111</td><td>0110 0001</td></tr>
<tr><td>-</td><td>0010 1101</td><td>0110 0000</td></tr>
<tr><td>*</td><td>0010 1010</td><td>0101 1100</td></tr>
<tr><td>+</td><td>0010 1011</td><td>0100 1110</td></tr>
<tr><td>,</td><td>0010 1100</td><td>0110 1011</td></tr>
<tr><td>.</td><td>0010 1110</td><td>0100 1011</td></tr>
<tr><td>:</td><td>0011 1010</td><td>0111 1010</td></tr>
<tr><td>;</td><td>0011 1011</td><td>0101 1110</td></tr>
<tr><td>&</td><td>0010 0110</td><td>0101 0000</td></tr>
<tr><td>\</td><td>0101 1100</td><td>1110 0000</td></tr>
<tr><td>$</td><td>0010 0100</td><td>0101 1011</td></tr>
<tr><td>%</td><td>0010 0101</td><td>0110 1100</td></tr>
<tr><td>=</td><td>0011 1101</td><td>0111 1110</td></tr>
<tr><td>></td><td>0011 1110</td><td>0110 1110</td></tr>
<tr><td><</td><td>0011 1100</td><td>0100 1100</td></tr>
<tr><td>!</td><td>0010 0001</td><td>0101 1010</td></tr>
<tr><td>|</td><td>0111 1100</td><td>0110 1010</td></tr>
<tr><td>?</td><td>0011 1111</td><td>0110 1111</td></tr>
<tr><td>@</td><td>0100 0000</td><td>0111 1100</td></tr>
<tr><td>_</td><td>0101 1111</td><td>0110 1101</td></tr>
<tr><td>`</td><td>0110 0000</td><td>1011 1001</td></tr>
<tr><td>{</td><td>0111 1011</td><td>1100 0000</td></tr>
<tr><td>}</td><td>0111 1101</td><td>1101 0000</td></tr>
<tr><td>~</td><td>0111 1110</td><td>1010 0001</td></tr>
<tr><td>[</td><td>0101 1011</td><td>0100 1010</td></tr>
<tr><td>]</td><td>0101 1101</td><td>0101 1010</td></tr>
</table>

Unicode

When consistent worldwide representation is needed, Unicode is typically used. Unicode can be used to represent every written language, as well as a variety of other symbols. Unicode codes are typically listed in hexadecimal notation—a sampling of Unicode is shown in Figure R-2.

The capability to display characters and other symbols using Unicode coding is incorporated into many programs. For instance, when the Symbol dialog box is opened using the Insert menu in Microsoft Office Word, the Unicode representation (as well as the corresponding ASCII code in either decimal or hexadecimal representation) can be viewed (see Figure R-3). Some programs allow you to enter a Unicode symbol using its Unicode hexadecimal value. For instance, in Microsoft Office programs you can use the Alt+X command when the insertion point is just to the right of a Unicode hex value to convert that hex value into the corresponding symbol. For example, the keystrokes

2264Alt+X

result in the symbol corresponding to the Unicode code 2264 (the less than or equal sign ≤) being inserted into the document; entering 27B2 and then pressing Alt+X inserts the symbol shown in the Word screen in Figure R-3.

A 0041	N 004E	a 0061	n 006E	0 0030	{ 007B	* 002A	■ 25A0	অ 0985
B 0042	O 004F	b 0062	o 006F	1 0031	| 007C	+ 002B	□ 25A1	গ 0997
C 0043	P 0050	c 0063	p 0070	2 0032	} 007D	, 002C	▲ 25B2	ে 09C7
D 0044	Q 0051	d 0064	q 0071	3 0033	~ 007E	- 002D	℅ 2105	৶ 09F6
E 0045	R 0052	e 0065	r 0072	4 0034	! 0021	. 002E	℞ 211E	څ 0685
F 0046	S 0053	f 0066	s 0073	5 0035	" 0022	/ 002F	⅓ 2153	ڴ 06B4
G 0047	T 0054	g 0067	t 0074	6 0036	# 0023	₤ 20A4	⅔ 2154	ڪ 06AA
H 0048	U 0055	h 0068	u 0075	7 0037	$ 0024	∑ 2211	♕ 2655	α 03B1
I 0049	V 0056	i 0069	v 0076	8 0038	% 0025	∅ 2205	☂ 2602	β 03B2
J 004A	W 0057	j 006A	w 0077	9 0039	& 0026	√ 221A	❐ 2750	Δ 0394
K 004B	X 0058	k 006B	x 0078	[005B	' 0027	∞ 221E	❂ 2742	Φ 03A6
L 004C	Y 0059	l 006C	y 0079	\\ 005C	(0028	≤ 2264	➲ 27B2	Ω 03A9
M 004D	Z 005A	m 006D	z 007A	] 005D	) 0029	≥ 2265	♥ 2665	Ϋ 03AB

FIGURE R-2
Selected Unicode codes.

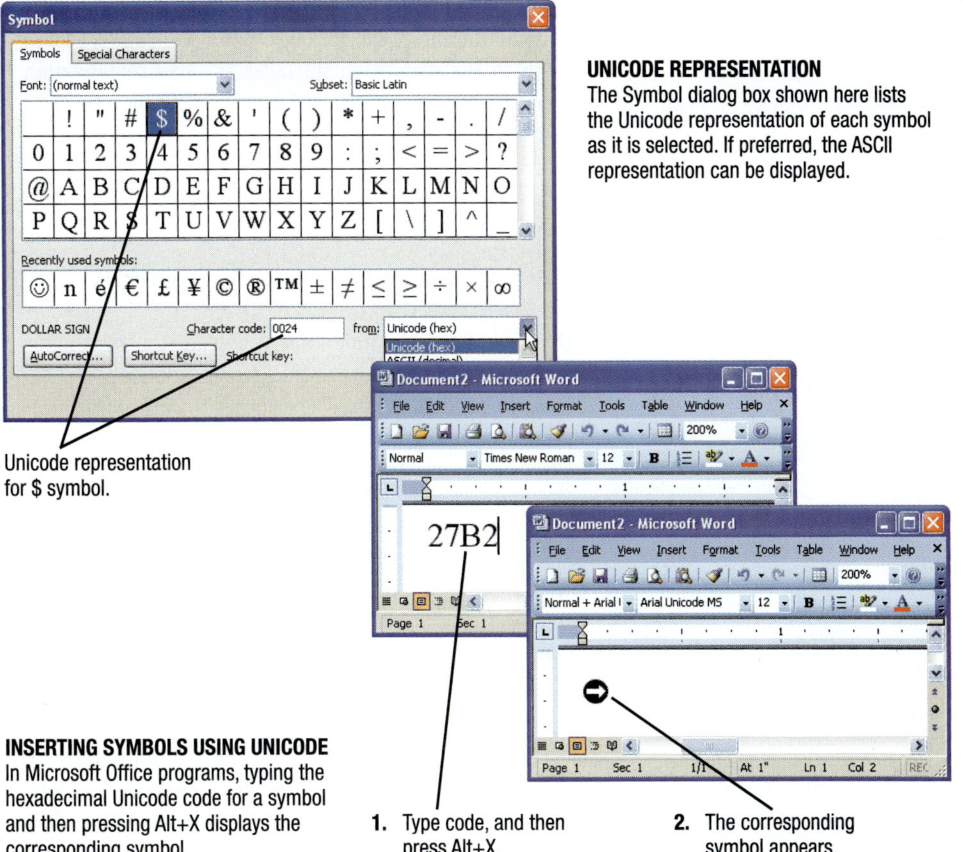

UNICODE REPRESENTATION
The Symbol dialog box shown here lists the Unicode representation of each symbol as it is selected. If preferred, the ASCII representation can be displayed.

Unicode representation for $ symbol.

INSERTING SYMBOLS USING UNICODE
In Microsoft Office programs, typing the hexadecimal Unicode code for a symbol and then pressing Alt+X displays the corresponding symbol.

1. Type code, and then press Alt+X.

2. The corresponding symbol appears.

FIGURE R-3
Using Unicode.

GUIDE TO BUYING A PC

Before buying a new PC, it is important to give some thought to what your needs are, including what software programs you wish to run, any other computers with which you need to be compatible, how you might want to connect to the Internet, and whether or not portability is important. This section of the References and Resources Guide explores topics related to buying and upgrading a PC. ■

Analyzing Needs

When referring to a computer system, a need refers to a functional requirement that the computer system must be able to meet. For example, at a video rental store, a computer system must be able to enter barcodes automatically from videos or DVDs being checked in and out, identify customers with overdue movies, manage movie inventories, and do routine accounting operations. Requiring portability is another example of a need. For example, if you need to take your computer with you as you travel or work out of the office, you will need a portable computer instead of a desktop computer.

Selecting a PC for home or business use must begin with the all-important question "What do I want the system to do?" Once you have determined what tasks the system will be used for, you can choose among the software and hardware alternatives available. Making a list of your needs in areas discussed in the next few sections can help you get a picture of what type of system you are shopping for. If you are not really sure what you want a system to do, you should think twice about buying one yet—you can easily make expensive mistakes if you are uncertain about what you want a system to do. Some common decision categories are discussed next; Figure R-4 provides a list of questions that can help you define the type of computer that will meet your needs.

FIGURE R-4 Questions to consider when getting ready to buy a PC.

POSSIBLE QUESTIONS
What tasks will I be using the computer for (writing papers, accessing the Internet, graphic design, composing music, playing games, etc.)?
Do I prefer a Mac or a PC-compatible? Are there any other computers I need my documents and storage media to be compatible with?
How fast do I need the system to be?
Do I need portability? If so, do I need the features of a conventional PC (notebook or tablet) or can I use a handheld PC?
What size and type of screen do I need?
What removable storage media will I need to use in the PC (such as standard floppy disks, CDs, DVDs, flash memory cards, or a USB flash memory drive)?
Do I need to be able to connect the PC to the Internet? If so, what type of Internet access will I be using (such as conventional dial-up, ISDN, DSL, cable, satellite, or wireless)?
Do I need to be able to connect the PC to a network? If so, is it a wired or wireless network and what type of network interface card is needed to connect to that network?
What additional hardware do I need (scanner, printer, or digital camera, for example)?
When do I need the computer?
Do I want to pay extra for a better warranty (such as a longer time period or on-site service)?

Operating Systems and Application Software

Determining what functions you want the system to perform will help you decide which application software is needed. Most users start with an application suite containing a word processor, spreadsheet, and other programs. In addition, specialty programs, such as tax preparation, drawing, home publishing, reference software, games, and more may be needed or desired.

Not all software is available for all operating systems. Consequently, if a specific piece of software is needed, that choice may determine which operating system you need to use. In addition, your operating system decision may already be made for you if your documents need to be compatible with those of another computer (such as other office computers or between a home and an office PC). The most widely used PC operating systems are Windows, Mac OS, and Linux.

Platforms and Configuration Options

If your operating system has already been determined, that is a good start in deciding the overall platform you will be looking for—most users will choose between the IBM-compatible and Apple Macintosh platform. IBM and compatible PCs usually run either Windows or Linux; Apple computers almost always use Mac OS.

Configuration decisions initially involve determining the size of the machine desired. For nonportable systems, you have the choice between tower, desktop, or all-in-one configurations; in addition, the monitor size and type (CRT or flat-screen) needs to be determined. Portable, fully functioning PCs can be notebook or tablet PCs. For tablet PCs, you need to decide if you will require keyboard use on a regular basis; if so, a convertible tablet PC would be the best choice. If a powerful, fully functioning PC is not required, you may decide to go with a more portable option, such as a handheld PC.

You should also consider any other specifications that are important to you, such as the size of the hard drive, type of other storage device needed, amount of memory required, and so forth. As discussed in the next section, these decisions often require reconciling the features you want with the amount of money you are willing to spend.

Power vs. Budget Requirements

As part of the needs analysis, you should look closely at your need for a powerful system versus your budgetary constraints. Most users do not need a state-of-the-art system. Those who do should expect to pay more than the average user. A PC that was top of the line six months or a year ago is usually reasonably priced and more than adequate for most users' needs. Individuals who just want a PC for basic tasks, such as using the Internet and word processing, can likely get by with an inexpensive PC designed for home use.

When determining your requirements, be sure to identify the features and functions that are absolutely essential for your primary PC tasks (such as a large hard drive and lots of memory for multimedia applications, a fast video card for gaming, a fast Internet connection, and so forth). After you have the minimum configuration determined, you can add optional or desirable components, as your budget allows.

Listing Alternatives

After you consider your needs and the questions mentioned in Figure R-4, you should have a pretty good idea of the hardware and software you will need. You will also know what purchasing options are available to you, depending on your time frame (while some retail stores have systems that can be purchased and brought home the same day, special orders or some systems purchased over the Internet may take a few weeks to arrive). The next step is to get enough information from possible vendors to compare and contrast a few alternative systems that satisfy your stated needs. Most often, these vendors are local stores (such as computer stores, warehouse clubs, and electronic stores) and/or online stores (such as manufacturer Web sites and e-tailers). To compare prices and specifications for possible computer systems, find at least three systems that meet or exceed your needs by looking through newspaper advertisements, configuring systems online via manufacturer and e-tailer Web sites, or calling or visiting local stores. A comparison sheet listing your criteria and the systems you are considering, such as the one in Figure R-5, can help you summarize your options. Although it is sometimes very difficult to compare the prices of systems since they typically have somewhat different configurations, you can assign an approximate dollar value to each extra feature a system has (such as $100 for an included printer or $50 for a larger hard drive). Be sure to also include any sales tax and shipping charges when you compare the prices of each total system.

If your budget is limited, you will have to balance the system you need with extra features you may want. But do not skimp on memory or hard drive space because sufficient memory can help your programs to run faster and with fewer problems and hard drive space is consumed quickly. Often for just a few extra dollars, you can get additional memory, a faster CPU, or a larger hard drive—significantly cheaper than trying to upgrade any of those features later. A good rule of thumb is to try to buy a little more computer than you

COMPONENT	EXAMPLE OF DESIRED SPECIFICATIONS	SYSTEM #1 VENDOR:	SYSTEM #2 VENDOR:	SYSTEM #3 VENDOR:
Operating System	Windows XP			
Manufacturer	HP or Dell			
Style	Tower			
CPU	AMD 2.4 GHz or higher			
RAM	512 MB or higher			
Hard drive	200 GB or higher			
Removable storage	8-in-1 flash memory card reader			
Optical drive	DVD-RW			
Monitor	Flat-panel 17-inch			
Video card and video RAM	Prefer dedicated video RAM			
Keyboard	Prefer speaker control keys			
Mouse	Optical with scroll wheel			
Sound card/speakers	Want subwoofer			
Modem	Cable			
Network card	Wi-Fi (802.11g)			
Printer	Ink-jet if get deal on price with complete system			
Scanner	Don't need			
Included software	Microsoft Office or Works			
Warranty	3 years min. (1 year onsite if not a local store)			
Other features	2 front USB ports minimum			
Price				
Tax				
Shipping				
TOTAL COST				

FIGURE R-5

Comparing PC alternatives. A checklist such as this one can help to organize your desired criteria and evaluate possible systems.

think you need. On the other hand, do not buy a top-of-the-line system, unless you fall into the power user category and really need it. Generally, the second or third system down from the top of the line is a very good system for a much more reasonable price. Some guidelines for minimum requirements for desktop PCs for most home users are as follows:

- 3 GHz Pentium 4 (or equivalent) CPU (generally, any CPU currently being sold today is fast enough for most users).
- 512 MB or more of memory (RAM).
- 160 GB or more hard drive space.
- Recordable or rewritable CD or DVD drive.
- Conventional dial-up modem plus a special modem, if needed, for an alternative type of Internet access.
- Sound card and external speakers.
- At least 2 USB ports.

System Troubleshooting and Upgrading

After your new system has been purchased and is up and running (refer to the Chapter 1 How it Works box for a review of how to set up a new PC), chances are at some point you will need to do some troubleshooting and upgrading.

Troubleshooting

Troubleshooting refers to actions taken to diagnose or solve a problem. Unfortunately, many problems are unique to specific types of hardware and software, so no simple troubleshooting remedy works all of the time. Nonetheless, the following simple steps and guidelines can help you to identify and correct a number of common problems.

- Try again. A number of procedures work when you try a second time. You may have pressed the wrong keys the first time, not pressed the keys hard enough, or have a special function activated (such as the ones activated by pressing the Caps Lock, Num Lock, or Insert key on the keyboard). If you have accidentally activated such a function, pressing the key again should turn the function off and correct the problem.
- Check to see that all the equipment is plugged in and turned on and that no cables are detached or loose.
- Reboot the system. Many software problems are corrected after the computer is restarted and the program is opened again. Some operating systems—such as Windows—will also try to reconfigure devices identified as having a problem when the system is restarted, as well as give you the option of temporarily disabling certain devices if your system crashed, to help you determine the device that is causing the problem. If for some reason the system does not boot at all, use your system startup disc (most systems either come with one or suggest you make one using a system option).
- Update your operating system and scan for viruses and spyware. A known bug or a virus or spyware program installed on your PC might be causing the problem and so installing the needed patch or removing the offending virus or spyware program might correct the problem.
- Recall exactly what happened between the time the system was operating properly and the time you began to encounter problems. For example, perhaps you installed a new piece of hardware or software during your last session, and it is affecting the way your current application works. If you can think of a recent change, try to undo it and see if that corrects the problem. Windows users can also try to use the System Restore option to roll their PC's settings back to a prior configuration.
- Be observant. If you heard a strange noise the last time you used your PC, it might be important. Even though solving the problem may be beyond your capabilities, the information may help the person who will assist you in figuring out the problem.
- Check the *documentation* that came with the system. Many products come with a hard-copy manual that includes a troubleshooting checklist; software programs usually have an online help feature that can help you solve many problems.
- Use diagnostic software. *Diagnostic utility programs* (discussed in Chapter 5) can be used to test your system to see if parts of it are malfunctioning or if it is just not performing well, for some reason. Sometimes when new hardware or software is installed, it creates a conflict with other hardware or software. Also, hard drives can get fragmented with use over time and may need to be defragmented; temporary Internet files need to be periodically deleted.

You should weigh the time that it takes to solve a problem yourself against the cost of outside help. It is not a personal failure to give up if the problem is more than you can handle. It is simply an admission that your time is valuable and that you are wise enough to know when to call in a professional for assistance. Options for technical assistance include:

- *Manufacturer*. Many manufacturers have toll-free phone numbers, fax numbers, e-mail addresses, and support information on their Web sites for users with technical assistance questions. If your system is still under warranty, you should contact the manufacturer before trying any other technical support options. Your PC manufacturer may also have recent software patches or updated drivers available via its Web site. These items are almost always available free of charge.
- *Third-party support*. If your system is out of warranty, you can get help from a third-party firm, such as a local computer repair company or a company that will provide assistance via the phone or Web. Typically you are charged by the minute or hour (with a minimum fee often assessed) for assistance acquired via a third party.
- *User support*. You can also get suggestions from other users via online discussion groups. To find an appropriate group, check the manufacturer's Web site to see if it has a link to a discussion group for the product in question, or locate an appropriate group from a third-party technical support Web site. The message you post might be read by literally hundreds of other users, and there is a good possibility that someone out there has encountered and solved the problem you are now wrestling with. While you may get the answer you are seeking without paying a dime, do not be surprised if you have to wait for a few days or more to have your plea for help read by the right person.

FIGURE R-6
Software updates.

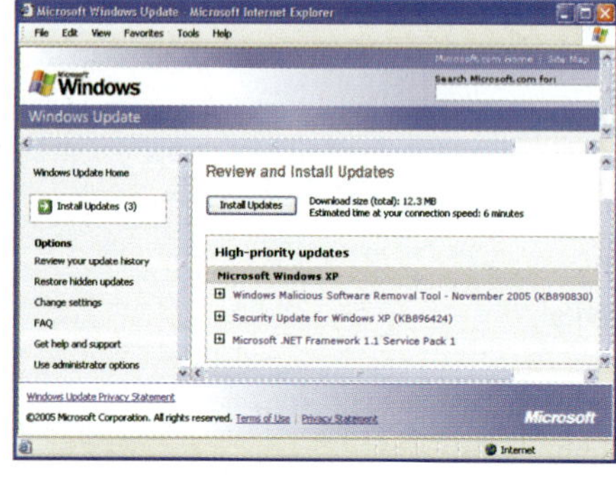

WINDOWS UPDATE
The Windows Update feature can be used to regularly locate and install patches and other updates for Windows and Internet Explorer.

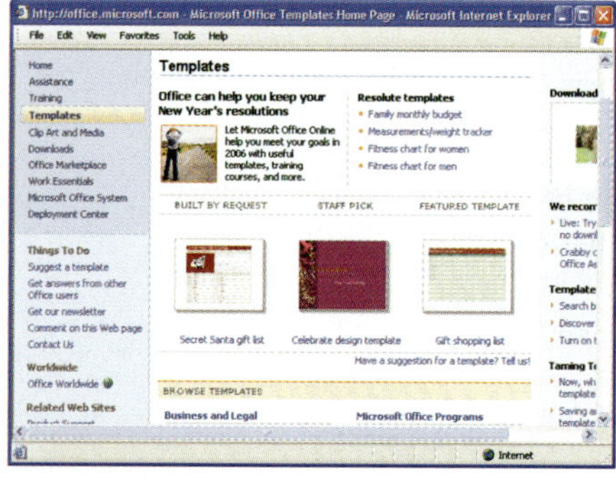

SOFTWARE WEB SITES
Support Web sites for specific software programs (such as the one for Microsoft Office shown here) can be used to locate free templates, clip art, and other resources to be used with that program.

Upgrading

Hardware and software generally need to be upgraded over time. *Upgrading* a computer system means buying new hardware or software components that extend the life of your current system. The question you must ask when considering an upgrade is the same one that you would ask when considering costly repairs to a car: Should I spend this money on my current system or start fresh and buy a completely new system? For example, it is usually not cost-effective to upgrade a computer that is more than three years old, since some new PCs today sell for $300 or less.

Upgrading Hardware

Some common hardware upgrades include adding more RAM or an additional storage device to a system, installing a different type of modem or additional memory, adding an expansion card to provide a new functionality, and adding new peripheral devices, such as a scanner or color printer.

Upgrading Software

Many PC software vendors enhance their products in some major way every year or two, prompting users to upgrade. Each upgrade—called a *version*—is assigned a number, such as 1.0, 2.0, 3.0, and so on. The higher the number, the more recent and more powerful the software is. Minor versions, called *releases*, typically increase their numbers in increments of 0.1—such as 1.1, 1.2, and 1.3—or .01. For example, release 3.11 might follow release 3.1, and release 7.1 might follow 7.0. Releases are usually issued in response to bugs or shortcomings in the version and are often free.

When a free update is available for a program that you use, or when a patch to fix a known problem becomes available, typically these are downloaded via the software publisher's Web site (see Figure R-6). Many software publishers also offer free templates, clip art, and other downloaded resources via their Web sites-one example is shown in Figure R-6. Full software upgrades are more often purchased in physical form and they generally cost less than buying the full version. Before upgrading to a new version, be sure to weigh the benefits against its costs. Unless the new version has a feature that you require, it may not be necessary to upgrade to that version.

E-MAIL FUNDAMENTALS

As discussed in Chapter 1, an e-mail program (such as Netscape Mail, Microsoft Outlook Express, Microsoft Outlook, or a proprietary mail program used by your ISP) is used to send conventional (non-Web-based) e-mail. You first need to set up the e-mail program with your name, e-mail address, incoming mail server, and outgoing mail server information and then you can begin to send and receive e-mail. This section of the References and Resources Guide includes the basic steps involved with sending, receiving, and managing e-mail. ■

Sending E-Mail

To send an e-mail message, first open your e-mail program and select the appropriate option to start a new message. Type one or more e-mail addresses in the To: box, enter an appropriate subject line, and then type the message in the appropriate area (see Figure R-7). Send the message using the Send toolbar button. To make it easier to send e-mails to people you contact frequently, you can add their names, nicknames, and their e-mail addresses to your e-mail program's *address book* (you can typically right-click on a sender's e-mail address to get an option to add that individual to your address book). When you begin to type a name or nickname in a To: box for which you have a related address book entry, the e-mail program will then fill in the appropriate e-mail address automatically.

Receiving E-Mail

In order to receive a new e-mail message, it must be retrieved from your ISP. To retrieve new e-mail messages waiting for you at your ISP's mail server, open your e-mail program. If your e-mail program does not then check for new messages, click the appropriate toolbar button, such as Get Msg or Send/Recv (refer to the bottom screens in Figure R-7). For convenience, you can typically select an option to have your e-mail program check for new messages on a regular basis; if you have a direct Internet connection, you can leave your e-mail program open at all times to have all new e-mail messages retrieved automatically. To read a specific e-mail message, click it; double-clicking an e-mail message typically opens the message in a new window for easier reading.

All new e-mail messages are usually placed in your *Inbox* folder. Once an e-mail message is displayed, it can be printed, replied to, forwarded to someone else, filed into a different folder, or deleted using your e-mail program's toolbar buttons.

Managing E-Mail

When you send e-mail, copies of the messages that you send are typically stored in a folder named Sent, Sent Items, Sent Messages, or something similar so that you can read them or resend them, if necessary. These messages remain there, and your retrieved e-mail messages remain in your Inbox folder, until you delete them or move them into a different folder (you can create new folders in most e-mail programs, as needed). Once an e-mail message is deleted, it is usually moved into a special folder for deleted items (called Trash, Deleted Items, Trash Can, or something similar). Messages in a deleted items folder typically remain there until you permanently delete them by selecting the appropriate option (such as *Empty Trash* from Netscape Mail's File menu or *Empty 'Deleted Items' Folder* from Outlook Express' Edit menu). Deleting unneeded messages frees up space on your hard drive.

FIGURE R-7
Sending and receiving e-mail.

SENDING E-MAIL
This example uses Netscape Mail.

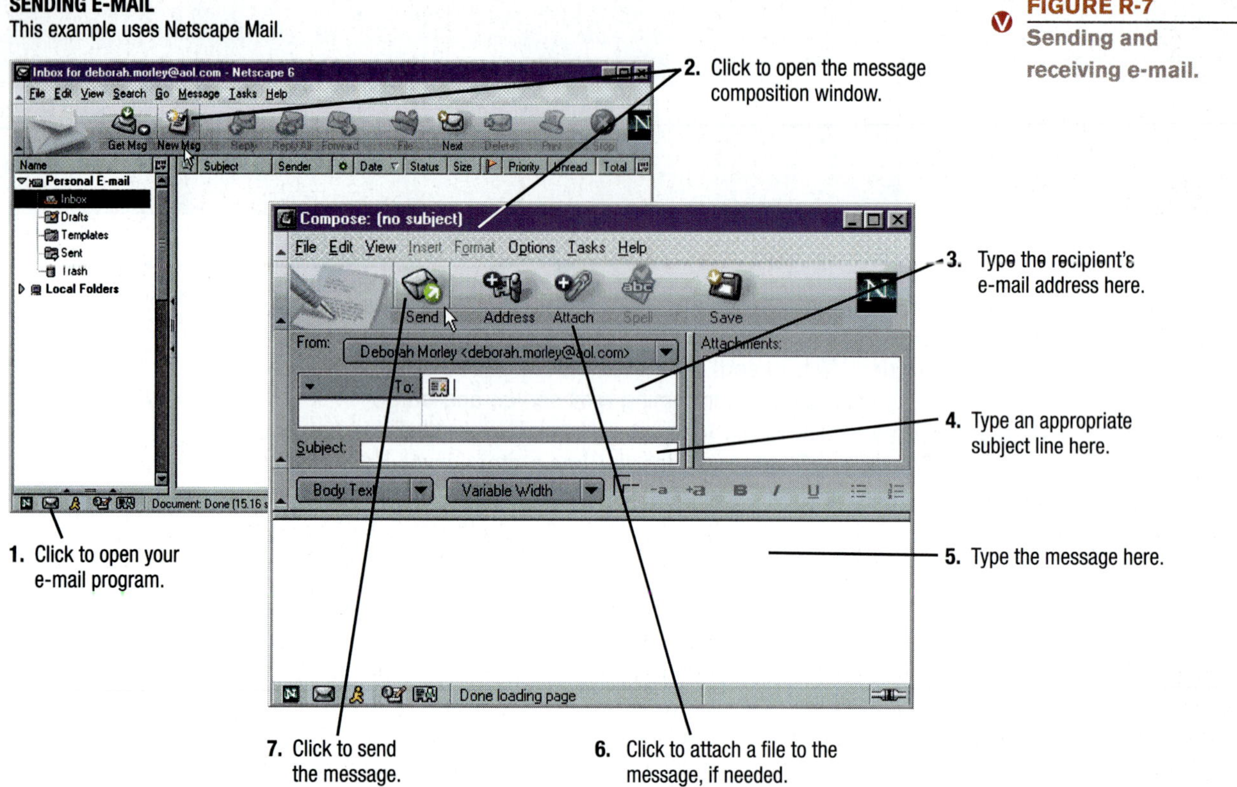

RECEIVING E-MAIL
This example uses Outlook Express.

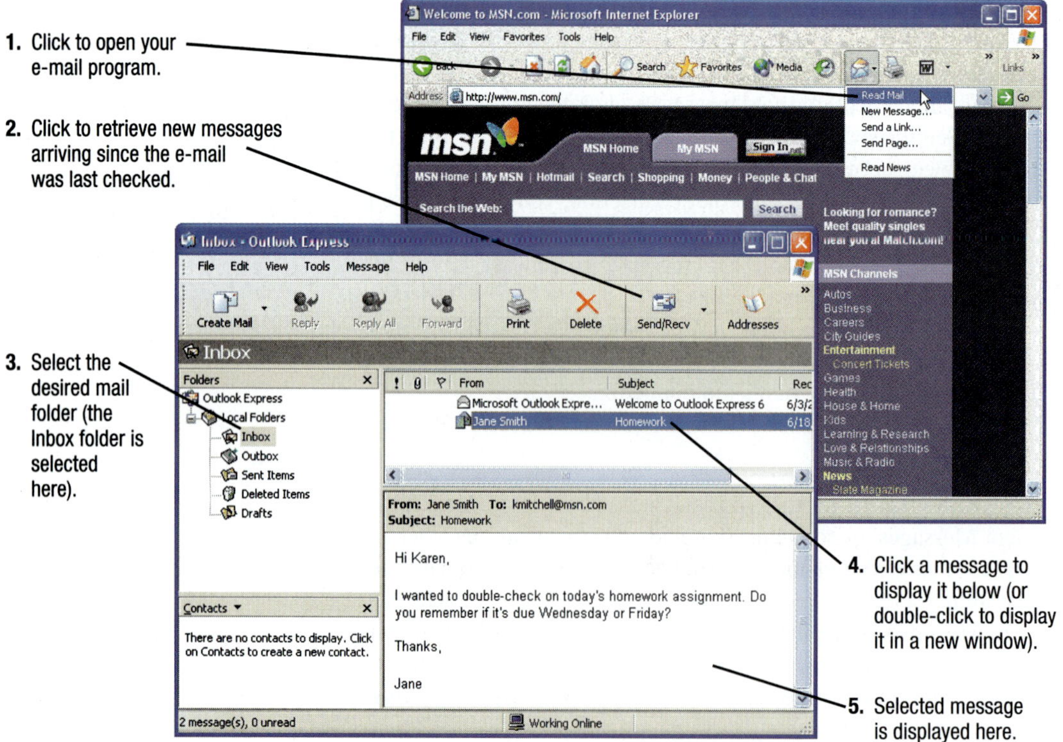

ANSWERS TO SELF-QUIZ

Chapter 1
1. T **2.** F **3.** F **4.** F **5.** T **6.** Input **7.** tablet **8.** hyperlinks **9.** electronic mail or e-mail **10. a.** 4 **b.** 2 **c.** 1 **d.** 3

Chapter 2
1. T **2.** F **3.** T **4.** T **5.** F **6.** 13 **7.** random access memory or RAM **8.** port **9.** pipelining **10. a.** 6 **b.** 2 **c.** 4 **d.** 9 **e.** 7 **f.** 1 **g.** 8 **h.** 5 **i.** 3

Chapter 3
1. F **2.** T **3.** F **4.** F **5.** T **6.** volatile **7.** 4.7 GB **8.** smart card **9.** flash memory **10. a.** 2 **b.** 3 **c.** 1

Chapter 4
1. F **2.** F **3.** T **4.** T **5.** F **6.** handwriting recognition **7.** scanner, optical scanner, flatbed scanner, or handheld scanner **8.** pixel **9.** flat-panel or LCD; cathode-ray tube or CRT **10. a.** 4 **b.** 3 **c.** 6 **d.** 2 **e.** 5 **f.** 1

Chapter 5
1. T **2.** F **3.** F **4.** F **5.** T **6.** operating system; utility **7.** Linux **8.** file compression **9.** back up **10. a.** 3 **b.** 6 **c.** 1 **d.** 2 **e.** 5 **f.** 4

Chapter 6
1. T **2.** T **3.** F **4.** F **5.** T **6.** open source **7.** insertion point **8.** function **9.** table **10. a.** 4 **b.** 3 **c.** 5 **d.** 2 **e.** 1

Chapter 7
1. F **2.** T **3.** F **4.** T **5.** F **6.** telecommuting **7.** bus **8.** satellite **9.** virtual private network or VPN **10. a.** 5 **b.** 4 **c.** 2 **d.** 1 **e.** 6 **f.** 3

Chapter 8
1. F **2.** F **3.** T **4.** T **5.** F **6.** Digital Subscriber Line or DSL **7.** keyword; directory **8.** instant messaging or IM **9.** online auction **10. a.** 2 **b.** 5 **c.** 3 **d.** 1 **e.** 6 **f.** 4

Chapter 9
1. F **2.** T **3.** F **4.** T **5.** F **6.** war driving **7.** biometric **8.** firewall **9.** public key or asymmetric key **10. a.** 4 **b.** 3 **c.** 6 **d.** 1 **e.** 5 **f.** 2

Chapter 10
1. F **2.** T **3.** F **4.** T **5.** F **6.** thumbnail **7.** Streaming **8.** intended audience; objectives **9.** Web site authoring **10. a.** 2 **b.** 1 **c.** 5 **d.** 4 **e.** 6 **f.** 3

Chapter 11
1. T **2.** F **3.** T **4.** T **5.** F **6.** B2G or business-to-government **7.** online payment service **8.** digital wallet **9.** banner ad **10. a.** 1 **b.** 3 **c.** 4 **d.** 2

Chapter 12
1. T **2.** F **3.** F **4.** T **5.** F **6.** inference engine **7.** systems analyst **8.** tangible **9.** prototype **10. a.** 3 **b.** 2 **c.** 4 **d.** 1

Chapter 13
1. F **2.** T **3.** T **4.** F 5. F **6.** program design **7.** interpreter **8.** logic **9.** visual **10. a.** 3 **b.** 5 **c.** 4 **d.** 1 **e.** 2

Chapter 14
1. T **2.** T **3.** F **4.** F **5.** T **6.** field or column; record or row **7.** integrity **8.** hashing **9.** client-server **10. a.** 3 **b.** 4 **c.** 2 **d.** 1

Chapter 15
1. F **2.** T **3.** T **4.** F **5.** F **6.** disaster-recovery **7.** digital counterfeiting **8.** filter **9.** opt out **10. a.** 4 **b.** 5 **c.** 2 **d.** 3 **e.** 1

Chapter 16
1. F **2.** T **3.** T **4.** F **5.** F **6.** copyright; trademark **7.** plagiarism **8.** computer/Internet addiction **9.** digital divide **10. a.** 2 **b.** 6 **c.** 1 **d.** 3 **e.** 5 **f.** 4

CREDITS

Throughout the modules: Screen shots of Microsoft Access®, Excel®, Paint®, PowerPoint®, Publisher®, Visual Basic®, Word®, and Windows® reprinted with permission from Microsoft Corporation. Copyright © Microsoft Explorer® reprinted with permission from Microsoft Corporation.

Chapter 1

Figure 1-1a, Photo courtesy of Nokia. Copyright © 2005 Nokia. All rights reserved. Nokia and Nokia Connecting People are registered trademarks of Nokia Corporation.; **Figure 1-1b**, Courtesy Alcatel; **Figure 1-2a**, Courtesy of Microsoft Corporation; **Figure 1-2b**, © Flying Colours Ltd/Getty Images; **Figure 1-2c**, © Fujitsu Siemens Computers; **Figure 1-2d**, Courtesy TMIO, Inc.; **Figure 1-3a**, Courtesy of Microsoft Corporation; **Figure 1-3b**, Courtesy Infocus Corporation; **Figure 1-3c**, Courtesy U.S. Marines; **You box**, Courtesy Stanford University Medical Center; **Figure 1-4a**, Courtesy of Siemens AG/Siemens press picture; **Figure 1-4b**, Courtesy of Symbol Technologies, Inc.; **Figure 1-4c**, Courtesy Xybernaut Corporation; **Figure 1-5ab**, Courtesy Deutsche Lufthansa AG; **Figure 1-5c**, Courtesy of Garmin Ltd. or its subsidiaries; **Figure 1-5d**, Courtesy of Siemens AG/Siemens press picture; **Figure 1-7ace**, Courtesy IBM Corporate Archives; **Figure 1-7b**, Courtesy U.S. Army; **Figure 1-7d**, Courtesy, Hewlett-Packard Company; **Figure 1-8a**, Courtesy of Gateway, Inc.; **Figure 1-8b**, Courtesy, Hewlett-Packard Company; **Figure 1-8c**, Courtesy of Logitech; **Figure 1-8d**, Courtesy SanDisk Corporation; **Figure 1-12c**, Courtesy of Microsoft Corporation/photo by Joanne Savio; **Figure 1-12e**, Courtesy RedLobster.com; **Figure 1-13a**, Photo courtesy of Nokia. Copyright © 2005 Nokia. All rights reserved. Nokia and Nokia Connecting People are registered trademarks of Nokia Corporation.; **Figure 1-13b**, Courtesy of Suunto; **Trend box**, Courtesy GoTV Networks; **Figure 1-14a**, Courtesy Acer America; **Figure 1-14b**, Courtesy of Lenovo; **Figure 1-14c**, Photo or screen shot(s) reprinted with permission from MPC Computers, LLC; **Figure 1-15a**, Courtesy Acer America; **Figure 1-15b**, Courtesy of Motion Computing®; **Figure 1-15cde**, Courtesy of ViewSonic Corporation; **Inside box a**, Courtesy of CrazyModders.be; **Inside box b**, Courtesy of Kurt Villcheck website: TrickedOutPC.net; **Inside box c**, Courtesy Tulip; **Inside box d**, Courtesy VoodooPC; **Figure 1-16a**, Courtesy of Research In Motion (RIM); **Figure 1-16b**, Courtesy OQO; **Figure 1-17a**, Courtesy of Symbol Technologies, Inc.; **Figure 1-17b**, Courtesy OQO; **Figure 1-18a**, © Fujitsu Siemens Computers; **Figure 1-18b**, Courtesy DataWind, Inc.; **Figure 1-18c**, MSN TV Set Top Box from Microsoft; **How box bd1**, Courtesy Acer America; **How box d2**, Courtesy of Symantec; **How box e**, Courtesy Kensington Technology Group, www.kensington.com; **Figure 1-19a**, Courtesy Sutter Gould Medical Foundation; **Figure 1-19b**, © Fujitsu Siemens Computers; **Figure 1-20**, © Corbis; **Figure 1-21**, LLNL photo; **Figure 1-22a**, Courtesy of Gateway, Inc.; **Figure 1-22bcd**, Courtesy Acer America; **Figure 1-22e**, Courtesy of IBM Corporation; **Figure 1-25a**, Courtesy Acer America; **Figure 1-25b**, ARTHUR Web site © 2005 WGBH; underlying ARTHUR TM/© Marc Brown.; **Figure 1-27**, BHG.com screen shot courtesy of Meredith Corporation; **Figure 1-28**, Courtesy Google; **Figure 1-29**, Courtesy Acer America; **Figure 1-30**, Courtesy of Symantec; **Expert Insight**, Photo courtesy of Nokia. Copyright © 2005 Nokia. All rights reserved. Nokia and Nokia Connecting People are registered trademarks of Nokia Corporation.

Chapter 2

Figure 2-7ac, Courtesy of Intel Corporation; **Figure 2-7b**, © 2003, 2005 Advanced Micro Devices, Inc., Reprinted with permission. AMD, the AMD logo, AMD Athlon, and combinations thereof are trademarks of Advanced Micro Devices, Inc.; **You box**, Courtesy adidas-Salomon AG; **Figure 2-9**, Courtesy Kingston Technology; **Figure 2-11**, © 2005 Spansion, LLC, Reprinted with permission. **Figure 2-12a**, Courtesy NETGEAR; **Figure 2-13a**, Courtesy of Intel Corporation; **Figure 2-13b**, Courtesy MSI.; **Figure 2-14a**, Courtesy Acer America; **Figure 2-14b**, Courtesy of Belkin Corporation; **Figure 2-15**, © Fujitsu Siemens Computers; **Figure 2-16**, Courtesy of Linksys; **Figure 2-17**, © Fujitsu Siemens Computers; **Figure 2-18**, Image provided by palmOne, Inc.; **Inside box**, Courtesy of Intel Corporation; **Trend box**, Courtesy TAEUS International Corporation; **Figure 2-21b**, Courtesy SimpleTech, Inc.; **Figure 2-24**, Courtesy Epson America Inc.; **Figure 2-26a**, Courtesy of Intel Corporation; **Figure 2-26b**, Courtesy Kingston Technology; **Figure 2-27**, Image reproduced by permission of IBM Research, Almaden Research Center. Unauthorized use not permitted.; **Exercise 5a**, Courtesy NETGEAR; **Exercise 5d**, Courtesy SimpleTech, Inc.

Chapter 3

Figure 3-1, © Fujitsu Siemens Computers; **Figure 3-7**, Courtesy of Seagate Technology LLC; **Inside box**, Courtesy of DriveSavers, Inc. www.drivesavers.com; **Figure 3-10a**, Courtesy SimpleTech, Inc.; **Figure 3-10b**, Courtesy of Intel Corporation; **Figure 3-10c**, Courtesy of Seagate Technology LLC; **Figure 3-11a**, Copyright © Iomega Corporation. All Rights Reserved. Iomega, the stylized "i" logo and all product images are property of Iomega Corporation in the United States and/or other countries. Zip and REV are registered trademarks of Iomega Corporation in the United States and/or other countries.; **Figure 3-11b**, Courtesy XIMETA, Inc.; **Figure 3-11c**, Courtesy of Seagate Technology LLC; **Figure 3-11d**, Courtesy of Toshiba Storage Device Division, a Division of Toshiba America Information Systems, Inc.; **Figure 3-12**, Copyright © Iomega Corporation. All Rights Reserved. Iomega, the stylized "i" logo and all product images are property of Iomega Corporation in the United States and/or other countries. Zip and REV are registered trademarks of Iomega Corporation in the United States and/or other countries.; **Figure 3-14**, Courtesy CD Digital Card www.cddigitalcard.com; **How box**, Courtesy RosArt Multimedia, Inc.; **Figure 3-15a**, Courtesy Memorex Products, Inc.; **Figure 3-15bc**, Courtesy of Maxell Corporation of America; **Figure 3-15d**, Courtesy of Sony Electronics Inc.; **Trend box**, Courtesy Imation Corp.; **Figure 3-16a**, Courtesy of Sony Electronics Inc.; **Figure 3-16bf**, Courtesy SanDisk Corporation; **Figure 3-16d**, Courtesy SimpleTech, Inc.; **Figure 3-16e**, Image provided by palmOne, Inc.; **Figure 3-17acd**, Courtesy SanDisk Corporation; **Figure 3-17b**, Courtesy of Lexar Media, Inc.; **Figure 3-17e**, Courtesy of Sony Electronics Inc.; **Figure 3-18ab**, Copyright © Iomega Corporation. All Rights Reserved. Iomega, the stylized "i" logo and all product images are property of Iomega Corporation in the United States and/or other countries. Zip and REV are registered trademarks of Iomega Corporation in the United States and/or other countries.; **Figure 3-18c**, Courtesy RememberUs.co.uk; **Figure 3-19a**, Courtesy Fotki, Inc. Fotki.com; **Figure 3-19b**, Courtesy Xdrive, Inc.; **You box**, Courtesy Pikeville College; **Figure 3-20a**, Courtesy of Siemens AG/Siemens press picture; **Figure 3-21**, Courtesy InPhase Technologies; **Figure 3-22**, Courtesy 3PARdata, Inc.; **Exercise 2b**, Courtesy of Seagate Technology LLC; **Exercise 2cd**, Courtesy SanDisk Corporation; **Exercise 2e**, Courtesy of Siemens AG/Siemens press picture; **Exercise 2f**, Courtesy of Maxell Corporation of America.

Chapter 4

Figure 4-1, Courtesy of Logitech; **Figure 4-2a**, Courtesy of Sierra Wireless; **Figure 4-2b**, Courtesy Digit Wireless; **Figure 4-2c**, Courtesy of Logitech; **Figure 4-3a**, Courtesy Optorite Inc.; **Figure 4-3b**, Courtesy Acer America; **Trend box**, Courtesy Virtual Devices; **Figure 4-4a**, Courtesy of Symbol Technologies, Inc.; **Figure 4-4b**, Courtesy of Microsoft Corporation; **Figure 4-4c**, Courtesy of Salton, Inc.; **Figure 4-5b**, Courtesy Active Ink Software; **Figure 4-6a**, Courtesy of C Technologies AB/Anoto Group AB (publ); **Figure 4-6b**, Courtesy Wacom Technology Co; **Figure 4-6c**, Courtesy of Hand Held Products, Inc.; **Figure 4-7a**, Courtesy Deutsche Lufthansa AG; **Figure 4-7b**, Courtesy PC America; **Figure 4-8ab**, Courtesy of Logitech; **Figure 4-8cd**, © Fujitsu Siemens Computers; **Figure 4-9**, Courtesy of Symbol Technologies, Inc.; **Figure 4-10a**, Courtesy, Hewlett-Packard Company; **Figure 4-10b**, Courtesy of C Technologies AB/Anoto Group AB (publ); **Figure 4-10c**, Courtesy of Visioneer, Inc.; **You box**, Courtesy INTELLIFIT; **Figure 4-11abd**, Courtesy of Symbol Technologies, Inc.; **Figure 4-11c**, Courtesy of Hand Held Products, Inc.; **Figure 4-12a**, Courtesy of Intermec Technologies Corporation; **Figure 4-12b**, Courtesy of Symbol Technologies, Inc.; **Figure 4-13**, Courtesy Chatsworth Data Corporation; **Figure 4-14**, Courtesy of Sierra Pacific; **Figure 4-15a**, Courtesy of NCR Corporation; **Figure 4-16a**, Courtesy of IR Recognition Systems, and Ingersoll-Rand Business; **Figure 4-16b**, © Fujitsu Siemens Computers; **Figure 4-17ac**, Courtesy of Sony Electronics Inc.; **Figure 4-17b**, Courtesy SanDisk Corporation; **Figure 4-17d**, Photo courtesy of Nokia. Copyright © 2005 Nokia. All rights reserved. Nokia and Nokia Connecting People are registered trademarks of Nokia Corporation.; **Inside box adefg**, Courtesy of Intermec Technologies Corporation; **Inside box bc**, Courtesy Texas Instruments; **Inside box hi**, Courtesy of NCR Corporation; **Figure 4-18a**, Courtesy of Sony Electronics Inc.; **Figure 4-18b**, Courtesy Apple Computer, Inc.; **Figure 4-19a**, Courtesy David Shopper/ScanSoft; **Figure 4-19b**, Courtesy Acer America; **Figure 4-20**, Courtesy Creative Labs; **Figure 4-21a**, © Fujitsu Siemens Computers; **Figure 4-21b**, Courtesy of Research In Motion (RIM); **Figure 4-21c**, Courtesy Alcatel; **Figure 4-21d**, Courtesy Creative Labs; **Figure 4-21e**, Courtesy Ceiva Logic, Inc.; **Figure 4-21f**, Courtesy of Garmin Ltd. or its subsidiaries; **Figure 4-22**, Courtesy Acer America; **Figure 4-23**, Courtesy of ViewSonic Corporation; **Inside box**, Courtesy Gyricon LLC; **Figure 4-24**, Courtesy Acer America; **Figure 4-25**, Copyright ATI Technologies Inc. 2006; **Figure 4-26a**, Courtesy PureDepth, Ltd; **Figure 4-26b**, Image courtesy of Actuality Systems, Inc. Bedford, MA USA (copyright 2004, David Shopper); **Figure 4-26c**, Courtesy of Eyeneo SAS; **Figure 4-27a**, Courtesy Acer America; **Figure 4-27b**, Courtesy Creative Labs; **Figure 4-27c**, Courtesy Samsung; **Figure 4-28a**, Courtesy of Sony Electronics Inc.; **Figure 4-29**, Courtesy of Universal Display Corporation; **Figure 4-30**, Courtesy of ViewSonic Corporation; **Figure 4-31a**, Courtesy Printek, Inc.; **Figure 4-32bc**, Courtesy, Hewlett-Packard Company; **Figure 4-33b**, Courtesy, Hewlett-Packard Company; **Figure 4-34a**, Courtesy Epson America Inc.; **Figure 4-34b**, Courtesy of Intermec Technologies Corporation; **Figure 4-34c**, Courtesy of Symbol Technologies, Inc.; **Figure 4-34d**, Courtesy, Hewlett-Packard Company; **Figure 4-35**, Courtesy of Altec Lansing; **Expert Insight**, Courtesy, Hewlett-Packard Company.

Chapter 5

Figure 5-1a, Courtesy Bluetooth SIG; **Figure 5-8a**, Courtesy of Seagate Technology LLC; **Figure 5-8b**, Courtesy SimpleTech, Inc.; **Inside box**, Courtesy Jellyvision www.jellyvision.com; **Figure 5-11ac**, Courtesy of Microsoft Corporation; **Figure 5-11bd**, Courtesy Apple Computer, Inc.; **Figure 5-12abc**, Courtesy Acer America; **Figure 5-12d**, Courtesy of IBM Corporation; **Figure 5-14**, Courtesy of Microsoft Corporation; **Figure 5-15**, Courtesy of Microsoft Corporation; **Figure 5-16**, Courtesy of Microsoft Corporation; **Figure 5-17**, Courtesy Apple Computer, Inc.; **Figure 5-18**, Courtesy Novell, Inc.; **You box**, Courtesy, Volvo Cars of North America, LLC; **Figure 5-19a**, Courtesy of Motorola; **Figure 5-19b**, Courtesy Creative Labs; **Figure 5-20a**, Image provided by palmOne, Inc.; **Figure 5-20bc**, Photo courtesy of Nokia. Copyright © 2005 Nokia. All rights reserved. Nokia and Nokia Connecting People are registered trademarks of Nokia Corporation.; **Figure 5-21**, Courtesy of Symantec; **How box**, Copyright 1991-2005 WinZip International LLC. WinZip® is a registered trademark of WinZip International LLC. WinZip is available from http://www.winzip.com. WinZip screen images reproduced with permission of WinZip International LLC.; **Figure 5-24**, Copyright 1991-2005 WinZip International LLC. WinZip® is a registered trademark of WinZip International LLC. WinZip is available from http://www.winzip.com. WinZip screen images reproduced with permission of WinZip International LLC.; **Trend box**, Courtesy Google.

Chapter 6

Figure 6-1a, Adobe product screen shot(s) reprinted with permission from Adobe Systems Incorporated.; **Inside box**, Courtesy OpenOffice.org; **Figure 6-3a**, Courtesy of Symantec; **Trend box**, Courtesy Protocall Technologies Incorporated; **Figure 6-4**, Courtesy of onProject, Inc. www.onproject.com; **Figure 6-5a**, Courtesy Microsoft Corporation; **Figure 6-5b**, Box shot reprinted with permission of Corel Corporation; **Figure 6-5c**, Courtesy of IBM Corporation; **Figure 6-5d**, Courtesy of Sun Microsystems; **Figure 6-6ad**, Courtesy DataViz, Inc.; **Figure 6-6b**, Image provided by palmOne, Inc.; **Figure 6-6cef**, Courtesy Microsoft Corporation; **Figure 6-20h**, © Fujitsu Siemens Computers; **Figure 6-23b**, Adobe product screen shot(s) reprinted with permission from Adobe Systems Incorporated.; **6-23c**, Courtesy Nero AG / Nero Inc.; **Figure 6-24**, Courtesy of Madison Media Software, Inc. and Sony Media Sound Forge 8 is/are [a] trademark/registered trademarks of Madison Media Software, Inc. All rights reserved.; **Figure 6-25**, Courtesy Sonic Solutions; **Figure 6-26**, Copyright © 1995-2002 RealNetworks, Inc. All rights reserved. RealNetworks, Real.com, RealAudio, RealVideo, RealSystem, RealPlayer, RealJukebox and RealMedia are trademarks or registered trademarks of RealNetworks, Inc.; Photo by Joanne Savio; **How box**, Courtesy Sonic Solutions; **Figure 6-27a**, Quark, QuarkXPress and other Quark, Inc. trademarks are the property of Quark, Inc. and all applicatable affiliated companies. Portions © 2000 Quark, Inc. All rights reserved.; **Figure 6-27b**, © 2005 Riverdeep Interactive Learning Limited, and its licensors www.riverdeep.net; **Figure 6-27c**, Courtesty of Sage Software SB, Inc. The Peachtree Logo is a registered trademark of Sage Software SB, Inc.; **Figure 6-27d**, Courtesy of Punch! Software, LLC. www.punchsoftware.com; **Figure 6-27e**, Courtesy Microsoft Corporation; **Figure 6-27f**, Courtesy FranklinCovey; **You box**, Courtesy Agilix Labs; **Expert Insight**, Courtesy Novell, Inc.

Chapter 7

Figure 7-2a, Courtesy Alcatel; **Figure 7-2b**, Photo courtesy of Globalstar LLC.; **Trend box a**, Courtesy Talking Street www.talkingstreet.com; **Trend box b**, Courtesy Office of Parking and Transportation, California State University, Fresno; **Figure 7-3**, Courtesy CommtechWireless; **Figure 7-4**, Courtesy Magellan Consumer Products; **Figure 7-5ab**, Courtesy Health Hero Network; **Figure 7-5c**, Courtesy of ViewSonic Corporation; **Figure 7-5d**, Courtesy of Panasonic; **Figure 7-6ac**, Courtesy XM Satellite Radio; **Figure 7-6b**, Courtesy SIRIUS Satellite Radio; **Figure 7-7a**, Courtesy SightSpeed www.sightspeed.com; **Figure 7-7b**, Courtesy of Motorola; **Inside box**, Courtesy Dust Networks; **Trend box a**, Courtesy Sling Media, Inc.; **Trend box b**, © Fujitsu Siemens Computers; **Figure 7-8a**, Courtesy InTouch Health, Inc.; **Figure 7-8b**, Courtesy, University of Rochester; **Figure 7-8c**, Photo made available by St. Joseph's Healthcare Hamilton; **Figure 7-9a**, Courtesy Acer America; **Figure 7-9b**, Courtesy of Linksys; Courtesy of IBM Corporation; **Figure 7-10a**, Courtesy Acer America; **Figure 7-10b**, Courtesy of Linksys; **Figure 7-10c**, Courtesy of IBM Corporation; **Figure 7-11a**, Courtesy Acer America; **Figure 7-11b**, Courtesy of Linksys; **Figure 7-11c**, Courtesy of IBM Corporation; **Figure 7-12**, Courtesy of SCOTTeVEST, www.scottevest.com; **Figure 7-15**, Courtesy Acer America; **Figure 7-16a**, Courtesy of Logitech; **Figure 7-16b**, Courtesy Acer America; **Figure 7-16c**, Courtesy of IBM Corporation; **Figure 7-17a**, Courtesy of Black Box Corporation; **Figure 7-17b**, Courtesy of Belkin Corporation; **Figure 7-18ac**, Photo(s) courtesy of Hughes Network Systems, LLC.; **Figure 7-18b**, Courtesy Alcatel; **Figure 7-18d**, Courtesy Acer America; **Figure 7-20**, Courtesy Acer America; **Figure 7-21**, Courtesy Acer America; **Figure 7-22a**, Photograph: Courtesy of the Information Services Publications and Marketing Team, University of Nottingham.; **Figure 7-22b**, Courtesy of Intel Corporation; **Figure 7-24**, Courtesy Bluetooth SIG; **Figure 7-25a**, Courtesy Acer America; **Figure 7-25b**, Courtesy Juniper Networks; **How box a**, Courtesy D-Link Systems; **How box b**, Courtesy NETGEAR; **How box c**, Courtesy of Belkin Corporation; **Figure 7-26af**, Courtesy NETGEAR; **Figure 7-26bc**, Courtesy of Linksys; **Figure 7-26de**, Courtesy D-Link Systems; **Figure 7-27ab**, Courtesy US Robotics; **Figure 7-27c**, Courtesy D-Link Systems; **Figure 7-27d**, Courtesy Spacenet Inc.; **Figure 7-28a**, Courtesy Acer America; **Figure 7-28b**, Courtesy D-Link Systems; **Figure 7-28c**, Courtesy Data Comm for Business Inc.; **Figure 7-28d**, Courtesy of Linksys; **Figure 7-28e**, Courtesy NETGEAR; **Figure 7-28f**, Courtesy Apple Computer, Inc.

Chapter 8

Figure 8-1a, Courtesy of ViewSonic Corporation; **Figure 8-1b**, CBS and the CBS Eye are registered trademarks of CBS Broadcasting Inc. The Survivor: Guatemala - The Maya Empire Logo is a registered trademark of Survivor Productions, LC. CBS.COM website contents © CBS Broadcasting Inc. Used by permission.; **Figure 8-2a**, Courtesy Sprint; **Figure 8-2b**, Courtesy Road Runner; **Figure 8-2c**, Courtesy EarthLink; **Figure 8-2d**, America Online, AOL and the Running Man icon are registered trademarks of America Online, Inc. The AOL Triangle logo is a trademark of America Online, Inc. AOL content © 2005 by America Online, Inc. The America Online content, name, icons and trademarks are used with permission; **Figure 8-2e**, Courtesy Cingular Wireless;; **Figure 8-2f**, Courtesy Spacenet Inc.; **Figure 8-2g**, Courtesy Pacific LightNet; **Figure 8-2h**, Courtesy Clearwire; **Figure 8-4**, Courtesy CoreFTP.com; **Figure 8-5a**, Courtesy Acer America; **Figure 8-5b**, Courtesy of Salton, Inc.; **Figure 8-5c**, Courtesy Danger, Inc.; **Figure 8-7ab**, Photo provided courtesy of the Wi-Fi Alliance; **Figure 8-7c**, Courtesy of Siemens AG/Siemens press picture; **Figure 8-7d**, Courtesy Bluetooth SIG; **Figure 8-9**, America Online, AOL and the Running Man icon are registered trademarks of America Online, Inc. The AOL Triangle logo is a trademark of America Online, Inc. AOL content © 2005 by America Online, Inc. The America Online content, name, icons and trademarks are used with permission; **Figure 8-10ab**, Courtesy Google; **Figure 8-11a**, Courtesy Yahoo!; **Figure 8-11b**, © 2006 InfoSpace, Inc. All rights reserved. Reprinted with permission of InfoSpace, Inc.; **Figure 8-11c**, Courtesy Ask Jeeves, Inc.; **Figure 8-12b**, Courtesy Google; **Figure 8-17c**, Courtesy SightSpeed www.sightspeed.com; **How box a**, Courtesy Vonage; **How box b**, Courtesy D-Link Systems; **Figure 8-18b**, These materials have been reproduced with the permission of eBay Inc. COPYRIGHT © EBAY INC. ALL RIGHTS RESERVED.; **Figure 8-19a**, Used by Permission of Clear Channel Radio.; **Figure 8-19b**, © 2000-2005, Wal-Mart.com USA, LLC and Wal-Mart Stores, Inc.; **Figure 8-19c**, © 2005 Movielink, LLC. All rights reserved. Paycheck © MMIII by PARAMOUNT PICTURES CORPORATION AND DREAMWORKS LLC. All rights reserved. Cruel Intentions 3 © 2004 Sony Pictures Television International. All rights reserved. Along Came Polly © 2004 Universal Studios. All rights reserved. Mystic River © 2003 Warner Bros. Entertainment Inc. All rights reserved. Osama © 2004 United Artists Films Inc. All rights reserved. Scary Movie 3 © 2003 Miramax Film Corp. All rights reserved. The Cooler © 2003 Cooler Productions, LLC. All rights reserved.; **Figure 8-19d**, Courtesy of IGN.com; **Figure 8-21**, Courtesy of Wurld Media, Inc.; **You box**, Napster logo and marks reprinted with the permission of Napster, LLC.; **Figure 8-22d**, The MapQuest.com logo is a registered trademark of MapQuest, Inc. MapQuest.com content © 2005 MapQuest, Inc. Used with permission.; **Trend box**, Courtesy of Edupodder; **Figure 8-26a**, Courtesy Yahoo!; **Figure 8-28**, Courtesy Bugnosis.org.

Chapter 9

Figure 9-1b, Courtesy Lance Fischer; **Figure 9-2a**, Courtesy Kensington Technology Group, www.kensington.com; **Figure 9-2b**, Courtesy Yahoo! Maps; **Figure 9-3**, Courtesy Jeff Bardin; **Figure 9-4**, Courtesy Acer America; **Figure 9-5**, Courtesy Acer America; **Figure 9-8**, Courtesy The CBORD Group, Inc.; **Figure 9-9ac**, Courtesy of Identix Inc. Minnetonka, MN, USA; **Figure 9-9b**, Courtesy of IR Recognition Systems, and Ingersoll-Rand Business; **Figure 9-9d**, Courtesy Diebold, Incorporated; **You box**, Joseph Mehling, Dartmouth College; **Figure 9-10a**, Courtesy of SURFnet; **Figure 9-11**, Copyright ©1999-2005 Zone Labs. All rights reserved.; **Figure 9-12**, Courtesy of Symantec; **Figure 9-15**, Netscape and the "N" logo are registered trademarks of Netscape Communications Corporation. Netscape content © 2005 Netscape. Used with permission.; **Trend box**, Courtesy of pharming.org and learnsecurity.com; **Inside box**, Courtesy Equifax; **Figure 9-18**, Courtesy RSA Security; **Figure 9-19**, These materials have been reproduced with the permission of eBay Inc. COPYRIGHT © EBAY INC. ALL RIGHTS RESERVED.; **Figure 9-21**, Courtesy Lavasoft AB; **Figure 9-22**, Netscape and the "N" logo are registered trademarks of Netscape Communications Corporation. Netscape content © 2005 Netscape. Used with permission.; **Expert Insight**, Courtesy Jeff Bardin.

Chapter 10

You box, Courtesy There; **Figure 10-2**, Courtesy of Meredith Corporation; **Figure 10-4b**, ©2005 JupiterImages Corporation. All rights reserved.; **Figure 10-8**, Courtesy of Jim McNew and Photoholic.com; **Figure 10-10a**, Courtesy of PBS and Thirteen/WNET New York. ©2005; **Figure 10-10b**, Screen shot courtesy of PBS. ARTHUR Web site © 2005 WGBH; underlying ARTHUR TM/© Marc Brown.; **Figure 10-11**, Courtesy Macromedia; **Trend box**, Courtesy Browse 3D; **Figure 10-12c**, Screen shot courtesy of PBS. ARTHUR Web site © 2005 WGBH; underlying ARTHUR TM/© Marc Brown.; **Inside box**, © 2004 Disney Enterprises, Inc./Pixar; **Figure 10-14a**, © Disney Enterprises, Inc. TOY STORY 2 © Disney Enterprises, Inc./Pixar; **Figure 10-15a**, Courtesy of Viewsonic Corporation; **Figure 10-15bc**, Courtesy Opera Software ASA; **Figure 10-16**, Courtesy of Stanford University; **Figure 10-17**, Bobby icon courtesy Watchfire; **Figure 10-18**, Courtesy Webpencil.com. Courtesy of TheUShack.com; **Figure 10-23**, Courtesy Macromedia.

Chapter 11

You box, Courtesy Telstra; **Figure 11-2**, Courtesy Pricegrabber.com; **Figure 11-3**, Courtesy of International Business Machines Corporation. Unauthorized use not permitted; **Figure 11-4a**, © 2005 Dell Inc. All Rights Reserved.; **Figure 11-5**, These materials have been reproduced with the permission of eBay Inc. COPYRIGHT © EBAY INC. ALL RIGHTS RESERVED.; **Figure 11-6**, Courtesy Quadrem; **How box**, Courtesy of Wurld Media, Inc.; **Figure 11-9a**, © 2005 Amazon.com, Inc. All Rights Reserved.; **Figure 11-9b**, Courtesy SimpleTech, Inc.; **Figure 11-10a**, © 2000-2005, Wal-Mart.com USA, LLC and Wal-Mart Stores, Inc.; **Figure 11-10b**, Courtesy K-Swiss, Inc.; **Figure 11-11**, Courtesy K-Swiss, Inc.; **Trend box**, Courtesy of Enpocket; **Figure 11-13**, Courtesy of Gemplus; **Figure 11-14a**, Courtesy Ilium Software; **Figure 11-14bc**, © 2005 Amazon.com, Inc. All Rights Reserved.; **Figure 11-15**, Courtesy MonsterCommerce.com; **Figure 11-16**, Reprinted with permission of TRUSTe; **Figure 11-18a**, Courtesy Milestone Mediaworks and webpencil.com; **Figure 11-18b**, Courtesy BizzToolz and webpencil.com; **Figure 11-18c**, Copyright © 2005 Yahoo! Inc. All Rights Reserved. Yahoo!, Y! and the Y! Music logo are the trademarks and/or registered trademarks of Yahoo! Inc. Banner Ad Courtesy of Yahoo! Inc. All Rights Reserved.; **Figure 11-18d**, Courtesy of TheUShack.com and webpencil.com; **Figure 11-18e**, Courtesy Group Travel Planet, LLC and webpencil.com; **Inside box**, Courtesy Dotomi Inc.; **Figure 11-19**, ©2005 Megaputer Intelligence Inc., www.megaputer.com. Published with the permission of Megaputer Intelligence Inc.; **Expert Insight**, Copyright © 2005 Yahoo! Inc. All Rights Reserved. Yahoo!, Y! and the Y! Music logo are the trademarks and/or registered trademarks of Yahoo! Inc. Banner Ad Courtesy of Yahoo! Inc. All Rights Reserved.

Chapter 12

You box, Courtesy Cedar Point; **Figure 12-3**, Adobe product screen shot(s) reprinted with permission from Adobe Systems Incorporated.; **Trend box**, Courtesy Pay By Touch Solutions; **Figure 12-4**, Courtesy Diebold, Incorporated; **Figure 12-7**, Huff Probability Model in Dallas Map is used herein with permission. Copyright © 2005 ESRI, Tele Atlas, and infoUSA. All rights reserved.; **Figure 12-8**, Screen shot from SimpleTech Web site courtesy of LivePerson, Inc and SimpleTech, Inc.; **Figure 12-9**, Courtesy of Provia Software; **How box**, These images are reproduced with permission of United Parcel Service of America, Inc. © Copyright 2006 United Parcel Service of America, Inc. All rights reserved. **Figure 12-10**, Courtesy of NCR Corporation; **Figure 12-11**, Courtesy AutoDesk, Inc.; **Inside box**, Courtesy of Dr. Huge Loebner; **Figure 12-12a**, Courtesy of IBM Corporation; **Figure 12-12b**, © AP Wide World Photos; **Figure 12-13**, Courtesy Agentland.com; **Figure 12-14a**, © Fujitsu Siemens Computers; **Figure 12-15**, Courtesy Bundesdruckerei GmbH; **Figure 12-16a**, Courtesy of iRobot; **Figure 12-16b**, Courtesy Berkeley Robotics and Human Engineering Laboratory; **Figure 12-16c**, Courtesy of Robowatch Technologies; **Figure 12-17a**, Courtesy of Sony Electronics Inc.; **Figure 12-17b**, Courtesy of American Honda Motor Co., Inc.; **Figure 12-17c**, Courtesy of Mitsubishi Heavy Industries, Ltd.; **Figure 12-17d**, Courtesy of iRobot; **Figure 12-19b**, Photo courtesy of Nokia. Copyright © 2005 Nokia. All rights reserved. Nokia and Nokia Connecting People are registered trademarks of Nokia Corporation.; **Figure 12-23ab**, Courtesy Acer America.

Chapter 13

Figure 13-3b, © PhotoDisc/Getty Images; **Figure 13-5b**, Courtesy of SmartDraw; to download a free trial of SmartDraw, visit www.smartdraw.com; **Inside box**, Courtesy U.S. Navy; **Figure 13-14**, Courtesy Visible Systems; **Figure 13-16**, Courtesy Wind River; **Trend box**, Courtesy Imagination Games; **You box**, Courtesy NOAA/NESDIS/NCDC; **Figure 13-24**, Java and the Java Coffee Cup logo are trademarks or registered trademarks of Sun Microsystems, Inc.

Chapter 14

Figure 14-1b, Courtesy Acer America; **Figure 14-7**, Courtesy Application Security, Inc.; **You box**, Courtesy of Gettysburg College; **Figure 14-8b**, Courtesy Acer America; **Figure 14-10**, Courtesy Acer America; **Figure 14-12b**, Courtesy of Linksys; **Figure 14-18a**, Courtesy of ViewSonic Corporation; **Figure 14-21**, Courtesy Astrophysical Research Consortium (ARC) and the Sloan Digital Sky Survey (SDSS) Collaboration, http://www.sdss.org; **Figure 14-22a**, © 2006 InfoSpace, Inc. All rights reserved. Reprinted with permission of InfoSpace, Inc.; **Figure 14-22b**, © 2005 Amazon.com, Inc. All Rights Reserved.; **Figure 14-23b**, Courtesy Acer America; **How box**, These images are reproduced with permission of United Parcel Service of America, Inc. © Copyright 2006 United Parcel Service of America, Inc. All rights reserved. **Expert Insight**, Courtesy Anthony Briggs.

Chapter 15

Figure 15-1, Courtesy of Verizon Communications; **Figure 15-2**, Courtesy Kensington Technology Group, www.kensington.com; **You box**, Courtesy Election Systems and Software; **Figure 15-3**, Courtesy Trekstor USA Inc.; **Figure 15-4**, Courtesy Itronix Corporation; **Figure 15-5**, Courtesy APC; **Figure 15-6**, Courtesy Getac Inc.; **How box**, Courtesy of Symantec; **Figure 15-8**, Photo courtesy of United States Secret Service; **Figure 15-9**, Photo courtesy of United States Secret Service; **Figure 15-10c**, © 2006 InfoSpace, Inc. All rights reserved. Reprinted with permission of InfoSpace, Inc.; **Trend box**, *MediNotes e* electronic medical record image courtesy MediNotes Corporation; **Figure 15-13b**, Courtesy Akonix Systems, Inc.; **Figure 15-14**, Privacy Bird® software was originally developed by AT&T Corp. It is now maintained by the CMU Usable Privacy and Security Laboratory at Carnegie Mellon University. Privacy Bird icons courtesy of Carnegie Mellon University.; **Figure 15-15**, Adobe product screen shot(s) reprinted with permission from Adobe Systems Incorporated.; **Figure 15-16a**, Courtesy Google; **Figure 15-17**, Netscape and the "N" logo are registered trademarks of Netscape Communications Corporation. Netscape content © 2005 Netscape. Used with permission.; **Figure 15-19**, Courtesy Fellowes, Inc.; **Figure 15-20**, Courtesy TrueActive Software; **Figure 15-21a**, © 2002 Cédric Laurant; **Inside box**, Courtesy LaserCard Corporation (www.lasercard.com); **Figure 15-22**, Courtesy HID Corporation; **Figure 15-23**, Courtesy Intellisync; **Figure 15-24**, Courtesy Omniquad Ltd.

Chapter 16

How box, Courtesy Digimarc Corporation; **Figure 16-1b**, Courtesy of Jim McNew and Photoholic.com.; **Figure 16-2b**, NBC logo reproduced courtes of NBC, Inc. **Figure 16-2c**, [eBay Mark] is a trademark of eBay Inc.; **Figure 16-2d**, Coca-Cola and the Contour Bottle design are registered trademarks of The Coca-Cola Company; **Figure 16-3**, Courtesy of United States Patent and Trademark Office; **Figure 16-5**, Courtesy of iParadigms, developers of Turnitin; **Figure 16-7**, Courtesy of University of Denver; **Figure 16-8**, Credit must be given to the University of California, Lawrence Livermore National Laboratory, and the Department of Energy under whose auspices the work was performed, when this information of a reproduction of it is used. Courtesy of CIAC (Computer Incident Advisory Capability); **Figure 16-9**, Courtesy PoliticsNJ.com; **Figure 16-12**, © AP World Wide Web Photos; **Figure 16-14a**, Courtesy APC; **Figure 16-15a**, Courtesy Microsoft Corporation; **Figure 16-15b**, Courtesy of 3M Company; **Figure 16-15cde**, Courtesy Kensington Technology Group, www.kensington.com; **Figure 16-15f**, Courtesy IMAK Products Corporation; **Figure 16-17a**, Courtesy Xybernaut Corporation; **Figure 16-17bd**, Courtesy Itronix Corporation; **Figure 16-17c**, Courtesy Sutter Gould Medical Foundation; **Figure 16-18**, Courtesy of Siemens AG/Siemens press picture; **Figure 16-19**, Courtesy of Maressa Hecht Orzack, Ph.D.; **Figure 16-21a**, Photo of "Encore Simputer" courtesy of Encore Software Limited, Bangalore; **Figure 16-21b**, Courtesy Design Continuum; **Figure 16-22a**, Courtesy Hooleon Corporation; **Figure 16-22b**, Courtesy of Maltron; **Figure 16-22c**, Courtesy of Prentke Romich, **Figure 16-22d**, Courtesy NaturalPoint, Inc.; **Figure 16-23abc**, Courtesy of Freedom Scientific, Inc.; **Figure 16-23d**, Courtesy of NanoPac, Inc. www.nanopac.com; **Trend box**, Courtesy Applied Digital Solutions, Inc.; **Figure 16-24a**, Courtesy of U.S. Environmental Protection Agency; **Figure 16-24b**, Courtesy of European Commission, Environment Directorate-General; **Figure 16-24c**, Directorate-General Courtesy of Korea Environmental Labeling Association (KELA); **Figure 16-24d**, Courtesy of ABNT - ASSOCIAÇÃO BRASILEIRA DE NORMAS TÉCNICAS; **Figure 16-25a**, Courtesy ICP Solar Technologies Inc.; **Figure 16-25b**, Courtesy IST Designs, Inc.; **Figure 16-26**, © Fujitsu Siemens Computers; **Inside box**, Courtesy of The Board of Trustees of The Leland Stanford Junior University; **Figure 16-27**, Courtesy of Silicon Valley Toxics Coalition; **Figure 16-28b**, Courtesy U.S. Marines; **Exercise 5a**, Courtesy of Prentke Romich; **Exercise 5b**, Courtesy IMAK Products Corporation; **Exercise 5c**, Courtesy Kensington Technology Group, www.kensington.com; **Exercise 5d**, Courtesy of U.S. Environmental Protection Agency; **Exercise 5e**, Courtesy of 3M Company; **Exercise 5f**, Courtesy Hooleon Corporation; **Expert Insight**, Courtesy of Dell Inc.; the Dell logo is a trademark of Dell Inc.

References and Resources Guide

Computer History Timeline: 1, **2**, **5**, **6**, **9**, **12**, **19**, Courtesy of IBM Archives; **3**, Courtesy Iowa State University; **4**, Courtesy Jim Bready; **7**, Courtesy Unisys Corporation ; **8**, Courtesy U.S. Navy; **10**, **37**, Courtesy Texas Instruments; **11**, Courtesy of Bootstrap Institute/Alliance; **13**, **22**, **28**, **32**, **34**, Courtesy of Intel Corporation; **14**, **15**, **36**, Courtesy Microsoft Corporation; **16**, Courtesy Dan Bricklin; **17**, Courtesy Cray Inc.; **18**, **23**, Courtesy Apple Computer, Inc.; **20**, **39**, Courtesy, Hewlett-Packard Company; **21**, Fabian Bachrach, courtesy W3C; **24**, Netscape and the "N" logo are registered trademarks of Netscape Communications Corporation. Netscape content © 2005 Netscape. Used with permission. **25**, Courtesy Larry Ewing lewing@isc.tamu.edu and The GIMP; **26**, Courtesy of Panasonic; **27**, **43**, Image provided by palmOne, Inc.; **29**, Courtesy Microsoft Museum; **30**, [eBay Mark] is a trademark of eBay Inc.; **31**, Java and the Java Coffee Cup logo are trademarks or registered trademarks of Sun Microsystems, Inc.; **33**, Courtesy Kingston Technology Company Inc.; **35**, **41**, Microsoft, Windows and the Windows logo are either registered trademarks or trademarks of Microsoft Corporation in the United States and/or other countries.; **38**, Courtesy GoTV Networks; **40**, © 2003, 2005 Advanced Micro Devices, Inc., Reprinted with permission. AMD, the AMD logo, AMD Athlon, and combinations thereof are trademarks of Advanced Micro Devices, Inc.; **42**, Courtesy Oakley; **R-7a**, Netscape and the "N" logo are registered trademarks of Netscape Communications Corporation. Netscape content © 2005 Netscape. Used with permission.

GLOSSARY/INDEX

Special Characters
$ (dollar sign), 239
* (asterisk), 237
+ (plus sign), 237
– (minus sign), 237
/ (slash), 237
^ (caret), 237

A

.aac file extension, 420
AAC (Advanced Audio Coding) format, 420
abacus, 13, R-2
ABC (Atanasoff-Berry Computer), R-2
ABC (Alcohol Beverages Control) Commission, 672
absolute cell referencing, 238–239
academic honor code, 668
Accelerated Graphics Port (AGP) bus, 70, 72
access control system, 372–376
access mechanism, 103
access provider, 314
access to technology, 682–688
assistive technology, 686–688
digital divide, 683–686
multimedia Web sites, 428–429
accounting software, 251, 252
accounting system A type of transaction system that deals with the financial transactions and financial recordkeeping for an organization. 494
accounts payable system, 494
accounts receivable system, 494
acronym, 40
active cell, 236
worksheet, 237
active data dictionary, 545
active RFID tag, 271
Active Service Pages (ASP), 34
ActiveX, 435
ad hoc network, 278
ADA (Americans with Disabilities Act), 686
adapter board. *See* expansion card
adaptive cruise control system, 202
Ad-Aware, 292
Add to Favorites option, 36
add-in board. *See* expansion card
addition operator (+), 237
address
memory, 68
storage, 98
Address bar, 35
address book, R-15
addressable media, 98
Adidas running shoe, CPU in, 64
Adobe Acrobat, 380, 492
Adobe AfterEffects, 419
Adobe Audition, 248
Adobe Authorware, 419, 420
Adobe GoLive, 436
Adobe Illustrator, 247
Adobe PhotoShop Elements, 247
Adobe Premiere Elements, 248
Adobe Reader, 339, 419, 492
Advance Research Projects Agency (ARPA), 312
Advanced Audio Coding (AAC) format, 420
Advanced Encryption Standard (AES), 379
Advanced Micro Devices (AMD), R-3
Advanced Micro Devices (AMD) microprocessor, 63
Advanced Micro Devices (AMD) Opteron Athlon 64, R-7
Advanced Micro Devices (AMD) Opteron server, R-7
Advanced Optical Disc (AOD), 113
adware, 352–353
AdWords, 472
AES (Advanced Encryption Standard), 379
Agilix Labs GoBinder, 253
AGP (Accelerated Graphics Port) bus, 70, 72
AI. *See* artificial intelligence (AI); artificial intelligence (AI) system
AIBO, 506, 507
AIFF (Audio Interchange Format File), 420
.aiff file extension, 420
airport security, 644
AJAX (Asynchronous JavaScript and XML), 435
Albertsons, 493
Alcohol Beverages Control (ABC) Commission, 672
algorithm
hashing, 589
program design, 535
align left option, 234
align right option, 234
alignment, formatting documents, 234
Allen, Christopher, 482–483
Allen, Paul, R-4
all-in-one desktop PC, 21, 22
ALM. *See* Application Lifecycle Management (ALM)
alpha test, 550
Altair, R-4
AltaVista, 343, 470
Alternate key, 134
alternative text description, 428–429
ALU. *See* arithmetic/logic unit (ALU)
always-on connection, 31–32, 319, 321
Amazon.com, 335, 456, 460, 472, 691, R-6
AMD. *See* Advanced Micro Devices *entries*
America Online (AOL), 31, 209, 314, 343, R-5
American Express, 672
American Standard Code for Information Interchange. *See* ASCII (American Standard Code for Information Interchange)
Americans with Disabilities Act (ADA), 686
analog signal, 281
Andreesen, Marc, R-5
animated GIF A group of GIF images saved as an animated GIF file that is inserted in a Web page; the individual images are displayed one after another to simulate movement. 418
animation The process by which a series of graphical images are displayed one after the other to simulate movement. 418–419
presentation graphics, 244–245
anonymity, 41
Anonymizer, 41, 637
anonymous Web browsing service, 637
Anticybersquatting Consumer Protection Act of 1999, 469
antiglare screen, 678
antiglare shield, 678
antipiracy technique, 629
antispam appliance, 638
antispy software, 647
antispyware program, 82, 211, 292, 626
antivirus software Software used to detect and eliminate computer viruses and other types of malware. 17, 39, 82, 210–211, 377–378, 626
AOD (Advanced Optical Disc), 113
AOL (America Online), 31, 209, 314, 343, R-5
AOL Instant Messenger, 333
AOP. *See* aspect-oriented programming (AOL)
API (application programming interface), 605
Apple, 662, R-4, R-6
Apple I, R-4
Apple iChat AV, 273
Apple II, R-4
Apple iPhoto, 247
Apple Macintosh. *See* Macintosh PC
Applebee's, 671
AppleWorks, 228
application assistant, 503
application generator, 552–553
Application Lifecycle Management (ALM) A broad term to describe complete systems that can be used to create and manage an application throughout its entire lifecycle-from design through testing. 551–552
application programming interface (API), 605
application service provider (ASP) A company that manages and distributes software-based services over the Internet. 225, 315–316
application software Programs that enable users to perform specific tasks on a computer, such as writing a letter or playing a game. 16, 18–19, 184, 220–255
accounting, 252
analyzing needs, R-10
audio editing, 248
CD and DVD burning, 249
collaboration, 253
common commands, 229–232
database. *See* database software
design, 251, 252
desktop publishing, 251, 252
desktop vs. mobile, 228–229

development. *See* program development; program development life cycle (PDLC)
DVD authoring, 248
edutainment, 251, 252
graphics (digital imaging), 246–247
graphics and multimedia for Web, 249
installed vs. Web-based, 224–226
media players, 249
note taking, 253
ownership rights, 221–224
personal finance, 252
personal productivity, 252, 253
personal publishing, 252
presentation graphics. *See* presentation graphics software
project management, 252, 253
reference, 252
spreadsheet. *See* spreadsheet software; spreadsheet
suites, 227–228
system software compared, 183–184
video editing, 248
word processing. *See* word processing software
architecture
improving, 83–84
networks, 278–279
archiving e-mail, 353
argument, functions, 237
arithmetic/logic unit (ALU) The part of the CPU that performs logical operations and integer arithmetic. 76
ARPA (Advance Research Projects Agency), 312
ARPANET The predecessor of the Internet, named after the Advanced Research Projects Agency (ARPA), which sponsored its development. 312, R-3
arrow, 18
arrow key, 133, 134
artificial intelligence (AI), 14, 502
expert systems, 504–505
intelligent agents, 503–504
neural networks, 505
robotics, 505–507
artificial intelligence (AI) system A system in which a computer performs actions that are characteristic of human intelligence. 490, 502–507, 503
ASCII (American Standard Code for Information Interchange) A fixed-length, binary coding system widely used to represent text-based data for computer processing on many types of computers. 57, 58
chart, R-8
ASIMO, 506, 507
Ask Jeeves, 209, 470
ASP. *See* application service provider (ASP)
.asp, 34
ASP (Active Service Pages), 34
aspect-oriented programming (AOP) An approach to program design in which different functions are clearly separated so program components can be developed and modified individually from one another, and the components can be easily reused with separate, nonrelated objects. 533–534
assembler, 547
assembly language A low-level programming language that uses names and other symbols to replace some of the 0s and 1s in machine language. 547, 554, R-2
assistive technology Hardware and software specifically designed for use by individuals with physical disabilities. 428–429, 686–688
input devices, 686–687
output devices, 687–688
asterisk (*), multiplication operator, 237
asymmetric encryption, 379
Asynchronous JavaScript and XML (AJAX), 435
asynchronous transmission, 282, 283
Atanasoff, John V. R-2
Atanasoff-Berry Computer (ABC), R-2
Athlon 64 microprocessor, 63, 65
Athlon 64 X2 microprocessor, 63, 65
Athlon 64-FX microprocessor, 65
Athlon XP microprocessor, 65
AT&T, 334, 637
AT&T Bell Laboratories, 199, R-3, R-4
AT&T WorldNet, 31
attribute A characteristic of an entity. 581
auction, online. *See* online auction *entries*
Audi, 202
audience, Web page, 423
audio Sound, such as music, spoken voice, and sound effects. 12, 420
coding system, 60–61
editing software, 248
input, 152–153
integrated, 69–70
output, 168–169
Audio Interchange Format File (AIFF), 420
audio port, 74
Audio-Video Interleave (AVI) format, 420
auditory learners, 413
authentication system, 372
AutoCAD, 501
Automated Biometric Identification System (IDENT), 644
automatic encryption, 379
.avi file extension, 420
AVI (Audio-Video Interleave) format, 420

B

back end, 590
backbone, 31
background color, transparent, 416
backlighting, 161
backside bus (BSB), 70
Backspace key, 133, 134
backup A duplicate copy of data or other computer content in case the original version is destroyed. 103, 105, 210, 625, 626, 627
databases, 586
backup utility, 210, 211
Baltimore, Maryland, 642
bandwidth The amount of data that can be transmitted over a communications medium at one time; higher bandwidth media deliver data faster than lower bandwidth media. 67, 281–282
high-bandwidth items on Web pages, 422
banking, online, 336
banner ad, 471, 472, 473
banner image, 422
barcode A machine-readable code that represents data as a set of bars. 144, 166
barcode printer An output device that prints barcoded documents. 166, 167
barcode reader An input device that reads barcodes. 144–145
Bardeen, John, R-3
Bardin, Jeff, 406–407
base 10 numbering system, 56
base number, 56
BASIC An easy-to-learn, high-level programming language that was developed to be used by beginning programmers. 18, 555, 559, 560, R-4
basic input/output system (BIOS), 69
batch processing, 575
BayTSP, 666
B2B. *See* business-to-business (B2) model
B2C. *See* business-to-consumer (B2C) model
BCI (brain-to-computer interfacing), 687, 688
BD (Blu-ray Disc), 113
Begaye, Kelsey, 623
Beginner's All-purpose Symbolic Instruction Code. *See* BASIC
behavioral targeting, 471, 472
Behziz, Nada, 664
Bell Labs, R-3, R-4
Ben Gurion Airport, 644
benchmark test A test that measures the performance of a computer system to evaluate certain hardware or software components. 66, 518
Berners-Lee, Tim, 312, 429, R-5
Berry, Clifford, R-2
BestBuy.com, 456
beta version, 550
Betamax, 665
B2G. *See* business-to-government (B2G) model
BI (business intelligence) system, 496
binary numbering system The numbering system that represents all numbers using just two symbols (0 and 1). 55, 56–57
biometric access system An access control system that uses one unique physical characteristic of an individual (such as a fingerprint, face, or voice) to authenticate that individual. 374–375
biometric data, 119–120, 373
biometric reader A device used to input biometric data. 148–149, 375
biometrics, 116, 187, 375
border control, 644
identification documents, 644
BIOS (basic input/output system), 69
bit, 55–56
bit depth, 58, 157
bitmap, 58
bit-mapped image, 246
bits per second (bps), 282
black hat hacker, 364
black-and-white printer, 163
Blackboard Learning System software, 253
blade, 20, 28
blade PC, 20, 28
blade server, 20, 28
Blair, Jason, 664
Blaster, 370
blind spot information system (BLIS), 202
block, worksheet, 236
blog A Web page that contains short, frequently updated entries in chronological order, typically by just one individual; also called a Web log. 345–346
blog aggregator, 346
blogosphere, 346
Blowfish, 379
Blue Gene/L computer, 29, 204
blue laser disc, 112, 113

Bluetooth A communications standard for very short-range wireless connections; the devices are automatically connected once they get within the allowable range. 281, 286, 293–294
Bluetooth port, 74
Bluetooth-compliant keyboard, 133
Blu-ray Disc (BD), 113
BMW, 202
Bobby service, 429
body, XHTML Web page, 433
body scanner, 144
Bolt, 343
book
  copyright protection, 664
  electronic. *See* e-book
Bookmarks feature, 36
Boolean operator, 329
boot To start up a computer. 17, 185
boot process, 17
border, 230
border control system, 644
BPL (broadband over power lines), 321
bps (bits per second), 282
Braille display, 688
Braille keyboard, 139, 428, 686
Braille printer, 688
brain-to-computer interfacing (BCI), 687, 688
Brattain, Walter, R-3
brick-and-mortar store A conventional store with a physical presence. 343, 450
bridge, 300
Briggs, Anthony, 614–615
Brigham Young University law school, 253
broadband Internet access, R-7
broadband over power lines (BPL), 321
broadcast flag, 666
broadcast radio transmission, 286
broker, online, 336
brokerage model, 459
brokerage site A type of Web site used to bring buyers and sellers together to facilitate transactions, such as online stock trading and exchanging goods, services, and commodities. 454–456
Brown, John Seely, 534
Brown, Michelle, 385
browser. *See* Web browser
browser hijacking, 389
BSA (Business Software Alliance), 627
BSB (backside bus), 70
buddy list, 333
budget, power vs., R-11
buffer An area in RAM or on the hard drive designated to hold input and output on their way in or out of the system. 190
buffering, audio files, 420
bug
  debugging programs, 545–549
  original, 546
Bugnosis, 352
Build option, Visual Basic, 561
burning a disc, 109
  CDs, 249
  DVDs, 248, 249
burnout A state of fatigue or frustration usually brought on by overwork. 675, 681
bus An electronic path on the motherboard or within the CPU or other computer component along which data is transferred. 66, 70–72
bus interface unit The part of the CPU where instructions and data flow in and out of the CPU. 76, 78
bus network A network consisting of a central cable to which all network devices are attached. 277
bus speed, 66, 67
bus width, 66–67
Bush, George W. 632, 683
business. *See also* e-commerce *entries*
  advantages of e-commerce, 450, 452
  disadvantages of e-commerce, 453
business analyst, information system development, 509
business auction site, 455
business card CD, 109–110
  increase in use, 111
business card scanner, 142
business ethics Standards of moral conduct that guide a business's policies, decisions, and actions. 663
business intelligence (BI) system, 496
business logic, 552
business model A description of how a company does business, such as its policies, operations, and technology. 456
  e-commerce, 456–459. *See also specific models*
business modeling tool, 552
business partners, security, 383
business practice, ethical, 671
business robot, 506
Business Software Alliance (BSA), 627
business-to-business (B2B) model An e-commerce model in which a business provides goods or services to other businesses. 458
  order-fulfillment companies, 466
  transaction processing, 466
business-to-consumer (B2C) model An e-commerce model in which a business provides goods or services to consumers. 456–457
business-to-government (B2G) model An e-commerce model in which a business provides goods and services to government organizations. 458–459
button, 17
  mouse, 135
  sizing, 18
  taskbar, 17, 18
  toolbar, 17
buyer protection program, 454
buying a PC, R-10—R-14
  analyzing needs, R-10—R-11
  listing alternatives, R-11—R-12
byte A group of 8 bits. 56

C

C A high-level structured programming language that has the executional efficiency of an assembly language. 555, 560
C++ A newer, object-oriented version of the C programming language. 18, 555, 560, 562, 564
C# The newest, object-oriented version of the C programming language. 555, 560
Cabir, 368
cable, 284–285
Cable Act of 1992, 649
Cable Communications Policy Act of 1984, 649
cable connection, 16
cable Internet access Fast, direct Internet access via cable TV lines. 320, 322
cable modem, 299
Cabronator, 370
cache, 638
  hard drives, 104–106
  internal, 71, 76, 78
cache memory A group of fast memory chips located on or near the CPU to help speed up processing. 66, 104–106
caching, 321
CAD. *See* computer-aided design (CAD) *entries*
CAD (computer addiction disorder). *See* computer/Internet addiction
CAM. *See* computer-aided manufacturing (CAM)
Campbell, Murray, 503
Cannondale Bicycle, 499
Canon, 629–630
CAN-SPAM Act of 2003, 636, 639, 649
Cantor Fitzgerald, 627
Caps Lock key, 134
captive marketing, 154
captive offshoring site, 511
CardBus, 72
CardSystems Solutions, 365
caret (^), exponentiation operator, 237
Carnivore, 641
carpal tunnel syndrome (CTS) A painful and crippling condition affecting the hands and wrist that can be caused by computer use. 675
carrier sense, 289
Carrier Sense Multiple Access with Collision Detection (CSMA/CD), 289
cartridge tape, 122
CASE (computer-aided software engineering), 552
case, HTML tags, 431
Category 3 twisted-pair cable, 284
Category 5 twisted-pair cable, 284
Category 6 twisted-pair cable, 284
cathode-ray tube (CRT), 155
C2C. *See* consumer -to-consumer (C2C) model
CD burning software, 249
CD disc, 15–16, 97. *See also* optical disc
CD drive, 97, 98, 110
CDA (community digital assistance), 685
CDMA (Code Division Multiple Access), 322
CDP (continuous data protection), 625
CD-R disc A recordable CD. 112, 123
CD-R drive, 112
CD-ROM (compact disc read-only memory) disc An optical disc, usually holding about 650 MB, that can be read, but not written to, by the user. 110
CD-ROM drive, 110
CD-RW A rewritable CD. 112, 123
Cedar Point Amusement Park, 490
celebrity tour guides, 269
Celeron microprocessor, 63, 65
cell The location at the intersection of a row and column on a worksheet into which data can be typed. 239
cell address, 236
cell formatting, spreadsheet program, 237
cell height, worksheet, 237
Cell microprocessor, 64
cell phone gas station, 690
cell pointer, 236
cell width, worksheet, 237
cellular network, 16
cellular (cell) phone, 268, 287–288, 451
  coupons, 464
  e911 mandate, 647

m-commerce, 451
TV shows and other media, R-7
cellular radio A form of broadcast radio that broadcasts using antennas located inside honeycomb-shaped cells. 287–288
cellular tower, 287
censorship, 347–348
Center for Democracy and Technology, 639
central processing unit (CPU) The chip located inside the system unit of a computer that performs the processing for a computer. 16, 62, 63–67
clock speed, 64, 66
operating system support, 193–194
quad-core, 83
centralized database system, 591
CERT (Computer Emergency Response Team), 382
Certificate Authority, 379, 394
C2G (consumer-to-government) site, 459
CGI (common gateway interface), 605
character, in data hierarchy, 581
Charles Schwab & Co. 200
chart, spreadsheet programs, 239
chat room A type of Internet communications that allows multiple users to exchange written messages in real time. 332
chat session, 35
chatterbot, 504
cheating, 668
check
electronic, 462
substitute, 494
Check Clearing for the 21st Century Act (Check 21) of 2004, 494
check processing system, 494
checklist, system design, 514
chess-playing program, 502–503, R-6
Chicago, Illinois, 642
chief information officer (CIO), 508
Child Internet Protection Act (CIPA), 348, 693
Children's Online Privacy Protection Act (COPA) of 1998, 348, 648–649, 693
chip
motherboard, 14, 63, 71, 84
RFID, high-frequency, 146
chipset, 70, 71
cigarettes, purchasing online, 672
CIO (chief information officer), 508
CIPA (Child Internet Protection Act), 348, 693
cipher, 378
circuit, 334
circuit board, 20, 28, 63
Citibank, 511
citing Internet resources, 331
Claflin, Bruce, 671
clamshell design, 24
Clark, James H. R-5
Clarke, Richard, 365
class, object-oriented programming, 533
class file, Java, 565
.class file extension, 562
classroom, 8
click through rate (CTR), 470
click-and-mortar store, 450
clicking, 135
clickstream data, 471
client, 30, 278
client-server database system, 590
client-server network, 278–279, 590
clip art Predrawn electronic images. 233, 235, 415
presentation graphics, 245
cloaking services, 637
clock speed, 64, 66
Close command, 229
cluster The part of a track on a disk that crosses a fixed number of contiguous sectors; it is the smallest addressable area of a disk. 101
CNAV (College Navigation) system, 587
coaxial cable A communications medium consisting of a center wire inside a grounded, cylindrical shield, capable of sending data at high speeds. 284, 285
COBOL A high-level programming language developed for transaction processing applications. 14, 18, 542, 546, 555, 556, 557–558, 564, R-3
Code 39 barcode, 145
code, reusable, 545
Code Division Multiple Access (CDMA), 322
code editing, 437
code generator, 552
code of conduct A policy, often for a school or business, that specifies allowable use of resources such as computers and other equipment. 364, 667
code of ethics A policy, often for an organization or industry, that specifies overall moral guidelines adopted by that organization or industry. 667
coding The process of writing the programming language statements to create a computer program. 542, 544–545
coding scheme, 55
coding standards, 544
coding system, 55
for audio data, 60–61
for graphics data, 58–60
text-based data, 57–58
for video data, 61
collaboration software, 253
collaboration tool, 274
collaborative computing, 273–274
College Navigation (CNAV) system, 587
college portal, 587
collision, 289–290, 589
collision detection, 289
color
background, transparent, 416
font, 230, 415
color display, 155
color image, 60
color printer, 163
column In a spreadsheet program, a vertical group of cells on a worksheet. In a database, a field. 575–576
in data hierarchy, 581
databases, 241
tables, 234
worksheets, 236, 237
column-level locking, 585
combination topology, 278
Comcast, 334
command, common, 229–232
command line interface A user interface in which commands are typed on a keyboard. 17, 191
comment, programming, 544
commercial software Copyrighted software that is developed, usually by a commercial company, for sale to others. 222–223
Commission of Federal Election Reform, 622
commodity broker, 456
commodity exchange, 456
COmmon Business-Oriented Language. *See* COBOL
common gateway interface (CGI), 605
communication device, 16
communications The transmission of data from one device to another. 12, 267
interception, 367
online, differences in, 40–41
Communications Decency Act of 1996, 348, 395, 693
communications network, 267, 268–276
collaborative computing, 273–274
digital data distribution, 274–275
GPSs, 270
messaging, 269
mobile phones, 268–269
monitoring systems, 270–271
paging, 269
satellite radio, 272
telecommuting, 274
telemedicine, 276
videoconferencing, 272–273
communications port address, 376
communications protocol, 288–297
Bluetooth, 293–294
Ethernet, 289–290
mesh networks, 292
mobile-Fi, 293
Phoneline, 297
Powerline, 297
TCP/IP, 294–295
Token Ring, 290
UWB, 294
WAP, 295
Wi-Fi, 291–292
WiMAX, 292–293
xMax, 293
communications satellite An earth-orbiting device that relays communications signals over long distances. 286–287
communications system, 492
community digital assistance (CDA), 685
Commwarrior, 368
compact disc read-only memory disc. *See* CD-ROM (compact disc read-only memory) disc
CompactFlash card, 115
Compaq Corporation, R-5
compiler A language translator that converts an entire program into machine language before executing it. 546–547
composite primary key, 576
computer A programmable, electronic device that accepts data input, performs processing operations on that data, and outputs and stores the results. 11
benefits and risks of computer-oriented society, 38–39
booting, 17, 185
categories, 20
copying photos to, 250
digital, 55
in education, 7–8
embedded, 5
faster, developments for building, 83–86
first-generation, 13–14
general-purpose, 5
handheld (pocket), 25
history, 12–14, R-2—R-7
home, 6, 7

importance, 6
improving performance, 81–83
locking, 621
mainframe, 20, 28, 29
massively parallel processor, 29
midrange, 20, 28
network, 26
notebook. *See* notebook computer
operations, 11–12
optical, 14, 87
opto-electronic, 87
organic, 86
personal. *See* personal computer (PC)
social impact, 38–41
system troubleshooting, R-13—R-14
upgrading, R-14
in workplace, 8–10
Computer Abuse Amendments Act, 397
computer addiction. *See* computer/Internet addiction
computer addiction disorder (CAD). *See* computer/Internet addiction
computer crime Any illegal act involving a computer. 363
protecting against, 389–392
Computer Emergency Response Team (CERT), 382
computer ethics Standards of moral conduct as they relate to computer use. 663
Computer Fraud and Abuse Acts of 1984 and 1986, 365–366, 397, 649
computer glasses, 679
computer hoax An inaccurate statement or story spread through the use of computers. 669
computer labs, 8
computer literacy The knowledge and understanding of basic computer fundamentals. 6
Computer Matching Privacy Act of 1988, 649
computer monitoring software Software that can be used to record an individual's computer usage, typically either by capturing images of the screen or by recording the actual keystrokes used. 640–641
computer name, 33
computer network A collection of computers and other hardware devices that are connected together to share hardware, software, and data, as well as to communicate electronically with one another. 14, 30, 266–303. *See also* Internet; network; Web
accessing, 31–34
overview, 267–268
computer operations personnel, 20
computer professional, 20
computer sabotage An act of malicious destruction to a computer or computer resource. 367–371
data or program alteration, 371
DoS attacks, 370–371
malware, 368–370. *See also* computer virus
computer user A person who uses a computer. 19–20. *See also* end-user *entries;* user
computer virus A software program installed without the user's knowledge and designed to alter the way a computer operates or to cause harm to the computer system. 39, 210–211, 363, 368–369
antivirus program, 17, 39, 82, 210–211, 377–378, 626
prevention strategies, 378
scanning for, 82
computer vision syndrome (CVS), 675
computer worm A malicious program designed to spread rapidly to a large number of computers by sending copies of itself to other computers. 369–370
computer-aided design (CAD) A general term applied to the use of computer technology to automate design functions. 501
computer-aided design (CAD) software, 252
computer-aided manufacturing (CAM) A general term applied to the use of computer technology to automate manufacturing functions. 501–502
computer-aided software engineering (CASE), 552
computer/Internet addiction The problem of overusing, or being unable to stop using, a computer or the Internet. 339, 675, 681–682
computing generation, 7–8
concentrator, 301
conductive e-ink, 156
configuration, options, R-11
configuring devices, 185–186
connector symbol, flowcharts, 538
constant value A numerical entry in a worksheet cell. 236–237
consumer auction site, 455
consumer credit bureaus, 389, 390
consumer-to-consumer (C2C) model An e-commerce model in which a consumer provides goods or services to other consumers. 458
consumer-to-government (G2G) site, 459
contextual advertising, 472
continuous data protection (CDP), 625
contrast, text, 415
control, animated films, 426
control, security, 383
Control key, 134
control processor, 85
control structure A pattern for controlling the flow of logic in a computer program. 539–541
control unit The part of the CPU that coordinates its operations. 76
conventional dial-up Internet access Dial-up Internet access via a conventional dial-up modem and standard telephone lines. 320, 321
conventional dial-up modem, 299
convergence trend, 6
convertible tablet PC, 23, 24–25
cookie A small file stored on a user's hard drive by a Web server; commonly used to identify personal preferences and settings for that user. 349–351
opt-out, 639
CoolSavings.com, 662–663
COPA (Children's Online Protection Act) of 1998, 648–649, 693
coprocessing, 188–189
coprocessor, 188
Copy command, 229
copying
files and folders, 207
spreadsheet cells, 239
text, 230
`**copyright** The legal right to sell, publish, or distribute an original artistic or literary work; is held by the creator of a work as soon as it exists in physical form. 221
online music, 337
peer-to-peer file sharing, 340, 342
copyright The legal right to sell, publish, or distribute an original artistic or literary work; is held by the creator of a work as soon as it exists in physical form. 659, 661
ethics, 664–666
Copyright Act of 1976, 661
Copyright Term Extension Act, 693
core, 63
Corel, 227
Corel Paint Shop Pro, 246
Corel Paradox, 241, 577
Corel Presentations, 243
Corel Quattro Pro, 236
Corel WordPerfect, 232
Corel WordPerfect Office, 227
CorelDRAW, 247
corporate information, online, 343
Corporate Responsibility Act. *See* Sarbanes-Oxley Act of 2002
cost, multimedia, 414
cost per click (CPC), 470
cost/benefit analysis, system design, 516
counterfeiting, digital, 628–629
country code TLD, 32
coupon
cell phone, 464
electronic, 464
coupon code, 464
CPC (cost per click), 470
C-Pen, 142
CPU. *See* central processing unit (CPU)
CPU clock speed, 64, 66
Cray, Seymour, R-4
Cray Research, R-4
credit card
fraud, 334, 384
for online purchases, 391, 392
processing, 461
RFID-enabled, 146
secure, 453
security, 586
credit report, obtaining, 390
criteria, queries, 242, 596
CRM. *See* customer relationship management (CRM)
crossbar latch, 87
crosscutting, 534
CRT monitor A display device that projects images onto a display screen using a technology similar to the one used with conventional TVs. 155
CSMA/CD (Carrier Sense Multiple Access with Collision Detection), 289
CTR (click through rate), 470
CTS. *See* carpel tunnel syndrome (CTS)
Cub Foods, 493
culture, ethical issues, 673–675
currency, counterfeiting, 628–630
current cell, 236
cursor, 135
CUseeMe, 273
customer
advantages of e-commerce, 452
disadvantages of e-commerce, 454
profiling, 473
customer information, ethical use, 667–668
customer relationship management (CRM) The process of building and managing good relationships with customers. 452, 468, 497–498
electronic, 460

customer service, e-commerce, 468
Cut command, 229
cutting text, 230
CVS (computer vision syndrome), 675
cybercrime, 363
cybersquatting, 469, 662
cyberstalking Repeated threats or harassing behavior via e-mail or another Internet communications method. 395, 396
cyberterrorism, 365
cybervandalism, 371
cylinder The collection of tracks located in the same location on a set of hard disk surfaces. 103

D

DARPA (Defense Advanced Research Projects Agency), 505
Dartmouth College, 375
data Raw, unorganized facts. 12
  hierarchy, 581
  test, 549
data collection, system development, 513
data cube, 601
data definition The process of describing the characteristics of data that is to be included in a database table. 582–584
data definition language (DDL), 584
data dictionary The repository of all data definitions in a database.
  data dictionary, 515, 516, 545, 584
data flow diagram, 513, 514
data integrity The accuracy of data. 584–585
data mining The process of using intelligent software to analyze data warehouses for patterns and relationships. 471, 472–473
data modeling, 538–539
data movement time, 104
data organization, 588–589
  direct, 589
  indexed, 588–589
  sequenced, 588
data privacy, 586
data processing, 508
data projector A display device that projects all computer output to a wall or projection screen. 16, 162
data recovery, 103
data recovery firm, 105
data security Protecting data in a database against destruction and misuse. 585–586
data storage company, 625
data theft, 384
data transmission over network, 281–288
  analog vs. digital, 281
  bandwidth, 281–282
  direction, 283
  serial vs. parallel, 282
  timing, 282–283
  wired transmission media, 284–285
  wired vs. wired connections, 283–284
  wireless transmission media, 286–288
data type, 241, 582
data validation The process of ensuring that data entered into a database matches the data definition. 585
data warehouse A comprehensive collection of data about a company and its customers. 471
database A collection of related data that is stored in a manner enabling information to be retrieved as needed; in a relational database, a collection of related tables. 239–243, 574–607
  advantages and disadvantages, 579, 581
  college portals, 587
  creating, 241–242
  data concepts and characteristics, 581–589
  in data hierarchy, 581
  electronic profiling, 631–634
  evolution, 578–579
  government, 631
  individuals involved with, 578
  in-memory, 591
  marketing, 631
  models. *See* database model
  relational, 576–577. *See also* relational database management system (RDBMS)
  Web sites, 243
database administrator (DBA), 578
database designer, 578
database developer, 578
database locking, 585
database management system (DBMS) A type of software program used to create, maintain, and access databases. 240, 575. *See also* relational database management system (RDBMS)
  advantages and disadvantages, 579
database model, 591–601
  hierarchical, 592, 593
  multidimensional, 601
  object-oriented, 599–600
  relational, 593–599
  Web. *See* Web database
database programmer, 578
database programming, 596
database software Application software that allows the creation and manipulation of an electronic database. 227, 240–241
database system
  centralized vs. distributed, 591
  client-server, 590
  N-tier, 590
  single-user vs. multiuser, 589
Datasheet view, 241
data/video projector, 162
David's Bridal, 144
DB-9 connector, 73
DB-25 connector, 73
DBA (database administrator), 578
DBMS. *See* database management system (DBMS)
DDL (data definition language), 584
DDoS (distributed denial of service) attack, 370–371
DDR (double-data rate) SDRAM, 68
DDR-II (double-data rate-II) SDRAM, 68
DDR-III (double-data rate-III) SDRAM, 68
Dean, Howard, 670
debit card, processing, 461
Debug option, Visual Basic, 561
debugging The process of ensuring a program is free of errors. 545–549
  preliminary, 547–549
Deceptive Duo, 365
decimal numbering system, 56
decision
  ethical, 671, 673–674
  make-or-buy, 516–517
  types made by managers, 489
decision support system (DSS) A type of information system typically used by upper management that provides people with the tools and capabilities to organize and analyze their decision making information. 490, 495–496
decision support tool, 556
decision symbol, flowcharts, 538
decision table, system design, 513–514
decision tree, system design, 514
declaration statement, XHTML Web page, 433
declarative programming language, 556
decode operation, 79
decode unit The part of the CPU that translates instructions into a form that can be processed by the ALU. 76, 77
decryption, 379
Deep Blue, 502–503, R-6
default value, database table, 241
Defense Advanced Research Projects Agency (DARPA), 505
Defense Department, 394
Delete key, 133, 134
deleting
  e-mail messages, R-15
  files and folders, 207
  restoring deleted file/folder, 207
  system files, inadvertently, 209
Delivery Information Acquisition Device (DIAD), 499, 501
Dell Computer, 335, 342
Delta Air Lines, 146
demo version, 223
denial of service (DoS) attack An act of sabotage that attempts to flood a network server or a Web server with so much activity that it is unable to function. 370–371
Dense WDM (DWDM), 301
Department of Defense, 146
Department of Health and Human Services, 394
Department of Homeland Security (DHS), 365, 644
design information system, 490, 501–502
design software, 251, 252
Design view, 241
desktop The background work area displayed on the screen inwhen using Microsoft Windows or another operating system with a graphical user interface. 17
desktop case, 21, 22
desktop PC A PC designed to fit on or next to a desk. 21–23
  accessing Internet, 319
  operating systems, 194–201
desktop publishing software, 251, 252
desktop software, 229
developer documentation, 550
device compatibility, access to Web sites, 428
device driver A program that enables an operating system to communicate with a specific hardware device. 185–186
device software development suite, 553
DHS (Department of Homeland Security), 365, 644
DHTML. *See* Dynamic HTML (DHTML)
DIAD (Delivery Information Acquisition Device), 499, 501
diagnostic program, 208, R-13
dialing program, 32
dialog box A window that requires the user to supply additional information to the computer about the task being requested. 17, 18

dial-up connection A type of Internet connection in which the PC or other device must dial up and connect to a service provider's computer via telephone lines before being connected to the Internet. 32, 319, 320–321
conventional, 320, 321
ISDN, 320, 321
dial-up modem, conventional, 299
digital camcorder, 152
digital camera An input device that takes pictures and records them as digital data (instead of film or videotaped) images. 10, 15–16, 141, 148–152
managing and archiving photos, 250
optical zoom specifications, 150
sales growth, R-7
still, 149–151
video, 152
digital camera watch, 149
digital cash, 119
digital certificate. A group of electronic data, such as encryption key pairs and a digital signature, that can be used to verify the identity of a person or organization. 387, 393, 394, 473
digital cinema, 274–275
digital communities, 413
digital computer, 55
digital counterfeiting The use of computers or other types of digital equipment to make illegal copies of currency, checks, collectibles, and other items. 628–629
protecting against, 629–630
digital data distribution, 274–275
digital data representation, 55–56
digital divide The gap between those who have access to technology and those who do not. 683–686
global, 684–686
in United States, 683–684
digital form, 137
digital health record, 631, 632
digital imaging software, 246–247
digital implant, 687, 688
digital manipulation The alteration of digital content, usually text or photographs. 669–670
digital media receiver, 274
Digital Millennium Copyright Act (DMCA), 693
digital note taking, 253
digital pen, 137
digital picture frame, 154
digital projector, 162
digital republishing, 690, 691
Digital Research, 194
digital rights management (DRM) software Software used to protect and manage the rights of creators of digital content, such as art, music, photographs, and movies. 660, 661
digital signal, 281
digital signature A unique digital code that can be attached to an e-mail message or document to verify the identity of the sender and guarantee the message or file has not been changed since it was signed. 393–394, 465, 473
Digital Subscriber Line (DSL) Internet access, 320, 322
Digital Subscriber Line (DSL) modem, 299
digital television (DTV), 158–159
digital versatile disc read-only memory disc. *See* DVD-ROM (digital versatile disc read-only memory disc)
Digital Video Interface (DVI) port, 158
digital video recorder (DVR), 102, 665
digital wallet An encrypted electronic file that holds information, such as electronic payment, billing, and shipping information, that can speed up online purchase transactions. 21, 451, 465–466
site-specific, 466
digital watermark A subtle alteration of digital content that is not noticeable under normal use, but that identifies the copyright holder. 630, 660, 661
digital writing system, 137, 138, 139
digital zoom, 150
digitizing tablet, 138
dimension
databases, 579
MDDB, 601
dingbats, 58
direct access, 98
direct connection An always-on type of Internet connection in which the PC or other device is continually connected to the Internet. 31–32, 319, 321
direct conversion, 518, 519
direct organization A method of arranging data on a storage medium that uses hashing to specify the exact storage location. 589
direct recording electronic (DRE) device, 622
directional key, 133, 134
directory search A type of Internet search in which categories are selected to locate information on the Internet. 327
disabilities. *See* assistive technology
disaster-recovery plan A written plan that describes the steps a company will take following the occurrence of a disaster. 627
databases, 586
discussion group A type of Internet communications that enables individuals to post messages on a particular topic for others to read and respond to. 35, 332
disgruntled employees, security concerns, 382–383
disintermediation, 459
disk. *See* floppy disk; hard disk
disk access time The time it takes to locate and read data from (or position and write data to) a storage medium. 104
disk cache A dedicated part of RAM used to store additional data adjacent to data retrieved during a disk fetch to improve system performance. 104–106
disk defragmentation, 208
disk management program, 208
disk mirroring, 122
Disk Operating System. *See* DOS (Disk Operating System)
disk striping, 121–122
diskette. *See* floppy disk
Disney, 426, 665, 671
display device An output device that contains a viewing screen. 154–162. *See also* monitor
Braille, 688
color vs. monochrome, 155
CRT vs. flat-panel, 155
data projector, 162
digital TV and HDTV, 159–160
flat-panel, 160–162
LCD, 160–161
multimedia projector, 162
OLED, 160, 161–162
plasma, 160, 162
screen resolution, 167
size, 167
2D vs. 3D, 159
video cards and ports, 157–158
wired vs. wireless, 158
Display method, 533
display screen A display device built into a notebook computer, handheld PC, or other device. 154
disposable e-mail address, 40, 636
disposal of computing equipment, 690–693
dissolving, presentation graphics, 244–245
distance learning A learning environment in which the student is physically located away from the instructor and other students; commonly, instruction and communications take place via the Internet. 8, 344–345, 669
distributed database system, 591
distributed denial of service (DDoS) attack, 370–371
dithering, 60
division operator (/), 237
DMCA (Digital Millennium Copyright Act), 693
DNS server, 296
pharming, 387
do until structure, 540, 541
do while structure, 540, 541
docking station A device that connects a portable PC to conventional hardware, such as a keyboard, mouse, monitor, and printer. 25, 676, 677
document, 99
creating, 233–234
editing, 230
formatting, 230, 234
fragmentation, 81
hyperlinks in, 235
saving, 210
document holder, 676, 678
document processing, 491–492
documentation
developer, 550
internal, 544
Java applet, 565
troubleshooting, R-13
user, 550
Documents to Go, 229
Dodge Viper, 202
dollar sign ($), cell references, 239
domain name A text-based Internet address used to uniquely identify a computer on the Internet. 32–33
checking availability, 32
e-commerce sites, 469
Do-Not-Call Implementation Act of 2003, 648, 649
Do-Not-E-Mail Registry, 639, 648
door lock, 621
DoS. *See* denial of service (DoS) attack
DOS (Disk Operating System) The operating system designed for and widely used on early IBM and IBM-compatible PCs. 194, 195
dot con A fraud or scam carried out through the Internet. 383–389
data theft, 384
identity theft. *See* identity theft
information theft, 384
Internet scams, 386
online auction fraud, 385–386
phishing, 386, 387
protecting against, 389–394

spoofing, 386–387
spyware, 388–389
dot-com An Internet-only store with no physical presence. 450
dot-matrix printer, 163
Dotomi, 472
dots per inch (dpi), 142, 164
DoubleClick, 351, 472
double-clicking, 135
double-data rate (DDR) SDRAM, 68
double-data rate-II (DDR-II) SDRAM, 68
double-data rate-III (DDR-III) SDRAM, 68
double-layer disc, 112
downloadable movies, 339
downloading, 205, 279
drive-by, 388
music, 457. *See also* music; music store, online
downward compatibility, 108
dpi (dots per inch), 142, 164
drag-and-drop operation, 135
drawing program, 246–247
Drawing toolbar, 235
drawn objects, presentation graphics, 245
DRE (direct recording electronic) device, 622
drive
CD, 97, 98, 110
CD-R, 112
CD-ROM, 110
DVD, 15–16, 110
DVD-R, 112
DVD-ROM, 110
flash memory, 69, 115, 116, 123
floppy disk. *See* floppy disk drive
hard disk. *See* hard disk drive
legacy, 100
logical, 106–107
tape, 99, 122
Zip, 108
drive-by download, 388
driver, 185–186
DriveSavers, 105
DRM. *See* digital rights management (DRM) software
drop-down menu, multimedia Web sites, 427
drum scanner, 142
DSL Internet access Fast, direct Internet access via standard telephone lines. 320, 322
DSL (Digital Subscriber Line) modem, 299
DSS. *See* decision support system (DSS)
DTV (digital television), 158–159
dual-channel memory architecture, 68
dual-core CPUs, 63
dumb terminal, 26
dummy print statement, 549
Dunkin' Donuts, 464
DVD authoring software, 248
DVD burning software, 249
DVD disc, 15–16, R-6. *See also* optical disc
burning, 248
increase in use, 111
DVD drive, 15–16, 110
DVD game programming, 563
DVD+R DL disc A dual-layer recordable DVD. 112, 123
DVD-R drive, 112
DVD-RAM disc, 112, 123
DVD-R/DVD+R discs Recordable DVDs. 112, 123
DVD-ROM (digital versatile disc read-only memory) disc An optical disc, usually holding 4.7 GB, that can be read from, but not written to, by the user. 110
DVD-ROM drive, 110
DVD-RW/DVD+RW/DVD-RAM discs Rewritable DVDs. 112, 123
DVI (Digital Video Interface) port, 158
DVR (digital video recorder), 102, 665
DWDM (Dense WDM), 301
dye-sublimation technology, 166
Dynamic HTML (DHTML) A form of HTML used to add dynamic capabilities and interactivity to Web pages. 433
dynamic pricing site, 455–456
dynamic Web page, 602, 603

E

e911 (enhanced 911), 334
E Ink, 156
EAI. *See* enterprise application integration (EAI)
Earnhardt, Dale, 628
EarthLink, 31, 314
EB. *See* Exabyte (EB)
eBay, 392, 454, 455, 672, R-6
EBCDIC (Extended Binary-Coded Decimal Interchange Code) A fixed-length, binary coding system widely used to represent text-based data on IBM mainframe computers. 57, 58
chart, R-8
e-book A book obtained in electronic format. 339–340
copyright protection, 664
e-clothing, 280
ECML (electronic Commerce Modeling Language), 465
eco-label A certification, often by a government agency, that identifies a device as meeting minimal environmental performance specifications. 689
e-commerce The act of doing business transactions over the Internet or similar technology. 334–337, 448–475, R-6
advantages, 450, 542
business models, 456–459, 460. *See also specific models*
cashless society, 451
disadvantages, 452–454
implementing. *See* implementing Web-based e-commerce
multimedia Web sites, 411–412
online auctions, 20, 336, 385–386, 454–456, 459
online banking, 336
online investing, 336–337
online shopping, 334–336
types of Web sites, 454–456
Web databases, 603, 604
e-commerce business model A description of the types of buyers and sellers involved in an e-commerce company, such B2B, B2G, and so forth. 456–459. *See also specific models*
selecting, 460
e-commerce merchant account, 461
e-commerce software, 316
e-commerce system, 449, 493
e-community, 498
ECP (Extended Capabilities Port), 74
eCRM (electronic customer relationship management), 460, 498, 604
EDGE (Enhanced Data Rates for Global Evolution), 323
EDI. *See* electronic data interchange (EDI)
editing documents, 230
education. *See also* school
computers in, 7–8
online, 344–345
to protect against software piracy and digital counterfeiting, 629
Education Privacy Act of 1974, 649
educational software, 252
edutainment software, 251, 252
EFT (electronic funds transfer), 449
e-fulfillment company, 466
e-government, 458
e-health network, 632
EHR (electronic health record), 632
802.11. *See* Wi-Fi (802.11)
802.11g, 291
802.11i, 375
802.11n, 291
802.16, 292–293
802.16e, 292–293
802.20, 293
e-ink (electronic ink), 156
EIS (executive information system), 495–496
Eisenhower, Dwight D. R-3
eject button, 101
electromechanical device, R-2
electron, 100
electronic check A check written and submitted electronically via the Internet. 462
electronic citation system, 492
Electronic Commerce Modeling Language (ECML), 465
Electronic Communications Policy Act of 1986, 649
electronic coupon, 464
electronic customer relationship management (eCRM), 460, 498, 604
electronic data interchange (EDI) The transfer of data between different companies using the Internet or another network. 497
electronic document management, 491
electronic funds transfer (EFT), 449
electronic gift card, 336, 463–464
electronic gift certificate, 463–464
electronic health record (EHR), 632
electronic ink (e-ink), 156
electronic mail (e-mail) Electronic messages sent from one user to another over the Internet or other network. 7, 37–38, R-15—R-16. *See also* e-mail *entries*
address, 32, 40, 636
address book, R-15
authentication, 378, 394
citing, 331
hoaxes, 41
humor in messages, 674
keeping inbox clean, 681
managing, R-15
privacy, 353
receiving, R-15, R-16
sending, R-15, R-16
spam, 40
video, 37
Web-based encrypted, 381
electronic monitoring, 640–641

electronic paper (e-paper), 154, 156
electronic pen An input device that is used to write electronically on the display screen; also called a stylus or digital pen. 15–16, 137–139
digital writing systems, 138, 139
graphics tablets, 138, 139
pen-based PCs, 137–138
signature capture device, 138, 139
electronic postage, 166
Electronic Privacy Information Center (EPIC), 351
Electronic Product Code (EPC), 150
electronic profiling Using electronic means to collect a variety of in-depth information about an individual, such as name, address, income, and buying habits. 631–634
electronic shelf label (ESL), 501
electronic storefront, 454
electrophosphorescence, 162
electrostatic plotter, 168
ellipsis, 18
e-mail. *See* electronic mail (e-mail)
e-mail address An Internet address consisting of a username and computer domain name that uniquely identifies a person on the Internet. 32
throw-away (disposable), 40, 636
e-mail authentication system, 639
e-mail filter A tool that automatically sorts your incoming e-mail messages based on specific criteria. 638
e-mail hoax, 671
e-mail program, 19, 37–38
e-marketplace, 456
embedded computer, 5
embedded Linux A version of Linux designed for handheld PCs and mobile devices. 203
embedded operating system, 193
emergency mail system provider, 627
emoticon, 40, 41
emotional health, 679–682
burnout, 681
computer/Internet addiction, 681–682
impact of always being on call, 680
information overload, 680–681
stress of ever-changing technology, 679–680
employee attacks, avoiding, 382–383
employee information, ethical use, 667–668
employee monitoring Observing or reviewing employees' actions while they are on the job. 643, 645–646, 673
employee policy, 647
employer, ethical use of resources, 667
encapsulated aggregate HTML document, 436
encapsulation, 533, 600
encryption A method of scrambling e-mail or files to make them unreadable if they are intercepted by an unauthorized user. 281, 372, 375, 378, 379–382
automatic, 379
e-mail, 353
key, 375
military-strength 2,048-bit, 381
private key (symmetric), 379, 380, 393
public key (asymmetric), 379, 393
smart cards, 119
strong 128-bit, 381
weak, 381
encryption algorithm, 379
end user, 19–20
end-user development, 521
end-user license agreement, 628
ENERGY STAR A program developed by the U.S. Department of Energy and the Environmental Protection Agency to encourage the development of energy-saving devices. 689
Engelbart, Doug, R-3
enhanced 911 (e911), 334, 647
Enhanced Data Rates for Global Evolution (EDGE), 323
Enhanced Parallel Port (EPP), 74
ENIAC, 13–134
e911 (enhanced 911), 334, 647
Enron, 671
Enter key, 134, 234
enterprise application integration (EAI) Exchanging information from an ERP or other internal system among different applications and organizations. 497
enterprise architecture A comprehensive framework used to describe and manage an organization's business functions and systems. 501
enterprise resource planning (ERP) A large integrated system that ties together all of a business's activities. 497
enterprise storage system, 120
enterprise-class server, 28
enterprise-wide system. A system that integrates activities throughout an entire enterprise. 490, 496–501
entertainment, multimedia Web sites, 412
entertainment bot, 503
entertainment software, 252
entity Something in a database system (such as a person, object, or event) that is of importance to the organization. 581
relationship, 581–582
environmental concerns, 689–693
digital republishing, 691
green computing, 689–690
recycling and disposal of equipment, 690–693
e-paper (electronic paper), 154, 156
EPC (Electronic Product Code), 150
EPIC (Electronic Privacy Information Center), 351
e-portfolio A collection of an individual's work accessible through a Web site. 345, 346
EPP (Enhanced Parallel Port), 74
Equifax, 389, 390
ergonomic hardware Hardware, typically input and output devices, that is designed to be more ergonomically correct than its nonergonomic counterparts. 677–678
ergonomic keyboard, 139, 677, 678
ergonomic mouse, 677, 678
ergonomics The science of fitting a work environment to the people who work there. 675–679
hardware, 677–678
user habits and precautions, 678–679
workspace design, 675–677
Ericcson, 204
ERP. *See* enterprise resource planning (ERP)
error
debugging programs, 545–549
loading Web pages, 35
logic, 542
logic (execution-time), 548, 549
reporting problems, 186
syntax, 548–549
tracing flowchart to find, 542, 543
Escape key, 134
escrow service, 392, 458
ESL (electronic shelf label), 501
ESPRIMO E computer, 690
e-stamp, 166
eSuds, 490
e-tailer An online retailer. 454
Ethernet A widely used communications protocol for a LAN. 289–290
ethics Overall standards of moral conduct. 663–675
business, 663
business practices and decision making, 671–675
code of, 667
computer, 663
computer hoaxes, 669
copyrighted material, 664–666
digital manipulation, 669–670
legislation regarding, 693
resources and information, 666–669
e-token, 373, 375
e-trash, 86, 690–693
EV-DO (Evolution Data Optimized), 323
event-drive programming language, 556
Evolution Data Optimized (EV-DO), 323
e-voting system, 621, 622–623
e-wallet. *See* digital wallet
e-waste, 690–693
exabyte (EB) Approximately 1,000 petabytes. 56
Excite, 470
executable file, 208
execute operation, 79
execution stage, 546
execution-time error. *See* logic error
executive information system (EIS), 495–496
executive manager, as information system users, 488, 489
ex-employees, security concerns, 382–383
exoskeleton suit, 505, 506
expansion bus A bus that connects the CPU to peripheral devices. 70
expansion card A circuit board that can be inserted into an expansion slot on a PC's motherboard to add additional functionality or to attach a peripheral device. 62, 63, 69–70
expansion slot A location on the motherboard into which expansion cards are inserted. 62, 63, 69–70
handheld PCs, 75
Experian, 389, 390
expert system A computer system that provides the type of advice that would be expected from a human expert. 504–505
expert system shell, 505
exponentiation operator (^), 237
ExpressCard PC Card, 72
ExpressCard port, 75
ExpressPay system, 451
Extended Binary-Coded Decimal Interchange Code. *See* EBCDIC (Extended Binary-Coded Decimal Interchange Code)
Extended Capabilities Port (ECP), 74
Extensible Hypertext Markup Language. *See* XHTML (Extensible Hypertext Markup Language)
Extensible Markup Language. *See* XML (Extensible Markup Language)
external cache, 66
external hard drive, 83, 102, 107
extranet An intranet that is at least partially accessible to authorized outsiders. 281

F

face reader, 375
Fair and Accurate Credit Transactions Act (FACTA) of 2003, 389, 390, 397
Fair Credit Reporting Act of 1970, 649
fair use, 661
Family Entertainment and Copyright Act of 2005 (FECA), 665, 666, 693
fan, 62, 69
Fanning, Shawn, R-6
Farm Fresh, 493
Fast Ethernet, 289
FAT32 file system, 106
fault tolerance, 121
Favorites feature, 35, 36
Favorites list, 36
FDM (Frequency Division Multiplexing), 301
feasibility study, system development life cycle, 512–513
FECA (Family Entertainment and Copyright Act of 2005), 665, 666, 693
Federal Electronic Signatures in Global and National Commerce Act of 2000, 393–394
FedEx, 604
FeliCa, 451
female connector, 72
fetch operation, 79
fiber-optic cable A communications medium that utilizes hundreds of hair-thin, transparent fibers over which lasers transmit data as light. 285
fiber-optic plug, 73
Fibre Channel over IP standard, 107
Fibre Channel standard, 107
field A single category of data to be stored in a database, such as a person's name or telephone number. Also called a column. 241, 575
in data hierarchy, 581
numeric, selecting type and size, 582
redundant, 580
size, 582–583
field name, database table, 241
field searching, 330
field size, database table, 241
field-programmable gate array (FPGA), 84
fifth normal form (5NF), 594
fifth-generation computer, 14
fifth-generation programming language, 556
file Something stored on a storage medium, such as a program, document, or image. 99
audio, formats, 420
copying, 207
deleting, 207
graphic, formats, 415–418
moving, 207
multiple formats for security, 627
renaming, 207
video, formats, 420–421
viewing, 206
file compression
lossless, 416
lossy, 417
file compression program, 208
file extension, 39, 186–187
file management, 186–187
file management program A utility program that enables the user to perform file management tasks, such as copying and deleting files. 187, 206–207
copying files and folders, 207
deleting files and folders, 207
moving files and folders, 207
renaming files and folders, 207
viewing contents of PC, 206
file management system, 580
file server, 278
file system, floppy disks, 101
File Transfer Protocol (FTP), 33, 318
publishing Web sites, 439
filename A name given to a file by the user that is used to retrieve the file at a later time. 99, 233
filter
e-mail, 638
Internet filtering, 348
financial brokerage site, 456
financial flow, 498
Financial Modernization Act of 1999, 649
financial reporting, fraud, 671–672
fingerprint payment system, 493
fingerprint reader, 15–16, 103, 148, 373, 375
Fins, Joseph, 688
Firefox, 31
firewall A collection of hardware and/or software intended to protect a computer or computer network from unauthorized access. 187, 211, 321, 372, 376–377
personal, 376
firewall program, 352
FireWire A bus standard often used to connect digital video cameras to a PC. 72
FireWire plug, 73
FireWire port, 74, 75
first-generation cell phone, 288
first-generation computer, 13–14, R-2—R-3
5NF (fifth normal form), 594
fixed barcode reader, 145
fixed wireless Internet access Fast, direct Internet access available in large metropolitan areas via the airwaves and a radio transceiver. 286, 320, 322
Flash A popular Web animation program. 419, 420
flash memory A type of nonvolatile memory that can be erased and reprogrammed; commonly implemented in the form of sticks or cards. 67, 68, 69
flash memory card A small, rectangular flash memory media, such as a CompactFlash or Secure Digital card. 15–16, 69, 75, 97, 115, 123
flash memory card reader, 15–16, 97, 98, 115
flash memory card slot, 74
flash memory drive A small drive that usually plugs into a PC's USB port and contains flash memory media. 69, 115, 116, 123, 623, R-6
flash memory hard drive, 116
flash memory media, 115
flash memory storage system A storage system that uses flash memory media. 114–116
flash RAM. *See* flash memory
flat file, 579
flatbed scanner An input device that scans flat objects one at a time. 142, 143
flat-panel display A slim type of display device that uses electronically charged chemicals or gases instead of an electron gun to display images. 155, 160–162
LCD, 160–161
OLED, 160, 161–162
plasma, 160, 162
flexible OLED (FOLED), 161–162
floating point operations per second, 64
floating point unit (FPU) The part of the CPU that performs decimal arithmetic. 76
floppy disk A low-capacity, removable magnetic disk made of flexible plastic permanently sealed inside a hard plastic cover. 15–16, 97, 100–102, 123
characteristics, 101
development, R-4
first, R-3
using, 101–102
floppy disk drive A storage device that reads from and writes to floppy disks. 15–16, 97, 98, 100–102
flowchart (programming) A program design tool that shows graphically step-by-step how a computer program will process data.
program, 536–538
tracing, 542, 543
flowchart (Web design) A tool that can be used during the Web design process to illustrate how the pages in a Web site relate to one another. 424–425
flowchart, system, 515
flowline, 419, 538
flying, presentation graphics, 244–245
folder A named place on a storage medium into which files can be stored to keep the files stored on that medium organized. 99, 186
copying, 207
deleting, 207
moving, 207
renaming, 207
viewing, 206
FOLED (flexible OLED), 161–162
font
color, 230, 415
size, 230, 233, 415
style, 230, 233
typefaces, 230, 233, 414–415
foot mouse, 428, 687
footer, 233, 234
Ford, 202
form, databases, 241, 575
form generator, 553
formatting
documents, 230, 234
floppy disks, 101
page, 234
paragraph, 234
storage media, caution regarding, 103
worksheet cells, 237
formula An entry in a worksheet cell that performs computations on worksheet data and displays the results. 236, 237
formula bar, spreadsheet program, 237
FORmula TRANslator. *See* FORTRAN
FORTRAN A high-level programming language used for mathematical, scientific, and engineering applications. 14, 555, 557, R-3
48-bit color, 143
Fotki, 637
419 scams, 387–388
4GL. *See* fourth-generation language (4GL)
fourth-generation (4G) cell phone, 288
fourth-generation computer, 13, 14, R-4
fourth-generation language (4GL) A class of programming languages that is closer to natural language and easier to work with than a high-level language. 555–556
FPGA (field-programmable gate array), 84

FPU. *See* floating point unit (FPU)
fragmentation, documents, 81
frame, 420
navigating multimedia Web sites, 426–427
fraud. *See* dot-con; phishing
credit card, 334, 384
financial reporting, 671–672
Internet auction, 385–386
legislation against, 365–366, 397, 649
Freedom of Information Act of 1970, 649
freeware Copyrighted software that may be used free of charge. 222, 224
Frequency Division Multiplexing (FDM), 301
front end, 590
frontside bus (FSB), 70, 71
FSB (Frontside bus), 70, 71
ftp://, 33
FTP (File Transfer Protocol), 33, 318
publishing Web sites, 439
FTP server, 318
fuel cell, 689
full mesh topology, 278
full-duplex transmission, 283
function A named formula that can be entered into a worksheet cell to perform some type of calculation or to extract information from other cells in the worksheet. 237, 238
function key, 133, 134
Function Lock key, 134
functional hub, 459
fusion biometrics, 375

G

Gaidano, Scott, 105
game, 19
game console, 102
game port, 74
game programming, 560
gamepad, 140
gaming, online, 339
gas station, cell phone, 690
Gates, Bill, 629, R-4, R-5
gateway, 300
GB. *See* gigabyte (GB)
gender, ports, 72
general ledger system, 494
general packet radio service (GPRS), 322
general-purpose computers, 5
generation, 13–14
geocaching, 270
geographic information system (GIS) An information system that combines geographic information with other types of data (such as information about your customers, sales, and so forth) in order to provide a better understanding of the relationships among the data. 490, 496
Geospatial Repository for Analysis and Safety Planning (GRASP), 564
geosynchronous (geostationary) orbit, 287
gesture-based input device, 136
Gettysburg College, 587
GHz (gigahertz), 64
GIF A graphics format that supports 256 colors and is commonly used for Web page line art images. 416, 417, 418
animated, 418
.gif file extension, 416
gift card, electronic, 463–464
gift certificate, electronic, 463–464
Gigabit Ethernet, 289
gigabyte (GB) Approximately 1 billion bytes. 56
gigaflop, 64, 66
gigahertz (GHz), 64
GIMP program, 223
GIS. *See* geographic information system (GIS)
global digital divide, 684–686
global positioning system (GPS) A system that uses satellites and a receiver to determine the exact geographic location of the receiver. 10, 11, 270
GPS receiver, 270
GPS satellite, 270
GPS-based monitoring system, 271
Global System for Mobile Communications (GSM), 322
Go stage, 546
goal seeking, 239
Google, 36, 209, 328, 470, 602
Google Gmail, 38
GoTV, 22
government. *See also* legislation; *specific laws*
influence on Internet, 316
online information, 343
government database A collection of data about people that is collected and maintained by the government. 631
GPRS (general packet radio service), 322
GPS. *See* global positioning system (GPS)
Gramm-Leach-Bliley Act of 1999, 649
graph, spreadsheet programs, 237, 239
graphic A digital representation of a photograph, drawing, chart, or other visual image. 12, 415–418. *See also* presentation graphics
coding system, 58–60
displaying Web pages, 415
file formats, 415–418
integrated, 69–70
presentation graphics, 245
SVG, 434
Web sites, 249
word processing, 235
graphical user interface (GUI) A graphically based interface that allows a user to communicate instructions to the computer easily. 17, 185, 191
graphics coprocessor, 188
Graphics Interchange Format (GIF), 416, 417, 418
animated, 418
graphics software Application software used to create or modify images. 246–247
for Web, 249
graphics tablet A flat, rectangular input device that is used in conjunction with a stylus to transfer drawings, sketches, and anything written on the device to a PC in graphic form. 138, 139
graphics-based user interface, 185
GRASP (Geospatial Repository for Analysis and Safety Planning), 564
grayscale image, 60
green computing The use of computers in an environmentally friendly manner. 689–690
grid computing, 29
Grokster, 340
Grolier's Electronic Encyclopedia, R-5
groove, optical disc, 109
GSM (Global System for Mobile Communications), 322
GUI. *See* graphical user interface (GUI)
GUI tool, 553
Gyricon Media, 156

H

hacker, 320, 364, 586
hacking Using a computer to break into another computer system. 364–367
Wi-Fi, 365–366
half-duplex transmission, 283
hand geometry reader, 148, 375
handheld computer A portable PC about the size of a paperback book or pocket calculator. 25
expansion slots, 75
medical student use, 9
handheld device, 6. *See also specific devices*
keyboards, 134–135
operating systems, 201–204
handheld scanner A small, handheld optical scanner. 142, 143
handshaking, 288
handwriting recognition The ability of a device to identify handwritten characters. 137
hanging of processes, 82
hard copy, 163
hard disk, 100
hard disk cartridge, 108
hard disk drive A storage system consisting of one or more metal magnetic disks permanently sealed with an access mechanism inside its drive. 15–16, 97, 98, 102–108
adding or increasing size, 83
caching, 104–106
characteristics, 102–104
development, R-4
external, 83, 102, 107
file systems, 106
flash memory, 116
hybrid, 116
internal, 102
partitioning, 106–107
portable, 107–108, 123
separate, for data, 210
speed, 104
wireless, 104
hard drive. *See* hard disk drive
hard drive interface standard, 107
hardware The physical parts of a computer system, such as the keyboard, monitor, printer, and so forth. 15–16. *See also specific devices*
damage, 620, 621–622
disposal, 639–640
ergonomic, 677–678
expert insight, 178–179
networking, 297–301
proper care, 624–625
protecting, 626
upgrading, R-14
hardware company, 316
hardware theft The theft of computer hardware. 620
protecting against, 621–622
hashing algorithm, 589
HD-capable broadcast, 160
HD-compatible monitor, 160
HD-DVD (high-definition DVD), 113
HD-integrated broadcast, 160
HD-ready monitor, 160
HDTV (high-definition television), 160
head crash, 103, 625
head mouse, 428, 687
head pointing system, 687
head statement, XHTML Web page, 433

header, 233, 234
head-mounted display, 158
headphone, 16, 169
voice input system, 152
headphone jack, 169
head-pointing system, 428
headset, 168, 169
voice input system, 152
health
emotional, 679–682
physical, 675–679
Health Insurance Portability and Accountability Act (HIPAA) of 2003, 397
Privacy Rule, 488, 632, 648, 649
heat sink, 69
Help system, 231–232
hertz (Hz), 79
HHD (hybrid hard drive), 116
hierarchical database management system, 592, 593
hierarchy chart, 536
high-definition DVD (HD-DVD), 113
high-definition television (HDTV), 160
high-end server, 28
high-frequency RFID chip, 146
high-level language A class of programming languages that is closer to natural language and easier to work with than a low-level language. 554–555
high-level programming language, R-2
high-speed dial-up access, 321
HIPAA (Health Insurance Portability and Accountability Act) of 2003, 397
Privacy Rule, 488, 632, 648, 649
History list, 36
hit, 326
Hoff, Ted, R-4
HOLAP (Hybrid OLAP), 601
Hollerith, Herman, 13
hologram, 158
to protect against software piracy and digital counterfeiting, 629
holographic storage An emerging type of storage technology that uses multiple blue laser beams to store data in three dimensions. 120
home computer, 6, 7
home network, 268
setting up, 296
home page, 35
link to, 427
Home Phoneline Networking Association (Home PNA), 298
Homeland Security Act of 2002, 397
HomePlug AV, 298
HomePNA 3.0, 298
Hopper, Grace, 546, R-3
horizontal hub, 459
hot site, 627
Hotmail, 38
hotspot, 291, 292, 323, 366
hot-swappable device, 74
HP, 200, 630
.htm file extension, 34, 430
.html, 33
HTML (Hypertext Markup Language) A markup language widely used for creating Web pages. 33, 235, 430–431
.html file extension, 430
HTML tag, 430–431
http://, 33
HTTP (Hypertext Transfer Protocol), 33, 318
https:, 33, 34, 379
HTTPS (Secure Hypertext Transfer Protocol), 33
hub A device that is a central location where data arrives and is then transferred in one or more directions. 277, 300
Huffman coding, 61
human cloning, 673
humanoid robot, 506–507
Hurricane Katrina
medical records lost in, 632
scams related to, 388
HushMail, 381
hybrid CD/DVD disc, 110
hybrid hard drive (HHD), 116
Hybrid OLAP (HOLAP), 601
hyperlink Text or an image located on a Web page or other document that is linked to a Web page or other type of document. 17, 18
in document, 235
navigating to Web pages, 35–36
Hypertext Markup Language. *See* HTML (Hypertext Markup Language)
Hypertext Transfer Protocol (HTTP), 33, 318
Hyper-Threading Technology, 86
HyperTransport bus, 72
Hz (hertz), 79

I

i2, 460
IAD (Internet addiction disorder). *See* computer/Internet addiction
IAFIS (Integrated Automated Fingerprint Identification System), 644
IBM, 13, 453, 460, 502–503, 663, R-2, R-4
Linux support, 200
operating systems, 204
PC-DOS, 194
quantum computing, 87
voice recognition system, 202
IBM DB2, 577
IBM Lotus Notes, 226
IBM Lotus SmartSuite, 227
IBM PC, 13, 14, R-5
IBM System/360 computer, R-3
IBM ViaVoice, 152
IBM Workplace, 226
IBM Workspace, 226
IBM-compatible PC, 21, 23
iBOT Mobility System, 507
IC (integrated circuit), 14, 63, R-2
ICANN (Internet Corporation for Assigned Names and Numbers), 32–33, 313, 316
iCi (Interactive Conversation Interface), 192
icon A small picture or other type of graphical image that represents a program, command, or document and invokes some action when selected. 17, 18
icon-based authoring program, 419
IDE standard, 107
IDENT (Automated Biometric Identification System), 644
identity, hiding, 41
identity theft Using someone else's identity to purchase goods or services, obtain new credit cards or bank loans, or otherwise illegally masquerade as that individual. 39, 210, 334, 384–385, 389–391, R-7
protecting against, 389–391
Identity Theft and Assumption Deterrence Act of 1998, 384, 397
Identity Theft Penalty Enhancement Act of 2004, 397
IEEE, 291
IEEE 1394 bus, 72
IEEE 1394 port, 74, 75
IEEE 1394 standard, 72
if-then-else structure, 539
Illium Software eWallet, 465
IM. *See* instant messaging (IM)
IM (instant messaging) program, 17
iMac, R-6
image. *See* graphics
image editing program, 142, 247
image map, 422
navigating multimedia Web sites, 426, 427
Imagination Entertainment, 563
IMDB (in-memory database), 591
impact printer, 163
implementation process, 550
implementing Web-based e-commerce, 459–473
designing and developing Web sites, 467–468
developing procedures for handling transactions, 461–466
sales and marketing strategies, 468–473
selecting business model and Web site type, 460
selecting desired applications, 460
Incredible technologies, 563
index A small table containing a primary key and the location of the record belonging to that key; used to locate records in a database. 588–589
index, Help feature, 231
indexed organization A method for organizing data on a storage medium or in a database that uses an index to specify the exact storage location. 588–589
inference engine, expert system, 504
infinite loop, 542
information Data that has been processed into a meaningful form. 12
delivery by multimedia, 411
ethical use, 666, 667–669
integrity, 41
retrieval using Web databases, 601, 602
retrieving from relational databases, 596–598, 599
information appliance, 26, 28, 319
information flow, 498
information hiding, 533
information overload, 680–681
information privacy The rights of individuals and companies to control how information about them is collected and used. 630–631
personal information, protecting, 636–640
information processing, 12
information processing cycle, 11
information reporting system, 490, 495
information system A system used to generate information to support users in an organization. 487–507
artificial intelligence, 490, 502–507
decision support, 490, 495–496
design and manufacturing, 490, 501–502
enterprise-wide and inter-enterprise, 490, 496–501
geographic, 490, 496
laundry room, 490
management, 490, 495
office, 490, 491–492
roller coaster, 490
transaction processing, 490, 492–494

types, 489–490
users, 488–489
information systems (IS) department, 508–509
information theft, 384
infrared capability, 25
Infrared Data Association (IrDA) port, 74
infrared laser disc, 112
infrared signal, 133
infrastructure company, 316
inheritance, object-oriented programming, 533
ink-jet printer An output device that sprays droplets of ink to produce images on paper. 163, 165–166, 168
in-memory database (IMDB), 591
input The process of entering data into a computer; can also refer to the data itself. 11–12
input device, 15–16. *See also specific devices*
assistive, 686–687
gesture-based, 136
input mask, 583–584
input/output (I/O) design, 515–516
Insert key, 134
insertion point An onscreen character that indicates the current location in a document, which is where the next change will be made to the document. 135, 233
installed software, 224–226
installing software, 16, 205
instance, object-oriented programming, 538
instant messaging (IM) A form of private chat set up to allow users to easily and quickly exchange real-time typed messages with the individuals they specify. 332, 333
instant messaging (IM) program, 17
instruction set, 79
instructions per cycle (IPC), 79
intangible benefit, 516
Integrated Automated Fingerprint Identification System (IAFIS), 644
integrated circuit (IC), 14, 63, R-2
integrated graphics, 69–70
integrated services digital network (ISDN)
Internet access, 320, 321
modem, 299
integrated software programs, 228
integrated sound, 69–70
integrity of information, 41
Intel, 292. *See also* Pentium *entries*
Intel 80286 CPU, R-5
Intel 4004 microprocessor, R-4
Intel386 chip, R-5
Intel486 chip, R-5
Intel Corporation, R-3, R-5, R-7
Intel Itanium CPU, R-7
Intel Pentium CPU
development, R-5, R-6
intellectual property, 628
intellectual property laws, 693
intellectual property rights The rights to which creators of original creative works (such as artistic or literary works, inventions, corporate logos, and more) are entitled. 659–663
copyrights, 659, 661
digital rights management, 660
patents, 662–663
trademarks, 661–662
Intellifit, 144
intelligent agent A program that performs specific tasks to help to make a user's work environment more efficient or entertaining and that typically modifies its behavior based on the user's actions. 503–504, 680
Interactive Conversation Interface (iCi), 192
interactive processing, 575
interactive TV (iTV), 160, 338
interactivity, Web-based multimedia, 411
interception of communications, 367
inter-enterprise system A system that links multiple enterprises, such as a business and its customers, suppliers, and partners. 490, 496–501
interface
command line, 191
graphical. *See* graphical user interface (GUI)
interface card. *See* expansion card
interlaced image, 416
intermediary hub, 456
intermediary hub model An e-commerce model in which a business brings buyers and sellers together, instead of directly selling goods or services. 459
internal bus, 71
internal cache, 66, 71, 76, 78
internal documentation, 544
internal mini hard drive, 107–108
International Business Machines. *See* IBM
internet, 312
Internet The largest and most well-known computer network, linking millions of computers all over the world. 14, 31, R-7. *See also* Web *entries*
accessing, 31–34
control, 318
cost, 317
devices for accessing, 318–319
evolution, 311–318
expert insight on, 406–407
future, 353
myths about, 317–318
searching. *See* searching the Internet
setting up to use, 318–325
users, 314
Web vs., 31, 318
Internet2 , 313–314
Internet access, broadband, R-7
Internet addiction. *See* computer/Internet addiction
Internet addiction disorder (IAD). *See* computer/Internet addiction
Internet address What identifies a computer, person, or Web page on the Internet, such as an IP address, domain name, or e-mail address. 32
pronouncing, 34
Internet appliance A specialized network computer designed primarily for Internet access and/or e-mail exchange. 26, 28, 319
Internet auction fraud, 385–386
Internet backbone, 313
Internet café, 10
Internet community, 314–316
Internet connection, upgrading, 83
Internet content provider A person or an organization that provides Internet content. 315
Internet Corporation for Assigned Names and Numbers (ICANN), 32–33, 313, 316
Internet Crime Complaint Center, 383
Internet device, 26, 28
Internet Explorer, 31
Internet filtering Using a software program or browser option to block access to particular Web pages or types of Web pages. 348
Internet merchant account, 461
Internet offer scam, 386
Internet peer-to-peer (P2P) computing, 279
Internet Protocol (IP), 32, 294
Internet radio station, 337
Internet scams, 386, 387
Internet SCSI (iSCSI) standard, 107
Internet search, 36
Internet Server Application Program Interface (ISAPI), 605
Internet service provider (ISP) A business or other organization that provides Internet access to others, typically for a fee. 31, 314
selecting, 323–324
Internet Society (ISOC), 313, 316
Internet tablet, 319
Internet telephony, 333–334
Internet-only store, 450
InterNIC, 32
interpreter A language translator that converts program statements line-by-line into machine language, immediately executing each one. 547
intranet A private network that is set up similar to the Internet and is accessed via a Web browser. 280–281
inventory control system, 499
inventory management system A system used to track and manage inventory. 499
investing online, 336–337
I/O (input/output) design, 515–516
IP (Internet Protocol), 32, 294
IP address A numeric Internet address used to uniquely identify a computer on the Internet. 32
IPC (instructions per cycle), 79
iPod, R-7
IPOS cycle, 11
IrDA (Infrared Data Association) port, 74
iris, 375
iris scanner, 375
iRobot PackBot Mobile Tactile Robot, 505, 506
IS (information systems) department, 508–509
ISAPI (Internet Server Application Program Interface), 605
iSCSI (Internet SCSI) standard, 107
ISDN Internet access Dial-up Internet access that is faster than conventional dial-up, but still uses standard telephone lines. 320, 321
ISDN (integrated services digital network) modem, 299
ISOC (Internet Society), 313, 316
isosynchronous transmission, 282, 283
ISP. *See* Internet service provider (ISP)
Itanium microprocessor, 65
Itanium 2 microprocessor, 64
iteration control structure, 541
iTunes, 662
iTunes Music Store, 337, 457, 660
iTV (interactive TV), 160, 338

J

Jacquard, Joseph-Marie, R-2
Janakiraman, John, 178–179
Java A high-level, object-oriented programming language frequently used for Web-based applications. 18, 419, 555, 562–565, R-6
personal safety systems, 564
Java applet A small program inserted into a Web page that performs a specific task, such as changing the values in a stock portfolio or scrolling text across the screen. 337, 418, 562, 564, 565
Java bytecode, 558, 562

Java Script, 434
Java Virtual Machine (Java VM), 562
JavaScript A scripting language widely used to add dynamic content to Web pages. 419
Jellyvision, 192
jewel case, 110
JIT. *See* just-in-time (JIT) system
job application, lying on, 669
Jobs, Steve, R-4, R-5
Joint Photographic Experts Group (JPEG) format, 417, 418
joystick An input device that resembles a car's gear shift and is often used for gaming. 15–16, 140
JPEG A graphics format that supports true color and is commonly used for photographs inserted in Web pages. 417, 418
.jpf file extension, 417
jump drive. *See* flash memory drive
Junk Fax Protection Act of 2005, 649
justify option, 234
just-in-time (JIT) system An inventory system in which inventory, other production resources, and finished products are limited to the right number at the right time as required to fill orders. 499

K

Kamen, Dean, 507
Kasparov, Garry, 502–503, R-6
KB. *See* kilobyte (KB)
Kbps (thousands of bits per second), 282
kernel, 185
key
  encryption, 375
  primary, 576, 577
  private, 379, 393
  public, 379, 393
  toggle, 133
key drive. *See* flash memory drive
key escrow system, 382
key ring feature, 380
keyboard An input device containing numerous keys, arranged in a configuration similar to that of a typewriter, that can be used to input letters, numbers, and other symbols. 15–16, 133–135
  Braille, 139, 428, 686
  ergonomic, 139, 677, 678
  one-handed, 686
  portable, 135
  travel, 676
  virtual, 136
keyboard buffer, 190
keyboard drawer, 677, 678
keyboard port, 73, 74
keyguard, 686
keyless entry and ignition system, 202
keystroke-logging program, 641
keyword A word typed in a search box on a search site to locate information on the Internet. 36, 326
  choosing, 329–330
  meta tags, 470
keyword search A type of Internet search in which keywords are typed in a search box to locate information on the Internet. 326–327
kilobyte (KB) 1,024 bytes. 56
kinesthetic learners, 413
Kinko, 316
kiosk, 11
  software, 226
  uses, 10
Kmart, 563
knowledge base, expert system, 504

L

LA Times, 670
label A text-based entry in a worksheet cell that identifies data on the worksheet.
  worksheet, 236
label printer, 166, 167
LAN. *See* local area network (LAN)
land, optical disc, 109
landline phone, 268
Lands' End, 144
landscape orientation, 234
Lane Bryant, 144
language. *See also* programming language
  accessibility of Web sites, 429
language translator A software program that converts program code to machine language. 62, 545–547
laptop computer, 23, 24–25
large-scale integration (LSI), R-4
laser mouse, 135
laser printer An output device that uses toner powder and technology similar to that of a photocopier to produce images on paper. 163, 164, 165
  recharged toner cartridges, 164, 692
laser visa, 644
LCD. *See* liquid crystal display (LCD)
learning styles, multimedia, 413
legacy database, 575
legacy drive, 100
legacy port, 73
legislation. *See also specific laws*
  ethics, 693
  intellectual property laws, 693
  security, 396–397, 648–649
  spyware, 392, 394
LEO (low earth orbit) satellite system, 287
Level 1 cache, 66
Level 2 cache, 66
Level 3 cache, 66
Levi's, 144
line art, 417
line of sight, 133
line printer, 164
line spacing, 230
  formatting documents, 234
linebusting, 9
link. *See also* hyperlink
  sponsored, 470
linkage editing, 546
link-edit stage, 546
linking, 228
Linux A version (flavor) of UNIX that is available without charge over the Internet and is increasingly being used with PCs, servers, mainframes, and supercomputers. 17, 199–200, 204
liquid crystal display (LCD) A type of flat-panel display that uses charged liquid crystals to display images. 160–161
LISP, 556
listing, sponsored, 470
literacy, accessibility of Web sites, 429
literary material, copyright protection, 664
lithography, 83
L.L. Bean, 335
load module, 546
local area network (LAN) A network that connects devices located in a small geographical area, such as within a building. 279
local storage, 117
lock, to protect against hardware loss, 621
Loebner, Hugh, 502
Loebner Prize, 502
logging on, 31
logic, business, 552
logic bomb, 368
logic error A programming error that occurs when running a program produces incorrect results. 542, 548, 549
logical drive, 106–107
logical storage, 99
login ID, 31
Logo, 556
logo, Web sites, 427
London subway, 642
Longhorn, 198
looping operation, 538
Los Angeles, California, 642
lossless file compression, 416
lossy file compression, 417
Lotus 1-2-3, 236
Lotus Approach, 241, 577
Lotus Freelance Graphics, 243
Lotus Notes, 226
Lotus SmartSuite, 227
Lotus WordPro, 232
low earth orbit (LEO) satellite system, 287
Lowe's Home Improvement store, 365–366
low-frequency RFID tag, 150
low-level language A class of programming languages that is highly detailed and machine-dependent. 554
LSI (large-scale integration), R-4
Lycos, 470

M

Mac OS X The most recent version of the operating system used on Apple computers. 17, 198–199
machine cycle The series of operations involved in the execution of a single machine level instruction. 79–81
machine dependent language, 554
machine language A low-level programming language in which the program code consists of 0s and 1s. 61–62, 554, R-2
Macintosh PC, 14, 21, 23, R-5
  CPU, 64
  operating system, 17, 198–199
macro, 552–553
macro programming language, 552–553
macro recorder, 552–553
Macromedia Director MX, 419, 420
Macromedia Dreamweaver, 436
Macromedia Fireworks, 419
Macromedia Flash, 419, 420
Macromedia Flash Player, 419
Macromedia Freehand, 247
Macromedia Shockwave Player, 419
Macy's, 144, 335
Madonna, 662
magnetic disk A storage medium that records data using magnetic spots on disks made of flexible plastic or rigid metal. 100–108. *See also* floppy disk; hard disk drive

magnetic ink character recognition (MICR) reader, 147–148
magnetic (magnetoresistive) RAM, 68
magnetic stripe technology, 119
magnetic tape A plastic tape with a magnetizable surface that stores data as a series of magnetic spots; typically comes as a cartridge. 122, R-2
mail server, 278
mainframe computer A computer used in large organizations (such as hospitals, large businesses, and colleges) that need to manage large amounts of centralized data and run multiple programs simultaneously. 20, 28, 29
operating systems, 204
storage, 120
maintaining multimedia Web sites, 438
make-or-buy decision, 516–517
male connector, 72
malware Any type of malicious software. 368–370. *See also* computer virus
MAN (metropolitan area network), 280
management information system (MIS) A type of information system that provides decision makers with preselected information that can be used to make middle-management decisions. 490, 495
Mandrell, Barbara, 105
manufacturing information system, 490, 501–502
many-to-many (M:M) entity relationship, 582
MapQuest, 343
margin, 230
formatting documents, 234
Mark I, R-2
Mark II computer, 546
markdown optimization software, 501
market exchange site, 456
marketing activities, 635–636
marketing database A collection of data about people that is stored in a large database and used for marketing purposes. 631
markup language A language that uses symbols or tags to describe what a document should look like when it is displayed in a Web browser. 430–434
DHTML, 433
HTML, 430–431
SVG format, 434
WML, 434
XHTML, 431–433
XML, 432
markup tag, 430
Massachusetts Institute of Technology Media Labs, 686
massive multiplayer online role-playing games (MMORPG), 681
massively parallel processing (MPP), 85, 86
massively parallel processor (MPP) computer, 29
master device, 294
MasterCard, 672
math coprocessor, 188
mathematical operator, 237
MB. *See* megabyte (MB)
MBps (megabytes per second), 71
Mbps (millions of bits per second), 282
MBWA (Mobile Broadband Wireless Access), 293
McCabe, Donald L. 668
McCarthy, John, 502
McDonald's, 10, 323, 464
m-commerce, 449–450, 451
MDDB. *See* multidimensional database (MDDB)
mechanical calculator, 13
mechanical mouse, 135
Medford, Oregon mesh network, 292
media player, 249, 337
portable, R-7
medical monitor, 270
medical school, handheld PCs, 9
medium earth orbit (MEO) satellite system, 287
megabyte (MB) Approximately 1 million bytes. 56
megabytes per second (MBps), 71
megaflop, 66
megahertz (MHz), 64, 79
megapixel, 150
Mehrotra, Vipul, 50–51
Melissa virus, 382
memory, 16, 62, 67–69
adding, 81
addressing, 68
cache, 66, 104–106
flash. *See* flash memory
RAM, 66, 67–68, 71, 97, 189–190
registers, 67, 68
ROM, 67, 69
storage vs., 67
video, 83
virtual, 189–190
memory leaking, 189
memory management, 189–190
memory module, 67
Memory Stick, 115
menu A set of options (usually text-based) used that can be displayed on the screen to enable the user to issue commands to the computer. 17, 18
drop-down, 427
pop-up, 427
spreadsheet program, 237
menu bar, 17
menu tab, multimedia Web sites, 427
MEO (medium earth orbit) satellite system, 287
Mercedes, 202
mesh network A network in which there are multiple connections between the devices on the network so that messages can take any of several possible paths. 278, 292
message board, 332
messaging, 269
meta tag, 470
metadata, 584
metamediary, 459
metasearch site, 327
method, OODBMS, 600
metropolitan area network (MAN), 280
MHTML (MIME HTML), 235, 436
MHz (megahertz), 64, 79
MICR (magnetic ink character recognition) reader, 147–148
microarchitecture, 75
microbrowser, 434
microcode, 79
microdisplay, 10
microphone, 15–16
voice input system, 152
microprocessor A central processing unit (CPU) for a microcomputer. Also called processor. 14. *See also* CPU (central processing unit)
Microsoft, 388–389, 636, 662, 674, R-4
MS-DOS, 194
Mydoom worm attack, 371
search tool, 209
Microsoft Access, 241, 577
Microsoft Database Engine (MSDE), 575
Microsoft Excel, 236
Microsoft FrontPage, 436
Microsoft Jet, 575
Microsoft MapPoint .NET Web service, 316
Microsoft Messenger, 273
Microsoft .NET framework, 542
Microsoft Office One of the most widely used office software suites. 227, 229, 380, 550, 646
Microsoft Office Online Web site, 235
Microsoft Office XP, R-7
Microsoft OneNote, 253
Microsoft Outlook, 37
Microsoft Outlook Express, 37
Microsoft Paint, 246
Microsoft Photo Editor, 247
Microsoft PowerPoint, 243
Microsoft Reader, 339
Microsoft Visual C++, 560
Microsoft Windows. *See* Windows *entries*
Microsoft Word, 232
Microsoft Works, 228
microwave, 286
microwave antenna, 286
microwave station An earth-based device that sends and receives high-frequency, high-speed radio signals. 286
middle manager, as information system users, 488–489
middleware Software used to connect two otherwise separate applications, such as a Web server and a database management system. 590, 605
MIDI (musical instrument digital interface) device, 74, 153
.midi file extension, 420
MIDI (Musical Instrument Digital Interface) format, 420
MIDI port, 74
midrange computer, 20, 28
midrange server A medium-sized computer used to host programs and data for a small network. 20, 28
storage, 120
migration, 595
millions of bits per second (Mbps), 282
MIME HTML (MHTML), 235, 436
MIMO (multiple in, multiple out) technology, 298
mini hard drive, 107
mini PC, 21
minicomputer, 20, 28
minus sign (–), subtraction operator, 237
MIS. *See* management information system (MIS)
M:M (many-to-many) entity relationship, 582
MMC (MultiMedia Card), 115
MMORPG (massive multiplayer online role-playing games), 681
MMX (Multimedia Extensions), 83
Mobile Broadband Wireless Access (MBWA), 293
mobile commerce, 449–450, 451
mobile device A very small device, usually based on a wireless phone, that has some type of built-in computing or Internet capability. 20–21. *See also specific devices*
growth in capabilities, R-7
keyboards, 134–135
operating systems, 201–204
mobile operating system, 193
mobile phone A cellular or satellite phone. 268–269. *See also* cellular (cell) phone
mobile software, 228–229

mobile TV, 21, 22
mobile video-on-demand, 22
mobile Web use, 319
mobile WiMAX, 292–293
mobile wireless Internet access Internet access via a wireless communications network, such as the ones used with cellular phones. 320, 322–323
Mobile-Fi, 293
mobisode, 22
MobiTV, 22
modem A communications device that enables digital computers to communicate over analog media, such as connecting to the Internet via telephone lines. 16, 281, 298–299
modem port, 73, 74, 75
module, 532
MOLAP (Multidimensional OLAP), 601
Molsberry, Frank, 712–713
Moneta, 451
monitor A display device for a desktop PC. 15–16, 154. *See also* display *entries*
  CRT, 155
  HD-compatible, 160
  HD-ready, 160
  HDTV, 160
  refreshing image, 155
  wired, 158
  wireless, 158
monitor plug, 73
monitor port, 73, 74, 75
monitoring
  electronic, 640–641
  employees, 643, 645–646, 673
monitoring system, 270–271
monochrome display, 155
monochrome graphic, 58
Moore, Gordon, 77, R-3
Moore's Law, 77
mote, 273
motherboard The main circuit board of a computer, located inside the system unit, to which all computer system components connect. 62, 63
Motion Picture Association of America (MPAA), 665, 666
Motion Picture Experts Group Audio Layer 3 format, 420
Motion Picture Experts Group Audio Layer 4 format, 420
Motion Picture Experts Group (MPEG) format, 61, 421
Motion Picture Laboratories Inc. 665
motion-controlled interface, 136
Motorola, 204
mouse A common pointing device that the user slides along a flat surface to move a pointer around the screen and clicks its buttons to make selections. 15–16, 135–136
  ergonomic, 677, 678
  first, R-3
  foot, 428, 687
  head, 428, 687
  operations, 135
  travel, 676
mouse button, 135
mouse pointer, 135
mouse port, 25, 73, 74
.mov file extension, 421
movie
  animated, creating, 426
  copyright protection, 665–666
  downloadable, 339
MovieLabs, 665
Movielink, 338
moving
  files and folders, 207
  text, 230
.mp3 file extension, 61, 420
MP3 format, 60, 61
MPAA (Motion Picture Association of America), 665, 666
MPEG Audio Layer 3, 61
.mpeg file extension, 421
MPEG (Motion Picture Experts Group) format, 61, 421
MP3-encoded file, 60
MPP (massively parallel processing), 85, 86
MPP (massively parallel processor) computer, 29
MSBlaster, 370
MSDE (Microsoft Database Engine), 575
MS-DOS, 194
MSN, 343
MSN Messenger, 273, 333
multidimensional database (MDDB) A type of database in which data can be viewed from multiple dimensions; commonly used with data warehousing. 601
Multidimensional OLAP (MOLAP), 601
multifunction device A device that offers multiple functions (such as printing, scanning, and faxing) in a single unit. 168
multimedia The integration of a variety of media, such as text, graphics, video, animation, and sound. 410–441
  place shifting, 275
  Web sites, 249
  Web-based. *See* Web-based multimedia
multimedia authoring software, 419
MultiMedia Card (MMC), 115
Multimedia Extensions (MMX), 83
multimedia program, 19
multimedia programming, 563
multimedia projector, 162
multimedia software, 316
  for Web, 249
multimedia Web site design, 421–429
  access considerations, 428–429
  basic principles, 421–423
  determining intended audience and objectives, 423–424
  flowcharts, page layouts, and storyboards, 424–425
  navigational considerations, 426–428
multimedia Web site development, 429–438
  ActiveX, 435
  AJAX, 435
  creating multimedia elements, 430
  maintaining sites, 438
  markup language, 430–434
  MHTML, 436
  publishing sites, 438, 439
  scripting languages, 430, 434–435
  testing sites, 437
  VRML, 436
  Web site authoring software, 430, 436–437
multiple access, 289
multiple in, multiple out (MIMO) technology, 298
multiplexer, 300–301
multiplication operator (*), 237
multiprocessing The capability of an operating system to use multiple processors in a single computer, usually to process multiple jobs at one time faster than could be performed with a single processor. 85–86, 188
multitasking The capability of an operating system to work with more than one programs at one time. 188
multithreading, 188
multiuser database system, 589
Munich, Germany, city of, 200
municipal Wi-Fi network, 292
music
  copyright protection, 664–665
  online, 249, 337–338, 457, 660
music input system, 153
music store, online, 457
  media players, 249
musical instrument digital interface (MIDI) device, 74, 153
Musical Instrument Digital Interface (MIDI) format, 420
Mydoom worm, 370, 371
Myfip, 370
MySimon.com, 452
MySQL, 223

N

NAI (Network Advertising Initiative), 351, 639
name box, spreadsheet program, 237
nanodot, 86
nanometer (nm), 83, 86
nanotechnology The science of creating tiny computers and components by working at the individual atomic and molecular levels. 83, 86
nanotube, 86
Napster, 337, 340, 342, 662, 664–665, R-6
Napster 2, 457
NARA (National Archives and Records Administration), 491
NAS. *See* network attached storage (NAS)
National Archives and Records Administration (NARA), 491
National Center for Supercomputing Applications (NCSA), 313
National Climatic Data Center (NCDC), 564
National Do-Not-Call Registry, 639, 648
National Electronic Product Stewardship Initiative, 692
National Information Infrastructure Protection Act of 1996, 397, 649
National Oceanic and Atmospheric Administration (NOAA), 564
The National Strategy to Secure Cyberspace, 365
National Threat Assessment Center (NTAC), 382
National White Collar Crime Center, 383
natural language, 56, 504
natural language search site, 327
natural programming language, 556
Navajo Nation, 623
navigation, multimedia Web pages, 426–428
navigation bar, multimedia Web sites, 427
NC (network computer), 26
NCDC (National Climatic Data Center), 564
NCSA (National Center for Supercomputing Applications), 313
NEC, 113
Neiman Marcus, 671
Nero Express, 249

Nero PhotoShow Elite, 247
Nero PhotoSnap, 247
nested if-then-else statement, 539, 541
netiquette An etiquette for guiding online behavior. 40
Net2Phone, 334
Netscape Mail, 37
Netscape Navigator, 31, R-5
Netscape Server API (NSAPI), 605
NetWare A widely used operating system for PC-based networks. 201
network, 267
architectures, 278–278
communications. *See* communications network
computer. *See* computer network
data transmission. *See* data transmission over network
expert insight on, 406–407
extranets, 281
gateway, 296
home, 268, 296
intranets, 280–281
LANs, 279
MANs, 280
PANs, 280
telephone, 267
topologies, 277–278
VPNs, 281
WANs, 279
wired, 283–284
wireless, 283–284
network adapter A network interface, such as an expansion card or external network adapter. 16, 297–298
Network Advertising Initiative (NAI), 351, 639
network attached storage (NAS) A high-performance storage server individually connected to a network to provide storage for computers on that network. 121
network computer (NC), 26
network database management system, 593
network interface card (NIC) An expansion card through which a computer can connect to a network. 297–298
network license, 223
network plug, 73
network port, 73, 74, 75
network printer, 164
network server, 30, 278
operating systems, 194–201
network storage, 117
networked economy, 39
networking hardware, 297–301
NetZero, 352
neural network An expert system in which the human brain's pattern-recognition process is emulated by the computer system. 505
New Document command, 229
New Slides button, presentation graphics software, 245
New York Times, 646
news, online, 340–342
newsgroup, 332
newsreader, 332
Newsweek magazine, 670
Nexrad (Next Generation Weather Radar), 564
Next Generation Internet (NGI), 314
Next Generation Weather Radar (Nexrad), 564
NIC. *See* network interface card (NIC)
Nigerian letter fraud scheme, 387–388
nm (nanometer), 83, 86
NOAA (National Oceanic and Atmospheric Administration), 564
Nokia, 203, 204
Nominet, 662
nonimpact printer, 163
nonmanagement worker, as information system users, 489
non-personally identifiable information (non-PII), 349
nonvolatile Describes a storage medium that retains its contents when the power is shut off. 98
normalization, 594
note, presentation graphics, 245
note taking, digital, 253
notebook computer A fully functioning portable PC that opens to reveal a screen and keyboard. 23, 24–25
accessing Internet, 319
ergonomics, 676–677
keyboards, 134
ports, 75
notebook stand, 25, 676, 677
Novell, 200
Novell NetWare, 191
Noyce, Robert, R-3
NSAPI (Netscape Server API), 605
NTAC (National Threat Assessment Center), 382
NTFS file system, 106
N-tier database system, 590
NTT DoCoMo, 451
Num Lock key, 134
number format, worksheet, 237
numbering system, 56
binary, 56–57
decimal (base 10), 56
numeric keypad, 133, 134
Nuvo, 507

O

OA. *See* office automation (OA)
OAKLEY THUMP sunglasses, R-7
object, OODBMS, 600
object code The machine language version of a computer program generated after the program's source code is compiled. 545
object linking and embedding (OLE), 228, 435
object query language (OQL), 600
object-based authoring program, 419
objectives, Web page, 423
object-oriented database management system (OODBMS) A type of database system in which multiple types of data are stored as objects along with their related code. 599–600
object-oriented programming (OOP) An approach to program design in which a program consists of a collection of objects that contain data and methods to be used with that data. 532–533
object-oriented programming language, 532
object-relations database management system (ORDBMS), 600
OCR. *See* optical character recognition (OCR)
Offica Watch, 451
office automation (OA) Computer-based office-oriented technologies, such as word processing, e-mail, workgroup computing, and the like. 491
office suite, 227–228
office system A type of system in which office automation hardware, software, and other resources are used to facilitate communications and enhance productivity. 490, 491–492
offshore outsourcing, 510
OFRO+detect, 506
OLAP (Online Analytical Processing), 601
OLE (object linking and embedding), 228, 435
OLED. *See* organic light emitting diode (OLED)
OLPC (One Laptop Per Child), 686
O:M (one-to-many) entity relationship, 582
OMR (optical mark reader), 147
1:1 (one-to-one) entity relationship, 581
One Laptop Per Child (OLPC), 686
one-entry-point/one-exit-point rule, 541–542
one-handed keyboard, 686
100Base-T, 289
1000Base-T, 289
one-to-many (O:M) entity relationship, 582
one-to-one (1:1) entity relationship, 581
Online Analytical Processing (OLAP), 601
online anonymity, 41
online auction An online activity for which bids are placed on items, and the highest bidder purchases the item. 20, 336
online auction fraud When an item purchased through an online auction is never delivered after payment, or the items is not as specified by the seller. 385–386
online auction site A Web site where potential buyers bid on an item and, at the end of a set time period, the highest bidder buys the item as long as all bidding criteria, such as minimum selling price, have been met. 454–456
escrow service, 392, 458
watching feature, 454
online banking Performing banking activities over the Internet. 252, 336
online broker, 336
online check, 462
online conferencing, 272–273
online education, 344–345
online entertainment, 337–340
e-books, 339–340
gaming, 339
music, 337–338
video, 338–339
online forum, 332
online fraud. *See* dot-con; fraud; phishing
online gaming Playing games over the Internet. 339
online investing Buying and selling stocks or other types of investments over the Internet. 334, 336–337
online music Music played or obtained via the Internet. 337–338, 660
online music store, 337, 338, 457
online news, 340–342
online payment account A type of payment account accessed via the Internet and used to make electronic payments to others, either from funds deposited into the account or by charging the appropriate amount to a credit card. 336, 462–463
online portfolio, 336
online portfolio management service, 252
online radio station, 337
online service provider, 314
online shopping Buying products or services over the Internet. 334–336, 335–336

online storage, 117
online storage system, 98
online testing, 344, 345
online voting, 622, 623
online writing, 344, 345–346
onsite paging, 269
OODBMS. *See* object-oriented database management system (OODBMS)
OOP. *See* object-oriented programming (OOP)
Open command, 229
Open Directory Project, 327
Open Enterprise Server, 201
open source software Software programs whose source code is made available to the general public. 199, 222, 223
opening the system unit, 81
OpenOffice.org office suite, 223, 227
Opera, 31
operating environment, 194
operating system The main component of system software that enables the computer to manage its activities and the resources under its control, run application programs, and interface with the user. 17, 184–204. *See also specific operating systems*
  analyzing needs, R-10
  automatic updates, 377
  command line vs. graphical user interface, 191
  for desktop PCs and servers, 194–201
  functions, 185–187
  future, 211
  for handheld PCs and mobile devices, 201–204
  intermediary role, 184
  larger computers, 204
  PC-DOS, R-4
  personal vs. server, 191–193
  processing techniques for increased efficiency, 188–191
  processors supported, 193–194
  security patches, 370
  spyware, 292
  updating, 377, 626
  upgrading, 185
Operation Web Snare, 389
operational decision, 489
operational manager, as information system users, 488, 489
operations personnel, information system development, 509
operator, relational, 536
opt out To request that you be removed from marketing activities or that your information not be shared with other companies. 638–639
Opteron microprocessor, 64, 65
optical character, 147
optical character recognition (OCR) The ability of a scanning device to recognize handwritten or typed characters and convert them to electronic form as text, not images. 142
optical character recognition (OCR) device, 147
optical computer A computer that uses light, such as from laser beams or infrared beams, to perform digital computations. 14, 87
optical disc A type of storage medium read from and written to using a laser beam. 109–114
optical mark reader (OMR), 147
optical mouse, 135
optical resolution, scanners, 142–143
optical scanner. *See* scanner
optical zoom, 150
opting in, 639
Options dialog box, 35
opto-electronic computer, 87
opt-out cookie, 639
OQL (object query language), 600
Oracle, 460, 575, 577
Oracle Database, 241
ORDBMS (object-relations database management system), 600
order entry system A type of transaction system that records and manages order processing. 493
order-fulfillment company, 466
organic computer, 86
organic light emitting diode (OLED) display A type of flat-panel display that uses emissive organic material to display brighter and sharper images. 160, 161–162
organizational chart, system development, 513
Orzack, Maressa Hecht, 681
Outline pane, presentation graphics software, 245
output The process of presenting the results of processing; can also refer to the results themselves. 11–12
output device, 16. *See also specific devices*
  assistive, 687–688
outsourcing Turning over specific business tasks to an outside vendor; increasingly, the vendor is located in a different country with lower labor costs. 414, 467
  information system development, 510–511
  offshore, 510
  privacy, 511
  security, 511
outsourcing company, 383
Overstock.com, 456
ownership rights, software, 221–224

P

package tracking, 604
Packet8, 334
packet switching, 294, 334
padlock icon, 34
page, memory, 189
Page Down key, 134
page formatting, 234
page layout A sketch of a Web page often developed during the Web design process to illustrate the basic layouts of the home page and the rest of the pages on a Web site. 425
page number, 230
page printer, 164
Page Setup command, 234
Page Up key, 134
pages per minute (ppm), 164
paging, 190, 269
painting program, 246
Palm Graffiti alphabet, 137
Palm handheld PC, 137, R-6
Palm LifeDrive, R-7
Palm OS The operating system designed for Palm handheld PCs. 203
Palm OS Cobalt 6.1, 203
Palm Reader, 339
PAN (personal area network), 280
paper, electronic, 154, 156
paperless office, 491, 690
paragraph formatting, 234
parallel ATA standard, 107
parallel conversion, 518, 519
parallel plug, 73
parallel port, 73, 74, 75
parallel processing A processing technique that uses multiple processors simultaneously in a single computer, usually to process a single job as fast as possible. 85, 86, 188
parallel transmission. Data transmission in which bytes of data are transmitted at one time, with the bits in each byte taking a separate path. 282
parameter, Java applet, 564, 565
Park-by-Phone, 269
partial dependency, 594
partial mesh topology, 278
partitioning a hard drive, 106–107
Pascal A structured, high-level programming language often used to teach structured programming, especially appropriate for use in math and science applications. 18, 555, 558–559
Pascal, Blaise, 558, R-2
Pascaline Arithmetic Machine, R-2
passive RFID tag, 271
password A secret combination of characters used to gain access to a computer, computer network, or other resource. 187, 372–373
  strong, 373
Paste command, 229
patent A form of protection that can be granted by the government for an invention; gives exclusive rights of an invention to its inventor for 20 years. 662–663
path, 186
Pay By Touch, 493
Payment Card Industry (PCI), 372
PayPal, 336, 463, 673
payroll system A type of transaction system that generates employee payroll amounts and reports. 494
PB. *See* petabyte (PB)
PC. *See* personal computer (PC)
PC cam, 152
PC Card, 72
PC Card hard drive, 108
PC modding, 21, 24
PC postage, 166
PC video camera, 152
PC video conference, 272–273
PC-compatible desktop PC, 21, 23
PC-DOS, 194, R-4
PCI (Payment Card Industry), 372
PCI (Peripheral Component Interconnect) bus, 70, 71
PCI Express (PCIe) One of the buses most commonly used to connect peripheral devices. 70, 71
PCIe. *See* PCI Express (PCIe)
PCIe x1 bus, 71
PCIe x16 bus, 71
PCMCIA (Personal Computer Memory Card International Association) card, 72
PCMCIA card slot, 72
PDA (personal digital assistant), 25
PDF (Portable Document Format), 492
PDF-Archive, 492
PDLC. *See* program development life cycle (PDLC)
Peer Cash, 457
Peer Impact, 457
peer-to-peer (P2P) file sharing The process of sharing resources directly between users via the Internet. 340, 342
peer-to-peer (P2P) MP3 file exchange, 249
peer-to-peer (P2P) network, 278, 279

pen-based PC, 137–138
Pentium 4 microprocessor, 63, 65
Pentium D microprocessor, 63, 65
Pentium 4EE microprocessor, 65
Pentium M microprocessor, 63, 65
PeopleSoft, 460
perceptual coding, 61
performance, improving, 81–83
Peripheral Component Interconnect (PCI) bus, 70, 71
peripheral device, 25, 62–63
Perl (Practical Extraction and Report Language), 435
permission-based advertising, 472
personal area network (PAN), 280
personal computer (PC) Another name for microcomputer. 20, 21–28. *See also* PC *entries*
  buying. *See* buying a PC
  desktop, 21–23
  environmentally friendly, 690
  expert insight, 50–51
  Internet appliances, 26, 28
  new, setting up, 27
  portable, 23–25
  protecting, 626
  setting up, 324–325
  thin clients, 26
Personal Computer Memory Card International Association (PCMCIA) card, 72
Personal Data Privacy and Security Act of 2005, 488, 648
personal digital assistant (PDA), 25
personal finance software, 252
personal firewall, 376
personal information, protecting privacy, 636–640
Personal Internet Communicator (PIC), 685
personal operating system A type of operating system designed to be installed on a PC. 191, 192
personal organizer, 253
personal planner, 253
personal printer, 164
personal productivity software, 251, 252, 253
personal publishing software, 252
personal robot, 506
personal safety systems, 564
personal safety tips, 396
personally identifiable information (PII), 349
person-to-person (P2P) model, 458
pervasive computing, 5
petabyte (PB) Approximately 1,000 terabytes. 56
PGP (Pretty Good Privacy), 379
pharming, 387
phase-change technology, 113–114
phased conversion, 518, 519
Philadelphia, Pennsylvania wireless network, 292
phishing The use of spoofed e-mail messages to gain credit card numbers and other personal data to be used for fraudulent purposes. 39, 210, 371, 378, 386, 387, R-7
PHOLED (phosphorescent OLED), 162
phone. *See also* telephone *entries*
  cellular (cell), 268, 287–288. *See* cellular (cell) phone
  landline, 268
  mobile, 268–269
  satellite, 268
  smart, 20, 204
  video, 152, 272–273
  wallet, 451
  WebPhone, 334
phone port, 73, 74
Phoneline, 298
phosphorescent OLED (PHOLED), 162
photo editing program, 247
photo printer An output device designed for printing digital photographs. 166, 167
photo-quality ink-jet printer, 166
PHP (PHP Hypertext Preprocessor), 605
PHP tag, 605
phrase searching, 328–329
physical disabilities
  assistive technology, 428–429
physical file representation, 99
physical health, 675–679
physical storage, 99
PIC (Personal Internet Communicator), 685
Pick 'n Save, 493
piconet, 294
picture element, 58, 143
Picture toolbar, 235
Picture trail, 637
Piggly Wiggly, 493
PII (personally identifiable information), 349
pilot conversion, 518, 519
pipelining A CPU feature designed to begin processing a new instruction as soon as the previous instruction completes the first stage of the machine cycle. 84–85
piracy, software, 627–628
  protecting against, 629
pit, optical disc, 109
Pixar, 426, R-5
pixel The smallest colorable area in an electronic image, such as a scanned document, digital photograph, or image displayed on a display screen. 58, 143, 155, 167
PL/1, 556
place shifting, multimedia, 275
plagiarism Presenting someone else's work as your own. 664
plagiarizing, 331
plasma display A type of flat-panel display that uses layers of gas to display images; most often used on large displays. 160, 162
platform, options, R-11
Platform for Privacy Preferences (P3P), 637
Play Station 3, 113
playlist, 249
Plexus, 370
PLM (product lifecycle management), 499
PLM software, 499
plotter, 168
Plug and Play, 73, 185
plug-in, 419
  Web pages, 422
plus sign (+), addition operator, 237
PNG A graphics format designed specifically for use with Web page images. 417
.png file extension, 417
PNG (Portable Network Graphic) format, 417, 418
pocket computer, 25
pocket hard drive, 107
Pocket Office, 229
podcasting, 346, 347
podcatching software, 347
point, 230
pointing, 135
pointing device An input device that moves an onscreen pointer, such as an arrow or insertion point, to allow the user to select objects on the screen. 135–141. *See also* electronic pen; mouse; touch screen
  assistive technology, 428
pointing stick An input device shaped like a pencil eraser that appears in the middle of some notebook computer keyboards and is used as a pointing device. 140, 141
point-of-sale (POS) system, 139, 493
policies, security, 383
polymorphism, object-oriented programming, 533
pop-under ad, 635
pop-up ad, 317, 635
pop-up menu, multimedia Web sites, 427
pornography, 395–396
port A connector on the exterior of a PC's system unit to which a device may be attached. 15–16, 70, 72–75
  display device, 157–158
port replicator, 75
portable barcode reader, 145
portable computer, 11
Portable Document Format (PDF), 492
portable hard drive, 107–108, 123
portable keyboard, 135
portable media player, 102, 154
Portable Network Graphic (PNG) format, 417, 418
portable PC A small personal computer, such as a notebook, tablet, or handheld PC, designed to be carried around easily. 23–25
portable printer, 167
portable thumb pad, 135
portal A Web site designed to be designated as a browser home page; typically can be customized to display personalized content.. 343
  college, 587
  vertical, 459
portal page, 341
portal RFID reader, 146
portfolio
  electronic, 345, 346
  online, 336
portrait orientation, 234
POS (point-of-sale) system, 139, 493
possessed knowledge access system An access control system that uses information that only an individual should know to identify that individual. 372–373
possessed object access system An access control system that uses physical objects that an individual has in his or her possession to identify that individual. 373
POST (power-on self test), 69
post-implementation review, 520
POSTNET code, 145
power, budget considerations vs., R-11
power connector, 73
Power5 microprocessor, 64
Power PC G5 microprocessor, 64, 65
power plug, 73
Powerline, 298
power-on self test (POST), 69
PowerPC microprocessor, 64
P2P. *See* peer-to-peer (P2P) file sharing
P2P (Internet peer-to-peer) computing, 279
P2P (person-to-person) model, 458

P2P (peer-to-peer) MP3 file exchange, 249
P2P (peer-to-peer) network, 278, 279
P3P (Platform for Privacy Preferences), 637
ppm (pages per minute), 164
Practical Extraction and Report Language (Perl), 435
precomputer, R-2
Preferences dialog box, 35
prefetch unit The part of the CPU that attempts to retrieve data and instructions before they are needed for processing, in order to avoid delays. 76, 77
preliminary investigation The phase of the system development life cycle in which a brief feasibility study is performed to assess whether or not a full-scale project should be undertaken. 512–513
presence management, 646–647
presence technology Technology that enables one computing device (such as a desktop PC, handheld computer, or smart phone) to locate and identify the current status of another device on the same network. 646–647
presentation graphic An image, such as a graph or text chart, designed to visually enhance a presentation. 243–246
  creating presentations, 244–245
  finishing presentations, 245–246
  Web sites, 246
presentation graphics software Application software used to create presentation graphics and online slide shows. 8, 227, 243
Pretty Good Privacy (PGP), 379
price optimization, 499, 501
PriceGrabber.com, 452
Priceline.com, 455–456, 460, 663
primary key A specific field in a database table that uniquely identifies the records in that table. 577
  composite, 576
print buffer, 190
Print command, 229
print queue, 190–191
print server, 278
print spooler, 82
printer An output device that produces output on paper. 15–16, 163–168
  barcode, 166, 167
  Braille, 688
  color vs. black-and-white, 163
  dot-matrix, 163
  impact vs. nonimpact, 163
  ink-jet, 163, 165–166
  label, 166, 167
  laser, 163, 164, 165
  multifunction devices, 168
  personal vs. network, 164
  photo, 166, 167
  plotters, 168
  portable, 167
  print resolution, 164
  print speed, 164
  wide-format, 167, 168
privacy The state of being concealed or free from unauthorized intrusion. 40, 349–353, 630
  adware, 352–353
  computer monitoring, 640–641
  cookies, 349–351
  data, 586
  disposing of equipment, 692–693
  e-mail, 353
  information, 630–631
  outsourcing, 511
  personal information, protecting, 636–640
  spyware, 352
  video surveillance, 641–643
  Web bugs, 352
  workplace, 647–648
Privacy Act of 1974, 649
Privacy Bird, 637
privacy policy A policy, commonly posted on a company's Web site, that explains how personal information provided to that company will be used. 40
  e-commerce sites, 469
  reading, 637
  Web sites, 634
privacy software, 637
PrivacyRightsNow!, 639
private key, 379
  digital signature, 393
private key encryption A type of encryption that uses a single key to encrypt and decrypt the file or message. 379, 380
problem analysis The step in the program development life cycle in which the problem is carefully considered and the program specifications are developed. 534–535
procedural programming language, 555
processing Performing operations on data that has been input into a computer to convert that input to output. 11–12
processing device, 16
processing speed, 66
processing symbol, flowcharts, 538
processing techniques, increasing efficiency, 188–191
processor Another name for central processing unit (CPU). 63. *See also* CPU (central processing unit)
product flow, 498
product information, online, 343
product lifecycle management (PLM), 499
product stewardship, 692
productivity software suite, 227
professional hacking, 364
profiling customers, 473
program. *See also* software; *specific programs*
  chess-playing, 502–503
  debugging, 545–549
  downloading, 205
  installing, 205
  keystroke-logging, 641
  upgrading, 196
  Web animation, 419
program design The step in the program development life cycle in which the program specifications are expanded into a complete design of the new program. 535–542
  algorithm, 535
  control structures, 539–541
  good, 541–542
  tools, 536–539
program development The process of creating application programs. 531–553
  aspect-oriented programming, 533–534
  life cycle. *See* program development life cycle (PDLC)
  object-oriented programming, 532–533
  structured programming, 531–534
  tools for facilitating, 551–553
program development life cycle (PDLC) The process containing the five steps of program development: analyzing, designing, coding, debugging and testing, and maintaining application software. 517, 534–550
  documentation, 535, 542, 545, 550
  problem analysis step, 534–535
  program coding step, 542, 544–545
  program debugging and testing step, 545–550
  program design step, 535–542
  program implementation and maintenance step, 550
program development process, 517
program flowchart, 425
program maintenance, 550
program package, 550
programmer A person whose job it is to write, test, and maintain computer programs. 20, 534
  database, 578
  information system development, 509
programming
  comments, 544
  multimedia, 563
programming language A set of rules, words, symbols, and codes used to write computer programs. 14, 18, 419, 531, 553–565. *See also specific languages*
  categories, 554–556
  choosing, 542, 544
  popular, 556–565
progressive image, 417
project, Visual Basic, 561
project folder, 520
Project Gutenberg, 691
project management software, 251, 252, 253, 519
project manager, information system development, 509
Prolog, 556
promotion, e-commerce sites, 470–471
property, object-oriented programming, 538
PROTECT Act of 2003, 397
protocol, 312
prototyping A system development alternative whereby a small model, or prototype, of the system is built before the full-scale systems development effort is undertaken. 521
proximity card An identification card with built-in smart card capabilities; used for access purposes, as well as for location monitoring. 645
proxy server, 296
PS/2 connector, 74
PS/2 plug, 73
pseudocode A program design tool that uses English-like statements to outline the logic of a program. 538
Psion, 204
public domain software Software that is not copyrighted and may be used without restriction. 222, 224
public hotspot, 323
public key, 379
  digital signature, 393
public key encryption A type of encryption that uses key pairs to encrypt and decrypt the file or message. 379
public keyserver, 380
publishing multimedia Web sites, 438, 439
punch card, R-2

Punch Card Tabulating Machine and Sorter, 13
punched card, 13

Q

quad-channel memory architecture, 68
quad-core CPU, 83
Quantum Computer Services, R-5
quantum computing A technology that applies the principles of quantum physics and quantum mechanics to computers to direct atoms or nuclei to work together as quantum bits (qubits), which function simultaneously as the computer's processor and memory. 87
qubit, 87
query A request to *see* information from a database that matches specific criteria.
  database, 596–598, 599
query, databases, 241, 242
query language, 575, 596
QuickTime, 420
QuickTime format, 421

R

RAD (rapid application development), 551
radio frequency identification (RFID) A technology used to store and transmit data located in RFID tags. 145–146, 150–151, 271
  m-commerce, 451
radio frequency (RF) transmission, 286
radio station, online, 337
radio wave, 133
RAID (redundant arrays of independent disks) A storage method that uses several small hard disks in parallel to do the job of a larger disk. 121–122
RAM. *See* random access memory (RAM)
Rambus in-line memory module (RIMM), 67
random access, 98
random access memory (RAM) Chips connected to the motherboard that provide a temporary location for the computer to hold data and program instructions while they are needed. 67–68, 71, 97
  flash. *See* flash memory
  memory management, 189–190
range, worksheet, 236, 237
rapid application development (RAD), 551
RDBMS. *See* relational database management system (RDBMS)
reader, 144–149
  barcode, 144–145
  biometric, 148–149
  MICR, 147–148
  OCR, 147
  OMR, 147
  RFID, 145–146
reading device, 141
read-only memory (ROM) Nonerasable chips located on the motherboard into which data or programs have been permanently stored. 67, 69
read-only storage media, 110
read/write head, 100
Real format, 421
Real ID Act of 2005, 644
Real Simple Syndication (RSS), 341
RealOne Player, 249, 337, 420
RealPlayer Music Store, 337, 457
real-time processing, 575
Recall Corporation, 627
receipt scanner, 142
receiver, wireless network transmission, 286
recharged toner cartridge, 164, 692
record A collection of related fields in a database. Also called a row. 576
  data hierarchy, 581
  databases, 241
recordable disc, 112
Recording Industry Association of America (RIAA), 342, 371
recovering deleted file/folder, 207
recovery partition, 106
recovery utility, 210
Recycle Bin, 207
  restoring deleted files and folders, 207
recycling computer equipment, 692
red laser disc, 112
redundant arrays of independent disks. *See* RAID (redundant arrays of independent disks)
redundant field, 580
reference site, 36, 343
reference software, 252
refreshing monitor image, 155
register High-speed memory built into the CPU that temporarily stores data during processing. 67, 68, 76, 78
Registered Traveler program, 644
registry, 185, 389
Rehabilitation Act, 429
  1998 amendment to, 693
reintermediation, 459
relational database, 240, 576–577
relational database management system (RDBMS) A type of database system in which data is stored in tables related by common fields; the most widely used database model today. 241, 593–599
  creating databases, 595–596, 597f
  database design, 594
  database maintenance, 598–599
  information retrieval, 596–598, 599
Relational OLAP (ROLAP), 601
relational operator, 536
relationship, entities, 581–582
relative cell referencing, 238
remarks, 544
remote diagnosis, 276
remote storage A storage device that is not directly a part of the PC being used, such as network storage or online storage. 117–118
renaming files and folders, 207
RenderMan computer system, 426
repeater, 300
repeating group, 594
repetition control structure, 541
repetitive stress injury (RSI) A type of injury, such as carpal tunnel syndrome, that is caused by performing the same physical movements over and over again. 675
report A formatted means of looking at a database table or the results of a query. 241, 243, 575, 596, 598, 599
report generator, 553
request for proposal (RFP), 517
request for quotation (RFQ), 517
resolution, print, 164
resources, ethical use, 666–667
restore disc, 27
restore point, 27
restoring deleted file/folder, 207
restricted TLD, 33
résumé padding, 669
reusable code, 545
REV hard drive cartridge, 123
reverse engineering, 78
rewritable disc, 112–114
rewritable optical media, 100
RF (radio frequency) transmission, 286
RFID. *See* radio frequency identification (RFID)
RFID tag A device containing tiny chips and radio antennas that is attached to objects that will be identified using RFID technology. 145, 271, R-7
RFID-enabled forklift, 146
RFP (request for proposal), 517
RFQ (request for quotation), 517
RIAA (Recording Industry Association of America), 342, 371
rich media ad, 471
Right to Financial Privacy Act of 1974, 649
right-clicking, 135
rights-management tool, 232
RIMM (Rambus in-line memory module), 67
ring network A network that connects devices in a closed loop. 277
ripping software, 248
Ritchie, Dennis, R-4
RJ-11 connector, 284
RJ-45 connector, 74, 284
RJ-45 plug, 73
.rm file extension, 421
RoadRunner, 31
robot A device, controlled by a human operator or a computer, that can move and react to sensory input. 502, 505
  business, 506
  humanoid, 506–507
  personal, 506
robot-assisted surgery, 276, 505
robotics The study of robot technology. 505–507
ROLAP (Relational OLAP), 601
ROM. *See* read-only memory (ROM)
root directory, 186
rotational delay, 104
router A device on a network that sends data via the most efficient route to travel to a specific location. 277, 300
row In a spreadsheet program, a horizontal group of cells on a worksheet. In a database program, a record. 576
  in data hierarchy, 581
  databases, 241
  tables, 234
  worksheets, 236, 237
row-level locking, 585
Roxio Easy Media Creator, 249
Roxio Easy Media Creator 7.5 Digital Media Suite, 250
royalty-free clip art, 415
RSI. *See* repetitive stress injury (RSI)
RSS (Real Simple Syndication), 341
RSS aggregator, 341
RSS feed, 341, 680
ruggedized PC, 624
Rutgers University, 382

S

sabotage. *See* computer sabotage; computer virus
Safari, 31
salami shaving, 384
Sales Support DSS, 495

sales tax, online purchases, 468–469
sample, audio data, 60
SAN. *See* storage area network (SAN)
sans serif typeface, 414–415
SAP, 460
Sarbanes-Oxley Act of 2002, 383, 397, 488, 645, 649, 667, 672, 693
SAS (serial attached SCSI) standard, 107
Sasser, 370
SATA (serial ATA) standard, 107
SATA II (serial ATA II) standard, 107
satellite, 286–287
satellite connection, 16
satellite dish, 286
satellite Internet access Fast, direct Internet access via the airwaves using a satellite dish and satellite modem. 320, 322
satellite modem, 299
satellite phone, 268
satellite radio, 272
Save command, 229
Save Toby Web site, 673
saving documents, 210
SC connector, 285
scalability, enterprise storage system, 120
Scalable Vector Graphics (SVG) format, 434
scanner An input device that reads printed text and graphics and transfers them to a computer in digital form. 15–16, 141–144
  body, 144
  scanning quality and resolution, 142–143
  types, 142
Scanner and Camera Wizard, 250
ScanSoft NaturallySpeaking, 152
scheduling routine, 185
school
  cheating, 668
  ethical use of resources, 667
  video surveillance, 642
Schundler, Bret, 670
SCM. *See* supply chain management (SCM)
SCO Group, 371
Scooba FloorWashing Robot, 507
screen painter, 553
screen reader, 428, 686, 687–688
screen resolution, 167
script, 605
scripting language, 430, 434–435
scroll wheel, 135
SCSI (small computer system interface) port, 74
SCSI (small computer system interface) standard, 107
SD (Secure Digital) flash memory card, 75, 115
SD slot, 75
SDLC. *See* system development life cycle (SDLC)
SDRAM (synchronous dynamic RAM), 68
SeaCode, 510
Seagate Technologies, R-4
search agent, 503
search box, multimedia Web sites, 427
search engine A software program used by a search site to retrieve matching Web pages from a search database. 326
search site A Web site designed to help users search for Web pages that match specified keywords or selected categories. 35, 36, 326–328, 601, 602
  directory searches, 327
  keyword searches, 326–327
  multiple, 329
  tools, 328
search tool A utility program designed to search for files on the user's hard drive. 208, 209
searching, Help feature, 231, 232
searching the Internet, 325–331
  citing Internet resources, 331
  evaluating search results, 330–331
  search sites, 326–328
  search strategies, 328–330
  Web, 36
second-generation (2G) cell phone, 288
second-generation computer, 13, 14, R-3
second-generation (2G) wireless standard, 322
Section 508, 429
sector A pie-shaped area on a disk surface. 101
Secure Digital (SD) flash memory card, 75, 115
Secure Hypertext Transfer Protocol (HTTPS), 33
secure server, personal information, 639–640
Secure Sockets Layer (SSL), 379
secure Web page, 33, 34, 378
secure Web server A Web server that uses encryption to protect information transmitted via the Web pages stored on that server. 334, 378–379
security, 39, 362–399
  access control systems, 372–376
  antivirus software, 17, 39, 82, 210–211, 377–378
  avoiding employee attacks, 382–383
  computer sabotage, 367–371
  cyberstalking, 395, 396
  data, 585–586
  data theft, 384
  digital certificates, 393, 394, 473
  digital counterfeiting, 628–630
  digital signatures, 393–394, 465, 473
  e-commerce, 473
  encryption. *See* encryption
  external, 586
  firewalls, 187, 211, 321, 372, 376–377
  hacking, 364–367
  hardware, 620–627
  identity theft, 39, 210, 334, 384–385, 389–391
  importance, 363, 619
  information theft, 384
  interception of communications, 367
  internet scams, 386, 387
  legislation, 396–397, 648–649
  multiple file formats, 627
  online auction fraud, 385–386
  operating system, 187
  outsourcing, 511
  personal safety tips, 396
  phishing, 39, 210, 371, 378, 386, 387
  pornography, 395–396
  protecting against crime, 389–392
  protecting against spyware, 392–393
  secure credit cards, 453
  secure Web servers, 378–379
  smart card, 465
  software piracy, 627–628, 629–630
  spoofing, 386–387
  spyware. *See* spyware
  unauthorized access, 364
  viruses. *See* computer virus
  Wi-Fi, 375, 376
security hole, 370
security patch, 187, 370
security utility program, 210–211
seek time, 104
segment, memory, 189
selection control structure, 539, 540–541
semirugged PC, 624
Sempron microprocessor, 63, 65
senior manager, as information system users, 488, 489
sensitivity analysis, 239
sequence control structure, 539
sequenced organization, 588
sequential access, 98–99
serial ATA (SATA) standard, 107
serial ATA II (SATA II) standard, 107
serial attached SCSI (SAS) standard, 107
serial connector, 73
serial plug, 73
serial port, 73
serial transmission Data transmission in which the bits in a byte travel down the same path one after the other. 282
serif typeface, 414
server
  blade, 20, 28
  client-server networks, 278–279
  DNS, 296, 387
  file, 278
  FTP, 318
  high-end (enterprise-class), 28
  mail, 278
  midrange, 20, 28, 120
  network, 30, 194–201, 278
  print, 278
  proxy, 296
  secure, 639–640
  storage, 120
  Web, 31, 278, 334, 378–379
server operating system A type of operating system designed to be installed on a network server. 191–193
service provider, 314
servlet, 564
set-top box, 26
shading, 230
shareware Copyrighted software that is distributed on the honor system; consumers should either pay for it or uninstall it after the trial period. 222, 224
sheetfed scanner A scanner that can accept a single sheet of paper at one time. 142, 143
shielding, twisted-pair cable, 284
Shift key, 134
Shockley, William, R-3
Shockwave, 419, 420
shopping bag, 335
shopping bot, 452, 503
shopping cart, 335
shopping cart software, 468
shortcut, 18
signature capture device, 138, 139
silicon on insulator (SOI), 84
SIMM (single in-line memory module), 67
simplex transmission, 283
Simpson, O. J. 670
Simputer, 685
single file Web page, 235
single in-line memory module (SIMM), 67
Single UNIX Specification, 199
single-user database system, 589
single-user license, 223
site license, 223
site map, navigating multimedia Web sites, 426, 427

site submission service, 470
site-specific digital wallet, 466
64-bit processor, 66
sizing button Small buttons located at the top-right corner of each a window used to resize the window. 17, 18
SK Telecom, 451
skimming, 384
Slammer worm, 370
slash (/), division operator, 237
slate tablet PC, 23, 24
slave device, 294
slide A one-page presentation graphic that can be displayed in a group with others to form an online slide show.
presentation graphics, 245
slide layout, 244–245
presentation graphics, 245
slide rule, 13, R-2
slide show, 245–246
slide sorter view, 245
Slides pane, presentation graphics software, 245
Slingbox, 275, 666
Small Computer System Interface (SCSI) port, 74
Small Computer System Interface (SCSI) standard, 107
SmallTalk, 556
smart appliance, 7
smart car, 202
smart card A credit card-sized piece of plastic containing a chip and other circuitry into which data can be stored. 10, 119–120, 336, 464–465, 662
digital signatures, 394, 465
smart card ID system, 118
smart card reader, 119
smart display, 158
smart dust, 271, 273
smart home, 7
smart phone, 20, 204
smart vending machine, 451
smart watch, 20–21
smiley, 41
Smith, David, 382
SMP (symmetric multiprocessing), 85–86
snapshot printer, 166
Sobig, 368
social engineering, 384
Social Security Administration (SSA), 146
society, expert insight, 712–713
soft copy, 154
software The instructions, also called computer programs, that are used to tell a computer what it should do. 15–19. *See also* program; *specific programs*
antispy, 647
application. *See* application software
commercial, 222–223
common commands, 229–232
computer monitoring, 640–641
demo version, 223
desktop, 229
DRM, 661
expert insight on, 262–263
installed, 224–226
installing, 16
markdown optimization, 501
mobile, 228–229
multimedia authoring, 419
open source, 199, 222, 223
ownership rights, 221–224
PLM, 499
price optimization, 499
privacy, 637
project management, 519
public domain, 222, 224
shopping cart, 468
storefront, 467–468
synchronization, 229
system, 16, 17–18. *See also* operating system; utility program; *specific operating systems*
trial version, 223
upgrading, R-14
videoconferencing, 273
Web-based, 225–226
software company, 316
software kiosk, 226
software license An agreement, either included in a software package or displayed on the screen during installation, that specifies the conditions under which a buyer of the program can use it. 221
network, 223
single-user, 223
site, 223
software piracy The unauthorized copying of a computer program. 627–628
protecting against, 629
software suite A collection of software programs bundled together and sold as a single software package. 227–228
software-asset management tool, 553
SoftwareToGo, 226
SOI (silicon on insulator), 84
solar panel, 689
solar power, 689
Solaris, 201, 204
solid state memory disk (SSD), 116
solid-state storage system, 114
Sony, 665, R-4
Sony Blu-ray Disc, 113
Sony Media Software ACID software products, 248
Sony Media Software Sound Forge 8 software, 248
Sony Media Software Vegas Movie Studio+ DVD, 248
Sony Play Station, 136
Sony Play Station 3, 64
sound clip, presentation graphics, 245
sound port, 73
source code A computer program before it is compiled. 545
source data automation, 141
source document, 141
space bar, 134
spam Unsolicited, bulk e-mail sent over the Internet. 40, 634–635
e-mail filters, 638
opting out, 638–639
speaker Output device that produces sound. 15–16, 168
special purpose key, 134
special-purpose printer, 166-168
specificity, good program design, 541
speech recognition system. *See* voice input system
speed, hard drive, 104
Speedpass, 451
Spelling and grammar command, 229
spider, 326
spim, 635
splash page, 419
sponsored link, 327, 470
sponsored listing, 470
spoofing Making it appear that an e-mail or a Web site originates from somewhere other than where it really does; typically used with dot cons. 386–387
spooling The process of placing items in a buffer so they can be retrieved by the appropriate device (such as a printer) when needed. 190–191
spreadsheet A group of values and other data organized into rows and columns. 236–239
charts, 239
crating, 236–239
Web pages, 239
what-if analysis, 239
spreadsheet software Application software used to create spreadsheets, which typically contain a great deal of numbers and mathematical computations and are organized into rows and columns. 19, 227, 236
Spyblock (Software Principles Yielding Better Levels of Consumer Knowledge), 392, 394
Spybot Search & Destroy, 292
spyware A software program installed without the user's knowledge that secretly collects information and sends it to an outside party via the user's Internet connection. 210, 342, 352, 363, 387, 388–389, R-7
antispyware program, 82, 211, 292, 626
legislation, 392, 394
protecting against, 392–393
scanning for, 82
SQL. *See* structured query language (SQL)
SQL (structured query language), 556, 596, 597
SSA (Social Security Administration), 146
SSD (solid state memory disk), 116
SSE2, 84
SSE3, 84
SSE (streaming SIMD extension), 84
SSL (Secure Sockets Layer), 379
SSTP (Streamlined Sales Tax Project), 468–469
ST connector, 285
stalking, online, 395, 396
star network A network that uses a host device connected directly to several other devices. 277
StarBand, 31
Starbucks, 323
StarOffice, 227
Start button, 17, 18
start/stop symbol, flowcharts, 636
static Web page, 603
status bar, 35, 233
presentation graphics software, 245
stealthware, 389
steering wheel, 140
stock photograph, 415
storage The operation of saving data, programs, or output for future use. 11–12, 96–125
address, 98
comparing alternatives, 122–123
flash memory. *See* flash memory
holographic, 120
large computer systems and networks, 120–122
local, 117
logical, 99
logical vs. physical representation, 00
magnetic disks. *See* hard disk drive; magnetic disk
magnetic tape, 122

memory vs., 67
NAS, 121
network, 117
online, 117
optical discs. *See* optical disc
physical, 99
RAID, 121–122
random vs. sequential access, 98–99
remote, 117–118
SANs, 121
smart cards, 119–120
volatility, 98

storage area network (SAN) A network of hard drives or other storage devices that provide storage for another network of computers. 121

storage device A piece of hardware, such as a floppy drive or CD drive, into which a storage medium is inserted to be read from or written to. 16, 97–98

storage medium The part of a storage system where data is stored, such as a floppy disk or CD disc. 16, 67, 97–98
formatting, caution regarding, 103
read-only, 110

storage server A hardware device containing multiple high-speed hard drives. 120

storage system, online, 98
StorCard, 119, 120, 662
store operation, 79

storefront software E-commerce software that allows facilitates the creation of an online store. 467–468

storyboard An ordered series of sketches that can be developed during the design process of an animated sequence or other multimedia component of a Web site that illustrates what each page or screen in the application will look like. 425

strained silicon, 84
strategic decision, 489
streaming media, 338
streaming SIMD extension (SSE), 84
streaming video, 421
Streamlined Sales Tax Project (SSTP), 468–469
stress, 675
strong 128-bit encryption, 381
strong password, 373
structure, database table, 241, 242
structure chart, 536

structured programming An approach to program design in which a program is separated into smaller subprograms, and step-by-step instructions are executed one after the other, accessing the subprograms when needed. 531–534

structured query language (SQL) A popular query language standard for information retrieval in relational databases. 556, 596, 597

student ID card, smart card, 118
Stuffit, 208
style, formatting documents, 233, 234

stylus Another name for electronic pen. 137. *See also* electronic pen

subclass, object-oriented programming, 533
subdirectory, 99
subfolder, 99, 186
submodule, 536
subnet mask, 296
subpixel, 161
subprogram, 532
substitute check, 494
subtraction operator (–), 237
Sun Microsystems, 200, 562, R-6
Sun Project Looking Glass, 423
Sun StarOffice, 227
Super Bowl (2001), 642

supercomputer The fastest, most expensive, and most powerful type of computer. 20, 28–29
operating systems, 204

supercomputing cluster, 29
superdiskette, 108
superscalar characteristic, 79

supply chain management (SCM) The oversight of materials, information, and finances as they move from the original supplier to the consumer. 498–499

surfing the Web, 35–36

surge suppressor A device that protects a computer system from damage due to electrical fluctuations. 624

SUSE Linux Enterprise Server, 201
SVG (Scalable Vector Graphics) format, 434
SVG image, 434
S-video port, 74, 75
swap file, 189
swapping, 190

switch A device on a network to which data is sent so it can be forwarded to the appropriate network node. 300, 686
star network, 277

Sybos/Cardtrap, 368

Symbian OS A leading operating system for smart phones. 203, 204

symmetric encryption, 379, 380
symmetric multiprocessing (SMP), 85–86
synchronization software, 229
synchronous dynamic RAM (SDRAM), 68
synchronous transmission, 282–283
synonym, searching the Internet, 330

syntax error A programming error that occurs when the programmer has not followed the rules of the programming language. 548–549

system A collection of elements and procedures that interact to accomplish a goal.
expert insight, 614–615

system acquisition The phase of the system development life cycle in which hardware, software, and other necessary system components are acquired. 516–518

system analysis The phase of the system development life cycle in which a problem area is thoroughly examined to determine what should be done. 513–515

system analysis and design group, 509
system board. *See* motherboard
system bus, 70, 71

system clock The timing mechanism within the computer system that synchronizes the computer's operations. 79

system design The phase of the system development life cycle in which a model of the new system and how it will work is formally established. 515–516

system development The process of designing and implementing a new or modified system. 488, 508–520
end-user development, 521
information systems department responsibility, 508–509
life cycle. *See* system development life cycle (SDLC)
outsourcing, 510–511
prototyping, 521
traditional, 520–521

system development life cycle (SDLC) The process consisting of the six phases of system development: preliminary investigation, system analysis, system design, system acquisition, system implementation, and system maintenance. 511–520
documentation, 511, 515, 516, 518, 519, 520
preliminary investigation phase, 512–513
system acquisition phase, 516–518
system analysis phase, 513–515
system design phase, 515–516
system implementation phase, 518–519
system maintenance phase, 520

system failure The complete malfunction of a computer system. 620–621
protecting against, 621–622

system file, caution about deleting, 209
system flowchart, system design, 515

system implementation The phase of the system development life cycle that encompasses activities related to making the system operational. 518–519

system maintenance The phase of the system development life cycle in which minor adjustments are made to the finished system to keep it operational until the end of the system's life or until the time that the system needs to be redesigned. 81–82, 520

system resources, managing, 185

system software Programs, such as the operating system, that control the operation of a computer and its devices, as well as enable application software to run on the PC. 16, 17–18, 182–213
application software compared, 183–184
operating system. *See* operating system
utility programs. *See* utility program

system unit The main box of a computer that houses the CPU, motherboard, memory, and other devices. 15–16, 54–89, 62–81. *See also* CPU (central processing unit)
buses, 70–72
components, 62–75, 75–81
cooling components, 62, 69
CPU, 62, 63–67
data and program representation, 55–62
expansion slots and cards, 9–70, 62, 63
memory, 62, 67–69
motherboard, 62, 63
opening, 81
performance, 81–87
ports, 72–75

systems analyst A person who studies systems in an organization in order to determine what work needs to be done and how this work may best be achieved. 20
information system development, 508–509
system development duties, 513

T

T1 line Fast, direct Internet access via a leased high-speed dedicated line. 321–322

T3 line, 322
tab, formatting documents, 234
Tab key, 134

table In a relational database, a collection of related records or rows. 233, 575–576
  in data hierarchy, 581
  databases, 241, 242
  word processing, 234–235
table of contents, Help feature, 231
table structure, 583
Tables and Borders toolbar, 235
tablet PC A portable PC about the size of a notebook that is designed to be used with an electronic pen. 23, 24–25
  accessing Internet, 319
  note taking, 253
Tacoda, 472
tactical decision, 489
Taeus International, 78
tag
  HTML, 430–431
  markup, 430
  meta, 470
  PHP, 605
  XHTML, 432
  XML, 431
tamper evident label, 623
tangible benefit, 516
tape drive, 99, 122
Target, 146, 563
task, 188
Task Manager screen, 185
task pane, 233
taskbar The bar located at the bottom of the Windows desktop that contains the Start button, task buttons, and the system tray. 17, 18
taskbar button, 17, 18
taskbar toolbar, 17
tax, online purchases, 468
TB. *See* terabyte (TB)
TCP (Transmission Control Protocol), 294
TCP/IP A communications protocol that uses packet switching to facilitate the transmission of messages; the protocol used with the Internet. 107, 294–295
technical assistance, R-14
technological change, stress due to, 679–680
telecommunications, 267
telecommuting The use of computer and electronic devices to enable an individual to work from his or her home. 7, 274
teleconferencing. *See* videoconferencing
telemarketing, 635–636
  preventing calls, 639
telemedicine The use of communications technology to provide medical information and services. 276
Telephone Anti-Spamming Amendments Act of 1998, 649
Telephone Consumer Protection Act of 1991, 649
telephone network, 267
telephone plug, 73
telesurgery A form of robot-assisted surgery in which the doctor is in a different physical location from the patient and controls the robot remotely over the Internet or another communications medium. 276
television
  high-definition, 160
  interactive, 338
Telnet, 318
template, word processing, 235
10Base-T, 289
10-Gigabit Ethernet, 289
terabyte (TB) Approximately 1 trillion bytes. 56
teraflop, 66
terminal emulation program, 318
terrorist attack of 9/11/2001, 621, 627
test, alpha, 550
test data, 549
testing, 549–550
  multimedia Web sites, 437
  online, 344, 345
  system for vulnerabilities, 626
text Alphanumeric characters kept in a text, not graphic, format. 12
  copying, 230
  cutting, 230
  Web sites, 414–415
text-based user interface, 185
text-to-speech system, 168–169
Thawte, 379
theft
  hardware, 620, 621–622
  identity, R-7
There (digital community), 413
thermal-transfer technology, 166
thermal-wax transfer, 166
thesaurus, 229
thin client A PC designed to access a network for processing and data storage, instead of performing those tasks locally; also called a network computer (NC). 26
third generation input output (3GIO) bus, 71
third normal form (3NF), 594
third-generation (3G) cell phone, 288
third-generation computer, 13, 14, R-3
third-generation programming language (3GL), 555
third-generation (3G) wireless standard, 322–323
third-party cookie, 350
32-bit processor, 66
thousands of bits per second (Kbps), 282
thread, 188, 332
3D browser, 423
3D (three-dimensional) chip, 87
3D desktop, 423
3D (three-dimensional) display screen, 158
3D online shopping, 454
3D projector, 158
3D (three-dimensional) scanner, 142
3G (third-generation) cell phone, 288
3G (third-generation) wireless standard, 322–323
3GIO (third generation input output) bus, 71
3GL (third-generation programming language), 555
3NF (third normal form), 594
three-tier database system, 590
Thriftway, 493
throughput, 67, 281–282
throw-away e-mail address An e-mail address used only for nonessential purposes and activities that may result in spam; the address can be disposed and replaced if spam becomes a problem. 40, 636
thumb drive. *See* flash memory drive
thumb pad, 134–135
thumbnail image A small image on a Web page that is linked to a larger, higher-resolution image. 418
Tiger. *See* Mac OS
time bomb, 368
TIME magazine, 670, R-5
time shifting, 665
Time Warner, 625
Time Warner Cable, 334
TLD (top-level domain), 32–33
toggle key, 133
token, 290
Token Ring A communications protocol that uses token passing to control the transmission of messages. 290
TOLED (transparent OLED), 162
toner cartridge, 165
  recharged, 164, 692
toner powder, 165
toolbar A set of icons or buttons displayed horizontally or vertically on the screen that can be used to issue commands to the computer. 18
  spreadsheet program, 237
  taskbar, 17
toolbar button, 17
Top Thrill Dragster, 490
top-down design, 536
top-level domain (TLD), 32–33
top-level manager, as information system users, 488, 489
topology, networks, 277–278
Torvalds, Linus, 199, R-6
Toshiba, 113
touch pad A small rectangular-shaped input device, often found on notebook computers, that is touched with the finger or thumb to control an onscreen pointer and make selections. 15–16, 140, 141
touch screen A display device that is touched with the finger to issue commands or otherwise generate input to the connected PC. 15–16, 139
touch stick, 140, 141
tower case, 21, 22
Toys R Us, 563
track A concentric path on a disk where data is recorded.
  floppy disks, 101
  optical disc, 109
trackball An input device, similar to an upside-down mouse, that can be used to control an onscreen pointer and make selections. 140
trademark A word, phrase, symbol, or design that identifies goods or services. 661–662
Trademark Cyberpiracy Prevention Act of 1999, 662
traditional system development An approach to system development whereby the six phases of the system development life cycle are carried out in a predetermined sequence. 520–521
training, Web-based, 412
transaction processing system A type of information system that processes and records data created by an organization's business transactions. 490, 492–494
transceiver, 63, 286
transistor, 14
  development, R-3
transition, presentation graphics, 244–245
transitive dependency, 594
Transmission Control Protocol (TCP), 294
transmitter, wireless network transmission, 286
transmitter-receiver, 286
transparent background color, 416
transparent OLED (TOLED), 162
transparent persistence, 600
Transportation DSS, 495

TransUnion, 389, 390
travel keyboard, 676
travel mouse, 676
trial version, 223
Trojan horse A malicious program that masquerades as something else. 370
troubleshooting, R-13—R-14
true color, 60
TRUSTe, 469
TSA (U.S. Transportation Security Administration), 644
tunneling, 281
Turing, Alan, 502
Turing Test, 502
Turion 64 microprocessor, 63, 65
turnaround document, 147
twisted-pair cable A communications medium consisting of wire strands twisted in sets of two and bound into a cable. 284, 285
2G (second-generation) cell phone, 288
2G (second-generation) wireless standard, 322
two-tier client-server database system, 590
two-way remote, 202
Tyco International, 671
typeface, 230
typing key, 134

U

ubiquitous computing, 5
u-commerce (universal commerce (universal commerce), 450, 451
Ulead DVD MovieFactory, 248
Ulead Photo Express, 247
Ultra Wideband (UWB), 294
ultra-high frequency RFID tag, 146
ultrarugged PC, 624
UltraSPARC microprocessor, 64
UMTO (Universal Mobile telecommunications System), 322
unauthorized access Gaining access to a computer, network, file, or other resource without permission. 364
unauthorized use Using a computer resource for unapproved activities. 364
Undo command, 229
Unicode A coding system for text-based data using any written language. 57, 58
  chart, R-9
uniform resource locator (URL) An Internet address, usually beginning with http://, that uniquely identifies a Web page. 32, 33–34
  e-commerce sites, 469
  navigating to Web pages, 35, 36
uninstall utility, 209
uninterruptible power supply (UPS) A device containing a built-in battery that provides continuous power to a PC and other connected components when the electricity goes out. 624, 625
United States Navy, 546
U.S. Anticybersquatting Act of 1999, 662, 693
U.S. Postal Service, 604
U.S. Transportation Security Administration (TSA), 644
UNIVAC, 13, 14
UNIVAC 1, R-3
Universal, 665
universal commerce (u-commerce), 450, 451
Universal Mobile telecommunications System (UMTO), 322
Universal Product Code (UPC), 145
Universal Serial Bus (USB) A universal bus used to connect up to 127 peripheral devices to a computer without requiring the use of additional expansion cards. 71, 72
University of Denver, 668
University of Vermont School of Business Administration, 253
UNIX An operating system developed in the 1970s for midrange servers and mainframes; many variations of this operating system are in use today. 199, 204, 560, R-3
unrestricted TLD, 33
unzipping, 208
UPC (Universal Product Code), 145
updating operating systems, 377, 626
upgrading, 196
  hardware, R-14
  operating system, 185
  software, R-14
uploading, 279
UPS. *See* uninterruptible power supply (UPS)
UPS (United Parcel Service), 499, 501, 604
URL. *See* uniform resource locator (URL)
USA Patriot Act (USAPA) of 2001, 365, 397, 641, 649
USB. *See* Universal Serial Bus (USB)
USB 2 standard, 72
USB flash drive. *See* flash memory drive
USB hub, 74
USB minidrive. *See* flash memory drive
USB plug, 73
USB port, 15–16, 73, 74, 122
USB security token, 373, 375
user. *See also* end-user *entries*
  database management system, 578
  ergonomics, 678–679
  information systems, 488–489
  Internet, 314
user documentation, 550
user ID, 31
user interface, 17, 185
  database, 575
user support, R-14
username A name that uniquely identifies a user on a particular network. 31
US-VISIT program, 644
utility program A type of software that performs a specific task, usually related to managing or maintaining the computer system. 82, 204–211
  backup and recovery utilities, 210, 211
  diagnostic, 208, R-13
  disk management, 208
  file compression programs, 208
  file management programs, 206–207
  search tools, 208, 209
  security programs, 210–211
  uninstall utilities, 209
UWB (Ultra Wideband), 294

V

vacuum tube, 13, R-2
value chain management The process of maximizing the flow of products, goods, services, and information through a value-added network of suppliers. 498
vaporware Software or hardware products that are announced or advertised, but that are not yet, and may never be, available. 673
variable
  Java applet, 564, 565
  object-oriented programming, 532, 538. *See also* comment
VBScript (Visual Basic Scripting Edition), 434
Vcast, 22
VCR, 665
vector-based image, 60
vein recognition system, 118
vendor rating system, 517–518
VeriChip, 451, 688
VeriSign, 379
Verizon, 334
vertical hub, 459
vertical portal, 459
very large-scale integration (VLSI), R-4
very-high-level language, 555–556
Veteran's Administration, 632
video A continuous stream of visual information broken into separate images or frames to be displayed one after the other to simulate the original visual event. 12, 420–421
  online, 338–339
  streaming, 421
video card, 71, 157–158
  upgrading, 83
video clip, presentation graphics, 245
video data, coding system, 61
video editing software, 248
video e-mail, 37
video memory, 83
video phone, 152, 272–273
Video Privacy Protection Act of 1988, 649
video RAM (VRAM), 158
video surveillance The use of video cameras to monitor activities of individuals, such as employees or individuals in public locations, for work-related or crime-prevention purposes. 641–643
videoconferencing The use of computers, video cameras, microphones, and other communications technologies to conduct face-to-face meetings over the Internet. 152, 272–273, 332, 333
video-on-demand (VOD) The process of downloading movies and televisions shows, on demand, via the Internet. 160, 338
viewable image size (VIS), 167
virtual account number, 462
virtual keyboard, 136
virtual memory A memory-management technique that uses hard drive space as additional RAM. 189–190
virtual model, 144
virtual private network (VPN) A group of secure paths over the Internet that provide authorized users a secure means of accessing a private network via the Internet. 281, 382
virtual reality (VR) The use of a computer to create three-dimensional environments that look like they do in the real world. 412
Virtual Reality Modeling Language (VRML), 436
virus. *See* computer virus
VIS (viewable image size), 167
Visa, 672
VisiCalc, R-4
vision system, 505
Visual Basic An object-oriented, fourth-generation version of the BASIC programming language. 18, 559, 561
Visual Basic for Applications, 552–553

Visual Basic Scripting Edition (VBScript), 434
visual learners, 413
visual programming language, 556
VLSI (very large-scale integration), R-4
VOD. *See* video-on-demand (VOD)
voice input system A system that enables a computer to recognize the human voice. 14, 137, 152–153, 202, 686
voice output, 168
Voice over Internet Protocol (VoIP) The process of placing telephone calls via the Internet. 333–334, 647
Voice over Wi-Fi, 292, 333
voice recognition system. *See* voice input system
VoIP. *See* Voice over Internet Protocol (VoIP)
volatile Describes a medium whose content is erased when the power is shut off. 98
Volvo, 202
Vonage, 334
vortal, 459
voting
  e-voting machines, 621, 622–623
  online, 622, 623
VPN. *See* virtual private network (VPN)
VR. *See* virtual reality (VR)
VRAM (video RAM), 158
VRML (Virtual Reality Modeling Language), 436

W

Wakamaru, 506–507
wallet, digital, Srr digital wallet, 451
wallet phone, 451
Wal-Mart, 146, 335, 469, 473, 563, R-7
Wal-Mart Music Downloads, 337, 457, 660
Walmart.com, 456, 461, 469
WAN. *See* wide area network (WAN)
WAP. *See* Wireless Application Protocol (WAP)
war driving Driving around an area with a Wi-Fi-enabled computer or mobile device to find a Wi-Fi network to access and use without authorization. 366–367
water cooling system, 69
.wav file extension, 420
Wave Division Multiplexing (WDM), 301
waveform format, 420
WBT. *See* Web-based training (WBT)
W3C (World Wide Web Consortium), 313, 316
WDM (Wave Division Multiplexing), 301
wearable PC, 9–10
wearable personal display, 158
Web
  graphics, 249
  Internet vs., 31
  multimedia, 249
  searching, 36
  surfing, 35–36
Web animation program, 419
Web browser A program used to view Web pages. 19, 31
  browser hijacking, 389
  displaying Web pages, 415
  home page, 35
  privacy settings, 350
  specific, features requiring, 422
  3D, 423
Web bug A very small (usually invisible) image on a Web page that transmits data about the Web page visitor to a Web server. 352
Web cam, 152
Web conferencing. *See* videoconferencing
Web database, 601–605
  examples, 601–604
  operation, 605
Web log, 345–346
Web mining, 473
Web pad, 26, 28, 319
Web page A document, typically containing hyperlinks to other documents, located on a Web server and available through the World Wide Web. 31
  citing articles, 331
  citing content, 331
  dynamic, 602, 603
  error messages when trying to load, 35
  portal, 343
  presentation graphics, 246
  secure, 33, 34, 335, 378
  size of content, 422
  static, 603
Web server A computer that is continually connected to the Internet and hosts Web pages that are accessible through the Internet. 31, 278
  secure, 334, 378–379
Web service A self-contained business application that operates over the Internet. 315–316
Web services provider, 316
Web site A collection of related Web pages usually belonging to an organization or individual. 31
  databases, 243
  e-commerce, types, 454–456
  home page, 35
  multimedia. *See* multimedia Web site *entries*
  presentation graphics, 246
  privacy policy, 634
  spreadsheets, 239
Web site authoring software A type of application program used to create Web pages and complete Web sites. 430, 436–437
Web site defacement, 371
Web site design
  e-commerce, 467–468
  multimedia. *See* multimedia Web site design
Web site development
  e-commerce, 467–468
  multimedia. *See* multimedia Web site development
  software. *See* Web site authoring software
Web site spoofing, 386–387
Web-based articles, copyright protection, 664
Web-based encrypted e-mail, 381
Web-based multimedia, 411–414
  advantages and disadvantages, 413–414
  animation, 418–419
  applications, 411–412
  audio, 420
  expert insight, 482–483
  future, 438
  graphics, 415–418
  text, 414–415
  video, 420–421
  Web site design. *See* Web site design
  Web site development. *See* multimedia Web site development
Web-based software, 225–226
Web-based training (WBT) Instruction delivered on an individual basis via the World Wide Web. 344–345, 412
webcrawler, 326
Weber, Aaron, 262–263
Webfolio, 345, 346
WebPhone, 334
WEP (Wired Equivalent Privacy), 375
what-if analysis, 239
white hat hacker, 364
wide area network (WAN) A network that connects devices located in a large geographical area. 279
wide-format ink-jet printer, 168
wide-format printer, 167, 168
widescreen display, 167
widgets, 198
Wi-Fi (802.11) A widely used communications protocol for wireless networks. 291–292
  security, 375, 376
Wi-Fi cloud, 292
Wi-Fi connection, 16
Wi-Fi finder, 366
Wi-Fi hacking, 365–366
Wi-Fi hotspot, 10
Wi-Fi network, 278
Wi-Fi Positioning System, 292
Wi-Fi Protected Access (WPA), 375
Wi-Fi technology, 281
Wi-Fi transmission, 286
wiki A collaborative Web page that is designed to be edited and republished by a variety of individuals. 345, 346
Wikipedia, 346
wildcard, searching the Internet, 330
Wi-MAXax An emerging wireless networking standard that is faster and has a greater range than Wi-Fi. 292–293
Wind River Workbench, 553
window A rectangular area in which programs, documents, and other content are displayed. 17, 18
Windows The primary PC operating system developed by Microsoft Corporation; the most recent version is Windows XP. 17, 688
  desktop, 17
  development, R-5
  large computers, 204
  registry, 185
  Start menu, 18
  system updates, 185
Windows 1.0, 194
Windows 3.x, 194
Windows 95, 195
Windows 98 Second Edition (SE), 195
Windows 2000, 196
Windows Automotive, 202
Windows Backup program, 210, 211
Windows Embedded A family of operating systems based on Windows and designed for nonpersonal computer devices, such as cash registers and consumer electronic devices. 201–202
Windows Explorer file management screen, 99
Windows key, 134
Windows ME, R-6
Windows Me (Millennium Edition), 196
Windows Media Player, 249, 337, 419, 420
Windows Messenger, 333
Windows Mobile A family of operating systems based on Windows and designed for handheld PCs, smart phones, and other mobile devices. 203
Windows NT (New Technology), 195
Windows PC, 21, 23
Windows Registry, 389

Windows Server 2003 The most recent version of Windows designed for server use. 196, 197
Windows Sound Recorder, 248
Windows System Restore program, 210
Windows Vista The upcoming version of Windows (previously known as Longhorn) that is designed to replace Windows XP. 196, 198, 646
Windows XP The latest personal version of Windows; designed to replace both Windows Me and Windows 2000. 196–197, R-7
Windows XP Embedded, 202
Windows 95, R-6
Windows 98, R-6
Windows 2000, R-6
WinZip, 208, 380
WIPO (World Intellectual Property Organization), 662
Wired Equivalent Privacy (WEP), 375
Wired for Health Care Quality Act of 2005, 632
wired monitor, 158
wired network A network in which computers and other devices are connected to the network via physical cables. 283–284
wired transmission media, 284–285
wireless access point A device used to connect wireless devices to a wired network. 291, 300
Wireless Application Protocol (WAP). A standard for delivering content, such as Web pages, to mobile devices. 295
wireless hard drive, 104
wireless hotspot, 8
wireless keyboard, 133
Wireless Markup Language (WML) A language similar to XML that is used with pages to be displayed on WAP-enabled devices. 428, 434
wireless mesh, 292
wireless monitor, 158
wireless mouse, 136
wireless network A network in which computers and other devices are connected to the network without physical cables; data is typically sent via radio waves. 283–284, R-7
  access, 375–376
  transmission media, 286–288
wireless networking technology, 25
wireless phone. *See* mobile phone
wireless projector, 162
wireless technology, 14
wireless USB standard, 294
wireless Web, 319, 320, 322–323
wizard, 235
WML. *See* Wireless Markup Language (WML)
word, size, 66
word processing Using a computer and word processing software to create, edit, save, and print written documents, such as letters, contracts, and manuscripts. 232–235
word processing software Application software used to create, edit, save, and print written documents. 19, 227, 232–233
  creating documents, 233–234
  graphics, 235
  tables, 234–235
  templates, 235
word processor, 8
word wrap The feature in a word processing program that automatically returns the insertion point to the next line when the end of the screen line is reached. 233
work for hire, 661
workbook A collection of worksheets saved in a single spreadsheet file. 236
workgroup computing, 273–274
workplace
  computers in, 8–10
  monitoring in, ethics, 673
  privacy in, 647–648
worksheet A document in a spreadsheet program. 236
worksheet area, spreadsheet program, 237
worksheet tab, 237
workspace design, 675–677
workstation, 64
World Intellectual Property Organization (WIPO), 662
World Wide Web The collection of Web pages available through the Internet. 31, 312–313. *See also* Internet; Web *entries*
  Internet vs., 318
World Wide Web Consortium (W3C), 313, 316
WorldCom, 671
worm, 369–370
Wozniak, Steve, R-4
WPA (Wi-Fi Protected Access), 375
WPA2 standard, 375
wrist rest, 678
writing
  online, 344, 345–346
  word processing software. *See* word processing software
.wrl file extension, 436
WWW. *See* World Wide Web
WYSIWYG editing, 437

X

xD card, 115
X3D Fritz, 503
Xeon microprocessor, 64, 65
Xeon MP microprocessor, 65
Xerox, 156
XHTML (Extensible Hypertext Markup Language) A newer, stricter version of HTML that is based on XML. 431–433
XHTML tag, 432
xMax, 293
XML (Extensible Markup Language) A set of rules used for exchanging data over the Web; addresses only the content, not the formatting; the content displays in an appropriate format based on the device being used. 198, 235, 341, 431
XML tag, 431

Y

Yahoo!, 209, 343, 454, 470
Yahoo! Auction, 672, 674
Yahoo! Mail, 38
Yahoo! Messenger, 333
Yahoo! Music, 337, 457
Yahoo! Photos, 637
YB. *See* yottabyte (YB)
yottabyte (YB) Approximately 1,000 zettabytes. 56
You Don't Know Jack trivia game, 192

Z

ZB. *See* zettabyte (ZB)
zero normal form (ZNF), 594
zettabyte (ZB) Approximately 1,000 exabytes. 56
Zip disk, 108, 123
Zip drive, 108
zipping, 208
ZNF (zero normal form), 594
zombie, 370–371